THESAURUS
OF WORDS AND PHRASES

THESAURUS
OF WORDS AND PHRASES

BY

PETER MARK ROGET, M.D., F.R.S.

ENLARGED BY

JOHN LEWIS ROGET, M.A.

NEW EDITION REVISED AND ENLARGED BY

SAMUEL ROMILLY ROGET, M.A.

REVISED AND AUTHORIZED AMERICAN EDITION

Grosset & Dunlap
PUBLISHERS
NEW YORK

ROGET: THESAURUS
AUTHORIZED EDITION
REVISED
1941
COPYRIGHT, 1941, 1947 BY
GROSSET & DUNLAP, INC.

By arrangement with Longmans, Green and Co.

WHAT ROGET CAN DO FOR YOU

As Mark Twain said: "The difference between the right word and the almost right word is the difference between lightning and the lightning bug." To find precisely the correct word is the problem of every writer and speaker— and that is where ROGET's THESAURUS is invaluable.

Suppose you are an advertising copywriter seeking a new substitute for the much over-used "fascination." How to go about finding a fresh eye-catching simile? It's quite simple. First look in the alphabetical index which occupies the last third of the book.

There on page 486 you find "fascinate: *influence* 615." Turn back in the body of the book to section 615, which you will easily find from the numbers on the upper corner of each page.

And here is a vast store of welcome variants for "fascination": *temptation, enticement, allurement, cajolery, blandishment, magnetism*—and any number of additional choices—including that dashing word *bewitchery*. Surely one of these will fit your needs better than the weary and outworn "fascination."

Perhaps you're a minister wrestling with the knotty problem of how to strengthen next Sunday's sermon on "sin." What to do about it? Look up "sin" in ROGET. You find in the index "sin: 945, 947." Back again to the body of the book (sections 945 & 947), and there is a magnificent collection of all the virtues and most of the vices arrayed in parallel columns: *Immorality, infamy, depravity, knavery, lust,* and *pollution* vie for space with *morality, integrity, nobleness,* and *self-control.* You find that sinners may range in degree from *naughty* and *undutiful* to *base, sinister, satanic, depraved,* and even *irreclaimable.*

But then you may be neither a preacher nor a copywriter. The problem may be that of a student confronted with an assignment to write a composition about the evolution of the modern dance. You know, of course, all about *jitterbugging,* the *Shag,* and the *Big Apple.* But, after all, these represent only the last ten years of popular dancing. What of the centuries before? What were the names of the dances your grandparents enjoyed? Before the dictionary or encyclopedia can be used, at least their names must be known.

So look again in the index of ROGET under "dance" and find on page 453 "dance: *sport* 840." Turning to section 840 you discover an all-inclusive list of dance-names. The *morris dance* of medieval England is here; the *fandango, pavan,* and the *polka.* The *bolero* and *tango* from Spain; the *Charleston,* the *cakewalk, jazz,* and the *blues.* The *gavotte, mazurka, quadrille,* and *lancers* are found in the merry company of the *turkeytrot, shimmy,* and *rhumba.* Here truly is a stimulating introduction to the dance in all its manifold varieties from the *polonaise* to the *cancan!*

When you run through this list, not only will the right word automatically catch your eye but the rich array of colorful names will suggest fresh ideas that are sure to help you in your thinking and writing.

Briefly, the simplest and best way to use ROGET is this:

1. Look up in the index at the back of the book the word for which you want a substitute.
2. Note the category number of the group which seems to fit your needs best.
3. Turn back to this number which you will find at the top of a page in the main part of the book. And there you will find the right word, the exact word for your purpose.

This, then, is *your* ROGET, a book you will want to keep al..ays in reach when writing or preparing a speech. You will be amazed at how easily you get the knack of its use—and how enormously valuable and profitable it will prove.

FOREWORD

AUTHORIZED AMERICAN EDITION

IT IS fitting that a new American edition of Roget's Thesaurus, issued by the American Company of its original London publishers, should have some account of its origin and progress.

Early in the nineteenth century the idea of the utility of a list of words classified according to the ideas that they express occurred to Dr. Peter Mark Roget, and his first draft was completed in 1805. It was added to from time to time, but it was not until Dr. Roget was over seventy years of age and had retired from the active secretaryship of the Royal Society that he was able to devote three or four years to the work of expansion.

It was first published in London by Longman, Brown, Green and Longmans in 1852, and went into a second edition in 1853. Two years later the "third and cheaper edition enlarged and improved" appeared, and was followed by the fourth edition in the same year. The fifth edition was issued in 1857, and since then edition has followed edition almost every year, and occasionally two or three times in one year, until seventy-seven printings have been called for, totalling more than two hundred thousand books.

The merits of the Thesaurus, its scholarship and erudition, were appreciated from the first, and successive improvements and enlargements by the author, the author's son and grandson, have caused it to maintain its great reputation.

In the course of years there have been several competing editions printed in America, all based on the London editions, but from none of these did the author or his representatives derive any pecuniary advantage.

The present edition, edited and revised by Willard Jerome Heggen, is the first one to be issued in America with the sanction and approval of Samuel Romilly Roget, the author's grandson, and holder of the existing British copyright.

It is worthy of note that it took three generations of the Roget family to compile and perfect this Thesaurus, and that after eighty years it is still published in London by the same firm, and from the same address in Paternoster Row, as when issued originally.

PREFACE

SINCE the preface of March 17, 1879, was written, Mr. John L. Roget continued to revise periodical reprints of the Thesaurus until his death in 1908. It then devolved upon the undersigned, his son, to carry on this task, and it has been his endeavour to follow the same lines in making such additions that have seemed suitable from time to time. The opportunity has now, however, presented itself for a rather more complete revision, owing to the necessity of resetting the entire work, and in the edition that is now presented not only have a few hitherto unnoticed errors been corrected but some hundreds of new words and phrases have been added throughout the book, some of which have only recently become a part of the language as the result of progress in the various arts of peace and the unfortunate necessities of war. Many additional entries of words already represented have also been made, where the meanings have widened out or where for other reasons it has been thought advisable, but in practically no case has a word been removed, as archaic and even obsolete words are often sought for by authors. A few examples of alternative and obsolete spelling have been removed, but no alteration whatever has been made with the general arrangement and classification of the categories.

The editor would at all times welcome practical suggestions from users of the Thesaurus, and would take this opportunity of expressing his thanks for much kind help already afforded in this direction.

S. R. ROGET

July 1925

PREFACE

TO

THE FIRST EDITION

(1852)

IT is now nearly fifty years since I first projected a system of verbal classification similar to that on which the present Work is founded. Conceiving that such a compilation might help to supply my own deficiencies, I had, in the year 1805, completed a classed catalogue of words on a small scale, but on the same principle, and nearly in the same form, as the Thesaurus now published. I had often during that long interval found this little collection, scanty and imperfect as it was, of much use to me in literary composition, and often contemplated its extension and improvement; but a sense of the magnitude of the task, amidst a multitude of other avocations, deterred me from the attempt. Since my retirement from the duties of Secretary of the Royal Society, however, finding myself possessed of more leisure, and believing that a repertory of which I had myself experienced the advantage might, when amplified, prove useful to others, I resolved to embark in an undertaking which, for the last three or four years, has given me incessant occupation, and has, indeed, imposed upon me an amount of labour very much greater than I had anticipated. Notwithstanding all the pains I have bestowed on its execution, I am fully aware of its numerous deficiencies and imperfections, and of its falling far short of the degree of excellence that might be attained. But, in a Work of this nature, where perfection is placed at so great a distance, I have thought it best to limit my ambition to that moderate share of merit which it may claim in its present form; trusting to the indulgence of those for whose benefit it is intended, and to the candour of critics who, while they find it easy to detect faults, can at the same time duly appreciate difficulties.

P. M. ROGET

April 29th, 1852

EDITOR'S PREFACE
(1879)
(*Slightly Abridged*)

THE FIRST EDITION of Dr. Roget's Thesaurus was published in the year 1852, and a second in the ensuing spring. On the issue of the third, in 1855, the volume was stereotyped. Since that time until now, the work has been reprinted in the same form and with little alteration, in rapidly succeeding editions, the printing of which has worn out the original plates.

During the last years of the author's life, which closed, at a very advanced age, in the month of September, 1869, he was engaged in the task of collecting additional words and phrases, for an enlarged edition which he had long projected. This he did not live to complete, and it became my duty, as his son, to attempt to carry the design into execution.

The result of the author's labours was embodied in a copy of the Thesaurus, in which the margins and spaces about the letterpress were closely covered with written words and phrases, without any very precise indication of the places in the text where additions or alterations were intended to be made. On a careful examination of these *addenda*, I came to the conclusion that, in order to introduce them with advantage, it would be necessary to make some slight changes; without, however, interfering at all with the framework of the book, and but little with the details of its system. In this proceeding my course has been mainly determined by the following considerations.

Any attempt at a philosophical arrangement under categories of the words of our language must reveal the fact that it is impossible to separate and circumscribe the several groups by absolutely distinct boundary lines. Many words, originally employed to express simple conceptions, are found to be capable, with perhaps a very slight modification of meaning, of being applied in many varied associations. Connecting links, thus formed, induce an approach between the categories; and a danger arises that the outlines of our classification may, by their means, become confused and eventually merged. Were we to disengage these interwoven ramifications, and seek to confine every word to its main or original import, we should find some secondary meaning has become so firmly associated with many words and phrases, that to sever the alliance would be to deprive our language of the richness due to an infinity of natural adaptations.

Were we, on the other hand, to attempt to include, in each category of the Thesaurus, every word and phrase which could by any possibility be appropriately used in relation to the leading idea for which that category was designed, we should impair, if not destroy, the whole use and value of the book. For, in the endeavour to enrich our treasury of expression, we might easily allow ourselves to be led imperceptibly onward by the natural association of one word with another, and to add word after word, until group after group would successively be absorbed under some single heading, and the fundamental divisions of the system be effaced. The small cluster of nearly synonymous words, which had formed the nucleus of a category, would be lost in a sea of phrases, and it would become difficult to recognize those which were peculiarly adapted to express the leading ideas.

These considerations were material in dealing with the new and multitudinous store of words and phrases which the author had accumulated. Many of these were altogether new to the Thesaurus. Many were merely repetitions in new places of words already included in its pages. With reference to cases similar to the latter, the author had declared it to have been a general rule with him 'to place words and phrases which appertain more especially to one head, also under other heads to which they have a relation,' whenever it appeared to him 'that this repetition would suit the convenience of the inquirer and spare him the trouble of turning to other parts of the work.' But, with the now increased mass of words, it became a question, in many cases, whether such repetition would still prove convenient. Where categories might by that course be unduly swollen, or where they might, by reason of their being separated from each other by subtle distinctions or faint lines of demarcation, be thereby too nearly assimilated, I thought it would often be better to confine words of the kind referred to to their primary headings. The necessity of keeping the book within reasonable dimensions had also to be borne in mind.

Under these circumstances, the best method of ensuring the ready accessibility of the multitude of words now to be dealt with, and at the same time preserving unimpaired the unity of the several categories, appeared to me to lie in the copious use of references from one place in the book to another. Relying on this contrivance as a means of opening more widely the resources of the collection, by making the groups of words mutually suggestive, and thereby leading not only to more varied forms of expression, but to kindred ideas, I have added largely to the references already inserted by the author. I have also ventured occasionally to substitute a reference for a group of words, when the identical group existed in another place, and could thus be made immediately available.

In order, at the same time, to make the value of the references more appreciable, I have (whenever it has appeared to me to be necessary) inserted, in a parenthesis, a word indicating the nature of the group or category referred to. Any one using the book will thereby be enabled to judge whether it will be worth his while to turn to the place in question.

The cross references may also be looked upon as indicating in some degree the natural points of connection between the categories, and the ramification of the ideas which they embody. As would be the case under any classification of language, a large proportion of the expressions, to find which recourse is had to the Thesaurus, lie on an ill-defined border land between one category and another; and it is not always easy, even with the aid of a carefully compiled index, to determine under which of several allied headings they should be sought. In the present edition, when the inquirer has once started on his voyage of discovery, the references enable him to pass freely from one division to another without recurring to the Index.

Many new words have also been inserted which were not contained in the author's manuscript.

Except in a very few cases, where distinct ideas were obviously united under one head, I have not had the presumption to meddle with the author's division into categories; but, within each category, I have endeavoured to carry somewhat further the sorting of words according to the ideas which they convey.

With these objects in view, I have supplied the work with a new and elaborate Index, much more complete than that which was appended to the previous editions. Although, in the original design of his work, the author appears to have conceived the process of search for a required expression as one in which the system of classification would be first consulted, and the Index afterwards called in aid if necessary, I believe that almost everyone who uses the book finds it more convenient to have recourse to the Index first.

From the peculiar nature and use of the Thesaurus, its Index will be found to differ, in some of its essential functions, from an alphabetical table of contents. The present Index does not merely afford an indication of the place where every given word or topic occurs or is dealt with in the text; but it is intended as a guide to other expressions which may be found there. The word we look out in this Index is not that which we require, but that which we wish to avoid. It is, therefore, not necessary that every word there given should be a repetition of one in the text. It may even happen that the word selected as a guide, though suggestive of the group wanted, is wholly unfit to be comprised within it.

The new Index contains not only all the *words* in the book (without needless repetition of conjugate forms), but likewise the *phrases*, all of which had been excluded from the Index to the previous editions. It is hoped that these additions, although they increase the bulk of the book, will have the effect of extending its usefulness in at least a corresponding degree.

Some changes of detail have also been made, where the form of the work seemed susceptible of improvement, and there was no reason to suppose that the author would have disapproved of the alteration. In the previous editions, the *phrases* were in general placed in separate paragraphs, under the heading **Phr.**, in each of the subdivisions assigned to the different grammatical parts of speech. In the present edition, *words* and *phrases* are placed together, and the heading **Phr.** is only employed in the case of phrases which have no convenient place in such an arrangement. Much space has been saved, and many repetitions have been avoided, by the use of lines and hyphens, where words or phrases in the same group have syllables or parts in common, and by references from one part of speech to another. These abbreviations may be best explained by examples, of which the following are a few:—

'with -relation, - reference, - respect, - regard- to'; is meant to include the phrases 'with relation to,' 'with reference to,' 'with respect to,' 'with regard to.'

'root -, weed -, grub -, rake- -up, - out;' includes 'root up,' 'root out,' 'weed up,' 'weed out,' 'grub up,' 'grub out,' 'rake up,' 'rake out.'

'away from -, foreign to -, beside- the -purpose, - question, - transaction, - point;' includes 'away from the purpose,' 'foreign to the purpose,' 'beside the purpose,' 'away from the question,' 'foreign to the question,' 'foreign to the transaction,' 'beside the question,' 'away from the point,' 'beside the transaction,' 'foreign to the point,' 'away from the transaction,' 'beside the point.'

'raze - to the ground'; includes 'raze,' and 'raze to the ground.'

'campan-iform, -ulate, -iliform;' includes 'campaniform,' 'campanulate,' and 'campaniliform.'

'goodness &c. *adj.*'; 'badly &c. *adj.*'; 'hindred &c. *v.*'; include all words similarly formed from synonyms of 'good,' 'bad,' and 'hinder,' respectively, given under the headings **Adj.** and **V.** in the same categories where the abbreviations occur.

The participle 'to' before a verb has in all cases been rejected, the heading **V.** being thought sufficiently distinctive; the use of capitals for the initial letters of the first words of paragraphs has been abandoned, as giving those words undue importance; and the title of each category has been kept distinct from the collection of words under its heading.

I should be ungrateful were I not to acknowledge the assistance derived, both by my father and myself, from various suggestions made by well-wishers to the work, some of whom have been personally unknown to either of us; and also to record my thanks to several kind friends, and to Messrs. Spottiswoode and Co.'s careful reader, for valuable aid during the passage of the sheets through the press.

JOHN L. ROGET

March 17th, 1879.

PLAN OF CLASSIFICATION

TABULAR SYNOPSIS OF CATEGORIES

Class I. ABSTRACT RELATIONS

I. EXISTENCE

1°. ABSTRACT	1. Existence.	2. Inexistence.
2°. CONCRETE	3. Substantiality.	4. Unsubstantiality.
3°. FORMAL	*Internal.*	*External.*
	5. Intrinsicality.	6. Extrinsicality.
4°. MODAL	*Absolute.*	*Relative.*
	7. State.	8. Circumstance.

II. RELATION

	9. Relation.	10. Irrelation.
	11. Consanguinity.	
1°. ABSOLUTE	12. Correlation.	
	13. Identity.	14. Contrariety.
	15. Difference.	
2°. CONTINUOUS	16. Uniformity.	16a. Non-uniformity.
	17. Similarity.	18. Dissimilarity.
3°. PARTIAL	19. Imitation.	20. Non-imitation.
	20a. Variation.	
	21. Copy.	22. Prototype.
4°. GENERAL	23. Agreement.	24. Disagreement.

III. QUANTITY

	Absolute.	*Relative.*
1°. SIMPLE	25. Quantity.	26. Degree.
	27. Equality.	28. Inequality.

2°. COMPARATIVE

29. Mean.
30. Compensation.
By Comparison with a Standard.
31. Greatness.   32. Smallness.
By Comparison with a similar Object.
33. Superiority.   34. Inferiority.
Changes in Quantity.
35. Increase.   36. Decrease.
37. Addition.   38. {Non-addition. / Subduction.}
39. Adjunct.   40. Remainder.
                40a. Decrement.

3°. CONJUNCTIVE

41. Mixture.   42. Simpleness.
43. Junction.   44. Disjunction.
45. Vinculum.
46. Coherence.   47. Incoherence.
48. Combination.   49. Decomposition.

4°. WITH REFERENCE TO DIRECTION—*cont*...

305. Ascent.	306. Descent.
307. Elevation.	308. Depression:
309. Leap.	310. Plunge.
311. Circuition.	
312. Rotation.	313. Evolution.
314. Oscillation.	
315. Agitation.	

CLASS III. MATTER

I. MATTER IN GENERAL......

316. Materiality.	317. Immateriality.
318. World.	
319. Gravity.	320. Levity.

II. INORGANIC MATTER

1°. SOLIDS............

321. Density.	322. Rarity.
323. Hardness.	324. Softness.
325. Elasticity.	326. Inelasticity.
327. Tenacity.	328. Brittleness.
329. Texture.	
330. Pulverulence.	
331. Friction.	332. Lubrication.

2°. FLUIDS

1. *In General*

333. Fluidity.	334. Gaseity.
335. Liquefaction.	336. Vaporization.
337. Water.	338. Air.
339. Moisture.	340. Dryness.

2. *Specific*...

341. Ocean.	342. Land.
343. { Gulf. / Lake.	
345. Marsh.	344. Plain.
	346. Island.

3. *In motion*

347. Stream.	
348. River.	349. Wind.
350. Conduit.	351. Air-pipe.
352. Semiliquidity.	353. Bubble.

3°. IMPERFECT FLUIDS...

354. Pulpiness.	355. Unctuousness.
	356. Oil.
	356a. Resin.

III. ORGANIC MATTER

1°. VITALITY

1. *In General*....

357. Organization.	358. Inorganization
359. Life.	360. Death.
	361. Killing.
	362. Corpse.
	363. Interment.

2. *Special*

364. Animality.	365. Vegetability.
366. Animal.	367. Vegetable.
368. Zoology.	369. Botany.
370. Cicuration.	371. Agriculture.
372. Mankind.	
373. Man.	374. Woman.

II. PROSPEC- 3°. *Precur-*
TIVE VOLI-   *sory Meas-*
TION—*cont.*   *ures* . . . . . .

673. Preparation.	674. Non-preparation:
675. Essay.	
676. Undertaking.	
677. Use.	678. Disuse.
	679. Misuse.
680. Action.	681. Inaction.
682. Activity.	683. Inactivity.
684. Haste.	685. Leisure.
686. Exertion.	687. Repose.
688. Fatigue.	689. Refreshment.
690. Agent.	
691. Workshop.	
692. Conduct.	
693. Direction.	
694. Director.	
695. Advice.	
696. Council.	
697. Precept.	
698. Skill.	699. Unskilfulness.
700. Proficient.	701. Bungler.
702. Cunning.	703. Artlessness.
704. Difficulty.	705. Facility.
706. Hindrance.	707. Aid.
708. Opposition.	709. Co-operation:
710. Opponent.	711. Auxiliary.
712. Party.	
713. Discord.	714. Concord.
715. Defiance.	
716. Attack.	717. Defence.
718. Retaliation.	719. Resistance.
720. Contention.	721. Peace.
722. Warfare.	723. Pacification:
724. Mediation.	
725. Submission.	
726. Combatant.	
727. Arms.	
728. Arena.	
729. Completion.	730. Non-completion:
731. Success.	732. Failure.
733. Trophy.	
734. Prosperity.	735. Adversity.
736. Mediocrity.	

III. ACTION

  1°. *Simple*. . .
  2°. *Complex* .

IV. ANTAGO-
NISM

  1°. *Condi-*
     tional. . . .
  2°. *Active*. . . .

Ϋ. RESULTS OF ACTION . . . . .

Division (II.). INTERSOCIAL VOLITION

737. Authority.	738. Laxity:
739. Severity.	740. Lenity.
741. Command.	
742. Disobedience.	743. Obedience:
744. Compulsion.	
745. Master.	746. Servant.
747. Sceptre.	
748. Freedom.	749. Subjection.
750. Liberation.	751. Restraint.
	752. Prison.
753. Keeper.	754. Prisoner.
755. Commission.	756. Abrogation.
	757 Resignation:
758. Consignee.	
759. Deputy.	

I. GENERAL. . . . .

CLASS VI. AFFECTIONS

II: PERSONAL

1°. PASSIVE

827. Pleasure.	828. Pain.
829. Pleasureableness.	830. Painfulness.
831. Content.	832. Discontent.
	833. Regret.
834. Relief.	835. Aggravation.
836. Cheerfulness.	837. Dejection.
838. Rejoicing.	839. Lamentation.
840. Amusement.	841. Weariness.
842. Wit.	843. Dulness.
844. Humorist.	

2°. DISCRIMINATIVE

845. Beauty.	846. Ugliness.
847. Ornament.	848. Blemish.
	849. Simplicity.
850. Taste.	851. Vulgarity.
852. Fashion.	
	853. Ridiculousness.
	854. Fop.
	855. Affectation.
	856. Ridicule.
	857. Laughing-stock.

3°. PROSPECTIVE

858. Hope.	859. Hopelessness.
	860. Fear.
861. Courage.	862. Cowardice.
863. Rashness.	864. Caution.
865. Desire.	866. Indifference.
	867. Dislike.
	868. Fastidiousness.
	869. Satiety.

4°. CONTEMPLATIVE

870. Wonder.	871. Expectance.
872. Prodigy.	

5°. EXTRINSIC

873. Repute.	874. Disrepute.
875. Nobility.	876. Commonalty.
877. Title.	
878. Pride.	879. Humility.
880. Vanity.	881. Modesty.
882. Ostentation.	
883. Celebration.	
884. Boasting.	
885. Insolence.	886. Servility.
887. Blusterer.	

III. SYMPATHETIC

1°. SOCIAL

888. Friendship.	889. Enmity.
890. Friend.	891. Enemy.
892. Sociality.	893. Seclusion.
894. Courtesy.	895. Discourtesy.
896. Congratulation.	
897. Love.	898. Hate.
899. Favourite.	
	900. Resentment.
	901. Irascibility.
	901a. Sullenness.
902. Endearment.	
903. Marriage.	904. Celibacy.
	905. Divorce.

SYNOPSIS OF CATEGORIES

2°. DIFFUSIVE .... {	906. Benevolence.
	910. Philanthropy.
	912. Benefactor.
3°. SPECIAL .... {	914. Pity.
	915. Condolence.
	916. Gratitude.
4°. RETROSPECTIVE .... {	918. Forgiveness.

907. Malevolence.
908. Malediction.
909. Threat.
911. Misanthropy.
913. Evil doer.
914a. Pitilessness.
917. Ingratitude.
919. Revenge.
920. Jealousy.
921. Envy.

IV. MORAL

1°. OBLIGATIONS .... {	922. Right.	923. Wrong.
	924. Dueness.	925. Undueness.
	926. Duty.	{ 927. Dereliction.
		{ 927a. Exemption.
	928. Respect.	929. Disrespect.
		930. Contempt.
2°. SENTIMENTS .... {	931. Approbation.	932. Disapprobation.
	933. Flattery.	934. Detraction.
	935. Flatterer.	936. Detractor.
	937. Vindication.	938. Accusation.
	939. Probity.	940. Improbity.
		941. Knave.
3°. CONDITIONS .... {	942. Disinterestedness.	943. Selfishness.
	944. Virtue.	945. Vice.
	946. Innocence.	947. Guilt.
	948. Good Man.	949. Bad Man.
	950. Penitence.	951. Impenitence.
	952. Atonement.	
	953. Temperance.	954. Intemperance.
		954a. Sensualist.
4°. PRACTICE .... {	955. Asceticism.	
	956. Fasting.	957. Gluttony.
	958. Sobriety.	959. Drunkenness.
	960. Purity.	961. Impurity.
		962. Libertine.
	963. Legality.	964. Illegality.
	965. Jurisprudence.	
	966. Tribunal.	
	967. Judge.	
5°. INSTITUTIONS ...... {	968. Lawyer.	
	969. Lawsuit.	
	970. Acquittal.	971. Condemnation.
	973. Reward.	{ 972. Punishment.
		{ 974. Penalty.
		975. Scourge.

RELIGIOUS

1°. SUPERHUMAN BE-	976. Deity.	
INGS AND REGIONS.. {	977. Angel.	978. Satan.
	979. Jupiter.	980. Demon.
	981. Heaven.	982. Hell.
2°. DOCTRINES .... {	983. Theology.	
	983a. Orthodoxy.	984. Heterodoxy.
	985. Revelation.	986. Pseudo-revelation.
3°. SENTIMENTS	987. Piety.	988. Impiety.
		989. Irreligion.

SYNOPSIS OF CATEGORIES

4°. ACTS.............
- 990. Worship.
- 991. Idolatry
- 992. Sorcery.
- 993. Spell.
- 994. Sorcerer.

5°. INSTITUTIONS......
- 995. Churchdom.
- 996. Clergy.
- 997. Laity.
- 998. Rite.
- 999. Canonicals.
- 1000. Temple.

ABBREVIATIONS, &c.

Adj.	*adj.*	Adjectives, Participles, and Words having the power of Adjectives.
Adv.	*adv.*	Adverbs and Adverbial Expressions.
Int.	*int.*	Interjections.
Phr.	*phr.*	Phrases.
V.	*v.*	Verbs.

The numbers are those of the headings, or Categories.

Words in italics within parentheses are not intended to explain the meanings of the words which precede them, but to indicate the nature of allied group of words under the numbers which follow them.

See also the Editor's Preface, p. xi.

THESAURUS

OF

WORDS AND PHRASES

CLASS I

WORDS EXPRESSING ABSTRACT RELATIONS

SECTION I. EXISTENCE

1°. BEING, IN THE ABSTRACT

1. Existence.—N. existence, being, entity, *ens, esse,* subsistence, quiddity.

reality, realness, actuality; positiveness &c. *adj.*; fact, matter of fact, sober reality; truth &c. 494; actual existence.

presence &c. (*existence in space*) 186; coexistence &c. 120.

stubborn fact; not a -dream &c. 515; no joke.

substance, essence, prime constituent, hypostatis.

[Science of existence], ontology.

V. exist, be; have -being &c. *n.*; subsist, live, breathe, stand, obtain, be the case; occur &c. (*event*) 151; have place, rank, prevail; find oneself, pass the time, vegetate.

consist in, lie in, reside in, inhere in; come into -existence &c. *n.*; arise &c. (*begin*) 66; come forth &c. (*appear*) 446.

become &c. (*be converted*) 144; bring into existence &c. 161; coexist, pre-exist, endure &c. 141.

Adj. existing &c. *v.*; existent, subsistent, under the sun; in -existence &c. *n.*; extant; afloat, on foot, current, prevalent, rife, in force, -vogue; undestroyed.

real, actual, positive, absolute; true &c. 494; substan-tial, -tive; self-existing, -ent,

2. Inexistence.—N. inexistence; non-existence, -subsistence; nonentity, *nil;* negativeness &c. *adj.*; nullity; nihil-ity, -ism; *tabula rasa,* blank; abeyance; absence &c. 187; no such thing &c. 4; nothingness, oblivion, *non esse.*

annihilation; extinction &c. (*destruction*) 162.

V. not -exist &c. 1; have no -existence &c. 1; be null and void; cease to -exist &c. 1; pass away, perish; be –, become-extinct &c. *adj.*; die out; disappear &c. 449; melt away, dissolve, leave not a rack behind, leave no trace; go, be no more; die &c. 360.

annihilate, render null, nullify; abrogate &c. 756; destroy &c. 162; take away; remove &c. (*displace*) 185.

Adj. inexistent, non-existent &c. 1; negative, blank, null and void; missing, omitted; absent &c. 187; visionary &c. 515.

unreal, potential, virtual; baseless, *in nubibus;* unsubstantial &c. 4; vain;

un-born, -created, -begotten, -conceived, -produced, -made.

perished, annihilated &c. *v.*; extinct, exhausted, gone, lost, departed; defunct &c. (*dead*) 360; *spurlos versenkt.*

fabulous, ideal &c. (*imaginary*) 515; supposititious &c. 514.

Adv. negatively, virtually, &c. *adj.*

[1]

&c. 12; analogy; similarity &c. 17; affinity, intimacy, friendship; homology, alliance, homogeneity, association, rapport; approximation &c. (*nearness*) 197; filiation &c. (*consanguinity*) 11; interest; relevancy &c. 23; relationship, relative position; relativity; interrelation &c. 12.

comparison &c. 464; ratio, proportion.

link, tie, bond, bond of union.

V. be-related &c. *adj.*; have a relation &c. *n.*; relate –, refer- to; bear upon, regard, concern, touch, affect, have to do with; pertain –, belong –, appertain- to; have respect to; answer to; interest.

bring -into relation with, – to bear upon; connect, associate, draw a parallel; link &c. 43.

Adj. relative; correlative &c. 12; cognate; relating to &c. *v.*; relative to, in relation with, referable *or* referrible to; belonging to &c. *v.*; appurtenant to, in common with.

related, connected; implicated, associated, affiliated, akin, allied to; collateral, cognate, congenial, kindred, affinitive, *en rapport*, in touch with.

approxima-tive, -ting; approaching; proportion-al, -ate, -able; allusive, comparable.

in the same -category &c. 75; like &c. 17; relevant &c. (*apt*) 23.

Adv. relatively &c. *adj.*; pertinently &c. 23.

thereof; as -to, – for, – respects, – regards; about; concerning &c. *v.*; anent; relating –, as relates- to; with -relation, – reference, – respect, – regard- to; in respect of; while speaking –, *à propos-* of; in connection with; by the -way, – by; whereas; for –, in -as much as; in point of, as far as; on the -part, – score- of; *quoad hoc; pro re natâ*; under the -head &c. (*class*) 75- of; in the matter of, *in re.*

Phr. 'thereby hangs a tale.'

junction) 44; inconsequence, independence; incommensurability; irreconcilableness &c. (*disagreement*) 24; heterogeneity; unconformity &c. 83; irrelevancy, impertinence, *nihil ad rem*; intrusion &c. 24.

V. have no -relation &c. 9 to, – bearing upon, – concern &c. 9 with, – business with; not -concern &c. 9; have -nothing to do with, – no business there; intrude, &c. 24.

bring –, drag –, haul –, lug- in head and shoulders.

Adj. irrelative, irrespective, unrelated, irrelated; arbitrary; independent, unallied; un-, dis-connected; adrift, isolated, insular; extraneous, strange, alien, foreign, outlandish, exotic.

not comparable, incommensurable, heterogeneous; unconformable &c. 83.

irrelevant; rambling &c. 279; inapplicable; not -pertinent, – to the purpose; impertinent, inapposite, beside the mark, *à propos de bottes*; away from –, foreign to –, beside- the -purpose, – question, – transaction, – point; misplaced &c. (*intrusive*) 24.

remote, far fetched, out of the way, forced, neither here nor there, quite another thing; detached, segregated, segregate.

multifarious; discordant &c. 24.

incidental, parenthetical, *obiter dictum*, episodic.

Adv. parenthetically &c. *adj.*; by the -way, – by; *en passant*, incidentally; irrespectively &c. *adj.*; without reference, – regard- to; in the abstract &c. 87; *a se.*

11. [Relations of kindred.] Consanguinity.—N. consanguinity, relationship, kindred, blood; parentage &c. (*paternity*) 166; filiation, affiliation; lineage, agnation, connection, cognation, alliance; family -connection, – tie; ties of blood; blood relationship; nepotism.

kins-man, -folk; people; kith and kin; rela-tion, -tive; connection; sib; next of kin; uncle, aunt, nephew, niece; cousin, -german; first –, second- cousin; cousin -once, – twice &c.- removed; near –, distant- relation; brother, sister, one's own flesh and blood.

family, patriarch, matriarch; fraternity; brother-, sister-, cousin-hood. race, stock, generation; sept &c. 166; stirps, side; strain; breed, clan, tribe.

V. be -related &c. *adj.* – to; claim -relationship &c. *n.*- with.

Adj. related, akin, consanguineous, matrilinear, patrilineal, of the blood, family, allied, collateral; cog-, ag-, con-nate; kindred; affiliated, affine; fraternal, avuncular.

intimately –, nearly –, closely –, remotely –, distantly- related, – allied; german.

12. [Double or reciprocal relation.] **Correlation.—N.** reciprocalness &c. *adj.*; recipro-city, -cality, -cation; mutuality, correlation, correspondence, interdependence; interchange &c. 148; exchange, barter; interrelation, interconnection; alternation, see-saw.

V. reciprocate, alternate; interchange &c. 148; exchange; counterchange; interact, correspond, mutualize, give and take.

Adj. reciprocal, mutual, commutual, correlative; alternate; interchangeable; international; correspondent, complementary, analogous.

Adv. *mutatis mutandis*; *vice versâ*; each other; by turns &c. 148; reciprocally &c. *adj.*; to and fro &c. 314.

13. Identity.—N. identity, sameness, oneness, ditto, homogeneity; unity, co-incidence, coalescence; convertibility; equality &c. 27; selfness, self, oneself; identification.

monotony, tautology &c. (*repetition*) 104.

synonym.

fac-simile &c. (*copy*) 21; *alter ego* &c. (*similar*) 17; *ipsissima verba* &c. (*exactness*) 494; same; self –, very –, one and the- same; very –, actual-thing; no other.

V. be -identical &c. *adj.*; match, coincide, coalesce.

treat as –, render- -the same, –identical; identify; recognize the identity of.

Adj. identical; self, ilk; the -same &c. *n.*; self same; synonymous; one and the same.

coincid-, coalesc-ent, -ing; indistinguishable; one; equivalent &c. (*equal*) 27; much -the same, – of a muchness; unaltered.

Adv. identically &c. *adj.*; on all fours; *ibid-, -em.*

14. [Non-coincidence.] **Contrariety. —N.** contrariety, contrast, foil, antithesis, oppositeness; counterpole; contradiction; antagonism &c. (*opposition*) 708; counteraction &c. 179.

inversion &c. 218; the -opposite, – reverse, – inverse, – converse, – antipodes, – other extreme &c. 237.

antonym.

V. be -contrary &c. *adj.*; contrast with, oppose; differ *toto cœlo*.

invert, reverse, turn the tables &c. 218.

contra-dict, -vene; antagonize &c. 708.

Adj. contrar-y, -ious, -iant; opposite, counter, dead against; ad-, con-, reverse; opposed, antithetical, contrasted, antipodean, antagonistic, opposing; conflicting, inconsistent, contradictory, at cross purposes; negative; hostile &c. 708.

differing *toto cœlo*; diametrically opposite; as opposite as -black and white, – light and darkness, – fire and water, – the poles, as different as chalk from cheese; 'Hyperion to a satyr'; quite the -contrary, – reverse; no such thing, just the other way, *tout au contraire*.

Adv. contrarily &c. *adj.*; *contra*, contrariwise, *per contra*, on the contrary, nay rather; topsy-turvy; *vice versâ*; on the other hand &c. (*in compensation*) 30.

15. Difference.—N. difference, unlikeness; heterogeneity; vari-ance, -ation, -ety; diversity, dissimilarity &c. 18; disagreement &c. 24; disparity &c. (*inequality*) 28; distinction, contradistinction; distinctness; discrepancy, divergence, contrast &c. 18; nonconformity, incompatibility, antithesis.

discord &c. 713.

modification, moods and tenses.

nice –, fine –, delicate –, subtle- distinction; shade of difference, *nuance;* discrimination &c. 465; *differentia.*

different thing, something else, variant, apple off another tree, horse of another colour, another pair of shoes; this that or the other.

V. be -different &c. *adj.;* differ, vary, ablude, mismatch, contrast; diverge –, depart –, deviate- -from; divaricate; differ *-toto cælo, – longo intervallo.*

disagree &c. 713.

vary, modify &c. (*change*) 140.

discriminate &c. 465.

Adj. differing &c. *v.;* different, diverse, divided, heterogeneous; distinguishable; varied, modified; divergent, incongruous, diversified, various; discrepant, dissentient, differential; divers, all manner of; variform &c. 81; discordant &c. 713.

other, another, not the same; unequal &c. 28; unmatched; widely apart.

distinctive, characteristic; discriminative; distinguishing.

Adv. differently &c. *adj.*

Phr. *il y a fagots et fagots; quot homines tot sententiæ;* one man's meat is another man's poison.

2°. CONTINUOUS RELATION

16. Uniformity. — N. uniformity; homogene-ity, -ousness; continuity, stability, consistency; connatural-ity, -ness; homology; accordance; conformity &c. 82; agreement &c. 23.

regularity, constancy, even tenor, routine; monotony, evenness, sameness, dead level; steadiness, equability, unity.

V. be -uniform &c. *adj.;* accord with &c. 23; run through.

become -uniform &c. *adj.;* conform to &c. 82.

render uniform &c. *adj.;* assimilate, level, smooth, dress.

Adj. uniform; homo-geneous, -logous; of a piece, consistent, steady; connatural; monotonous, changeless, dreary, even, invariable, equable, level, regular, stereotyped, unchanged, unvarying; methodical &c. 60; habitual &c. 613.

Adv. uniformly &c. *adj.;* uniformly with &c. (*conformably*) 82; in harmony with &c. (*agreeing*) 23; in a -rut, – groove.

always, ever &c. 112; invariably, without exception, never otherwise; by clock-work; endlessly &c. 112.

Phr. *ab uno disce omnes.*

16a. [Absence or want of uniformity.] **Non-uniformity. — N.** diversity irregularity, unevenness; multiformity &c. 81; unconformity &c. 83; roughness &c. 256; heterogeneity, heteromorphism.

Adj. diversified, varied, irregular, uneven, rough &c. 256; multifarious; multiform &c. 81; of various kinds; all -manner, – sorts, – kinds- of.

Adv. in all manner of ways, here there and everywhere.

3°. PARTIAL RELATION

17. Similarity.—N. similarity, resemblance, likeness, similitude, sem-

18. Dissimilarity.—N. dissimil-arity, -itude; unlikeness, diversity, disparity

blance; affinity, approximation, parallelism; parity; agreement &c. 23; ana-logy, -logicalness; correspondence, equality &c.

connatural-ness, -ity; brotherhood, family likeness.

alliteration, rhyme, pun.

repetition &c. 104; sameness &c. (*identity*) 13; uniformity &c. 16.

analogue; the like; match, *pendant*, fellow, companion, pair, mate, twin, double, counterpart, brother, sister; one's second self, *alter ego*, chip of the old block, *par nobile fratrum*, *Arcades ambo*, birds of a feather, *et hoc genus omne*.

parallel; simile; type &c. (*metaphor*) 521; image &c. (*representation*) 554; photograph; close -, striking -, speaking -, faithful &c. *adj.* - likeness, - resemblance.

V. be -similar &c. *adj.*; look like, resemble, bear resemblance, favour; savour -, smack- of; approximate; parallel, match, rhyme with; take after; imitate &c. 19; run in pairs.

render -similar &c. *adj.*; assimilate, approximate, bring near; connaturalize, make alike; rhyme, pun.

Adj. similar; resembling &c. *v.*; like, alike; twin.

analog-ous, -ical; parallel, of a piece; such as, so.

connatural, congeneric, allied to; corresponding, cognate; akin to &c. (*consanguineous*) 11.

approximate, much the same, near, close, something like, such like; a show of; mock, *pseudo*, simulating, representing.

exact &c. (*true*) 494; lifelike, faithful, realistic; true to -nature, - the life; the -very image - picture- of; for all the world like, *comme deux gouttes d'eau*; as like as -two peas, - it can stare; *instar omnium*, cast in the same mould, ridiculously like.

Adv. as if, so to speak; as -, as if- it were; *quasi*, just as, *veluti in speculum*.

dissemblance; divergence, inequality, difference &c. 15; novelty; variation, variety, originality, disguise.

V. be -unlike &c. *adj.*; vary &c. (*differ*) 15; bear no resemblance to, differ *toto cœlo*.

render -unlike &c. *adj.*; vary &c. (*diversify*) 140.

Adj. dissimilar, unlike, disparate; of a different kind &c. (*class*) 75; unmatched, unique; new, novel; unprecedented &c. 83; original.

nothing of the kind; no such -, quite another- thing; far from it, other than, cast in a different mould, *tertium quid*, as like as a dock as a daisy, 'very like a whale'; as different as -chalk from cheese, - Macedon and Monmouth; *lucus a non lucendo*.

diversified &c. 16a.

Adv. otherwise, *alias*.

---

19. Imitation.

N. imitation; copying &c. *v.*; transcription; repetition, mimeograph, mimeotype, duplication, reduplication; quotation; reproduction.

mockery, mimicry, mime, simulation, impersonation; representation &c. 554; semblance, simulacrum; pretence; copy &c. 21; assimilation.

paraphrase, parody &c. 21.

plagiarism; forgery &c. (*falsehood*) 544.

imitator, echo, cuckoo, parrot, ape, monkey, mocking-bird, mimic, impersonator; copyist.

V. imitate, copy, mirror, reflect, reproduce, repeat, borrow; do like, echo, re-echo, catch; transcribe; match, parallel.

20. Non-Imitation.

N. no imitation, genuineness, originality; creativeness.

Adj. unimitated, uncopied; unmatched, unparalleled; inimitable &c. 33; *unique*, original, primordial, primary, pristine, underived, first-hand, archetypal, prototypal.

---

mock, take off, mimic, ape, simulate, personate, impersonate; forge; act &c. (*drama*) 599; represent &c. 554; counterfeit, duplicate; portray, parody, travesty, caricature, burlesque.

follow –, tread- in the- -steps, – footsteps, – wake- of; pattern after, take pattern by; follow -suit, – the example of; walk in the shoes of, take a leaf out of another's book, strike in with; take –, model -after; emulate.

Adj. imitated &c. *v.*; mock, mimic; counterfeit, false, pseudo; modelled after, moulded on, paraphrastic; literal; imitative, apish; second-hand; imitable; sham &c. 545.

Adv. literally, to the letter, strictly, precisely, *verbatim, literatim, sic, totidem verbis*, word for word, *mot à mot*.

Phr. like master like man.

20a. **Variation.**—**N.** variation; alteration &c. (*change*) 140.
modification, moods and tenses; modulation.
divergency &c. 291; deviation &c. 279; aberration; innovation.
V. vary &c. (*change*) 140; deviate &c. 279; diverge &c. 291.
Adj. varied &c. *v.*; modified; dissimilar &c. 18; diversified &c. 16*a*.

21. [Result of imitation.] Copy.—N.
copy, fac-simile, counterpart, *effigies*, effigy, symbol, image, form, likeness, similitude, semblance, resemblance, cast, electrotype, stereotype, tracing, ectype; imitation &c. 19; model, representation, adumbration, study; counterfeit presentment, portrait &c. (*representment*) 554.

duplicate; transcript, -ion; reflex, -ion; shadow, echo; chip of the old block; reprint, reproduction, casting, engraving, replica; transfer; second edition &c. (*repetition*) 104; *réchauffé*; apograph, fair copy, revise.

parody, caricature, cartoon, burlesque, travesty, paraphrase.
servile -copy, – imitation; counterfeit &c. (*deception*) 545; *pasticcio*.
Adj. faithful; lifelike &c. (*similar*) 17.

22. [Thing copied.] Prototype.—N.
prototype, original, model, pattern, founding, precedent, standard, scantling, type, arche-, anti-type; protoplast, copy-book, module, exemplar, example, ensample, specimen; paradigm; guide; templet; lay-figure.

text, copy, manuscript, MS., design; fugleman, keynote.

die, mould; matrix, engraving, last, plasm; pro-, proto-plasm; mint; seal, punch, *intaglio*, negative, stamp.

V. be –, set- an example; set a copy; standardize.

4°. GENERAL RELATION

23. Agreement. — N. agreement; ac-cord, -cordance; unison, harmony, syntony; concord &c. 714; concordance, concert, understanding, convention, *entente -cordiale, consortium*, consensus of opinion, pact, mutual understanding, unanimity.

conformity &c. 82; conformance; uniformity &c. 16; consonance, consentaneousness, consistency; congruity, -ence; keeping; congeniality; correspondence, concinnity, parallelism, apposition, union.

fitness, aptness &c. *adj.*; relevancy;

24. Disagreement. — N. disagreement; dis-cord, -cordance; disunion, dissonance, dissidence, discrepancy; unconformity &c. 83; incongru-ity, -ence; discongruity, *mésalliance*, oxymoron; jarring &c. *v.*; clash, collision, dissension &c. 713; conflict &c. (*opposition*) 708; controversy &c. 720; falling out, wrangle, argument.

disparity, mismatch, misfit, disproportion; disproportionateness &c. *adj.*; variance, divergence, repugnance.

unfitness &c. *adj.*; inaptitude, impropriety; inapplicability &c. *adj.*; in-

pertinen-ce, -cy; sortance; case in point; aptitude, coaptation, propriety, applicability, admissibility, commensurability, compatibility, suitability; cognation &c. (*relation*) 9.

adaptation, adjustment, arrangement, graduation, accommodation; reconcil-iation -ement; assimilation; attunement.

consent &c. (*assent*) 488; concurrence &c. 178; co-operation &c. 709.

right man in the right place, very thing; quite –, just- the thing.

V. be -accordant &c. *adj.*; agree, accord, harmonize; correspond, tally, respond; meet, suit, fit, befit, do, adapt itself to; fall in –, chime in –, square –, quadrate –, consort –, comport- with; dovetail, assimilate; fit like a glove; fit to a -tittle, – T; match &c. 17; become one.

consent &c. (*assent*) 488.

render -accordant &c. *adj.*; fit, suit, adapt, accommodate; graduate; adjust &c. (*render equal*) 27; dress, regulate, readjust; accord, harmonize, reconcile; fadge, dovetail, square.

Adj. agreeing, suiting &c. *v.*; in accord, accordant, concordant, consonant, congruous, consentaneous, correspondent, corresponding, homologous, congenial; becoming; harmonious, reconcilable, conformable; in -accordance, – harmony, – keeping, – unison, &c. *n.*- with; at one with, of one mind, of a piece; consistent, compatible, proportionate, answerable; commensurate; on all fours.

apt, apposite, pertinent, pat; to the -point, – purpose; happy, felicitous, germane, *ad rem*, in point, bearing upon, applicable, relevant, admissible.

fit, adapted, *in loco*, *à propos*, appropriate, seasonable, sortable, suitable, idoneous, deft; meet &c. (*expedient*) 646.

at home, in one's proper element.

Adv. *à propos of*; pertinently &c. *adj.*; *pro rata*.

Phr. *rem acu tetigisti*, the cap fits.

consistency, inconcinnity; irrelevancy &c. (*irrelation*) 10.

misjoin-ing, -der; syncretism, intrusion, interference; *concordia discors*.

fish out of water.

V. disagree; clash, quarrel, jar &c. (*discord*) 713; interfere, intrude, come amiss; not concern &c. 10; mismatch; *humano capiti cervicem jungere equinam.*

Adj. disagreeing &c. *v.*; discordant, discrepant; at -variance, – war; hostile, antagonistic, repugnant, factious, contradictory, dissentious, incompatible, irreconcilable, inconsistent with; unconformable, exceptional &c. 83; intrusive, incongruous; disproportionate, -ed; unharmonious; unconsonant; divergent, repugnant to.

inapt, unapt, inappropriate, inept, infelicitous, improper; unsuit-ed, -able; inapplicable; un-fit, -fitting, -befitting; unbecoming; ill-timed, ill-adapted, unseasonable, *mal à propos*, inadmissible; inapposite &c. (*irrelevant*) 10.

uncongenial; ill-assorted, -sorted, -matched; mis-matched, -mated, -joined, -placed; unaccommodating, irreducible, uncommensurable, unsympathetic.

out of -character, – keeping, – proportion, – joint, – tune, – place, – season, – its element; at -odds, – variance with.

Adv. in -defiance, – contempt, – spite-of; discordantly &c. *adj.*; *à tort et à travers.*

___

Section III.   QUANTITY

1°. Simple Quantity

25. [Absolute quantity.] **Quantity.—**
N. quantity, magnitude; size &c. (*dimensions*) 192; amplitude, mass,

26. [Relative quantity.] **Degree.—**
N. degree, grade, extent, measure, proportion, amount, ratio, stint, standard

amount, *quantum*, measure, measurement, substance, strength.

[Science of quantity.] Mathematics, Mathesis.

[Definite or finite quantity] arm-, hand-, mouth-, spoon-, thimble-, capful; stock, batch, lot, dose, ration, quotum, quota, pittance, driblet, part, portion &c. 51.

Adj. quantitative, some, any, more or less.

Adv. to the tune of.

———

height, pitch; reach, amplitude, range, scope, size, calibre; gradation, shade; tenor, compass; sphere, station, rank, standing; rate, way, sort.

point, mark, step, stage &c. (*term*) 71; intensity, strength &c. (*greatness*) 31.

V. compare, graduate, calibrate, measure.

Adj. comparative; gradual, shading off, gradational; within the bounds &c. (*limit*), 233.

Adv. by degrees, gradually, inasmuch, *pro tanto*; how-ever, -soever; step by step, bit by bit, little by little, inch by inch, drop by drop, gradatim; by -inches, – slow degrees, – little and little; in some -degree, – measure to some extent; just a bit.

2°. COMPARATIVE QUANTITY

27. [Sameness of quantity or degree.] **Equality.—N.** equality, parity, co-extension, symmetry, balance, poise; evenness, monotony, level.

equivalence; equi-pollence, -poise, -librium, -ponderance; par, quits; not a pin to choose; distinction without a difference, six of one and half a dozen of the other; identity &c. 13; similarity &c. 17; isotropism; coequality.

equalization, equation; equilibration, co-ordination, adjustment, readjustment.

drawn -game, -battle, draw, stalemate; neck and neck race; tie, dead heat.

match, peer, compeer, equal, mate, fellow, brother; equivalent.

V. be -equal &c. *adj.*; equal, match, reach, keep pace with, run abreast; come –, amount –, come up-to; be –, lie- on a level with; balance; cope with; come to the same thing; level off.

render -equal &c. *adj.*; equalize, level, dress, balance, equate, handicap, give points, trim, adjust, poise; fit, accommodate; adapt &c. (*render accordant*) 23; strike a balance; establish –, restore-equality, – equilibrium; readjust; stretch on the bed of Procrustes.

Adj. equal, even, level, monotonous, coequal, symmetrical, co-ordinate; on a -par, – level, – footing- with; up to the mark; equi parent.

equivalent, tantamount; quits; homologous; synonymous &c. 522; resolvable into, convertible, much at one, as broad as long, neither more nor less; much the same –, the same thing –, as good-as; all -one, – the same; equi-pollent, -ponderant, -ponderous, -balanced; equalized &c. *v.*; drawn; half and half; isochronous; isoperimetrical.

28. [Difference of quantity or degree.] **Inequality.—N.** inequality; dis-, im-parity; odds; difference &c. 15; ill-balanced; unevenness; inclination of the balance, partiality; shortcoming; casting – make- weight; superiority &c. 33; inferiority &c. 34.

V. be -unequal &c. *adj.*; countervail; have –, give the advantage; turn the scale; kick the beam; topple, -over; over-match &c. 33; not come up to &c. 34.

Adj. unequal, uneven, disparate, partial; un-, over-balanced; top-heavy, lop-sided.

Adv. *haud passibus æquis.*

———

Adv. equally &c. *adj.*; *pari passu, ad eundem, cæteris paribus*; *in equilibrio*; to all intents and purposes.

Phr. it -comes, -adds up, – amounts- to the same thing.

29. Mean.—N. mean, medium, intermedium, average, run of the mill, normal, balance; mediocrity, generality, rule, ordinary -run, -ruck; golden mean &c. (*mid-course*) 628; middle &c. 68; compromise &c. 774; neutrality; middle point, middle course.

V. split the difference; take the -average &c. *n.*; reduce to a -mean &c. *n.*; strike a balance, pair off.

Adj. mean, intermediate; medial; middle &c. 68; average, normal, standard; neutral; middling, moderate.

mediocre, middle-class; *bourgeois*, commonplace &c. (*unimportant*) 643.

Adv. on an average, in the long run; taking -one with another, – all things together, – it for all in all; *communibus annis*, in round numbers.

30. Compensation.—N. compensation, equation; commutation; indemnification; compromise &c. 774; neutralization, nullification; counteraction &c. 179; reaction; measure for measure; retaliation &c. 718; equalization &c. 27; redemption, recoupment, recompense.

set-off, offset; make- casting-weight; counterpoise, equipoise, ballast; indemnity, reparation &c. 790; equivalent, *quid pro quo*; bribe, hush-money, tribute &c. 784; amends &c. (*atonement*) 952; counterclaim, counterbalance, equiponderance, countervail, cross demand.

V. make -amends, – compensation; com-pensate, -pense; indemnify; counter-act, -vail, -poise; equiponderate; balance; out-, over-, counter-balance; set off, offset, cancel; hedge, square, give and take; make up -for, – lee way; cover, fill up, neutralize, nullify; equalize &c. 27; make good; redeem &c. (*atone*) 952; recoup, pay &c. 973.

Adj. compensat-ing, -ory; amendatory, reparative, countervailing &c. *v.*; in the opposite scale; equivalent &c. (*equal*) 27.

Adv. in -return, – consideration; but, however, yet, still, notwithstanding; neverthe-, nath-less; although, though; al-, how-beit; in spite of, despite; maugre; at -all events, – any rate; be that as it may, for all that, even so, on the other hand, at the same time, *quoad minus, quand même*, however that may be; after all, – is said and done; taking one thing with another &c. (*average*) 29.

QUANTITY BY COMPARISON WITH A STANDARD

31. Greatness.—N. greatness &c. *adj.*; magnitude; size &c. (*dimensions*) 192; multitude &c. (*number*) 102; immensity, enormity; infinity &c. 105; might, strength, intensity, fulness; importance &c. 642; fame &c. 873.

great quantity, quantity, deal, power, sight, pot, volume, world; mass, heap &c. (*assemblage*) 72; stock &c. (*store*) 636; peck, bushel, load, cargo; cart -, wagon -, car -, truck -, ship- load; flood, spring tide; abundance &c. (*sufficiency*) 639.

principal -, chief -, main -, greater -,

32. Smallness.—N. smallness &c. *adj.*; littleness &c. (*small size*) 193; tenuity; paucity; fewness &c. (*small number*) 103; meanness, insignificance &c. (*unimportance*) 643; mediocrity, moderation.

small quantity, *modicum, minimum*; vanishing point; material point, electron, atom, particle, molecule, corpuscle, point, dab, fleck, speck, dot, mote, jot, iota, ace; *minutiæ*, details; look, thought, idea, *soupçon*, whit, tittle, shade, shadow; spark, *scintilla*, gleam; touch, cast; grain, scruple,

major –, best –, essential- part; bulk, mass &c. (*whole*) 50.

V. be -great &c. *adj.*; run high, soar, loom up, tower, bulk large, transcend; rise –, carry- to a great height; know no bounds; scale, overtop, ascend.

enlarge &c. (*increase*) 35, (*expand*) 194.

Adj. great; greater &c. 33; large, considerable, fair, above par; big, massive, huge &c. (*large in size*) 192; ample; abundant &c. (*enough*) 639; Herculean &c. 159; full, intense, strong, sound, passing, heavy, plenary, deep, high; signal, at its height, in the zenith.

world-wide, wide-spread, extensive; wholesale; many &c. 102.

goodly, noble, precious, mighty; sad, grave, serious; far gone, arrant, down-right; utter, -most; crass, gross, arch, profound, intense, consummate; rank, unmitigated, red-hot, desperate; glaring, flagrant, stark staring; thorough-paced, -going; roaring, thumping, thundering, strapping, whacking; extraordinary; important &c. 642; unsurpassed &c. (*supreme*) 33; complete &c. 52.

vast, immense, enormous, extreme; inordinate, excessive, extravagant, exorbitant, outrageous, preposterous, unconscionable, swingeing, monstrous, over-grown; towering, stupendous, prodigious, astonishing, incredible; terrific, frightful; marvellous &c. (*wonder*) 870; grand.

unlimited &c. (*infinite*) 105; unapproachable, unutterable, indescribable, ineffable, unspeakable, inexpressible, beyond expression, fabulous.

un-diminished, -abated, -reduced, -restricted.

absolute, positive, stark, decided, unequivocal, essential, perfect, finished.

remarkable, of mark, marked, pointed, veriest; noticeable, uncommon, noteworthy, eminent &c. 873.

Adv. [in a positive degree] truly &c. (*truth*) 494; decidedly, unequivocally, purely, absolutely, seriously, essentially, fundamentally, radically, downright, in all conscience; for the most part, in the main.

[in a complete degree] entirely &c. (*completely*) 52; abundantly, &c. (*suf-*

granule, globule, minim, sup, sip, sop, spice, drop, droplet, sprinkling, dash, smack, tinge, tincture; inch, patch, scantling, dole; scrap, shred, tag, splinter, rag, tatter, cantlet, flitter, gobbet, mite, bit, morsel, crumb, seed, fritter, shive; snip, -pet; snick, snack, snatch, slip, scrag; chip, -ping; shiver, sliver, driblet, clipping, paring, shaving, hair.

nutshell; thimble-, spoon-, hand-, cap-, mouth-ful; fragment; fraction &c. (*part*) 51; drop in the ocean, drop in the bucket.

animalcule &c. 193.

trifle &c. (*unimportant thing*) 643; mere –, next to- nothing; hardly anything; just enough to swear by; the shadow of a shade.

finiteness, finite quantity.

V. be -shall &c. *adj.*; lie in a nutshell.

diminish &c. (*decrease*) 36, (*contract*) 195.

Adj. small, little, tiny, weeny; diminutive &c. (*small in size*) 193; minute; minikin, fine, inconsiderable, dribbling, paltry &c. (*unimportant*) 643; faint &c. (*weak*) 160; slender, light, slight, scanty, scant, limited; meagre &c. (*insufficient*) 640; sparing; few &c. 103; low, so-so, middling, tolerable, no great shakes; below –, under- -par, – the mark; at a low ebb; half-way; moderate, modest; tender, subtle; petty, shallow, skin-deep.

inappreciable, evanescent, infinitesimal, homœopathic, very small, atomic, molecular, ultra-, -microscopic.

petty, shallow &c. 499.

mere, simple, sheer, stark, bare; near run.

Adv. [in a small degree] to a small extent, on a small scale; a -little, – wee, – tiny bit; slightly &c. *adj.*; imperceptibly; miserably, wretchedly; insufficiently &c. 640; imperfectly; faintly &c. 160; passably, pretty well, well enough.

[in a certain or limited degree] partially, in part; in –, to a certain degree; to a certain extent; comparatively; some, rather; in some -degree, -measure; some-thing, -what; simply, only, purely, merely; at –, at the- -least,

ficiently) 639; widely, far and wide. [in a great or high degree] greatly &c. *adj.*; much, muckle, well, indeed, very, very much, a deal, no end of, most, not a little; pretty, – well; enough, in a great measure, passing richly; to a -large, – great, – gigantic-extent; on a large scale; so; never –, ever- so; ever so much; by wholesale; mightily, mighty, powerfully; with a witness, *ultra*, in the extreme, extremely, exceedingly, intensely, exquisitely, acutely, indefinitely, immeasurably; beyond -compare, – comparison, – measure, – all bounds; incalculably, infinitely.

[in a supreme degree] pre-eminently, superlatively &c. (*superiority*) 33.

[in a too great degree] immoderately, unduly, monstrously, grossly, preposterously, inordinately, exorbitantly, excessively, enormously, out of all proportion, with a vengeance.

[in a marked degree] particularly, remarkably, singularly, curiously, uncommonly, unusually, peculiarly, notably, signally, strikingly, pointedly, mainly, chiefly; famously, egregiously, prominently, glaringly, emphatically, strangely, wonderfully, amazingly, surprisingly, astonishingly, incredibly, marvellously, awfully, stupendously.

[in an exceptional degree] peculiarly &c. (*unconformity*) 83.

[in a violent degree] furiously &c. (*violence*) 173; severely, desperately, tremendously, extravagantly, confoundedly, deucedly, devilishly, with a vengeance; *à –, à toute- outrance*.

[in a painful degree] painfully, sadly, grossly, sorely, bitterly, piteously, grievously, miserably, cruelly, woefully, lamentably, shockingly, frightfully, dreadfully, fearfully, terribly, horribly, distressingly, balefully.

– most; ever so little, as little as may be, *tant soit peu*, in ever so small a degree; thus far, *pro tanto*, within bounds, in a manner, after a fashion.

almost, nearly, well nigh, short of, not quite, all but; near –, close- upon; *peu s'en faut*, near the mark; within an ·ace, – inch- of; on the brink of; scarcely, hardly, barely, only just, no more than.

[in an uncertain degree] about, thereabouts, somewhere about, nearly, say; be the same -more, – little more- or less.

[in no degree] no- ways, – wise; not -at all, – in the least, – a bit, – a bit of it, – a whit, – a jot, – a shadow; in no -wise, – respect; by no -means, – manner of means; on no account, at no hand.

QUANTITY BY COMPARISON WITH A SIMILAR OBJECT

33. Superiority.—N. supremacy, superiority, majority; greatness &c. 31; advantage, odds, pull; preponderance, -ation; predominance, vantage ground, coign of vantage, prevalence, partiality; personal superiority; sovereignty &c. 737; nobility &c. (*rank*) 875; Triton among the minnows, *primus inter pares, nulli secundus*, superman; captain &c. 745.

supremacy, pre-eminence; primacy, lead, *maximum*; record; climax, crest, top; culmination &c. (*summit*) 210; transcendence; *ne plus ultra*; lion's share, Benjamin's mess; excess; bisque,

34. Inferiority.—N. inferiority, minority, subordinancy; shortcoming, deficiency; handicap; *minimum*; smallness &c. 32; imperfection, shabbiness.

[personal inferiority] commonalty &c. 876; subordinate, substitute, sub.

V. be -inferior &c. *adj.*; fall –, come- short of; not -pass, – come up to; want.

become –, render- smaller &c. (*decrease*) 36, (*contract*) 195; hide its diminished head, retire into the shade, yield the palm, play second fiddle, take a back seat; bow.

Adj. inferior, smaller; small &c. 32;

surplus &c. (*remainder*) 40, (*redundance*) 641.

V. be -superior &c. *adj.*; exceed, excel, transcend; out-do, -balance, -weigh, -rival, -Herod, outrank, pass, surpass, surmount, get ahead of; over-top, -ride, -pass, -balance, -weigh, -match; top, o'er-top, cap, beat, win out, cut out; beat hollow; outstrip &c. 303; eclipse, throw into the shade, take the shine out of, put one's nose out of joint; have the -upper hand, – whip hand of, – advantage; turn the scale, play first fiddle &c. (*importance*) 642; preponderate, predominate, prevail; precede, take precedence, come first; come to a head, culminate; beat &c. all others, bear the palm; break the record, take the cake.

minor, less, lesser, deficient, minus, lower, subordinate, secondary; secondrate &c. (*imperfect*) 651; sub, subaltern; thrown into the shade; weighed in the balance and found wanting; not fit to hold a candle to.

least, smallest &c. (*see* little, small &c. 193); lowest.

diminished &c. (*decreased*) 36; reduced &c. (*contracted*) 195; unimportant &c. 643.

Adv. less; under –, below- -the mark, – par; at -the bottom of the scale, – a low ebb, – a disadvantage; short of, under.

become –, render- -larger, &c. (*increase*) 35, (*expand*) 194.

Adj. superior, greater, major, higher; exceeding &c. *v.*; great &c. 31; distinguished, *ultra*; vaulting; more than a match for.

supreme, greatest, maximal, maximum, utmost, paramount, pre-eminent, foremost, crowning; first-rate &c. (*important*) 642, (*excellent*) 648; unrivalled; peer-, match-less; none such, second to none, *sans pareil*; un-paragoned, -paralleled, -equalled, -approached, -surpassed; superlative, inimitable, *facile princeps*, incomparable, sovereign, without parallel, *nulli secundus, ne plus ultra*; beyond -compare, – comparison; culminating &c. (*topmost*) 210; transcendent, -ental; *plus royaliste que le Roi*.

increased &c. (*added to*) 35; enlarged &c. (*expanded*) 194.

Adv. beyond, more, over; over –, above- the mark; above par; upwards –, in advance- of; over and above; at the top of the scale, on the crest, at its height.

[in a superior or supreme degree] eminently, egregiously, pre-eminently, surpassing, prominently, superlatively, supremely, above all, of all things, the most, to crown all, *par excellence*, principally, especially, particularly, peculiarly, *a fortiori*, even, yea, still more.

Phr. 'we shall not look upon his like again.'

CHANGES IN QUANTITY

35. Increase—N. increase, augmentation, addition, enlargement, extension; dilatation &c. (*expansion*) 194; multiplication; increment, accretion; accession &c. 37; production &c. 161; development, growth; aggrandizement, aggravation, intensification; rise; ascent &c. 305; anabasis; ex-aggeration, -acerbation; spread &c. (*dispersion*) 73; flood-, spring-, -tide; gain, produce, profit &c. 618; booty, plunder &c. 793.

V. increase, augment, add to, en-large; dilate &c. (*expand*) 194; grow,

36. Non-Increase, Decrease.—N. decrease, diminution; lessening &c. *v.*; subtraction &c. 38; reduction, abatement, declension; shrinkage &c. (*contraction*) 195; coarctation; abridgment &c. (*shortening*) 201; extenuation.

subsidence, catabasis, wane, ebb-, neap-tide, decline; descent &c. 306; decrement, reflux, depreciation; erosion, wear and tear, deterioration &c. 659; anticlimax; mitigation &c. (*moderation*) 174.

V. decrease, diminish. lessen: abridge

wax, mount, swell, get ahead, gain strength; advance; run –, shoot- up; rise; ascend &c. 305; sprout &c. 194.

aggrandize; raise, exalt; deepen, **heighten; lengthen; thicken;** strengthen; intensify, enhance, inflate, magnify, double, redouble; multiply; aggravate, exaggerate; ex-asperate, -acerbate; add fuel to the flame, *oleum addere camino,* superadd &c. (*add*) 37; spread &c. (*disperse*) 73.

Adj. increased &c. *v.*; on the increase, undiminished; additional &c. (*added*) 37; increasing &c. *v.*; growing, crescent, intensive, cumulative.

Adv. *crescendo,* increasingly.

Phr. *vires acquirit eundo.*

&c. (*shorten*) 201; shrink &c. (*contract*) 195; drop –, fall –, tail- off; fall away, waste, wear, erode; wane, ebb, decline; descend &c. 306; subside; deliquesce, melt –, die -away; retire into the shade, hide its diminished head, fall to a low ebb, run low, languish, decay, crumble, consume away.

bate, abate, dequantitate; discount; depreciate; extenuate, lower, weaken, attenuate, fritter away; mitigate &c. (*moderate*) 174; belittle, minimize; dwarf, throw into the shade; keep down, reduce &c. 195; shorten &c. 201; subtract &c. 38.

Adj. unincreased &c. (*see* increase &c. 35); decreased &c. *v.*; decreasing &c. *v.*; on the -wane &c. *n.*; deliquescent.

Adv. *diminuendo, decrescendo,* decreasingly.

3°. CONJUNCTIVE QUANTITY

37. Addition.—N. addition, annexation, adjection; junction &c. 43; super-position, -addition, -junction, -fetation; accession, reinforcement; increase &c. 35; increment, supplement; accompaniment &c. 88; interposition &c. 228; insertion &c. 300; summation &c. 85; adjunct &c. 39.

V. add, annex, adject, affix, attach, superadd, subjoin, superpose; clap –, saddle- on; tack to, postfix, append, tag; ingraft; saddle with; sprinkle; introduce &c. (*interpose*) 228; insert &c. 300.

become added, accrue; ad-, supervene; add up &c. 85.

reinforce, strengthen, swell the ranks of; augment &c. 35.

Adj. added &c. *v.*; additional; supplement, -al, -ary; suppletory, subjunctive; adjec-, adsci-, asci-titious; additive, extra, spare, further, fresh, more, new, ulterior, other, auxiliary, supernumerary, accessory.

Adv. in addition, more, plus, extra; and, also, likewise, too, furthermore, further, item; and -also, – eke; else, besides, to boot, *et cætera;* &c.; and so -on, – forth; into the bargain, *cum multis aliis,* over and above, moreover.

with, withal; including, inclusive, as well as, not to mention, let

38. Non-Addition. Subduction.—N. sub-traction, -duction; deduction, retrenchment; removal; ab-, sub-lation; abstraction &c. (*taking*) 789; garbling &c. *v.*; mutilation, detruncation; amputation, severance; abs-, ex-, re-cision; curtailment &c. 201; minuend, subtrahend; decrease &c. 36; abrasion.

V. sub-tract, -duct; rebate, de-duct, -duce; bate, retrench; remove, withdraw; take -from, – away; detract.

garble, mutilate, amputate, sever, detruncate; cut -off, – away, – out; expurgate; abscind, excise; pare, thin, prune, decimate; abrade, scrape, file; geld, castrate, emasculate, unman, spay, caponize; eliminate.

diminish &c. 36; curtail &c. (*shorten*) 201; deprive of &c. (*take*) 789; weaken-

Adj. subtracted &c. *v.*; subtractive-tailless, acaudal.

Adv. in -deduction &c. *n.*; less, short of; minus, without, except, excepting, with the exception of, barring, bar, save, exclusive of, save and except, with a reservation.

alone; together –, along –, coupled –, in conjunction- with; con-jointly; jointly &c. 43.

39. [Thing added.] Adjunct.—N. adjunct; addit-ion, -ament; *additum,* affix, appendage, annex; augment, -ation; increment, reinforcement, supernumerary, accessory, item; garnish, sauce; accompaniment &c. 88; adjective, *addendum,* accession, complement, supplement; continuation; extension, subscript, tag, appendix, postscript, interlineation, interpolation, insertion.

rider, codicil, off-shoot, episode, side issue, corollary; piece; flap, lapel, label, tab, strip, fold, lappet, apron, skirt, embroidery, trappings, *cortège;* tail, suffix &c. (*sequel*) 65; wing.

Adj. additional &c. 37.

Adv. in addition &c. 37.

40. [Thing remaining.] Remainder•—N. remainder, residue; remains, *remanet,* remnant, rest, relic, relict; leavings, heel-tap, odds and ends, cheese-parings, candle ends, orts; *residuum;* dottle, dregs &c. (*dirt*) 653; refuse &c. (*useless*) 645; stubble, result, educt; fag-end, stub; ruins, wreck, skeleton, stump; *alluvium.*

surplus, overplus, excess; balance, complement; superfluity &c. (*redundance*) 641; surviv-al, -ance; afterglow.

V. remain; be -left &c. *adj.;* exceed, survive; leave.

Adj. remaining, left; left -behind, – over; residu-al, -ary; over, odd; unconsumed, sedimentary; surviving; net; exceeding, over and above; out-lying, -standing; cast off &c. 782; superfluous &c. (*redundant*) 641.

40a. [Thing deducted.] Decrement.—N. decrement, discount, rebate, defect, loss, deduction, eduction, tare; drawback; waste, wastage; reprise.

41. [Forming a whole without coherence.] Mixture.—N. mix-, admix-, commix-ture, -tion, mingling; commixion, immixture, interfusion, intermixture, alloyage, matrimony; junction &c. 43; combination &c. 48; entanglement, interlacing; miscegenation, inter-breeding.

impregnation; in-, dif-, suf-, trans fusion: infiltration; seasoning, sprinkling, interlarding; interpolation &c. 228; adulteration, sophistication.

[Thing mixed] tinge, tincture, touch, dash, smack, sprinkling, spice, seasoning, infusion, *soupçon.*

[Compound resulting from mixture] alloy, brass, bronze, pewter &c.; amalgam, *magma,* blend, half-and-half, *mélange, tertium quid,* miscellany, *ambigu,* medley, mess, hash, hotchpotch, hodgepodge, *pasticcio,* patchwork, odds and ends, all sorts; jumble &c. (*disorder*) 59; salad, sauce, mash, *omnium gatherum,* gallimaufry, ragout, *olla podrida, olio,* salmagundi, *potpourri,* Noah's ark; texture, mingled yarn; mosaic &c. (*variegation*) 440.

half-blood, -caste, -breed, Eurasian; mulatto; terc-, quart-, quint-eron &c.; quad-, octo-roon; *griffo, zambo;* cross, hybrid, mongrel &c. 83.

42. [Freedom from mixture.] Simpleness.—N. simpleness &c. *adj.;* purity, homogeneity.

elimination; sifting &c. *v.;* purification &c. (*cleanness*) 652.

V. render -simple &c. *adj.;* simplify. sift, winnow, bolt, eliminate; narrow down; get rid of, exclude &c. 55; clear; purify &c. (*clean*) 652; disentangle &c. (*disjoin*) 44.

Adj. simple, uniform, of a piece, homogeneous, single, pure, clear, sheer, neat; Attic.

un-mixed, -mingled, -blended, -combined, -compounded; elementary, undecomposed; un-adulterated, -sophisticated, -alloyed, -tinged, -fortified; pure and simple.

free –, exempt- from; exclusive.

Adv. simply &c. *adj.;* only.

V. mix; join &c. 43; combine &c. 48; com-, im-, inter-mix; mix up with, mingle; com-, inter-, be-mingle; shuffle &c. (*derange*) 61; pound together; hash -, stir- up; knead, brew; impregnate with; interlard &c. (*interpolate*) 228; inter-twine, -weave &c. 219; associate with, miscegenate, interbreed.

be mixed &c.; get among, be entangled with.

instil, imbue; in-, suf-, trans-fuse; infiltrate, dash, tinge, tincture, season, sprinkle, besprinkle, attemper, medicate, blend, cross; alloy, amalgamate, compound, adulterate, sophisticate, infect.

Adj. mixed &c. *v.*; implex, composite, half-and-half, linsey-wolsey, hybrid, mongrel, heterogeneous; motley &c. (*variegated*) 440; miscellaneous, promiscuous, indiscriminate; miscible.

Adv. among, amongst, amid, amidst, with; in the midst of, in the crowd.

43. Junction.—N. junction; joining &c. *v.*; joinder, union; con-nection, -junction, -jugation, compendency, annex-ion, -ation, -ment; coalition; astriction, attachment, compagination, vincture, ligation, alligation; accouplement; marriage &c. (*wedlock*) 903; infibulation, inosculation, symphysis, anastomosis, confluence, communication, concatenation; concurrence, meeting, reunion; assemblage &c. 72.

copulation, coition, intercourse.

joint, joining, juncture, chiasma, pivot, hinge, articulation, commissure, seam, suture, gusset, stitch, splice; link &c. 45; mitre, mortise.

closeness, tightness &c. *adj.*; coherence &c. 46; combination &c. 48.

V. join, unite; con-join, -nect; associate; put -, lay -, clap -, hang -, lump -, hold -, piece -, tack -, fix -, bind up- together; embody, re-embody; roll into one.

attach, fix, affix, saddle on, fasten, bind, paste, secure, clinch, twist, make -fast &c. *adj.*; tie, pinion, string, strap, sew, lace, stitch, tack, baste, knit, button, buckle, hitch, lash, truss, bandage, braid, splice, swathe, gird, tether, moor, picket, harness, chain; fetter &c. (*restrain*) 751; lock, latch, belay, brace, hook, grapple, leash, couple, accouple, link, yoke, bracket; marry &c. (*wed*) 903; bridge over, span.

pin, nail, bolt, hasp, clasp, clamp, screw, rivet; impact, solder, braze, cement, set; weld -, fuse- together; wedge, rabbet, mortise, mitre, jam, dovetail, enchase; graft, ingraft, in-osculate; en-, in-twine; inter-link, -lace,

44. Disjunction.—N. dis-junction, -connection, -unity, -union, -association, -engagement, -sociation; discontinuity &c. 70; inconnection; abstraction, -edness; isolation; insul-arity, -ation; oasis; separateness &c. *adj.*; severalty; *disjecta membra*; dispersion &c. 73; apportionment &c. 786.

separation; parting &c. *v.*; detachment, segregation; divorce, sejunction, seposition, diduction, diremption, discerption; elision; *cæsura*, division, subdivision, break, fracture, rupture; compartition; dis-memberment, -integration, -location; luxation; sever-, dis-sever-ance; scission; re-, ab-scission; circumcision; lacer-, dilacer-ation; dis-, ab-ruption; avulsion, divulsion; section, resection, cleavage; fission; separability; separatism.

fissure, breach, rent, split, rift, crack, slit, slot, incision.

dissection, anatomy; decomposition &c. 49; cutting instrument &c. (*sharpness*) 253; saw.

V. be -disjoined &c.; come -, fall--off, - to pieces; peel off; get loose.

dis-join, -connect, -engage, -unite, -sociate, -pair; divorce, part, dispart, detach, uncouple, separate, cut off, rescind, segregate; set -, keep- apart; insulate, isolate; throw out of gear; cut adrift; loose; un-loose, -do, -bind, -tie, -hitch, -chain, -lock &c. (*fix*) 43, -pack, -ravel; disentangle; set free &c. (*liberate*) 750.

sunder, divide, subdivide, sectionalize, sever, dissever, abscind; cut; segment; in-cide, -cise; circumcise; saw, snip, nib, nip, cleave, rive, rend, slit,

-twine, -twist, -weave; entangle; twine round, belay; tighten; trice –, screw-up.

be -joined &c.; hang –, hold- together; cohere &c. 46.

Adj. joined &c. *v.*; joint; con-joint, -junct; corporate, compact; hand in hand.

firm, fast, close, tight, taut, taught, tense, secure, set, intervolved; in-separable, -dissoluble, -secable, -severable.

Adv. jointly &c. *adj.*; in conjunction with &c. (*in addition to*) 37; fast, firmly &c. *adj.*; intimately.

split, splinter, chip, crack, snap, break, tear, burst; rend &c. -asunder, – in twain; wrench, rupture, shatter, shiver, cranch, crunch, craunch, chop; rip up; hack, hew, slash; whittle; haggle, hackle, discind, lacerate, scamble, mangle, gash, hash, slice, shave.

cut up, carve, quarter, dissect, anatomize; take –, pull –, pick –, tear- to pieces; tear to tatters, – piecemeal; divellicate; skin &c. 226; dis-integrate, -member, -branch, -band; disperse &c. 73; dis-locate, -joint; break up; mince; comminute &c. (*pulverize*) 330; distribute, apportion &c. 786.

part, – company; separate, leave; alienate, estrange.

Adj. disjoined &c. *v.*; discontinuous &c. 70; bipartite, multipartite, abstract; digitate; disjunctive; isolated &c. *v.*; insular, separate, disparate, discrete, apart, asunder, far between, loose, free; unattached, -annexed, -associated, -connected; distinct; adrift; straggling; rift, reft, cleft, split.

[capable of being divided] scissile, partible, divisible, separable, severable, detachable.

Adv. separately &c. *adj.*; one by one, severally, apart; adrift, asunder, in twain; in the abstract, abstractedly.

45. [Connecting medium.] **Vinculum.—N.** vinculum, link, *nexus*; connec-tive, -tion; junction &c. 43; bond of union, copula, intermedium, hyphen; bracket; bridge, stepping-stone, isthmus.

bond, tendon, tendril; fibre; cord, -age; riband, ribbon, rope, guy, cable, line, halser, hawser, painter, moorings, wire, chain; string &c. (*filament*) 205.

fastening, tie; liga-ment, -ture; strap; bowline, halliard, tackle, lanyard, rigging, shrouds; standing –, running- rigging; traces, harness; yoke; band, -age; brace, roller, fillet; inkle; with. withe, withy; thong, braid; girder, tie-beam; girt, cinch, girth, girdle, cestus, garter, braces, suspenders, halter, noose, lasso, lariat, surcingle, knot, hitch, running knot, frog.

pin, corking pin, nail, brad, tack, skewer, staple, cleat, clamp; cramp, screw, button, buckle, clasp, hasp, hinge, hank, catch, latch, bolt, ring, latchet, pawl, tag; tooth; stud; hook, – and eye; morse, lock, holdfast, padlock, rivet; anchor, grappling-iron, drawbar, coupler, drawhead, coupling, treenail, trennel, stake, pale, pile, post, bollard.

cement, glue, gum, paste, size, wafer, solder, lute, putty, bird--lime, mortar, stucco, plaster, grout.

shackle, rein &c. (*means of restraint*) 752; suspender &c. 214; prop &c. (*support*) 215.

V. bridge over, span; connect &c. 43; hang &c. 214.

46. Coherence.—N. co-, ad-herence, -hesion, -hesiveness; concretion, accretion; con-, ag-glutination, -glomeration; aggregation; consolidation, set, cementation; sticking, soldering &c. *v.*; connection.

47. [Want of adhesion, non-adhesion, immiscibility.] **Incoherence.—N.** non-adhesion; immiscibility; incoherence; looseness &c. *adj.*; laxity; relaxation; loosening &c. *v.*; freedom; disjunction &c. 44; rope of sand.

tenacity, toughness; stickiness &c. 352; insepara-bility, -bleness; bur, remora.

conglomerate, concrete &c. (*density*) 321.

V. cohere, adhere, stick, cling, cleave, hold, take hold of, hold fast, close with, embrace, clasp, hug; grow –, hang-together; twine round &c. (*join*) 43.

stick like -a leech, – wax; stick close; cling like -ivy, – a bur; adhere like -a remora, – Dejanira's shirt.

glue; ag-, con-glutinate; cement, lute, paste, gum; solder, weld; cake, coagulate, consolidate &c. (*solidify*) 321; agglomerate.

Adj. co-, ad-hesive, -hering &c. *v.*; tenacious, tough; sticky &c. 352.

united, unseparated, sessile, inseparable, inextricable, infrangible; compact &c. (*dense*) 321.

48. Combination.—N. combination; mixture &c. 41; alloy; junction &c. 43; union, unification, synthesis, incorporation, amalgamation, embodiment, coalescence, crasis, fusion, blend, blending, absorption, centralization, federation.

compound, amalgam, composition, *tertium quid*; resultant, impregnation.

V. combine, unite, incorporate, alloy, intertwine &c. 41; amalgamate, embody, absorb, re-embody, blend, merge, fuse, melt into one, consolidate, coalesce, centralize, impregnate; put –, lump- together; federate, associate; fraternize; cement a union, marry, wed, couple, pair, ally.

Adj. combined &c. *v.*; conjunctive, conjugate, conjoint, allied, confederate; impregnated with, ingrained, inoculated.

49. Decomposition.—N. decomposition, analysis, diæresis, dissection, resolution, catalysis, electrolysis, hydrolysis, photolysis, dissolution; dispersion &c. 73; disjunction &c. 44; disintegration, decay, rot, putrefaction, putrescence, caries, necrosis, corruption &c. (*uncleanness*) 653.

V. decom-pose, -pound; analyze, disembody, dissolve; resolve –, separate-into its elements; electrolyze; dissect, decentralize, break up; disintegrate; disperse &c. 73; unravel &c. (*unroll*) 313; crumble into dust; decay &c. *n.*; deteriorate &c. 659.

Adj. decomposed &c. *v.*; catalytic analytical.

4°. Concrete Quantity

50. Whole. [Principal part.]—N. whole, totality, integrity; totalness &c. *adj.*; entirety, *ensemble*, collectiveness; unity &c. 87; completeness &c. 52; indivisibility, indiscerptibility; integration, embodiment; integer, integral.

all, the whole, total, aggregate, one and all, gross amount, sum, sum-total, *tout ensemble*, length and breadth of, Alpha and Omega, 'be all and end all,' lock, stock and barrel.

bulk, mass, lump, tissue, staple, body, torso, *compages*; trunk, bole, hull, hulk, skeleton; greater –, major

51. Part.—N. part, portion; dose, item, particular; aught, any; division, ward; subdivision, section; chapter, verse; article, clause, count, paragraph, passage; phrase; number, volume, book, fascicle; sector, segment; fraction, fragment; cantle, -t; frustum; detachment, parcel, unit, class &c. 75.

piece, lump, bit; cut, -ting; chip, chunk, collop, slice, scale, shard; lamina &c. 204; moiety; small part; morsel, scrap, crumb; particle &c. (*smallness*) 32; instalment, dividend; share &c. (*allotment*) 786.

-, best -, principal -, main- part; essential part &c. (*importance*) 642; lion's share, Benjamin's mess; the long and the short; nearly -, almost- all.

V. form -, constitute- a whole; integrate, embody, amass; aggregate &c. (*assemble*) 72; amount to, come to.

Adj. whole, total, integral, entire; complete &c. 52; one, individual.

un-broken, -cut, -divided, -severed, -clipped, -cropped, -shorn; seamless; undiminished; un-demolished, -dissolved, -destroyed, -bruised.

in-divisible, -dissoluble, -dissolvable, -discerptible.

wholesale, sweeping, comprehensive.

Adv. wholly, altogether; totally &c. (*completely*) 52; entirely, all, all in all, considering all things, in a body, collectively, all put together; in the -aggregate, - lump, - mass, - gross, - main, - long run; *en masse*, on the whole, as a whole, bodily, *en bloc*, *in extenso*, throughout, every inch; substantially.

52. Completeness.—N. completeness &c. *adj.*; completion &c. 729; integration; integrality.

entirety; universality; totality; perfection &c. 650; solid-ity, -arity; unity; all; *ne plus ultra*, ideal, limit.

complement, supplement, make-weight; filling up &c. *v.*

impletion; satur-ation, -ity; high water; high -, flood -, spring- tide; fill, load, bumper, bellyful; brimmer; sufficiency &c. 639.

V. be -complete &c. *adj.*; come to a head.

render -complete &c. *adj.*; complete &c. (*accomplish*) 729; fill, charge, load, replenish; make-up, - good; piece -, eke- out; supply deficiencies; fill -up, - in, - to the brim, - the measure of; saturate &c. 869.

go the whole -hog, - length, go all lengths.

Adj. complete, entire; whole &c. 50; perfect &c. 650; full, good, absolute, thorough, plenary; solid, undivided; with all its parts.

exhaustive, radical, sweeping, thorough-going; dead.

regular, consummate, unmitigated, sheer, unqualified, unconditional, free; abundant &c. (*sufficient*) 639.

débris, odds and ends, oddments, detritus; excerpta; member, limb, lobe, lobule, arm, wing, scion, branch, bough, joint, link, offshoot, ramification, twig, stipule, tendril, bush, spray, sprig; runner; leaf, -let; stump; constituent, ingredient, component part &c. 56.

compartment; department &c. (*class*) 75; county &c. (*region*) 181.

V. part, divide, break &c. (*disjoin*) 44; partition &c. (*apportion*) 786.

Adj. fractional, fragmentary; sectional, aliquot; divided &c. *v.*; in compartments, multifid, incomplete, partial, divided &c. 44.

Adv. partly, in part, partially; piecemeal, part by part; by -instalments, - snatches, - inches, - driblets; bit by bit, inch by inch, foot by foot, drop by drop; in -detail, - lots.

53. Incompleteness.—N. incompleteness &c. *adj.*; deficiency, short -measure, - weight; shortcoming &c. 304; insufficiency &c. 640; imperfection &c. 651; immaturity &c. (*non-preparation*) 674; half measures.

[part wanting] defect, deficit, shortage, ullage, defalcation, omission, caret; interval &c. 198; break &c. (*discontinuity*) 70; non-completion &c. 730; missing link.

V. be -incomplete &c. *adj.*; fall short of &c. 304; lack &c. (*be insufficient*) 640; neglect &c. 460.

Adj. incomplete; imperfect &c. 651; unfinished; uncompleted &c. (*see complete* &c. 729); defective, deficient, wanting; failing; in -default, - arrear; short, - of; hollow, meagre, lame, half-and-half, perfunctory, sketchy; crude &c. (*unprepared*) 674.

mutilated, garbled, mangled, docked, lopped, truncated; bobtailed, cropped, bobbed, shingled.

in -progress, - hand; going on, proceeding.

Adv. incompletely &c. *adj.*; by halves.

Phr. *cætera desunt; caret.*

brimming; brim-, top-ful; chock –, choke- full; as full as -an egg is of meat, – a vetch, – a tick; saturated, crammed; replete &c. (*redundant*) 641; fraught, laden; full-laden, -fraught, -charged; heavy laden.

completing &c. *v.*; supplement-al, -ary; ascititious.

Adv. completely &c. *adj.*; altogether, outright, wholly, totally, *in toto*, quite; over head and ears; effectually, for good and all, nicely, fully, through thick and thin, head and shoulders; neck and -heel, – crop; all out; in -all respects, – every respect; at all points, out and out, to all intents and purposes; *toto cœlo*; utterly, clean, – as a whistle; to the -full, – utmost, – backbone; hollow, stark; heart and soul, root and branch; down to the ground.

to the top of one's bent, as far as possible, *à outrance*.

throughout; from -first to last, – beginning to end, – end to end, – one end to the other, – Dan to Beersheba, – head to foot, – head to heels, – top to toe, – top to bottom; *de fond en comble*; *à fond, a capite ad calcem, ab ovo usque ad mala,* fore and aft; every -whit, – inch; *cap-à-pie,* to the end of the chapter; up to the -brim, – ears, – eyes; as . . . as can be.

on all accounts; *sous tous les rapports*; with a -vengeance, – witness.

---

54. Composition.—**N.** composition, constitution, crasis, synthesis; make-up; combination &c. 48; inclusion, admission, comprehension, reception; embodiment, formation, conformation, production.

compilation &c. 72; (*musical*) composition &c. 415; painting &c. 556; writing &c. 590; typography &c. 591.

V. be -composed, – made, – formed, – made up- of; consist of, be resolved into.

include &c. (*in a class*) 76; subsume; synthesize; contain, hold, comprehend, take in, admit, embrace, embody; involve; implicate, drag into.

compose, constitute, form, make; make –, fill –, build- up; weave, construct, fabricate; compile; write, draw; set up (*printing*); enter into the composition of &c. (*be a component*) 56.

Adj. containing, constituting &c. *v.*

---

56. Component.—**N.** component; component –, integral –, integrant-part; element, constituent, ingredient, leaven, part and parcel; contents; appurtenance; feature; member &c. (*part*) 51; personnel.

V. enter into, – the composition of; be a -component &c. *n.*; be –, form-part of; merge –, be merged- in; be

55. Exclusion.—**N.** exclusion, non-admission, omission, exception, rejection, repudiation; exile &c. (*seclusion*) 893; preclusion, lock out, ostracism, prohibition; disbarment, expulsion, ban;

separation, segregation, seposition, elimination, coffer-dam.

V. be excluded from &c.

exclude, bar, ban; leave –, shut –, thrust –, bar- out; reject, repudiate, spurn, blackball; ostracize, boycott; lay –, put –, set -apart, – aside; relegate, segregate; throw overboard; strike -off, – out; neglect &c. 460; banish &c. (*seclude*) 893; separate &c. (*disjoin*) 44.

pass over, omit; garble; eliminate, weed, winnow.

Adj. excluding &c. *v.*; exclusive.

excluded &c. *v.*; unrecounted, not included in; inadmissible; preventive, interdictive.

Adv. exclusive of, barring; except; with the exception of; save, bating.

---

57. Extraneousness.—**N.** extraneousness &c. *adj.*; extrinsicality &c. 6; exteriority &c. 220; alienism.

foreign -body, – substance, – element; alien, stranger, intruder, interloper, foreigner, tramontane, *novus homo,* new comer, immi-, emi-grant; creole, Afrikander; outsider, outlander, tenderfoot.

implicated in; share in &c. (*participate*) 778; belong –, appertain- to.

form, make, constitute, compose.

Adj. forming &c. *v.*; inclusive; inherent &c. 5.

_____

Adj. extraneous, foreign, alien, ulterior; exterior, external, outside, outlandish; oversea; tra-, ultra-montane; excluded &c. 55; inadmissible; exceptional.

Adv. in foreign -parts, – lands; abroad, beyond seas, overseas.

SECTION IV. ORDER

1°. ORDER IN GENERAL

58. Order.—**N.** order, regularity &c. 80; uniformity, symmetry, *lucidus ordo*; harmony, music of the spheres.

gradation, progression; series &c. (*continuity*) 69.

subordination; course, even tenor, routine; method, disposition, arrangement, array, system, economy, discipline; orderliness &c. *adj.*

rank, place, &c. (*term*) 71.

V. be –, become- in order &c. *adj.*; form, fall in, draw up; arrange –, range –, place- itself; adjust; fall into –, take- -one's place, – rank; rally round; arrange &c. 60.

Adj. orderly, regular; in -order, – trim, – apple-pie order, according to Cocker, – its proper place, neat, neat as a pin, tidy, *en règle*, well regulated, correct, methodical, uniform, symmetrical, ship-shape, business-like, systematic; habitual; unconfused &c. (*see* confuse &c. 61) arranged &c. 60.

Adv. in order; methodically &c. *adj.*; in -turn, – its turn; step by step; by regular -steps, – gradations, – stages, – intervals; *seriatim*, systematically, by clockwork, *gradatim*; at stated periods &c. (*periodically*) 138; O.K.

_____

59. [Absence, or want of Order, &c.] **Disorder.**—**N.** disorder; derangement &c. 61; irregularity; anomaly &c. (*unconformity*) 83; anar-chy, -chism; want of method; dishevelment, untidiness &c. *adj.*; disunion; discord &c. 24.

confusion; confusedness &c. *adj.*; disarray, jumble, mix-up, huddle, litter, lumber; *cahotage*; farrago; mess, muss, mash, muddle, hash; hotchpotch; *imbroglio*, chaos, *omnium gatherum*, medley; mere -mixture &c. 41; fortuitous concourse of atoms, *disjecta membra*, *rudis indigestaque moles.*

complexity; complexness &c. *adj.*; com-, im-plication; intri-cacy, -cation; perplexity; network, maze, labyrinth; wilderness, jungle; involution, ravelling, entanglement; coil &c. (*convolution*) 248; sleave, tangled skein, knot, Gordian knot, kink, web; wheels within wheels.

turmoil; ferment, &c. (*agitation*) 315; to do, trouble, pudder, pother, row, disturbance, convulsion, tumult, pandemonium, uproar, riot, rumpus, stour, scramble, *fracas*, embroilment, *mêlée*, spill and pelt, rough and tumble; whirlwind &c. 349; bear garden, Babel, Saturnalia, Donnybrook Fair, confusion worse confounded, most admired disorder, *concordia discors*; Bedlam –,

hell- broke loose; bull in a china shop; all the fat in the fire, *diable à quatre*, Devil to pay; pretty kettle of fish; pretty piece of -work, – business.

slattern, slut, sloven, draggle-tail.

V. be -disorderly &c. *adj.*; ferment, play at cross purposes.

put out of order; derange &c. 61; ravel &c. 219; ruffle, rumple; bungle, botch.

Adj. disorderly, orderless; out of -order, – place, – gear, – whack; irregular, desultory; anomalous &c. (*unconformable*) 83; acephalous, disorganized. straggling; un-, im-methodical; unsymmetric; unsystematic; untidy, slovenly, bedraggled, messy; dislocated; out of sorts; promiscuous, indiscriminate; chaotic, anarchical, lawless; unarranged &c. 60; confused, tumultuous, turbulent, tempestuous; deranged &c. 61; topsy turvy &c. (*inverted*) 218; shapeless &c. 241; disjointed, out of joint.

com-plex, -plexed; intricate, complicated, perplexed, involved, ravelled, entangled, knotted, tangled, inextricable; irreducible.

troublous; riotous &c. (*violent*) 173.

Adv. irregularly &c. *adj.*; by fits and -snatches, – starts; pell-mell; higgledy-piggledy; helter-skelter, harum-scarum; in a ferment; at -sixes and sevens, – cross purposes; upside down &c. 218.

Phr. the cart before the horse, chaos is come again.

---

60. [Reduction to Order.] **Arrangement.—N.** arrangement; plan &c. 626; preparation &c. 673; dispos-al, -ition; col-, al-location; distribution; sorting &c. *v.*; assortment, allotment; grouping; apportionment, *taxis*, taxonomy, *syn-taxis*, graduation, organization, grading; re-organization, rationalization.

analysis, classification, division, digestion; systematism.

[Result of arrangement] order, orderliness, form, array; digest, synopsis &c. (*compendium*) 596; *syntagma*, table, atlas; register &c. (*record*) 551; score &c. 415; cosmos, organism, architecture.

[Instrument for sorting] sieve &c. 260; file, card index.

V. reduce to –, bring into- order; introduce order into; rally.

arrange, dispose, place, form; put –, – place- in order; straighten up, – up; set out, collocate, allocate, pack, marshal, range, size, rank, array, group, parcel out, allot, space, distribute, deal; cast –, assign- the parts; dispose of, assign places to; assort, sort; sift, riddle; put –, set- -to rights, – into shape, – in trim, – in array.

class, -ify; divide; file, string together, thread; register &c. (*record*) 551; list, catalogue, tabulate, index, alphabeticize, graduate, digest, grade, codify; orchestrate, score.

methodize, regulate, systematize, standardize, co-ordinate, organize, settle, fix, apportion.

unravel, disentangle, ravel, card; disembroil.

Adj. arranged &c. *v.*; embattled, in battle array; cut and dried; methodical. orderly, regular, systematic, tabular.

61. [Subversion of Order; bringing into disorder.] **Derangement.—N.** derangement &c. *v.*; disorder &c. 59; evection, discomposure, disturbance; dis-, de-organization; involvement; dislocation; perturbation, interruption; shuffling &c. *v.*; inversion &c. 218; corrugation &c. (*fold*) 258; insanity &c. 503.

V. derange; dis-, mis-arrange; dis-, mis-place; mislay, discompose, disorder, de-, dis-organize; embroil, unsettle, disturb, confuse, trouble, perturb, jumble, tumble; huddle, shuffle, muddle, toss, hustle, fumble, riot; bring –, put –, throw- into -disorder &c. 59; break the ranks, disconcert, convulse; break in upon.

unhinge, dislocate, put out of joint, throw out of gear.

turn topsy-turvy &c. (*invert*) 218; bedevil; complicate, involve, perplex, confound; im-, em-brangle; tangle, en-tangle, ravel, tousle, dishevel, ruffle, rumple &c. (*fold*) 258; dement.

litter, scatter; mix &c. 41.

Adj. deranged &c. *v.*; syncre-tic, -tistic.

2°. Consecutive Order

62. Precedence.—N. precedence; coming before &c. *v.*; the lead, *le pas*; superiority &c. 33; importance &c. 642; anteced-ence, -ency; anteriority &c. (*front*) 234; precursor &c. 64; priority &c. 116; precession &c. 280; anteposition, preference.

V. precede; come -before, – first; forerun, head, lead, take the lead; lead the -way, – dance; introduce, usher in; have the *pas*; set the fashion &c. (*influence*) 175; lead off, kick off, open the ball; take –, have- precedence; outrank; have the start &c. (*get before*) 280.

place before; prefix; premise, prelude, preface.

Adj. preceding &c. *v.*; pre-, antecedent; anterior; prior &c. 116; before; former, foregoing; before-, above-mentioned; aforesaid, said; precurs-ory, -ive; prevenient, preliminary, prefatory, introductory; prelus-ive, -ory; proemial, preparatory.

Adv. before; in advance &c. (*precession*) 280.

Phr. *seniores priores.*

63. Sequence.—N. sequence, coming after; going after &c. (*following*) 281; consecution, succession; posteriority &c. 117.

continuation; prolongation, order of succession; successiveness; Elijah's mantle.

secondariness; subordinancy &c. (*inferiority*) 34.

V. succeed; come -after, – on, – next; follow, ensue, step into the shoes of; alternate.

place after, suffix, append.

Adj. succeeding &c. *v.*; sequent; sub-, con-sequent; sequacious, proximate, next; consecutive &c. (*continuity*) 69; alternate, amœbæan.

latter; posterior &c. 117.

Adv. after, subsequently; behind &c. (*rear*) 235.

---

64. Precursor.—N. precursor, antecedent, precedent, predecessor; forerunner, van-courier, *avant-coureur*, pioneer, prodrome, *prodromos*, outrider; leader, bell-wether; herald, harbinger; dawn.

prelude, preamble, preface, prologue, foreword, *avant-propos*, *protasis*, prolusion, proem, *prolepsis*, *prolegomena*, prefix, introduction; lead, heading, frontispiece, groundwork; preparation &c. 673; overture, voluntary, *exordium*, symphony, *ritornello*; premises.

prefigurement &c. 511; omen &c. 512.

Adj. precursory; prelu-sive, -sory, -dious; proemial, introductory, prefatory, prodromous, inaugural, preliminary; precedent &c. (*prior*) 116.

65. Sequel.—N. sequel, suffix, successor; tail, queue, train, wake, trail, rear; retinue, suite; appendix, postscript, subscript; epilogue; conclusion; peroration; codicil; continuation, sequela; appendage &c. 39; tail –, heelpiece; tag, more last words; colophon, *feliciter explicit.*

follower, after-glow, -growth, -crop, -taste, -math.

after-part, -piece, -course, -thought, -game; *arrière pensée*, second thoughts.

---

66. Beginning.—N. beginning, commencement, opening, outset, incipience, inception, inchoation; introduction &c. (*precursor*) 64; *alpha*; initial; foundation; inauguration, *début*, le premier pas, embarcation, rising of the curtain; zero hour; exordium, curtain raiser; maiden speech; prelude; outbreak, onset, brunt; initiative, move, first move; gambit, narrow –, thin-

67. End.—N. end, close, termination; desinence, conclusion, *finis*, *finale*, period, term, *terminus*, last, *omega*; extreme, -tremity; gable –, butt –, fagend; tip, nib, point; tail &c. (*rear*) 235; verge &c. (*edge*) 231; tag, epilogue, peroration; *bonne bouche*; bitter end, tail end; terminal; *apodosis*; appendix.

consummation, *dénouement*; finish &c. (*completion*) 729; fate; doom, -sday;

end of the wedge; fresh start, new departure; forefront.

origin &c. (*cause*) 153; source, rise; bud, germ &c. 153; egg, rudiment; genesis, birth, nativity, cradle, infancy, incunabula; start, starting-point &c. 293; dawn &c. (*morning*) 125.

title-page; head, -ing, caption; van &c. (*front*) 234, *feliciter incipit.*

en-trance, -try; inlet, orifice, mouth, chops, lips, porch, portal, portico, *propylon*, door; gate, -way; postern, wicket, threshold, vestibule; skirts, border &c. (*edge*) 231; tee.

first -stage, – blush, – glance, – impression, – sight.

rudiments, elements, outlines, *principia*, grammar, *protasis*; alphabet, ABC.

V. begin, commence, inchoate, rise, arise, originate, institute, conceive, initiate, open, dawn, set in, take its rise, enter upon, start; enter; set out &c. (*depart*) 293; embark in.

usher in; lead -off, – the way; take the -lead, – initiative; inaugurate, head; stand -at the head, – first, – for; lay the foundations &c. (*prepare*) 673; found &c. (*cause*) 153; set -up, – on foot, – agoing, – abroach, – the ball in motion; apply the match to a train; launch, broach; open -up, – the door to; set -about, – to work; make a -beginning, – start; handsel; take the first step, lay the first stone, cut the first turf; break -ground, – the ice, – cover; pass -, cross- the Rubicon; open -fire, – the ball; ventilate, air; undertake &c. 676.

come into -existence, – the world; make one's *début*, take birth; burst forth, break out; spring -, crop- up.

begin -at the beginning, – *ab ovo*, – again, – *de novo*; start afresh, make a fresh start, shuffle the cards, resume, recommence.

Adj. beginning &c. *v.*; initi-al, -atory, -ative; inceptive, introductory, incipient; proemial, inaugural; incho-ate, -ative; embryonic, rudimental; primogenial; primeval &c. (*old*) 124; rudimentary, aboriginal; natal, nascent.

first, foremost, front, leading, head; maiden.

begun &c. *v.*; just -begun &c. *v.*

Adv. at -, in- the beginning &c. *n.*; first, in the first place, *imprimis*, first and foremost; *in limine*; in -the bud, – embryo, – its infancy; from -the beginning, – its birth; *ab -initio, – ovo, – incunabulis*, primarily, originally.

crack of doom, day of Judgement, fall of the curtain, wind-up; goal, destination; limit, stoppage, end all, determination; expiration, expiry; death &c. 360; end of all things; finality; eschatology.

break up, *commencement de la fin*, last stage, turning point; *coup de grâce*, death-blow; knock-out.

V. end, close, finish, terminate, conclude, be all over; expire; die &c. 360; come -, draw- to a -close &c. *n.*; have run its course; run out, pass away.

bring to an -end &c. *n.*; put an end to, make an end of; determine; get through; achieve &c. (*complete*) 729; stop &c. (*make to cease*) 142; shut up shop.

Adj. ending &c. *v.*; final, terminal, definitive, conclusive; crowning &c. (*completing*) 729; last, ultimate; hindermost; rear &c. 235; caudal.

contermin-ate, -ous, -able.

ended &c. *v.*; at an end; settled, decided, over, played out, set at rest.

penultimate; last but -one, – two, &c.

unbegun, uncommenced; fresh.

Adv. finally &c. *adj.*; in fine; at the last; once for all.

———

68. Middle.—N. middle, midst, mediety; mean &c. 29; medium, middle term; centre &c. 222, mid-course &c. 628; *mezzo termine*; *juste milieu* &c. 628; half-way house, nave, navel, omphalos; nucle-us, -olus.

equidistance, bisection, half-distance; middle-distance, equator, diaphragm, midriff; interjacence &c. 228.

Adj. middle, medial, mesial, mean, mid; middle-, mid-most; middling; mediate; intermediate &c. (*interjacent*) 228; equidistant; central &c. 222; mediterranean, equatorial.

Adv. in the middle; in the thick; mid-, half-way; midships, *in medias res*.

69. [Uninterrupted sequence.] **Continuity.**—**N.** continuity; consecu-tion, -tiveness &c. *adj.*; succession, round, suite, progression, series, train, chain; cat-, concat-enation; catena; scale; gradation, course, constant flow, perpetuity.

procession, column; retinue, *cortège*, cavalcade, rank and file, line of battle, array.

pedigree, genealogy, lineage, race &c. 166.

rank, file, line, row, range, tier, string, thread, team; suit; colonnade.

V. follow in –, form- a series &c. *n.*; fall in.

arrange in a -series &c. *n.*; string together, catenate, file, thread, graduate, tabulate.

Adj. continu-ous, -ed; consecutive; progressive, gradual; serial, successive; immediate, unbroken, entire; linear; in a -line, – row &c. *n.*; uninter-rupted, -mitting; unremitting; perennial, evergreen; constant.

Adv. continuously &c. *adj.*; *seriatim*; in a -line &c. *n.*; in -succession, – turn; running, gradually, step by step, *gradatim*, at a stretch; in -file, – column, – single file, – Indian file.

70. [Interrupted sequence.] **Discontinuity.**—**N.** discontinuity; disjunction &c. 44; anacoluthon, *non sequitur*; interruption, break, fracture, flaw, fault, split, crack, cut; gap &c. (*interval*) 198; solution of continuity; *cæsura*; broken thread; parenthesis, episode; rhapsody, patchwork; intermission; alternation &c. (*periodicity*) 138; dropping fire.

V. be -discontinuous &c. *adj.*; alternate, intermit.

discontinue, pause, interrupt; intervene; break, – in upon; interpose &c. 228; break –, snap- the thread; disconnect &c. (*disjoin*) 44.

Adj. discontinuous, unsuccessive, broken, interrupted, *décousu*; dis-, un-connected, discrete, disjunctive; fitful &c. (*irregular*) 139; spasmodic, desultory, intermit-ting &c. *v.*, -tent; alternate; recurrent &c. (*periodic*) 138; few and far between.

Adv. at intervals; by -snatches, – jerks, – skips, – catches, – fits and starts; skippingly, *per saltum*; *longo intervallo*.

---

71. Term.—**N.** term, rank, station, stage, step; degree &c. 26; scale, remove, grade, link, peg, round –, rung- of the ladder, *status*, position, place, point, mark, *pas*, period, pitch; stand, -ing; footing, range.

V. hold –, occupy –, fall into- a place &c. *n.*

3°. COLLECTIVE ORDER

72. Assemblage.—**N.** assemblage; col-lection, -location, -ligation; compilation, levy, gathering, ingathering, mobilization, meet, foregathering, muster, *attroupement*; con-course, -flux, -gregation, -tesseration, -vergence &c. 290; meeting, *levée*, *réunion*, drawing room, at home; conversazione &c. (*social gathering*) 892; assembly, congress, eisteddfod; conven-tion, -ticle;

73. Non-assemblage. Dispersion.—**N.** dispersion; disjunction &c. 44; divergence &c. 291; scattering &c. *v.*; dissemination, broadcasting, diffusion, dissipation, distribution; apportionment &c. 786; spread, respersion, circumfusion, interspersion, spargefaction.

waifs and estrays, flotsam and jetsam, *disjecta membra*.

V. disperse, scatter, sow, dissemi-

gemote; conclave, &c. (*council*) 696; posse, *posse comitatûs*; Noah's ark.

miscellany, *collectanea*, symposium; museum, menagerie, &c. (*store*) 636.

crowd, throng, multitude; flood, rush, deluge; rout, rabble, mob, press, crush, *cohue*, jam, horde, body, tribe; crew, gang, knot, squad, band, party; swarm, shoal, school, covey, flock, herd, drove, kennel; array, bevy, galaxy; *corps*, company, troop, *troupe*; army, force, regiment, &c. (*combatants*) 726; host &c. (*multitude*) 102; populousness.

clan, brotherhood, association &c. (*party*) 712.

volley, shower, storm, cloud.

group, cluster, Pleiades, clump, pencil; set, batch, lot, pack; budget, *dossier*, assortment, bunch; parcel; pack-et, -age; bundle, *fasciculus*, fascine, bale; ser-on, -oon; faggot, wisp, truss, tuft; shock, rick, fardel, stack, sheaf, swath, gavel, haycock, stook.

accumulation &c. (*store*) 636; congeries, heap, lump, pile, *rouleau*, tissue, mass, pyramid; drift; snow-ball, -drift; acervation, cumulation; amassment, glom-, agglom-eration; conglobation; conglomeration, -ate; coacervation, coagmentation, aggregation, concentration, congestion, *omnium gatherum*, *spicilegium*, black hole of Calcutta; quantity &c. (*greatness*) 31.

collector, gatherer; whip, -per in.

V. [be or come together] assemble, collect, muster; meet, unite, join, rejoin; cluster, flock, swarm, surge, stream, herd, crowd, throng, associate; con-gregate, -glomerate, -centrate; centre round, rendezvous, resort; come –, flock –, get –, pig- together; forgather; huddle; reassemble.

[get or bring together] assemble, muster, mobilize; bring –, get –, put –, draw –, scrape –, lump- together; col-lect, -locate, -ligate; get –, whip- in; gather; hold a meeting; con-vene, -voke, -vocate; rake up, dredge; heap, mass, pile; pack, put up, truss, cram; acervate; ag-glomerate, -gregate; compile; group, aggroup, concentrate, unite; collect –, bring- into a focus; amass, accumulate &c. (*store*) 636; collect in a drag-net; heap Ossa upon Pelion.

Adj. assembled &c. *v.*; closely packed, dense, serried, crowded to suffocation, teeming, swarming, populous; as thick as hops; all of a heap, fasciculated; cumulative.

Phr. the plot thickens.

74. [Place of meeting.] **Focus.—N.** focus; point of- convergence &c; 290; corradiation; centre &c. 222; gathering-place, resort; haunt; retreat; *venue, rendezvous*; rallying point, headquarters, home, club; *dépôt* &c. (*store*) 636; tryst, trysting-place; place of -meeting, – resort, – assignation; *point de –, lieu de- réunion*; issue.

V. bring to- a point, – a focus, – an issue; focus.

4°. DISTRIBUTIVE ORDER

75. Class.—N. class, category, *categorema*, head, order, sec

nate, radiate, diffuse, shed, spread, ted, bestrew, overspread, dispense, disband, disembody, demobilize, dismember, distribute; apportion &c. 786; blow off, let out, dispel, cast forth, draught off; strew, straw, strow; spirtle, cast, sprinkle, spatter; issue, deal out, retail, utter; re-, inter-sperse; set abroach, circumfuse.

turn –, cast- adrift; scatter to the winds; sow broadcast.

spread like wildfire, disperse themselves.

Adj. unassembled &c. (*see* assemble &c. 72); dispersed &c. *v.*; sparse, dispread, broadcast, sporadic, widespread; far-flung; epidemic &c. (*general*) 78; adrift, stray; dishevelled, streaming.

Adv. *sparsim*, here and there, *passim*

tion; division, subdivision; department, province, domain, sphere.

kind, sort, genus, species, variety, branch, family, race, tribe, caste, sept, clan, breed; *clique, coterie*; type, kit, sect, set; assortment; feather, kidney; suit; range; gender, sex, kin.

manner, description, denomination, persuasion, connection, designation, character, stamp; predicament; conviction &c. 484.

similarity &c. 17.

76. Inclusion. [Comprehension under, or reference to a class.]—**N.** inclusion, admission, incorporation, comprehension, reception.

composition &c. (*inclusion in a compound*) 54.

V. be -included in &c.; come –, fall –, range- under; belong –, pertain- to; range with; merge in.

include, compromise, comprehend, contain, admit, embrace, receive; enclose &c. (*circumscribe*) 229; incorporate, cover, embody, encircle.

reckon –, enumerate –, number- among; refer to; place –, arrange- under, – with; take into account.

Adj. includ-ed, -ing &c. *v.*; inclusive; comprehensive, all-embracing; congen-er, -erous: of the same -class &c. 75.

Phr. *el hoc genus omne*, &c.; *et cætera.*

77. Exclusion.*—N. exclusion &c. 55.

---

78. Generality. — N. general-ity, -ization; universality; catholic-ity, -ism; miscel-lany, -laneousness; drag-net.

every-one, -body; all hands, all the world and his wife; any body, N or M, all sorts; *tout le monde.*

prevalence, run.

V. be -general &c. *adj.*; prevail, obtain, be going about, stalk abroad.

render -general &c. *adj.*; generalize; spread, broadcast.

Adj. general, usual, current, generic, collective; broad, comprehensive, sweeping; encyclopedical, panoramic, widespread &c. (*dispersed*) 73.

universal; catho-lic, -lical; common, world-wide; œ-, e-cumenical; transcendental; prevalent, prevailing, rife, epidemic, besetting; all over, covered with.

every, all; indeterminate, indefinite, unspecified, impersonal.

customary &c. (*habitual*) 613.

Adv. what-ever, -soever; to a man, one and all, without exception.

generally &c. *adj.*; always, for better

79. Speciality.—N. speciality, *spécialité*; individ-uality, -uity; particularity, peculiarity; idiocrasy &c. (*tendency*) 176; personality, characteristic, mannerism, idiosyncrasy, attribute, specificness &c. *adj.*; singularity &c. (*unconformity*) 83; reading, version, lection; state; *trait*; distinctive feature; technicality; *differentia.*

particulars, details, minutiæ, items, counts.

I, self, I myself, *ego*; my-, him-, her-, it-self.

V. specify, particularize, individualize, realize, specialize, designate, differentiate, determine, define, denote, indicate, itemize, detail.

descend to particulars, enter into detail, come to the point.

Adj. special, particular, individual, specific, proper, personal, intimate, original, private, respective, definite, concrete, determinate, especial, certain, esoteric, endemic, partial, party, peculiar, marked, appropriate, several, characteristic, diagnostic, exact, exclusive; singular &c. (*exceptional*) 83;

for worse; in general, generally speaking; speaking generally; for the most part; in the long run &c. (*on an average*) 29.

idiomatic; typical, representative, distinctive.

this, that; yon, -der.

Adv. specially &c. *adj.*; in particular, *in propriâ personâ*; *ad hominem*; for my part.

each, apiece, one by one; severally, respectively, each to each; *seriatim*, in detail, bit by bit; *pro hac vice, – re natâ*.

namely, that is to say, *videlicet*, viz.; to wit; i.e., e.g.

5°. ORDER AS REGARDS CATEGORIES

80. Rule.—N. regularity, uniformity &c. 16; clock-work precision; punctuality &c. (*exactness*) 494; routine &c. (*custom*) 613; formula; system; rut; canon, convention, maxim; rule &c. (*form, regulation*) 697; key-note, standard, model; precedent &c. (*prototype*) 22; conformity &c. 82.

nature, principle; law; order of things; normal –, natural –, ordinary –, model- -state, – condition; standing -dish, – order; normality; Procrustean law; law of the Medes and Persians; hard and fast rule.

Adj. regular, uniform, symmetrical, constant, steady; according to rule &c. (*conformable*) 82; customary &c. 613; orderly &c. 58.

82. Conformity.—N. conform-ity, -ance; observance.

naturalization; conventionality &c. (*custom*) 613; agreement &c. 23.

example, instance, specimen, sample, quotation; exemplification, illustration, case in point; object lesson.

conventionalist, formalist, Philistine.

pattern &c. (*prototype*) 22.

V. conform to, - rule; accommodate –, adapt- oneself to; rub off corners.

be -regular &c. *adj.*; move in a groove; follow –, observe –, go by –, bend to –, obey- -rules, – precedents; comply –, tally –, chime in –, fall in-with; be -guided, – regulated- by; fall into a -custom, – usage; follow the -fashion, – multitude; pass muster, do as others do, *hurler avec les loups*; do at Rome as the Romans do; go –, swim- with the -stream, – current, – tide; tread the beaten track &c. (*habit*) 613; rubber-stamp; keep one in countenance.

exemplify, illustrate, cite, quote, put

81. Multiformity.—N. multi-, omniformity; variety, diversity; multifariousness &c. *adj.*

Adj. multi-form, -fold, -farious, -generous; multiplex, variform, manifold, many-sided, multiplicate; omni-form, -genous, -farious; polymorphic; protean; heterogeneous, motley, mosaic; epicene, indiscriminate, desultory, irregular, diversified, different, divers; all manner of; of -every description, – all sorts and kinds; *et hoc genus omne*; and what not? *de omnibus rebus et quibusdam aliis*.

83. Unconformity.—N. non-conformity &c. 82; un-, dis-conformity; unconventionality, informality, abnormity, anomaly; anomalousness &c. *adj.*; exception, peculiarity, &c. 79; infraction –, breach –, violation –, infringement- of -law, – custom, – usage; eccentricity, *bizarrerie*, oddity, *je ne sais quoi*, monstrosity, rarity; freak of Nature.

individuality, idiosyncrasy, singularity, originality, mannerism.

aberration; irregularity; variety; singularity; exemption; salvo &c. (*qualification*) 469.

nonconformist; nondescript, character, original, nonsuch, monster, prodigy, wonder, miracle, curiosity, missing link, flying fish, black swan, *lusus naturæ, rara avis*, queer fish; mongrel; half-caste, -blood, -breed; *métis*, cross breed, hybrid, mule, mulatto, sacatra, marabou; *tertium quid*, hermaphrodite, gynander, androgyn.

phœnix, chimera, hydra, sphinx, minotaur; griff-in, -on; centaur; hippo-

a case; produce an- instance &c. *n.*
Adj. conformable to rule, adaptable, compliant, consistent, agreeable; regular &c. 80; according to -regulation, – rule, – Cocker; *en règle, selon les règles,* well regulated, orderly; symmetric &c. 242.

conventional, commonplace &c. (*customary*) 613; of -daily, – every day-occurrence; in the natural order of things; ordinary, common, – or garden, prosaic, habitual, usual.

in the order of the day; naturalized.

typical, normal, formal; canonical, orthodox, sound, strict, rigid, positive, uncompromising, Procrustean; point device.

secundum artem, ship-shape, technical.

exemplary, illustrative, in point.

Adv. conformably &c. *adj.*; by rule; agreeably to; in -conformity, – accordance, – keeping- with; according to; consistently with; as usual, *ad instar, instar omnium; more -solito, – majorum.*

for the sake of conformity; of –, as a matter of- course; *pro formâ,* for form's sake, by the card; according to plan.

invariably &c. (*uniformly*) 16.

for -example, – instance; *exempli gratiâ; e.g.; inter alia.*

Phr. *cela va sans dire; ex pede Herculem, noscitur a sociis.*

griff, -centaur; sagittary; kraken, cockatrice, wyvern, roc, liver, dragon, sea-serpent; mermaid; unicorn; Cyclops, 'men whose heads do grow beneath their shoulders'; Teratology.

fish out of water; neither -one thing nor another, – fish flesh nor fowl nor good red herring; one in a -way, – thousand; out-cast, -law; Ishmael, pariah; oasis.

V. be -unconformable &c. *adj.*; leave the beaten -track, – path; infringe –, break –, violate- a -law, – habit, – usage, – custom; drive a coach and six through; stretch a point; have no business there; baffle –, beggar- all description.

Adj. unconformable, exceptional; abnorm-al, -ous; anomal-ous, -istic; out of -order, – place, – keeping, – tune, – one's element; irregular, arbitrary; lawless, informal, aberrant, stray, wandering, wanton; peculiar, exclusive, unnatural, eccentric, crotchety, egregious; out of the -beaten track, – common, – common run, – pale of; misplaced; funny.

un-usual, -accustomed, -customary, -wonted, -common; rare, singular, unique, curious, odd, extraordinary, strange, monstrous; wonderful &c. 870; unexpected, unaccountable; *outré,* out of the way, remarkable, noteworthy; queer, quaint, nondescript, none such, *sui generis;* original, unconventional, Bohemian, unfashionable; un-described, -precedented, -paralleled, -exampled, -heard of, -familiar; fantastic, new-fangled, grotesque, *bizarre;* outlandish, exotic, *tombé des nues,* preternatural; denaturalized.

heterogeneous, heteroclite, amorphous, mongrel, amphibious, epicene, half-blood, hybrid; androgyn-ous, -al; unsymmetric &c. 243. qualified &c. 469.

Adv. unconformably &c. *adj.*; except, unless, save, barring, beside, without, save and except, let alone.

however, yet, but.

Int. what -on earth! – in the world!

Phr. never was -seen, – heard, – known- the like.

Section V. NUMBER

1°. NUMBER, IN THE ABSTRACT

84. Number.—**N.** number, symbol, numeral, figure, cipher, digit, integer; counter; round number; formula; function; series.

sum, total, aggregate, difference, complement, subtrahend; product; multipli-cand, -er, -cator; coefficient, multiple; dividend, divisor, factor, quotient, sub-multiple, fraction; mixed number; numerator denomi nator; decimal, circulating decimal, repetend, common measure, aliquot part; reciprocal; prime number; totitive, totient.

permutation, combination, variation; election.

ratio, proportion; progression; arithmetical -, geometrical -, harmonical- progression; percentage.

figurate -, pyramidal -, polygonal- numbers.

power, root, exponent, index, logarithm, antilogarithm; modulus; differential, integral, fluxion, fluent.

Adj. numeral, complementary, divisible, aliquot, reciprocal, prime, fractional, decimal, figurate, incommensurable.

proportional, exponential, logarithmic, logometric, differential, fluxional, integral.

positive, negative; rational, irrational; surd, radical, real, imaginary, impossible.

85. Numeration.—N. numeration; numbering &c. *v.*; pagination; tale, tally, recension, enumeration, summation, reckoning, computation, supputation; calcu-lation, -lus; algorithm, rhabdology, dactylonomy; measurement &c. 466; statistics.

arithmetic, analysis, algebra, fluxions; differential -, integral -, infinitesimal- calculus; calculus of differences.

[Statistics] dead reckoning, muster, poll, census, capitation, roll-call, recapitulation; account &c. (*list*) 86.

[Operations] notation, addition, subtraction, multiplication, division, proportion, rule of three, practice, equations, extraction of roots, reduction, involution, evolution, approximation, interpolation, differentiation, integration.

[Instruments] abacus, swan-pan, logometer, sliding -, slide- rule, tallies, Napier's bones, calculating -, adding- machine, difference engine; cash register.

arithmetician, calculator, abacist; mathematician, actuary, statistician, surveyor, geodesist.

V. number, count, tell; call -, run- over, take an account of, enumerate, call the roll, muster, poll, recite, recapitulate; sum; sum -, cast- up; tell off, score, cipher, compute, calculate, set a price, reckon, - up, estimate; suppute, add, subtract, multiply, divide, extract roots.

check, prove, demonstrate, balance, audit, overhaul, take stock; affix numbers to, page, foliate, paginate.

amount -, come- to.

Adj. numer-al, -ical; arithmetical, analytic, algebraic, statistical, numerable, computable, calculable; commensur-able, -ate; incommensur-able, -ate.

86. List.—N. list, catalogue, enumeration, inventory, schedule; register &c. (*record*) 551; account; bill, - of costs; syllabus; terrier, tally, file; almanac, calendar, index, table, atlas, contents, card index; rota, ticket; book, ledger; synopsis, *catalogue raisonné; tableau;* scroll, manifest, invoice, bill of lading; prospectus, *programme;* bill of fare, *menu, carte;* score, census, statistics, returns; Red -, Blue -, Domesday- book; *cadastre;* directory, gazetteer, dictionary, glossary, lexicon, thesaurus, gradus.

roll; check -, chequer -, bead- roll, - of honour; muster -roll, - book; roster, panel; cartulary, diptych.

V. list, enrol, schedule, register &c. *n.*; indent, post, docket; matriculate.

Adj. cadastral, listed &c. *v.*

2°. DETERMINATE NUMBER

87. Unity.—**N.** unity; oneness &c. *adj.*; individuality; solitude &c. (*seclusion*) 893; isolation &c. (*disjunction*) 44; unification &c. 48.

one, unit, ace; item; individual; solo, none else, no other, naught beside.

V. be -one, – alone &c. *adj.*; dine with Duke Humphrey.

isolate &c. (*disjoin*) 44.

render one; unite &c. (*join*) 43, (*combine*) 48.

Adj. one, sole, single, solitary, only-begotten; individual, apart, alone; kithless.

un-accompanied, -attended; *solus*, single-handed; singular, odd, unique, unrepeated, azygous, first and last; isolated &c. (*disjoined*) 44; insular; unitary.

lone; lone-ly, -some; desolate, dreary.

in-secable, -severable, -discerptible; compact, irresolvable.

Adv. singly &c. *adj.*; alone, by itself, *per se*, only, apart, in the singular number, in the abstract; one -by one, – at a time; simply; one and a half, *sesqui-*.

Phr. *natura il fece, e poi roppe la stampa.*

88. Accompaniment.—**N.** accompaniment; appurtenance, adjunct &c. 39; context.

coexistence, concomitance, company, association, companionship; part-, co-part-nership; coefficiency.

concomitant, accessory, coefficient; companion, attendant, fellow, associate, consort, spouse, colleague, *fidus Achates*; part-, co-part-ner; satellite, hanger on, shadow; escort, *entourage*, suite, *cortège*; convoy, follower &c. 65; attribute.

V. accompany, coexist, attend, convoy, chaperon; hang –, wait- on; go hand in hand with; synchronize &c. 120; bear –, keep- company; row in the same boat; bring in its train, associate –, couple- with.

Adj. accompanying &c. *v.*; concomitant, fellow, twin, joint; associated –, coupled- with; accessory, attendant, *obbligato*.

Adv. with, withal; together –, along –, in company- with; hand in hand, side by side; cheek by -jowl, – jole; arm in arm; there-, here-with; and &c. (*addition*) 37.

together, in a body, collectively.

---

89. Duality.—**N.** dual-ity, -ism; duplicity; bi-plicity, -formity; span, polarity.

two, deuce, couple, couplet, doublet, brace, pair, cheeks, twins, Castor and Pollux, *gemini*, Siamese twins; fellows; yoke, conjugation, dyad, distich.

V. [unite in pairs] pair, couple, bracket, yoke; conduplicate, mate.

Adj. two, twain; dual, -istic; binary, binomial; twin, biparous; dyadic; conduplicate; duplex &c. 90; *tête-à-tête*; paired; dihedral.

coupled &c. *v.*; conjugate.

both, – the one and the other.

90. Duplication.—**N.** duplication; doubling &c. *v.*; gemi-, ingemi-nation; reduplication; iteration &c. (*repetition*) 104; renewal.

V. double; re-double, -duplicate; geminate; repeat &c. 104; renew &c. 660; duplicate, copy &c. 21.

Adj. double; doubled &c. *v.*; bicameral, bicapital, bi-fold, -form, -lateral,

91. [Division into two parts.] Bisection.—**N.** bi-section, -partition; di-, subdi-chotomy; halving &c. *v.*; dimidiation; *hendiadys*.

bifurcation, forking, branching, furcation, ramification, divarication; fork, prong; fold.

half, moiety.

V. bisect, halve, divide, split, cut **in**

-farious, -facial; two-fold, -sided, -headed, -edged &c.; duplex; double-faced; twin, duplicate, ingeminate; second; dual &c. 89.

Adv. twice, once more; over again &c. (*repeatedly*) 104; as much again, twofold.

secondly, in the second place, again.

two, cleave, dimidiate, dichotomize, divaricate.

go halves, divide with.

separate, fork, bifurcate; branch -off, ~ out; ramify.

Adj. bisected &c. *v.*; cloven, cleft; bipartite, biconjugate, bicuspid, bifid; bifur-cous, -cate, -cated; semi-, demi-hemi-.

92. Triality.—N. triality, trinity,* triplicity.

three, triad, triplet, trey, trio, ternion, trinomial, leash; tierce; triennium; trefoil, triangle, trident, tripod, triumvirate, *troika.*

third power, cube.

Adj. three; tri-form, -nal, -nomial; tertiary; triune.

93. Triplication.—N. tripli-cation, -city; trebleness, trine, trilogy.

V. treble, triple, triplicate, cube.

Adj. treble, triple; tern, -ary; triplex, triplicate, threefold, trilogistic; third; trinal; trihedral.

Adv. three -times, - fold; thrice, in the third place, thirdly; trebly &c. *adj.*

94. [Division into three parts.] **Trisection. — N.** tri-section, -partition, -chotomy; third, - part.

V. trisect, divide into three parts trifurcate.

Adj. trifid; trisected &c. *v.*; tri partite, -chotomous, -sulcate.

95. Quaternity.—N. quaternity, four, tetrad, quartet, quaternion, square, quadrature, quarter, quadruplet; quadrilateral, quadrangle, quatrefoil; *quadriga.*

V. reduce to a square, square.

Adj. four; quat-ernary, -ernal; quadratic; quartile, quartic, tetractic, tetrad, tetrahedral; quadrennial; quadrivalent.

96. Quadruplication.—N. quadruplication.

V. multiply by four, quadruplicate, biquadrate.

Adj. fourfold; quad-ruple, -ruplicate, -rible; quadruplex; fourth.

Adv. four times; in the fourth place, fourthly.

97. [Division into four parts.] **Quadrisection.—N.** quadri-section, -partition; quartering &c. *v.*; fourth; quart, -er, -ern; farthing (*i.e.* fourthing); quarto.

V. quarter, divide into four parts, quadrisect.

Adj. quartered &c. *v.*; quadri-fid, -partite.

98. Five, &c.—N. five, cinque, quint, quincunx, quintuplet, quintet, pentagon, pentameter, Pentateuch; six, half-a-dozen, sextet, hexagon, hexameter; seven, Heptarchy; eight, octet, octagon, octave; nine, three times three; ten, decade; eleven; twelve, dozen; thirteen; long -, baker's- dozen.

twenty, score; twenty-four, four and twenty, two dozen; twenty-five, five

99. Quinquesection, &c.—N. division by -five &c. 98; quinquesection &c.; fifth &c.; decimation.

V. decimate, quinquesect.

Adj. quinque-fid, -partite; quinquarticular; octifid; decimal, tenth, tithe, teind; duodecimal, twelfth; sexa-gesimal, -genary; hundredth, centesimal; millesimal &c.

and twenty, quarter of a hundred; forty, two score; fifty, half a hundred; sixty, three score, sexagenarian; seventy, three score and ten, septuagenarian; eighty, four score, octogenarian; ninety, four score and ten, nonagenarian.

* *Trinity* is hardly ever used except in a theological sense; *see* Deity 976.

hundred, centenary, hecatomb, century; hundredweight, cwt.; one hundred and forty-four, gross; bicentenary, tercentenary &c.

thousand, chiliad; myriad, millennium, ten thousand; lac, lakh, one hundred thousand, plum; million; thousand million, *milliard*.

billion, trillion &c.

V. centuriate.

Adj. five, quinary, quintuple; fifth; senary, sextuple; sixth; seventh; octuple; eighth; ninefold, ninth; tenfold, decimal, denary, decuple, tenth; eleventh; duo-denary, -denal; twelfth; in one's 'teens, thirteenth.

vices-, viges-imal; twentieth; twenty-fourth &c. *n.*

cent-uple, -uplicate, -ennial, -enary, -urial; secular, hundredth; thousandth; millenary &c.

3°. INDETERMINATE NUMBER

100. [More than one.] **Plurality.—N.** plurality; a -number, – certain number; one or two, two or three &c.; a few, several; multitude &c. 102.

Adj. plural, more than one, upwards of, some, certain; not -alone &c. 87.

Adv. *et cætera*, &c., etc.

Phr. *non deficit alter.*

102. Multitude.—N. multitude; numerousness &c. *adj.*; numer-osity, -ality; multiplicity; profusion &c. (*plenty*) 639; legion, host; great –, large –, round –, enormous- number; a quantity, numbers, array, sight, army, sea, galaxy; scores, peck, bushel, school, shoal, swarm, draft, bevy, cloud, flock, herd, drove, flight, covey, hive, brood, litter, farrow, fry, nest; mob, crowd &c. (*assemblage*) 72; lots, loads, heaps; all the world and his wife.

[Increase of number] greater number, majority; multiplication, multiple.

V. be -numerous &c. *adj.*; swarm –. teem –, crawl –, creep -with; crowd, swarm, come thick upon; outnumber, multiply; people; swarm like -locusts, – bees; be alive with.

Adj. many, several, sundry, divers, various, not a few; a -hundred, – thousand, – myriad, – million, – thousand and one; some -ten or a dozen, – forty or fifty &c.; half a -dozen, – hundred &c.; very –, full –, ever so- many; numer-ous, -ose; profuse, in profusion; manifold, multiplied, multitudinous, multiferous, multiple, multinomial, teeming, crawling, populous, peopled, crowded, thick, studded; galore.

thick coming, many more, more than one can tell, a world of; no end -of, – to; *cum multis aliis*; thick as -hops, – hail; plenty as blackberries; numerous as the -stars in the firmament, – sands on

100a. [Less than one.] **Fraction.—N.** fraction, fractional part, fragment; part &c. 51.

Adj. fractional, fragmentary, partial.

101. Zero.—N. zero, nothing naught, nought, duck's egg, goose egg; cipher, none, nobody; not a soul; *âme qui vive*; absence &c. 187; unsubstantiality &c. 4.

Adj. not -one, – any.

103. Fewness.—N. fewness &c. *adj.*; paucity, small number; small quantity &c. 32; scarcity, sparsity, rarity; infrequency &c. 137; handful; maniple; minority, exiguity.

[Diminution of number] reduction; weeding &c. *v.*; elimination, sarculation, decimation.

V. be -few &c. *adj.*

render -few &c. *adj.*; reduce, diminish the number, weed, eliminate, thin decimate.

Adj. few; scarce; scant, -y; thin, rare, thinly scattered, few and far between; exiguous; infrequent &c. 137; *rari nantes*; hardly –, scarcely-any; to be counted on one's fingers; reduced &c. *v.*; unrepeated.

Adv. here and there.

⟡e sea-shore, – hairs on the head; and -what not, – heaven knows
⟡at; endless &c. (*infinite*) 105.
Phr. their name is 'Legion.'

104. Repetition.—N. repetition, iteration, reiteration, duplication,
ding-dong, alliteration; *epistrophe*; harping, recurrence, succession, run;
batto-, tauto-logy; monotony, tautophony; rhythm &c. 138; pleonasm,
redundancy, diffuseness.

chimes, repetend, echo, *ritornello*, burden of a song, *refrain*; rehearsal;
encore; *réchauffé*, *rifacimento*, recapitulation.

cuckoo &c. (*imitation*) 19; reverberation &c. 408; drumming &c.
(*roll*) 407; renewal &c. (*restoration*) 660.

twice-told tale; old -story, – song, chestnut; second –, new- edition;
reprint, new impression; return game, return match, reappearance,
reproduction; periodicity &c. 138.

V. repeat, iterate, reiterate, reproduce, parrot, echo, re-echo, drum,
harp upon, battologize, hammer, redouble.

recur, revert, return, reappear; renew &c. (*restore*) 660.

rehearse; do –, say- over again; ring the changes on; harp on the
same string; din –, drum- in the ear; conjugate in all its moods, tenses
and inflexions, begin again, go over the same ground, go the same round,
never hear the last of; resume, return to, recapitulate, reword.

Adj. repeated &c. *v.*; repetition-al, -ary; recur-rent, -ring; ever
recurring, thick coming; frequent, incessant, redundant, pleonastic,
tautological.

monotonous, harping, iterative; mocking, chiming; retold; aforesaid,
-named; above-mentioned, said; habitual &c. 613; another.

Adv. repeatedly, often, again, afresh, anew, over again, once more;
ditto, *encore, de novo, bis, da capo.*

again and again; over and over, – again; many times over; time-
and again, – after time; year after year; day by day &c.; many –,
several –, a number of- times; many –, full many- a time; times out of
number, year in and year out, morning, noon and night; frequently
&c. 136.

Phr. *ecce iterum Crispinus, toujours perdrix,* cut and come again;
tomorrow and tomorrow.'

105. Infinity.—N. infini-ty, -tude, -teness &c. *adj.*; perpetuity &c. 112.

V. be -infinite &c. *adj.*; know –, have- no -limits, – bounds; go on
for ever.

Adj. infinite; immense; number-, count-, sum-, measure-less; in
numer-, immeasur-, incalcul-, illimit-, intermin-, unfathom-, unap-
proach-able; exhaustless, inexhaustible, indefinite; without -number,
– measure, – limit, – end; incomprehensible; limit-, end-, bound-, termless; un-told, -numbered, -measured, -bounded, -limited; illimited;
perpetual &c. 112.

Adv. infinitely &c. *adj.*; *ad infinitum.*

Section VI.   TIME

1°. Absolute Time

106. Time.—N. time, duration;
period, term, stage, space, span, spell,
season; the whole -time, – period;
course &c. 109.

107. Neverness.*—N. 'neverness'
absence of time, no time; *dies non,*
Tib's eve; Greek Kalends.

Adv. never; at no -time, – period;

* A term introduced by Bishop Wilkins.

intermediate time, while, *interim*, interval, bit, pendency; inter-vention, -mission, -mittence, -regnum, -lude; respite.

on no occasion, never in all one's born days, nevermore, *sine die*.

era, epoch, æon, cycle; time of life, age, year, date; decade &c. (*period*) 108; moment, &c. (*instant*) 113; reign &c. 737.

glass –, ravages –, whirligig –, noiseless foot- of time; scythe. **V.** continue, last, endure, go on, hold out, remain, stay, persist, abide, run; intervene; elapse &c. 109.

take –, take up –, fill –, occupy- time.

pass –, pass away –, spend –, while away –, consume –, talk against –, kill- time; tide over; use –, employ- time; tarry &c. 110; seize an opportunity &c. 134; waste time &c. (*be inactive*) 683.

Adj. continuing &c. *v.*; on foot; permanent &c. (*durable*) 110.

Adv. while, whilst, during, pending; during the -time, – interval; in the course of; for the time being, day by day; in the time of, when; mean-time, -while; in the -meantime, – *interim*; *ad interim, pendente lite*; *de die in diem*; from -day to day, – hour to hour &c.; hourly, always; for a -time, – season; till, until, up to, yet; the whole –, all the- time; all along; throughout &c. (*completely*) 52; for good &c. (*diuturnity*) 110.

here-, there-, where-upon; then; *anno*, – *Domini*; A.D.; *ante Christum*; A.C.; before Christ; B.C.; *anno urbis conditæ*; A.U.C.; *anno regni*; A.R.; once upon a time, one fine morning.

Phr. time -runs, – runs against; *tempus fugit*.

---

108. [Definite duration, or portion of time.] **Period.**—**N.** period; second, minute, hour, day, week, sennight, octave, month, moon, quarter, semester, year, *lustrum, quinquennium*, decade, *decennium*, indiction, lifetime, generation, epoch, era, cycle.

century, age, *millennium; annus magnus*.

Adj. horary; hourly, annual &c. (*periodical*) 138.

108a. Contingent Duration.—**Adv.** during -pleasure, – good behaviour; *quamdiu se bene gesserit*.

---

109. [Indefinite duration.] **Course.** —**N.** course –, progress –, process –. succession –, lapse –, flow –, flux –, effluxion, stream –, tract –, current –, sweep –, tide –, march –, step –, flight- of time; duration &c. 106.

[Indefinite time] aorist.

V. elapse, lapse, flow, run, proceed, advance, pass; roll –, wear –, press –, drag- on; flit, fly, slip, slide, glide, crawl; run -its course.

out; expire; go –, pass- by; be -past &c. 122.

Adj. elapsing &c. *v.*; aoristic; progressive, transient &c. 111.

Adv. in due -time, – season; in -course, – process, – the fulness- of time; in time.

Phr. *labitur et labetur*; *truditur dies die*; *fugaces labuntur anni*; 'tomorrow and tomorrow and tomorrow creeps in this petty pace from day to day.'

---

110. [Long duration.] **Diuturnity.** —**N.** diuturnity; a -long –, length of- time; an age, a century, an eternity,

111. [Short duration.] **Transientness.** —**N.** transientness &c. *adj.*; evanescence, impermanence, fugacity, transi-

æons; slowness &c. 275; perpetuity &c. 112; blue moon.

dura-bleness, -bility; persistence, lastingness &c. *adj.*; continuance, assiduity, endurance, standing; permanence &c. (*stability*) 150; survi-val, -vance; longevity &c. (*age*) 128; distance of time.

protraction –, prolongation –, extension- of time; delay &c. (*lateness*) 133.

V. last, endure, stand, remain, abide, continue, brave a thousand years.

tarry &c. (*be late*) 133; drag -on, – its slow length along, – a lengthening chain; protract, prolong; spin –, eke –, draw –, lengthen- out; temporize; gain –, make –, talk against- time.

out-last, -live; survive; live to fight again.

Adj. durable; perdurable; lasting &c. *v.*; of long -duration, – standing; permanent, chronic, long-standing; intransi-ent, -tive; intransmutable, persistent; life-, live-long; longeval, long-lived, macrobiotic, diuturnal, sempervirent, evergreen, perennial; unin-, ter-, unre-mitting; perpetual &c. 112.

lingering, protracted, prolonged, spun out &c. *v.*; long-pending, -winded; slow &c. 275.

Adv. long; for -a long time, – an age, – ages, – ever so long, – many a long day; long ago &c. (*in a past time*) 122; *longo intervallo.*

all the -day long, – year round; the livelong day, as the day is long, morning, noon and night; hour after hour, day after day, &c.; for good; permanently &c. *adj.*

112. [Endless duration.] **Perpetuity.**
—**N.** perpetuity, eternity, timelessness; everness,* aye, sempiternity, immortality, athanasia; everlastingness &c. *adj.*; perpetuation; infinite duration.

V. last –, endure –, go on- for ever; have no end.

eternize, eternify, perpetuate, immortalize.

Adj. perpetual, eternal, eterne; everlasting, -living, -flowing; continual, constant, sempiternal; co-eternal; endless, unending; ceaseless, incessant, uninterrupted, indesinent, unceasing; interminable, having no end; unfad-

toriness, volatility, caducity, mortality, span; flash in the pan, nine days' wonder, bubble, May-fly; spurt; temporary arrangement, interregnum.

velocity &c. 274; suddenness &c. 113; changeableness &c. 149.

V. be -transient &c. *adj.*; flit, pass away, fly, gallop, vanish, fade, fleet, melt away, evaporate; pass away like a -cloud, – summer cloud, – shadow, – dream.

Adj. transi-ent, -tory, -tive; passing, evanescent, fleeting; flying &c. *v.*; fug-acious, -itive; shifting, slippery; spasmodic.

tempor-al, -ary; provis-ional, -ory; cursory, short-lived, ephemeral, deciduous; perishable, mortal, precarious; impermanent.

brief, quick, brisk; cometary, meteoric, extemporaneous, summary; pressed for time &c. (*haste*) 684; sudden, momentary &c. (*instantaneous*) 113.

Adv. temporarily &c. *adj.*; *pro tempore*; for -the moment, – a time; awhile, *en passant, in transitu*; in a short time; soon &c. (*early*) 132; briefly &c. *adj.*; at short notice; on the -point, – eve -of; *in articulo*; between cup and lip.

Phr. one's days are numbered; the time is up; here to-day and gone to-morrow; *non semper erit æstas; eheu! fugaces labuntur anni; sic transit gloria mundi.*

_____

113. [Point of time.] **Instantaneity.**
—**N.** instantane-ity, -ousness; sudden-, abrupt-ness.

moment, instant, second, minute; twinkling, trice, flash, breath, crack, jiffy, *coup*, burst, flash of lightning, stroke of time.

epoch, time; time of -day, – night; hour, minute; very -minute &c., – time, – hour; present –, right –, true –, exact –, correct- time.

V. be -instantaneous &c. *adj.*: twinkle, flash.

Adj. instantaneous, momentary, extempore, sudden, instant, abrupt;

ing, evergreen, amaranthine; never-ending, -dying, -fading; deathless, immortal, undying, imperishable.

Adv. perpetually &c. *adj.*; always, ever, evermore, aye; for -ever, – aye, – evermore, – ever and a day, – ever and ever; in all ages, from age to age; without end; world –, time- without end; *in sæcula sæculorum*; to the -end of time, – crack of doom, – 'last syllable of recorded time'; till doomsday; constantly &c. (*very frequently*) 136.

Phr. *esto perpetua!; labitur et labetur in omne volubilis ævum.*

subitaneous, hasty; quick as -thought,[*] – lightning, – a flash; rapid as electricity.

Adv. instantaneously &c. *adj.*; in –, in less than- no time; *presto, subito, instanter,* suddenly, at a stroke, like a shot, – greased lightning; in a trice, in a moment &c. *n.*; eftsoons, in the twinkling of -an eye, – a bed post; at one jump, in the same breath, *per saltum, uno saltu*; at –, all at- once; in one's tracks; plump, slap; 'at one fell swoop'; at the same -instant &c. *n.*; immediately &c. (*early*) 132; extempore, on the -spot, – spur of the moment, – dot; just then; slap- dash &c. (*haste*) 684; before you could -turn

round, – say -knife, – Jack Robinson.
Phr. touch and go; no sooner said than done.

---

114. [Estimation, measurement, and record of time.] **Chronometry.—N.** chrono-, horo-metry, -logy; date, epoch; style, era, age.

almanac, calendar, ephemeris; register, -try; chronicle, annals, journal, diary, chronogram.

[Instruments for the measurement of time] clock, watch; chrono-meter, -scope, -graph; repeater, alarum; time-keeper, -piece; dial, sun-dial, *gnomon, pendule,* horologe, pendulum, hourglass, water clock, clepsydra.

mean –, Greenwich –, solar –, sidereal –, local –, summer- time; daylight saving.

chrono-grapher, -loger, -logist; annalist.

V. fix –, mark- the time; date, register, chronicle; measure –. beat –, mark- time; bear date.

Adj. chrono-logical, -metrical, -grammatical; isochronal.

Adv. o'clock; *a.m., p.m.*

115. [False estimate of time.] **Anachronism.—N.** ana-, meta-, para-, prochronism; *prolepsis,* misdate; anticipation, antichronism.

disregard –, neglect –, oblivion- of time.

intempestivity &c. 135.

V. mis-, ante-, post-, over-date; anticipate; take no note of time.

Adj. misdated &c. *v.*; undated; overdue; out of date; anachronous &c. *n.*

2°. RELATIVE TIME

1. *Time with reference to Succession*

116. Priority.—N. priority, antecedence, anteriority, pre-existence, precedence &c. 62; precession &c. 280; precursor &c. 64; the past &c. 122; premises.

V. precede, come before; forerun; antecede, go before &c. (*lead*) 280; pre-exist; dawn; premise, presage &c. 511.

be -beforehand &c. (*be early*) 132;

117. Posteriority.—N. posteriority; succession, sequence; following &c. 281; subsequence, supervention; futurity &c. 121; successor; sequel &c. 65; remainder, reversion.

V. follow &c. 281 –, come –, go-after; ensue, result; succeed, supervene; step into the shoes of.

Adj. subsequent, posterior, following, after, later, succeeding, postliminious,

steal a march upon, anticipate, forestall; have –, gain- the start.

Adj. prior, previous; preced-ing, -ent; anterior, antecedent; pre-existing, -existent; foresighted; former, foregoing; afore –, before-, above-mentioned; aforesaid, said; introductory &c. (*precursory*) 64; pre-war.

Adv. before, prior to; earlier; previously &c. *adj.*; afore, ere, theretofore, erewhile; ere –, before- -then, – now; erewhile, already, yet, beforehand; aforetime, on the eve of, in anticipation.

118. The Present Time.—N. the present -time, – day, – moment, – juncture, – occasion; the times, existing time, time being; twentieth century; nonce, crisis, epoch, day, hour.

age, time of life.

Adj. present, actual, instant, current, latest, existing, that is.

Adv. at this -time, – moment &c. 113; at the -present time &c. *n.*; now, at present.

at this time of day, to-day, now-a-days; already; even –, but –, just-now; on the present occasion; for the -time being, – nonce; *pro hâc vice*; on the -nail, – spot; on the spur of the -moment, – occasion.

until now; to -this, – the present day.

120. Synchronism.—N. synchronism; coexistence, coincidence; simultaneousness &c. *adj.*; concurrence, concomitance, unity of time, interim.

[Having equal times] isochronism, syntony.

contemporary, coetanian.

V. coexist, concur, accompany, go hand in hand, keep pace with; synchronize, isochronize.

Adj. synchron-ous, -al, -ical, -istical; simultaneous, coexisting, coincident, concomitant, concurrent; coev-al, -ous; contempora-ry, -neous; coetaneous; coterminous, coeternal; isochronous.

Adv. at the same time; simultaneously &c. *adj.*; together, in concert, during the same time; in the same breath; *pari passu*; in the interim.

at the -very moment &c. 113; just as, as soon as; meanwhile &c. (*while*) 106.

121. [Prospective time.] **Futurity. —N.** futur-ity, -ition; future, hereafter, time to come; approaching –, coming –, after- -time, – age, – days, – hours, – years, – ages, – life; morrow, to-morrow, by and by; millennium, doomsday, day of judgment, crack of doom, remote future.

postnate; successive &c. 63; postdiluvial, -an; *puisné*; posthumous; post-war, future &c. 121.

Adv. subsequently, after, afterwards, since, later; at a -subsequent, – later-period; next, in the sequel, close upon, thereafter, thereupon, upon which, eftsoons; from that -time, – moment; after a -while, – time; in process of time.

postcenal, postcibal, postprandial, after-dinner.

119. [Time different from the present.] **Different Time.—N.** different –, other- time.

[Indefinite time] aorist.

Adj. aoristic.

Adv. at that –, at which- -time, – moment, – instant; then, on that occasion, upon.

when; when-ever, -soever; upon which, on which occasion; at -another, – a different, – some other, – any- time; at various times; some –, one- -of these days, – fine morning, – day; sooner or later; some time or other; once upon a time, once.

122. [Retrospective time.] **Preterition.—N.** preterition; priority &c. 116; the past, past time; days –, times- -of yore, – of old, – past, – gone by; bygone days, good old days; old –, ancient –, former -times; fore time; yesterdays; the olden –, good old-time; auld lang syne; eld.

approach of time, advent, time draw-ing on, womb of time; destiny &c. 152; eventuality.

heritage, heirs, posterity, descend-ants.

prospect &c. (*expectation*) 5C7; fore-sight &c. 510.

V. look forwards; anticipate &c. (*ex-pect*) 507, (*foresee*) 510; forestall &c. (*be early*) 132.

come –, draw- on; draw near; ap-proach, await, threaten; impend &c. (*be destined*) 152.

Adj. future, to come; coming &c. (*impending*) 152; next, near; near –, close- at hand; eventual, ulterior; ex-pectant, prospective, in prospect &c. (*expectation*) 507.

Adv. prospectively, hereafter, on the knees of the gods, in future; to-morrow, the day after to-morrow; in -course, – process, – the fulness- of time; even-tually, ultimately, sooner or later; *proximo*; *paulo post futurum*; in after time; one of these days; after a -time, – while.

from this time; hence-forth, -for-wards; thence; thence-forth, -forward; whereupon, upon which.

soon &c. (*early*) 132; on the -eve, – point, – brink- of; about to; close upon.

---

antiquity, antiqueness, *status quo*; time immemorial; distance of time; remote -age, – time; ancient history; remote past; rust of antiquity; ancient-ness.

pale-ontology, -ography, -ology; pa-lætiology,* archæology; archaism, an-tiquarianism, mediævalism, pre-Raph-aelitism; retrospection, looking back, memory &c. 505.

laudator temporis acti; mediævalist, pre-Raphaelite; antiqu-ary, -arian; archæologist &c.; Oldbuck, Dryasdust.

ancestry &c. (*paternity*) 166.

V. be -past &c. *adj.*; have -expired &c. *adj.*, – run its course, – had its day; pass; pass –, go- -by, – away, – off; lapse, blow over.

look –, trace –, cast the eyes- back; exhume.

Adj. past, gone, gone by, over, passed away, bygone, foregone; elapsed, lapsed, preterlapsed, expired, no more, run out, blown over, that has been, whilom, extinct, never to return, exploded, forgotten, irrecover-able; obsolete &c. (*old*) 124; extinct as the dodo.

former, pristine, *quondam*, *ci-devant*, late; ancestral.

foregoing; last, latter; recent, over-night; past, preterite, preter-perfect, -pluperfect, past perfect.

looking back &c. *v.*; retro-spective, -active; archæological &c. *n.*

Adv. formerly; of -old, – yore; erst, whilom, erewhile, time was ago, over; in -the olden time &c. *n.*; anciently, long -ago, – since; a long -while, – time- ago; years –, ages- ago; some time -ago, – since, – back.

yesterday, the day before yesterday; last -year, – season, – month &c.; *ultimo*; lately &c. (*newly*) 123.

retrospecti~ely, ere –, before –, till- now; hitherto, heretofore; no longer; once, – upon a time; from time immemorial; in the memory of man; time out of mind; already, yet, up to this time; *ex post facto*.

Phr. time was; the time -has, – hath- been.

2. *Time with reference to a particular Period*

123. Newness.—N. newness &c. *adj.*; neologism, neoterism; novelty, recency; immaturity; youth &c. 127; gloss of novelty.

124. Oldness.—N. oldness &c. *adj.*; age, antiquity; cobwebs of antiquity; maturity, ripeness; decline, decay; senility &c. 128.

* Whewell.

innovation; renovation &c. (*restoration*) 660.

modernist, neologist, neoteric.

modernism, modernity; mushroom; latest fashion, *dernier cri*.

upstart, *parvenu, nouveau riche*.

V. renew &c. (*restore*) 660; modernize.

Adj. new, novel, recent, fresh, green; young &c. 127; evergreen; raw, immature; virgin; un-tried, -handseled, -used, -trodden, -beaten; fledgling.

late, modern, neoteric; new-born, -fashioned, -fangled, -fledged; of yesterday; just out, brand –, span-new, up to date, topical; vernal, renovated; innovatory.

fresh as -a rose, – a daisy, – paint; spick and span.

Adv. newly &c. *adj.*; afresh, anew, lately, just now, only yesterday, the other day; latterly, of late.

not long –, a short time- ago.

seniority, eldership, primogeniture; archaism &c. (*the past*) 122; thing –, relic- of the past; megatherium.

tradition, prescription, custom, folklore, immemorial usage, common law.

V. be -old &c. *adj.*; have -had, – seen- its day; become -old &c. *adj.*; age, fade.

Adj. old, olden, ancient, antique; of long standing, time-honoured, venerable; eld-er, -est; first-born.

prime; prim-itive, -eval, -igenous; primordi-al, -nate; aboriginal &c. (*beginning*) 66; diluvian, antediluvian; pre-historic; patriarchal, preadamite; palæocrystic; fossil, paleozoic, preglacial, ante-mundane; archaic, classic, mediæval, pre-Raphaelite, ancestral, black-letter.

immemorial, traditional, prescriptive, customary, whereof the memory of man runneth not to the contrary; inveterate, rooted.

antiquated, of other times, rococo, of the old school, after-age, obsolete; fusty, moth-eaten; out of -date, – fashion; stale, old-fashioned, behind the -age, – times; exploded; gone out, – by; *passé*, outworn, run out; disused; senile &c. 128; time-worn; crumbling &c. (*deteriorated*) 659; second-hand.

old as -the hills, – Methuselah, – Adam, – history; Anno Domini.

Adv. since the -world was made, – year one, – days of Methuselah;

---

125. Morning. [Noon.]—**N.** morning, morn, matins, forenoon, *a.m.*, prime, dawn, daybreak, daylight, sun-up, peep –, break- of day; aurora, Eos; first blush –, prime- of the morning; twilight, crepuscule, sunrise, cockcrow.

spring; vernal equinox.

noon; mid-, noon-day; noontide, meridian, prime.

summer, midsummer; summer solstice.

Adj. matin, matutinal; vernal, æstival.

Adv. at -sunrise &c. *n.*; with the lark, when the morning dawns

127. Youth.—N. youth; juven- -ility, -escence; juniority; infancy; baby-, child-, boy-, girl-, youth-hood; *incunabula*; minority, immaturity, nonage, teens, tender age, bloom.

cradle, nursery, leading-strings, pupilage, puberty, *pucelage*.

126. Evening. [Midnight.]—**N.** evening, eve; decline –, fall –, close- or day; eventide, evensong, vespers; candlelight; nightfall, curfew, dusk, twilight, blind man's holiday; eleventh hour; sun-set, -down; going down of the sun, cock-shut, dewy eve, gloaming, bed-time.

afternoon, *post meridiem, p.m.*

autumn; fall, – of the leaf; autumnal equinox, Indian summer, harvest-time.

midnight; dead –, witching time- of nighv; winter, – solstice.

Adj. vespertine, autumnal, nocturnal, wintry, brumal, hiemal.

128. Age.—N. age; oldness &c. *adj.*; old –, advanced- age; sen-ility, -escence; years, anility, grey hairs, climacteric, grand climacteric, declining years, decrepitude, hoary age, caducity, superannuation; second childhood, -ishness; dotage; vale of years,

prime –, flower –, spring-tide –, seed-time –, golden season- of life; heyday of youth, school days; rising generation, younger generation.

Adj. young, youthful, juvenile, green, callow, budding, sappy, *puisné*, beardless, unfledged, unripe, under age, in one's teens; *in statu pupillari*; younger, junior.

decline of life, 'sear and yellow leaf'; three-score years and ten; green old age, ripe old age; longevity; time of life.

seniority, eldership; elders &c. (*veteran*) 130; firstling; *doyen*, dean, father; primogeniture; nostology.

V. be -aged &c. *adj.*; grow –, get-old &c. *adj.*; age; decline, wane.

Adj. aged; old &c. 124; elderly, senile; matronly, anile; in years; ripe, mellow, run to seed, declining, waning, past one's prime; grey, -headed; hoar, -y; venerable, time-worn, antiquated, *passé*, effete, doddering, decrepit, superannuated; advanced in -life, – years; stricken in years; wrinkled, marked with the crow's foot; having one foot in the grave; doting &c. (*imbecile*) 499.

old-, eld-er, -est; senior; first-born.

turned of, years old; of a certain age, no chicken, old as Methuselah; gerontic; ancestral; patriarchal &c. (*ancient*) 124.

129. Infant.—N. infant, babe, baby; nurse-, suck-, year-, wean-ling; *papoose*, *bambino*.

child, bairn, little- one, – tot, – mite, chick, brat, chit, pickaninny, kid, urchin; bant-, brat-ling; elf.

youth, boy, lad, slip, sprig, stripling, youngster, cub, unlicked cub, younker, callant, whipster, whipper-snapper, schoolboy, hobbledehoy, hopeful, cadet, minor, master.

scion; sap-, seed-ling; tendril, olive-branch, nestling, chicken, duckling; larva, caterpillar, chrysalis, cocoon; tadpole, whelp, cub, pullet, fry, callow; codlin, -g; *fœtus*, calf, colt, pup, foal, kitten; lamb, -kin.

girl; lass, -ie; wench, miss, damsel, *demoiselle*, damozel; maid. -en; virgin; nymph; colleen; minx, baggage, school-girl; tomboy, flapper, hoyden.

Adj. infant-ine, -ile; puerile; boy-, girl-, child-, baby-, kitten-ish; baby; new-born, unfledged, new-fledged, callow.

in -the cradle, – swaddling clothes, – long clothes, – arms, – leading strings; at the breast; in one's teens; young &c. 127.

130. Veteran.—N. veteran, old man, seer, patriarch, greybeard, dugout, grand-father, -sire; grandam, beldam; gaffer, gammer; hag, crone; pantaloon; sexage-, octoge-, nonage-, cente-narian; old stager; dotard &c. 501.

preadamite, Methuselah, Nestor, Rip van Winkle, old Parr; elders; fore-fathers &c. (*paternity*) 166.

131. Adolescence.—N. adolescence, pubescence, majority; adultness &c. *adj.*; manhood, virility, maturity; flower of age; prime –, meridian- of life.

man &c. 373; woman &c. 374; adult, no chicken.

V. come -of age, – to man's estate, – to years of discretion; attain majority, assume the *toga virilis*; have -cut one's eye-teeth, – sown one's wild oats, settle down.

Adj. adolescent, pubescent, of age; of -full, – ripe- age; out of one's teens, grown up, mature, full- blown, – grown, in one's prime, in full bloom, manly, virile, adult; womanly, matronly; marriageable, nubile.

3. *Time with reference to an Effect or Purpose*

132. Earliness.—N. earliness &c. *adj.*; morning &c. 125.

punctuality; promptitude &c. (*activity*) 682; haste &c. (*velocity*) 274; suddenness &c. (*instantaneity*) 113.

prematurity, precocity, precipitation, anticipation; prevenience, a stitch in time.

V. be -early &c. *adj.*, - beforehand &c. *adv.*; keep time, take time by the forelock, anticipate, forestall; have -, gain- the start; steal a march upon; gain time, draw on futurity; bespeak, secure, engage, pre-engage.

accelerate; expedite &c. (*quicken*) 274; make haste &c. (*hurry*) 684.

Adj. early, prime, timely, in time, punctual, forward; prompt &c. (*active*) 682; summary.

premature, precipitate, precocious; prevenient, anticipatory; rathe.

sudden &c. (*instantaneous*) 113; unexpected &c. 508; impending, imminent; near, - at hand; immediate.

Adv. early, soon, anon, betimes, rathe; eft, -soons; ere -, before- long; punctually &c. *adj.*; to the minute; in time; in -good, - military, - pudding, - due- time; time enough.

beforehand; prematurely &c. *adj.*; precipitately &c. (*hastily*) 684; too soon; before -its, - one's- time; in anticipation; unexpectedly &c. 508.

suddenly &c. (*instantaneously*) 113; before one can say 'Jack Robinson,' at short notice, extempore; on the spur of the -moment, - occasion; at once; on the -spot, - instant; at sight; off -, out of- hand; à vue d'œil; straight, -way, -forth; forthwith, incontinently, summarily, instanter, immediately, briefly, shortly, quickly, speedily, apace, before the ink is dry, almost immediately, presently, at the first opportunity, in no long time, by and by, in a while, directly.

Phr. touch and go, no sooner said than done.

134. Occasion.—N. occasion, opportunity, opening, room, scope, field; suitable -, proper- -time, - season; high time; opportuneness &c. *adj.*; tempestivity.

133. Lateness.—N. lateness &c. *adj.*; tardiness &c. (*slowness*) 275.

de-lay, -lation; cunctation, procrastination; detention; deferring &c. *v.*; filibuster, postponement, adjournment, prorogation, retardation, respite, reprieve, stay; protraction, prolongation, moratorium; contango; demurrage; remand; Fabian policy, *médecine expectante*, chancery suit; leeway; high time.

V. be -late &c. *adj.*; tarry, wait, stay, bide, take time; dawdle &c. (*be inactive*) 683; linger, loiter, saunter, lag behind; bide -, take- one's time; hang -about, - around, - back, - in the balance; gain time; hang fire; stand -, lie-over.

put off, defer, delay, lay over, suspend; shift -, stave- off; waive, retard, remand, postpcne, adjourn; procrastinate; dally; prolong, protract; spin -, draw -, lengthen- out; prorogue; keep back; tide over; push -, drive- to the last; let the matter stand over; reserve &c. (*store*) 636; temporize; consult one's pillow, sleep upon it.

shelve, table, lay on the table.

lose an opportunity &c. 135; be kept waiting, dance attendance; kick -, cool- one's heels; *faire antichambre*; wait impatiently; await &c. (*expect*) 507; sit up, - at night.

Adj. late, tardy, slow, behindhand, belated, postliminious, posthumous, backward, unpunctual; dilatory &c. (*slow*), overdue 275; delayed &c. *v.*; in abeyance.

Adv. late; late-, back-ward; late in the day; at -sunset, - the eleventh hour, - length, - last, - long; ultimately; after -, behind- time; too late; too late for &c. 135.

slowly, leisurely, deliberately, at one's leisure; *ex post facto*; *sine die*.

Phr. *nonum prematur in annum.*

_____

135. Intempestivity.—N. intempestivity; unseasonableness; unsuitable -, improper-time; unreasonableness &c. *adj.*; evil hour; *contretemps*; intrusion; anachronism &c. 115.

crisis, turn, juncture, emergency, conjuncture; turning point, given time.

nick of time; golden -, well-timed -, fine -, favourable- opportunity; clear stage, fair field; *mollia tempora*; *fata Morgana*; spare time &c. (*leisure*) 685.

V. seize &c. (*take*) 789 -, use &c. 677 -, give &c. 784- an -opportunity, - occasion; improve the occasion.

suit the occasion &c. (*be expedient*) 646.

strike the iron while it is hot, *battre le fer sur l'enclume*, make hay while the sun shines, take time by the forelock, *prendre la balle au bond*.

Adj. opportune, timely, well-timed, timeous, timeful, seasonable.

providential, lucky, fortunate, happy, favourable, propitious, auspicious, critical; suitable &c. 23; *obiter dicta*.

Adv. opportunely &c. *adj.*; in ·proper, - due- -time, - course, - season; for the nonce; in the -nick, - fulness- of time; all in good time; just in time, at the eleventh hour, now or never.

by the -way, - by; *en passant, à propos; pro -re natâ, - hac vice; par parenthèse*, parenthetically, by way of parenthesis; while -speaking of, - on this subject; extempore; on the spur of the -moment, - occasion; on the spot &c. (*early*) 132.

Phr. *carpe diem; occasionem cognosce;* one's hour is come, the time is up; that reminds me.

V. be -ill timed &c. *adj.*; mistime, intrude, come amiss, break in upon; have other fish to fry; be -busy, - engaged, - tied up, - occupied.

lose -, throw away -, waste -, neglect &c. 460- an opportunity; allow -, suffer- the -opportunity, - occasion- to -pass, - slip, - go by, - escape, - lapse; waste time &c. (*be inactive*) 683; let slip through the fingers, lock the stable door when the steed is stolen.

Adj. ill-, mis-timed; untimely, intrusive, unseasonable; out of -date, - season; inopportune, timeless, untoward, *mal à propos*, unlucky, inauspicious, unpropitious, unfortunate, unfavourable; unsuited &c. 24; inexpedient &c. 647.

unpunctual &c. (*late*) 133; too late for; premature &c. (*early*) 132; too soon for; wise after the event.

Adv. inopportunely &c. *adj.*; as ill luck would have it, in an evil hour, the time having gone by, a day after the fair.

Phr. after meat mustard, after death the doctor.

3°. Recurrent Time

136. Frequency.—**N.** frequency, oftness; repetition, &c. 104.

V. recur &c. 104; do nothing but; keep, - on.

Adj. frequent, many times, not rare, thickcoming, incessant, perpetual, continual, constant, recurrent, repeated &c. 104; habitual &c. 613; hourly, &c. 138.

Adv. often, often to be met with, oft; oft-, often-times; frequently; repeatedly &c. 104; unseldom, not unfrequently; in -quick, - rapid- succession; many a time and oft; daily, hourly &c.; every -day, - hour, - moment &c.

perpetually, continually, constantly, incessantly, without ceasing, at all times, daily and hourly, night and day,

137. Infrequency.—**N.** infrequency, infrequence, rareness, rarity; fewness &c. 103; seldomness, uncommonness.

V. be -rare &c. *adj.*

Adj. un-, in-frequent; uncommon, sporadic, rare, - as a blue diamond; few &c. 103; scarce; almost unheard of, unprecedented, which has not occurred within the memory of the oldest inhabitant, not within one's previous experience.

Adv. seldom, rarely, scarcely, hardly; not often, unfrequently, infrequently, unoften; scarcely -, hardly- ever; once in a blue moon.

once; once -for all, - in a way; *pro hac vice*; like angels' visits, few and far between.

----

day and night, day after day, morning noon and night, ever and anon.

most often; commonly &c. (*habitually*) 613.

sometimes, occasionally, at times, now and then, from time to time, there being times when, *toties quoties*, often enough, again and again &c. 104.

138. Regularity of recurrence. Periodicity.—N. periodicity, intermittence; beat; oscillation &c. 314; pulse, pulsation; rhythm; alter-nation, -nateness, -nativeness, -nity.

bout, round, revolution, rotation, turn.

anniversary, birthday, jubilee, centenary, bi-, ter-centenary.

[Regularity of return] rota, cycle, period, stated time, routine; days of the week; Sunday, Monday &c.; months of the year; January &c.; feast, fast, saint's day &c.; Christmas, Easter, New Year's Day &c. 998; quarter-, Lady-, Midsummer-, Michaelmas-day; May Day, the King's Birthday; leap year; seasons.

punctuality, regularity, steadiness.

V. recur in regular -order, – succession; return, revolve, rotate; come -again, – in its turn; come round, – again; beat, pulsate; alternate; intermit.

Adj. periodic, -al; serial, recurrent, cyclic-, -al, rhythmic-, -al, even; recurring &c. *v.*; inter-, re-mittent; alternate, every other.

hourly; diurnal, daily; quotidian, tertian, weekly; hebdomad-al, -ary; bi-weekly, fortnightly; monthly, menstrual, catamenial; yearly, annual; biennial, triennial, &c.; bissextile; centennial, secular; paschal, lenten, &c.

regular, steady, punctual, constant, methodical, regular as clockwork.

Adv. periodically &c. *adj.*; at -regular intervals, – stated times; at -fixed, – established- periods; punctually &c. *adj.*; *de die in diem*; from day to day, day by day.

by turns; in -turn, – rotation; alternately, every other day, off and on, ride and tie, round and round.

139. Irregularity of recurrence.—N. irregularity, uncertainty, unpunctuality; fitfulness &c. *adj.*

Adj. irregular, uneven, uncertain, unpunctual, capricious, erratic, desultory, fitful, flickering; rambling, rhapsodical; spasmodic, unsystematic, unequal, variable, halting.

Adv. irregularly &c. *adj.*; by fits and starts &c. (*discontinuously*) 70.

Section VII. CHANGE

1°. Simple Change

140. [Difference at different times.] **Change.—N.** change, alteration, mutation, permutation, variation, modification, modulation, inflexion, mood, qualification, innovation, *metastasis*, deviation, shift, turn; diversion; break.

transformation, transfiguration; metamorphosis; metabolism; transmutation; transubstantiation; metagenesis, transanimation, transmigration, me-

141. [Absence of change.] **Permanence.—N.** stability &c. 150; quiescence &c. 265; obstinacy &c. 606.

permanence, -cy, persistence, fixity, fixity of purpose, endurance, durability; standing, *status quo*; maintenance, preservation, conservation; conservatism; *laissez-faire*; law of the Medes and Persians; standing dish.

V. let -alone, – be; persist, remain,

tempsychosis; version; metathesis; transmogrification; catalysis; *avatar*; alterative.

conversion &c. (*gradual change*) 144; revolution &c. (*sudden or radical change*) 146; inversion &c. (*reversal*) 218; displacement &c. 185; transference &c. 270.

changeableness &c. 149; tergiversation &c. (*change of mind*) 607.

V. change, alter, vary, wax and wane; modulate, diversify, qualify, tamper with; turn, shift, veer, jibe, tack, chop, shuffle, swerve, dodge, warp, deviate, turn aside, evert, intervert; pass to, take a turn, turn the corner, resume.

work a change, modify, vamp, revamp, superinduce; trans-form, –mute, -ume, –figure &c. *n.*; metamorphose, ring the changes; convert, resolve; revolutionize; chop and change; patch, re-shape.

innovate, introduce new blood, shuffle the cards, spin the wheel; give a -turn, – colour- to; influence, turn the scale; shift the scene, turn over a new leaf.

recast &c. 146; reverse &c. 218; disturb &c. 61; convert into &c. 144.

Adj. changed &c. *v.*; new-fangled; changeable &c. 149; transitional; modifiable; alterative.

Adv. *mutatis mutandis.*

Int. *quantum mutatus!*

Phr. 'a change came o'er the spirit of my dream'; *nous avons changé tout cela; tempora mutantur et nos mutamur in illis; non sum qualis eram.*

stay, tarry, rest; hold, – on; last, endure, bide, abide, aby, dwell, maintain, keep; stand, – still, – fast; subsist, live, outlive, survive; hold –, keep-one's -ground, – footing; hold good.

Adj. stable &c. 150; persisting &c. *v.*; permanent; established, fixed; durable; unchanged &c. (change &c. 140); unrenewed; intact, inviolate; persistent; monotonous, uncheckered; unfailing.

un-destroyed, -repealed, -suppressed; conservative, *qualis ab incepto*; prescriptive &c. (*old*) 124; stationary &c. 265.

Adv. *in statu quo*; for good, finally; at a stand, -still; *uti possidetis*; without a shadow of turning.

Phr. as you were!; *j'y suis j'y reste; esto perpetua; nolumus leges Angliæ mutari*; let sleeping dogs lie.

---

142. [Change from action to rest.] **Cessation.—N.** cessation, discontinuance, desistance, desinence.

inter-, re-mission; sus-pense, -pension; interruption, hitch; hartal; stop; stopping &c. *v.*; closure, stoppage, halt; arrival &c. 292.

pause, rest, lull, respite, truce, armistice, drop; interregnum, abeyance.

closure &c. 261.

dead -stop, – stand, – lock; checkmate; comma, colon, semicolon, period, full stop; end &c. 67; death &c. 360; *cæsura.*

V. cease, discontinue, desist. stay; break –, leave- off; hold, stop, pull up. stall, stop short, check; stick, deadlock, hang fire; halt; pause, rest.

have done with, give over, surcease,

143. Continuance in action.—**N.** continu-ance, -ation; run; extension, prolongation; maintenance, perpetuation; persistence &c. (*perseverance*) 604a; repetition &c. 104.

V. continue, persist; go –, jog –, keep –, carry –, run – hold- on; abide, keep, pursue, stick to; endure; take –, maintain- its course; keep up.

sustain, uphold, hold up, keep on foot; follow up. perpetuate, prolong; maintain; preserve &c. 604a; harp upon &c. (*repeat*) 104.

keep going, – alive, – at it, – the pot boiling, – the ball rolling, – up the ball; plod-, plug- along; slog on; die in harness; hold on –, pursue- the even tenor of one's way.

let be; *stare super antiquas vias;*

shut up shop; give up &c. (*relinquish*) 624.

hold –, stay- one's hand; rest on one's oars, repose on one's laurels.

come to a -stand, – standstill, – dead lock, – full stop; arrive &c. 292; go out, die away, peter out; wear -away, – off; pass away &c. (*be past*) 122; be at an end.

intromit, interrupt, suspend, interpel; inter-, re-mit; put -an end, – a stop, – a period- to; bring to a stand, -still; stop, cut out, cut short, arrest, avast; stem the -tide, – torrent; pull the check string; switch off.

Int. halt! hold! stop! enough! avast! have done! a truce to! scft! leave off! shut up! give over! chuck it!

quieta non movere; let things take their course.

Adj. continuing &c. *v.*; uninterrupted, unintermitting, unremitting, unvarying, unshifting; unreversed, unstopped, unrevoked, unvaried; sustained; undying &c. (*perpetual*) 112; inconvertible.

follow-up.

Int. carry on! right away!

Phr. *vestigia nulla retrorsum*; *labitur et labetur.*

144. [Gradual change to something different.] **Conversion.**—N. conversion, reduction, transmutation, transformation, development, resolution, assimilation; assumption; naturalization.

chemistry, alchemy; progress, growth, lapse, flux.

passage; transit, -ion; transmigration, shifting &c. *v.*; conjugation; convertibility.

crucible, alembic, caldron, retort, test tube &c.

convert, neophyte, proselyte, pervert, renegade, deserter, apostate, turncoat.

V. be converted into; become, get, wax; come –, turn- -to, – into; turn out, lapse, shift; run –, fall –, pass –, slide –, glide –, grow –, ripen –, open –, resolve itself –, settle –, merge- into; melt, grow, come round to, mature, mellow; assume the -form, – shape, – state, – nature, – character- of; illapse; assume a new phase, undergo a change.

convert –, resolve- into; make, render; mould, form &c. 240; re-model, new model, refound, reform, reorganize; assimilate –, bring –, reduce- to; transform.

Adj. converted into &c. *v.*; convertible, resolvable into; transitional; naturalized.

Adv. gradually &c. (*slowly*) 275; *in transitu* &c. (*transference*) 270.

145. **Reversion.**—N. reversion, return; revulsion; reaction.

turning point, turn of the tide; *status quo ante bellum*; calm before a storm.

alternation &c. (*periodicity*) 138; inversion &c. 218; recoil &c. 277; regression &c. 283; restoration &c. 660; relapse &c. 661; vicinism, atavism, throwback.

V. revert, turn back, return; relapse &c. 661; recoil &c. 277; retreat &c. 283; restore &c. 660; undo, unmake; turn the -tide, – scale; escheat.

Adj. reverting &c. *v.*; revulsive, reactionary.

Adv. *à rebours*, wrong side out.

146. [Sudden or violent change.] **Revolution.**—N. revolution, *bouleversement*, subversion, break up; destruction &c. 162; sudden –, radical –, sweeping –, organic- change; clean sweep, *coup d'état*, overthrow, *débâcle*; counter-revolution, rebellion &c. 742.

transilience, jump, leap, plunge, jerk, start; explosion; spasm, convulsion, throe, revulsion; storm, earthquake, eruption, upheaval, cataclysm; legerdemain &c. (*trick*) 545.

V. revolutionize; new model, remodel, recast; strike out something new, break with the past; change the face of, unsex; revert &c. 742.
Adj. unrecognizable.
Revolutionary, Bolshevik &c. 742.

147. [Change of one thing for another.] **Substitution.—N.** substitution, subrogation, commutation; supplanting &c. *v.*, supersession, metonymy &c. (*figure of speech*) 521.

[Thing substituted] substitute, *succedaneum*, make-shift, temporary expedient, shift, *pis aller*, stop-gap, jury-mast, *locum tenens*, warming-pan, dummy, goat, scape-goat; double; changeling; *quid pro quo*, alternative; remount; representative &c. (*deputy*) 759; palimpsest.

price, purchase-money, consideration, equivalent.

V. substitute, put in the place of, change for; make way for, give place to; supply –, take- the place of; supplant, supersede, replace, cut out, serve as a substitute; step into –, stand in- the shoes of; make a shift –, put up- with; borrow of Peter to pay Paul; commute, redeem, compound for.

Adj. substituted &c. *v.*; vicarious, subdititious; substitutional.

Adv. instead; in -place, – lieu, – the stead, – the room- of; *faute de mieux*;

148. [Double or mutual change.] **Interchange.—N.** inter-, ex-change; com-, per-, inter-mutation; reciprocation, transposal, transposition, shuffling; reciprocity, castling [at chess]; hocus-pocus.

interchange-ableness, -ability.

barter &c. 794; tit for tat &c. (*retaliation*) 718; cross fire, battledore and shuttlecock; *quid pro quo*.

V. inter-, ex-, counter-change; bandy, transpose, shuffle, change hands, swap, trade, permute, reciprocate, commute; give and take, return the compliment; play at -puss in the corner, – battledore and shuttlecock; retaliate &c. 718; barter &c. 794.

Adj. interchanged &c. *v.*; reciprocal, mutual, commutative, interchanged &c. *v.*; interchangeable, intercurrent.

Adv. in exchange, *vice versâ, mutatis mutandis*, backwards and forwards, by turns, turn and turn about, turn about; each –, every one- in his turn.

2°. COMPLEX CHANGE

149. Changeableness.—N. changeableness &c. *adj.*; mutability, inconstancy; versatility, mobility; instability, unstable equilibrium; vacillation &c. (*irresolution*) 605; fluctuation, vicissitude; alternation &c. (*oscillation*) 314.

restlessness &c. *adj.*; fidgets, disquiet; dis-, in-quietude; unrest; agitation &c. 315.

moon, Proteus, chameleon, kaleidoscope, quicksilver, shifting sands, weathercock, harlequin, Cynthia of the minute, April showers; wheel of Fortune; transientness &c. 111.

V. fluctuate, vary, waver, flounder, flicker, flitter, flit, flutter, shift, shuffle, shake, totter, tremble, vacillate, wamble, turn and turn about, ring the changes; sway –, shift- to and fro; change and change about; oscillate

150. Stability.—N. stability; immutability &c. *adj.*; unchangeableness &c. *adj.*; constancy; stable equilibrium, immobility, soundness, vitality, stabiliment, stabilization, stiffness, ankylosis, solidity, *aplomb*.

establishment, fixture; rock, pillar, tower, foundation, leopard's spots, Ethiopian's skin, law of the Medes and Persians.

stabilimeter, stabilizator.

permanence &c. 141; obstinacy &c. 606.

V. be -firm &c. *adj.*; stick fast; stand –, keep –, remain- firm; weather the storm.

settle, establish, stablish, ascertain, fix, set, stabilitate, stabilize; retain, stet, keep hold; make -good, – sure; fasten &c. (*join*) 43; set on its legs; float; perpetuate.

&c. 314; vibrate –, oscillate- between two extremes; alternate; have as many phases as the moon.

Adj. change-able, -ful; changing &c. 140; mutable, variable, checkered, ever changing, kaleidoscopic, prote-an, -iform; versatile.

unstaid, inconstant; un-steady, -stable, -fixed, -settled; fluctuating &c. *v.*; restless; mercurial; agitated &c. 315; erratic, fickle; irresolute &c. 605; capricious &c. 608; touch-and-go; inconsonant, fitful, spasmodic; vibratory; vagrant, wayward, wavering; desultory; afloat; alternating; alterable, plastic, mobile; fleeting, transient &c. 111.

Adv. see-saw &c. (*oscillation*) 314; off and on.

settle down; strike –, take- root; take up one's abode &c. 184; build one's house on a rock.

Adj. unchangeable, immutable; un-alter-ed, -able; not to be changed, constant; permanent &c. 141; invariable, undeviating; stable, durable; perennial &c. (*diuturnal*) 110.

fixed, steadfast, firm, fast, steady, balanced; confirmed, valid, fiducial, immovable, irremovable, riveted, rooted; settled, established &c. *v.*; vested; incontrovertible, stereotyped, indeclinable.

tethered, anchored, moored, at anchor, on a rock, firm as a rock; firmly -seated, – established &c. *v.*; deep-rooted, ineradicable; inveterate; obstinate &c. 606.

transfixed, stuck fast, aground, high and dry, stranded.

indefeasible, irretrievable, intransmutable, incommutable, irresoluble, irrevocable, irreversible, reverseless, inextinguishable, irreducible; indissol-uble, -vable; indestructible, undying, imperishable, indelible, indeciduous; insusceptible, – of change.

Int. *stet.*

Present Events

151. Eventuality.—N. eventuality, event, occurrence, incident, affair, transaction, proceeding, fact; matter of –, naked- fact; phenomenon; advent.

business, concern; circumstance, particular, casualty, happening, accident, adventure, passage, crisis, pass, emergency, contingency, consequence &c. 154.

the world, life, things, doings, affairs, matters; things –, affairs- in general; the times, state of affairs, order of the day; course –, tide –, stream –, current –, run –, march- of -things, – events; ups and downs of life; chapter of accidents &c. (*chance*) 156; situation &c. (*circumstances*) 8.

V. happen, occur; take -place, – effect; come, become of; come -off, – about, – round, – into existence, – forth, – to pass, – on; pass, present itself; fall; fall –, turn- out; run, be on foot, fall in; be-fall, -tide, -chance; prove, eventuate, draw on; turn –, crop –, spring –, cast- up; super-, sur-vene; issue, emanate, arrive, ensue,

Future Events

152. Destiny.—N. destiny &c. (*necessity*) 601; hereafter, future –, post-existence; future state, next world, world to come, after life; futurity &c. 121; everlasting -life, – death; prospect &c. (*expectation*) 507.

V. impend; hang –, lie –, hover-over; threaten, loom, await, come on, approach, stare one in the face; fore-, pre-ordain; predestine, doom, fore-doom, foreshadow, have in store for.

Adj. impending &c. *v.*; destined; about to -be, – happen; coming, in store, to come, going to happen, instant, at hand, near; near –, close- at hand; overhanging, hanging over one's head, imminent; brewing, preparing, forthcoming; in the wind, on the cards, in reserve; that -will, – is to- be; in prospect &c. (*expected*) 507; looming in the -distance, – horizon, – future; unborn, in embryo; in the womb of -time; – futurity; on the knees of the gods; pregnant &c. (*producing*) 161.

Adv. in -time, – the long run; all in good time; eventually &c. 151; what-

arise, start, hold, take its course; pass off &c. (*be past*) 122.

meet with; experience; fall to the lot of; be one's -chance, – fortune, – lot; find; encounter, undergo; pass –, go-through; endure &c. (*feel*) 821.

Adj. happening &c. *v.*; going on, doing, current; in the wind, afloat; on -foot, – the *tapis*; at issue, in question; incidental.

eventful, momentous, signal; stirring, bustling, full of incident.

Adv. eventually, ultimately, in -the event of, – case; in the course of things; in the -natural, – ordinary- course of things; as -things, – times- go; as the world -goes, – wags; as the -tree falls, – cat jumps; as it may -turn out, – happen.

Phr. the plot thickens.

ever may happen &c. (*certainly*) 474; as -chance &c. 156- would have it.

Section VIII. CAUSATION

1°. Constancy of Sequence in Events

153. [Constant antecedent.] Cause.
—N. cause, origin, source, principle, element; occasioner, prime mover, engine, turbine, motor, *primum mobile*; *vera causa*; author &c. (*producer*) 164; main-spring, agent; dynamo, generator, battery (electric); leaven; groundwork, foundation &c. (*support*) 215.

spring, fountain, well, font; foun-tain -, spring- head; *fons et origo*, genesis; descent &c. (*paternity*) 166; remote cause; influence.

pivot, hinge, turning-point, lever; key; kernel, core; proximate cause, *causa causans*; last straw that breaks the camel's back.

ground; reason, – why; why and wherefore, rationale, occasion, deriva-tion; final cause &c. (*intention*) 620; *le dessous des cartes*; undercurrents.

rudiment, egg, germ, embryo, fœtus bud, root, *radix*, radical, etymon, nucleus, seed, stem, stalk, stock, *stirps*, trunk, tap-root; latent organism.

nest, cradle, nursery, womb, *nidus*, birth-, breeding-place, hot-bed.

caus-ality, -ation; origination; pro-duction &c. 161.

V. be the -cause &c. *n.*- of; originate; give -origin, – rise, – occasion- to; cause, occasion, sow the seeds of, kindle, suscitate; bring -on, – to pass, – about; produce; create &c. 161; set -up, – afloat, – on foot; found, broach,

154. [Constant sequent.] Effect.—N.
effect, consequence, sequela; deriva-tive, -tion; result; result-ant, -ance; upshot, issue, *dénouement*; outcome; termination, end &c. 67; development, outgrowth, fruit, crop, harvest, prod-uct, bud, blossom, florescence, ear.

production, produce, product, fin-ished product, work, handiwork, fabric, performance; creature, creation; off-spring, -shoot; first-fruits, -lings; *prémices*.

V. be the -effect &c. *n.*- of; be -due, – owing- to; originate -in, – from; rise -, arise -, take its rise -, spring -, proceed -, emanate -, come -, grow -, bud -, sprout -, germinate -, issue -, flow -, result -, follow -, derive its origin -, accrue- from; come -to, – of, – out of; depend -, hang -, hinge -, turn- upon.

take the consequences, sow the wind and reap the whirlwind.

Adj. owing to; resulting from &c. *v.*; resultant; derivable from; due to; caused &c. by, 153; dependent upon; derived -, evolved- from; derivative; hereditary.

Adv. of course, it follows that, natu-rally, consequently; as a -, in- con-sequence; through all, all along of, necessarily, eventually.

Phr. *cela va sans dire*, thereby hangs a tale.

institute, lay the foundation of, inaugurate; lie at the root of.

procure, induce, draw down, open the door to, superinduce, evoke, entail, operate; elicit, provoke.

conduce to &c. (*tend to*) 176; contribute; promote; have a -hand in, – finger in- the pie; determine, decide, turn the scale, give the casting vote; have a common origin; derive its origin &c. (*effect*) 154.

Adj. caused &c. *v.*; causal, original; prim-ary, -itive, -ordial; aboriginal; radical; inceptive, embry-onic, -otic; *in -embryo, – ovo*; seminal, germinal; formative, productive &c. 168; at the bottom of; connate, having a common origin.

Adv. because &c. 155; behind the scenes.

155. [Assignment of cause.] **Attribution.—N.** attribution, theory, etiology, ascription, reference to, rationale; accounting for &c. *v.*; palaetiology,* imputation, derivation from.

fil-, affil-iation; pedigree &c. (*paternity*) 166.

explanation &c. (*interpretation*) 522; reason why &c. (*cause*) 153.

V. attribute –, ascribe –, impute –, refer –, lay –, point –, trace –, bring home- to; put –, set- down- to; charge –, ground- on; invest with, assign as cause, charge with, blame, lay at the door of, father upon; saddle with; affiliate; account for, derive from, point out the -reason &c. 153; theorize; tell how it comes; put the saddle on the right horse.

Adj. attributed &c. *v.*; attributable &c. *v.*; refer-able, -rible; due to, derivable from; owing to &c. (*effect*) 154; putative.

Adv. hence, thence, therefore, for, since, on account of, because, owing to; on that account; from -this, – that- cause; thanks to, forasmuch as; whence, *propter hoc.*

why? wherefore? whence? how -comes, – is, – happens- it? how does it happen?

in -some, – some such- way; somehow, – or other.

Phr. that is why; *hinc illæ lachrymæ; cherchez la femme.*

156. [Absence of assignable cause.] **Chance.†—N.** chance, indetermination, accident, fortune, hazard, hap, haphazard, chance-medley, random, luck, *raccroc*, casualty, fortuity, contingence, coincidence, adventure, hit; fate &c. (*necessity*) 601; equal chance; lottery, raffle, tombola. sweepstake; toss up &c. 621; turn of the -table, – cards; hazard of the die, chapter of accidents; cast –, throw- of the dice; heads or tails, wheel of Fortune, whirligig of chance; *sortes, – Virgilianæ, -biblicæ.*

probability, possibility, contingency, odds, long odds, run of luck; main-chance.

theory of -probabilities, – chances; book-making; assurance; speculation, gamble, gaming &c. 621.

V. chance, hap, turn up; fall to one's lot; be one's -fate &c. 601; stumble on, light –, blunder –, hit- upon; take one's chance &c. 621.

Adj. casual, fortuitous, accidental, haphazard, random, stray, adventitious, adventive, causeless, incidental. contingent, uncaused, undetermined, indeterminate; possible &c. 470; unintentional &c. 621.

Adv. by -chance, – accident; casually; perchance &c. (*possibly*) 470; for aught one knows; as -good, – bad, – ill-luck &c. *n.*- would have it; as it may -be, – chance, – turn up, – happen; as the case may be.

2°. CONNECTION BETWEEN CAUSE AND EFFECT

157. Power.—N. power; poten-cy, -tiality; puissance, might, force; energy &c. 171; dint; right -hand, – arm;

158. Impotence.—N. impotence; in-, dis-ability; disablement, impuissance, imbecility, caducity; incapa-city,

* Whewell, 'History of the Inductive Sciences,' book xviii, vol. iii., p. 397 (3rd edit.).

† The word *Chance* has two distinct meanings: the first, the absence of assignable *cause*, as above; and the second, the absence of *design*—for the latter see 621.

ascendency, sway, control; pre-potency, -pollence; almightiness, omnipotence; authority &c. 737; strength &c. 159.

ability; ableness &c. *adj.*; competency; effi-ciency, -cacy; validity, cogency; enablement; vantage ground; influence &c. 175; horse power; dynamometer.

pressure; elasticity; gravity, electricity, magnetism, galvanism, voltaic electricity, voltaism, electro-magnetism, electrostatics, electrification, electric current &c.; attraction, repulsion; *vis -inertiæ, – mortua, – viva*; potential –, dynamic –, kinetic –, electrical –, chemical –, atomic- energy; friction, suction.

capability, capacity; *quid valeant humeri quid ferre recusent*; faculty, quality, attribute, endowment, virtue, gift, property, qualification, susceptibility.

V. be -powerful &c. *adj.*; gain -power &c. *n.*

belong –, pertain- to; lie –, be- in one's power; can.

give –, confer –, exercise- power &c. *n.*; empower, enable, invest; in-, en-due; endow, arm; strengthen &c. 159; compel &c. 744.

Adj. powerful, puissant; potent, -ial; capable, able; equal –, up- to; cogent, valid; effect-ive, -ual; efficient, efficacious, adequate, competent; multi-, pleni-, omni-, armi- potent; mighty, ascendent; almighty.

electric, electrical &c.

forcible &c. *adj.* (*energetic*) 171; influential &c. 175; productive &c. 168.

Adv. powerfully &c. *adj.*; by -virtue, – dint- of.

-bility; inapt-, inept-itude; indocility; invalidity, inefficiency, incompetence, disqualification.

telum imbelle, brutum fulmen, blank cartridge, flash in the pan, *vox et præterea nihil,* dead letter, bit of waste paper, dummy; scrap of paper.

inefficacy &c. (*inutility*) 645; failure &c. 732.

helplessness &c. *adj.*; prostration, paralysis, palsy, ataxia, apoplexy, syncope, sideration, *deliquium,* collapse, exhaustion, softening of the brain, emasculation, inanition, senility &c. 128; castrato, eunuch.

cripple, old woman, muff, mollycoddle, milksop.

V. be -impotent &c. *adj.*; not have a leg to stand on.

vouloir -rompre l'anguille au genou, – prendre la lune avec les dents.

collapse, faint, swoon, fall into a swoon, drop; go by the board; end in smoke &c. (*fail*) 732.

render -powerless &c. *adj.*; deprive of power; decontrol; dis-able, -enable; disarm, incapacitate, disqualify, unfit, invalidate, undermine, deaden, cramp, tie the hands; double up, prostrate, paralyze, muzzle, cripple, becripple, maim, lame, hamstring, draw the teeth of; throttle, strangle, *garrotte*; ratten, silence, sprain, clip the wings of, render *hors de combat,* spike the guns; take the wind out of one's sails, scotch the snake, put a spoke in one's wheel; break the -neck, – back; un-hinge, -fit; put out of gear.

unman, unnerve, devitalize, attenuate, enervate; emasculate, spay, caponize, castrate, geld; effeminize.

shatter, exhaust; weaken &c. 160.

Adj. powerless, impotent, unable, incapable, incompetent; ineff-icient, -ective; inept; un-fit, -fitted; un-, dis-qualified; unendowed; in-, un-apt; crippled, decrepit, dis-, abled &c. *v.*; armless.

harmless, unarmed, weaponless, defenceless, *sine ictu,* unfortified, indefensible, vincible, pregnable, untenable.

para-lytic, -lyzed; palsied, imbecile; nerve-, sinew-, marrow-, pith-, lust-less; emasculate, disjointed; out of -joint, – gear; un-nerved, -hinged; water-logged, on one's beam ends, rudderless; laid on one's back; done up, dead beat, exhausted, shattered, demoralized; gravelled &c. (*in difficulty*) 704; helpless, unfriended, fatherless; without a leg to stand on, *hors de combat,* laid on the shelf.

null and void, nugatory, inoperative, good for nothing; dud, invertebrate; ineffectual &c. (*failing*) 732; inadequate &c. 640; inefficacious &c. (*useless*) 645.

159. [Degree of power.] **Strength.**
—**N.** strength; power &c. 157; energy &c. 171; vigour, force; main -, physical -, brute- force; spring, elasticity, tone, tension, tonicity.

stoutness &c. *adj*; lustihood, stamina, nerve, muscle, sinew, thews and sinews, *physique*; pith, -iness; virility, vitality.

athlet-ics, -icism; gymnastics, feats of strength.

adamant, steel, iron, oak, heart of oak; iron grip; grit, bone.

athlete, gymnast, tumbler, acrobat; Atlas, Hercules, Antæus, Samson, Cyclops, Goliath, Titan; tower of strength; giant refreshed.

strengthening &c. *v.*; invigoration, refreshment, refocillation.

[Science of forces] dynamics, statics.
V. be -strong &c. *adj.*, - stronger; overmatch.

render -strong &c. *adj.*; give -strength &c. *n.*; strengthen, invigorate, brace, nerve, fortify, buttress, sustain, harden, case-harden, steel; gird; screw -, wind -, set- up; gird -, brace- up one's loins; recruit, set on one's legs; vivify; refresh &c. 689; refect; reinforce &c. (*restore*) 660.

Adj. strong, mighty, vigorous, forcible, hard, adamantine, stout, robust, sturdy, hardy, powerful, potent, puissant, valid.

resistless, irresistible, invincible, proof against, impregnable, unconquerable, indomitable, inextinguishable, unquenchable; incontestable; more than a match for; over-powering, -whelming; all-powerful; sovereign.

able-bodied; athletic, gymnastic; Herculean, Cyclopean, Atlantean; muscular, husky, brawny, wiry, well-knit, broad-shouldered, sinewy, strapping, stalwart, gigantic.

man-ly, -like, -ful; masculine, male, virile, in the prime of manhood.

un-weakened, -allayed, -withered, -shaken, -worn, -exhausted; in full -force, - swing; in the plenitude of power.

160. Weakness.—N. weakness &c, *adj.*; debility, atony, relaxation, languor, enervation; impotence &c. 158 infirmity; effeminacy, feminality; fragility, flaccidity; inactivity &c. 683.

declension -, loss -, failure- of strength; delicacy, invalidation, decrepitude, asthenia, adynamy, cachexy, *cachexia*, anæmia, bloodlessness, sprain, strain.

reed, thread, rope of sand, broken reed, house -of cards, - built on sand.

soft-, weak-ling; infant &c. 129; youth &c. 127.

V. be -weak &c. *adj.*; drop, crumble, give way, totter, tremble, shake, halt, limp, fade, languish, decline, flag, fail, have one foot in the grave.

render -weak &c. *adj.*; weaken, enfeeble, debilitate, shake, deprive of strength, relax, enervate; un-brace, -nerve; cripple, unman, &c. (*render powerless*) 158; cramp, reduce, sprain, strain, blunt the edge of; dilute, impoverish; decimate; extenuate; reduce -in strength, - the strength of; invalidate; *mettre de l'eau dans son vin.*

Adj. weak, feeble, debile; impotent &c. 158; relaxed, unnerved &c. *v.*; sap-, strength-, power-less; weakly, unstrung, flaccid, adynamic, asthenic; nervous.

soft, effeminate, feminate, womanish.

frail, fragile, shattery, frangible, brittle &c. 328; flimsy, unsubstantial, gimcrack, gingerbread; rickety, cranky; creachy; drooping, tottering &c. *v.*; broken, lame, halt, game, withered, shattered, shaken, crazy, shaky, tumble-down; palsied &c. 158; decrepit; C3.

languid, poor, poorly, infirm; faint, -ish; sickly &c. (*disease*) 655; dull, slack, evanid, spent, short-winded, effete; weatherbeaten; decayed, rotten, worn, seedy, languishing, wasted, washy, wishy-washy, laid low, pulled down, the worse for wear.

un-strengthened &c. 159, -supported, -aided, -assisted; aidless, defenceless &c. 158.

stubborn, thick-ribbed, made of iron, deep-rooted; strong as -a lion, - a horse, - brandy; sound as a roach; in -fine, - high- feather; in fine fettle; like a giant refreshed.

Adv. strongly &c. adj.; by -force &c. n.; by main force &c. (by compulsion) 744.

Phr. 'our withers are unwrung.'

on its last legs; weak as a -child, - baby, - chicken, - cat, - rat; weak as -water, - water gruel, - gingerbread, - milk and water; colourless &c. 429.

Phr. non sum qualis eram.

3°. Power in Operation

161. Production.—**N.** production, creation, construction, formation, fabrication, manufacture; building, architecture, erection, edification; coinage; organization; nisus formativus; putting together &c. v.; establishment; workmanship, performance; achievement &c. (completion) 729; effect &c. 154.

flowering, fructification, fruition.

bringing forth &c. v.; parturition, birth, birth-throe, child-birth, delivery, confinement, accouchement, travail, labour, midwifery, obstetrics; geniture; gestation &c. (maturation) 673; evolution, development, growth; genesis, fertilization, breeding, conception, germination, generation, epigenesis, pro-creation, -generation, -pagation; fecundation, impregnation; spontaneous generation; arche-genesis, -biosis; bio-, abio-, homo-, xeno-genesis.*

authorship, publication; works, œuvre, opus.

edifice, building, structure, fabric, erection, pile, tower, flower, fruit.

V. produce, perform, operate, do, make, gar, form, construct, fabricate, frame, contrive, manufacture; weave, forge, coin, carve, chisel; build, raise, edify, rear, erect, put together; set -, run- up; establish, constitute, compose, organize, institute, get up; achieve, accomplish &c. (complete) 729.

flower, sprout, blossom, burgeon, bear fruit, fructify, spawn, teem, ean, yean, farrow, drop, calf, pup, whelp, kitten, kindle; bear, lay, bring forth, give birth to, lie in, be brought to bed of, evolve, pullulate, usher into the world.

make productive &c. 168; create; beget, conceive, get, generate, fecun-

162. [Non-production.] **Destruction.** —**N.** destruction; waste, dissolution, breaking up; di-, dis-ruption; consumption; disorganization.

fall, downfall, ruin, perdition, crash, smash, havoc, délabrement, débâcle; break -down, - up; prostration; desolation, bouleversement, wreck, crack-up, crash, wrack, shipwreck, cataclysm; Caudine Forks, Sedan.

extinction, annihilation; destruction of life &c. 361; knock-out, knock-down blow; doom, crack of doom.

destroying &c. v.; demo-lition, -lishment; biblioclasm; overthrow, subversion, suppression; abolition &c. (abrogation) 756; sacrifice; ravage, devastation, sabotage, razzia; incendiarism; revolution &c. 146; extirpation &c. (extraction) 301; commencement de la fin, road to ruin; dilapidation &c. (deterioration) 659.

V. be -destroyed &c.; perish; fall, - to the ground; tumble, topple; go -, fall- to pieces; break up; crumble, - to dust; go to -the dogs, - the wall, - smash, - shivers, - wreck, - pot, - wrack and ruin; go -by the board, - all to smash, - to pieces, - under; be all -over, - up- with; totter to its fall.

destroy; do -, make- away with; nullify; annul &c. 756; sacrifice, demolish; tear up; over-turn, -throw, -whelm; upset, subvert, put an end to; seal the doom of, do for, dish, undo; break -, cut- up; break -, cut -, pull -; mow -, blow -, beat- down; suppress, quash, put down; cut short, take off, blot out; dispel, dissipate, dissolve; consume; abolish.

smash, - to smithereens, quell, squash, squelch, crumple up, shatter,

* Huxley.

date, impregnate; pro-create, -generate, -pagate; engender; bring –, call- into -being, – existence; breed, hatch, develop, bring up.

induce, superinduce; suscitate; cause &c. 153; acquire &c. 775.

Adj. produc-ed, -ing &c. *ɔ.*; productive of; prolific &c. 168; creative; formative; gen-etic, -ial, -ital; fertile, pregnant; *enceinte*, big –, fraught-with; with child, in the family way, teeming, parturient, in the straw, brought to bed of; puerper-al, -ous.

architectonic; constructive.

shiver; batter; tear –, crush –, cut –, shake –, pull –, pick- to pieces; nip; tear to -rags, – tatters; crush –, knock-to atoms; pulverize; ruin; strike out; throw –, knock- -down, – over; lay by the heels; fell, sink, swamp, scuttle, wreck, crash, shipwreck, engulf, submerge; lay in -ashes, – ruins; sweep away, erase, expunge, strike out, delete, efface, raze; level, – with the -ground, – dust.

deal destruction, lay waste, ravage, gut; disorganize; dismantle &c. (*render useless*) 645; devour, swallow up, desolate, devastate, sap, mine, blast, confound; exterminate, extinguish, quench, annihilate; snuff –, put –, stamp –, trample- out; lay –, trample- in the dust; prostrate; tread –, crush –, trample- under foot; lay the axe to the root of; make -short work, – a clean sweep, – mince-meat- of; cut up root and branch; fling –, scatter- to the winds; throw overboard; strike at the root of, sap the foundations of, spring a mine, blow up; ravage with fire and sword; cast to the dogs; eradicate &c. 301.

Adj. destroyed &c. *v.*; perishing &c. *v.*; trembling –, nodding –, tottering- to its fall; in course of -destruction &c. *n.*; extinct.

destructive, subversive, ruinous, incendiary, deletory; destroying &c. *v.*; suicidal; deadly &c. (*killing*) 361.

Adv. with -crushing effect, – a sledge-hammer.

Phr. *delenda est Carthago.*

---

163. Reproduction.—N. reproduction, renovation; restoration &c. 660; renewal; new edition, reprint &c. 21; revival, regeneration, palingenesia, revivification; apotheosis; resuscitation, reanimation, resurrection, resurgence, reappearance, atavism; Phœnix; reincarnation.

generation &c. (*production*) 161; multiplication.

V. reproduce; restore &c. 660; revive, renovate, renew, regenerate, revivify, resuscitate, reanimate, refashion, stir the embers, put into the crucible; multiply, repeat, resurge.

crop up, spring up like mushrooms.

Adj. reproduced &c. *v.*; renascent, reappearing; reproductive; resurgent; progenitive; Hydra-headed.

164. Producer.—N. producer, creator, deviser, designer, originator, inventor, author, founder, generator, mover, architect; grower, constructor, maker &c. (*agent*) 690.

166. Paternity.—N. paternity; parentage; fatherhood; consanguinity &c. 11.

parent, father, sire, dad, daddy, papa, governor, *pater*, *paterfamilias*, *abba*; genitor, progenitor, procreator, begetter; ancestor; grand-sire, -father; great-grandfather.

165. Destroyer.—N. destroyer &c. (destroy &c. 162); cankerworm &c. (*bane*) 663; iconoclast; assassin &c. (*killer*) 361; executioner &c. (*punish*) 975; Hun, Vandal, nihilist, anarchist.

167. Posterity.—N. posterity, progeny, breed, issue, offspring, brood, litter, seed, farrow, spawn, spat; family, children, grandchildren, heirs; great-grandchild.

child, son, daughter; kid; infant &c. 129; bantling, scion; shoot, sprout, olive branch, sprit, branch; off-shoot,

house, stem, trunk, tree, stock, *stirps*, pedigree, lineage, line, family, tribe, sept, race, clan; genealogy, descent, extraction, birth, ancestry; forefathers, forbears, patriarchs.

motherhood, maternity; mother, dam, mamma, *materfamilias*; grandmother; matriarch.

Adj. paternal, parental; maternal; matrilinear, patrilineal, patriarchal.

-set; ramification; descendant; heir, -ess; heir -apparent, – presumptive; chip of the old block; heredity; rising generation.

straight descent, sonship, line, lineage, filiation, primogeniture.

Adj. filial.

family, ancestral, linear,

168. Productiveness.—N. productiveness &c. *adj.*; fecundity, fertility, luxuriance, uberty.

pregnancy, pullulation, fructification, multiplication, propagation, procreation; superfetation.

milch cow, rabbit, hydra, warren, seed-plot, land flowing with milk and honey; second crop, after-crop, -growth, -math; fertilization.

V. make -productive &c. *adj.*; fructify; procreate, generate, fertilize, spermatize, impregnate; fecund-ate, -ify; teem, pullulate, multiply; produce &c. 161; conceive.

Adj. productive, prolific; teem-ing, -ful; fertile, fruitful, frugiferous, fruit-bearing; fructiferous; fecund, luxuriant; pregnant, uberous.

procre-ant, -ative; generative, life-giving, spermatic; originative; multiparous; omnific; propagable.

parturient &c. (*producing*) 161; profitable &c. (*useful*) 644.

169. Unproductiveness.—N. unproductiveness &c. *adj.*; infertility, sterility, infecundity; impotence &c. 158 unprofitableness &c. (*inutility*) 645.

waste, desert, Sahara, wild, wilderness, howling wilderness.

V. be -unproductive &c. *adj.*; hang fire, flash in the pan, come to nothing.

Adj. unproductive, inoperative, barren, addle, unfertile, unprolific, arid, sterile, unfruitful, acarpous, infecund; *sine prole*; fallow; teem-, issue-, fruitless; unprofitable &c. (*useless*) 645; null and void, of no effect.

170. Agency.—N. agency, operation, force, working, strain, function, office, maintenance, exercise, work, swing, play; inter-working, -action, procuration, procurement.

causation &c. 153; instrumentality &c. 631; influence &c. 175; action &c. (*voluntary*) 680; *modus operandi* &c. 627.

quickening –, maintaining- power; home stroke.

V. be -in action &c. *adj.*; operate, work; act, – upon; perform, play, support, sustain, strain, maintain, take effect, quicken, strike.

come –, bring- into -operation, – play; have -play, – free play; bring to bear upon.

Adj. operative, efficient, efficacious, practical, effectual.

at work, on foot; acting &c. (*doing*) 680; in -operation, – force, – action, – play, – exercise; acted –, wrought- upon.

Adv. by the -agency &c: *n.*- of; through &c. (*instrumentality*) 631; by means of &c. 632.

171. Physical Energy.—N. energy, physical energy, force; keenness &c. *adj.*; intensity, vigour, strength, elasticity; go; pep, live wire, high pressure; backbone, mettle, fire, vim.

acri-mony, -tude, -dity; causticity,

172. Physical Inertness.—N. inertness, dulness &c. *adj.*; inertia, *vis inertiæ*, inertion, inactivity, torpor, languor; dormancy, quiescence &c. 265; latency, inaction, passivity.

mental inertness; sloth &c. (*inac-*

virulence, poignancy; harshness &c. *adj.*; severity, edge, point; pungency &c. 392.

cantharides; Spanish fly; seasoning &c: (*condiment*) 393, stimulant, excitant.

activity, agitation, effervescence; ferment, -ation; ebullition, splutter, perturbation, stir, bustle; voluntary energy &c. 682; quicksilver.

resolution &c. (*mental energy*) 604; exertion &c. (*effort*) 686; excitation &c. (*mental*) 824.

V. give -energy &c. *n.*; energize, stimulate, kindle, excite, activate, exert; sharpen, pep up, intensify; inflame &c. (*render violent*) 173; wind up &c. (*strengthen*) 159.

strike, – into, – hard, – home; make an impression.

Adj. strong, energetic, forcible, active; strenuous, forceful, mettlesome, enterprising, go ahead; intense, deep-dyed, severe, keen, vivid, sharp, acute, incisive, trenchant, brisk, vigorous, live.

rousing, irritating; poignant; virulent, caustic, corrosive, mordant, harsh, stringent; double-edged, – shotted, – distilled; drastic, escharotic; racy &c. (*pungent*) 392; sarcastic &c. 932; irenic: potent &c. (*powerful*) 157; radio-active.

Adv. strongly &c. *adj.*; *fortiter in re*; with telling effect.

Phr. the steam is up; *vires acquirit eundo.*

173. Violence.—N. violence, inclemency, vehemence, might, impetuosity; boisterousness &c. *adj.*; effervescence, ebullition; turbulence, bluster; uproar, riot, row, rumpus, *le diable à quatre*, devil to pay, all the fat in the fire.

severity &c. 739; ferocity, rage, berserk, fury; exacerbation, exasperation, malignity; fit, paroxysm, orgasm; force, brute force; outrage; *coup de main*; strain, shock, shog; spasm, convulsion, throe; hysterics, passion &c. (*state of excitability*) 825.

out-break, -burst; burst, bounce, dissilience, discharge, volley, explosion, blow up, blast, detonation, rush, eruption, displosion, torrent.

turmoil &c. (*disorder*) 59; ferment &c. (*agitation*) 315; storm, tempest, rough weather; squall &c. (*wind*) 349; earthquake, volcano, thunderstorm.

fury, dragon, demon, tiger, beldame, Tisiphone, Megæra, Alecto, madcap, wild beast; fire-eater &c. (*blusterer*) 887.

V. be -violent &c. *adj.*; run high; ferment, effervesce; romp, rampage; run -wild, – riot; break the peace;

tivity) 683; inexcitability &c. 826; irresolution &c. 605; obstinacy &c: 606; permanence &c. 141.

V. be -inert &c. *adj.*; hang fire, smoulder.

Adj. inert, inactive, passive, pacific; torpid &c. 683; sluggish, stagnant, dull, heavy, flat, slack, tame, slow, blunt; lifeless, dead, uninfluential.

latent, dormant, smouldering, unexerted.

Adv. inactively &c. *adj.*; in -suspense, -abeyance.

---

174. Moderation.—N. moderation; lenity &c. 740; temperance, temperateness, gentleness &c. *adj.*; sobriety; quiet; mental calmness &c. (*inexcitability*) 826.

moderating &c. *v.*; relaxation, remission, mitigation &c. 834; tranquillization, alleviation, assuagement, appeasement, contemporation, pacification.

measure, *juste milieu*, golden mean &c. 29.

moderator; lullaby, sedative, lenitive, demulcent, rose-water, balm, soothing syrup, poppy, opiate, anodyne, milk, opium, laudanum, 'poppy or mandragora'; wet blanket; palliative, calmative.

V. be -moderate &c. *adj.*; keep within -bounds, – compass; sober –, settle down; keep the peace, remit, relent; shorten sail.

moderate, soften, mitigate, temper, accoy; at-, con-temper; mollify, lenify, dull, take off the edge, blunt, obtund, sheathe, subdue, chasten; sober –, tone –, smooth- down; censor, blue-

rush, tear; rush head-long, -foremost; run amuck, raise a storm, make a riot; make –, kick up- a row, – a fuss; bluster, rage, roar, riot, storm; boil, – over; fume, foam, come in like a lion, wreak, bear down, ride rough-shod, out-Herod Herod; spread like wildfire.

break –, fly –, burst- out; bounce, shock, strain; break-, pry-, force-, prize- open.

render -violent &c. *adj.*; sharpen, stir up, quicken, excite, incite, urge, lash, stimulate; irritate, inflame, ex-acerbate, kindle, suscitate, foment; accelerate, aggravate, exasperate, convulse, infuriate, madden, lash into fury; fan –, add fuel to- the flame; *oleum addere camino.*

explode, go off, displode, fly, detonate, thunder, blow up, flash, flare, erupt, burst; let -off, – fly; discharge, detonize, fulminate.

Adj. violent, vehement, forcible; warm; acute, sharp; rough, rude, ungentle, bluff, boisterous, wild, vicious; brusque, abrupt, waspish; impetuous; rampant.

turbulent; disorderly; blustering, raging &c. *v.*; troublous, riotous; tumultu-ary, -ous; obstreperous, uproarious; extravagant, unmitigated; ravening, tameless; frenzied &c. (*insane*) 503; desperate &c. (*rash*) 863; infuriate, towering, furious, outrageous, frantic, hysteric, in hysterics.

fiery, flaming, scorching, hot, red-hot, ebullient.

savage, fierce, ferocious, fierce as a tiger.

excited &c. *v.*; un-quelled, -quenched, -extinguished, -repressed, -bridled, -ruly; headstrong; un-governable, -appeasable, -mitigable; un-, in-controllable; insup-, irre-pressible.

spasmodic, convulsive, explosive; detonating &c. *v.*; volcanic, meteoric; stormy &c. (*wind*) 349.

Adv. violently &c. *adj.*; amain; by -storm, – force, – main force; with might and main; tooth and nail, *vi et armis*, at the point of the -sword, – bayonet; at one fell swoop; with a high hand, through thick and thin; in desperation, with a vengeance; *à –, à toute-outrance*; head-long, -foremost, -first; like a bull at a gate.

pencil, weaken &c. 160; lessen &c. (*decrease*) 36; check; palliate.

tranquillize, assuage, appease, dulcify, swage, lull, soothe, compose, still, calm, cool, quiet, hush, quell, sober, pacify, tame, damp, lay, allay, rebate, slacken, smooth, alleviate, rock to sleep, deaden, smother; throw -cold water on, – a wet blanket over; slake; curb &c. (*restrain*) 751; tame &c. (*subjugate*) 749; smooth over; pour oil on the -waves, – troubled waters; pour balm into, *mettre de l'eau dans son vin.*

go out like a lamb, 'roar you as gently as any sucking dove.'

Adj. moderate; lenient &c. 740; gentle, mild; cool, sober, temperate, reasonable, measured; tempered &c. *v.*; calm, unruffled, quiet, tranquil, still; slow, smooth, untroubled; tame; peaceful, -able; pacific, halcyon.

un-exciting, -irritating; soft, bland, oily, demulcent, lenitive, anodyne; hypnotic &c. 683; sedative; assuaging.

mild as mother's milk; milk and water; gentle as a lamb.

Adv. moderately &c. *adj.*; gingerly; *piano*; under easy sail, at half speed; within -bounds, – compass; in reason.

Phr. *est modus in rebus.*

———

4°. INDIRECT POWER

175. Influence.—N. influence; importance &c. 642; weight, pressure, preponderance, prevalence, sway, pull; predomi-nance, -nancy; ascendency; control, dominance, reign; authority

175a. Absence of Influence.—N. impotence &c. 158; inertness &c. 172; irrelevancy &c. 10.

V. have no -influence &c. 175.

Adj. uninfluential; unconduc-ing,

&c. 737; capability &c. (*power*) 157; interest; spell, magic, magnetism.

footing; purchase &c. (*support*) 215; play, leverage, vantage ground.

tower of strength, host in himself; protection, patronage, auspices.

V. have -influence &c. *n.*; be -influential &c. *adj.*; carry weight, actuate, sway, bias, weigh, tell; have a hold upon, magnetize, bear upon, gain a footing, work upon; take -root, – hold; strike root in.

run through, pervade; prevail, dominate, predominate, subject; out-, over-weigh; over-ride, -bear, – come; gain head; rage; be -rife &c. *adj.*; spread like wildfire; have –, get –, gain- -the upper hand, – full play.

be -recognized, – listened to; make one's voice heard, gain a hearing; play a -part, – leading part- in; lead, control, rule, master; get the mastery over; make one's influence felt, cut ice with; take the lead, pull the strings; turn –, throw one's weight into- the scale; set the fashion, lead the dance.

Adj. influential; important &c. 642; weighty; prevailing &c. *v.*; prevalent, rife, rampant, dominant, regnant, predominant, in the ascendant, hegemonical; authoritative, recognized, telling, with authority.

Adv. with telling effect.

-ive, -ting to; powerless &c. 158; irrelevant &c. 10.

---

176. Tendency.—N. tendency; apt-ness, -itude; proneness, proclivity, bent, turn, tone, bias, set, warp, leaning to, predisposition, inclination, conat's, propensity, susceptibility; liability &c. 177; quality, nature, temperament; characteristic, idio-crasy, -syncrasy; cast, vein, grain; humour, mood; drift &c. (*direction*) 278; con-duciveness, -ducement; applicability &c. (*utility*) 644; subservience &c. (*instrumentality*) 631.

V. tend, contribute, conduce, lead, dispose, incline, verge, bend to, warp, turn, trend, affect, carry, redound to, bid fair to, gravitate towards; promote &c. (*aid*) 707.

Adj. tending &c. *v.*; conducive, working towards, in a fair way to, calculated to; liable &c. 177; subservient &c. (*instrumental*) 631; useful &c. 644; subsidiary &c. (*helping*) 707.

Adv. for, whither.

177. Liability.—N. lia-bility, -bleness; possibility, contingency; suscepti-vity, -bility.

V. be -liable &c. *adj.*; incur, lay oneself open to; run the –, stand a- chance; lie under, expose oneself to, open a door to.

Adj. liable, subject; in danger &c. 665; open –, exposed –, obnoxious-to; answerable, responsible, accountable, amenable; unexempt from; apt to; dependent on; incident to.

contingent, incidental, possible, on the cards, within range of, at the mercy of.

5°. COMBINATIONS OF CAUSES

178. Concurrence.—N. concurrence, co-operation, coagency; coincidence, consilience; union; agreement &c. 23; consent &c. (*assent*) 488; alliance; con-cert &c. 709; partnership &c. 712; collaboration, co formity.

V. con-cur, -duce, -spire, -tribute;

179. Counteraction.—N. counterac-tion, opposition; contrariety &c. 14; antagonism, polarity; clashing &c. *v.*; collision, interference, resistance, re-nitency, friction; reaction; retroaction; repercussion &c. (*recoil*) 277; counter-blast; neutralization &c. (*compensa-*

agree, unite, harmonize; hang –, pull-together &c. (*co-operate*) 709; help to &c. (*aid*) 707.

keep pace with, run parallel to; go –, go along –, go hand in hand- with.

Adj. concurring &c. *v.*; concurrent, conformable, joint, co-operative, concordant, coincident, concomitant, harmonious; in alliance with, banded together, of one mind, at one with; parallel.

Adv. with one consent.

tion) 30; *vis inertiæ*; check &c. (*hindrance*) 706.

voluntary -opposition &c. 708, - resistance &c. 719; repression &c. (*restraint*) 751.

V. counteract; run counter, clash, cross; interfere –, conflict- with; jostle; go –, run –, beat –, militate- against; stultify; antagonize, frustrate, oppose &c. 708; withstand &c. (*resist*) 719; hinder &c. 706; repress &c. (*restrain*) 751; react &c. (*recoil*) 277.

undo, neutralize, cancel; counterpoise &c. (*compensate*) 30; overpoise.

Adj. counteracting &c. *v.*; antagonistic, conflicting, retroactive, renitent, reactionary; contrary &c. 14.

Adv. although &c. 30; in spite of &c. 708; *malgré*; against.

CLASS II

WORDS RELATING TO SPACE

SECTION I.   SPACE IN GENERAL

1°. ABSTRACT SPACE

180. [Indefinite space.] **Space.—N.** space, extension, extent, superficial extent, expanse, stretch; capacity, room, accommodation, scope, range, latitude, field, way, expansion, compass, sweep, play, swing, spread.

spare -, elbow -, house- room; stowage, roomage, margin; opening, sphere, arena; lee-, sea-, head-way.

open -, free- space; wide open spaces; void &c. (*absence*) 187; waste; wild-, wilder-ness; up-, bottom-, moor -land; *campagna*, *veld*, prairie, steppe.

abyss &c. (*interval*) 198; unlimited space; infinity &c. 105; world, wide world; ubiquity &c. (*presence*) 186; length and breadth of the land.

proportions, acreage; acres, - roods and perches; square -inches, - yards &c.

Adj. spacious, roomy, extensive, expansive, capacious, ample; wide-spread, vast, world-wide, uncircumscribed; boundless &c. (*infinite*) 105; shore-, track-, path-less; large &c. 192.

Adv. extensively &c. *adj.*; wherever; everywhere; far and -near, - wide; right and left, all over, all the world over; throughout the -world, - length and breadth of the land; under the sun, in every quarter; in all -quarters, - lands; here, there and everywhere; from -pole to pole, - China to Peru, - Indus to the pole, - Dan to Beersheba, - end to end; on the face of the earth, in the wide world, from all points of the compass; to the -four winds, - uttermost parts of the earth.

180a. Inextension.—N. in-, non-extension; point; atom &c. (*smallness*) 32; pinprick; limitation &c. 229.

181. [Definite space.] **Region.—N.** region, sphere, sphere of influence, corridor, ground, soil, area, realm, hemisphere, quarter, district, beat, orb, circuit, circle; pale &c. (*limit*) 233; com-, de-partment; domain, tract, territory, terrain, country, canton, county, shire, province, *arrondissement*, diocese, parish, township, borough, constituency, *commune*, ward, wapentake, hundred, riding, lathe, garth, soke, tithing, bailiwick; empire, kingdom, principality, duchy, grand -, arch- duchy, palatinate; republic, commonwealth, dominion, colony, state, island.

arena, precincts, *enceinte*, walk, march; patch, plot, enclosure, &c. 232; close, *enclave*, field, court; street &c. (*abode*) 189.

clime, climate, zone, meridian, latitude.

Adj. territorial, local, parochial, provincial, insular.

182. [Limited space.] **Place.—N.** place, lieu, spot, point, dot; niche, nook, &c. (*corner*) 244; hole; pigeon-hole &c. (*receptacle*) 191; compartment; premises, precinct, station, confine; area, court, yard, court-yard, quadrangle, square, compound; abode &c. 189; locality &c. (*situation*) 183.

ins and outs; every hole and corner.

Adv. somewhere, in some place, wherever it may be, here and there, in various places, *passim*.

2°. RELATIVE SPACE

183. Situation.—N. situation, position, locality, *locale*, *status*, latitude and longitude; footing, standing, standpoint, post; stage; aspect, attitude, posture, *pose*.

place, site, base, station, seat, *venue*, whereabouts, environment, neighbourhood; bearings &c. (*direction*) 278; spot &c. (*limited space*) 182.

top-, ge-, chor-ography; map &c. 554.

V. be -situated, – situate; lie; have its seat in.

Adj. situ-ate, -ated; local, topical, topographical &c. *n.*

Adv. *in -situ*, – *loco*; here and there, *passim*; here-, there-, whereabouts; in place, here, there.

in –, amidst- such and such- -surroundings, – *environs*, – *entourage*.

184. Location.—N. loca-tion, -lization; lodgment; de-, re-position; stow-, pack-age; collocation; packing, lading; establishment, settlement, installation; fixation; insertion &c. 300.

anchorage, roadstead, mooring, mooring mast, encampment, camp, bivouac.

plantation, colony, settlement, cantonment, encampment, reservation; colonization, domestication, situation; habitation &c. (*abode*) 189; cohabitation; 'a local habitation and a name'; indenization, naturalization.

V. place, situate, locate, localize, make a place for, put, lay, set, seat, station, lodge, quarter, post, install; store, house, stow; establish, fix, pin, root; graft; plant &c. (*insert*) 300; shelve, pitch, camp, lay down, deposit, reposit; cradle; moor, tether, picket; pack, tuck in; embed; vest, invest in.

billet on, quarter upon, saddle with; load, lade, freight; pocket, put up, bag.

inhabit &c. (*be present*) 186; domesticate, colonize, populate, people; take –, strike- root; anchor; cast –, come to an- anchor; sit –, settle-down; settle; take up one's -abode, – quarters; plant –, establish –, locate- oneself; squat, perch, hive, *se nicher*, bivouac, burrow, get a footing; encamp, pitch one's tent; put up -at, – one's horses at; keep house.

indenizen, naturalize, adopt.

put back, replace &c. (*restore*) 660.

Adj. placed &c. *v.*; situate, posited, ensconced, embedded, embosomed, rooted; domesticated; vested in, unremoved.

moored &c. *v.*; at anchor.

185. Displacement.—N. displacement, elocation, transposition.

ejectment &c. 297; exile &c. (*banishment*) 893; removal &c. (*transference*) 270; unshipment.

misplacement, dislocation &c. 61; fish out of water.

V. dis-place, -plant, -lodge, -nest, -establish; misplace, unseat, disturb; exile &c. (*seclude*) 893; ablegate, set aside, remove; take –, cart- away; take –, draft- off; lade &c. 184, unship.

unload, empty &c. (*eject*) 297; transfer &c. 270; dispel.

vacate; depart &c. 293.

Adj. displaced &c. *v.*; un-placed, -housed, -harboured, -established, -settled; house-, home-less; out of -place, – a situation.

misplaced, out of its element.

3°. EXISTENCE IN SPACE

186. Presence.—N. presence; occupancy, -ation; attendance; whereness.

permeation, pervasion; diffusion &c. (*dispersion*) 73.

187. [Nullibiety.*] **Absence.** — N absence; inexistence &c. 2; non-residence, absenteeism; non-attendance, *alibi*.

* Bishop Wilkins.

ubi-ety, -quity, -quitariness; omni-presence.

bystander &c. (*spectator*) 444.

V. exist in space, be -present &c. *adj.*; assist at; make one -of, – at; look on, attend, remain; find –, present- one-self; show one's face; fall in the way of, occur in a place; lie, stand; occupy.

people; inhabit, dwell, reside, stay, sojourn, live, room, abide, bunk, lodge, nestle, roost, perch; take up one's abode &c. (*be located*) 184; tenant, occupy.

resort to, frequent, haunt; revisit.

fill, pervade, permeate; be -diffused, – disseminated- through; over-spread, -run; run through; meet one at every turn.

Adj. present; occupying, inhabiting &c. *v.*; moored &c. 184; residential, resi-ant, -dent, -dentiary; domiciled.

ubiquit-ous, -ary; omnipresent.

peopled, populous, full of people, inhabited.

Adv. here, there, where, everywhere, aboard, on board, at home, afield; on the spot; here, there and everywhere &c. (*space*) 180; in presence of, before; under the -eyes, – nose- of; in the face of; *in propriâ personâ*.

188. Inhabitant. — N. inhabitant; habitant, resident, -iary; dweller, in-dweller; occup-ier, -ant, farmer, planter; householder, lodger, boarder, paying guest; inmate, tenant, renter, incumbent, sojourner, *locum tenens*, commorant; settler, squatter, backwoodsman, colonist; islander; denizen, citizen; burgher, oppidan, cockney, cit, townsman, burgess; villager; cot-tager, -tier, -ter; compatriot.

native, indigene, aboriginal, aborigines, autochthones; Briton, Englishman, John Bull; new comer &c. (*stranger*) 57.

garrison, crew; population; people &c. (*mankind*) 372; colony, settlement; household.

V. inhabit &c. (*be present*) 186; in-denizen &c. (*locate oneself*) 184.

Adj. indigenous; enchorial; national, nat-ive, -al; autochthonous; British, English; colonial; domestic; domicil-

emptiness &c. *adj.*; void, *vacuum*; vac-uity, -ancy; *tabula rasa*; exemption; *hiatus* &c. (*interval*) 198; no man's land.

truant, absentee.

nobody; nobody -present, – on earth; no one; not a soul; *âme qui vive*.

V. be -absent &c. *adj.*; keep -away, – out of the way; play truant, absent oneself, stay away.

withdraw, make oneself scarce, va-cate; go away, slip out, slip away, retreat &c. 293.

Adj. absent, not present, away, non-resident, gone, from home; missing; lost; wanted, wanting; omitted; no where to be found; inexistent &c. 2.

empty, void; blank, vac-ant, -uous; untenanted, -occupied, -inhabited; ten-antless; desert, -ed; devoid; un-, unin-habitable.

exempt from, not having.

Adv. without, *minus*, nowhere; else-where; neither here nor there; in default of; *sans*; behind one's back.

Phr. the bird has flown, *non est inventus*.

189. [Place of habitation, or resort.] **Abode.—N.** abode, dwelling, lodging, -s; diggings, domicile, residence, ad-dress, habitation, where one's lot is cast, local habitation, berth, seat, lap, sojourn, housing, quarters, headquar-ters, resiance, tabernacle, throne, ark.

home, fatherland, mother country, country &c. 181; home-stead, -stall; fireside, chimney corner; hearth, – stone; household gods, *lares et penates*; roof, household, housing, *dulce domum*; paternal domicile; native -soil, – land, blighty.

nest, *nidus*, snuggery; arbour, bower &c. 191; lair, den, cave, hole, hiding-place, cache, cell, *sanctum sanctorum*, aerie, eyry, rookery, hive; *habitat*, haunt, covert, resort, retreat, perch, roost; nidification.

bivouac, camp, encampment, can-tonment, castrametation; barrack, casemate, casern.

lated, -ed; naturalized, vernacular, domesticated; domiciliary.

in the occupation of; garrisoned –,
•ccupied- by.

tent &c. (*covering*) 223; building &c. (*construction*) 161; chamber &c. (*receptacle*) 191.

tenement, messuage, farm, farm-house, grange, *hacienda*.

cot, cabin, log cabin, shack, hut, *châlet*, croft, shed, booth, stall, hovel, bothy, shanty, igloo, tepee, wigwam; pen &c. (*inclosure*) 232; barn, bawn; kennel, sty, dog-hole, cote, coop, hutch, byre; cow-house, -shed; stable, dove-cote, shippen.

house, mansion, place, villa, cottage, box, lodge, hermitage, *rus in urbe*, folly, rotunda, tower, *château*, castle, pavilion, hotel, court, manor-house, capital messuage, hall, palace, alcazar; country seat; kiosk, bungalow; temple &c. 1000; home of rest, alms-, poor-, work-house, asylum; boarding-, lodging-house; flat, maisonette, duplex, penthouse, suite of rooms, apartments, rooms, room, building &c. 161; Mansion House, town hall, Capitol.

assembly-room, auditorium, coliseum, meeting-house, pump-room, spa, health resort, watering-place; club; theatre &c. 840; drill hall, gymnasium, church &c. 1000; Houses of Parliament &c. 696; school &c. 542; inn; hostel, -ry; hotel, tavern, caravansary, khan, hospice; public-, ale-, pot-, mug-house; gin-palace, gin-mill; coffee-, eating-house; canteen, *restaurant, rôtisserie*, cafeteria, grill-room, *buffet, café, estaminet, posada, bodega*; bar; saloon, speakeasy, shebeen.

hamlet, village, thorp, dorp, ham, kraal; borough, burgh, town, county-seat, – town, city, capital, metropolis; suburb, quarter, parish &c. 181; ghetto; province, country.

street, place, terrace, parade, esplanade, promenade, pier, em-bankment, road, villas, row, walk, lane, alley, court, quadrangle, quad, wynd, close, yard, passage, rents, mansions, buildings, mews.

square, polygon, circus, crescent, mall, *piazza*, arcade, colonnade, peristyle, cloister; gardens, grove, residences; block of buildings, market-place, *place*.

anchorage, roadstead, roads; dock, basin, wharf, quay, port, harbour; dry-, graving-, floating-dock.

garden, park, pleasure-ground, pleasance, demesne.

V. take up one's abode &c. (*locate oneself*) 184; inhabit &c. (*be present*) 186.

Adj. urban, oppidan, metropolitan; suburban; provincial, rural, rustic; countrified; regional, parochial, domestic; cosmopolitan; palatial.

190. [Things contained.] **Contents.—N.** contents; cargo, lading, freight, shipment, load, bale, burden; cart-, ship-load; cup –, basket –, &c. (*receptacle*) 191- of; inside &c. 221; stuffing, ullage.

V. load, lade, ship, charge, fill, stuff.

191. Receptacle.—N. receptacle, container; inclosure &c. 232; re-cipient, receiver, reservatory.

compartment; cell, -ule; follicle; hole, corner, niche, recess, nook; crypt, stall, pigeon-hole, cove, oriel; cave &c. (*concavity*) 252.

capsule, vesicle, cyst, pod, calyx, *cancelli*, utricle, bladder, udder.

stomach, paunch, *venter*, abdomen, ventricle, crop, craw, ingluvies, maw, gizzard, bread-basket, belly, little Mary; mouth.

pocket, pouch, fob, sheath, scabbard, socket, bag, vanity bag, com-

pact, sac, sack, saccule, despatch –, attaché-, tachy- case, wallet,
scrip, card-, note- case, billfold, poke, kit, knap-, haver-, ruck-sack,
sachel, satchel, reticule, budget, net; ditty-, -box, -bag, kitbag; portfolio; saddlebags, holster; quiver &c. (*magazine*) 636.

chest, box, coffer, caddy, case, casket, pyx, pix, *caisson*, desk, *bureau*,
reliquary, shrine; trunk, portmanteau, band-box, *valise*, suitcase, hand-,
traveling-, overnight-, Gladstone-, carpet-bag, brief case; boot, imperial;
vache; cage, manger, rack.

vessel, vase, bushel, barrel; canister, jar; pottle, basket, punnet,
pannier, buck-basket, hopper, maund, creel, cran, crate, cradle, bassinet,
wisket, whisket, *jardinière*, *corbeille*, hamper, wastepaper basket, dosser,
dorser, tray, hod, scuttle, utensil, spittoon, cuspidor.

[For liquids] cistern &c. (*store*) 636; vat, caldron, barrel, cask,
puncheon, keg, rundlet, tun, butt, firkin, hogshead, kilderkin, carboy,
amphora, ampulla, bottle, jar, leather bottle, decanter, ewer, cruse,
carafe, crock, kit, canteen, flagon; demijohn; flask, -et; stoup, noggin,
vial, phial, *ampoule*, cruet, caster; gourd; urn, *épergne*, salver, *patella*,
tazza, *patera*; pig-, big-gin; tea-, coffee-pot, percolator, *samovar*; tyg,
nipperkin. pocket-pistol; tub, bucket, pail, skeel, pot, tankard, jug,
pitcher, toby, mug, pipkin; gal-, gall-ipot, pannikin; matrass, receiver,
retort, alembic, bolthead, can, kettle; bowl, basin, jorum, punch-bowl,
cup, goblet, chalice, tumbler, glass, wineglass, rummer, beaker, tass,
horn, saucepan, skillet, posnet, tureen, terrine, *casserole*, sauce-, gravy-
boat.

plate, platter, paten, dish, vegetable –, *entrée-* dish, trencher, calabash,
porringer, potager, saucer, pan, crucible.

shovel, trowel, spoon; table-, dessert-, tea-, egg-, salt-spoon; spatula,
ladle; dipper; baler; watch-glass, thimble.

closet, commode, cupboard, cellaret, *chiffonnière*, locker, bin, bunker.
buffet, press, safe, sideboard, drawer, chest of drawers, till, *scrutoire*,
secrétaire, *éscritoire*, davenport, book-case, cabinet, canterbury; corner
cupboard, wardrobe.

chamber, apartment, room, cabin; office, court, hall, atrium; suite of
rooms, flat, story; saloon, *salon*, parlour; presence-chamber; sitting-,
drawing-, reception-, state-, living-, work-room; gallery, cabinet, closet,
cubicle; pew, box; *boudoir*; *adytum*, *sanctum*; bed-room, dormitory,
dressing-room; refectory, dining-room, *salle-à-manger*; nursery, schoolroom; library, study; studio; billiard-, bath-, smoking-room; den,
canteen, mess, officers' mess; gun-, ward-, mess-room.

attic, loft, garret, cockloft, clerestory; cellar, vault, hold, cockpit;
entresol; mezzanine floor; ground-floor, *rez-de-chaussée*; basement,
kitchen, cook-house, galley, pantry, scullery, offices; store-room &c.
(*depository*) 636; lumber-room; dust-hole, -bin; dairy, laundry, coach-
house; *garage*; *hangar*; out-, pent-house; lean-to.

portico, porch, piazza, verandah, lobby, court, hall, vestibule,
corridor, passage; ante-room, -chamber; lounge; *foyer*, *loggia*.

conservatory, green-house, glass-house, vinery, bower, arbour,
summer-house, alcove, grotto, hermitage, pergola.

lodging &c. (*abode*) 189; bed &c. (*support*) 215; carriage &c. (*vehicle*)
272.

Adj. capsular; saccu-lar, -lated; recipient; ventricular, cystic, vascular, vesicular, cellular, camerated, locular, multilocular, poly-gastric;
marsupial; siliqu-ose, -ous.

Section II.   DIMENSIONS

1°. General Dimensions

192. Size.—**N.** size, magnitude, dimension, bulk, volume; largeness &c. *adj.*; greatness &c. (*of quantity*) 31; expanse &c. (*space*) 180; amplitude, mass; proportions.

capacity; ton-, tun-nage; calibre, scantling.

turgidity &c. (*expansion*) 194; corpulence, obesity; plumpness, &c. *adj.*; *embonpoint*, corporation, flesh and blood, lustihood.

hugeness &c. *adj.*; enormity, immensity, monstrosity.

giant, Brobdingnagian, Antæus, Goliath, Gog and Magog, Gargantua, monster, mammoth, Cyclops; whale, porpoise, behemoth, leviathan, elephant, hippopotamus; colossus; tun, lump, bulk, block, loaf, mass, clod, nugget, bushel, thumper, whopper, spanker, strapper; Triton among the minnows.

mountain, mound; heap &c. (*assemblage*) 72.

largest portion &c. 50; full-, life-size.

V. be- large &c. *adj.*; become -large &c. (*expand*) 194.

Adj. large, big; great &c. (*in quantity*) 31; considerable, bulky, voluminous, ample, massive, massy; capacious, comprehensive; spacious &c. 180; mighty towering, fine, magnificent.

corpulent, stout, fat, plump, squab, full, lusty, strapping, bouncing; portly, burly, well-fed, full-grown; stalwart, brawny, fleshy; goodly; in good -case, - condition; in condition; chopping, jolly; chub-, chubby-faced.

lubberly, hulky, unwieldy, lumpish, gaunt, spanking, whacking, whopping, thumping, thundering, hulking; overgrown; puffy &c. (*swollen*) 194.

huge, immense, enormous, mighty; vast, -y; amplitudinous, stupendous; monst-er, -rous; gigantic, elephantine;

193. Littleness.—**N.** littleness &c. *adj.*; smallness &c. (*of quantity*) 32; exiguity, inextension; parvi-tude, -ty; duodecimo; Elzevir edition, epitome, microcosm; rudiment; vanishing point; thinness &c. 203.

dwarf, pigmy, atomy, Liliputian, midget, chit, pigwidgeon, urchin, elf; doll, puppet; Tom Thumb, Hop-o'-my thumb, Humpty-dumpty; man-, mannikin; *homunculus*, dapperling, fingerling, dandiprat, cock-sparrow, scalawag.

animalcule, monad, mite, insect, emmet, fly, midge, gnat, shrimp, minnow, worm, maggot, entozoon; *bacillus*, microbe, micro-organism, *bacteria*; *infusoria*; microbe; grub; tit, tomtit, runt, mouse, small fry; millet-, mustard-seed; barley-corn; pebble, grain of sand; mole-hill, button, bubble.

point; atom &c. (*small quantity*) 32; fragment &c. (*small part*) 51; powder &c. 330; point of a pin, mathematical point; *minutiæ* &c. (*unimportance*) 643.

micro-graphy, -meter, -scope; vernier; scale.

V. be -little &c. *adj.*; lie in a nutshell; become small &c. (*decrease*) 36, (*contract*) 195.

Adj. little; small &c. (*in quantity*) 32; minute, diminutive, microscopic; inconsiderable &c. (*unimportant*) 643; exiguous, puny, tiny, wee, petty, minikin, miniature, pigmy, elfin; under sized; dwarf, -ed, -ish; spare, stunted, limited; cramp, -ed; pollard, Liliputian, dapper, pocket; port-ative, -able; duodecimo; dumpy, squat; compact, handy; short &c. 201.

impalpable, intangible, evanescent, imperceptible, invisible, inappreciable, infinitesimal, homœopathic; atomic, corpuscular, molecular; rudiment-ary, -al; embryonic.

weazen, scant, scraggy, scrubby;

giant, -like; colossal, Cyclopean, Brobdingnagian, Gargantuan, Titanic; infinite &c. 105.

large as life; plump as a -dumpling,
– partridge; fat as -a pig, – a quail,
– butter, – brawn, – bacon.

194. Expansion. — N. expansion;
increase &c. 35 -of size; enlargement,
extension, augmentation; ampli-fica-
tion, -ation; aggrandizement, spread,
increment, growth, development, pullulation, swell, dilation, dilatation, rarefaction; turg-escence, -idness, -idity;
obesity &c. (size) 192; dropsy, tumefaction, intumescence, swelling, tumour, diastole, distension; puff-ing,
-iness; inflation; pandiculation.

dilatability, expansibility.

germination, growth, upgrowth; accretion &c. 35.

over-growth, -distension; hypertrophy, tympany.

bulb &c. (convexity) 250; plumper;
superiority of size.

V. become -larger &c. (large &c. 192);
expand, widen, enlarge, extend, grow,
increase, incrassate, swell, gather; fill
out; deploy, take open order, dilate,
stretch, spread; mantle, wax; grow –,
spring- up; bud, bourgeon, shoot,
sprout, germinate, put forth, vegetate,
pullulate, open, burst forth, flower,
blow &c. 734; gain –, gather- flesh;
outgrow; spread like wildfire, overrun.

be larger than; surpass &c. (be superior) 33.

render -larger &c. (large &c. 192);
expand, spread, extend, aggrandize,
distend, develop, amplify, spread out,
widen, magnify, rarefy, inflate, puff,
puff out, blow up, stuff, pad, cram;
exaggerate; fatten; bloat, augment.

Adj. expanded &c. v.; larger &c.
(large &c. 192); swollen; expansive;
wide-open, -spread; fan-shaped; fla-
belliform; overgrown, exaggerated,
bloated, fat, turgid, tumid, hyper-
trophied, dropsical; pot-, swag-bellied;
œdematous, obese, puffy, pursy,
blowzy, distended; patulous; bulbous &c. (convex) 250; full-blown,
-grown, -formed; big &c. 192.

thin &c. (narrow) 203; granular &c.
(powdery) 330; shrunk &c. 195.

Adv. in a -small compass, – nutshell;
on a small scale.

---

195. Contraction.—N. contraction,
reduction, diminution; decrease &c. 36-
of size; defalcation, decrement; lessening, shrinkage; collapse, emaciation,
attenuation, tabefaction, consumption,
marasmus, atrophy; systole, neck,
hour-glass.

condensation, compression, constraint, compactness; compendium &c.
596; squeezing &c. v.; strangulation;
corrugation; astringency, constrin-
gency; astringents, sclerotics; contrac-
tility, compressibility; coarctation.

inferiority in size.

V. become -small, – smaller; lessen,
decrease &c. 36; grow less, dwindle,
shrink, contract, narrow, shrivel, collapse, wither, lose flesh, wizen, fall
away, waste, wane, ebb; decay &c.
(deteriorate) 659.

be smaller than, fall short of; not
come up to &c. (be inferior) 34.

render smaller, lessen, diminish, contract, draw in, narrow, coarctate; constrict, constringe; condense, compress,
boil down, deflate, exhaust, empty;
squeeze, corrugate, crush, crumple up,
warp, purse up, pack, stow; pinch,
tighten, strangle; cramp; dwarf, bedwarf; shorten &c. 201; circumscribe
&c. 229; restrain &c. 751; fold &c. 258.

pare, reduce, attenuate, rub down,
scrape, file, grind, chip, shave, shear.

Adj. contracting &c. v.; astringent;
shrunk, contracted &c. v.; strangulated,
tabid, wizened, stunted; tabescent;
marasmic; waning &c. v.; neap; compact.

unexpanded &c. (expand &c. 194);
inswept; contractile; compressible;
smaller &c. (small &c. 193).

---

196. Distance.—N. distance; space
180: remoteness, farness; far- cry

197. Nearness.—N. nearness &c.
adj.; proximity, propinquity; vicinity,

to; longinquity, elongation; offing, background; removedness; parallax; reach, span, stride; drift.

out-post, -skirt; horizon, sky-line; aphelion; foreign parts, *ultima Thule, ne plus ultra,* antipodes; long range, giant's stride.

dispersion &c. 73.

V. be -distant &c. *adj.*; extend -, stretch -, reach -, spread -, go -, get -, stretch away- to; range, outrange, outreach.

remain at a distance; keep -, stand- -away, - off, - aloof, - clear of.

Adj. distant; far -off, - away; remote, telescopic, distal, wide of; stretching to &c. *v.*; yon, -der; ulterior; trans-marine, -pontine, -atlantic, -alpine; tramontane; ultra-montane, -mundane; hyperborean, antipodean; inaccessible, out of the way; unapproach-ed, -able; incontiguous.

Adv. far -off, - away; afar, -off; off; away; a -long, - great, - good- way off; wide away, aloof; wide -, clear- of; out of -the way, - reach; abroad, yonder, farther, further, beyond; *outre mer,* over the border, far and wide, over the hills and far away; from pole to pole &c. (*over great space*) 180; to the -uttermost parts, - ends- of the earth; out of -hearing, - range, nobody knows where, *à perte de vue,* out of the sphere of, wide of the mark; a far cry to.

apart, asunder; wide -apart, - asunder; *longo intervallo*; at arm's length.

-age; neighbourhood, adjacency; contiguity &c. 199.

short -distance, - step, - cut; earshot, close quarters, stone's throw; bow -, gun -, pistol- shot; hair's breadth, span; close-up.

purlieus, neighbourhood, vicinage, *environs, alentours,* suburbs, confines, *banlieue,* borderland; whereabouts.

bystander: neighbour, borderer.

approach &c. 286; convergence &c. 290; perihelion.

V. be -near &c. *adj.*; adjoin, hang about, trench on; border -, verge upon; stand by, approximate, tread on the heels of, cling to, clasp, hug; cuddle, huddle; hang upon the skirts of, hov over; burn; abut.

bring -, draw- -near &c. 286; con-. verge &c. 290; crowd &c. 72; place -side by side &c. *adv.*

Adj. near, nigh; close -, near- at hand; close, neighbouring, propinquent, bordering upon; adjacent, adjoining, limitrophe; proxim-ate, -al; at hand, handy; near the mark, near run; home, intimate.

Adv. near, nigh; hard -, fast- by; close -to, - upon, - up; at the point of; next door to; within -reach, - call, - hearing, - earshot, - range; within an ace of; but a step, not far from, at no great distance; on the -verge, - brink, - skirts- of; in the -environs &c. *n.*; at one's -door, - feet, - elbow, - finger's end, - side; on the tip of one's tongue; under one's nose; within a -stone's throw &c. *n.*; in -sight, - presence- of; at close quarters; cheek by -jole, - jowl; beside, alongside, side by side, *tête-à-tête*; in juxtaposition &c. (*touching*) 199; yard-arm to yard-arm; at the heels of; on the confines of, at the threshold, bordering upon, verging to; in the way.

about; here-, there-abouts; roughly, in round numbers; approxim- -ately, -atively; as good as, well nigh.

---

198. Interval.—**N.** interval, interspace; separation &c. 44; break, gap, opening; hole &c. 260; chasm, *hiatus,* cæsura; inter-ruption, -regnum; interstice, *lacuna,* cleft, mesh, crevice, chink, rime, creek, cranny, crack, chap, slit, slot, fissure, scissure, rift, flaw, breach, fracture, rent, gash, cut, leak, dike, ha-ha.

199. Contiguity.— **N.** contiguity, contact, proximity, apposition, juxtaposition, touching &c. *v.*; abutment, osculation; meeting, appulse, appulsion, *rencontre,* rencounter, syzygy, coincidence, conjunction, coexistence; adhesion &c. 46.

border-land; frontier &c. (*limit*) 233; tangent.

gorge, defile, ravine, cañon, *crevasse,* abyss, abysm; gulf; inlet, frith, strait, gully, gulch, nullah; pass; notch; furrow &c. 259; yawning gulf; *hiatus -maxime, – valde- deflendus;* parenthesis &c. (*interjacence*) 228; void &c. (*absence*) 187; incompleteness &c. 530.

V. gape &c. (*open*) 260.

Adj. with an interval, far between.

Adv. at intervals &c. (*discontinuously*) 70; *longo intervallo.*

V. be -contiguous &c. *adj.*; join, ad join, abut on, march with, border; tick, graze, touch, meet, osculate, kiss, come in contact, coincide; coexist; adhere &c. 46.

Adj. contiguous; touching &c. *v.*; in -contact &c. *n.*; conterminous, end to end, osculatory; pertingent; tangential.

hand to hand; close to &c. (*near*) 197; with no -interval &c. 198.

2°. Linear Dimensions

200. Length.—**N.** length, longitude, span, extent, mileage.

line, bar, rule, stripe, streak, spoke, radius.

lengthening &c. *v.*; pro-longation, -duction, -traction; ten-sion, -sure; extension.

[Measures of length] line, nail, inch, hand, palm, foot, cubit, yard, ell, fathom, rod, pole, perch, furlong, mile, league; chain, metre, kilo-, centi-, milli- &c. -metre.

pedometer, perambulator, odometer, odograph, speedometer, cyclometer, log, telemeter, range finder; scale &c. (*measurement*) 466.

V. be -long &c. *adj.*; stretch out, sprawl, extend –, reach –, stretch- to; make a long arm, 'drag its slow length along.'

render -long &c. *adj.*; lengthen, extend, elongate; stretch; pro-long, -duce, -tract; let –, pay –, draw –, spin- out; drawl.

enfilade, look along, view in perspective.

Adj. long, -some; lengthy, lank, wire-drawn, outstretched; lengthened &c. *v.*; sesquipedalian &c. (*words*) 577; interminable, no end of.

line-ar, -al; longitudinal, oblong.

as long as -my arm, – to-day and to-morrow; unshortened &c. (shorten &c. 201).

Adv. lengthwise, at length, longitudinally, endlong, along; *tandem;* in a line &c. (*continuously*) 69; in perspective.

from -end to end, – stem to stern, – head to foot, – the crown of the head to the sole of the foot. – top to toe, – head to heels; fore and aft.

201. Shortness.—**N.** shortness &c. *adj.*; brevity; littleness &c. 193; a span.

shortening &c. *v.*; abbrevia-tion, -ture; abridgment, concision, retrenchment, curtailment, decurtation; reduction &c. (*contraction*) 195; epitome &c. (*compendium*) 596.

abridger, abstractor, epitomiser.

elision, ellipsis; conciseness &c. (*in style*) 572.

V. be -short &c. *adj.*; render -short &c. *adj.*; shorten, curtail, abridge, abbreviate, take in, reduce; compress &c. (*contract*) 195; epitomize &c. 596.

retrench, cut short, obtruncate; scrimp, cut, chop up, hack, hew; cut –, pare- down; clip, snip, dock, lop, prune; shear, shave, mow, reap, crop; snub; truncate, pollard, stunt, nip, nip in the bud, check the growth of; [in drawing] foreshorten.

Adj. short, brief, curt; compendious, compact; stubby, scrimp; shorn, stubbed; stumpy, thickset, podgy, stocky, pug; squab, -by; squat, dumpy; little &c. 193; curtailed of its fair proportions; short by; oblate; concise &c. 572; summary.

Adv. shortly &c. *adj.*; in short &c. (*concisely*) 572.

202. Breadth. Thickness.—N.
breadth, width, latitude, amplitude;
'diameter, bore, calibre, radius; superficial extent &c. (*space*) 180.

. thickness, crassitude; corpulence &c.
(*size*) 192; dilatation &c. (*expansion*)
194.

V. be -broad &c. *adj.*; become –,
render- -broad &c. *adj.*; expand &c.
194; thicken, widen.

Adj. broad, wide, ample, extended;
discous; fan-like; out-spread, -stretched;
wide as a church-door.

thick, dumpy, squab, squat, thickset, tubby; thick as a rope, stubby &c.
201.

203. Narrowness. Thinness. —N.
narrowness &c. *adj.*; closeness, exility;
exiguity &c. (*little*) 193.

line; hair's –, finger's -breadth; strip,
streak, vein.

thinness &c. *adj.*; tenuity; emaciation, macilency, *marcor*.

shaving, slip &c. (*filament*) 205;
threadpaper, skeleton, shadow, scrag,
anatomy, spindle-shanks, barebones,
lantern jaws, mere skin and bone.

middle constriction, stricture, neck,
waist, isthmus, wasp, hour-glass; ridge,
ghaut, pass; ravine &c. 198.

narrowing, coarctation, angustation,
tapering; contraction &c. 195.

V. be -narrow &c. *adj.*; narrow, taper,
contract &c. 195; render -narrow &c.
adj.

Adj. narrow, close; slender, thin, fine; *svelte*; thread-like &c.
(*filament*) 205; finespun, taper, slim, gracile, slight, slight-made;
scant, -y; spare, delicate, incapacious; contracted &c. 195; unexpanded &c. (expand &c. 194); slender as a thread, capillary.

emaciated, lean, meagre, gaunt, macilent; lank, -y; weedy, skinny,
scrawny, scraggy; starv-ed, -eling; attenuated, shrivelled, wizened,
pinched, peaky, skeletal, spindling, spindle- -legged, -shanked;
extenuated, tabid, marcid, bare-bone, raw-boned; herring-gutted;
worn to a shadow, lean as a rake; thin as a -lath, – whipping post,
– wafer; hatchet-faced; lantern-jawed.

204. Layer.—N. layer, stratum,
course, bed, zone, *substratum*, floor,
flag, stage, story, tier, slab, escarpment,
table, tablet, panel, plaque; board,
plank; trencher, platter.

plate; lam-ina, -ella; sheet, flake,
foil, wafer, scale, coat, peel, pellicle,
ply, thickness, membrane, film, leaf,
slice, shive, cut, rasher, shaving, integument &c. (*covering*) 223.

stratification, lamination, scaliness,
nest of boxes, coats of an onion.

V. slice, shave, pare, peel; plate,
coat, veneer; cover &c. 223.

Adj. lamell-ar, -ated, -iform; lamin-
ated, -iferous; micaceous; schist-ose,
-ous; scaly, filmy, membranous, flaky,
squamous; folia-ted, -ceous; strati-
fied, -form; tabular, discoid, spathic.

205. Filament.—N. filament, line;
fibre, fibril; funicle, vein, hair, capillament, *cilium*, tendril, gossamer; hair-
stroke; harl.

wire, string, thread, packthread,
cotton, sewing-silk, twine, twist, whipcord, cord, rope, cable, yarn, hemp,
oakum, jute, wool, worsted.

strip, shred, slip, spill, list, band,
fillet, *fascia*, ribbon, riband, tape, roll,
lath, slat, strake, splinter, shiver,
shaving.

beard &c. (*roughness*) 256; ramification; strand.

Adj. fil-amentous, -aceous, -iform;
fibr-ous, -illous; thread-like, wiry,
stringy, ropy; capill-ary, -iform; funicular, wire-drawn; anguilliform; flagelliform; hairy &c. (*rough*) 256; ligulate;

206. Height.—N. height, altitude,
elevation, ceiling; eminence. pitch;
loftiness &c. *adj.*; sublimity.

tallness &c. *adj.*; stature, procerity;
prominence &c. 250.

207. Lowness.—N. lowness &c. *adj.*;
debasement, depression; prostration
&c. (*horizontal*) 213; depression &c.
(*concave*) 252.

molehill; lowlands; bottomlands;

colossus &c. (*size*) 192; giant, grenadier, giraffe.

mount, -ain; hill, butte, monticle, fell, knap; cape; head-, fore-land; promontory; ridge, hog's back, dune; rising -, vantage- ground; down; moor, -land; Alp; up-, high-lands; heights &c. (*summit*) 210; knoll, hummock, hillock, barrow, mound, mole, *kopje*; steeps, bluff, cliff, craig, tor, peak, pike, clough; escarpment, edge, ledge, brae; dizzy height.

tower, pillar, column, pylon, obelisk, monument, steeple, spire, minaret, *campanile*, belfry, turret, roof, dome, cupola, pagoda, pyramid; sky scraper; Eiffel tower.

pole, pikestaff, maypole, flagstaff; mast, top -, topgallant- mast.

ceiling &c. (*covering*) 223.

high water; high -, flood -, spring- tide.

altimetry &c. (*angle*) 244; altimeter, height-finder, hypsometer, barograph.

V. be -high &c. *adj.*; tower, soar. command; hover; cap, culminate; overhang, hang over, impend, beetle; bestride, ride, mount; perch, surmount; cover &c. 223; overtop &c. (*be superior*) 33; stand on tiptoe.

become -high &c. *adj.*; grow, - higher, - taller; upgrow; rise &c. (*ascend*) 305.

render -high &c. *adj.*; heighten &c. (*elevate*) 307.

Adj. high, elevated, eminent, exalted, lofty, supernal; tall; gigantic &c. (*big*) 192; Patagonian; towering, beetling, soaring, hanging [gardens]; elevated &c. 307; upper; highest &c. (*topmost*) 210; monticolous, perching, hill-dwelling.

up-, moor-land; hilly, mountainous, alpine, sub-alpine, heaven-kissing; cloud-topt, -capt, -touching; aerial.

overhanging &c. *v.*; incumbent, overlying; super-incumbent, -natant, -imposed; prominent &c. 250.

tall as a -maypole, - poplar, - steeple; lanky &c. (*thin*) 203.

Adv. on high, high up, aloft, up, above, aloof, overhead; up -, above- stairs; in the clouds; on -tiptoe, - stilts, - the shoulders of; over head and ears; breast high.

over, upwards; from top to bottom &c. (*completely*) 52.

basement, ground-floor; *rez-de-chaussée* &c. 211; hold; feet, heels.

low water; low -, ebb -, neap -, spring- tide.

V. be -low &c. *adj.*; lie -low, - flat; underlie; crouch, slouch, wallow, grovel; lower &c. (*depress*) 308.

Adj. low, neap, debased; nether, -most; flat, level with the ground; lying low &c. *v.*; crouched, subjacent, squat, prostrate &c. (*horizontal*) 213.

Adv. under; be-, under-neath; below; down, -wards; adown, at the foot of; under-foot, -ground; down -, below-stairs; at a low ebb; below par.

---

208. Depth.—**N.** depth; deepness &c. *adj.*; profundity, depression &c. (*concavity*) 252.

hollow, pit, shaft, well, crater, abyss; gulf &c. 198; bowels of the earth, bottomless pit, hell.

soundings, depth of water, water, draught, submersion; plummet, sound, probe; sounding -rod, - line, - machine; lead; submarine, diving bell, bathysphere; diver.

V. be -deep &c. *adj.*; render -deep &c. *adj.*; deepen.

plunge &c. 310; sound, heave the lead, take soundings; dig &c. (*excavate*) 252.

209. Shallowness.—**N.** shallowness &c. *adj.*; shoals; mere scratch.

Adj. shallow, superficial; skin -, ankle -, knee- deep; just enough to wet one's feet; shoal, -y

Adj. deep, -seated; profound, sunk, buried; submerged &c. 310; sub-aqueous, -marine, -terranean, -terrene; underground.

bottom-, sound-, fathom-less; unfathom-ed, -able; abysmal; deep as a well, deep-sea.

knee-, ankle-deep.

Adv. beyond –, out of- one's depth; over head and ears, over one's head.

210. Summit.—N. summit, -y; top, vertex, apex, zenith, pinnacle, acme, acropolis, culmination, meridian, utmost height, *ne plus ultra*, height, pitch, maximum, climax, apogee; culminating –, crowning –, turning- point; turn of the tide, fountain head; water-shed, -parting; sky, pole.

tip, -top; crest, crow's nest, cap, truck, peak, nib; end &c. 67; crown, brow; head, nob, noddle, pate.

high places, heights.

top-, top-gallant mast, sky scraper; quarter –, hurricane- deck.

architrave, frieze, cornice, coping, coping-stone, zoophorus, capital, headpiece, capstone, epistyle, sconce, pediment, entablature; tympanum; ceiling &c. (*covering*) 223.

attic, loft, garret, house-top, upper story, roof.

V. culminate, cap, crown, top; overtop &c. (*be superior to*) 33.

Adj. highest &c. (high &c. 206); top; top-, upper-most; tip-top; culminating &c. *v.*; meridi-an, -onal; capital, head, polar, supreme, supernal, top-gallant.

Adv. a-top, at the top of – the tree, – the heap.

211. Base.—N. base, -ment; plinth, dado, wainscot, baseboard; foundation &c. (*support*) 215; substructure, substratum, sump, ground, earth, pavement, floor, paving, flag, carpet, ground-floor, deck; footing, groundwork, basis; hold, bilge, orlop deck.

bottom, nadir, foot, sole, toe, hoof, keel, kelson, root.

Adj. bottom; under-, nether-most; fundamental; founded –, based –, grounded –, built- on.

---

212. Verticality. — N. verticality; erectness &c. *adj.*; perpendicularity; right angle, normal; azimuth circle.

wall, palisade, precipice, cliff, steep, bluff.

elevation, erection; square, plumbline, plummet.

V. be -vertical &c. *adj.*; stand -up, – on end, – erect, – upright; stick –, cock-up.

render -vertical &c. *adj.*; set –, stick –, raise –, cock- up; erect, rear, raise, pitch, raise on its legs.

Adj. vertical, upright, erect, perpendicular, normal, plumb, straight, bolt upright; rampant; straight –, standing-up &c. *v.*; rectangular, orthogonal.

Adv. vertically &c. *adj.*; up, on end; up –, right- on end; *à plomb*, endwise; on one's legs; at right angles.

---

213. Horizontality.—N. horizontality; flatness; level, plane; stratum &c. 204; dead -level, – flat; level plane.

recumbency; lying down &c. *v.*; reclination, decumbence; de-, discumbency; proneness &c. *adj.*; accubation, supination, resupination, prostration; azimuth.

plain, floor, platform, bowling-green; cricket-ground; court; gridiron; baseball diamond; hockey rink; tennis-, croquet-ground, – lawn; billiard table; terrace, estrade, esplanade, *parterre*, table-land, *plateau*, ledge.

spirit-, level; T-square.

V. be -horizontal &c. *adj.*; lie, recline, couch; lie -down, – flat, – prostrate; sprawl, loll; sit down.

render -horizontal &c. *adj.*; lay, – down, – out; level, flatten, even, raze, equalize, smooth, align; prostrate, knock down, floor, fell, ground.

Adj. horizontal, level, even, plane;

flat &c. 251; flat as a -billiard table, – bowling green; alluvial; calm, – as a mill-pond; smooth, – as glass.

re-, de-, pro-, ac-cumbent; lying &c. *v.*; prone, supine, couchant, jacent, prostrate.

Adv. horizontally &c. *adj.*; on -one's back. – all fours, – its beam ends.

214. Pendency.—N. pend-, dependency; suspension, hanging &c. *v.*

pendant, drop, tippet, tassel, lobe, tail, train, flap, lappet, skirt, pig-tail, queue, pendulum.

peg, knob, button, hook, nail, stud, ring, staple, tenterhook; davit; fastening &c. 45; spar, horse.

chande-, gase-, electro-lier.

V. be -pendent &c. *adj.*; hang, depend, swing, dangle, droop, sag; swag; daggle, flap, trail, flow.

suspend, hang, sling, hook up, hitch, fasten to, append.

Adj. pend-ent, -ulous; pensile; hanging &c. *v.*; dependent; suspended &c. *v.*; lowering, overhanging, beetling, decumbent; loose, flowing.

having a -peduncle &c. *n.*; pedunculate, tailed, caudate.

215. Support.—N. support, ground, foundation, base, basis; *terra firma*; bearing, fulcrum, *point d'appui*, caudex, purchase, footing, hold, -*locus standi*; landing, – stage, – place; stage, platform; block; rest, resting-place; groundwork, *substratum*, sustentation, subvention; floor &c. (*basement*) 211.

supporter; aid &c. 707; prop, stand, anvil, fulciment; hod, stay, shore, skid, rib, sprag, truss, bandage; sleeper; stirrup, stilts, shoe, sole, heel, splint, lap; bar, rod, boom, sprit, outrigger.

staff, stick, crutch, alpenstock, bourdon; *bâton*, maulstick, colstaff, cowlstaff, staddle; stalk, ped-icel, -icle, – uncle.

post, pillar, shaft, column, pilaster; pediment, pedestal; plinth, shank, leg, socle, zocle; buttress, jamb, mullion, abutment; pile, baluster, banister, stanchion, king post; balustrade.

frame, -work, body, *chassis, fuselage*; scaffold, skeleton, beam, rafter, girder, lintel, joist, cantilever, travis, trave, corner-stone, summer, transom; rung, round, step, sill.

columella, back-bone; key-stone; axle, -tree; axis; arch, ogive, mainstay.

trunnion, pivot, rowlock; peg &c. (*pendency*) 214; tie-beam &c. (*fastening*) 45; thole pin.

board, ledge, shelf, hob, bracket, trevet, trivet, arbor, rack, hatrack; mantel, -piece, -shelf; slab, console; counter, dresser; flange, corbel; table, trestle, teapoy; shoulder; perch; horse; easel, desk; retable, predella.

seat, throne, dais; divan, musnud; chair, bench, form, stool, camp-stool, sofa, settee, davenport, stall, miserere, arm –, easy –, elbow –, rocking- chair; couch, day bed, *fauteuil*, woolsack, ottoman, settle, squab, bench, box, dicky; saddle, pannel, pillion; side –, pack- saddle; pommel.

bed, berth, pallet, tester, crib, cot, bassinet, hammock, shakedown, camp bed, bunk, truckle-bed, cradle, litter, stretcher, bedstead; four-poster, French bed; bedding, mattress, *paillasse*; pillow, bolster; mat, rug, cushion.

stool, footstool, hassock, faldstool, *prie-dieu*; tabouret; tripod; Atlas, Persides, Atlantes, Caryatides, Hercules.

V. be -supported &c.; lie –, sit –, recline –, lean –, loll -, rest – stand –, step –, repose –, abut –, bear –, be based &c.- on; have at one's back; be-stride, -straddle.

support, bear, carry, hold, sustain, shoulder; hold –, back –, bolster –, shore- up; up-hold, -bear; prop; under-prop, -pin, -set; bandage, &c. 43; brace, truss; cradle, pillow.

give –, furnish –, afford –, supply –, lend- -support, – foundations; bottom, found, base, ground, embed.

maintain, keep on foot; aid &c. 707.

Adj. support-ing, -ed, &c. *v.*; atlantean, columellar; sustentative, fundamental, basal.

Adv. astride on, astraddle; pick-a-back.

216. Parallelism.—N. parallelism; coextension, concentricity, collimation.

V. be –, lie- parallel to; collimate.

Adj. parallel; coextensive, collateral, concentric, concurrent.

Adv. alongside, abreast &c. (*laterally*) 236.

---

217. Obliquity.—N. obliquity, inclination, skew, slope, slant; crookedness &c. *adj.*; slopeness; leaning &c. *v.*; bevel, bezel, ramp, tilt; bias, list, twist, swag, cant, lurch; distortion &c. 243; bend &c. (*curve*) 245; tower of Pisa.

acclivity, rise, ascent, grade, gradient, *glacis*, rising ground, hill, bank, declivity, downhill, dip, fall, devexity; gentle –, rapid- slope; easy -ascent, – descent; shelving beach; *talus*; *montagne Russe*; *facilis descensus Averni*.

steepness &c. *adj.*; cliff, precipice &c. (*vertical*) 212; escarpment, scarp.

[Measure of inclination] clinometer, theodolite, level sextant, quadrant, protractor; angle, sine, cosine, tangent &c. hypothenuse; diagonal; zigzag, chevron.

V. be -oblique &c. *adj.*; slope, slant, lean, incline, shelve, stoop, decline, descend, bend, heel, careen, sag, swag, seel, slouch, cant sidle.

render -oblique &c. *adj.*; sway, bias; slope, slant; incline, bend, crook; cant, tilt; distort &c. 243.

Adj. oblique, inclined; sloping &c. *v.*; tilted &c. *v.*; recumbent, clinal, skew, askew, slant, aslant, bias, plagiedral, indirect, wry, awry, ajee, crooked; knock-kneed &c. (*distorted*) 243; bevel, out of the perpendicular.

uphill, rising, ascending, acclivous; downhill, falling, descending; declining, declivous, devex, anticlinal; steep, abrupt, precipitous, break-neck.

diagonal; trans-verse, -versal; athwart, antiparallel; curved &c. 245.

Adv. obliquely &c. *adj.*; on –, all on- one side; askew, askant, askance, aslope, asquint, edgewise, at an angle; side-long, -ways; slope-, slant-wise; by a side wind.

218. Inversion.—N. in-, e-, sub-, re-, retro-, intro-version; contraposition &c. 237; contrariety &c. 14; reversal; turn of the tide.

overturn; somer-sault, -set; summerset; *culbute*; revulsion; *pirouette*.

transposition, transposal, anastrophy, *metastasis, hyperbaton, anastrophe, hysteron-proteron*, hypallage, *synchysis, tmesis*, parenthesis; *metathesis*; palindrome; Spoonerism.

pronation and supination.

V. be -inverted &c.; turn –, go –, wheel- -round, – about, – to the right about; turn –, go –, tilt –, topple-over; capsize, turn turtle.

in-, sub-, retro-, intro-vert; reverse; up-, over-turn, -set; turn -topsy turvy &c. *adj.*; *culbuter*; transpose, put the cart before the horse, turn the tables.

Adj. inverted &c. *v.*; wrong side -out, – up; inside out, upside down; bottom –, keel- upwards; supine, on one's head, topsy turvy, *sens dessus sens dessous.*

inverse; reverse &c. (*contrary*) 14; opposite &c. 237.

topheavy, unstable.

Adv. inversely &c. *adj.*; hirdie-girdie; heels over head, head over heels.

219. Crossing.—N. crossing &c. *v.*; inter-section, – lacement, – twine-ment, -digitation; decussation, transversion; convolution &c. 248.

reticulation, meshwork, network; inosculation, anastomosis, inter-texture, mortise.

net, *plexus*, web, mesh, twill, skein, sleeve, felt, lace; wicker; mat, -ting; plait, trellis, wattle, lattice, grating, *grille*, gridiron, tracery, fretwork, filigree, reticle; tissue, netting, mokes.

cross, crucifix, rood, crisscross, crux; chain, wreath, braid, cat's cradle, knot; entanglement &c. (*disorder*) 59.

[woven fabrics] cloth, linen, muslin, cambric, drill, homespun, tweed, broadcloth &c.

V. cross, decussate; inter-sect, -lace, -twine, -twist, -weave, -digitate, -link.

twine, entwine, weave, inweave, twist, wreathe; anastomose, inoscu-late, dovetail, splice, link.

mat, plait, plat, braid, felt, twill; tangle, entangle, ravel; net, knot; dishevel, raddle.

Adj. crossing &c. *v.*; crossed, matted &c. *v.*; transverse.

cross, cruciform, crucial; reti-form, -cular, -culated; areolar, cancel-lated, mullioned, latticed, grated, barred, streaked; textile, secant, plexal; interfretted.

Adv. across, thwart, athwart, transversely, crosswise.

3°. Centrical Dimensions*

1. *General*

220. Exteriority. — N. exteriority; outside, exterior; surface, superficies; skin &c. (*covering*) 223; *superstratum*; disk, disc; face, facet.

excentricity; circumjacence &c. 227.

V. be -exterior &c. *adj.*; lie around &c. 227.

place -exteriorly, – outwardly, – out-side; put –, turn- out.

Adj. exter-ior, -nal; extraneous, outer, -most; out-ward, -lying, -side, -door; round about &c. 227; extra-mural.

superficial, skin-deep; frontal, dis-coid.

extraregarding; eccentric; outstand-ing; extrinsic &c. 6.

Adv. externally &c. *adj.*; out, with-out, over, outwards, *ab extra*, out of doors; *extra muros.*

221. Interiority.—N. interiority; in-side, interior, endocrine; interspace, subsoil, *substratum.*

contents &c. 190; substance, pith, marrow; backbone &c. (*centre*) 222; heart, bosom, breast, abdomen; vitals, viscera, entrails, bowels, belly, intes-tines, guts, chitterlings, womb, lap; gland, cell; internal organs, *penetralia,* recesses, innermost recesses; cave &c. (*concavity*) 252.

inhabitant &c. 188.

V. be -inside &c. *adj.*, – within &c. *adv.*

place –, keep- within; enclose &c. (*circumscribe*) 229; intern; embed &c. (*insert*) 300.

Adj. inter-ior, -nal; inner, inside, intimate, inward, intraregarding; in-, inner-most; deep-seated; visceral, intes-

* That is, Dimensions having reference to a centre.

in the open air; *sub -Jove*, – *dio*; à *la belle étoile, al fresco*.

tine, -tinal; inland; subcutaneous; interstitial &c. (*interjacent*) 228; inwrought &c. (*intrinsic*) 5; enclosed &c. *v.*

home, domestic, indoor, intramural, vernacular; endemic.

Adv. internally &c. *adj.*; inwards, within, in, inly; here-, there-, where-in; *ab intra*, withinside; in –, within- doors; at home, in the bosom of one's family.

222. Centrality.—**N.** centrality, centricalness, centre; middle &c. 68; focus &c. 74.

core, kernel; nucleus, nucleolus; heart, pole, axis, pivot, fulcrum, bull's eye; hub, nave, navel; *umbilicus*, spine, backbone, marrow, pith; hot-bed; concentration &c. (*convergence*) 290; centralization; symmetry.

centre of -gravity, – pressure, – percussion, – oscillation, – buoyancy &c. metacentre.

V. be -central &c. *adj.*; converge &c. 290.

render central, centralize, concentrate; bring to a focus.

Adj. centr-al, -ical; middle &c. 68; axial, pivotal, focal, umbilical, concentric; middlemost, nuclear, centric, centraidal; spinal, vertebral.

Adv. middle; midst; centrally &c. *adj.*

223. Covering.—**N.** covering, cover; canopy, tilt, awning, baldachin, tent, marquee, *tente d'abri*, umbrella, parasol, sunshade; veil (*shade*) 424; shield &c. (*defence*) 717; pall.

roof, dome, cupola, mansard roof; ceiling; thatch, tile; pan-, pen-tile; tiling, shingles, slates, slating, leads; shed &c. (*abode*) 189.

top, lid, covercle, door, *operculum*, eyelid, blind, curtain.

bandage, plaster, lint, wrapping, dossil, finger stall.

coverlet, counterpane, sheet, quilt, comforter, eiderdown; tarpaulin, blanket, rug, drugget, linoleum, oilcloth; housing.

in-, tegument; skin, pellicle, fleece, fell, fur, ermine, miniver, sable, sealskin &c.; leather, morocco, calf, pigskin, elk, kid, cowhide &c.; shagreen, hide; pelt, -ry; cuticle, *dermis*, scarf-skin, *epidermis*.

clothing &c. 225; mask &c. (*concealment*) 530.

peel, crust, bark, rind, *cortex*, husk, shell, coat.

capsule; ferrule; sheath, -ing; pod, cod; casing, case, theca, *elytron*; *involucrum*; wrapp-ing, -er, envelope, vesicle; dermatology, conchology.

armour, -plate, armouring; veneer, facing; pavement; scale &c. (*layer*) 204; coating, paint, stain; varnish &c. (*resin*) 356a; anointing &c. *v.*; inunction; incrustation, superposition, obduction, ground, enamel, whitewash, plaster, stucco, rough cast, pebble dash, compo; rendering; cerement; ointment &c. (*grease*) 356.

V. cover; super-pose, -impose; over-lay, -spread; wrap &c. 225; incase; face, case, veneer, pave, paper; tip, cap, bind, revet.

coat, paint, varnish, pay, incrust, stucco, cement, dab, plaster, tar; wash; be-, smear; be-, daub; anoint, do over; gild, plate,

224. Lining.—**N.** lining, inner coating; coating &c. (*covering*) 223; stalactite, -agmite.

filling, stuffing, wadding, padding, bushing.

wainscot, *parietes*, wall, brattice.

V. line, stuff, incrust, wad, pad, fill.

Adj. lined &c. *v.*

electroplate, japan, lacquer, lacker, enamel, whitewash; lay it on thick.

over-lie, -arch; conceal &c. 528.

Adj. covering &c. *v.*; cutaneous, dermal, cortical, cuticular, tegumentary, skinny, scaly, squamous; covered &c. *v.*; imbricated, loricated, armour-plated, iron-clad; under cover, hooded, cloaked, cowled.

---

225. Investment.—N. investment; covering &c. 223; dress, clothing, raiment, drapery, costume, attire, guise, toilet, *toilette*, trim; habiliment; vesture, -ment; garment, garb, palliament, apparel, wardrobe, wearing apparel, clothes, things.

array; tailoring, millinery; best bib and tucker; finery &c. (*ornament*) 847; full dress &c. (*show*) 882; garniture; theatrical properties.

outfit, equipment, *trousseau*; uniform, khaki, regimentals; academicals, canonicals &c. 999; livery, gear, harness, turn out, accoutrement, caparison, suit, rigging, trappings, traps, slops, togs, toggery; masquerade.

dishabille, morning dress, lounge suit, tea-gown, *kimono*, *négligé*, dressing-gown, *peignoir*, wrapper, undress; shooting-coat; smoking-jacket, mufti; rags, tatters, old clothes; mourning, weeds; duds; slippers.

robe, tunic, dolman, *paletot*, habit, gown, coat, coatee, frock, blouse, middy, sagum, *toga*, smock-frock; frock-, dress-, morning-, tail-coat; dress-suit, – clothes, swallow-tail coat, dinner-, Eton-jacket.

cloak, pall; mantle, mantlet, mantua, shawl, *pelisse*, veil, yashmak; cape, tippet, kirtle, plaid, muffler, comforter,

226. Divestment.—N. divestment; taking off &c. *v.*

nudity; bareness &c. *adj.*; undress; dishabille &c. 225, altogether; nu-, denu-dation; decortication, depilation, excoriation, desquamation; moulting; exfoliation.

baldness, alopecia, acomia.

V. divest; uncover &c. (*cover* &c. 223); denude, bare, strip; undress, unclothe, disrobe &c. (dress, enrobe, &c. 225); uncoif; dismantle; uncase; put –, take –, cast- off; shed, doff; husk, peel, pare, decorticate, desquamate, excoriate, skin, scalp, flay, bark, expose, lay open; exfoliate, moult, mew; cast the skin.

Adj. divested &c. *v.*; bare, naked, nude; un-dressed, -draped, -clad, -clothed, -appareled; exposed; in dishabille; *décolleté*; bald, threadbare, ragged, callow, roofless.

in -a state of nature, – nature's garb, – buff, – native buff, – birthday suit; *in puris naturalibus*; with nothing on, stark naked; bald as a coot, bare as the back of one's hand; out at elbows; barefoot; bareback; leaf-, nap-, hairless, shaved, clean shaven, tonsured, beardless, bald-headed, acomous.

Balaclava helmet, haik, huke, chlamys, mantilla, tabard, housing, horse-cloth, burnous, *roquelaure*; *houppelande*; sur-, top , over-, great-coat; *surtout*, spencer, cardigan, sweater, blazer; mackintosh, waterproof, slicker, raincoat, oilskin, trench coat, ulster, monkey-, pea-, pilot-jacket, redingote; wraprascal, poncho, cardinal, pelerine, talma.

jacket, jumper, vest, jerkin, waistcoat, doublet, *camisole*, gabardine; stays, *corsage*, corset, corselet, bodice; stomacher; skirt, petticoat, slip, farthingale, kilt, jupe, crinoline, bustle, hobble skirt, *panier*, apron, pinafore; loin cloth.

trousers; breeches, trews, pantaloons, unmentionables, inexpressibles, overalls, pyjamas, smalls, small-clothes; tights, pants, shorts, drawers; knickerbockers, knickers, plus fours, bloomers, divided skirt; phil-, fill-ibeg.

head-dress, -gear; cap, *béret,* tam o' shanter, glengarry, topee, sombrero; hat; cocked –, high –, tall –, top –, silk –, opera –, crush -hat, *gibus,* beaver, castor, bonnet, tile, wideawake, billy-cock; bowler; soft felt –, straw –, leghorn -hat, panama; toque; wimple; night-, mob-, skull-cap, biretta; hood, cowl, coif; capote, calach; scull-cap; kerchief, snood; head, *coiffure;* crown &c. (*circle*) 247; *chignon,* pelt, wig, front, peruke, periwig; caftan, turban, fez, *tarboosh,* taj, shako, csako, busby; *képi,* forage cap, bearskin; helmet &c. 717; mask, domino.

body clothes; linen; shirt, sark, smock, shift, *chemise, lingerie;* night-gown, -shirt; bed-gown, *sac de nuit;* jersey, guernsey; underwear, undies, underclothing, -waistcoat.

neck-erchief, -cloth; tie, ruff, collar, cravat, stock, handkerchief, bandana, scarf; bib, tucker; dicky; boa; girdle &c. (*circle*) 247; cummerbund.

shoe, pump, brogue, boot, slipper, sandal, galoche, goloshes, arctics, rubber boots, overshoes, patten, clog, sabot; high-low; Blücher –, Wellington –, Hessian –, jack –, top- boot; Balmoral; legging, puttee, buskin, greave, galligaskin, moccasin, *gamache,* gambado, gaiter, spatter-dash, spat, antigropelos; stocking, hose, gaskins, trunk-hose, sock, hosiery.

glove, gauntlet, mitten, cuff, muffettee, wristband, sleeve.

swaddling cloth, baby-linen, *layette;* pocket-handkerchief.

shroud &c. 363.

clothier, tailor, milliner, *costumier,* sempstress, seamstress, snip; dress-, habit-, breeches-, shoe-maker; cordwainer, cobbler, Crispin, hosier, hatter; draper, linendraper, haberdasher, mercer.

V. invest; cover &c. 223; envelop, lap, involve; in-, en-wrap; wrap; fold –, wrap –, lap –, muffle- up; overlap; sheathe, swathe, swaddle, roll up in, shroud, circumvest.

vest, clothe, array, dress, dight, drape, robe, enrobe, attire, tire, garb, habilitate, apparel, accoutre, rig, fit out; bedizen, deck &c. (*ornament*) 847; perk; equip, harness, caparison; dress up.

wear; don; put –, huddle –, slip- on; mantle.

Adj. invested &c. *v.;* habited; dight, -ed; clad, *costumé,* shod, *chaussé; en grande tenue* &c. (*show*) 882.

sartorial.

227. Circumjacence.—N. circumjacence, -ambience; environment, encompassment; atmosphere, medium; surroundings, *entourage.*

outpost; border &c. (*edge*) 231; girdle &c. (*circumference*) 230; outskirts, *boulevards,* suburbs, purlieus, precincts, *faubourgs, environs, banlieue,* neighbourhood, vicinity.

V. lie -around &c. *adv.;* surround, beset, compass, encompass, environ, inclose, enclose, encircle, circle, embrace, circumvent, lap, gird; begird, girdle, engird; skirt; twine round; hem in &c. (*circumscribe*) 229; besiege, invest, blockade.

Adj. circum-jacent, -ambient, -fluent;

228. Interjacence.—N. inter-jacence, -currence, -venience, -location, -digitation, -penetration; permeation.

inter-jection, -polation, -lineation, -spersion, -calation; embolism.

inter-vention, -ference, -position; in-, ob-trusion; insinuation; insertion &c. 300; dovetailing; infiltration; intromission.

intermedi-um, -ary; go-between, agent, middleman, medium, bodkin, intruder, interloper; parenthesis, episode; fly-leaf.

partition, *septum,* diaphragm, midriff; party-wall, panel, vail, bulkhead, brattice, *cloison;* half-way house.

V. lie –, come –, get- between; inter-

ambient; surrounding &c. *v.*; circumferential, surburban.

Adv. around, about; without; on -every side, – all sides; right and left, all round, round about; in the neighbourhood.

vene, slide in, interpenetrate, permeate. put between, introduce, intromit. import; throw –, wedge –, edge –, jam –, worm –, foist –, run –, plough –, work- in; inter-pose, -ject, -calate, -polate, -line, -leave, -sperse, -weave, -lard, -digitate; let in, dovetail, splice, mortise; insinuate, smuggle; infiltrate, ingrain.

interfere, put in an oar, thrust one's nose in; intrude, obtrude; have a finger in the pie; introduce the thin end of the wedge; thrust in &c. (*insert*) 300.

Adj. inter-jacent, -current, -venient, -vening &c. *v.*, -mediate, -mediary, -calary, -stitial, -costal, -mural, -planetary, -stellar; embolismal.

parenthetical, episodic; mediterranean; intrusive; embosomed; merged, mean, middle, medium, median.

Adv. between, betwixt; 'twixt; among, -st; amid, -st; 'mid, -st; in the thick of; betwixt and between; sandwich-wise; parenthetically, *obiter dictum*.

229. Circumscription.—N. circumscription, limitation, inclosure; confinement &c. (*restraint*) 751; circumvallation, encincture; envelope &c. 232.

V. circumscribe, limit, bound, confine, enclose; surround &c. 227; compass about; imprison &c. (*restrain*) 751; hedge –, wall –, rail- in; fence –, hedge- round; embar; picket, corral.

enfold, bury, incase, pack up, enshrine, inclasp; wrap up &c. (*invest*) 225; embosom.

Adj. circumscribed &c. *v.*; begirt, lapt; circumambient; buried –, immersed- in; embosomed, in the bosom of, imbedded, encysted, mewed up; imprisoned &c. 751; land-locked, in a ring fence.

230. Outline.—N. outline, circumference; peri-meter, -phery; ambit, circuit, lines, *tournure*, *contour*, profile, *silhouette*, lineaments; bounds, coastline.

zone, belt, girth, band, baldric, zodiac, girdle, tire, cingle, clasp, girt; *cordon* &c. (*inclosure*) 232; circlet &c. 247.

V. outline, delineate, *silhouette*, circumscribe &c. 229; profile, block out.

Adj. outlined &c. *v.*; circumferential, perimetric, peripheral.

231. Edge.—N. edge, verge, brink, brow, brim, margin, border, confines, skirt, rim, felloe, felly, flange, side, mouth; jaws, chops, chaps, *fauces*; lip, muzzle.

threshold, door, porch; portal &c. (*opening*) 260; coast, shore, strand, beach, bank, wharf, quay, dock.

frame, fringe, flounce, frill, list, trimming, edging, skirting, hem, selvedge, welt; furbelow, valance, exergue.

Adj. border, marginal, skirting; labial, labiated, marginated.

232. Inclosure.—N. inclosure, enclosure, envelope; case &c. (*receptacle*) 191; wrapper; girdle &c. 230.

pen, fold, croft, sty; pen-, in-, sheep-fold; paddock, pound, corral, kraal; yard, compound; net, seine net.

wall; hedge, -row; *espalier*; fence &c. (*defence*) 717; pale, paling, balustrade, rail, railing, gunwale; quickset hedge, park paling, circumvallation, *enceinte*, ring fence.

barrier, barricade; gate, -way; door, hatch, *cordon*; prison &c. 752.
dike, dyke, ditch, fosse, moat, trench.

V. inclose; circumscribe &c. 229.

233. Limit.—N. limit, boundary, bounds, confine, *enclave*, term, bourn, verge, kerb-stone, curbstone, but, pale; termin-ation, -us; stint, frontier, precinct, marches.

boundary line, landmark, benchmark; line of -demarcation, - circumvallation; pillars of Hercules; Rubicon, turning-point; *ne plus ultra*; sluice, flood-gate.

V. limit, bound, confine, define, circumscribe, demarcate, delimit, encompass.

Adj. definite; contermin-ate, -able, terminable, limitable; terminal, frontier, border, bordering, boundary.

Adv. thus far, - and no further.

2. *Special*

234. Front.—N. front; fore, - part; foreground; forefront, face, disk, disc, frontage, *façade*, *proscenium*, facia, frontispiece; priority, anteriority; obverse [of a medal].

fore -, front- rank, first line; van, -guard; advanced guard; outpost, scout.

brow, forehead, visage, physiognomy, phiz, features, countenance, map, mug; rostrum, beak, bow, stem, prow, prore, jib, bowsprit; forecastle.

pioneer &c. (*precursor*) 64; metoposcopy.

V. be -, stand- in front &c. *adj.*; front, face, confront, breast, brave; bend forwards; come to the -front, ⁓ fore.

Adj. fore, forward, anterior, front, frontal.

Adv. before; in -front, - the van, - advance; ahead, right ahead; fore-, head-most; in the foreground; before one's -face, - eyes; face to face, *vis-à-vis*.

236. Laterality.—N. laterality; side, flank, beam, quarter, lee; hand; cheek, jowl, jole, wing; profile; temple, *parietes*, loin, haunch, hip.

gable, -end; broadside; lee side.

points of the compass; East, Orient, Levant; West, occident; orientation.

V. be -on one side &c. *adv.*; flank, outflank; sidle; skirt, border.

Adj. lateral, sidelong; collateral;

235. Rear.—N. rear, back, posteriority; rear -rank, - guard; background, *hinterland*.

occiput, nape, scruff, chine; heels; tail, rump, croup, buttock, posteriors, bottom, seat, backside, scut, breech, *dorsum*, loin; dorsal -, lumbar- region; hind quarters.

stern, poop, after-part, counter; postern, heel-, tail-piece, crupper.

wake; train &c. (*sequence*) 281.

reverse; other side of the shield.

V. be -behind &c. *adv.*; fall astern; bend backwards; bring up the rear; follow &c. 622; tail, shadow.

Adj. back, rear; hind, -er, -most, -ermost; post-ern, -erior; dorsal, after; caudal, lumbar; mizzen.

Adv. behind; in the -rear, - ruck, - back-ground; behind one's back; at the -heels, - tail, - back- of; back to back.

after, -most, aft, abaft, astern, sternmost, aback, rear-, hind-, back-ward.

237. Contraposition.—N. contraposition, opposition; polarity; inversion &c. 218; opposite side; antithesis; reverse, inverse; counterpart; antipodes; opposite poles, North and South.

V. be -opposite &c. *adj.*; subtend.

Adj. opposite; reverse, inverse; antipodal, subcontrary; fronting, facing, diametrically opposite.

Northern, Septentrional, Boreal, aro

parietal, flanking, skirting; flanked; sideling.

many-sided; multi-, bi-, tri-, quadrilateral.

East-ern, -ward, -erly; orient, -al, auroral, Levantine; West-ern, -ward, -erly; occidental, Hesperian; equatorial.

Adv. side-ways, -long; broadside on; on one side, abreast, abeam, alongside, beside, aside; by, – the side of; side by side; cheek by jowl &c. (*near*) 197; to -windward, – leeward; laterally &c. *adj.*; right and left; on her beam ends.

tic; Southern, Austral, antarctic, polar,

Adv. over, – the way, – against; against; face to face, *vis-à-vis*; as poles asunder.

---

238. Dextrality. — N. dextrality; right, – hand; dexter, offside, starboard.

Adj. dextral, right-handed; ambidextral, dexterous, dextrorsal &c.

239. Sinistrality.—N. sinistrality; left, – hand; *sinister*, nearside, larboard, port.

Adj. sinistral, sinister, sinistrorsal &c., left-handed, sinistromanual, sinistrous.

Section III. FORM

1°. General Form

240. Form.—N. form, figure, shape; con-formation, -figuration; make, formation, frame, construction, design, cut, set, build, trim, cut of one's jib; stamp, type, cast, mould; fashion; contour &c. (*outline*) 230; structure &c. 329.

feature, lineament, outline, turn; phase &c. (*aspect*) 448; posture, attitude, *pose.*

[Science of form] morphology.

[Similarity of form] isomorphism.

forming &c. *v.*; form-, figur-, efformation; sculpture.

V. form, shape, figure, fashion, efform, carve, cut, chisel, hew, cast; rough-hew, -cast; sketch; block –, hammer- out; trim; lick –, put- into shape; model, knead, work up into, set, mould, sculpture; cast, stamp; build &c. (*construct*) 161.

Adj. formed &c. *v.*

[Receiving form] plastic, fictile, full-fashioned &c.

[Giving form] plasmic &c.

[Similar in form] isomorphous &c.

241. [Absence of form.] Amorphism. —N. amorphism, informity, uncouthness; unlicked cub, rough diamond; *rudis indigestaque moles*; disorder &c. 59; deformity &c. 243.

disfigure-, deface-ment, deformation; mutilation.

V. [Destroy form] deface, disfigure, deform, mutilate, truncate; derange &c. 61.

Adj. shapeless, amorphous, malformed, formless; un-formed, -hewn, -fashioned, -shapen; rough, rude, Gothic, barbarous, rugged, in the rough; misshapen &c. 243.

---

242. [Regularity of form.] Symmetry. —N. symmetry, shapeliness, finish; beauty &c. 845; proportion, eurythmy, eurythmic, uniformity, parallelism; bi-, tri-, multi-lateral symmetry; centrality &c. 222.

243. [Irregularity of form.] Distortion.—N. dis-, de-, con-tortion; knot, mop, warp, buckle, screw, twist; crookedness &c. (*obliquity*) 217; grimace; deformity; mal-, malcon-formation; monstrosity, misproportion, want

arborescence, branching, ramification.

Adj. symmetrical, shapely, well set, finished; beautiful &c. 845; classic, chaste, severe.

regular, uniform, balanced; equal &c. 27; parallel, coextensive.

arbor-escent, -iform; dendr-iform, -oid; branching; ramous, ramose.

---

of symmetry, *anamorphosis*; ugliness &c. 846; teratology.

V. distort, contort, twist, warp &c. *n.;* wrest, writhe, make faces, deform, misshape.

Adj. distorted &c. *v.*; out of shape, irregular, unsymmetric, awry, wry, askew, crooked, sinuous; anamorphous; not -true, – straight; on one side, crump, deformed; mis-shapen, -begotten; mis-, ill-proportioned; ill-made; grotesque, crooked as a ram's horn; hump-, hunch-, bunch-, crook-backed; bandy; bandy-, bow-legged; bow-, knock-kneed; splay-, club-footed; taliped; round-shouldered; snub-nosed; curtailed of one's fair proportions; scalene, stumpy &c. (*short*) 201; gaunt &c. (*thin*) 203; bloated &c. 194.

Adv. all manner of ways.

2°. SPECIAL FORM

244. Angularity.—N. angular-ity, -ness; aduncity; angle, cusp, bend; fold &c. 258; notch &c. 257; fork, bifurcation.

elbow, knee, knuckle, ankle, groin, crotch, crutch, crane, fluke, scythe, sickle, zigzag, kimbo.

corner, nook, recess, niche, oriel.

right angle &c. (*perpendicular*) 212; obliquity &c. 217; angle of 45°, mitre; acute –, obtuse –, salient –, re-entrant –, spherical –, solid –, dihedral- angle.

angular -measurement, – elevation, – distance, – velocity; trigon-, goni-ometry; altimetry; clin-, graph-, goni-ometer; theodolite; transit circle; sextant, quadrant; dichotomy.

triangle, trigon, wedge; rectangle, square, lozenge, diamond; rhomb, -us; quadr-angle, -ilateral; parallelogram; quadrature; poly-, penta-, hexa-, hepta-, octa-, deca-gon.

Platonic bodies; cube, rhomboid; tetra-, penta-, hexa-, octa-, dodeca-, icosa-hedron; prism, pyramid; parallelopiped.

V. bend, fork, bifurcate, crinkle, divaricate, branch, ramify.

Adj. angular, bent, crooked, aduncous, uncinated, aquiline, jagged, serrated; falc-iform, -ated; furcular, furcated, forked, bifurcate, crotched; zigzag; dovetailed; knock-kneed, crinkled, akimbo, kimbo, geniculated; oblique &c. 217.

fusiform, wedge-shaped, cuneiform; tri-angular, -gonal, -lateral; quadr-angular, -ilateral; rectangular, square, foursquare, multilateral; polygonal &c. *n.*; cubical, rhomboidal, pyramidal.

245. Curvature.—N. curv-ature, -ity, -ation; incurv-ity, -ation; bend; flexure, -ion; conflexure; crook, hook, bought, bending; de-, inflexion; arcuation, devexity, turn; deviation, *détour*, sweep; curl, -ing; bough; recurv-ity, -ation; sinuosity &c. 248; aduncity.

curve, arc, arch, arcade, vault, dome, bow, crescent, *meniscus*, half-moon, lunule, horse-shoe, loop, crane-neck;

246. Straightness.—N. straightness, rectilinearity, directness; inflexibility &c. (*stiffness*) 323; straight –, right –, direct-, bee- line; short cut.

V. be -straight &c. *adj.*; have no turning; not -incline, – bend, – turn, – deviate- to either side; go straight; steer for &c. (*direction*) 278.

render straight, straighten, rectify; set –, put- straight; un-bend, -fold.

para-, hyper-bola; catenary, festoon; conch-, cardi-oid; caustic, instep; tracery.

V. be -curved &c. *adj.*; sweep, swag, sag; deviate &c. 279; turn; re-enter.

render -curved &c. *adj.*; bend, curve, incurvate; de-, in-flect; crook; turn, round, arch, arcuate, arch over, loop the loop, concamerate; bow, coil, curl, recurve, frizzle.

Adj. curved &c. *v.*; curvi-form, -lineal, -linear; devex, devious; recurv-ed, -ous; *retroussé*; crump; bowed &c. *v.*; vaulted; hooked; falc-iform, -ated; semicircular, crescentic; lun-iform, -ular; semi-lunar, meniscal; conchoidal; cord-iform, -ated; cardioid; heart-, bell-, pear-, fig-shaped; reniform; lenti-form, -cular; bow-legged &c. (*distorted*) 243; oblique &c. 217; circular &c. 247.

-curl &c. 248, -ravel &c. 219, -wrap.

Adj. straight; rectiline-ar, -al; direct, even, right, true, in a line; unbent &c. *v.*; un-deviating, -turned, -distorted. -swerving; straight as an arrow &c. (*direct*) 278; inflexible &c. 323.

---

247. [Simple circularity.] **Circularity.** —N. circularity, roundness; rotundity &c. 249.

circle, circlet, clasp, ring, washer, areola, hoop, roundlet, *annulus*, am-ulet, bracelet, armlet, armilla; ringlet; eye, loop, wheel; cycle, orb, orbit, rundle, zone, belt, *cordon*, band; sash, girdle, cestus, cincture, baldric, fillet, *fascia*, wreath, garland; crown, corona, coronet, chaplet, snood, necklace, collar; noose, lasso, lariat.

ellipse, oval, ovule; ellipsoid, cycloid; epi-cycloid, -cycle; semi-circle; quad-rant, sextant, sector.

V. make -round &c. *adj.*; round.

go round; encircle &c. 227; describe -a circle &c. 311.

Adj. round, rounded, circular, annu-lar, orbicular; oval, ovate; elliptic, -al; ovoid, egg-shaped; pear-shaped &c. 245; cycloidal &c. *n.*; spherical &c. 249.

248. [Complex circularity.] **Convolu-tion.**—N. winding &c. *v.*; con-, in-circum-volution; wave, undulation, tortuosity, anfractuosity; sinu-osity, -ation, sinuousness; meandering, cir-cuit, circumbendibus, twist, twirl, windings and turnings, *ambages*; tor-sion; inosculation; reticulation &c. (*crossing*) 219.

coil, roll, curl, buckle, spire, spiral, helix, corkscrew, worm, volute, whorl, rundle; tendril; scollop, scallop, es-calop; kink.

serpent, snake, eel, maze, labyrinth

V. be -convoluted &c. *adj.*; wind, twine, turn and twist, twirl; wave, undulate, meander; inosculate; en-twine, intwine; twist, coil, roll; wrinkle, curl, crisp, twill; frizz, -le; crimp, crape, indent, scollop, scallop; wring, intort; contort; wreathe &c. (*cross*) 219.

Adj. convoluted; winding, twisted &c. *v.*; tortile, tortive; wavy; und-ated, -ulatory; circling, snaky, snake-like, serpentine; serpent-, anguill-, verm-iform; vermicular; mazy, tortu-ous, anfractuous, sinuous, flexuous, wavy, sigmoidal.

involved, intricate, complicated, perplexed; labyrinth-ic, -ian, -ine; circuitous; peristaltic; dædalian, curly.

wreathy, frizzly, crapy, buckled; ravelled &c. (*in disorder*) 59. spiral, coiled, helical, turbinated.

Adv. in and out, round and round.

249. Rotundity.—N. rotundity; roundness &c. *adj.*; cylindricity; spher-icity, -oidity; globosity.

cylin-der, -droid; barrel, drum; roll, -er; *rouleau*, column, rolling-pin, rundle; chimney-pot, drain-pipe.

cone, conoid; pear-, egg-, bell-shape.

sphere, globe, ball, boulder, bowlder; spher-, ellips-, ɡe-, glob-oid, oblong –, oblate- spheroid; drop, spherule, globule, vesicle, bulb, bullet, pellet, *pelote*, clew, pill, marble, pea, knob, pommel, knot.

V. render -spherical &c. *adj.*; form into a sphere, sphere, roll into a ball; give -rotundity &c. *n.*; round.

Adj. rotund; round &c. (*circular*) 247; cylindr-ic, -ical, -oid; columnar, lumbriciform; conic, -al; spher-ical, -oidal; glob-ular, -ated, -ous, -ose; egg-, bell-, pear-shaped; ov-oid, -iform; gibbous; campaniform, -ulate, -iliform; fungiform, bead-like, moniliform, pyriform, bulbous; *teres atque rotundus*; round as -an orange, – an apple, – a ball, – a billiard ball, – a cannon ball.

3°. SUPERFICIAL FORM

250. Convexity. — N. convexity, prominence, projection, swelling, gibbosity, bilge, bulge, protuberance, protrusion; excrescency, camber.

intumescence; tumour, tumor; tubercle, -osity; excrescence; hump, hunch, bunch, gnarl, lump.

tooth, knob, elbow, process, *apophysis*, condyle, bulb, node, nodule, nodosity, tongue, *dorsum*, boss, embossment, bump, clump; sugar-loaf &c. (*sharpness*) 253; bow; mamelon.

pimple, wen, wheal, *papula*, postule, pock, proud flesh, growth, goitre, *sarcoma*, carbuncle, corn, bunion, wart, furnuncle, polypus, adenoid, fungus, fungosity, *exostosis*, bleb, blister, blain; boil &c. (*disease*) 655; bubble, blob.

papilla, nipple, teat, pap, breast, dug, mammilla; proboscis, nose, neb, beak, snout, nozzle, snozzle; Adam's apple; belly, paunch, corporation; withers, back, shoulder, lip, flange.

peg, button, stud, ridge, rib, jutty, trunnion, snag.

cupola, dome, bee-hive; arch, balcony, eaves; pilaster.

relief, relievo, *cameo*; *basso-*, *mezzo-*, *alto-rilievo*; low-, bas-, high-relief.

hill &c. (*height*) 206; cape, promontory, mull; fore-, head-land; point of land, naze, ness, mole, jetty, hummock, ledge, spur.

V. be -prominent &c. *adj.*; project, bulge, protrude, bag, belly, pout, bouge, bunch; jut –, stand –, stick –, poke- out; stick –, bristle –, start –, cock –, shoot- up; swell –, hang –, pend- over; beetle.

render -prominent &c. *adj.*; raise emboss, chase.

251. Flatness.—N. flatness &c. *adj.*; smoothness &c. 255.

plane; level &c. 213; plate, platter, table, tablet, slab.

V. render flat, flatten, squash; level &c. 213.

Adj. flat, plane, even, flush, scutiform, discoid; level &c. (*horizontal*) 213; smooth; flat as -a pancake, – a fluke, – a flounder, – a board, – my hand.

252. Concavity.—N. concavity, depression, dip; hollow, -ness; indentation, *intaglio*, cavity, antrum, dent, dint, dimple, follicle, pit, *sinus*, *alveolus*, *lacuna*; excavation, trench, sap, mine, tunnel, burrow; trough &c. (*furrow*) 259; honeycomb.

cup, basin, crater, punch-bowl; cell &c. (*receptacle*) 191; socket, faucet.

valley, vale, dale, dell, gap, dingle, combe, bottom, slade, strath, glade, grove, glen, cave, cavern, cove; grot, -to; alcove, *cul-de-sac*, blind alley; gully &c. 198; arch &c. (*curve*) 245; bay &c. (*of the sea*) 343.

excavator, sapper, miner.

V. be -concave &c. *adj.*; retire, cave in.

render -concave &c. *adj.*; depress hollow; scoop, – out; gouge, dig, delve, excavate, dent, dint, mine, sap, undermine, burrow, tunnel, stave in.

Adj. depressed &c. *v.*; concave, hollow, stove in; dished; spoon-like; retiring; retreating; cavernous; porous &c. (*with holes*) 260; cellular, spongy, spongious; honeycombed, alveolar; infundibul-ar, -iform; funnel-, bell-shaped; campaniform, capsular; vaulted, arched. ──────

Adj. convex, prominent, protuberant, underhung, undershot; projecting &c. *v.*; bossed, bossy, nodular, bunchy; clav-ate, -ated; hummocky, *moutonné*, mammiform; papul-ous, -ose; hemispheric, bulbous; bowed, arched; bold; bellied; tuber-ous, -culous; tumorous; cornute, knobby, odontoid; lenti-form, -cular; gibbous.

salient, in relief, raised, *repoussé*; bloated &c. (*expanded*) 194.

253. Sharpness.—N. sharpness &c. *adj.*; acuity, acumination; spinosity.

point, spike, spine, *spiculum*, tine; needle, pin; tack, nail; prick, -le; spur, rowel, barb; spit, cusp; horn, antler; snag; tag; thorn, bristle.

nib, tooth, incisor, tusk; spoke, cog, ratchet.

crag. crest, *arête*, cone, peak, sugar-loaf, pike, *aiguille*; spire, pyramid, steeple.

beard, *chevaux de frise*, porcupine, hedgehog, brier, bramble, thistle; comb, awn, bur.

wedge; knife-, cutting- edge; blade, edge-tool, cutlery, knife, penknife, whittle, razor; scalpel, bistoury, lancet; chisel; ploughshare, coulter; hatchet, axe, pick-axe, mattock, pick, adze, bill; bill-hook, cleaver, cutter; skiver; scythe, sickle, scissors, shears; sword &c. (*arms*) 727; bodkin &c. (*perforator*) 262.

sharpener, hone, strop; grind-, whet-stone; steel, emery.

V. be -sharp &c. *adj.*; taper to a point; bristle with.

render -sharp &c. *adj.*; sharpen, point, aculeate, acuminate, whet, barb, spiculate, set, strop, grind.

cut &c. (*sunder*) 44.

Adj. sharp, keen; acute; aci-cular, -form; acu-leated, -minated; pointed; tapering; conical, pyramidal; mucron-ate, -ated; spindle-, needle-shaped; spiked, spiky, ensiform, peaked, salient, cusp-ed; -idate, -idated; corn-ute, -uted, -iculate; prickly; spiny, spinous; thorny, bristling, muricated, pectinated, studded, thistly, briery; craggy &c. (*rough*) 256; snaggy; digitated, two-edged, fusiform; denti-form, -culated; toothed; odontoid; star-like; stell-ated, -iform; arrow-headed; arrowy, barbed, spurred, sagittal; spear-shaped, hastate; horned; conical.

cutting; sharp-, knife-edged; sharp -, keen- as a razor; sharp as a needle; sharpened &c. *v.*; set.

254. Bluntness.—N. bluntness &c. *adj.*

V. be -, render- blunt &c. *adj.*; obtund, dull; take off the -point, - edge; turn.

Adj. blunt, obtuse, dull, bluff.

255. Smoothness.—N. smoothness &c. *adj.*; polish, gloss; lubric-ity, -ation.

down, velvet, silk, satin; slide; bowling green &c. (*level*) 213; glass, ice; asphalt, pavement, flags.

roller, steam-roller; iron, flat-iron, tailor's goose; sand-, emery-paper; burnisher, turpentine and bees-wax.

V. smooth, -en; plane; file; mow, shave; level, roll; macadamize; polish, burnish, planish, levigate, calender, glaze; iron, hot-press, mangle; lubricate &c. (*oil*) 332.

256. Roughness.—N. roughness &c. *adj.*; tooth, grain, texture, ripple; asperity, rugosity, salebrosity, corrugation, nodosity; arborescence &c. 242.

brush, hair, beard, shag, mane, whisker, mutton-chops, *moustache*, *mustachio*, imperial, Van Dyke, tress, lock, curl, ringlet, *fimbriæ*, *cilia*, *villi*; eyelashes, eye-brows, love-lock.

plum-age, -osity; plume, *panache*, crest; feather, tuft, tussock, fringe, toupee.

wool, velvet, plush, nap, pile, floss,

Adj. smooth; polished &c. *v.*; even; level &c. 213; plane &c. (*flat*) 251; sleek, glossy; silken, silky; lanate, downy, velvety; glabrous, slippery, glassy, lubricous, oily, soft; unwrinkled; smooth as -glass, – ice, – velvet, – oil; slippery as an eel; woolly &c. (*feathery*) 256.

fluff, fur, down; byssus. moss, bur.

V. be -rough &c. *adj.*; go against the grain.

render -rough &c. *adj.*; roughen, rough cast, knurl; ruffle, crisp, crumple, crinkle, corrugate, engrail; set on edge, stroke –, rub- the wrong way, rumple.

Adj. rough, uneven; scabrous, knotted; nodular; rug-ged, -ose, -ous; asperous, crisp, salebrous, gnarled, unpolished, unsmooth, rough-hewn; knurled, cross-grained, crag-gy, -ged; crankling, scraggy, jagged, unkempt, prickly &c. (*sharp*) 253; arborescent &c. 242; leafy, well wooded; feathery; plum-ose, -igerous; tufted, fimbriated, hairy, bristly, ciliated, filamentous, hirsute; crin-ose, -ite; bushy, hispid, villous, pappous, bearded, pilous, shaggy, shagged; fringed, befringed; set-ous, -ose, -aceous; 'like quills upon the fretful porcupine'; rough as a -nutmeg grater; – bear.

downy, velvety, flocculent, woolly; lan-ate, -ated; lanugin-ous, -ose; tomentous.

Adv. against the grain, in the rough, on edge.

257. Notch.—N. notch, dent, nick, cut; indent, -ation; serration; dimple.

embrasure, battlement, machicolation; saw, tooth, crenelle, scallop, scollop, vandyke.

V. notch, nick, cut, pink, mill, score, dent, indent, jag, scarify, scotch, crimp, scollop, crenulate, vandyke.

Adj. notched &c. *v.*; crenate, -d; dentate, -d; denticulate, -d; toothed, palmated, serrated.

258. Fold.—N. fold, plicature, pleat, plait, ply, crease; tuck, gather; flexion, flexure, joint, elbow, doubling, duplicature, wrinkle, rimple, crinkle, crankle, crumple, rumple, rivel, ruck, ruffle, dog's ear, corrugation, frounce, flounce, lapel; pucker, crow's feet.

V. fold, double, plicate, pleat, plait, crease, wrinkle, crinkle, crankle. curl, smock, cockle up, crocker, rimple, rumple, frizzle, frounce, rivel, twill, corrugate, ruffle, crimple, crumple, pucker; turn –, double- -down, – under; tuck, ruck, hem, gather.

Adj. folded &c. *v.*

259. Furrow.—N. furrow, groove, rut, *sulcus*, scratch, streak, *striæ*, crack, score, incision, slit; chamfer, fluting.

channel, gutter, trench, ditch, dike, dyke, moat, fosse, trough, kennel; ravine &c. (*interval*) 198.

V. furrow &c. *n.*; flute, groove, carve, corrugate, plough; incise, chase, enchase, grave, engrave, etch, bite in, cross-hatch.

Adj. furrowed &c. *v.*; ribbed, striated, sulcated, fluted, canaliculated; bisulc-ous, -ate; trisulcate; corduroy.

260. Opening.—N. hole, foramen; puncture, blow-out, perforation; pin-, key-, loop-, port-, peep-, mouse-, pigeon-hole; eye, – of a needle; eyelet; slot.

opening; apert-ure, -ness; hiation,

261. Closure.—N. closure, occlusion, blockade; shutting up &c. *v.*; obstruction &c. (*hindrance*) 706; gag; embolism; contraction &c. 195; infarction; con-ob-stipation; blind -alley, – corner; *cul-de-sac*, *cæcum*; imper-foration

yawning, oscitancy, dehiscence, patefaction, pandiculation; gap, chasm &c;
(*interval*) 198.

embrasure, window, casement, light;
sky-, fan-light; lattice; bay-, bow-
window; oriel; dormer, lantern, *abat-
jour*.

out-, in-let; vent, vomitory; *embouchure*; orifice, mouth, sucker, muzzle,
throat, gullet, placket, weasand, wizen,
nozzle, *œsophagus*.

portal, porch, gate, ostiary, postern,
wicket, trap-door, hatch, door; arcade;
gate-, door-, hatch-, gang-way; lich-
gate.

way, path &c. 627; thoroughfare;
channel, passage, tube, pipe; water-
pipe &c. 350; air-pipe &c. 351; vessel,
tubule, canal, gut, fistula; adjutage,
ajutage; chimney, smoke stack, flue,
tap, funnel, gully, tunnel, main; mine,
pit, adit, shaft; gallery.

alley, aisle, glade, lane, vista.

bore, calibre; pore; blind orifice.

por-ousness, -osity; sieve, cullender, colander; grater, shredder;
cribble, riddle, screen; honeycomb.

apertion, perforation; piercing &c. *v.*; terebration, empalement,
pertusion, puncture, acupuncture, penetration.

opener, key, master-key, *passe-partout*.

V. open, ope, gape, dehisce, yawn, bilge; fly open.

perforate, pierce, empierce, tap, bore, drill; mine &c. (*scoop out*)
252; tunnel; trans-pierce, -fix; enfilade, impale, spike, spear, gore,
spit, stab, pink, puncture, lance, trepan, trephine, stick, prick,
riddle, punch; stave in.

cut a passage through; make -way, – room- for.

un-cover, -close, -rip; lay –, cut –, rip –, throw- open.

Adj. open; perforated &c. *v.*; perforate; wide open, agape, **ajar;**
un-closed, -stopped; oscitant, gaping, yawning; patent.

tubular, cannular, fistulous; per-vious, -meable; foraminous;
vesi-, vas-cular; porous, follicular, cribriform, honeycombed, in-
fundibular, riddled; tubul-ous, -ated, piped.

opening &c. *v.*; aperient.

Int. open sesame!

262. Perforator. — N. perforator,
piercer, borer, auger, gimlet, stylet,
drill, wimble, awl, bradawl, scoop,
terrier, corkscrew, dibble, trocar, tre-
pan, trephine, probe, bodkin, needle,
stiletto, broach, reamer, rimer, warder,
lancet; punch, -eon; spikebit, gouge;
spear &c. (*weapon*) 727.

-viousness &c. *adj.*, -meability; stopper
&c. 263; *operculum*.

V. close, occlude, plug; block –,
stop –, fill –, bung –, cork –, button –,
stuff –, shut –, dam- up, obturate;
blockade; obstruct &c. (*hinder*) **706;**
bar, bolt, stop, seal, plumb; choke,
throttle; ram down, tamp, dam, cram;
trap, clinch; put to –, shut- the door;
batten down the hatches.

Adj. closed &c. *v.*; shut, operculated;
unopened.

unpierced, imporous, cæcal; imperforate, -vious, -meable; impenetrable;
un-, im-passable; invious; path-, wayless; untrodden.

unventilated; air-, water-tight; hermetically sealed; tight, snug.

———

263. Stopper.—N. stopper, stopple;
plug, cork, bung, spike, spill, stop-cock,
tap; rammer; ram, -rod; piston; stop-
gap; wadding, stuffing, padding, stopping, dossil, pledget, tompion, tourniquet. obturator; wad.

cover &c. 223; valve, slide valve;
vent-peg, spigot.

janitor, door –, gate- keeper, porter,
commissionaire, *concierge*, warder.
beadle, Cerberus, usher, guard, sentry
sentinel; ostiary.

SECTION IV. MOTION

1°. MOTION IN GENERAL

264. [Successive change of place.*]
Motion.—N. motion, movement, move;
motivity, motility, going &c. *v.*; unrest.

stream, current, flow, flux, run,
course, stir; conduction, evolution;
kinematics.

step, rate, pace, tread, stride, gait,
clip, port, footfall, cadence, carriage,
velocity, angular velocity; progress,
locomotion; journey &c. 266; voyage
&c. 267; transit &c. 270.

restlessness &c. (*changeableness*) 149;
mobility; movableness, motive power;
laws of motion; mobilization.

V. be -in motion &c. *adj.*; move, go,
hie, gang, budge, stir, pass, flit; hover
-round, – about; shift, slide, slither,
glide; roll, – on; flow, stream, run,
drift, sweep along; wander &c. (*deviate*)
279; walk &c. 266; change –, shift-
one's -place, – quarters; dodge; keep
-going, – moving.

put –, set- in motion; move; impel
&c. 276; propel &c. 284; render movable, mobilize.

Adj. moving &c. *v.*;in motion;motile,
transitional; motory, motive; shifting,
movable, mobile, mercurial, unquiet;
restless &c. (*changeable*) 149; nomadic
&c. 266; erratic &c. 279.

Adv. under way; on the -move, –
wing, – tramp, – march.

---

265. Quiescence.—N. rest; stillness
&c. *adj.*; quiescence; stag-nation,
-nancy; fixity, immobility, catalepsy;
indisturbance; quietism.

quiet, tranquillity, calm; repose &c.
687; peace; dead calm, anticyclone;
statue-like repose; silence &c. 403; not
a -breath of air, – mouse stirring; sleep
&c. (*inactivity*) 683.

pause, lull &c. (*cessation*) 142; stand,
– still; standing still &c. *v.*; lock; dead
-lock, – stop, – stand; full stop; fix;
embargo.

resting-place; bivouac; home &c.
(*abode*) 189; pillow &c. (*support*) 215;
haven &c. (*refuge*) 666; goal &c.
(*arrival*) 292.

V. be -quiescent &c. *adj.*; stand –,
lie- still; keep quiet, repose, hold the
breath.

remain, stay; stand, lie to, ride at
anchor, remain *in situ*, mark time,
tarry; bring –, heave –, lay- to; pull
–, draw- up; hold, halt; stop, – short;
rest, pause, anchor; cast –, come to
an- anchor; rest on one's oars; repose
on one's laurels, take breath; stop &c.
(*discontinue*) 142.

stagnate, vegetate; *quieta non movere*;
let -alone, – well alone; abide, rest and
be thankful; keep within doors, stay
at home, go to bed.

dwell &c. (*be present*) 186; settle &c.
(*be located*) 184; alight &c. (*arrive*) 292.

stick, – fast; stand, – like a post; not stir a -peg, – step; be at
a -stand &c. *n.*

quell, becalm, hush, stay, lull to sleep, lay an embargo on; put
the brake on.

Adj. quiescent, still; motion-, move-less; fixed; stationary; at
-rest, – a stand, – a stand-still, – anchor; stock-still; immotile;
standing still &c. *v.*; sedentary, untravelled, stay-at-home; becalmed,
stagnant, quiet; un-moved, -disturbed, -ruffled; calm, restful;
cataleptic; immovable &c. (*stable*) 150; sleeping &c. (*inactive*) 683;
silent &c. 403; still as -a statue, – a post, – a mouse, – death.

Adv. at a stand &c. *adj.*; *tout court*; at the halt.

Int. stop! stay! avast! halt! hold, – hard! whoa!

Phr. *requiescat in pace.*

* A thing cannot be said to *move* from one place to another, unless it passes in succession through every intermediate place; hence motion is only such a change of place
as is *successive*. 'Rapid, swift, &c., as thought' are therefore incorrect expressions.

266. [Locomotion by land.] **Journey.**
—**N.** travel; travelling &c. *v.*; wayfaring, campaigning.

journey, excursion, expedition, tour, trip, grand tour, circuit, peregrination, discursion, ramble, pilgrimage, *trek*, course, ambulation, màrch, walk, hike, promenade, constitutional, stroll, saunter, tramp, jog-trot, turn, stalk, perambulation; noctambulation; somnambulism, sleep walking; outing, ride, drive, airing, jaunt.

equitation, horsemanship, riding, *manège*, ride and tie.

roving, vagrancy, pererration; marching and countermarching; nomadism; vagabond-ism, -age; gadding; flit, -ting; migration; e-, im-, de-, inter-migration.

plan, itinerary, guide; hand-, road-book; Baedeker, Murray, Bradshaw, time table.

procession, parade, cavalcade, caravan, file, *cortège*, column.

[Organs and instruments of locomotion] vehicle &c. 272; locomotive &c. 271; legs, feet, pegs, pins, trotters.

traveller &c. 268.

V. travel, journey, course; tour; take -, go- a journey; take -, go out for- -a walk &c. *n.*; have a run; take the air.

flit, take wing; migrate, emigrate, *trek*; rove, prowl, roam, range, patrol, pace up and down, traverse; scour -, traverse- the country; peragrate; per-, circum-ambulate; nomadize, wander, ramble, stroll, saunter, hover, go one's rounds; straggle; gad, - about; expatiate.

walk, march, step, tread, pace, plod, wend; promenade; trudge, tramp; stalk, stride, straddle, strut, foot it, stump, bundle, bowl along, toddle; paddle; tread -, follow -, pursue- a path.

take horse, ride, drive, trot, amble, canter, prance, fisk, frisk, *caracoler*; gallop &c. (*move quickly*) 274; motor, cycle, taxi; go by -car, - train, - tram, - bus, - plane.

peg -, jog -, wag -, shuffle- on; stir one's stumps; bend one's -steps, - course; make -, find -, wend -, pick -, thread -, plough-one's way; coast, slide, glide, skim, skate, ski; march in procession, tle off, defile.

go -, repair -, resort -, hie -, betake oneself- to.

Adj. travelling &c. *v.*; ambulatory, itinerant, peripatetic, peram-

267. [Locomotion by water or air.] **Navigation.**—**N.** navigation; aquatics; boating, cruising, yachting; ship &c. 273; oar, scull, sweep, punt-pole, paddle, - wheel, screw, propeller, stern wheel, sail, canvas.

natation, swimming; fin, flipper, fish's tail.

aerial navigation, air service, airways, airmanship, aero-donetics, -dynamics, -mechanics, -station, -statics, -nautics; ballooning, balloonry; balloon &c. 273; flying, flight, aviation, volitation; wing, pinion, *aileron*.

voyage, sail, cruise, passage, circumnavigation, *periplus*; head-, stern-, lee-way.

mariner, aeronaut &c. 269.

V. sail; put to sea &c. (*depart*) 293; take ship, get under way; spread -sail, - canvas; gather way, have way on; make -, carry- sail; plough the -waves, - deep, - main, - ocean; walk the waters.

navigate, warp, luff, scud, boom, kedge; drift, course, cruise, coast; hug the -shore, - land; circumnavigate.

ply the oar, row, paddle, pull, scull, punt, steam.

swim, float; buffet the waves, ride the storm, skim, *effleurer*, dive, wade;

fly, aviate, be wafted, hover, soar, drift, glide, plane, sideslip, *volplane*, pique, dive, spin, roll, loop, flutter; take -wing, - a flight; wing one's -flight, - way.

Adj. sailing &c. *v.*; seafaring, nautical, maritime, naval; sea-going, coasting; afloat; navigable, aquatic, natatory.

volitant, volant, aerostatic, aerial, aeronautic; alar, alate, pennate.

Adv. under -way, - sail, - canvas, - steam; on the wing.

bulatory, roving, rambling, gadding, discursive, vagrant, migratory, nomadic; circumforane-an, -ous; somnambular, nocti-, mundi-vagant; locomotive, automotive, self-moving.

way-faring, -worn; travel-stained.

Adv. on -foot, – horseback, – Shanks's mare; by the Marrowbone stage; *in transitu* &c. 270; *en route* &c. 282.

Int. come along!

268. Traveller.—N. traveller, way-farer, voyager, itinerant, passenger.

tourist, excursionist, globe-trotter; explorer, adventurer, mountaineer, Alpine Club; peregrinator, wanderer, rover, straggler, rambler; bird of passage; gad-about, -ling; vagrant, scatterling, landloper, waifs and estrays, wastrel, stray; loafer; tramp, -er, hobo, beachcomber, vagabond, nomad, Bohemian, gipsy, Arab, Wandering Jew, Hadji, pilgrim, palmer; peripatetic; somnambulist, sleep walker, noctambulist; emigrant, fugitive, refugee, *émigré*.

runner, courier, King's messenger; Mercury, Iris, Ariel, comet.

pedestrian, walker, foot-passenger; cyclist; wheelman.

rider, horseman, equestrian, cavalier, jockey, rough rider, trainer, breaker, huntsman.

driver, coachman, whip, Jehu, charioteer, postilion, post-boy, carter, wagoner, drayman, truckman; cab-man, -driver; *voiturier*, *vetturino*, *condottiere*; engine-driver; stoker, fireman, guard, brake-man, conductor; chauffeur, automobilist, motorist, motor –, truck –, taxi- driver.

269. Mariner.—N. sailor, mariner, navigator, argonaut; sea-man, -farer, -faring man; yachtsman; tar, jack tar, salt, gob, sea-dog, shellback, able seaman, A.B.; man-of-war's man, blue-jacket, marine, jolly; midshipman, middy, reefer; captain, commander, master mariner, skipper, mate; ship-, boat-, ferry-, water-, lighter-, barge-, longshore- man, hoveller; bargee, gondolier; oar-, -sman; rower; boat-, cock-swain; coxswain; steersman, helmsman, pilot; crew; lascar.

aerial navigator, aeronaut, balloonist, Icarus, aviator, pilot, observer, flyer, airman.

270. Transference.—N. transfer, -ence; trans-, e-location; displacement; *meta-stasis*, *-thesis*; removal; re-, a-motion; relegation; de-, as-portation; extradition, conveyance, draft; carrying, carriage; convection, -duction, -tagion, infection; transfusion; transfer &c. (*of property*) 783.

transit, transition; passage, ferry, gestation; portage, porterage, carting, cartage; shovelling &c. *v.*; vect-ion, -ure, -itation; shipment, freight, wafture; trans-mission, -port, -portation, -umption, -plantation, -lation; shift-, dodg-ing; dispersion &c. 73; transposition &c. (*interchange*) 148; traction &c. 285.

[Thing transferred] drift, alluvium, detritus, *moraine*; gift, legacy, bequest, lease; freight, mails, cargo, luggage, baggage, goods.

V. trans-fer, -mit, -port, -place, -plant; convey, assign, carry, bear, fetch and carry; carry –, ferry- over; hand, pass, forward; shift; conduct, convoy, bring, fetch, reach.

send, delegate, consign, mail, post, relegate, turn over to, pass the buck, deliver; ship, embark; waft; switch, shunt; transpose &c. (*interchange*) 148; displace &c. 185; throw &c. 284; drag &c. 285.

shovel, lade, dip, ladle, bale, decant, draft off, transfuse.

Adj. transferred &c. *v.*; drifted; movable; port-able, -ative; conductive; contagious, infectious.

transferable, assignable, conveyable, devisable, negotiable, transmissible.

Adv. from -hand to hand, – pillar to post.

on –, by- the way; on the -road, – wing; as one goes; *in transitu, en route, chemin faisant, en passant,* in mid-progress.

271. Carrier.—N. carrier, porter, red cap, bearer, messenger, postman, tranter, conveyer; stevedore; coolie; conductor, locomotive, tractor, caterpillar tractor, motor.

beast of burden, cattle, horse, steed, nag, palfrey, Arab, blood horse, thorough-bred, galloway, charger, courser, racer, hunter, jument, pony, filly, colt, foal, barb, roan, jade, hack, *bidet*, pad, cob, tit, punch, roadster, goer; race-, pack-, draft-, cart-, dray-, post-horse, mount; Shetland pony, sheltie; garran; jennet, genet, bayard, mare, stallion, gelding; stud.

Pegasus, Bucephalus, Rozinante.

ass, donkey, jackass, mule, hinny; sumpter -horse, – mule; reindeer; camel, dromedary, mehari, llama, elephant; carrier pigeon.

carriage &c. (*vehicle*) 272; ship &c. 273.

Adj. equine, asinine.

272. Vehicle.—N. vehicle, conveyance, carriage, car, caravan, van, furniture van, pantechnicon; wagon, wain, dray, cart, lorry.

carriole; sledge, sled, sleigh, bobsleigh, toboggan, *luge*, truck, tram; limber, tumbrel, pontoon; barrow; wheel-, hand- -barrow, – cart, trolley; perambulator; Bath -, wheel -, sedanchair, jinriksha, rickshaw; ekka; chaise; palan-keen, -quin; litter, horse-litter, brancard, crate, hurdle, stretcher, ambulance; velocipede, hobby-horse, coaster, scooter, go-cart; cycle; bi-, tri-, quadri-cycle; tandem, safety; skate, roller skate; ski, snow-shoe.

equipage, turn-out; coach, chariot, *quadriga*, chaise, phaëton, break, brake, mail-phaëton, wagonette, drag, curricle, tilbury, whisky, landau, *barouche*, victoria, brougham, clarence, calash, *calèche*, britzska, *araba*, kibitka; berlin; sulky, *désobligeant*, sociable, *vis-à-vis, dormeuse*; jaunting –, outside- car; *tarantass*; runabout; shay.

post-chaise; diligence, stage; stage –, mail –, hackney –, glass- coach; stage-wagon; car, omnibus, bus, fly, *cabriolet*, cab, hansom, shofle, four-wheeler, growler, *droshki*, drosky.

dog-cart, trap, gig, whitechapel, buggy, four-in-hand, unicorn, random, tandem; shandredhan, *char-à-banc*.

automobile, motor-, auto-, touring-, racing-, cycle-, side-, steam-, electric-

273. Ship.—N. ship, vessel, sail; craft, bottom.

navy, marine, fleet, flotilla, squadron; shipping.

man of war &c. (*combatant*) 726; transport, tender, store-ship; merchant ship, merchantman; packet, liner; whaler, slaver, collier, coaster, tanker, freighter, freight steamer, cargo boat, lighter; fishing-, pilot- boat; trawler, drifter; cable ship; hulk; yacht; floating palace, ocean greyhound.

ship, bark, barque, brig, snow, hermaphrodite brig; brigantine, barquentine; schooner; topsail -, fore and aft –, three masted- schooner; *chasse-marée*; sloop, cutter, corvette, clipper, foist, yawl, dandy, ketch, smack, lugger, barge, hoy, cat-, -boat, buss; sail-er, -ing vessel, wind-jammer; steam-er, -boat, -ship; mail –, paddle -, screw -, sternwheel- steamer; tug; train-ferry; line of steamers &c.

boat, pinnace, launch, motor-boat, picket-boat; hydroplane; life-, long-, jolly-, bum-, fly-, cock-, ferry-, canal-boat, dory, dugout, galliot; shallop, gig, funny, skiff, dingy, scow, cockle-shell, wherry, coble, punt, cog, lerret; eight-, four-, pair- oar; randan; outrigger; float, raft, pontoon; prame, ice-yacht.

state barge, bucentaur.

catamaran, coracle, gondola, carvel, caravel; felucca, caique, canoe; trireme;

car; motor-, -omnibus, – bus, – cab, – cycle; limousine, landaulette, cabriolet, *coupé, voiturette,* runabout, electromobile, taxi, -cab.

train; passenger –, express –, freight -, subway –, special –, corridor –, parliamentary –, luggage –, goods-train, *train de luxe*; 1st-, 2nd-, 3rd-class- -train, – carriage, – compartment; Pullman –, sleeping-, club-, observation-, dining-, restaurant-car; mail-, luggage-, brake-van, coach, car, carriage; rolling stock; horse-box, cattle-truck.

tramcar, trolley-omnibus, trackless trolley.

shovel, spoon, spatula, ladle, hod, hoe; spade, spaddle, loy; spud; pitch-fork.

Adj. vehicular.

galley, – foist, oilander, dogger, hooker, howker; argosy, carack; galliass, galleon; galliot, polacca, polaere, corsair, tartane, junk, lorcha, praam, proa, prahu, saick, sampan, xebec, dhow; dahabeah; nuggar, cayak, pirogue.

submarine, submersible.

aircraft (*combatant*) &c. 726; flying machine, air mail, aero-, air-, mono-, bi-, tri-, hydroplane, plane, cabin plane, transport plane, *avion,* flying boat, glider, *aviette,* helicopter; balloon, air-, fire-, gas-, Mongolfier-, pilot-, captive-, free-, kite-, dirigible- balloon, air-ship, *Zeppelin,* blimp; kite, parachute.

nacelle, car, gondola, aileron; hangar, airport, landing field, airdrome; cat-walk, controls, rudder, tail.

Adj. marine, maritime, naval, nautical, seafaring, sea-, ocean going, seaworthy.

aerial, aeronautical, air-worthy, flying &c. *n.*

Adv. afloat, aboard; on -board, – ship board, – board ship.

2°. DEGREES OF MOTION

274. Velocity.—N. velocity, speed, celerity; swiftness &c. *adj.*; rapidity, eagle speed; expedition &c. (*activity*) 682; pernicity; acceleration; haste &c. 684.

spurt, rush, dash, race, steeplechase; smart –, lively –, swift &c. *adj.* –, rattling –, spanking –, strapping- -rate, – pace; round pace; flying, flight.

gallop, canter, trot, round trot, run, scamper; hand –, full- gallop; swoop.

lightning, light, electricity, wind; cannon-ball, rocket, arrow, dart, quick-silver; telegraph, express train; torrent; swallow flight.

eagle, antelope, courser, race-horse, gazelle, greyhound, hare, doe, squirrel.

Mercury, Ariel, Camilla, Harlequin.

[Measurement of velocity] speed-ometer, log, -line, tachometer.

V. move quickly, trip, fisk; speed, hie, hasten, sprint, spurt, post, spank, scuttle; scud, -dle, scurry; scour, – the plain; scamper; run, – like mad; fly, race, run a race, cut away, cut and run, shoot, tear, whisk, whiz, sweep, skim, brush; cut –, bowl- along; rush

275. Slowness.—N. slowness &c. *adj.*; languor &c. (*inactivity*) 683; drawl; creeping &c. *v.*, lentor.

retardation; slackening &c. *v.*; delay &c. (*lateness*) 133; claudication.

jog-, dog-trot, walk; mincing steps; slow -march, – time.

slow -goer, – coach, – back; lingerer, loiterer, sluggard, tortoise, snail; dawdle &c. (*inactive*) 683.

V. move -slowly, &c. *adv.*; creep, crawl, lag, slug, walk, drawl, linger, loiter, saunter; plod, trudge, stump along, lumber; trail; drag; dawdle &c. (*be inactive*) 683; grovel, worm one's way, steal along; jog –, rub –, bundle-on; toddle, waddle, wabble, slug; traipse, slouch, shuffle, halt, hobble, limp, claudicate, shamble; flag, falter, totter, stagger; mince, step short; march in -slow time, – funeral procession; take one's time; hang fire &c. (*be late*) 133.

retard, relax; slacken, check, moderate, rein in, curb; reef; strike –, shorten –, take in- sail; put on the drag, apply the brake; clip the wings; reduce the

&c. (*be violent*) 173; dash -on, – off, – forward; bolt; trot, gallop, bound, flit, spring, dart, boom; march in double-time; ride hard, get over the ground, scorch.

hurry &c. (*hasten*) 684; accelerate, put on; quicken; quicken –, mend one's pace; clap spurs to one's horse; make -haste, – rapid strides, – forced marches, – the best of one's way; put one's best leg foremost, stir one's stumps, wing one's way, set off at a score; carry –, crowd- sail; go off like a shot, go ahead, gain ground; outstrip the wind, fly on the wings of the wind.

keep -up, – pace- with; outstrip &c. 303.

Adj. fast, speedy, swift, rapid, quick, fleet; nimble, agile, expeditious; express; active &c. 682; flying, galloping &c. *v.*; light-, nimble-footed; winged, eagle-winged, mercurial, electric, tele-graphic; light-legged, light of heel; swift as -an arrow &c. *n.*; quick as -lightning &c. *n.*, – thought.*

Adv. swiftly &c. *adj.*; with -speed &c. *n.*; apace; at -a great rate, – full speed, – railway speed; full -drive, – gallop; post-haste, in full sail, tantivy; trippingly; instantaneously &c. 113; like a shot.

under press of -sail, – canvas, – sail and steam; *velis et remis*, on eagle's wing, in double quick time; with -rapid, – giant- strides; *à pas de géant*; in seven league boots; whip and spur; *ventre à terre*; as fast as one's -legs, – heels- will carry one; as fast as one can lay feet to the ground, at the top of one's speed; by leaps and bounds; with haste &c. 684; in- high – gear, – speed.

Phr. *vires acquirit eundo.*

speed, decelerate; slacken -speed, – one's pace, lose ground; back -water, – pedal, put the engines astern, throttle down.

Adj. slow, slack; tardy; dilatory &c. (*inactive*) 683; gentle, easy; leisurely; deliberate, gradual; insensible, imperceptible; languid, sluggish, apathetic, phlegmatic, slow-paced, tardigrade, snail-like; creeping &c. *v.*

Adv. slowly &c. *adj.*; leisurely; *piano, adagio*; *largo, larghetto*; at half speed, under easy sail; at a -foot's, – snail's, – funeral- pace; slower than molasses in January; in slow time; with -mincing steps, – clipped wings; *haud passibus æquis*; in- low –, gear, – speed.

gradually &c. *adj.*; *gradatim*; by -degrees, – slow degrees, – inches, – little and little; step by step; inch by inch, bit by bit, little by little, *seriatim*; consecutively.

3°. MOTION CONJOINED WITH FORCE

276. Impulse.—**N.** impulse, impulsion, impetus; momentum; push, pulsion, thrust, shove, jog, jolt, brunt, booming, boost, throw; explosion &c. (*violence*) 173; propulsion &c. 284.

percussion, concussion, collision, occursion, clash, encounter, cannon, *carambole*, appulse, shock, crash, bump; impact; *élan*; charge &c. (*attack*) 716; beating &c. (*punishment*) 972.

blow, dint, stroke, knock, tap, rap, slap, smack, pat, dab; fillip; slam, bang; hit, whack, thwack, clout; cuff &c. 972; squash, dowse, whap, swap, punch, thump, swipe, jab, pelt, kick, punce, calcitration; *ruade*; arietation; cut, thrust, lunge, yerk.

277. Recoil.—**N.** recoil; re-, retro-action; revulsion; rebound, *ricochet*; re-percussion, -calcitration; kick, *contrecoup*; springing back &c. *v.*; elasticity &c. 325; reflection, reflex, reflux; reverberation &c. (*resonance*) 408; rebuff, repulse; return.

ducks and drakes; boomerang; spring; reactionist, reactionary.

V. recoil, resile, react; spring –, fly –, bound- back; rebound, reverberate, repercuss, recalcitrate, echo, *ricochet*.

Adj. recoiling &c. *v.*; re-fluent, -percussive, -calcitrant, -actionary; retroactive.

Adv. on the -recoil &c. *n.*

* See note on 264.

hammer, sledge-hammer, mall, maul, mallet, flail; ram, -mer; battering-ram, monkey, pile-driver, punch, bat, tamper, tamping iron; cudgel &c. (*weapon*) 727; axe &c. (*sharp*) 253.

[Science of mechanical forces] mechanics, dynamics &c.

V. give an -impetus &c. *n.*; impel, push; start, give a start to, set going; drive, urge, boom; thrust, prod, foin; cant; elbow, shoulder, jostle, justle, hustle, hurtle, shove, jog, jolt, bean, encounter; run -, bump -, butt- against; knock -, run- one's head against; impinge.

strike, knock, hit, bash, tap, rap, bat, slap, flap, dab, pat, thump, beat, bang, slam, dash; punch, thwack, whack; hit -, strike- hard; swap, batter, dowse, baste; pelt, patter, skelter, buffet, belabour, tamp; fetch one a blow, swat; poke at, pink, lunge, yerk; kick, calcitrate; butt; strike at &c. (*attack*) 716; whip &c. (*punish*) 972; propel &c. 284.

come -, enter- into collision; collide; foul; fall -, run- foul of.

throw &c. (*propel*) 284.

Adj. impelling &c. *v.*; im-pulsive, -pellent; booming; dynamic, -al; impelled &c. *v.*

4°. MOTION WITH REFERENCE TO DIRECTION

278. Direction.—N. direction, bearing, course, set, drift, tenor; tendency &c. 176; incidence; bending, trending &c. *v.*; dip, tack, aim, collimation; steer-ing, -age.

point of the compass, cardinal -, half -, quarter- points; North, East, South, West; N by E, ENE, NE by N, NE &c.; rhumb, azimuth, line of collimation.

line, path, road, range, quarter, line of march; alignment; straight shot, bee-line.

V. tend -, bend -, point- towards; conduct -, go- to; point -to, - at; bend, trend, verge, incline, dip, determine.

steer -, make- -for, - towards; aim -, level- at; take aim; keep -, hold- a course; be bound for; bend one's steps towards; direct -, steer -, bend -, shape- one's course; align -, one's march; go straight, - to the point; march -on, - on a point.

ascertain one's -direction &c. *n.*; *s'orienter*, see which way the wind blows; box the compass.

Adj. directed &c. *v.*, - towards; pointing towards &c. *v.*; bound for; aligned -, alligned- with; direct, straight; un-deviating, -swerving; straightforward; North, -ern, -erly, &c. *n.*

directable &c. *v.*

Adv. towards; on the -road, - high

279. Deviation. — N. deviation; swerving &c. *v.*; obliquation, warp, refraction; flection, flexion; sweep; de-flection, -flexure; declination.

diversion, digression, departure from, aberration, drift, sheer; divergence &c. 291; zigzag; *détour* &c. (*circuit*) 629.

[Desultory motion] wandering &c. *v.*, vagrancy, evagation; by-paths and crooked ways.

[Motion sideways, oblique motion] sidling &c. *v.*; *échelon*, leeway; knight's move (at chess).

V. alter one's course, deviate, depart from, turn, trend; bend, curve &c. 245; swerve, heel, bear off.

intervert; deflect; divert, - from its course; put on a new scent, shift, shunt, switch, wear, draw aside, crook, warp short circuit.

stray, straggle; sidle, edge; diverge &c. 291; tralineate, digress, divagate, wander; wind, twist, meander, meander around Robin Hood's barn; veer, tack, sheer; turn -aside, - a corner, - away from; wheel, steer clear of; ramble, rove, drift; go -astray, - adrift; yaw, dodge; step aside, ease off, make way for, shy.

fly off at a tangent; glance off; turn, wheel -, face- about; turn -, face- to the right about; wabble &c. (*oscillate*) 314; go out of one's way &c. (*perform a circuit*) 629: lose one's way.

road- to; *versus*, to; hither, thither, whither; directly; straight, – forwards, – as an arrow; point blank; in a -direct, – straight- line -to, – for, – with; in a line with; full tilt at, as the crow flies.

before –, near –, close to –, against- the wind; windwards, in the wind's eye.

through, *via*, by way of; in all -directions, – manner of ways; *quaqua-versum*, from the four winds.

280. [Going before.] **Precession.—N.** precession, leading, heading; preced-ence &c. 62; priority &c. 116; the lead, *le pas*; van &c. (*front*) 234; precursor &c. 64.

V. go -before, – ahead, – in the van, – in advance; precede, forerun; usher in, introduce, herald, head, take the lead; lead, – the way, – the dance; get –, have- the start; steal a march; get -before, – ahead, – in front of; outstrip &c. 303; take precedence &c. (*first in order*) 62.

Adj. foremost, first, leading &c. *v.*

Adv. in advance, before, ahead, in the van; fore-, head-most; in front.

Phr. *seniores priores*.

282. [Motion forwards; progressive motion.] **Progression.—N.** progress, -ion, -iveness; advancing &c. *v.*; ad-vance, -ment; ongoing; flood-tide, headway; march &c. 266; rise; improve-ment &c. 658.

V. advance; proceed, progress; get -on, – along, – over the ground; gain ground; jog –, rub –, wag- on; go with the stream; keep –, hold on- one's course; go –, move –, come –, get –, pass –, push –, press- -on, – forward, – forwards, – ahead; press onwards, step forward; make –, work –, carve –, push –, force –, edge –, elbow- one's way; make -progress, – head, – way, - headway; – advances, – strides, – rapid strides &c. (*velocity*) 274; go –, shoot- ahead; distance; make up leeway.

Adj. advancing &c. *v.*; pro-gressive, -fluent; advanced.

Adj. deviating &c. *v.*; aberrant, errant; ex-, dis-cursive; devious, de-sultory, loose; rambling; stray, erratic, vagrant, undirected; circuitous, indi-rect, zigzag; crab-like.

Adv. astray from, round about, wide of the mark; to the right about; all manner of ways; circuitously &c. 629.

obliquely, sideling, like the move of the knight on a chessboard.

281. [Going after.] **Sequence.—N.** sequence, run; coming after &c. (*order*) 63; (*time*) 117; following; pursuit &c. 622.

follower, attendant, satellite, shad-ow, dangler, train.

V. follow; pursue &c. 622; go –, fly- after.

attend, beset, dance attendance on, dog, be-dog; tread -in the steps of, – close upon; be –, go –, follow- in the -wake, – trail. – rear- of; trail, follow as a shadow, hang on the skirts of; tread –, follow- on the heels of, tag after.

lag, get behind.

Adj. following &c. *v.*

Adv. behind; in the -rear &c. 235, – train of, wake of; after &c. (*order*) 63, (*time*) 117.

283. [Motion backwards.] **Regres-sion.—N.** regress, -ion; retro-cession, -gression, -gradation, -action; *reculade*; retreat, withdrawal, retirement, re-migration; recession &c. (*motion from*) 287; recess; crab-like motion.

re-fluence, -flux; backwater, regur-gitation, ebb, return; resilience; re-flexion (*recoil*) 277; *volte-face*.

counter -motion, – movement, march; veering, tergiversation, re-cidivation, backsliding, fall, relapse; deterioration &c. 659.

turning-point &c. (*reversion*) 145.

V. re-cede, -grade, -turn, -vert, -treat, -tire; retro-grade, -cede; back, – down, – out, crawl; withdraw; rebound &c. 277; go –, come –, turn –, hark –, draw –, fall –, get –, put –, run- back; lose ground; fall –, drop- astern; back water, put about; veer, – round; double,

Adv. forward, onward; forth, on ahead, under way, *en route* for, on -one's way, – the way, – the road, – the high road- to; in -progress, – mid progress; *in transitu* &c. 270.

Int. Forward, march!

Phr. *vestigia nulla retrorsum.*

---

wheel, counter-march; ebb, regurgitate; jib, shrink, shy.

turn -tail, – round, – upon one's heel, – one's back upon; retrace one's steps, dance the back step; sound –, beat- a retreat; go home.

Adj. receding &c. *v.*; retro-grade, -gressive; re-gressive, -fluent, -flex, -cidivous, -silient; crab-like; reactionary &c. 277; counter-clockwise.

Adv. back, -wards; reflexively, to the right about; *à reculons, à rebours.*

Phr. *revenons à nos moutons,* as you were.

284. [Motion given to an object situated in front.] **Propulsion.—N.** pro-pulsion, -jection; *vis a tergo*; push &c. (*impulse*) 276; e-, jaculation; ejection &c. 297; throw, fling, toss, shot, discharge, shy.

[Science of propulsion] gunnery, ballistics, archery.

missile, projectile, ball, *discus*, javelin, hammer, quoit, brickbat, shot, bullet; arrow, shaft; gun &c. (*arms*) 727.

shooter, shot; gunner, gun-layer; archer, toxophilite; bow-, rifle-, marksman; good –, crack- shot; sharpshooter &c. (*combatant*) 726.

V. propel, project, throw, fling, cast, pitch, chuck, toss, jerk, heave, shy, hurl; flirt, fillip.

dart, lance, tilt; e-, jaculate; fulminate, bolt, drive, sling, pitchfork.

send; send –, let –, fire- off; discharge, shoot; launch, send forth, let fly; dash.

put –, set- in motion; set agoing, start; give -a start, – an impulse-to; push, impel &c. 276; trundle &c. (*set in rotation*) 312; expel &c. 297.

carry one off one's legs; put to flight.

Adj. propelled &c. *v.*; propelling &c. *v.*; pro-pulsive, -jectile.

285. [Motion given to an object situated behind.] **Traction.—N.** traction; drawing &c. *v.*; draught, pull, haul; rake; 'a long pull, a strong pull and a pull all together'; towage, haulage.

V. draw, pull, haul, lug, rake, drag, draggle, tug, tow, trail, trawl, train, take in tow.

wrench, jerk, twitch.

Adj. drawing &c. *v.*; tractive, tractile; ductile.

---

286. [Motion towards.] **Approach.— N.** approach, approximation, appropinquation; access; appulse; afflux, -ion; advent &c. (*approach of time*) 121; pursuit &c. 622; convergence &c. 290.

V. approach, approximate; near; get –, go –, draw- near; come, – near, – to close quarters; move –, set in- towards; drift; make up to; gain upon; pursue &c. 622; tread on the heels of; bear up; make the land; hug the -shore, -coast, – land.

Adj. approaching &c. *v.*; approximative; convergent; affluent; impending, imminent &c. (*destined*) 152.

287. [Motion from.] **Recession.—N.** recession, retirement, withdrawal; retreat; retrocession &c. 283; departure &c. 293; recoil &c. 277; flight &c. (*avoidance*) 623.

V. recede, go, move from, retire, ebb, withdraw, shrink; come –, move –, go –, get –, drift- away; depart &c. 293; retreat &c. 283; move –, stand –, sheer- off; swerve from; fall back, stand aside; run away &c. (*avoid*) 623.

remove, shunt, side track, switch off.

Adj. receding &c. *v.*

Adv. on the road.
Int. come hither! approach! here! come! come near!

288. [Motion towards, actively.] **Attraction.—N.** attract-ion, -iveness; pull; drawing to, pulling towards, adduction, magnetism, gravity, attraction of gravitation; lure, bait, decoy.

loadstone, -star; magnet, siderite, magnetite.

V. attract; draw –, pull –, drag- towards; adduce.

lure, bait, decoy.

Adj. attracting &c. *v.*; attrahent, attractive, adducent, adductive.

289. [Motion from, actively.] **Repulsion.—N.** repulsion; driving from &c. *v.*; repulse; abduction.

V. repel; push –, drive – &c. 276; from; chase, dispel; retrude; abduce, abduct; send away, repulse, dismiss.

keep at arm's length, turn one's back upon, give the cold shoulder; send packing; send -off, – away- with a flea in one's ear, – about one's business.

Adj. repelling &c. *v.*; repellant, repulsive; abducent, abductive.

290. [Motion nearer to.] **Convergence. —N.** con-vergence, -fluence, -course, -flux, -gress, -currence, -centration; appulse, meeting; corradiation.

assemblage &c. 72; resort &c. (*focus*) 74; asymptote.

V. converge, concur; come together, unite, meet, fall in with; close -with, – in upon; centre -round, – in; enter in; pour in.

gather together, unite, concentrate, bring into a focus.

Adj. converging &c. *v.*; con-vergent, -fluent, -current; centripetal; asymptotical.

291. [Motion further off.] **Divergence. —N.** diverg-ence, -ency; divarication, ramification, radiation; separation &c. (*disjunction*) 44; dispersion &c. 73; deviation &c. 279; aberration, declination.

V. diverge, divaricate, radiate; ramify; branch –, glance –, file- off; fly off, – at a tangent; spread, scatter, disperse &c. 73; deviate &c. 279; part &c. (*separate*) 44; splay apart.

Adj. diverging &c. *v.*; divergent, radiant, centrifugal; aberrant.

---

292. [Terminal motion at.] **Arrival. —N.** arrival, advent; landing; de-, disem-barkation; reception, welcome, *vin d'honneur.*

home, goal, bourn; landing-place, -stage; resting –, stopping -place; destination, harbour, haven, port; terminal, terminus, railway station, depot, airport; halt, halting -place, – ground; anchorage &c. (*refuge*) 666.

return, recursion, remigration; meeting; ren-, en-counter.

completion &c. 729.

V. arrive; get to, come to; come; reach, attain; come up, – with, – to; overtake; make, fetch; complete &c. 729; join, rejoin.

light, alight, dismount; land, go ashore; debark, disembark; put -in, – into; visit, cast anchor, pitch one's tent; sit down &c. (*be located*) 184; get to one's journey's end; make the

293. [Initial motion from.] **Departure.—N.** departure, decession, decampment; embarkation; take-off; outset, start; removal; exit &c. (*egress*) 295; exodus, Hejira, flight.

leave-taking, congé, valediction, valedictory, adieu, farewell, good-bye, stirrup-cup.

starting -point, – post; point –, place- of -departure, – embarkation; port of embarkation.

V. depart; go, – away; take one's departure, set out; set –, march –, put –, start –, be –, move –, get –, whip –, pack –, go –, take oneself- off; start, issue, march out, debouch; go –, sally-forth; sally, set forward; be gone.

leave a place, quit, vacate, evacuate, abandon; go off the stage, make one's exit; retire, withdraw, remove; go -one's way, – along, – from home; take -flight, – wing; spring, fly, flit, wing

land; be in at the death; come –, get- -back, – home; return; come in &c. (*ingress*) 294; make one's appearance &c. (*appear*) 446; drop in; detrain; outspan.

come to hand; come -at, – across; hit; come –, light –, pop –, bounce –, plump –, burst –, pitch- upon; meet; en- ren-counter; come in contact.

Adj. arriving &c. *v.*; homeward-bound; terminal.

Adv. here, hither.

Int. welcome! hail! all hail! good-day, – morrow; greetings! hullo! well!

one's flight; fly –, whip- away; take off, hop off; embark; go -on board, – aboard; set sail; put –, go- to sea; sail, take ship; hoist blue Peter; get under way, weigh anchor; strike tents, break camp, decamp; walk one's chalks, make tracks, cut one's stick; cut and run; take leave; say –, bid- -good-bye &c. *n.*; disappear &c. 449; abscond &c. (*avoid*) 623; entrain, saddle –, harness –, hitch- up; inspan.

Adj. departing &c. *v.*; valedictory; outward bound.

Adv. whence, hence, thence; with a foot in the stirrup; on the -wing, – move.

Int. begone! &c. (*ejection*) 297; to horse! all aboard! farewell!! adieu! good-bye, – day! *au revoir! auf Wiedersehen!* fare you well! so long! God -bless you, – speed! *bon voyage!*

---

294. [Motion into.] **Ingress.—N.** ingress; entrance, entry; introgression; influx; intrusion, inroad, incursion, invasion, irruption; pene-, interpenetration; illapse, import, importation, infiltration; immigration; admission &c. (*reception*) 296; insinuation &c. (*interjacence*) 228; insertion &c. 300.

inlet; way in; mouth, door &c. (*opening*) 260; path &c. (*way*) 627; conduit &c. 350; immigrant, visitor, incomer, newcomer, colonist.

V. have the *entrée*; enter; go –, come –, pour –, flow –, creep –, slip –, pop –, break –, burst- -into, – in; set foot on; burst –, break- in upon; invade, intrude, butt in, horn in, crash; insinuate itself; inter-, penetrate; infiltrate; find one's way –, wriggle –, worm oneself- into.

give entrance to &c. (*receive*) 296; insert &c. 300.

Adj. incoming, ingressive &c. *n.*; inward bound.

Adv. inward.

---

295. [Motion out of.] **Egress.—N.** egress, exit, issue; emer-sion, -gence; disemboguement; out-break, -burst; e-, pro-ruption; emanation; evacuation; ex-, trans-udation; extravasation, perspiration, sweating, leakage, percolation, distillation, oozing; gush &c. (*water in motion*) 348; outpour, -ing; effluence, effusion; efflux, -ion; drain; dribbling &c. *v.*; defluxion; drainage; out-come, -put; discharge &c. (*excretion*) 299.

export; expatriation; e-, re-migration; *débouche*; exodus &c. (*departure*) 293; emigrant, migrant, *émigré*, colonist.

outlet, vent, spout, tap, sluice, floodgate; pore; vomitory, out-gate, sally-port; way out; mouth, door &c. (*opening*) 260; path &c. (*way*) 627; conduit &c. 350; air-pipe &c. 351.

V. emerge, emanate, issue; go –, come –, move –, pass –, pour –, flow-out of; pass off, evacuate; migrate.

ex-, trans-ude; leak; run, – out, – through; per-, trans-colate; seep; strain, distil; perspire, sweat, drain, ooze; filter, filtrate; dribble, gush, spout, flow out; well, – out; pour, trickle &c. (*water in motion*) 348; effuse, extravasate, disembogue, discharge itself, debouch; come –, break- forth; burst- out, – through; find vent, escape &c. 671.

Adj. effused &c. *v.*; outgoing, outward bound.

Adv. outward.

296. [Motion into, actively.] Reception. —N. reception; admission, admittance, *entrée*, importation; initiation; intro-duction, -mission, -ception; im-mission, ingestion, imbibition, absorption, ingurgitation, inhalation; suction, sucking; eating, drinking &c. (*food*) 298; insertion &c. 300; interjection &c. 228.

V. give -entrance to, – admittance to, – the *entrée*; intro-duce, -mit; usher, admit, receive, import, initiate, bring in, open the door to, throw open, ingest, absorb, imbibe, inhale, infiltrate; let –, take –, suck- in; re-admit, -sorb, -absorb; snuff up; swallow, ingurgitate; engulf, engorge; gulp; eat, drink &c. (*food*) 298.

Adj. admit-ting &c. *v.*, -ted &c. *v.*; admissible; absorbent; introductory, introceptive, intromittent, initiatory.

297. [Motion out of, actively.] Ejection.—N. ejection, emission, effusion, rejection, expulsion, eviction, extrusion, trajection; discharge.

egestion, evacuation, vomition, dis-gorgement, voidance, eruption, eruptiveness; ruc-, eruc-tation, blood-letting, venesection, phlebotomy, paracentesis; tapping, drainage; clear-ance, -age, voidance; vomiting, excretion &c. 299.

deportation; banishment &c. (*punishment*) 972; rogue's march; relegation, extradition; dislodgment.

V. give -exit, – vent- to; let –, give –, pour –, send- out; des-, dis-patch; exhale, excern, excrete, disembogue; secrete, secern; extravasate, shed, void, evacuate, egest, emit; open the -sluices, – floodgates; turn on the tap; extrude, detrude; effuse, spend, expend; pour forth; squirt, spirt, spill, slop; perspire &c. (*exude*) 295; breathe, blow &c. (*wind*) 349.

tap, draw off; bale –, lade- out; let blood, broach.

eject, reject; expel, discard; cut, send to Coventry, boycott, ostracize; *chasser*; banish &c. (*punish*) 972; throw &c. 284 -out, – up, – off, – away, – aside; push &c. 276 -out, – off, – away, – aside; shovel –, sweep- -out, – away; brush –, whisk –, turn –, send- -off, – away; discharge; send –, turn –, cast- adrift; turn –, bundle- out; throw overboard; give the sack to; send -packing, – about one's business, – to the right about; strike off the roll &c. (*abrogate*) 756; turn out- neck and heels, – head and shoulders, – neck and crop; pack off; send away with a flea in the ear; send to Jericho; bow out, show the door to, dismiss, fire, sack.

turn out of -doors, – house and home; evict, oust; exorcise, un-house, -kennel; dislodge; un-, dis-people; depopulate; relegate, deport.

empty; drain, – to the dregs; sweep off; clear, – off, – out, – away; suck, draw off, extract; clean out, make a clean sweep of, clear decks, purge.

em-, dis-, disem-bowel; eviscerate, gut; unearth, root -out, – up; averruncate; weed –, get out; eliminate, get rid of, do away with, shake off; exenterate.

vomit, spew, puke, keck, retch; belch, – out, eruct, eructate; cast –, bring- up; disgorge; expectorate, salivate, clear the throat, hawk, spit, sputter, splutter, slobber, drool, drivel, slaver, slabber.

unpack, unlade, unload, unship; break bulk.

be let out; ooze &c. (*emerge*) 295.

Adj. emitt-ing, -ed &c. *v.*

Int. begone! get you gone! get –, go- -away, – along, – along with you! go your way! away, – with! off with you! go, – about your business! be off! avaunt! aroynt! get out! beat it!

298. [Eating.] Food.—N. eating &c. *v.*; deglutition, gulp, epulation, mastication, manducation, rumination, gastronomy, gastrology; panto-, hippo-, ichthyo-phagy &c.; gluttony &c. 957; carnivorousness, vegetarianism.

mou:.h, jaws, mandible, mazard, chops.

drinking &c. *v.*; potation, draught, libation; carousal &c. (*amusement*) 840; drunkenness &c. 959.

food, *pabulum*; aliment, nourishment, nutriment; susten-ance, -tation; nurture, subsistence, provender, feed, fodder, provision, ration, keep, commons, board; commissariat &c. (*provision*) 637; prey, forage, pasture, pasturage; fare, cheer; diet, -ary; regimen; belly timber, staff of life; bread, -and cheese; proteins, carbohydrates, vitamines.

comestibles, eatables, victuals, edibles, *ingesta*; grub, prog, tack, hard tack, meat; bread, -stuffs; cereals; viands, cates, delicacy, dainty, creature comforts, contents of the larder, flesh-pots; festal board; ambrosia; good -cheer, – living.

hors-d'œuvre; soup, pottage, *potage*, broth, *bouillon*, *consommé*, *purée*, *borsch*, stock, skilly, gumbo; fish, – cakes, – pie; joint, *rôti*, *pièce de résistance*, *relevé*, hash, *réchauffé*, stew, *ragoût*, fricassee, mince, *salmi*, *goulash*, *bouillabaisse*, remove, *entrée*, *croquette*, *rissole*, sausage, curry, bubble and squeak; haggis, collops, giblets; poultry, game &c.; biscuit, bun, scone, rusk, pancake, pie, pastry, pasty, patty, *patisserie*, tart, turnover, *vol-au-vent*, *soufflé*, dumpling, pudding, duff, *compote*, fritters, cake, napoleon, *blancmange*, custard, jelly, jam, sweets &c. 396; *entremet*; oatmeal, porridge, hasty pudding, gruel; eggs, omelet, cheese, matzoon, savoury; vegetable, salad, *mayonnaise*, fruit; sauce, condiment &c. 393; kickshaws.

table, *cuisine*, bill of fare, *menu*, *prix fixe*, ordinary, *à la carte*; cover.

meal, repast, feed, spread; mess; dish, plate, course, side dish; regale; regale-, refresh-, entertain-ment; refection, collation, picnic, feast, banquet, junket, breakfast·· lunch, -eon; *déjeuner*, bever, tiffin, tea, dinner, supper, snack, whet, bait, dessert; pot-luck, *table d'hôte*, *déjeuner à la fourchette*; hearty –, square –, substantial –, full- -meal; blow out; light -efreshment: pemmican.

mouthful, bolus, gobbet, ti.-oit, morsel, sop, sippet.

drink, beverage, liquor, broth, soup; potion, dram, draught, drench, swill; nip, peg, sip, sup, gulp.

wine, champagne, spirits, *liqueur*, beer, porter. stout, ale, malt liquor, julep, Sir John Barleycorn, stingo, heavy wet, bitter, lager-beer, cider; grog, toddy, flip, purl, punch, negus, cup, bishop, posset, wassail; bitters, *apéritif*, high-ball, cocktail; whisky, rum, absinthe; gin &c. (*intoxicating liquor*) 959; coffee, chocolate, cocoa tea, *maté*, the cup that cheers but not inebriates.

eating-house &c. 189.

299. Excretion.—N. excretion, discharge, emanation; ejection &c. 297; exhalation, extrusion, secretion, effusion, extravasation, *ecchymosis*, evacuation, cacation, defecation, dysentery, dejection, *fæces*, excrement; perspiration, sweat; sud-, exud-ation; *diaphoresis*; sewage.

saliva, spittle, rheum; ptyalism, salivation, catarrh, diarrhœa; *ejecta, egesta, sputum, sputa*; *excreta*; lava; *exuviæ* &c. (*uncleanness*) 653.

hemorrhage, bleeding; catamenia, menses; outpouring &c. (*egress*) 295; leucorrhea.

V. excrete &c. (*eject*) 297; emanate &c. (*come out*) 295.

Adj. excretory, fæcal, secretory; ejective, eliminant.

V. eat, feed, fare, devour, swallow, take; gulp, bolt, snap; fall to; despatch, dispatch; discuss; take –, get –, gulp-down; lay –, tuck- in; lick, pick, peck; gormandize &c. 957; bite, champ, munch, cranch, craunch, crunch, chew, masticate, nibble, gnaw, mumble.

live on; feed –, batten –, fatten –, feast- upon; browse, graze, crop, regale; carouse &c. (*make merry*) 840; eat heartily, do justice to, play a good knife and fork, banquet.

break -bread, – one's fast; breakfast, lunch, dine, take tea, sup.

drink, – in, – up, – one's fill; quaff, sip, sup; suck, – up; lap; swig; swill, tipple &c. (*be drunken*) 959; empty one's glass, drain the cup; toss -off, – one's glass; wash down, crack a bottle, wet one's whistle.

cater, purvey &c. 637.

Adj. eatable, edible, esculent, comestible, alimentary; cereal, cibarious; dietetic; culinary; nutri-tive, -tious; succulent; drinkable, pot-able, -ulent; bibulous.

omn-, carn-, herb-, frug-, gran-, gramin-, phyt-ivorus; ichthyophagous.

prandial.

300. [Forcible ingress.] **Insertion.—**
N. insertion, implantation, intercalation, embolism, introduction; interpolation, insinuation &c. (*intervention*) 228; planting &c. *v.*; injection, inoculation, importation, infusion; forcible -ingress &c. 294; immersion; submersion, -gence; dip, plunge; bath &c. (*water*) 337; interment &c. 363.

V. insert; intro-duce, -mit; put –, run- into; import; inject; interject &c. 228; infuse, instil, inoculate, impregnate, imbue, imbrue.

graft, ingraft, bud, plant, implant; dovetail.

obtrude; thrust –, stick –, ram –, stuff –, tuck –, press –, drive –, pop –, whip –, drop –, put- in; impact; empierce &c. (*make a hole*) 260.

embed; immerse, immerge, merge; bathe, soak &c. (*water*) 337; dip, plunge &c. 310.

bury &c. (*inter*) 363.

insert &c.- itself; plunge *in medias res.*
Adj. inserted &c. *v.*

301. [Forcible egress.] **Extraction.—**
N. extraction; extracting &c. *v.*; removal, elimination, extrication, eradication, evolution.

evulsion, avulsion; wrench; expression, squeezing; extirpation, extermination; ejection &c. 297; export &c. (*egress*) 295; distillation.

extractor, corkscrew, forceps, pliers.

V. extract, draw, pit; take –, draw –, pull –, tear –, pluck –, pick –, get- out; wring from, wrench; extort; root –, weed –, grub –, rake- up, – out; eradicate; pull –, pluck- up by the roots; averruncate; unroot; uproot, pull up, extirpate, dredge.

remove; educe, elicit; evolve, extricate; eliminate &c. (*eject*) 297; eviscerate &c. 297.

express, squeeze –, press- out; distil.
Adj. extracted &c. *v.*

---

302. [Motion through.] **Passage.—N.** passage, transmission; permeation; pene-, interpene-tration; transudation, infiltration; *osmosis,* osmose, endos-, exos-mose; intercurrence; ingress &c. 294; egress &c. 295; path &c. 627; conduit &c. 350; opening &c. 260; journey &c. 266; voyage &c. 267.

V. pass, – through; perforate &c. (*hole*) 260; penetrate, permeate, thread, thrid, enfilade; go -through, – across; go –, pass- over; cut across; ford, cross; pass and repass, work; make –, thread –. worm –, force- one's way; make –, force- a passage; cut one's way through;

find its -way, – vent; transmit. make way, clear the course; traverse, go over the ground.

Adj. passing &c. *v.*; intercurrent; osmotic &c. *n.*

Adv. *en passant* &c. (*transit*) 270.

303. [Motion beyond.] **Overstep.—**
N. trans-cursion, -ilience, -gression; infraction, intrusion; trespass; encroach-, infringe-ment; extravagation, transcendence; redundance &c. 641; ingress &c. 294.

V. transgress, surpass, pass; go- beyond, – by; show in –, come to the-front; shoot ahead of; steal a march –, gain- upon.

over-step, -pass, -reach, -go, -ride, -leap, -jump, -skip, -lap, -shoot the mark; out-strip, -leap, -jump, -go, -step, -run, -ride, -rival, -do; beat, – hollow; distance; leave in the -lurch, – rear; go one better, throw into the shade; exceed, transcend, surmount; soar &c. (*rise*) 305.

encroach, intrude, trespass, infringe, invade, trench upon, intrench on; strain; stretch –, strain- a point; pass the Rubicon.

Adj. surpassing &c. *v.*

Adv. beyond the mark, ahead.

305. [Motion upwards.] **Ascent.—N.** ascent, ascension; rising &c. *v.*; rise, upgrowth; leap &c. 309; acclivity, hill &c. 217; stair, stairs, stair-case, -way, flight of -steps, – stairs; ladder, companion, – way; lift, elevator &c. 307.

rocket, lark; sky-rocket, -lark; Alpine Club.

V. ascend, rise, mount, arise, uprise; go –, get –, work one's way –, start –, spring –, shoot- up; zoom; aspire.

climb, clamber, ramp, scramble, swarm, *escalade*, surmount; scale, – the heights.

tower, soar, hover, spire, plane, swim, float, surge; leap &c. 309.

Adj. rising &c. *v.*; scandent, buoyant; super-natant, -fluitant; excelsior.

Adv. uphill.

304. [Motion short of.] **Shortcoming.**
—N. shortcoming, failure; delinquency; falling short &c. *v.*; de-fault, -falcation; leeway; labour in vain, no go.

incompleteness &c. 53; imperfection &c. 651; insufficiency &c. 640; non-completion &c. 730; failure &c. 732.

V. come –, fall –, stop- -short, – short of; not reach; want; keep within -bounds, – the mark, – compass.

break down, stick in the mud, collapse, come to nothing; fall -through, – to the ground, – down; cave in, end in smoke, fizzle out, miss the mark, fail; lose ground; miss stays, slump.

Adj. unreached; deficient; short, – of; *minus*; out of depth; perfunctory &c. (*neglect*) 460.

Adv. within -the mark, – compass, – bounds; behindhand; *re infectâ*; to no purpose; far from it.

Phr. the bubble burst.

306. [Motion downwards.] **Descent.**
—N. descent, descension, declension, declination; fall; falling &c. *v.*; drop, cadence; subsidence, lapse; come-down, downfall, tumble, slip, tilt, trip, lurch, cropper, *culbute*; titubation, stumble; fate of Icarus; dive. nose-dive, *volplane.*

avalanche, *débâcle*, land-slip, -slide.

declivity, dip, hill; decline, drop.

V. descend; go –, drop –, comedown; fall, gravitate, drop, slip, slide, glissade, dive, plunge, settle; decline, slump, set, sink, droop, come down a peg.

dismount, alight, light, get down; swoop; stoop &c. 308; fall prostrate, precipitate oneself; let fall &c. 308.

tumble, trip, stumble, titubate, lurch, pitch, swag, topple; topple –, tumble- -down, – over; tilt, sprawl, plump down, come a cropper.

Adj. descending &c. *v.*; descendent, declivitous; downcast; decur-rent, -sive; labent, deciduous; nodding to its fall.

Adv. down. -hill, -wards.

307. Elevation.—N. elevation; raising &c. *v.*; erection, lift; sublevation, upheaval; sublimation, exaltation; prominence &c. (*convexity*) 250.

lever &c. 633; crane, derrick, windlass, capstan, winch, dredger, lift, elevator, escalator, dumb waiter.

V. heighten, elevate, raise, lift, erect; set –, stick –, perch –, perk –, tilt- up; rear, hoist, heave; up-lift, -raise, -rear, -bear, -cast, -hoist, -heave; buoy, weigh, mount, give a lift; exalt, sublimate; place –, set- on a pedestal.

take –, drag –, fish- up; dredge.

stand –, rise –, get –, jump- up; spring to one's feet; hold -oneself, – one's head- up; draw oneself up to his full height.

Adj. elevated &c. *v.*; standing up; stilted, attollent, rampant.

Adv. on -stilts, – the shoulders of, – one's legs, – one's hind legs.

308. Depression.—N. lowering &c. *v.*; depression; dip &c. (*concavity*) 252; abasement; detrusion; reduction.

over-throw, -set, -turn; upset; prostration, subversion, precipitation.

bow; courtesy, curtsy; genuflexion, *kowtow*, obeisance, *salaam*.

V. depress, lower; let –, take- -down, – down a peg; cast; let -drop, – fall; sink, debase, bring low, abase, slash, reduce, detrude, pitch, precipitate.

over-throw, -turn, -set; upset, subvert, prostrate, level, fell; cast –, take –, throw –, fling –, dash –, pull –, cut –, knock –, hew- down; raze, – to the ground; humiliate, trample in the dust, pull about one's ears.

sit, – down; couch, squat, crouch, stoop, bend, bow, courtsey, curtsy; bob, duck, dip, genuflect, kneel; *kowtow*, *salaam*, make obeisance, prostrate oneself; bend, bow- the -head, – knee; incline the head; bow down; cower; recline &c. (*be horizontal*) 213.

Adj. depressed &c. *v.*; at a low ebb; prostrate &c. (*horizontal*) 213; detrusive.

309. Leap.—N. leap, jump, hop, spring, bound, vault, saltation.

dance, caper, gambol; curvet, caracole; *gam-bade, -bado*; capriole, demivolt; buck, – jump; hop, skip and jump.

kangaroo, jerboa, chamois, goat, frog, grasshopper, flea.

V. leap; jump -up, – over the moon; hop, spring, bound, vault, ramp, cut capers, gambol, trip, skip, dance, caper; curvet, *caracole*; foot it, bob, bounce, flounce, start, frisk &c. (*amusement*) 840; jump about &c. (*agitation*) 315; trip it on the light fantastic toe, dance oneself off one's legs.

Adj. leaping &c. *v.*; saltatory, frisky.

Adv. on the light fantastic toe.

310. Plunge.—N. plunge, dip, dive, header; ducking &c. *v.*; submergence, immersion, diver.

V. plunge, dip, souse, duck; dive, plump; take a -plunge, – header, make a plunge; bathe &c. (*water*) 337.

sub-merge, -merse; immerse, douse, sink, engulf, send to -the bottom, – Davy Jones' locker.

get out of one's depth; go -to the bottom, – down like a stone; founder, welter, wallow.

311. [Curvilinear motion.] **Circuition.—N.** circuition, circulation; turn, curvet; excursion; circum-vention, -navigation, -ambulation; north-west passage; ambit, gyre, lap, circuit &c. 629.

turning &c. *v.*; wrench; evolution; coil, helix, spiral; corkscrew.

V. turn, bend, wheel; go –, put- about; heel; go –, turn -round, – to the right about; turn on one's heel; make –, describe- a -circle, – complete circle; encircle; go –, pass- through -180°, – 360°.

circum-navigate, -aviate, -ambulate, -vent; put a girdle round the earth, go the round, make the round of.

turn –, round- a corner; double a point.

wind, circulate, meander; whisk, twirl; twist &c. (*convolution*) 248; make a *détour* &c. (*circuit*) 629.

Adj. turning &c. *v.*; circuitous; circum-foraneous, -fluent; devious, roundabout, circum-ambient, -flex, -navigable.

Adv. round about.

312. [Motion in a continued circle.] **Rotation.—N.** rotation, revolution, gyration, circulation, roll; circum-rotation, -volution, -gyration; volutation, circination, turbination, *pirouette*, convolution.

verticity; whir, whirl, swirl, eddy, vortex, whirlpool, gurge; cyclone, tornado; surge; *vertigo*, dizzy round; Maelstrom, Charybdis; Ixion; wheel of Fortune.

313. [Motion in a reverse circle.] **Evolution.—N.** evolution, unfolding, development; eversion &c. (*inversion*) 218.

V. evolve; un-fold, -roll, -wind, -coil, -twist, -furl, -twine, -ravel; disentangle; develop.

Adj. evolving &c. *v.*; evolved &c. *v.*

wheel, screw, propeller, whirligig, rolling stone, windmill; top, teetotum, merry-go-round; roller; cog-, fly-wheel, spit; jack; caster.

axis, axle, spindle, spool, pivot, pin, hinge, pole, swivel, gimbals, arbor, bobbin, mandrel, shaft.

[Science of rotatory motion] trochilics, gyrostatics.

V. rotate; roll, – along; revolve, spin; turn, – round; circumvolve; circulate, gyre, gyrate, wheel, whirl, swirl, twirl, trundle, troll, bowl; slew round.

roll up, furl; wallow, welter; box the compass; spin like a -top, – teetotum.

Adj. rotating &c. *v.*; rota-tory, -ry; circumrotatory, trochilic, vertiginous, gyratory; vortic-al, -ose.

Adv. head over heels, round and round, like a horse in a mill.

314. [Reciprocating motion, motion to and fro.] **Oscillation.—N.** oscillation; vibration, libration; motion of a pendulum; nutation; undulation; pulsation; pulse; throb; seismic disturbance.

alternation; coming and going &c. *v.*; ebb and flow, flux and reflux, ups and downs; wave, vibratiuncle, swing, beat, shake, wag, see-saw, dance, lurch, dodge; fluctuation; vacillation &c. (*irresolution*) 605.

seismometer, vibroscope, seismograph.

V. oscillate; vi-, li-brate; alternate, undulate, wave; sway, rock, swing; pulsate, beat; wag, -gle; nod, bob, courtesy, curtsy; tick; play; chatter, wamble, wabble; teeter, dangle, swag.

fluctuate, dance, curvet, reel, quake; quiver, quaver, shake, flicker; wriggle; roll, toss, pitch; flounder, stagger, totter, waddle; move –, bob- up and down &c. *adv.*; pass and repass, ebb and flow, come and go, shuttle; vacillate &c. 605.

brandish, shake, flourish.

Adj. oscillating &c. *v.*; oscill-, undul-, puls-, libr-atory; vibrat-ory, -ile; pendulous, shutterwise, seismic.

Adv. to and fro, up and down, backwards and forwards, see-saw, zig-zag, wibble-wabble, in and out, from side to side, like buckets in a well.

315. [Irregular motion.] **Agitation.—N.** agitation, stir, tremor, shake, ripple, jog, jolt, jar, jerk, shock, succussion, trepidation, quiver, quaver, dance; jactit-ation, -ance; shuffling &c. *v.*; twitter, flicker, flutter.

disquiet, perturbation, commotion, turmoil, turbulence; tumult, -uation; hubbub, rout, bustle, fuss, racket, *subsultus,* staggers, megrims, epilepsy, fits, twitching, vellication, St. Vitus' dance.

spasm, throe, throb, palpitation, convulsion, paroxysm; tetanus.

disturbance &c. (*disorder*) 59; restlessness &c. (*changeableness*) 149.

ferment, -ation; ebullition, effervescence, hurly-burly, *cahotage;* tempest, storm, ground swell, heavy sea, whirlpool, vortex &c. 312, whirlwind &c. (*wind*) 349.

V. be -agitated &c.; shake; tremble, – like an aspen leaf; quiver, quaver, quake, shiver, twitter, twire, dither, dodder; twitch, writhe, toss, shuffle, tumble, stagger, bob, reel, sway; wag, -gle, wiggle; wriggle, – like an eel; squirm; dance, stumble, shamble, flounder, totter, flounce, flop, curvet, prance.

throb, pulsate, beat, palpitate, go pit-a-pat; flutter, flitter, flicker, bicker; bustle.

ferment, effervesce, foam; boil, – over; bubble, – up; simmer.

toss –, jump- about; jump like a parched pea; shake to its -centre, – foundations; be the sport of the winds and waves; reel to and fro like a drunken man; move –, drive- from post to pillar and from pillar to post; keep between hawk and buzzard.

agitate, shake, convulse, toss, tumble, bandy, wield, brandish, flap, flourish, whisk, jerk, hitch, jolt; jog, -gle; jostle, buffet, hustle, disturb, stir, shake up, churn, jounce, wallop, whip, vellicate.

Adj. shaking &c. *v.*; agitated, tremulous; de-, sub-sultory; shambling; giddy-paced, saltatory, convulsive, jerky, unquiet, restless, all of a twitter.

Adv. by fits and starts; subsultorily &c. *adj.*; *per saltum*; hop, skip and jump; in -convulsions, – fits, pit-a-pat.

CLASS III

Words relating to MATTER

Section I. MATTER IN GENERAL

316. Materiality.—N. material-ity, -ness; materialization; corpor-eity, -ality; substantiality, material existence, incarnation, flesh and blood, *plenum*; physical condition.

matter, body, substance, brute matter, stuff, element, principle, protoplasm, plasma, *parenchyma*, material, *substratum*, hyle, *corpus*, *pabulum*; frame.

object, article, thing, something; still life; stocks and stones; materials &c. 635.

[Science of matter] physics; somatology, -ics; natural –, experimental-philosophy; physical science, *philosophie positive*, materialism, hylism; materialist, physicist.

V. materialize, incorporate, incarnate, substantiate, embody.

Adj. material, bodily; corpor-eal, -al; physical; somat-ic, -oscopic; sensible, tangible, ponderable, palpable, substantial; fleshly incarnate.

objective, impersonal, neuter, unspiritual, materialistic.

317. Immateriality.—N. immaterial ity, -ness; incorporeity, dematerialization, unsubstantiality, spirituality; in. extension; astral plane.

personality; I, myself, me; *ego*, spirit &c. (*soul*) 450; astral body; immaterialism; spiritual-ism, -ist; subliminal –, subconscious- self.

V. disembody, spiritualize, dematerialize.

Adj. immateri-al, -ate; incorpor-eal, -al; asomatous, unextended; un-, disembodied; extramundane, supersensible, unearthly; pneumatoscopic; spiritual &c. (*psychical*) 450; aery.

personal, subjective.

---

318. World.—N. world, creation, nature, universe; earth, globe, wide world; *cosmos*; terraqueous globe, sphere; macro-, mega-cosm; music of the spheres.

heavens, sky, welkin, empyrean; starry -heaven, – host; firmament; vault –, canopy- of heaven; celestial spaces.

heavenly bodies, stars, luminaries, nebulæ; galaxy, milky way, galactic circle, *via lactea*.

sun, orb of day, Apollo, Phœbus; photo-, chromo-sphere; solar system; planet, -oid, asteroid; comet; satellite; moon, orb of night, Diana, Luna; aerolite, meteor; falling –, shooting- star; meteorite.

constellation. zodiac, signs of the zodiac, Charles's wain, Great Bear Southern Cross, Orion's belt, Cassiopeia's chair, Pleiades &c.

colures, equator, ecliptic, orbit.

[Science of heavenly bodies] astronomy; urano-graphy, -logy; cosmo-logy, -graphy, -gony; *eidouranion*, orrery; geography; geodesy

&c. (*measurement*) 466; star-gazing, -gazer; astronomer; cosmogonist, geodesist, geographer; observatory.

Adj. cosmic, cosmical, mundane; terr-estrial, -estrious, -aqueous, -ene, -eous; telluric, earthly, geotic, geodetic, cosmogonal, under the sun; sub-lunary, -astral.

solar, heliacal; lunar; celestial, heavenly, empyreal, sphery; starry, stellar; sider-eal, -al; astral; nebular.

Adv. in all creation, on the face of the globe, here below, under the sun.

319. Gravity.—N. gravi-ty, -tation; weight; heaviness &c. *adj.*; specific gravity; ponderosity, pressure, load; bur-den, -then; ballast, counterpoise; lump –, mass –, weight- of.

lead, millstone, mountain, Ossa on Pelion.

weighing, ponderation, trutination; weights; avoirdupois –, troy –, apothecaries'- weight; grain, scruple, drachm, ounce, pound, lb., load, stone, hundredweight, cwt., ton, quintal, carat, pennyweight, tod, gramme, kilogramme &c.

[Weighing instrument] balance, scales, steelyard, beam, weighbridge. spring balance, weighing machine.

[Science of gravity] statics.

V. be -heavy &c. *adj.*; gravitate, weigh, press, cumber, load.

[Measure the weight of] weigh, poise.

Adj. weighty; weighing &c. *v.*; heavy, – as lead; ponder-ous, -able; lump-ish, -y; cumber-, burden-some; cumbrous, unwieldy, massive. in-, superin-cumbent.

320. Levity.—N. levity; lightness &c; *adj.*; imponderability, imponderableness, buoyancy, volatility.

feather, dust, mote, down, thistledown, flue, cobweb, gossamer, straw, cork, bubble; float, buoy; ether, air.

leaven, ferment, barm, yeast, enzyme.

V. be -light &c. *adj.*; float, swim, be buoyed up.

render -light &c. *adj.*; lighten, levitate; leaven.

Adj. light, subtile, subtle, airy; imponder-ous, -able; astatic, weightless, ethereal, sublimated; uncompressed, volatile; buoyant, floating &c. *v.*; barmy, frothy; portable.

light as -a feather, – thistle down, – air.

fermenting &c. *n.*

Section II.   INORGANIC MATTER

1°. Solid Matter

321. Density.—N. density, solidity; solidness &c. *adj.*; impenetra-, impermea-bility; incompressibility; imporosity; cohesion &c. 46; constipation, consistence, spissitude.

specific gravity; hydro-, areo-meter.

condensation; solid-ation, -ification; consolidation; concretion, caseation, coagulation; petrifaction &c. (*hardening*) 323; crystallization, precipitation; deposit, precipitate, silt; inspissation; thickening &c. *v.*

indivisibility, indiscerptibility, indissolvableness.

solid body, mass, block, knot, lump; con-cretion, -crete, -glomerate; cake.

322. Rarity.—N. rarity; tenuity; absence of -solidity &c. 321; subtility; sponginess, compressibility.

rarefaction, expansion, dilatation, inflation, subtilization.

ether &c. (*gas*) 334.

V. rarefy, expand, dilate, subtilize, attenuate, thin.

Adj. rare, subtile, thin, fine, tenuous, compressible, flimsy, slight; light &c. 320; cavernous, spongy &c. (*hollow*) 252.

rarefied &c. *v.*; unsubstantial; uncom-pact, -pressed.

clot, stone, curd, coagulum, grume; bone, gristle, cartilage.

V. be -dense &c. *adj.*; become -, render- solid &c. *adj.*; solid-ify, -ate; concrete, set, take a set, consolidate, congeal, coagulate; curd, -le; fix, clot, cake, candy, precipitate, deposit, cohere, crystallize; petrify &c. (*harden*) 323.

condense, thicken, inspissate, incrassate; compress, squeeze, ram down, constipate.

Adj. dense, solid; solidified &c. *v.*; cohe-rent, -sive &c. 46; compact, close, serried, thickset; substantial, massive, lumpish; impenetrable, impermeable, imporous; incompressible; constipated; concrete &c. (*hard*) 323; knot-ted, -ty; gnarled; crystal-line, -lizable; thick, grumous, stuffy.

un-dissolved, -melted, -liquefied, -thawed.

in-divisible, -discerptible, -frangible, -dissolvable, -dissoluble, -soluble, -fusible.

323. Hardness.—N. hardness &c. *adj.*; rigidity, renitence, inflexibility, temper, callosity, durity.

induration, petrifaction; lapid-ification, -escence; vitri-, ossi-, corni-fication; crystallization.

stone, pebble, flint, marble, rock, fossil, crag, crystal, quartz, granite, adamant; bone, cartilage; heart of oak, block, board, deal board; iron. steel; cast -, wrought- iron; nail; brick, concrete; cement.

V. render -hard &c. *adj.*; harden, stiffen, indurate, petrify, temper, ossify, vitrify.

Adj. hard, rigid, stubborn, stiff, firm; starch, -ed; stark, unbending, unlimber, unyielding; inflexible, tense; indurate, -d; gritty, proof.

adamant-ine, -ean; concrete, stony, rocky, lithic, granitic, vitreous; crystalline; horny, corneous; bony;oss-eous, -ific; cartilaginous; hard as a -stone &c. *n.*; stiff as -buckram, - a poker.

324. Softness.—N. softness, pliableness &c. *adj.*; flexibility; pli-ancy, -ability; sequacity, malleability; flabbiness; duct-, tract-ility; extend-, extensibility; plasticity; inelasticity, flaccidity, laxity.

clay, wax, butter, dough, pudding; cushion, pillow, feather-bed, pad, down, padding, wadding.

mollification; softening &c. *v.*

V. render -soft &c. *adj.*; soften, mollify, mellow, relax, temper; mash, knead, squash, *massage*.

bend, yield, relent, relax, give.

Adj. soft, tender, supple; pli-ant, -able; flex-ible, -ile; lithe, -some; lissom, limber, plastic; ductile; tract-ile, -able; malleable, extensile, sequacious, inelastic, mollient.

yielding &c. *v.*; flabby, limp, flimsy.

flaccid, flocculent, downy; spongy, œdematous, medullary, doughy, argillaceous, mellow.

soft as -butter, - down, - silk; yielding as wax; tender as a chicken.

325. Elasticity. — N. elasticity, springiness, spring, resilience, renitency, buoyancy.

india-rubber, caoutchouc, gutta-percha, whalebone, gum elastic.

V. be -elastic &c. *adj.*; spring back &c. (*recoil*) 277.

Adj. elastic, tensile, springy, ductile, resilient, renitent, buoyant.

326. Inelasticity.—N. want of -, absence of- elasticity &c. 325; inelasticity &c. (*softness*) 324.

Adj. inelastic &c. (*soft*) 324.

327. Tenacity.—N. tenacity, toughness, strength; cohesion &c. 46; sequacity; stubbornness &c. (*obstinacy*) 606; viscidity &c. 352.

leather; gristle, cartilage.

328. Brittleness.—N. brittleness &c. *adj.*; frag-, friab-, frangib-, fiss-ility; frailty; house of -cards, - glass.

V. be -brittle &c. *adj.*; live in a glass house.

V. be -tenacious &c. *adj.*; resist fracture.

Adj. tenacious, tough, cohesive, adhesive, strong, resisting, sequacious, stringy, gristly, cartilaginous, leathery, coriaceous, tough as whit-leather; stubborn &c. (*obstinate*) 606.

break, crack, snap, split, shiver, splinter, crumble, break short, burst, fly, give way; fall to pieces; crumble -to, – into- dust.

Adj. breakable, brittle, frangible, fragile, frail, friable, delicate, gimcrack, shivery, fissile; splitting &c. *v.*; lacerable, splintery, crisp, crimp, short brittle as glass.

329. [Structure.] **Texture.—N.** structure, organization, anatomy, frame, mould, fabric, construction; frame-work, carcass, architecture; stratification, cleavage.

substance, stuff, *compages, parenchyma*; constitution, staple, organism.

[Science of structures] organ-, oste-, my-, splanchn-, neur , angi-, aden-ology; angi-, aden-ography.

texture; inter-, con-texture; tissue, grain, web, surface; warp and -woof, – weft; tooth, nap &c. (*roughness*) 256; fineness –, coarseness-of grain.

[Science of tissues] histology.

Adj. structural, organic; anatomic, -al.

text-ural, -ile; fine-, coarse-grained; fine, delicate, subtile, gossamery, filmy; coarse; home-spun; linsey-woolsey.

330. Pulverulence.—N. [State of powder.] pulverulence; sandiness &c. *adj.*; efflorescence; friability.

powder, dust, sand, shingle; sawdust; grit; attrition; meal, bran, flour, *farina*, spore, sporule; crumb, seed, grain; particle &c. (*smallness*) 32; thermion; limature, filings, *débris, detritus*, scobs, magistery, fine powder; *flocculi*.

smoke; cloud of -dust, – sand, – smoke; puff –, volume -of smoke; sand –, dust- storm.

[Reduction to powder] pulverization, comminution, attenuation, granulation, disintegration, subaction, contusion, trituration, levigation, abrasion, detrition, multure; limation; filing &c. *v.*

[Instruments for pulverization] mill, millstone, grater, rasp, file, pestle and mortar, nutmeg-grater, teeth, molar, grinder, chopper, grindstone, kern, quern, muller.

V. come to dust; be -disintegrated, – reduced to powder &c.

reduce –, grind- to powder; pulverize, comminute, granulate, triturate, levigate; scrape, file, abrade, rub down, grind, grate, rasp, pound, bray, bruise; con-tuse, -tund; beat, crush, cranch, craunch, crunch, muller, scranch, crumble, disintegrate; attenuate &c. 195.

Adj. powdery, pulverulent, granular, mealy, floury, farinaceous, branny, furfuraceous, flocculent, dusty, sandy, sabulous; aren-ose, -arious, -aceous; gritty; efflorescent, impalpable.

pulverizable; friable, crumbly, shivery; pulverized &c. *v.*; attrite; in pieces.

331. Friction.—N. friction, attrition; rubbing &c. *v.*; erasure; con-frication, -trition; affriction, abrasion, arrosion, limature, frication, rub; elbow-grease; rosin; massage.

V. rub, scratch, abrade, scrape, scrub,

332. [Absence of friction. Prevention of friction.] **Lubrication.—N.** smoothness &c. 255; unctuousness &c. 355.

lubri-cation, -fication; anointment; oiling &c. *v.*

fray, rasp, graze, curry, scour, polish, rub out, erase, gnaw; nie, grind &c. (*reduce to powder*) 330; *massage.*
set one's teeth on edge; rosin.
Adj. anatriptic, abrasive.

synovia; lubricant, graphite, glycerine, oil &c. 356; saliva; lather.
V. lubri-cate, -citate; oil, grease lather, soap; wax.
Adj. lubricated &c. *v.*

2°. FLUID MATTER

1. *Fluids in General*

333. Fluidity.—N. fluidity, liquidity; liquidness &c. *adj.*; gaseity &c. 334; liquefaction &c. 334.

fluid, inelastic fluid; liquid, liquor; lymph, humour, juice, sap, serum, blood, serosity, gravy, rheum, ichor, sanies.

solu-bility, -bleness.

[Science of liquids] hydro-logy, -statics, -dynamics, hydraulics &c.

V. be -fluid &c. *adj.*; flow &c. (*water in motion*) 348; liquefy &c. 335.

Adj. liquid, fluid, serous, juicy, succulent, sappy; fluent &c. (*flowing*) 348.

liquefied &c. 335; uncongealed; soluble, hydrostatic &c. *n.*

335. Liquefaction.—N. liquefaction; liquescen-ce, -cy, deliquescence; melting &c. (*heat*) 384; colliqu-ation, -efaction; thaw; de-, liquation; lixiviation, dissolution.

solution, apozem, lixivium, infusion, decoction, flux.

solvent, diluent, menstruum, alkahest, *aqua fortis.*

V. render -liquid &c. 333; liquefy, run, deliquesce; melt &c. (*heat*) 384; solve; dissolve, resolve; liquate; hold in solution; leach, lixiviate.

Adj. lique-fied &c. *v.*, -scent, -fiable; deliquescent, soluble, colliquative; solvent.

334. Gaseity.—N. gaseity, gaseousness; vapourousness &c. *adj.*; flatulence, -lency; volatility, aeration, gasification.

elastic fluid, gas, air, vapour, ether, steam, fume, reek, *effluvium, flatus;* cloud &c. 353.

[Science of elastic fluids] pneumat-ics, -ostatics; aero-statics, -dynamics &c.

gas-, gaso-meter.

V. gassify, aerate, aerify; emit vapour &c. 336.

Adj. gaseous, aeriform, ethereal, aerial, airy, vaporous, volatile, evaporable; flatulent; aerostatic &c. *n.*

336. Vaporization. — N. vapor-, volatil-ization; gasification; e-, vaporation; distillation, cohobation, sublimation, exhalation; volatility.

vaporizer, still, retort, spray, atomizer; fumigation, steaming.

V. render -gaseous &c. 334; vaporize, volatilize; distil, sublime; evaporate, exhale, smoke, transpire, emit vapour, fume, reek, steam, fumigate.

Adj. volatilized &c. *v.*; reeking &c. *v.*; volatile; evaporable, vaporizable.

---

2. *Specific Fluids*

337. Water.—N. water; serum, serosity; lymph; rheum; diluent.

dilution, maceration, lotion; washing &c. *v.*; im-, mersion; humectation, infiltration, spargefaction, affusion, irrigation, *douche,* balneation, bath.

deluge &c. (*water in motion*) 348; high water, flood-, spring-tide

338. Air.—N. air &c. (*gas*) 334; common -, atmospheric- air; atmosphere, stratosphere, isothermal layer, troposphere, Heaviside layer.

open, - air; sky, welkin; blue, - sky; cloud &c. 353.

weather, climate, rise and fall of the barometer, isobar.

V. be -watery &c. *adj.*; reek.

add water, water, wet; moisten &c. 339; dilute, dip, immerse; merge; im-, sub-merge; plunge, souse, duck, drown; soak, steep, macerate, pickle, wash, sprinkle, sparge, lave, bathe, affuse, splash, swash, douse, slosh, drench; dabble, slop, slobber, irrigate, inundate, deluge; syringe, inject, gargle; infiltrate, percolate.

Adj. watery, aqueous, aquatic, lymphatic; balneal, diluent; drenching &c. *v.*; diluted &c. *v.*; weak; wet &c. (*moist*) 339.

Phr. the waters are out.

339. Moisture.—N. moisture; moistness &c. *adj.*; hum-idity, -ectation; madefaction, dew; *serein*; marsh &c. 345; Hygromet-ry, -er.

V. moisten, wet; humect, -ate; sponge, damp, dampen, bedew; imbue, imbrue, infiltrate, saturate; seethe, sop; soak, drench &c. (*water*) 337.

be -moist &c. *adj.*; not have a dry hread; perspire &c. (*exude*) 295.

Adj. moist, damp; watery &c. 337; undried, humid, wet, dank, muggy, dewy; roric; roscid; juicy.

wringing wet; wet -through, – to the skin; saturated &c. *v.*

swashy, soggy, dabbled; reeking, seething, dripping, soaking, soft, sodden, sloppy, muddy; swampy &c. (*marshy*) 345; irriguous.

341. Ocean.—N. sea, ocean, main, deep, brine, salt water, waters, waves, billows, high seas, offing, great waters, watery waste, 'vasty deep,' briny ocean, herring pond, steamer track, the seven seas; wave, tide &c. (*water in motion*) 348.

hydrograph-y, -er, oceanography; Neptune, Thetis, Triton, Naiad, Nereid; sea-nymph, Siren, mer-maid, -man; trident, dolphin.

Adj. oceanic; mar-ine, -itime; pelagic, -ian; sea-going, -worthy; hydrographic.

Adv. at –, on- sea; afloat, on the high seas.

[Science of air] pneumatics, aero-logy, -scopy, -graphy; meteorology, climatology; eudio-, baro-, aero-meter; aneroid baro-graph, -scope; weather-gauge, -glass, -cock.

exposure to the -air, – weather; ventilation; aero-station, -nautics, -naut &c. 267 and 269.

V. air, ventilate; fan &c. (*wind*) 349.

Adj. containing air, flatulent, effervescent; windy &c. 349.

atmospheric, airy; aeri-al, -form; pneumatic; meteorological; weatherwise.

Adv. in the open air, out of doors, *à la belle étoile, al fresco; sub -Jove, – dio.*

340. Dryness.—N. dryness &c. *adj.*; siccity, aridity, drought, ebb-, neaptide, low water.

drying, ex-, de-siccation; evaporation; dehydration; arefaction, dephlegmation, drainage.

drier, desiccator.

V. be -dry &c. *adj.*; render -dry &c. *adj.*; dry; dry –, soak- up; sponge swab, wipe; ex-, de-siccate, dehydrate, anhydrate; drain, parch.

be fine, hold up.

Adj. dry, anhydrous, arid, waterless; dried &c. *v.*; undamped; juice-, sapless; sear; husky; rainless, without rain, fine; dry as -a bone, – dust, – a stick, – a mummy, – a biscuit; desiccated; dehydrated; water-proof, -tight.

342. Land.—N. land, earth, ground, dry land, *terra firma*.

continent, mainland, peninsula, delta; tongue –, neck- of land; isthmus, oasis; promontory &c. (*projection*) 250; highland &c. (*height*) 206.

coast, shore, scar, strand, beach; bank, lea; sea- board, -side, -shore, -bank, -coast, -beach; rock-, iron-bound coast; loom of the land; derelict; innings; *alluvium*, alluvion.

soil, glebe, clay, loam, marl, cledge, chalk, gravel, mould, subsoil, clod, clot; rock, crag, cliff.

acres; real estate &c. (*property*) 780; landsman, land-lubber, farmer.

geography &c. 318; agriculture &c. 371.

V. land, come to land; set foot on -the soil, – dry land; come –, go- ashore.

Adj. earthy; continental, midland; littoral, riparian, ripuarian; alluvial; terrene &c. (*world*) 318; landed, predial, territorial.

Adv. ashore; on -shore, – land.

343. Gulf. Lake.—N. land covered with water, gulf. gulph, bay, inlet, bight, estuary, arm of the sea, fiord, armlet; frith, firth, ostiary, mouth; lagune, lagoon; indraught; cove, creek; natural harbour; roads; strait, narrows; Euripus; sound, belt, gut, kyles.

lake, loch, lough, mere, tarn, plash, broad, pond, pool, lin, puddle, well, artesian well, tank, sump; standing –, dead –, sheet of- water; fish -, mill-pond; race; ditch, dike, dyke, dam; reservoir &c. (*store*) 636.

Adj. lacustrine; land locked.

344. Plain.—N. plain, table land, mesa, face of the country; open –, country; basin, downs, waste, weary waste, desert, tundra, wild, steppe, pampas, savanna, prairie, champaign, heath, common, wold, veld; moor, -land, uplands, fell; bush; *plateau* &c. (*level*) 213; *campagna*.

meadow, mead, haugh, pasturage, park, field, lawn, green, plat, plot, grass-plat, greensward, sward, grass, turf, sod, heather; lea, ley, lay; grounds.

Adj. campestrian, champaign, alluvial.

345. Marsh.—N. marsh, swamp, morass, marish, moss, fen, bog, quagmire, slough, sump, wash; mud, squash, slush.

Adj. marsh, -y; swampy, boggy, plashy, poachy, quaggy, soft; muddy, sloppy, squashy, spongy; paludal; moor-ish, -y; fenny.

346. Island.—N. island, isle, islet, eyot, ait, holm, reef, atoll, breaker; archipelago; islander.

Adj. insular, sea-girt.

---

3. *Fluids in Motion*

347. [Fluid in motion.] **Stream.—N.** stream &c. (*of water*) 348, (*of air*) 349.

V. flow &c. 348; blow &c. 349.

348. [Water in motion.] **River.—N.** running water.

jet, spirt, squirt, spout, splash, swash, rush, gush, *jet d'eau*; sluice, chute.

water-spout, -fall: fall, cascade, force, foss; lin, -n; ghyll, Niagara; cata-ract, -dupe, -clysm; *débâcle*, inundation, deluge.

rain, -fall; *serein*; shower, scud; downpour, cloud burst; driving –, pouring –, drenching- rain; hyeto-logy, -graphy; rainy season, monsoon; predominance of Aquarius, reign of St. Swithin; mizzle, drizzle, *stillicidium*, plash; dropping &c. *v.*

stream, course, flux, flow, profluence; effluence &c. (*egress*) 295; defluxion; flowing &c. *v.*; current, tide, race.

spring; fount, -ain; rill, rivulet, gill,

349. [Air in motion.] **Wind.—N.** wind, draught, *flatus*, *afflatus*, air; breath, – of air; puff, whiff, zephyr; blow, drift; *aura*; stream, current; under-current.

gust, blast, breeze, squall, gale, half a gale, storm, tempest, hurricane, whirlwind, tornado, samiel, cyclone, typhoon; simoon; harmattan, monsoon, trade wind, sirocco, *mistral*, bise, *föhn*, tramontane, levanter; capful of wind; fresh –, stiff- breeze; keen blast; blizzard.

windiness &c. *adj.*; ventosity; rough –, dirty –, ugly –, stress of- weather; dirty-, windy-, mackerel- sky; mare's tail; thick –, black –, white- squall.

anemography, aerodynamics; wind-gauge, anemometer. weather-cock, vane.

gullet, rillet; stream-, brook-let; runnel, sike, burn, beck, brook, stream, river; reach; tributary.

body of water, torrent, rapids, flush, flood, swash, spate; spring -, high -, full-tide; bore; eagre, *hygre*; fresh, -et; undertow, indraught, reflux, undercurrent, eddy, vortex, gurge, whirlpool, Maelstrom, regurgitation, overflow; confluence, corrivation.

wave, billow, surge, swell, ripple; roller, ground swell, surf, breaker, white horses; comber, beach-comber; rough -, heavy -, cross -, long -, short -, chopping -, choppy- sea, choppiness; tidal wave.

[Science of fluids in motion] Hydrodynamics; Hydraul-ics &c.; rain-gauge &c.

water-bearer, - carrier, Aquarius.

irrigation &c. (*water*) 337; pump; watering-pot, - cart; hydrant, standpipe, hose, sprinkler, drencher; fire engine, squirt, syringe.

V. flow, run; meander; gush, pour, spout, roll, jet, well, issue; drop, drip, dribble, plash, squirt, spurt, spirtle, trill, trickle, distil, percolate; stream, overflow, inundate, deluge, flow over, splash, swash; guggle, murmur, babble, bubble, purl, gurgle, sputter, regurgitate; ooze flow out &c. (*egress*) 295.

rain, - hard, - in torrents, - cats and dogs, - pitchforks; come down in sheets; pour with rain, drizzle, mizzle, spit, sprinkle, set in.

flow -, fall -, open -, drain- into; discharge itself, disembogue.

[Cause a flow] pour; pour out &c. (*discharge*) 297; shower down; irrigate, drench &c. (*wet*) 337; spill, splash.

[Stop a flow] stanch; dam, -up &c. (*close*) 261; obstruct &c. 706.

Adj. fluent; dif-, pro-, af-fluent; tidal; flowing &c. *v.*; meand-ering, -ry, -rous; fluvi-al, -atile; streamy, showery, rainy drizzly, drizzling, pluvial, pluviose, stillicidous.

suf-, insuf-, per-, in-, af-flation; blowing, fanning &c. *v.*; ventilation.

sneezing &c. *v.*; sternutation; hiccup, -cough; catching of the breath; breathing &c.

Eolus, Eurus, Boreas, Zephyr, cave of Eolus.

air-pump, lungs, bellows, blow-pipe, fan, blower; pulmotor, ventilator, punkah, aspirator, exhauster, ejector.

V. blow, waft; blow -hard, - great guns, - a hurricane &c. *n.*; whistle, roar, howl, ring in the shrouds; stream, issue.

respire, breathe, in-, ex-hale, puff; whif, -fle; gasp, wheeze; snuff, -le; sniff, -le; sneeze, cough, belch.

fan, ventilate; in-, per-flate; blow -, pump- up.

Adj. blowing &c. *v.*; windy, airy, æolian, flatulent; breezy, gusty, squally; stormy, tempestuous, blustering; boisterous &c. (*violent*) 173.

pulmon-ic, -ary.

---

350. [Channel for the passage of water.] **Conduit.**—**N.** conduit, channel, duct, watercourse, race; head -, tail-race; adit, aqueduct, canal, trough, flume, gutter, pantile; dike, canyon, ravine, gorge, hollow, main, gully, moat, ditch, drain, sewer, culvert, *cloaca*, sough, kennel, siphon, *piscina*; pipe &c. (*tube*) 260; funnel; tunnel &c. (*passage*) 627; water -, waste- pipe; emunctory, gully-hole, artery, aorta, vein, blood vessel; lymphatic; throat, alimentary canal, intestine; pore, spout, scupper; ad-, a-jutage;

351. [Channel for the passage of air.] **Air-pipe.**—**N.** air-pipe, - shaft, - way, - passage, - tube; shaft, flue, chimney, funnel, vent, blow-hole, nostril, nozzle, throat, weasand, *trachea*; *bronch-us, -ia*; larynx, tonsils, wind-pipe, spiracle; venti-duct, -lator; louvre, blow-pipe &c. (*wind*) 349; pipe &c. (*tube*) 260.

---

hose; gar-, gur-goyle; penstock, weir; flood-. water-gate; sluice,
lock, valve; rose; waterworks.
Adj. vascular &c. (*with holes*) 260.

3°. IMPERFECT FLUIDS

352. Semiliquidity.—N. semiliquidity; stickiness &c. *adj.*; visc-idity,
-osity; gumm-, glutin-, muc-osity;
spiss-, crass-itude; lentor; adhesive-
ness &c. (*cohesion*) 46.

inspiss-, incrass-ation; thickening,
coagulation.

jelly, aspic, mucilage, gelatin, isin-
glass; colloid, mucus, phlegm; pituite,
lava; glair, starch, gluten, albumen,
milk, cream, protein; syrup, treacle;
gum, size, glue, paste; wax, bee's-wax;
emulsoid, emulsion, soup; squash, mud,
slush, slime, ooze; moisture &c. 339;
marsh &c. 345.

V. inspiss-, incrass-ate; coagulate,
gelatinize, gelatinify, gel, jell, emulsify,
thicken; mash, squash, churn, beat up.

Adj. semi-fluid, -liquid; half-melted,
-frozen; milky, muddy &c. *n.*; lact-eal,
-ean, -eous, -escent, -iferous; emulsive,
curdled, thick, succulent, uliginous.

gelat-, album-, mucilag-, glut-inous;
gelatine, mastic, amylaceous, ropy,
clammy, clotted; vis-cid, -cous; sticky,
tacky; slab, -by; lentous, pituitous;
mu-cid, -culent, -cous.

353. [Mixture of air and water.]
Bubble. [Cloud.]—N. bubble; foam,
froth, head, fume, spume, lather, suds,
spray, surf, yeast, barm, spindrift.

cloud, vapour, fog, mist, haze,
steam; scud, rack, *nimbus*; *cumulus*,
woolpack, *cirrus*, *stratus*; *cirro-*, *cumulo-
stratus*; *cirro-cumulus*; mackerel sky,
mare's tail, dirty sky.
[Science of clouds] nephelognosy,
nephology.

effervescence, fermentation; bubbling &c. *v.*

nebula; cloudiness &c. (*opacity*) 426;
nebulosity &c. (*dimness*) 422.

V. bubble, boil, foam, froth, spume,
mantle, sparkle, guggle, gurgle; effervesce, ferment, fizzle; aerate; cloud,
overcast, befog.

Adj. bubbling &c. *v.*; frothy, nappy,
effervescent, sparkling, *mousseux*, up-
fizzy, with a head on.

cloudy &c. *n.*; vaporous, nebulous,
overcast; nubiferous, nephological;
foggy, brumous.

---

354. Pulpiness.—N. pulpiness &c.
adj.; pulp, paste, dough, sponge, curd,
pap, rob, jam, pudding, mush, fool,
poultice, grume, *papier mâché.*
Adj. pulpy &c. *n.*; pultaceous,
grumous.
V. pulp, pulpify, mash.

355. Unctuousness.—N. unctuousness &c. *adj.*; unctuosity, lubricity;
ointment &c. (*oil*) 356; anointment;
lubrication &c. 332.
V. oil &c. (*lubricate*) 332.
Adj. unctuous, oily, oleaginous, adipose, sebaceous; fat, -ty; greasy; waxy,
butyraceous, soapy, saponaceous, pin-
guid, lardaceous; slippery.

---

356. Oil.—N. oil, fat, butter, cream, grease, tallow, suet, lard,
dripping, margarine, oleomargarine, exunge, blubber; glycerine, stearine,
elaine, oleagine; soap; soft soap, wax, cerement; paraffin, spermaceti,
adipocere; petroleum, mineral –, rock –, crystal- oil, kerosene, vegetable –, colza –, olive –, linseed –, cotton seed –, rape –, nut –, fusel- oil;
animal –, neat's foot –, signal –, train- oil; ointment, unguent, liniment,
salve, pomade, pomatum, brilliantine, spike –, nard.

356a. Resin.—N. resin, rosin, colophony; gum; lac, shellac, sealing-
wax; amber, -gris; bitumen, pitch, tar, asphalt, -e, -um; varnish, copal,
mastic, magilp, lacquer, japan.
V. varnish &c. (*overlay*) 223.
Adj. resinous, bituminous, pitchy, tarry.

Section III. ORGANIC MATTER

1°: Vitality

1. *Vitality in general*

357. Organization.—N. organized -world, – nature; living –. animated-nature; living beings; organic remains, organism; fossils; animal and vegetable kingdom, *fauna* and *flora*, biota.

prot-oplasm, -ein; albumen; structure &c. 329; organ-ization, -ism.

[Science of living beings] biology; natural history,* organic –, bio-chemistry, anatomy, physiology, embryology, morphology, evolution, Darwinism, Lamarkism, zoology &c. 368; botany &c. 369; naturalist, biologist &c.

Adj. organ-ic, -ized.

359. Life.—N. life; vi-tality, -ability; animation; vital -spark, – flame, – force.

respiration, wind; breath -of life, – of one's nostrils; life-blood; Archeus; existence &c. 1.

vivification, vitalization; revivification &c. 163; Prometheus; life to come &c. (*destiny*) 152.

[Science of life] physiology, etiology, embryology, biology; animal economy.

nourishment, staff of life &c. (*food*) 298.

V. be -alive &c. *adj.*; live, breathe, respire; subsist &c. (*exist*) 1; walk the earth; strut and fret one's hour upon a stage; be spared.

see the light, be born, come into the world; fetch –, draw- -breath, – the breath of life; quicken; revive; come to, – life.

give birth to &c. (*produce*) 161; bring to life, put life into, vitalize; vivi-fy, -ficate; reanimate &c. (*restore*) 660; keep -alive, – body and soul together, – the wolf from the door; support life.

have nine lives like a cat.

358. Inorganization. — N. mineral -world, – kingdom; unorganized –, inorganic –, brute –, inanimate- matter.

[Science of the mineral kingdom] mineralogy; geo-logy, -gnosy, -scopy; metall-urgy, -ography; lithology; orycto-logy, -graphy.

V. turn to dust, pulverize.

Adj. in-organic, -animate; unorganized; azoic; mineral.

———

360. Death.—N. death, dying &c. *v.*; de-cease, -mise; dissolution, departure, *obit*, release, rest, *quietus*, fall; loss, bereavement.

end &c. 67 –, cessation &c. 142 –, loss –, extinction –, ebb- of -life &c. 359.

death-warrant, -watch, -rattle, -bed; stroke –, agonies –, shades –, valley of the shadow –, jaws –, hand- of death; last -breath, – gasp, – agonies; dying -day, – breath, – agonies; swan song, *chant du cygne*; *rigor mortis*; Stygian shore; crossing the bar, the great adventure.

King -of terrors, – Death; Death, Angel of Death; mortality; doom &c. (*necessity*) 601.

euthanasia; happy release; break up of the system; natural -death, – decay; sudden –, violent- death; untimely end, watery grave; suffocation, *asphyxia*; heart failure; fatal disease &c. (*disease*) 655; death-blow &c. (*killing*) 361.

necrology, bills of mortality, obituary; death-song &c. (*lamentation*) 839.

V. die, expire, perish; meet one's -death, – end; pass away, be taken; yield –, resign- one's breath; resign

* The term *Natural History* is also used as relating to all the objects in Nature whether organic or inorganic, and including therefore *Mineralogy, Geology, Meteorology,* &c.

Adj. living, alive; in -life, – the flesh, – the land of the living; on this side of the grave, above ground, breathing, quick, animated, viable; lively &c. (*active*) 682; alive and kicking; tenacious of life.

vital; vivi-fying, -fied &c. *v.*; Promethean.

Adv. *vivendi causâ.*

———

one's -being, – life; end one's -days, – life, – earthly career; breathe one's last; cease to -live, – breathe; depart this life; be -no more &c. *adj.*; go –, drop –, pop -off; lose –, lay down –, relinquish –, surrender- one's life; drop -, sink- into the grave; close one's eyes; fall –, drop- dead, – down dead; break one's neck; give –, yield- up the ghost; be all over with one.

pay the debt to nature, shuffle off this mortal coil, take one's last sleep; go the way of all flesh; join the -greater number, – majority, – choir invisible; awake to life immortal; come –, turn- to dust; cross the Stygian ferry; go to -one's long account, – one's last home, – Davy Jones's locker, – the wall; receive one's death warrant, make one's will, die a natural death, go out like the snuff of a candle; come to an untimely end; catch one's death; go off the hooks, kick the bucket, peg out; go West; hop the twig, turn up one's toes; die a violent death &c. (*be killed*) 361; make the supreme sacrifice.

Adj. dead, lifeless; deceased, demised, departed, defunct; late, gone, no more; ex-, in-animate; out of the world, taken off, released; departed this life &c. *v.*; dead and gone; bereft of life, stone dead, dead as -a door nail, – a door post, – mutton, – a herring, – nits; launched into eternity, gathered to one's fathers, numbered with the dead, gone to a better land, behind the veil, beyond the grave, – mortal ken.

dying &c. *v.*; mori-bund, -ent, Acherontic; hippocratic; *in -articulo, – extremis*; in the -jaws, – agony- of death; going, - off; *aux abois*; on one's -last legs, – death bed; at -the point of death, – death's door, – the last gasp; near one's end, given over, booked, fey; with one foot in –, tottering on the brink of- the grave.

still-born; mortuary; deadly &c. (*killing*) 361.

Adv. *post -obit, – mortem.*

Phr. life -ebbs, – fails, – hangs by a thread; one's -days are numbered, – hour is come, – race is run, – doom is sealed; Death -knocks at the door, – stares one in the face; the breath is out of the body; the grave closes over one; *sic itur ad astra.*

---

361. [Destruction of life; violent death.] **Killing.—N.** killing &c. *v.*; homicide, manslaughter, murder, assassination, trucidation, occision; lynching, effusion of blood; blood, -shed; gore, slaughter, carnage, butchery; *battue*, gladiatorial combat.

massacre; *fusillade, noyade, pogrom*; Thuggee, thuggism.

death blow, finishing stroke, *coup de grâce, quietus*; execution &c: (*capital punishment*) 972; judicial murder; martyrdom.

butcher, slayer, murderer, Cain, assassin. cut-throat, garrotter, *bravo*, thug, racketeer, gunman, mobster, gangster, Moloch, *matador, sabreur*; *guet-à-pens*; gallows, executioner &c. (*punishment*) 975; man-eater.

regicide, parricide, fratricide, infanticide, aborticide &c.

suicide, *felo-de-se, suttee, hara-kiri*, Juggernaut; immolation, holocaust. suffocation, strangulation, garrotte; hanging &c. *v.*

deadly weapon &c. (*arms*) 727; Aceldama; the potter's field, the field of blood.

fatal accident, violent death, casualty.

[Destruction of animals] slaughtering; phthiozoics;* sport, -ing; the chase, venery; hunting, coursing, shooting, fishing; pig-sticking; sports-, hunts-, fisher-man; hunter, Nimrod; slaughterer, knacker, slaughter-house, shambles, *abattoir.*

V. kill, put to death, slay, shed blood; murder, assassinate, butcher, slaughter; victimize, immolate; massacre; take away –, deprive of-life; make away with, put an end to; despatch, decimate; burke, settle do, – to death, – for.

strangle, garrotte, hang, lynch, throttle, choke, stifle, suffocate, stop the breath, smother, asphyxiate, drown.

sabre; cut -down, – to pieces, – the throat; jugulate; stab, run through the body, bayonet; put to the -sword, – edge of the sword.

shoot, – dead; blow one's brains out; brain, knock on the head; stone, lapidate; give –, deal- a death blow; give a -*quietus*, – *coup de grâce.*

behead, bowstring &c. (*execute*) 972.

hunt, shoot &c. *n.*

cut off, nip in the bud, launch into eternity, send to one's last account, bump off, rub out, sign one's death warrant, strike the death knell of.

give no quarter, pour out blood like water; run amuck, wade knee-deep –, imbrue one's hands- in blood.

die a violent death, welter in one's blood; dash –, blow- out one's brains; commit suicide; kill –, -make away with –, put an end to- oneself.

Adj. killing &c. *v.*; murd-, slaught-erous; sanguin-ary, -olent; blood-stained, -thirsty; homicidal, red-handed; bloody, -minded; ensanguined, gory, sanguineous.

mortal, fatal, lethal; dead-, death-ly; mort-, leth-iferous; unhealthy &c. 657; internecine; suicidal.

sporting; piscator-ial, -y.

Adv. in at the death.

362. Corpse.—N. corpse, corse, carcass, bones, skeleton, dry-bones; defunct, relics, *reliquiæ,* remains, mortal remains, dust, ashes, earth, clay; mummy; carrion; food for- worms, – fishes; tenement of clay, this mortal coil.

shade, ghost, *manes,* apparition &c. 980.

organic remains, fossils.

Adj. cadaverous, corpse-like; unburied &c. 363.

363. Interment.—N. interment, burial, sepulture, entombment; in-, humation; obs-, ex-equies; funeral, wake, pyre, funeral pile; crema-tion.

funeral -rite, – solemnity; knell, passing bell, tolling; dirge &c. (*lamentation*) 839; cypress; *obit,* dead march, muffled drum; coroner, mortician, undertaker, mute, mourner, professional mourner, pall-bearer; elegy; funeral -oration, – sermon; epitaph.

grave clothes, shroud, winding-sheet, cere-cloth; cerement.

coffin, shell, sarcophagus, urn, pall, bier, hearse, catafalque, cinerary urn.

grave, pit, sepulchre, tomb, vault, crypt, catacomb, mausoleum, *Golgotha,* house of death, narrow house, long home; cemetery, necropolis, boneyard; burial-place, -ground; grave-, church-yard; God's acre; mortuary, tope, cromlech, dolmen, menhir, barrow, tumulus, cairn;

* Bentham, 'Chrestomathia.'

ossuary; bone-, charnel-, dead-house; *morgue*; lich-gate; crematorium. sexton, grave-digger.

monument, memorial, cenotaph, shrine; grave-, head-, tomb-stone: *memento mori*; hatchment, stone, cross.

exhumation, disinterment; necropsy, autopsy, *post-mortem* exami- nation.

V. inter, bury; lay in –, consign to- the -grave, – tomb; en-, in-tomb; inhume; lay out, prepare for burial, embalm, mummify; conduct a funeral, hold services; toll the knell; put to bed with a shovel.

exhume, disinter, unearth.

Adj. buried &c. *v.*; burial; fune-real, -brial; mortuary, sepulchral, cinerary; elegiac; necroscopic.

Adv. *in memoriam*; *post-obit, -mortem*; beneath –, under- the sod.

Phr. *hic jacet, ci-gît, requiescat in pace.*

2. *Special Vitality*

364. Animality.—N. animal life; anima-tion, -lity, -lization; breath.

flesh, – and blood; corporeal nature; *physique*; strength &c. 159.

V. animalize, incorporate.

Adj. fleshly, incarnate, carnal, cor- poreal, human.

365. Vegetability.—N. vegetable life; vegeta-tion, -bility; herbage.

V. vegetate, germinate, sprout, shoot; cultivate.

Adj. vegetable &c. 367; rank, lush.

---

366. Animal.*—N. animal, – king- dom; *fauna*; brute creation.

beast, brute, creature, created being; creeping –, living- thing; dumb -animal, – creature.

flocks and herds, live stock; domes- tic –, wild- animals; game, *feræ naturæ*; beasts of the field, fowls of the air, denizens of the day.

vertebrate, bi-, quadru-ped, mam- mal, marsupial, bird, reptile, batra- chian, amphibian, fish, crustacean, shell fish, articulate, mollusc, worm, insect, zoophyte; protozoon, animal- cule &c. 193.

horse &c. (*beast of burden*) 271; cattle, kine, ox; bull, -ock; steer, stot; cow, milch cow, calf, heifer, shorthorn; sheep; lamb, -kin; ewe –, pet- lamb; ewe, ram, tup; pig, swine, boar, hog, shoat, sow; tag, teg, wether.

dog, bitch, hound; pup, -py; whelp, cur, mutt, mongrel; house-, watch-, sheep-, shepherd's-, sporting-, fancy-, lap-, toy-, bull-, badger-dog; mastiff; blood-, grey-, stag-, deer-, fox-, otter- hound; harrier, beagle, spaniel, pointer,

367. Vegetable.*— N. vegetable, – kingdom; *flora*, verdure.

plant; tree, shrub, bush; creeper; vine; herb, -age; grass.

annual; per-, bi-, tri-ennial; exotic.

timber; primeval –, virgin- forest; wood, -lands; hurst, frith, holt, weald, park, chase, greenwood, brake, grove, copse, coppice, *bocage, tope,* clump of trees, thicket, spinet, spinney; under-. brush-wood; boscage, scrub; the oak and the ash and the bonny ivy tree.

bush, jungle, prairie; heath, -er; fern, bracken; furze, gorse, whin, broom; grass, turf, grassland, green- sward, green, lawn, meadow; pas-ture, -turage; turbary; sedge, rush, weed; fungus, mushroom, toadstool; lichen, moss, conferva, mould; seaweed &c.; growth, crop.

foliage, leafage, branch, bough, ram- age; spray &c. 51; leaf, frond, flag, petal, shoot, tendril.

flower, blossom, bud, bloom, bine; flowering plant; tree, sapling, pollard; timber-, fruit-tree; palm-, gum-tree; pulse, legume.

* Extended lists of names of specific varieties of animals, vegetables, &c., are beyond the scope of this work; see Introduction, p. xxv.

setter, retriever; Newfoundland; water -dog, – spaniel; pug, poodle; dachshund; Pinscher; turnspit; terrier; fox –, Skye-terrier; Dandie Dinmont; collie.

cat; puss, -y; kitten; grimalkin; gib-, tom-cat; mouser; fox, Reynard, vixen, stag, deer, hart, buck, doe, roe, ante-lope.

bird; poultry, fowl, cock, hen, chicken, chanticleer, partlet, rooster, dunghill cock, barn-door fowl; feathered -tribes, – songster; sing-ing –, dicky- bird; canary; finch; auk, dodo, moa, roc, phœnix.

snake, serpent, viper, adder; newt, eft; asp, vermin.

Adj. animal, zoological.

equine, bovine, vaccine, canine, feline; fishy; piscator-y, -ial; molluscous, porcine, vermicular.

Adj. veget-able, -ous; herb-aceous, -al; botanic; sylvan, silvan; arbor- ary, -eous, -escent, -ical; dendritic, dendri-form; woody, grassy; ver-dant,-durous; floral, mossy; lign-ous, -eous; wooden, leguminous; end-, ex-ogenous.

---

368. [The science of animals.] Zool-ogy.—N. zoo-logy, -nomy, -graphy, -tomy; anatomy; comparative ana-tomy; animal –, comparative- physi-ology; morphology.

anthrop-, ornith-, ichthy-, herpet-, ophi-, malac-, helminth-, entom-, oryct-, paleont-ology; ichthy- &c. -otomy; taxidermy.

zo- &c. -ologist.

Adj. zoological &c. n.

369. [The science of plants.] Botany, —N. botany; phyto-graphy, -logy, -tomy; vegetable physiology, herbori-zation, dendr-, myc-, fung-, alg-ology; flora, pomona; botanist &c.; botanic garden &c. (garden) 371; hortus siccus, herbarium, herbal.

herb-ist, -arist, -alist, -orist, -arian &c.

V. botanize, herborize.

Adj. botanical &c. n.

370. [The economy or management of animals.] Cicuration.—N. taming &c. v.; cicuration, zoohygiantics; domestic-ation, -ity; manège; veterinary art; breeding, pisciculture, apiculture &c.

menagery, vivarium, zoological gar-den, zoo; bear-pit; aviary, apiary, hive; aquarium, fishery, fish hatchery; duck-, fish-pond; stud-farm; stock farm, dairy.

[Destruction of animals] phthisozo-ics* &c. (killing) 361.

neat-, cow-, shep-herd, shepherdess; grazier, drover, cowboy, cowkeeper; trainer, breeder, groom, ostler &c. 746; veterinary surgeon, vet, horse doctor; farrier; keeper; gamekeeper.

cage &c. (prison) 752; hen-coop, bird-cage, cauf; sheep-fold &c. (inclo-sure) 232.

V. tame, domesticate, acclimatize, breed, tend, break in, train, corral, round up; cage, bridle &c. (restrain) 751; ride &c. 266.

drive, yoke, harness, hitch; groom,

371. [The economy or management of plants.] Agriculture.—N. agricul-ture, cultivation, husbandry, farming; georgics, geoponics; tillage, tilth, agron-omy, gardening, spade husbandry, vintage; hort-, arbor-, silv-, citr-, vit-, flor-iculture; intensive culture; land-scape gardening; forestry, afforesta-tion.

husbandman, horticulturist, citri-culturist, gardener, florist; agricult-or, -urist; yeoman, farmer, cultivator, tiller of the soil, ploughman, sower, reaper; woodcutter, backwoodsman, forester; vine grower, vintager; Boer; Triptolemus.

field, meadow, garden; botanic –, winter –, ornamental –, flower –, kit-chen –, truck –, market –, hop- garden; nursery; green-, hot-, glass-house; conservatory, cucumber frame, cloche, bed, border, seed-plot; grass-plat, lawn; park &c. (pleasure ground) 840; parterre, shrubbery, plantation, avenue,

---

* Bentham.

curry-comb; milk; shear; hatch; incubate.

Adj. pastoral, bucolic; tame, domestic, domesticated, broken in, gentle, docile.

arboretum, pinery, *pinetum*, orchard; vineyard, vinery; orangery; farm &c. (*abode*) 189.

V. cultivate; till, – the soil; farm, garden; sow, plant; reap, mow, cut; manure, dress the ground, dig, delve, dibble, hoe, plough, plow, harrow, rake, weed, lop and top, force, transplant, thin out, bed out, prune, graft.

Adj. agr-icultural, -arian, -estic.

arable; predial, rural, rustic, country, bucolic, Bœotian; horticultural.

---

372. Mankind.—N. man, -kind; human -race, – species, – nature; humanity, mortality, flesh, generation.

[Science of man] anthropo-logy, -graphy, -sophy; ethno-logy, -graphy; humanitarianism.

human being; person, -age; individual, creature, fellow creature, mortal, body, somebody, one; such a –, some- one; soul, living soul; earthling; party, head, hand; *dramatis personæ*.

people, persons, folk, public, society, world; community, – at large; general public; nation, -ality; state, realm; common-weal, -wealth; republic, body politic; million &c. (*commonalty*) 876; population &c. (*inhabitant*) 188.

cosmopolite; lords of the creation; ourselves.

Adj. human, mortal, personal, individual, national, civic, public, cosmopolitan; anthropoid.

---

373. Man.—N. man, male, he; manhood &c. (*adolescence*) 131; gentleman, sir, master; yeoman, wight, swain, fellow, guy, blade, *beau*, chap, gaffer, goodman; husband &c. (*married man*) 903; Mr., mister, *monsieur, sahib, Herr, señor, signor*; boy &c. (*youth*) 129; Adonis.

[Male animal] cock, drake, gander, dog, boar, stag, hart, buck, horse, entire horse, stallion; gib-, tom-cat; he-, Billy-goat; ram, tup; bull, -ock; capon, ox, gelding; steer, stot.

Adj. male, he, masculine; manly, virile; un-womanly, -feminine.

374. Woman.—N. woman, she, female, petticoat, skirt, moll, broad.

feminality, feminity, muliebrity; womanhood &c. (*adolescence*) 131; feminism; gynecology, gyniatrics, gynics.

womankind; the -sex, – fair; fair –, softer- sex; weaker vessel; the distaff side.

dame, madam, *madame*, mistress, Mrs., lady, *mem-sahib, Frau, señora, signora, donna, belle*, matron, dowager, goody, gammer; good -woman, – wife; squaw; wife &c. (*marriage*) 903; matron-age, -hood.

Venus, nymph, wench, *grisette*; little bit of fluff; girl &c. (*youth*) 129.

inamorata (love) &c. 897; courtesan &c. 962.

spinster, old maid, virgin, bachelor girl, new woman, Amazon.

[Female animal] hen, slut, bitch, sow, doe, roe, mare; she-, Nannygoat; ewe, cow; lioness, tigress; vixen.

gynecæum, harem, *seraglio, zenana, purdah*.

Adj. female, she; feminine, womanly, ladylike, matronly, maidenly; womanish, effeminate, unmanly, gynecic.

2°. SENSATION

(1.) *Sensation in general*

375. Physical Sensibility.—N. sensibility; sensitiveness &c. *adj.*; physical sensibility, feeling, perceptivity, anaphylaxis, susceptibility, æsthetics; moral sensibility &c. 822.

sensation, impression, effect; consciousness &c. (*knowledge*) 490.

external senses.

V. be -sensible &c. *adj.* -of; feel, perceive.

render, -sensible &c. *adj.*; excite, stir, sharpen, cultivate, tutor.

cause sensation, impress; excite -, produce- an impression.

Adj. sens-ible, -itive, -uous; æsthetic, perceptive, sentient; conscious &c. (*aware*) 490; impressionable, responsive, alive to.

acute, sharp, keen, vivid, lively, impressive, thin-skinned.

Adv. to the quick.

_____

377. Physical Pleasure.—N. pleasure; physical -, sensual -, sensuous-pleasure; bodily enjoyment, animal gratification, sensuality; hedonism, luxuriousness &c. *adj.*; dissipation, round of pleasure; titillation, *gusto*, creature comforts, comfort, ease; pillow &c. (*support*) 215; luxury, lap of luxury; purple and fine linen; bed of ·down, - roses; velvet, clover; cup of Circe &c. (*intemperance*) 954.

treat; diversion, divertisement, entertainment; refreshment, regale; feast; *délice*; dainty &c. 394; *bonne bouche*.

source of pleasure &c. 829; happiness &c. (*mental enjoyment*) 827.

V. feel -, experience -, receive-pleasure; enjoy, relish; luxuriate -, revel -, riot -, bask -, swim -, wallow-in; feast on; gloat -over, - on; smack the lips.

live -on the fat of the land, - in comfort &c. *adv.*; bask in the sunshine, *faire ses choux gras*.

give pleasure &c. 829.

376. Physical Insensibility.—N. insensibility, physical insensibility; obtuseness &c. *adj.*; palsy, paralysis, *anæsthesia, analgesia, narcosis, hypnosis,* twilight sleep, stupor, coma, trance, catalepsy; sleep &c. (*inactivity*) 683; moral insensibility &c. 823; numbness &c. 381.

anæsthetic agent, general -, local-anæsthetic, opium, ether, chloroform, cocaine, novocaine, chloral; nitrous oxide, laughing gas; refrigeration.

V. be -insensible &c. *adj.*; have a -thick skin, - rhinoceros hide.

render -insensible &c. *adj.*; blunt, pall, obtund, benumb, deaden, paralyze; anæsthetize, drug, dope; put under the influence of -chloroform &c. *n.*; hypnotize; stupefy, stun, narcotize.

Adj. insensible, unfeeling, senseless, comatose, dazed, impercipient, callous, thick-skinned, pachydermatous; hard, -ened; case-hardened; proof; obtuse, dull; anæsthetic; paralytic, palsied, numb, dead.

378. Physical Pain.—N. pain; suffering, -ance; bodily - physical- -pain, - suffering; mental suffering &c. 828; dolour, ache; aching &c. *v.*; smart; shoot, -ing; twinge, twitch, gripe, head-, ear-, tooth-ache; *migraine*, neuralgia, neuritis, lumbago, gout, sciatica; hurt, cut; sore, -ness; discomfort, *malaise*; *tic douloureux*.

spasm, cramp; nightmare, *ephialtes*; crick, stitch, kink; thrill, convulsion, throe; throb &c. (*agitation*) 315; pang.

sharp -, piercing -, throbbing -, shooting -, gnawing -, burning- pain; anguish, agony.

torment, torture; rack; cruci-ation, -fixion; martyrdom; martyr, toad under a harrow, vivisection.

V. feel -, experience -, suffer -, undergo- pain &c. *n.*; suffer, ache, smart, bleed; tingle. shoot; twinge, twitch, lancinate; writhe, wince, make a wry face; sit on -thorns, - pins and needles.

give -, inflict- pain; pain, hurt, chafe, sting, bite, gnaw, gripe, stab, grind;

Adj. enjoying &c. *v.*; luxurious, voluptuous, sensual, hedonistic, comfortable, cosy, snug, in comfort, at ease.

agreeable &c. 829; grateful, refreshing, comforting, cordial, genial; sensuous; palatable &c. 394; sweet &c. (*sugar*) 396; fragrant &c. 400; melodious &c. 413; lovely &c. (*beautiful*) 845.

Adv. in -comfort &c. *n.*; on -a bed of roses &c. *n.*; at one's ease.

pinch, tweak; grate, gall, fret, prick, pierce wring, convulse; torment, torture; rack, agonize; crucify; ex-, cruciate; break on the wheel, put to the rack; flog &c. (*punish*) 972; grate on the ear &c. (*harsh sound*) 410.

Adj. in -pain &c. *n.*, – a state of pain; pained &c. *v.*

painful; aching &c. *v.*; biting, poignant; sore, raw, tender, with exposed nerve.

(2.) *Special Sensation*

1. *Touch*

379. [Sensation of pressure.] **Touch.—N.** touch; tact, -ion, -ility; feeling; palp-ation, -ability; manipulation; brush, tick, graze, contact &c. 199.

[Organ of touch] hand, finger, fore-finger, thumb, paw, feeler, *antenna*.

V. touch, feel, handle, finger, thumb, paw, fumble, grope, grabble; twiddle, tweedle; pass –, run- the fingers over, massage, rub, knead; palpate, stroke, manipulate, wield; throw out a feeler.

Adj. tact-ual, -ile; tangible, palpable; lambent.

380. Sensations of Touch.—N. itching &c. *v.*; titillation, formication, *aura*.

V. itch, tingle, creep, thrill, sting; prick, -le; tickle, titillate.

Adj. itching &c. *v.*

381. [Insensibility to touch.] **Numbness.—N.** numbness &c. (*physical insensibility*) 376; pins and needles.

local anæsthetic, cocaine, novocaine &c.; morphia.

V. benumb &c. 376; freeze, dull deaden.

Adj. numb; benumbed &c. *v.*; intangible, impalpable.

2. *Heat*

382. Heat.—N. heat, caloric; temperature, warmth, fervour, calidity; incal-, incand-, recal-, decal-escence; glow, flush, blush; fever, hectic.

phlogiston; fire, spark, scintillation, flash, flame, blaze; arc; bonfire; firework, pyrotechny; wild-fire; sheet of fire, lambent flame; devouring element; conflagration.

summer, dog-days, canicule; baking &c. 384 –, white –, tropical –, Afric –, Bengal –, summer –, blood- heat; heat wave, sirocco, simoon; broiling sun; isolation; warming &c. 384.

sun &c. (*luminary*) 423; fire worshipper &c. 991; furnace &c. 386.

geyser, hot spring, volcano.

[Science of heat] pyrology; therm-

383. Cold.—N. cold, -ness &c. *adj.*; frigidity, gelidity, algidity, inclemency, *fresco*.

winter; depth of –, hard- winter; Siberia, Nova Zembla; Ant-, arctic, North –, South- Pole.

ice; snow, – flake, – crystal, – drift; sleet; hail, -stone; rime, frost; hoar –, white –, hard –, sharp- frost; icicle, thick-ribbed ice; fall of snow, snow storm, heavy fall, *avalanche*; ice-berg, -floe; floe, berg; *glacier*; *névé, serac*.

[Sensation of cold] chilliness &c. *adj.*; chill; shivering &c. *v.*; gooseskin, -flesh; *rigor*, horripilation, chattering of teeth; frostbite, chilblain.

V. be -cold &c. *adj.*; shiver, starve, quake, shake, tremble, shudder, didder,

ology, -otics; thermometer &c. 389.

V. be -hot &c. *adj.*; glow, incandesce, flush, sweat, swelter, bask, smoke, reek, stew, simmer, seethe, boil, burn, singe, scorch, scald, grill, broil, blaze, flame; smoulder; parch, fume, pant.

heat &c. (*make hot*) 384; thaw, fuse, melt, give.

Adj. hot, heated, warm, mild, genial, tepid, lukewarm, unfrozen; therm-al, -ic; calorific; ferv-ent, -id; ardent; aglow.

sunny, torrid, tropical, estival, canicular; close, sultry, stifling, stuffy, suffocating, oppressive; reeking &c. *v.*; baking &c. 384.

red -, white - smoking -, burning &c. *v.* -, piping- hot; like -a furnace, - an oven; hot as -fire, - pepper; hot enough to roast an ox.

fiery; incand-, incal-escent; candent, ebullient, glowing, smoking; on fire; blazing &c. *v.*; in -flames, - a blaze; alight, afire, ablaze; un-quenched, -extinguished; smouldering; in a -heat, - glow, - fever, - perspiration, - sweat; sudorific; swelter-ing, -ed; blood-hot, -warm; warm as -a toast, - wool; recalescent, thermogenic, pyrotechnic, feverish, febrile, inflamed.

volcanic, plutonic, igneous; isother-mal, -mic, -al.

Phr. Not a breath of air.

384. Calefaction.—N. increase of temperature; heating &c. *v.*; cale-, tepe-, torre-faction; melting, fusion; liquefaction &c. 335; burning &c. *v.*; kindling, combustion; in-, ac-cension; con-, cremation; scorification; cauter-y, -ization; ustulation, calcination; in-, cineration; cupellation; carbonization.

ignition, inflammation, adustion, flagration; de-, con-flagration; empyrosis, incendiarism; arson; *auto-dafé*; suttee.

boiling &c. *v.*; coction, ebullition, estuation, elixation, decoction.

furnace &c. 386; blanket, flannel, fur, muffler, wrap; wadding &c. (*lining*) 224; clothing &c. 225.

match &c. (*fuel*) 388; incendiary, pyromaniac; *pétroleur, pétroleuse*; cauterant, caustic, lunar caustic, apozem, moxa.

sunstroke, *coup de soleil*; insolation, sunburn.

pottery, ceramics, crockery, porcelain, china; earthen-, stone-ware; pot

quiver; perish with cold; chill &c. (*render cold*) 385.

Adj. cold, cool; chill, -y; gelid, frigid, algid; fresh, keen, bleak, raw, inclement, bitter, biting, niveous, cutting, nipping, piercing, pinching; clay-cold; starved &c. (*made cold*) 385; shivering &c. *v.*; aguish, *transi de froid*; frostbitten, -bound, -nipped.

cold as -a stone, - marble, - lead, - iron, - a frog, - charity, - Christmas; cool as -a cucumber, - custard.

icy, glacial, frosty, freezing, wintry, brumal, hibernal, boreal, arctic, antarctic, polar, Siberian, hyemal; hyperbore-an, -al; ice-bound; frozen out.

un-warmed, -thawed, -heated; isocheimal, -chimenal.

Adv. coldly, bitterly &c. *adj.*; *à pierre fendre.*

---

385. Refrigeration.—N. refrigeration, infrigidation, reduction of temperature; cooling &c. *v.*; con-gelation, -glaciation; ice &c. 383; solidification &c. (*density*) 321; refrigerator &c. 387.

V. cool, fan, refrigerate, refresh, ice; congeal, freeze, glaciate; benumb. starve, pinch, chill, petrify, chill to the marrow, nip, cut, pierce, bite, make one's teeth chatter; damp.

Adj. cooled &c. *v.*; frozen out; cooling &c. *v.*; frigorific.

Extinction.—N. *extincteur*; fire, - engine, - extinguisher, - annihilator. - brigade, - man; sprinkler, hose, hydrant, standpipe.

incombusti-bility, -bleness &c. *adj.*

V. Quench, damp; blow-, put-, stamp - out; extinquish.

go -, burn-out.

Adj. incombustible; un-, unin-flammable; fire-proof.

---

mug, *terra-cotta*, brick, clinker; cinder, ash, *scoriæ*; embers, dross, slag, products of combustion, coke, carbon, charcoal.

inflamma-, combusti-bility.

[Transmission of heat] diathermancy, transcalency.

V. heat, warm, chafe, stive, foment; make -hot &c. 382; sun oneself, bask in the sun.

fire; set -fire to, – on fire; kindle, enkindle, light, ignite, strike a light; apply the -match, – torch- to; re-kindle, -lume; fan –, add fuel to- the flame; poke –, stir –, blow- the fire; make a bonfire of; burn at the stake.

melt, thaw, fuse; liquefy &c. 335.

burn, inflame, roast, toast, fry, grill, singe, parch, bake, torrefy, scorch; brand, cauterize, sear, burn in; corrode, char, carbonize, calcine, incinerate; smelt, cupel, scorify; reduce to ashes; burn to ɪ cinder; commit –, consign- to the flames.

boil, digest, stew, cook, seethe, scald, parboil, simmer; do to rags. take –, catch- fire; blaze &c. (*flame*) 382.

Adj. heated &c. *v.*; molten, sodden; *réchauffé*; heating &c. *v.* inflammable, burnable, inflammatory, combustible; diatherm-al -anous; burnt &c. *v.*; volcanic.

---

386. Furnace.—N. furnace, blast furnace, fire-box, stove, incinerator, destructor, crematorium, crematory, kiln, oven, oast-house; hot-, bake-, wash-house; laundry; conservatory; hearth, focus; athanor, hypocaust, reverberatory; volcano; forge, fiery furnace; *tuyère*, brasier, salamander,

heater, warming-pan, foot-warmer, hot-water bottle; radiator; boiler, geyser, caldron, seething caldron, pot; urn, kettle; chafing-dish; retort, crucible, alembic, still; saggar.

fire-place, -dog, -irons; hearth, ingle, grate, range, kitchener; kitchen range; oil-, gas-, electric, -cooker, -stove; fireless cooker; fire; galley; ca-, cam-boose; poker, tongs, shovel, hob, trivet; and-, grid-iron; frying-, stew-pan &c.

hot –, Turkish –, Russian –, vapour –, shower –, warm- bath; *calidarium, tepidarium, sudatorium*, sudatory; *hammam.*

387. Refrigerator.—N. refrigerator, -y; *frigidarium*; cold storage; refriger-ating-plant, – machine; ice-house, -pail, -bag, -chest, -pack; cooler, damper; wine-cooler, freezing mixture.

See 385.

---

388. Fuel.—N. fuel, firing, combustible, coal, wallsend, anthracite, bituminous coal, slack, culm, cannel coal, lignite, briquette, coke, carbon, charcoal; turf, peat, fire-wood, bobbing, faggot, log, Yule log ember, cinder &c. (*products of combustion*) 384; kindling wood, tinder, touch-wood; fumigator, sulphur, brimstone; incense; port-fire; fire-barrel, -ball, -brand

fuel oil gas, gasoline.

brand, torch, fuse; wick; spill, match, safety match, light, lucifer; congreve, vesuvian, vesta, fusee, locofoco; linstock; illuminant.

candle &c. (*luminary*) 423; oil &c. (*grease*), 356; petrol, gasoline, methylated –, spirit; gas, acetylene.

Adj. carbonaceous; combustible, inflammable.

V. stoke, fire, feed, add fuel to the flames.

389. Thermometer.—N. thermo-meter, -scope, -stat, -pile, differential thermometer; pyro-, calori-meter; radio micrometer &c.

3. *Taste*

390. Taste.—N. taste, flavour, gust, *gusto*, relish, savour; sapor, sapidity; twang, smack, smatch; after-taste, tang.

tasting; de-, gustation.

palate, tongue, tooth, stomach.

V. taste, savour, smatch, smack, flavour, twang; tickle the palate &c. (*savoury*) 394; smack the lips.

Adj. sapid, saporific; gusta-ble, -tory; strong; flavoured, spiced, savoury; palatable &c. 394.

391. Insipidity.—N. insipidity; tastelessness &c. *adj.*

V. be -tasteless &c. *adj.*

Adj. void of -taste &c. 390; insipid; jejune; taste-, gust-, savour-less; ingustible, mawkish. milk and water, weak, stale, flat, vapid, *fade*, wishy-washy, mild; untasted.

---

392. Pungency.—N. pungency, piquancy, poignancy, *haut-goût*, strong taste, twang, race, tang.

sharpness &c. *adj.*; acrimony, acridity; roughness &c. (*sour*) 397; unsavouriness &c. 395.

nitre, saltpetre; mustard, cayenne, caviare; seasoning &c. (*condiment*) 393; brine.

dram, cordial, nip, pick-me-up, bracer, potion.

nicotine, tobacco, snuff, quid; segar; cigar, -ette, gasper, fag; cheroot; weed; fragrant -, Indian- weed; pipe, clay pipe, churchwarden, brier, meerschaum, hookah, hubble-bubble.

V. be -pungent &c. *adj.*; bite the tongue.

render -pungent &c. *adj.*; season, spice, salt, pepper, pickle, brine, devil, curry.

smoke, chew, take snuff.

Adj. pungent, strong; high-, full-flavoured; high-tasted, -seasoned; gamy; sharp, stinging, rough, *piquant*, racy; biting, mordant; spicy; seasoned &c. *v.*; hot, – as pepper; peppery, vellicating, escharotic, meracious; acrid, acrimonious, bitter; rough &c. (*sour*) 397; unsavoury &c. 395.

salt, saline, brackish, briny; salt as -brine, – a herring, – Lot's wife.

393. Condiment.—N. condiment, flavouring, salt, mustard, pepper, cayenne, curry, seasoning, sauce, spice, cinnamon, chillies, relish, *sauce piquante*, caviare, pot-herbs, onion, garlic, pickle, chutney, nutmeg &c.

V. season &c. (*render pungent*) 392.

394. Savouriness.—N. savouriness &c. *adj.*; relish, zest.

tit-bit, dainty, delicacy, ambrosia, nectar, *bonne bouche*; game, turtle, venison.

V. taste good, be -savoury &c. *adj.*; tickle the -palate, – appetite; flatter the palate.

render -palatable &c. *adj.*

relish, like, smack the lips.

Adj. savoury, well-tasted, to one's taste, tasty, good, palatable, nice, dainty, delectable; tooth-ful, -some;

395. Unsavouriness.—N. unsavouriness &c. *adj.*; amaritude; acri-mony, -tude; roughness &c. (*sour*) 397; acerbity, austerity; gall and worm-wood, rue, quassia, aloes; sickener.

V. be -unpalatable &c. *adj.*; sicken, disgust, nauseate, pall, turn the stomach.

Adj. un-savoury, -palatable, -sweet; ill-flavoured, un-appetizing, -eatable, inedible; bitter, – as gall; acrid, acrimonious; rough.

offensive, repulsive, nasty; sickening

gustful, appetizing, lickerish, delicate, delicious, exquisite, rich, luscious, ambrosial.

Adv. *per amusare la bocca.*

Phr. *cela se laisse manger.*

396. Sweetness.—N. sweetness, dulcitude, saccharinity.

sugar, cane-, beet-sugar; saccharine, glucose, syrup, treacle, molasses, honey, manna; confection, -ery; sweets, grocery, conserve, preserve, *confiture,* jam, marmalade, julep; sugar-candy, -plum; licorice, liquorice, plum, lollipop, *bonbon, jujube,* comfit, sweetmeat, caramel, toffee, butterscotch.

nectar; hydromel, mead, metheglin, honeysuckle, *liqueur,* sweet wine.

pastry, pie, tart, puff, pudding, cake. dulc-ification, -oration.

V. be -sweet &c. *adj.*

render -sweet &c. *adj.*; sugar, saccharize, sweeten; edulcorate; dulc-orate, -ify; candy; mull.

Adj. sweet, sugary; sacchar-ine, -iferous; dulcet, honied, candied, luscious, nectarious, melliferous; sweetened &c. *v.*

sweet as -a nut, – sugar, – honey.

&c. *v.*; nauseous; loath-, ful-some; unpleasant &c. 830.

_____

397. Sourness.—N. sourness &c.; *adj.*; acid, -ity; acetous fermentation; acerbity.

vinegar, verjuice, crab, alum.

V. be –, turn- -sour &c. *adj.*; set the teeth on edge.

render -sour &c. *adj.*; acid-ify, -ulate.

Adj. sour; acid, -ulous, -ulated; acerb; tart, crabbed; acet-ous, -ose; sour as vinegar, sourish, acescent, sub-acid; styptic, hard, rough; unripe, green.

_____

4. *Odour*

398. Odour.—N. odour, smell, odorament, scent, effluvium; eman-, exhal-ation; fume, essence, trail, nidor, redolence.

sense of smell; scent; act of -smelling &c. *v.*

V. have an -odour &c. *n.*; smell, – of, – strong of; exhale; give out a -smell &c. *n.*; scent.

smell, scent; snuff, – up; sniff, nose, inhale.

Adj. odor-ous, -iferous; smelling, strong-scented; redolent, graveolent, nidorous, pungent.

[Relating to the sense of smell] olfactory, quick-scented.

399. Inodorousness.—N. inodorousness; absence –, want- of smell.

V. be -inodorous &c. *adj.*; not smell. deodorize.

Adj. inodor-ous, -ate; scentless; without –, wanting- smell &c. 398. deodoriz-ed, -ing.

_____

400. Fragrance. — N. fragrance, aroma, redolence, perfume, *bouquet;* sweet smell, aromatic perfume.

perfumery; incense; musk, frankincense; pastil, -le; myrrh, perfumes of Arabia, chypre; otto, ottar, attar; bergamot, balm, civet, *pot-pourri,* pulvil; nosegay, *boutonnière;* scent, -bag; *sachet,* scent-bottle, smelling bottle, *vinaigrette;* toilet water, *eau de Cologne;* thurible, censer, thurification.

perfumer; incense bearer.

401. Fetor.—N. fetor, fetidness; bad &c. *adj.*; -smell, – odour; stench, stink; mephitis, foul -, mal- odour; *empyreuma;* mustiness &c. *adj.*; rancidity; foulness &c. (*uncleanness*) 653.

stoat, polecat, skunk; assafœtida, fungus, garlic; stink-pot, -bomb.

V. have a -bad smell &c. *n.*; smell; stink, – in the nostrils, – like a polecat; smell -strong &c. *adj.*, – offensively.

Adj. fetid; strong-smelling; high, bad, strong, fulsome, offensive, noisome, rank, rancid, reasty, tainted, musty

V. be -fragrant &c. *adj.*; have a -perfume &c. *n.*; smell sweet, scent, perfume, thurify, embalm.

Adj. fragrant, aromatic, redolent, spicy, balmy, scented; sweet-smelling, -scented; perfum-ed, -atory; thuriferous; fragrant as a rose, muscadine, ambrosial.

fusty, frouzy; olid, -ous; nidorous; smelling, stinking; putrid &c. 653; suffocating, mephitic; empyreumatic.

---

5. Sound

(i.) SOUND IN GENERAL

402. Sound.—N. sound, noise, strain; accent, twang, intonation, tone, tune; cadence; sonority, sonorousness &c *adj.*; audibility; resonance &c. 408; voice &c. 580.

[Science of sound] acou-, acu-stics; catacoustics, cataphonics; phon-ics, -etics, -ology, -ography; dia-coustics, -phonics.

telephone, phonograph &c. 418.

V. produce sound; sound, make a noise; give out –, emit- sound; phonetize, phonate; resound &c. 408.

Adj. sounding; soniferous; sonorific; resonant, audible, acoustic, auditory; distinct; stertorous; phonic, sonant; phonetic.

403. Silence.—N. silence; stillness &c. (*quiet*) 265; peace, hush, lull, rest; muteness &c. 581; solemn –, awful –, dead –. deathlike- silence.

V. be -silent &c. *adj.*; hold one's tongue &c. (*not speak*) 585.

render -silent &c. *adj.*; silence, still, hush; stifle, muffle, gag, stop; muzzle, put to silence &c. (*render mute*) 581.

Adj. silent; still, -y; calm, quiet; noise-, sound-, speech-less; hushed &c. *v.*; mute &c. 581; aphonic.

soft, solemn, awful, deathlike, silent as the grave; inaudible &c. (*faint*) 405.

Adv. silently &c. *adj.*; *sub silentio*; in perfect silence.

Int. hush! 'sh! silence! soft! whist! tush! chut! tut! *pax!* mum's the word! hold your tongue! shut up! be silent! be quiet! stop that noise! hold your row! dry up! peace, be still!

Phr. one might hear a -feather, – pin- drop.

---

404. Loudness.—N. loudness, power; loud noise, din; clang, -or; clatter, noise, bombilation, roar, uproar, racket, static, grinders, hubbub, *fracas, charivari,* trumpet blast, blare, flourish of trumpets, fanfare, *tintamarre,* peal, swell, blast, alarum, boom; resonance &c. 408.

vociferation; pandemonium, hullaballoo &c. 411; lungs; Stentor; megaphone; siren.

artillery, cannon, gunfire, shellburst, bomb; thunder.

V. be -loud &c. *adj.*; peal, swell, clang, boom, thunder, fulminate, roar; resound &c. 408; speak up, shout &c. (*vociferate*) 411; bellow &c. (*cry as an animal*) 412; give tongue.

rend the -air, – skies; fill the air; din –, ring –, thunder- in the ear;

405. Faintness.—N. faintness &c. *adj.*; faint sound, whisper, breath; under-tone, -breath; murmur, hum, rustle, buzz, purr; plash; sough, moan, sigh, susurration; tinkle; 'still small voice.'

hoarseness &c. *adj.*; raucity.

silencer, soft pedal, damper, mute, *sourdine.*

V. whisper, breathe, murmur, purl, hum, gurgle, ripple, babble, flow; tinkle; mutter &c. (*speak imperfectly*) 583.

steal on the ear; melt in –, float on- the air.

muffle, mute, deaden, damp, stifle.

Adj. inaudible; scarcely –, just-audible; low, dull; stifled, muffled; hoarse, husky; gentle, soft, faint; floating; purling, flowing &c. *v.*;

pierce –, split –, rend- the -ears, – head; deafen, stun; *faire le diable à quatre*; make one's windows shake; awaken –, startle- the echoes; make the welkin ring.

Adj. loud, sonorous; high-, big-sounding; blatant; deep, full, powerful, noisy, clangorous, multisonous, *fortissimo*; thundering, deafening &c. *v.*; trumpet-tongued; ear-splitting, -rending, -deafening; piercing; obstreperous, rackety, uproarious; enough to wake the -dead, – seven sleepers.

shrill &c. 410; clamorous &c. (*vociferous*) 411; stentor-ian, -ophonic.

Adv. loudly &c. *adj.*; aloud; at the top of one's voice, lustily, in full cry.

Phr. the air rings with.

whispered &c. *v.*; liquid; soothing; dulcet &c. (*melodious*) 413.

Adv. in a whisper, with bated breath, *sotto voce*, between the teeth, aside; *pian-o*, *-issimo*; *à la sourdine*; *con sordine*; out of earshot, inaudibly &c. *adj.*

(ii.) SPECIFIC SOUNDS*

406. [Sudden and violent sounds.] **Snap.—N.** snap &c. *v.*; rapping &c. *v.*; de-, crepitation; smack, clap, report; thud; burst, explosion, discharge, detonation, blow-out, back-fire, firing, salvo, volley, pistol-shot.

squib, cracker, gun, rifle, pop-gun.

V. rap, snap, tap, knock; click; clash; crack, -le; crash; pop; slam, bang, clap, thump, plump; toot; back-fire, explode, burst on the ear.

Adj. rapping &c. *v.*

Int. crash! bang!

407. [Repeated and protracted sounds.] **Roll.—N.** roll &c. *v.*; drumming &c. *v.*; tattoo; ding-dong; tantara; rataplan; whirr; rat-a-tat; rub-a-dub; pit-a-pat; quaver, clutter, *charivari*, racket; cuckoo; repetition &c. 104; peal of bells, devil's tattoo; reverberation &c. 408.

drumfire, barrage.

machine gun.

V. roll, drum, rumble, rattle, clatter, rustle, roar, drone, patter, clack.

hum, trill, shake; chime, peal, toll; tick, beat.

drum –, din- in the ear.

Adj. rolling &c. *v.*; monotonous &c. (*repeated*), 104; like a bee in a bottle.

---

408. Resonance.—N. resonance; ring &c. *v.*; ringing &c. *v.*; tintinnabulation; reflection, reverberation, clangor.

low –, base –, bass –, flat –, grave –, deep –, pedal- note; bass; *basso*, – *profondo*; bari-, bary-tone; *contralto*.

V. re-sound, -verberate, -echo; ring, ding, sing, jingle, gingle, chink, clink; tink, -le; chime; gurgle &c. 405; plash, guggle, echo, ring in the ear.

Adj. resounding &c. *v.*; resonant, tinnient, tintinnabulary; deep-toned, -sounding, -mouthed; hollow, sepulchral; gruff &c. (*harsh*) 410.

408a. Non-resonance. — N. thud, thump, dead sound; non-resonance; muffled drums, cracked bell; silencer, damper; mute, *sourdine*.

V. sound dead; stop –, damp- the -sound, – reverberations; deaden, muffle.

Adj. non-resonant, dead, muted, muffled.

---

409. [Hissing sounds.] **Sibilation.—N.** sibilation; hiss &c. *v.*; sternutation; high note &c. 410.

goose, serpent, snake.

---

* [The author's classification of sounds has been retained, though it does not entirely accord with the theories of modern science.—ED.]

V. hiss, buzz, whiz, rustle; fizz, -le, sizzle, swish; wheeze, whistle, snuffle; squash; sneeze.

Adj. sibilant; hissing &c. *v.*; wheezy.

410. [Harsh sounds.] Stridor.—N. creak &c. *v.*; creaking &c. *v.*; discord &c. 414; stridor; harshness, roughness, sharpness &c. *adj.*; cacophony.

acute –, high- note; *soprano*, treble, tenor, *alto*, falsetto, *voce di testa*; shriek, cry &c. 411.

piccolo, fife, penny -whistle, – trumpet.

V. creak, grate, jar, burr, pipe, twang, jangle, clank, clink; scream &c. (*cry*) 411; yelp &c. (*animal sound*) 412; buzz &c. (*hiss*) 409.

set the teeth on edge, *écorcher les oreilles*; pierce –, split- the -ears, – head; offend –, grate upon –, jar upon- the ear.

Adj. creaking &c. *v.*; strident, stridulous, harsh, coarse, hoarse, horrisonous, raucous, metallic, rough, gruff, grum, sepulchral.

sharp, high, acute, shrill, high-pitched; trumpet-toned; piercing, ear-piercing; cracked; discordant &c. 414; cacophonous.

411. Cry.—N. cry &c. *v.*; voice &c. (*human*) 580; bark &c. (*animal*) 412.

vociferation, outcry, hullaballoo, chorus, clamour, hue and cry, plaint; lungs; stentor.

V. cry, roar, shout, bawl, brawl, halloo, halloa, hail, hoop, whoop, yell, bellow, howl, scream, screech, screak, shriek, shrill, squeak, squeal, squall, whine, whinny, pule, pipe, yaup.

cheer, hurrah; hoot; grumble, moan, groan.

snore, snort; grunt &c. (*animal sounds*) 412.

vociferate; raise –, lift up- the voice; call –, sing –, cry- out; exclaim; rend the air; thunder –, shout- at the -top of one's voice, – pitch of one's breath; *s'égosiller*; strain the -throat, – voice, – lungs; give a -cry &c.

Adj. crying &c. *v.*; clam-ant, -orous; vociferous; stentorian &c. (*loud*) 404; open-mouthed.

412. [Animal sounds.] Ululation.—N. cry &c. *v.*; crying &c. *v.*; ululation, latration, belling; reboation; call, note; bark, howl, yelp; twittering, woodnote; insect cry, fritinancy, drone; screech; cuckoo.

V. cry, ululate, howl, roar, bellow, blare, rebellow, bark, yelp; bay, – the moon; yap, growl, yarr, yawl, snarl, howl; grunt, -le; snort, squeak; neigh, bray; mew, mewl; purr, caterwaul, pule; bleat, low, moo; troat, croak, crow, screech, caw, coo, gobble, quack, cackle, gaggle, guggle; chuck, -le; cluck; clack; cheep, chirp, chirrup, twitter, sing, cuckoo; pout, wail, hum, buzz; hiss, blatter; hoot.

Adj. crying &c. *v.*; blatant, latrant; re-, mugient; deep-, full-mouthed.

Adv. in full cry.

(iii.) Musical Sounds

413. Melody. Concord.—N. melody, rhythm, measure; rhyme &c. (*poetry*) 597.

pitch, *timbre*, intonation, tone, over-tone.

scale, gamut; diapason; diatonic –, chromatic –, enharmonic- scale; key, clef, chords,

modulation, temperament, syncope, syncopation, preparation, suspension, resolution.

414. Discord.—N. discord, -ance; dissonance, cacophony, caterwauling; harshness &c. 410; consecutive fifths.

[Confused sounds] Babel, pandemonium; Dutch –, cat's- concert, marrow-bones and cleavers.

V. be -discordant &c. *adj.*; jar &c. (*sound harshly*) 410.

Adj. discordant; dis-, ab-sonant; out of tune, tuneless; un-musical, -tunable; un-, im-melodious; un-, in-harmonious;

staff, stave, line, space, brace; bar, rest; *avpogia-to*, *-tura*; *acciaccatura*, shake, *arpeggio*.

sing-song; cacophonous; jarring, harsh &c. 410.

note, musical note, notes of a scale; sharp, flat, natural; high note &c. (*shrillness*) 410; low note &c. 408; interval; semitone; second, third, fourth &c.; diatessaron.

breve, semibreve, minim, crotchet, quaver; semi-, demisemiquaver; sustained note, drone, burden.

tonic; key-, leading-, fundamental- note; supertonic, mediant, dominant; sub-mediant, -dominant, organ-, pedal-point; octave, tetrachord; major –, minor- -mode, – scale, – key; Doric mode, passage, phrase.

concord, harmony; unison, -ance; chime, homophony; euphon-y, -ism; tonality; consonance; concent; part.

orchestration, harmonization, – phrasing.

[Science of harmony] harmon-y, -ics; thorough-, fundamental-bass; counterpoint; faburden.

piece of music &c. 415; composer, harmonist, contrapuntist.

V. be -harmonious &c. *adj.*; harmonize, chime, symphonize, transpose; put in tune, tune, accord, string; score, arrange, orchestrate.

Adj. harmoni-ous, -cal; in -concord &c. *n.*, – tune, – concert; unisonant, concentual, symphonizing, isotonic, homophonous, assonant, consonant.

measured, rhythmical, diatonic, chromatic, enharmonic.

1 elodious, musical; tuneful, tunable; sweet, dulcet, canorous; mell-ow, -ifluous; soft; clear, – as a bell; silvery; euphon-ious, -ic, -ical; symphonious; enchanting &c. (*pleasure-giving*) 829; fine-, full-, silver-toned.

Adv. harmoniously &c. *adj.*

---

415. Music.—**N.** music, classical –, modern –, descriptive- music; concert, recital; strain, tune, air, *motif*; melody &c. 413; *aria, arietta*; piece of music, *sonata*; *rond-o, -eau*; *pastorale, cavatina*, roulade, *fantasia, toccata, concerto*, overture, symphony, symphonic poem, tone poem, prelude, voluntary, *intermezzo*, variations, *cadenza*; cadence; fugue, canon, serenade, *nocturne, notturno*, rhapsody, romance, *aubade*, dithyramb; opera, operetta; oratorio; composition, movement; stave.

instrumental music; full-, orchestral- score; minstrelsy, tweedledum and tweedledee, band, orchestra &c. 416; concerted piece, *potpourri*, medley, *capriccio*, incidental music; improvisation; peal.

vocal music, vocalism; chaunt, chant; psalm, -ody; hymn; song &c. (*poem*) 597; canticle, canzonet, *cantata, bravura, coloratura*; lay, ballad, ditty, carol, barcarolle, pastoral, recitative, *recitativo, solfeggio*, tonic sol-fa.

Lydian measures; slow -music, – movement; *adagio* &c. *adv.*; minuet; siren strains, soft music, lullaby; *berceuse*, cradle song, dump; dirge &c. (*lament*) 839; pibroch; martial music, march, funeral-, dead- march; dance music; waltz &c. (*dance*) 840; rag-time, syncopation, jazz.

solo, duet, *duo, trio*; quartet; quintet, sextet, septet; part song, descant, glee, madrigal, catch, round, chorus, *chorale*; antiphon, -y; accompaniment, second –, alto –, tenor –, bass- part; score, thorough bass; counterpoint.

composer &c. 413; musician &c. 416.

V. compose, perform &c. 416; attune.

Adj. musical; instrumental, orchestral, vocal, choral, lyric, operatic; harmonious &c. 413.

Adv. *adagio; largo, larghetto, andan-te, -tino; alla capella; maestoso, moderato; allegr-o, -etto; spiritoso, vivace, veloce; prest-o, -issimo; pian-o, -issimo, fort-e, -issimo, sforzando; con brio; capriccioso; scherz-o, -ando; legato, sostenuto, staccato, crescendo, diminuendo, rallentando, affettuoso, arioso; parlante, cantabile; obbligato; pizzicato, tremolo, vibrato.*

416. Musician. [Performance of Music.]—**N.** musician, *artiste, virtuoso,* performer, player, minstrel; bard &c. (*poet*) 597; instrumental-, organ-, accompan-, pian-, violin-, flaut-, harp-ist; harper, fiddler, fifer, trumpeter, piper, drummer; catgut scraper.

band, orchestra, waits.

vocal-, melod-ist; singer, warbler; songst-, chaunt-er, -ress; *diva, cantatrice,* coloratura, soprano, mezzo-soprano, alto, contralto, tenor, baritone, bass, *basso, -profondo.*

choir, quire, chorister; chorus, – singer; choral society, festival, *eisteddfod.*

nightingale, philomel, thrush; siren; Orpheus, Apollo, the Muses, Erato, Euterpe, Terpsichore; tuneful -nine, – quire.

composer &c. 413.

performance, virtuosity, execution, touch, expression, solmization.

V. play, pipe, strike –, tune- up, sweep the chords, tickle –, paw- the ivories, vamp, tweedle, fiddle; strike the lyre, beat the drum; blow –, sound –, wind- the horn; grind the organ; touch the -guitar &c. (*instruments*) 417; thrum, strum, twang, drum, beat –, keep- time, conduct.

execute, perform; accompany; sing –, play- a second; compose, write music, set to music, arrange, harmonize, orchestrate.

sing, chaunt, chant, hum, warble, carol, chirp, chirrup, lilt, purl, quaver, trill, shake, twitter, whistle; sol-fa; intone.

have -an ear for music, – a musical ear, – a correct ear, – absolute pitch.

Adj. playing &c. *v.*; musical, lyric.

Adv. *adagio, andante* &c. (*music*) 415.

417. Musical Instruments.—**N.** musical instruments; band; string-, brass-, drum and fife-, military-, bugle-, German-, dance-, jazz-band; orchestra, string quartet; orchestrion, orchestrelle.

[Stringed instruments] mono-, poly-chord; harp, lyre, lute, archlute, theorbo; mandol-a, -in, -ine; guitar; *ukulele;* psaltery, zither; bandore, cither, -n; gittern, rebeck, *bandurria,* banjo, zither banjo, *balalaika, samisen;* plectrum.

viol, -in, Cremona, Stradivarius; fiddle, kit; *vielle, viola, – d'amore, – di gamba;* tenor, *violoncello,* cello; bass, bass-, base-viol; double-bass, *contrabasso, violone,* hurdy-gurdy; strings, catgut; bow, fiddlestick.

piano, -forte; grand –, concert grand –, baby –, upright –, cottage-piano; pianino, pianette; harpsi-, clavi-, clari-, mani-chord; *clavier,* spinet, virginals; dulcimer, *cymbalo;* Eolian harp; piano-organ, -player, electric piano, player-piano, pianola.

[Wind instruments] organ, church –, pipe –, American- organ; harmoni-um, -phon; accordion, seraphina, concertina; melodeon; barrel-organ; humming top.

flute, fife, piccolo, flageolet, penny-whistle, reed instrument; clari-net, -onet; bass clarionet; saxophone; basset horn, *corno di bassetto*; musette, shawm, oboe, hautboy, *cor Anglais, corno Inglese*, bassoon, double bassoon, *contrafagotto*; bag-, union-pipes; ocarina, Pandean pipes; calliope; sirene, pipe, pitch-pipe; sourdet; whistle, catcall.

horn, bugle, key bugle, cornet, *cornet-à-pistons*, cornopean, clarion, trumpet, trombone, ophicleide, serpent; English-, French-, bugle-, sax-, flugel-, alt-, helicon-, post-horn; sackbut, euphonium, bombardon, tuba, bass tuba.

[Vibrating surfaces] cymbal, bell, gong, peal of bells, *carillon*; tambour, -ine; drum, tom-tom, tab-or, -ret, -ourine, -orin; *sistrum*; *grande caisse*, bass-, big-, side-, kettle-drum; *tympani*; war drums; tymbal, timbrel, castanet, bones; musical-glasses, -stones; harmonica, sounding-board, rattle; gramophone, phonograph.

[Vibrating bars] reed, tuning-fork, triangle, Jew's harp, musical box, harmonicon, xylophone, marimba, *celeste*.

sord-ine, -et; *sourd-ine, -et*; mute.

(iv.) PERCEPTION OF SOUND

418. [Sense of sound.] **Hearing.—N.** hearing &c. *v.*; audition, auscultation; eavesdropping; audibility; acoustics &c. 402.

acute -, nice -, delicate -, quick -, sharp -, correct -, musical -ear; ear for music.

ear, auricle, lug, acoustic organs, auditory apparatus, ear-drum, tympanum; ear-, speaking-trumpet, megaphone; telephone, radiophone, stethoscope, phonograph, gramophone, microphone.

hearer, auditor, listener, eavesdropper; audi-tory, -ence.

V. hear, overhear; hark, -en; list, -en; give -, lend -, bend- an ear; give attention; catch a sound, prick up one's ears; give -a hearing, - audience- to.

hang upon the lips of, be all ear, listen with both ears.

become audible; meet -, fall upon -, catch -, reach- the ear; be heard; ring in the ear &c. (*resound*) 408.

Adj. hearing &c. *v.*; auditory, auricular, aural, auditive, acoustic.

Adv. *arrectis auribus.*

Int. hark. - ye! bea-r! list, -en! *Oyez!* attention! lend me your ears!

419. Deafness.—N. deafness, hardness of hearing, surdity; inaudibility.

V. be -deaf &c. *adj.*; have no ear; shut -, stop -, close- one's ears; turn a deaf ear to.

render deaf, stun, deafen.

Adj. deaf, earless, surd; hard -, dull- of hearing; deaf-mute. stunned, deafened; stone deaf; deaf as -a post, - an adder, - a beetle, - a trunk-maker.

inaudible &c. 405; out of hearing.

6. *Light*

(i.) LIGHT IN GENERAL

420. Light.—N. light, ray, beam, stream, gleam, streak, pencil; sun-, moon-beam; dawn, aurora.

day; sunshine; light of -day, - heaven; sun &c. (*luminary*) 423, day-, broad day-, noontide- light; noon-tide, -day; glare.

421. Darkness.—N. darkness &c. *adj.*; blackness &c. (*dark colour*) 431; obscurity, gloom, murk; dusk &c. (*dimness*) 422; tenebrosity, umbrageousness.

Cimmerian -, Stygian -, Egyptian-darkness; night; midnight; dead of -.

glow &c. *v.*; afterglow, sunset; glimmering &c. *v.*; glint; play –, flood- of light; phosphorescence, lambent flame.

flush, halo, glory, nimbus, aureole, *aureola.*

spark, *scintilla*; *facula*; sparkling &c. *v.*; emication, scintillation, flash, blaze, coruscation, fulguration; flame &c. (*fire*) 382; lightning, *ignis fatuus*, &c. (*luminary*) 423, radio-activity.

lustre, sheen, shimmer, reflection; gloss, tinsel, spangle, brightness, brilliancy, splendour; ef-, re-fulgence; ful-gor, -gidity; dazzlement, resplendence, transplendency; luminousness &c. *adj.*; luminosity; lucidity; renitency; radi-ance, -ation; irradiation, illumination, phosphorescence, luminescence.

radiation, radiant heat, infra-red rays, visible radiation, ultra-violet –, actinic- rays, actinism; X –, Roentgen-rays; phot-, heli-ography; optical instruments &c. 445.

[Science of light] optics; photo-logy, -metry; di-, cat-optrics.

[Distribution of light] *chiaroscuro, clair-obscur,* clear-obscure, breadth, light and shade, black and white, tonality, half-tone, mezzotint.

reflection, refraction, dispersion, double refraction, polarization, diffraction, interference.

illuminant &c. 423.

V. shine, glow, glitter, phosphoresce; glis-ter, -ten; twinkle, gleam; flare, – up; glare, beam, shimmer, glimmer, flicker, sparkle, scintillate, coruscate, flash, fulgurate, blaze; be -bright &c. *adj.*; reflect light, daze, dazzle, bedazzle, radiate, shoot out beams.

clear up, brighten.

lighten, enlighten; light, – up; irradiate, shine upon; give –, hang out- a light; cast –, throw –, shed- -lustre, – light- upon; illum-e, -ine, -inate; relume, strike a light; kindle &c. (*set fire to*) 384.

Adj. shining &c. *v.*; lumin-ous, -iferous; luc-id, -ent, -ulent, -ific, -iferous; illuminating, light, -some; bright, vivid, splendent, nitid, lustrous, shiny, brilliant, beamy, scintillant, radiant, lambent; sheen, -y; glossy,

witching time of- night; blind man's holiday; darkness -visible, – that can be felt; palpable, obscure; Erebus.

shade, shadow, umbra, penumbra; sciagraphy; *silhouette*; radiograph, skiagraph.

obscuration; ad-, ob-umbration; obtenebration, offuscation, caligation; extinction; eclipse, total eclipse; gathering of the clouds.

shading; distribution of shade; *chiaroscuro* &c. (*light*) 420.

noctivagation, noctograph, noctuary; obscurantist.

V. be -dark &c. *adj.*

darken, obscure, shade; dim; tone down, lower; over-cast, -shadow; cloud, eclipse; ob-, of-fuscate; ob-, ad-umbrate, cast into the shade; be-cloud, -dim, -darken; cast –, throw –, spread- a -shade, – shadow, – gloom.

extinguish; put –, blow –, snuff- out; doubt.

Adj. dark, -some, -ling; obscure, tenebrous, tenebrious, sombrous, pitch dark, pitchy; caliginous; black &c. (*in colour*) 431.

sunless, lightless &c. (*see* sun, light, &c. 423); sombre, dusky; unilluminated &c. (*see* illuminate &c. 420); nocturnal; dingy, lurid, gloomy; murk-y, -some; shady, umbrageous; overcast &c. (*dim*) 422; cloudy &c. (*opaque*) 426; darkened &c. *v.*

dark as -pitch, – a pit, – Erebus.

benighted; noctivag-ant, -ous.

Adv. in the -dark, – shade; at night.

422. Dimness.—N. dimness &c. *adj.*; darkness &c. 421; paleness &c. (*light colour*) 429.

half-light, *demi-jour*; partial -shadow, – eclipse; shadow of a shade; glimmer, -ing; nebulosity; cloud &c. 353; eclipse.

aurora, dusk, twilight, gloaming, blind man's holiday, shades of evening, crepuscule, cockshut time; break of day, daybreak, dawn.

moon-light, -beam, -shine; star-, owl's-, candle-, rush-, fire-light; farthing candle.

V. be –, grow- -dim &c. *adj.*; flicker, twinkle, glimmer; loom, lower; fade; darken; pale, – its ineffectual fire.

burnished, glassy, sunny, orient, meridian; noon-day, -tide; cloudless, clear; un-clouded, -obscured.

garish; re-, tran-splendent; re-, effulgent; ful-gid, -gent; relucent, splendid, blazing, in a blaze, ablaze, rutilant, meteoric, phosphorescent; aglow.

bright as silver; light -, bright- as -day, - noonday, - the sun at noonday.

optical, actinic; photo-genic, -graphic; heliographic, radioactive.

423. [Source of light &c.] **Luminary.** —**N.** luminary; light &c. 420; flame &c. (*fire*) 382.

spark, *scintilla*; phosphorescence.

sun, orb of day, day star, Phœbus, Apollo, Helios, Phaethon, Hyperion, Ra, Aurora; star, orb, meteor; falling -, shooting- star; blazing -, dog- star; Sirius, canicula, Aldebaran; morning star, Lucifer, Phosphor, evening star; Hesperus, Venus, planet, moon &c. 318; constellation, galaxy; northern light, *aurora -borealis*, - *australis*, zodiacal light; mock sun, parhelion.

lightning; fork -, sheet -, summer- lightning, St. Elmo's fire; phosphorus; *ignis fatuus*; Jack o' -, Friar's- lantern; Will o' the wisp, fire-drake, *Fata Morgana*.

glow-worm, fire-fly.

radium, luminous paint.

[Artificial light] gas; gas -, lime -, electric -, head -, search -, spot -, flash -, flood -, foot-light; lamp, oil -, gas -, arc -, incandescent- lamp; flare; lant-ern, -horn; dark lantern, bull's eye, projector; candle, *bougie*, tallow -, wax- candle; dip, farthing dip; taper, rush-light; oil &c. (*grease*) 356; wick, burner; Argand, moderator, duplex; torch, *flambeau*, link, brand; cresset; gase-, chande-, electro-lier; candelabrum, *girandole*, sconce, lustre, candle-stick.

firework, fizgig; pyrotechnics; Roman candle, Véry light, star shell, parachute light; rocket, lighthouse &c. (*signal*) 550.

V. illuminate &c. (*light*) 420.

Adj. self-luminous, incandescent; phosphor-ic, -escent; luminescent, fluorescent, radiant &c. (*light*) 420.

render -dim &c. *adj.*; dim, bedim, obscure.

Adj. dim, dull, lack-lustre, dingy, darkish, shorn of its beams; dark 421.

faint, shadowed forth; glassy; bleary; cloudy; misty &c. (*opaque*) 426; muggy, fuliginous; nebul-ous, -ar; obnubilated, overcast, crepuscular, twilight, muddy, lurid, leaden, dun, dirty; looming &c. *v.*

pale &c. (*colourless*) 429; confused &c. (*invisible*) 447.

424. Shade.—N. shade; awning &c. (*cover*) 223; parasol, sunshade, umbrella; screen, curtain, shutter, blind, gauze, veil, mantle, mask; cloud, mist, gathering of clouds; smoke screen; smoked glasses, coloured spectacles; blinkers, blinders.

umbrage, glade; shadow &c. 421.

V. draw a curtain; put up -, close- a shutter; veil &c. *v.*; cast a shadow &c. (*darken*) 421; screen, obstruct the view.

Adj. shady, umbrageous, bowery.

425. Transparency. — N. transparen-ce, -cy; translucen-ce, -cy; diaphaneity; luc-, pelluc-, limp-idity.

transparent medium, glass, crystal, mica; lymph, water.

V. be -transparent &c. *adj.*; transmit light.

Adj. transparent, pellucid, lucid, diaphanous; trans-, tra-lucent; limpid, clear, serene, crystalline, clear as crys-

426. Opacity.—N. opacity; opaqueness &c. *adj.*

film; cloud &c. 353.

V. be -opaque &c. *adj.*; obstruct the passage of light; ob-, of-fuscate.

Adj. opaque, impervious to light.

dim &c. 422; turbid, thick, muddy, opacous, obfuscated, fuliginous, cloudy, hazy, foggy, vaporous, nubiferous, muggy.

tal, vitreous, transpicuous, glassy, hyaline.

smoky, fumid, murky, dirty.

---

427. Semitransparency.—N. semi-transparency, opalescence, milkiness, pearliness; gauze, muslin; film; mist &c. (*cloud*) 353; frosted glass.

Adj. semi-transparent, -pellucid, -diaphanous, -opacous, -opaque; opal-escent, -ine; pearly, milky, frosted, mat; misty.

(ii.) SPECIFIC LIGHT

428. Colour.—N. colour, hue, tint, tinge, dye, complexion, shade, tincture, cast, livery, coloration, chromatism, glow, flush; tone, key.

pure -, positive -, primary -, primitive -, complementary- colour; three primaries; spectrum, chromatic dispersion; broken -, secondary -, tertiary-colour.

local colour, colouring, keeping, tone, value, aerial perspective.

[Science of colour] chromatics, spectrum analysis; prism, spectroscope.

pigment, colouring matter, paint, dye, wash, distemper, stain; medium; mordant; oil-paint &c. (*painting*) 556.

V. colour, dye, tinge, stain, tint, tinct, tone, paint, wash, ingrain, grain, illuminate, emblazon, imbue; paint &c. (*fine art*) 556; daub.

Adj. coloured &c. *v.*; colorific, tingent, tinctorial; chromatic, prismatic; full-, high-, deep-coloured; doubly-dyed; polychromatic.

bright, vivid, intense, deep; fresh, unfaded; rich, gorgeous; highly coloured; gay; variegated &c. 440.

gaudy, florid; garish; showy, flaunting, flashy; raw, crude; glaring, flaring; discordant, inharmonious.

mellow, harmonious, pearly, sweet, delicate, tender, refined.

429. [Absence of colour.] Achromatism.—N. achromatism; de-, discoloration; pall-or, -idity; paleness &c. *adj.*; etiolation; neutral tint, monochrome, black-and-white.

V. lose -colour &c. 428; fade, fly, go; become -colourless &c. *adj.*; turn pale, pale, whiten.

deprive of colour, decolorize, bleach, tarnish, achromatize, blanch, etiolate, wash out, tone down.

Adj. uncoloured &c. (*see* colour &c. 428); colourless, achromatic, hueless, pale, pallid; pale-, tallow-faced; faint, dull, cold, muddy, leaden, dun, wan, sallow, dead, dingy, ashy, ashen, ghastly, cadaverous, glassy, lack-lustre; discoloured &c. *v.*

light-coloured, fair, *blond*; white &c. 430.

pale as -death, - ashes, - a witch, - a ghost, - a corpse.

---

430. Whiteness.—N. whiteness &c. *adj.*; argent.

albification, albescence, albinism, etiolation.

snow, paper, chalk, milk, lily, ivory, silver, alabaster; white lead, chinese -, flake-, ivory -, zinc- white, white-wash, -ning, whiting.

V. be -white &c. *adj.*

render -white &c. *adj.*; whiten-bleach, blanch, etiolate, whitewash, silver, frost.

Adj. white; milky, milk-, snow-white; snowy, niveous, candid, chalky; hoar,

431. Blackness.—N. blackness &c. *adj.*; darkness &c. (*want of light*) 421; swarthness, lividity, dark colour, tone, colour; *chiaroscuro* &c. 420.

nigrification, infuscation, denigration.

jet, ink, ebony, coal, pitch, soot, smudge, charcoal, sloe, raven, crow; negro, blackamoor, man of colour, nigger, darky, Ethiopian, black.

[Pigments] lamp -, ivory -, blue-black; writing -, printing -, printer's -, Indian- ink.

V. be -black &c. *adj.*

-y; frosted, silvery; argent, -ine; canescent.

whitish, creamy, pearly, ivory, fair, *blond*, ash-blond, platinum blond; blanched &c. *v.*; high in tone, light.

white as -a sheet, – driven snow, – a lily – silver; like -ivory &c. *n.*

render -black &c. *adj.*; blacken, infuscate, denigrate; blot, -ch; smutch; smirch; darken &c. 421.

Adj. black, sable, swarthy, sombre, dark, inky, ebon, atramentous, jetty; coal-, jet-black; fuliginous, pitchy, sooty, swart, dusky, dingy, murky, Ethiopic; low-toned, low in tone; of the deepest dye.

black as -jet &c. *n.*, – my hat, – a shoe, – a tinker's pot, – November, – thunder, – midnight; nocturnal &c. (*dark*) 421; nigrescent; gray &c. 432; obscure &c. 421.

Adv. in mourning.

432. Gray.—N. gray &c. *adj.*; neutral tint, silver, pepper and salt, *chiaroscuro, grisaille*, grayness.

[Pigments] Payne's gray; black &c. 431.

Adj. gray, grey; steel –, iron- gray, dun, drab, dingy, leaden, livid, sombre, sad, pearly; silver, -y, -ed; ash-en, -y; ciner-eous, -itious; grizzl-y, -ed; dove-, slate-, stone-, mouse-, ash-coloured; mole; cool.

433. Brown.—N. brown &c. *adj.* [Pigments] bistre, ochre, sepia, Vandyke brown.

Adj. brown, adust, bay, dapple, auburn, chestnut, nutbrown, cinnamon, hazel, fawn, puce, *écru*, russet, tawny, fuscous, chocolate, maroon, foxy, tan, brunette, whitey-brown; snuff-, liver-coloured; brown as -a berry, – mahogany; reddish brown; copper-, rust- coloured; henna, bronze, khaki; roan, sorrel.

sun-burnt; tanned &c. *v.*

V. render -brown &c. *adj.*; tan, embrown, bronze.

Primitive Colours*

434. Redness.—N. red, scarlet, vermilion, cardinal, Post Office red, carmine, crimson, pink, lake, *cerise*, cherry red, maroon, carnation, *couleur de rose*, *rose du Barry*; magenta, damask; flesh -colour, – tint; colour; fresh –, high-colour; warmth; gules.

ruby, garnet, carbuncle; rose; rust, iron-mould.

[Dyes and pigments] cinnabar, cochineal; fuchsine; ruddle, madder, red-lead; Indian –, light –, Venetian- red; red ink, annotto.

redness &c. *adj.*; rub-escence, -icundity, -ification; erubescence, blush.

V. be –, become- -red &c. *adj.*; blush, flush, colour up, mantle, redden.

render -red &c. *adj.*; redden, rouge; rub-ify, -ricate; incarnadine; ruddle.

Adj. red &c. *n.*, -dish; rufous, ruddy, florid, incarnadine, sanguine, bloody, gory; ros-y, -eate; blowz-y, -ed; burnt; rubi-cund, -form;

Complementary Colours

435. Greenness.—N. green &c. *adj.*; blue and yellow; vert.

emerald, verd antique, verdigris, malachite, beryl, aquamarine, reseda.

[Pigments] *terre verte*, verditer, bice-chlorophyl.

greenness, verdure, verdancy; viridity, -escence.

Adj. green, verdant; glaucous, olive; porraceous; green as grass.

emerald –, pea –, grass –, apple –, sea –, olive –, bottle –, leaf- green.

greenish; vir-ent, -escent.

* The author's classification of colours has been retained, though it does not entirely accord with the theories of modern science: Complete lists of shades or pigments are beyond the scope of this work.

lurid, stammel, blood-red; russet, murrey, carroty, sorrel, lateritious.

rose-, ruby-, cherry-, claret-, wine-, plum-, flame-, flesh-, peach-, salmon-, brick-, brickdust-coloured, reddish brown &c. 433.

blushing &c. *v.*; erubescent; reddened &c. *v.*

red as -fire, – blood, – scarlet, – a turkeycock, – a lobster; warm, hot; foxy.

436. Yellowness.—N. yellow &c. *adj.*; or.

[Pigments] gamboge; cadmium –, chrome –, Indian –, lemon- yellow; orpiment, yellow ochre, Claude tint, aureolin.

crocus, saffron, topaz, gold.

jaundice; London fog; yellowness &c. *adj.*

Adj. yellow, aureate, gold, golden, gilt, gilded, flavous, citrine, fallow; fulv-ous, -id; sallow, luteous, tawny, creamy, sandy; xanth-ic, -ous; jaundiced.

gold-, citron-, saffron-, lemon-, sulphur-, amber-, straw-, primrose-, cream-coloured; flaxen, yellowish, buff.

yellow as a -quince, – guinea, – crow's foot.

437. Purple.—N. purple &c. *adj.*; blue and red, bishop's purple; aniline dyes, gridelin, amethyst; purpure.

livid-ness, -ity.

V. empurple.

Adj. purple, violet, plum-coloured. lavender, lilac, puce, *mauve*; livid.

438. Blueness.—N. blue &c. *adj.*; garter-blue; watchet.

[Pigments] ultramarine, smalt, cobalt, cyanogen; Prussian –, syenite-blue; bice, indigo, woad.

lapis lazuli, sapphire, turquoise.

blue-, bluish-ness; bloom.

Adj. blue, azure, cerulean; sky-blue, -coloured, -dyed; navy-blue, aquamarine, electric blue, royal blue, cyanic; bluish; atmospheric, retiring; cold.

439. Orange.—N. orange, red and yellow; gold; or; flame &c. colour, *adj.*

[Pigments] ochre, Mars orange, cadmium.

V. gild, warm.

Adj. orange; ochreous; orange-, gold-, flame-, copper-, brass-, apricot-coloured; warm, hot, glowing.

440. Variegation.—N. variegation; di-, tri-chroism; iridescence, irisation, play of colours, polychrome, maculation, spottiness, striæ.

spectrum, rainbow, iris, tulip, peacock, chameleon, butterfly, tortoise-shell; mackerel, – sky; zebra, leopard, mother-of-pearl, nacre, opal, marble, batik.

check, plaid, tartan, patchwork; mar-, par-quetry; mosaic, *tesseræ,* tesselation, chess-board, checkers, chequers; harlequin; Joseph's coat; tricolour; patches, bands, stripes, spots &c. of colour.

V. be -variegated &c. *adj.*; variegate, stripe, streak, checker, chequer; be-, speckle, fleck; be-, sprinkle; stipple, maculate, dot, bespot; tattoo, inlay, tesselate, damascene; embroider, braid, quilt.

Adj. variegated &c. *v.*; many-coloured, -hued; divers-, parti-coloured; di-, poly-chromatic; bi-, tri-, versi-colour; of all -the colours of the rainbow, – manner of colours; kaleidoscopic.

iridescent; opal-ine, -escent; prismatic, nacreous, pearly, shot, *gorge de pigeon, chatoyant,* irisated.

pied, piebald, skewbald; motley; mottled, marbled; pepper and salt, paned, dappled, clouded, cymophanous.

mosaic, tesselated, chequered, plaid; tortoiseshell &c. *n.*

spott-ed, -y; punctated, powdered; speckled &c. *v.*; freckled, flea-bitten, studded; fleck-ed, -ered; striated, barred, veined; brind-ed, -led; tabby; watered; grizzled; listed; embroidered &c. *v.*; dædal.

(iii.) PERCEPTIONS OF LIGHT

441. Vision.—N. vision, sight, optics, eye-sight.

view, look, espial, glance, ken, *coup d'œil*; glimpse, peep, glint; gaze, stare, leer; perlustration, contemplation; conspect-ion, -uity; regard, survey; in-, intro-spection; *reconnaissance*, speculation, watch, espionage, *espionnage*, autopsy; ocular -inspection, – demonstration; sight-seeing.

macrography, micrography.

point of view; view-, stand-point; gazebo, loop-hole, *belvedere*, watchtower.

field of view; theatre, amphitheatre, arena, vista, horizon; commanding –, bird's eye –, panoramic- view; periscope.

visual organ, organ of vision; eye; naked –, unassisted- eye; eye-ball, retina, pupil, iris, cornea, white; optics, orbs; saucer –, goggle –, gooseberry-eyes.

short sight &c. 443; clear –, sharp –, quick –, eagle –, piercing –, penetrating–sight, – glance, – eye; perspicacity, discernment; catopsis.

eagle, hawk; cat, lynx; Argus.

evil eye; basilisk, cockatrice.

spectacles, telescope &c. 445.

V. see, behold, discern, perceive, have in sight, descry, sight, make out, discover, distinguish, recognize, spy, espy, ken; get –, have –, catch- a -sight, – glimpse- of; command a view of; witness, contemplate, speculate; cast –, set- the eyes on; be a -spectator &c. 444- of; look on &c. (*be present*) 186; see sights &c. (*curiosity*) 455; see at a glance &c. (*intelligence*) 498.

look, view, eye; lift up the eyes, open one's eye; look -at, – on, – upon, – over, – about one, – round; survey, scan, inspect; run the eye -over, – through; reconnoitre, glance -round, – on, – over; turn –, bend- one's looks upon; direct the eyes to, turn the eyes on, cast a glance, make eyes at.

observe &c. (*attend to*) 457; watch &c. (*care*) 459; see with one's own eyes; watch for &c. (*expect*) 507; peek, peep, peer, pry, take a peep; play at bo-peep.

look -full in the face, – hard at, – intently; strain one's eyes; fix –, rivet- the eyes upon; stare, gaze; pore over, gloat -over, – on; leer, ogle, glare; goggle; cock the eye, squint, gloat, look askance; give the glad eye.

Adj. seeing &c. *v.*; visual, ocular, -al; ophthalmic.

far-, clear-sighted &c. *n.*; eagle-, hawk-, lynx-, keen-, Argus-eyed visible &c. 446.

442. Blindness.—N. blindness, anopsia, cecity, excecation, *amaurosis*, cataract, ablepsy, prestriction; dim-sightedness &c. 443.

V. be -blind &c. *adj.*; not see; lose sight of; have the eyes bandaged; grope in the dark.

not look; close –, shut –, turn away –, avert- the eyes; look another way; wink &c. (*limited vision*) 443; shut the eyes –, be blind- to; wink –, blink- at.

render -blind &c. *adj.*; blind, -fold; hoodwink, dazzle; put one's eyes out; throw dust into one's eyes; *jeter de la poudre aux yeux*; screen from sight &c. (*hide*) 528.

Adj. blind; eye-, sight-, vision-less; dark; stone-, sand-, stark-blind; undiscerning; dim-sighted &c. 443.

blind as -a bat, – a buzzard, – a beetle, – a mole, – an owl; wall-eyed.

blinded &c. *v.*

Adv. blind-ly, -fold; darkly.

Adv. visibly &c. 446; in sight of, with one's eyes open.

at -sight, – first sight, – a glance, – the first blush; *primâ facie*.

Int. look! &c. (*attention*) 457.

Phr. the scales falling from one's eyes.

443. [Imperfect vision.] Dim-sightedness. [Fallacies of vision.]—**N.** dim –, dull –, half –, short –, near –, long –, double –, astigmatic –, failing- sight; dim &c. -sightedness; snow blindness; purblindness, lippitude; my-, presby-opia; confusion of vision; astigmatism, nystagmus; colour-blindness, dichromism, chromato-pseudo-blepsis, Daltonism; nyctalopy; *strabismus*, strabism, squint, cast in the eye, swivel eye, goggle eyes; obliquity of vision.

winking &c. *v.*; nictitation; blinkard, albino.

dizziness, swimming, scotomy; cataract; ophthalmia.

[Limitation of vision] eye shade, blinker, blinder; screen &c. (*hider*) 530.

[Fallacies of vision] *deceptio visûs*; refraction, distortion, illusion, false light, *anamorphosis*, virtual image, *spectrum*, *mirage*, looming, phasma; phant-asm, -asma, -om; vision; spectre, apparition, ghost; *ignis fatuus* &c. (*luminary*) 423; spectre of the Brocken; magic mirror; magic lantern &c. (*show*) 448; mirror, lens &c. (*instrument*) 445.

V. be -dim-sighted &c. *n.*; see double; have a -mote in the eye, – mist before the eyes, – film over the eyes; see through a -prism, – glass darkly; wink, blink, nictitate; squint; look ask-ant, -ance; screw up the eyes, glare, glower.

dazzle, glare, blur, swim, loom.

Adj. dim-sighted &c. *n.*; my-, presby-opic; astigmatic; moon-, mope-, blear-, goggle-, gooseberry-, one-eyed; blind of one eye, monoculous; half-, pur-, colour-blind; dichromatic.

blind as a bat &c. (*blind*) 442; winking &c. *v.*

444. Spectator.—**N.** spectator, beholder, observer, inspector, viewer, looker-on, onlooker, witness, eye-witness, bystander, passer by; sight-seer.

spy, scout; sentinel &c. (*warning*) 668.

V. witness, behold &c. (*see*) 441; look on &c. (*be present*) 186.

445. Optical Instruments.—**N.** optical instruments; lens, meniscus, magnifier, reading –, burning- glass; micro-, mega-, teino-scope; spectacles, glasses, barnacles, goggles, giglamps, eyeglass, *pince-nez*, monocle; periscopic lens; telescope, glass, lorgnette, binocular; spy-, opera-, field-glass, periscope, range finder.

mirror, reflector, speculum; looking-, pier-, cheval-, hand-glass.

prism; camera, *camera-lucida*, *-obscura*; projector, stereopticon, magic lantern &c. (*show*) 448; chro-, thau-matrope; stereo-, pseudo-, poly-, kaleido-scope.

photo-, opto-, erio-, actino-, luci-, radio-, spectro-meter; polari-, polemo-, spectro-scope, diffraction grating.

optics, optician, optometry, optometrist; microscop-y, -ist; photometry, photography; photographer.

446. Visibility.—**N.** visibility, perceptibility; conspicuousness, distinctness &c. *adj.*; conspicuity; appearance &c. 448; exposure; manifestation &c. 525; ocular -proof, – evidence, – demonstration; field of view &c. (*vision*) 441.

447. Invisibility.—**N.** invisibility, non-appearance, imperceptibility; indistinctness &c. *adj.*; mystery, delitescence.

concealment &c. 528; latency &c. 526.

V. be -, become- -visible &c. *adj.*; appear, emerge, open to the view; meet -, catch- the eye; present -, show -, manifest -, produce -, discover -, reveal -, expose -, betray-itself; stand -forth, - out; show; arise; peep -, peer -, crop- out; start -, spring -, show -, turn -, crop- up; glimmer, glitter, glow, loom; glare; burst forth, scintillate; burst upon the -view, - sight; heave in sight; come -in sight, - into view, - out, - forth, - forward; see the light of day; break through the clouds; make its appearance, show its face, materialize, appear to one's eyes, come upon the stage, enter; float before the eyes, speak for *itself* &c. (*manifest*) 525; attract the attention &c. 457; reappear; live in a glass house.

expose to view &c. 525.

Adj. visible, perceptible, perceivable, discernible, apparent; in -view, - full view, - sight; exposed to view, *en évidence*; unclouded.

obvious &c. (*manifest*) 525; plain, clear, distinct, definite; well-defined, -marked; in focus; recognizable, palpable, autoptical; glaring, staring, conspicuous; stereoscopic; in -bold, - strong, - high- relief.

periscopic, panoramic.

before -, under- one's eyes; before one, *à vue d'œil*, in one's eye, *oculis subjecta fidelibus.*

Adv. visibly &c. *adj.*; in sight of; before one's eyes &c. *adj.*; *veluti in speculum.*

V. be -invisible &c. *adj.*; be hidden &c. (*hide*) 528; lurk &c. (*lie hidden*) 526; escape notice.

render -invisible &c. *adj* ; conceal &c. 528; put out of sight.

not see &c. (*be blind*) 442; lose sight of.

Adj. invisible, imperceptible; un-, in-discernible; un-, non-apparent; out of -, not in- sight; *à perte de vue*; behind the -scenes, - curtain; view-, sight-less; in-, un-conspicuous; unseen &c. (*see* see &c. 441); covert &c. (*latent*) 526; eclipsed, under an eclipse.

dim &c. (*faint*) 422; mysterious, dark, obscure, confused; indistin-ct, -guishable; shadowy, indefinite, undefined; ill-defined, -marked; blurred, fuzzy, out of focus; misty &c. (*opaque*) 426; veiled &c. (*concealed*) 528; delitescent.

---

448. Appearance.—N. appearance, phenomenon, sight, spectacle, show, premonstration, scene, species, view, *coup d'œil*; look-out, out-look, prospect, vista, perspective, bird's-eye view, scenery, landscape, picture, *tableau*; display, exposure, *mise en scène*; scenery, *décor*; rising of the curtain.

phant-asm, -om &c. (*fallacy of vision*) 443.

pageant, *spectacle*; peep-, raree-, gallanty-show; *ombres chinoises*; projector, optical -, magic- lantern, phantasmagoria, dissolving views; cinema, -tograph; bio-scope. -graph; moving pictures, movies, film, screen &c.; pan-, di-, cosm-, ge-orama; *coup -, jeu- de théâtre*; pageantry &c. (*ostentation*) 882; insignia &c. (*indication*) 550.

aspect, phase, *phasis*, seeming; shape &c. (*form*) 240; guise, look,

449. Disappearance.—N. disappearance, evanescence, eclipse, occultation.

departure &c. 293; exit, vanishing point; dissolving views.

V. disappear, vanish, dissolve, fade, melt away, pass, go, avaunt; be -gone &c. *adj.*; leave -no trace, - 'not a rack behind'; go off the stage &c. (*depart*) 293; suffer -, undergo- an eclipse; be lost to -, retire from- -sight, - view.

lose sight of.

efface &c. 552.

Adj. disappearing &c. *v.*; evanescent; missing, lost; lost to -sight, - view; gone; *spurlos versenkt.*

Int. vanish! disappear! avaunt! &c. (*ejection*) 297.

---

complexion, colour, image, mien, air, cast, carriage, port, demeanour; presence, expression, first blush, face of the thing; point of view, light.

lineament, feature, trait, lines; out-line, -side; contour, *silhouette*, face, countenance, physiognomy, visage, phiz, mug, cast of countenance, profile, *tournure*, cut of one's jib, metoposcopy; outside &c. 220.

V. appear; be –, become- visible &c. 446; seem, look, show; present –, wear –, carry –, have –, bear –, exhibit –, take –, take on –, assume- the -appearance, – semblance- of; look like; cut a figure, figure; present to the view; show &c. (*make manifest*) 525.

Adj. apparent, seeming, ostensible; on view.

Adv. apparently; to all -seeming, – appearance; ostensibly, seemingly, as it seems, on the face of it, *primâ facie*; at the first blush, at first sight; in the eyes of; to the eye.

CLASS IV

WORDS RELATING TO THE INTELLECTUAL FACULTIES

DIVISION (I.) FORMATION OF IDEAS

Section I. OPERATIONS OF INTELLECT IN GENERAL

450. Intellect.—N. intellect, mind, understanding, reason, thinking principle; rationality; cogitative -, cognitive -, intellectual- faculties; faculties, senses, consciousness, observation, percipience, apperception, mentality, intelligence, intellection, intuition, association of ideas, instinct, flair, conception, judgement, wits, parts, capacity, intellectuality, reasoning power, brains, genius; wit &c. 498; ability &c. (*skill*) 698; wisdom &c. 498.

soul, spirit, ghost, inner man, heart, breast, bosom, *penetralia mentis, divina particula auræ,* heart's core; ego, psyche, pneuma, subconsciousness, subconscious, subliminal self; dual personality.

organ -, seat- of thought; *sensorium,* sensory, brain, gray matter; head, -piece; pate, noddle, skull, scull, *pericranium, cerebrum, cranium,* brain-pan, -box; sconce, upper story.

[Science of mind] metaphysics; psychics, psycho-logy, -metry, -genesis, -analysis, -physics, psychi-atry, -cal research, thought reading &c. 992; ideology; mental -, moral- philosophy; philosophy of the mind; pneumat-, phren-ology; no -, cranio-logy, -scopy.

ideal-ity, -ism; transcendental-, spiritual-ism; immateriality &c. 317.

metaphysician, psychologist &c.

V. note, notice, mark; take -notice, - cognizance- of; be -aware, - conscious- of; realize; appreciate; ruminate &c. (*think*) 451; fancy &c. (*imagine*) 515; conceive, reason, understand.

Adj. [Relating to intellect] intellectual, mental, rational, subjective, metaphysical, nooscopic, spiritual; ghostly; psych-ical, -ological; cerebral.

immaterial &c. 317; endowed with reason.

Adv. *in petto.*

450a. Absence or want of Intellect.—N. absence -, want- of -intellect &c. 450; imbecility &c. 499; brutality; brute -instinct, - force.

Adj. unendowed with reason.

———

451. Thought.—N. thought; exercitation -, exercise- of the intellect; reflection, cogitation, consideration, meditation, study, lucubration, speculation, deliberation, pondering; head-,

452. [Absence or want of thought.] Incogitancy.—N. incogitancy, vacancy, inunderstanding; inanity, fatuity &c. 499; thoughtlessness &c. (*inattention*) 458.

brain-work; cerebration; mentation, deep reflection; close study, application &c. (*attention*) 457.

abstract thought, abstraction, contemplation, musing; brown study &c. (*inattention*) 458; reverie, Platonism; depth of thought, workings of the mind, thoughts, inmost thoughts; self-counsel, -communing, -consultation.

association –, succession –, flow –, train –, current- of -thought, – ideas.

after –, mature- thought; reconsideration, second thoughts; retrospection &c. (*memory*) 505; excogitation; examination &c. (*inquiry*) 461; invention &c. (*imagination*) 515.

thoughtfulness &c. *adj.*

V. think, reflect, reason, cogitate, excogitate, consider, deliberate; bestow -thought, – consideration- upon; speculate, contemplate, meditate, ponder, muse, dream, ruminate; brood –, con- over; animadvert, study; bend –, apply- the mind &c. (*attend*) 457; digest, discuss, hammer at, weigh, perpend; realize, appreciate; fancy &c. (*imagine*) 515; trow.

take into consideration; take counsel &c. (*be advised*) 695; commune with –, bethink- oneself; collect one's thoughts; revolve –, turn over –, run over- in the mind; chew the cud –, sleep- upon; take counsel of –, advise with- one's pillow.

rack –, ransack –, crack –, beat –, cudgel- one's brains; set one's -brain, – wits- to work.

harbour –, entertain –, cherish –, nurture- an -idea &c. 453; take into one's head; bear in mind; reconsider.

occur; present –, suggest- itself; come –, get- into one's head; strike one, flit across the view, come uppermost, run in one's head; enter –, pass in –, cross –, flash on –, flash across –, float in –, fasten itself on –, be uppermost in –, occupy- the mind; have in one's mind.

make an impression; sink –, penetrate- into the mind; engross the thoughts.

Adj. thinking &c. *v.*; thoughtful, pensive, meditative, reflective, cogitative, museful, wistful, contemplative, speculative, deliberative, studious, sedate, introspective, Platonic, philosophical.

lost –, engrossed –, rapt –, absorbed- in thought &c. (*inattentive*) 458; deep musing &c. (*intent*) 457.

in the mind, under consideration, in contemplation.

Adv. all things considered; taking everything into account.

Phr. the mind being on the stretch; the -mind, – head- -turning, running- upon.

V. not -think &c. 451; not think of; dismiss from the -mind, – thoughts &c. 451.

indulge in reverie &c. (*be inattentive*) 458.

put away thought; unbend –, relax –, divert- the mind.

Adj. vacant, unintellectual, unideal, unoccupied, unthinking, inconsiderate, thoughtless; absent &c. (*inattentive*) 458; diverted; irrational &c. 499; narrow-minded &c. 481.

un-thought of, -dreamt of, -considered; off one's mind; incogitable, not to be thought of, inconceivable.

---

453. [Object of thought.] **Idea.**—**N.** idea, notion, conception, thought, apprehension, impression, perception, image, sentiment, reflection, observation, consideration; abstract idea, principle; archetype.

view &c. (*opinion*) 484; theory &c.

454. [Subject of thought.] **Topic.**— **N.** subject of –, material for- thought; food for the mind, mental *pabulum*.

subject, -matter; matter, theme, topic, what it is about, *thesis*, text, business, affair, matter in hand, argument; motion, resolution; head, chap-

514; conceit, fancy; phantasy &c. (*imagination*) 515.

point of view &c. (*aspect*) 448; field of view.

———

ter; case, point; proposition, theorem; field of inquiry; moot point, problem, &c. (*question*) 461.

V. float –, pass- in the mind &c. 451.

Adj. thought of; uppermost in the mind; *in petto*.

Adv. under -discussion, – consideration, – advisement; in -question, – the mind; on -foot, – the carpet, – the *tapis*; before the house, relative to &c. 9.

Section II. PRECURSORY CONDITIONS AND OPERATIONS

455. [The desire of knowledge.] **Curiosity.** — **N.** interest, thirst for knowledge; curi-osity, -ousness; inquiring mind; inquisitiveness.

sight-seer, quidnunc, newsmonger, Paul Pry, peeping Tom, eavesdropper; gossip &c. (*news*) 532; questioner, *enfant terrible*.

V. be -curious &c. *adj.*; take an interest in, stare, gape; prick up the ears, see sights, lionize; pry, speer; dig up.

Adj. curious, inquisitive, burning with curiosity, overcurious, nosey; inquiring &c. 461; prying; inquisitorial; agape &c. (*expectant*) 507; attentive &c. 457.

Phr. what's the matter? what next?

456. [Absence of curiosity.] **Incuriosity.**—**N.** incuriosity; incuriousness &c. *adj.*; *insouciance* &c. 866; indifference, apathy.

V. be -incurious &c. *adj.*; have no -curiosity &c. 455; take no interest in &c. 823; mind one's own business.

Adj. incurious, uninquisitive, uninterested, indifferent, bored; impassive &c. 823.

———

457. Attention.—**N.** attention; mindfulness &c. *adj.*; intent-ness, -iveness; thought &c. 451; adverten-ce, -cy; observ-ance, -ation; consideration, reflection, perpension; heed; particularity; notice, regard &c. *v.*; circumspection &c. (*care*) 459; study, scrutiny, once-over; in-, intro-spection; revision, -al.

active –, diligent –, exclusive –, minute –, close –, intense –, deep –, profound –, abstract –, laboured –, deliberate- -thought, – attention, – application, – study.

minuteness, attention to detail &c. 459.

absorption of mind &c. (*abstraction*) 458.

indication, calling attention to &c. *v.*

V. be -attentive &c. *adj.*; attend, advert to, observe, look, see, view, remark, notice, regard, take notice, mark; give –, pay- -attention, – heed- to; listen in, incline –, lend- an ear to; trouble one's head about: give a

458. Inattention.—**N.** in-attention, -consideration; inconsiderateness &c. *adj.*; oversight; inadverten-ce, -cy; non-observance, disregard.

supineness &c. (*inactivity*) 683; *étourderie*; want of thought; heedlessness &c. (*neglect*) 460; *insouciance* &c. (*indifference*) 866.

abstraction; absence –, absorption- of mind; preoccupation, distraction, reverie, brown study, deep musing, fit of abstraction, woolgathering.

V. be -inattentive &c. *adj.*; overlook, disregard; pass by &c. (*neglect*) 460; not -observe &c. 457; think little of; close –, shut- one's eyes to; wink at; pay no attention to; dismiss –, discard –, discharge- from one's -thoughts, – mind; drop the subject, think no more of; set –, turn –, put- aside; turn -away from, – one's attention from, – a deaf ear to, – one's back upon.

abstract oneself, dream, indulge in reverie.

escape -notice, – attention; come in

thought –, animadvert- to; occupy oneself with; contemplate &c. (*think of*) 451; look -at, – to, – after, – into, – over; see to; turn –, bend –, apply –, direct –, give- the -mind, – eye, – attention- to; have -an eye to, – in one's eye; bear in mind; take into -account, – consideration; keep in -sight, – view; have regard to, heed, mind, take cognizance of, be engaged in, entertain, recognize; make –, take-note of; note.

examine cursorily; glance -at, – upon, – over; cast –, pass- the eyes over; run over, turn over the leaves, dip into, perstringe; skim &c. (*neglect*) 460; take a cursory view of.

examine, – closely, – intently; scan, scrutinize, consider; give –, bend- one's mind to; overhaul, revise, pore over; inspect, review, pass under review; take stock of; fix –, rivet –, focus –, devote- the -eye, – mind, – thoughts, – attention- on *or* to; hear –, think- out; mind one's business.

revert –, hark back- to; watch &c. (*expect*) 507, (*take care of*) 459; hearken –, listen- to; prick up the ears; have –, keep- the eyes open; come to the point.

meet with attention; fall under one's -notice, – observation; be -under consideration &c. (*topic*) 454.

catch –, strike- the eye; attract notice; catch –, awaken –, wake –, invite –, solicit –, attract –, claim –, excite –, engage –, occupy –, strike –, arrest –, fix –, engross –, absorb –, rivet- the- attention, – mind, – thoughts; be -present to, – uppermost in- the mind.

bring under one's notice; point -out, – to, – at, – the finger at; lay the finger on, indigitate, indicate; direct –, call- attention to; show; put a -mark &c. (*sign*) 550- upon; call soldiers to 'attention'; bring forward &c. (*make manifest*) 525.

Adj. attentive, mindful, heedful, observant, regardful; alive –, awake- to, alert; observing &c. *v.*; taken up –, occupied- with; engaged –, engrossed –, interested –, wrapped- in; absorbed, rapt; breathless; pre-occupied &c. (*inattentive*) 458; watchful &c. (*careful*) 459; intent on, open-eyed, undistracted, upon the stretch; on the watch &c. (*expectant*) 507.

steadfast.

Int. see! look, – here, – out, – alive, – you, ·· to it; mark! lo!

at one ear and go out at the other; forget &c. (*have no remembrance*) 506.

call off –, draw off –, call away –, divert –, distract- the -attention, – thoughts, – mind; put out of one's head; dis-concert, -compose; put out, confuse, perplex, bewilder, moider, fluster, muddle, dazzle; throw a sop to Cerberus.

Adj. inattentive; un-observant, -mindful, -heeding, -discerning; inadvertent; mind-, regard-, respect-less; listless &c. (*indifferent*) 866; blind, deaf; flighty, hand over head; cur-, percur-sory; giddy-, scatter-, hare-brained; unreflecting, écervelé, inconsiderate, off-hand, thoughtless, dizzy, muzzy, brainsick; giddy, – as a goose; wild, harum-scarum, rantipole, high-flying; heed-, care-less &c. (*neglectful*) 460.

absent, absent-minded, abstracted, *distrait*; lost; lost –, wrapped- in thought, woolgathering; rapt, in the clouds, bemused; dreaming –, musing-on other things; pre-occupied; en-grossed &c. (*attentive*) 457; in a -reverie &c. *n.*; off one's guard &c. (*inexpectant*) 508; napping; dreamy.

disconcerted, put out &c. *v.*; rattled.

Adv. inattentively, inadvertently &c. *adj.*; per incuriam, sub silentio.

Int. stand -at ease, – easy!

Phr. the attention wanders; one's wits gone a -woolgathering, – bird's nesting; it never entered into one's head; the mind running on other things; one's thoughts being elsewhere; had it been a bear it would have bitten you.

———

behold! soho! hark, – ye! mind! halloo! observe! lo and behold! attention! *nota bene*; N.B.; *, †; I'd have you to know; notice! take notice! O yes! *Oyez!*

Phr. this is –, these are- to give notice.

459. Care. [Vigilance.]—**N.** care, solicitude, heed; heedfulness &c. *adj.*; scruple &c. (*conscientiousness*) 939.

watchfulness &c. *adj.*; vigilance, *surveillance*, eyes of Argus, watch, vigil, look out, watch and ward, *l'œil du maître*.

alertness &c. (*activity*) 682; attention &c. 457; prudence &c., circumspection &c. (*caution*) 864; forethought &c. 510; precaution &c. (*preparation*) 673; tidiness &c. (*order*) 58, (*cleanliness*) 652; accuracy &c. (*exactness*) 494; minuteness, attention to detail; meticulousness, nicety, circumstantiality.

V. be -careful &c. *adj.*; reck; take care &c. (*be cautious*) 864; pay attention to &c. 457; take care of; look –, see- -to, – after; keep -an eye, – a sharp eye- upon; keep -watch, – watch and ward; mount guard, set watch, watch; keep in -sight, – view; chaperon, play gooseberry; mind, – one's business.

look -sharp, – about one; look with one's own eyes; keep a -good, – sharp-look-out; have all one's -wits, – eyes-about one; watch for &c. (*expect*) 507; stand to; keep one's eyes –, have the eyes –, sleep with one eye- open.

take precautions &c. 673; protect &c. (*render safe*) 664.

do one's best &c. 682; mind one's Ps and Qs, speak by the card, pick one's steps.

Adj. care-, regard-, heed-ful; taking care &c. *v.*; particular; prudent &c. (*cautious*) 864; considerate; thoughtful &c. (*deliberative*) 451; provident &c. (*prepared*) 673; alert &c. (*active*) 682; sure-footed.

guarded, on one's guard; on the *-qui vive*, – alert, – watch, – look-out; awake, broad awake, vigilant; watch-, wake-, wist-ful; Argus-, lynx- eyed; wide awake &c. (*intelligent*) 498; on the watch for &c. (*expectant*) 507.

tidy &c. (*orderly*) 58, (*clean*) 652; accurate &c. (*exact*) 494; scrupulous

460. Neglect.—**N.** neglect; carelessness &c. *adj.*; trifling &c. *v.*; negligence; omission, laches, default; remissness, slackness, procrastination; supineness &c. (*inactivity*) 683; inattention &c. 458; nonchalance &c. (*insensibility*) 823; imprudence, recklessness &c. 863; slovenliness &c. (*disorder*) 59, (*dirt*) 653; improvidence &c. 674; non-completion &c. 730; inexactness &c. (*error*) 495.

paraleipsis [in rhetoric].

trifler, slacker, waster, waiter on Providence; Micawber.

V. be -negligent &c. *adj.*; take no care of &c. (take care of &c. 459); neglect; let -slip, – go; lay –, set –, cast –, put- aside; keep –, leave- out of sight; lose sight of.

overlook, disregard; pass -over, – by; let pass; blink; wink –, connive- at; gloss over; take no -note, – notice, - thought, – account- of; pay no regard to; *laisser aller*; allow to lie on the table.

scamp; trifle, fribble; do by halves; skimp; cut; slight &c. (*despise*) 930; play –, trifle- with; slur; skim, – the surface; *effleurer*; take a cursory view of &c. 457.

slur –, slip –, skip –, jump- over; pretermit, miss, skip, jump, omit, give the go-by to, push aside, throw into the background, shelve, sink; ignore, shut one's eyes to, refuse to hear, turn a deaf ear to; leave out of one's calculation; not -attend to &c. 457, – mind; not trouble -oneself, – one's head- -with, –about; forget &c. 506; be caught napping &c. (*not expect*) 508; leave a loose thread; let the grass grow under one's feet.

render -neglectful &c. *adj.*; put –, throw- off one's guard.

Adj. neglecting &c. *v.*; unmindful, negligent, neglectful; heedless, careless, thoughtless; perfunctory, remiss, slack.

inconsiderate; un-, in-circumspect;

&c. (*conscientious*) 939; *cavendo tutus* &c. (*safe*) 664.

Adv. carefully &c. *adj.*; with care, gingerly.

Phr. *quis custodiet ipsos custodes?*

----

off one's guard; un-wary, -watchful, -guarded; offhand.

supine &c. (*inactive*) 683; inattentive &c. 458; *insouciant* &c. (*indifferent*) 823; imprudent, reckless &c. 863; slovenly &c. (*disorderly*) 59, (*dirty*) 653; inexact &c. (*erroneous*) 495; improvident &c. 674.

neglected &c. *v.*; un-heeded, -cared for, -perceived, -seen, -observed, -noticed, -noted, -marked, -attended to, -thought of, -regarded, -remarked, -missed; shunted, shelved.

un-examined, -studied, -searched, -scanned, -weighed, -sifted, -explored.

abandoned; buried in a napkin, hid under a bushel.

Adv. negligently &c. *adj.*; hand over head, anyhow; in an unguarded moment &c. (*unexpectedly*) 508; *per incuriam*.

Int. never mind, no matter, let it pass; it will be all the same a hundred years hence.

----

461. Inquiry. [Subject of Inquiry. Question.]—**N.** inquiry; request &c. 765; search, research, quest; pursuit &c. 622.

examination, review, scrutiny, investigation, indagation; per-quisition, -scrutation, -vestigation; inqu-est, -isition; exploration; *exploitation*, ventilation.

sifting; calculation, analysis, dissection, resolution, induction; Baconian method.

strict –, close –, searching –, exhaustive- inquiry; narrow –, strict-search; study &c. (*consideration*) 451.

scire facias, ad referendum; trial.

questioning &c. *v.*; interroga-tion, -tory; third degree; interpellation; challenge, examination, cross-examination, catechism; feeler, Socratic method, zetetic philosophy; leading question; discussion &c. (*reasoning*) 476; questionnaire, questionary.

reconnoitering, *reconnaissance*; prying &c. *v.*; espionage, *espionnage*; domiciliary visit, peep behind the curtain; lantern of Diogenes.

question, query, problem, *desideratum*, point to be solved, porism; subject –, field- of -inquiry, – controversy; point –, matter- in dispute; moot-point; issue, question at issue; bone of contention &c. (*discord*) 713; plain –, fair –, open- question; enigma &c. (*secret*) 533; knotty point &c. (*difficulty*) 704; *quodlibet*; threshold of an inquiry.

inquirer, investigator, experimenter, inquisitor, inspector, querist,

462. Answer.—**N.** answer, response, reply, replication, *riposte*, rejoinder, surrejoinder, rebutter, surrebutter, counter-evidence &c. 468, countercharge, defence, plea; retort, repartee; contradiction &c. 536; rescript, -iont antiphon, -y; acknowledgment; password; echo.

discovery &c. 480a; solution &c; (*explanation*) 522; rationale &c. (*cause*) 153; clue &c. (*indication*) 550.

Œdipus; oracle &c. 513; return &c (*record*) 551.

V. answer, respond, reply, rebut, retort, rejoin; give –, return for-answer; acknowledge, echo.

explain &c. (*interpret*) 522; solve &c; (*unriddle*) 522; discover &c. 480a; fathom, hunt out &c. (*inquire*) 461; satisfy, set at rest, determine.

Adj. answering &c. *v.*; respon-sive, -dent; oracular; antiphonal; conclusive.

Adv. because &c. (*cause*) 153; on the -scent, – right scent.

Int. *eureka!*

----

examiner, catechist; scrut-ator, -ineer; analyst; quidnunc &c. (*curiosity*) 455.

V. make -inquiry &c. *n*.; inquire, seek, search, frisk, speer, look -for, – about for, – out for; scan, reconnoitre, explore, sound, rummage, ransack, pry, peer, look round; look –, go- -over, – through; spy, over-haul.

scratch the head, slap the forehead.

look –, peer –, pry- into every hole and corner; look behind the scenes; trace up; hunt –, fish –, dig –, ferret- out; unearth; leave no stone unturned.

seek a -clue, – clew; hunt, track, trail, shadow, mouse, dodge, trace; follow the -trail, – scent; pursue &c. 622; beat up one's quarters; fish for; feel for &c. (*experiment*) 463.

investigate; take up –, institute –, pursue –, follow up –, conduct –, carry on –, prosecute- -an inquiry &c. *n*.; look -at, – into; pre-examine; discuss, canvass, agitate.

examine, study, consider, calculate; dip –, dive –, delve –, go deep- into; make sure of, probe, sound, fathom; probe to the -bottom, – quick; scrutinize, analyze, anatomize, dissect, parse, resolve, sift, winnow; view –, try- in all its phases; thresh out.

bring in question, subject to examination; put to the proof &c. (*experiment*) 463; audit, tax, pass in review; take into consideration &c. (*think over*) 451; take counsel &c. 695.

ask, question, demand; put –, pop –, propose –, propound –, moot –, start –, raise –, stir –, suggest –, put forth –, ventilate – grapple with –, go into- a question.

put to the question, interrogate, catechize, pump, grill; cross-question, -examine; dodge; require an answer; pick –, suck- the brains of; feel the pulse.

be -in question &c. *adj*.; undergo examination.

Adj. inquiring &c. *v*.; inquisitive &c. (*curious*) 455; requisit-ive, -ory; catechetical, inquisitorial, analytic; in -search, – quest- of; on the look-out for, interrogative, zetetic: all-searching.

un-determined, -tried, -decided; in -question, – dispute, – issue, – course of inquiry; under -discussion, – consideration, – investigation &c. *n*., *sub judice*, moot, proposed; doubtful &c. (*uncertain*) 475.

Adv. what? why? wherefore? whence? whither? where? *quare?* how -comes, – happens, – is- it? what is the reason? what's -the matter, – up, – in the wind? what on earth? when? who?

463. Experiment.—N. experiment; essay &c. (*attempt*) 675; research &c. (*investigation*) 461; trial, tentative method, *tâtonnement*.

verification, probation, *experimentum crucis*, proof, criterion, diagnostic, test, tryout, crucial test, acid test.

crucible, reagent, check, touchstone, pix; assay, ordeal; ring.

empiricism, rule of thumb.

feeler; pilot –, messenger- balloon, *ballon d'essai*; pilot engine; scout; straw to show the wind.

speculation, random shot, leap in the dark.

analy-zer, -st; adventurer, explorer, sourdough, prospector; experiment-er, -ist, -alist; assayer.

V. experiment; essay &c. (*endeavour*) 675; try, assay, sample; make -an experiment, – trial of; give a trial to; put upon –, subject to- trial; experiment upon; rehearse; put –, bring –, submit- to the -test, – proof; prove, verify, test, touch, practise upon, try one's strength.

grope; feel –, grope- -for, – one's way; fumble; *tâtonner, aller à tâtons*; put –, throw- out a feeler; send up a pilot balloon; see how the -land lies, – wind blows; consult the barometer; feel the pulse; fish –, bob- for; cast –, beat- about for; angle, trawl, cast one's net, beat the bushes.

venture, try one's fortune &c. (*adventure*) 675; explore &c. (*inquire*) 461.

Adj. experimental; probat-ive, -ory, -ionary; analytic, docimastic; tentative; empirical; speculative.

under probation, on one's trial, on trial, on approval.

464. Comparison.—N. comparison, collation, contrast; identification. sim-ile, -ilitude; allegory &c. (*metaphor*) 521.

V. compare -to, – with; collate, confront; place side by side &c. (*near*) 197; set –, pit- against one another; contrast, balance.

identify, draw a parallel, parallel.

compare notes; institute a comparison; *parva componere magnis*.

Adj. comparative, relative; metaphorical &c. 521.

compared with &c. *v.*; comparable.

Adv. relatively &c. (*relation*) 9; as compared with &c. *v.*

465. Discrimination.—N. discrimination, distinction, differentiation, diagnosis, diorism; nice perception; perception –, appreciation- of difference; acuteness; estimation &c. 466; nicety, refinement; taste &c. 850; *critique*, judgement, tact; insight, discernment &c. (*intelligence*) 498; *nuances*.

V. discriminate, distinguish, differentiate, severalize; separate; draw the line, sift; separate –, winnow- the chaff from the wheat; split hairs.

465a. Indiscrimination.—N. indiscrimination; promiscuity; indistinctness, -ion; uncertainty &c. (*doubt*) 475; obtuseness.

V. not -indiscriminate &c. 465; overlook &c. (*neglect*) 460- a distinction; con-found, -fuse, jumble; swallow whole.

Adj. indiscriminate, undiscriminating, promiscuous; undistinguish-ed, -able, -ing; unmeasured.

estimate &c. (*measure*) 466; know -which is which, – one's stuff, – one's way about, – what is what, – 'a hawk from a handsaw.'

take into -account, – consideration; give –, allow- due weight to; weigh carefully.

Adj. discriminating &c. *v.*; dioristic, discriminative, critical, distinctive; nice.

Phr. *il y a fagots et fagots; rem acu tetigisti.*

466. Measurement.—N. measurement, admeasurement, mensuration, survey, valuation, appraisement, assessment, assize; estim-ate, -ation; dead reckoning; reckoning &c. (*numeration*) 85; gauging &c. *v.*

metrology, weights and measures, compound arithmetic.

measure, yard measure, standard, rule, foot-rule, chain, tape, staff, compass, callipers; dividers; gage, gauge, planimeter; meter, line, rod, check.

volt, kilowatt, ampere, candle power; horse power; axle load; foot pound.

flood –, high water- mark; Plimsoll mark; index &c. 550.

scale; gradu-ation, -ated scale; nonius; vernier &c. (*minuteness*) 193; pedo (*length*)- 200, sounding line &c. (*depth*)- 208, thermo (*heat* &c. 389)-, baro (*air* &c. 338)-, dynamo (*power*)- 276, anemo (*wind* 349)-, gonio (*angle* 244)- meter; landmark &c. (*limit*) 233; balance &c. (*weight*) 319; optical instruments &c. 445.

co-ordinates, ordinate and abscissa, polar co-ordinates, latitude and longitude, declination and right ascension, altitude and azimuth.

geo-, stereo-, hypso-metry; metage; surveying, land surveying; geo-desy, -detics, -desia; ortho-, alti-metry; *cadastre.*

astrolabe, armillary sphere.

land, -surveyor; geometer, topographer, cartographer, hydrographer.

V. measure, meter, mete; value, assess, rate, appraise, estimate, form an estimate, set a value on; appreciate; standardize.

span, pace, step; apply the -compass &c. *n.*; gauge, plumb, probe, calliper, sound, fathom &c. 208; heave the -log, – lead; weigh &c. 319; survey.

take an average &c. 29; graduate.

Adj. measuring &c. *v.*; metric, -al; measurable; geodetical, cadastral, topographical.

Section III. Materials for Reasoning

467. Evidence [on one side.]—**N.** evidence; facts, premises, *data, præcognita,* grounds.

indication &c. 550; criterion &c. (*test*) 463.

testi-mony, -fication; attestation; deposition &c. (*affirmation*) 535; examination.

admission &c. (*assent*) 488; authority, warrant, credential, diploma, voucher, certificate, docket; record &c. 551; document, muniments; *pièce justificative;* deed, warranty &c. (*security*) 771; signature, seal &c. (*identification*) 550; exhibit, citation, reference.

witness, indicator; eye-, ear-witness; deponent; sponsor.

oral –, documentary –, hearsay –, external –, extrinsic –, internal –, intrinsic –, circumstantial –, cumulative –, *ex parte* –, presumptive –, collateral –, constructive- evidence; proof &c. (*demonstration*) 478; evidence in chief; finger prints, dactylogram.

secondary evidence; confirmation, corroboration, adminicle, support; ratification &c. (*assent*) 488; authentication, verification; compurgation, wager of law, comprobation.

citation, reference.

V. be -evidence &c. *n.*; evince, show, betoken, tell of; indicate &c. (*denote*) 550; imply, involve, argue, bespeak, breathe.

have –, carry- weight; tell, speak

468. [Evidence on the other side, on the other hand.] **Counter-evidence.— N.** counter-evidence; evidence on the other -side, – hand; disproof; refutation &c. 479; negation &c. 536; conflicting evidence.

plea &c. 617; vindication &c. 937; counter-protest; *tu quoque* argument; other side –, reverse- of the shield.

V. countervail, oppose; run counter; rebut &c. (*refute*) 479; subvert &c. (*destroy*) 162; check, weaken; contravene; contradict &c. (*deny*) 536; tell another story, turn the -tables, – scale; alter the case; cut both ways; prove a negative.

audire alteram partem.

Adj. countervailing &c. *v.*; contradictory, in rebuttal.

un-attested, -authenticated, -supported by evidence; supposititious, trumped up.

Adv. *per contra,* conversely, on the other hand.

469. Qualification.—N. qualification, limitation, modification, colouring.

allowance, grains of allowance, consideration, extenuating circumstances.

condition, proviso, exception; exemption; salvo, saving clause; discount &c. 813.

V. qualify, limit, modify, affect, temper, leaven, give a colour to, introduce new conditions.

allow –, make allowance- for; ad-

volumes; speak for itself &c. (*manifest*)
525.

rest –, depend- upon; repose on.

bear -witness &c. *n.*; give -evidence
&c. *n.*; testify, depose, witness, vouch
for; sign, seal, undersign, set one's
hand and seal, sign and seal, deliver as
one's act and deed, certify, attest;
acknowledge &c. (*assent*) 488.

make absolute, confirm, ratify, corroborate, endorse, countersign, support, bear out, vindicate, uphold,
warrant.

adduce, attest, cite, quote; refer –,
appeal- to; call, – to witness; bring
-forward, – into court; allege, plead;
produce –, confront- witnesses; collect
–, bring together –, rake up- evidence.

have –, make out- a case; establish,
circumstantiate, authenticate, substantiate, verify, make good, quote chapter
and verse; bring -home to, – to book.

Adj. showing &c. *v.*; evidential, indica-tive, -tory; deducible &c.
478; grounded –, founded –, based- on; first hand, authentic, veri-
fiable; corroborative, confirmatory; significant, conclusive.

Adv. by inference; according to, witness, *a fortiori*; still -more,
– less; *raison de plus*; in corroboration &c. *n.* of; *valeat quantum*;
under -seal, – one's hand and seal.

mit exceptions, take into account.
take exception, object.

Adj. qualifying &c. *v.*; conditional;
extenuatory; exceptional &c. (*unconformable*) 83.

hypothetical &c. (*supposed*) 514;
contingent &c. (*uncertain*) 475.

Adv. provided, – always; if, unless,
but, yet; according as; conditionally,
admitting, supposing; on the supposition of &c. (*theoretically*) 514; with the
understanding, even, although, though,
for all that, after all, at all events.

with grains of allowance, *cum grano
salis*; *exceptis excipiendis*; wind and
weather permitting; if possible &c. 470.
subject to; with this -proviso &c. *n.*

Degrees of Evidence

470. Possibility.—N. possibility, po-
tentiality; what -may be, – is possible
&c. *adj.*; compatibility &c. (*agreement*)
23.

practicability, feasibility; practi-
cableness &c. *adj.*

contingency, chance &c. 156.

V. be -possible &c. *adj.*; stand a
chance, have a leg to stand on; admit
of, bear.

render -possible &c. *adj.*; put in the
way of.

Adj. possible; on the -cards, – dice;
in posse, within the bounds of possibility, conceivable, credible, imaginable; compatible &c. 23.

practicable, feasible, workable, performable, achievable; within -reach, –
measurable distance; accessible, superable, surmountable; at-, ob-tainable;
contingent &c. (*doubtful*) 475.

Adv. possibly, by possibility; perhaps, -chance, -adventure; may be,
haply, mayhap.

471. Impossibility.—N. impossibility
&c. *adj.*; what -cannot, – can never- be;
sour grapes; infeasibility, impracticability, hopelessness &c. 859.

V. be -impossible &c. *adj.*; have no
chance whatever.

attempt impossibilities; square the
circle; discover the -philosopher's stone,
– elixir of life, – secret of perpetual
motion; wash a blackamoor white;
skin a flint; make -a silk purse out of
a sow's ear, – bricks without straw;
have nothing to go upon; weave a rope
of sand, build castles in the air, *prendre
la lune avec les dents*, extract sunbeams
from cucumbers, set the Thames on
fire, milk a he-goat into a sieve, catch
a weasel asleep, *rompre l'anguille au
genou*, be in two places at once.

Adj. impossible; not -possible &c.
470; absurd, contrary to reason; unlikely, at variance with facts; unreasonable &c. 477; incredible &c. 485; beyond the bounds of -reason, – possi-

if possible, wind and weather permitting, God willing, *Deo volente,* D.V.

---

bility; from which reason recoils; visionary; inconceivable &c. (*improbable*) 473; prodigious &c. (*wonderful*) 870; un-, in-imaginable, unthinkable, not a Chinaman's chance.

impracticable, unachievable; un-, in-feasible; insuperable; un-, in-surmountable; unat-, unob-tainable; out of -reach, – the question; not to be -had, – thought of; beyond control; desperate &c. (*hopeless*) 859; incompatible &c. 24; inaccessible, uncomeatable, impassable impervious, innavigable, inextricable.

out of –, beyond- one's -power, – depth, – reach, – grasp; too much for; *ultra crepidam.*

Phr. the grapes are sour; *non possumus; non nostrum tantas componere lites.*

472. Probability.—N. probability, likelihood; likeliness &c. *adj.*

vraisemblance, verisimilitude, plausibility; colour, semblance, show of; presumption; presumptive –, circumstantial- evidence; credibility.

reasonable –, fair –, good –, favourable- -chance, – prospect; prospect, well-grounded hope; chance &c. 156.

V. be -probable &c. *adj.*; give –, lend- colour to; point to; imply &c. (*evidence*) 467; bid fair &c. (*promise*) 511; stand fair for; stand –, run- a good chance.

presume, infer, suppose, take for granted.

think likely, dare say, flatter oneself; expect &c. 507; count upon &c. (*believe*) 484.

Adj. probable, likely, hopeful, to be expected, in a fair way.

plausible, specious, ostensible, colourable, *ben trovato,* well-founded, reasonable, credible, easy of belief, presumable, presumptive, apparent.

Adv. probably &c. *adj.*; belike; in all -probability, – likelihood; very –, most- likely; as likely as not; like enough; ten &c. to one; apparently, seemingly, according to every reasonable expectation; *primâ facie*; to all appearance &c. (*to the eye*) 448.

Phr. the -chances, – odds- are; appearances –, chances- are in favour of; there is reason to -believe, – think, – expect; I dare say; all Lombard Street to a China orange.

473. Improbability.—N. improbability, unlikelihood; unfavourable –, bad –, little –, small –, poor –, scarcely any –, no –, not a ghost of a- chance; bare possibility; long odds; incredibility &c. 485.

V. be -improbable &c. *adj.*; have a -small chance &c. *n.*

Adj. improbable, unlikely, contrary to all reasonable expectation, implausible.

rare &c. (*infrequent*) 137; unheard of inconceivable; un-, in-imaginable; incredible &c. 485; more than doubtful

Int. not likely! no fear!

Phr. the chances are against.

474. Certainty.—N. certainty; necessity &c. 601; certitude, certainness, surety, assurance, sureness; dead –, moral- certainty; infallibleness &c. *adj.*; infallibility, reliability.

gospel, scripture, church, pope, court of final appeal; *res judicata, ultimatum.*

positiveness; dogmat-ism, -ist, -izer; *doctrinaire,* know-all, bigot, -ry; opin-

475. Uncertainty.—N. uncertaint; incertitude, doubt; doubtfulness &c; *adj.*; dubi-ety, -tation, -tancy, -ousness.

hesitation, suspense; perplexity, embarrassment, dilemma, quandary, Morton's fork, bewilderment; timidity &c. (*fear*) 860; indecision, vacillation &c. 605; *diaporesis,* indetermination.

vagueness &c. *adj.*; haze, fog; ob-

ionist, Sir Oracle; *ipse dixit*; zealot.

fact; positive –, matter of- fact; *fait accompli.*

V. be -certain &c. *adj.*; stand to reason.

render -certain &c. *adj.*; in-, en-, assure; clinch, make sure; determine, decide, set at rest, 'make assurance double sure'; know &c. *(believe)* 484; dismiss all doubt.

dogmatize, lay down the law.

Adj. certain, sure; assured &c. *v.*; solid, well-founded.

unqualified, absolute, positive, determinate, definite, clear, unequivocal, categorical, unmistakable, decisive, decided, ascertained.

inevitable, unavoidable, ineluctable, avoidless.

unerring, infallible; unchangeable &c. 150; to be depended on, trustworthy, reliable, bound.

un-impeachable, -deniable, -questionable; in-disputable, -contestable, -controvertible, -defeasible, -dubitable; irrefutable &c. *(proven)* 478; conclusive, without power of appeal, final.

indubious; without –, beyond a –, without a shade or shadow of- -doubt – question; past dispute; beyond all -question, – dispute; un-doubted, -contested, -questioned, -disputed; question-, doubt-less.

bigoted, fanatical, dogmatic, opinionat-ed, -ive, *doctrinaire.*

authoritative, authentic, official.

sure as -fate, – death and taxes, – a gun.

evident, self-evident, axiomatic; clear, – as day, – as the sun at noonday; obvious.

Adv. certainly &c. *adj.*; for certain, certes, sure, no doubt, doubtless, and no mistake, *flagrante delicto*, sure enough, to be sure, of course, as a matter of course, *à coup sur*, to a certainty, undoubtedly; in truth &c. *(truly)* 494; at -any rate, – all events; without fail; *coûte que coûte*; whatever may happen, if the worst come to the worst; come –, happen- what -may, – will; sink or swim; rain or shine.

Phr. *cela va sans dire*; there is ·no question, – not a shadow of doubt;

scurity &c. *(darkness)* 421; ambiguity &c. *(double meaning)* 520; contingency, double contingency, possibility upon a possibility; conjecture; open question &c. *(question)* 461; *onus probandi*; blind bargain, pig in a poke, leap in the dark, something or other; needle in a bottle of hay; roving commission.

fallibility, unreliability, untrustworthiness, precariousness.

V. be -uncertain &c. *adj.*; wonder whether.

lose the -clue, – clew, – scent; miss one's way.

not know -what to make of &c. *(unintelligibility)* 519, – which way to turn, – whether one stands on one's head or one's heels; float in a sea of doubt, hesitate, flounder; lose -oneself, – one's head, – one's way, wander aimlessly; muddle one's brains.

render -uncertain &c. *adj.*; put out, pose, puzzle, perplex, embarrass; confuse, -found; bewilder, mystify, bother, moider, nonplus, addle the wits, throw off the scent; *spargere voces in vulgum ambiguas*; keep in suspense.

doubt &c. *(disbelieve)* 485; hang –, tremble- in the balance; depend.

Adj. uncertain; casual; random &c. *(aimless)* 621; changeable &c. 149.

doubtful, dubious; indecisive; unsettled, -decided, -determined; in suspense, open to discussion; controvertible; in question &c. *(inquiry)* 461; insecure, unstable.

vague; in-determinate, -definite; ambiguous, equivocal; undefin-ed, -able; confused &c. *(indistinct)* 447; mystic, mysterious, veiled, obscure, cryptic, oracular.

perplexing &c. *v.*; enigmatic, paradoxical, apocryphal, problematical, hypothetical; experimental &c. 463.

fallible, questionable, precarious, slippery, ticklish, debatable, disputable; un-reliable, -trustworthy.

contingent, – on, dependent on; subject to; dependent on circumstances; occasional; provisional.

unauth-entic, -enticated, -oritative; un-ascertained, -confirmed; undemonstrated; un-told, -counted.

in a -state of uncertainty, – cloud.

the die is cast &c. (*necessity*) 601.

―fault, ― a loss, ― one's wit's end, ― a *nonplus*; puzzled &c. *v.*; lost, abroad, *désorienté*; dis-tracted, -traught.

Adv. *pendente lite*; *sub spe rati.*

Phr. Heaven knows; who can tell? who shall decide when doctors disagree?

‒ maze; ignorant &c. 491; on the horns of a dilemma; afraid to say; out of one's reckoning, astray, adrift; at -sea, ― maze; ignorant &c. 491; on the horns

Section IV. REASONING PROCESSES

476. Reasoning. — N. reasoning; ratio-cination, -nalism; dialectics, in-duction, generalization.

discussion, comment; ventilation; inquiry &c. 461.

argumentation, controversy, debate; polemics, wrangling; contention &c. 720; logomachy; dis-putation, -cepta-tion; paper war.

art of reasoning, logic.

process ‒, train ‒, chain- of reason-ing; de-, in-duction; synthesis, analysis.

argument; case, plea, *plaidoyer*, opening; *lemma*, proposition, terms, premises, postulate, *data*, starting point, principle; inference &c. (*judg-ment*) 480.

pro-, syllogism; enthymeme, sorites, dilemma, *perilepsis, a priori* reasoning, *reductio ad absurdum*, horns of a di-lemma, *argumentum ad hominem*, com-prehensive argument.

reasoner, logician, dialectician; dis-putant; controver-sialist, -tist; wrang-ler, arguer, debater, polemic, casuist, rationalist; scientist.

logical sequence; good case; correct ‒, just ‒, sound ‒, valid ‒, cogent ‒, logical ‒, forcible ‒, persuasive ‒, per-suasory ‒, consectary ‒, conclusive &c. 478 ‒, subtle- reasoning; force of argu-ment; strong -point, ‒ argument.

arguments, reasons, pros and cons.

V. reason, argue, discuss, debate, dispute, wrangle; bandy -words, ‒ arguments; chop logic; hold ‒, carry on- an argument; controvert &c. (*deny*) 536; canvass; comment ‒, moralize-upon; consider &c. (*examine*) 461.

open a -discussion, ‒ case; join ‒, be at- issue; moot; come to the point; stir ‒, agitate ‒, ventilate ‒, torture- a question; try conclusions; take up a -side, ‒ case.

477. [The absence of reasoning.] **Intuition.** [False or vicious reasoning; show of reason.] **Sophistry.—N.** intui-tion, instinct, association; presenti-ment; rule of thumb.

sophistry, paralogy, perversion, casu-istry, jesuitry, equivocation, evasion, mental reservation; chicane, -ry; quid-dit, quiddity; mystification; special pleading; speciousness &c. *adj.*; non-sense &c. 497; word-, tongue-fence.

false ‒, vicious- reasoning; *petitio principii, ignoratio elenchi*; *post hoc ergo propter hoc*; *non sequitur, ignotum per ignotius.*

misjudgment &c. 481; false teaching &c. 538.

sophism, solecism, paralogism; quib-ble, quirk, *elenchus*, elench, fallacy, *quodlibet*, subterfuge, subtlety, quillet; inconsistency, antilogy; 'a mockery, a delusion and a snare'; claptrap, mere words; 'lame and impotent conclusion.'

meshes ‒, cobwebs- of sophistry; flaw in an argument; weak point, bad case.

over-refinement; hair-splitting &c. *v.* sophist, casuist, paralogist.

V. judge -intuitively, ‒ by intuition; hazard a proposition, talk at random.

reason -ill, ‒ falsely &c. *adj.*; paralo-gize; misjudge &c. 481.

pervert, quibble; equivocate, mysti-fy, evade, elude; gloss over, varnish; misteach &c. 538; mislead &c. (*error*) 495; cavil, refine, subtilize, split hairs; misrepresent &c. (*lie*) 544.

beg the question, reason in a circle, cut blocks with a razor, beat about the bush, play fast and loose, blow hot and cold, prove that black is white and white black, travel out of the record, *parler à tort et à travers*, put oneself out of court, not have a leg to stand on.

Adj. intuitive, instinctive, impulsive;

contend, take one's stand upon, insist, lay stress on; infer &c. 480.

follow from &c. (*demonstration*) 478.

Adj. rational; reasoning &c. *v.*; rationalistic; argumentative, controversial, dialectic, polemical; discursory, -ive; disputatious.

debatable, controvertible.

logical; in-, de-ductive; synthetic, analytic; relevant &c. 23.

Adv. for, because, hence, whence, seeing that, since, sith, then, thence, so; for -that, – this, – which- reason; for-, inasmuch as; whereas, *ex concesso*, considering, in consideration of; there-, where-fore; consequently, *ergo*, thus, accordingly; *a fortiori*.

in -conclusion, – fine; finally, after all, *au bout du compte*, on the whole, taking one thing with another.

rationally &c. *adj.*

---

478. Demonstration.—N. demonstration, proof; conclusiveness &c. *adj.*; *apodixis*, probation, comprobation.

logic of facts &c. (*evidence*) 467; *experimentum crucis* &c. (*test*) 463; argument &c. 476; irrefragability.

V. demonstrate, prove, establish, make good; show; evince &c. (*be evidence of*) 467; verify &c. 467; settle the question, reduce to demonstration, set the question at rest.

make out, – a case; prove one's point, have the best of the argument; draw a conclusion &c. (*judge*) 480.

follow, – of course; stand to reason; hold -good, – water.

Adj. demonstra-ting &c. *v.*, -tive, -ble; probative, unanswerable, conclusive; apodictic, -al; irre-sistible, -futable, -fragable, undeniable.

categorical, decisive, crucial.

demonstrated &c. *v.*; proven; un-confuted, -answered, -refuted; evident &c. 474.

deducible, consequential, consectary, inferential, following.

Adv. of course, in consequence, consequently, as a matter of course.

Phr. *probatum est*: there is nothing more to be said, Q.E D., it must follow.

independent of –, anterior to- reason; gratuitous, hazarded; unconnected.

unreasonable, illogical, false, unsound, invalid; unwarranted, not following; inconsequent, -ial; inconsistent, incongruous; abson-ous, -ant; unscientific; untenable, inconclusive, incorrect; fall-acious, -ible; groundless, unproved.

deceptive, sophistical, sophisticated, casuistical, jesuitical; illus-ive, -ory; specious, hollow, plausible, *ad captandum*, evasive; irrelevant &c. 10.

weak, feeble, poor, flimsy, loose, vague, irrational; nonsensical &c. (*absurd*) 497; foolish &c. (*imbecile*) 499; frivolous, pettifogging, quibbling; fine-spun, over-refined.

at the end of one's tether, *au bout de son latin*.

Adv. intuitively &c. *adj.*; by intuition; illogically &c. *adj.*

Phr. *non constat*; that goes for nothing.

---

479. Confutation.—N. con-, re-futation; answer, complete answer; disproof, conviction, redargution, invalidation; expos-ure, -ition; clincher; retort; *reductio ad absurdum*; knock down –, *tu quoque*- argument.

V. con-, re-fute; parry, negative, disprove, redargue, expose, show the fallacy of, rebut, defeat; demolish &c. (*destroy*) 162; over-throw, -turn; scatter to the winds, explode, invalidate; silence; put –, reduce- to silence; clinch -an argument, – a question; give one a set down, stop the mouth, shut up; have, – on the hip; get the better of; confound, convince.

not leave a leg to stand on, cut the ground from under one's feet.

be confuted &c.; fail; expose –, show- one's weak point.

Adj. confut-ing, -ed &c. *v.*; capable of refutation; re-, con-futable.

condemned -on one's own showing, – out of one's own mouth.

Phr. the argument falls to the ground. *cadit quæstio*, it does not hold water, '*suo sibi gladio hunc jugulo.*'

Section V. Results of Reasoning

480. Judgement. [Conclusion.]—**N.** result, conclusion, upshot; deduction, inference, ergotism, illation; corollary, porism; moral.

estimation, valuation, appreciation, judication; di-, ad-judication; arbitrament, -ement, -ation; assessment, ponderation.

award, estimate; review, criticism, *critique*, notice, report.

decision, determination, judgment, finding, verdict, sentence, decree, – nisi, – absolute, – interlocutory; *dictum*; *res judicata*.

plébiscite, referendum, voice, casting vote; vote &c. (*choice*) 609; opinion &c. (*belief*) 484; good judgment &c. (*wisdom*) 498.

judge, jurist, umpire; arbi-ter, -trator; assessor, referee; censor, reviewer, critic; *connoisseur*; commentator &c. 524; inspector, inspecting officer.

V. judge, conclude; come to –, draw –, arrive at- a conclusion; ascertain, determine, make up one's mind.

deduce, derive, gather, collect, draw an inference, make a deduction, weet, ween.

form an estimate, estimate, size up, appreciate, value, count, assess, rate, rank, account; regard, consider, think of; look upon &c. (*believe*) 484.

settle; pass –, give- an opinion; decide, try, pronounce. rule; pass -judgment, – sentence; sentence, doom; find; give –, deliver- judgment; adjud-ge, -icate; arbitrate, award, report; bring in a verdict; make absolute, set a question at rest; conf*rm &c. (*assent*) 488.

comment, criticize; review, pass under review &c. (*examine*) 457; investigate &c. (*inquire*) 461.

hold the scales, sit in judgment; try –, hear- a cause.

Adj. judging &c. *v.*; judicious &c. (*wise*) 498; determinate, conclusive, censorious, critical &c. 932.

Adv. on the whole, all things considered.

481. Misjudgment. — N. misjudgment, obliquity of –, warped- judgment; mis-calculation, -computation, -conception &c. (*error*) 495; hasty conclusion.

prejud-gment, -ication, -ice; foregone conclusion; pre-notion, -vention, -conception, -dilection, -possession, -apprehension, -sumption, -sentiment; fixed –, preconceived- idea; *idée fixe*; *mentis gratissimus error*; fool's paradise.

esprit de corps, party spirit, race –, class- prejudice, partisanship, clannishness, *prestige*.

bias, warp, twist; hobby, fad, whim, craze, quirk, crotchet, partiality, infatuation, blind side, mote in the eye.

one-sided –, partial –, narrow –, confined –, superficial- -views, – ideas, – conceptions, – notions; narrow mind; bigotry &c. (*obstinacy*) 606; *odium theologicum*; pedantry; hypercriticism. *doctrinaire* &c. (*positive*) 474.

V. mis-judge, -estimate, -think, -conjecture, -conceive &c. (*error*) 495; fly in the face of facts; mis-calculate, -reckon, -compute.

overestimate &c. 482; underestimate &c. 483.

pre-, fore-judge; pre-suppose, -sume, -judicate; dogmatize; have a -bias &c. *n.*; have only one idea; *jurare in verba magistri*, run away with the notion; jump –, rush- to a conclusion; look only at one side of the shield; view -with jaundiced eye, – through distorting spectacles; not see beyond one's nose; *dare pondus fumo*; get the wrong sow by the ear &c. (*blunder*) 699.

give a -bias; – twist; bias, warp, twist; pre-judice, -possess.

Adj. misjudging &c. *v.*; ill-judging, wrong-headed; prejudiced, prejudicial, &c. *v.*; jaundiced; short-sighted, purblind; partial, one-sided, superficial.

narrow-minded; confined, insular, provincial, parochial, illiberal, intolerant, narrow, besotted, infatuated, fanatical, cracked, warped, *entêté*, positive, dogmatic, dictatorial; conceited; opin-, opini-ative; opinion-ed, -ate, -ative, -ated; self-opinioned, wedded to an opinion, *opiniâtre*; bigoted &c. (*obstinate*) 606; crotchety, fussy, impracticable; unreason-able, -ing; stupid &c. 499; credulous &c. 486.

misjudged &c. *v.*

Adv. *ex parte.*

Phr. nothing like leather; the wish the father to the thought,

480a. [Result of search or inquiry.] **Discovery.—N.** discovery, invention, detection, disenchantment, disclosure, find, ascertainment, revelation.

trover &c. 775.

V. discover, find, determine, evolve; fix upon; find –, trace –, make –, hunt –, fish –, worm –, ferret –, root- out; fathom; bring –, draw- out; educe, elicit, bring to light, invent; dig –, grub –, fish- up; unearth, disinter.

solve, resolve; un-riddle, -ravel, -lock; pick –, open- the lock; find a -clue, – clew- to; interpret &c. 522; disclose &c. 529.

trace, get at; hit it, have it; lay one's -finger, – hands- upon; spot; get –, arrive- at the -truth &c. 494; put the saddle on the right horse, hit the right nail on the head.

be near the truth. burn; smoke, scent, sniff, smell a rat.

open the eyes to; see -through, – daylight, – in its true colours, – the cloven foot; detect; catch, – tripping.

pitch –, fall –, light –, hit –, stumble –, pop- upon; come across; meet –, fall in- with.

recognize, realize, verify, make certain of, identify.

Int. *eureka!*

482. Overestimation.—N. overestimation &c. *v.*; exaggeration &c. 549; vanity &c. 880; optim-, pessim-ism, -ist; megalomania.

much -cry and little wool, – ado about nothing; storm in a teacup; fine talking, rodomontade, gush, hot air, gas, bombast.

egotism &c. 880; boasting &c. 884.

V. over-estimate, -rate, -value, -prize, -weigh, -reckon, -strain, -praise; estimate too highly, attach too much importance to, make mountains of mole-hills, catch at straws; strain, magnify; exaggerate &c. 549; set too high a value upon; think –, make- -much, – too much- of; outreckon.

extol, – to the skies; make the -most, – best, – worst- of, eulogize, panegyrize, gush, puff, boost; make two bites of a cherry.

have too high an opinion of oneself &c. (*vanity*) 880.

Adj. overestimated &c. *v.*; oversensitive &c. (*sensibility*) 822; inflated, puffed up, exaggerated &c. 549.

Phr. all his geese are swans; *parturiunt montes.*

483. Underestimation.—N. underestimation; depreciation &c. (*detraction*) 934; pessim-ism, -ist; undervaluing &c. *v.*; modesty &c. 881.

V. under-rate, -estimate, -value, -reckon; depreciate; disparage &c. (*detract*) 934; not do justice to; mis-, dis-prize; ridicule &c. 856; slight &c. (*despise*) 930; neglect &c. 460; slur over, under-state.

make -light, – little, – nothing, – no account- of; minimize, belittle, run down, think nothing of; set -no store by, – at naught; shake off as dew-drops from the lion's mane.

Adj. depreciat-ing, -ed, -ive, -ory, &c. *v.*; un-appreciated, -valued, -prized; pejorative.

484. Belief.—N. belief; credence; credit; assurance; faith, trust, troth, confidence, presumption, sanguine expectation &c. (*hope*) 858; dependence on, reliance on.

persuasion, conviction, convincement, plerophory, self-conviction; certainty &c. 474; opinion, mind, view; conception, thinking; impression &c. (*idea*) 453; surmise &c. 514; conclusion &c. (*judgment*) 480.

tenet, dogma, principle, way of thinking; popular belief &c. (*assent*) 488.

firm –, implicit –, settled –, fixed –, rooted –, deep-rooted –, staunch –, unshaken –, steadfast –, inveterate –, calm –, sober –, dispassionate –, impartial –, well-founded- -belief, – opinion &c.; *uberrima fides*.

system of opinions, school, doctrine, articles, canons; declaration –, profession- of faith; tenets, *credenda*, creed; thirty-nine articles &c. (*orthodoxy*) 983*a*; catechism; assent &c. 488; *propaganda* &c. (*teaching*) 537.

credibility &c. (*probability*) 472.

V. believe. credit; give -faith, – credit, – credence- to; see, realize; assume, receive; set down –, take- for; have –, take- it; consider, esteem, presume.

count –, depend –, calculate –, pin one's faith –, reckon –, lean –, build –, rely –, rest- upon; lay one's account for; make sure of.

make oneself easy -about, – on that score; take on -trust, – credit; take for -granted, –gospel; allow –, attach-some weight to.

know, – for certain; have –, make-no doubt; doubt not; be – rest- -assured &c. *adj.*; persuade –, assure –, satisfy-oneself; make up one's mind.

give one credit for; confide –, believe –, put one's trust- in; place –, repose- implicit confidence in; take -one's word for, – at one's word; place reliance on, rely upon, swear by, pay regard to.

think, hold; take, – it; opine, be of opinion, conceive, trow, ween, fancy, apprehend; have –, hold –, possess –, entertain –, adopt –, imbibe –, embrace

485. Unbelief. Doubt.—N. un-, dis-, mis-belief; discredit, miscreance; infidelity &c. (*irreligion*) 989; dissent &c. 489; change of -opinion &c. 484; retraction &c. 607.

doubt &c. (*uncertainty*) 475; skepticism, misgiving, demur; dis-, mis-trust; misdoubt, suspicion, jealousy, scruple, qualm; *onus probandi.*

incredib-ility, -leness; incredulity; unbeliever &c. 487.

V. dis-believe, -credit; not -believe &c. 484; misbelieve; refuse to admit &c. (*dissent*) 489; refuse to believe &c. (*incredulity*) 487.

doubt; be -doubtful &c. (*uncertain*) 475; doubt the truth of; be -skeptical as to &c. *adj.*; diffide; dis-, mis-trust; suspect, smoke, scent, smell a rat; have –, harbour –, entertain- -doubts, – suspicions; have one's doubts.

demur, stick at, pause, hesitate, scruple, waver, stop and consider.

hang in -suspense, – doubt.

throw doubt upon, raise a question; bring –, call- in question; question, challenge, query; dispute; deny &c. 536; cavil; cause –, raise –, start –, suggest –, awake- a -doubt, – suspicion; ergotize.

startle, stagger; shake –, stagger-one's faith, – belief.

Adj. unbelieving; incredulous –, skeptical- as to; distrustful –, shy –, suspicious- of; doubting &c. *v.*

doubtful &c. (*uncertain*) 475; disputable; unworthy –, undeserving- of -belief &c. 484; questionable; sus-pect, -picious; open to -suspicion, – doubt; staggering, hard to believe, incredible, not to be believed, inconceivable.

fallible &c. (*uncertain*) 475; undemonstrable; controvertible &c. (*untrue*) 495.

Adv. *cum grano salis.*

Phr. *fronti nulla fides; nimium ne crede colori;* '*timeo Danaos et dona ferentes*'; *credat Judæus Apella;* let those believe who may.

–, get hold of –, hazard –, foster –, nurture –, cherish- -a belief, – an opinion &c. *n.*

view –, consider –, take –, hold –, conceive –, regard –. esteem –, deem –, look upon –, account –, set down- as; surmise &c. 514.

get –, take- it into one's head; come round to an opinion; swallow &c. (*credulity*) 486.

cause to -be believed &c. *v.*; satisfy, persuade, have the ear of, gain the confidence of, assure; con-vince, -vict, -vert; put across, sell; wean, bring round; bring –, put –, win- over; indoctrinate &c. (*teach*) 537; cram down the throat; produce –, carry- conviction; bring –, drive- home to.

go down, find credence, pass current; be -received &c. *v.*, – current &c. *adj.*; possess –, take hold of –, take possession of- the mind.

Adj. believing &c. *v.*; certain, sure, assured, positive, cocksure, satisfied, confident, unhesitating, convinced, secure.

under the impression; impressed –, imbued –, penetrated- with.

confiding, trustful, suspectless; unsusp-ecting, -icious; void of suspicion; credulous &c. 486; wedded to.

believed &c. *v.*; accredited, putative; unsuspected.

worthy of –, deserving of –, commanding- -belief, – confidence; credible, reliable, trusted, trustworthy, to be depended on, un-doubted; satisfactory; probable &c. 472; fiduci-al, -ary; persuasive, impressive.

relating to belief, doctrinal.

Adv. in the -opinion, – eyes- of; *me judice*; me-seems, -thinks; to the best of one's belief; I -dare say, – doubt not, – have no doubt, – am sure; in my opinion; sure enough &c. (*certainty*) 474; depend –, rely- upon it; be –, rest- assured; I'll warrant you &c. (*affirmation*) 535.

---

486. Credulity.—N. credul-ity, -ous-ness &c. *adj.*; gull-, cull-ibility; gross credulity, infatuation; self-delusion, -deception; blind reasoning; supersti-tion; one's blind side; bigotry &c. (*obstinacy*) 606; hyper-orthodoxy &c. 984; misjudgment &c. 481.

credulous person &c. (*dupe*) 547.

V. be -credulous &c. *adj.*; *jurare in verba magistri*; follow implicitly; swal-low, – whole, gulp down; take on trust; take for -granted, – gospel; run away with -a notion, – an idea; jump –, rush- to a conclusion; think the moon is made of green cheese; take –, grasp- the shadow for the substance; catch at straws.

impose upon &c. (*deceive*) 545.

Adj. credulous, gullible; easily -de-ceived &c. 545; simple, green, soft, childish, silly, stupid; over-credulous, -confident; infatuated, superstitious, &c.

Phr. the wish the father to the thought; *credo quia impossibile.*

487. Incredulity.—N. incredul-ous-ness, -ity; skepticism, pyrrhonism; want of faith &c. (*irreligion*) 989.

suspiciousness &c. *adj.*; scrupulosity; suspicion &c. (*unbelief*) 485; dissent &c. 489.

unbeliever, skeptic, aporetic; atheist, agnostic, infidel, disbeliever, misbe-liever, pyrrhonist &c. 989; heretic &c. (*heterodox*) 984.

V. be -incredulous &c. *adj.*; distrust &c. (*disbelieve*) 485; refuse to believe; shut one's -eyes, – ears- to; turn a deaf ear to; hold aloof; ignore; *nullius jurare in verba magistri.*

Adj. incredulous, skeptical, unbeliev-ing, inconvincible; hard –, shy- of belief; suspicious, scrupulous, distrust-ful, heterodox &c. 984.

---

confiding &c. (*believing*) 484.

488. Assent.—N. assent, -ment; acquiescence, admission; nod; ac-, con-cord, -cordance; agreement &c. 23; affirm-ance, -ation; recognition, acknowledgment, avowal; confession, – of faith.

unanimity, common consent, *consensus*, acclamation, chorus, *vox populi*; popular –, current- -belief, – opinion; public opinion; concurrence &c. (*of causes*) 178; co-operation &c. (*voluntary*) 709.

ratification, confirmation, corroboration, approval, acceptance, *visa*; indorsement, &c. (*record*) 551; O.K.

consent &c. (*compliance*) 762.

affirmant, consenter, covenanter, subscriber, endorser, upholder.

V. assent; give –, yield –, nod- assent; acquiesce; agree &c. 23; receive, accept, accede, accord, concur, lend oneself to, consent, coincide, reciprocate, go with; be -at one with &c. *adj.*; go along –, chime in –, strike in –, close- with; echo, enter into one's views, agree in opinion; vote –, give one's voice- for; recognize; subscribe -, conform –, defer- to; say -yes, – ditto, – amen, – aye- to; to O.K.

acknowledge, own, admit, allow, avow, confess; concede &c. (*yield*) 762; come round to; abide by; permit &c. 760.

come to –, arrive at- -an understanding, – terms, – an agreement.

con-, af-firm; ratify, approve, endorse, countersign; visa; corroborate &c. 467.

go –, swim- with the stream, float with the current; be in the fashion, join in the chorus; be in every mouth.

Adj. assenting &c. *v.*; of one -accord, – mind; of the same mind, at one with, agreed, acquiescent, content; willing &c. 602.

un-contradicted, -challenged, -questioned, -controverted.

carried –, agreed- -*nem. con.* &c. *adv.*; unanimous; agreed on all hands, carried by acclamation.

affirmative &c. 535.

Adv. yes, yea, ay, aye, true; good; well; very -well, – true; well and good; granted; *placet*; even –, just- so; to be sure, surely, 'thou hast said'; truly, exactly, precisely,

489. Dissent.—N. dissent; discordance &c. (*disagreement*) 24; difference –, diversity- of opinion.

non-conformity &c. (*heterodoxy*) 984; protestantism, recusancy, schism; disaffection; secession &c. 624; recantation &c. 607.

dissension &c. (*discord*) 713; discontent &c. 832; cavilling.

protest; contradiction &c. (*denial*) 536; non-compliance &c. (*rejection*) 764; disapprobation &c. 932; hartal.

dissent-ient, -er; non-juror, -content; recusant, sectary, schismatic, protestant, non-conformist, separatist, nonco-operator, conscientious objector, passive resister.

V. dissent, demur; call in question &c. (*doubt*) 485; differ in opinion, disagree; say -no &c. 536; refuse -assent, – to admit, cavil, protest, raise one's voice against, make bold to differ; repudiate; contradict &c. (*deny*) 536; agree to differ.

have no notion of, differ *toto cælo*: revolt -at, – from the idea.

shake the head, shrug the shoulders; look -askance, – askant.

secede; recant &c. 607.

Adj. dissenting &c. *v.*; negative &c. 536; diss-ident, -entient; unconsenting &c. (*refusing*) 764; non-content, -juring; protestant, recusant; uncon-vinced, -verted.

unavowed, unacknowledged; out of the question.

discontented &c. 832; unwilling &c. 603; extorted.

sectarian, denominational, schismatic, heterodox, intolerant.

Adv. no &c. 536; at -variance, – issue- with; under protest; *non placet.*

Int. God forbid! not for the world; not on your life; I beg to differ; I'll be hanged if; never tell me; your humble servant, pardon me; tell that to the marines.

Phr. many men many minds; *quot homines tot sententiæ*; *tant s'en faut*; *il s'en faut bien.*

that's just it, indeed, certainly, certes, *ex concesso*; of course, un-questionably, assuredly, no doubt, doubtless, undoubtedly.

be it so; so -be it, – let it be, so mote it be; amen; with all my heart; willingly &c. 602.

affirmatively, in the affirmative.

with one -consent, – voice, – accord; unanimously, *unâ voce*, by common consent, in chorus, to a man, *nem. con.*; *nemine -contradi-cente*, – *dissentiente*; without a dissentient voice; as one man, one and all, on all hands.

---

490. Knowledge.—N. knowledge; cogn-izance, -ition, -oscence; acquaint-ance, experience, ken privity, insight, familiarity; com-, ap-prehension; re-cognition; appreciation &c. (*judgment*) 480; intuition; consci-ence, -ousness; perception, precognition; acroamatics.

light, enlightenment; glimpse, ink-ling; side light; glimmer, -ing; dawn; scent, suspicion; impression &c. (*idea*) 453; discovery &c. 480a.

system –, body- of knowledge; science, philosophy, pansophy; theory, etiology; circle of the sciences; pan-dect, doctrine, body of doctrine; cy-, ency-clopædia; school &c. (*system of opinions*) 484.

tree of knowledge; republic of letters &c. (*language*) 560.

erudition, learning, lore, scholarship, reading, letters; literature; book-learning, bookishness; biblio-mania, -latry; information, general informa-tion; store of -knowledge &c.; educa-tion &c. (*teaching*) 537; culture, attain-ments; acqui-rements, -sitions; ac-complishments, proficiency; practical knowledge &c. (*skill*) 698; higher edu-cation, liberal education; dilettantism; rudiments &c. (*beginning*) 66.

deep –, profound –, solid –, accurate –, acroatic –, acroamatic –, vast –, ex-ensive –, encyclopædical- -knowledge, – learning; omniscience, pantology.

march of intellect; progress –, ad-vance- of -science, – learning; school-master abroad.

V. know, ken, scan, wot; wot –, be aware &c. *adj.*- of; ween, weet, trow, have, possess.

conceive; ap-, com-prehend; take, realize, understand, appreciate; fathom, make out; recognize, discern, perceive, see, get a sight of, experience.

491. Ignorance. — N. ignorance, nescience, *tabula rasa*, crass ignorance, *ignorance crasse*; unacquaintance; un-consciousness &c. *adj.*; dark-, blind-ness; incomprehension, inexperience, simplicity.

unknown quantities, x, y, z.

sealed book, *terra incognita*, virgin soil, unexplored ground; dark ages.

[Imperfect knowledge] smattering, superficiality, half-learning, sciolism, glimmering; bewilderment &c. (*uncer-tainty*) 475; incapacity.

[Affectation of knowledge] pedantry; charlatan-ry, -ism.

V. be -ignorant &c. *adj.*; not -know &c. 490; know -not, – not what, – no-thing of; have no -idea, – notion, – conception; not have the remotest idea; not know chalk from cheese.

ignore, be blind to; keep in ignorance &c. (*conceal*) 528.

see through a glass darkly; have a -film over the eyes, – glimmering &c. *n.*; wonder whether; not know what to make of &c. (*unintelligibility*) 519; not pretend –, not take upon oneself- to say.

Adj. ignorant, nescient; un-knowing, -aware, -acquainted, -apprized, -wit-ting, -weeting, -conscious; wit-, weet-less; a stranger to; unconversant.

un-informed, -cultivated, -versed, -instructed, -taught, -initiated, -tu-tored, -schooled, -guided, -enlightened; Philistine; behind the age.

shallow, superficial, green, rude, empty, half-learned, illiterate; un-read, -informed, -educated, -learned, -let-tered, -bookish; empty-headed; low-brow; pedantic.

in the dark; be-nighted, -lated; blind-ed, -fold; hoodwinked; misin-formed; *au bout de son latin*, at the

know full well; have –, possess- some knowledge of; be -*au courant* &c. *adj.*; have -in one's head, – at one's fingers' ends; know by -heart, – rote; be master of; *connaître le dessous des cartes*, know what's what &c. 698.

see one's way; learn, discover &c. 480*a*.

come to one's knowledge &c. (*information*) 527.

Adj. knowing &c. *v.*; cognitive; acroamatic.

aware –, cognizant –, conscious- of; acquainted –, made acquainted- with; privy –, no stranger- to; *au -fait*, – *courant*; in the secret; up –, alive- to; sensible of; behind the ·scenes, – curtain; let into; apprised –, informed- of; undeceived.

proficient –, versed –, read –, forward –, strong –, at home- in; conversant –, familiar- with.

erudite, instructed, learned, lettered, educated; high-brow; well-conned, -informed, -read, -grounded, -educated; enlightened, shrewd, insightful, *savant*, blue, bookish, scholastic, solid, profound, deep-read, book-learned; accomplished &c. (*skilful*) 698; omniscient; self-taught, -educated.

known &c. *v.*; ascertained, well-known, recognized, received, notorious, noted; proverbial; familiar, – as household words, to every schoolboy; hackneyed, trite, commonplace.

knowable, cogn-oscible, -izable.

Adv. to –, to the best of- one's knowledge.

Phr. one's eyes being opened &c. (*disclosure*) 529.

end of his tether; at fault; at sea &c. (*uncertain*) 475; caught tripping.

un-known, -apprehended, -explained, -ascertained, -investigated, -explored, -heard of, -perceived; concealed &c. 528; novel.

Adv. ignorantly &c. *adj.*; unawares; for -anything, – aught- one knows; not that one knows.

Int. God –, Heaven –, the Lord –, nobody- knows.

Phr. a little learning is a dangerous thing.

---

492. Scholar—N. scholar, *connoisseur, savant*, pundit, schoolman, professor, graduate, wrangler, moonshee; academ-ician, -ist; fellow, don, post graduate, advanced student; master –, bachelor- of arts; doctor, licentiate, gownsman; philo-sopher, -math; scientist, clerk; soph, -ist, -ister; linguist, classicist; glosso-, etymo-, philologist; philologer; lexico-, glosso-grapher; scholiast, commentator, annotator, grammarian; *littérateur, literati, dilettanti, illuminati*; Mezzofanti, admirable Crichton, Mæcenas.

book-worm, *helluo librorum*, biblio-phile, -maniac; blue-stocking, *bas-bleu*; big-wig, learned Theban.

learned –, literary- man; *homo multarum literarum*; man of -learning, – letters, – education; high-brow, intelligentsia.

antiquar-ian, -y; archæologist; sage &c. (*wise man*) 500.

pedant, *doctrinaire*; pedagogue, Dr. Pangloss; pantologist.

teacher &c. 540; schoolboy &c. (*learner*) 541.

Adj. learned &c. 490; brought up at the feet of **Gamaliel.**

493. Ignoramus.—N. ignoramus, illiterate, moron, dunce, numskull, wooden spoon; no scholar.

sciolist, smatterer, dabbler, half-scholar; *charlatan*; wiseacre.

novice, griffin; greenhorn &c. (*dupe*) 547; tyro &c. (*learner*) 541.

lubber &c. (*bungler*) 701; fool &c. 501; pedant &c. 492.

Adj. bookless, shallow, simple, dense, dumb, thick, dull, ignorant &c. 491.

494. [Object of knowledge.] Truth.
—**N.** fact, reality &c. (*existence*) 1; plain matter of fact; nature &c. (*principle*) 5; truth, verity; gospel; orthodoxy &c. 983*a*; authenticity; veracity &c. 543.

accuracy, exactitude; exact-, precise-ness &c. *adj.*; precision, delicacy; rigour, mathematical precision, punctuality; clockwork precision &c. (*regularity*) 80.

orthology; *ipsissima verba*; letter of the law, realism.

plain -, honest -, sober -, naked -, unalloyed -, unqualified -, stern -, exact -, intrinsic- truth; *nuda veritas*; the very thing; not an -illusion &c. 495; real Simon Pure; unvarnished tale; the truth, the whole truth and nothing but the truth; just the thing.

V. be -true &c. *adj.*, – the case; stand the test; have the true ring; hold -good, – true, – water; conform to rule.

render -, prove- -true &c. *adj.*; substantiate &c. (*evidence*) 467.

get at the truth &c. (*discover*) 480*a*.

Adj. real, actual &c. (*existing*) 1; veritable, true; certain &c. 474; substantially -, categorically- true &c.; true -to the letter, – to life, – to scale, – the facts, – as gospel; unimpeachable; veracious &c. 543; unre-, uncon-futed; un-ideal, -imagined; realistic.

exact, accurate, definite, precise, well defined, just, right, correct, strict, severe; close &c. (*similar*) 17; literal; rigid, rigorous; scrupulous &c. (*conscientious*) 939; religiously exact, punctual, mathematical, scientific; faithful, constant, unerring; curious, particular, punctilious, meticulous, nice, delicate, fine.

genuine, authentic, legitimate, pukka; orthodox &c. 983*a*; official, *ex officio*.

pure, natural, sound, sterling; unsophisticated, -adulterated, -varnished, -coloured; in its true colours.

well-grounded, -founded; solid, substantial, tangible, valid; undis-torted, -guised; un-affected, -exaggerated, -romantic, -flattering.

Adv. truly &c. *adj.*; verily, indeed, in reality; as a matter of fact; beyond

495. Error.—**N.** error, fallacy; misconception, -apprehension, -understanding; inexactness &c. *adj.*; laxity; misconstruction &c. (*misinterpretation*) 523; miscomputation &c. (*misjudgment*) 481; *non-sequitur* &c. 477; misstatement, -report; anachronism; malapropism.

mistake; miss, fault, blunder, boner, bloomer, howler, *quid pro quo*, cross purposes, oversight, misprint, *erratum, corrigendum*, slip, blot, flaw, loose thread; trip, stumble &c. (*failure*) 732; botchery &c. (*want of skill*) 699; slip of the -tongue, – pen; *lapsus -linguæ, – calami*, clerical error; bull &c. (*absurdity*) 497.

il-, de-lusion; false -impression, – idea; bubble; self-deceit, -deception; warped notion; mists of error; superstition, exploded notion.

heresy &c. (*heterodoxy*) 984; hallucination &c. (*insanity*) 503; false light &c. (*fallacy of vision*) 443; dream &c; (*fancy*) 515; fable &c. (*untruth*) 546; bias &c. (*misjudgment*) 481; misleading &c. v.

V. be -erroneous &c. *adj.*

cause error; mis-lead, -guide; lead -astray, – into error; beguile, misinform &c. (*misteach*) 538; delude; give a false -impression, – idea; falsify, garble, misstate; deceive &c. 545; lie &c. 544.

err; be -in error &c. *adj.*, – mistaken &c. v.; be deceived &c. (*duped*) 547; mistake, receive a false impression, deceive oneself; fall into -, lie under -, labour under- -an error &c. *n.*; be in the wrong, blunder; mis-apprehend, -conceive, -understand, -reckon, -count, -calculate &c. (*misjudge*) 481.

play -, be- at cross purposes &c; (*misinterpret*) 523.

trip, stumble; lose oneself &c. (*uncertainty*) 475; go astray; fail &c. 732; take the wrong sow by the ear &c; (*mismanage*) 699; put the saddle on the wrong horse; reckon without one's host; take the shadow for the substance &c. (*credulity*) 486; dream &c; (*imagine*) 515.

Adj. erroneous, untrue, false, devoid of truth, fallacious, faulty, apocryphal,

-doubt, – question; with truth &c. (*veracity*) 543; certainly &c. (*certain*) 474; actually &c. (*existence*) 1; in effect &c. (*intrinsically*) 5.

exactly &c. *adj.*; *ad amussim*; *verbatim*, – *et literatim*; word for word, literally, *literatim*, *totidem verbis*, *sic*, to the letter, chapter and verse, *ipsissimis verbis*; *ad unguem*; to an inch; to a -nicety, – hair, – tittle, – turn, – T; *au pied de la lettre*; neither more nor less; in -every respect, – all respects; *sous tous les rapports*; at -any rate, – all events; strictly speaking.

Phr. the -truth, – fact- is; *rem acu tetigisti*.

_____

scent; in the wrong box; at cross purposes, all in the wrong, all abroad, at sea.

Adv. more or less.

496. Maxim.—N. maxim, aphorism; apo-, apoph-thegm; *dictum*, saying, gnome, adage, saw, proverb, epigram; sentence, *mot*, motto, word, by-word, precept, moral, phylactery, *protasis*, brocard.

axiom, postulate, theorem, *scholium*, truism.

reflection &c. (*idea*) 453; conclusion &c. (*judgment*) 480; golden rule &c. (*precept*) 697; principle, *principia*; profession of faith &c. (*belief*) 484; formula.

wise –, sage –, received –, admitted –, recognized- maxim &c.; true –, common –, hackneyed –, trite –, commonplace- saying &c.

Adj. aphoristic, proverbial, phylacteric; axiomatic, gnomic.

Adv. as -the saying is, – they say.

_____

unreal, ungrounded, groundless; unsubstantial &c. 4; heretical &c. (*heterodox*) 984; unsound; illogical &c. 477; wrong.

in-, un-exact; in-accurate, -correct; indefinite &c. (*uncertain*) 475.

illus-ive, -ory; delusive; mock; ideal &c. (*imaginary*) 515; spurious &c. 545; deceitful &c. 544; perverted.

controvertible, unsustain-able, -ed; unauthenticated, untrustworthy.

exploded, refuted, discarded.

in –, under an- error &c. *n.*; mistaken &c. *v.*; tripping &c. *v.*; out, – in one's reckoning; aberrant; beside –, wide of the- -mark, – truth; astray &c. (*at fault*) 475; on -a false, – the wrong-

497. Absurdity.—N. absurd-ity, -ness &c. *adj.*; imbecility &c. 499; alogy, nonsense, paradox, inconsistency; stultiloqu-y, -ence, futility.

blunder, muddle, bull; Irish-, Hibernic-ism; slip-slop; anticlimax, bathos; sophism &c. 477.

farce, burlesque, *galimatias, amphigouri*, rhapsody; farrago &c. (*disorder*) 59; extravagance, romance; sciomachy.

joke, catch, sell, pun, verbal quibble, macaronic.

jargon, fustian, twaddle &c. (*no meaning*) 517; exaggeration &c. 549; moonshine, stuff; mare's nest.

vagary, tomfoolery, mummery, monkey trick, practical joke, *boutade, escapade*.

V. play the fool &c. 499; stultify, blunder, muddle; joke; talk nonsense, *parler à tort et à travers*; *battre la campagne*; be -absurd &c. *adj.*

Adj. absurd, nonsensical, preposterous, egregious, senseless, farcical, inconsistent, ridiculous, extravagant, quibbling, futile; macaronic, punning, paradoxical.

foolish &c. 499; sophistical &c. 477; unmeaning &c. 517; without rhyme or reason; fantastic.

Int. fiddle-de-dee! pish! pish and tush! pho! stuff and nonsense! rubbish! rot! bosh! in the name of the Prophet—figs!

Phr. *credat Judæus Apella*; tell it to the marines.

Faculties

498. Intelligence. Wisdom.—N. intelligence, capacity, comprehension,

499. Imbecility. Folly.—N. want of -intelligence &c. 498, – intellect &c.

understanding; intellect &c. 450; nous, parts, sagacity, mother wit, wit, *esprit*, gumption, quick parts, grasp of intellect; acuteness &c. *adj.*; acumen, subtlety, penetration; perspica-cy, -city; discernment, long-headedness, due sense of, good judgement; discrimination &c. 465; craftiness, cunning &c. 702; refinement &c. (*taste*) 850.

head, brains, gray matter, headpiece, upper story, long head; eagle -eye, – glance; eye of a -lynx, – hawk.

wisdom, sapience, sense; good –, common –, plain –, horse- sense; clear thinking; rationality, reason; reasonableness &c. *adj.*; judgement; solidity, depth, profundity, calibre; enlarged views; reach –, compass- of thought; enlargement of mind.

genius, inspiration, *Geist*, fire of genius, heaven-born genius, soul; talent &c. (*aptitude*) 698.

[Wisdom in action] prudence &c. 864; vigilance &c. 459; tact &c. 698; foresight &c. 510; sobriety, self-possession, *aplomb*, ballast, mental -poise, – balance.

a bright thought, inspiration, brain-wave, not a bad idea.

V. be -intelligent &c. *adj.*; have all one's wits about one; understand &c. (*intelligible*) 518; catch –, take in- an idea; take a -joke, – hint.

see -through, – at a glance, – with half an eye, – far into, – through a millstone; penetrate; discern &c. (*descry*) 441; foresee &c. 510.

discriminate &c. 465; know what's what &c. 698; listen to reason.

Adj. [Applied to persons] intelligent, quick of apprehension, keen, acute, alive, brainy, awake, bright, quick, sharp; quick-, keen-, clear-, sharp--eyed, -sighted, -witted; wide awake; canny, shrewd, astute; clear-headed; far-sighted &c. 510; discerning, perspicacious, penetrating, piercing; argute; nimble-, needle-witted; sharp as a needle; alive to &c. (*cognizant*) 490; clever &c. (*apt*) 698; arch &c. (*cunning*) 702; *pas si bête* &c. 682.

wise, sage, sapient, sagacious, reasonable, rational, sound, in one's right

450; shallow-, silli-, foolish-ness &c. *adj.*; imbecility, incapacity, vacancy of mind, poverty of intellect, clouded perception, poor head, apartments to let; stup-, stol-idity; hebetude, dull understanding, meanest capacity; short-sightedness; incompetence &c. (*unskilfulness*) 699.

one's weak side; bias &c. 481; infatuation &c. (*insanity*) 503.

simplicity, puerility, babyhood; dotage, anility, second childishness, senile dementia, fatuity; idio-cy, -tism; drivelling.

folly, frivolity, desipience, irrationality, trifling, ineptitude, nugacity, inconsistency, lip-wisdom, conceit; sophistry &c. 477; giddiness &c. (*inattention*) 458; eccentricity &c. 503; extravagance &c. (*absurdity*) **497;** rashness &c. 863.

act of folly &c. 699.

V. be -imbecile &c. *adj.*; have no -brains, – sense &c. 498.

trifle, drivel, *radoter*, dote; ramble &c. (*madness*) 503; play the -fool, – monkey, – goat, take leave of one's senses; not see an inch beyond one's nose; stultify oneself &c. 699; talk nonsense &c. 497.

Adj. [Applied to persons] un-intelligent, -intellectual, -reasoning; mind-, wit-, reason-, brain-less; having no -head &c. 498; not -bright &c. 498; inapprehensible.

weak-, addle-, puzzle-, blunder-, muddle-, muddy-, pig-, beetle-, maggoty-, gross-headed; beef-, fat- -witted, -headed.

weak-, feeble-minded; dull-, shallow-, rattle-, lack-brained; half-, nit-, short-, dull-, blunt-witted; shallow-, clod-, addle-pated; dim-, short-sighted; thick-skulled; weak in the upper story.

shallow, *borné*, weak, wanting, soft, nutty, sappy, spoony; dull, – as a beetle; stupid, heavy, insulse, obtuse, blunt, stolid, doltish, asinine; inapt &c. 699; prosaic &c. 843.

child-ish, -like; infant-ine, -ile; baby-, bab-ish; puerile, anile; simple &c. (*credulous*) 486.

fatuous, idiotic, imbecile, moronic

mind, sensible, *abnormis sapiens*, judicious, strong-minded.

un-prejudiced, -biassed, -bigoted, -prepossessed; un-dazzled, -perplexed; of unwarped judgment, impartial, equitable, fair, broad-minded.

cool; cool-, long-, hard-, strong-headed; long-sighted, calculating, thoughtful, reflecting; solid, deep, profound.

oracular; heaven-directed, -born.

prudent &c. (*cautious*) 864; sober, staid, solid; considerate, politic, wise in one's generation; watchful &c. 459; provident &c. (*prepared*) 673; in advance of one's age; wise as -a serpent, - Solomon, - Solon.

[Applied to actions] wise, sensible, reasonable, judicious; well-judged, -advised; prudent, politic; expedient &c. 646.

---

500. Sage.—N. sage, wise man; pundit; master -mind, - spirit of the age; longhead, thinker, philosopher.

authority, oracle, mentor, luminary, shining light, *esprit fort*, *magnus Apollo*, Solon, Solomon, Nestor, Magi, 'second Daniel.'

man of learning &c. 492; expert &c. 700; wizard &c. 994.

[Ironically] wiseacre, bigwig.

Adj. wise, learned; authoritative, oracular; erudite &c. 490; venerable, reverenced, revered, *emeritus*.

---

drivelling; blatant, babbling; vacant; sottish; bewildered &c. 475.

blockish, unteachable; Bœot-ian, -ic; bovine; un-gifted, -discerning, -enlightened, -wise, -philosophical; apish.

foolish, silly, senseless, irrational, insensate, nonsensical, inept; maudlin.

narrow-minded &c. 481; bigoted &c. (*obstinate*) 606; giddy &c. (*thoughtless*) 458; rash &c. 863; eccentric &c. (*crazed*) 503.

[Applied to actions] foolish, unwise, indiscreet, injudicious, improper, unreasonable, without reason, ridiculous, silly, stupid, asinine; ill-imagined, -advised, -judged, -devised; inconsistent, irrational, unphilosophical; extravagant &c. (*nonsensical*) 497; sleeveless, idle; useless &c. 645; inexpedient &c. 647; frivolous &c. (*trivial*) 643; absurd &c. 497.

Phr. *Davus sum non Œdipus.*

501. Fool.—N. fool, idiot, tomfool, wiseacre, simpleton, Simple Simon, nit-wit, witling, dizzard, donkey, ass; ninny, -hammer; moron, dolt, booby, Tom Noddy, looby, hoddy-doddy, noddy, nonny, noodle, nizy, owl; goose, -cap; *imbécile*; gaby, *radoteur*, nincompoop, *badaud*, zany; trifler, babbler; pretty fellow; natural, *niais*.

child, baby, infant, innocent, milksop, sop.

oaf, lout, loon, lown, dullard, doodle, calf, colt, buzzard, block, put, stick, stock, numps, tony.

bull-, dunder-, addle-, block-, dull-, logger-, jolt-, jolter-, beetle-, gross-, thick-, giddy-head; num-, thick-skull; lack-, shallow-brain; half-, lack-wit; dunder-pate; fat-head, poor stick.

sawney, gowk; clod, -hopper; clod-, clot-poll, -pate; bull-calf; men of Bœotia, wise men of Gotham.

un sot à triple étage, sot; jobbernowl, changeling, mooncalf, *gobemouche*.

dotard, driveller; old -fogey, - woman; crone, grandmother.

greenhorn &c. (*dupe*) 547; dunce &c. (*ignoramus*) 493; lubber &c. (*bungler*) 701; madman &c. 504.

one who -will not set the Thames on fire, - did not invent gunpowder; *qui n'a pas inventé la poudre*; no conjuror.

502. Sanity.—N. sanity; soundness &c. *adj.*; rationality, normality, sobriety, lucidity, lucid interval; senses, sober senses, sound mind, *mens sana*.

503. Insanity.—N. disordered -reason, - intellect; diseased -, unsound -, abnormal- mind; derangement, unsoundness.

V. be -sane &c. *adj.*; retain one's senses, – reason.

become -sane &c. *adj.*; come to one's senses, sober down.

render -sane &c. *adj.*; bring to one's senses, sober.

Adj. sane, rational, reasonable, *compos mentis*, of sound mind; sound, -minded.

self-possessed; sober, -minded.

in one's -sober senses, – right mind; in possession of one's faculties.

Adv. sanely &c. *adj.*

insanity, lunacy; madness &c. *adj.*; mania, *rabies*, *furor*, mental alienation, paranoia, aberration; *amentia*, dementation, -tia, -cy; *dementia præcox*; *morosis*, idiocy, phrenitis, frenzy, raving, incoherence, wandering, delirium, calenture of the brain, delusion, hallucination; lycanthropy, brain storm, *delirium tremens*, D.T's.

vertigo, dizziness, swimming; sunstroke, *coup de soleil*, siriasis.

fanaticism, infatuation, craze; oddity, eccentricity, twist, monomania; klepto-, dipso-mania; hypochondriasis &c. (*low spirits*) 837; *melancholia*, hysteria.

screw –, tile –, slate- loose; bee in one's bonnet, rats in the upper story; dotage &c. (*imbecility*) 499.

V. be –, become- -insane &c. *adj.*; lose one's senses, – reason, – faculties, – wits; go –, run- mad, run amuck; rave, dote, ramble, wander; drivel &c. (*be imbecile*) 499; have a -screw loose &c. *n.*, – devil; *avoir le diable au corps*; lose one's head &c. (*be uncertain*) 475.

derange, render –, drive- -mad &c. *adj.*; madden, dementate, addle the wits, derange the head, infatuate, befool; turn -the brain, – one's head.

Adj. insane, mad, lunatic; crazy, crazed, *aliéné*, *non compos mentis*; not right, cracked, touched; bereft of reason; unhinged, deranged, unsettled in one's mind; insensate, reasonless, beside oneself, demented, daft; phren-, fren-zied, -etic; possessed, – with a devil; far gone, maddened, moonstruck; shatterpated; barmy; mad-, scatter-, shatter-, crack-brained; off one's head; bug-house, *loco*.

maniacal; manic, manic-depressive; delirious, light-headed, incoherent, rambling, doting, wandering; frantic, raving, stark staring mad, amok, amuck, berserk.

corybantic, dithyrambic; rabid, giddy, vertiginous, dizzy, wild, haggard, mazed; flighty; distr-acted, -aught; bewildered &c. (*uncertain*) 475.

mad as a -March hare, – hatter; of -unsound mind &c. *n.*; touched –, wrong –, not right- in one's -head, – mind, – wits, – upper story; out of one's -mind, – senses, – wits; not in one's right mind.

fanatical, infatuated, odd, eccentric; hipp-ed, -ish.

imbecile, silly &c. 499.

Adv. like one possessed.

Phr. the mind having lost its balance; the reason under a cloud; *tête -exaltée, -montée.*

504. Madman.—**N.** madman, lunatic, maniac, bedlamite, candidate for Bedlam, raver, madcap; energumen; paranoiac; auto-, mono-, pyro-, megalo-, dipso-, klepto-maniac; hypochondriac &c. (*low spirits*) 837.

dreamer &c. 515; rhapsodist, seer, high-flier, enthusiast, crank, eccentric, nut, fanatic, *fanatico*; *exalté*; knight errant, Don Quixote.

idiot &c. 501.

Section VI. Extension of Thought

1°. *To the Past*

505. Memory.—N. memory, remembrance; reten-tion, -tiveness; tenacity; *veteris vestigia flammæ*; tablets of the memory; readiness.

reminiscence, recognition, recurrence, recollection, rememoration; retrospect, -ion; after-thought.

suggestion &c. (*information*) 527; prompting &c. *v.*; hint, reminder, token of remembrance, *memento, souvenir*, keepsake, relic, *memorandum*; remembrancer, flapper; memorial &c. (*record*) 551; commemoration &c. (*celebration*) 883.

things to be remembered, *memorabilia*.

art of –, artificial- memory; *memoria technica*; mnemo-nics, -technics; phrenotypics; Mnemosyne; memorandum-, note-, engagement-, prompt-book.

retentive –, tenacious –, green –, trustworthy –, capacious –, faithful –, correct –, exact –, ready –, prompt-memory.

V. remember, mind; retain the -memory, – remembrance- of; keep in view.

have –, hold –, bear –, carry –, keep –, retain- in *or* in the -thoughts, – mind, – memory, – remembrance; be in –, live in –, remain in –, dwell in –, haunt –, impress- one's -memory, – thoughts, – mind.

sink in the mind; run in the head; not be able to get it out of one's head; be deeply impressed with; rankle &c. (*revenge*) 919.

recur to the mind; flash -on the mind, – across the memory.

recognize, recollect, bethink oneself, recall, call up, conjure up, retrace; look –, trace- -back, – backwards; think –, look back- upon; review; call –, recall –, bring- to mind; remembrance; carry one's thoughts back; rake up the past.

suggest &c. (*inform*) 527; prompt; put –, keep- in mind; remind; fan the embers; call –, summon –, rip- up; renew; *infandum renovare dolorem*; task –, tax –, jog –, flap –, refresh –, rub up –, awaken-the memory; pull by the sleeve; bring back to the memory, put in remembrance, memorialize.

get –, have –, learn –, know –, say –, repeat- by -heart – rote; drive –, get- into -one's head; say one's lesson; repeat, – as a parrot; have at one's fingers' ends.

506. Oblivion.—N. oblivion; forgetfulness &c. *adj.*; obliteration &c. 552, of –, insensibility &c. 823 to- the past.

short –, treacherous –, loose –, slippery –, failing- memory; decay –, failure –, lapse- of memory; memory like a sieve; waters of -Lethe, – oblivion, *amnesia*.

pardon, acquittal, amnesty, oblivion; absolution.

V. forget; be -forgetful &c. *adj.*; fall –, sink- into oblivion; have -a short memory &c. *n.*, – no head.

forget one's own name, have on the tip of one's tongue, come in at one ear and go out at the other.

slip –, escape –, fade from –, die away from- the memory; lose, – sight of.

unlearn; efface &c. 552 –, discharge-from the memory; consign to -oblivion, – the tomb of the Capulets; think no more of &c. (*turn the attention from*) 458; cast behind one's back, wean one's thoughts from; let bygones be bygones &c. (*forgive*) 918.

Adj. forgotten &c. *v.*; unremembered, past recollection, bygone, out of mind; buried –, sunk- in oblivion; clean forgotten; gone out of one's -head, – recollection.

forgetful, oblivious, mindless, heedless, Lethean; insensible &c. 823- to the past.

Phr. *non mi ricordo*; the memory -failing, – deserting one, – being at (*or* in) fault.

commit to memory; memorize; con, – over; fix –, rivet –, imprint –, impress –, stamp –, grave –, engrave –, store –, treasure up –, bottle up –, embalm –, enshrine- in the memory; load –, store –, stuff –, burden- the memory with.

redeem from oblivion; keep the memory -alive, – green; *tangere ulcus*; keep up the memory of; commemorate &c. (*celebrate*) 883.

make a note of &c. (*record*) 551.

Adj. remember-ing, -ed &c. *v.*; mindful, reminiscential; retained in the memory &c. *v.*; pent up in one's memory; fresh; green, – in remembrance, still vivid; unforgotten, present to the mind; within one's -memory &c. *n.*; indelible; not to be forgotten, unforgettable, enduring; uppermost in one's thoughts; memorable &c. (*important*) 642.

Adv. by -heart, – rote; without book, *memoriter*.

in memory of; *in memoriam*; suggestive.

Phr. *manet altâ mente repostum; forsan et hæc olim meminisse juvabit.*

2°. To the Future

507. Expectation.—N. expect-ation, -ance, -ancy; anticipation, reckoning, calculation; contingency; foresight &c. 510.

contemplation, prospection, look out; prospect, perspective, horizon, vista; destiny &c. 152.

suspense, waiting, abeyance; curiosity &c. 455; anxious –, ardent –, eager –, breathless –, sanguine- expectation; torment of Tantalus.

presumption, hope &c. 858; trust &c. (*belief*) 484; prognostication, auspices &c. (*prediction*) 511.

V. expect; look -for, – out for, – forward to; hope for, anticipate; have in -prospect, – contemplation; keep in view; contemplate, promise oneself; not -wonder &c. 870 -at, – if.

wait –, tarry –, lie in wait –, watch –, bargain- for; keep a -good, – sharp- look-out for; await; stand at 'attention,' abide, bide one's –, mark- time, watch.

foresee &c. 510; prepare for &c. 673; forestall &c. (*be early*) 132; count upon &c. (*believe in*) 484; think likely &c. (*probability*) 472; make one's mouth water.

lead one to expect &c. (*predict*) 511; have in store for &c. (*destiny*) 152.

prick up one's ears, hold one's breath.

Adj. expectant; expecting &c. *v.*; in -expectation &c. *n.*; on the watch &c. (*vigilant*) 459; open -eyed, -mouthed;

508. Inexpectation.—N. in-, non-expectation; false expectation &c. (*disappointment*) 509; miscalculation &c. 481; unforeseen contingency, the unforeseen, the unexpected.

surprise, sudden burst, thunderclap, blow, shock; bolt out of the blue; eye-opener; wonder &c. 870.

V. not -expect &c. 507; be taken by surprise; start; miscalculate &c. 481; not bargain for; come –, fall- upon.

be -unexpected &c. *adj.*; come -unawares &c. *adv.*; turn up, pop, drop from the clouds; come –, burst –, flash –, bounce –, steal –, creep- upon one; come –, burst- like a thunderclap, -bolt; take –, catch- -by surprise, – unawares, – napping.

pounce –, spring a mine- upon.

surprise, startle, take aback, electrify, stun, stagger, take away one's breath, throw off one's guard; astonish &c. (*strike with wonder*) 870.

Adj. non-expectant; surprised &c. *v.*; un-warned, -aware; off one's guard; inattentive &c. 458.

un-expected, -anticipated, -prepared for, -looked for, -foreseen, -hoped for; dropped from the clouds; beyond –, contrary to –, against- expectation; out of one's reckoning; unheard of &c. (*exceptional*) 83; startling; sudden &c. (*instantaneous*) 113.

Adv. abruptly, unexpectedly, plump, pop, *à l'improviste*, unawares; without

agape, gaping, all agog; on -tenter-
hooks, – tiptoe, – the tiptoe of expectation; *aux aguets*; ready; curious &c.
455; looking forward to; prepared for;
on the rack.

   expected &c. *v.*; long expected, foreseen; in prospect &c. *n.*; prospective;
in -one's eye, – view, – the horizon;
impending &c. (*destiny*) 152.

-notice, – warning, – saying 'by your
leave'; like a -thief in the night, –
thunderbolt; in an unguarded moment;
suddenly &c. (*instantaneously*) 113.

   Int. heyday! &c. (*wonder*) 870.

   Phr. little did one -think, – expect;
nobody would ever -suppose, – think,
– expect; who would have thought?

   Adv. expectantly; in the event of; on the watch &c. *adj.*; with
-breathless expectation &c. *n.*, – bated breath, – eyes, – ears strained;
rrectis auribus; on edge.

   Phr. we shall see; *nous verrons.*

      509. [Failure of expectation.] **Disappointment.**—**N.** disappointment,
disillusionment; blighted hope, balk; blow; slip 'twixt cup and lip;
non-fulfilment of one's hopes; sad –, bitter- disappointment; trick of
fortune; afterclap; false –, vain- expectation; miscalculation &c. 481;
fool's paradise; much cry and little wool.

   V. be disappointed; look -blank, – blue; look –, stand- -aghast &c.
(*wonder*) 870; find to one's cost; laugh on the wrong side of one's
mouth; find one a false prophet.

   disappoint; crush –, dash –, balk –, disappoint –, blight –, falsify –,
defeat –, not realize- one's -hope, – expectation; balk, jilt, bilk; play one
-false, – a trick; dash the cup from the lips; tantalize; dumb-found,
-founder; disillusion, -ize; dissatisfy, disgruntle.

   Adj. disappointed &c. *v.*; disconcerted, aghast; out of one's reckoning; disgruntled.

   Phr. the mountain brought forth a mouse; *nascitur ridiculus mus*;
parturiunt montes; *dis aliter visum*, the bubble burst; one's countenance
falling.

      510. Foresight.—**N.** foresight, prospicience, prevision, longsighted-
ness; anticipation; providence &c. (*preparation*) 673.

   fore-thought, -cast; pre-deliberation, -surmise; foregone conclusion
&c. (*prejudgment*) 481; prudence &c. (*caution*) 864.

   foreknowledge; *prognosis*; pre-cognition, -science, -notion, -sentiment;
second sight; sagacity &c. (*intelligence*) 498.

   prospect &c. (*expectation*) 507; foretaste; prospectus &c. (*plan*) 626.

   V. foresee; look -forwards to, – ahead, – beyond; scent from afar;
feel in one's bones; look –, pry –, peep- into the future.

   see one's way; see how the -land lies, – wind blows, – cat jumps.

   anticipate; expect &c. 507; be beforehand &c. (*early*) 132; predict
&c. 511; fore-know, -judge, -cast; surmise; have an eye to the -future,
– main chance; *respicere finem*; keep a sharp look-out &c. (*vigilance*)
459; forewarn &c. 668.

   Adj. foreseeing &c. *v.*; prescient; anticipatory; far-seeing, -sighted;
sagacious &c. (*intelligent*) 498; weather-wise; provident &c. (*prepared*)
673; prospective &c. 507.

   Adv. against the time when.

      511. Prediction.—**N.** prediction, announcement; program, programme
&c. (*plan*) 626; premonition &c. (*warning*) 668; *prognosis*, prophecy,
vaticination, mantology, prognostication, premonstration, augur-y,
·ation; a-, ha-riolation; fore-, a-boding; bode-, abode-ment; omin-ation,

-ousness; auspices, forecast; sign, presage, prognostic; omen &c. 512; horoscope, nativity; sooth, -saying; fortune-telling; divination; crystal gazing, necromancy &c. 992; prophet &c. 512.

[Divination by the stars] astrology, horoscopy, astromancy, judicial astrology.*

[Place of prediction] *adytum*.

prefigur-ation, -ement; prototype, type.

V. predict, prognosticate, prophesy, vaticinate, divine, foretell, sooth-say, augurate, tell fortunes; cast a -horoscope, – nativity; advise; forewarn &c. 668.

presage, augur, bode; a-, fore-bode, -cast; fore-, be-token; pre-figure, -show; portend; fore-show, -shadow, shadow forth, typify, ominate, signify, point to, precurse.

usher in, herald, premise, announce; lower.

hold out –, raise –, excite- -expectation, – hope; bid fair, promise, lead one to expect; be the -precursor &c. 64.

Adj. predicting &c. *v.*; predictive, prophetic, fatidical, vaticinal, oracular, Sibylline, haruspical, weatherwise.

ominous, presageful, portentous; augur-ous, -al, -ial; auspici-al, -ous; prescious, monitory, extispicious, premonitory, precursory, significant of, pregnant with, big with the fate of.

Phr. 'coming events cast their shadows before.'

512. Omen.—N. omen, portent, presage, prognostic, augury, auspice; sign &c. (*indication*) 550; herald, forerunner, harbinger &c. (*precursor*) 64.

bird of ill omen; signs of the times; gathering clouds; warning &c. 668.

prefigurement &c. 511.

513. Oracle.—N. oracle; prophet, -ess; seer, soothsayer, augur, fortune-teller, palmist, medium, clairvoyant, crystal gazer, witch, geomancer, *aruspex*; a-, ha-ruspice; Sibyl; Python, -ess; Pythia; Pythian –, Delphian- oracle; Monitor, Sphinx, Tiresias, Cassandra, Sibylline leaves; Zadkiel, Old Moore; sorcerer &c. 994; interpreter &c. 524.

Section VII. Creative Thought

514. Supposition.—N. supposition, assumption, postulation, condi-tion, pre-supposition, hypothesis, postulate, *postulatum*, theory, *data*; pro-, position; *thesis*, theorem; proposal &c. (*plan*) 626.

---

* The following terms, expressive of different forms of divination, have been col-lected from various sources, and are here given as a curious illustration of bygone superstitions:

Divination *by oracles*, Theomancy; *by the Bible*, Bibliomancy; *by ghosts*, Psycho-mancy; *by spirits seen in a magic lens*, Cristallomantia; *by shadows or manes*, Scio-mancy; *by appearances in the air*, Aeromancy, Chaomancy; *by the stars at birth*, Genethliacs; *by meteors*, Meteoromancy; *by winds*, Austromancy; *by sacrificial ap-pearances*, Aruspicy (*or* Haruspicy), Hieromancy, Hieroscopy; *by the entrails of animals sacrificed*, Hieromancy; *by the entrails of a human sacrifice*, Anthropomancy; *by the entrails of fishes*, Ichthyomancy; *by sacrificial fire*, Pyromancy; *by red-hot iron*, Sidero-mancy; *by smoke from the altar*, Capnomancy; *by mice*, Myomancy; *by birds*, Orniscopy, Ornithomancy; *by a cock picking up grains*, Alectryomancy (*or* Alectoromancy); *by fishes*, Ophiomancy; *by herbs*, Botanomancy; *by water*, Hydromancy; *by fountains*

bare –, vague –, loose- -supposition, – suggestion; conceit; conjecture; guess, – work; rough guess, shot; conjecturality; surmise, suspicion, inkling, suggestion, suggestiveness, association of ideas, hint; presumption &c. (*belief*) 484; divination, speculation.

theorist, speculator, doctrinarian, hypothesist.

V. suppose, conjecture, surmise, suspect, guess, divine; theorize; pre-sume, -surmise, -suppose; assume, fancy, wis, take it; give a guess, speculate, believe, dare say, take it into one's head, take for granted.

put forth; pro-pound, -pose; moot; hypothesize; start, put a case, submit, move, make a motion; hazard –, throw out –, put forward- a - suggestion, – conjecture.

allude to, suggest, hint, put it into one's head.

suggest itself &c. (*thought*) 451; run in the head &c. (*memory*) 505; marvel –, wonder- -if, – whether.

Adj. supposing &c. *v.*; given, mooted, postulatory; assumed &c. *v.* supposit-ive, -itious; gratuitous, speculative, conjectural, hypothetical, suppositional, theoretical, academic, supposable, presumptive, putative.

suggestive, allusive, stimulating.

Adv. if, – so be; an; on the -supposition &c. *n.*; *ex hypothesi*; in -case, – the event of; *quasi*, as if, provided; perhaps &c. (*by possibility*) 470; for aught one knows.

515. Imagination.—N. imagination; originality; invention; fancy; inspiration; *verve*; empathy.

warm –, heated –, excited –, sanguine –, ardent –, fiery –, boiling –, wild –, bold –, daring –, playful –, lively –, fertile- -imagination, – fancy.

'mind's eye'; 'such stuff as dreams are made of.'

ideal-ity, -ism; romanticism, utopianism, castle-building; dreaming; frenzy; ecs-, ex-tasy; calenture &c. (*delirium*) 503; reverie, brown study, trance; somnambulism.

conception, *vorstellung*, excogitation, 'a fine frenzy,' poetic frenzy, divine afflatus; cloud-, dream-land; flight –, fumes- of fancy; 'thick-coming fancies'; creation –, coinage- of the brain; imagery, word painting.

conceit, maggot, figment, myth, dream, vision, shadow, chimera; phan-tasm, -tasy; fantasy, fancy; whim, -sey; vagary, rhapsody, romance, *extravaganza*; air-drawn dagger, bugbear, nightmare; flying Dutchman, great sea-serpent, man in the moon, castle in the air, *châteaux en Espagne*; Utopia, Atlantis, happy valley, millennium, fairy land; land of Prester John, kingdom of Micomicon; work of fiction &c. (*novel*) 594; poetry &c. 597; drama &c. 599; Arabian nights; *le pot au lait*; dream of Alnaschar &c. (*hope*) 858; day –, golden- dream.

illusion &c. (*error*) 495; phantom &c. (*fallacy of vision*) 443; *Fata*

Pegomancy; *by a wand*, Rhabdomancy; *by dough of cakes*, Crithomancy; *by meal.* Aleuromancy, Alphitomancy; *by salt*, Halomancy; *by dice*, Cleromancy; *by arrows*, Belomancy; *by a balanced hatchet*, Axinomancy; *by a balanced sieve*, Coscinomancy; *by a suspended ring*, Dactyliomancy; *by dots made at random on paper*, Geomancy; *by precious stones*, Lithomancy; *by pebbles*, Pessomancy; *by pebbles drawn from a heap*, Psephomancy; *by mirrors*, Catoptromancy; *by writings in ashes*, Tephramancy; *by dreams*, Oneiromancy; *by the hand*, Palmistry, Chiromancy; *by nails reflecting the sun's rays*, Onychomancy; *by finger rings*, Dactylomancy; *by numbers*, Arithmancy; *by drawing lots*, Sortilege; *by passages in books*, Stichomancy; *by the letters forming the name of the person*, Onomancy, Nomancy; *by the features*, Anthroposcopy; *by the mode of laughing*, Geloscopy; *by ventriloquism*, Gastromancy; *by walking in a circle*, Gyromancy; *by dropping melted wax into water*, Ceromancy; *by currents*, Bletonism.

Morgana &c. (*ignis fatuus*) 423; vapour &c. (*cloud*) 353; stretch of the imagination &c. (*exaggeration*) 549.

idealist, romanticist, visionary; mopus; romancer, dreamer; som-nambulist; rhapsodist &c. (*fanatic*) 504.

V. imagine, fancy, conceive; ideal-, real-ize; dream, – of; 'give to airy nothing a local habitation and a name.'

create, originate, devise, invent, coin, fabricate; improvise, strike out something new.

set one's wits to work; strain –, crack- one's invention; rack –, ransack –, cudgel- one's brains; excogitate.

give -play, – the reins, – a loose- to the -imagination, – fancy; empathize; indulge in reverie.

conjure up a vision; fancy –, represent –, picture –, figure- to one-self; envisage.

float in the mind; suggest itself &c. (*thought*) 451.

Adj. imagined &c. *v.*; *ben trovato*; air-drawn, -built.

imagin-ing &c. *v.*, -ative; original, inventive, creative, fertile, pro-ductive; ingenious.

romantic, high-flown, flighty, extravagant, fanatic, enthusiastic, Uto-pian, Quixotic; preposterous, rhapsodical.

ideal, unreal; in the clouds, *in nubibus*; unsubstantial &c. 4; illusory &c. (*fallacious*) 495; fictitious, theoretical, hypothetical.

fabulous, legendary; myth-ic, -ological; chimerical; imagin-, vision-ary; notional; fan-cy, -ciful, -tastic, -tastical; whimsical; fairy, -like.

dreamy, entranced, vaporous.

Division (II.) COMMUNICATION OF IDEAS
Section I. Nature of Ideas Communicated

516. [Idea to be conveyed.] **Meaning.** [Thing signified.]—N. meaning; signific-ation, -ance; sense, expression; im-, pur-port; drift, tenor, implication, connotation, essence, force, spirit, bear-ing, colouring; scope.

matter; subject, -matter; argument, text, sum and substance; gist &c. 5.

general –, broad –, substantial –, colloquial –, literal –, plain –, simple –, accepted –, natural –, unstrained –, true &c. (*exact*) 494 –, honest &c. 543 –, *primâ facie* &c. (*manifest*) 525- meaning.

literality; literal interpretation; after acceptation; allusion &c. (*latency*) 526; suggestion &c. (*information*) 527; syn-onym; figure of speech &c. 521; acceptation &c. (*interpretation*) 522.

V. mean, signify, express, connote, denote; im-, pur-port; convey, imply, breathe, indicate, bespeak, bear a sense; tell –, speak- of; touch on; point –, allude- to; drive at; involve &c. (*latency*) 526; declare &c. (*affirm*) 535.

517. [Absence of meaning.] **Unmean-ingness.**—N. unmeaningness &c. *adj.*; scrabble, scribble, scrawl, daub, (*paint-ing*), strumming (*music*).

empty sound, dead letter, *vox et præterea nihil*; 'a tale told by an idiot, full of sound and fury, signifying nothing'; 'sounding brass and a tinkling cymbal.'

nonsense, jargon, gibberish, jabber, mere words, hocus-pocus, fustian, rant, bombast, balderdash, palaver, patter, flummery, verbiage, babble, *bavardage, baragouin*, platitude, *niaiserie*; inanity; rigmarole, rodomontade; truism; *nugæ canoræ*; twaddle, twattle, fudge, trash; stuff, – and nonsense; bosh, rubbish, rot, drivel, moonshine, wish-wash, fiddle-faddle, flapdoodle; absurdity &c. 497; vagueness &c. (*unintelligibility*) 519.

V. mean nothing; be -unmeaning &c. *adj.*; twaddle, quibble, rant, gabble, scrabble &c. *n.*

Adj. unmeaning; meaning-, sense-less;

understand by &c. (*interpret*) 522.

Adj. meaning &c. *v.*; expressive, suggestive, meaningful, allusive; signific-ant, -ative, -atory; pithy; full of –, pregnant with- meaning.

declaratory &c. 535; intelligible &c. 518; literal, metaphrastic; synonymous; tantamount &c. (*equivalent*) 27; implied &c. (*latent*) 526; explicit &c. 525; literal &c. 562.

Adv. to that effect; that is to say &c. (*being interpreted*) 522.

literally; evidently, from the context.

518. Intelligibility.—N. intelligibility, clearness, clarity, explicitness &c. *adj.*; lucidity, perspicuity; legibility, plain speaking &c. (*manifestation*) 525; precision &c. 494; a word to the wise.

V. be -intelligible &c. *adj.*; speak -for itself, – volumes; tell its own tale, lie on the surface.

render -intelligible &c. *adj.*; popularize, simplify, clear up; elucidate &c. (*explain*) 522.

understand, comprehend; take, – in; catch, grasp, recognize, follow, collect, master, make out; see -with half an eye, – daylight, – one's way; enter into the ideas of; come to an understanding.

Adj. intelligible; clear, – as -day, – crystal, – noonday; lucid; per-, transpicuous; luminous, transparent; comprehensible.

easily understood, easy to understand, for the million, intelligible to the meanest capacity, popularized.

plain, distinct, explicit, clear-cut; positive; definite &c. (*precise*) 494.

graphic, vivid, telling; expressive &c. (*meaning*) 516; illustrative &c. (*explanatory*) 522.

un-ambiguous, -equivocal, -mistakable &c. (*manifest*) 525, -confused; legible, recognizable; obvious &c. 525.

Adv. in plain -terms, – words, – English.

Phr. he that runs may read &c. (*manifest*) 525.

nonsensical; void of -sense &c. 516; in-, un-expressive; vacant, fatuous; not significant; insignificant.

trashy, washy, inane, vague, trumpery, trivial, fiddle-faddle, twaddling, quibbling.

unmeant, not expressed; tacit &c. (*latent*) 526.

inexpressible, undefinable, incommunicable.

Int. rubbish! &c. 497.

---

519. Unintelligibility.—N. unintelligibility, incomprehensibility, imperspicuity; inconceivableness, vagueness &c. *adj.*; obscurity; ambiguity &c. 520; doubtful meaning; uncertainty &c. 475; perplexity &c. (*confusion*) 59; spinosity; *obscurum per obscurius*; mystification &c. (*concealment*) 528; latency &c. 526; transcendentalism.

paradox; enigma, riddle &c. (*secret*) 533; *dignus vindice nodus*; sealed book; steganography, Freemasonry.

pons asinorum, asses' bridge; double –, high- Dutch, Greek, Hebrew; jargon &c. (*unmeaning*) 517.

obscurantist.

V. be -unintelligible &c. *adj.*; require -explanation &c. 522; have a doubtful meaning, pass comprehension.

render -unintelligible &c. *adj.*; conceal &c. 528; darken &c. 421; confuse &c. (*derange*) 61; perplex &c. (*bewilder*) 475.

not -understand &c. 518; lose, – the clue; miss; not know what to make of, be able to make nothing of, give it up; not be able to -account for, – make either head or tail of; be at sea &c. (*uncertain*) 475; wonder &c. 870; see through a glass darkly &c. (*ignorance*) 491.

not understand one another; play at cross purposes &c. (*misinterpret*) 523.

Adj. un-intelligible, -accountable, -decipherable, -discoverable, -knowable, -fathomable; in-cognizable, -explicable, -scrutable; inap-, incomprehensible; insol-vable, -uble; impenetrable.

illegible, indecipherable, as Greek to one, unexplained, para-doxical; enigmatic, -al; puzzling, baffling.

obscure, dark, muddy, clear as mud, seen through a mist, dim, nebulous, shrouded in mystery; undiscernible &c. (*invisible*) 447; misty &c. (*opaque*) 426; hidden &c. 528; latent &c. 526.

indefinite &c. (*indistinct*) 447; perplexed &c. (*confused*) 59; undetermined, vague, loose, ambiguous; mysterious; mystic, -al; transcendental; occult, recondite, esoteric, abstruse, crabbed.

incon-ceivable, -ceptible; searchless; above –, beyond –, past-comprehension; beyond one's depth; unconceived.

inexpressible, undefinable, incommunicable, unutterable, ineffable, unpronounceable.

520. [Having a double sense.] **Equivocalness.**—**N.** equivocalness &c. *adj.*; double -meaning &c. 516; ambiguity, *double entendre*, pun, para-gram, *calembour*, quibble, *équivoque*, anagram; conundrum &c. (*riddle*) 533; word-play &c. (*wit*) 842; homonym, -y; amphibo-ly, -logy; am-biloquy.

Sphinx, Delphic oracle.

equivocation &c. (*duplicity*) 544; white lie, mental reservation &c. (*concealment*) 528.

V. be -equivocal &c. *adj.*; have two -meanings &c. 516; equivocate &c. (*palter*) 544.

Adj. equivocal, ambiguous, amphibolous, homonymous; double-tongued &c. (*lying*) 544.

521. Metaphor.—**N.** figure of speech; *façon de parler*, way of speaking, colloquialism.

phrase &c. 566; figure, trope, metaphor, tralatition, metonymy, enallage, *catachresis, synecdoche, antonomasia*; irony, satire, figurative-ness &c. *adj.*; image, -ry; *metalepsis*, type, anagoge, simile, personifica-tion, *prosopopæia*, allegory, apologue, parable, fable; allusion, adum-bration; application; euphemism; euphuism.

V. employ -metaphor &c. *n.*; personify, allegorize, adumbrate, shadow forth, apply, allude –, refer- to.

Adj. metaphorical &c. *n.*; figurative, catachrestical, typical, tralati-tious, parabolic, allegorical, allusive, anagogical; ironical; colloquial.

Adv. so to -speak, – say, – express oneself; as it were.

Phr. *mutato nomine de te fabula narratur.*

522. Interpretation.—**N.** interpreta-tion, definition; explan-, explic-ation; solution, answer; rationale; plain –, simple –, strict- interpretation; mean-ing &c. 516.

translation; rend-ering, -ition; red-dition; literal –, free- translation; key, crib; secret; clew &c. (*indication*) 550; Rosetta stone.

exegesis; ex-pounding, -position; Hermeneutics; comment, -ary; infer-ence &c. (*deduction*) 480; illustration, exemplification; gloss, annotation, scholium, note; e-, di-lucidation, enucle-ation; *éclaircissement, mot de l'énigme.*

symptomat-, semei-ology; metopo-scopy, physiognomy; diagnosis, prog-

523. Misinterpretation. — **N.** mis-interpretation, -apprehension, -under-standing, -acceptation, -construction, -application; *catachresis*; cross -read-ing, – purposes; mistake &c. 495.

misrepresentation, perversion, exag-geration &c. 549; false -colouring, – construction; abuse of terms; parody, travesty; falsification &c. (*lying*) 544.

V. mis-interpret, -apprehend, -under-stand, -conceive, -judge, -doubt, -spell, -translate, -construe, -apply; mistake &c. 495.

misrepresent, pervert; garble &c. (*falsify*) 544; distort, detort; travesty, play upon words; stretch –, strain –, wrest- the -sense, – meaning; explain

nosis; paleography &c. (*philology*) 560;
accept-ion, -ation, -ance; light, reading, lection, construction, version.

equivalent, – meaning &c. 516;
synonym; para-, meta-phrase; convertible terms, apposition; dictionary
&c. 562; polyglot.

V. interpret, explain, define, con-
strue, translate, render; do –, turn-
into; transfuse the sense of.

find out &c. 480a- -the meaning &c. 516- of; read; spell –, figure –,
make- out; decipher, decode, unravel, disentangle, puzzle out; find
the key of, enucleate, resolve, solve; read between the lines.

account for; find –, tell- the cause &c. 153- of; throw –, shed-
-light, – new light, – a fresh light- upon; clear up, elucidate.

illustrate, exemplify; unfold, expound, comment upon, annotate;
popularize &c. (*render intelligible*) 518.

take –, understand –, receive –, accept- in a particular sense;
understand by, put a construction on, be given to understand.

Adj. explanatory, expository; explica-tive, -tory; exegetical;
hermeneutic, interpretive, illustrative, elucidative, annotative
scholiastic.

polyglot; literal; para-, meta-phrastic; cosignificative, synonymous; equivalent &c. 27.

Adv. in -explanation &c. *n.*; that is to say, *id est, videlicet,* to wit,
namely, in other words.

literally, strictly speaking; in -plain, – plainer- -terms, – words,
- English; more simply.

524. Interpreter.—N. interpreter, translator, ex-positor, -pounder,
-ponent, -plainer; demonstrator.

scholiast, commentator, annotator; meta-, para-phrast.

spokesman, speaker, mouthpiece, prolocutor; diplomat &c. 758.

guide, courier, dragoman, *valet de place, cicerone,* showman; oneirocritic; Œdipus; oracle &c. 513.

away; put a -bad, - false- construction
on; give a false colouring, look through
-rose coloured -, - dark - spectacles
be –, play- at cross purposes.

Adj. misinterpreted &c. *v.*; untrans-
lat-ed, -able.

Adv. at cross purposes.

Section II. Modes of Communication

525. Manifestation.—N. manifestation; unfolding; plainness &c. *adj.*;
plain speaking; expression; showing &c.
v.; exposition, demonstration, *séance*;
exhibition, production; display, showing off &c. 882, premonstration.
[Thing shown] exhibit, show.

indication &c. (*calling attention to*)
457; publicity &c. 531; disclosure &c.
529; openness &c. (*honesty*) 543, (*artlessness*) 703; *épanchement,* prominence.

V. make –, render- -manifest &c. *adj.*;
bring -forth, – forward, – to the front,
- into view; give notice; express;
represent, set forth, exhibit; show,
- up; expose; produce; hold up –,
expose- to view: set –, place –, lay-

526. Latency.—N. latency, inexpres-
sion; hidden –, occult- meaning; occult-
ness, occultism, mysticism, mystery,
cabala, symbolism, anagoge; silence &c.
(*taciturnity*) 585; concealment &c. 528;
more than meets the -eye, – ear;
Delphic oracle; *le dessous des cartes,*
undercurrent.

allusion, insinuation, implication;
innuendo &c. 527; adumbration; 'something rotten in the state of Denmark.'

snake in the grass &c. (*pitfall*) 667;
secret &c. 533.

darkness, invisibility, imperceptibility.

latent influence, power behind the
throne; friend at court, wire puller.

before -one, – one's eyes; tell to one's face; trot out, put through one's paces, unfold, show off, show forth, unveil, bring to light, display, demonstrate, unroll; lay open; draw –, bring- out; bring out in strong relief; call –, bring-into notice; hold up the mirror; wear one's heart upon his sleeve; show one's -face, – colours; manifest oneself; speak out; make no -mystery, – secret- of; unfurl the flag; proclaim &c. (*publish*) 531.

indicate &c. (*direct attention to*) 457; disclose &c. 529; elicit &c. 480*a*; interpret &c. 522.

be -manifest &c. *adj.*; appear &c. (*be visible*) 446; transpire &c. (*be disclosed*) 529; speak for itself, stand to reason; stare one in the face; loom large, appear on the horizon, rear its head; give -token, – sign, – indication of; tell its own tale &c. (*intelligible*) 518; go without saying.

Adj. manifest, apparent; salient, striking, demonstrative, prominent, in the foreground, notable, pronounced.

flagrant; notorious &c. (*public*) 531; arrant; stark staring; unshaded, glaring.

defin-ed, -ite; distinct, conspicuous &c. (*visible*) 446; obvious, evident, incontestable, unmistakable, not to be mistaken, plain, clear, palpable, self-evident, autoptical; intelligible &c. 518; clear as -day, – daylight, – noonday; plain as -a pikestaff, – the sun at noonday, – the nose on one's face, – the way to the parish church.

ostensible; open, – as day; overt, patent, express, explicit; naked, bare, literal, downright, undisguised, exoteric.

V. be -latent &c. *adj.*; lurk, smoulder, underlie, make no sign; escape -observation, – detection, – recognition; lie hid &c. 528.

laugh in one's sleeve; keep back &c. (*conceal*) 528.

involve, imply, implicate, connote, import, understand, allude to, infer, leave an inference; symbolize; whisper &c. (*conceal*) 528.

Adj. latent; lurking &c. *v.*; secret &c. 528; occult, symbolic, mystic; implied &c. *v.*; dormant.

un-apparent, -known, -seen &c. 441; in the background; invisible &c. 447; indiscoverable, dark; impenetrable &c. (*unintelligible*) 519; un-spied, -suspected.

un - said, - written, - published, -breathed, -talked of, -told &c. 527, -sung, -exposed, -proclaimed, -disclosed &c. 529, -pronounced, -mentioned, -expressed; not expressed, tacit.

un-developed, -solved, -explained, -traced, -discovered &c. 480*a*, -tracked. -explored, -invented.

indirect, crooked, inferential; by -inference, – implication; implicit; constructive; allusive, covert, muffled; steganographic; under-stood, -hand, -ground; concealed &c. 528; delitescent.

Adv. by a side wind; *sub silentio*; in the background; behind -the scenes, – one's back, – the veil; below the surface; on the tip of one's tongue; secretly &c. 528; between the lines; by a mutual understanding.

Phr. 'thereby hangs a tale.' 'that is another story.'

———

unreserved; frank, plain spoken &c. (*artless*) 703; barefaced, brazen, bold, shameless, daring, flaunting, loud.

manifested &c. *v.*; disclosed &c. 529; expressible, capable of being shown, producible; in-, un-concealable.

Adv. manifestly, openly &c. *adj.*; before one's eyes, under one's nose, to one's face, face to face, above board, *cartes sur table*, on the stage, in plain sight, in open court, in the open, – streets; at the cross roads; in market overt; in the face of -day, – heaven; in -broad –, open- daylight; without reserve; at first blush, *primâ facie*, on the face of; in set terms.

Phr. *cela saute aux yeux*; he that runs may read; you can see it with half an eye; it needs no ghost to tell us; the meaning lies on the surface; *cela va sans dire*; *res ipsa loquitur*.

527. Information.—N. information, enlightenment, acquaintance, knowledge &c. 490; publicity &c. 531.

communication, intimation; not-ice, -ification; e-, an-nunciation; announcement; representation, round robin, presentment.

case, estimate, specification, report, advice, monition; news &c. 532; return &c. (*record*) 551; account &c. (*description*) 594; statement &c. (*affirmation*) 535.

mention; acquainting &c. *v.*; instruction &c. (*teaching*) 537; outpouring; intercommunication, communicativeness.

informant, authority, teller, announcer, annunciator, harbinger, herald, intelligencer, commentator, columnist, reporter, exponent, mouthpiece; informer, keek, eavesdropper, delator, detective, sleuth; *mouchard,* spy stool pigeon, newsmonger; messenger &c. 534; *amicus curiæ.*

valet de place, cicerone, pilot, guide; guide-, hand-book; *vade mecum;* manual; map, plan, chart, gazetteer; itinerary &c. (*journey*) 266.

hint, suggestion, wrinkle, innuendo, inkling, whisper, passing word, word in the ear, subaudition, cue, by-play; gesture &c. (*indication*) 550; gentle -broad- hint; *verbum sapienti*; word to the wise; insinuation &c. (*latency*) 526.

V. tell; inform, - of; acquaint, - with; impart, - to; make acquainted with, bring to the ears of, apprise, advise, enlighten, awaken.

let fall, mention, express, intimate, represent, communicate, make known; publish &c. 531; notify, signify, specify, convey the knowledge of.

let one -, have one to- know; serve notice, give one to understand; give notice; set -, lay -, put- before; point out, put into one's head; put one in possession of; instruct &c. (*teach*) 537; direct the attention to &c. 457.

an-nounce, -nunciate; report, - progress; bring -, send -, leave -, write-word; tele-graph, -phone; ring -, call-up; wire; retail, render an account; give an account &c. (*describe*) 594; state &c. (*affirm*) 535.

528. Concealment.—N. concealment; hiding &c. *v.*; occultation, mystification.

seal of secrecy; screen &c. 530; disguise &c. 530; masquerade; masked battery; hiding place &c. 530; cipher, code, crypt-, stegan-ography; invisible -, sympathetic- ink; palimpsest; Freemasonry.

stealth, -iness; obreption; slyness &c; (*cunning*) 702.

latit-ancy, -ation; seclusion &c. 893; privacy, secrecy, secretness; *incognita.*

reticence; reserve; mental -, reservation, aside; *arrière pensée,* suppression, evasion, white lie, misprision; silence &c. (*taciturnity*) 585; suppression of truth &c. 544; underhand dealing; close-, secretive-ness &c. *adj.*; mystery.

latency &c. 526; snake in the grass; secret &c. 533.

V. conceal, hide, secrete, stow away, put out of sight; lock -, seal -, bottle-up.

cover, screen, cloak, veil, shroud; screen from -sight, - observation; draw the veil; draw -, close- the curtain; curtain, shade, eclipse, throw a veil over; be-cloud, -fog, -mask; mask, disguise; ensconce, muffle, smother; whisper.

keep -from, - back, - to oneself; keep -snug, - close, - secret, - dark; bury; sink, suppress; keep -from, - out of- -view, - sight; keep in -, throw into- the -shade, - background; cover up one's tracks; stifle, hush up, withhold, reserve; fence with a question; ignore &c. 460.

code, codify, use a cipher.

keep -a secret, - one's own counsel; hold one's tongue &c. (*silence*) 585; make no sign, not let it go further; not breathe a -word, - syllable- about; not let the right hand know what the left is doing; hide one's light under a bushel, bury one's talent in a napkin.

keep -, leave- in -the dark, - ignorance; blind, - the eyes; blindfold, hoodwink, mystify; puzzle &c. (*render uncertain*) 475; bamboozle &c. (*deceive*) 545.

be -concealed &c. *v.*; suffer an eclipse;

disclose &c. 529; show cause; explain &c. (*interpret*) 522.

hint; give an inkling of; give –, drop –, throw out- a hint; insinuate; allude –, make allusion- to; glance at; tip off, tip the wink &c. (*indicate*) 550; suggest, prompt, give the cue, breathe; whisper, – in the ear.

give a bit of one's mind; tell one plainly, – once for all; speak volumes.

un-deceive, -beguile; set right, correct, open the eyes of, disabuse.

be -informed of &c.; know &c. 490; learn &c. 539; get scent of, gather from; awaken –, open one's eyes- to; become -alive, – awake- to; keep posted; hear, overhear, understand.

come to one's -ears, – knowledge; reach one's ears.

Adj. informed &c. *v.*; *communiqué*; reported &c. *v.*; published &c. 531; advisory.

expressive &c. 516; explicit &c. (*open*) 525, (*clear*) 518; plain-spoken &c. (*artless*) 703.

declara-, nuncupa-, exposi-tory; declarative, enunciative, communicat-ive, -ory; oral.

Adv. from information received; according to -rumour, – report; in the air; from what one can gather.

Phr. a little bird told me.

---

retire from sight, couch; hide oneself; lie -hid, – in ambush, – low, – *perdu*, – snug, – close; seclude oneself &c. 893; lurk, sneak, skulk, slink, pussy-foot, prowl; steal -into, – out of, – by, – along; play at -bopeep, – hide and seek; hide in holes and corners.

Adj. concealed &c. *v.*; hidden; veiled, secret, recondite, mystic, cabalistic, occult, dark; cryptic, -al; private, privy, *in petto*, auricular, clandestine, close, inviolate.

behind a -screen &c. 530; under -cover, – an eclipse; in -ambush, – hiding, – disguise; in a -cloud, – fog, – mist, – haze, – dark corner; in the -shade, – dark; clouded, wrapt in clouds; invisible &c. 447; buried, underground, *perdu*; incommunicado; secluded &c. 893.

un-disclosed &c. 529, -told &c. 527; covert &c. (*latent*) 526; mysterious &c. (*unintelligible*) 519.

irrevealable, inviolable; confidential; esoteric; not to be spoken of.

obreptitious, furtive, stealthy, feline; skulking &c. *v.*; surreptitious, underhand, hole and corner; sly &c. (*cunning*) 702; secretive, evasive, non-committal, reserved, reticent, uncommunicative, buttoned up; close, – as wax; taciturn &c. 585.

Adv. secretly &c. *adj.*; in -secret, – private, – one's sleeve, – holes and corners; in the dark &c. *adj.*

januis clausis, with closed doors, *à huis clos*; hugger-mugger, *à la dérobée*; under the -cloak of, – rose, – table; *sub rosâ, en tapinois*, in the background, aside, on the sly, with bated breath, *sotto voce*, in a whisper, without beat of drum, *à la sourdine*.

in –, strict- confidence; confidentially &c. *adj.*; between -ourselves, – you and me; *entre nous, inter nos*, under the seal of secrecy; in -code, – cipher.

underhand, by stealth, like a thief in the night; stealthily &c. *adj.*; behind -the scenes, – the curtain, – one's back, – a screen &c. 530; *incognito; in camerâ*.

Phr. it -must, – will- go no further; 'tell it not in Gath,' nobody the wiser.

529. Disclosure.—N. disclosure; retection; unveiling &c. *v.*; deterration, revealment, revelation; divulgence, expos-ition, -ure; *exposé*; whole truth; tell-tale &c. (*news*) 532.

acknowledgment, avowal; confession, -al; shrift.

530. Ambush. [Means of conceal-ment.]—**N.** hiding-place; secret -place. – drawer; recess, hole, funk hole, holes and corners; closet, crypt, *adytum*, abditory, *oubliette*, safe, – deposit; cache. am-bush, -buscade; stalking horse; lurking-hole, -place; secret path,

bursting of a bubble; *dénouement.*

V. dis-close, -cover, -mask; draw –, draw aside –, lift –, raise –, lift up –, remove –, tear- the -veil, – curtain; un-mask, -veil, -fold, -cover, -seal, -kennel; take off –, break- the seal; lay -open, – bare; expose; open, – up; bare, bring to light; evidence; make - clear, – evident, – manifest; evince.

divulge, reveal, break; let into the secret; reveal the secrets of the prison-house; tell &c. (*inform*) 527; breathe, utter, blab, peach; let -out, – fall, – drop, – the cat out of the bag; betray; tell tales, – out of school; come out with; give -v∍nt, – utterance- to; open the lips, blurt out, vent, whisper about; speak out &c. (*make manifest*) 525; make public &c. 531; unriddle &c. (*find out*) 480a; split; blow the gaff; break the news.

acknowledge, allow, concede, grant, admit, own, confess, avow, throw off all disguise, turn inside out, make a clean breast; show one's -hand, – cards; unburden –, disburden- one's -mind, – conscience, – heart; open –, lay bare –, tell a piece of- one's mind; unbosom oneself, own to the soft impeachment; say –, speak- the truth; turn -King's, –Queen's, –State's- evidence.

raise –, drop –, lift –, remove –, throw off- the mask; expose; debunk; lay open; un-deceive, -beguile; disabuse, set right, correct, open the eyes of; *désillusionner.*

be -disclosed &c.; transpire, come to light; come in sight &c. (*be visible*) 446; become known, escape the lips; come –, ooze –, creep –, leak –, peep –, crop- out; show its -face, – colours; discover &c. itself; break through the clouds, flash on the mind.

Adj. disclosed &c. *v.*

Int. out with it!

Phr. the murder is out; a light breaks in upon one; the scales fall from one's eyes; the eyes are opened.

backstairs; retreat &c. (*refuge*) 666. screen, cover, shade, blinker; veil, curtain, blind, *purdah*, cloak, cloud.

mask, vizor, visor, disguise, masquerade dress, domino; *camouflage.*

pitfall &c. (*source of danger*) 667; trap &c. (*snare*) 545.

V. ambush, ambuscade, lie in ambush &c. (*hide oneself*) 528; lie in wait for; set a trap for &c. (*deceive*) 545.

Adv. *aux aguets.*

531. Publication.—N. publication; public -announcement &c. 527; promulgation, propagation, proclamation, pronouncement, encyclical, *pronunciamento*; circulation, indiction, edition, imprint, impression, printing; hue and cry.

publicity, notoriety, currency, flagrancy, cry, *bruit*; *vox populi*; report &c. (*news*) 532.

the Press, fourth estate, public press, newspaper, periodical, journal, gazette; house organ, trade publication, tabloid; daily, weekly, monthly, quarterly, annual, magazine, monograph, book; review; news sheet, special edition, supplement, feature, rotogravure, comic strips; leaflet, pamphlet; telegraphy; publisher &c. *v.*

circular, – letter; manifesto, advertisement, puff, placard, bill, *affiche*, broadside, poster; notice &c. 527; programme.

V. publish; make -public, – known &c. (*information*) 527; speak –, talk- of; broach, utter; put forward; circulate, propagate, promulgate; spread –, abroad; rumour, diffuse, disseminate, evulgate; put –, give –, send- forth; emit, edit, get out; issue; cover, report; bring –, lay –, drag- before the public; give -out, – to the world; put –, bandy –, hawk –, buzz –, whisper –, bruit –, blaze- about; drag into the -open day, – limelight; voice.

proclaim, herald, blazon; blaze –, noise- abroad; sound a trumpet; trumpet –, thunder- forth; give tongue; announce with -beat of drum, – flourish of trumpets; proclaim -from the housetops, – at Charing Cross, at the cross roads; declare, declaim.

advertise, placard; post, – up; *afficher*, publish in the Gazette, send round the crier.

raise a -cry, – hue and cry, – report; set news afloat.

telegraph, cable, wireless, broadcast.

be -published &c.; be –, become- public &c. *adj.*; come out; go –, fly –, buzz –, blow- about; get -about, – abroad, – afloat, – wind; find vent; see the light; go forth, take air, acquire currency, pass current; go -the rounds, – the round of the newspapers, – through the length and breadth of the land; *virum volitare per ora*; pass from mouth to mouth; spread; run –, spread- like wildfire.

Adj. published &c. *v.*; current &c. (*news*) 532; in circulation, public; notorious; flagrant, arrant; open &c. 525; trumpet-tongued; encyclical, promulgatory; exoteric.

Adv. publicly &c. *adj.*; in open court, with open doors; in the limelight.

Int. *Oyez!* O yes! notice!

Phr. notice is hereby given; this is –, these are- to give nctice.

532. News.—N. news; information &c. 527; piece –, budget- of -news, – information; report, story, yarn, copy, filler, intelligence, tidings; stop press news.

word, advice, *aviso*, message; dis-, des-patch; radio, telegram, cablegram, wireless telegram, radiogram, marconi-gram, communication, errand, em-bassy; *bulletin, petit bleu.*

rumour, hearsay, *on dit*, flying rumour, news stirring, cry, buzz, *bruit*, fame; talk, *oui-dire*, scandal, eaves-dropping; town –, table- talk; tittle-tattle; *canard*, topic of the day, idea afloat.

fresh –, stirring –, old –, stale- news; glad tidings; old –, stale- story.

533. Secret.—N. secret; dead –, profound- secret; *arcanum*, mystery; latency &c. 526; Asian mystery; sealed book, secrets of the prison-house; *le dessous des cartes.*

enigma, riddle, puzzle, nut to crack, conundrum, charade, rebus, logogriph; mono-, ana-gram; acrostic, cross-word puzzle; Sphinx; *crux criticorum.*

maze, labyrinth, Hyrcynian wood.

problem &c. (*question*) 461; paradox &c. (*difficulty*) 704; unintelligibility &c. 519; *terra incognita* &c. (*ignorance*) 491.

Adj. secret &c. (*concealed*) 528.

narrator &c. (*describe*) 594; news-, scandal-monger; tale-bearer; tell-tale, gossip, tattler, busy-body, chatterer; informer.

V. transpire &c. (*be disclosed*) 529; rumour &c. (*publish*) 531.

Adj. many-tongued; rumoured; publicly –, currently- -rumoured, – reported; rife, current, floating, afloat, going about, in circulation, in everyone's mouth, all over the town.

Adv. as the story -goes, – runs; as they say, it is said.

534. Messenger.—N. messenger, envoy, emissary, legate; nuncio, internuncio; intermediary; ambassador &c. (*diplomatist*) 758.

marshal, flag-bearer, herald, crier, trumpeter, bellman, pursuivant, *parlementaire, apparitor.*

courier, runner, dawk, *estafette*; Hermes, Mercury, Iris, Ariel.

postman, letter carrier, telegraph boy, messenger boy, district mes-senger; despatch rider, commissionaire, errand-boy.

mail; post, -office; letter-bag; mail -boat, – train, – coach, – van, air mail; tele-graph, -phone; cable, wire; carrier-pigeon; wireless tele-graph, -phone; radiotele-graph, -phone.

journalist, newspaperman, reporter; gentleman –, representative- of the press; sob sister; penny-a-liner; special –, war –, own- correspondent; spy, scout; informer &c. 527.

535. Affirmation.—N. affirm-ance, -ation; statement, allegation, assertion, predication, declaration, word, averment.

asseveration, adjuration, swearing, oath, affidavit; deposition &c. (*record*) 551; avouchment, assurance; protest, -ation; profession; acknowledgment &c. (*assent*) 488; pledge.

vote, voice, suffrage, ballot.

remark, observation; position &c. (*proposition*) 514; saying, *dictum*, sentence, *ipse dixit*.

emphasis, positiveness, peremptoriness; dogmatism &c. (*certainty*) 474; dogmatist &c. 887.

V. assert; make -an assertion &c. *n.*; have one's say; say, affirm, predicate, declare, state, represent; protest, profess.

put -forth, – forward; advance, allege, propose, propound, enunciate, enounce, broach, set forth, hold out, maintain, contend, pronounce, pretend.

depose, depone, aver, avow, avouch, asseverate, swear; make –, take one's-oath; make –, swear –, put in- an affidavit; take one's Bible oath, kiss the book, vow, *vitam impendere vero*; swear till -one is black in the face, – all's blue; be sworn, call Heaven to witness; vouch, warrant, certify, assure, swear by bell, book and candle.

swear by &c. (*believe*) 484; insist –, take one's stand- upon; emphasize, lay stress on; assert -roundly, – positively; lay down, – the law; raise one's voice, dogmatize, have the last word; rap out; repeat; re-assert, -affirm.

536. Negation.—N. ne-, abne-gation; denial; dis-avowal, -claimer; abjuration; contra-diction, -vention; recusation, protest; rebuttal; recusancy &c. (*dissent*) 489; flat –, emphatic- -contradiction, – denial; *démenti*.

qualification &c. 469; repudiation &c. 610; retractation &c. 607; confutation &c. 479; refusal &c. 764; prohibition &c. 761.

V. deny; contra-dict, -vene; controvert, give denial to, gainsay, negative, shake the head.

dis-own, -affirm, -claim, -avow; recant &c. 607; revoke &c. (*abrogate*) 756.

dispute, impugn, traverse, rebut, join issue upon; bring –, call- in question &c. (*doubt*) 485.

deny -flatly, – peremptorily, – emphatically, – absolutely, – wholly, – entirely; give the lie to, belie.

repudiate &c. 610; set aside, ignore &c. 460; rebut &c. (*confute*) 479; qualify &c. 469; refuse &c. 764.

Adj. denying &c. *v.*; denied &c. *v.*; contradictory; negat-ive, -ory; revocatory; recusant &c. (*dissenting*) 489; at issue upon.

Adv. no, nay, not, nowise; not a -bit, – whit, – jot; not -at all, – in the least, – so; no such thing; nothing of the -kind, – sort; quite the contrary, *tout au contraire*, far from it; *tant s'en faut*; on no account, in no respect; by -no, – no manner of- means; negatively.

Phr. there never was a greater mistake; I know better; *non hæc in fœdera*.

announce &c. (*information*) 527; acknowledge &c. (*assent*) 488; attest &c. (*evidence*) 467; adjure &c. (*put to one's oath*) 768.

Adj. asserting &c. *v.*; declaratory, predicatory, pronunciative, affirmative, *soi-disant*; positive; certain &c. 474; express, explicit &c. (*patent*) 525; absolute, emphatic, flat, broad, round, pointed, marked, distinct, decided, confident, assertive, insistent, trenchant, dogmatic, definitive, formal, solemn, categorical, peremptory; unretracted; predicable, affirmable.

Adv. affirmatively &c. *adj.*; in the affirmative.

with emphasis, *ex cathedrâ*, without fear of contradiction.

I must say, indeed, i' faith, let me tell you, why, give me leave to say, marry, you may be sure, I'd have you to know; upon my -word, – honour; by my troth, egad, I assure you; by -jingo, – Jove, – George, – &c.; troth, seriously, sadly; in –, in sober- -sadness, – truth, – earnest; of a truth, truly, pardi, perdy; in all conscience, upon oath; be assured &c. (*belief*) 484; yes &c. (*assent*) 488; I'll -warrant, – warrant you, – engage, – answer for it, – be bound, – venture to say, – take my oath; in fact, as a matter of fact, forsooth, joking apart; so help me God; not to mince the matter.

Phr. quoth he; *dixi*.

537. Teaching.—N. teaching &c. *v.*; instruction; edification; education; pedagogy; tuition; tutor-, tutel-age; direction, guidance.

qualification, preparation; train-, school-ing &c. *v.*; discipline; exer-cise, -citation; drill, practice.

persuasion, proselytism, propagandism, *propaganda*; in-doctrination, -culcation, -oculation.

explanation &c. (*interpretation*) 522; lesson, lecture, sermon, homily; apologue, parable; discourse, prelection, preachment, disquisition.

exercise, task; *curriculum*; course, – of study; grammar, three R's, initiation, A. B. C. &c. (*beginning*) 66.

elementary –, primary –, secondary –, grammar school –, high school –, college –, university –, technical –, liberal –, classical –, religious –, denominational –, moral –, secular- education; technical –, vocational- training; university extension lectures; propædeutics, moral tuition; evening classes, correspondence course.

physical education, gymnastics, calisthenics, eurythmics; *sloyd*.

V. teach, instruct, edify, school, tutor; cram, prime, coach; enlighten &c. (*inform*) 527.

in-culcate, -doctrinate, -oculate, -fuse, -stil, -fix, -graft, -filtrate; imbue, -pregnate, -plant; graft, sow the seeds of, disseminate, propagandize.

give an idea of; put -up to, – in the way of; set right.

sharpen the wits, enlarge the mind; give new ideas, open the eyes, bring forward, 'teach the young idea how to shoot'; improve &c. 658.

538. Misteaching.—N. mis-teaching, -information, -intelligence, -guidance, -direction, -persuasion, -instruction, -leading &c. *v.*; perversion, false teaching; sophistry &c. 477; college of Laputa; the blind leading the blind.

V. mis-inform, -teach, -direct, -guide, -instruct, -correct; pervert; put on a false –, throw off the- scent; deceive &c. 545; mislead &c. (*error*) 495; misrepresent; lie &c. 544; *spargere voces in vulgum ambiguas*, preach to the wise, teach one's grandmother to suck eggs.

render unintelligible &c. 519; bewilder &c. (*uncertainty*) 475; mystify &c. (*conceal*) 528; unteach.

Adj. misteaching &c. *v.*; unedifying.

Phr. *piscem natare doces*.

539. Learning.—N. learning; acquisition of -knowledge &c. 490, – skill &c. 698; acquirement, attainment; edification, scholarship, erudition; lore; information; self-instruction; study, reading, perusal; inquiry &c. 461.

ap-, prenticeship; pupil-age, -arity; tutelage, novitiate, matriculation.

docility &c. (*willingness*) 602; aptitude &c. 698.

V. learn; acquire –, gain –, receive –, take in –, drink in –, imbibe –, pick up –, gather –, get –, obtain –, collect –, glean- -knowledge, – information, - learning.

acquaint oneself with, master; make oneself -master of, – acquainted with; grind, cram; get –, coach- up; learn by -heart, – rote.

read, spell, peruse; con –, pore –, thumb- over; wade through; dip into;

expound &c. (*interpret*) 522; lecture; prelect; read –, give- a -lesson,– lecture, – sermon, – discourse; hold forth, preach; sermon-, moral-ize; point a moral.

train, discipline; bring up, – to; educate, form, ground, prepare, qualify, drill, exercise, practice, habituate, familiarize with, nurture, dry-nurse, breed, rear, take in hand; break, – in; tame; pre-instruct; initiate; inure &c. (*habituate*) 613.

put to nurse, send to school.

direct, guide; direct attention to &c. (*attention*) 457; impress upon the -mind, – memory; beat into, – the head; convince &c. (*belief*) 484.

Adj. teaching &c. *v.*; taught &c. *v.*; educational; scholastic, academic, doctrinal; disciplinal; instructive, didactic, hortative, pedagogic, tutorial.

Phr. the schoolmaster abroad.

540. Teacher.—N. teacher, trainer, instructor, institutor, master, tutor, don, director, Corypheus, dry nurse, coach, grinder, crammer; governor, bear-leader; governess, duenna; disciplinarian.

professor, lecturer, reader, prelector, prolocutor, preacher; Boanerges; pastor &c. (*clergy*) 996; schoolmaster, dominie, usher, pedagogue, abecedarian; schoolmistress, dame, monitor, proctor, pupil-teacher.

expositor &c. 524; preceptor, guide; mentor &c. (*adviser*) 695; pioneer, apostle, missionary, propagandist, moonshee; example &c. (*model for imitation*) 22.

professorship &c. (*school*) 542.

tutelage &c. (*teaching*) 537.

Adj. professorial, tutorial &c. 537.

run the eye -over, – through; turn over the leaves.

study; be -studious &c. *adj.*; consume the midnight oil, mind one's book.

go to -school, – college, – the university; serve -an (*or* one's) apprenticeship, – one's time; learn one's trade; be -informed &c. 527; be -taught &c. 537.

Adj. studious; schol-astic, -arly; teachable; docile &c. (*willing*) 602; apt &c. 698, industrious &c. 682; learned, erudite.

Adv. at one's books; *in statu pupillari* &c. (*learner*) 541.

―――――

541. Learner.—N. learner, scholar, student, *alumnus*, *élève*, pupil; ap-, prentice; articled clerk; school-boy, -girl, beginner, tyro, abecedarian, alphabetarian.

recruit, novice, neophyte, tenderfoot, inceptor, *débutant*, catechumen, probationer; undergraduate; freshman, frosh; sophomore, junior, senior; junior –, senior- soph; sophister, questionist, fellow-, commoner, pensioner, exhibitioner, sizar, scholar, fellow, advanced –, post graduate –, research- student.

class, form, grade, standard, remove; pupilage &c. (*learning*) 539.

disciple, follower, apostle, proselyte; fellow student, school-mate, -fellow, class mate, condisciple.

Adj. *in statu pupillari*, in leading strings, sophomoric.

542. School.—N. school, academy, university, *alma mater*, college, seminary, Lyceum; instit-ute, -ution, *conservatoire*; *palæstra, gymnasium*.

day –, boarding –, public –, preparatory –, elementary –, primary –, infant –, dame's –, grammar –, middle class –, Board –, County –, Council –, parochial –, denominational –, Sunday –, National –, British and Foreign –, collegiate –, secondary –, continuation –, night –, correspondence –, secretarial –, military –, law –, medical –, business –, technical- school; technical –, training- college; Polytechnic; training ship; *Kindergarten*, nursery, *crèche*, reformatory.

pulpit, desk, reading desk, ambo, class-, lecture-room, theatre, amphitheatre, forum, stage, rostrum, platform, hustings, tribune.

school –, horn –, text- book; grammar, primer, abecedary, rudiments, manual, *vade mecum*, Lindley Murray, Cocker.

professor-, lecture-, reader-ship; chair; schoolmaster &c. 540.

School Board, Council of Education; *propaganda*.

Adj. scholastic, academic, collegiate; educational.

Adv. *ex cathedrâ*.

543. Veracity.—N. veracity; truthfulness, frankness &c. *adj.*; truth, sooth, sincerity, candour, honesty, fidelity; plain dealing, *bona fides*; love of truth; probi̇ty &c. 939; ingenuousness &c. (*artlessness*) 703.

the truth the whole truth and nothing but the truth; honest –, sobertruth &c. (*fact*) 494; unvarnished tale; light of truth.

V. speak –, tell- the truth; speak by the card; paint in its –, show oneself in one's-true colours; make a clean breast &c. (*disclose*) 529; speak one's mind &c. (*be blunt*) 703; not -lie &c. 544, – deceive &c. 545.

Adj. truthful, true; ver-acious, -edi̇al; scrupulous &c. (*honourable*) 939; sincere, candid, frank, open, straight-forward, unreserved; open-, true-, simple- hearted; honest, trustworthy; undissembling &c. (dissemble &c. 544); guileless, pure; unperjured, true blue, as good as one's word; unaffected, unfeigned, *bonâ fide*; outspoken, ingenuous &c. (*artless*) 703; undisguised &c. (*real*) 494.

Adv. truly &c. (*really*) 494; on oath; in plain words &c. 703; in –, with –, of a –, in good –, very- truth; as the -dial to the sun, – needle to the pole; honour bright; troth; in good -sooth, – earnest; unfeignedly, with no nonsense, in sooth, sooth to say, *bonâ fide*, *in foro conscientiæ*; without equivocation; *cartes sur table*, from the bottom of one's heart; by my troth &c. (*affirmation*) 535.

544. Falsehood. — N. false-hood, -ness; fals-ity, -ification; misrepresentation; deception &c. 545; untruth &c. 546; guile; bad faith; lying &c. *v.*; misrepresentation; mendacity, perjury, false swearing; forgery, invention, fabrication; subreption; covin.

perversion –, suppression- of truth; *suppressio veri*; perversion, distortion, false colouring; exaggeration &c. 549; prevarication, equivocation, shuffling, fencing, evasion, fraud; *suggestio falsi* &c. (*lie*) 546; mystification &c. (*concealment*) 528; simulation &c. (*imitation*) 19; dis-simulation, -sembling; deceit.

sham; pretence, pretending, malingering.

lip -homage, – service; mouth honour; hollowness; mere -show, – outside, eye-wash, window dressing; duplicity, double dealing, insincerity, hypocrisy, cant, humbug, casuistry; jesuit-ism, -ry; pharisaism; Machiavellism, 'organized hypocrisy'; crocodile tears, mealy-mouthedness, quackery; charlatan-ism, -ry; gammon; bun-kum, -come; flam, bam, ñim-flam, cajolery, flattery; Judas kiss; perfidy &c. (*bad faith*) 940; *il volto sciolto i pensieri stretti.*

unfairness &c. (*dishonesty*) 940; art-fulness &c. (*cunning*) 702; misstatement &c. (*error*) 495.

V. be -false &c. *adj.*, – a liar &c. 548; speak -falsely &c. *adv.*; tell -a lie &c. 546; lie, fib; lie like a trooper; swear falsely, forswear, perjure oneself, bear false witness.

mis-state, -quote, -cite, -report, -represent; belie, falsify, pervert, distort; put a false construction upon &c. (*misinterpret*) 523.

prevaricate, equivocate, quibble; palter, – to the understanding; *répondre en Normand*; trim, shuffle, fence, mince the truth, beat about the bush, blow hot and cold, play fast and loose.

garble, gloss over, disguise, give a colour to; give –, put- a -gloss, – false colouring- upon; colour, varnish, cook, dress up, embroider; varnish right and puzzle wrong, exaggerate &c. 549.

invent, fabricate; trump -, get- up; forge, hatch, concoct; romance &c. (*imagine*) 515; cry 'wolf!'

dis-semble, -simulate; feign, assume, put on, pretend, make be-lieve; play -false, - a double game; coquet; act -, play- a part; affect &c. 855; simulate, pass off for; counterfeit, fake, sham, make a show of; malinger; swing the lead; say the grapes are sour.

cant, play the hypocrite, sham Abraham, *faire pattes de velours*, put on the mask, clean the outside of the platter, lie like a con-juror; hang out -, hold out -, sail under- false colours; 'commend the poisoned chalice to the lips'; *spargere voces in vulgum ambiguas*; deceive &c. 545.

Adj. false, deceitful, mendacious, unveracious, fraudulent, un-truthful, dishonest; faith-, truth-, troth-less; un-fair, -candid; evasive; un-, dis-ingenuous; hollow, insincere, *Parthis mendacior*; forsworn.

canting; hypocrit-, jesuit-, pharisa-ical; tartuffish; Machiavelian; double-tongued, -faced, -handed, -minded, -hearted, -dealing; two-faced, bare-faced; Janus-faced; smooth-faced, -spoken, -tongued; plausible; mealy-mouthed; affected &c. 855.

collus-ive, -ory; artful &c. (*cunning*) 702; perfidious &c. 940, spurious &c. (*deceptive*) 545; untrue &c. 546; falsified &c. *v.*; covinous.

Adv. falsely &c. *adj.*; *à la Tartufe*, with a double tongue; out of whole cloth; slily &c. (*cunning*) 702.

545. Deception.—N. deception; falseness &c. 544; untruth &c. 546; impos-ition, -ture; fraud, deceit, guile; fraudulen-ce, -cy; covin; knavery &c. (*cunning*) 702; misrepresentation &c. (*falsehood*) 544.

delusion, gullery, bluff, spoof, *blague*; juggl-ing, -ery; sleight of hand, legerdemain; presti-giation, -digitation; magic &c. 992; conjur-ing, -ation; hocus-pocus, jockeyship; trickery, coggery, hanky-panky, chicanery, pettifogging, sharp practice; *supercherie*, cozenage, circum-vention, ingannation, collusion; treachery &c. 940; practical joke.

trick, cheat, wile, ruse, blind, feint, plant, bubble, fetch, catch, chicane, juggle, reach, hocus, bite; thimble-rig, card-sharping, artful dodge, machination, swindle, hoax; tricks upon travellers; confidence trick; stratagem &c. (*artifice*) 702; theft &c. 791.

snare, trap, pitfall, decoy, gin; sprin-ge, -gle; noose, hook; bait, decoy-duck, tub to the whale, baited trap, *guet-à-pens*; cobweb, net, meshes, toils, mouse-trap, bird-lime; ambush &c. 530; trap-door, sliding panel, false bottom; spring-net, -gun; mask, -ed battery; mine booby trap.

Cornish hug; wolf in sheep's clothing &c. (*deceiver*) 548; disguise, -ment; false colours, masquerade, mummery, borrowed plumes; *pattes de velours*.

mockery &c. (*imitation*) 19; copy &c. 21; counterfeit, sham, Brum-magem, make-believe, forgery, fraud, fake; lie &c. 546; 'a mockery, a delusion, and a snare,' hollow mockery.

whited -, painted- sepulchre; tinsel, paste, false jewellery, scagliola, ormolu, German silver, Britannia metal, paint; jerry building; man of straw.

illusion &c. (*error*) 495; *ignis fatuus* &c. 423; *mirage* &c. 443.

V. deceive, take in; defraud, cheat, jockey, do, cozen, diddle, nab, gyp, chouse, double cross, play one false, bilk, cully, jilt, bite, pluck, swindle, victimize; abuse; mystify; blind one's eyes; blindfold, hoodwink, spoof, bluff; throw dust into the eyes, 'keep the word of promise to the ear and break it to the hope,' 'draw a herring across the trail.'

impose –, practise –, play –, put –, palm –, foist- upon; snatch a verdict.

circumvent, overreach; out-reach, -wit, -manœuvre; steal a march upon, give the go-by to, leave in the lurch.

set –, lay- a -trap, – snare- for; bait the hook, forelay, spread the toils, lime; decoy, waylay, lure, beguile, delude, inveigle; tra-, tre-pan; kidnap; let-, hook-in; trick; en-, in-trap, -snare, entoil, benet; nick, springe; catch, – in a trap; sniggle, entangle, illaqueate, hocus, practise on one's credulity, dupe, gull, hoax, fool, befool, bamboozle; hum, -bug; gammon, stuff up, dope, sell; play a -trick, – practical joke- upon one; balk, trip up, throw a tub to a whale; fool to the top of one's bent, send on -a wild goose chase, – a fool's errand; make -game, – a fool, – an April fool, – an ass- of; trifle with, cajole, flatter; come over &c. \(influence) 615; gild the pill, make things pleasant, divert, put a good face upon; dissemble &c. 544.

cog, – the dice, play with marked cards; live by one's wits, play at hide and seek; obtain money under false pretences &c. (*steal*) 791; conjure, juggle, practise chicanery; gerrymander.

play –, palm –, foist –, fob- off.

lie &c. 544; misinform &c. 538; mislead &c. (*error*) 495; betray &c; 940; be -deceived &c. 547.

Adj. deceived &c. *v.*; deceiving &c. *v.*; cunning &c. 702; prestigi-ous, -atory; decept-ive, -ious; deceitful, covinous; delus-ive, -ory; illus-ive, -ory; elusive, insidious, *ad captandum vulgus*.

untrue &c. 546; mock, sham, make-believe, counterfeit, faked, pseudo, spurious, so-called, pretended, feigned, trumped up, bogus, scamped, fraudulent, tricky, factitious, artificial, bastard; surreptitious, illegitimate, contraband, adulterated, sophisticated; unsound, rotten at the core; colourable; disguised; meretricious; tinsel, pinchbeck, plated; catch-penny; Brummagem; simulated &c. 544.

Adv. under -false colours, – the garb of, – cover of; over the left.
Phr. *fronti nulla fides.*

546. Untruth.—N. untruth, falsehood, lie, story, thing that is not, fib, bounce, crammer, taradiddle, whopper.

forgery, fabrication, invention; mis-statement, -representation; perversion, falsification, gloss, *suggestio falsi*; exaggeration &c. 549.

fiction; fable, nursery tale; romance &c. (*imagination*) 515; untrue –, false –, trumped up- -story, – statement; thing devised by the enemy; *canard*; shave, sell, hum, yarn, traveller's tale, Canterbury tale, cock and bull story, fairy tale, clap-trap.

myth, moonshine, bosh, all my eye, -and Betty Martin, mare's nest, farce.

irony; half truth, white lie, pious fraud; mental reservation &c. (*concealment*) 528.

pretence, pretext; false -plea &c. 617; subterfuge, evasion, shift, shuffle, make-believe; sham &c. (*deception*) 545.

profession, empty words; Judas kiss &c. (*hypocrisy*) 544; disguise &c. (*mask*) 530.

V. have a false meaning; not ring true.

pretend, sham, feign, counterfeit, make believe.

Adj. untrue, false, trumped up; void of –, without- foundation; far from the truth, false as dicer's oaths; unfounded, *ben trovato*, invented, fabulous, fabricated, forged; fict-, fact-, supposit-, surrept-itious; e-, il-lusory; ironical; satirical; evasive; *soi-disant* &c. (*misnamed*) 565.

Phr. *se non è vero è ben trovato.*

547. Dupe.— N. dupe, gull, gudgeon, *gobemouche*, cull, cully, victim, sucker, pigeon, April fool; laughing stock &c. 857; Cyclops, simple Simon, flat, mug, greenhorn; fool &c. 501; puppet, cat's paw.

V. be -deceived &c. 545, – the dupe of; fall into a trap; swallow –, nibble at- the bait; bite; catch a Tartar.

Adj. credulous &c. 486; mistaken &c. (*error*) 495.

548. Deceiver.—N. deceiver &c. (deceive &c. 545); dissembler, hypocrite; sophist, Pharisee, Jesuit, Mawworm, Pecksniff, Joseph Surface, Tartufe, Janus; serpent, snake in the grass, cockatrice, Judas, wolf in sheep's clothing; Molly Maguire; jilt; shuffler.

liar &c. (lie &c. 544); story-teller, perjurer, false-witness, *menteur, -à triple etage, -à payer patente*; Scapin.

impostor, pretender, capper, decoy, fraud, *soi-disant*, humbug; adventurer; Cagliostro, Fernam Mendez Pinto; ass in lion's skin &c. (*bungler*) 701; actor &c. (*stage player*) 599.

quack, *charlatan*, mountebank, saltimbanco, *saltimbanque*, empiric, quacksalver, medicaster.

conjuror, juggler, magician, necromancer, trickster, prestidigitator, medium, jockey; crimp; decoy-duck, stool pigeon; rogue, knave, cheat; swindler &c. (*thief*) 792; jobber.

549. Exaggeration.—N. exaggeration; expansion &c. 194; hyperbole, stretch, strain, colouring; high colouring, caricature, *caricatura*; extravagance &c. (*nonsense*) 497; Baron Munchausen; men in buckram, yarn, fringe, embroidery, traveller's tale; Ossa upon Pelion.

storm in a teacup; much ado about nothing &c. (*over-estimation*) 482; puffery &c. (*boasting*) 884; rant &c. (*turgescence*) 577.

figure of speech, *façon de parler*; stretch of -fancy, – the imagination; flight of fancy &c. (*imagination*) 515.

false colouring &c. (*falsehood*) 544; aggravation &c. 835.

V. exaggerate, magnify, pile up, aggravate; amplify &c. (*expand*) 194; overestimate &c. 482; hyperbolize; over-charge, -state, -draw, -lay, -shoot the mark, -praise; make -much, – the most- of; strain, – a point; stretch, – a point; go great lengths; spin a long yarn; draw –, shoot with- a long-bow; deal in the marvellous.

out-Herod Herod, run riot, talk at random.

heighten, overcolour; colour -highly, – too highly; embroider, *broder*; flourish; colour &c. (*misrepresent*) 544; puff &c. (*boast*) 884.

Adj. exaggerated &c. *v.*; overwrought; bombastic &c. (*magniloquent*) 577; hyperbolical, on stilts; fabulous, extravagant, preposterous, egregious, *outré*, high-flying.

Adv. hyperbolically &c. *adj.*

Section III. Means of Communicating Ideas

1.° *Natural Means*

550. Indication.—N. indication; symbol-ism, -ization; semeio-logy, -tics; sign of the times.

lineament, feature, *trait*, characteristic, trick, diagnostic; divining-rod; cloven hoof; footfall; means of recognition; earmark.

sign, symbol; ind-ex, -ice, -icator; point, -er; marker; exponent, note, token, symptom.

type, figure, emblem, cipher, device; representation &c. 554; epigraph, motto, posy.

gest-ure, -iculation; pantomime; wink, glance, leer; nod, shrug, beck; touch, nudge; grip; dactylo-logy, -nomy; Freemasonry, telegraphy, chirology, by-play, dumb-show; cue; hint &c. 527; clue, clew, key, scent, track &c. 551.

signal, -post; rocket, blue light; watch-fire, -tower; telegrapL, semaphore, flag-staff; cresset, fiery cross; calumet; heliograph, signal-, flash-lamp.

mark, line, stroke, dash, score, stripe, streak, scratch, tick, dot, point, notch, nick, blaze; asterisk, red letter, italics, heavy type, inverted commas, quotation marks, sublineation, underlining, jotting; print; impr-int, -ess, -ession; note, annotation, mark of exclamation.

[For identification] badge, criterion; counter-check, -mark, -sign, -foil; duplicate, tally; label, tab, ticket, stub, billet, letter, counter, *tessera*, card, bill, check; witness, voucher; stamp; *cachet*; trade -, hall- mark; broad arrow; signature; address -, visiting- card; *carte de visite*; credentials &c. (*evidence*) 467; passport, indentity book, *carte d' identité*; attestation; hand, - writing, sign-manual; cipher; monogram, - mark, seal, sigil, signet; autograph, -y; paraph, brand; superscription; in-, en-dorsement· title, heading, rubric, docket; *mot -de passe, – du guet*; *passe-parole*; shibboleth; watch-, catch-, pass-word; *open sesame!*

insignia; banner, -et, -ol; bandrol; flag, colours, streamer, standard, eagle, labarum, oriflamb, *oriflamme*; figure-head; ensign; pen-non, -nant, -dant; burgee, blue Peter, jack, ancient, gonfalon, Union jack; tricolour, stars and stripes; bunting, Jolly Roger, *drapeau, pavillon*.

heraldry, crest; coat of -, arms; armorial bearings, hatchment; e-, scutcheon; shield, supporters; livery, uniform; cockade, *epaulette*, brassard, chevron; garland, chaplet, love-knot, fillet, favour.

[Of locality] beacon, cairn, post, staff, flagstaff, hand, pointer, vane, cock, weathercock; guide-, hand-, finger-, directing-, sign-post; pillars of Hercules, pharos, signal fire; bench-, land-, sea-mark; lighthouse, balize; pole-, load-, lode-star; cynosure, guide; address, direction, name; sign, -board.

[Of the future] warning &c. 668; omen &c. 512; prefigurement &c. 511. [Of the past] trace record &c. 551. [Of danger] warning &c. 668; alarm &c. 669. [Of authority] sceptre &c. 747. [Of triumph] trophy &c. 733. [Of quantity] gauge &c. 466. [Of distance] mile-stone, -post. [Of disgrace] brand, fool's cap, stigma, mark of Cain. [For detection] check, tell-tale; test &c. (*experiment*) 463.

notification &c. (*information*) 527; advertisement &c. (*publication*) 531.

word of command, call; bugle-, trumpet-call; reveille, taps; bell, alarum, cry; battle -, rallying- cry.

church, bell, angelus, sacring bell; muezzin.

exposition &c. (*explanation*) 522; proof &c. (*evidence*) 467; pattern &c. (*prototype*) 22.

V. indicate; be the -sign &c. *n.*- of; denote, betoken; argue, testify &c. (*evidence*) 467; bear the -impress &c. *n.*- of; con-note, -notate.

represent, stand for; typify &c. (*prefigure*) 511; symbolize.

put -an indication, - a mark, - &c. *n.*; note, mark, tick, blaze, stamp, earmark; set one's seal upon; label, ticket, docket; dot, spot, score, dash, trace, chalk; print; im-print, -press, surprint; engrave, stereotype. electrotype.

make a -sign &c. *n.*; signalize; give –, hang out- a signal; beck, -on; gesture; nod; wink, glance, leer, nudge, shrug, tip the wink; gesticulate; raise –, hold up- the -finger, – hand; saw the air, suit the action to the word.

wave –, unfurl –, hoist –, hang out- a banner &c. *n.*; wave -the hand, – a kerchief; give the cue &c. (*inform*) 527; show one's colours; give –, sound- an alarm; beat the drum, sound the trumpets, raise a cry.

sign, seal, attest &c. (*evidence*) 467; underline &c. (*give importance to*) 642; call attention to &c. (*attention*) 457; give notice &c. (*inform*) 527.

Adj. indicat-ing &c. *v.*, -ive, -ory; de-, con-notative; diacritical, representative, typical, symbolic, pantomimic, pathognomonic, symptomatic, ominous, characteristic, demonstrative, diagnostic, exponential, emblematic, armorial; individual &c. (*special*) 79.

known –, recognizable- by; indicated &c. *v.*; pointed, marked.

[Capable of being denoted] denotable; indelible.

Adv. in token of; symbolically &c. *adj.*; in dumb show.

Phr. *ecce signum; ex ungue leonem, ex pede Herculem.*

---

551. Record.—**N.** trace, vestige, relic, remains; scar, *cicatrix;* foot-step, -mark, -print; track, mark, wake, trail, spoor, scent, *piste.*

monument, hatchment, escutcheon, slab, tablet, trophy, achievement; obelisk, pillar, column, monolith, cromlech, dolmen; memorial; *memento* &c. (*memory*) 505; testimonial, medal, ribbon, order; commemoration &c. (*celebration*) 883.

record, note, minute; *dossier;* register, -try; census, roll &c. (*list*) 86; cartulary, diptych, Domesday book; entry, memorandum, indorsement, inscription, copy, duplicate, docket; notch &c. (*mark*) 550; muniment, deed &c. (*security*) 771; document; deposition, *procès-verbal;* affidavit; certificate &c. (*evidence*) 467.

552. [Suppression of sign.] **Obliteration.**—**N.** obliteration; erasure, rasure; effacement; cancel, -lation; cassation; circumduction; deletion, blot; *tabula rasa.*

V. efface, obliterate, erase, rase, expunge, cancel; blot –, take –, rub –, scratch –, strike –, wipe –, wash –, sponge- out; wipe –, rub- off; wipe away; deface, render illegible; draw the pen through, apply the sponge.

be -effaced &c.; leave no -trace &c. 449; 'leave not a rack behind.'

Adj. obliterated &c. *v.*; out of print; printless; leaving no trace; intestate; un-recorded, -registered, -written.

Int. *dele;* out with it!

---

note-, memorandum-, pocket-, commonplace-book; portfolio; scoring-board, -sheet; bulletin board; card index, file; pigeon-holes, *excerpta, adversaria,* jottings, dottings.

gazette, -er; newspaper, magazine &c. 531; alman-ac, -ack; calendar, ephemeris, noctuary, diary, log, journal, account-, cash-, day-book, ledger.

archive, scroll, state-paper, Congressional Record, return, blue-book; statistics &c. 86; *compte rendu;* Acts –, Transactions –, Proceedings- of; Hansard's Debates; chronicle, annals; legend; history, biography &c. 594.

registration; en-, in-rolment; tabulation; entry, booking; signature &c. (*identification*) 550; recorder &c. 553; journalism.

drawing, photograph &c. 554; phonograph –, gramophone-record; music roll.

V. record; put –, place- upon record; go on record; chronicle, calendar, hand down to posterity; keep up the memory of &c. (*remember*) 505; commemorate &c. (*celebrate*) 883; report &c. (*inform*) 527; commit to –, reduce to- writing; put –, set down- -in writing, – in black and white; put –, jot –, take –, write –, note –, set- down; note, minute, put on paper; take –, make- a -note, – minute, – memorandum; make a return.

mark &c. (*indicate*) 550; sign &c. (*attest*) 467.

enter, book; post, – up; insert, make an entry of; mark –, tick-off; register, list, docket, enroll, inscroll; file &c. (*store*) 636.

Adv. on record.

553. Recorder.—N. recorder, notary, clerk; regis-trar, -trary, -ter; prothonotary; amanuensis, secretary, scribe, stenographer, remem-brancer, book-keeper, *custos rotulorum*, Master of the Rolls.

annalist; histori-an, -ographer; chronicler, journalist, reporter, columnist; biographer &c. (*narrator*) 594; antiquary &c. (*antiquity*) 122; memorialist.

draughtsman &c. 559; engraver 558; photographer, cinematographer, camera man.

Recording instrument, recorder, camera, phonograph, gramophone, dictaphone, telegraphone, telautograph, printing telegraph, tape machine, ticker, time recorder, cash register, turnstile, speedometer, voting machine, seismograph, photostat.

554. Representation.—N. represent--ation, -ment; imitation &c. 19; illus-tration, delineation, depictment, por-trayal; imagery, portraiture, iconog-raphy; design, -ing; art, fine arts; painting &c. 556; sculpture &c. 557; engraving &c. 558; photography, radi-ography, skiagraphy.

person-ation, -ification; impersona-tion; drama &c. 599.

picture, drawing, sketch, draught,

555. Misrepresentation.—N. mis-representation, distortion, exaggera-tion; daubing &c. *v.*; bad likeness, daub, sign-painting; scratch, carica-ture; *anamorphosis*.

V. misrepresent, distort, overdraw, travesty, parody, burlesque, exagger-ate, caricature, daub.

Adj. misrepresented &c. *v.*

draft; tracing; copy &c. 21; photo-, helio-graph; daguerreo-, talbo-, calo-, helio-type; cabinet, *carte-de-visite*, snapshot; X-ray photo-graph; radio-gram, -graph, skia-graph, -gram.

image, likeness, icon, portrait; striking –, speaking- likeness; very image; effigy, fac-simile.

figure, – head; puppet, doll, *figurine*, aglet, manikin, lay-figure, model, *marionnette*, *fantoccini*, bust; waxwork, statue, -tte, auto-maton, Robot.

hieroglyphic, anaglyph; dia-, mono-gram, -graph.

map, plan, chart; ground plan, projection, elevation; ichno-, carto-graphy; atlas; outline, scheme; view &c. (*painting*) 556.

artist, draughtsman &c. 559.

V. represent, delineate; depict, -ure; portray; picture; take –, catch- a likeness &c. *n.*; hit off, photograph, daguerreotype; figure; shadow -forth, – out; adumbrate; body forth; describe &c. 594; trace, copy; mould.

dress up; illustrate, symbolize.

paint &c. 556; carve &c. 557; engrave &c. 558.

person-ate, -ify; impersonate; assume a character; pose as; act;

play &c. (*drama*) 599; mimic &c. (*imitate*) 19; hold the mirror up to nature.

Adj. represent-ing &c. *v.*, -ative; illustrative; represented &c. *v* ; imitative, figurative.

like &c. 17; graphic &c. (*descriptive*) 594.

556. Painting.—N. painting; depicting; drawing &c. *v.*; design; perspective, skiagraphy; *chiaroscuro* &c. (*light*) 420; composition; treatment, values, atmosphere, tone, technique.

historical –, portrait –, miniature –, battle-, *genre* -, landscape –, marine –, fruit and flower –, scene- painting; scenography.

school, style; the grand style, high art, *genre*, portraiture; ornamental art &c. 847.

mono-, poly-chrome; *grisaille*.

pallet, palette; easel; brush, pencil, stump; blacklead, charcoal, crayons, chalk, pastel; paint &c. (*colouring matter*) 428; water-, body-, oil-colour; oils, oil-paint; varnish &c. 356*a*; *gouache*, tempera, distemper, fresco; enamel; encaustic painting; *graffito*, *gesso*; mosaic; tapestry.

picture, painting, piece, *tableau*, canvas; oil &c.- painting; cartoon; easel –, cabinet- picture; drawing, draught, draft; pencil &c. –, water-colour- drawing; sketch, outline; study.

portrait &c. (*representation*) 554; whole –, full –, half- length; kitcat. head; miniature; shade, *silhouette*; profile.

landscape, sea-piece, -scape; view, scene, prospect; interior; bird's-eye view; pan-, di-orama; still life.

picture –, art- gallery; studio, *atelier*.

V. paint, design, limn, draw, sketch, pencil, scratch, shade, stipple, hatch, dash off, chalk out, square up; colour, dead-colour, wash, varnish; draw in -pencil &c. *n.*; paint in -oils &c. *n.*; stencil; depict &c. (*represent*) 554.

Adj. painted &c. *v.*; pictorial, graphic, picturesque, decorative; classical, romantic, pre-Raphaelite, modern, cubist, futurist, vorticist, post-, impressionist.

pencil, oil &c. *n.*

Adv. in -pencil &c. *n.*

Phr. *fecit, delineavit, pinxit.*

557. Sculpture.—N. sculpture, insculpture; carving &c. *v.*; statuary, ceramics, plastic arts.

high –, low –, bas- relief; relievo; *basso-, alto-, mezzo-rilievo*; *intaglio*, anaglyph; medal, -lion; *cameo*.

marble, bronze, terracotta; ceramic ware, pottery, porcelain, china, earthenware, faïence, enamel, *cloisonné*.

statue &c. (*image*) 554; cast &c. (*copy*) 21; glyptotheca.

V. sculpture, carve, cut, chisel, model, mould; cast.

Adj. sculptured &c. *v.*; in relief, anaglyptic, ceroplastic, ceramic; parian; marble &c. *n.* **Phr.** *sculpsit.*

558. Engraving.—N. engraving, chalcography; line –, mezzotint –, stipple –, chalk- engraving; dry-point, bur; etching, aquatinta; plate –, copper-plate –, steel –, wood-, process-, photo-engraving; xylo-, ligno-, glypto-, cero-, litho-, chromolitho-, photolitho-, zinco-, glypho- -graphy, -graph.

impression, print, engraving, plate; steel-, copper-plate; etching; mezzo-, aqua-, litho-tint; cut, woodcut, block; stereo-, grapho-, auto-, helio-type; half-tone; *photogravure, rotogravure.*

graver, *burin*, etching-point, style; plate, stone, wood-block, negative; die, punch, stamp.

printing; plate –, copper-plate –, intaglio –, anastatic –, lithographic –, colour –, three or four colour- printing; type-printing &c. 591.

illustr-, illumin-ation; *vignette*, initial letter, *cul de lampe*, tail-piece.

V. engrave, grave, stipple, scrape, etch; bite, – in; lithograph &c. *n.*; print.

Adj. insculptured; engraved &c. *v.*

Phr. *fecit, sculpsit, imprimit, incisit.*

559. Artist.—**N.** artist; painter, limner, drawer, sketcher, delineator; cartoon-, caricatur-ist, designer, engraver; draughtsman; copyist; enamel-ler, -list.

historical –, landscape –, battle-, *genre* –, marine –, fruit and flower –, portrait –, miniature –, scene –, sign- painter; engraver; Apelles; sculptor, carver, chaser, modeller, lapidary, *figuriste*, statuary; Phidias, Praxiteles; Royal Academician.

photographer, retoucher.

2°. *Conventional Means*
1. *Language generally*

560. Language.—**N.** language; phraseology &c. 569; speech &c. 582; tongue, lingo, vernacular, slang; mother –, vulgar –, native- tongue; household words; King's *or* Queen's English; idiom; dialect &c. 563.

Volapuk, Esperanto, Ido, occidental, Ro.

confusion of tongues, Babel, *pasigraphie*; pantomime &c. (*signs*) 550; *onomatopœia.*

phil-, gloss-, glott-ology; linguistics, chrestomathy; paleo-logy; -graphy; comparative grammar.

literature, letters, polite literature, *belles lettres*, muses, humanities. *literæ humaniores*, republic of letters, dead languages, classics; genius of a language; scholarship &c. (*knowledge*) 490.

linguist &c. (*scholar*) 492.

V. speak, say, express by words &c. 566.

Adj. lingu-al, -istic; dialectic; vernacular, current, colloquial, slangy; bilingual, polyglot; literary.

561. Letter.—**N.** letter; character; hieroglyphic &c. (*writing*) 590; type &c. (*printing*) 591; capitals; majus-, minus-cule; alphabet, ABC, abecedary, Christ-cross-row.

consonant, vowel, diphthong; mute, surd; sonant, liquid, labial, dental, palatal, guttural.

syllable; mono-, dis-, poly-syllable; affix, prefix, suffix.

spelling, orthography; phon-ography, -etic spelling; ana-, meta-grammatism.

cipher, monogram, anagram; double –, acrostic.

V. spell.

Adj. literal; alphabetical, abecedarian; syllabic; uncial &c. (*writing*) 590; phonetic, voiced, mute &c. *n.*

562. Word.—**N.** word, term, vocable; name &c. 564; phrase &c. 566; root, etymon; derivative; part of speech &c. (*grammar*) 567.

dictionary, vocabulary, word book,

563. Neology.—**N.** neolo-gy, -gism; new-fangled expression; barbarism; caconym; archaism, black letter, monkish Latin; corruption; missaying, antiphrasis.

lexicon, index, glossary, thesaurus, *gradus, delectus,* concordance.

etymology, lexicology, derivation; phonology, orthoepy; gloss-, termin-, orism-ology; paleology &c. (*philology*) 560; comparative philology.

lexicograph-er, -y; glossographer &c. (*scholar*) 492; etymologist; logolept.

verbosity, verbiage, loquacity &c. 584.

Adj. verbal, literal; titular, nominal. [Similarly derived] conjugate, paronymous; derivative.

Adv. verbally &c. *adj.*; *verbatim* &c. (*exactly*) 494.

---

paronomasia, play upon words; word·play &c. (*wit*) 842; pun; *double-entendre* &c. (*ambiguity*) 520; palindrome, paragram, clinch; abuse of -language, – terms.

dialect, brogue, *patois,* provincialism, broken English, *lingua franca*; Brit-, Gall-, Scott-, Hibern-icism; Americanism; Gipsy lingo, Romany, pidgin English.

dog Latin, macaronics, gibberish, confusion of tongues, Babel; jargon.

colloquialism &c. (*figure of speech*) 521; by-word; technicality, lingo, slang, cant, *argot,* St. Giles's Greek, thieves' Latin, peddler's French, flash tongue, Billingsgate, Wall Street slang.

pseudonym &c. (*misnomer*) 565; Mr. So-and-so; what d'ye call 'em, what's his name; N. N.; *Monsieur Un Tel*; thingum-my, -bob; gadget, dooflicker, do-funny, *oo-ja-ka-pi-vi*; *je ne sais quoi.*

neologist, coiner of words.

V. coin words.

Adj. neologic, -al; rare; archaic; obsolete &c. (*old*) 124; colloquial, dialectic, slang, cant.

Phr. *Il a passé par Marseille.*

564. Nomenclature. — N. nomenclature; naming &c. *v.*; nuncupation, nomination, baptism; orismology; *onomatopœia*; antonomasia.

name; appella-tion, -tive; designation; title; head, -ing, caption; denomination; by-name, epithet.

style, proper name; præ-, ag-, cognomen; patronymic, surname; cognomination; compellation, description; empty -title, – name; handle to one's name; namesake, eponym.

synonym, antonym.

term, expression, noun; by-word; convertible terms &c. 522; technical term; cant &c. 563.

V. name, call, term, denominate, designate, style, entitle, intitule, clepe, dub, christen, baptize, nickname, characterize, specify, define, distinguish by the name of; label &c. (*mark*) 550.

be -called &c. *v.*; take –, bear –, go (*or* be known) by –, go (*or* pass) under –, rejoice in- the name of.

Adj. named &c. *v.*; hight, yclept, known as; what one may -well, – fairly, – properly, – fitly- call.

nuncupa-tory, -tive; cognominal, titular, nominal; orismological.

565. Misnomer.—N. misnomer; *lucus a non lucendo*; Mrs. Malaprop; what d'ye call 'em &c. (*neologism*) 563.

nickname, *sobriquet,* by-name, handle, moniker; assumed -name, – title; *alias*; *nom de -guerre,* – *plume,* – *théâtre*; pseudonym, pen name, stage name.

V. mis-name, -call, -term; nickname; assume -a name, – an alias.

Adj. misnamed &c. *v.*; pseudonymous; *soi-disant*; self-called, -styled, -christened; so-called.

nameless, anonymous; without a –, having no- name; innominate, unnamed.

Adv. in no sense.

---

566. Phrase.—N. phrase, expression, set phrase; sentence, paragraph; figure of speech &c. 521; idi-om, -otism; turn of expression.

paraphrase &c. (*synonym*) 522; periphrase &c. (*circumlocution*) 573; motto &c. (*proverb*) 496; phraseology &c. 569.

V. express, phrase; word, – it; give -words, – expression- to; voice; arrange in –, clothe in –, put into –, express by- words; couch in terms; find words to express; speak by the card.

Adj. expressed &c. *v.*; idiomatic.

Adv. in -round, – set, – good, set- terms; in set phrases.

567. Grammar.—N. grammar, accidence, syntax, *praxis*, analysis, paradigm; punctuation; parts of speech; inflexion, case, declension, conjugation; *jus et norma loquendi*; Lindley Murray &c. (*school-book*) 542; correct style; philology &c. (*language*) 560.

V. parse, analyze; decline, conjugate; punctuate.

Adj. grammatical; syntactic; inflexional.

568. Solecism.—N. solecism; bad –, false –, faulty- grammar; slip, error; slip of the -pen, – tongue; *lapsus calami-*, – *linguæ*; *faux pas*; slip-slop; bull.

V. use -bad, – faulty- grammar; solecize, commit a solecism; murder the -King's, – Queen's- English; break Priscian's head.

Adj. ungrammatical; in-correct, -accurate; faulty, improper, incongruous, abnormal.

569. Style.—N. style, diction, phraseology, wording; manner, strain; composition; mode of expression, choice of words, literary power, ready pen, pen of a ready writer; command of language &c. (*eloquence*) 582; authorship; *la morgue littéraire*.

V. express by words &c. 566; write.

Various Qualities of Style

570. Perspicuity.—N. perspicuity &c. (*intelligibility*) 518; plain speaking &c. (*manifestation*) 525; defin-iteness, -ition; exactness &c. 494; perspicuousness, logical acuteness.

Adj. lucid &c. (*intelligible*) 518; explicit &c. (*manifest*) 525; exact &c. 494.

571. Obscurity.—N. obscurity &c. (*unintelligibility*) 519; involution; hard words; ambiguity &c. 520; vagueness &c. 475, inexactness &c. 495; what d'ye call 'em &c. (*neologism*) 563; cloudiness, confusion.

Adj. obscure &c. *n.*; crabbed, involved, confused.

572. Conciseness.—N. conciseness &c. *adj.*; brevity, 'the soul of wit,' laconism; Tacitus; ellipsis; syncope; abridgment &c. (*shortening*) 201; compression &c. 195; epitome &c. 596; monostitch; portmanteau word, telescope word, protogram.

V. be -concise &c. *adj.*; condense &c. 195; abridge &c. 201; abstract &c. 596; come to the point.

Adj. concise, brief, short, terse, close; to the point, exact; neat, compact, condensed, pointed; laconic, curt, pithy, trenchant, summary; pregnant; compendious &c. (*compendium*) 596; succinct; elliptical, epigrammatic, crisp, sententious.

Adv. concisely &c. *adj.*; briefly,

573. Diffuseness.—N. diffuseness &c. *adj.*; amplification &c. *v.*; dilating &c. *v.*; verbosity, verbiage, wordiness, cloud of words, *copia verborum*; flow of words &c. (*loquacity*) 584.

poly-, tauto-, batto-, perisso-logy; pleonasm, exuberance, redundance; thrice-told tale; prolixity; circumlocution, *ambages*; periphra-se, -sis; roundabout phrases; episode; expletive; penny-a-lining; padding, drivel, twaddle, rigmarole; richness &c. 577.

V. be -diffuse &c. *adj.*; run out on, descant, expatiate, enlarge, dilate, amplify, expand, inflate, pad; launch –, branch- out; rant.

maunder, prose; harp upon &c. (*repeat*) 104; dwell on, insist upon.

summarily; in -brief, – short, – a word, – few words, – a nutshell; for shortness sake; to -come to the point, – make a long story short, – cut the matter short, – be brief; it comes to this, the long and the short of it is.

digress, ramble, *battre la campagne*, beat about the bush, perorate, spin a, long yarn, protract; spin –, swell –, draw- out, drivel.

Adj. dif-, pro-fuse; wordy, verbose, largiloquent, copious, exuberant, effusive, pleonastic, lengthy; long, -some, -winded, -spun, -drawn out; diffusive, spun out, protracted, prolix, prosing, maundering; circumlocutory, periphrastic, ambagious, roundabout; digressive; dis-, ex-cursive; rambling, episodic; flatulent, frothy.

Adv. diffusely &c. *adj.*; at large, *in extenso*; about it and about it.

574. Vigour.—N. vigour, power, force; boldness, raciness &c. *adj.*; spirit, point, antithesis, piquancy; *verve*, glow, fire, warmth, ardour, enthusiasm; 'thoughts that breathe and words that burn'; strong language; punch; gravity, sententiousness; elevation, loftiness, sublimity.

eloquence; command of -words, – language.

Adj. vigorous, nervous, powerful, forcible, trenchant, mordant, biting, incisive, impressive; sensational.

spirited, lively, glowing, sparkling, racy, bold, slashing; pungent, *piquant*, full of point, pointed, pithy, antithetical; sententious.

lofty, elevated, sublime, grand, weighty, ponderous; eloquent; vehement, petulant, impassioned; poetic.

Adv. in -glowing, – good set, – no measured- terms.

575. Feebleness.—N. feebleness &c. *adj.*

Adj. feeble, bald, tame, meagre, insipid, nerveless, jejune, vapid, trashy, cold, frigid, poor, dull, dry, languid; pros-ing, -y, -aic; unvaried, monotonous, weak, frail, washy, wishy-washy, sloppy; sketchy, slight; careless, slovenly, loose, lax; slip-shod, -slop; inexact; dis-jointed, -connected; puerile, childish; flatulent; rambling &c. (*diffuse*) 573.

576. Plainness.—N. plainness &c. *adj.*; simplicity, severity; plain -terms, – English; Saxon English; household words.

V. speak plainly; call a spade 'a spade'; plunge *in medias res*; come to the point.

Adj. plain, simple; un-ornamented, -adorned, -varnished; home-ly, -spun; neat; severe, chaste, pure, Saxon; commonplace, matter of fact, natural, prosaic, sober, unimaginative.

dry, unvaried, monotonous &c. 575.

Adv. in plain -terms, – words, – English, – common parlance; point blank.

577. Ornament. — N. ornament; floridness &c. *adj.*; turg-idity, -escence; altiloquence &c. *adj.*; orotundity; declamation, teratology; well-rounded periods; elegance &c. 578.

inversion, antithesis, alliteration, *paronomasia*; figurativeness &c. (*metaphor*) 521.

flourish; flowers of -speech, – rhetoric; euph-uism, -emism.

big-, high-sounding words; macrology, *sesquipedalia verba*, sesquipedalianism; Alexandrine; inflation, pretension; rant, bombast, fustian, bunkum, balderdash, prose run mad; fine writing; Minerva press.

phrasemonger; euph-uist, -emist.

V. ornament, overlay with ornament, overcharge; smell of the lamp.

Adj. ornamented &c. *v.*; beautified &c. 847; ornate, florid, rich, flowery; euph-uistic, -emistic; sonorous; high-, big-sounding; inflated, swelling, tumid; turg-id, -escent; pedantic, pompous, stilted;

high-flown, -flowing; sententious, rhetorical, declamatory; grandiose; grand-, magn-, alt-iloquent; sesquipedal, -ian; Johnsonian, mouthy; bombastic; fustian; frothy, flashy, flaming, flamboyant.

antithetical, alliterative; figurative &c. 521; artificial &c. (*inelegant*) 579.

Adv. *ore rotundo*; with rounded phrase.

578. Elegance.—N. elegance, purity, grace, ease, felicity, distinction, gracefulness, refinement, readiness &c. *adj.*; concinnity, euphony, numerosity, balance, rhythm, symmetry, proportion; restraint; good taste, propriety.

well rounded –, well turned –, flowing- periods; the right word in the right place; antithesis &c. 577.

purist, stylist.

V. point an antithesis, round a period.

Adj. elegant, polished, classical, Attic, correct, Ciceronian, artistic; chaste, pure, Saxon, academical.

graceful, easy, readable, fluent, flowing, tripping; unaffected, natural, unlaboured; mellifluous; euph-onious, -emistic; rhythmical, balanced, symmetrical.

felicitous, happy, neat; well –, neatly- -put, – expressed.

579. Inelegance. — N. inelegance; vulgarity, bad taste; stiffness &c. *adj.*; unlettered Muse; barbarism; slang &c. 563; solecism &c. 568; mannerism &c. (*affectation*) 855; euphuism; fustian &c. 577; cacophony; want of balance; words that -break the teeth, – dislocate the jaw.

V. be -inelegant &c. *adj.*

Adj. inelegant, graceless, ungraceful, unpolished; harsh, abrupt; dry, stiff, cramped, formal, *guindé*; forced, laboured, awkward; artificial, mannered, ponderous; turgid &c. 577; affected, euphuistic; barbarous, uncouth, grotesque, rude, crude, halting; vulgar, offensive to ears polite.

---

2. Spoken Language

580. Voice.—N. voice; vocality; organ, lungs, bellows: good –, fine –, powerful &c. (*loud*) 404 ·-, musical &c. 413- voice; intonation; tone &c. (*sound*) 402- of voice.

vocalization; cry &c. 411; strain, utterance, prolation; exclam-, ejacul-, vocifer-ation; enunci-, articul-ation; articulate sound, distinctness; clearness, – of articulation; stage whisper; delivery; attack.

accent, -uation; emphasis, stress; broad –, strong –, pure –, native –, for-eign- accent; pronunciation.

[Word similarly pronounced] homonym.

orthoepy; euphony &c. (*melody*) 413.

gastri-, ventri-loquism; ventriloquist; polyphon-ism, -ist.

[Science of voice] phonology &c. (*sound*) 402.

V. sing, speak. utter, breathe, voice; give -utterance, – tongue; cry &c.

581. Aphony.—N. aphony, *aphonia*; dumbness &c. *adj.*; obmutescence; absence –, want- of voice; dysphony; silence &c. (*taciturnity*) 585; raucity; harsh &c. 410 –, unmusical &c. 414- voice; *falsetto*, 'childish treble'; mute, dummy, deaf mute.

V. keep silence &c. 585; speak -low, – softly; whisper &c. (*faintness*) 405.

silence; render -mute, – silent &c. 403; muzzle, muffle, suppress, smother, gag, strike dumb, dumb-found, -founder; drown the voice, put to silence, stop one's mouth, cut one short; stick in the throat.

Adj. aphon-ous, -ic, dumb, mute; deaf-mute, – and dumb; mum; tongue-tied; breath-, tongue-, voice-, speech-, word-less; mute as a -fish, – stockfish, – mackerel; silent &c. (*taciturn*) 585; muzzled; in-articulate, -audible.

croaking, raucous, hoarse, husky,

(*shout*) 411; ejaculate, rap out; vocalize, prolate, articulate, enunciate, enounce, pronounce, accentuate, aspirate, deliver, mouth; emit, murmur, whisper, – in the ear, croon, yodel.

Adj. vocal, phonetic, oral; ejaculatory, articulate, distinct, stertorous; enunciative; accentuated, aspirated; euphonious &c. (*melodious*) 413.

582. Speech.—N. speech, faculty of speech; locution, talk, parlance, verbal intercourse, prolation, oral communication, word of mouth, *parole*, palaver, prattle; effusion.

oration, recitation, delivery, say, address, speech, lecture, harangue, sermon, *tirade*, screed, formal speech, salutatory, peroration; prelection; speechifying; soliloquy &c. 589; allocution &c. 586; interlocution &c. 588.

oratory; elo-cution, -quence; rhetoric, declamation; grandi-, multiloquence; burst of eloquence; facundity; talkativeness; flow –, commandof -words, – language; *copia verborum*; power of speech, gift of the gab; *usus loquendi*.

speaker &c. *v.*; spokesman; pro-, inter-locutor; mouthpiece, Hermes; ora-tor, -trix, -tress; Demosthenes, Cicero; rhetorician; stump –, platform-orator, tub-thumper; elocutionist; speech-maker, patterer, *improvisatore*.

V. speak, – of; say, utter, pronounce, deliver, give utterance to; utter –, pour- forth; breathe, let fall, come out with; rap –, blurt- out; have on one's lips; have at the -end, – tip- of one's tongue.

break silence; open one's -lips, – mouth; lift –, raise- one's voice; give –, wag the- tongue; talk, outspeak; put in a word or two.

hold forth; make –, deliver- -a speech &c. *n.*; speechify, harangue, declaim, stump, flourish, spout, rant, recite, lecture, preach, sermonize, discourse, be on one's legs; have –, say- one's say; expatiate &c. (*speak at length*) 573; speak one's mind.

soliloquize &c. 589; tell &c. (*inform*) 527; speak to &c. 586; talk together &c. 588.

be -eloquent &c. *adj.*; have -a tongue in one's head, – the gift of the gab &c. *n.*

pass –, escape- one's lips; fall from the -lips, – mouth.

Adj. speaking &c., spoken &c. *v.*; oral, lingual, phonetic, not written, unwritten, outspoken; elo-quent, -cutionary; orat-, rhet-orical; declamatory; grandiloquent &c. 577; talkative &c. 584.

dry, hollow, sepulchral, hoarse as a raven.

Adv. with -bated breath, – the finger on the lips; *sotto voce*; in a -low tone, – cracked voice, – broken voice; in an aside.

Phr. *vox faucibus hæsit.*

583. [Imperfect Speech.] Stammering.—N. inarticulateness; stammering &c. *v.*; hesitation &c. *v.*; impediment in one's speech; aphasia, titubancy, traulism; whisper &c. (*faint sound*) 405; lisp, drawl, tardiloquence; nasal -tone, – accent; twang; *falsetto* &c. (*want of voice*) 581; broken -voice, – accents, – sentences.

brogue &c. 563; slip of the tongue, *lapsus linguæ*.

V. stammer, stutter, hesitate, falter, hammer; balbu-tiate, -cinate; haw, hum and haw, be unable to put two words together.

mumble, mutter; maund, -er; whisper &c. 405; mince, lisp; jabber, gabble, gibber; sp-, spl-utter; muffle, mump; drawl, mouth; croak; speak -thick, – through the nose; snuffle, clip one's words; murder the -language, – King's (*or* Queen's) English; mis-pronounce, -say.

Adj. stammering &c. *v.*; inarticulate, guttural, nasal; tremulous.

Adv. *sotto voce* &c. (*faintly*) 405.

Adv. orally &c. *adj.*; by word of mouth, *vivâ voce*, from the lips of.
Phr. quoth –, said- he &c.

584. Loquacity. — N. loquac-ity, -iousness; talkativeness &c. *adj.*; garrulity; multiloquence, much speaking, effusion, wordiness.

jaw; gab, -ble; jabber, chatter; prate, prattle, cackle, clack; twaddle, twattle, rattle; *caquet, -terie*; blabber, *bavardage*, bibble-babble, gibble-gabble; small talk &c. (*converse*) 588.

fluency, flippancy, volubility, flowing tongue; flow, – of words; *flux de -bouche, – mots, – paroles*; *copia verborum, cacoëthes loquendi*; verbosity &c. (*diffuseness*) 573; gift of the gab &c. (*eloquence*) 582.

talker; chatter-er, -box; babbler &c. *v.*; rattle; ranter; sermonizer, proser, driveller; windbag; gossip &c. (*converse*) 588; magpie, jay, parrot, poll, Babel; *moulin à paroles*.

V. be -loquacious &c. *adj.*; talk glibly, pour forth, patter; prate, palaver, prose, chatter, prattle, clack, jabber, jaw; rattle, – on; twaddle, twattle; babble, gabble; out-talk; talk oneself -out of breath, – hoarse; maunder, gush, blather; talk a donkey's hind leg off; expatiate &c. (*speak at length*) 573; gossip &c. (*converse*) 588; din in the ears &c. (*repeat*) 104; talk -at random, – nonsense &c. 497; be hoarse with talking.

Adj. loquacious, talkative, conversational, garrulous, linguacious, multiloquous; chattering &c. *v.*; chatty &c. (*sociable*) 892; declamatory &c. 582; open-mouthed.

fluent, voluble, glib, flippant; long-tongued, -winded &c. (*diffuse*) 573.

Adv. trippingly on the tongue; glibly &c. *adj.*
Phr. the tongue running -fast, – loose, – on wheels.

585. Taciturnity.—N. silence, muteness, obmutescence; taciturnity, pauciloquy, costiveness, curtness; reserve, reticence &c. (*concealment*) 528; *aposiopesis*.

man of few words.

V. be -silent &c. *adj.*; keep silence; hold one's -tongue, – peace, – jaw; not speak &c. 582; say nothing; seal –, close –, put a padlock on- the -lips, – mouth; put a bridle on one's tongue; keep one's tongue between one's teeth; make no sign, not let a word escape one; keep a secret &c. 528; not have a word to say; lay –, place- the finger on the lips; render mute &c. 581.

stick in one's throat.

Adj. silent, mute, mum; silent as -a post, – a stone, – the grave &c. (*still*) 403; dumb &c. 581.

taciturn, sparing of words; close, – mouthed, – tongued; laconic, costive, inconversable, curt; reserved; reticent &c. (*concealing*) 528.

Int. tush! silence! mum! hush! *chut!* hist! tut! &c. 403.

586. Allocution. — N. allocution, alloquy, address; speech &c. 582; apostrophe, interpellation, appeal, invocation, salutation; word in the ear.

[Feigned dialogue] dialogism.

platform &c. 542; audience &c. (*interview*) 588.

V. speak to, address, accost, make up to, apostrophize, appeal to, invoke; hail, salute; call to, halloo.

take -aside, – by the button, button-hole; talk to in private.

lecture &c. (*make a speech*) 582.

Int. soho! halloo! hey! hist! hi!

587. Response &c., *see* Answer 462.

588. Interlocution.—N. interlocution; collocution, colloquy, converse, conversation, confabulation, talk, discourse, verbal intercourse; communion, oral communication, commerce; dia-, duo-, tria-logue.

causerie, chat, chit-chat; small –, table –, tea-table –, town –, village –, idle- talk; tattle, gossip, tittle-tattle; babble, -ment; *tripotage*, cackle, prittle-prattle, *on dit*; talk of the -town, – village.

conference, parley, interview, audience, *pourparler*; *tête-à-tête*; reception, *conversazione*; congress &c. (*council*) 696; pow-wow.

hall of audience, *durbar*, coliseum, assembly hall, auditorium.

palaver, debate, logomachy, war of words, controversy.

talker, gossip, tattler; Paul Pry; tabby; chatterer &c. (*loquacity*) 584; interlocutor &c. (*spokesman*) 582; conversation-ist, -alist; dialogist.

'the feast of reason and the flow of soul'; *mollia tempora fandi.*

V. talk together, converse, confabulate; hold –, carry on –, join in –, engage in- a conversation; put in a word; shine in conversation; bandy words; parley; palaver; chat, gossip, tattle; prate &c. (*loquacity*) 584.

discourse –, confer –, commune –, commerce- with; hold -converse, – conference, – intercourse; talk it over; be closeted with; talk with one -in private, – *tête-à-tête.*

Adj. conversing &c. *v.*; interlocutory; convers-ational, -able; discursive, -coursive; chatty &c. (*sociable*) 892; colloquial, *tête-à-tête*, confabulatory.

589. Soliloquy.—N. soliloquy, monologue, apostrophe.

solilo-quist, -quizer, monologist.

V. soliloquize; say –, talk- to oneself; say aside, think aloud, apostrophize.

Adj. soliloquizing &c. *v.*

Adv. aside.

---

3. *Written Language*

590. Writing.—N. writing &c. *v.*; chiro-, stelo-, cero-graphy, graphology; stylography; pen-craft, -script, -manship; quill-driving; typewriting.

writing, manuscript, MS., *literæ scriptæ*; these presents.

stroke –, dash- of the pen; *coup de plume*; line; pen and ink.

letter &c. 561; uncial writing, cuneiform character, arrow-head, Ogham, Runes, futhorc; hieroglyphic, hieratic, demotic; script; contraction.

short-hand; steno-, brachy-, tachy-graphy; secret writing, writing in cipher; crypt-, stegan-ography: phono-, pasi-, poly-, logo-graphy.

copy; tran-, re-script; draft, rough –, fair- copy; handwriting; signature. sign-manual; auto-, mono-, holo-graph; hand, fist; mark.

calligraphy; good –, running –,

591. Printing.—N. printing; block –, type- printing, lino-, mono-type; plate printing &c. (*engraving*) 558; the press &c. (*publication*) 531; composition.

print, letterpress, text, matter, standing type; context, note, page, column; over-running; head-, foot-line, title.

typography; stereo-, electro-, apro-type; type, black letter, heavy type, font, fount; pi, pie; capitals &c. (*letters*) 561; diamond, pearl, nonpareil, minion, brevier, bourgeois, long primer, small pica, pica, english, great primer.

folio &c. (*book*) 593; copy, impression, pull, proof, galley –, author's –, page- proof, revise.

printer, compositor, reader; printer's devil.

V. print; compose; put –, go- to press; pass –, see- through the press:

flowing –, cursive –, legible –, copper-plate –, round –, bold- hand.

cacography, *griffonage, barbouillage*; bad –, cramped –, crabbed –, illegible-hand; scribble &c. *v.; pattes de mouche;* ill-formed letters; pot-hooks and hangers.

publish &c. 531; bring out; appea* in –, rush into- print.

Adj. printed &c. *v.*; in type; typo graphical &c. *n.*

stationery; pen, quill, goose-quill, reed; stylographic-, fountain-pen; pencil, style, stylus; paper, foolscap, parchment, vellum, papyrus, pad, tablet, block, note-book, slate, marble, pillar, table, black board.

ink-bottle, -pot, -stand, -well, -horn; typewriter.

transcription &c. (*copy*) 21; inscription &c. (*record*) 551; super-scription &c. (*indication*) 550.

composition, authorship; *cacoëthes scribendi.*

writer, scribe, amanuensis, scrivener, secretary, clerk, penman, copyist, transcriber, quill-driver; writer for the press &c. (*author*) 593.

shorthand writer, stenographer; typewriter, typist.

V. write, pen; copy, engross; write out, – fair; transcribe; scribble, scrawl, scrabble, scratch; interline; stain paper; write down &c. (*record*) 551; sign &c. (*attest*) 467; take down, – in shorthand; typewrite, type.

compose, indite, draw up, redact, draft, formulate; dictate; in-scribe, throw on paper, dash off; concoct.

take -up the pen, – pen in hand; shed –, spill –, dip one's pen in- ink.

Adj. writing &c. *v.*; written &c. *v.*; in -writing, – black and white; under one's hand.

uncial, Runic, cuneiform, hieroglyphical &c. *n.*

Adv. *currente calamo;* pen in hand.

592. Correspondence. — N. corre-spondence, letter, epistle, note, *billet,* post-, letter-card, missive, circular, form letter; favour, *billet-doux;* des-, dis-patch; *bulletin,* communication &c. 532; these presents; rescript, -ion; post &c. (*messenger*) 534; letter writer, correspondent.

V. correspond, – with; write –, send a letter- to; keep up a correspondence; drop a line to; despatch; communicate with; circularize.

Adj. epistolary.

593. Book.—N. book, -let; writing, work, volume, tome, opuscule; tract, -ate; *livret; brochure, libretto,* hand-book, treatise, text-book, codex, man-ual, pamphlet, monograph, enchiridion, circular, publication; book of poems; novel; chap-book.

part, issue, number, *livraison;* album, portfolio; periodical, serial, magazine, ephemeris, annual, journal.

paper, bill, sheet, broadsheet, screed; leaf, -let; fly-leaf, page; quire, ream.

chapter, section, head, article, para-graph, passage, clause, supplement, appendix; *feuilleton.*

folio, quarto, octavo; duo-, sexto-, octo-decimo.

en-, cyclopædia, dictionary, lexicon, thesaurus, concordance, an-thology, bibliography; compilation, compendium, catalogue &c. 86; library, bibliotheca; the press &c. (*publication*) 531.

writer, author, *littérateur, homme de lettres,* essayist, journalist, publicist; scribe, penman, war –, special –, correspondent; pen, scribbler, the scribbling race; ghost, hack, literary hack, Grub-street writer; writer for –, gentleman of –, representative of- the press; reporter, penny-a-liner; editor, sub-editor; literary agent; playwright &c. 599; poet &c. 597.

bookseller, publisher; biblio-pole, -polist, -grapher; librarian; book -collector, – worm.

book -shop, – club, circulating –, lending –, public- library; publishing house.

knowledge of books, bibliography; book-learning &c. (*knowledge*) 490.

594. Description.—N. description, account, statement, report; *exposé* &c. (*disclosure*) 529; specification, particulars, scenario, plot; state –, summary- of facts; brief &c. (*abstract*) 596; return &c. (*record*) 551; catalogue raisonné &c. (*list*) 86; guide-book &c. (*information*) 527.

delineation &c. (*representation*) 554; sketch, vignette; monograph; minute –, detailed –, particular –, circumstantial –, graphic- account; narration, recital, rehearsal, relation.

histori-, chron-ography; historic Muse, Clio; history; bi-, autobi-ography; necrology, obituary.

narrative, history; memoir, memorials; annals &c. (*chronicle*) 551; tradition, legend, saga, epic, epos, story, tale, historiette; personal narrative, journal, letters, life, adventures, fortunes, experiences, confessions; anecdote, ana, *trait*.

work of fiction, short story, novelette, novel, romance, penny dreadful shilling shocker, Minerva press; fairy –, nursery- tale; fable, allegory, parable, apologue.

relator &c. *v.*; *raconteur*; historian &c. (*recorder*) 553; biographer, fabulist, novelist, story teller, romancer, teller of tales, spinner of yarns, anecdotist.

V. describe; set forth &c. (*state*) 535; draw a picture, picture; portray &c. (*represent*) 554; characterize, particularize; narrate, relate, recite, recount, sum up, run over, recapitulate, rehearse, fight one's battles over again.

unfold &c. (*disclose*) 529- a tale; tell; give –, render- an account of; report, make a report, draw up a statement.

detail; enter into –, descend to- -particulars, – details.

Adj. descriptive, graphic, narrative, epic, suggestive, well-drawn; historic; auto-, biographical, realistic, expository, tradition-al, -ary; legendary; fabulous, mythical; anecdotic, storied; described &c. *v.*

595. Dissertation.—N. dissertation, treatise, essay; *thesis*, theme; tract, -ate, -ation, excursus; discourse, memoir, disquisition, lecture, sermon, homily, pandect.

commentary, review, *critique*, criticism, article; lead-er, -ing article, editorial; argument, running commentary.

investigation &c. (*inquiry*) 461; study &c. (*consideration*) 451; discussion &c. (*reasoning*) 476; exposition &c. (*explanation*) 522.

commentator, critic, essayist, pamphleteer; publicist, reviewer, leader writer, editor, annotator.

V. dissert –, descant –, write –, touch- upon a subject; dissertate; treat of –, take up –, ventilate –, discuss –, deal with –, go into –, canvass –, handle –, do justice to- a subject; comment, criticize, interpret &c. 522; argue.

Adj. dis-cursive, -coursive; disquisitional, disquisitionary; expository, critical.

596. Compendium.—N. compend, -ium; abstract, *précis*, epitome, *multum in parvo*, analysis, pandect, digest, sum and substance, brief, abridgment, summary, *aperçu*, draft, minute, note; synopsis, text-book, *conspectus*, outlines, syllabus, contents, heads, prospectus.

album; scrap –, note –, memorandum –, commonplace- book; extracts, *excerpta*, cuttings; fugitive -pieces, – writings; *spicilegium*, flowers, anthology, miscellany, *collectanea, analecta*; compilation.

recapitulation, *résumé*, review.

abbrevia-tion, -ture; contraction; shortening &c. 201; compression &c. 195.

V. abridge, abstract, epitomize, summarize; make –, prepare –, draw –, compile- an abstract &c. *n.*

recapitulate, review, skim, run over, sum up.

abbreviate &c. (*shorten*) 201; condense &c. (*compress*) 195; compile &c. (*collect*) 72; edit, blue pencil.

Adj. compendious, synoptic, analectic, analytical; abridged &c. *v.*

Adv. in -short, – epitome, – substance, – few words.

Phr. it lies in a nutshell.

---

597. Poetry.—N. poetry, poetics, poesy, Muse, Calliope, tuneful Nine, Parnassus, Helicon, Pierides, Pierian spring, afflatus, inspiration.

versification, rhyming, making verses; prosody, scansion, orthometry.

poem; epic, – poem; epopee, *epopæa,* ode, epode, idyl, lyric, eclogue, pastoral, bucolic, georgic, dithyramb,

598. Prose.—N. prose, – writer, pros-aism, -aist, -er.

V. prose, write prose.

write -prose, – in prose.

Adj. pros-y, -aic; unpoetical.

rhymeless, unrhymed, in prose, not in verse.

---

anacreontic, sonnet, roundelay, *rondel, rondoletto, rondeau, rondo,* triolet; madrigal, canzonet, *cento,* monody, elegy, palinode; rhapsody.

dramatic –, lyric- poetry; opera; posy, anthology.

song, ballad, lay; love –, drinking –, war –, folk –, sea- song; lullaby; music &c. 415; nursery rhymes.

[Bad poetry] doggerel, Hudibrastic verse, prose run mad; maca-ronics; macaronic –, leonine- verse; runes.

canto, stanza, distich, verse, line, couplet, triplet, quatrain, sestet; *strophe, antistrophe,* refrain, chorus, burden.

verse, rhyme, assonance, crambo, metre, measure, foot, numbers, strain, rhythm; accentuation &c. (*voice*) 580; iambus, dactyl, spondee, trochee, anapæst &c.; hex-, pent-ameter; Alexandrine; blank verse, alliteration.

elegiacs &c. *adj.*; elegiac &c. *adj.* -verse, – metre, – poetry.

poet, – laureate; laureate; minor poet, bard, lyrist, scald, troubadour, *trouvère*; minstrel; minne-, meister-singer; *improvisatore*; versifier, sonneteer; ballad monger; rhym-er, -ist, -ester; poetaster.

V. poetize, sing, versify, make verses, rhyme, scan.

Adj. poetic, -al; lyric, -al; tuneful; epic; dithyrambic &c. *n.*; metrical; a-, catalectic; elegiac, iambic, trochaic, spondaic, dactylic, anapæstic; Ionic, Sapphic, Alcaic, Pindaric.

---

599. The Drama.—N. the -drama, – stage, – theatre, – play; theatricals, dramaturgy, histrionic art, buskin, sock, *cothurnus,* Melpomene and Thalia, Thespis.

play, drama, stage-play, piece, five-act play, tragedy, comedy, opera, comic opera, *vaudeville, comedietta, lever de rideau,* curtain raiser, interlude, afterpiece, exode, farce, *divertissement, extravaganza,* burletta, harlequinade, pantomime, mimodrama, burlesque, *opéra bouffe*, musical comedy, review, revue, intimate revue, variety, cabaret entertainment, *ballet, spectacle*, masque, *drame, comédie drame*; melo-drama, -drame; *comédie larmoyante*, emotional drama, sensation drama, tragi-, farcical-comedy; mono-drame, -logue; duologue; trilogy; charade, *proverbe*; mystery, miracle –, morality- play.

act, scene, *tableau*; in-, intro-duction; pro-, epi-logue, curtain; *libretto*, book, script.

performance, representation, show, *mise en scène*, stagery, *jeu de théâtre*, stage-craft; acting; gesture &c. 550; impersonation &c. 554; stage business, gag, patter, buffoonery.

theatre; play-, opera-house; house; music hall; *cabaret*; amphitheatre, circus, hippodrome; puppet-show, *fantoccini*; *marionnettes*, Punch and Judy.

cinema, -tograph-, picture –, theatre, the pictures, the movies, the talkies.

auditory, *auditorium*, front of the house, stalls, boxes, balcony, dress –, upper- -circle, – boxes, amphitheatre, pit, gallery; *foyer*; green-room; dressing rooms, *coulisses*.

flat; drop, – scene; wing, screen, side-scene; transformation scene, curtain, act-drop, safety –, fire- curtain; *proscenium*, forestage.

stage, revolving stage, scene, the boards; star –, grave –, trap, mezzanine floor; flies; gridiron, floats, battens, footlights; lime –, spot –, flood –, bunch-lights; scenery, set, *décor*; orchestra;

theatrical -costume, – properties, props.

part, *rôle*, character, cast, *dramatis personæ*; *répertoire*.

actor, player; stage –, strolling- player; old –, stager, performer; mime, -r; *artiste*; com-, trag-edian, straight man; *tragédienne*, Thespian, Roscius, star.

pantomimist, clown, harlequin, *buffo*, buffoon, *farceur, grimacier*, pantaloon, columbine; *Pierrot, Pierrette*; punch, -inello; *pulcinell-o*, -a; mute, *figurante*, general utility; super, -numerary, extra.

mummer, guiser, guisard, gysart, masque.

mountebank, Jack Pudding; tumbler, posture-master, acrobat, equilibrist, juggler, contortionist; *danseuse, ballerina*, ballet -dancer, – girl, *coryphée; bayadère, geisha*; chorus -singer, – girl.

company; first tragedian, *prima donna*, lead, leading lady, protagonist; *jeune premier*; juvenile lead, *débutant, -e*; light –, genteel –, low- -comedy, – comedian; *soubrette*, walking gentleman, *amoroso*, heavy, heavy father, *ingénue, jeune veuve, commère, compère*.

property man, *costumier*, machinist, stage hand, electrician, prompter, call-boy; director, manager; stage –, acting –, business- manager; *entrepreneur, impresario*, producer, press agent.

dramatic -author, – writer; play-writer, -wright; dramatist, mimographer; dramatic critic.

V. act, play, perform; stage, produce, put on the stage; personate &c. 554; mimic &c. (*imitate*) 19; enact; play –, act –, go through –, perform- a part; rehearse, spout, gag, rant; 'strut and fret one's hour upon a stage'; tread the -stage, – boards; come out; star.

Adj. dramatic; theatric, -al; scenic, histrionic, comic, tragic, buskined, farcical, tragi-comic, melodramatic, operatic; stagey, spectacular; stagestruck.

Adv. on the -stage, – boards; before -the floats, – an audience; in the limelight, behind the footlights; behind the scenes.

CLASS V

WORDS RELATING TO THE VOLUNTARY POWERS*

DIVISION (I.) INDIVIDUAL VOLITION

Section I. VOLITION IN GENERAL

1°. *Acts of Volition*

600. Will.—N. will, volition, co-rationǂ, velleity; will and pleasure, free-will; freedom &c. 748; discretion; choice, inclination, intent, purpose, option &c. (*choice*) 609; voluntariness; spontane-ity, -ousness; originality.

pleasure, wish, desire, mind; frame of mind &c. (*inclination*) 602; intention &c. 620; predetermination &c. 611; self-control &c. determination &c. (*resolution*) 604; will-power.

V. will, list; see –, think- fit; deter-mine &c. (*resolve*) 604; settle &c. (*choose*) 609; volunteer.

have a will of one's own; do what one chooses &c. (*freedom*) 748; have it all one's own way; have one's -will, – own way.

use –, exercise- one's discretion; take -upon oneself, – one's own course, – the law into one's own hands; do -of one's own accord, – upon one's own -responsibility, – authority; take the bit between one's teeth; take responsi-bility; originate &c. (*cause*) 153.

Adj. voluntary, volitive, volitional, wilful; free &c. 748; optional; discre-tion-al, -ary; volitient; dictatorial.

minded &c. (*willing*) 602; prepense &c. (*predetermined*) 611; intended &c. 620; autocratic; unbidden &c. (bid &c. 741); spontaneous; original &c. (*causal*) 153.

Adv. voluntarily &c. *adj.*; at -will, – pleasure; à -volonté, – discrétion; al piacere; ad -libitum, – arbitrium; as one thinks proper, – it seems good to.

* Conative powers or faculties (Hamilton).

601. Necessity.—N. involuntariness, instinct, blind –, natural- impulse; inborn –, innate- proclivity; the force of circumstances.

necessi-ty, -tation, necessarianism; obligation; compulsion &c. 744; sub-jection &c. 749; stern –, hard –, dire –, imperious –, inexorable –, iron –, ad-verse- -necessity, – fate; what must be.

desti-ny, -nation; fatality, fate, *kis-met*, doom, foredoom, election, pre-destination; pre-, fore-ordination; lot, fortune; fatalism, determinism; in-evitableness &c. *adj.*; spell &c. 993.

star, -s; planet, -s; astral influence; sky, Fates, Norns, *Parcæ*, Sisters three, Clotho, Lachesis, Atropos; book of fate; God's will, will of Heaven; wheel of Fortune, Ides of March, Hobson's choice.

last -shift, – resort; *dernier ressort; pis aller* &c. (*substitute*) 147; necessaries &c. (*requirement*) 630.

necess-arian, -itarian; fatalist, deter-minist; automaton.

V. lie under a necessity; be -fated, – doomed, – destined &c., – in for, – under the necessity of; have no -choice, – alternative; be- obliged –, forced –, driven –; one's -fate &c. *n.*-to; be -pushed to the wall, – driven into a corner, – unable to help.- – drawn irresistibly.

destine, doom, foredoom, devote; pre-destine, -ordain; cast a spell &c: 992; necessitate; compel &c. 744.

ǂHamilton.

of one's own -accord, – free will; *proprio* –, *suo* –, *ex mero- motu*; out of one's own head; by choice &c. 609; purposely &c. (*intentionally*) 620; deliberately &c. 611.

Phr. *stet pro ratione voluntas*; *sic volo sic jubeo*.

Adj. necessary; needful &c. (*requisite*) 630.

fated; destined &c. *v.*; fateful; elect; spell-bound.

compulsory &c. (*compel*) 744; uncontrollable, inevitable, unavoidable, irresistible, irrevocable, inexorable, binding; avoid-, resist-less; written in the book of fate.

involuntary, instinctive, automatic, blind, mechanical; un-conscious, -witting, -thinking; unintentional &c. (*undesigned*) 621; impulsive &c. 612.

Adv. necessarily &c. *adv.*; of -necessity, – course; *ex necessitate rei*; needs must; perforce &c. 744; *nolens volens*; will he nil he, willy nilly, *bon gré mal gré*, willing or unwilling, *coûte que coûte*, forcefully; *faute de mieux*; by stress of; if need be.

Phr. it cannot be helped; there is no- help for, – helping- it; it -will, – must, – must needs- be, – be so, – have its way; the die is cast; *jacta est alea*; *che sarà sarà*; 'it is written'; one's- days are numbered, – fate is sealed; *Fata obstant*; *dis aliter visum*.

---

602. Willingness.—N. willingness, voluntariness &c. *adj.*; willing mind, heart.

disposition, inclination, leaning, *animus*; frame of mind, humour, mood, vein; bent &c. (*turn of mind*) 820; *penchant* &c. (*desire*) 865; aptitude &c. 698.

doc-ility, -ibleness, tractability; persuasi-bleness, -bility; pliability &c. (*softness*) 324.

geniality, cordiality; goodwill; alacrity, readiness, earnestness, forwardness, enthusiasm; zeal, eagerness &c. (*desire*) 865.

assent &c. 488; compliance &c. 762; pleasure &c. (*will*) 600.

labour of love, self-appointed task; volunteer, -ing, gratuitous service; unpaid worker, amateur.

V. be -willing &c. *adj.*; incline, lean to, mind, propend; had as lief; lend –, give –, turn- a willing ear; have -a, – half a, – a great- mind to; hold –, cling- to; desire &c. 865.

see –, think- -good, – fit, – proper; acquiescence &c. (*assent*) 488; comply with &c. 762.

swallow –, nibble at- the bait; gorge the hook; swallow hook, line and sinker; have –, make- no scruple of; make no bones of; jump –, catch- at; meet half way; volunteer, offer oneself &c. 763.

603. Unwillingness.—N. unwillingness &c. *adj.*; indispos-ition, -edness; disinclination, aversation, aversion; nolleity, nolition; renitence; reluctance; indifference &c. 866; backwardness &c. *adj.*; slowness &c. 275; want of -alacrity, – readiness; indocility &c. (*obstinacy*) 606.

scrupul-ousness, -osity; qualms of conscience, delicacy, demur, scruple, qualm, shrinking, recoil; hesitation &c. (*irresolution*) 605; fastidiousness &c. 868.

averseness &c. (*dislike*) 867; dissent &c. 489; refusal &c. 764.

slacker, scrimshanker, *embusqué*, unwilling worker, forced labour.

V. be -unwilling &c. *adj.*; nill; dislike &c. 867; grudge, begrudge; not be able to find it in one's heart to, not have the stomach to.

demur, stick at, scruple, stickle; hang fire, run rusty, slack, shirk, scamp, give up, fight shy of, not pull fair; recoil, shrink, swerve; hesitate &c. 605; avoid &c. 623.

oppose &c. 708; dissent &c. 489; refuse &c. 764.

Adj. unwilling; not in the vein, loth, shy of, disinclined, indisposed, averse, reluctant, not content; adverse &c. (*opposed*) 708; laggard, backward, remiss, slack, slow to; renitent; indifferent &c. 866; scrupulous; squeamish

Adj. willing, minded, fain, disposed, inclined, favourable; favourably-minded, -inclined, -disposed; nothing loth; in the -vein, – mood, – humour, – mind.

ready, forward, enthusiastic, earnest, eager; bent upon &c. (*desirous*) 865; predisposed, propense.

' docile; persua-dable, -sible; suasible, easily persuaded, facile, easy-going; amenable; tractable &c. (*pliant*) 324; genial, gracious, cordial, hearty; content &c. (*assenting*) 488.

voluntary, gratuitous, spontaneous; unasked &c. (ask &c. 765); unforced &c. (*free*) 748.

Adv. willingly &c. *adj.*; fain, freely, as lief, heart and soul; with -pleasure, – all one's heart, – open arms; with -good, – right good- will; *de bonne volonté, ex animo*; *con amore*, heart in hand, nothing loth, without reluctance, of one's own accord, graciously, with a good grace, without demur.

à la bonne heure; by all -means, – manner of means; to one's heart's content; yes &c. (*assent*) 488.

Int. sure, -ly! of course!

&c. (*fastidious*) 868; repugnant &c. (*dislike*) 867; rest-iff, -ive; demurring &c. *v.*; unconsenting &c. (*refusing*) 764; involuntary &c. 601; grudging, irreconcilable.

Adv. unwillingly &c. *adj.*; grudgingly, with a heavy heart; with -a bad, – an ill- grace; against –, sore against- -one's wishes, – one's will, – the grain; *invitâ Minervâ*; *à contre cœur*; *malgré soi*; in spite of -one's teeth, – oneself; *nolens volens* &c. (*necessity*) 601; perforce &c. 744; under protest; no &c. 536; not for the world, far be it from me; not if I can help it; if I must I must.

---

604. Resolution.—**N.** determination, will; iron –, unconquerable- will; will of one's own, decision, resolution, backbone, grit; strength of -mind, – will; resolve &c. (*intent*) 620; intransigeance: firmness &c. (*stability*) 150; energy, manliness, vigour; game, pluck; resoluteness &c. (*courage*) 861; zeal &c. 682; *aplomb*; desperation; devot-ion, -edness.

mastery over self; self-control, -command, -mastery, -possession, -reliance, -government, -restraint, -conquest, -denial; moral -courage, – strength, – fibre; perseverance &c. 604a; tenacity; obstinacy &c. 606; bull-dog; British lion.

V. have -determination &c. *n.*; know one's own mind; be -resolved &c. *adj.*; make up one's mind, will, resolve, determine; decide &c. (*judgment*) 480; form –, come to- a -determination, – resolution, – resolve; conclude, fix, seal, determine once for all, bring to a crisis, drive matters to an extremity; take a decisive step &c. (*choice*) 609; take upon oneself &c. (*undertake*) 676.

devote oneself –, give oneself up- to; throw away the scabbard, kick down

605. Irresolution.—**N.** irresolution, infirmity of purpose, indecision; in-, un-determination, loss of will power; unsettlement; uncertainty &c. 475; demur, suspense; hesi-tating &c. *v.*, -tation, -tancy; vacillation; ambivalence; changeableness &c. 149; fluctuation; alternation &c. (*oscillation*) 314; caprice &c. 608; lukewarmness.

fickleness, levity, *légèreté*; pliancy &c. (*softness*) 324; weakness; timidity &c. 860; cowardice &c. 862; half measures.

waverer, ass between two bundles of hay; shuttlecock, butterfly; time-server, opportunist, turn coat.

V. be -irresolute &c. *adj.*; hang –, keep- in suspense; leave '*ad referendum*'; think twice about, pause; dawdle &c. (*inactivity*) 683; remain neuter; dilly-dally, hesitate, boggle, hover, wobble, shilly-shally, hum and haw, demur, not know one's own mind; debate, balance; dally –, coquet- with; will and will not, *chasser-balancer*; go half-way, compromise, make a compromise; be thrown off one's balance, stagger like a drunken man; be afraid &c. 860; let 'I dare not' wait upon 'I would': falter, waver.

the ladder, nail one's colours to the mast, set one's back against the wall, set one's teeth, put one's foot down, burn one's bridges, take one's stand; stand firm &c. (*stability*) 150; steel oneself; stand no nonsense, not listen to the voice of the charmer.

buckle to; put –, lay –, set- one's shoulder to the wheel; put one's heart into; run the gauntlet, make a dash at, take the bull by the horns; beard the lion in his den; rush –, plunge- *in medias res*; go in for; insist upon, make a point of; set one's heart, – mind- upon.

stick at nothing; make short work of &c. (*activity*) 682; not stick at trifles; go -all lengths, – the whole hog; persist &c. (*persevere*) 604a; go down with colours flying, die game; go through fire and water, ride in the whirlwind and direct the storm.

Adj. resolved &c. *v.*; determined; strong-willed, -minded; resolute &c. (*brave*) 861; self-possessed, plucky, tenacious; decided, definitive, peremptory; un-hesitating, -flinching, -shrinking; firm, cast iron, indomitable, game to the backbone; inexorable relentless, not to be -shaken, – put down; *tenax propositi*; inflexible &c. (*hard*) 323; obstinate &c. 606; steady &c. (*persevering*) 604a; unbending, un-yielding, irrevocable; firm as a rock; grim.

earnest, serious; set –, bent –, intent- upon.

steeled –, proof- against; *in utrumque paratus.*

Adv. resolutely &c. *adj.*; in –, in good- earnest; seriously, joking apart, earnestly, heart and soul; on one's metal; manfully, like a man, with a high hand; with a strong hand &c. (*exertion*) 686.

at any -rate, – risk, – hazard, – price, – cost, – sacrifice; at all -hazards, – risks, – events; cost what it may; *coûte que coûte*; *à tort et à travers*; once for all; neck or nothing; rain or shine; with colours nailed to the mast.

Phr. *spes sibi quisque.*

vacillate &c. 149; change &c. 140; retract &c. 607; fluctuate; alternate &c. (*oscillate*) 314; keep off and on, play fast and loose; blow hot and cold &c. (*caprice*) 608.

shuffle, palter, blink; trim.

Adj. irresolute, infirm of purpose, double-minded, half-hearted; un-decided, -resolved, -determined; drifting; shilly-shally; fidgety, tremulous; wobbly; hesitating &c. *v.*; off one's balance; at a loss &c. (*uncertain*) 475.

vacillating &c. *v.*; unsteady &c. (*changeable*) 149; unsteadfast, fickle, unreliable, irresponsible, unstable, without ballast; capricious &c. 608; volatile, frothy; light, -some, -minded; giddy; fast and loose.

weak, feeble-minded, frail; timid &c. 860; cowardly &c. 862; facile; pliant &c. (*soft*) 324; unable to say 'no.' easy-going.

revocable, reversible.

Adv. irresolutely &c. *adj.*; irresolvedly; in faltering accents; off and on; from pillar to post; see-saw &c. 314.

Int. 'how happy could I be with either!'

————

504a. Perseverance.—N. perseverance; continuance &c. (*inaction*) 143; permanence &c. (*absence of change*) 141; firmness &c. (*stability*) 150.

constancy, steadiness; singleness –, tenacity- of purpose; persistence, plodding, patience; sedulity &c. (*industry*) 682; pertina-cy, city, -ciousness; iteration &c. 104.

bottom, game, pluck, stamina, backbone, grit; indefatiga-bility, -bleness; bulldog courage.

V. persevere, persist; hold -on, – out; die in the last ditch, be in at the death; stick –, cling –, adhere- to; stick to one's text, keep on; keep to –, maintain- one's -course, – ground; bear –, keep –, hold-up; plod; stick to work &c. (*work*) 686; continue &c. 143; follow up; die -in harness, – at one's post.

Adj. persevering, constant; stead-y, -fast; un-deviating, -wavering, -faltering, -swerving, -flinching, -sleeping, -flagging, -drooping; steady as time; uninter-, un-remitting; plodding; industrious &c. 682; strenuous &c. 686; pertinacious; persist-ing, -ent.

solid, sturdy, staunch, stanch, true to oneself; unchangeable &c. 150; unconquerable &c. (*strong*) 159; indomitable, game to the last, indefatigable, untiring, unwearied, never tiring.

Adv. through -evil report and good report, – thick and thin, – fire and water; *per fas et nefas*; without fail, sink or swim, at any price, *vogue la galère*; in sickness and in health.

Phr. never say die; *vestigia nulla retrorsum*.

606. Obstinacy.—N. obstinateness &c. *adj.*; obstinacy, tenacity; perseverance &c. 604a; immovability; old school; inflexibility &c. (*hardness*) 323; obdur-acy, -ation; dogged resolution; resolution &c. 604; ruling passion; blind side.

self-will, contumacy, perversity; pervica-cy, -city; indocility.

bigotry, intolerance, dogmatism; opinia-try, -tiveness; fixed idea &c.; intractability, incorrigibility; (*prejudgment*) 481; fanaticism, zealotry, infatuation, monomania, opinionativeness.

mule; opin-ionist, -ionatist, -iator, -ator; stickler, dogmatist, die-hard, bitter-ender; bigot; zealot, enthusiast, fanatic.

V. be -obstinate &c. *adj.*; stickle, take no denial, fly in the face of facts; opinionate, be wedded to an opinion, hug a belief; have one's own way &c. (*will*) 600; persist &c. (*persevere*) 604a; have –, insist on having- the last word.

die -hard, – fighting, fight -against destiny, – to the last ditch; not yield an inch, stand out.

Adj. obstinate, tenacious, stubborn, obdurate, case-hardened; inflexible &c. (*hard*) 323; immovable, not to be moved, inert &c. 172; unchangeable &c. 150; inexorable &c. (*determined*) 604; mulish, obstinate as a mule, pig-headed.

dogged; sullen, sulky; un-moved, -influenced, -affected.

wilful, self-willed, perverse; res-ty, -tive, -tiff; pervicacious, wayward, refractory, unruly; head-y, -strong; *entêté*; contumacious; cross-grained.

607. Tergiversation.—N. change of -mind, – intention, – purpose; afterthought.

tergiversation, recantation; palinode, -ody; renunciation; abjur-ation, -ement; defection &c. (*relinquishment*) 624; going over &c. *v.*; apostasy; retract-ion, -ation; withdrawal, disavowal &c. (*negation*) 536; revo-cation, -kement; reversal; repentance &c. 950; *redintegratio amoris*.

coquetry, flirtation; vacillation &c. 605; back-sliding, recidivation.

turn-coat, -tippet; rat, apostate, renegade, mugwump; con-, per-vert; proselyte, deserter; backslider, recidivist; black leg.

time-server, -pleaser; timist, Vicar of Bray, trimmer, ambidexter; weathercock &c. (*changeable*) 149; Janus.

V. change one's -mind, – intention, – purpose, – note; abjure, renounce; withdraw from &c. (*relinquish*) 624; wheel –, turn –, veer- round; turn a *pirouette*; go over –, pass –, change –, skip- from one side to another; go to the right about; box the compass, shift one's ground, go upon another tack; back down, crawl, crawfish.

apostatize, change sides, go over, rat; recant, retract; revoke; rescind &c. (*abrogate*) 756; recall, forswear, abjure, unsay; come -over, – round- to an opinion.

draw in one's horns, eat one's words; eat –, swallow- the leek; swerve, flinch, back out of, retrace one's steps, think better of it; come back –, return- to one's first love; turn over a new leaf &c. (*repent*) 950.

arbitrary, dogmatic, opinionated, positive, bigoted; prejudiced &c. 481; prepossessed, infatuated; stiff-backed, -necked, -hearted; hard-mouthed, hide-bound; unyielding; im-pervious, -prac-ticable, -persuasible; unpersuadable; in-, un-tractable; incorrigible, deaf to advice, impervious to reason; crotchety &c. 608.

Adv. obstinately &c. *adj.*

Phr. *non possumus*; no surrender.

---

trim, shuffle, play fast and loose, blow hot and cold, coquet, flirt, hold with the hare but run with the hounds; straddle; *nager entre deux eaux*; wait to see how the -cat jumps, – wind blows.

Adj. changeful &c. 149; irresolute &c. 605; ductile, slippery as an eel, trimming, ambidextrous, timeserving; coquetting &c. *v.*

revocatory, reactionary.

Phr. 'a change came o'er the spirit of my dream.'

608. Caprice.—N. caprice, fancy, humour; whim, -sey, -wham; crotchet, *capriccio*, quirk, freak, maggot, fad, vagary, prank, fit, flim-flam, *escapade*, *boutade*, wild-goose chase; capriciousness &c. *adj.*; kink.

V. be -capricious &c. *adj.*; have a maggot in the brain; take it into one's head, strain at a gnat and swallow a camel; blow hot and cold; play -fast and loose, – fantastic tricks.

Adj. capricious; erratic, eccentric, fitful, hysterical; full of -whims &c. *n.*; maggoty; inconsistent, fanciful, fantastic, whimsical, crotchety, particular, humoursome, freakish, skittish, wanton, wayward; contrary; captious; arbitrary; unrestrained, undisciplined; not amenable to reason; uncomfortable &c. 83; penny- wise and pound foolish; fickle &c. (*irresolute*) 605; frivolous, sleeveless, giddy, volatile.

Adv. by fits and starts, without rhyme or reason, at one's own sweet will.

Phr. *nil fuit unquam sic impar sibi*; the deuce is in him.

---

609. Choice.—N. choice, option; dis-cretion &c. (*volition*) 600; preoption; alternative; dilemma; *embarras de choix*; adoption, co-optation; novation; decision &c. (*judgment*) 480.

election, poll, ballot, vote, voice, suffrage, plumper, cumulative vote; *plebiscitum*, *plébiscite*, *vox populi*; refer-endum, electioneering; voting &c. *v.*; franchise; ballot box; slate, ticket.

selection, excerption, gleaning, eclec-ticism; *excerpta*, gleanings, cuttings, scissors and paste; pick &c. (*best*) 650.

preference, prelation; predilection &c. (*desire*) 865.

V. offer for one's choice, set before; hold out –, present –; offer- the alterna-tive; put to the vote.

use –, exercise –, one's- -discretion, – option; adopt, take up, embrace, es-pouse; choose, elect, co-opt; take –, make- one's choice; make choice of, fix upon.

vote, poll, hold up one's hand; divide.

settle; decide &c. (*adjudge*) 480; list

609a. Absence of Choice.—N. no –, Hobson's- choice; first come, first served; necessity &c. 601; not a pin to choose &c. (*equality*) 27; any, the first that comes.

neutrality, indifference; indecision &c. (*irresolution*) 605.

V. be -neutral &c. *adj.*; have no choice; waive, not vote; abstain –, refrain- from voting; leave undecided; make a virtue of necessity.

Adj. neu-tral, -ter; indifferent; un-decided &c. (*irresolute*) 605.

Adv. either &c. (*choice*) 609.

610. Rejection.—N. rejection, re-pudiation, exclusion; declination; re-fusal &c. 764.

V. reject; set –, lay- aside; give up; decline &c. (*refuse*) 764; exclude, ex-cept, eliminate; pluck, spin; cast.

repudiate, scout, set at naught; fling –, cast –, thrown –, toss- -to the winds, – to the dogs, – overboard, – away; send to the right about; dis-

&c. (*will*) 600; make up one's mind &c. (*resolve*) 604.

select; pick, – and choose; pick –, single- out, excerpt; cull, glean, winnow; sift –, separate –, winnow- the chaff from the wheat; pick up, pitch upon; pick one's way; indulge one's fancy.

set apart, reserve, mark out for; mark &c. 550.

prefer; have -rather, – as lief; fancy &c. (desire) 865; be persuaded &c. 615.

take a -decided, – decisive- step; commit oneself to a course; pass –, cross- the Rubicon; cast in one's lot with; take for better or for worse.

Adj. optional; co-optative; discretional &c. (*voluntary*) 600; on approval.

eclectic; choosing &c. *v.*; preferential; chosen &c. *v.*; choice &c. (*good*) 648.

Adv. optionally &c. *adj.*; at pleasure &c. (*will*) 600; either, – the one or the other; or; at the option of; whether or not; once for all; for one's money.

by -choice, – preference; in preference; rather, before.

claim &c. (*deny*) 536; discard &c. (*eject*) 297, (*have done with*) 678.

Adj. rejected &c. *v.*; reject-aneous, -itious; not -chosen &c. 609, – to be thought of; out of the question.

Adv. neither, – the one nor the other; no &c. 536.

Phr. *non hæc in fœdera.*

———

611. Predetermination. — **N.** premeditation, -deliberation, -determination, -destination; foreordination; foregone conclusion; *parti pris*; resolve, propendency; intention &c. 620; project &c. 626.

V. pre-determine, -destine, -meditate, -resolve, -concert; foreordain; resolve beforehand.

Adj. pre-pense, -meditated &c. *v.*, -designed; advised, studied, designed, calculated; aforethought; intended &c. 620; foregone.

well-laid, -devised, -weighed; maturely considered; cut and dried; cunning.

Adv. advisedly &c. *adj.*; with premeditation, deliberately, all things considered, with eyes open, in cold blood; intentionally &c. 620.

612. Impulse.—**N.** impulse, sudden thought; *impromptu*, improvisation; inspiration, hunch, flash, spurt.

improvisatore, improvisatrice, improviser, extemporizer; creature of impulse.

V. flash on the mind.

say what comes uppermost; improvise, extemporize; rise to the occasion; spurt.

Adj. extemporaneous, impulsive, indeliberate; improvis-ed, -ate, -atory; un-, unpre-meditated; *improvisé*; unprompted, -guided; natural, unguarded; spontaneous &c. (*voluntary*) 600; instinctive &c. 601.

Adv. extem-pore, -poraneously; offhand, *impromptu, à l'improviste*; improviso; on the spur of the -moment, – occasion.

613. Habit.—**N.** habit, -ude; assuetude, -faction; wont; run, way.

common –, general –, natural –, ordinary –, habitual- -course, – run, – state- of things; matter of course; beaten -path, – track, – ground.

prescription, custom, use, usage, immemorial usage, practice; tradition; prevalence, observance; conventional-

614. Desuetude.—**N.** desuetude, disusage; disuse &c. 678; want of -habit, – practice; inusitation; newness to; new brooms.

infraction of usage &c. (*unconformity*) 83; non-prevalence; 'a custom more honoured in the breach than the observance.'

V. be -unaccustomed &c. *adj.*; leave

ism, -ity; mode, fashion, vogue; *éti-quette* &c. (*gentility*) 852; order of the day, cry; conformity &c. 82.

habitué, addict.

one's old way, old school, consuetude, *veteris vestigia flammæ; laudator temporis acti.*

rule, standing order, precedent, routine; red-tape, -tapism; pipe-clay; rut, groove.

cacoëthes; bad –, confirmed –, inveterate –, intrinsic &c. 5- habit; addiction, trick.

training &c. (*education*) 537; seasoning, hardening, inurement; radication; second nature, acclimatization; knack &c. (*skill*) 698.

V. be -wont &c. *adj.*

fall into a custom &c. (*conform to*) 82; tread –, follow- the beaten -track, – path; *stare super antiquas vias;* move in a rut, run on in a groove, go round like a horse in a mill, go on in the old jog-trot way.

habituate, inure, harden, season, caseharden; accustom, familiarize; naturalize, acclimatize; keep one's hand in; train &c. (*educate*) 537.

get into the -way, – knack- of; learn &c. 539; cling –, adhere- to; repeat &c. 104; acquire –, contract –, fall into- a -habit, – trick; addict oneself –, take- to; accustom oneself to.

be -habitual &c. *adj.*; prevail; come into use, become a habit, take root; gain –, grow- upon one.

Adj. habitual; ac-, customary; prescriptive; accustomed &c. *v.*; traditional; of -daily, – every-day- occurrence; wonted, usual, general, ordinary, common, frequent, every-day, household, jog-trot; well-trodden, -known; familiar, vernacular, trite, commonplace, banal, bromidic, conventional, regular, set, stock, officinal, established, stereotyped; pre-vailing, -valent; current, received, acknowledged, recognized, accredited; of course, admitted, understood.

conformable &c. 82; according to -use, – custom, – routine; in -vogue, – fashion; fashionable &c. (*genteel*) 852.

wont; used – given – addicted –, attuned –, habituated &c. *v.*- to; in the habit of; *habitué;* at home in &c. (*skilful*) 698; seasoned; permeated –, imbued- with; devoted –, wedded- to; never free from.

hackneyed, fixed, rooted, deep-rooted, ingrafted, permanent, inveterate, besetting; naturalized; ingrained &c. (*intrinsic*) 5.

Adv. habitually &c. *adj.*; always &c. (*uniformly*) 16.

as -usual, – is one's wont, – things go, – the world goes, – the sparks fly upwards; *more -suo, – solito.*

as a rule, for the most part; generally &c. *adj.*; most often, – frequently.

Phr. *cela s'entend.*

off –, cast off –, break off –, wean oneself of –, violate –, break through –, infringe- -a habit, – a custom, – a usage; break one's fetters; disuse &c. 678; wear off.

Adj. un-accustomed, -used, -wonted, -seasoned, -inured, -habituated, -trained; new; green &c. (*unskilled*) 699; fresh, original, unhackneyed.

unusual &c. (*unconformable*) 83; unconventional, non-observant; disused &c. 678.

Adv. just for once.

2°. *Causes of Volition*

615. Motive.—N. motive, springs of action.

reason, ground, call, principle; main-

615a. Absence of Motive.—N. absence of motive; caprice &c. 608; chance &c. (*absence of design*) 621₂

spring, *primum mobile*, key-stone; the why and the wherefore; *pro* and *con*, reason why; secret –, ulterior- motive, *arrière-pensée*; intention &c. 620.

inducement, consideration; attraction &c. 288; loadstone; magnet, -ism, -ic force; allect-ation, -ive; temptation, enticement, *agacerie*, allurement, witchery; bewitch-ment, -ery; charm; spell &c. 993; fascination, blandishment, cajolery; seduc-tion, -ement; honeyed words, voice of the tempter, song of the Sirens; forbidden fruit, golden apple.

persuasi-bility, -bleness; attractability; impress-, suscept-ibility; softness; persuas-, attract-iveness; tantalization.

influence, prompting, dictate, instance; impuls-e, -ion; incit-ement, -ation; press, instigation; provocation &c. (*excitation of feeling*) 824; inspiration; per-, suasion; encouragement, advocacy; exhortation, advice &c. 695; solicitation &c. (*request*) 765; lobbying.

incentive, stimulus, spur, fillip, whip, goad, rowel, provocative, whet, dram.

bribe, lure; decoy, – duck; bait, trail of a red herring; bribery and corruption; sop, – for Cerberus.

prompter, tempter; seduc-er, -tor; suggester, coaxer, wheedler; instigator, firebrand, incendiary; Siren, Circe; *agent provocateur*; lobbyist.

V. induce, move; draw, – on; bring in its train, give an -impulse &c. *n.*-to; inspire; put up to, prompt, call up; attract, beckon.

stimulate &c. (*excite*) 824; spirit up, inspirit; a-, rouse; ecphorize; animate, incite, provoke, instigate. set on, actuate; act –, work –, operate- upon; encourage; pat –, clap- on the -back, – shoulder.

influence, weigh with, bias, sway, incline, dispose, predispose, turn the scale, inoculate; lead, – by the nose; have –, exercise-influence- -with, – over, – upon; go –, come- round one; turn the head, magnetize.

persuade; prevail -with, – upon; overcome, carry; bring -round, – to one's senses; draw –, win –, gain –, come –, talk- over; procure, enlist, engage; invite, court.

tempt, seduce, overpersuade, entice, allure, captivate, fascinate, intrigue, bewitch, carry away, charm, conciliate, wheedle, coax, lure, suggest; inveigle; tantalize; cajole &c. (*deceive*) 545.

tamper with, bribe, suborn, grease the palm, bait with a silver hook, gild the pill, make things pleasant, put a sop into the pan, throw a sop to, bait the hook.

V. have no motive; scruple &c. (*be unwilling*) 603.

Adj. without rhyme or reason; aimless &c. (*chance*) 621.

Adv. capriciously; out of mere caprice.

616. Dissuasion.—N. dissuasion, dehortation, expostulation, remonstrance; deprecation &c. 766.

discouragement, damper, wet blanket; warning.

cohibition &c. (*restraint*) 751; curb &c. (*means of restraint*) 752; check &c. (*hindrance*) 706.

reluctance &c. (*unwillingness*) 603; contraindication.

V. dissuade, dehort, cry out against, remonstrate, expostulate, warn, contraindicate.

disincline, indispose, shake, stagger; dispirit; dis-courage, -hearten, -enchant; deter; hold –, keep- back &c. (*restrain*) 751; render -averse &c. 603; repel; turn aside &c. (*deviation*) 279; wean from; act as a drag &c. (*hinder*) 706; throw cold water on, damp, cool, chill, blunt, calm, quiet, quench; deprecate &c. 766.

Adj. dissuading &c. *v.*; dissuasive; dehortatory, expostulatory; monit-ive, -ory.

dissuaded &c. *v.*; uninduced &c. (induce &c. 615); unpersuadable &c. (*obstinate*) 606; averse &c. (*unwil'ing*) 603; repugnant &c. (*dislike*) 867.

enforce, force; impel &c. (*push*) 276; propel &c. 284; whip, lash, goad, spur, prick, urge; egg –, hound –, hurry- on; drag &c. 285; exhort; advise &c. 695; call upon &c., press &c. (*request*) 765; advocate.

set -an example, – the fashion; keep in countenance; back up.

be -persuaded &c.; yield to temptation, come round; concede &c. (*consent*) 762; obey a call; follow -advice, – the bent, – the dictates of; act on principle.

Adj. impulsive, motive; suas-, persuas-, hortat-ive, -ory; protreptical; inviting, tempting &c. *v.*; seductive, attractive, irresistible; fascinating &c. (*pleasing*) 829; provocative &c. (*exciting*) 824.

induced &c. *v.*; disposed; persuadable &c. (*docile*) 602; spellbound; instinct –, smitten- with; inspired &c. *v.*- by.

Adv. because, therefore &c. (*cause*) 155; from -this, – that-motive; for -this, – that- reason; for; by reason –, for the sake –, on the score –, on account- of; out of, from, as, forasmuch as.

for all the world; on principle.

617. [Ostensible motive, ground, or reason assigned.] **Plea.**—N plea, pretext; allegation, advocation; ostensible -motive, – ground, – reason; excuse &c. (*vindication*) 937; colour; gloss, guise.

loop-, starting-hole; how to creep out of, salvo, come off.

handle, peg to hang on, room, *locus standi*; stalking-horse, *cheval de bataille*, cue.

pretence &c. (*untruth*) 546; put off, subterfuge, dust thrown in the eyes; blind; moonshine; mere –, shallow- pretext; lame -excuse, – apology; tub to a whale; false plea, sour grapes; makeshift, shift, white lie; special pleading &c. (*sophistry*) 477; soft sawder &c. (*flattery*) 933.

V. plead, allege; shelter oneself under the plea of; excuse &c. (*vindicate*) 937; gloss over; lend a colour to; furnish a -handle &c. *n.*; make a -pretext, – handle- of; use as a plea &c. *n.*; take one's stand upon, make capital out of; pretend &c. (*lie*) 544.

Adj. ostensible &c. (*manifest*) 525; excusing; alleged, apologetic; pretended &c. 545.

Adv. ostensibly; under -colour, – the plea, – the pretence- of.

3°. *Objects of Volition*

618. Good.—N. good, benefit, advantage; improvement &c. 658; interest, service, behoof, behalf; weal; main chance, *summum bonum*, common weal; 'consummation devoutly to be wished'; gain, boot; profit, harvest.

boon &c. (*gift*) 784; good turn; blessing, benison; world of good; piece of good -luck, – fortune; nuts, prize, windfall, godsend, waif, treasure trove.

good fortune &c. (*prosperity*) 734; happiness &c. 827.

[Source of good] goodness &c. 648; utility &c. 644; remedy &c. 662; pleasure-giving &c. 829.

Adj. commendable &c. 931; useful &c. 644; good &c., beneficial &c. 648.

619. Evil.—N. evil, ill, harm, hurt, mischief, nuisance; machinations of the devil, Pandora's box, ills that flesh is heir to.

blow, buffet, stroke, scratch, bruise, wound, gash, mutilation; mortal -blow, – wound; *immedicabile vulnus*; damage, loss &c. (*deterioration*) 659.

disadvantage, prejudice, drawback; disaster, accident, casualty; mishap &c. (*misfortune*) 735; bad job, devil to pay; calamity, bale, woe, catastrophe, tragedy; ruin &c. (*destruction*) 162; adversity &c. 735.

mental suffering &c. 828. [Evil spirit] demon &c. 980. [Cause of evil] bane &c. 663. [Production of evil]

V. benefit, profit, advantage, serve, help, avail; do good to, gain, prosper, flourish.

Adv. well, aright, satisfactorily, favourably, not amiss; all for the best; to one's -advantage &c. *n.*; in one's -favour, - interest &c. *n.*

Phr. so far so good.

---

badness &c. 649; painfulness &c. 830; evil doer &c. 913.

outrage, wrong, injury, foul play; bad -, ill- turn; disservice; spoliation &c. 791; grievance, crying evil.

V. be in trouble &c. (*adversity*) 735; harm, injure, hurt, do disservice to.

Adj. disastrous, bad &c. 649; awry, out of joint; disadvantageous, injurious, harmful.

Adv. amiss, wrong, ill, to one's cost;

Section II. Prospective Volition*

1°. *Conceptional Volition*

620. Intention.—N. intent, -ion, -ionality; purpose; *quo animo*; project &c. 626; undertaking &c. 676; predetermination &c. 611; design, ambition.

contemplation, mind, *animus*, view, purview, proposal; study; look out.

final cause; *raison d'être*; *cui bono*; object, aim, end; 'the be all and the end all'; drift &c. (*meaning*) 516; tendency &c. 176; destination, mark, point, butt, goal, target, bull's-eye, quintain; prey, quarry, game.

decision, determination, resolve; set -, settled- purpose; *ultimatum*; resolution &c. 604; wish &c. 865; *arrière-pensée*; motive &c. 615.

[Study of final causes] teleology.

V. intend, purpose, design, mean; have to; propose to oneself; harbour a design; have in -view, - contemplation, - one's eye, - *petto*; have an eye to.

bid -, labour- for; be -, aspire -, endeavour- after; be -, aim -, drive -, point-, level - at; take aim; set before oneself; study to.

take upon oneself &c (*undertake*) 676; take into one's head; meditate, contemplate; think - dream -, talk- of; premeditate &c. 611; compass, calculate; dest-ine, -inate: propose.

project &c. (*plan*) 626; have a mind to &c. (*be willing*) 602; desire &c. 865; pursue &c. 622.

Adj. intended &c. *v.*; intentional, advised, express, determinate; pre-pense &c. 611; bound for; intending &c. *v.*; minded, disposed, inclined;

621. [Absence of purpose in the succession of events.] **Chance.†—N.** chance &c. 156; lot, fate &c. (*necessity*) 601; luck; good luck &c. (*good*) 618; bad luck &c. 735; wheel of fortune; mascot; swastika.

speculation, venture, stake, flutter, flier, gamble, game of chance; mere -, random- shot; blind bargain, leap in the dark; pig in a poke &c. (*uncertainty*) 475; fluke, pot-luck.

drawing lots; sorti-legy, -tion; *sortes, - Virgilianæ, -biblicæ; rouge et noir,* hazard, *roulette,* pitch and toss, chuck-farthing, cup-tossing, heads or tails, cross and pile, wager; bet, -ting; risk, stake, plunge; gambling; the turf.

stock exchange, bourse, board of trade (U.S.A.), curb exchange.

gaming-, gambling-, betting-house; hell; betting ring, totalisator; dice, - box; dicer; gam-bler, -ester, plunger, stock operator, manipulator, punter; man of the turf; adventurer, speculator; bookmaker, layer, backer.

V. chance &c. (*hap*) 156; stand a chance &c. (*be possible*) 470.

toss up; cast -, draw- lots; leave -, trust- -to chance, - to the chapter of accidents; tempt fortune; chance it, take one's chance; run -, incur -, en-counter- the -risk, - chance; stand the hazard of the die.

speculate, try one's luck, set on a cast, raffle, put into a lottery, buy a pig in a poke, shuffle the cards.

risk, venture, hazard, stake; lay, - a wager; make a bet, wager, bet, gamble,

---

* That is, volition having reference to a future object.   † See note on 156.

bent upon &c. (*earnest*) 604; at stake, on the -anvil, – *tapis*; in -view; – prospect, – the breast of; *in petto*; teleological.

Adv. intentionally &c. *adj.*; advisedly, wittingly, knowingly, designedly, purposely, on purpose, by design, studiously, pointedly; with -intent &c. *n.*; deliberately &c. (*with premeditation*) 611; with one's eyes open in cold blood.

for; with -a view, – an eye- to; in order -to, – that; to the end –, with the intent- that; for the purpose –, with the view –, in contemplation –, on account- of.

in pursuance of, pursuant to; *quo animo*; to all intents and purposes.

game, play for; play at chuck-farthing.

Adj. fortuitous &c. 156; unintentional, -ded; accidental; not meant; un-designed, -purposed; unpremeditated &c. 612; never thought of.

indiscriminate, promiscuous; undirected, random; aim-, drift-, design-, purpose-, cause-less; without purpose; possible &c. 470.

Adv. casually &c. 156; unintentionally &c. *adj.*; unwittingly.

en passant, by the way, incidentally; as it may happen; at -random, – a venture, – haphazard; as luck would have it, by -chance, – good fortune; un-, -luckily.

---

622. [Purpose in action.] **Pursuit.—**
N. pursuit; pursuing &c. *v.*; prosecution; pursuance; enterprise &c. (*undertaking*) 676; business &c. 625; adventure &c. (*essay*) 675; quest &c. (*search*) 461; scramble, hue and cry, game; hobby.

chase, hunt, *battue*, race, steeplechase, hunting, coursing; ven-ation, -ery; fox-chase; sport, -ing; shooting, angling, fishing, hawking.

pursuer; hunt-er, -sman; sportsman, Nimrod, the field; hound &c. 366.

V. pursue, prosecute, follow; run –, make –, be –, hunt –, prowl- after; shadow; carry on &c. (*do*) 680; engage in &c. (*undertake*) 676; set about &c. (*begin*) 66; endeavour &c. 675; court &c. (*request*) 765; seek &c. (*search*) 461; aim at &c. (*intention*) 620; follow the trail &c. (*trace*) 461; fish for &c. (*experiment*) 463; press on &c. (*haste*) 684; run a race &c. (*velocity*) 274.

chase, give chase, course, dog, hunt, hound, stalk; tread –, follow- on the heels of &c. (*sequence*) 281.

rush upon; rush headlong &c. (*violence*) 173; ride –, run- full tilt at; make a leap –, jump –, snatch- at; run down; start game.

tread a path; take –, hold- a course; shape –, direct –, bend- one's -steps, – course; play a game; fight –, elbow- one's way; follow up; take -to, – up; go in for; ride one's hobby.

Adj. pursuing &c. *v.*; in quest of &c.

623. [Absence of pursuit.] **Avoidance.**
—N. abst-ention, -inence; forbearance; refraining &c. *v.*; inaction &c. 681; neutrality.

avoidance, evasion, elusion; seclusion &c. 893.

avolation, flight; escape &c. 671; retreat &c. 287; recoil &c. 277; departure &c. 293; rejection &c. 610

shirker &c. *v.*; slacker; truant; fugitive, refugee; runa-way, -gate; renegade; deserter.

V. abstain, refrain, spare, not attempt; not do &c. 681; maintain the even tenor of one's way.

eschew, keep from, let alone, have nothing to do with; keep –, stand –, hold- -aloof, – off; take no part in, have no hand in.

avoid, shun; steer –, keep- clear of; fight shy of; keep -one's, – at a respectful- distance; keep –, get- out of the way; evade, elude, turn away from; set one's face against &c. (*oppose*) 708; deny oneself.

shrink; hang –, hold –, draw- back; recoil &c. 277; retire &c. (*recede*) 287; flinch, blink, blench, shy, shirk, dodge, parry, make way for, give place to.

beat a retreat; turn -tail, – one's back; take to one's heels; run, -away, – for one's life; cut and run; be off, – like a shot; fly, flee; fly –, flee –, run away- from; take –, take to- flight; desert, elope; make –, scamper –, sneak –, shuffle –, sheer- off; break –,

(inquiry) 461; in -pursuit, – full cry, – hot pursuit; on the scent.

Adv. in pursuance of &c. *(intention)* 620; after.

Int. tally-ho! yoicks! so-ho!

———

burst –, tear oneself –, slip –, slink –, steal- -away, – away from; slip cable, part company, turn on one's heel; sneak out of, play truant, give one the go by, give leg bail, take French leave, slope, decamp, flit, bolt, abscond, levant, skedaddle, absquatulate, cut one's stick, walk one's chalks, show a light pair of heels, make oneself scarce; escape &c. 671; go away &c. *(depart)* 293; abandon &c. 624; reject &c. 610.

lead one a -dance, – a merry chase, – pretty dance; throw off the scent, play at hide and seek.

Adj. unsought, unattempted; avoiding &c. *v.*; neutral; shy of &c. *(unwilling)* 603; elusive, evasive, distant; fugitive, runaway; shy, wild.

Adj. lest, in order to avoid.

Int. forbear! keep –, hands- off! *sauve qui peut!* devil take the hindmost!

624. Relinquishment.—N. relinquish-, abandon-ment; desertion, defection, secession, withdrawal; cave of Adullam; *nolle prosequi.*

discontinuance &c. *(cessation)* 142; renunciation &c. *(recantation)* 607; abrogation &c. 756; resignation &c. *(retirement)* 757; desuetude &c. 614; cession &c. *(of property)* 782.

V. relinquish, give up, abandon, desert, forsake, leave in the lurch; depart –, secede –, withdraw- from; back – out of, – down from, leave, go back on one's word, quit, take leave of, bid a long farewell; vacate &c. *(resign)* 757.

renounce &c. *(abjure)* 607; forego, have done with, drop; write off; disuse &c. 678; discard &c. 782; wash one's hands of; drop all idea of; *nolle-pros.*; lose interest in.

break –, leave- off; desist; stop &c. *(cease)* 142; hold –, stay- one's hand; quit one's hold; give over, shut up shop.

throw up the -game, – cards; give up the -point, – argument; pass to the order of the day, move the previous question, table the motion.

Adj. unpursued; relinquished &c. *v.*; relinquishing &c. *v.*

Int. avast &c.! *(stop)* 142.

625. Business.—N. business, occupation, employment; pursuit &c. 622; what one is doing-, – about; affair, concern, matter, case, undertaking.

matter in hand, irons in the fire; thing to do, *agendum*, task, work, job, chore, errand, transaction, commission, mission, charge, care; duty &c. 926.

part, *rôle*, cue; province, function, look-out, department, capacity, sphere, orb, field, line; walk, – of life; beat, round, routine; race, career.

office, place, post, incumbency, living; situation, appointment, billet, berth, employ; service &c. *(servitude)* 749; engagement; undertaking &c. 676.

vocation, calling, profession, *métier*, cloth, faculty; industry, art; industrial arts; craft, mystery, handicraft; trade &c. *(commerce)* 794.

exercise; work &c. *(action)* 680; avocation; press of business &c. *(activity)* 682.

V. pass –, employ –, spend- one's time in; employ oneself -in, – upon;

occupy –, concern- oneself with; make it one's -business *&c. n.*; undertake &c. 676; enter a profession; betake oneself to, turn one's hand to; have to do with &c. (*do*) 680.

drive a trade; carry on –, do –, transact- -business, – a trade &c: *n.*; keep a shop; ply one's task, – trade; labour in one's vocation; pursue the even tenor of one's way; attend to -business, – one's work.

officiate, serve, act; act –, play- one's part; do duty; serve –, discharge –, perform- the -office, – duties, – functions- of; hold –, fill- -an office, – a place, – a situation; hold a portfolio.

be -about, – doing, – engaged in, – employed in, – occupied with, – at work on; have one's hands in, have in hand; have on one's -hands, – shoulders; bear the burden; have one's hands full &c. (*activity*) 682.

be -in the hands of, – on the stocks, – on the anvil; pass through one's hands.

Adj. business-like; work-a-day; professional; official, functional; busy &c. (*actively employed*) 682; on –, in- -hand, – one's hands; afoot; on -foot, – the anvil; going on; acting.

Adv. in the course of business, all in a day's work; professionally &c. *adj.*

626. Plan.—N. plan, scheme, design, project; propos-al, -ition; suggestion; resolution; motion; precaution &c. (*provision*) 673; deep-laid &c. (*premeditated*) 611- plan &c.; racket.

system &c. (order) 58; organization &c. (*arrangement*) 60; germ &c. (*cause*) 153; Five Year Plan.

sketch, skeleton, outline, draught, draft, *ébauche, brouillon*; rough -cast, – draft, – draught, – copy; copy; proof, revise.

forecast, *programme*, prospectus, scenario; *carte du pays*; card; bill, protocol; order of the day, list of agenda, *memorandum*; bill of fare &c. (*food*) 298; base of operations; platform, plank.

rôle; policy &c. (*line of conduct*) 692.

contrivance, invention, expedient, receipt, nostrum, artifice, device, gadget; stratagem &c. (*cunning*) 702; trick &c. (*deception*) 545; alternative, loophole, shift &c. (*substitute*) 147; last shift &c. (*necessity*) 601.

measure, step; stroke, – of policy; master stroke; trump-, court-card; *cheval de bataille*, great gun; *coup*, – *d'état*; clever –, bold –, good- -move, – hit, – stroke; bright -thought, – idea, great idea.

intrigue, cabal, plot, frame-up, conspiracy, complot, machination; under-, counter-plot.

schem-ist, -atist; strategist, machinator, schemer; projector, author, builder, artist, promoter, designer &c. *v.*; conspirator; *intrigant* &c. (*cunning*) 702.

V. plan, scheme, design, frame, contrive, project, forecast, sketch; conceive, devise, invent &c. (*imagine*) 515; set one's wits to work &c. 515; spring a project; fall –, hit- upon; strike –, chalk –, cut –, lay –, map-out; lay down a plan; shape –, mark- out a course; predetermine &c. 611; concert, preconcert, preestablish; prepare &c. 673; hatch, – a plot; concoct; take -steps, – measures.

cast, recast, systematize, organize; arrange &c. 60; digest, mature.

plot, counter-plot, -mine; dig a mine; lay a train; intrigue &c: (*cunning*) 702.

Adj. planned &c. *v.*; strategic, -al; planning &c. *v.*; in course of preparation &c. 673; under consideration; on the -*tapis*, – carpet, – table.

627. Method. [Path.]—N. method, way, manner, wise, gait, form, mode, fashion, tone, guise; *modus operandi*; procedure &c. (*line of conduct*) 692.

path, road, route, course; line of -way, – road; trajectory, orbit, track, beat, tack.

steps; stair, -case; flight of stairs, ladder, stile.

bridge, viaduct, gauntry, pontoon, stepping stone, plank, gangway, catwalk, drawbridge; pass, ford, ferry, tunnel, subway, elevated; pipe &c. 260.

door; gateway &c. (*opening*) 260; channel, passage, avenue, means of access, approach, perron, adit, entrance; artery, lane, alley, aisle, lobby, corridor, cloister; back- door, -stairs; secret passage; covert-way.

road-, path-, stair-way; thoroughfare; highway, pike, turnpike, trail, parkway, *boulevard*; turnpike -, royal -, coach- road; broad -, King's -, Queen's- highway; beaten -track, – path; horse -, bridle- road, – track, – path; pathway; walk, *trottoir*, foot-path, pavement, flags, side-walk; by -, cross- -road, – path, – way; cut; short -cut &c. (*mid-course*) 628; *carrefour*; private -, occupation- road; highways and byways; rail-, tram-road, -way; funicular, ropeway, causeway; defile, cutting; canal &c. (*conduit*) 350; street &c. (*abode*) 189.

Adv. how; in what -way, – manner; by what mode; so, in this way, after this fashion, on these lines.

one way or another, anyhow; somehow or other &c. (*instrumentality*) 631; by way of; *viâ*; in *transitu* &c. 270; on the high road to.

Phr. hæ tibi erunt artes.

---

628. Mid-course.—N. middle-, mid-course; moderation, mean &c. 29: middle &c. 68; *juste milieu*, *mezzo termine*, golden mean, *aurea mediocritas*.

straight &c. (*direct*) 278 -course, – path; short -, cross- cut; short-circuit; great circle sailing.

neutrality; half -, half and half-measures; compromise.

V. keep in -, steer -, preserve- -a middle, – an even- course; go straight &c. (*direct*) 278.

go half way, compromise, make a compromise.

Adj. neutral, average, even, impartial, moderate, straight &c. (*direct*) 278.

629. Circuit.—N. circuit, round-about way, digression, divagation, *détour*, circum-ambience, -ambulation, -bendibus, *ambages*, loop; winding &c. (*circuition*) 311; zigzag &c. (*deviation*) 279.

V. perform -, make- a circuit; go -round about, – out of one's way; make a *détour*; meander &c. (*deviate*) 279; circumambulate.

lead a pretty dance; beat about, – the bush; make two bites of a cherry.

Adj. circuitous, indirect, round-about; zig-zag &c. (*deviating*) 279; circum-ambient, -ambulatory.

Adv. by -a side wind, – an indirect course; in a roundabout way; from pillar to post.

---

630. Requirement.—N. requirement, need, wants, necessities; necessaries, – of life; stress, exigency, pinch, *sine quâ non*, matter of necessity; case of -need, – life or death.

needfulness, essentiality, necessity, indispensability, urgency, prerequisite.

requisition &c. (*request*) 765, (*exaction*) 741; run upon; demand -, call- for.

desideratum &c. (*desire*) 865; want &c. (*deficiency*) 640.

charge, claim, command, injunction, requisition, mandate, order, *ultimatum*.

V. require, need, want, have occasion for, entail; not be able to -do without, – dispense with; prerequire.

render necessary, necessitate, create a necessity for, call for, put in requisition; make a requisition &c. (*ask for*) 765, (*demand*) 741.

stand in need of; lack &c. 640; desiderate; desire &c. 865; be -necessary &c. *adj.*

Adj. required &c. *v.*; requisite, needful, necessary, imperative, essential, indispensable, prerequisite; called for; in -demand, – request.

urgent, exigent, pressing, instant, crying, absorbing.

in want of; destitute of &c. 640.

Adv. *ex necessitate rei* &c. (*necessarily*) 601; of –, out of stern- necessity; at a pinch.

Phr. there is no time to lose; it cannot be -spared, – dispensed with.

2° *Subservience to Ends*
1. *Actual Subservience*

631. Instrumentality.—N. instrumentality; aid &c. 707; subservien-ce, -cy; mediation, inter-vention, -mediacy, medium, inter-medium, -mediary, vehicle, hand; agency &c. 170.

minister, handmaid, servant, slave, maid, valet; midwife, *accoucheur,* obstetrician; go-between; cat's paw; stepping-stone.

key; master –, pass –, latch- key; 'open sesame'; passport, *passe-partout*, safe-conduct; influence.

instrument &c. 633; expedient &c. (*plan*) 626; means &c. 632.

V. subserve, minister, tend, mediate, intervene; come –, go- between, interpose; pull the strings; be -instrumental &c. *adj.*; pander to.

Adj. instrumental; useful &c. 644; ministerial, subservient, mediatorial, inter-mediate, -vening; conducive.

Adv. througn, by, *per*; where-, there-, here-by; by the -agency &c. 170- of; by dint of; by –, in- virtue of; through the -medium &c. *n.*-of; along with; on the shoulders of; by means of &c. 622; by –, with--the aid &c. (*assistance*) 707- of.

per fas et nefas. by fair means or foul; somehow, – or other; by hook or by crook.

632. Means.—N. means, resources, revenue, wherewithal, ways and means, income; capital &c. (*money*) 800; stock in trade &c. 636; provision &c. 637; a shot in the locker; appliances &c. (*machinery*) 633; means and appliances; conveniences; cards to play; expedients &c. (*measures*) 626; two strings to one's bow; sheet anchor &c. (*safety*) 666; aid &c. 707; medium &c. 631.

V. find –, have –, possess- means &c. *n.*; provide the wherewithal.

Adj. instrumental &c. 631; mechanical &c. 633.

Adv. by means of, with; by -what, – all, – any, – some- means; where-, here-, there-with; wherewithal.

how &c. (*in what manner*) 627; through &c. (*by the instrumentality of*) 631; with –, by- the aid &c. (*assistance*) 707- of; by the -agency &c. 170- of.

633. Instrument.—N. machinery, mechanism, engineering.

instrument, organ, tool, implement, utensil, contrivance, machine, motor, engine, lathe, gin, mill, pump.

gear; tack-le, -ling, trice, rigging, gear, apparatus, appliances; plant, *matériel*; harness, trappings, fittings, accoutrements; equip-ment, -age:

appointments, furniture, upholstery; chattels; paraphernalia &c. (*belongings*) 780; *impedimenta*.

mechanical powers; lever, -age; mechanical advantage; crow, -bar; handspike, gavelock, jemmy, arm, limb, wing; oar, paddle; pulley, sheave; parbuckle; wheel and axle; wheel-, clock-work; wheels within wheels; pinion, gear wheel, spur –, bevel- gearing, chains, belting, crank, winch, capstan, windlass, crane, derrick, hoist, lift &c. 307; cam; pedal; wheel &c. (*rotation*) 312; inclined plane; wedge; screw; jack; spring, mainspring.

handle, hilt, haft, shaft, heft, shank, blade, trigger, tiller, helm, treadle, key; turnscrew, screwdriver, spanner, wrench.

hammer &c. (*impulse*) 276; edge tool &c. (*cut*) 253; borer &c. 262; vice, teeth &c. (*hold*) 781; nail, rope &c. (*join*) 45; peg &c. (*hang*) 214; support &c. 215; spoon &c. (*vehicle*) 272; arms &c. 727; oar &c. (*navigation*) 267.

Adj. instrumental &c. 631; mechanical, machinal, automatic, self-acting; brachial.

634. Substitute.—**N.** substitute &c. 147; deputy &c. 759; proxy, alternative, understudy.

635. Materials.—**N.** material, raw material, stuff, stock, staple; building materials, bricks and mortar; metal; stone; clav. brick; crockery &c. 384; compo, -sition; reinforced –, ferro-, concrete; cement; wood, ore, timber; gravel, cobbles, macadam, asphalt, tarmac.

materials; supplies, munition, fuel, grist, household stuff; *pabulum* &c. (*food*) 298; ammunition &c. (*arms*) 727; contingents; relay, reinforcement; baggage &c. (*personal property*) 780; means &c. 632.

Adj. raw &c. (*unprepared*) 674; wooden &c. *n.*

636. Store.—**N.** stock, fund, mine, vein, lode, quarry; spring; fount, -ain; well, -spring; milch cow

stock in trade, supply; heap &c. (*collection*) 72; treasure; reserve, *corps de réserve*, reserve fund, nest-egg, savings, *bonne bouche*.

crop, harvest, mow, vintage; yield, product, gleanings.

store, accumulation, hoard, rick, stack; lumber; relay &c. (*provision*) 637.

store-house, -room, -closet; depository, depot, *cache*, safe deposit, vault, pantechnicon, re-pository, -servatory, -pertory; *repertorium*; promptuary, warehouse, *entrepôt*, magazine, dump, buttery, larder, pantry, panary, lanary, still-room, spence; crib, garner, granary, silo, barn; bunker; thesaurus; bank &c. (*treasury*) 802; armoury; arsenal; dock; gallery, museum, library, conservatory, hot-house; menag-ery, -erie, aquarium, zoological gardens.

reservoir, cistern, tank, sump, pond, mill-pond; gasometer.

budget, quiver, bandolier, portfolio; coffer &c. (*receptacle*) 191.

conservation; storing &c. *v.*; storage.

dictionary &c. 562; list &c. 86.

V. store; put –, lay –, set- by; stow away; set –, lay- apart; store –, hoard –, treasure –, lay –, heap –, put –, garner –, save- up; *cacher*; accumulate, amass, hoard, fund, garner, save, bank.

conserve, reserve; keep –, hold- back; husband, – one's resources.

deposit; stow, stack, load, dump; harvest; heap, collect &c. 72; lay -in, – down, – by, store &c. *adj.*; keep, file [papers]; lay in &c. (*provide*) 637; preserve &c. 670; put by for a rainy day.

Adj. stored &c. *v.*; in -store, – reserve, – ordinary; spare, supernumerary.

637. Provision.—N. provision, supply; grist, – to the mill; subvention &c. (*aid*) 707; resources &c. (*means*) 632.

providing &c. *v.*; purveyance; reinforcement; commissary, commissariat.

rations; iron –, emergency- rations; provender &c. (*food*) 298; *viaticum*; ensilage.

caterer, purveyor, commissary, quartermaster, steward, housekeeper, manciple, feeder, batman, victualler, storekeeper, provision merchant, green-, grocer, *comprador*, *restaurateur*; sutler &c. (*merchant*) 797; innkeeper, publican, confectioner, baker, butcher, wine merchant, vintner.

V. provide; make -provision, – due provision for; lay in, – a stock, – a store.

sup-ply, -peditate; furnish; find, – one in; arm.

cater, victual, provision, purvey, forage; beat up for; stock, – with; make good, replenish; fill, – up; recruit, feed, ration.

have in -store, – reserve; keep, – by one, – on foot; have to fall back upon; store &c. 636; provide against a rainy day &c. (*economy*) 817.

639. Sufficiency.—N. sufficiency, adequacy, enough, withal, *quantum sufficit*, satisfaction, competence; no less.

mediocrity &c. (*average*) 29.

fill; fulness &c. (*completeness*) 52; plen-itude, -ty; abundance; copiousness &c. *adj.*; amplitude, galore, lots, profusion; full measure; 'good measure pressed down, shaken together and running over.'

luxuriance &c. (*fertility*) 168; affluence &c. (*wealth*) 803; fat of the land; 'a land flowing with milk and honey'; cornucopia; horn of -plenty, – Amalthæa; mine &c. (*stock*) 636.

outpouring; flood &c. (*great quantity*) 31; tide &c. (*river*) 348; repletion &c. (*redundance*) 641; satiety &c. 869; rich man &c. 803.

638. Waste.—N. consumption, expenditure, exhaustion; dispersion &c. 73; ebb; leakage &c. (*exudation*) 295; loss &c. 776; wear and tear; waste; prodigality &c. 818; misuse &c. 679; wasting &c. *v.*; rubbish &c. (*useless*) 645.

mountain in labour.

V. spend, expend, use, consume, swallow up, exhaust, deplete; impoverish; spill, drain, empty; disperse &c. 73.

cast –, throw –, fling –, fritter- away; burn the candle at both ends, waste; squander &c. 818.

'waste its sweetness on the desert air'; cast -one's bread upon the waters, – pearls before swine; employ a steam hammer to crack a nut, waste powder and shot, break a butterfly on a wheel; labour in vain &c. (*useless*) 645; cut a whetstone with a razor, pour water into a sieve; tilt at windmills.

leak &c. (*run out*) 295; run to waste; ebb; melt away, run dry, dry up.

Adj. wasted &c. *v.*; at a low ebb.

wasteful &c. (*prodigal*) 818; penny wise and pound foolish.

Phr. *magno conatu magnas nugas; le jeu n'en vaut pas la chandelle.*

640. Insufficiency.—N. insufficiency; inadequa-cy, -teness; incompetence &c. (*impotence*) 158; deficiency &c. (*incompleteness*) 53; imperfection &c. 651; shortcoming &c. 304; paucity; stint; scantiness &c. (*smallness*) 32; none to spare; bare subsistence.

scarcity, dearth; want, need, lack, poverty, exigency; inanition, starvation, famine, drought.

dole, pittance, mite; short -allowance, – commons; half-rations; banyan –, fast- day. Lent.

emptiness, poorness &c. *adj.*; depletion, vacancy, flaccidity; ebb-tide; low water; 'a beggarly account of empty boxes'; indigence &c. (*poverty*) 804; insolvency &c. (*non-payment*) 808; poor man &c. 804; bankrupt &c. 808.

V. be -insufficient &c. *adj.*; not -suf-

V. be -sufficient &c. *adj.*; suffice, do, just do, satisfy, pass muster; have -enough &c. *n.*; eat –, drink –, have-one's fill; roll –, swim- in; wallow in &c. (*superabundance*) 641.

abound, exuberate, teem, flow, stream, rain, shower down; pour, – in; swarm; bristle with.

render -sufficient &c. *adj.*; replenish &c. (*fill*) 52.

Adj. sufficient, enough, adequate, up to the mark, commensurate, competent, satisfactory, valid, tangible.

measured; moderate &c. (*temperate*) 953.

full &c. (*complete*) 52; ample; plen-ty, -tiful, -teous; plenty as blackberries; copious, abundant; abounding &c. *v.*; replete, enough and to spare, flush; choke-full; well-stocked, -provided; liberal; unstint-ed, -ing; stintless; without stint; un-sparing, -measured; lavish &c. 641; wholesale.

rich; luxuriant &c. (*fertile*) 168; affluent &c. (*wealthy*) 803; wantless; big with &c. (*pregnant*) 161.

un-exhausted, -wasted; exhaustless, inexhaustible.

Adv. sufficiently, amply &c. *adj.*; full; in -abundance &c. *n.*; with no sparing hand; to one's heart's content, *ad libitum*, without stint.

Phr. cut and come again.

---

fice &c. 639; come short of &c. 304; run dry.

want, lack, need, require; *caret*; be in want &c. (*poor*) 804; live from hand to mouth.

render- insufficient &c. *adj.*; drain of resources; impoverish &c. (*waste*) 638; stint &c. (*begrudge*) 819; put on short -commons, – allowance.

do -insufficiently &c. *adv.*; scotch the snake.

Adj. insufficient, inadequate; too -little &c. 32; not -enough &c. 639; unequal to; incompetent &c. (*impotent*) 158; 'weighed in the balance and found wanting'; perfunctory &c. (*neglect*) 460; deficient &c. (*incomplete*) 53; wanting &c. *v.*; imperfect &c. 651; ill-furnished, -provided, -stored, -off.

slack, at a low ebb; empty, vacant, bare; short –, out –, destitute –, devoid –, bereft &c. 776 –, denuded- of; dry, drained.

un -provided, -supplied, -furnished; un-replenished, -fed; un-stored, -treasured; empty-handed.

meagre, poor, thin, scrimp, sparing, spare, stinted, stunted; skimpy; starv-ed, -eling; half-starved, emaciated, famine-stricken, famished, underfed, undernourished; jejune.

scant &c. (*small*) 32; scarce; not to be had, – for love or money, – at any price; scurvy; stingy &c. 819; at the end of one's tether; without -resources &c. 632; in want &c. (*poor*) 804; in debt &c. 806.

Adv. insufficiently &c. *adj.*; in default –, for want- of; failing.

---

641. Redundance.—N. redundance; too -much, – many; super-abundance, -fluity, -fluence, -saturation; nimiety, transcendency, exuberance, profuseness; profusion &c. (*plenty*) 639; repletion, enough in all conscience, *satis superque*, lion's share; more than -enough &c. 639; plethora, engorgement, congestion, load, surfeit, sickener; turgescence &c. (*expansion*) 194; over-dose, -measure, -supply, -flow; inundation &c. (*water*) 348; avalanche.

accumulation &c. (*store*) 636; heap &c. 72; drug, – in the market, glut; crowd; burden.

excess; sur-, over-plus, epact; margin; remainder &c. 40; duplicate; surplusage, expletive; work of –, supererogation; *bonus, bonanza*.

luxury; intemperance &c. 954; extravagance &c. (*prodigality*) 818; exorbitance, lavishment.

pleonasm &c. (*diffuseness*) 573; too many irons in the fire; embarrassment of riches; money to burn.

V. super-, over-abound; know no bounds, swarm; meet one at every turn; creep –, bristle- with; overflow; run –, flow –, well –, brim-over; run riot; over-run, -stock, -lay, -charge, -dose, feed, burden, -load -do, -whelm, -shoot the mark &c. (*go beyond*) 303; surcharge, supersaturate, gorge, glut, load, drench, whelm, inundate, deluge, flood; drug, – the market.

choke, cloy, accloy, suffocate; pile up, lay it on, – with a trowel, lay on thick; impregnate with; lavish &c. (*squander*) 818.

send –, carry- coals to Newcastle, – owls to Athens; teach one's grandmother to suck eggs; *pisces natare docere*; kill the slain, 'gild refined gold,' 'paint the lily'; butter one's bread on both sides, put butter upon bacon; employ a steam-hammer to crack a nut &c. (*waste*) 638.

exaggerate &c. 549; wallow in; roll in &c. (*plenty*) 639; remain on one's hands, hang heavy on hand, go a begging.

Adj. redundant; too -much, – many; exuberant, inordinate, superabundant, excessive, overmuch, replete, profuse, lavish; prodigal &c. 818; exorbitant; overweening; extravagant; overcharged &c. *v.*; supersaturated, drenched, overflowing; running -over, – to waste, – down.

crammed –, filled- to overflowing; gorged, stuffed, ready to burst; dropsical, turgid, plethoric, full-blooded; obese &c. 194; voluminous.

superfluous, unnecessary, needless, supervacaneous, uncalled for, to spare, in excess; over and above &c. (*remainder*) 40; de trop; adscititious &c. (*additional*) 37; supernumerary &c. (*reserve*) 636; on one's hands, spare, duplicate, supererogatory, expletive; *un peu fort*.

Adv. over, too, over and above; over –, too- much; too far; without –, beyond –, out of- measure; with . . . to spare; over head and ears; up to one's -eyes, – ears; *extra*; beyond the mark &c. (*transcursion*) 303; over one's head.

Phr. it never rains but it pours.

2. *Degree of Subservience*

642. Importance.—N. importance, consequence, moment, prominence, consideration, mark, materialness.

import, significance, concern; emphasis, interest.

greatness &c. 31; superiority &c. 33; notability &c. (*repute*) 873; weight &c. (*influence*) 175; value &c. (*goodness*) 648; usefulness &c. 644.

gravity, seriousness, solemnity; no -joke, – laughing matter; pressure, urgency, stress; matter of life and death.

memorabilia, notabilia, great doings; red-letter day.

great -thing, – point; main chance, 'the be all and end all,' cardinal point, outstanding feature; substance, gist &c. (*essence*) 5; sum and substance, *gravamen*, head and front; important –, principal –, prominent –, essential-part; half the battle; *sine quâ non*; breath of one's nostrils &c. (*life*) 359; cream, salt, core, kernel, heart, nucleus:

643. Unimportance.—N. unimportance, insignificance, nothingness, immateriality.

triviality, trivia, fribble, levity, frivolity; paltriness &c. *adj.*; poverty; smallness &c. 32; vanity &c. (*uselessness*) 645; matter of -indifference &c. 866; no object; side issue.

nothing, – to signify, – worth speaking of, – particular, – to boast of, – to speak of; small –, no great –, trifling &c. *adj.* -matter; mere -joke, – nothing; hardly –, scarcely- anything; nonentity, cipher, figurehead; no great shakes, *peu de chose*; child's play; small beer.

toy, plaything, popgun, paper pellet, gimcrack, gewgaw, bauble, trinket, *bagatelle*, kickshaw, knicknack, whimwham, trifle, 'trifles light as air.'

trumpery, trash, rubbish, stuff, *fatras*, frippery; 'leather or prunello'; chaff, drug, froth, bubble, smoke, cob-

key, -note, -stone; corner stone; trump-card &c. (*device*) 626; salient points.

top-sawyer, first fiddle, *prima donna*, chief, big-wig; triton among the minnows.

V. be -important &c. *adj.*, – some-body, – something; import, signify, matter, be an object; carry weight &c. (*influence*) 175; make a figure &c. (*repute*) 873; be in the ascendant, come to the front, lead the way, take the lead, play first fiddle, throw all else into the shade; lie at the root of; de-serve –, merit –, be worthy- -of notice, – regard, – consideration.

attach –, ascribe –, give- importance &c. *n.*- tc; value, care for; set store -upon, – by; mark &c. 550; mark with a white stone, underline; write –, put –, print- in -italics, – capitals, – large letters, – large type, – letters of gold; accentuate, emphasize, lay stress on.

make -a fuss, – a stir, – a piece of work, – much ado- about; make -of, – much of.

Adj. important; of -importance &c. *n.*; momentous, material; to the point; not to be -overlooked, – despised, – sneezed at; egregious; weighty &c. (*influential*) 175; of note &c. (*repute*) 873; notable, prominent, salient, signal; memorable, remarkable; worthy of -remark, – notice; never to be forgot-ten; stirring, eventful.

grave, serious, earnest, noble, grand, solemn, impressive, commanding, im-posing.

urgent, pressing, critical, instant.

paramount, essential, vital, all-ab-sorbing, radical, cardinal, chief, main, prime, primary, principal, leading, capital, foremost, overruling; of vital &c. importance.

in the front rank, first-rate, A1; superior &c. 33; considerable &c. (*great*) 31; marked &c. *v.*; rare &c. 137.

significant, telling, trenchant, em-phatic, pregnant; *tanti*.

Adv. materially &c. *adj.*; in the main; above all, *par excellence*, to crown all.

web; weed; refuse &c. (*inutility*) 645; scum &c. (*dirt*) 653.

joke, jest, snap of the fingers; fudge &c. (*unmeaning*) 517; fiddlestick, – end; pack of nonsense, mere farce.

straw, pin, fig, continental, button, rush; bulrush, feather, halfpenny, farthing, brass farthing, doit, pepper-corn, jot, rap, pinch of snuff, old song.

minutiæ, details, minor details, small fry; dust in the balance, feather in the scale, drop in the ocean, flea-bite, molehill; fingle-fangle.

nine days' wonder, *ridiculus mus*; flash in the pan &c. (*impotence*) 158; much ado about nothing &c. (*over-estimation*) 482; storm in a teacup.

V. be -unimportant &c. *adj.*; not -matter &c. 642; go for –, matter –, signify- -little, – nothing, – little or nothing; not matter a -straw &c. *n.*

make light of &c. (*underestimate*) 483; catch at straws &c. (*overestimate*) 482.

Adj. unimportant; of -little, – small, – no- -account, – importance &c. 642; immaterial; un-, non-essential; not vital; irrelevant, incidental, indifferent.

subordinate &c. (*inferior*) 34; *médi-ocre* &c. (*average*) 29; passable, fair, respectable, tolerable, commonplace; uneventful, mere, common; ordinary &c. (*habitual*) 613; inconsiderable, so-so, insignificant, inappreciable, nu-gatory.

trifling, trivial; slight, slender, light, flimsy, frothy, idle; puerile &c. (*fool-ish*) 499; airy, shallow; weak &c. 160; powerless &c. 158; frivolous, petty, niggling; pid-, ped-dling; fribble, inane, ridiculous, farcical; fini-cal, -kin; fiddle-faddle, namby-pamby, wishy-washy, milk and water.

poor, paltry, pitiful; contemptible &c. (*contempt*) 930; sorry, mean, meagre, shabby, miserable, wretched, vile, scrubby, scrannel, weedy, nig-gardly, scurvy, putid, beggarly, worth-less, twopenny-halfpenny, cheap, trashy, catchpenny, gimcrack, trump-ery, one-horse; toy.

not worth -the pains, – while, – men-tioning, – speaking of, – a thought, – a curse, – a straw, – rap &c. *n.*; be-

[225]

neath –, unworthy of- -notice, – regard, – consideration, – contempt; *de lanâ caprinâ*; vain &c. (*useless*) 645.

Adv. slightly &c. *adj.*; rather, somewhat, pretty well, fairly well, tolerably.

for aught one cares.

Int. no matter! pish! tush! tut! pshaw! pugh! pooh, -pooh! fudge! bosh! humbug! fiddle-stick, – end! fiddlededee! never mind! *n'importe!* what -signifies, – matter, – boots it, – of that, –'s the odds! a fig for! stuff! nonsense! stuff and nonsense!

Phr. *magno conatu magnas nugas*; *le jeu n'en vaut pas la chandells*; it -matters not, – does not signify; it is of no -consequence, – importance.

644. Utility.—N. utility; usefulness &c. *adj.*; efficacy, efficiency, adequacy; service, use, stead, avail; help &c. (*aid*) 707; applicability &c. *adj.*; subservience &c. (*instrumentality*) 631; function &c. (*business*) 625; value; worth &c. (*goodness*) 648; money's worth; productiveness &c. 168; *cui bono* &c. (*intention*) 620; utilization &c. (*use*) 677; step in the right direction.

common weal, public good; utilitarianism &c. (*philanthropy*) 910.

V. be -useful &c. *adj.*; avail, serve; subserve &c. (*be instrumental to*) 631; conduce &c. (*tend*) 176; answer –, serve- -one's turn, – a purpose.

act a part &c. (*action*) 680; perform –, discharge- -a function &c. 625; do –, render- -a service, – good service, – yeoman's service; bestead, stand one in good stead; be the making of; help &c. 707.

bear fruit &c. (*produce*) 161; bring grist to the mill; profit, remunerate; benefit &c. (*do good*) 648.

find one's -account, – advantage- in; reap the benefit of &c. (*be better for*) 658.

render useful &c. (*use*) 677.

Adj. useful; of -use &c. *n.*; serviceable, usable, proficuous, good for; subservient &c. (*instrumental*) 631; conducive &c. (*tending*) 176; subsidiary &c. (*helping*) 707.

advantageous &c. (*beneficial*) 648; profitable, gainful, remunerative, worth one's salt; in-, valuable; prolific &c. (*productive*) 168.

adequate; ef-ficient, -ficacious; effect-ive, -ual; practicable, expedient &c. 646.

645. Inutility.—N. inutility; uselessness &c. *adj.*; inefficacy, futility; inep-, inap-titude; unsubservience; inadequacy &c. (*insufficiency*) 640; inefficiency &c. (*incompetence*) 158; unskilfulness &c. 699; disservice; unfruitfulness &c. (*unproductiveness*) 169; labour -in vain, – lost, – of Sisyphus; lost -trouble, – labour; work of Penelope; sleeveless errand, wild goose chase, mere farce.

tautology &c. (*repetition*) 104; supererogation &c. (*redundance*) 641.

vanitas vanitatum, vanity, inanity, worthlessness, nugacity; triviality &c. (*unimportance*) 643.

caput mortuum, waste paper, dead letter; blunt tool.

litter, rubbish, lumber, odds and ends, cast-off clothes; button-top; shoddy; rags, orts, trash, refuse, sweepings, scourings, off-scourings, dross, slag, waste, rubble, dottle, drast, *débris*; stubble, leavings; broken meat; dregs &c. (*dirt*) 653; weeds, tares; rubbish heap, dust hole; *rudera*, deads.

fruges consumere natus &c. (*drone*) 683.

V. be -useless &c. *adj.*; go a begging &c. (*redundant*) 641; fail &c. 732.

seek –, strive- after impossibilities; use vain efforts, labour in vain, roll the stone of Sisyphus, beat the air, lash the waves, *battre l'eau avec un bâton, donner un coup d'épée dans l'eau*, fish in the air, milk the ram, drop a bucket into an empty well, sow the sand; bay the moon; preach –, speak- to the winds; whistle jigs to a milestone; kick against the pricks, *se battre contre des moulins*; lock the stable door

applicable, available, ready, handy, at hand, tangible; commodious, adaptable; of all work.

Adv. usefully &c. *adj.*; *pro bono publico.*

___

render -useless &c. *adj.*; dis-mantle, -mast, -mount, -qualify, -able; unrig; cripple, lame &c. (*injure*) 659; spike guns, clip the wings; put out of gear.

Adj. useless, inutile, inefficacious, futile, unavailing, bootless; inoperative &c. 158; inadequate &c. (*insufficient*) 640; in-, un-sub-servient; inept, inefficient &c. (*impotent*) 158; of no -avail &c. (*use*) 644; ineffectual &c. (*failure*) 732; incompetent &c. (*unskilful*) 699; 'stale, flat and unprofitable'; superfluous &c. (*redundant*) 641; dispensable; thrown away &c. (*wasted*) 638; abortive &c. (*immature*) 674.

worth-, value-less; unsaleable; not worth a straw &c. (*trifling*) 643; dear at any price.

vain, empty, inane; gain-, profit-, fruit-less; un-serviceable, -profitable; ill-spent; unproductive &c. 169; *hors de combat*; barren, sterile, impotent, unproductive; effete, past work &c. (*impaired*) 659; obsolete &c. (*old*) 124; fit for the -dust-hole, - wastepaper basket; good for nothing; of no earthly use; not worth -having; - powder and shot; leading to no end, uncalled for; un-necessary, -needed, superfluous.

Adv. uselessly &c. *adj.*; to -little, - no, - little or no- purpose. Int. *cui bono?* what's the good!

when the steed is stolen &c. (*too late*) 135; hold a farthing candle to the sun; cast pearls before swine &c. (*waste*) 638; carry coals to Newcastle &c. (*redundance*) 641; wash a blackamoor white &c. (*impossible*) 471.

___

646. [Specific subservience.] **Expedience.**—N. expedien-ce, -cy; desirableness, -bility &c. *adj.*; fitness &c. (*agreement*) 23; utility &c. 644; propriety; advantage; opportunism, pragmatism.

high time &c. (*occasion*) 134.

V. be -expedient &c. *adj.*; suit &c. (*agree*) 23; befit; suit -, befit- the -time, season, - occasion.

conform &c. 82.

Adj. expedient; desir-, advis-, accept-able; convenient; worth while, meet; ut, -ting; due, proper, eligible, seemly, becoming; befitting &c. *v.*; opportune &c. (*in season*) 134; *in loco*; suitable &c. (*accordant*) 23; applicable &c. (*useful*) 644; practical, effective, pragmatical; suitable, handy; appropriate.

Adv. in the right place; conveniently &c. *adj.*; in the nick of time.

Phr. *operæ pretium est.*

___

647. Inexpedience.—N. inexpedien-ce, -cy; undesira-bleness, -bility &c. *adj.*; discommodity, impropriety; unfitness &c. (*disagreement*) 24; in-utility &c. 645; inconvenience, inadvisability; disadvantage.

V. be -inexpedient &c. *adj.*; come amiss &c. (*disagree*) 24; embarrass &c. (*hinder*) 706; put to inconvenience; pay too dear for one's whistle.

Adj. inexpedient, undesirable; un-, in-advisable; objectionable; troublesome, in-apt, -eligible, -admissible, -convenient; in-, dis-commodious; disadvantageous; inappropriate, unsuitable, unfit &c. (*inconsonant*) 24.

ill-contrived, -advised; unsatisfactory; unprofitable &c., unsubservient &c. (*useless*) 645; inopportune &c. (*unseasonable*) 135; out of -, in the wrong-place; improper, unseemly.

clumsy, awkward; cum-brous, -bersome; lumbering, unwieldy, hulky; un-manageable &c. (*impracticable*) 704; impedient &c. (*in the way*) 706; unnecessary &c. (*redundant*) 641.

Phr. it will never do.

648. [Capability of producing good. Good qualities.] **Goodness.—N.** goodness &c. *adj.*; excellence, merit; virtue &c. 944; value, worth, price.

super-excellence, -eminence; superiority &c. 33; perfection &c. 650; *coup de maître*; master-piece, *chef d'œuvre*, prime, flower, cream, *élite*, pick, A1, none such, *nonpareil*, *crème de la crème*, flower of the flock, cock of the roost, salt of the earth; champion.

tid-bit; gem, – of the first water; *bijou*, precious stone, jewel, pearl, diamond, ruby, brilliant, treasure; good thing; *rara avis*, one in a thousand.

beneficence &c. 906; good man &c. 948.

V. be -beneficial &c. *adj.*; produce -, do- -good &c. 618; profit &c. (*be of use*) 644; benefit; confer a -benefit &c. 618.

be the making of, do a world of good, make a man of.

produce a good effect; do a good turn, confer an obligation; improve &c. 658.

do no harm, break no bones.

be -good &c. *adj.*; excel, transcend &c. (*be superior*) 33; bear away the bell stand the -proof, – test; pass -muster, – an examination.

challenge comparison, vie, emulate, rival.

Adj. harm-, hurt-less; unobnoxious; un-nocuous, -nocent, -offensive.

beneficial, valuable, of value; serviceable &c. (*useful*) 644; advantageous, profitable, edifying; salutary &c. (*healthful*) 656.

favourable; propitious &c. (*hope-giving*) 858; fair.

good, – as gold; excellent; better; superior &c. 33; above par; nice, fine; genuine &c. (*true*) 494.

best, choice, select, picked, elect, eximious, *recherché*, rare, priceless; unpara-goned, -lleled &c. (*supreme*) 33; superlatively &c. 33; good; super-fine, -excellent; bonzer; of the first water; first-rate, -class; high-wrought; exquisite, very best, crack, prime, tip-top, gilt-edged, capital, cardinal; standard &c. (*perfect*) 650; inimitable.

admirable, estimable; praiseworthy &c. (*approve*) 931; pleasing &c. 829; *couleur de rose*, precious, of great price;

649. [Capability of producing evil. Bad qualities.] **Badness.—N.** hurtfulness &c. *adj.*; virulence

evil doer &c. 913; bane &c. 663; plague-spot &c. (*insalubrity*) 657; evil star, ill wind; snake in the grass, skeleton in the closet; *amari aliquid*, thorn in the side; Jonah, jinx, hoodoo.

malignity; malevolence &c. 907; tender mercies [ironically].

ill-treatment, annoyance, molestation, abuse, oppression, persecution, outrage; misusage &c. 679; injury &c. (*damage*) 659.

badness &c. *adj.*; peccancy, abomination; painfulness &c. 830; pestilence &c. (*disease*) 655; guilt &c. 947; depravity &c. 945.

V. be -hurtful &c. *adj.*; cause -, produce -, inflict -, work -, do- evil &c. 619; damnify, endamage, hurt, harm, scathe; injure &c. (*damage*) 659; pain &c. 830.

wrong, aggrieve, oppress, persecute; trample -, tread -, bear hard -, put-upon; overburden; weigh -down, - heavy on; victimize; run down; molest &c. 830.

maltreat, abuse; ill-use, -treat; thwart, buffet, bruise, scratch, maul; smite &c. (*scourge*) 972; do -violence, – harm, – a mischief; stab, pierce, outrage.

do -, make- mischief; bring -, get-into trouble.

destroy &c. 162.

Adj. hurt-, harm-, scath-, bane-, baleful; injurious, deleterious, detrimental, noxious, pernicious, mischievous, full of mischief, mischief-making, malefic, malignant, nocuous, noisome; prejudicial; dis-serviceable, -advantageous; wide-wasting.

unlucky, sinister; obnoxious, untoward, disastrous.

oppressive, burdensome, onerous; malign &c. (*malevolent*) 907.

corrupting &c. (corrupt &c. 659); virulent, venomous, envenomed, corrosive; poisonous &c. (*morbific*) 657; deadly &c. (*killing*) 361; destructive &c. (*destroying*) 162; inauspicious &c. 859.

bad, ill, arrant, as bad as bad can be, dreadful; hor-rid, -rible; dire; rank.

costly &c. (*dear*) 814; worth -its weight in gold, – a Jew's eye, – a king's ransom; matchless, peerless, invaluable, inestimable, precious as the apple of the eye.

tolerable &c. (*not very good*) 651; up to the mark, un-exceptionable, -objectionable; satisfactory, tidy.

in -good, – fair- condition; fresh; unspoiled; sound &c. (*perfect*) 650.

Adv. beneficially &c. *adj.*; well &c. 618.

peccant, foul, fulsome; rotten, – at the core.

vile, base, villainous; mean &c. (*paltry*) 643; injured &c., deteriorated &c. 659; unsatisfactory, exception, -able indifferent; below par &c. (*imperfect*) 651; ill-contrived, -conditioned; wretched, sad, grievous, deplorable, lamentable; piti-ful, -able, woeful &c. (*painful*) 830.

evil, wrong; depraved &c. 945; shocking; reprehensible &c. (*disapprove*) 932.

hateful, – as a toad: abominable, detestable, execrable, cursed, accursed, confounded; damn-ed, -able; infernal; diabolic &c. (*malevolent*) 907. inadvisable &c. (*inexpedient*) 647· unprofitable &c. (*useless*) 645; incompetent &c. (*unskilful*) 699; irremediable &c. (*hopeless*) 859. **Adv.** badly &c. *adj.*; wrong, ill; to one's cost; where the shoe pinches.

Phr. bad is the best; the worst come to the worst.

---

650. Perfection. — N. perfection; perfectness &c. *adj.*; indefectibility; impecc-ancy, -ability.

pink, *beau idéal*, phœnix, paragon; pink –, acme- of perfection; *ne plus ultra*; summit &c. 210.

cygne noir; philosopher's stone; chrysolite, Koh-i-noor, black tulip.

model, standard, pattern, mirror, admirable Crichton; trump; very prince of.

master-piece, -stroke, super-excellence &c. (*goodness*) 648; transcendence &c. (*superiority*) 33.

V. be -perfect &c. *adj.*; transcend &c. (*be supreme*) 33.

bring to perfection, perfect, ripen, mature; consummate, complete &c. 729; put in trim &c. (*prepare*) 673; put the finishing touch to.

Adj. perfect, faultless, ideal; inde-fective, -ficient, -fectible; immaculate, spotless, impeccable; free from -imperfection &c. 651; un-blemished, -injured &c. 659; sound, – as a roach; in perfect condition; scathless, intact, harmless; seaworthy &c. (*safe*) 644; right as a trivet; *in seipso totus teres atque rotundus*; consummate &c. (*complete*) 52; finished &c. 729; complete in itself.

best &c. (*good*) 648; model, standard, inimitable, unparagoned, unparalleled &c. (*supreme*) 33; superhuman, divine;

651. Imperfection.—N. imperfection; imperfectness &c. *adj.*; deficiency; in-adequacy &c. (*insufficiency*) 640; pee-cancy &c. (*badness*) 649; immaturity &c. 674.

fault, defect, weak point; screw loose; rift within the lute; fly in the ointment; flaw &c. (*break*) 70; gap &c. 198; twist &c. 243; taint, attainder; bar sinister, hole in one's coat; blemish &c. 848; weakness &c. 160; half-blood, touch of the tar brush; shortcoming &c. 304; drawback; seamy side.

mediocrity; no great -shakes, – catch; not much to boast of.

V. be -imperfect &c. *adj.*; have a -defect &c. *n.*; lie under a disadvantage; spring a leak.

not –, barely- pass muster; fall short &c. 304.

Adj. imperfect; not -perfect &c. 650; de-ficient, -fective; faulty, unsound, mutilated, tainted; out of -order, – tune; cracked, leaky; sprung; warped &c. (*distort*) 243; lame; injured &c. (*deteriorated*) 659; peccant &c. (*bad*) 649; frail &c. (*weak*) 160; inadequate &c. (*insufficient*) 640; crude &c. (*unprepared*) 674; incomplete &c. 53; found wanting; below par; short-handed; below –, under- its full -strength, – complement.

indifferent, middling, ordinary, medi-

beyond all praise &c. (*approbation*) 931; *sans peur et sans reproche*.

Adv. to perfection, to the limit; perfectly &c. *adj.*; *ad unguem*; clean, – as a whistle.

---

ocre; average &c. 29; so-so; *così-così*, milk and water; tolerable, fair, passable, pretty -well, – good; rather –, moderately- good; good –, well- enough; decent; not -bad, – amiss; unobjectionable, admissible, bearable, only better than nothing.

secondary, inferior; second-rate, -best, one-horse.

Adv. almost &c.; to a limited extent, rather &c. 32; pretty, moderately; only; considering, all things considered, enough.

Phr. *surgit amari aliquid.*

652. Cleanness.—N. cleanness &c. *adj.*; purity; cleaning &c. *v.*; purification, defecation &c. *v.*; purgation, lustration; de-, abs-tersion; epuration, mundation, ablution, lavation, colature; disinfection &c. *v.*; drain-, sewerage.

lavatory, bath, -room; swimming pool, natatorium; public baths; hot –, cold –, Turkish –, Swedish –, Russian –, vapour- bath; *hammam*, laundry, washhouse; washerwoman, laundress, laundryman; scavenger, cleaner, sweeper, goody; crossing sweeper, white wings, dustman, sweep.

brush; broom, besom, carpet-sweeper, vacuum-cleaner, mop, squilgee, rake, shovel, sieve, riddle, screen, filter; scraper, strigil.

napkin, *serviette*, cloth, table-, carving-cloth, table-linen, napery, maukin, handkerchief, towel, sudary; doyley, doily, duster, sponge, mop, swab.

cover, drugget, mat, doormat.

soap, wash, lotion, detergent, cathartic, purgative; purifier &c. *v.*; dentifrice, tooth-powder, -paste; mouth wash; disinfectant.

V. be –, render- clean &c. *adj.*

clean, -se; mundify, rinse. wring, flush, full, wipe, mop, sponge, scour, swab, scrub, holystone, brush up.

wash, shampoo, lave, launder, buck; abs-, de-terge; clear, purify; de-purate, -spumate, -fecate; purge, expurgate; Bowdlerize; elutriate, lixiviate, edulcorate, clarify, refine, rack; fil-ter, -trate; drain, strain.

disinfect, sterilize, pasteurize, fumigate, ventilate, deodorize; whitewash.

sift, winnow, screen, riddle, pick, weed. comb, rake, brush, sweep.

653. Uncleanness.—N. uncleanness &c. *adj.*; impurity; immundi-ty, -city; impurity &c. [of mind] 961.

defilement, contamination &c. *v.*; defœdation; soil-ure, -iness; abomination; leaven; taint, -ure; fetor &c. 401.

decay; putre-scence, -faction; corruption; mould, must, mildew, dry-rot, *mucor*, rubigo, caries.

slovenry; slovenliness &c. *adj.*; squalor.

dowdy, drab, slut, malkin, slattern, sloven, slammerkin, scrub, draggletail, mudlark, dustman, sweep; beast.

dirt, filth, soil, slop; dust, cobweb, flue; smoke, soot, smudge, smut, grime, raff.

sordes, dregs, grounds, lees; sedi-, settle-ment; heel-tap; dross, -iness; mother, precipitate, *scoriæ*, ashes, cinders, recrement, slag; scum, froth.

hog-wash, swill, ditch-, dish-, bilge-water; rinsings, cheese-parings; sweepings &c. (*useless refuse*) 645; off-, out- scourings; off-scum; *caput mortuum*, *residuum*, sprue, feculence, clinker, draff; scurf, -iness; *exuviæ*, morphew; fur, -fur; dandruff; tartar.

riffraff; vermin, louse, cootie, flea, bug.

mud, mire, quagmire, *alluvium*, silt, sludge, slime, slush, slosh.

spawn, offal, garbage, carrion; *excreta* &c. 299; slough, peccant humour, pus, matter, suppuration, *lienteria*; *fæces*, excrement, ordure, dung; sew-, sewer-age; muck, coprolite; guano, manure, compost.

dunghill, *coluvies*, mixen, midden, bog, laystall, sink, w.c., water-, earth-closet, latrine, privy, jakes, John's; cess, -pool; sump, sough, *cloaca*, drain,

rout –, clear –, sweep &c.- out; make a clean sweep of.

Adj. clean, -ly; pure; immaculate; spot-, stain-, taint-less; without a stain, un-stained, -spotted, -soiled, -sullied, -tainted, -infected, -adulterated; aseptic; sweet, – as a nut.

neat, spruce, tidy, trim, gimp, clean as a new penny, like a cat in pattens; cleaned &c. *v.*; kempt.

Adv. neatly &c. *adj.*; clean as a whistle.

sewer, common sewer; Cloacina; dust-hole.

sty, pig-sty, lair, den, Augean stable, sink of corruption; slum, rookery.

V. be –, become- unclean &c. *adj.*; rot, putrefy, fester, rankle, reek; stink &c. 401; mould, -er; go -bad &c. *adj*₁ render -unclean &c. *adj.*; dirt, -y; soil, smoke, tarnish, slaver, spot, smear, daub, blot, blur, smudge, smutch. smirch; d-, dr-abble, -aggle; spatter, slubber; be-smear &c., -mire, -slime, -grime, -foul; splash, stain, distain, maculate, sully, pollute, defile, debase, corrupt &c. (*injure*) 659; cover with -dust &c. *n.*; drabble in the mud.

wallow in the mire; slob-, slab-ber.

Adj. unclean, dirty, filthy, grimy; soiled &c. *v.*; not to be handled with kid gloves; dusty, snuffy, smutty, sooty, smoky; thick, turbid, dreggy; slimy.

uncleanly, slovenly, untidy, sluttish, dowdy, slatternly, draggle-tailed; un-combed, -kempt, -scoured, -swept, -wiped, -washed, -strained, -purified; squalid.

nasty, coarse, foul, impure, offensive, abominable, beastly, reeky, reechy; fetid &c. 401.

mouldy, lentiginous, musty, mildewed, rusty, moth-eaten, mucid, rancid, bad, gone bad, touched, fusty, reasty, rotten, corrupt, tainted, high, fly-blown, maggoty; putr-id, -escent, -efied; purulent, carious, peccant, fec-al, -ulent; stercoraceous, excrementitious; scurfy, impetiginous; gory, bloody; rotting &c. *v.*; rotten ᴜs -a pear, – cheese.

crapulous &c. (*intemperate*) 954; gross &c. (*impure in mind*) 961₁

---

654. Health.—N. health, sanity; soundness &c. *adj.*; vigour; good –, perfect –, excellent –, rude –, robust-health; bloom, *mens sana in corpore sano*; Hygeia; incorrupti-on, -bility; good state –, clean bill- of health, eupepsia.

V. be in health &c. *adj.*; bloom, flourish.

keep -body and soul together, – on one's legs; enjoy -good, – a good state of- health; have a clean bill of health.

return to health; recover &c. 660; get better &c. (*improve*) 658; take a -new, – fresh- lease of life; convalesce, be convalescent, recruit; restore to health; cure &c. (*restore*) 660.

Adj. health-y, -ful; in -health &c. *n.*; well, sound, strong, fit, hearty, hale, fresh, blooming, green, whole; florid, flush, hardy, stanch, staunch,

655. Disease.*—N. disease; illness, sickness &c. *adj.*; ailing &c. *v.*; 'the ills that flesh is heir to'; morb-idity, -osity; infirmity, ailment, indisposition; complaint, disorder, malady; distemper, -ature.

visitation, attack, seizure, stroke, fit, epilepsy, apoplexy, shock, shell-shock.

delicacy, loss of health, valetudinarianism, invalidism, cachexy; *cachexia*, atrophy, *marasmus*; indigestion, *dyspepsia*; decay &c. (*deterioration*) 659; malnutrition, decline, consumption, palsy, paralysis, prostration; occupational diseases.

taint, pollution, infection, contagion, septicity, septicæmia, blood poisoning, pyæmia, epi-, en-demic; murrain, plague, pestilence, virus, pox.

sore, ulcer, abscess, fester, boil; pimple &c. (*swelling*) 250; carbuncle,

* Extended lists of different diseases are beyond the scope of this work.

brave, robust, vigorous, weather-proof; convalescent.

un-scathed, -injured, -maimed, -marred, -tainted; sound of wind and limb, safe and sound; without a scratch.

on one's legs; sound as a -roach, - bell; fresh as -a daisy, - a rose, - April; picture of health; bursting with health; fit as a fiddle; hearty as a buck; in -fine, - high- feather; in -good case, - full bloom; in fine fettle; pretty bobbish, tolerably well, as well as can be expected.

sanitary &c. (*health-giving*) 656; sanatory &c. (*remedial*) 662.

gathering, whitlow, imposthume, peccant humour, issue; rot, canker, cancer, *carcinoma, caries*, mortification, corruption, gangrene, *sphacelus*, leprosy, eruption, rash, breaking out, venereal disease.

fever, calenture; inflammation.

fatal &c. (*hopeless*) 859- -disease &c.; dangerous illness, galloping consumption, churchyard cough; general breaking up, break up of the system.

[Disease of mind] neurasthenia; idiocy &c. 499; insanity &c. 503.

martyr to disease; cripple; 'the halt, the lame and the blind'; valetudinar-y, -ian; invalid, patient, case; sick-room, -chamber, hospital &c. 662.

[Science of disease] path-, eti-, nos-ology, therapeutics, diagnosis, prognosis.

V. be -ill &c. *adj.*; ail, suffer, labour under, be affected with, complain of; droop, flag, languish, halt; sicken, peak, pine, waste away, fail, lose strength; gasp.

keep one's bed; feign sickness &c. (*falsehood*) 544, malinger.

lay -by, - up; take -, catch- -a disease &c. *n.*, - an infection; be stricken by; break out.

Adj. diseased; ailing &c. *v.*; ill, - of; taken ill, seized with; indisposed, unwell, sick, squeamish, poorly, seedy; affected -, afflicted-with illness; laid up, confined, bed-ridden, invalided, in hospital, on the sick list; out of -health, - sorts; valetudinary.

un-sound, -healthy; sickly, morbose, healthless, infirm, chlorotic, unbraced, drooping, flagging, lame, halt, crippled, halting.

morbid, tainted, vitiated, peccant, contaminated, poisoned, septic, tabid, mangy, leprous, cankered; rotten, - to, - at- the core; withered, palsied, paralytic, tuberculous; dyspeptic.

touched in the wind, broken-winded, spavined, gasping; *hors de combat* &c. (*useless*) 645.

weak-ly, -ened &c. (*weak*) 160; decrepit; decayed &c. (*deteriorated*) 659; incurable &c. (*hopeless*) 859; in declining health; cranky; in a bad way, in danger, prostrate; moribund &c. (*death*) 360.

morbific, epidemic &c. 657.

---

656. Salubrity.—N. salubrity, salubriousness; healthiness &c. *adj.*

fine -air, - climate; eudiometer.

[Preservation of health] *hygiène*; valetudinarian, -ism, preventorium, sanitarian; *sanitarium, sanitorium*, immunity.

V. be -salubrious &c. *adj.*; agree with, be good for; assimilate &c. 23.

Adj. salu-brious, -tary, -tiferous; wholesome; health-y, -ful; sanitary, prophylactic, benign, bracing, tonic,

657. Insalubrity.—N. insalubrity; unhealthiness &c. *adj.*; non-naturals; plague spot; malaria &c. (*poison*) 663; death in the pot, contagion.

Adj. insalubrious; un-healthy, -wholesome; noxious, noisome, foul; morbi-fic, -ferous; mephitic, septic, azotic, deleterious; pesti-lent, -ferous, -lential; virulent, venomous, envenomed, poisonous, toxic, narcotic.

contagious, infectious, catching, taking, communicable, epidemic, zymotic;

invigorating, good for, nutritious, hyg-eian, -ienic.

in-noxious, -nocuous, -nocent; harmless, uninjurious, uninfectious; immune.

sanative &c. (*remedial*) 662; restorative &c. (*reinstate*) 660; useful &c. 644.

658. Improvement.—N. improvement; a-, melioration; betterment; mend, amendment, emendation; mending &c. *v.*; advancement; advance &c. (*progress*) 282; ascent &c. 305; promotion, preferment; elevation &c. 307; increase &c. 35.

cultiv-, civiliz-ation; menticulture, culture, march of intellect; eugenics, euthenics, meliorism, telesis.

reform, -ation; revision, radical reform; second thoughts, correction, *limæ labor*, refinement, elaboration; purification &c. 652; repair &c. (*restoration*) 660; recovery &c. 660.

revise; revised -, new- edition.

reformer, radical, progressive.

V. improve; be -, become -, get-better; mend, amend.

advance &c. (*progress*) 282; ascend &c. 305; increase &c. 35; fructify, ripen, mature; pick up, come about, rally; take a favourable turn; turn -over a new leaf, - the corner; raise one's head, sow one's wild oats; recover &c. 660.

be -better &c. *adj.*, - improved by; turn to -right, - good, - best- account; profit by, reap the benefit of; make -good use of, - capital out of; place to good account; take advantage of.

render better, improve, emend, make over, better; a-, meliorate; correct.

improve -, refine- upon; rectify; enrich, mellow, elaborate, fatten.

promote, cultivate, advance, forward, enhance; bring -forward, - on; foster &c. 707; invigorate &c. (*strengthen*) 159.

touch -. rub -, brush -, furbish -, bolster -, vamp -, brighten -, warm-up; polish, cook, make the most of, set off to advantage; prune; repair &c. (*restore*) 660; put in order &c. (*arrange*) 60.

review, revise, edit, redact; make -corrections, - improvements &c. *n.*; doctor &c. (*remedy*) 662; purify &c. 652.

sporadic, endemic, pandemic, epizoötic.

innutritious, indigestible, ungenial; uncongenial &c. (*disagreeing*) 24.

deadly &c. (*killing*) 361.

---

659. Deterioration.—N. deterioration, debasement; want, ebb; recession &c. 287; retrogradation &c. 283; decrease &c. 36.

degenera-cy, -tion, -teness; degradation; deprav-ation, -ement; depravity &c. 945; demoralization, retrogression.

impairment, inquination, injury, damage, loss, detriment, delaceration, outrage, havoc, inroad, ravage, scath; perversion, prostitution, vitiation, discoloration, oxidation, pollution, defœdation, poisoning, venenation, leaven, contamination, canker, corruption, adulteration, alloy.

decl-ine, -ension, -ination; decadence, -cy; falling off &c. *v.*; caducity, decrepitude, senility.

decay, dilapidation, ravages of time, wear and tear; cor-, e-rosion; mouldi-, rotten-ness; moth and rust, dry-rot, blight, marasmus, atrophy, collapse; disorganization; *délabrement* &c. (*destruction*) 162.

wreck, mere wreck, honeycomb, *magni nominis umbra.*

V. be -, become--worse,-deteriorated &c. *adj.*; have seen better days, deteriorate, degenerate, fall off; wane &c. (*decrease*) 36; ebb; retrograde &c. 283; decline, droop; go down &c. (*sink*) 306; go -downhill, - on from bad to worse, - farther and fare worse; jump out of the frying pan into the fire.

run to -seed, - waste; swale, sweal; lapse, be the worse for; break, - down; spring a leak, crack, start; shrivel &c. (*contract*) 195; fade, go off, wither, moulder, rot, rankle, decay, go bad; go to -, fall into- decay; 'fall into the sear and yellow leaf,' rust, crumble, shake; totter, - to its fall; perish &c. 162; die &c. 360.

[Render less good] deteriorate; weaken &c. 160; put back; taint, infect, contaminate, poison, empoison,

relieve, refresh, revive, infuse new blood into, recruit, re-invigorate, renew, revivify, freshen, build -afresh, – anew; uplift, inspire.

re-form, -model, -organise; new model, civilize.

view in a new light, think better of, appeal from Philip drunk to Philip sober.

palliate, mitigate; lessen &c. 36- an evil.

Adj. improving &c. *v.*; progressive, improved &c. *v.*; better, – off, – for; all the better for; better advised.

reform-, emend-atory; reparatory &c. (*restorative*) 660; remedial &c. 662.

corrigible, improvable, curable, accultural.

Adv. on -consideration, – reconsideration, – second thoughts, – better advice; *ad melius inquirendum*; on the -mend, – up grade.

envenom, canker, corrupt, exulcerate, pollute, vitiate, inquinate; de-, embase; denaturalize, leaven; de-flower, -bauch, -file, -prave, -grade; stain &c. (*dirt*) 653; discolour; alloy, adulterate, sophisticate, tamper with, prejudice.

pervert, prostitute, demoralize, brutalize; render vicious &c. 945; compromise.

embitter, ex-, acerbate, aggravate.

injure, impair, labefy, damage, harm, hurt, shend, scathe, spoil, mar, despoil, dilapidate, waste; overrun; ravage; pillage &c. 791.

wound, stab, pierce, maim, lame, surbate, cripple, hough, hamstring, hit between wind and water, scotch, mangle, mutilate, disfigure, blemish, deface, warp.

blight, rot; cor-, e-rode, eat away; wear -away, – out; gnaw, – at the root of; sap, mine, undermine, shake, sap the foundations of, break up; dis-organize, -mantle, -mast; destroy &c. 162.

damnify &c. (*aggrieve*) 649; do one's worst; knock down; deal a blow to; play -havoc, – sad havoc, – the mischief, – the deuce, – the very devil- -with, – among; decimate.

Adj. ·nimproved &c. (improve &c. 658); deteriorated &c. *v.*; altered, – for the worse; injured &c. *v.*; sprung; withering, spoiling, &c. *v.*; on the -wane, – decline; tabid; degenerate; worse; the –, all the- worse for; out of -repair, – tune; imperfect &c. 651; the worse for wear; battered; weather-ed, -beaten; stale, *passé*, shaken, dilapidated, frayed, faded, wilted, shabby, second-hand, second-rate, threadbare; worn, – to- -a thread, – a shadow, – the stump, rags; reduced, – to a skeleton, skeletonized; far gone.

decayed &c. *v.*; moth-, worm-eaten; mildewed, rusty, mouldy, spotted, seedy, time-worn, moss-grown; discoloured; effete, wasted, crumbling, mouldering, rotten, cankered. blighted, tainted; depraved &c. (*vicious*) 945; decrep-id, -it; broken down; done, – for, – up; worn out, used up; fit for the -dust-hole, – wastepaper basket; past work &c. (*useless*) 645.

at a low ebb, in a bad way, on one's last legs, washed -up, – out; undermined, deciduous; nodding to its fall &c. (*destruction*) 162; tottering &c. (*dangerous*) 665; past cure &c. (*hopeless*) 859; fatigued &c. 688; backward, retrograde &c. (*retrogressive*) 283; deleterious &c. 649; behind the times.

Adv. on the down grade; beyond hope.

Phr. out of the frying pan into the fire; *ægrescit medendo*.

660. Restoration.—N. restor-ation, -al; re-instatement, -placement, -habilitation, -establishment, -construction; reproduction &c. 163; re-novation, -newal; reviv-al, -escence; refreshment

661. Relapse.—N. relapse, lapse; falling back &c. *v.*; retrogradation &c. (*retrogression*) 283; deterioration &c. 659.

[Return to, or recurrence of a bad

&c. 689; re-suscitation, -animation, -vivification, -viction; Phœnix; reorganization.

renaissance, renascence, rebirth, second youth, rejuvenation, rejuvenescence, new birth; regenera-tion, -cy, -teness; palingenesis, reconversion, resurgence, resurrection.

state] backsliding, recidivation, recrudescence.

V. relapse, lapse; fall -, slide -, sinkback; have a relapse; return; retrograde &c. 283; recidivate; fall off &c. 659, again.

redress, retrieval, reclamation, recovery; convalescence; resumption, *résumption.*

recurrence &c. (*repetition*) 104; *réchauffé, rifacimento.*

cure, recure, sanation; healing &c. *v.;* redintegration; rectification, instauration.

repair, reparation, mending; recruiting &c. *v.;* cicatrization; disinfection; tinkering.

reaction; redemption &c. (*deliverance*) 672; restitution &c. 790; relief &c. 834.

mender, repairer, renewer; tinker, cobbler; doctor &c. 662; *vis medicatrix* &c. (*remedy*) 662.

curableness.

V. return to the original state; recover, rally, revive; come -to, – round, – to oneself; pull through, weather the storm, be oneself again; get -well, – round, – the better of, – over, – about; rise from -one's ashes, – the grave; resurge, resurrect; survive &c. (*outlive*) 110; resume, reappear; come to, – life again; live -, rise- again; relive.

heal, skin over, cicatrize; right itself.

restore, put back, place *in statu quo;* re-instate, -place, -seat, -habilitate, -establish, -estate, -install.

re-construct, -build, -organize, -constitute; reconvert; re-new, -novate; recondition; regenerate; rejuvenate.

re-deem, -claim, -cover, -trieve; rescue &c. (*deliver*) 672.

redress, recure; cure, heal, remedy, doctor, physic, medicate; break of; bring round, set on one's legs.

re-suscitate, -vive, -animate, -vivify, -call to life; reproduce &c. 163; warm up; reinvigorate, refresh &c. 689.

redintegrate, make whole; recoup &c. 790; make -good, – all square; rectify; put -, set- -right, – to rights, – straight; set up, correct; put in order &c. (*arrange*) 60; refit, recruit; fill up, – the ranks; reinforce.

repair, mend; put in -repair, – thorough repair, – complete repair; retouch, botch, vamp, tinker, doctor, cobble; do -, patch -, plaster -, vamp- up; darn, fine-draw, heel-piece; stop a gap, stanch, staunch, caulk, calk, careen, splice, bind up wounds.

Adj. restored &c. *v.; redivivus,* convalescent; in a fair way; none the worse; rejuvenated, renascent.

restoring &c. *v.;* restorative, recuperative; sana-, repara-tive, -tory; curative, remedial.

restor-, recover-, san-, remedi-, retriev-, cur-able.

Adv. *in statu quo;* as you were.

Phr. *revenons à nos moutons.*

---

662. Remedy.—N. remedy, help, redress; antidote, anti-toxin, anti-,

663. Bane.—N. bane, curse, thorn ir the -side, -flesh, bugbear, *bête noire;*

counter-poison, prophylactic, antiseptic, germicide, bactericide, corrective, restorative, stimulant, pick-me-up, tonic; sedative &c. 174; palliative; febrifuge; alter-ant, -ative; specific; emetic, carminative; narcotic &c. *adj.*; Nepenthe, Mithridate.

cure; radical -, perfect -, certain-cure; sovereign remedy.

physic, medicine, patent medicine, Galenicals, simples, drug, potion, draught, dose, pill, bolus, lozenge, tablet, tabloid, capsule; electuary; linct-us, -ure; medicament.

nostrum, receipt, recipe, prescription; catholicon, panacea, elixir, *elixir vitæ*, philosopher's stone; balm, balsam, cordial, theriac, ptisan.

salve, ointment, cerate, oil, lenitive, lotion, cosmetic; plaster; epithem, embrocation, liniment, cataplasm, sinapism, arquebusade, traumatic, vulnerary, pepastic, poultice, collyrium, depilatory.

compress, pledget; bandage &c. (*support*) 215.

treatment, medical treatment, regimen; diet-ary, -etics; *vis medicatrix, naturæ*; *medicine expectante*; seton, blood-letting, bleeding, venesection, phlebotomy, cupping, leeches; operation, surgical operation; tonsillectomy, appendectomy; injection, electrolysis, massage.

pharma-cy, -cology, -ceutics; acology; materia medica, pharmacopœia, therapeutics, therapy, posology, pathology &c. 655; homœ-, heter-, all-, hydr-opathy; cold water -, open air- cure; dietetics; sur-, chirur-gery, osteopathy; healing art, leechcraft, practice of medicine; ortho-pædy, -praxy; dentistry, midwifery, obstetrics, gynæcology.

faith -cure, - healing; psycho-therapy, -analysis, psychiatry.

hospital, infirmary, clinic; pest-, lazar-house; lazaretto, lazaret; lock hospital; *maison de santé*; *ambulance*; dispensary; *sanatorium, sanitarium*, spa, baths, pump-room, well; *hospice*; Red Cross; nursing home; asylum.

doctor, physician, surgeon; medical -, general- practitioner, consultant, specialist; medical attendant; medical student, medico; chemist, apothecary, pharmacopolist, druggist; leech; Æsculapius, Hippocrates, Galen; *accoucheur*, gynæcologist, midwife, oculist, aurist, dentist; operator; osteopath, bonesetter; nurse, monthly nurse, sister; dresser; *masseur, masseuse*.

V. apply a -remedy &c. *n.*; doctor, dose, physic, nurse, minister to, attend, dress the wounds, plaster, bandage, poultice; heal, cure, work a cure, kill or cure, remedy, stay (disease), snatch from the jaws of death; prevent &c. 706; relieve &c. 834; palliate &c. 658·

evil &c. 619; hurtfulness &c. (*badness*) 649; painfulness &c. (*cause of pain*) 830; scourge &c. (*punishment*) 975; *damnosa hereditas*; white elephant.

sting, fang, thorn, tang, bramble, brier, nettle.

poison, leaven, virus, venom; intoxicant; arsenic, Prussic acid, antimony, tartar emetic, strychnine, nicotine, cyanide of potassium, corrosive sublimate; curare; hyoscine &c.; poison-, mustard-, tear-gas; carbon di-, monoxide; ptomaine poisoning, botulism; miasm, mephitis, malaria, azote, sewer gas; pest, stench &c. 401.

rust, worm, moth, moth and rust, fungus, mildew; dry-rot; canker, -worm; cancer; torpedo; viper &c. (*evil-doer*) 913; demon &c. 980.

hemlock, hellebore, nightshade, *belladonna*, henbane, aconite; Upas tree.

drugs, dope, opium, morphia, morphine, cocaine, heroin, hashish, bhang; [Science of poisons] Toxicology.

Adj. baneful &c. (*bad*) 649; poisonous &c. (*unwholesome*) 657.

restore &c. 660; drench with physic; consult, operate, extract, deliver; bleed, cup, let blood, transfuse; electrolyse; psycho-analyse.

Adj. remedial; restorative &c. 660; corrective, palliative, healing; sana-tory, -tive; prophylactic; salutiferous &c. (*salutary*) 656; medic-al, -inal; therapeutic, surgical, chirurgical, orthopedic, epulotic, paregoric, tonic, corroborant, analeptic, balsamic, anodyne, hypnotic, neurotic, narcotic, sedative, lenitive, demulcent, emollient; depuratory; deter-sive, -gent; abstersive, disinfectant, febrifugal, alternative; traumatic, vulnerary.

dietetic, alimentary; nutrit-ious, -ive; peptic; alexi-pharmic, -teric; remedi-, cur-able.

3. *Contingent Subservience*

664. Safety.—N. safety, security, impregnability; invulnera-bility, -bleness &c. *adj.*; danger -past, – over; storm blown over; coast clear; escape &c. 671; means of escape, safety-valve; safeguard, palladium, sheet anchor, rock, tower of strength.

guardian-, ward-, warden-ship; tutelage, custody, safe keeping; preservation &c. 670; protection, auspices.

safe-conduct, escort, convoy; guard, shield &c. (*defence*) 717; guardian angel, tutelary -god, – deity, – saint; *genius loci.*

protector, guardian; ward-en, -er; preserver, custodian, *duenna, chaperon*, third person.

watch-, ban-dog; Cerberus; watch-, patrol-, police-man, constable, peeler, bobby, copper, cop, bull, flat-foot, detective, armed guard; sentinel, sentry, scout &c. (*warning*) 668; garrison; guard-ship.

[Means of safety] refuge &c., anchor &c. 666; precaution &c. (*preparation*) 673; quarantine, *cordon sanitaire.* [Sense of security] confidence &c. 858.

V. be -safe &c. *adj.*; keep one's head above water, tide over, save one's bacon; ride out –, weather- the storm; light upon one's feet; bear a charmed life; escape &c. 671; possess nine lives.

make –, render- -safe &c. *adj.*; protect, watch over; take care of &c. (*care*) 459; preserve &c. 670; cover, screen, shelter, shroud, flank, ward; guard &c. (*defend*) 717; secure &c. (*restrain*) 751; intrench, fence round &c. (*circumscribe*) 229; house, nestle, ensconce; take charge of.

665. Danger.—N. danger, peril, il security, jeopardy, risk, hazard, venture, precariousness, slipperiness; instability &c. 149; defencelessness &c. *adj.*

exposure &c. (*liability*) 177; vulnerability; vulnerable point, heel of Achilles; forlorn hope &c. (*hopelessness*) 859.

[Dangerous course] leap in the dark &c. (*rashness*) 863; road to ruin, *facilis descensus Averni*, hair-breadth escape;

cause for alarm; source of danger &c. 667. [Approach of danger] rock –, breakers- ahead; storm brewing; clouds -in the horizon, – gathering; warning &c. 668; alarm &c. 669. [Sense of danger] apprehension &c. 860.

V. be -in danger &c. *adj.*; be exposed to –, run into –, incur –, encounter-danger &c. *n.*; run a risk; lay oneself open to &c. (*liability*) 177; lean on –, trust to- a broken reed; feel the ground sliding from under one, have to run for it; have the -chances, – odds- against one.

hang by a thread, totter; tremble on the -verge, – brink; sleep –, stand -on a volcano; sit on a barrel of gunpowder, live in a glass house.

bring –, place –, put- in -danger &c. *n.*; endanger, expose to danger, imperil; jeopard, -ize, compromise; sail too near the wind &c. (*rash*) 863; put one's head in the lion's mouth.

adventure, risk, hazard, venture, stake, set at hazard; run the gauntlet &c. (*dare*) 861; engage in a forlorn hope.

threaten &c 909- danger; run one

escort, convoy; garrison; watch, mount guard, patrol, scout, spy.

make assurance double sure &c. (*caution*) 864; take up a loose thread; take precautions &c. (*prepare for*) 673; take in a reef; double reef topsails.

seek safety; take –, find- shelter &c. 666; run into port.

Adj. safe, secure, sure; in -safety, – security; have an anchor to windward; on the safe side; under the -shield of, – shade of, – wing of, – shadow of one's wing; under -cover, – lock and key; out of -danger, – the meshes, – harm's way; in -harbour, – port; on sure ground, at anchor, high and dry, above water. on *terra firma*; unthreatened, -molested; protected &c. *v.*; *cavendo tutus*; panoplied &c. (*defended*) 717.

snug, sea-, air-worthy; weather-, water-, fire-, bomb-proof.

defensible, tenable, proof against, invulnerable; un-assailable, -attackable; im-pregnable, -perdible; founded on a rock; inexpugnable.

safe and sound &c. (*preserved*) 670; harmless; scathless &c. (*perfect*) 650; unhazarded; not -dangerous &c. 665.

protecting &c. *v.*; guardian, tutelary; preservative &c. 670; trustworthy &c. 939.

Adv. *ex abundanti cautelâ*; with impunity.

Phr. all's well; all clear; *salva res est*; *suave mari magno*; safety first.

———

hard; lay a trap for &c. (*deceive*) 545.

Adj. in -danger &c. *n.*; endangered &c. *v.*; fraught with danger; danger-, hazard-, peril-, parl-, pericul-ous; un-safe, unprotected &c. (safe, protect &c. 664); insecure, untrustworthy, unreliable; built upon sand, on a sandy basis.

defence-, fence-, guard-, harbour-less; unshielded; vulnerable, expugnable, unsheltered, exposed; open to &c. (*liable*) 177.

aux abois, at bay; on -the wrong side of the wall, – a lee shore, – the rocks.

at stake, in question; precarious, aleatory, critical, ticklish; slip-pery, -py; hanging by a thread &c. *v.*; with a halter round one's neck; between -the hammer and the anvil, – Scylla and Charybdis, – two fires; on the -edge, – brink, – verge of a- -precipice, – volcano; in the lion's den, on slippery ground, under fire; not out of the wood.

un-warned, -admonished, -advised; unprepared &c. 674; off one's guard &c. (*inexpectant*) 508.

tottering; un-stable, -steady; shaky, top-heavy, tumble-down, ramshackle, crumbling, waterlogged; help-, guide-less; in a bad way; reduced to –, at-the last extremity; trembling in the balance; nodding to its fall &c. (*destruction*) 162.

threatening &c. 909; ominous, ill-omened; alarming &c. (*fear*) 860; explosive; poisonous &c. 657.

adventurous &c. (*rash*) 863, (*bold*) 861.

Int. stop! look out! beware! take care!

Phr. *incidit in Scyllam qui vult vitare Charybdim; nam tua res agitur paries dum proximus ardet.*

666. [Means of safety.] **Refuge.—N.** refuge, sanctuary, retreat, fastness; stronghold, keep, last resort; ward; prison &c. 752; asylum, ark, home, almshouse, refuge for the destitute; hiding-place &c. (*ambush*) 530; *sanctum sanctorum* &c. (*privacy*) 893; cache.

roadstead, anchorage; breakwater, mole, port, haven; harbour, – of refuge; sea-port; pier, jetty, embankment, quay.

667. [Source of danger.] **Pitfall.—N.** rocks, reefs, coral reef, sunken rocks, snags; sands, quicksands, Goodwin sands, sandy foundation; slippery ground; breakers, shoals, shallows, bank, shelf, flat, lee shore, iron-bound coast; rock –, breakers- ahead; derelict.

precipice; abyss, chasm, pit, crevasse; maelstrom, whirlpool, eddy, vortex, rapids, current, bore, tidal wave; storm, squall, hurricane, whirl-

covert, shelter, abri, screen, lee-wall, wing, shield, umbrella; splash-, dash-board, mudguard.

wall &c. (*inclosure*) 232; fort &c. (*defence*) 717.

anchor, kedge; grap-nel, -pling iron; sheet-, mushroom-anchor, main-stay; support &c. 215; check &c. 706; ballast.

jury-mast; vent-peg; safety -valve, - lamp; lightning conductor.

means of escape &c. (*escape*) 671; life-boat, swimming belt, cork jacket; life preserver, breeches buoy; parachute, plank, stepping-stone. safeguard &c. (*protection*) 664.

wind; volcano; ambush &c. 530; pit-fall, trap-door; trap &c. (*snare*) 545.

sword of Damocles; wolf at the door, snake in the grass, viper in one's bosom, death in the pot; latency &c. 526.

ugly customer, dangerous person, le chat qui dort; firebrand, hornet's nest.

Phr. *latet anguis in herbâ; proximus ardet Ucalegon.*

V. seek -, take -, find- refuge &c. *n.*; seek -, find- safety &c. 664; throw oneself into the arms of; claim sanctuary; take to the -hills, - woods; make port, reach shelter, bar -, bolt -, lock -the door, - gate; let the portcullis down; raise the drawbridge.

668. Warning.—N. warning, caution, caveat; notice &c. (*information*) 527; premoni-tion, -shment; prediction &c. 511; contraindication; symptom; lesson, dehortation; admonition, monition; alarm &c. 669.

handwriting on the wall, *tekel upharsin*, yellow flag; fog-signal, -horn; siren; monitor, warning voice, Cassandra, signs of the times, Mother Carey's chickens, stormy petrel, bird of ill omen, gathering clouds, clouds in the horizon, cloud no bigger than a man's hand, death-watch.

watch-tower, beacon, signal-post; light-house &c. (*indication of locality*) 550.

sent-inel, -ry; watch, -man; watch and ward; watch-, ban-, house-dog; patrol, vedette, picket, bivouac, scout, spy, spial; advanced -, rear-guard, lookout, flagman.

cautiousness &c. 864.

V. warn, caution; fore-, pre-warn; ad-, pre-monish; give -notice, - warning; menace &c. (*threaten*) 909; put on one's guard; sound the alarm &c. 669; croak.

beware, ware; take -warning, - heed at one's peril; watch out for; keep watch and ward &c. (*care*) 459.

Adj. warning &c. *v.*; premonitory, monitory, cautionary; admonitory, -tive; ominous, threatening, lowering, minatory, symptomatic, warned &c. *v.*; on one's guard &c. (*careful*) 459, (*cautious*) 864.

Adv. *in terrorem* &c. (*threat*) 909.

Int. beware! ware! take care! mind -, take care-what you are about; mind! look out!

Phr. *ne reveillez pas le chat qui dort; fœnum habet in cornu.*

669. [Indication of danger.] Alarm.—N. alarm; alarum, larum, alarm bell, tocsin, *alerte*, beat of drum, sound of trumpet, note of alarm, hue and cry, signal of distress, S.O.S.; blue-lights; war-cry, -whoop; warning &c. 668; fog-signal, -horn; siren; yellow flag; danger signal; red -light, - flag; fire -bell, - alarm; burglar alarm, police whistle, watchman's rattle.

false alarm, cry of wolf; bugbear, -aboo.

V. give -, raise -, sound -, beat- the *or* an -alarm &c. *n.*; alarm; warn &c. 668; ring the tocsin; *battre la générale*; cry wolf.

Adj. alarming &c. *v.*

Int. *sauve qui peut! qui vive?* who goes there?

670. Preservation.—N. preservation; safe keeping; conservation &c. (*storage*) 636; maintenance, upkeep, support, sustentation, conservatism; *vis conservatrix*; salvation &c. (*deliverance*) 672; drying &c. *v.*

[Means of preservation] prophylaxis; preserv-er, -ative; canned goods; cold pack; hygi-astics, -antics; cover, drugget; *cordon sanitaire.* [Superstitious remedies] charm &c. 993.

V. preserve, maintain, keep, sustain, support; keep -up, – alive; not willingly let die; shore –, bank- up; nurse; save, rescue; be –, make- -safe &c. 664; take care of &c. (*care*) 459; guard &c. (*defend*) 717.

stare super antiquas vias; hold one's own; hold –, stand- -one's ground &c. (*resist*) 719.

embalm, dry, cure, smoke, salt, pickle, season, kyanize, bottle, pot, tin, can; husband &c. (*store*) 636.

Adj. preserving &c. *v.*; conservative; prophylactic; preserva-tory, -tive; hygienic.

preserved &c. *v.*; un-impaired, -broken, -injured, -hurt, -singed, -marred; safe, – and sound; intact, with a whole skin, without a scratch.

Phr. *nolumus leges Angliæ mutari.*

671. Escape.—N. escape, scape; avolation, elopement, flight, get-away; evasion &c. (*avoidance*) 623; retreat; narrow –, hairbreadth-escape; close –, rear- shave; come off, impunity.

[Means of escape] loophole &c. (*opening*) 260; path &c. 627; secret -door, – passage; refuge &c. 666; vent, – peg; safety-valve; draw-bridge, fire-escape.

reprieve &c. (*deliverance*) 672; liberation &c. 750.

refugee &c. (*fugitive*) 623.

V. escape, scape; make –, effect –, make good- one's escape, make a get-away; get -off, – clear off, – well out of; *échapper belle*, save one's bacon; weather the storm &c. (*safe*) 664; escape scot-free.

elude &c., make off &c. (*avoid*) 623; march off &c. (*go away*) 293; give one the slip; slip through the -hands, – fingers; slip the collar, wriggle out of; break -loose, – from prison; break –, slip –, get- away; find -vent, – a hole to creep out of.

Adj. escap-ing, -ed &c. *v.*; stolen away, fled.

Phr. the bird has flown.

672. Deliverance.—N. deliverance, extrication, rescue; repriev-e, -al; respite; ransom; liberation &c. 750; truce, armistice; redemption; salvation; riddance; gaol delivery; exemption, day of grace; redeem-ableness.

V. deliver, extricate, rescue, save, redeem, ransom, free, liberate, release, set free, redeem, emancipate; bring -off, – through; *tirer d'affaire*, get the wheel out of the rut; snatch from the jaws of death. come to the rescue; rid; retrieve &c. (*restore*) 660; be –, get- rid of.

Adj. saved &c. *v.*; extric-, redeem-, rescu-able.

Phr. to the rescue!

3°. *Precursory Measures*

673. Preparation.—N. preparation; providing &c. *v.*; provi-sion, -dence; anticipation &c. (*foresight*) 510; pre-caution, -concertation, -disposition;

674. Non-Preparation. — N. non-. absence of –, want of- preparation; un-preparedness; inculture, inconcoction, improvidence.

forecast &c. (*plan*) 626; rehearsal, note of preparation.

[Putting in order] arrangement &c. 60; clearance; adjustment &c. 23; tuning; equipment, outfit, accoutrement, armament, array.

ripening &c. *v.*; maturation, evolution; elaboration, concoction, digestion; gestation, hatching, incubation, sitting.

groundwork, datum, first stone, cradle, stepping-stone; foundation, scaffold &c. (*support*) 215; scaffolding, *échafaudage*.

[Preparation -of men] training &c. (*education*) 537; inurement &c. (*habit*) 613; novitiate; [- of food] cook-ing, -ery; brewing, culinary art; [- of the soil] till-, plough-, sow-ing; semination, cultivation.

[State of being prepared] prepared-, readi-, ripe-, mellow-ness; maturity; *un impromptu fait à loisir*.

[Preparer] preparer, teacher, coach, trainer, pioneer; *avant-courrier*, -*coureur*; sappers and miners, paviour, navvy; packer, stevedore; warming-pan; precursor &c. 64.

V. prepare; get -, make- ready; make preparations, settle preliminaries, get up, sound the note of preparation; address oneself to.

set -, put- in order &c. (*arrange*) 60; forecast &c. (*plan*) 626; prepare -, plough -, dress- the ground; till -, cultivate- the soil; predispose, sow the seed, lay a train, dig a mine; lay -, fix- the -foundations, - basis, -groundwork; dig the foundations, erect the scaffolding; lay the first stone &c. (*begin*) 66.

rough-hew; cut out work; block -, hammer- out; lick into shape &c. (*form*) 240.

elaborate, mature, ripen, mellow, season, bring to maturity; nurture &c. (*aid*) 707; hatch, cook, brew; temper; anneal, smelt; dry, cure &c. 670.

equip, arm, man; fit-out, -up; furnish, rig, dress, garnish, betrim, accoutre, array, fettle, fledge; dress -, furbish -, brush -, vamp- up; refurbish; sharpen one's tools, trim one's foils, set, prime, attune; whet the -knife, - sword; wind -, screw- up; adjust &c. (*fit*) 27; put in -trim, - train, - gear, - working order, - tune, - a groove for, - harness; pack, stow away, store.

immaturity, crudity; rawness &c. *adj.*; abortion; disqualification.

[Absence of art] nature, state of nature; virgin soil, unweeded garden; rough diamond, neglect &c. 460.

rough copy &c. (*plan*) 626; germ &c. 153; raw material &c. 635.

improvisation &c. (*impulse*) 612.

V. be -unprepared &c. *adj.*; want -, lack- preparation; lie fallow; *s'embarquer sans biscuits*; live from hand to mouth.

[Render unprepared] dismantle &c (*render useless*) 645; undress &c. 226 extemporize, improvise.

surprise, pay a surprise visit, take by surprise, drop in upon, take unawares; take pot-luck.

Adj. un-prepared &c. [prepare &c. 673]; without -preparation &c. 673; incomplete &c. 53; rudimental, embryonic, abortive; immature, unripe, raw, green, crude; coarse; rough, -cast, -hewn; in the rough; un-hewn, -formed, -fashioned, -wrought, -laboured, -blown, -cooked, -boiled, -concocted, -cut -polished.

callow, un-hatched, -fledged, -nurtured, -licked, -taught, -educated, -cultivated, -trained, -tutored, -drilled, -exercised; precocious, premature; un-, in-digested; un-mellowed, -seasoned, -leavened.

fallow; un-sown, -tilled; natural, in a state of nature; undressed; in dishabille, *en déshabillé, en négligé*.

un-, dis-qualified; unfitted; ill-digested; un-begun, -ready, -arranged -organized, -furnished, -provided -equipped, -trimmed; out of -gear - order; dismantled &c. *v.*

shiftless, improvident, unthrifty thoughtless, unguarded; happy-go-lucky; caught napping &c. (*inexpectant*) 508; unpremeditated &c. 612.

Adv. extempore &c. 612.

train &c. (*teach*) 527; inure &c. (*habituate*) 613; breed; prepare &c.- for; rehearse; make provision for; take -steps, – measures, – precautions; provide, – against; beat up for recruits; open the door to &c. (*facilitate*) 705.

set one's house in order, make all snug; clear -decks, – for action; close one's ranks; shuffle the cards.

prepare oneself; serve an apprenticeship &c. (*learn*) 539; lay oneself out for, get into harness, gird up one's loins, buckle on one's armour, *reculer pour mieux sauter*, prime and load, shoulder arms, get the steam up, put the horses to.

guard –, make sure- against; forearm, make sure, prepare for the evil day, have a rod in pickle, provide against a rainy day, feather 'one's nest; lay in provisions &c. 637; make investments; keep on foot.

be -prepared, – ready &c. *adj.*; hold oneself in readiness, watch and pray, keep one's powder dry; lie in wait for &c. (*expect*) 507; anticipate &c. (*foresee*) 510; *principiis obstare; veniente occurrere morbo.*

Adj. preparing &c. *v.*; in -preparation, – course of preparation, – agitation, – embryo, – hand, – train; afoot, afloat; on -foot, – the stocks, – the anvil; under consideration &c. (*plan*) 626; brewing, hatching, forthcoming, brooding; in -store for, – reserve.

precautionary, provident; prepara-tive, -tory; provisional, in-choate, under revision; preliminary &c. (*precedent*) 62.

prepared &c. *v.*; in readiness; ready, – to one's hand, – made, cut and dried; ready for use, reach me down; made to one's hand, handy, on the table, made to order; in gear; in working -order, – gear; snug; in practice.

ripe, mature, mellow; practised &c. (*skilled*) 698; laboured, elab-orate, highly-wrought, smelling of the lamp, worked up.

in -full feather, – best bib and tucker; in –, at- harness; in – the saddle, – arms, – battle array, – war paint; up in arms; armed -at all points, – to the teeth, – *cap-à-pie*; sword in hand; booted and spurred.

in utrumque –, semper- paratus; on the alert &c. (*vigilant*) 459; at one's post.

Adv. in -preparation, – anticipation of; afoot, astir, abroad; abroach.

675. Essay.—N. essay, trial, endeavour, aim, attempt; venture, ad-venture, speculation, *coup d'essai, début*; probation &c. (*experiment*) 463.

V. try, essay; experiment &c. 463; endeavour, strive; tempt, tackle, take on, attempt, make an attempt; venture, adventure, speculate, take one's chance, tempt fortune; try one's -fortune, – luck, – hand; use one's endeavour; feel –, grope –, pick- one's way.

try hard, push, make a bold push, use one's best endeavour; do one's best &c. (*exertion*) 686.

Adj. essaying &c. *v.*; experimental &c. 463; tentative, empirical, probationary.

Adv. experimentally &c. *adj.*; on trial, at a venture; by rule of thumb. if one may be so bold.

676. Undertaking.—N. undertaking; compact &c. 769; engagement &c. (*promise*) 768; enter-, em-prise; venture &c. 675; pilgrimage; mat-ter in hand &c. (*business*) 625; move; first move &c. (*beginning*) 66.

V. undertake; engage -. embark- in; launch –, plunge- into; volunteer; apprentice oneself to; engage &c. (*promise*) 768; contract &c. 769; take upon -oneself, – one's shoulders; devote oneself to &c. (*determination*) 604.

take -up, – in hand; tackle; set –, go- about; set –, fall- -to, – to work; launch forth; set up shop; put in -hand, – execution; set forward; break the neck of a business, be in for; put one's hand to; betake oneself to, turn one's hand to, go to do; begin &c. 66; broach, institute, &c. (*originate*) 153; put –, lay- one's -hand to the plough, – shoulder to the wheel.

have in hand &c. (*business*) 625; have many irons in the fire &c. [*activity*) 682.

Adj. undertaking &c. *v.*; on the anvil &c. 625; adventurous, venturesome.

Int. here goes!

677. Use.—N. use; employ, -ment; exer-cise, -citation; appli-cation, -ance; adhibition, disposal; consumption; agency &c. (*physical*) 170; usufruct; usefulness &c. 644; recourse, resort, avail, pragmatism.

[Conversion to use] utilization, service, wear.

[Way of using] usage.

V. use, make use of, employ, put to use; apply, put in -action, – operation, – practice; set -in motion, – to work.

ply, work, wield, handle, manipulate; play, – off; exert, exercise, practise, avail oneself of, profit by; resort –, have recourse –, recur –, take –, betake oneself- to; take -up with, – advantage of; lay one's hands on, try.

render useful &c. 644; mould; turn to -account, – use; convert to use, utilize, administer; work up; call –, bring- into play; put into requisition; call –, draw- forth; press –, enlist- into the service; bring to bear upon, devote, dedicate, consecrate, apply, adhibit, dispose of; make a -handle, – cat's paw- of.

fall back upon, make a shift with; make the -most, – best- of.

use –, swallow- up; consume, absorb, expend; tax, task, wear, put to task.

Adj. in use; used &c. *v.*; well-worn, -trodden.

useful &c. 644; subservient &c. (*instrumental*) 631; utilitarian; pragmatical.

678. Disuse.—N. forbearance, abstinence; disuse; relinquishment &c 782; desuetude &c. (*want of habit*) 614

V. not use; do without, dispense with, let alone, not touch, forbear, abstain, spare, waive, neglect; keep back, reserve.

lay -up, – by, – on the shelf, – up in a napkin; shelve; set –, put –, lay- aside; disuse, leave off, have done with; supersede; discard &c. (*eject*) 297; dismiss, give warning.

throw aside &c. (*relinquish*) 782; make away with &c. (*destroy*) 162; cast –, heave –, throw- overboard; cast to the -dogs, – winds; dismantle &c. (*render useless*) 645.

lie , remain unemployed &c. *adj.*

Adj. not used &c. *v.*; un-employed, -applied, -disposed of, -spent, -exercised, -touched, -trodden, -essayed, -gathered, -culled; uncalled for, not required.

disused &c. *v.*; done with; run down, used up, cast off.

679. Misuse.—N. mis-use, -usage, -employment, -application, -appropriation.

abuse, profanation, prostitution, desecration; waste &c. 638.

V. mis-use, -employ, -apply, -appropriate.

desecrate, abuse, profane, prostitute; waste &c. 638; over-task, -tax, -work; squander &c. 818.

cut a whetstone with a razor, employ a steam-engine to crack a nut; catch at a straw.

Adj. misused &c. *v.*

Section III. Voluntary Action

1°. *Simple Voluntary Action*

680. Action.—N. action, perform-ance; doing &c. *v.*; perpetration; exer-cise, -citation; movement, operation, evolution, work; labour &c. (*exertion*) 686; *praxis*, execution; procedure &c. (*conduct*) 692; handicraft; business &c. 625; agency &c. (*power at work*) 170.

deed, act, overt act, stitch, touch, gest; transaction, job, doings, dealings, proceeding, measure, step, manœuvre, bout, passage, move, stroke, blow; *coup*, – *de main*, – *d'état*; *tour de force* &c. (*display*) 882; feat, exploit, stunt; achievement &c. (*completion*) 729; handiwork, workmanship. craftsman-ship; manufacture; stroke of policy &c. (*plan*) 626.

actor &c. (*doer*) 690.

V. do, perform, execute; achieve &c. (*complete*) 729; transact, enact; com-mit, perpetrate, inflict; exercise, prose-cute, carry on, work, practise, play.

employ oneself, ply one's task; offi-ciate, have in hand &c. (*business*) 625; labour &c. 686; be at work; pursue a course; shape one's course &c. (*con-duct*) 692.

act, operate; take -action, – steps; strike a blow, lift a finger, stretch forth one's hand; take in hand &c. (*under-take*) 676; put oneself in motion; put in practice; carry into execution &c. (*complete*) 729; act upon.

be -an actor &c. 690; take –, act –, play –, perform- a part in; participate in; have a -hand in, – finger in the pie; have to do with; be a -party to, – participator in; bear –, lend- a hand; pull an oar, run in a race; mix oneself up with &c. (*meddle*) 682.

be in action; come into operation &c. (*power at work*) 170.

Adj. doing &c. *v.*; acting; in action; in harness; on duty; at work; in opera-tion &c. 170; up to one's ears in work, in the midst of things.

Adv. in the -act, – midst of, – thick of; red-handed, *in flagrante delicto*; while one's hand is in.

681. Inaction.—N. inaction, passive-ness, abstinence from action; non-interference; Fabian –, conservative- policy; neglect &c. 460; stagnation, vegetation; loafing.

inactivity &c. 683; rest &c. (*repose*) 687; quiescence &c. 265; want of –, in- occupation; unemployment; idle hours, time hanging on one's hands, *dolce far niente*; sinecure.

V. not -do, – act, – attempt; be -in-active &c. 683; abstain from doing, do nothing, hold, spare; not -stir, – move, – lift- a -finger, – foot, – peg; fold one's -arms, – hands; leave –, let- alone; let -be, – pass, – things take their course, – it have its way, – well alone; *quieta non movere*; *stare super antiquas vias*; rest and be thankful, live and let live; lie –, rest- upon one's oars; *laisser -aller*, – *faire*; stand aloof; refrain &c. (*avoid*) 623; keep oneself from doing; remit –, relax- one's efforts; desist &c. (*relinquish*) 624; stop &c. (*cease*) 142; pause &c. (*be quiet*) 265.

wait, lie in wait, bide one's time, take time, tide it over.

cool –, kick- one's heels; loaf, while away the -time, – tedious hours; pass –, fill up –, beguile- the time; talk against time; waste time &c. (*inactive*) 683.

lie -by, – on the shelf, – in ordinary, – idle, – to, – fallow; keep quiet, slug; have nothing to do, whistle for want of thought; twiddle one's thumbs.

undo, do away with; take -down, – to pieces; destroy &c. 162.

Adj. not doing &c. *v.*; not done &c. *v.*; undone; passive; un-occupied, -em-ployed; out of -employ, – work, – a job; fallow; *désœuvré*.

Adv. *re infectâ*, at a stand, *les bras croisés*, with folded arms; with the hands -in the pockets, – behind one's back; *pour passer le temps*.

Int. so let it be! stop! &c. 142; hands off!

Phr. nothing doing; *cunctando resti-tuit rem*.

682. Activity.— N. activity; briskness, liveliness &c. *adj.*; animation, life, vivacity, spirit, verve, dash, energy, go.

nimbleness, agility; smartness, quickness &c. *adj.*; velocity &c. 274; alacrity, promptitude; des-, dis-patch; expedition; haste &c. 684; punctuality &c. (*early*) 132.

eagerness, zeal, ardour, *perfervidum ingenium, empressement,* earnestness, intentness; *abandon;* vigour &c. (*physical energy*) 171; devotion &c. (*resolution*) 604; exertion &c. 686.

industry, assiduity; assiduousness &c. *adj.*; sedulity; laboriousness; drudgery &c. (*labour*) 686; painstaking, diligence; perseverance &c. 604*a*; indefatigation; habits of business.

vigilance &c. 459; wakefulness; sleep-, rest-lessness; *pervigilium, insomnia;* racketing.

movement, bustle, hustle, stir, fuss, ado, bother, pottering; fidgets, -iness; flurry &c. (*haste*) 684.

officiousness; dabbling, meddling; inter-ference, -position, -meddling, butting in, intrusiveness; tampering with, intrigue.

press of business, no sinecure, plenty to do, many irons in the fire, great doings, busy hum of men, battle of life, thick of -things, – the action; the madding crowd.

housewife, busy bee; new brooms; sharp fellow, blade; hustler, devotee, enthusiast, fan, zealot, fanatic; meddler, intermeddler, intriguer, busybody, kibitzer, pickthank.

V. be -active &c. *adj.*; busy oneself in; stir, -about, – one's stumps; bestir –, rouse- oneself; speed, hasten, peg away, lay about one, bustle, fuss; raise –, kick up- a dust; push; make a -push, – fuss, – stir; go ahead, push forward; fight –, elbow- one's way; make progress &c. 282; toil &c. (*labour*) 686; drudge, plod, persist &c. (*persevere*) 604*a*; keep -up the ball, – the pot boiling.

look sharp; have all one's eyes about one &c. (*vigilance*) 459; rise, arouse oneself, get up early, hustle, push; be about, keep moving, steal a march, kill two birds with one stone; seize the opportunity &c. 134: lose no time, not

683. Inactivity.—N. inactivity; inaction &c. 681; inertness, inertia &c. 172; obstinacy &c. 606.

lull &c. (*cessation*) 142; quiescence &c. 265; rust, -iness.

idle-, remiss-ness &c. *adj.*; sloth, indolence, indiligence; otiosity, dawdling &c. *v.*

dullness &c. *adj.*; languor; segni-ty, -tude; lentor; sluggishness &c. (*slowness*) 275; procrastination &c. (*delay*) 133; torp-or, -idity, -escence; stupor &c. (*insensibility*) 823; somnolence; drowsiness &c. *adj.*; nodding &c. *v.*; oscit-ation, -ancy; pandiculation, hypnotism, lethargy; heaviness, heavy eye-lids, sand in the eyes.

sleep, slumber; sound –, heavy –, balmy- sleep; Morpheus, dreamland; coma, trance, catalepsy, hypnosis, ecstasis, dream, hibernation, nap, doze, snooze, *siesta,* wink of sleep, forty winks, snore; Hypnology.

dull work; pottering; relaxation &c. (*loosening*) 47; Castle of Indolence.

[Cause of inactivity] lullaby, *berceuse;* anæsthetic, sedative &c. 174; torpedo.

idler, drone, droil, dawdle, mopus; do-little, *fainéant,* dummy, sleeping partner; afternoon farmer; truant &c. (*runaway*) 623; lounger, *lazzarone,* floater, loafer, tramp, beggar, cadger; lub-ber, -bard; slow-coach &c. (*slow*) 275; opium –, lotus- eater; slug; lag-, slug-gard, lie-abed; slumberer, dormouse, marmot; waiter on Providence, *fruges consumere natus.*

V. be -inactive &c. *adj.*; do nothing &c. 681; move slowly &c. 275; let the grass grow under one's feet; take one's time, dawdle, poke, drawl, droil, lag, hang back, slouch; loll, -op; lounge, loaf, loiter; go to sleep over; sleep at one's post, *ne battre que d'une aile.*

take -it easy, – things as they come; lead an easy life, vegetate, swim with the stream, eat the bread of idleness; loll in the lap of -luxury, – indolence; waste –, consume –, kill –, lose- time; burn daylight, waste the precious hours.

idle –, trifle –, fritter –, fool- away time; spend –, take- time in; ped-, pid-dle· potter, putter, dabble, faddle,

lose a moment, make the most of one's time, not suffer the grass to grow under one's feet, improve the shining hour, make short work of; dash off; make haste &c. 684; do one's best, take pains &c. (*exert oneself*) 686; do –, work- wonders.

have -many irons in the fire, – one's hands full, – much on one's hands; have other -things to do, – fish to fry; be busy; not have a moment -to spare, – that one can call one's own.

have one's fling, run the round of; go all lengths, stick at nothing, run riot.

outdo; over-do, -act, -lay, -shoot the mark; make a toil of a pleasure.

have a hand in &c. (*act in*) 680; take an active part, put in one's oar, have a finger in the pie, mix oneself up with, trouble one's head about, intrigue; agitate.

tamper with, meddle, moil; inter-meddle, -fere, -pose; obtrude; poke –, thrust- one's nose in, butt in.

Adj. active; brisk, – as a lark, – as a bee; lively, animated, vivacious; alive, – and kicking; frisky, spirited, stirring.

nimble, – as a squirrel; agile; light-, nimble-footed; featly, tripping.

quick, prompt, yare, instant, ready, alert, spry, sharp, smart, slick, go-ahead; fast &c. (*swift*) 274; quick as a lamplighter, expeditious; awake, broad awake; wide awake &c. (*intelligent*) 498.

forward, eager, ardent, strenuous, zealous, enterprising, pushing, in earnest; resolute &c. 604.

industrious, assiduous, diligent, sedulous, notable, painstaking; intent &c. (*attention*) 457; indefatigable &c. (*persevering*) 604a; unwearied; unsleeping, sleepless, never tired; plodding, hard-working &c. 686; business-like, workaday.

bustling; restless, – as a hyæna; fussy, fidgety, pottering; busy, – as a hen with one chicken.

working, labouring, at work, on duty, in harness; up in arms; on one's legs, at call; up and -doing, – stirring.

busy, occupied; hard at -work, – it; up to one's ears in, full of business, busy as a bee.

meddling &c. *v.*; meddlesome, pushing, officious, overofficious, *intrigant*.

astir, stirring; a-going, -foot; on foot; in full swing; eventful; on the alert &c. (*vigilant*) 459.

fribble, fiddle-faddle; dally, dilly-dally.

sleep, slumber, be asleep; hibernate; oversleep; sleep like a -top, – log, – dormouse; sleep -soundly, – heavily; doze, drowze, snooze, nap; take a -nap &c. *n.*; dream; snore; settle –, go –, go off- to sleep; drop off; fall –, drop-asleep; close –, seal up- -the -eyes, – eyelids; weigh down the eyelids; get sleepy, nod, yawn; go to bed, turn in.

languish, expend itself, flag, hang fire; relax.

render -idle &c. *adj.*; sluggardize; mitigate &c. 174.

Adj. inactive; motionless &c. 265; unoccupied &c. (*doing nothing*) 681.

indolent, lazy, slothful, idle, otiose, lusk, remiss, slack, inert, torpid, sluggish, languid, supine, heavy, dull, leaden, lumpish; exanimate, soulless; listless; dron-y, -ish; lazy as Ludlam's dog.

dilatory, laggard; lagging &c. *v.*; slow &c. 275; rusty, flagging; lackadaisical, maudlin, fiddle-faddle; pottering &c. *v.*; shilly-shally &c. (*irresolute*) 605.

sleeping &c. *v.*; asleep; fast –, dead –, sound- asleep; in a sound sleep; sound as a top, dormant, comatose; in the -arms, – lap- of Morpheus.

sleep-y, -ful; dozy, drowsy, somnolent, torpescent; lethargic, -al; heavy, – with sleep; napping; somni-fic, -ferous; sopor-ous, -ific, -iferous; hypnotic; balmy, dreamy; un-, una-wakened.

sedative &c. 174.

Adv. inactively &c. *adj.*; at leisure &c. 685.

Phr. the eyes begin to draw straws.

———

Adv. actively &c. *adj.*; with -life and spirit, – might and main &c. 686, – haste &c. 684, – wings; full tilt, *in mediis rebus.*

Int. be –, look- -alive, – sharp! move –, push- on! keep moving! go ahead! stir your stumps! *age quod agis!*

Phr. *carpe diem* &c. (*opportunity*) 134; *nulla dies sine lineâ*; *nec mora nec requies*; no sooner said than done &c. (*early*) 132; catch a weasel asleep.

---

684. Haste.—N. haste, urgency; des-, dis-patch; acceleration, spurt, spirt, forced march, rush, dash; velocity &c. 274; precipit-ancy, -ation, -ousness &c. *adj.*; impetuosity; *brusquerie*; hurry, scurry, scuttle, drive, scramble, push, hustle, bustle, fuss, fidgets, flurry, flutter, splutter.

V. haste, hasten; make -haste, – a dash &c. *n.*; hurry –, dash –, whip –, push –, press- -on, – forward; hurry, skurry, scuttle along, bundle on, dart to and fro, bustle, flutter, scramble; plunge, – headlong; run, race, speed; dash off; rush &c. (*violence*) 173.

bestir oneself &c. (*be active*) 682; lose -no time, – not a moment, – not an instant; make short work of; make the best of one's -time, – way.

be -precipitate &c. *adj.*; jump at; be in -haste, – a hurry &c. *n.*; have -no time, – not a moment- -to lose, – to spare; work -under pressure, – against time.

quicken &c. 274; accelerate, expedite, put on, precipitate, urge, whip, spur, flog, goad.

Adj. hasty, hurried, *brusque*; scrambling, cursory, precipitate, headlong, furious, boisterous, impetuous, hot-headed; feverish, fussy; pushing.

in -haste, – a hurry &c. *n.*; in -hot, – all- haste; breathless, pressed for time, hard pressed, urgent.

Adv. with -haste, – all haste, – breathless speed; in haste &c. *adj.*; apace &c. (*swiftly*) 274; amain; all at once &c. (*instantaneously*) 113; at short notice &c., immediately &c. (*early*) 132; posthaste; by -express, – telegraph, – wire, – wireless, – air mail.

hastily, precipitately &c. *adj.*; helter-skelter, hurry-skurry, holus-bolus; slap-dash, -bang; full-tilt, -drive; heels over head, head and shoulders, headlong, *à corps perdu.*

by -fits and starts, – spurts; hop, skip and jump.

Phr. *sauve qui peut*, devil take the hindmost, no time to be lost; no sooner said than done &c. (*early*) 132; a word and a blow.

Int. hurry up! look alive! get a move on! buck up! double march! rush! urgent!

685. Leisure.—N. leisure; spare -time, – hours, – moments; vacant hour; time, – to spare, – on one's hands; holiday &c. (*rest*) 687; *otium cum dignitate*, ease.

V. have -leisure &c. *n.*; take one's -time, – leisure, – ease; repose &c. 687; move slowly &c. 275; while away the time &c. (*inaction*) 681; be -master of one's time, – an idle man; *desipere in loco.*

Adj. leisurely; slow &c. 275; deliberate, quiet, calm, undisturbed; at -leisure, – one's ease, – a loose end.

Phr. time hanging heavy on one's hands.

---

686. Exertion.—N. exertion, effort, strain, tug, pull, stress, force, pressure, throw, stretch, struggle, spell, spurt, spirt; stroke –, stitch- of work.

687. Repose.—N. repose, rest, silken repose; sleep &c. 683.

relaxation, breathing time; halt pause &c. (*cessation*) 142; respite.

'a strong pull, a long pull and a pull all together'; dead lift; heft; gymnastics, sports; exer-cise, -citation; wear and tear; ado; toil and trouble; uphill -, hard -, warm- work; harvest time.

labour, work, toil, travail, manual labour, sweat of one's brow, swink, operoseness, drudgery, slavery, fagging, hammering; limæ labor.

trouble, pains, duty; resolution &c. 604; energy &c. (physical) 171.

V. exert oneself; exert -, tax- one's energies; use exertion.

labour, work, toil, moil, sweat, fag, drudge, slave, drag a lengthened chain, wade through, strive, strain; make -, stretch- a long arm; pull, tug, ply; ply -, tug at- the oar; do the work; take the labouring oar.

bestir oneself (be active) 682; take trouble, trouble oneself.

work hard; rough it; put forth -one's strength, - a strong arm; fall to work, bend the bow; buckle to, set one's shoulder to the wheel &c. (resolution) 604; work like a -Briton, - horse, - carthorse, - galley-slave, - coalheaver; labour -, work- day and night; redouble one's efforts; do double duty; work double -hours, - tides; sit up, burn the -midnight oil, - candle at both ends; stick to &c. (persevere) 604a; work -, fight- one's way; lay about one, hammer at.

take pains; do one's -best, - level best, - utmost; do -the best one can, - all one can, - all in one's power, - as much as in one lies, - what lies in one's power; use one's -best, - utmost- endeavour; try one's -best, - utmost; play one's best card; put one's -best, - right- leg foremost; have one's whole soul in one's work, put all one's strength into, strain every nerve; spare no -efforts, - pains; go all lengths; go through fire and water &c. (resolution) 604; move heaven and earth, leave no stone unturned.

Adj. labouring &c. v.

laborious, operose, elaborate; strained; toil-, trouble-, burden-, weari-some; uphill; herculean, gymnastic, athletic, palestric.

hardworking, painstaking, strenuous, energetic.

hard at work, on the stretch.

Adv. laboriously &c. adj.; lustily; with -might and main, - all one's might, - a strong hand, - sledge-hammer, - much ado; to the best of one's abilities, totis viribus, vi et armis, manibus pedibusque, tooth and nail, unguibus et rostro, hammer and tongs, heart and soul; through thick and thin &c. (perseverance) 604a.

by the sweat of one's brow, suo Marte.

day of rest, dies non, Sabbath, Lord's day, holiday, red-letter day, vacation, recess.

V. repose; rest, - and be thankful; take -rest, - one's ease.

relax, unbend, slacken; take breath &c. (refresh) 689; rest upon one's oars; pause &c. (cease) 142; stay one's hand.

lie down; recline, - on a bed of down, - on an easy chair; go to -rest, - bed, - sleep &c. 683.

take a holiday, shut up shop; lie fallow &c. (inaction) 681.

Adj. reposing &c. v.; unstrained.

Adv. at rest.

---

688. Fatigue.—**N.** fatigue; weariness &c. 841; yawning, drowsiness &c. 683; lassitude, tiredness, fatigation, exhaustion; sweat.

anhelation, shortness of breath, pant-faintness; collapse, prostration.

689. Refreshment.—**N.** bracing &c. v.; recovery of -strength &c. 159; restoration, revival &c. 660; repair, refection, refocillation, refreshment, regalement, bait; relief &c. 834.

V. brace &c. (strengthen) 159; rein-

swoon, fainting, *deliquium*, syncope, lipothymy.

V. be -fatigued &c. *adj.*; yawn &c. (*get sleepy*) 683; droop, sink, flag; lose -breath, – wind; gasp, pant, puff, blow, drop, swoon, faint, succumb.

fatigue, tire, weary, bore, irk, fag, jade, harass, exhaust, knock up, wear out, prostrate.

tax, task, strain; over-task, -work, -burden, -tax, -strain.

Adj. fatigued &c. *v.*; weary &c. 841; drowsy &c. 683; drooping &c. *v.*; haggard; toil-, way-worn; footsore, surbated, weatherbeaten; faint; done –, used –, knocked- up; exhausted, prostrate, spent; over-tired, -spent, -fatigued; forspent; unre-freshed, -stored.

worn, – out; battered, shattered, pulled down, seedy, altered.

breath-, wind-less; short of –, out of -breath, – wind; blown, puffing and blowing; short-breathed; anhelous; broken-, short-winded.

ready to drop, more dead than alive, dog -tired, – weary, walked off one's legs, tired to death, on one's last legs, played out, *hors de combat.*

fatiguing &c. *v.*; tire-, irk-, weari-some; weary; trying.

vigorate; air, freshen up, refresh, recruit; repair &c. (*restore*) 660; fan, refocillate.

breathe, respire; draw –, take –, gather –, take a long –, regain –, re-cover- breath; get better, raise one's head; recover –, regain –, renew- one's strength &c. 159; perk up.

come to oneself &c. (*revive*) 660; feel like a giant refreshed.

Adj. refreshing &c. *v.*; recuperative &c. 660.

refreshed &c. *v.*; un-tired, -wearied.

---

690. Agent.—**N.** doer, actor, agent, performer, perpetrator, operator; execu-tor, -trix; practitioner, worker, stager.

bee, ant, working bee, labouring oar, shaft horse, servant –, maid-of all work, general servant, factotum.

workman, artisan; crafts-, handicrafts-man; mechanic, operative; working –, labouring- man; hewers of wood and drawers of water, labourer, navvy; hand, man, day labourer, journeyman, hack; mere -tool &c. ˉ33; porter, docker, stevedore, beast of burden, drudge, fag.

maker, artificer, artist, wright, manufacturer, architect, contractor, builder, mason, bricklayer, smith, forger, Vulcan; black-, tin-smith; carpenter; ganger, platelayer.

machinist, mechanician, engineer, electrician, plumber, gasfitter &c.

semp-, sem-, seam-stress; needle-, char-, work-woman; tailor, cord-wainer.

minister &c. (*instrument*) 631; servant &c. 746; representative &c; (*commissioner*) 758, (*deputy*) 759.

co-worker, fellow-worker, party to, participator in, co-operator, col-league, associate, collaborator, *particeps criminis, dramatis personæ; personnel.*

Phr. '*quorum pars magna fui.*'

---

691. Workshop.—**N.** work-shop, -house; laboratory; manufactory, mill, factory, armoury, arsenal, mint, forge, loom; cabinet, studio, *bureau, atelier*; hive, – of industry; nursery; hot-house, -bed; kitchen, kitchenette; dock, -yard; slip, yard, wharf; found-ry, -ery; furnace; vineyard, orchard, farm, kitchen garden.

melting pot, crucible, alembic, caldron, mortar, *matrix.*

2°. *Complex Voluntary Action*

692. Conduct.—N. dealing, transaction &c. (*action*) 680; business &c. 625.

tactics, game, policy, polity; general-, statesman-, seaman-ship; strate-gy, -gics; plan &c. 626.

husbandry; house-keeping, -wifery; stewardship; *ménage*; regimen, *régime*; econom-y, -ics; political economy; management; government &c. (*direction*) 693.

execution, manipulation, treatment, campaign, career, life, course, walk, race.

conduct; behaviour; de-, com-portment; carriage, *maintien*, demeanour, guise, bearing, manner, mien, air, observance.

course –, line- of -conduct, – action, – proceeding; *rôle*; process, ways, practice, procedure, *modus operandi*; method &c., path &c. 627.

V. transact, execute; des-, dis-patch; proceed with, discharge; carry -on, – through, – out, – into effect; work out; go –, get- through; enact; put into practice; officiate &c. 625.

behave –, comport –, demean –, carry -, bear –, conduct –, acquit-oneself.

run a race, lead a life, play a game; take –, adopt- a course; steer –, shape- one's course; play one's- -part, – cards; shift for oneself; paddle one's own canoe.

conduct; manage &c. (*direct*) 693.

deal –, have to do- with; treat, handle a case; take -steps, – measures.

Adj. conducting &c. *v.*; strategical, business-like, practical, economic, executive.

693. Direction.—N. direction; manage-ment, -ry; government, guber-, nation, conduct, legislation, regulation, guidance; steer-, pilot-age; reins, – of government; helm, rudder, controls, joy stick, needle, compass, binnacle; guiding –, load –, lode –, pole- star; cynosure.

super-vision, -intendence; *surveillance*, oversight; eye of the master; control, charge, auspices; board of control &c. (*council*) 696; command &c. (*authority*) 737.

premier-, senator-ship; director &c. 694; chair, seat, portfolio. statesmanship; state-, king-craft.

minis-try, -tration; administration; steward-, proctor-ship; agency.

V. direct, manage, govern, conduct; order, prescribe, cut out work for; head, lead; lead –, show- the way; take the lead, lead on; regulate, guide, steer, pilot; take –, be at- the helm; have –, handle –, hold –, take- the reins, handle the ribbons; drive, tool; tackle.

super-intend, -vise; overlook, control, keep in order, look after, see to, oversee, legislate for; administer, ministrate; patronize; have the -care, – charge- of; have –, take- the direction; pull the -strings, – wires; rule &c. (*command*) 737; have –, hold- -office, – the portfolio; preside, – at the board; take –, occupy –, be in- the chair; pull the stroke oar.

Adj. directing &c. *v.*; executive, supervisory, hegemonic.

Adv. at the -helm, – head of, in charge of; under the auspices of.

694. Director.—N. director, manager, governor, rector, comptroller; super-intendent, -visor; intendant; over-seer, -looker; foreman, boss, straw boss; supercargo, husband, inspector, visitor, ranger, surveyor, ædile, moderator, monitor, taskmaster; master &c. 745; leader, ring-leader, demagogue, corypheus, conductor, fugleman, precentor, bell-wether, agitator.

guiding star &c. (*guidance*) 693; adviser &c. 695; guide &c. (*information*) 527; pilot; helmsman; steers-man, -mate; man at the wheel; wire-puller;

driver, whip. Jehu, charioteer; coach-, car-, cab-man, jarvey; postilion, *vetturino*, muleteer, teamster; whipper in; engineer, engine driver, motorman, *chauffeur*.

head, – man; principal, president, speaker; chair, -man; captain &c. (*master*) 745; superior; dean; mayor &c. (*civil authority*) 745; vice-president, prime minister, premier, vizier, grand vizier; dictator.

officer, functionary, minister, official, red-tapist, bureaucrat; man –, Jack- in office; office-bearer; person in authority &c. 745.

statesman, strategist, legislator, lawgiver, politician, administrator, statist, statemonger; Minos, Draco; arbiter &c. (*judge*) 967; king maker, power behind the throne.

board &c. (*council*) 696.

secretary, – of state; Reis Effendi; vicar &c. (*deputy*) 759; steward, factor; agent &c. 758; bailiff, middleman; ganger, clerk of works; landreeve; factotum, major-domo, seneschal, housekeeper, shepherd, *croupier*; proctor, procurator, curator, librarian.

Adv. *ex officio*.

695. Advice.—**N.** advice, counsel, adhortation; word to the wise; suggestion, submonition, recommendation, advocacy, consultation.

exhortation &c. (*persuasion*) 615; expostulation &c. (*dissuasion*) 616; admonition &c. (*warning*) 668; guidance &c. (*direction*) 693.

instruction, charge, injunction.

adviser, prompter; counsel, -lor; monitor, mentor, Nestor, *magnus Apollo*, senator; teacher &c. 540.

guide, manual, chart &c. (*information*) 527.

physician, leech, archiater; arbiter &c. (*judge*) 967.

refer-ence, -ment; consultation, conference, parley, *pourparler* &c. 696.

V. advise, counsel; give -advice, – counsel, – a piece of advice; suggest, prompt, submonish, recommend, prescribe, advocate; exhort &c. (*persuade*) 615.

enjoin, enforce, charge, instruct, call; call upon &c. (*request*) 765; dictate.

expostulate &c. (*dissuade*) 616; admonish &c. (*warn*) 668.

advise with; lay heads –, consult- together; compare notes; hold a council, deliberate, be closeted with.

confer, consult, refer to, call in; take –, follow- advice; follow implicitly; be advised by, have at one's elbow, take one's cue from.

Adj. recommendatory; hortative &c. (*persuasive*) 615; dehortatory &c. (*dissuasive*) 616; admonitory &c. (*warning*) 668; consultative.

Int. go to!

696. Council.—**N.** council, committee, subcommittee, *comitia*, court, chamber, cabinet, board, bench, staff; consultation.

senate, *senatus*, parliament, House, – of Lords, – Peers, – Commons, legislature, legislative assembly, federal council, chamber of deputies, directory, *Reichsrath*, *rigsdag*, *cortes*, storthing, witenagemote, *junta*, divan, *musnud*, *sanhedrim*, Amphictyonic council; *duma*, *zemstvo*, *soviet*, *cheka*, *ogpu*; *Dail Eireann*; caput, consistory, chapter, syndicate; court of appeal &c. (*tribunal*) 966; Doard of -control, – works; vestry; county –, borough –, district –, parish –, town- council, local board.

cabinet –, privy- council, royal commission; cockpit, convocation, synod, congress, congregation, convention, diet, states-general, aulic council.

League of Nations, assembly, *caucus*, conclave, *clique*, conventicle; meeting, sitting, *séance*, conference, session, hearing, palaver, *pourparler*, *durbar*, pow-wow, house; *quorum*.

senator; member, – of parliament; councillor, M.P., representative of the people.

Adj. senatorial, curule, parliamentary.

697. Precept.—N. precept, direction, instruction, charge; prescript, -ion; *recipe*, receipt; golden rule; maxim &c. 496.

commandment, rule, ruling, canon, law, code, *corpus juris*, *lex scripta*, common –, unwritten –, canon-law; the Ten Commandments; act, statute, convention, rubric, stage direction, regulation; form, -ula, -ulary; technicality; nice point.

order &c. (*command*) 741.

698. Skill.—N. skill, skilfulness, address; dexter-ity, -ousness; adroitness, expertness &c. *adj.*; proficiency, competence, craft, callidity, facility, knack, trick, sleight; master-y, -ship; excellence, panurgy; ambidext-erity, -rousness; sleight of hand &c. (*deception*) 545.

sea-, air-, marks-, horse-manship; tight-, rope-dancing.

accomplish-, acquire-, attain-ment; art, science; techn-icality, -ology, -ique; practical –, technical- knowledge; technocracy; finish, technic.

knowledge of the world, world wisdom, *savoir-faire*; tact; mother wit &c. (*sagacity*) 498; discretion &c. (*caution*) 864; *finesse*; craftiness &c. (*cunning*) 702; management &c. (*conduct*) 692; *ars celare artem*; self-help.

cleverness, talent, ability, ingenuity, capacity, parts, talents, faculty, endowment, *forte*, turn, gift, genius, flair, feeling; intelligence &c. 498; sharpness, readiness &c. (*activity*) 682; invention &c. 515; apt-ness, -itude; turn –, capacity –, genius- for; felicity, capability, *curiosa felicitas*, qualification, habilitation.

proficient &c. 700.

masterpiece, *coup de maître*, *chef-d'œuvre*, *tour de force*; good stroke &c. (*plan*) 626.

V. be -skilful &c. *adj.*; excel in, be master of; have -a turn for &c. *n.*

know -what's what, – a hawk from a handsaw, – what one is about, – on

699. Unskilfulness.—N. unskilfulness &c. *adj.*; want of -skill &c. 698; incompeten-ce, -cy; in-ability, -felicity, -dexterity, -experience; clumsiness; disqualification, unproficiency; quackery.

folly, stupidity &c. 499; indiscretion &c. (*rashness*) 863; thoughtlessness &c. (*inattention*) 458, (*neglect*) 460.

mis-management, -conduct; impolicy; maladministration; mis-rule, -government, -application, -direction, -feasance.

absence of rule, rule of thumb; bungling &c. *v.*; failure &c. 732; screw loose; too many cooks.

blunder &c. (*mistake*) 495; *étourderie*, *gaucherie*, act of folly, *balourdise*; botch, -ery; bad job, sad work.

sprat sent out to catch a whale, much ado about nothing, wildgoose chase.

bungler &c. 701; fool &c. 501.

layman, amateur.

V. be -unskilful &c. *adj.*; not see an inch beyond one's nose; blunder, bungle, boggle, fumble, muff, botch, bitch, flounder, loppet, stumble, trip; hobble &c. 275; put one's foot in it; make a -mess, – hash, – sad work- of; overshoot the mark.

play -tricks with, – Puck; mismanage, -conduct, -direct, -apply, -send.

stultify –, make a fool of –, commit-oneself; act foolishly; play the fool; put oneself out of court; lose one's -head, – cunning.

begin at the wrong end; do things

which side one's bread is buttered, – what's o'clock, – a thing or two; have cut one's -eye, – wisdom- teeth.

see -one's way, – where the wind lies, – which way the wind blows; have -all one's wits about one, – one's hand in; *savoir-vivre*; *scire quid valeant humeri quid ferre recusent.*

look after the main chance; cut one's coat according to one's cloth; live by one's wits; exercise one's discretion, feather the oar, sail near the wind; stoop to conquer &c. (*cunning*) 702; play one's -cards well, – best card; hit the right nail on the head, put the saddle on the right horse.

take advantage of, make the most of; profit by &c. (*use*) 677; make a hit &c. (*succeed*) 731; make a virtue of necessity; make hay while the sun shines &c. (*occasion*) 134.

Adj. skilful, dexterous, adroit, expert, apt, slick, handy, quick, deft, ready, resourceful, gain; smart &c. (*active*) 682; proficient, good at, up to, at home in, master of, a good hand at, *au fait,* thoroughbred, masterly, crack, accomplished; conversant &c. (*knowing*) 490.

experienced, practised, skilled; up –, well up- in; in -practice, – proper cue; competent, efficient, qualified, capable, fitted, fit for, up to the mark, trained, initiated, prepared, primed, finished.

clever, able, ingenious, felicitous, gifted, talented, endowed, cute, inventive &c. 515; shrewd, sharp &c. (*intelligent*) 498; cunning &c. 702; alive to, up to snuff, not to be caught with chaff; discreet.

neat-handed, fine-fingered, ambidextrous, sure-footed; cut out –, fitted-for.

technical, artistic, scientific, dædalian, shipshape; workman-, business-, statesman-like.

Adv. skillfully &c. *adj.*; well &c. 618; artistically; with -skill, – consummate skill; *secundum artem, suo Marte;* to the best of one's abilities &c. (*exertion*) 686; like a machine.

---

by halves &c. (*not complete*) 730; make two bites of a cherry; play at cross purposes; strain at a gnat and swallow a camel &c. (*caprice*) 608; put the cart before the horse; lock the stable door when the horse is stolen &c. (*too late*) 135.

not know -what one is about, – one's own interest, – on which side one's bread is buttered; stand in one's own light, quarrel with one's bread and butter, throw a stone in one's own garden, kill the goose which lays the golden eggs, pay dear for one's whistle, cut one's own throat, burn one's fingers; knock –, run- one's head against a stone wall; fall into a trap, catch a Tartar, bring the house about one's ears; have too many -eggs in one basket (*imprudent*) 863, – irons in the fire.

mistake &c. 495; take the shadow for the substance &c. (*credulity*) 486; be in the wrong box, aim at a pigeon and kill a crow; take –, get- the wrong sow by the ear, – the dirty end of the stick; put -the saddle on the wrong horse, – a square peg into a round hole, – new wine into old bottles.

cut a whetstone with a razor; hold a farthing candle to the sun &c. (*useless*) 645; fight with –, grasp at- a shadow; catch at straws, lean on a broken reed, reckon without one's host, pursue a wildgoose chase; go on a fool's –, sleeveless- errand; go further and fare worse; loose –, miss- one's way; fail &c. 732.

Adj. un-skilful &c. 698; unskilled, inexpert; bungling &c. *v.*; awkward, clumsy, unhandy, lubberly, *gauche, maladroit*; left-, heavy-handed; slovenly, slatternly; gawky.

adrift, at fault.

in-, un-apt; inhabile; un-tractable, -teachable; giddy &c. (*inattentive*) 458; inconsiderate &c. (*neglectful*) 460; stupid &c. 499; inactive &c. 683; incompetent; un-, dis-, ill-qualified; unfit; quackish; raw, green, inexperienced, rusty, out of practice.

un-accustomed, -used, -trained &c. 537, -initiated, -conversant &c. (*ignorant*) 491; shiftless; unbusinesslike, unpractical; unstatesmanlike.

un-, ill-, mis-advised; ill-devised, -imagined, -judged, -contrived, -conducted; un-, mis-guided; misconducted, foolish, wild; infelicitous; penny wise and pound foolish &c. (*inconsistent*) 608.

Phr. one's fingers being all thumbs; the right hand forgets its cunning.

il se noyerait dans une goutte d'eau.

incidit in Scyllam qui vult vitare Charybdim; out of the frying pan into the fire.

---

700. Proficient.—N. proficient, expert, adept, dab; *connoisseur* &c. (*scholar*) 492; master, -hand; topsawyer, *prima donna*, first fiddle, *cordon bleu*; protagonist; past master; profess-or, -ional, specialist.

picked man; medallist, prizeman.

veteran; old -stager, – campaigner, – soldier, – file, – hand; man of -business, – the world.

nice –, good –, clean- hand; practised –, experienced- -eye, – hand; marksman; good –, dead –, crack- shot; rope-dancer, funambulist, acrobat, contortionist; cunning man; conjuror &c. (*deceiver*) 548; wizard &c. 994.

genius; master-mind, – head, – spirit; cunning –, sharp -blade, – fellow; jobber; cracksman &c. (*thief*) 792; politician, tactician, diplomat, -ist, strategist.

pantologist, admirable Crichton, Jack of all trades; prodigy of learning; walking encyclopædia; mine of information.

701. Bungler.—N. bungler; blunderer, -head; marplot, fumbler, lubber, lout, oaf, duffer, stick, clown; bad –, poor- -hand, – shot; butter-fingers.

no conjuror, flat, muff, slow coach, looby, lubber, swab; clod, yokel, hick, awkward squad, novice, greenhorn, jaywalker, *blanc-bec*.

land lubber; fresh water –, fair weather- sailor; horse-marine; fish out of water, ass in lion's skin, jackdaw in peacock's feathers; quack &c. (*deceiver*) 548; Lord of Misrule.

sloven, slattern, trapes.

Phr. *il n'a pas inventé la poudre*; h · will never set the Thames on fire.

---

702. Cunning.—N. cunning, craft; cunningness, craftiness &c. *adj.*; subtlety, artificiality; manœuvring &c. *v.*; temporization; circumvention.

chicane, -ry; sharp practice, knavery, jugglery; concealment &c. 528; nigger in the woodpile; guile, duplicity &c. (*falsehood*) 544; foul play.

diplomacy, politics; Machiavellism; jobbery, back-stairs influence, gerrymandering.

art, -ifice; device, machination; plot &c. (*plan*) 626; manœuvre, stratagem, dodge, artful dodge, wile; trick, -ery &c. (*deception*) 545; *ruse, – de guerre*; *finesse*, side-blow, thin end of the wedge, shift, go by, subterfuge, evasion; white lie &c. (*untruth*) 546; juggle, *tour de force*; tricks -of the trade, – upon travellers; imposture, deception; *espièglerie*; net, trap &c. 545.

Ulysses, Machiavel, sly boots, fox,

703. Artlessness.—N. artlessness &c. *adj.*; nature, simplicity; innocence &c. 946; *bonhomie, naïveté, abandon*, candour, sincerity; singleness of -purpose, – heart; honesty &c. 939; plain speaking; *épanchement.*

rough diamond, matter of fact man; *le palais de vérité; enfant terrible.*

V. be -artless &c. *adj.*; look one in the face; wear one's heart upon his sleeve for daws to peck at; think aloud; speak -out, – one's mind; be free with one, call a spade a spade.

Adj. artless, natural, pure, native, simple, plain, inartificial, untutored, unsophisticated, *ingénue*, unaffected, *naïve*; sincere, frank; open, – as day; candid, ingenuous, guileless, unsuspicious, childlike; honest &c. 939; innocent &c. 946; Arcadian; undesigning, straightforward, unreserved, unvarnished, above-board; simple-, single-

reynard; Scotch-, Yorkshire-man; Jew, Greek, Yankee; intriguer, *intrigant,* schemer, trickster.

V. be -cunning &c. *adj.*; have cut one's eye-teeth; contrive &c. *(plan)* 626; live by one's wits; manœuvre; intrigue, gerrymander, *finesse,* double, temporize, stoop to conquer, *reculer pour mieux sauter,* circumvent, steal a march upon; overreach &c. 545; throw off one's guard; surprise &c. 508; out-do, get the better of, snatch from under one's nose; snatch a verdict; waylay, undermine, introduce the thin end of the wedge; play -a deep game, - tricks with; have an axe to grind; *spargere voces in vulgum ambiguas;* flatter, make things pleasant.

Adj. cunning, crafty, artful; skilful &c. 698; subtle, feline, vulpine; cunning as a -fox, - serpent; deep, - laid; profound; designing, contriving; intriguing &c. *v.*; strategic, diplomatic, politic, Machiavellian, time-serving; artificial; trick-y, -sy; wily, sly, slim, insidious, stealthy, foxy; underhand &c. *(hidden)* 528; subdolous; deceitful &c. 545; double-tongued, -faced; shifty; crooked; arch, pawky, shrewd, acute; sharp, - as a needle; canny, astute, leery, knowing, up to snuff, too clever by half, not to be caught with chaff.

Adv. cunningly &c. *adj.*; slily, on the sly, by a side wind.

Phr. diamond cut diamond.

minded; frank-, open-, single-, simple-hearted; open and above-board.

free-, plain-, out-spoken; blunt, downright, direct, matter of fact, unpoetical; unflattering.

Adv. in plain -words, - English; without mincing the matter; not to mince the matter &c. *(affirmation)* 535.

Phr. *Davus sum non Œdipus; liberavi animam meam.*

Section IV. ANTAGONISM

1°. *Conditional Antagonism*

704. Difficulty.—N. difficulty; hardness &c. *adj.*; impracticability &c. *(impossibility)* 471; tough -, hard -, uphill- work; hard -, Herculean -, Augean- task; task of Sisyphus, Sisyphean labour, tough job, teaser, rasper, dead lift.

dilemma, embarrassment; perplexity &c. *(uncertainty)* 475; involvement; intricacy; entanglement &c. 59; cross fire; awkwardness, delicacy, ticklish card to play, deadlock, knot, Gordian knot, *dignus vindice nodus,* net, meshes, maze; coil &c. *(convolution)* 248; crooked path.

nice -, delicate -, subtle -, knotty-point; vexed question, *vexata quæstio* poser; puzzle &c. *(riddle)* 533; paradox; hard -, nut to crack; bone to pick, *crux, pons asinorum,* where the shoe pinches.

nonplus, quandary, strait, pass, pinch, pretty pass, stress, brunt; criti-

705. Facility. — N. facility, ease; easiness &c. *adj.*; capability; feasibility &c. *(practicability)* 470; flexibility, pliancy &c. 324; smoothness &c. 255; convenience.

plain -, smooth -, straight- sailing; mere child's play, holiday task.

smooth water, fair wind; smooth - royal- road; clear -coast, - stage; *tabula rasa;* full play &c. *(freedom)* 748.

disen-cumbrance, -tanglement; de-oppilation; permission &c. 760.

V. be -easy &c. *adj.*; go on -, run-smoothly; have -full play &c. *n.*; go -, run- on all fours; obey the helm, work well.

flow -, swim -, drift -, go- with the--stream, - tide; see one's way; have -it all one's own way, - the game in one's own hands; walk over the course, win -at a canter, - hands down; make -light of, - nothing of; be at home in &c. *(skilful)* 698.

cal situation, crisis; trial, rub, emergency, exigency, scramble.

scrape, hobble, slough, quagmire, hot water, hornet's nest; sea –, peck- of troubles; pretty kettle of fish; pickle, stew, *imbroglio*, mess, muddle, botch, fuss, bustle, ado; false position; set fast, stand; dead -lock, – set; fix, horns of a dilemma, *cul de sac*; hitch; stumbling block &c. (*hindrance*) 706.

V. be -difficult &c. *adj.*; run one hard, go against the grain, try one's patience, put one out; put to one's -shifts, – wit's end; go hard with –, try- one; pose, perplex &c. (*uncertain*) 475; bother, nonplus, gravel, bring to a dead lock; be -impossible &c. 471; be in the way of &c. (*hinder*) 706.

meet with –, labour under –, get into –, plunge into –, struggle with –, contend with –, grapple with- difficulties; labour under a disadvantage; be -in difficulty &c. *adj.*

fish in troubled waters, buffet the waves, swim against the stream, scud under bare poles.

have -much ado with, – a hard time of it; come to the -push, – pinch; bear the brunt.

grope in the dark, lose one's way, weave a tangled web, walk among eggs.

get into a -scrape &c. *n.*; bring a hornet's nest about one's ears; be put to one's shifts; flounder, boggle, struggle; not know which way to turn &c. (*uncertain*) 475; get -tangled up, – wound up; *perdre son latin*; stick - at, – in the mud, – fast; come to a -stand, – dead lock; hold the wolf by the ears.

render -difficult &c. *adj.*; encumber, embarrass, ravel, entangle; put a spoke in the wheel &c. (*hinder*) 706; lead a pretty dance.

Adj. difficult, not easy, hard, tough; trouble-, toil-, irk-some; operose, laborious, onerous, arduous, Herculean, formidable; sooner –, more easily- said than done; difficult –, hard- to deal with; ill-conditioned, crabbed; not -to be handled with kid gloves, – made with rosewater.

awkward, unwieldy, unmanageable; intractable, stubborn &c. (*obstinate*) 606; perverse, refractory, plaguy, trying, thorny, rugged; knot-ted, -ty; invious; path-, track-less; labyrinthine &c. (*convoluted*) 248; intricate, complicated &c. (*tangled*) 59; impracticable &c. (*impossible*) 471; not -feasible &c. 470; desperate &c. (*hopeless*) 859.

embarrassing, perplexing &c. (*uncertain*) 475; delicate, ticklish,

render -easy &c. *adj.*; facilitate, smooth, ease; popularize; lighten, – the labour; free, clear; dis-encumber, -embarrass, -entangle, -engage; deobstruct, unclog, extricate, unravel; untie –, cut- the knot; disburden, unload, exonerate, emancipate, free from, deoppilate; humour &c. (*aid*) 707; lubricate &c. 332; relieve &c. 834.

leave -a hole to creep out of, – a loophole, – the matter open; give -the reins to, – full play, – full swing; make way for; open the -door to, – way; prepare –, smooth –, clear- the -ground, – way, – path, – road; pave the way, bridge over; permit &c. 760.

Adj. easy, facile; feasible &c. (*practicable*) 470; easily -managed, – accomplished; within reach, accessible, easy of access, for the million, open to.

manageable, wieldy; towardly, tractable; submissive; yielding, ductile; pliant &c. (*soft*) 324; glib, slippery; smooth &c. 255; on -friction wheels, – velvet; convenient.

un-, dis-burdened, -encumbered, -embarrassed; exonerated; un-loaded, -obstructed, -trammelled, - impeded, -restrained &c. (*free*) 748; at ease, light.

at –, quite at- home; in -one's element, – smooth water.

Adv. easily &c. *adj.*; readily, smoothly, swimmingly, *ad lib.*, on easy terms, single-handed.

Phr. touch and go.

Int. all clear!

critical; beset with –, full of –, surrounded by –, entangled by –, encompassed with- difficulties.

under a difficulty; in -difficulty, – hot water, – the suds, – a cleft stick, – a fix, – the wrong box, – a scrape &c. *n.*, – deep water, – a fine pickle; *in extremis*; between -two stools, – Scylla and Charybdis; surrounded by -shoals, – breakers, – quicksands; at cross purposes; not out of the wood.

reduced to straits; hard –, sorely- pressed; run hard; pinched, put to it, straitened; hard -up, – put to it, – set; put to one's shifts; puzzled, at a loss &c. *(uncertain)* 475; at -the end of one's tether, – one's wit's end, – a nonplus, – a standstill; gravelled, nonplussed, stranded, aground; stuck –, set- fast; up a tree, at bay, *aux abois*, driven -into a corner, – from post to pillar, – to extremity, – to one's wit's end, – to the wall; *au bout de son latin*; out of one's -depth, – reckoning; put –, thrown -out.

accomplished with difficulty; hard-fought, -earned.

Adv. with -difficulty, – much ado; hardly &c. *adj.*; uphill; against the -stream, – grain; *à rebours*; *invitâ Minervâ*; in the teeth of; at –, upon- a pinch; at long odds.

Phr. ay there's the rub; *hic labor hoc opus*; things are come to a pretty pass.

2°. *Active Antagonism*

706. Hindrance. — N. prevention, preclusion, obstruction, stoppage; prohibition; inter-ruption, -ception, -clusion; hindrance, impedition; retardment, -ation; constriction; embarrassment, oppilation; coarctation, stricture, restriction; anchor &c. 666; restraint &c. 751 & 752; inhibition &c. 761; blockade &c. *(closure)* 261; picketing.

inter-ference, -position; obtrusion; dis-couragement, -countenance, -approval, -approbation; opposition &c. 708.

impediment, let, obstacle, obstruction, knot, knag; check, hitch, *contretemps, impasse,* screw loose, grit in the oil.

bar, stile, barrier; turn-stile, -pike; gate, portcullis; bulwark, parapet, barricade &c. *(defence)* 717; wall, dead wall, breakwater, groyne; bulkhead, block, buffer; stopper &c. 263; boom, dam, weir, burrock.

drawback, objection; stumbling-block, -stone; lion in the path; snag; snags and sawyers.

en-, in-cumbrance; clog, skid, shoe, spoke; brake, drag, – chain, – weight; stay, stop; preventive, prophylactic; contraception; load, burden, fardel,

707. Aid.—N. aid, -ance; assistance, help, opitulation, succour; support, lift, advance, furtherance, promotion; coadjuvancy &c. *(co-operation)* 709.

patronage, championship, countenance, favour, interest, advocacy, auspices.

sustentation, subvention, subsidy, bounty, alimentation, nutrition, nourishment, maintenance; manna in the wilderness; food &c. 298; means &c. 632.

ministr-y, -ation; subministration; accommodation.

relief, rescue; help at a dead lift; supernatural aid; *deus ex machinâ*.

supplies, reinforcements, succours, contingents, recruits; support &c. *(physical)* 215; adjunct, ally &c. *(helper)* 711.

V. aid, assist, help, succour, lend one's aid; come to the aid &c. *n.*- of; contribute, subscribe to; bring –, give –, furnish –, afford –, supply- -aid &c. *n.*; render assistance; give –, stretch –, lend –, bear –, hold out- a -hand, – helping hand; give one a -lift, – cast, – turn; take -by the hand, – in tow; help a lame dog over a stile, lend wings to.

onus, millstone round one's neck, *impedimenta*; dead weight; lumber, pack; nightmare, Ephialtes, incubus, old man of the sea; remora.

difficulty &c. 704; insuperable &c. 471- obstacle; estoppel; ill wind; head wind &c. (*opposition*) 708; trammel, tether &c. (*means of restraint*) 752; hold back, counterpoise; damper, wet blanket, hinderer, marplot, kill-joy, dog in the manger, interloper; trail of a red herring; opponent &c. 710.

V. hinder, impede, impedite, embarrass.

keep -, stave -, ward- off; picket; obviate; a-, ante-vert; turn aside, draw off, prevent, forefend, nip in the bud; retard, slacken, check, let; counter-act, -check; preclude, debar, foreclose, estop; inhibit &c. 761; shackle &c. (*restrain*) 751; restrict, restrain, cohibit.

obstruct, filibuster, stop, stay, bar, bolt, lock; block, - up; belay, barricade; block -, stop- the way; dam up &c. (*close*) 261; put on the -brake &c. *n.*; scotch -, lock -, put a spoke in- the wheel; put a stop to &c. 142; traverse, contravene; inter-rupt, -cept; oppose &c. 708; hedge -in, - round; cut off; interclude.

inter-pose, -fere, -meddle &c. 682.

cramp, hamper; clog, - the wheels; cumber; en-, in-cumber; handicap; choke; saddle -, load- with; over-load, -lay; lumber, trammel, tie one's hands, put to inconvenience; in-, discommode; discompose; hustle, drive into a corner; choke off.

run -, fall- foul of; cross the path of, break in upon.

thwart, frustrate, disconcert, balk, foil, baffle, snub, override, circumvent; defeat &c. 731; spike guns &c. (*render useless*) 645; spoil, mar, clip the wings of; cripple &c. (*injure*) 659; put an extinguisher on; damp; dishearten &c. (*dissuade*) 616; discountenance, throw cold water on, spoil sport; lay -, throw- a wet blanket on; cut the ground from under one, take the wind out of one's sails, undermine; be -, stand- in the way of; act as a drag; hang like a millstone round one's neck.

relieve, rescue; set -up, - agoing, - on one's legs; bear -, pull- through; give new life to, be the making of; reinforce, recruit; set -, put -, push-forward; give -a lift, - a shove, - an impulse- to; promote, further, forward, advance; speed, expedite, quicken, hasten.

support, sustain, uphold, prop, hold up, bolster.

cradle, nourish; nurture, nurse, dry nurse, suckle, put out to nurse; manure, cultivate, force; foster, cherish, foment; feed -, fan- the flame.

serve; do service to, tender to, pander to; ad-, sub-, minister to; tend, attend, wait on; take care of &c. 459; entertain; smooth the bed of death.

oblige, accommodate, consult the wishes of; humour, cheer, encourage; second, stand by; back, - up; pay the piper, abet; work -, make interest -, stick up -, take up the cudgels- for; take up -, espouse -, adopt- the cause of; advocate, beat up for recruits, press into the service; squire, give moral support to, keep in countenance, countenance, patronize; lend -oneself, - one's countenance- to; smile -, shine-upon; favour, befriend, take up, take in hand, enlist under the banners of; side with &c. (*co-operate*) 709.

be of use to; subserve &c. (*instrument*) 631; benefit &c. 648; render a service &c. (*utility*) 644; conduce &c. (*tend*) 176.

Adj. aiding &c. *v.*; auxiliary, adjuvant, helpful; coadjuvant &c. 709; subservient, ministrant, ancillary, accessory, subsidiary.

at one's beck; friendly, amicable, favourable, propitious, well-disposed; neighbourly; obliging &c. (*benevolent*) 906.

Adv. with -, by- -the aid &c. *n.*- of; on -, in- behalf of; in -aid, - the service, - the name, - favour, - furtherance- of; on account of; for the sake of, on the part of; *non obstante*.

Int. help! save us! to the rescue. SOS! *à moi!*

Adj. hindering &c. *v.*; obstr-uctive, -uent; impedi-tive, -ent; intercipient; prophylactic &c. (*remedial*) 662.

in the way of, unfavourable; onerous, burdensome; cumb-rous, -ersome; obtrusive.

hindered &c. *v.*; wind-bound, water-logged, heavy laden; hard pressed.

unassisted &c. (*see* assist &c. 707); single-handed, alone; deserted &c. 624.

708. Opposition.—N. opposition, antagonism; oppug-nancy, -nation; impugnation; contravention; counteraction &c. 179; counterplot, obstacle.

cross-fire, under-current, head-wind.

clashing, collision, conflict, lack of harmony, contest.

competition, two of a trade, rivalry, emulation, race; war to the knife.

absence of -aid &c. 707; resistance &c. 719; restraint &c. 751; hindrance &c. 706.

V. oppose, counteract, run counter to; withstand &c. (*resist*) 719; control &c. (*restrain*) 751; hinder &c. 706; antagonize, oppugn, fly in the face of, go dead against, kick against, fall foul of; set -, pit- against; face, confront, cope with; make a -stand, - dead set-against; set -oneself, one's face- against; protest -, vote -, raise one's voice-against; disfavour, turn one's back upon; set at naught, slap in the face, slam the door in one's face.

be -, play- at cross purposes; counter-work, -mine; thwart, overthwart.

stem, breast, encounter; stem -, breast- the -tide, - current, - flood; buffet the waves; beat up -, make head- against; grapple with; kick against the pricks &c. (*resist*) 719; contend &c. 720 -, do battle &c. (*warfare*) 722- -with, - against.

contra-dict, -vene; belie; go -, run -, beat -, militate- against; come in conflict with.

emulate &c. (*compete*) 720; rival, spoil one's trade.

Adj. oppos-ing, -ed &c. *v.*; adverse, antagonistic; ambivalent; contrary &c. 14; at variance &c. 24; at issue, at war with; in opposition: 'agin the Government.'

un-favourable, -friendly; hostile, inimical, cross, unpropitious.

709. Co-operation.—N. co-operation; coadju-vancy, -tancy; coagency, co-efficiency; concert, concurrence, complicity, participation; union &c. 43; amalgamation, combination &c. 48; collusion.

association, alliance, colleagueship, jointstock, copartnership, trust, cartel, pool, ring, combine, interlocking directorate; confederation &c. (*party*) 712; federation, coalition, fusion; a long pull, a strong pull and a pull all together; log-rolling, Freemasonry.

unanimity &c. (*assent*) 488; *esprit de corps*, party spirit; clan-, partisan-ship; reciprocity, concord &c. 714.

V co-operate, co-adjute, concur; conduce &c. 178; combine, cartelize, unite one's efforts; keep -, draw -, pull -, club -, hang -, hold -, league -, band -, be banded- together; stand -, put-shoulder to shoulder; act in concert, join forces, fraternize, cling to one another, conspire, concert, lay one's heads together; confederate, be in league with; collude, understand one another, play into the hands of, hunt in couples.

side -, take side -, go along -, go hand in hand -, join hands -, make common cause -, strike 'n -, unite -, join -, mix oneself up - take part -, play along -, cast in one's lot- with; join -, enter into- partnership with; rally round, follow the lead of; come to, pass over to, come into the views of; be -, row -, sail- in the same boat; sail on the same tack.

be a party to, lend oneself to; participate; have a -hand in, - finger in the pie; take -, bear- part in; second &c. (*aid*) 707; take the part of, play the game of; espouse a -cause, - quarrel.

Adj. co-operating &c. *v.*; in -co-operation &c. *n.*, - league &c. (*party*) 712;

in hostile array, front to front, with crossed bayonets, at daggers drawn; up in arms; resistant &c. 719.

competitive, emulous.

Adv. against, *versus*, counter to, in conflict with, at cross purposes.

against the -grain, – current, – stream, – wind, – tide; with a head-wind; with the wind -ahead, – in one's teeth.

coadju-vant, -tant; hand and glove with.

favourable &c. 707- to; un-opposed &c. 708.

Adv. as one man &c. (*unanimously*) 488; shoulder to shoulder; in co-operation with.

_____

in spite, in despite, in defiance; in the -way, – teeth, – face- of; across; a-, over-thwart; where the shoe pinches.

though &c. 30; even; *quand même*; *per contra*.

Phr. *nitor in adversum*.

_____

710. Opponent.—N. opponent, antagonist, adversary; adverse party, opposition; enemy &c. 891; assailant.

oppositionist, obstructive; obscurantist; brawler, wrangler, brangler, disputant, extremist, irreconcilable, diehard, bitter-ender.

malcontent; Jacobin, Fenian &c. 742; demagogue, reactionist.

passive resister, conscientious objector.

rival, competitor, contestant.

_____

711. Auxiliary.—N. auxiliary; recruit; assistant; adju-vant, -tant; adjunct; help, -er, -mate, -ing hand; midwife; colleague, partner, mate, *confrère*, co-operator; coadju-tor, -trix; collaborator.

ally; friend &c. 890, confidant, *fidus Achates*, pal, chum, buddy, *alter ego*.

confederate; ac-, complice; accessory, – after the fact; *particeps criminis*.

aide-de-camp, secretary, clerk, associate, marshal; right-hand; candle-, bottle-holder; hand-maid; servant &c. 746; puppet, cat's-paw, stooge, dependent, creature, jackal; tool, *âme damnée*; satellite, adherent, parasite.

votary, disciple; secta-rian, -ry; seconder, backer, upholder, supporter, abettor, advocate, partisan, champion, patron, friend at court, mediator.

friend in need, Jack at a pinch, *deus ex machinâ*, guardian angel, fairy godmother; special providence, tutelary genius.

712. Party.—N. party, faction, side, denomination, class, communion, set, crowd, crew, band, horde, posse, phalanx; regiment &c. 726; family, clan &c. 166.

Tories, Conservatives, Unionists, Whigs, Liberals, Radicals, Labour party, Socialists, Communists &c.; Republicans, Democrats, Farmer-Labor; *Fascisti*, Revolutionaries &c. 742.

community, body, fellowship, sodality, solidarity; con-, fraternity; sorority; brother-, sister-hood.

Freemasons, Knights Templars, Odd Fellows, Ku Klux Klan, Rosicrucians; knot, gang, *clique*, ring, circle; *coterie*, club, *casino*.

corporation, corporate body, guild; establishment, company; co-partnership; firm, house; joint concern, joint-stock company, trust, investment trust, combine &c. 709.

society, association; instit-ute, -ution; union; trade-union; league, syndicate, alliance, *Verein*, *Bund*, *Zollverein*, combination; league –, alliance- offensive and defensive; coalition; federation; confedera -tion, -cy; junto, cabal, *camarilla*, *Camorra*, *brigue*; Freemasonry; party spirit &c. (*co-operation*) 709.

[260]

staff; cast, *dramatis personæ*.
V. unite, join; club together &c. (*co-operate*) 709; cement –, form- a party &c. *n.*; associate &c. (*assemble*) 72.
Adj. in -league, – partnership, – alliance &c. *n.*
bonded –, banded –, linked &c. (*joined*) 43- together; embattled; confederated, federative, joint, corporate, leagued, fraternal, Masonic, cliquish.
Adv. hand in hand, side by side, shoulder to shoulder, *en masse*, in the same boat.

713. Discord.—N. disagreement &c. 24; dis-cord, -accord, -sidence, -sonance; jar, clash, shock; jarring, jostling &c. *v.*; screw loose.

variance, difference, dissension, misunderstanding, cross purposes, odds, *brouillerie*; division, split, rupture, disruption, division in the camp, house divided against itself, rift within the lute; disunion, breach; schism &c. (*dissent*) 489; feud, faction.

quarrel, dispute, rippet, spat, tiff, *tracasserie*, squabble, altercation, words, high words; wrangling &c. *v.*; jangle, brabble, cross questions and crooked answers, snip-snap; family jars.

polemics; litigation; strife &c. (*contention*) 720; warfare &c. 722; outbreak, open rupture; breaking off of negotiations, recall of ambassadors; declaration of war.

broil, brawl, row, racket, hubbub, rixation; embroilment, embranglement, *imbroglio, fracas*, breach of the peace, pi ce of work, scrimmage, rumpus; bree:e, squall; riot, disturbance &c. (*disorder*) 59; commotion &c. (*agitation*) 315; bear garden, Donnybrook Fair.

subject of dispute, ground of quarrel, battle ground, disputed point; bone -of contention, – to pick; apple of discord, *casus belli*; question at issue &c. (*subject of inquiry*) 461; vexed question, *vexata quæstio*, brand of discord.

troublous times; cat-and-dog life; contentiousness &c. *adj.*; enmity &c. 889; hate &c. 898; Kilkenny cats; disputant &c. 710; strange bedfellows.

V. be -discordant &c. *adj.*; disagree, come amiss &c. 24; clash, jar, jostle, pull different ways, conflict, have no measures with, misunderstand one another; live like cat and dog; differ; dissent &c. 489; have a -bone to pick, – crow to pluck- with.

fall out, quarrel, dispute; litigate; controvert &c. (*deny*) 536;

714. Concord.—N. concord, accord, harmony, symphony, homology; agreement &c. 23; sympathy &c. (*love*) 897; response; union, unison, unity; bonds of harmony; peace &c. 721; unanimity &c. (*assent*) 488; league &c. 712; happy family.

rapprochement; réunion; amity &c. (*friendship*) 888; reciprocity; alliance, *entente cordiale*, good understanding, conciliation, arbitration, peacemaker &c. 724.

V. agree &c. 23; accord, harmonize with; fraternize; be -concordant &c. *adj.*; go hand in hand; blend –, tone in- with; run parallel &c. (*concur*) 178; understand one another; pull together &c. (*co-operate*) 709; put up one's horses together, sing in chorus.

side –, sympathize –, go –, chime in –, fall in- with; come round; be pacified &c. 723; assent &c. 488; enter into the -ideas, – feelings- of; reciprocate.

hurler avec les loups; go –, swim- with the stream.

pour oil on troubled waters, keep in good humour, render accordant, put in tune; come to an understanding, meet half-way; keep the –, remain at- peace.

Adj. concordant, congenial; agreeing &c. *v.*; in- accord &c. *n.*; harmonious, united, cemented; banded together &c. 712; allied; friendly &c. 888; fraternal; conciliatory; at one with; of one mind &c. (*assent*) 488.

at peace, in still water; tranquil &c. (*pacific*) 721.

Adv. with one voice &c. (*assent*) 488; in concert with, hand in hand; on one's side, unanimously.

squabble, wrangle, jangle, brangle, bicker, nag; spar &c. (*contend*) 720; have -words &c. *n.* with; fall foul of.

split; break –, break squares –, part company- with; declare war, try conclusions; join –, put in- issue; pick a quarrel, fasten a quarrel on; sow –, stir up- -dissension &c. *n.*; embroil, estrange, entangle, disunite, widen the breach; set -at odds, – together by the ears; set –, pit- against; rub up the wrong way.

get into hot water, fish in troubled waters, brawl; kick up a -row. – dust; turn the house out of window.

Adj. discordant; disagreeing &c. *v.*; out of tune, dissonant, inharmonious, harsh, grating, jangling, ajar, on bad terms; dissentient &c. 489; inconsistent, contradictory, incongruous, discrepant; un- -reconciled, -pacified.

quarrelsome, unpacific; gladiatorial, controversial, polemic, disputatious; factious; liti-gious, -gant; pettifogging.

at odds, at loggerheads, at daggers drawn, at variance, at issue, at cross purposes, at sixes and sevens, at feud, at high words; up in arms, together by the ears, in hot water, embroiled.

torn, disunited.

Phr. *quot homines tot sententiæ*; no love lost between them, *non nostrum tantas componere lites.*

715. Defiance.—N. defiance; daring &c. *v.*; dare, challenge, *cartel*; threat &c. 909; war-cry, -whoop.

V. defy, dare, beard; brave &c. (*courage*) 861; bid defiance to; set at -defiance, – naught; hurl defiance at; dance the war dance; snap the fingers at, laugh to scorn; disobey &c. 742.

show -fight, – one's teeth, – a bold front; bluster, look big, stand akimbo; double –, shake- the fist; threaten &c. 909.

challenge, call out; throw –, fling- down the -gauntlet, – gage, – glove.

Adj. defiant; defying &c. *v.*; with arms akimbo; rebellious, insolent; reckless, greatly daring.

Adv. in -defiance, – the teeth- of; under one's very nose.

Int. do your worst! come if you dare! come on! marry come up! hoity toity!

Phr. *noli me tangere; nemo me impune lacessit.*

716. Attack.—N. attack; assault, – and battery; onset, onslaught, charge.

aggression, drive, offence; incursion, inroad, invasion; irruption; outbreak; *estrapade, ruade; coup de main*, sally, *sortie, camisade*, raid, foray; run -at, – against; dead set at.

storm, -ing; boarding, *escalade*; siege, investment, obsession, bombardment, cannonade; air raid.

fire, volley; platoon –, file –, rapid-fire; *fusillade*; sharp-shooting, sniping; broadside; raking –, cross –, machine gun- fire; volley of grapeshot, *feu d'enfer*; salvo.

cut, thrust, lunge, pass, *passado*, *carte* and *tierce*, home thrust; *coup de pied*; kick, punch &c. (*impulse*) 276.

717. Defence.—N. defence, protection. guard, ward; shielding &c. *v.*; propugnation; preservation &c. 670; guardianship.

self-defence, -preservation; resistance &c. 719.

safeguard &c. (*safety*) 664; screen &c. (*shelter*) 666, (*concealment*) 530; barrage; fortification; muni-tion, -ment; bulwark, fosse, moat, ditch, intrenchment, trench, dugout, gas mask; dike, dyke; parapet, parados, sunk fence, embankment, mound, mole, bank; earth- field-work, gabions; fence, wall, dead wall, contravallation; paling &c; (*inclosure*) 232; palisade, ha-ha, stockade, *stoccado, laager, sangar*; barri-er, -cade; boom; portcullis, *chevaux de*

[262]

battue, razzia, Jacquerie, dragonnade; devastation &c. 162.

assailant, aggressor, invader.

base of operations, point of attack.

V. attack, assault, assail; set –, fall-upon; charge, impugn, break a lance with, enter the lists.

assume –, take- the offensive; be –, become- the aggressor; strike the first blow, fire the first shot, throw the first stone at; lift a hand –, draw the sword- against; take up the cudgels; advance –, march- against; march upon, invade, harry; come on, show fight.

strike at, poke at, thrust at; aim –, deal- a blow at; give –, fetch- one a -blow, – kick; have a -cut, – shot, – fling, – shy- at; be down –, pounce-upon; fall foul of, pitch into, launch out against· bait, slap on the face; make a -thrust, – pass, – set, – dead set- at; dunt; bear down upon.

close with, come to close quarters, bring to bay.

ride full tilt against; let fly at, dash at, run a tilt at, rush at. tilt at, run at, fly at, hawk at, have at, let out at; make a -dash, – rush at; attack tooth and nail; strike home; drive –, press-one hard; be hard upon, run down, strike at the root of.

lay about one, run amuck.

fire -upon, – at, – a shot at; shoot at, pop at, level at, let off a gun at; open fire, pepper, bombard, shell, pour a broadside into; fire -a volley, – red-hot shot; spring a mine.

throw -a stone, – stones- at; stone, lapidate, pelt; hurl -at, – against, – at the head of.

beset, besiege, beleaguer; lay siege to, invest, open the trenches, plant a battery, sap, mine; storm, board, scale the walls.

cut and thrust, bayonet, butt; kick, strike &c. *(impulse)* 276; whip &c. *(punish)* 972.

Adj. attacking &c. *v.;* aggressive, offensive, obsidional.

up in arms; on the warpath; over the top.

Adv. on the offensive.

Int. 'up and at them!'

___

frise; aba-, abat-, abba-tis; *vallum,* circumvallation, battlement, rampart, scarp; e-, counter-scarp; glacis, case-mate, obstacle.

mine, countermine.

buttress, abutment; shore &c. *(support)* 215.

breastwork, *banquette,* curtain, mant-let, bastion, demilune, redan, ravelin; advanced –, horn –, out- work, lunette; barb-acan, -ican; redoubt; fort-elage, -alice; lines; coast defence.

loop-hole, machicolation; sally-port, postern gate.

hold, stronghold, fastness; asylum &c. *(refuge)* 666; keep, donjon, fort-ress, citadel; capitol, castle; tower, – of strength; fort, barracoon, pah, sconce, martello tower, peel-house, block-house, rath; wooden walls; turret, barbette.

buffer, corner-stone, fender, apron, mask, gauntlet, thimble, carapace, armour, shield, buckler; target, targe, ægis, breastplate, cuirass, plastron, habergeon, mail, coat of mail, brigan-dine, hauberk, lorication, helmet, helm, basinet, sallet, salade, heaume, morion, murrion, armet, cabaset, vizor, cas-quetel, siege-cap, head-piece, casque, steel helmet, tin hat; *Pickelhaube,* csako; shako &c. *(dress)* 225; bearskin; panoply; truncheon &c. *(weapon)* 727.

garrison, picket, piquet; defender, protector; guardian &c. *(safety)* 664; trabant, body guard, champion; knight-errant, Paladin; propugner.

V. defend, forfend, fend; shield, screen, shroud; fence round &c. *(cir-cumscribe)* 229; fence, intrench; guard &c. *(keep safe)* 664; guard against; take care of &c. *(vigilance)* 459; bear harm-less; keep –, ward –, beat- off; hinder &c. 706.

parry, repel, propugn, put to flight; give a warm reception to [*ironical*]; hold –, keep- at -bay, – arm's length.

stand –, act- on the defensive; show fight; maintain –, stand- one's ground; stand by; hold one's own; bear –, stand- the brunt; fall back upon, hold, stand in the gap.

Adj. defending &c. *v.;* defensive; mural; armed, – at all points, – *cap-à-pie,* – to the teeth; panoplied, accoutred, harnessed; iron-plated, -clad; loop-holed, castellated, machicolated, casemated; defended &c. *v.*; proof against, bomb-, bulletproof; protective.

Adv. defensively; on the -defence, – defensive; in defence; at bay, *pro aris et focis.*

Int. no surrender! *ils ne passeront pas!*

Phr. defence not defiance.

718. Retaliation. — N. retaliation, reprisal, retort; counter-stroke, -blast, -plot, -project; retribution, *lex talionis*; reciprocation &c. (*reciprocity*) 12.

requital, desert, tit for tat, give and take, blow for blow, *quid pro quo*, a Roland for an Oliver, measure for measure, an eye for an eye, diamond cut diamond, the biter bit, a game at which two can play; boomerang.

recrimination &c. (*accusation*) 938; revenge &c. 919; compensation &c. 30; reaction &c. (*recoil*) 277.

V. retaliate, retort, turn upon; pay -off, – back; pay in -one's own, – the same- coin; cap; reciprocate &c. 148; turn the tables upon, return the compliment; give -a *quid pro quo* &c. *n.*, – as much as one takes; give and take, exchange -blows, – fisticuffs; be -quits, – even- with; pay off old scores.

serve one right, be hoist on one's own petard, throw a stone in one's own garden, catch a Tartar.

Adj. retaliating &c. *v.*; retalia-tory, -tive; retributive, recriminatory, reciprocal.

Adv. in retaliation; *en revanche.*

Phr. *mutato nomine de te fabula narratur; par pari refero; tu quoque*; you're another; *suo sibi gladio hunc jugulo.*

719. Resistance. — N. resistance, stand, front, oppugnation; opposition &c. 708; renitence, reluctation, recalcitration, recalcitrance; repugnance; kicking &c. *v.*

repulse, rebuff.

insurrection &c. (*disobedience*) 742; strike; turn –, lock –, barring- out; *levée en masse, Jacquerie*; riot &c. (*disorder*) 59.

V. resist; not -submit &c. 725; repugn, reluctate, withstand; stand up –, strive –, bear up –, be proof –, make head- against; stand, – firm, – one's ground, – the brunt of, – out; hold -one's ground, – one's own, – out.

breast the -wave, – current; stem the -tide, – torrent; face, confront, grapple with; show a bold front &c. (*courage*) 861; present a front; make a –, take one's- stand.

kick, – against; recalcitrate, kick against the pricks; oppose &c. 708; fly in the face of; lift the hand against &c. (*attack*) 716; rise up in arms &c. (*war*) 722; strike, turn out; draw up a round robin &c. (*remonstrate*) 932; revolt &c. (*disobey*) 742; make a riot.

prendre le mors aux dents; take the bit between the teeth; sell one's life dearly, die hard, keep at bay; repel repulse.

Adj. resisting &c. *v.*; resist-ive, -ant; refractory &c. (*disobedient*) 742; recalcitrant, re-nitent, -pulsive, -pellant; up in arms.

proof against; unconquerable &c. (*strong*) 159; stubborn, unconquered; indomitable &c. (*persevering*) 604a; unyielding &c. (*obstinate*) 606.

Int. hands off! keep off!

720. Contention. — N. contention, strife; contest, -ation; struggle; belligerency; opposition &c. 708.

controversy, polemics; debate &c. (*discussion*) 476; war of words, logomachy, litigation; paper war, ink slinging; high words &c. (*quarrel*) 713; sparring &c. *v.*

721. Peace.—N. peace; amity &c; (*friendship*) 888; harmony &c. (*concord*) 714; tranquillity &c. (*quiescence*) 265; truce &c. (*pacification*) 723; pacificism; pipe –, calumet- of peace.

piping time of peace, quiet life; neutrality.

V. be at peace; keep the peace &c;

competition, rivalry; corrival-ry, -ship; agonism, *concours*, match, race, horse-racing, heat, steeple chase, point-to-point race, handicap; boat race, regatta; field-day; sham fight, Derby day; turf, sporting, bull-fight, tauro-machy, *gymkhana*, rodeo, Olympiad.

wrestling, *ju-jitsu*, pugilism, boxing, fisticuffs, spar, mill, set-to, scrap, round, bout. event; prize-fighting; quarter-staff, single stick; gladiatorship, gymnastics; athletic-s. – sports; games of skill &c. 840.

shindy; *fracas* &c. (*discord*) 713; clash of arms; tussle, scuffle, broil, fray; affray, -ment; velitation; col-, luctation; brabble, *brigue*, scramble, *mêlée*, scrimmage, stramash, bush-fighting.

free –, stand up –, hand to hand –, running- fight.

conflict, skirmish; ren-, en-counter; *rencontre*, collision, affair, brush, fight; battle, – royal; combat, action, engagement, joust, tournament; tilt, -ing; tourney, list; pitched battle, guerilla warfare.

death-struggle, struggle for life or death, Armageddon; hard knocks, sharp contest, tug of war.

naval -engagement, – battle; *naumachia*, sea-fight.

duel, -lo; single combat, monomachy, satisfaction, *passage d'armes*, passage of arms, affair of honour; triangular duel; hostile meeting, digladiation; appeal to arms &c. (*warfare*) 722.

deeds –, feats- of arms; pugnacity; combativeness &c. *adj.*; bone of contention &c. 713.

V. contend; contest, strive, struggle, scramble, wrestle; spar, square; exchange -blows, – fisticuffs; scrap, mix with, fib, justle, tussle, tilt, box, stave, fence; skirmish; fight &c. (*war*) 722; wrangle &c. (*quarrel*) 713.

contend &c. –, grapple –, engage –, close –, buckle –, bandy –, try conclusions –, have a brush &c. *n.* –, tilt- with; encounter, fall foul of, pitch into, clapperclaw, run a tilt at; oppose &c. 708; reluct.

join issue, come to blows, be at loggerheads, set-to, come to the scratch, exchange shots, measure swords, meet hand to hand; take up the -cudgels, – glove, – gauntlet; enter the lists; couch one's lance; give satisfaction; appeal to arms &c. (*warfare*) 722.

lay about one; break the peace.

compete –, cope –, vie –, race- with; outvie, emulate, rival; run a race; contend &c. –, stipulate –, stickle- for; insist upon, make a point of.

Adj. contending &c. *v.*; together by the ears, at loggerheads, at war, at issue.

competitive, rival; belligerent; contentious, combative, bellicose, unpeaceful; warlike &c. 722; quarrelsome &c. 901; pugnacious; pugilistic, gladiatorial; palestric, -al; irenic.

Phr. *a verbis ad verbera*; a word and a blow

(*concord*) 714; make peace &c. 723.

Adj. pacific; peace-able, -ful; calm, tranquil, untroubled, halcyon; blood-less; neutral.

Phr. the storm blown over; the lion lies down with the lamb.

---

722. Warfare.—N. warfare; fighting &c. *v.*; hostilities; war, arms, the sword; Mars, Bellona, grim visaged war, *horrida bella*, Armageddon.

appeal to -arms, – the sword: ordeal

723. Pacification.—N. pacification, conciliation; reconcil-iation, -ement; shaking of hands, accommodation, ar-rangement, adjustment; terms, com-promise; amnesty, deed of release.

–, wager- of battle; *ultima ratio regum*, arbitrament of the sword.

battle array, campaign, crusade, expedition; mobilization; state of siege; battle-field &c. (*arena*) 728; warpath.

art of war, tactics, strategy, castrametation; general-, soldier-ship; aerial –, submarine –, naval –, chemical- warfare; military evolutions, ballistics, gunnery; chivalry; poison gas; gunpowder, shot, – and shell.

battle, tug of war &c. (*contention*) 720; service, campaigning, active service, tented field; fiery cross, trumpet, clarion, bugle, pibroch, slogan; warcry, -whoop; battle cry, beat of drum, rappel, tom-tom; word of command; pass-, watch-word.

war to the -death, – knife; *guerre à -mort, – outrance*; open –, internecine –, civil- war.

V. arm; raise –, mobilize- troops; rise up in arms; take up the cudgels &c. 720; take up –, fly to –, appeal to- -arms, – the sword; draw –, unsheathe- the sword; dig up the hatchet; go to –, declare –, wage –, let slip the dogs of- war; cry havoc; kindle –, light- the torch of war; raise one's banner, send round the fiery cross; hoist the black flag; throw –. fling- away the scabbard; enrol, enlist, join up; take the field; take the law into one's own hands; do –, give –, join –, engage in –, go to- battle; flesh one's sword; set to, fall to, engage, measure swords with, draw the trigger, cross swords; come to -blows, – close quarters; fight; combat; contend &c. 720; battle –, break a lance- with.

serve; see –, be on- -service, – active service; campaign; wield the sword, shoulder a musket, smell powder, be under the fire; spill –, imbrue the hands in- blood; be on the warpath.

carry on -war, – hostilities; keep the field; fight the good fight; go over the top; cut one's way through; fight -it out, – like devils, – one's way, – hand to hand; sell one's life dearly.

Adj. conten-ding, -tious &c. 720; armed, – to the teeth, – cap-à-pie; sword in hand; in –, under –, up in- arms; at war with; bristling with arms; in -battle array, – open arms, – the field; embattled.

unpacific, unpeaceful; belligerent, combative, armigerous, bellicose, martial, warlike; mili-tary, -tant; soldier-like, -ly; chivalrous; strategical, internecine.

Adv. *flagrante bello*, in the -thick of the fray. – cannon's mouth; at the -sword's point, – point of the bayonet.

Int. *væ victis!* to arms! to your tents O Israel!

Phr. the battle rages

peace-offering; olive-branch; overtures; pipe –, calumet –, preliminaries- of peace.

truce, armistice; suspension of -arms, – hostilities; breathing-time; convention; *modus vivendi*; flag of truce, white flag, *parlementaire, cartel*.

hollow truce, *pax in bello*; drawn battle.

V. pacify, tranquillize, compose; allay &c. (*moderate*) 174; reconcile, propitiate, placate, conciliate, meet half way, hold out the olive-branch, heal the breach, make peace, restore harmony, bring to terms.

settle –, arrange –, accommodate- -matters, – differences; set straight; make up a quarrel, *tantas componere lites*; come to -an understanding, – terms; bridge over, hush up; make -it, – matters- up; shake hands.

raise a siege; put up –, sheathe- the sword; bury the hatchet, lay down one's arms, turn swords into ploughshares; smoke the calumet of peace, close the temple of Janus; keep the peace &c. (*concord*) 714; be -pacified &c.; come round.

Adj. conciliatory, pacificatory; composing &c. *v.*; pacified &c. *v.*

Phr. *requiescat in pace.*

724. Mediation.—N. media-tion, -torship, -tization; inter-vention, -position, -ference, -meddling, -cession; parley, negotiation, arbitration; flag of truce &c. 723; good offices, peace-offering; diploma-tics, -cy; compromise &c. 774.

mediator, intercessor, peacemaker, make-peace, negotiator, go-between; diplomatist &c. (*consignee*) 758; moderator, propitiator, umpire, arbitrator.

V. media-te, -tize; inter-cede, -pose, -fere, -vene; step in, negotiate: meet half-way; arbitrate; *magnas componere lites*.

Adj. mediatory, propitiatory, diplomatic.

725. Submission.—N. submission, yielding, acquiescence, compliance; non-resistance; obedience &c. 743; submissiveness, deference.

surrender, cession, capitulation, resignation.

obeisance, homage, kneeling, genuflexion, courtesy, curtsy, *salaam*, *kowtow*, prostration.

V. succumb, submit, yield, bend, resign, defer to, accede.

lay down -, deliver up- one's arms; hand over one's sword; lower -, haul down -, strike- one's flag, - colours; deliver the keys of the city; surrender, - at discretion; cede, capitulate, come to terms, retreat, beat a retreat; draw in one's horns &c. (*humility*) 879; give -way, - ground, - in, - up; cave in; suffer judgment by default; bend, - to one's yoke, - before the storm; reel back; bend -, knuckle- -down, - to, - under; knock under.

humble oneself; eat -dirt, - the leek, - humble pie; bite -, lick- the dust; be -, fall- at one's feet; craven; crouch before, throw oneself at the feet of; swallow the -leek, - pill; kiss the rod; turn the other cheek; *avaler des couleuvres*, gulp down.

obey &c. 743; kneel to, bow to, pay homage to, cringe to, truckle to; bend the -neck, - knee; kneel, fall on one's knees, bow submission, courtesy, curtsy, *kowtow*; make obeisance.

pocket the affront; make -the best of, - a virtue of necessity; grin and abide, shrug the shoulders, resign oneself; submit with a good grace &c. (*bear with*) 826.

Adj. surrendering &c. *v.*; submissive, resigned, crouching; down-trodden; down on one's marrow bones; on one's bended knee; weak-kneed, un-, non-resisting; pliant &c. (*soft*) 324; undefended.

untenable, indefensible; humble &c. 879.

Phr. have it your own way; it can't be helped; amen &c. (*assent*) 488.

726. Combatant.—N. combatant; disputant, controversialist, polemic, litigant, belligerent; competitor, rival, corrival; fighter, assailant, aggressor; champion, Paladin; moss-trooper, swashbuckler, fire-eater, duellist, bully, bludgeon-man, rough, fighter, fighting-man, prize-fighter, pugilist, pug, boxer, bruiser, the fancy, gladiator, athlete, wrestler; fighting-, game-cock; swordsman, *sabreur*.

warrior, soldier, Amazon, man-at-arms, armigerent; campaigner, veteran; red-coat, military man, *rajpoot*, brave.

armed force, troops, soldiery, military, forces, sabaoth, the army, standing army, regulars, the line, troops of the line, militia, territorials, yeomanry, volunteers, trainband, fencible; auxiliary -, reserve- forces, reserves, *posse comitatus*, national guard, *gendarme*, beefeater; guards, -man; yeoman of the guard, life guards, household troops.

ianissary; myrmidon; Mama-, Mame-luke; spahee, *spahi*, Cossack,

726—727 VOLITION V. (I.) iv

Croat, Pandour; irregular, free lance, *franc-tireur*, *bashi-bazouk*, *guerilla*, *condottiere*; mercenary.

levy, draught, commando; *Land-wehr*, *-sturm*; conscript, recruit, rookie, cadet, raw levies.

private, – soldier; Tommy Atkins, rank and file, peon, trooper, doughboy, sepoy, *askari*, *légionnaire*, legionary, food for powder, cannon fodder; officer &c. (*commander*) 745; subaltern, ensign, shave-tail, standard bearer, non-com; spear-, pike-man; halberdier, lancer; musketeer, carabineer, rifleman, sharpshooter, yager, skirmisher; grenadier, fusileer; archer, bowman.

horse and foot; horse –, foot- soldier; cavalry, horse, artillery, horse –, field –, heavy –, mountain- artillery, infantry, light horse, *voltigeur*, *Uhlan*, mounted rifles, dragoon, hussar, trooper; light –, heavy-dragoon; heavy; *cuirassier*; gunner, cannoneer, bombardier, artilleryman, matross; sapper. – and miner; engineer; light infantry, rifles, *chasseur*, *zouave*; military train, supply and transport, coolie.

army, – corps, *corps d'armée*, host, division, column, wing, detachment, *escadrille*, garrison, flying column, brigade, regiment, *corps*, battalion, squadron, company, platoon, battery, subdivision, section, squad; piquet, picket, guard, rank, file; legion, phalanx, cohort; cloud of skirmishers; impi.

war-horse, charger, *destrier*.

armoured -train, – car; tank.

marine, man of war's man &c. (*sailor*) 269; navy, first line of defence, wooden walls; naval forces, fleet, flotilla, armada, squadron.

man-of-war, warship; H.M.S., U.S.S.; capital ship; line-of-battle ship, battle ship; super-, dreadnought, battle –, armoured –, protected – light- cruiser; scout, flotilla leader; destroyer, torpedo boat; submarine, submersible, U-boat; submarine chaser, eagle boat, mystery ship, Q-boat; mine-layer, -sweeper; ship of the line, iron-clad, turret-ship, ram, Monitor, floating battery; first-rate, frigate, sloop of war, corvette, gunboat, bomb-vessel, fire-boat; flag ship, guard ship, cruiser; aircraft carrier; privateer; tender; depot --, parent- ship; store –, troop- ship; transport, catamaran.

aircraft &c. 273, air force, scout, fighter, bomber, troop carrier, aerial patrol, seaplane, flying boat, torpedo plane; airship, Zeppelin; rigid –, semi-rigid –, non-rigid- airship; dirigible –, free –, captive –, kite –, observation- balloon.

anti-aircraft guns, searchlights, sound locators; catapult.

727. Arms.—N. arm, -s; weapon, deadly weapon; arma-ment, -ture; panoply, stand of arms; armour &c. (*defence*) 717; armoury &c. (*store*) 636.

ammunition; powder, – and shot; explosive; propellant; gun-powder, -cotton; dynam-, melin-, cord-, lydd-ite; trinitrotoluene, T.N.T., ammonal; cartridge; ball cartridge, *cartouche*, fire-ball; dud, black Maria; 'villainous saltpetre'; poison –, mustard –, lachrymatory –, tear- gas.

sword, sabre, broadsword, cutlass, falchion, scimitar, cimeter, brand, whinyard, bilbo, glaive, glave, rapier, skean, Toledo, Ferrara, tuck, claymore, creese, kris, *kukri*, dagger, dirk, hanger, poniard, stiletto, stylet, dudgeon, bayonet; sword-bayonet, -stick; side arms, foil, blade, steel; axe, bill; pole-, battle-axe; gisarm, halberd, partisan, tomahawk, bowie-knife; at-, att-, yat-aghan; yatachan; good –, trusty –, naked-sword; cold –, naked- steel.

[268]

club, mace, truncheon, staff, bludgeon, cudgel, life-preserver, shillelagh, sprig; hand-, quarter-staff; bat, cane, stick, knuckle-duster, sand bag.

gun, piece; fire-arms; artillery, ordnance; siege -, battering-train; park, battery; cannon, gun of position, heavy -, siege -, field -, mountain -, anti-aircraft -, breech loading -, quick firing- gun; field piece, mortar, trench mortar, mine thrower, howitzer, carronade, culverin. basilisk; falconet, jingal, swivel, *pederero*, *bouche à feu*; smooth bore. rifled cannon; Armstrong -, Lancaster -, Paixhan -, Whitworth -, Parrott -, Krupp -, Gatling -, Maxim -, Vickers -, Hotchkiss -, Lewis -, machine- gun; tommy gun, Thompson submachine gun; *mitrailleu-r, -se*; pom-pom; blow pipe.

small arms; musket, -ry, firelock, flintlock, fowling-piece, shot gun, rifle, *fusil*, caliver, carbine, blunderbuss, musketoon, Brown Bess, matchlock, harquebuss, *arquebuse*, haguebut; petronel; smallbore; breech-, muzzle-loader; Miniè -, Enfield -, Westley Richards -, Snider -, Springfield -, Martini-Henry -, Lee-Metford -, Lee-Enfield -, Mauser -, Männlicher -, magazine -, repeating- rifle; needle-gun, *chassepot*; pistol, -et; revolver, automatic pistol, automatic; wind-, air-gun; flame -, gas-projector.

bow, cross-bow, arbalest, balister, catapult, sling; battering-ram &c. *(impulse)* 276; gunnery; ballistics &c. *(propulsion)* 284.

missile, bolt, projectile, shot, pellet, ball; grape; grape -, canister -, bar -, cannon -, langrel -, langrage -, round -, chain- shot; explosive; incendiary -, expanding -, soft-nosed -, dum-dum- bullet; slug, stone, brickbat; hand -, rifle- grenade; high explosive -, incendiary -, star -, gas- shell; depth -, gas -, incendiary -, stink- bomb; petard, torpedo, carcass, rocket; congreve, - rocket; shrapnel, *mitraille*; thunderbolt; mine, land mine, infernal machine.

pike, lance, spear, spontoon, javelin, assagai, throwing stick, dart, djerrid, arrow, reed, shaft, bolt, boomerang, harpoon, gaff.

728. Arena.—N. arena, field, platform; scene of action, theatre; walk, course; hustings; stage, boards &c. *(playhouse)* 599; amphitheatre; Coli-, Colos-seum; Flavian amphitheatre, hippodrome, circus, race-course, track, *stadium*, *corso*, turf, cockpit, bear-garden, playground, playing fields, *gymnasium*, *palæstra*, ring, lists; tilt-yard, -ing ground; *Campus Martius*, *Champ de Mars*; aerodrome, airport, air base, flying field.

theatre -, seat- of war; battle-field, -ground; field of -battle, - slaughter; no man's land; Aceldan a, camp; the enemy's camp; trysting-place &c. *(place of meeting)* 74.

Section V. Results of Voluntary Action

729. Completion.—N. completion; accomplish-, achieve-, fulfil-ment; performance, execution; des-, dis-patch; consummation, culmination, climax; finish, conclusion, effectuation; close &c. *(end)* 67; terminus &c. *(arrival)* 292; winding up; *finale*, *dénouement*, catastrophe, issue, upshot, result; final -, last -, crowning -, finishing- -touch, - stroke; last finish, *coup de grâce*;

730. Non-Completion.—N. non-completion, -fulfilment; shortcoming &c. 304; incompleteness &c. 53; drawn -battle, - game; work of Penelope, task of Sisyphus.

non-performance, inexecution; neglect &c. 460.

V. not -complete &c. 729; leave -unfinished &c. *adj.*, - undone; neglect &c. 460; let -alone, - clip; lose sight of.

crowning of the edifice; coping-, key-stone; missing link &c. 53; superstructure, *ne plus ultra*, work done, *fait accompli*.

elaboration; finality; completeness &c. 52.

V. effect, -uate; accomplish, achieve, compass, consummate, hammer out; bring to -maturity, – perfection; perfect, complete; elaborate.

do, execute, make; go –, get- through; work out, enact; bring -about, – to bear, – to pass, – through, – to a head.

des-, dis-patch; knock –, finish –, polish- off; make short work of; dispose of, set at rest; perform, discharge, fulfil, realize; put in -practice, – force; – into execution; make good; be as good as one's word.

do thoroughly, not do by halves, go the whole hog; drive home; be in at the death &c. (*persevere*) 604a; carry through, play out, exhaust, deliver the goods, fill the bill.

finish, bring to a close &c. (*end*) 67; wind up, stamp, clinch, seal, set the seal on, put the seal to; give the -final touch &c. *n.* to; put the -last, – finishing- hand to; crown, – all; cap.

ripen, culminate; come to a -head, – crisis; come to its end; die -a natural death, – of old age; run -its course, – one's race; touch –, reach –, attain- the goal; reach &c. (*arrive*) 292; get in the harvest.

Adj. completing, final; conclu-ding, -sive; crowning &c. *v.*; exhaustive, complete, mature, perfect, consummate.

done, completed &c. *v.*; done for, sped, wrought out; highly wrought &c. (*preparation*) 673; thorough &c. 52; ripe &c. (*ready*) 673.

Adv. completely &c. (*thoroughly*) 52; to crown all, out of hand.

Phr. the race is run; *actum est*; *finis coronat opus*; *consummatum est*; *c'en est fait*; it is all over; the game is played out, the bubble has burst.

fall short of &c. 304; do things by halves; scotch the snake, not kill it; hang fire; be slow to; collapse &c. 304.

Adj. not completed &c. *v.*; incomplete &c. 53; uncompleted, unfinished, unaccomplished, unperformed, unexecuted; sketchy, addle.

in progress, in hand; going on, proceeding; on one's hands; on the fire; on the stocks; in preparation; lacking the finishing touch.

Adv. *re infectâ*.

_____

carry -out, – into effect, – into execution.

---

731. Success.—N. success, -fulness; speed; advance &c. (*progress*) 282.

trump card; hit, stroke; lucky –, fortunate –, good- -hit, – stroke; bold –, master- stroke; *coup de maître*, checkmate; half the battle, prize; profit &c. (*acquisition*) 775; best seller.

continued success; good fortune &c. (*prosperity*) 734; time well spent.

advantage over; edge; upper-, whip-hand; ascendancy, mastery; expugnation, conquest, victory, subdual; subjugation &c. (*subjection*) 749.

triumph &c. (*exultation*) 884; proficiency &c. (*skill*) 698; conqueror, victor, winner, champion; master of the -situation, – position.

V. succeed; be -successful &c. *adj.*;

732. Failure. — N. failure; non-success, -fulfilment; dead failure, successlessness; abortion, miscarriage; *brutum fulmen* &c. 158; labour in vain &c. (*inutility*) 645; no go; inefficacy; inefficaciousness &c. *adj.*; vain –, ineffectual –, abortive- -attempt, – efforts; flash in the pan, 'lame and impotent conclusion'; frustration; slip 'twixt cup and lip &c. (*disappointment*) 509.

blunder &c. (*mistake*) 495; fault, omission, miss, oversight, slip, trip, stumble, claudication, footfall; false –, wrong- step; *faux pas*, titubation, *bévue*, *faute*, lurch; botchery &c. (*want of skill*) 699; scrape, jam, mess, muddle, foozle, *fiasco*, breakdown.

mishap &c. (*misfortune*) 735; split,

gain one's -end, – ends; crown with success.

gain –, attain –, carry –, secure –, win- -a point, – an object; put over; make a go of; manage to, contrive to; accomplish &c. (*effect, complete*) 729; do –, work- wonders.

come off -well, – successfully, – with flying colours; make short work of; take –, carry- by storm; bear away the bell; win -one's spurs, – the battle; win –, carry –, gain- the -day, – prize, - palm; climb on the bandwagon; have -the best of it, – it all one's own way, – the game in one's own hands, – the ball at one's feet, – one on the hip; walk over the course; carry all before one, remain in possession of the field; score a success, win hands down.

speed; make progress &c. (*advance*) 282; win –, make –, work –, find- one's way; strive to some purpose; prosper &c. 734; drive a roaring trade; make profit &c. (*acquire*) 775; reap –, gather- the -fruits, – benefit of, – harvest; make one's fortune, get in the harvest, turn to good account; turn to account &c. (*use*) 677.

triumph, be triumphant; gain –, obtain- -a victory, – an advantage; chain victory to one's car.

surmount –, overcome –, get over- -a difficulty, – an obstacle &c. 706; *se tirer d'affaire*; make head against; stem the -torrent, – tide, – current; weather -the storm, – a point; turn a corner, keep one's head above water, tide over; master; get –, have –, gain- the -better of, – best of, – upper hand, – ascendancy, – whip hand, – start of; distance; surpass &c. (*superiority*) 33.

defeat, conquer, vanquish, discomfit; over-come, · throw, -power, -master, -match, -set, -ride, -reach; out-wit, -do, -flank, -manœuvre, -general, -vote; take the wind out of one's adversary's sails; beat, – hollow; rout, lick, drub, floor, worst; put -down, – to flight, – to the rout, – *hors de combat*, – out of court.

silence, quell, nonsuit, checkmate, upset, confound, nonplus, trump; baffle &c. (*hinder*) 706; circumvent; elude; trip up, – the heels of; drive

collapse, smash, blow, explosion; repulse, rebuff, defeat, rout, over-throw, discomfiture; beating, drubbing; *quietus*, nonsuit, subjugation; check-, fool's-mate.

fall, downfall, ruin, perdition; wreck &c. (*destruction*) 162; death-blow; bankruptcy &c. (*non-payment*) 808.

losing game, *affaire flambée*.

victim, prey; bankrupt.

V. fail; be -unsuccessful &c. *adj.*; not -succeed &c. 731; make -vain efforts &c. *n.*; do –, labour –, toil- in vain; lose one's labour, take nothing by one's motion; bring to naught; make nothing of; wash a blackamoor white &c. (*impossible*) 471; roll the stone of Sisyphus &c. (*useless*) 645; do by halves &c. (*not complete*) 730; lose ground &c. (*recede*) 283; flunk; fall short of &c. 304.

miss, – one's aim, – the mark, – one's footing, – stays; slip, trip, stumble; make a -slip &c. *n.*, – blunder &c. 495, – mess of, – botch of; bitch it, mis-carry, abort, go up like a rocket and come down like the stick, reckon with-out one's host; get the wrong sow by the ear &c. (*blunder, mismanage*) 699.

limp, halt, hobble, titubate; fall, tumble; lose one's balance; fall -to the ground, – between two stools; flounder, falter, stick in the mud, run aground, split upon a rock; run –, knock –, dash- one's head against a stone wall; break one's back; break down, sink, drown, founder, have the ground cut from under one; get into -trouble, – a mess, – a scrape; come to grief &c. (*adversity*) 735; go to -the wall, – the dogs, – pot; lick –, bite- the dust; be -defeated &c. 731; have the worst of it, lose the day, come off second best, lose; fall a prey to; succumb &c. (*submit*) 725; not have a leg to stand on.

come to nothing, end in smoke; fall -to the ground, – through, – dead, – still-born, – flat; slip through one's fingers; hang –, miss- fire; flash in the pan, collapse; topple down &c. (*descent*) 305; go to wrack and ruin &c. (*destruction*) 162.

go amiss, go wrong, go cross, go hard with, go on a wrong tack; go on –,

-into a corner, – to the wall; run hard, put one's nose out of joint.

settle, do for; break the -neck of, – back of; capsize, sink, shipwreck, drown, swamp; subdue; subjugate &c. (*subject*) 749; reduce; make the enemy bite the dust; victimize, roll in the dust, trample under foot, put an extinguisher upon.

answer, – the purpose; avail, prevail, take effect, do, turn out well, work well, take, tell, bear fruit; hit -it, – the mark, – the right nail on the head; nick it; turn up trumps, make a hit; find one's account in.

Adj. succeeding &c. *v.*; successful; prosperous &c. 734; triumphant; flushed –, crowned- with success; victorious; set up; in the ascendant; unbeaten &c. (*see* beat &c. *v.*); well-spent; felicitous, effective, in full swing.

Adv. successfully &c. *adj.*; with flying colours, in triumph, swimmingly; *à merveille*, beyond all hope; to some –, good- purpose; to one's heart's content.

Phr. *veni vidi vici*, the day being one's own, one's star in the ascendant; *omne tulit punctum.*

come off –, turn out –, work- ill; take -a wrong, – an ugly- turn; gang agley.

be all -over with, – up with; explode; dash one's hopes &c. (*disappoint*) 509; defeat the purpose; upset the apple cart; sow the wind and reap the whirlwind, jump out of the frying pan into the fire.

Adj. unsuccessful, successless; failing, tripping &c. *v.*; at fault; unfortunate &c. 735.

abortive, addle, still-born; fruitless, sterile, bootless; ineffect-ual, -ive; inefficient &c. (*impotent*) 158; inefficacious; lame, hobbling, *décousu*; insufficient &c. 640; unavailing &c. (*useless*) 645; of no effect.

aground, grounded, swamped, stranded, cast away, wrecked, foundered, capsized, shipwrecked, nonsuited; foiled; defeated &c. 731; struck –, borne –, broken- down; down-trodden; over-borne, -whelmed; all up with; beaten to a frazzle.

lost, undone, ruined, broken; bankrupt &c. (*not paying*) 808; played out; done -up, – for; dead beat, ruined root and branch, *flambé*, knocked on the head; destroyed &c. 162.

frustrated, thwarted, crossed, unhinged, disconcerted, dashed; thrown -off one's balance, – on one's back, – on one's beam ends; unhorsed, in a sorry plight; hard hit.

stultified, befooled, dished, hoist on one's own petard; victimized, sacrificed.

wide of the mark &c. (*error*) 495; out of one's reckoning &c. (*inexpectation*) 508; left in the lurch; thrown away &c. (*wasted*) 638; unattained; uncompleted &c. 730.

Adv. unsuccessfully &c. *adj.*; to little or no purpose, in vain, *re infectâ*.

Phr. the bubble has burst, the game is up, all is lost; the devil to pay; *parturiunt montes* &c. (*disappointment*) 509.

733. Trophy.—N. trophy; medal, prize, palm; ribbon, blue ribbon, *cordon bleu*; citation; cup; laurel, -s; bays, crown, chaplet, wreath, civic crown; Victoria Cross, V.C., *Croix de Guerre*, Iron Cross; Distinguished Service Cross, Medal of Honor, Congressional Medal; insignia &c. 550; feather in one's cap &c. (*honour*) 873; decoration &c. 877; garland, triumphal arch.

triumph &c. (*celebration*) 883; flying colours &c. (*show*) 882.

monumentum ære perennius.

734. Prosperity.—N. prosperity, welfare, well-being; affluence &c. (*wealth*) 803; success &c. 731; thrift, roaring

735. Adversity.—N. adversity, evil &c. 619; failure &c. 732; bad –, ill –, evil –, adverse –, hard- -fortune, – hap,

trade; chicken in every pot, the full dinner pail; good –, smiles of- fortune; blessings, godsend.

luck; good –, run of- luck; sunshine; fair -weather, – wind; palmy –, bright –, halcyon- days; piping times, tide, flood, high tide.

Saturnia regna, Saturnian age; golden *time, – age; bed of roses; fat of the land, milk and honey, loaves and fishes, fleshpots of Egypt.

made man, lucky dog, *enfant gâté*, spoiled child of fortune.

upstart, *parvenu, nouveau riche*, profiteer, skipjack, mushroom.

V. prosper, thrive, flourish; be -prosperous &c. *adj.*; drive a roaring trade; go on -well, – smoothly, – swimmingly; sail before the wind, swim with the tide; run -smooth, – smoothly, – on all fours.

rise –, get on- in the world; work –, make- one's way; look up; lift –, raise- one's head, make one's -fortune, – pile, feather one's nest.

flower, blow, blossom, bloom, fructify, bear fruit, fatten, batten.

keep oneself afloat; keep –, hold- one's head above water; light –, fall- on one's -legs, – feet; drop into a good thing; bear a charmed life; bask in the sunshine; have a -good, – fine- time of it; have a run, – of luck; have the -good fortune &c. *n.* to; take a favourable turn; live -on the fat of the land, – in clover.

Adj. prosperous; thriving &c. *v.*; in a fair way, buoyant; well -off, – to do, – to do in the world; set up, at one's ease; rich &c. 803; in good case; in -full, – high- feather; fortunate, lucky, in luck; born -with a silver spoon in one's mouth, – under a lucky star; on the sunny side of the hedge.

auspicious, propitious, providential. palmy, halcyon; agreeable &c. 829; *couleur de rose.*

Adv. prosperously &c. *adj.*; swimmingly; as good luck would have it; beyond all -expectation, – hope, – one's wildest dreams.

Phr. one's star in the ascendant, all for the best, one's course runs smooth.

–––––––––

– luck, – lot; frowns of fortune; evil -dispensation, – star, – genius; ups and downs of life, broken fortunes; hard -case, – lines, – life; sea –, peck- of troubles; hell upon earth; slough of despond; jinx.

trouble, humiliation, hardship, curse, blight, blast, load, pressure, plight.

pressure of the times, iron age, evil day, time out of joint; hard –, bad –, sad- times; rainy day, cloud, dark cloud, gathering clouds, ill wind; visitation, infliction; affliction &c. (*painfulness*) 830; bitter -pill, – cup; care, trial; the sport of fortune.

mis-hap, -chance, -adventure, -fortune; disaster, calamity, catastrophe; accident, casualty, cross, reverse, check, *contretemps*, rub, pinch, setback.

losing game; falling &c. *v.*; fall, down-fall, come-down; ruin-ation, -ousness; undoing; extremity; ruin &c. (*destruction*) 162.

V. be -ill off &c. *adj.*; go hard with; fall on evil, – days; go on ill; not -prosper &c. 734.

go -downhill, – to rack and ruin &c. (*destruction*) 162, – to the dogs; fall, – from one's high estate; decay, sink, decline, go down in the world; have seen better days; bring down one's grey hairs with sorrow to the grave; come to grief; be all -over, – up- with; bring a -wasp's, – hornet's- nest about one's ears.

Adj. unfortunate, unblest, unhappy, unlucky; im-, un-prosperous; luck-, hap-less; out of luck; in trouble, in a bad way, in an evil plight; under a cloud; clouded; ill –, badly- off; in adverse circumstances; poor &c. 804; behindhand, down in the world, decayed, undone; on the road to ruin, on its last legs, on the wane; in one's utmost need.

planet-struck, devoted; born -under an evil star, – with a wooden ladle in one's mouth; ill-fated, -starred, -omened; inconspicuous, ominous, doomed, unpropitious.

adverse, untoward; disastrous, calamitous, ruinous, dire, deplorable.

Adv. if the worst come to the worst, as ill luck would have it, from bad to worse, out of the frying pan into the fire.

Phr. one's star is on the wane; one's luck -turns, – fails; the game is up, one's doom is sealed, the ground crumbles under one's feet, *sic transit gloria mundi, tant va la cruche à l'eau qu'à la fin elle se casse.*

736. Mediocrity.—N. moderate –, average- circumstances; respectability; middle classes, *bourgeoisie*; mediocrity; golden mean &c. (*midcourse*) 628, (*moderation*) 174.

V. jog on; go –, get on- -fairly, – quietly, – peaceably, – tolerably, – respectably; steer a middle course &c. 628.

Adj. middling, so-so, fair, medium, moderate, mediocre, second-, third- &c. -rate.

DIVISION (II). INTERSOCIAL VOLITION*

Section I. GENERAL INTERSOCIAL VOLITION

737. Authority.—N. authority; influence, patronage, power, preponderance, credit, *prestige*, prerogative, jurisdiction; right &c. (*title*) 924.

divine right, dynastic rights, authoritativeness; absolut-eness, -ism; despotism, tyranny; *jus nocendi.*

command, empire, sway, rule; domin-ion, -ation; sovereignty, supremacy, suzerainty; lord-, head-ship; chiefdom; seignior-y, -ity, hegemony, patriarchate, patriarchy; master-y, -ship, -dom; government &c. (*direction*) 693; dictation, control.

hold, grasp; grip, -e; reach; iron sway &c. (*severity*) 739; fangs, clutches, talons; rod of empire &c. (*sceptre*) 747.

reign, regnancy, *régime*, dynasty; director-, dictator-ship; protector-ate, -ship; caliphate, pashalic, electorate; presiden-cy, -tship; administration; pro-, consulship; prefecture; seneschalship; magistra-ture, -cy; raj.

empire; monarchy; king-hood, -ship; royalty, regality, autocracy, monocracy, arist-archy, -ocracy; oligarchy, democracy, demogogy; republic, -anism, federalism; socialism, collectivism; communism, bolshevism, syndicalism; mob law, mobocracy, ochlocracy, ergatocracy; *vox populi, imperium in imperio*; bureaucracy; beadle-, bumble-dom; stratocracy; martial law, military -power, – government; feodality, feudal system, feudalism.

Thearchy, dinarchy, diarchy; du-, tri-, heter-archy; du-, tri-umvirate; auto-cracy, -nomy; limited monarchy; constitutional -government, – monarchy; home rule, self-government, -determination; representative government; Soviet government.

738. [Absence of authority.] Laxity. —N. laxity; lax-, loose-, slack-ness; toleration &c. (*lenity*) 740; freedom &c. 748.

anarchy, interregnum; relaxation; loosening &c. *v.*; remission; dead letter, *brutum fulmen*, misrule; licence, licentiousness; insubordination &c. (*disobedience*) 742; lynch law &c. (*illegality*) 964; nihilism.

[Deprivation of power] dethronement, deposition, usurpation, abdication.

V. be -lax &c. *adj.*; *laisser -faire, – aller*; hold a loose rein; give -the reins to, – rope enough, – a loose to; tolerate; relax; misrule.

go beyond the length of one's tether; have one's -swing, – fling; act without -instructions, – authority; act on one's own responsibility, usurp authority.

dethrone, depose; abdicate.

Adj. lax, loose; slack; remiss &c. (*careless*) 460; weak.

relaxed; licensed; reinless, unbridled; anarchical; unauthorized &c. (*unwarranted*) 925.

*Implying the action of the will of one mind over the will of another.

gyn-archy, -ocracy, -æocracy; petticoat government, matri-
archate, matriarchy.

[Vicarious authority] commission &c. 755; deputy &c. 759; permission &c. 760.

country, state, realm, commonwealth, canton, constituency,
toparchy, municipality, polity, body politic, *posse comitatus.*

person in authority &c. (*master*) 745; judicature &c. 965; cabinet
&c. (*council*) 696; usurper; seat of -government, - authority;
headquarters.

[Acquisition of authority] accession; installation &c. 755; usurpation.

V. authorize &c. (*permit*) 760; warrant &c. (*right*) 924; dictate
&c. (*order*) 741; have -, hold -, possess -, exercise -, exert -, wield-
-authority &c. *n.*

be -at the head of &c. *adj.*; hold -, be in -, fill an- office; hold -,
occupy- a post; be -master &c. 745.

rule, sway, command, control, administer; govern &c. (*direct*)
693; lead, preside over, reign; possess -, be seated on -, occupy-
the throne; sway -, wield- the sceptre; wear the crown.

have -, get- the -upper, - whip- hand; gain a hold upon, preponderate, dominate, boss, rule the roost; over-ride, -rule, -awe;
lord it over, hold in hand, keep under, make a puppet of, lead by
the nose, hold in the hollow of one's hand, turn round one's little
finger, bend to one's will, hold one's own, wear the breeches; have
-the ball at one's feet, - it all one's own way, - the game in one's
own hand, - on the hip, - under one's thumb; be master of the
situation; take the lead, play first fiddle, set the fashion; give the
law to; carry with a high hand; lay down the law; 'ride in the whirlwind and direct the storm'; rule with a rod of iron &c. (*severity*) 739.

ascend -, mount- the throne, take the reins, - into one's hand;
assume -authority &c. *n.*, - the reins of government; take -, assume
the- command.

be -governed by, - in the power of; be under -the rule of, - the
domination of.

Adj. ruling &c. *v.*; regnant, at the head, dominant, paramount,
supreme, predominant, preponderant, in the ascendant, influential;
gubernatorial; imperious; authoritative, executive, administrative,
clothed with authority, official, *ex officio,* ministerial, bureaucratic,
departmental, imperative, peremptory, overruling, absolute; hegemonic, -al; arbitrary; compulsory &c. 744; stringent.

regal, sovereign; royal, -ist; monarchical, kingly; imperial, -istic;
princely; feudal; aristo-, auto-cratic; oligarchic &c. *n.*; democratic,
republican, dynastic.

at one's command; in one's -power, - grasp; under control;
authorized &c. (*due*) 924.

Adv. in the name of, by the authority of, *de par le Roi,* in virtue
of; under the auspices of, in the hands of.

at one's pleasure; by a -dash, - stroke- of the pen; *ex mero motu;
ex cathedrâ.*

Phr. the grey mare the better horse; 'every inch a king.'

---

739. Severity.—**N.** severity; strictness, formalism, harshness &c. *adj.;*
rigour, stringency, austerity; inclem-

740. Lenity. — N. leni-ty, -ence,
-ency; moderation &c. 174; toler-ance,
-ation; mildness, gentleness; favour;

ency &c. (*pitilessness*) 914*a*; arrogance &c. 885.

arbitrary power; absolut-, despotism; dictatorship, autocracy, tyranny, domineering, oppression; assumption, usurpation; inquisition, reign of terror, martial law; iron -heel, – rule, – hand, – sway; tight grasp; brute -force, – strength; coercion &c. 744; strong –, tight- hand.

hard -lines, – measure; tender mercies [ironical]; sharp practice; bureaucracy, red tape; pipe-clay, officialism.

tyrant, disciplinarian, martinet, stickler, formalist, bashaw, despot, hard master, Draco, oppressor, inquisitor, extortioner, harpy, vulture, bird of prey.

indulgen-ce, -cy; clemency, mercy, forbearance, quarter; compassion &c. 914.

V. be -lenient &c. *adj.*; tolerate, bear with; *parcere subjectis*, give quarter.

indulge, allow one to have his own way, spoil.

Adj. lenient; mild, – as milk; gentle, soft; tolerant, indulgent, easy-going; clement &c. (*compassionate*) 914; forbearing; complaisant, long-suffering.

V. be -severe &c. *adj.*

assume, usurp, arrogate, take liberties; domineer, bully &c. 885; tyrannize, inflict, wreak, stretch a point, put on the screw; be hard upon; bear –, lay- a heavy hand on; be –, come- down upon; ill-treat; deal -hardly with, – hard measure to; rule with a rod of iron, chastise with scorpions; dye with blood; oppress, override; trample –, tread- -down, – upon, – under foot; crush under an iron heel, ride roughshod over; rivet the yoke; hold –, keep- a tight hand; force down the throat; coerce &c. 744; give no quarter &c. (*pitiless*) 914*a*.

Adj. severe; strict, hard, harsh, dour, rigid, stiff, stern, rigorous, uncompromising, exacting, exigent, *exigeant*, inexorable, inflexible, obdurate, austere, relentless, Spartan, Draconian, stringent, strait-laced, puritanical, prudish, searching, unsparing, ironhanded, hard-headed, peremptory, absolute, positive, arbitrary, imperative; coercive &c. 744; tyrannical, despotic, masterful, extortionate, grinding, withering, oppressive, inquisitorial; inclement &c. (*ruthless*) 914*a*; cruel &c. (*malevolent*) 907; haughty, arrogant &c. 885.

Adv. severely &c. *adj.*; with a -high, – strong, – tight, – heavy-hand.

at the point of the -sword, – bayonet.

Phr. *Delirant reges plectuntur Achivi.*

---

741. Command.—**N.** command, order, ordinance, act, *fiat*, bidding, *dictum*, hest, behest, call, beck, nod.

des-, dis-patch; message, direction, injunction, charge, instructions; appointment, fixture.

demand, exaction, imposition, requisition, claim, reclamation, revendication; *ultimatum* &c. (*terms*) 770; request &c. 765; requirement.

dictation; dict-, mand-ate; *caveat*, decree, decree -nisi, – absolute, *senatus consultum*; precept; pre-, re-script; writ, ordination, bull, edict, decretal, dispensation, prescription, brevet, placet, ukase, *firman*, hatti-sheriff, warrant, passport, *mittimus*, *mandamus*, summons; subpœna, –*duces tecum*, *nisi prius*, interpellation, citation; word, – of command; *mot d'ordre*; bugle –, trumpet- call; beat of drum, tattoo; order of the day; enactment &c. (*law*) 963; *plebiscite* &c. (*choice*) 609.

V. command, order, decree, enact, ordain, dictate, direct, give orders.

prescribe, set, appoint, mark out; set –, prescribe –, impose- a task; set to work, put in requisition &c. 926.

bid, enjoin, charge, call upon, instruct; require, – at the hands of; exact, impose, tax, task; demand; insist on &c. (*compel*) 744.

claim, lay claim to, revendicate, reclaim.

cite, summon; call –, send- for; subpœna; beckon.

issue a command; make –, issue –, promulgate- -a requisition, – a decree, – an order &c. *n.*; give the -word of command, – word, – signal; call to order; give –, lay down- the law; assume the command &c. (*authority*) 737; remand.

be -ordered &c.; receive an order &c. *n.*

Adj. commanding &c. *v.*; authoritative &c. 737; decret-ory, -ive, -al; imperative, jussive, decisive, final.

Adv. in a commanding tone; by a -stroke, – dash- of the pen; by order, at beat of drum, on the first summons; at the word of command.

Phr. the decree is gone forth; *sic volo sic jubeo; le Roi le veut.*

---

742. Disobedience.—N. disobedience, insubordination, contumacy; infraction, -fringement; violation, non-compliance; non-observance &c. 773.

revolt, rebellion, mutiny, outbreak, rising, uprising, putsch, insurrection, *émeute*; riot, tumult &c. (*disorder*) 59; strike &c. (*resistance*) 719; barring out; defiance &c. 715.

mutinousness &c. *adj.*; mutineering; sedition, treason; high –, petty –, misprision of- treason; *premunire; lèse-majesté*; violation of law &c. 964; defection, secession, revolution, sabotage, bolshevism, *Sinn Fein.*

insurgent, mutineer, rebel, revolter, rioter, traitor, *carbonaro, sansculottes,* red republican, communist, Fenian, chartist, *frondeur*; seceder, runagate, brawler, anarchist, demagogue; suffragette; Spartacus, Masaniello, Wat Tyler, Jack Cade; bolshevist, bolshevik, maximalist, ringleader.

V. disobey, violate, infringe; shirk; set at defiance &c. (*defy*) 715; set authority at naught, run riot, fly in the face of, bolt, take the law into one's own hands; kick over the traces.

turn –, run- restive; champ the bit; strike &c. (*resist*) 719; rise, – in arms; secede; mutiny, rebel.

Adj. disobedient; uncompl-ying, -iant; unsubmissive, unruly, ungovernable; insubordinate, impatient of control; rest-iff, -ive; refractory, contumacious; recusant &c. (refuse) 764; recalcitrant; resisting &c. 719; lawless, mutinous, seditious, insurgent, riotous, revolutionary.

disobeyed, unobeyed; unbidden.

743. Obedience.—N. obedience; observance &c. 772; compliance; submission &c. 725; subjection &c. 749; non-resistance; passiveness, passivity, resignation.

allegiance, loyalty, fealty, homage, deference, devotion, fidelity, constancy.

submiss-ness, -iveness; ductility &c. (*softness*) 324; obsequiousness &c. (*servility*) 886.

V. be -obedient &c. *adj.*; obey, bear obedience to; submit &c. 725; comply, answer the helm, come at one's call; do -one's bidding, – what one is told, – suit and service; attend to orders, serve -devotedly, – loyally, – faithfully.

follow, – the lead of, – to the world's end; serve &c. 746; play second fiddle.

Adj. obedient; compl-ying, -iant; law-abiding, loyal, faithful, leal, devoted; at one's -call, – command, – orders, – beck and call; under -beck and call, – control.

restrainable; resigned, passive; submissive &c. 725; henpecked; pliant &c. (*soft*) 324.

unresist-ed, -ing.

Adv. obediently &c. *adj.*; in compliance with, in obedience to.

Phr. to hear is to obey; as –, if- you please; at your service.

---

744. Compulsion.—N. compulsion, coercion, coaction, constraint, eminent domain, duress, enforcement, press, conscription.

force; brute –, main –, physical- force; the sword, *ultima ratio*; club –, mob –, lynch- law; *argumentum ad baculum, le droit du plus fort*, martial law.

restraint &c. 751; necessity &c. 601; *force majeure*; Hobson's choice; the spur of necessity.

V. compel, force, make, drive, coerce, constrain, enforce, necessitate, oblige.

force upon, press; cram –, thrust –, force- down the throat; say it must be done, make a point of, insist upon, take no denial; put down, dragoon.

extort, wring from; put –, turn- on the screw; drag into; bind, – over; pin –, tie- down; require, tax, put in force; commandeer; restrain &c. 751.

Adj. compelling &c. *v.*; coercive, coactive; inexorable &c. 739; compuls-ory, -atory; obligatory, stringent, peremptory, binding.

forcible, not to be trifled with; irresistible &c. 601; compelled &c. *v.*; fain to.

Adv. by -force &c. *n.*, – force of arms; on compulsion, perforce; *vi et armis*, under the lash; at the point of the -sword, – bayonet; forcibly; by a strong arm.

under protest, in spite of one's teeth; against one's will &c. 603; *nolens volens* &c. (*of necessity*) 601; by stress of -circumstances, – weather; under press of; *de rigueur*.

745. Master.—N. master, *padrone*; lord, – paramount; command-er, -ant; captain; chief, -tain; *sahib*, sirdar, sachem, sheik, head, senior, governor, *duce*, ruler, dictator; leader &c. (*director*) 694.

lord of the ascendant; cock of the -walk, – roost; grey mare; mistress.

potentate; liege, – lord; suzerain, sovereign, monarch, autocrat, despot, tyrant, oligarch, overlord.

crowned head, emperor, king, anointed king, majesty, *imperator*, protector, president, stadtholder, judge.

cæsar, kaiser, czar, sultan, grand Turk, caliph, imaum, shah, padishah, sophi, mogul, great mogul, khan, cham; lama, tycoon, mikado, inca, cazique; domn; vaivode; wai-, way-wode; landamman; seyyid, cacique.

prince, duke &c. (*nobility*) 875; archduke, doge, elector; seignior; mar-, land-grave; rajah, emir, nizam, nawab, negus.

empress, queen, sultana, czarina, princess, infanta, duchess, margravine, begum, maharani.

regent, viceroy, exarch, palatine,

746. Servant.—N. subject, liegeman; servant, retainer, follower, henchman, servitor, domestic, menial, help, lady help, *employé, attaché*; official.

retinue, suite, *cortège*, staff, court.

attendant, squire, usher, page, buttons, donzel, footboy; dog robber; train-, cup-bearer; waiter, busboy, tapster, butler, livery servant, lackey, footman, flunkey, valet, *valet de chambre*; boots; scout, gyp; equerry, groom; jockey, hostler, ostler, tiger, orderly, messenger, cad, gillie, caddie; *wallah*; journeyman, herdsman, swineherd.

bailiff, castellan, seneschal, chamberlain, *major-domo*, groom of the chambers.

secretary; under –, assistant- secretary; clerk; clerical staff, stenographer, subsidiary; agent &c. 758; subaltern; under-ling, -strapper; man.

maid, -servant, waitress; handmaid; *confidente*, lady's maid, abigail, *soubrette*; nurse, *bonne, ayah*; nurse-, nursery-, house-, parlour-, waiting-, chamber-, kitchen-, scullery-, between –, laundry –, dairy-maid; *femme –, fille- de chambre; camarista; chef de cuisine*,

khedive, hospodar, beglerbeg, three-tailed bashaw, pasha, pashaw, bashaw, bey, beg, dey, scherif, tetrarch, satrap, mandarin, subahdar, Nabob, maharajah; burgrave; laird &c. (*proprietor*) 779; High Commissioner.

the -authorities, – powers that be, – government; staff, *état major*, aga, official, man in office, person in authority.

[Naval authorities] admiral, -ty, – of the fleet; rear-, vice-, port-admiral; senior-, naval officer, S.N.O., commodore, captain, commander, lieutenant-commander, lieutenant, sub-lieutenant, midshipman, warrant –, petty- officer, leading seaman; skipper, mate, master.

[Military authorities] marshal, field-marshal, *maréchal*; general, -issimo; commander-in-chief, *seraskier*, *hetman*; lieutenant-, major-general; commandant; colonel, lieutenant-colonel, major, captain, centurion, skipper, lieutenant, second-lieutenant, officer, staff-officer, aide-de-camp, brigadier, brigade-major, adjutant, *jemidar*, ensign, cornet, cadet, subaltern, warrant officer, quartermaster, noncommissioned officer, N.C.O.; sergeant, -major; top-sergeant, troop-sergeant, colour sergeant; corporal, -major; lance-, acting-corporal; drum major; shavetail.

[Air authorities] air -marshal, – commodore; group captain, squadron leader, wing commander, flight lieutenant, flying –, pilot-officer.

[Civil authorities] judge &c. 967; mayor, -alty; prefect, chancellor, archon, provost, magistrate, syndic; alcalde, alcaid; burgomaster, *corregidor*, seneschal, alderman, warden, constable, portreeve; lord mayor, sheriff; officer &c. (*executive*) 965.

cordon bleu, cook, scullion, Cinderella; maid –, servant- of all work, tweeny, general servant, girl, slavey; laundress, bed-maker, goody, char-woman &c. (*worker*) 690.

serf, vassal, slave, negro, helot; bondsman, -woman; bondslave; *âme damnée*, odalisque, ryot, *adscriptus glebæ*; vill-ain, -ein; bead-, bede-sman; sizar; pension-er, -ary; client; dependant, -ent; hanger on, stooge, satellite; parasite &c. (*servility*) 886; led captain; *protégé*, ward, hireling, mercenary, puppet, creature.

badge of slavery; bonds &c. 752.

V. serve; minister to, wait –, attend –, dance attendance –; pin oneself-upon; squire, tend, hang on the sleeve of, char, do for; fag; valet.

Adj. in the train of; in one's -pay, – employ; at one's call &c. (*obedient*) 743; in bonds.

---

747. [Insignia of authority.] **Sceptre.—N.** sceptre, regalia, rod of empire, sword of state, mace, *fasces*, wand; staff, – of office; *bâton*, truncheon; flag &c. (*insignia*) 550; ensign –, emblem –, badge –, insignia- of authority, rank marks, brassard, badge, sash; cocked –, brass- hat.

epaulette, *aiguillette*, crown, star, eagle, bar, double bar, pip, stripe, chevron, curl, ring, anchor, shoulder-strap, tab.

throne, chair, musnud, divan, dais, woolsack.

toga, pall, mantle, robes of state, ermine, purple.

crown, coronet, diadem, tiara, triple crown, mitre, crozier, cardinal's hat &c.; cap of maintenance; decoration; title &c. 877; portfolio.

key, signet, seals, talisman; helm; reins &c. (*means of restraint*) 752.

---

748. Freedom.—N. freedom, liberty, independence; licence &c. (*permission*) 760; facility &c. 705.

scope, range, latitude, play; free –, full- -play, – scope; free stage and no

749. Subjection. — N. subjection; depend-ence, -ance, -ency; subordination; thrall, thraldom. enthralment, subjugation, bondage, serfdom; feudal--ism, -ity; vassalage, villenage; slavery,

favour; swing, full swing, elbow-room, margin, rope, wide berth; Liberty Hall.

franchise, denization; free –, freed-, livery- man; denizen.

autonomy, self-government, home-rule, self-determination, liberalism, free trade; non-interference &c. 706.

immunity, exemption; emancipation &c. (*liberation*) 750; en-, af-franchisement; rights, privileges.

free land, freehold; allodium; frank-almoigne, mortmain.

independent, free-lance, -thinker, -trader.

V. be -free &c. *adj.*; have -scope &c. *n.*, – the run of, – one's own way, – a will of one's own, – one's fling; do what one -likes, – wishes, – pleases, – chooses; go at large, feel at home, paddle one's own canoe; stand on one's -legs, – rights; shift for oneself.

take a liberty; make -free with, – oneself quite at home; use a freedom; take -leave, – French leave.

set free &c. (*liberate*) 750; give the reins to &c. (*permit*) 760; allow –, give-scope &c. *n.* to; give a horse his head.

make free of; give the -freedom of, – franchise; en-, af-franchise.

laisser -faire, – aller; live and let live; leave to oneself; leave –, let- alone; mind one's own business.

Adj. free, – as air; out of harness, independent, at large, loose, scot free; left -alone, – to oneself.

in full swing; uncaught, unconstrained, unbuttoned, unconfined, unrestrained, unchecked, unprevented, unhindered, unobstructed, unbound, uncontrolled, untrammelled.

unsubject, ungoverned, unenslaved, unenthralled, unchained, unshackled, unfettered, unreined, unbridled, uncurbed, unmuzzled, unimpeded.

enslavement, involuntary servitude.

service; servi-tude, -torship; tendence, employ, tutelage, clientship; liability &c. 177; constraint &c. 751; oppression &c. (*severity*) 739; yoke &c. (*means of restraint*) 752; submission &c 725; obedience &c. 743.

V. be -subject &c. *adj.*; be –, lie- at the mercy of; depend –, lean –, hang-upon; fall -a prey to, – under; play second fiddle.

be a -mere machine, – puppet, – football; not dare to say one's soul is his own; drag a chain.

serve &c. 746; obey &c. 743; submit &c. 725.

break in, tame; subject, subjugate; master &c. 731; tread -down, – under foot; weigh down; drag at one's chariot wheels; reduce to -subjection, – slavery; en-, in-, be-thral; enslave, lead captive; take into custody &c. (*restrain*) 751; rule &c. 737; drive into a corner, hold at the sword's point; keep under; hold in -bondage, – leading strings, – swaddling clothes.

Adj. subject, dependent, subordinate; feud-al, -atory; in subjection to, under control; in -leading strings, – harness; subjected, enslaved &c. *v.*; constrained &c. 751; subservient, servile, fawning, slavish, obsequious, cringing; down-trodden; over-borne, -whelmed; under the lash, on the hip, led by the nose, henpecked; the -puppet, – sport, – plaything- of; under one's -orders, – command, – thumb; like dirt under one's feet; a slave to; at the mercy of; in the -power, – hands, – clutches- of; at the feet of; at one's beck and call &c. (*obedient*) 743; **liable** &c. 177; parasitical; stipendiary.

Adv. under.

_____

unrestricted, unlimited, unconditional; absolute; discretionary &c. (*optional*) 600.

unassailed, unforced, uncompelled.

unbiassed, unprejudiced, uninfluenced, spontaneous.

free and easy; at –, at one's- ease; *dégagé*, quite at home; wanton, rampant, irrepressible, unvanquished.

exempt; freed &c. 750; freeborn; autonomous, freehold, allodial; *gratis* &c. 815.

unclaimed, going a begging.

Adv. freely &c. *adj.*; *ad libitum* &c. (*at will*) 600.

750. Liberation.—N. liberation, disengagement, release, disenthrallment, enlargement, emancipation; af-, enfranchisement; manumission; discharge, dismissal.

deliverance &c. 672; redemption, extrication, acquittance, absolution; acquittal &c. 970; escape &c. 671.

V. liberate, free; set -free, – clear, – at liberty; render free, emancipate, release; en-, af-franchise; manumit; enlarge; dis-band, -charge, -miss, -enthral; let -go, – loose, – out, – slip; cast –, turn- adrift; deliver &c. 672; absolve &c. (*acquit*) 970; reprieve.

unfetter &c. 751; untie &c. 44; loose &c. (*disjoin*) 44; loosen, relax; un-bolt, -bar, -close, -cork, -clog, -hand, -bind, -latch, -chain, -harness; dis-engage, -entangle; clear, extricate, unloose.

gain –, obtain –, acquire- one's -liberty &c. 748; get -rid, – clear- of; deliver oneself from; shake off the yoke, slip the collar; break -loose, – prison; tear asunder one's bonds, cast off trammels; escape &c. 671.

Adj. at -liberty, – large, free, liberated &c. *v.*; out of harness &c. 748; adrift.

Int. unhand me! let me go!

751. Restraint.—N. restraint; hindrance &c. 706; coercion &c. (*compulsion*) 744; cohibition, constraint, repression; discipline, control, self-restraint &c. 604.

confinement; durance, duress; im-, prisonment; incarceration, coarctation, entombment, mancipation, durance vile, thrall, -dom, limbo, captivity; blockade; quarantine; detention.

arrest, -ation; custody, keep, care, charge, ward, restringency.

curb &c. (*means of restraint*) 752; lettre de cachet.

limitation, restriction, protection, monopoly; prohibition &c. 761; economic pressure.

prisoner &c. 754.

V. restrain, check; put –, lay- under restraint; en-, in-, be-thral; restrict; debar &c. (*hinder*) 706; constrain; coerce &c. (*compel*) 744; curb, control; hold –, keep- -back, – from, – in, – in check, – within bounds; hold in -leash, – leading strings; withhold.

keep under; repress, suppress; smother; pull in, rein in; hold, – fast; keep a tight hand on; prohibit &c. 761; in-, co-hibit.

enchain; fasten &c. (*join*) 43; fetter, shackle; en-, trammel; bridle, muzzle, gag, pinion, manacle, handcuff, tie one's hands, hobble, bind hand and foot; swathe, swaddle; pin –, peg- down; tether, picket; tie, – up, – down; secure; forge fetters; belay.

confine; shut –, clap –, lock –, box –, mew –, bottle –, cork –, seal –, button- up; shut –, hem –, bolt –, wall –, rail- in; impound, pen, coop; enclose &c. (*circumscribe*) 229; cage; in-, en-cage; close the door upon, cloister; imprison, immure; incarcerate, entomb; clap –, lay- under hatches; put in -irons, – a strait waistcoat; throw –, cast- into prison; put into bilboes.

arrest; take -up, – charge of, – into custody; take –, make- -prisoner, – captive; captivate; lead -captive, – into captivity; send –, commit- to prison; commit; give in -charge, – custody; subjugate &c. 749.

Adj. re-, con-strained; imprisoned &c. *v.*; pent up; jammed in, wedged in; under -restraint, – lock and key, – hatches; serving –, doing- time; in swaddling clothes; on *parole*; in custody &c. (*prisoner*) 754; cohibitive; coactive &c. (*compulsory*) 744.

stiff, restringent, straitlaced, hide-bound.

ice-, wind-, weather-bound; 'cabined, cribbed, confined'; in Lob's pound, laid by the heels.

Adv. in captivity, under arrest, behind the bars, in -prison, – jail, – durance vile.

752. [Means of restraint.] Prison.—N. prison, -house; jail, gaol, cage, coop, den, death house, condemned –, cell; stronghold, fortress, keep, donjon, dungeon, *Bastille, oubliette*, bridewell, house of correction, hulks, toll-booth, panopticon, penitentiary, guard-room, clink, can, stir, tronk, jug, lock-up, hold; round –, watch –, station –, sponging-house; station; house of detention, black hole, pen, fold, pound; enclosure &c. 232; penal settlement; chain gang; debtors' prison; reformatory; federal penitentiary, state prison; criminal lunatic asylum; bilboes, stocks, limbo, quod.

Dartmoor, Newgate, Fleet, Marshalsea; King's (*or* Queen's) Bench; Sing Sing, Dannemora.

bond; strap, bandage, splint, tourniquet; irons, pinion, gyve, fetter, shackle, trammel, manacle, handcuff, bracelets, darbies, strait waistcoat, strait-jacket.

yoke, collar, halter, harness; muzzle, gag, bit, brake, curb, snaffle, bridle; rein, -s; ribbons, lines, bearing-rein; martingale, leading string; tether, picket, band, guy, chain; cord &c. (*fastening*) 45.

bolt, bar, lock, padlock, rail, wall; paling, palisade; fence; barrier, barricade.

brake, drag &c. (*hindrance*) 706.

753. Keeper.—N. keeper, custodian, *custos*, ranger, warder, jailer, gaoler, turnkey, castellan, guard; watch, -dog, -man; Charley; sen-try, -tinel; watch and ward; *concierge,* coast-guard, *guarda costa*, gamekeeper.

escort, body guard, convoy.

protector, governor, duenna; guardian; governess &c. (*teacher*) 540; nurse, *bonne, ayah, amah.*

754. Prisoner.—N. prisoner, captive, *détenu*, close prisoner.

jail-bird, ticket-of-leave man.

V. stand committed; be -imprisoned &c. 751.

Adj. imprisoned &c. 751; in -prison., – quod, – durance vile, – limbo, – custody, – charge, – chains; under -lock and key, – hatches; on *parole*; detained at his Majesty's pleasure.

755. [Vicarious authority.] Commission.—N. commission, delegation; con-, as-signment; procuration; deputation, legation, mission, embassy; agency, agentship; power of attorney, proxy; clerkship.

errand, charge, *brevet*, diploma, *exequatur*, permit &c. (*permission*) 760.

appointment, nomination, return; charter; ordination; installation, inauguration, investiture; accession, coronation, enthronement.

vicegerency; regency, regentship.

viceroy &c 745; consignee &c. 758; deputy &c. 759.

V. commission, delegate, depute; consign, assign; charge; in-, en-trust; turn over to; commit, – to the hands of; authorize &c. (*permit*) 760.

put in commission, accredit, engage, hire, bespeak, appoint, name, nominate, return, ordain; install, induct,

756. Abrogation.—N. abrogation, annulment, nullification; cancelling &c. *v.*; cancel; revo-cation, -kement; repeal, rescission, defeasance.

dismissal, *congé*, demission; depos-al, -ition; sack, dethronement; disestablish-, disendow-ment; deconsecration; aboli-tion, -shment; dissolution.

counter-order, -mand; repudiation, retractation; recantation &c. (*tergiversation*) 607.

V. abrogate, annul, cancel; destroy &c. 162; abolish; revoke, repeal, rescind, reverse, retract, recall; over-rule, -ride; set aside; disannul, dissolve, quash, nullify, declare null and void; dis-establish, -endow; deconsecrate.

disclaim &c. (*deny*) 536; ignore, repudiate; recant &c. 607; divest oneself, break off.

counter-mand, -order; do away with; sweep –, brush- away: throw -over-

inaugurate, invest, crown; en-roll, -list. employ, empower; give power of attorney to; set –, place- over; send out.

be commissioned, be accredited; represent, stand for; stand in the -stead, – place, – shoes- of.

Adj. commissioned &c. v.

Adv. per procuratione.

———————

board, – to the dogs; scatter to the winds, cast behind.

dismiss, discard; cast –, turn- -off, – out, – adrift, – out of doors, – aside, – away; send -off, – away, – about one's business; discharge, get rid of, fire out, fire &c. (eject) 297; jilt.

cashier; break; oust; set down, unseat, -saddle; un-, de-, disen-throne; depose, uncrown; unfrock, strike off the roll; dis-bar, -bench.

be -abrogated &c.; receive its quietus.

Adj. abrogated &c. v.; functus officio.

Int. get along with you! begone! go about your business! away with!

757. Resignation.—N. resignation, retirement, abdication, renunciation, abjuration, disclaimer, abandonment, relinquishment.

V. resign; give –, throw- up; lay down, throw up the cards, wash one's hands of, abjure, renounce, forego, disclaim, abandon, relinquish, retract, demit; deny &c. 536.

abrogate &c. 756; desert &c. (relinquish) 624; get rid of &c. 782.

abdicate; vacate, – one's seat; apply for –, accept- the stewardship of the Chiltern Hundreds; retire; tender –, send in –, hand in- one's resignation.

Adj. abdicant, renunciatory &c. v. Phr. 'Othello's occupation's gone.'

758. Consignee.—N. consignee, trustee, nominee, committee.

delegate; commiss-ary, -ioner; emissary, envoy, commissionaire; messenger &c. 534.

diplomatist, diplomat, corps diplomatique, embassy; am-, em-bassador; representative, resident, consul, legate, nuncio, internuncio, chargé d'affaires, attaché.

vicegerent &c. (deputy) 759; plenipotentiary.

functionary, placeman, curator; treasurer &c. 801; agent, factor, bailiff, steward, clerk, secretary, attorney, solicitor, proctor, broker, underwriter, commission agent, auctioneer, one's man of business; factotum &c. (director) 694; caretaker.

negotiator, go between; middleman; under agent, employé; servant &c. 746.

salesman; commercial, – traveller; bagman, commis-voyageur, touter. newspaper –, own –, war –, special- correspondent; reporter.

759. Deputy.—N. deputy, substitute, vice, proxy, locum tenens, delegate, representative, next friend, surrogate, secondary.

regent, vicegerent, vizier, minister, vicar; premier &c. (director) 694; chancellor, prefect, provost, warden, lieutenant, archon, consul, procon sul; viceroy &c. (governor) 745; commissioner &c. 758; plenipotentiary, alter ego.

team, eight, eleven; champion.

V. be -deputy &c. n.; stand –, appear –, hold a brief –, answer- for; represent; stand –, walk- in the shoes of; stand in the stead of.

substitute, ablegate, accredit; commission, empower, delegate &c. 755.

Adj. acting; vice, -regal; accredited to.

Adv. in behalf of, by proxy.

Section II. Special Intersocial Volition

760. Permission.—N. permission, leave; allow-, suffer-ance; toler-ance, -ation; liberty, law, licence, concession, grace; indulgence &c. (*lenity*) 740; favour, dispensation, exemption, release; connivance; vouchsafement.

authorization, warranty, accordance, admission.

permit, warrant, *brevet*, precept, sanction, authority, *firman*; pass, -port; furlough, licence, *carte blanche*, ticket of leave; grant, charter, patent.

V. permit; give -permission &c. *n.*, - power; let, allow, admit; suffer, bear with, tolerate, recognize; concede &c. 762; accord, vouchsafe, favour, humour, gratify, indulge, stretch a point; wink at, connive at; shut one's eyes to.

grant, empower, charter, enfranchise, privilege, confer a privilege, license, authorize, warrant; sanction; entrust &c. (*commission*) 755.

give -*carte blanche*, - the reins to, - scope to &c. (*freedom*) 748; leave -alone, - it to one, - the door open; open the -door to, - floodgates; give a loose to.

let off; absolve &c. (*acquit*) 970; release, exonerate, dispense with.

ask -, beg -, request- -leave, - permission.

761. Prohibition.—N. pro-, in-hibition; *veto*, disallowance; interdict, -ion; injunction; embargo, ban, *verboten*, taboo, proscription; *index expurgatorius*; restriction &c. (*restraint*) 751; hindrance &c. 706; forbidden fruit.

V. pro-, in-hibit; forbid, put one's *veto* upon, disallow; bar; debar &c. (*hinder*) 706, forefend.

keep -in, - within bounds; restrain &c. 751; cohibit, withhold, limit, circumscribe, clip the wings of, restrict, narrow; interdict, taboo; put -, place-under -an interdiction, - the ban; proscribe, censor; exclude, shut out; shut -, bolt -, show- the door; warn off; dash the cup from one's lips; forbid the banns.

Adj. prohibit-ive, -ory; interdictive; proscriptive; restrictive, exclusive; forbidding &c. *v.*

prohibited &c. *v.*; not -permitted &c. 760; unlicensed, contraband, under the ban of; illegal &c. 964; unauthorized, not to be thought of.

Adv. on no account &c. (*no*) 536.

Int. forbid it heaven! &c. (*deprecation*) 766.

hands -, keep- off! hold! stop! avast!

Phr. that will never do.

Adj. permitting &c. *v.*; permissive, indulgent; permitted &c. *v.*; patent, chartered, permissible, allowable, lawful, legitimate, legal; legalized &c. (*law*) 963; licit; unforbid, -den; unconditional.

Adv. permissibly; by -, with -, on- -leave &c. *n.*; *speciali gratiâ*; under favour of; *pace*; *ad libitum* &c. (*freely*) 748, (*at will*) 600; by all means &c. (*willingly*) 602; yes &c. (*assent*) 488.

---

762. Consent.—N. consent; assent &c. 488; acquiescence; approval &c. 931; compliance, agreement, concession; yield-ance, -ingness; accession, acknowledgment, acceptance, agnition.

settlement, ratification, confirmation, adjustment.

permit &c. (*permission*) 760; promise &c. 768.

V. consent; assent &c. 488; yield assent, admit, allow, concede, grant, yield; come -over, - round; give in to, acknowledge, agnize, give consent, comply with, acquiesce, agree to, fall in with, accede, accept, embrace an offer, close with, take at one's word, have no objection.

satisfy, meet one's wishes, settle, come to terms &c. 488; not -refuse &c. 764; turn a willing ear &c. (*willingness*) 602; jump at; deign, vouchsafe; promise &c. 768.

Adj. consenting &c. *v.*; agreeable, compliant; agreed &c. (*assent*) 488; unconditional.

Adv. yes &c. (*assent*) 488; by all means &c. (*willingly*) 602; if –, as-you please; be it so, so be it, well and good, of course.

763. Offer.—N. offer, proffer, pre-sentation, tender, bid, overture; pro-pos-al, -ition; motion, invitation; can-didature; offering &c. (*gift*) 784.

V. offer, proffer, present, tender; bid; propose, move; make -a motion, – advances; start; invite, hold out, place- at one's disposal, – in one's way, put forward.

hawk about; offer for sale &c. 796; press &c. (*request*) 765; lay at one's feet.

offer –, present- oneself; volunteer, come forward, be a candidate; stand –, bid- for; seek; be at one's service; go a begging; bribe &c. (*give*) 784.

Adj. offer-ing, -ed &c. *v.*; in the market, for sale, to let, disengaged, on hire.

764. Refusal.—N. refusal, rejection; non-, in-compliance; denial; declining &c. *v.*; declension; peremptory –, flat –, point blank- refusal; repulse, rebuff; discountenance.

recusancy, renunciation, abnegation. negation, protest, disclaimer; dissent &c. 489; revocation &c. 756.

V. refuse, reject, deny, decline; nill, negative; refuse –, withhold- one's assent; shake the head; close the -hand, – purse; grudge, begrudge, be slow to, hang fire.

be deaf to; turn -a deaf ear to, – one's back upon; set one's face against, discountenance, not hear of, have nothing to do with, wash one's hands of, stand aloof, forswear, set aside, cast behind one; not yield an inch &c. (*obstinacy*) 606.

resist, cross; not -grant &c. 762; repel, repulse; shut –, slam- the door in one's face; rebuff; send -back, – to the right about, – away with a flea in the ear; deny oneself, not be at home to; discard &c. (*repudiate*) 610; rescind &c. (*revoke*) 756; disclaim, protest; dissent &c. 489.

Adj. refusing &c. *v.*; rest-ive, -iff; recusant; uncomplying, non-compliant, unconsenting, uncomplaisant, protestant; not willing to hear of, deaf to.

refused &c. *v.*; ungranted, out of the question, not to be thought of, impossible.

Adv. no &c. 536; on no account, not for the world; no thank you.

Phr. *non possumus*; [ironically] your humble servant; *bien obligé*.

765. Request.—N. requ-est, -isition; claim &c. (*demand*) 741; petition, suit, prayer; begging letter, round-robin.

motion, overture, application, can-vass, address, appeal, apostrophe; im-precation; rogation; proposal, propo-sition.

orison &c. (*worship*) 990; incanta-tion &c. (*spell*) 993.

mendicancy; asking, panhandling, begging &c. *v.*; postulation, solicita-tion, invitation, entreaty, importunity, supplication, instance, impetration, imploration, obsecration, obtestation, invocation, interpellation.

V. request, ask; beg, crave, sue, pray, petition, solicit, invite, pop the question, make bold to ask; beg -leave, – a boon; apply to, call to, put to; call -upon, – for; make –, address –, prefer –, put up- a -request, – prayer, – petition;

766. [Negative request.] Depreca-tion.—N. deprecation, expostulation; remonstrance; intercession, mediation.

V. deprecate, protest, expostulate, enter a protest, intercede for.

Adj. deprecatory, expostulatory, in-tercessory, mediatorial.

deprecated, protested.

un-, unbe-sought; unasked &c. (*see* ask &c. 765).

Int. cry you mercy! God forbid! forbid it Heaven! Heaven -forefend, – forbid! far be it from! hands off! &c. (*prohibition*) 761.

make -application, – a requisition; ask –, trouble- one for; claim &c. (*demand*) 741; offer up prayers &c. (*worship*) 990; whistle for.

beg hard, entreat, beseech, plead, supplicate, implore, apostrophize; conjure, adjure; obtest; cry to, kneel to, appeal to; invoke, evoke; impetrate, imprecate, ply, press, urge, beset, importune, dun, tax, clamour for; cry -aloud, – for help; fall on one's knees; throw oneself at the feet of; come down on one's marrow-bones.

beg from door to door, send the hat round, go a begging; mendicate, mump, cadge, panhandle, beg one's bread.

dance attendance on, besiege, knock at the door.

bespeak, canvass, tout, make interest, court; seek, bid for &c. (*offer*) 763; publish the banns.

Adj. requesting &c. *v.*; precatory; suppli-ant, -cant, -catory; invoc-, imprec-, rog-atory; postulant, mendicant.

importunate, clamorous, urgent; solicitous; cap in hand; on one's -knees, – bended knees, – marrow-bones.

Adv. prithee, do, please, pray; be so good as, be good enough; have the goodness, vouchsafe, will you, I pray thee, if you please.

Int. for -God's, – heaven's, – goodness', – mercy's- sake.

767. Petitioner.—**N.** petitioner, solicitor, applicant; suppli-ant, -cant; suitor, candidate, claimant, postulant, aspirant, competitor, bidder; place –, pot –, mug- hunter; prizer.

beggar, mendicant, mumper, sturdy beggar, cadger, panhandler; canvasser, barker, touter &c. 758.

sycophant, parasite &c. 886.

Section III. Conditional Intersocial Volition

768. Promise.—**N.** promise, undertaking, word, troth, plight, pledge, *parole*, word of honour, vow; oath &c. (*affirmation*) 535; profession, assurance, warranty, guarantee, insurance, obligation; contract &c. 769.

engagement, pre-engagement: affiance; betroth, -al, -ment; marriage -compact, – vow.

V. promise; give a -promise &c. *n.*; undertake, engage; make –, form- an engagement; enter -into, – on- an engagement; bind –, tie –, pledge –, commit –, take upon- oneself; vow; swear &c. (*affirm*) 535, give –, pass –, pledge –, plight- one's -word, – honour, – credit, – troth; betroth, plight faith; take the vows.

assure, warrant, guarantee, vouch for, avouch, covenant &c. 769; attest &c. (*bear witness*) 467.

hold out an expectation; contract an obligation; become -bound to, – sponsor for; answer –, be answerable- for; secure; give security &c. 771; underwrite.

adjure, administer an oath, put to one's oath, swear a witness.

Adj. promising &c. *v.*; promissory; votive; under hand and seal; upon -oath, – affirmation.

promised &c. *v.*; affianced, pledged, bound; committed, compromised; in for it.

Adv. as one's head shall answer for; upon my honour.

Phr. in for a penny, in for a pound.

768a. Release from engagement.—**N.** release &c. (*liberation*) 750.

Adj. absolute; unconditional &c. (*free*) 748.

769. Compact.—N. compact, contract, agreement, bargain, deal, transaction; affidation; pact, -ion; bond, covenant, indenture.

stipulation, settlement, convention; compromise, *cartel*.

protocol, treaty, *concordat, Zollverein, Sonderbund,* charter, *Magna Charta,* Pragmatic Sanction.

negotiation &c. (*bargaining*) 794; diplomacy &c. (*mediation*) 724: negotiator &c. (*agent*) 758.

ratification, completion, signature, seal, sigil, signet.

V. contract, covenant, agree for, engage &c. (*promise*) 768.

treat, negotiate, stipulate, make terms; bargain &c. (*barter*) 794.

make –, strike- a bargain; come to -terms, – an understanding; compromise &c. 774; set at rest; close, – with; conclude, complete, settle; confirm, ratify, clench, subscribe, underwrite; en-, in-dorse; put the seal to; sign, seal &c. (*attest*) 467; indent.

take one at one's word, bargain by inch of candle.

Adj. contractual, agreed &c. *v.*; conventional; under hand and seal; signed, sealed and delivered.

Phr. *caveat emptor.*

770. Conditions.—N. conditions, terms; articles, – of agreement.

clauses, provisions; proviso &c. (*qualification*) 469; covenant, stipulation, obligation, *ultimatum, sine quâ non; casus fœderis.*

V. make –, come to- -terms &c. (*contract*) 769; make it a condition, stipulate, insist upon, make a point of; bind, tie up.

Adj. conditional, provisional, guarded, fenced, hedged in.

Adv. conditionally &c. (*with qualification*) 469; provisionally, *pro re natâ*; on condition; with a reservation.

771. Security.—N. security; guaran-ty, -tee; gage, warranty, bond, tie, pledge, plight, mortgage, debenture, hypothecation, bill of sale, lien, pignus, pawn, pignoration; real security; bottomry; collateral, vadium.

stake, deposit, earnest, handsel, caution.

promissory note; bill, – of exchange; I.O.U.; personal security, covenant, specialty; *parole* &c. (*promise*) 768.

acceptance, indorsement, signature, execution, stamp, seal.

spon-sor, -sion, -sorship; surety, bail; mainpernor, hostage.

recognizance; deed –, covenant- of indemnity.

authentication, verification, warrant, certificate, voucher, docket, doquet; record &c. 551; probate, attested copy.

receipt; ac-, quittance; discharge, release.

muniment, title-deed, instrument; deed, – poll; assurance, insurance, indenture; charter &c. (*compact*) 769; charter-poll; paper, parchment, settlement, will, testament, last will and testament, codicil.

V. give -security, – bail, – substantial bail; go bail; pawn, impawn, hock, spout, mortgage, hypothecate, impignorate.

guarantee, warrant, assure; accept, indorse, underwrite, insure.

execute, stamp; sign, seal &c. (*evidence*) 467.

let, sett; grant –, take –, hold- a lease; hold in pledge; lend on security &c. 787.

Adj. secure, -ed; pledged &c. *v.*; in pawn, on deposit.

772. Observance.—N. observance, performance, compliance; obedience

773. Non-observance. — N. non-observance &c. 772: evasion, inob-

&c. 743; fulfilment, satisfaction, discharge; acquit-tance, -tal.

adhesion, acknowledgment; fidelity &c. (*probity*) 939; exact &c. 494- observance.

V. observe, comply with, respect, acknowledge, abide by; cling to, adhere to, be faithful to, act up to; meet, fulfil; carry -out, – into execution; execute, perform, keep, satisfy, discharge; do one's office.

perform –, fulfill –, discharge –, acquit oneself of- an obligation; make good; make good –, keep- one's -word, – promise; redeem one's pledge; keep faith with, stand to one's engagement.

Adj. observant, faithful, true, loyal; honourable &c. 939; true as the -dial to the sun, – needle to the pole; punct-ual, -ilious; meticulous; literal &c. (*exact*) 494; as good as one's word.

Adv. faithfully &c. *adj.*

servance, failure, omission, neglect, laches, laxity, informality.

infringement, infraction; violation. transgression.

retractation, repudiation, nullification; protest; forfeiture.

lawlessness; disobedience &c. 742; bad faith &c. 940.

V. fail, neglect, omit, elude, evade, give the go by to, cut, set aside, ignore; shut –, close- one's eyes to, avoid.

infringe, transgress, pirate, violate, break, trample under foot, do violence to, drive a coach and six through.

discard, protest, repudiate, fling to the winds, set at naught, nullify, declare null and void; cancel &c. (*wipe off*) 552.

retract, go back from, be off, forfeit, go from one's word, palter; stretch -, strain- a point.

Adj. violating &c. *v.*; lawless, transgressive; elusive, evasive; lax, casual; non-observant.

unfulfilled &c. (*see* fulfil &c. 772).

---

774. Compromise.—N. com-promise, -mutation, -position; middle term, *mezzo termine*; compensation &c. 30; adjustment, mutual concession.

V. com-promise, -mute, -pound; take the mean; split the difference, meet one half way, give and take; come to terms &c. (*contract*) 769; submit to –, abide by- arbitration; patch up, bridge over, fix up, arrange; adjust, – differences; agree; make -the best of, – a virtue of necessity; take the will for the deed.

Section IV. POSSESSIVE RELATIONS*

1°. *Property in general*

775. Acquisition.—N. acquisition; gaining &c. *v.*; obtainment; procuration, -ement; purchase, descent, inheritance; gift &c. 784.

recovery, retrieval, revendication, replevin; redemption, salvage, trover; find, *trouvaille*, foundling.

gain, thrift; money-making, -grubbing: lucre, filthy lucre, loaves and fishes, the main chance, pelf; emolument &c. 973: wealth &c. 803.

profit, earnings, winnings, innings, clean-up, pickings, perquisite, net profit; income &c. (*receipt*) 810; proceeds, -duce, -duct; out-come, -put;

776. Loss.—N. loss: de-, perdition ; forfeiture, lapse.

privation, bereavement; deprivation &c. (*dispossession*) 789; riddance.

V. lose; incur –, experience –, meet with- a loss; miss; mislay, let slip, allow to slip through the fingers, squander; be without &c. (*exempt*) 777*a*; forfeit.

get rid of &c. 782; waste &c. 638.

be lost, lapse.

Adj. losing &c. *v.*; not having &c. 777*a*.

shorn of, deprived of; denuded, bereaved, bereft, *minus*, cut off; dispos-

* That is, relations which concern property.

return, fruit, crop, harvest, tilth; second crop, aftermath; benefit &c. (*good*) 618.

sweepstakes, trick, prize, pool.

[Fraudulent acquisition] subreption: theft, stealing &c. 791.

V. acquire, get, gain, win, earn, obtain, procure, gather, annex; collect &c. 72; pick, – up; glean, take &c. 789.

find; come –, pitch –, light- upon; scrape -up, – together; get in, reap and carry, net, bag, sack, bring home, secure, come across, derive, draw, get in the harvest.

profit; make –, draw- profit; turn to -profit, – account; make -capital out of, – money by; obtain a return, reap the fruits of; reap –, gain- an advantage; turn -a penny, – an honest penny; make the pot boil, bring grist to the mill; make –, coin –, raise-money; raise -funds, – the wind; fill one's pocket &c. (*wealth*) 803.

treasure up &c. (*store*) 636; realize, clear; produce &c. 161; take &c. 789.

get back, recover, regain, retrieve, revendicate, replevy, redeem, come by one's own.

come -by, – in for; receive &c. 785; inherit; step into, – a fortune, – the shoes of; succeed to.

get -hold of, – between one's finger and thumb, – into one's hand, – at; take –, come into –, enter into- possession.

be -profitable &c. *adj.*; pay, answer.

accrue &c. (*be received*) 785.

Adj. acquir-ing, -ed &c. *v.*; acquisitive; productive, profitable, advantageous, gainful, remunerative, paying, lucrative.

sessed &c. 789; rid of, quit of; out of pocket.

lost &c. *v.*; long lost; irretrievable &c. (*hopeless*) 859; irredentist; off one's hands.

Int. farewell to! adieu to! good riddance!

---

777. Possession.—N. possession, seisin; ownership &c. 780; occupancy; hold, -ing; tenure, tenancy, feodality, dependency; villenage, socage, chivalry, knight service.

exclusive possession, impropriation, monopoly, corner; retention &c. 781; pre-possession, -occupancy; nine points of the law.

future possession, heritage, inheritance, heirship, reversion, fee, seigniority, feud, fief.

bird in hand, *uti possidetis*, *chose* in possession.

V. possess, have, hold, occupy, enjoy; be -possessed of &c. *adj.*; have -in hand &c. *adj.*; own &c. 780; command.

inherit; come -to, – in for.

engross, monopolize, forestall, regrate, impropriate, have all to oneself, corner; have a firm hold of &c. (*retain*) 781; get into one's hand &c. (*acquire*) 775.

belong to, appertain to, pertain to; be -in one's possession &c. *adj.*; vest in.

Adj. possessing &c. *v.*; worth; possessed of, seized of, master of, in possession of; endowed –, blest –, instinct –, fraught –, laden –, charged –, instilled –, with.

possessed &c. *v.*; on hand, by one; in hand, in store, in stock; in one's -hands, – grasp, – possession; at one's -command, – disposal; one's own &c. (*property*) 780.

unsold; unshared.

777a. Exemption.—N. exemption; exception, immunity, privilege, release &c. 927*a*; absence &c. 187.

V. not -have &c. 777; be -without &c. *adj.*

Adj. exempt from, devoid of, without, unpossessed of, unblest with, immune from.

not -having &c. 777; unpossessed; untenanted &c. (*vacant*) 187; without an owner.

unobtained, unacquired.

778. [Joint possession.] Participation.—N. participation; co-, joint-tenancy; possession –, tenancy- in common; joint –, common- stock; co-, partnership; communion; community of -possessions, – goods; communalism, communism, socialism, collectivism; co-operation &c. 709; profit sharing.

snacks, co-portion, picnic, hotchpotch; co-heirship, -parceny, -parcenary; gavelkind.

participator, sharer; co-, partner; shareholder; co-, joint-tenant; tenants in common; co-heir, -parcener.

communist, socialist.

V. par-ticipate, -take; share, – in; come in for a share; go -shares, – snacks, – halves; share and share alike.

have –, possess –, be seized- -in common, – as joint tenants &c. *n*ı join in; have a hand in &c. (*co-operate*) 709.

Adj. partaking &c. *v.*; communistic, socialistic, co-operative, profit sharing.

Adv. share and share alike.

779. Possessor.—N. possessor, holder; occup-ant, -ier; tenant; person –, man- -in possession &c. 777; renter, lodger, lessee, under-lessee; zemindar, ryot; tenant -on sufferance, – at will, – from year to year, – for years, – for life.

owner; propriet-or, -ress, -ary; impropriator, master, mistress, lord. land-holder, -owner, -lord, -lady; lord -of the manor, – paramount; heritor, laird, vavasour, landed gentry, mesne lord.

cestui-que-trust, beneficiary, mortgagor.

grantee, feoffee, relessee, devisee; legat-ee, -ary.

trustee; holder &c.- of the legal estate; mortgagee.

right –, rightful- owner.

[Future possessor] heir, – apparent; – presumptive; heiress; inherit-or, -ress, -rix; reversioner, remainder-man.

780. Property.—N. property, possession, *suum cuique, meum et tuum.*

owner-, proprietor-, lord-ship; seignority; empire &c. (*dominion*) 737.

interest, stake, estate, right, title, claim, demand, holding; tenure &c. (*possession*) 777; vested –, contingent –, beneficial –, equitable-interest; use, trust, benefit; legal –, equitable- estate; seisin.

absolute interest, paramount estate, freehold; fee, – simple, – tail; ˋstate -in fee, – in tail, – tail; estate in tail -male, – female, – general.

limitation, term, lease, settlement, strict settlement, particular estate; ˋstate -for life, – for years, – *pur autre vie*; remainder, reversion, expectancy, possibility.

dower, dowry, *dot*, jointure, marriage portion, appanage, inheritance, heritage, patrimony, alimony; legacy &c. (*gift*) 784.

assets, belongings, means, resources, circumstances; wealth &c. 803; money &c. 800; what one -is worth, – will cut up for; estate and effects.

landed –, real- -estate, – property; realty; land, -s; subdivision; plot, site; tenements; hereditaments; corporeal –, incorporeal- hereditaments; acres; ground &c. (*earth*) 342; acquest; messuage.

territory, state, kingdom, principality, realm, empire, protectorate, margravate, dependancy, colony, sphere of influence, mandate.

manor, honour, domain, demesne; farm, ranch, plantation, *hacienda*; allodium &c. (*free*) 748; fief, feoff, feud, zemindary, dependency.

free-, copy-, lease-holds; chattels real; fixtures, plant, heirloom easement; folkland; right of -common, – user.

personal -property, – estate, – effects; personalty, chattels, goods, effects, movables; stock, – in trade; things, traps, rattle-traps, paraphernalia; equipage &c. 633.

parcels, appurtenances.

impedimenta; lug-, bag-gage; bag and baggage; pelf; cargo, lading.

rent-roll; income &c. (*receipts*) 810.

patent, copyright; *chose* in action; credit &c. 805; debt &c. 806.

V. possess &c. 777; be the -possessor &c. 779- of· own; have for one's own, – very own; come in for, inherit; enfeoff.

savour of the realty.

be one's -property &c. *n.*; belong to; ap-, pertain to.

Adj. one's own; landed, predial, manorial, allodial, seigniorial; free-, copy-, lease-hold; feu-, feo-dal; hereditary, entailed, personal.

Adv. to one's -credit, – account; to the good.

to one and -his heirs for ever, – the heirs of his body, – his heirs and assigns, – his executors, administrators and assigns.

781. Retention.—N. retention; retaining &c. *v.*; keep, detention, custody; tenacity, firm hold, grasp, gripe, grip, iron grip.

fangs, teeth, claws, talons, nail, hook, tentacle, *tenaculum*; bond &c. (*vinculum*) 45.

clutches, tongs, forceps, pincers, nippers, pliers, tweezers, vice.

paw, hand, finger, wrist, fist, neaf, neif.

bird in hand; captive &c. 754.

V. retain, keep; hold, – fast, – tight, – one's own, – one's ground; clinch, clench, clutch, grasp, gripe, hug, have a firm hold of.

secure, withold, detain; hold –, keep-back; keep close; husband &c. (*store*) 636; reserve; have –, keep- in stock &c. (*possess*) 777; entail, tie up, settle.

Adj. retaining &c. *v.*; retentive, tenacious.

unforfeited, undeprived, undisposed, uncommunicated.

incommunicable, inalienable; in mortmain; in strict settlement.

Phr. *uti possidetis.*

782. Relinquishment. — N. relinquishment, abandonment &c. (*of a course*) 624; renunciation, expropriation, dereliction; cession, surrender, dispensation; resignation &c. 757; riddance.

derelict &c. *adj.*; jetsam; waif, foundling, orphan.

V. relinquish, give up, surrender, yield, cede; let -go, – slip; spare, drop, resign, forego, renounce, abjure, abandon, expropriate, give away, dispose of, part with; lay -aside, – apart, – down, – on the shelf &c. (*disuse*) 678; set –, put- aside; make away with, cast behind; discard, cast off, dismiss; maroon.

give -notice to quit, – warning; supersede; be –, get- -rid of, – quit of; eject &c. 297.

rid –, disburden –, divest –, dispossess- oneself of; wash one's hands of; divorce, desert; disinherit, cut off.

cast –, throw –, pitch –, fling- -away, – aside, – overboard, – to the dogs; cast –, throw –, sweep- to the winds; put –, turn –, sweep- away; jettison; quit one's hold.

Adj. relinquished &c. *v.*; cast off, derelict; unowned, unappropriated, un-

culled; left &c. (*residuary*) 40; divorced; disinherited.
Int. away with!

2°. *Transfer of Property*

783. Transfer.—N. transfer, conveyance, assignment, alienation, abalienation; demise, limitation; conveyancing; transmission &c. (*transference*) 270; enfeoffment, bargain and sale, lease and release; exchange &c. (*interchange*) 148; barter &c. 794; substitution &c. 147.

succession, reversion; shifting -use, – trust; devolution.

V. transfer, convey; alien, -ate; assign; grant &c. (*confer*) 784; consign; make –, hand- over; pass, hand, transmit, negotiate; hand down; exchange &c. (*interchange*) 148.

change -hands, – from one to another; devolve, succeed; come into possession &c. (*acquire*) 775; take over.

abalienate; disinherit; dispossess &c. 789; substitute &c. 147.

Adj. alienable, negotiable, transferable, reversional.

Phr. estate coming into possession.

784. Giving.—N. giving &c. *v.*; bestowal, donation; present-ation, -ment; accordance; con-, cession; delivery, consignment, dispensation, communication, endowment; invest-ment, -iture; award.

almsgiving, charity, liberality, generosity; philanthropy &c. 910.

[Thing given] gift, donation, present, *cadeau*; fairing; free gift, boon, favour, benefaction, grant, offering, oblation, sacrifice, immolation.

grace, act of grace, *bonus, bonanza*.

allowance, contribution, subscription, subsidy, tribute, subvention.

bequest, legacy, devise, will, dotation, appanage; dowry; voluntary -settlement, – conveyance &c. 783; amortization.

alms, largess, bounty, dole, sportule, donative, help, oblation, offertory, Peter's pence, *honorarium*, gratuity, Maundy money, Christmas box, Easter offering, vail, tip, *douceur*, drink money, *pourboire, Trinkgeld, backsheesh*; fee &c. (*recompense*) 973; consideration.

bribe, bait, ground-bait; peace-offering, handsel.

giver, grantor &c. *v.*; donor, feoffer, settlor; almoner; testator; investor, subscriber, contributor; fairy godmother; Santa Claus, benefactor &c. 816.

V. deliver, hand, pass, put into the hands of; hand –, make –, deliver –, pass –, turn- over.

present, give away, dispense, dispose of; give –, deal –, dole –, mete –, fork –, shell –, squeeze- out.

pay &c. 807; render, impart, communicate.

785. Receiving.—N. receiving &c. *v.*; acquisition &c. 775; reception &c. (*introduction*) 296; suscipiency, acceptance, admission.

re-, ac-cipient; assignee, devisee; lega-tee, -tary; grantee, feoffee, donee, relessee, lessee.

sportulary, stipendiary; beneficiary; pension-er, -ary; almsman.

income &c. (*receipt*) 810.

V. receive; take &c. 789; acquire &c. 775; admit.

take in, catch, touch; pocket; put into one's -pocket, – purse; accept; take off one's hands.

be received; come -in, – to hand; pass –, fall- into one's hand; go into one's pocket; fall to one's -lot, – share; come –, fall- to one; accrue; have -given &c. 784 to one.

Adj. receiving &c. *v.*; re-, suscipient; received &c. *v.*; given &c. 784; second-hand.

not given, unbestowed &c. (*see give*, bestow &c. 784).

concede, cede, yield, part with, shed cast; spend &c. 809.
give, bestow, confer, grant, accord, award, assign.
entrust, consign, vest in.
make a present; allow, contribute, subscribe, donate, furnish its quota.
invest, endow, settle upon; bequeath, leave, devise.
furnish, supply, help; ad-, minister to; afford, spare; accommo·date -, indulge -, favour with; shower down upon; lavish, pour on, thrust upon; tip, bribe; tickle -, grease- the palm; offer &c. 763; sacrifice, immolate.
Adj. giving &c. *v.*; given &c. *v.*; allow-ed, -able; concessional; communicable; charitable, eleemosynary, sportulary, tributary; *gratis* &c. 815.

786. Apportionment.—N. apportion-, allot-, consign-, assign-, appointment; appropriation; dis-pensation, -tribution; allocation, division, deal; repartition; administration.
dividend, portion, contingent, share, allotment, lot, cut, split, measure, dose; dole, meed, pittance; *quantum*, ration; ratio, proportion, quota, *modicum*, mess, allowance.
V. apportion, divide; cut, split, divvy; distribute, administer, dispense; billet, allot, detail, cast, share, mete; portion -, parcel -, dole out; deal, carve.
partition, assign, appropriate, appoint.
come in for one's share &c. (*participate*) 778.
Adj. apportioning &c. *v.*; respective.
Adv. respectively, each to each.

787. Lending.—N. lending &c. *v.*; loan, advance, accommodation, feneration; mortgage &c. (*security*) 771; investment.
mont-de-piété, pawnshop, hock shop, spout, my uncle's.
lender, pawnbroker, money-lender, usurer, Jew, Shylock.
V. lend, advance, loan, accommodate with; lend on security; pawn &c. (*security*) 771.
intrust, invest; place -, put- out to interest; sink, risk.
let, demise, lease, sett, under-, sub-let.
Adj. lending &c. *v.*; lent &c. *v.*; un-borrowed &c. (*see* borrowed &c. 788).
Adv. in advance; on -loan, - security.

788. Borrowing. — N. borrowing pledging, pawning.
borrowed plumes; plagiarism &c. (*thieving*) 791.
replevin.
V. borrow, desume; pawn.
hire, rent, farm; take a -lease, - demise; take -, hire- by the -hour, - mile, - year &c.
raise -, take up- money; float bonds; raise the wind; fly a kite, borrow of Peter to pay Paul; run into debt &c. (*debt*) 806.
make use of, plagiarize, pirate.
replevy.

789. Taking.—N. taking &c. *v.*; reception &c. (*taking in*) 296; deglutition &c. (*taking food*) 298; appropriation, prehension, prensation; capture, caption; ap-, de-prehension; abreption; seizure; ab-duction, -lation; subtraction &c. (*subduction*) 38; abstraction, a-demption.

790. Restitution.—N. restitution, return; ren-, red-dition; reinstatement, restoration; reinvestment, recuperation; repatriation; rehabilitation &c. (*reconstruction*) 660; reparation, atonement, indemnity, compensation, recompense.
release, replevin, redemption; recov-

˙ dispossession; depriv-ation, -ement; bereavement; divestment; disherison; distraint, distress; sequestration, confiscation, attachment, execution; eviction &c. 297.

rapacity, extortion, vampirism, predacity, blood-sucking; theft &c. 791.

resumption; repris-e, -al; recovery &c. 775.

clutch, swoop, wrench; grip &c. (*retention*) 781; haul, take, catch; scramble.

taker, captor, capturer; vampire; extortioner.

V. take, catch, hook, nab, bag, sack, pocket, put into one's pocket, scrounge; receive; accept.

reap, crop, cull, pluck; gather &c. (*get*) 775; draw.

ap-, im-propriate; assume, possess oneself of; take possession of; commandeer; lay –, clap- one's hands on; help oneself to; make free with, dip one's hands into, lay under contribution; intercept; scramble for; deprive of.

take –, carry –, bear- -away, – off; abstract; hurry off –, run away- with; abduct; steal &c. 791; ravish; seize; pounce –, spring-upon; swoop -to, – down upon; take by -storm, – assault; snatch, reave.

snap up, nip up, whip up, catch up; kidnap, crimp, capture, lay violent hands on.

get –, lay –, take –, catch –, lay fast –, take firm- hold of; lay by the heels, take prisoner; fasten upon, grip, grapple, embrace, gripe; clasp, grab, clutch, collar, throttle, take by the throat, claw, clinch, clench, make sure of; apprehend.

catch at, jump at, make a grab at, snap at, snatch at; reach, make a long arm, stretch forth one's hand.

take -from, – away from; deduct &c. 38; retrench &c. (*curtail*) 201; dispossess, ease one of, snatch from one's grasp; tear –, tear away –, wrench –, wrest –, wring- from; extort; deprive of, bereave; disinherit, cut off with a shilling.

oust &c. (*eject*) 297; divest; levy, distrain, confiscate; sequest-er, -rate, accroach; usurp; despoil, strip, fleece, shear, displume, impoverish, eat out of house and home; drain, – to the dregs; gut, dry, exhaust, swallow up; absorb &c. (*suck in*) 296; draw off; suck, – like a leech, – the blood of.

retake, resume; recover &c. 775.

Adj. taking &c. *v.*; privative, prehensile; pred-aceous, -al, -atory, -atorial; rap-acious, -torial; ravenous: parasitic; all-devouring, -engulfing.

bereft &c. 776.

Adv. at one fell swoop.

Phr. give an inch and take an ell.

ery &c. (*getting back*) 775; remitter, reversion.

V. return, restore; recondition; give –, carry –, bring- back; render, – up; give up; let go, unclutch; dis-, re-gorge; regurgitate; recoup, reimburse, repay, indemnify, reinvest, remit, rehabilitate; repair &c. (*make good*) 660.

redeem, recover &c. (*get back*) 775; take back again; revest, revert.

Adj. restoring &c. *v.*; recuperative &c. 660; in full restitution, to compensate for.

Phr. *suum cuique.*

---

791. Stealing.—N. stealing &c. *v.*; theft, thievery, robbery, latrociny, direption; abstraction, appropriation; plagiar-y, -ism; rape, kidnapping, depredation; raid, hold up.

spoliation, plunder, pillage; sack, -age; rapine, *brigandage*, highway robbery, foray, *razzia*; black-mail; piracy, privateering, buccaneering; filibuster-ing, -ism; burglary; house-breaking; cattle-stealing, -rustling, -lifting.

peculation, embezzlement; fraud &c. 545; larceny, petty larceny, pilfering, shop-lifting.

thievishness, rapacity, kleptomania, Alsatia; den of -Cacus, – thieves licence to plunder, letters of marque.

V. steal, thieve, rob, purloin, pilfer, filch, lift, prig, bag, nim, cri cabbage, palm; abstract; appropriate, plagiarize.

convey away, carry off, abduct, kidnap, shanghai, impress, crimp, make –, walk –, run- off with; run away with; spirit away; seize &c. (*lay violent hands on*) 789.

plunder, pillage, rifle, sack, loot, ransack, spoil, spoliate, despoil, strip, sweep, gut, forage, levy black-mail, pirate, pickeer, maraud, lift cattle, rustle, poach, smuggle, run.

stick –, hold- up.

swindle, peculate, embezzle; sponge, mulct, rook, bilk, pluck, pigeon, skin, fleece, diddle; defraud &c. 545; obtain under false pretences; live by one's wits.

rob –, borrow of- Peter to pay Paul; set a thief to catch a thief.

disregard the distinction between *meum* and *tuum*.

Adj. thieving &c. *v.*; thievish, light-fingered; fur-acious, -tive; piratical; pred-aceous, -al, -atory, -atorial; raptorial &c. (*rapacious*) 789.

stolen &c. *v.*

Phr. *sic vos non vobis.*

792. Thief.—N. thief, robber, *homo trium literarum*, pilferer, rifler, filcher, plagiarist.

spoiler, depredator, pillager, marauder; harpy, shark, land-shark, falcon, moss-trooper, bushranger, Bedouin, brigand, freebooter, bandit, thug, dacoit, pirate, corsair, viking, Paul Jones; buccan-eer, -ier; piqu-, pick-eerer; rover, ranger, privateer, filibuster; rapparee, wrecker, picaroon; smuggler, poacher, plunderer; racketeer.

highwayman, Dick Turpin, Claude Duval, Macheath, knight of the road, footpad, sturdy beggar; abductor, kidnapper.

cut-, pick-purse; pick-pocket, light-fingered gentry; sharper; card-, skittle-sharper; crook; thimble-rigger; rook, Greek, blackleg, leg, welsher, defaulter; Autolycus, Cacus, Barabbas, Jeremy Diddler, Robert Macaire, artful dodger, trickster; swell mob, *chevalier d'industrie*; shop-lifter.

swindler, peculator; forger, coiner, counterfeiter, shoful; fence, receiver of stolen goods, duffer; smasher.

burglar, housebreaker; cracks-, mags-man; Bill Sikes, Jack Sheppard, Jonathan Wild, Raffles, cat burglar.

793. Booty.—N. booty, spoil, plunder, prize, loot, graft, swag, pickings, boodle; *spolia opima*, prey; blackmail; stolen goods.

Adj. looting &c. *n.*; manubial, spoliative.

3°. *Interchange of Property*

794. Barter.—N. barter, exchange, scorse, truck system; interchange &c. 148.

a Roland for an Oliver; *quid pro quo*; com-mutation, -position.

trade, commerce, mercature, buying and selling, bargain and sale; traffic, business, nundination, custom, shopping; commercial enterprise, speculation, jobbing, stock-jobbing, *agiotage*, brokery, arbitrage.

dealing, transaction, negotiation, bargain.

free trade.

V. barter, exchange, truck, scorse, swop; interchange &c. 148; commutate &c. (*substitute*) 147; compound for.

trade, traffic, buy and sell, give and take, nundinate; carry on -, ply -, drive- a trade; be in -business, - the city; keep a shop, deal in, employ one's capital in.

trade -, deal -, have dealings- with; transact -, do- business with; open -, keep- an account with.

bargain; drive -, make- a bargain; negotiate, bid for; dicker, haggle, higgle; chaffer, huckster, cheapen, beat down; stickle, - for; out-, under-bid; ask, charge; strike a bargain &c. (*contract*) 769.

speculate, give a sprat to catch a herring; buy in the cheapest and sell in the dearest market; rig the market.

Adj. commercial, mercantile, trading; interchangeable, marketable, staple, in the market, for sale.

wholesale, retail.

Adv. across the counter; on 'change.

795. Purchase.—N. purchase, emption; buying, purchasing, shopping; pre-emption, refusal.

coemption, bribery; slave trade.

buyer, purchaser, *emptor*, vendee; patron, employer, client, customer, *clientèle*.

V. buy, purchase, invest in, procure; rent &c. (*hire*) 788; repurchase, buy in.

keep in one's pay, bribe, suborn; pay &c. 807; spend &c. 809.

make -, complete- a purchase; buy over the counter; pay cash for.

shop, market, go a shopping.

Adj. purchased &c. *v.*

Phr. *caveat emptor.*

796. Sale.—N. sale, vent, disposal; auction, roup, Dutch auction; custom &c. (*traffic*) 794.

vendi-bility, -bleness.

seller, salesman; peddler, smous; vender, vendor, consignor; merchant &c. 797; auctioneer.

V. sell, vend, dispose of, effect a sale; sell -over the counter, - by auction &c. *n.*; dispense, retail; deal in &c. 794; sell -off, - out; turn into money; realize; bring -to, - under- the hammer; put up to auction; auction, offer -, put up- for sale; hawk, peddle, bring to market; offer &c. 763; undersell; dump, unload.

let; mortgage &c. (*security*) 771.

Adj. under the hammer, in the market, for sale.

saleable, marketable, vendible, in demand, having a ready sale; unsaleable &c., unpurchased, unbought; on one's hands.

797. Merchant.—N. merchant, trader, dealer, monger, chandler, salesman; changer; regrater; shop-keeper, -man; trades-man, -people, -folk.

retailer; chapman, hawker, huckster, higgler; peddler, smous, pedlar, colporteur, cadger, Autolycus; sutler, *vivandière*; coster-man, -monger; market woman; cheap jack; caterer &c. 637; tallyman.

money-broker, -changer, -lender; stock-broker, -jobber; cambist, usurer, moneyer, banker.

jobber; broker &c. (*agent*) 758; buyer &c. 795; seller &c. 796. concern; firm &c. (*partnership*) 712.

798. Merchandise. — N. merchandise, ware, commodity, effects, goods, article, stock, produce, staple commodity; stock in trade &c. (*store*) 636; cargo &c. (*contents*) 190.

799. Mart.—N. mart; market, -place, *forum*; fair, bazaar, staple; stock –, exchange; 'change, *bourse*, Wall Street, Rialto, hall, guildhall; toll-booth, custom-house; Tattersalls.

shop, stall, booth; wharf; office, chambers, counting-house, *bureau*; coun-, comp-ter.

ware-house, -room; depot, interposit, *entrepôt, emporium*, establishment; store &c. 636.

open market, market-overt.

4°. *Monetary Relations*

800. Money.—N. money -matters, – market; finance; accounts &c. 811; funds, treasure; capital, stock; assets &c. (*property*) 780; wealth &c. 803; supplies, ways and means, wherewithal, sinews of war, almighty dollar, needful, cash.

sum, amount; balance, -sheet; sum total; proceeds &c. (*receipts*) 810.

currency, circulating medium, specie; coin, – of the realm; piece, hard cash, dollar, sterling coin; pounds shillings and pence; £ s. d., guineas; pocket, breeches pocket, purse; money in hand; the best, ready, – money; filthy lucre, shekels, roll, jack, rhino, blunt, dust, bawbees, brass, dibs, dough, mopus, tin, salt, chink, oof, spondulics, pile, wads.

precious metals, gold, silver, copper, nickel; bullion, bar, ingot, nugget.

petty cash; pocket-, pin-money; small –, change; small coin, loose cash; doit, stiver, rap, mite, farthing, *sou*, penny, shilling, bob, tanner, tester, groat, guinea, ducat; *rouleau; wampum*; good –, round –, lump-sum; power –, mint –, tons- of money; plum, lac of rupees, millions, money-bags, miser's hoard, stocking, mine of wealth &c. 803.

[Science of coins] numismatics, chrysology.

paper-money; money –, postal –, Post Office- order; note, – of hand; bank –, treasury- note; Bradbury; promissory note; I O U., bond; bill, – of exchange; draft, cheque, order, warrant, coupon, debenture, exchequer bill, *assignat*, greenback, gold –, silver- certificate.

copper, nickel, dime, quarter, two bits, half a dollar, dollar, buck, simoleon, fiver, tenner, a twenty, a sawbuck, a century, a grand; eagle, double eagle.

gold standard, bimetallism, fiat money; rate of –, exchange; in-, de-flation.

remittance &c. (*payment*) 807; credit &c. 805; liability &c. 806; solvency &c. 803.

draw-er, -ee; oblig-or, -ee; moneyer, coiner, counterfeiter, forger.

false –, bad- money; base –, counterfeit- coin, flash note, slip, kite; Bank of Elegance.

argumentum ad crumenam.

V. amount to, come to, mount up to; touch the pocket; draw, – upon; endorse &c. (*security*) 771; issue, utter, circulate; discount &c. 813.

forge, counterfeit, coin, circulate –, pass- bad money.

Adj. monetary, pecuniary, crumenal, fiscal, financial, sumptuary, numismatical; sterling; solvent &c. 803.

801. Treasurer.—N. treasurer; bursar, -y; purser, purse-bearer; cash-keeper, banker; depositary; questor, receiver, steward, trustee, chartered –, accountant; Accountant-General, almoner, liquidator, paymaster, cashier, teller; cambist; money-changer &c. (*merchant*) 797. financier, Chancellor of the Exchequer, minister of finance; Secretary of the Treasury, Director of the Budget, Controller of Currency.

802. Treasury.—N. treasury, thesaurus, bank, exchequer, almonry, fisc, hanaper, bursary; safe; strong-box, -hold, -room; coffer; chest &c. (*receptacle*) 191; depository &c. 636; till, -er; cash-box, -register, purse, pocket-book, wallet; money-bag, -belt, -box; *porte-monnaie*.

purse-strings; pocket, breeches pocket.

sinking fund; stocks; government –, public –, parliamentary- -stocks, – funds, – securities, bonds; gilt-edged securities; Consols, Liberty bonds, government bonds, *crédit mobilier*.

803. Wealth.—N. wealth, riches, fortune, handsome fortune, opulence, affluence; good –, easy- circumstances; independence; competence &c. (*sufficiency*) 639; solvency, soundness, solidity.

provision, livelihood, maintenance; alimony, dowry; means, resources, substance; property &c. 780; command of money.

income &c. 810; capital, money; round sum &c. (*treasure*) 800; mint of money, mine of wealth, El Dorado, Pactolus, Golconda, Potosi, *bonanza*; philosopher's stone.

long –, full –, well lined –, heavy-purse; purse of Fortunatus.

pelf, Mammon, lucre, filthy lucre; loaves and fishes; fleshpots of Egypt.

rich –, moneyed –, warm- man; man of substance; capitalist, millionaire, Nabob, Crœsus, Midas, Plutus, Dives, Timon of Athens; Timo-, Pluto-cracy; Danaë.

V. be -rich &c. *adj.*; roll –, wallow-in -wealth, – riches; have money to burn.

afford, well afford; command -money, – a sum; make both ends meet, hold one's head above water.

become -rich &c. *adj.*; fill one's -pocket &c. (*treasury*) 802; feather one's nest, clean up –, make- a fortune; make money &c. (*acquire*) 775.

enrich, imburse.

worship -Mammon, – the golden calf.

Adj. wealthy, rich, affluent, opulent, moneyed, monied, worth -a great deal,

804. Poverty.—N. poverty, indigence, penury, pauperism, destitution, want; need, -iness; lack, necessity, privation, distress, difficulties, wolf at the door.

bad –, poor –, needy –, embarrassed –, reduced –, straitened- circumstances; slender –, narrow- means; straits; hand to mouth existence, *res angusta domi*, low water, impecuniosity.

beggary; mendi-cancy, -city; broken –, loss of- fortune; insolvency &c. (*nonpayment*) 808.

empty -purse, – pocket; light purse; beggarly account of empty boxes.

poor man, pauper, mendicant, mumper, beggar, starveling; *pauvre diable*.

V. be -poor &c. *adj.*; want, lack, starve, live from hand to mouth, have seen better days, go down in the world, be on one's uppers, come upon the parish; go to -the dogs, – wrack and ruin; not have a -penny &c. (*money*) 800, – shot in one's locker; beg one's bread; *tirer le diable par la queue*; run into debt &c. (*debt*) 806.

render -poor &c. *adj.*; impoverish; reduce, – to poverty; pauperize, fleece, ruin, bring to the parish.

Adj. poor, indigent; poverty -stricken; badly –, poorly –, ill- off; poor as -a rat, – a church mouse, – Job's turkey, – Job; fortune-, dower-, money-, penni-less; unportioned, unmoneyed; impecunious; broke, flat; out –, short- of -money, – cash; without –, not worth- a rap &c. (*money*) 800; *qui n'a pas le sou*, out of pocket, hard up; out at

– much; well -to do, – off; warm; well –, provided for.

made of money; rich as Crœsus; rolling in -riches, – wealth.

flush, – of -cash, – money, – tin; in -funds, – cash, – full feather; solvent, solid, sound, pecunious, out of debt, all straight; able to pay 20s in the £.

Phr. one's ship coming in.

___

elbows, down at heels; seedy, bare-root, beggar-ly, -ed; destitute; fleeced, strapped, stripped; bereft, bereaved; reduced.

in -want &c. *n.*; needy, necessitous, distressed, pinched, straitened; put to one's -shifts, – last shifts; unable to -keep the wolf from the door, – make both ends meet; embarrassed, under hatches; involved &c. (*in debt*) 806; insolvent &c. (*not paying*) 808.

Adv. *in formâ pauperis.*

Phr. *zonam perdidit.*

___

805. Credit.—N. credit, trust, tick, score, tally, account.

letter of credit, circular note; duplicate; mortgage, lien, debenture, paper credit, floating capital; draft; securities.

creditor, lender, lessor, mortgagee; dun; usurer.

V. keep –, run up- an account with; entrust, credit, accredit.

place to one's -credit, – account; give –, take- credit; fly a kite.

Adj. credit-ing, -ed; accredited.

Adv. on -credit &c. *n.*; to the -account, - credit- of.

___

806. Debt.—N. debt, obligation, liability, indebtment, debit, score.

arrears, deferred payment, deficit, default; insolvency &c. (*non-payment*) 808; bad debt.

interest; usance, usury; premium; floating -debt, – capital.

debtor, debitor; mortgagor; defaulter &c. 808; borrower.

V. be -in debt &c. *adj.*; owe; incur –, contract- a debt &c. *n.*; run up -a bill, – a score, – an account; go on tick, put on the cuff; borrow &c. 788; run –, get- into debt; outrun the constable, answer –, go bail- for; back one's note.

Adj. indebted; liable, chargeable, answerable for.

in -debt, – embarrassed circumstances, – difficulties; incumbered, involved; involved –, plunged –, deep –, over head and ears- in debt; deeply involved; fast tied up; insolvent &c. (*not paying*) 808; *minus*, out of pocket.

unpaid; unrequited, unrewarded; owing, due, in arrear, outstanding.

___

807. Payment.—N. pay-, defrayment; discharge; ac-, quittance; settlement, clearance, liquidation, satisfaction, reckoning, arrangement.

acknowledgment, release; receipt, – in full, – in full of all demands; voucher.

repayment, reimbursement, retribution; pay &c. (*reward*) 973; money paid &c. (*expenditure*) 809.

ready money &c. (*cash*) 800; stake, remittance, instalment.

payer, liquidator &c. 801.

V. pay, defray, make payment; pay -down, – on the nail, – ready money, – at sight, – in advance; cash, honour a bill, acknowledge; redeem; pay in kind.

___

808. Non-payment.—N. non-payment; default, defalcation; protest, repudiation; application of the sponge; whitewashing.

insolvency, bankruptcy, failure; overdraft, overdrawn account; insufficiency &c. 640; run upon a bank.

waste paper bonds; dishonoured –, protested- bills; bogus cheque.

bankrupt, insolvent debtor, lame duck, man of straw, welsher, stag, defaulter, absconder, levanter.

V. not -pay &c. 807; fail, break, stop payment; become -insolvent, – bankrupt; be gazetted; abscond.

protest, dishonour, repudiate, nullify.

pay under protest; button up one's

pay one's -way, - shot, - footing; pay -the piper, - sauce for all, - costs; do the needful; come across; shell -, fork- out; come down with, - the dust; tickle -, grease- the palm; expend &c. 809; put -, lay- down.

discharge, settle, quit, acquit oneself of; account -, reckon -, settle -, be even -, be quits- with; strike a balance; settle -, balance -, square- accounts with; quit scores; foot the bill; wipe -, clear- off old scores; satisfy; pay in full; satisfy -, pay in full of- all demands; clear, liquidate; pay -up, - old debts.

disgorge, make repayment; repay, refund, reimburse, retribute; make compensation &c. 30.

Adj. paying &c., paid &c. *v.*; owing nothing, out of debt, all straight, clear of -debt, - encumbrance; unowed, never indebted.

Adv. to the tune of; on the nail; money -, cash- down; cash on delivery.

pockets, draw the purse strings; apply the sponge; pay over the left shoulder, get whitewashed; swindle &c. 791; run up bills, fly kites.

Adj. not paying; in debt &c. 806; behindhand, in arrear; beggared &c. (*poor*) 804; unable to make both ends meet; *minus*; worse than nothing.

insolvent, bankrupt, in the gazette, gazetted, ruined.

unpaid &c. (*outstanding*) 806; *gratis* &c. 815; unremunerated.

---

809. Expenditure.—**N.** expenditure, money going out; out-goings, -lay; expenses, disbursement; prime cost &c. (*price*) 812; circulation; run upon a bank.

[Money paid] payment &c. 807; pay &c. (*remuneration*) 973; bribe &c. 973; fee, footing, garnish; subsidy; tribute, Peter's pence; contingent, quota; donation &c. 784.

pay in advance, earnest, handsel, deposit, instalment.

investment; purchase &c. 795.

V. expend, spend; run -, get- through; pay, disburse; open -, loose -, untie- the purse strings; lay -, shell -, fork- out; bleed; make up a sum, invest, sink money.

fee &c. (*reward*) 973; pay one's way &c. (*pay*) 807; subscribe &c. (*give*) 784; subsidize, bribe.

Adj. expend-ing, -ed &c. *v.*; sumptuary, liberal &c. 816; open-handed, lavish &c. 818; expensive &c. 814.

810. Receipt.—**N.** receipt, account-able -, conditional -, binding -, return-receipt; value received, money coming in; income, incomings, innings, reve-nue, return, proceeds; gross receipts, net profit; earnings &c. (*gain*) 775.

rent, - roll; rent-al, -age; rack-rent; premium, *bonus*; sweepstakes, ton-tine, prize, drawing.

pension, annuity; jointure &c. (*prop-erty*) 780; alimony, pittance; emolu-ment &c. (*remuneration*) 973.

V. receive &c. 785; take money; draw -, derive- from; get, be in receipt of, acquire &c. 775; take &c. 789.

bring in, yield, afford, pay, return; accrue &c. (*be received from*) 785.

Adj. receiv-ing, -ed &c. *v.*; profitable &c. (*gainful*) 775.

---

811. Accounts.—**N.** accounts, accompts; commercial -. monetary-arithmetic; statistics &c. (*numeration*) 85; money matters, finance, budget, bill, score, reckoning, account.

books, account book, ledger; day -, cash -, pass- book; journal; debtor and creditor -, cash -, petty cash -, running- account; account-current; balance, - sheet; *compte rendu*, account settled.

book-keeping, audit; double -, single- entry; reckoning &c. 85.

chartered -, certified public -, accountant; auditor, actuary, book-keeper; financier &c. 801; accounting party.

V. keep accounts, enter, post, book, credit, debit, carry over; take stock; balance –, make up –, square –, settle –, wind up –, cast up –, add up –, tot up- accounts; make accounts square.

bring to book, audit, tax, surcharge and falsify.

falsify –, garble –, cook –, doctor- an account.

Adj. monetary &c. 800; account-able, -ing; statistical.

812. Price.—N. price, amount, cost, expense, prime cost, charge, figure, demand, damage, fare, hire; wages &c. (*remuneration*) 973.

dues, duty, toll, tax, impost, cess, sess, tallage, levy, capitation-, poll-, income-, sur-, sales-, super-tax; gabel, *gabelle*; gavel, *octroi*, custom, tariff, excise, assessment, taxation, benevolence, tithe, tenths, exactment, ransom, salvage; broker-, wharf-, lighter-, ton-, freight-age.

worth, rate, value, valuation, appraisement, money's worth, par value; penny &c. -worth; price current, market price, quotation; what it will -fetch &c. *v.*

bill &c. (*account*) 811; shot.

V. bear –, set –, fix- a price; appraise, assess, price, charge, demand, ask, require, exact, run up; distrain; run up a bill &c. (*debt*) 806; have one's price; liquidate.

amount to, come to, mount up to; stand one in.

fetch, sell for, cost, bring in, yield, afford.

Adj. priced &c. *v.*; to the tune of, *ad valorem*; mercenary, venal.

Phr. no penny, no paternoster; *point d'argent, point de Suisse*; no longer pipe, no longer dance; no song, no supper.

one may have it for.

813. Discount.—N. discount, abatement, concession, reduction, depreciation, allowance, qualification, set off, drawback, poundage, *agio*, percentage; rebate, -ment; backwardation, contango; salvage; tare and tret.

V. discount, bate; a-, re-bate; deduct, reduce, mark down, take off, allow, give, make allowance; tax, depreciate.

Adj. discounting &c. *v.*

Adv. at a discount, below par.

---

814. Dearness. — N. dearness &c. *adj.*; high –, famine –, fancy- price; overcharge; extravagance; exorbitance, extortion; heavy pull upon the purse; Pyrrhic victory.

V. be -dear &c. *adj.*; cost -much, – a pretty penny; rise in price, look up.

overcharge, bleed, fleece, skin, extort.

pay -too much, – through the nose, – too dear for one's whistle.

Adj. dear; high, -priced; of great price, expensive, costly, precious, worth a Jew's eye, dear bought; unreasonable, extravagant, exorbitant, extortionate.

at a premium; not to be had, – for love or money; beyond –, above- price; priceless, of priceless value.

Adv. dear, -ly; at great –, heavy-cost; *à grands frais.*

Phr. prices looking up; *le jeu n'en vaut pas la chandelle.*

815. Cheapness.—N. cheapness, low price; depreciation; bargain; good penny &c.- worth, *bon marché.*

[Absence of charge] gratuity; free -quarters, – seats, – admission, – warren; pass, Annie Oakley; run of one's teeth; nominal price, peppercorn rent; labour of love.

drug in the market.

V. be -cheap &c. *adj.*; cost little; come down –, fall- in price.

buy for -a mere nothing, – an old song; have one's money's worth; cheapen, beat down.

Adj. cheap; low, – priced; moderate, reasonable; in-, un-expensive; well –, worth the money; *magnifique et pas cher*; good –, cheap- at the price; dirt –, dog- cheap; cheap, -as dirt, – and nasty; catchpenny.

reduced, marked down, half-price, depreciated, unsaleable.

gratuitous, *gratis*, free, for love,

– nothing; cost-, expense-less; without charge, not charged, un-taxed; scot –, shot –, rent- free; free of -cost, – expense; honorary, unbought, unpaid, complimentary.

Adv. for a mere song; at -cost price, – prime cost, – a reduction, – a bargain; on the cheap.

816. Liberality.—N. liberality, gener-osity, munificence; bount-y, -eousness, -ifulness; hospitality; charity &c. (*beneficence*) 906.

benefactor, free giver, Lady Bountiful.

V. be -liberal &c. *adj.*; spend –, bleed- freely; shower down upon; open one's purse strings &c. (*disburse*) 809; spare no expense, give -with both hands, – *carte blanche*.

Adj. liberal, free, generous; charitable &c. (*beneficent*) 906; hospitable; bount-iful, -eous; handsome; unsparing, ungrudging; open-, free-, full-handed; open-, large-, free-hearted; munificent, princely, unstinting.

overpaid.

Adv. liberally, ungrudgingly, with open hand.

818. Prodigality.—N. prodi-gality, -gence; unthriftiness, waste, -fulness; profus-ion, -eness; extravagance; squandering &c. *v.*; lavishness; malversation.

prodigal; spend-, waste-thrift; losel, play-boy, spender, squanderer, locust.

V. be -prodigal &c. *adj.*; squander, lavish, sow broadcast; pour forth like water; pay through the nose &c. (*dear*) 814; spill, waste, dissipate, exhaust, drain, eat out of house and home, overdraw, outrun the constable; run -out, – through; misspend; throw -good money after bad, – the helve after the hatchet; burn the candle at both ends; make ducks and drakes of one's money; squander one's substance, spend money like water; fool –, potter –, muddle –, fritter –, throw- away one's money; pour water into a sieve, kill the goose that lays the golden eggs; *manger son blé en herbe.*

Adj. prodigal, profuse, thriftless, un-thrifty, improvident, wasteful, losel,

817. Economy.—N. economy, fru-gality; thrift, -iness; prudence, care, husbandry, good housewifery, saving-ness, retrenchment.

savings; prevention of waste, save-all; cheese parings and candle ends; parsimony &c. 819.

V. be -economical &c. *adj.*; econo-mize, save; retrench; cut- down expenses, – one's coat according to one's cloth, make both ends meet, keep within compass, meet one's expenses, pay one's way; keep one's head above water; husband &c. (*lay by*) 636; save –, invest- money; put out to interest; provide –, save- -for, – against- a rainy day; feather one's nest; look after the main chance.

Adj. economical, frugal, careful, thrifty, saving, chary, spare, sparing; parsimonious &c. 819.

underpaid.

Adv. sparingly &c. *adj.*; *ne quid nimis*.

819. Parsimony. — N. parsimony, parcity; parsimoniousness, stinginess &c. *adj.*; stint; illiberality, avarice, tenacity, avidity, rapacity, extortion, venality, cupidity; selfishness &c. 943; *auri sacra fames.*

miser, niggard, churl, screw, tight-wad, skinflint, crib, codger, muckworm, money-grubber, pinchfist, scrimp, lick-penny, hunks, curmudgeon, *Harpagon*, Silas Marner, harpy, extortioner, Jew, usurer.

V. be -parsimonious &c. *adj.*; grudge, begrudge, stint, skimp, pinch, gripe, screw, dole out, hold back, withhold, starve, famish, live upon nothing, skin a flint.

drive a -bargain, – hard bargain; cheapen, beat down; stop one hole in a sieve; have an itching palm, grasp, grab.

Adj. parsimonious, penurious, stingy, miserly, mean, shabby, peddling, scrubby, pennywise, near, niggardly,

[302]

extravagant, lavish, dissipated, over liberal; full-handed &c. (*liberal*) 816.
penny wise and pound foolish.

Adv. with an unsparing hand: money burning one's pocket; recklessly profuse.

Int. hang the expense!

———

frugal to excess; close; fast-, close-, strait-handed; close-, hard-, tight-fisted; tight, sparing; chary; grudging, griping &c. *v.*; illiberal, ungenerous, churlish, hidebound, sordid, mercenary, venal, covetous, usurious, avaricious, greedy, extortionate, rapacious.

Adv. with a sparing hand.

CLASS VI

WORDS RELATING TO THE SENTIENT AND MORAL POWERS.

~~~~~~~~~~

SECTION I. AFFECTIONS IN GENERAL

820. Affections.—N. affections, character, qualities, disposition, nature, spirit, tone; temper, -ament; *diathesis*, idiosyncrasy; cast -, habit -, frame- of -mind, - soul; predilection, turn; natural -, turn of mind; bent, bias, predisposition, proneness, proclivity; propen-sity, -sedness, -sion, -dency; vein, humour, mood, grain, mettle; sympathy &c. (*love*) 897.

soul, heart, breast, bosom, inner man; heart's -core, - strings, - blood; heart of hearts, *penetralia mentis*; secret and inmost recesses of the -, .ockles of one's- heart; inmost -heart, - soul; back-bone.

passion, pervading spirit; ruling -, master- passion; *furore*; fulness of the heart, heyday of the blood, flesh and blood, flow of soul, force of character.

V. have -, possess- -affections &c. *n.*; be of a -character &c. *n.*; be -affected &c. *adj.*; breathe.

Adj. affected, characterized, formed, moulded, cast; at-, tempered; framed; pre-, disposed; prone, inclined; having a -bias &c. *n.*; tinctured -, imbued -, penetrated -, eaten up- with.

inborn, inbred, ingrained, in the grain, congenital, inherent, bred in the bone; deep-rooted, ineffaceable, inveterate; pathoscopic.

Adv. in one's -heart &c. *n.*; at heart; heart and soul &c. 821; in the -vein, - mood.

821. Feeling.—N. feeling; suffering &c. *v.*; endurance, tolerance, sufferance, supportance, experience, response; sympathy &c. (*love*) 897; impression, inspiration, affection, sensation, emotion, pathos, deep sense.

fire, warmth, glow, unction, *gusto*, vehemence; ferv-our, -ency; heartiness, cordiality; earnestness, eagerness; *empressement*, ardour, zeal, passion, enthusiasm, *verve, furore*, fanaticism; excitation of feeling &c. 824; fulness of the heart &c. (*disposition*) 820; passion &c. (*state of excitability*) 825; ecstasy &c. (*pleasure*) 827.

blush, suffusion, flush; hectic; tingling, thrill, kick, turn, shock; agitation &c. (*irregular motion*) 315; quiver, heaving, flutter, flurry, fluster, twitter, tremor; throb, -bing; pulsation, palpitation, panting; trepid-, perturb-ation; ruffle, hurry of spirits, pother, stew, ferment.

V. feel; receive an -impression &c. *n.*; be -impressed with &c. *adj.*; entertain -, harbour -, cherish- -feeling &c. *n.*

respond; catch the -flame, - infection; enter the spirit of.

bear, suffer. support, sustain, endure, brook, thole, aby; abide &c.

(*be composed*) 826; experience &c. (*meet with*) 151; taste, prove; labour –, smart- under; bear the brunt of, brave, stand.

swell, glow, warm, flush, blush, change colour, mantle; turn -colour, – pale, – red, – black in the face; blench, crimson, whiten, pale, tingle, thrill, heave, pant, throb, palpitate, go pit-a-pat, tremble, quiver, flutter, twitter; stagger, reel; shake &c. 315; be -agitated, – excited &c. 824; look -blue, – black; wince, draw a deep breath.

impress &c. (*excite the feelings*) 824.

Adj. feeling &c. *v.*; sentient; sensuous; sensor-ial, -y; emo-tive, -tional; of –, with- feeling &c. *n.*

warm, quick, lively, smart, strong, sharp, acute, cutting, piercing, incisive; keen, – as a razor; trenchant, pungent, racy, *piquant*, poignant, caustic.

impressive, deep, profound, indelible; deep-, home-, heart-felt; swelling, soul-stirring, deep-mouthed, heart-expanding, electric, thrilling, rapturous, ecstatic.

earnest, wistful, eager, breathless; fer-vent, -vid; gushing, passionate, warmhearted, hearty, cordial, sincere, zealous, enthusiastic, glowing, ardent, burning, red-hot, fiery, flaming; boiling, – over.

pervading, penetrating, absorbing; rabid, raving, feverish, fanatical, hysterical; impetuous &c. (*excitable*) 825; overmastering.

impressed –, moved –, touched –, affected –, penetrated –, seized –, imbued &c. 820- with; devoured by; wrought up &c. (*excited*) 824; struck all of a heap; rapt; in a -quiver &c. *n.*; enraptured &c. 829.

Adv. heart and soul, from the bottom of one's heart, *ab imo pectore*, *de profundis*, at heart, *con amore*, heartily, devoutly, over head and ears.

Phr. the heart -big, – full, – swelling, – beating, – pulsating, – throbbing, – thumping, – beating high, – melting, – overflowing, – bursting, – breaking.

---

822. Sensibility. — N. sensi-bility, -bleness, -tiveness; moral sensibility; impress-, affect-ibility; suscepti-ble-ness, -bility, -vity; mobility; viva-city, -ciousness; tender-, soft-ness; sentimental-ity, -ism.

excitability &c. 825; fastidiousness &c. 868; physical sensibility &c. 375.

sore -point, – place; where the shoe pinches.

V. be -sensible &c. *adj.*; have a -tender, – warm, – sensitive- heart.

take to –, treasure up in the- heart; shrink.

'die of a rose in aromatic pain'; touch to the quick.

Adj. sensi-ble, -tive; impressi-ble, -onable; suscepti-ve, -ble; alive to, impassion-able, -ed; gushing; warm-, tender-, soft-hearted; tender –, as a chicken; soft, sentimental, romantic; enthusiastic, highflying, spirited, mettlesome, vivacious, lively, expressive, mobile, tremblingly alive; excitable

823. Insensibility.—N. insensi-bility, -bleness; moral insensibility; inertness, *inertia*, *vis inertiæ*; impassi-bility, -bleness; inappetency, apathy, phlegm, dulness, hebetude, supineness, lukewarmness, insusceptibility, unimpress-ibility.

cold -fit, – blood, – heart; cold-, cool-ness; frigidity, *sang-froid*; stoicism, imperturbation &c. (*inexcitability*) 826; *nonchalance*, unconcern, dry eyes; *insouciance* &c. (*indifference*) 866; recklessness &c. 863; callousness; heart of stone, stock and stone, marble, deadness.

torp-or, -idity; obstupefaction, lethargy, coma, trance; sleep &c. 683; suspended animation; stup-or, -efaction; paralysis, palsy; numbness &c. (*physical insensibility*) 376.

neutrality; quietism, vegetation.

V. be -insensible &c. *adj.*; have a rhinoceros hide; show -insensibility &c. *n.*; not -mind, – care, – be affected

&c. 825, over-sensitive, without skin, thin-skinned; fastidious &c. 868.

Adv. sensibly &c. *adj.*; to the -quick, - inmost core.

———————

by; have no desire for &c. 866; have -, feel -, take- no interest in; *nil admirari*; not care a -straw &c. (*unimportance*) 643 for; disregard &c. (*neglect*) 460; set at naught &c. (*make light of*) 483; turn a deaf ear to &c. (*inattention*) 458; vegetate.

render -insensible, - callous; blunt, obtund, numb, benumb, paralyze, chloroform, deaden, hebetate, stun, stupefy; brut-ify, -alize.

inure; harden, - the heart; steel, case-harden, sear.

Adj. insensible, unconscious; impassi-ve, -ble; blind to, deaf to, dead to; un-, in-susceptible; unimpress-ionable, -ible; passion-, spirit-, heart-, soul-less; unfeeling, unmoral.

apathetic; leuco-, phlegmatic; dull, frigid; cold, -blooded, -hearted; unemotional; cold as charity; flat, obtuse, inert, supine, sluggish, torpid; sleepy &c. (*inactive*) 683; languid, half-hearted, tame; numb, -ed; comatose; anæsthetic &c. 376; stupefied, chloroformed, palsy-stricken.

indifferent, lukewarm; Laodicean; careless, mindless, regardless; inattentive &c. 458; neglectful &c. 460; disregarding.

unconcerned, *nonchalant, pococurante, insouciant, sans souci*; unambitious &c. 866.

un-affected, -ruffled, -impressed, -inspired, -excited, -moved, -stirred, -touched, -shocked, -struck; unblushing &c. (*shameless*) 885; unanimated; vegetative.

callous, thick-skinned, pachydermatous, impervious; hard, -ened; inured, case-hardened; steeled -, proof- against; imperturbable &c. (*inexcitable*) 826; unfelt.

Adv. insensibly &c. *adj.*; *æquo animo*; without being -moved, - touched, - impressed; in cold blood; with -dry eyes, - withers unwrung.

Phr. never mind; it is of no consequence &c. (*unimportant*) 643: it cannot be helped; nothing coming amiss; it is all -the same, - one- to.

824. Excitation.—N. excitation of feeling; mental -, excitement; suscitation, galvanism, stimulation, piquancy, provocation, inspiration, calling forth, infection; interest, animation, agitation, perturbation; subjugation, fascination, intoxication; en-, ravishment; entrancement, high pressure.

unction, impressiveness &c. *adj.*; emotional appeal; melodrama; psychological moment, crisis; sensationalism.

trial of temper, *casus belli*; irritation &c. (*anger*) 900; passion &c. (*state of excitability*) 825; thrill &c. (*feeling*) 821; repression of feeling &c. 826.

V. excite, affect, touch, move, impress, strike, interest, intrigue, animate, inspire, impassion, smite, infect; stir -, fire -, warm- the blood; set astir; a-, wake; a-, waken; call forth; e-, pro-voke; raise up, summon up, call up, wake up, blow up, get up, light up; raise; get up steam, rouse, arouse, stir, fire, kindle, enkindle, apply the torch, set on fire, inflame, illuminate.

stimulate; ex-, suscitate; inspirit; spirit up, stir up, work up; infuse life into, give new life to: bring -. introduce- new blood; quicken;

sharpen, whet; work upon &c. (*incite*) 615; hurry on, give a fillip, put on one's mettle.

fan the -fire, – flame; blow the coals, stir the embers; fan, – into a flame; foster, heat, warm, foment, raise to a fever heat; keep -up, – the pot boiling; revive, rekindle; rake up, rip up.

stir –, play on –, come home to- the feelings; touch -a string, – a chord, – the soul, – the heart; go to one's heart, penetrate, pierce, go through one, touch to the quick, open the wound; possess –, pervade –, penetrate –, imbrue –, absorb –, affect –, disturb- the soul.

absorb, rivet the attention; sink into the -mind, – heart; prey on the mind; intoxicate; over-whelm, -power; *bouleverser*, upset, turn one's head.

fascinate; enrapture &c. (*give pleasure*) 829.

agitate, perturb, ruffle, fluster, flutter, shake, disturb, faze, startle, shock, stagger; give one a -shock, – turn; strike -dumb, – all of a heap; stun, astound, electrify, galvanize, petrify.

irritate, sting; cut, – to the -heart, – quick; try one's temper; fool to the top of one's bent, pique; infuriate, madden, make one's blood boil; lash into fury &c. (*wrath*) 900.

be -excited &c. *adj.*; flash up, flare up; catch the infection; thrill &c. (*feel*) 821; mantle; work oneself up; seethe, boil, simmer, foam, fume, flame, rage, rave; run mad &c. (*passion*) 825.

Adj. excited &c. *v.*; wrought up, on the *qui vive*, astir, sparkling; in a -quiver &c. 821, – fever, – ferment, – blaze, – state of excitement; in hysterics; black in the face, over-wrought; hot, red-hot, flushed, feverish; all -of a twitter, – of a flutter, – of a dither, – in a pucker; with -quivering lips, – tears in one's eyes.

flaming; boiling, – over; ebullient, seething; foaming, – at the mouth; fuming, raging, carried away by passion, wild, raving, frantic, mad, distracted, distraught, beside oneself, out of one's wits, amuck, ready to burst, *bouleversé*, demoniacal.

lost, *éperdu*, tempest-tossed; haggard; ready to sink.

stung to the quick, up, on one's high ropes.

exciting &c. *v.*; impressive, warm, glowing, fervid, swelling, impos-ing, spirit-stirring, thrilling; high-wrought; soul-stirring, -subduing; heart-swelling, -thrilling; agonizing &c. (*painful*) 830; telling, sensa-tional, melodramatic, hysterical; over-powering, -whelming; more than flesh and blood can bear.

piquant &c. (*pungent*) 392; spicy, appetizing, provocative, *provoquant*, tantalizing.

Adv. till one is black in the face.

Phr. the heart -beating high, – going pit-a-pat, – leaping into one's mouth; the blood -being up, – boiling in one's veins; the eye -glisten-ing, – 'in a fine frenzy rolling'; the head turned.

---

825. [Excess of sensitiveness.] **Excit-ability.**—**N.** excitability, impetuosity, vehemence; boisterousness &c. *adj.*; turbulence; impatience, intolerance, non-endurance; irritability &c. (*irasci-bility*) 901; itching &c. (*desire*) 865; wincing; disquiet, -ude; restlessness; fidgets, fidgetiness; agitation &c. (*ir-regular motion*) 315.

826. [Absence of excitability, or of excitement.] **Inexcitability.**—**N.** inex-cit-, imperturb-, inirrit-ability; even temper, tranquil mind, dispassion; tol-erance, toleration, patience.

passiveness &c. (*physical inertness*) 172; hebet-ude, -ation; impassibility &c. (*insensibility*) 823; stupefaction.

coolness, calmness &c. *adj.*; compo-

trepidation, perturbation, ruffle, hurry, -skurry, fuss, flurry; fluster, flutter; pother, stew, ferment; whirl; thrill &c. (*feeling*) 821; state –, fever-of excitement; transport.

passion, excitement, flush, heat; fever, -heat; fire, flame, fume, blood boiling; tumult; effervescence, ebullition; boiling, – over; whiff, gust, storm, tempest; scene, breaking out, burst, fit, paroxysm, explosion; out-break, -burst; agony.

violence &c. 173; fierceness &c. *adj.*; rage, fury, *furor*, *furore*, desperation, madness, distraction, raving, delirium, brain storm; frenzy, hysterics; intoxication; tearing –, raging- passion, towering rage; anger &c. 900.

fascination, infatuation, fanaticism; Quixot-ism, -ry; *tête montée*.

V. be -impatient &c. *adj.*; not be able to -bear &c. 826; bear ill, wince, chafe, champ the bit; be in a -stew &c. *n.*; be out of all patience, fidget, fuss, not have a wink of sleep; toss, – on one's pillow.

lose one's temper &c. 900; break –, burst –, fly- out; go –, fly- -off, – off the handle, – off at a tangent; explode; flare up, flame up, fire up, burst into a flame, take fire, fire, burn; boil, – over; foam, fume, rage, rave, rant, tear; go –, run- -wild, – mad; go into hysterics; run -riot, – amuck; *battre la campagne, faire le diable à quatre*, play the deuce; raise -Cain, – the devil.

Adj. excitable, easily excited, in an excitable state; highly strung; irritable &c. (*irascible*) 901; impatient, intolerant.

feverish, febrile, hysterical; delirious, mad, moody, maggoty-headed.

unquiet, mercurial, electric, galvanic, hasty, hurried, restless, fidgety, fussy; chafing &c. *v.*

startlish, mettlesome, high mettled, skittish.

vehement, demonstrative, violent, wild, furious, fierce, fiery, hot-headed, mad-cap.

over-zealous, enthusiastic, impassioned, fanatical; rabid &c. (*eager*) 865.

rampant, clamorous, uproarious, tur-

sure, placidity, indisturbance, imperturbation, *sang-froid*, tranquillity, serenity; quiet, -ude; peace of mind, mental calmness.

staidness &c. *adj.*; gravity, sobriety, Quakerism; philosophy, equanimity, stoicism, command of temper; self-possession, -control, -command, -restraint; presence of mind.

submission &c. 725; resignation; suffer-, support-, endur-, long-suffer-, forbear-ance; longanimity; fortitude; patience -of Job, – 'on a monument,' – 'sovereign o'er transmuted ill'; moderation; repression –, subjugation- of feeling; restraint &c. 751.

tranquillization &c. (*moderation*) 174.

V. be -composed &c. *adj.*

laisser -faire, – aller; take things -easily, – as they come; take it easy, run on, live and let live; take -easily, – coolly, – in good part; *æquam servare mentem*.

bear -well, – the brunt; go through, support, endure, brave, disregard.

tolerate, suffer, stand, bide; abide, aby; bear –, put up –, abide- with; acquiesce; submit &c. (*yield*) 725; submit with a good grace; resign –, reconcile- oneself to; brook, digest, eat, swallow, pocket, stomach; make -light of, – the best of, – a virtue of necessity; put a good face on, keep one's countenance; carry -on, – through; check &c. 751- oneself.

compose, appease &c. (*moderate*) 174; propitiate; repress &c. (*restrain*) 751; render insensible &c. 823; overcome –, allay –, repress- one's -excitability &c. 825; master one's feelings.

make -oneself, – one's mind- easy; set one's mind at -ease, – rest.

calm –, cool- down; thaw, grow cool; be -borne, – endured; go down.

Adj. in-, un-excitable; imperturbable; unsusceptible &c. (*insensible*) 823; un-, dis-passionate; cold-blooded, inirritable; enduring &c. *v.*; stoical, Platonic, philosophic, staid, stayed; sober, – minded; grave; sober –, grave- as a judge; sedate, demure, cool-, level-headed; steady.

easy-going, peaceful, placid, calm; quiet, – as a mouse; tranquil, serene;

bulent, tempestuous, tumultuary, boisterous.

impulsive, impetuous, passionate;
uncontroll-ed, -able; ungovernable,
irrepressible, stanchless, inextinguishable, burning, simmering, volcanic,
ready to burst forth.

excit-ed, -ing &c. 824.

Int. pish! pshaw!

Phr. *noli me tangere.*

cool, – as -a cucumber, – custard; un-
demonstrative.

temperate &c. (*moderate*) 174; composed, collected; un-excited, -stirred,
-ruffled, -disturbed, -perturbed, -im-
passioned; unoffended; unresisting.

meek, tolerant; patient, – as Job;
submissive &c. 725; tame; content,
resigned, chastened, subdued, lamb-
like; gentle, – as a lamb; *suaviter in
modo*; mild, – as mother's milk; soft
as peppermint; armed with patience, bearing with, clement, for-
bearant, long-suffering.

Adv. 'like patience on a monument smiling at grief'; *æquo animo*,
in cold blood &c. 823; more in sorrow than in anger.

Int. patience! and shuffle the cards.

SECTION II. PERSONAL AFFECTIONS*

1°. PASSIVE AFFECTIONS

827. Pleasure.—N. pleasure, gratification, enjoyment, fruition; ob-, delectation; relish, zest; *gusto* &c.
(*physical pleasure*) 377; satisfaction
&c. (*content*) 831; complacency.

well-being; good &c. 618; snugness,
comfort, ease; cushion &c. 215; *sans
souci*, mind at ease.

joy, gladness, delight, glee, cheer,
sunshine; cheerfulness &c. 836.

treat, refreshment; frolic, fun, lark,
gambol, merry-making; amusement
&c. 840; luxury &c. 377; hedonism.

mens sana in corpore sano.

happiness, felicity, bliss; beati-tude,
-fication; enchantment, transport, rapture, ravishment, ecstasy; *summum
bonum*; paradise, elysium &c. (*heaven*)
981; third –, seventh- heaven; unalloyed -happiness &c.

honeymoon; palmy –, halcyon- days;
golden -age, – time; *Saturnia regna*,
Eden, Arcadia, happy valley, Agapemone; Cockaigne.

V. be pleased &c. 829; feel –, experi-
ence- pleasure &c. *n.*; joy; enjoy –,
hug- oneself; be in -clover &c. 377,
– elysium &c. 981; tread on enchanted
ground; fall –, go- into raptures.

feel at home, breathe freely, bask in
the sunshine.

be -pleased &c. 829- with; receive –,
derive- pleasure &c. *n.*- from; take
-pleasure &c. *n.*- in; delight in, rejoice

828. Pain. — N. mental suffering,
pain, dolour; suffer-ing, -ance; ache,
smart &c. (*physical pain*) 378; passion.

displeasure, dissatisfaction, discomfort, discomposure, disquiet; *malaise*;
inquietude, uneasiness, vexation of
spirit; taking; discontent &c. 832.

dejection &c. 837; weariness &c. 841.

annoyance, irritation, worry, infliction, visitation; plague, bore; bother,
-ation; stew, vexation, mortification,
chagrin, *esclandre*; *mauvais quart
d'heure.*

care, anxiety, solicitude, trouble,
trial, ordeal, fiery ordeal, shock, blow,
cark, dole, fret, burden, load.

concern, grief, sorrow, distress, affliction, woe, bitterness, gloom, heartache;
heavy –, aching –, bleeding –, broken-
heart; heavy affliction, gnawing grief.

unhappiness, infelicity, misery, tribulation, wretchedness, desolation; despair &c. 859; extremity, prostration,
depth of misery.

nightmare, *ephialtes*, incubus.

anguish, agony; throe, tor-ture,
-ment; crucifixion, martyrdom; pang,
twinge, stab; the rack, the stake;
purgatory &c. (*hell*) 982.

hell upon earth; iron age, reign of
terror; slough of despond &c. (*adversity*) 735; peck –, sea- of troubles; ills
that flesh is heir to &c. (*evil*) 619;

* Or those which concern one's own state of feeling.

in, indulge in, luxuriate in; gloat over &c. (*physical pleasure*) 377; enjoy, relish, like; love &c. 897; take -to, – a fancy to; have a liking for; enter into the spirit of.

take in good part.

treat oneself to, solace oneself with.

Adj. pleased &c. 829; not sorry; glad, -some; pleased as Punch.

happy, blest, blessed, blissful, beatified; happy as -a king, – the day is long; thrice happy, *ter quaterque beatus*; enjoying &c. *v.*; joyful &c. (*in spirits*) 836; hedonic.

in -a blissful state, – paradise &c. 981, – raptures, – ecstasies, – a transport of delight; rapturous.

comfortable &c. (*physical pleasure*) 377; at ease; content &c. 831; *sans souci*, in clover.

overjoyed, entranced, enchanted; enraptured; en-, ravished; transported; fascinated, captivated.

with -a joyful face, – sparkling eyes.

pleasing &c. 829; ecstatic, beat-ic, -ific; painless, unalloyed, without alloy, cloudless.

Adv. happily &c. *adj.*; with pleasure &c. (*willingly*) 602; with -glee &c. *n.*

Phr. one's heart leaping with joy.

---

miseries of human life; unkindest cut of all.

sufferer, victim, prey, martyr, object of compassion, wretch, shorn lamb.

V. feel –, suffer –, experience –, undergo –, bear –, endure- pain &c. *n.*; smart, ache &c. (*physical pain*) 378; suffer, bleed, ail; be the victim of; bear –, take up- the cross.

labour under afflictions; quaff the bitter cup, have a bad time of it; fall on evil days &c. (*adversity*) 735; go hard with, come to grief, fall a sacrifice to, drain the cup of misery to the dregs, sup full of horrors.

sit on thorns, be on pins and needles, wince, fret, chafe, worry oneself, be in a taking, fret and fume, take -on, – to heart.

grieve; mourn &c. (*lament*) 839; yearn, repine, pine, droop, languish, sink; give way; despair &c. 859; break one's heart; weigh upon the heart &c. (*inflict pain*) 830.

Adj. in –, in a state of –, full of- pain &c. *n.*; suffering &c. *v.*; pained, afflicted, worried, displeased &c. 830; aching, griped, sore &c. (*physical pain*) 378; on the rack, in limbo; between hawk and buzzard.

un-comfortable, -easy; ill at ease; in a -taking, – way; disturbed; discontented &c. 832; out of humour &c. 901*a*; weary &c. 841.

heavy laden, stricken, crushed, a prey to, victimized, ill-used.

unfortunate &c. (*hapless*) 735; to be pitied, doomed, devoted, accursed, undone, lost, stranded.

unhappy, infelicitous, poor, wretched, miserable, woe-begone; cheerless &c. (*dejected*) 837; careworn.

concerned, sorry; sorrow-ing, -ful; cut up, chagrined, horrified, horror-stricken; in –, plunged in –, a prey to- grief &c. *n.*; in tears &c. (*lamenting*) 839; steeped to the lips in misery; heart-stricken, -broken, -scalded; broken-hearted; in despair &c. 859.

Phr. 'the iron entered into the soul'; '*hæret lateri lethalis arundo*'; one's heart bleeding.

---

829. [Capability of giving pleasure; cause or source of pleasure.] **Pleasurableness.—N.** pleasurable-, pleasant-, agreeable-ness &c. *adj.*; pleasure giving, jocundity, delectability; amusement &c. 840.

attraction &c. (*motive*) 615; attractiveness, -ability; invitingness &c. *adj.*; charm, fascination, captivation, en-

830. [Capability of giving pain; cause or source of pain.] **Painfulness.** **—N.** painfulness &c. *adj.*; trouble, care &c. (*pain*) 828; trial; af-, in-fliction; cross, blow, stroke, burden, load, curse; bitter -pill, – draught, – cup; waters of bitterness.

annoyance, grievance, nuisance, vexation, mortification, sickener; bore

chantment, witchery, seduction, winsomeness, winning ways, amenity, amiability, sweetness.

loveliness &c. (*beauty*) 845; sunny -, bright- side; sweets &c. (*sugar*) 396; goodness &c. 648; manna in the wilderness, land flowing with milk and honey.

treat; regale &c. (*physical pleasure*) 377; dainty; tit-, tid-bit; nuts, *sauce piquante.*

V. cause -, produce -, create -, give -, afford -, procure -, offer -, present -, yield- pleasure &c. 827.

please, charm, delight; gladden &c. (*make cheerful*) 836; take, captivate, fascinate; enchant, entrance, enrapture, transport, bewitch; en-, ravish.

bless, beatify; satisfy; gratify, - desire &c. 865; slake, satiate, quench; indulge, humour, flatter, tickle; tickle the palate &c. (*savoury*) 394; regale, refresh; enliven; treat; amuse &c. 840; take -, tickle -, hit- one's fancy; meet one's wishes; win -, gladden -, rejoice -, warm the cockles of- the heart; do one's heart good.

attract, allure &c. (*move*) 615; stimulate &c. (*excite*) 824; interest, intrigue.

make things pleasant, popularize, gild the pill, sweeten.

Adj. causing pleasure &c. *v.*; pleasure-giving; pleas-ing, -ant, -urable; agreeable, cushy; grat-eful, -ifying; leef, lief, acceptable; welcome, - as the roses in May; welcomed; favourite; to one's -taste, - mind, - liking, - heart's content; satisfactory &c. (*good*) 648.

refreshing; comfortable; cordial; genial; glad, -some; sweet, delectable, nice, dainty; delic-ate, -ious; dulcet; luscious &c. 396; palatable &c. 394; luxurious, voluptuous; sensual &c. 377.

attractive &c. 615; inviting, prepossessing, engaging; win-ning, -some; taking, fascinating, captivating, killing; seduc-ing, -tive; alluring, enticing; appetizing &c. (*exciting*) 824; cheering &c. 836; bewitching; interesting, absorbing, enchanting, entrancing, enravishing.

charming; delightful, felicitous, exquisite; lovely &c. (*beautiful*) 845;

bother, pother, hot water, sea of troubles, hornet's nest, plague, pest.

cancer, ulcer, sting, thorn; canker &c. (*bane*) 663; scorpion &c. (*evil-doer*) 913; dagger &c. (*arms*) 727; scourge &c. (*instrument of punishment*) 975; carking -, canker worm of- care.

mishap, misfortune &c. (*adversity*) 735; désagrément, esclandre, ɪub.

source of -irritation, - annoyance; wound, sore subject, skeleton in the closet; thorn in -the flesh, - one's side; where the shoe pinches, gall and wormwood.

sorry sight, heavy news, provocation; affront &c. 929; head and front of one's offending.

infestation, molestation; malignity &c. (*malevolence*) 907; acrimony.

V. cause -, occasion -, give -, bring -, induce -, produce -, create -, inflict-pain &c. 828; pain, hurt, wound.

pinch, prick, gripe &c. (*physical pain*) 378; pierce, lancinate, cut.

hurt -, wound -, grate upon -, jar upon- the feelings; wring -, pierce -, lacerate -, break -, rend- the heart; make the heart bleed; tear -, rend- the heart-strings; draw tears from the eyes.

sadden; make -unhappy &c. 828; plunge into sorrow, grieve, fash, afflict, distress; cut -up, - to the heart.

displease, annoy, incommode, discommode, discompose, trouble, disquiet, disturb, thwart, cross, perplex, molest, tease, rag, tire, irk, vex, mortify, wherret, worry, plague, bother, pester, bore, pother, harass, harry, badger, heckle, bait, beset, infest, persecute, importune, be troublesome.

wring, harrow, torment, torture; put to the -rack, - question; break on the wheel, rack, scarify; cruci-ate, -fy; convulse, agonize; barb the dart; plant a -dagger in the breast, - thorn in one's side.

irritate, provoke, sting, nettle, try the patience, pique, fret, rile, tweak the nose, chafe, gall; sting -, wound -, cut- to the quick; aggrieve, affront, enchafe, enrage, ruffle, sour the temper; give offence &c. (*resentment*) 900.

ravishing, rapturous; heartfelt, thrilling, ecstatic; beat-ic, -ific; seraphic; empyrean; elysian &c. (*heavenly*) 981. palmy, halcyon, Saturnian.

Phr. *decies repetita placebit.*

maltreat, bite, snap at, assail, bully; smite &c. (*punish*) 972.

sicken, disgust, revolt, nauseate, disenchant, repel, offend, shock, stink in the nostrils; go against –, turn- the stomach; make one sick, set the teeth on edge, go against the grain, grate on the ear; stick in one's -throat, – gizzard; rankle, gnaw, corrode, horrify, appal, freeze the blood; chill the spine; make the -flesh creep, – hair stand on end; make the blood -curdle, – run cold; make one shudder.

haunt, – the memory; weigh –, prey- on the -heart, – mind, – spirits; bring one's grey hairs with sorrow to the grave; add a nail to one's coffin.

Adj. causing pain, hurting &c. *v.*; hurtful &c. (*bad*) 649; painful; dolor-ific, -ous; unpleasant; un-, dis-pleasing; disagreeable, unpalatable, bitter, distasteful; uninviting; unwelcome; undesir-able, -ed; obnoxious; unacceptable, unpopular, thankless.

unsatisfactory, untoward, unlucky, uncomfortable.

distressing; afflict-ing, -ive; joy-, cheer-, comfort-less; dismal, disheartening; depress-ing, -ive; dreary, melancholy, grievous, piteous; woeful, rueful, mournful, deplorable, pitiable, lamentable; sad, affecting, touching, pathetic.

irritating, provoking, stinging, annoying, aggravating, mortifying, galling; unaccommodating, invidious, vexatious; trouble-, tire-, irk-, weari-some; plagu-ing, -y; awkward.

importunate; teas-, pester-, bother-, harass-, worry-, torment-, cark-ing.

in-toler-, -suffer-, -support-able; un-bear-, -endur-able; past bearing; not to be -borne, – endured; more than flesh and blood can bear; enough to -drive one mad, – provoke a saint, – make a parson swear, – try the patience of Job.

shocking, terrific, grim, appalling, crushing; dreadful, fearful, frightful; thrilling, tremendous, dire; heart-breaking, -rending, -wounding, -corroding, -sickening; harrowing, rending.

odious, hateful, execrable, repulsive, repellent, abhorrent; horri-d, -ble, -fic, -fying; offensive; nause-ous, -ating; disgust-, sicken-, revolt-ing; nasty; loath-some, -ful; fulsome; vile &c. (*bad*) 649; hideous &c. 846.

sharp, acute, sore, severe, grave, hard, harsh, cruel, biting, acrimonious, caustic; cutting, corroding, consuming, racking, excruciating, searching, searing, grinding, grating, agonizing; envenomed.

ruinous, disastrous, calamitous, tragical; desolating, withering; burdensome, onerous, oppressive; cumb-rous, -ersome.

Adv. painfully &c. *adj.*; with -pain &c. 828; deuced.

Int. *hinc illæ lachrymæ!* woe is me!

Phr. *surgit amari aliquid*; the place being too hot to hold one; the iron entering into the soul.

---

831. Content.—**N.** content, -ment, -edness; complacency, satisfaction, entire satisfaction, ease, heart's ease, peace of mind; serenity &c. 826; cheer-

832. Discontent. — **N.** discontent, -ment; dissatisfaction; dissent &c. 489; labour unrest.

disappointment, mortification; cold

fulness &c. 836; ray of comfort; comfort &c. (*well-being*) 827.

re-, conciliation; resignation &c. (*patience*) 826.

waiter on Providence.

V. be -content &c. *adj.*; rest -satisfied, – and be thankful; take the good the gods provide, let well alone, feel oneself at home, hug oneself, lay the flattering unction to one's soul.

take -up with, – in good part; assent &c. 488; be reconciled to, make one's peace with; get over it; take -heart, – comfort; put up with &c. (*bear*) 826.

render -content &c. *adj.*; set at ease, comfort; set one's -heart, – mind- at -ease, – rest; speak peace; conciliate, reconcile, win over, propitiate, disarm, beguile; content, satisfy; gratify &c. 829.

be -tolerated &c. 826; go down, – with; do.

Adj. content, -ed; satisfied &c. *v.*; at -ease, – one's ease, – home; with the mind at ease, *sans souci, sine curâ*, easy-going, not particular; conciliatory; unrepining, of good comfort; resigned &c. (*patient*) 826; cheerful &c. 836.

un-afflicted, -vexed, -molested, -plagued; serene &c. 826; at rest; snug, comfortable; in one's element.

satisfactory, satisfying, ample, sufficient, adequate, tolerable.

Adv. to one's heart's content; *à la bonne heure*; all for the best.

Int. amen &c. (*assent*) 488; very well, so much the better, well and good; it –, that- will do; it cannot be helped.

Phr. nothing comes amiss.

comfort; regret &c. 833; repining, taking on &c. *v.*; inquietude, vexation of spirit, soreness; heart-burning, -grief; querulousness &c. (*lamentation*) 839; hypercriticism.

malcontent, grumbler, growler, croaker, *laudator temporis acti*; censurer, complainer, faultfinder, murmurer, Adullamite, Diehard, Bitterender.

the Opposition, cave of Adullam, indignation meeting, 'winter of our discontent.'

V. be -discontented &c. *adj.*; quarrel with one's bread and butter; repine; regret &c. 833; wish one at the bottom of the Red Sea; take -on, – to heart; shrug the shoulders; make a wry –, pull a long- face; knit one's brows; look -blue, – black, – black as thunder, – blank, – glum.

take -in bad part, – ill; fret, chafe, make a piece of work; grumble, croak, grouse; lament &c. 839.

cause -discontent &c. *n.*; dissatisfy, disappoint, mortify, put out, disconcert; cut up; dishearten.

Adj. discontented; dissatisfied &c. *v.*; unsatisfied, ungratified; dissident; dissentient &c. 489; malcontent, exigent, exacting, hypercritical.

repining &c. *v.*; regretful &c. 833; down in the mouth &c. (*dejected*) 837.

in -high dudgeon, – a fume, – the sulks, – the dumps, – bad humour; glum, sulky; sour, – as a crab; soured, sore; out of -humour, – temper.

disappointing &c. *v.*; unsatisfactory.

Int. so much the worse!

Phr. that –, it- will never do.

---

833. Regret.—N. regret, repining; home sickness, nostalgia; *mal –, maladie-du pays*; lamentation &c. 839, contrition, compunction, penitence &c. 950.

bitterness, heart-burning.

laudator temporis acti &c. (*discontent*) 832.

V. regret, deplore; bewail &c. (*lament*) 839; repine, cast a longing lingering look behind; rue, – the day; repent &c. 950; *infandum renovare dolorem*.

prey –, weigh –, have a weight- on the mind; leave an aching void.

Adj. regretting &c. *v.*; regretful; home-sick.

regretted &c. *v.*; much to be regretted, regrettable; lamentable &c. (*bad*) 649.

Int. what a pity! hang it!
Phr. 'tis -pity, – too true.

834. Relief.—N. relief; deliverance; refreshment &c. 689; easement, softening, alleviation, mitigation, palliation &c. 174; soothing, lullaby; cradle song, *berceuse.*

solace, consolation, comfort, encouragement.

lenitive, *restorative* &c. (*remedy*) 662; poultice &c. *v.*; cushion &c. 215; crumb of comfort, balm in Gilead; aspirin.

V. relieve, ease, alleviate, mitigate, palliate, soothe, addulce; salve; soften, – down; foment, stupe, poultice; assuage, allay.

cheer, comfort, console; encourage, bear up, pat on the back, give comfort, set at ease; enliven, gladden –, cheerthe heart.

remedy; cure &c. (*restore*) 660; refresh; pour -balm into, – oil on.

smooth the ruffled brow of care, temper the wind to the shorn lamb, lay the flattering unction to one's soul.

disburden &c. (*free*) 705; take off a load of care.

be relieved; breathe more freely, draw a long breath; take comfort; dry –, wipe- the -tears, – eyes.

Adj. relieving &c. *v.*; consolatory, soothing; assua-ging, -sive; bal-my, -samic; lenitive, palliative; anodyne &c. (*remedial*) 662; curative &c. 660.

835. Aggravation.—N. aggravation, heightening; exacerbation; exasperation; overestimation &c. 482; exaggeration &c. 549.

V. aggravate, render worse, heighten, embitter, sour; ex-, acerbate; exasperate, envenom; tease, provoke, enrage.

add fuel to the -fire, – flame; fan the flame &c. (*excite*) 824; go from bad to worse &c. (*deteriorate*) 659.

Adj. aggravated &c. *v.*; worse, unrelieved; aggravable; aggravating &c. *v.*

Adv. out of the frying pan into the fire, from bad to worse, worse and worse.

Int. so much the worse!

836. Cheerfulness.—N. cheerfulness &c. *adj.*; geniality, gaiety, *l'allegro*, cheer, good humour, spirits; high –, animal –, flow of- spirits; glee, high glee, light heart; sunshine of the -mind, – breast; *gaieté de cœur, bon naturel.*

liveliness &c. *adj.*; life, alacrity, vivacity, animation, *allégresse*; jocundity, joviality, jollity; levity; jocularity &c. (*wit*) 842.

mirth, merriment, hilarity, exhilaration; laughter &c. 838; merry-making &c. (*amusement*) 840; heyday, rejoicing &c. 838; marriage bells.

nepenthe, Euphrosyne.

optimism &c. (*hopefulness*) 858; self-complacency.

V. be -cheerful &c. *adj.*; have the mind at ease, smile, put a good face upon, keep up one's spirits; view -the bright side of the picture, – things *en couleur de rose*; *ridentem dicere verum*,

837. Dejection.—N. dejection; dejectedness &c. *adj.*; depression, prosternation; lowness –, depression- of spirits; weight –, oppression –, dampon the spirits; low –, bad –, drooping –, depressed- spirits; heart sinking; heaviness –, failure- of heart.

heaviness &c. *adj.*; infestivity, gloom; weariness &c. 841; tædium vitæ, disgust of life; *mal du pays* &c. (*regret*) 833.

melancholy; sadness &c. *adj.*; *il penseroso, melancholia,* dismals, mumps, mopes, lachrymals, dumps, blues, blue devils, doldrums, vapours, megrims, spleen, horrors, hypochondriasis, pessimism; despondency, slough of Despond; disconsolateness &c. *adj.*; hope deferred, blank despondency.

prostration, – of soul; broken heart; despair &c. 859; cave of -despair, – Trophonius.

cheer up, brighten up, light up, bear up; chirp, take heart, cast away care, drive dull care away, perk up.

rejoice &c. 838; carol, chirrup, lilt; frisk, rollick, give a loose to mirth.

cheer, enliven, elate, exhilarate, gladden, inspirit, animate, raise the spirits, inspire; put in good humour; cheer –, rejoice- the heart; delight &c. (*give pleasure*) 829.

Adj. cheerful; happy &c. 827; cheery, -ly; of good cheer, smiling; blithe; in –, in good- spirits; in high -spirits, – feather; happy as -the day is long, – a king; gay, – as a lark; *allegro*; light, -some, -hearted; buoyant, *débonnaire*, bright, free and easy, airy; janty, jaunty, canty; spright-ly, -ful; spry; spirit-ed, -ful; lively; animated, breezy, vivacious; brisk, – as a bee; sparkling; sportive; full of -play, – spirit; all alive.

sunny, palmy; hopeful &c. 858.

merry, – as a -cricket, – grig, – marriage bell; joyful, joyous, jocund, jovial; jolly, – as a thrush, – as a sandboy; blithesome; glee-ful, -some; hilarious, rattling.

winsome, bonny, hearty, buxom.

play-ful, -some; *folâtre*, playful as a kitten, tricksy, frisky, frolicsome; gamesome; jocose, jocular, waggish; mirth-, laughter-loving; mirthful, rollicking.

elate, -d; exulting, jubilant, flushed; rejoicing &c. 838; cock-a-hoop.

cheering, inspiriting, exhilarating; cardiac, -al; pleasing &c. 829; flourishing, halcyon.

Adv. cheerfully &c. *adj.*

Int. never say die! come! cheer up! hurrah! &c. 838; 'hence loathed melancholy!' begone dull care! away with melancholy!

demureness &c. *adj.*; gravity, solemnity; long –, grave- face.

hypochondriac, seek-sorrow, self-tormentor, *heautontimorumenos, malade imaginaire, médecin tant pis*; croaker, pessimist; mope, mopus.

[Cause of dejection] affliction &c. 830; sorry sight; *memento mori*; damper, wet blanket, Job's comforter; death's head, skeleton at the feast.

V. be -dejected &c. *adj.*; grieve; mourn &c. (*lament*) 839; take on, give way, lose heart, despond, droop, sink.

lower, look downcast, frown, pout; hang down the head; pull –, make- a long face; laugh on the wrong side of the mouth; grin a ghastly smile; look -blue, – like a drowned man; lay –, take- to heart.

mope, brood over; fret; sulk; pine, – away; yearn; repine &c. (*regret*) 833; despair &c. 859.

refrain from laughter, keep one's countenance; be –, look- grave &c. *adj.*; repress a smile, keep a straight face.

depress; dis-courage, -hearten; dispirit; damp, dull, deject, lower, sink, dash, knock down, unman, prostrate, break one's heart; frown upon; cast a -gloom, – shade- on; sadden; damp –, dash –, wither- one's hopes; weigh –, lie heavy –, prey- on the -mind, – spirits; damp –, depress- the spirits.

Adj. cheer-, joy-, spirit-less; uncheerful, -y; unlively; unhappy &c. 828; melancholy, dismal, sombre, dark, gloomy, adust, *triste*, clouded, murky, lowering, frowning, lugubrious, Acherontic, funereal, mournful, lamentable, dreadful.

dreary, flat; dull, – as -a beetle, – ditchwater; depressing &c. *v.*

'melancholy as a gib cat'; oppressed with –, a prey to- melancholy; downcast, -hearted; down -in the mouth, – on one's luck; heavy-hearted; in the -dumps, – suds, – sulks, – doldrums; in doleful dumps, in bad humour; sullen; mumpish, dumpish; mopish, moping; moody, glum; sulky &c. (*discontented*) 832; out of -sorts, – humour, – heart, – spirits; ill at ease, low-spirited, in low spirits, a cup too low; weary &c. 841; dis-couraged, -heartened; desponding; chop-, jaw-, crest-fallen.

sad, pensive, *penseroso*, tristful; dole-some, -ful; woebegone lachrymose, in tears, melancholic, hipped, hypochondriacal, bil ious, jaundiced, atrabilious, saturnine, splenetic; lackadaisical; serious, sedate, staid, stayed; grave, – as -a judge, – an undertaker, – a mustard pot; sober, solemn, demure; grim; grim-faced, -visaged; rueful, wan, long-faced.

disconsolate; un-, in-consolable; forlorn, comfortless, desolate, désolé, sick at heart; soul-, heart-sick; au désespoir; in despair &c. 859; lost.

overcome; broken-, borne-, bowed-down; heart-stricken &c. (mental suffering) 828; cut up, dashed, sunk; unnerved, unmanned; down-fallen, -trodden; broken-hearted; care-worn.

Adv. with -a long face, – tears in one's eyes; sadly &c. adj.

Phr. the countenance falling; the heart -failing, – sinking within-one.

838. [Expression of pleasure.] **Rejoicing.**—**N.** rejoicing, exultation, triumph, jubilation, heyday, flush, revelling; merry-making &c. (amusement) 840; jubilee &c. (celebration) 883; pæan, Te Deum &c. (thanksgiving) 990; congratulation &c. 896; applause &c. 931.

smile, simper, smirk, grin; broad –, sardonic- grin.

laughter, giggle, titter, crow, cheer, chuckle, snicker, snigger, shout; Homeric laughter, horse –, hearty- laugh; guffaw; burst –, fit –, shout –, roar –, peal- of laughter; cachinnation.

risibility; derision &c. 856.

Momus; Democritus the Abderite; rollicker; Laughter holding both his sides.

V. rejoice; thank –, bless- one's stars; congratulate –, hug- oneself; rub –, clap- one's hands; smack the lips, fling up one's cap; dance, skip, caleer; sing, carol, chirrup, chirp; hurrah; cry for –, leap with- joy; exult &c. (boast) 884; triumph; hold jubilee &c. (celebrate) 883; make merry &c. (sport) 840; sing a pæan of joy.

smile, simper, smirk; grin, – like a Cheshire cat; mock, laugh in one's sleeve; laugh, – outright; giggle, titter, snigger, crow, smicker, chuckle, snicker, cackle; burst -out, – into a fit of laughter; shout, split, roar.

shake –, split –, hold both- one's sides; roar –, die- with laughter.

raise laughter &c. (amuse) 840.

Adj. rejoicing &c. v.; jubilant, exultant, triumphant; flushed, elated; laughing &c. v.; risible; ready to -burst, – split, – die with laughter; convulsed with laughter.

839. [Expression of pain.] **Lamentation.**—**N.** lament, -ation; wail, complaint, plaint, murmur, mutter, grumble, groan, moan, whine, whimper, sob, sigh, suspiration, heaving, deep sigh.

cry &c. (vociferation) 411; scream, howl; outcry, wail of woe, frown, scowl.

tear; weeping &c. v.; flood of tears, fit of crying, lachrymation, melting mood, weeping and gnashing of teeth.

plaintiveness &c. adj.; languishment; condolence &c. 915.

mourning, weeds, willow, cypress, crêpe, crape, deep mourning; sackcloth and ashes; knell &c. 363; dump, death-song, dirge, coronach, keen, nenia, requiem, elegy, epicedium; threne; mon-, thren-ody; jeremiad; ululation.

mourner, professional mourner, keener; grumbler &c. (discontent) 832; Niobe; Heraclitus.

V. lament, mourn, deplore, grieve, weep over; be-wail, -moan; keen; condole with &c. 915; fret &c. (suffer) 828; wear –, go into –, put on- mourning; wear -the willow, – sackcloth and ashes; infandum renovare dolorem &c. (regret) 833; give sorrow words.

sigh; give –, heave –, fetch- a sigh; 'waft a sigh from Indus to the pole'; sigh 'like furnace'; wail.

cry, weep, sob, greet, blubber, pipe, snivel, bibber, whimper, pule; pipe one's eye; drop –, shed- -tears, – a tear; melt –, burst- into tears; fondre en larmes; cry -oneself blind, – one's eyes out.

scream &c. (cry out) 411; mew &c. (animal sounds) 412; groan, moan,

laughable &c. (*ludicrous*) 853.

Int. hip, hip, -hurrah! huzza! aha! hail! tolderolloll! tra-la la! Heaven be praised! *io triumphe! tant mieux!* so much the better.

Phr. the heart leaping with joy.

————

whine, yammer; roar; roar –, bellow-like a bull; cry out lustily, rend the air, yell.

frown, scowl, make a wry face, grimace, gnash one's teeth, wring one's hands, tear one's hair, beat one's breast, roll on the ground, burst with grief.

complain, murmur, mutter, grumble, growl, clamour, make a fuss about, croak, grunt, maunder; deprecate &c. (*disapprove*) 932.

cry out before one is hurt, complain without cause.

Adj. lamenting &c. *v.*; in mourning, in sackcloth and ashes; crying, sorrowing, -ful &c. (*unhappy*) 828; mourn-, tear-ful; lachrymose; plaint-ive, -ful, quer-ulous, -imonious; in the melting mood.

in tears, with tears in one's eyes; with -moistened, – watery-eyes; bathed –, dissolved- in tears; 'like Niobe all tears.'

elagiac, epicedial, threnetic.

Adv. *de profundis; les larmes aux yeux.*

Int. heigh-ho! alas! alack! O dear! ah –, woe is- me! lackadaisy! well –, lack –, alack- a day! well-a-way! alas the day! *O temporal O mores!* what a pity! *miserabile dictu!* O lud lud! too true!

Phr. tears -standing in, – starting from- the eyes; eyes -suffused. – swimming, – brimming –, overflowing- with tears.

840. Amusement.—N. amuse-, entertain-ment; diver-sion, -tissement; recreation, relaxation, solace; pastime, *passetemps*, sport; labour of love; pleasure &c. 827.

fun, frolic, merriment, whoopee, jollity; jovial-ity, -ness; heyday; laughter &c. 838; jocos-ity, -eness; droll-, buffoon-, tomfool-ery; mummery, masquing, pleasantry; wit &c. 842; quip, quirk.

play; game, – at romps; gambol, romp, prank, antic, rig, lark, spree, skylarking, vagary, trick, monkey trick, *gambade, fredaine, escapade, échappée,* bout, *espièglerie*; practical joke &c. (*ridicule*) 856.

dance; round -, square –, solo -, step -, tap -, clog –, skirt –, sand -, folk –, morris- dance, *pas seul,* step, turn, *chassé,* cut, shuffle, double shuffle; hop, reel, rigadoon, saraband, hornpipe, bolero, fandango, pavan, tarantella, minuet, waltz, polka; galop, -ade; schottische, *pas de quatre,* Boston, one-, two-step, rumba, tango, maxixe, fox-, turkey-trot, shimmy, ragtime, cakewalk, jazz, blues, Charleston; jig, breakdown, fling, strathspey; *alle-*

841. Weariness.—N. weariness, defatigation, boredom, *ennui*; lassitude &c. (*fatigue*) 688; drowsiness &c. 683.

disgust, nausea, loathing, sickness; satiety &c. 869; *tædium vitæ* &c. (*dejection*) 837.

wearisome-, tedious-ness &c. *adj.*; dull work, tedium, monotony, twice told tale.

bore, button-holer, proser, wet blanket; heavy hours, 'the enemy' [time].

V. weary, tire &c. (*fatigue*) 688; bore; bore –, weary –, tire- -to death, – out of one's life, – out of all patience; set –, send- to sleep; buttonhole.

pall, sicken, nauseate, disgust.

harp on the same string; drag its -slow, – weary- length along.

never hear the last of; be -tired &c. *adj.* -of, – with; yawn; die with *ennui.*

Adj. wearying &c. *v.*; wearing; weari-, tire-, irk-some; uninteresting, stupid, bald, devoid of interest, dry, monotonous, dull, arid, tedious, humdrum, mortal, flat; pros-y, -ing; slow; soporific, somniferous, dormitive.

disgusting &c. *v.*; unenjoyed.

weary; tired &c. *v.*; drowsy &c (*sleepy*) 683; uninterested, flagging

mande; gavot, -te; mazurka, morisco; quadrille, lancers, country dance, *cotillon*, polonaise, Sir Roger de Coverley, Swedish dance; *ballet* &c. (*drama*) 599; ball; *bal, – masqué, – costumé*; masquerade, fancy dress ball; *thé dansant*; Terpsichore, choreography, Russian ballet, classical dancing; eurythmics; nautch dance, *danse du ventre*, cancan.

used up, worn out, *blasé*, life-weary, weary of life; sick of.
Adv. wearily &c. *adj.*; *usque ad nauseam.*
Phr. time hanging heavily on one's hands; *toujours perdrix*; *crambe repetita.*

festivity, merry-making; party &c. (*social gathering*) 892; *fête*, festival, gala, *ridotto*; revel-s, -ry, -ling; carnival, brawl, saturnalia, high jinks; feast, banquet &c. (*food*) 298; regale, *symposium*, wassail; carous-e, -al; jollification, junket, wake, picnic, *fête champêtre*, garden party, gymkhana, regatta, track meet, fieldday, jamboree, treat.

round of pleasures, dissipation, a short life and a merry one, racketing, holiday making, high jinks.

rejoicing &c. 838; jubilee &c. (*celebration*) 883.

bonfire, fireworks, *feu-de-joie*, rocket, Catherine wheel, roman candle &c.

holiday; gala –, red letter –, play- day; high days and holidays; high –, Bank- holiday; May –, Derby- day; Saint –, Easter –, Whit- Monday; King's birthday, Empire Day; *mi-carême*; *Bairam*; wayzgoose, beanfeast, beano.

place of amusement, theatre &c. 599; concert-, ball-, assemblyroom; music-hall, cinema, movies, talkies, vaudeville; hippodrome, circus, rodeo; *casino, kursaal*; winter garden; park, pleasance, arbour; garden &c. 371; pleasure-, play-, cricket-, football-, polo-, croquet-, archery-, hunting-ground; golf links, race course, stadium, gridiron, bowl, speedway, racing track, ring; gymnasium, swimming pool; shooting gallery; tennis-, racket-court; bowling-green, -alley; croquet-lawn, rink, skating rink; roller-coaster, roundabout, carousel, merry-go-round; swing; *montagne russe*; switchback, scenic railway &c.

game, – of -chance, – skill; athletic sports, gymnastics; fencing; archery, rifle-shooting; tournament, pugilism &c. (*contention*) 720; sporting &c. 622; horse-racing, the turf; aquatics &c. 267; skating, roller skating; ski-running, -joring, -jumping, bobsleighing, luging, tobogganing, winter sports; sliding; cricket, tennis, lawn –, table –, deck- tennis, rackets, fives, squash, ping-pong, trap bat and ball, battledore and shuttlecock, badminton, *la grâce*; pall mall, tip-cat, croquet, golf, curling, hockey, basketball, soccer, football, Rugby, Association, *pallone*, polo; tent-pegging, tilting at the ring, quintain, greasy pole; quoits, *discus*; throwing the hammer, putting the -weight, – shot, tossing the caber; knurr and spell; leap-frog, hop, skip and jump; French and English, tug of war; blind man's buff, hunt the slipper, hide-and-seek, kiss in the ring; snapdragon; cross questions and crooked answers; jig-saw puzzle; rounders, base-ball, lacrosse &c.; angling; swimming, diving, water-polo.

billiards, pool, pyramids, snooker, bagatelle; bowls, skittles, ninepins, kail, American bowls.

cards; bridge, auction, contract, whist, rubber; round game, coon-can, loo, cribbage, *bésique*, pinocle, euchre, drole, *écarté*, skat, picquet, all-fours, quadrille, ombre, reverse, Pope Joan, commit;

bo-, boa-ston; *vingt-et-un*; *quinze*, thirty-one, put-and-take, speculation, connections, brag, cassino, lottery, commerce, snip-snap-snorem,
lift smoke, blind hookey, Polish bank, poker, banker; faro; Earl of
Coventry, Napoleon, nap, patience, pairs; old maid, fright, beggar-
my-neighbour; *baccarat, chemin de fer, monte;* craps.

chess, draughts, backgammon, dominoes, checkers, mah jong.
merelles, nine men's morris, go-bang, solitaire; game of –, fox and-
geese; lotto; &c.*

morra; gambling &c. (*chance*) 621; roulette.

toy, plaything, bauble; doll &c. (*puppet*) 554; teetotum; knick-
knack &c. (*trifle*) 643; magic lantern &c. (*show*) 448; peep-. puppet-,
raree-, gallanty-show; marionnettes, Punch and Judy; toy-shop;
'quips and cranks and wanton wiles, nods and becks and wreathèd
smiles.'

sportsman, gamester, gambler &c. 621; reveller, master of the
-ceremonies, – revels; *arbiter elegantiarum.*

V. amuse, entertain, divert, enliven; tickle, – the fancy; titillate,
raise a smile, put in good humour; cause –, create –, occasion –,
raise –, excite –, produce –, convulse with- laughter; set the table
in a roar, be the death of one.

recreate, solace, cheer, rejoice; please &c. 829; interest; treat,
regale.

amuse oneself; game; play, – a game, – pranks, – tricks; sport,
disport, toy, wanton, revel, junket, feast, carouse, banquet, make
merry; drown care; drive dull care away; frolic, gambol, frisk,
romp; caper; dance &c. (*leap*) 309; keep up the ball; run a rig,
sow one's wild oats, have one's fling, paint the town red, take
one's pleasure; see life; *desipere in loco*, play the fool.

make –, keep- holiday; go a Maying.

while away –, beguile- the time; kill time, dally.

Adj. amusing, entertaining, diverting &c. *v.*; recreative, lusory;
pleasant &c. (*pleasing*) 829; laughable &c. (*ludicrous*) 853; witty
&c. 842; fest-ive, -al; jovial, jolly, jocund, roguish, rompish; sporting; playful, – as a kitten; sportive, ludibrious.

amused &c. *v.*; 'pleased with a feather, tickled with a straw.'

Adv. 'on the light fantastic toe,' at play, in sport.

Int. *vive la bagatelle! vogue la galère!*

Phr. *Deus nobis hæc otia fecit; dum vivimus vivamus.*

---

842. Wit.—N. wit, -tiness; attic
-wit, – salt; atticism; salt, *esprit*, point,
fancy, whim, humour, drollery, pleasantry.

farce, buffoonery, fooling, tomfoolery; harlequinade &c. 599; broad
-farce, – humour; fun, *espièglerie; vis
comica.*

jocularity; jocos-ity, -eness; face-
tiousness; wagg-ery, -ishness; whim-
sicality; comicality &c. 853.

smartness, ready wit, banter, *badi-*

843. Dulness.—N. dulness, heaviness, flatness; infestivity &c. 837;
stupidity &c. 499; want of originality,
dearth of ideas.

prose, matter of fact; heavy book,
conte à dormir debout; platitude.

V. be -dull &c. *adj.*; prose, plati-
tudinize, take *au sérieux*, be caught
napping.

render -dull &c. *adj.*; damp, depress,
throw cold water on, lay a wet blanket
on; fall flat upon the ear; hang fire.

---

* A curious list of games is given in Sir Thomas Urquhart's translation of Rabelais'
Life of Gargantua, book i. chapter 22.

nage, persiflage, retort, repartee, *quid pro quo;* ridicule &c. 856.

facetiæ, quips and cranks; jest, joke, capital joke; standing -jest, – joke; conceit, quip, quirk, crank, quiddity, *concetto, plaisanterie,* brilliant idea; merry –, bright –, happy- thought; sally; flash, – of wit, – of merriment; scintillation; *mot, – pour rire;* witticism, smart saying, *bon mot, jeu d'esprit,* epigram; jest book; dry joke, *quodlibet,* cream of the jest.

word-play, *jeu de mots;* play -of, – upon- words; pun, -ning; *double entendre* &c. (*ambiguity*) 520; quibble, verbal quibble; conundrum &c. (*riddle*) 533; anagram, acrostic, double acrostic, *nugæ canoræ,* trifling, idle conceit, *turlupinade.*

old joke, Joe Miller, chestnut, hoary-headed jest.

V. joke, jest, cut jokes; crack a joke; perpetrate a -joke, – pun; make -fun of, – merry with; set the table in a roar &c. (*amuse*) 840; scintillate.

retort, flash back; banter &c. (*ridicule*) 856; *ridentem dicere verum;* joke at one's expense.

Adj. witty, attic, salty; quick-, nimble-witted; keen, clever, smart, brilliant, pungent, jocular, jocose, funny, waggish, facetious, whimsical, humorous, Gilbertian; playful &c. 840; merry and wise; pleasant, sprightly, *spirituel,* sparkling, epigrammatic, full of point, *ben trovato;* comic &c. 853.

Adv. in joke, in jest, in sport, in play.

844. Humorist.—N. humorist, wag, wit, reparteeist, epigrammatist, gag-man, punster; *bel esprit,* life of the party; wit-snapper, -cracker, -worm; joker, jester, jokesmith, Joe Miller, *drôle de corps, gaillard,* spark, *persifleur,* banterer.

buffoon, *farceur,* merry-andrew, mime, tumbler, acrobat, mountebank, charlatan, posturemaster, harlequin, punch, *pulcinella,* scaramouch, clown; wearer of the -cap and bells, – motley; motley fool; pantaloon, gipsy; jack -pudding, – in the green, – a dandy; zany; mad-cap, pickle-herring, witling, caricaturist, *grimacier.*

2°. DISCRIMINATE AFFECTIONS

845. Beauty.—N. beauty, the beautiful, *le beau idéal,* loveliness.

[Science of the perception of beauty] Callæsthetics.*

form, elegance, grace, beauty unadorned; symmetry &c. 242; comeliness, fairness &c. *adj.;* pulchritude, polish, gloss; good -effect, – looks; *belle tournure;* bloom, brilliancy, radiance, splendour, gorgeousness, magnificence; sublimi-ty, -fication.

Adj. dull, – as ditch water; dry, insipid, jejune; unentertaining, uninteresting, unlively, unimaginative; heavisome, heavy-gaited; insulse; dry as dust; pros-y, -ing, -aic; matter of fact, commonplace, banal, pointless; 'weary. flat, stale and unprofitable.'

stupid, slow, flat, sluggish, ponderous, humdrum, monotonous; melancholic &c. 837; stolid &c. 499; plodding.

Phr. *Davus sum non Œdipus.*

---

846. Ugliness.—N. ugliness &c. *adj.;* deformity, inelegance; disfigurement &c. (*blemish*) 848; want of symmetry, inconcinnity; distortion &c. 243; squalor &c. (*uncleanness*) 653.

forbidding countenance, vinegar aspect, hanging look, wry face, '*spretæ injuria formæ.*'

eyesore, object, figure, sight, fright, spectre, scarecrow, hag, harridan, satyr, witch, toad, baboon, monster,

* Whewell, 'Philosophy of the Inductive Sciences.'

concinnity, delicacy, refinement; charm, *je ne sais quoi*, style, *chic*, swank.

Venus, – of Milo; Aphrodite, Hebe, the Graces, Peri, Houri, Cupid, Apollo, Hyperion, Adonis, Antinous, Narcissus; Helen of Troy.

, peacock, butterfly; flower, flow'ret gay, rose, lily, asphodel; garden; flower of, pink of; *bijou*; jewel &c. (*ornament*) 847; work of art.

pleasurableness &c. 829.

beautifying; landscape gardening; decoration &c. 847; calisthenics.

V. be -beautiful &c. *adj.*; shine, beam, bloom; become one &c. (*accord*) 23; set off, grace, flatter one.

render -beautiful &c. *adj.*; beautify; polish, burnish; gild &c. (*decorate*) 847; set out.

'snatch a grace beyond the reach of art.'

Adj. beaut-iful, -eous; handsome; pretty; lovely, graceful, elegant; delicate, dainty, refined, exquisite; fair, personable, comely, seemly; bonny; good-looking; well-favoured, -made, -formed, -proportioned; proper, shapely; symmetrical &c. (*regular*) 242; harmonious &c. (*colour*) 428; sightly. fit to be seen, passable, not amiss.

goodly, dapper, tight, jimp; gimp; janty, jaunty; natty, quaint, trim, tidy, neat, spruce, smart, tricksy.

bright, -eyed; rosy-, cherry-cheeked; rosy, ruddy; blooming, in full bloom.

brilliant, shining; beam-y, -ing; sparkling, swanky, splendid, resplendent, dazzling, glowing; glossy, sleek.

showy, specious; rich, gorgeous, superb, magnificent, grand, fine, sublime, imposing; majestic 873.

artistic, -al; æsthetic; pict-uresque, -orial; *fait à peindre*, paintable; well-composed, -grouped, -varied; curious.

Caliban, Æsop, '*monstrum horrendum informe ingens cui lumen ademptum.*'

V. be -ugly &c. *adj.*; look ill, grin horribly a ghastly smile, make faces, render -ugly &c. *adj.*; deface; dis-, de-figure; deform, spoil, distort &c 243; blemish &c. (*injure*) 659; soil &c, (*render unclean*) 653.

Adj. ugly, – as -sin, – a toad, – a scarecrow, – a dead monkey; plain, bald &c. 226; homely &c. (*unadorned*) 849; ordinary, unornamental, inartistic; unsightly, unseemly, uncomely, unshapely, unlovely; sightless, seemless; not fit to be seen; unbeaut-eous, -iful; beautiless; shapeless &c. (*amorphous*) 241; course; garish, over-decorated &c. 882.

mis-shapen, -proportioned; monstrous; gaunt &c. (*thin*) 203; dumpy &c. (*short*) 201; curtailed of its fair proportions; ill-made, -shaped, -proportioned; crooked &c. (*distorted*) 243; hard-featured, -visaged; ill-, hard-, evil-favoured; ill-looking; unprepossessing.

graceless, inelegant; ungraceful, ungainly, uncouth; stiff; rugged, rough, gross, rude, awkward, clumsy, slouching, rickety; gawky; lump-ing, -ish; lumbering; hulk-y, -ing; unwieldy.

squalid, haggard; grim, -faced, -visaged; grisly, ghastly; ghost-, death-like; cadaverous, gruesome.

frightful, hideous, odious, uncanny, forbidding, repellant, repulsive; horri-d, -ble; shocking &c. (*painful*) 830. foul &c. (*dirty*) 653; dingy &c. (*colourless*) 429; gaudy &c. (*colour*) 428; disfigured &c. *v.*; discoloured (*blemished*) &c. 848.

enchanting &c. (*pleasure-giving*) 829; attractive &c. (*inviting*) 615; becoming &c. (*accordant*) 23; ornamental &c. 847.

undeformed, undefaced, unspotted; spotless &c. (*perfect*) 650.

847. Ornament. — N. ornament, -ation, -al art; ornat-ure, -eness; adorn-ment, decoration, embellishment; architecture.

garnish, polish, varnish, French pol-

848. Blemish.—N. blemish, disfigurement, deformity; defect &c. (*imperfection*) 651; flaw; injury &c. (*deterioration*) 659; spots on the sun; eyesore.

ish, gilding, japanning, lacquer, ormolu,
enamel.

cosmetics, rouge, powder, lipstick,
lip salve, mascara; manicure, nail polish; permanent –, Marcel –, finger-
wave.

pattern, diaper, powdering, panelling, graining, pargeting, inlay, detail;
texture &c. 329; richness; tracery,
moulding, beading, reeding, fillet, listel,
strapwork, *coquillage*, ficurish, *fleur-de-
lis*, arabesque, fret, *anthemion*; egg and
-tongue, – dart; *astragal*, zigzag, *acan-
thus*, *cartouche*; pilaster &c. (*projection*)
250; cyma, ogee.

em-, broidery, needlework; knitting,
crochet, tatting, brocade, *brocatelle*,
beads, bugles; galloon, lace, gimp,
guipure, fringe, trapping, border, edging, insertion, *motif*, trimming; *passementerie*; drapery, hanging, tapestry,
arras; millinery, ermine.

wreath, festoon, garland, lei, chaplet,
flower, nosegay, *bouquet*, posy, 'daisies
pied and violets blue.'

tassel, knot; shoulder-knot, *épaulette*,
epaulet, aigulet, *aiguillette*, frog; star,
rosette, bow; feather, plume, *panache*,
aigrette.

jewel, -ry, -lery; bijoutry; *bijou*,
-terie; diadem, tiara; pendant, trinket,
locket, necklace, armilla, bracelet,
bangle, armlet, anklet, ear-, nose- ring,
carcanet, chain, *châtelaine*, albert,
brooch, torque.

gem, precious stone; diamond, brilliant, beryl, aquamarine, alexandrite,
cat's eye, emerald, calcedony, chrysoprase, cornelian, jasper, blood-
stone, agate, heliotrope; girasol, -e; onyx, plasma; sard, -onyx;
garnet, lapis-lazuli, opal, peridot, chrysolite, sapphire, ruby; spinel,
-le; balais; oriental –, topaz; turquois, -e; zircon, jacinth, hyacinth,
carbuncle, amethyst; moonstone; pearl, coral.

finery, frippery, gewgaw, gimcrack, knick-knack, tinsel, spangle,
sequin, *clinquant*, pinch-beck, paste; excess of ornament &c. (*vulgarity*) 851; gaud, pride, ostentation; frills and furbelows.

illustration, illumination, *vignette*; *fleuron*; head-, tail-piece; *cul-
de-lampe*; flowers of rhetoric &c. 577; work of art, article of vertu,
bric-à-brac, curio, *bibelot*.

V. ornament, embellish, enrich, decorate, adorn, beautify, ado-
nize.

smarten, furbish, polish, gild, varnish, whitewash, enamel, japan,
lacquer, paint, grain.

garnish, trim, dizen, bedizen, prink, prank; trick –, fig- out;
deck, bedeck, dight, bedight, array; dress, – up, preen, spruce up,

stain, blot, slur; spot, -tiness; speck,
-le; blur, freckle, mole, *macula*, patch,
blotch, birthmark, blain, maculation,
tarnish, smudge, smear; dirt &c. 653;
bruise, black eye, scar, wem; pustule;
excrescence, pimple &c. (*protuberance*)
250.

V. disfigure &c. (*injure*) 659; speckle;
render ugly &c. 846.

Adj. pitted, freckled, discoloured,
bloodshot, bruised, disfigured; stained
&c. *n.*; imperfect &c. 651; injured &c.
(*deteriorated*) 659.

849. Simplicity. — N. simplicity;
plain-, homeli-ness; undress, nudity,
nakedness, beauty unadorned, chas
tity, chasteness.

V. be -simple &c. *adj.*
render -simple &c. *adj.*; simplify,
chasten, strip of ornament.

Adj. simple, plain; home-ly, -spun,
ordinary, household.

natural, unaffected; free from -affec-
tation, – ornament; *simplex munditiis*;
sans façon, *en déshabillé*, nude, naked.

chaste, inornate, severe.

un-adorned, -ornamented, -decked,
-garnished, -arranged, -trimmed, -var
nished.

bald, flat, dull, blank.

titivate; spangle, bespangle, powder; embroider, work; chase, tool, emboss, fret; emblazon, blazon, illuminate; illustrate.

become &c. (*accord with*) 23.

Adj. ornamented, beautified &c. *v.*; ornate, rich, gilt, begilt, tesselated, enamelled, inlaid; festooned; topiary.

smart, gay, tricksy, flowery, glittering; new-gilt, -spangled; fine, – as -a Mayday queen, – fivepence, – a carrot fresh scraped; pranked out, bedight, well-groomed.

in full dress &c. (*fashion*) 852; en grande -tenue, – toilette; in best bib and tucker, in Sunday best, *endimanché*; dressed to advantage.

showy, flashy; gaudy &c. (*vulgar*) 851; garish; gorgeous.

ornamental, decorative; becoming &c. (*accordant*) 23.

850. [Good taste.] **Taste.—N.** taste; good –, refined –, cultivated- taste; delicacy, refinement, fine feeling, gust, *gusto*, tact, *finesse*; nicety &c. (*discrimination*) 465; polish, elegance, grace.

virtu; dilettanteism, virtuosity; fine art; cul-ture, -ivation.

[Science of taste] æsthetics.

man of -taste &c.; *connoisseur*, judge, critic, *conoscente*, *virtuoso*, *amateur*, *dilettante*, Aristarchus, Corinthian, *arbiter elegantiarum*, stagirite, euphemist.

'caviare to the general.'

V. appreciate, judge, criticize, discriminate &c. 465.

Adj. in good taste; tasteful, tasty; unaffected, pure, chaste, classical, attic; cultivated, refined; dainty; æsthetic, artistic; elegant &c. 578; euphemistic.

to one's -taste, – mind; after one's fancy; *comme il faut*; *tiré à quatre épingles*.

Adv. elegantly &c. *adj.*

Phr. *nihil tetigit quod non ornavit.*

852. Fashion.—N. fashion, style, *ton*, *bon ton*, society; good –, polite-society; drawing room, civilized life, civilization, town, *beau monde*, high life; court; world; fashionable –, gay-world; Vanity Fair; show &c. (*ostentation*) 822.

manners, breeding &c. (*politeness*) 894; air, demeanour &c. (*appearance*) 448; *savoir-faire*; gentlemanliness, gentility, decorum, propriety, *bienséance*; conventions –, dictates- of society; Mrs. Grundy; convention, -ality; punctilio; form, -ality; etiquette, point of

851. [Bad taste.] **Vulgarity.—N.** vulgar-ity, -ism; barbar-, Vandal-, Gothic-ism; *mauvais goût*, bad taste; Babbittry; *gaucherie*, awkwardness, want of tact; ill-breeding &c. (*discourtesy*) 895; ungentlemanly behaviour.

coarseness &c. *adj.*; indecorum, misbehaviour.

low-, homeli-ness; low life, *mauvais ton*, rusticity; boorishness &c. *adj.*; brutality; rowdy-, ruffian-, blackguard-ism; ribaldry; slang &c. (*neology*) 563.

bad joke, *mauvaise plaisanterie.*

[Excess of ornament] gaudi-, tawdri-ness; false ornament; finery, frippery, trickery, tinsel, gewgaw, *clinquant*.

rough diamond, tomboy, hoyden, cub, unlicked cub; clown &c. (*commonalty*) 876; Hun, Goth, Vandal, Bœotian; vulgarian; snob, cad, bounder, gent; *parvenu* &c. 876; frump, dowdy; slattern &c. 653.

V. be -vulgar &c. *adj.*; misbehave; talk –, smell of the- shop.

Adj. in bad taste, vulgar, unrefined, gutter.

coarse, indecorous, ribald, gross; unseemly, unbeseeming, unpresentable; *contra bonos mores*; ungraceful &c. (*ugly*) 846.

dowdy; slovenly &c. (*dirty*) 653; ungenteel, shabby genteel; low &c. (*plebeian*) 876; uncourtly; uncivil &c. (*discourteous*) 895; ill-bred, -mannered; underbred; ungentleman-ly, -like; unladylike, unfeminine; wild, – as an unbacked colt.

unkempt, uncombed, untamed, unlicked, unpolished, uncouth, plebeian;

etiquette; custom &c. 613; mode, vogue, style, go; rage &c. (*desire*) 865; prevailing taste, *dernier cri*, dress &c. 225.

man –, woman- of -fashion, – the world; height –, pink –, star –, glass –, leader- of fashion; *arbiter elegantiarum* &c. (*taste*) 850; upper ten thousand &c. (*nobility*) 875; *élite* &c. (*distinction*) 873.

V. be -fashionable &c. *adj.*, – the rage &c. *n.*; have a run, pass current. follow –, conform to –, fall in with- the fashion &c. *n.*; go with the stream &c. (*conform*) 82; *savoir -vivre*, – *faire*; keep up appearances, behave oneself.

set the –, bring into- fashion; give a tone to –, cut a figure in- society, rub shoulders with nobility, keep one's carriage.

incondite; heavy, rude, awkward; home-ly, -spun, -bred; provincial, hick, countrified, rustic, uncultivated, fresh-water; boorish, clownish; savage, brut-ish, blackguard, rowdy, snobbish; barbar-ous, -ic; Gothic, unclassical, doggerel, heathenish, tramontane, out-landish; Bohemian.

obsolete &c. (*antiquated*) 124; un-fashionable, old-fashioned, out of date; new-fangled &c. (*unfamiliar*) 83; fan-tastic, odd &c. (*ridiculous*) 853.

particular; affected &c. 855; mere-tricious; extravagant, monstrous, hor-rid; shocking &c. (*painful*) 830.

gaudy, tawdry, bedizened, tricked out, gingerbread; obtrusive, flaunting, loud, flashy, garish, showy.

Adj. fashionable; in -fashion &c. *n.*; *à la mode*, *comme il faut*; admitted –, admissible- in -society &c. *n.*; presentable, decorous, punctilious, conventional &c. (*customary*) 613; genteel; well-bred, -mannered, -behaved, -spoken; gentleman-like, -ly; ladylike; civil, polite &c. (*courteous*) 894.

polished, refined, thoroughbred, courtly; *distingué*, aristocratic, unembarrassed, poised, *dégagé*; ja-, jau-nty; dashing, fast, showy, high toned, toney.

modish, stylish, in the latest style, *recherché*; new-fangled &c. (*unfamiliar*) 83.

in -court, – full, – evening- dress; *en grande tenue* &c. (*ornament*) 847.

Adv. fashionably &c. *adj.*; for fashion's sake.

---

853. Ridiculousness.—N. ridiculousness &c. *adj.*; comical-, odd-ity &c. *adj.*; extravagance, drollery.

farce, comedy; burlesque &c. (*ridicule*) 856; buffoonery &c. (*fun*) 840; frippery; doggerel verses; Irish bull, Hibernianism, Hibernicism; Spoonerism; absurdity &c. 497; bombast &c. (*unmeaning*) 517; anti-climax, bathos; monstrosity &c. (*unconformity*) 83; laughing stock &c. 857.

V. be -ridiculous &c. *adj.*; pass from the sublime to the ridiculous; make one laugh; play the fool, make a fool of oneself, commit an absurdity.

play a joke on, make a -fool of, – sucker of, – monkey of.

Adj. ridiculous, ludicrous; comic, -al; droll, funny, laughable, *pour rire*, grotesque, farcical, odd; whimsical, – as a dancing bear; fanciful, fantastic, queer, rum, quizzical, waggish, quaint, *bizarre*; eccentric &c. (*unconformable*) 83; strange, outlandish, out of the way, *baroque*, *rocaille*, rococo; awkward &c. (*ugly*) 846.

absurd, extravagant, *outré*, monstrous, preposterous, bombastic, inflated, stilted, burlesque, mock heroic.

drollish; serio-, tragic-comic; gimcrack, contemptible &c. (*unimportant*) 643; doggerel; ironical &c. (*derisive*) 856; risible.

Phr. 'risum teneatis amici?' rideret Heraclitus.

854. Fop.—N. fop, fine gentleman; swell; dand-y, -iprat; exquisite, coxcomb, toff, beau, macaroni, blade, blood, buck, man about town, fast man; fribble, jemmy, spark, popinjay, puppy, prig, petit maître; jacka-napes, -dandy; man milliner; Jemmy Jessamy, carpet-knight, masher, Dundreary, Johnnie, dude.

belle, fine lady, coquette, flirt.

855. Affectation.—N. affectation; affectedness &c. adj.; acting a part -xc. v.; pretence &c. (falsehood) 544, (ostentation) 882; boasting &c. 884.

charlatanism, quackery, shallow profundity, humbug, pretension, airs, ₚedantry, purism, precisianism, euphuism, prunes and prisms; teratology &c. (altiloquence) 577.

mannerism, simagrée, grimace.

conceit, foppery, dandyism, man millinery, coxcombry, puppyism.

stiffness, formality, buckram; prudery, demureness, coquetry, mock modesty, minauderie, sentimentalism; mauvaise honte, false shame.

affector, performer, actor; pedant, pedagogue, doctrinaire, purist, euphuist, mannerist; shoneen; grimacier; lump of affectation, précieuse ridicule, bas bleu, blue stocking, poetaster; prig, hypocrite; charlatan &c. (deceiver) 548; petit maître &c. (fop) 854; flatterer &c. 935; coquette, prude, puritan; precisian, formalist.

V. affect, act a part, put on; give oneself airs &c. (arrogance) 885; boast &c. 884; coquet; simper, mince, attitudinize, strike a pose, pose; flirt a fan; over-act, -play, -do.

Adj. affected, full of affectation, pretentious, pedantic, stilted, stagey, theatrical, big-sounding, ad captandum, canting, insincere.

not natural, unnatural; self-conscious; maniéré; artificial; over-wrought, -done, -acted; euphuistic &c. 577.

stiff, starch, formal, prim, smug, demure, tiré à quatre épingles, quakerish, puritanical, prudish, pragmatical, priggish, conceited, cox-comical, foppish, dandified; fini-cal, -kin, -cky, mincing, simpering, namby-pamby, sentimental, languishing.

856. Ridicule.—N. ridicule, derision; sardonic -smile, – grin; irrision; snigger; scoffing &c. (disrespect) 929; mockery, quiz, banter, irony, persiflage, raillery, chaff, badinage; quizzing &c. v.

squib, satire, skit, quip, quib, grin.

parody, burlesque, travesty; farce &c. (drama) 599; caricature, take-off.

buffoonery &c. (fun) 840; practical joke, horseplay.

V. ridicule, deride; laugh at, grin at, smile at; snigger; laugh in one's sleeve; banter, rally, chaff, joke, twit, quiz, poke fun at, jolly, roast, rag; fleer; play –, play tricks- upon; fool, – to the top of one's bent; show up.

satirize, parody, caricature, burlesque, travesty.

turn into ridicule; make merry with; make -fun, – game, – a fool, – an April fool- of; rally; scoff &c. (disrespect) 929.

raise a laugh &c. (amuse) 840; play the fool, make a fool of oneself. be ridiculous &c. 853.

Adj. deris-ory, -ive; mock; sarcastic, ironical, quizzical, burlesque, Hudibrastic; scurrilous &c. (disrespectful) 929.

Adv. in -ridicule &c. n.

857. [Object and cause of ridicule.] **Laughing-stock.—N.** laughing-, jesting-, gazing-stock; butt, game, fair game; April fool &c. (*dupe*) 547.

original, oddity; queer –, odd- fish; quiz, square-toes; old –, fogey *or* fogy.

monkey; buffoon &c. (*jester*) 844; pantomimist &c. (*actor*) 599. jest &c. (*wit*) 842.

3°. PROSPECTIVE AFFECTIONS

858. Hope.—N. hope, -s; desire &c. 865; fervent hope, sanguine expectation, trust, confidence, reliance; faith &c. (*belief*) 484; affiance, assurance; secur-eness, -ity; reassurance.

good -omen, – auspices; promise, well-grounded hopes; good –, bright-prospect; clear sky.

as-, pre-sumption; anticipation &c. (*expectation*) 507.

hopefulness, buoyancy, optimism, enthusiasm, heart of grace, aspiration; optimist, utop-ian, -ist; Pollyanna.

castles in the air, *châteaux en Espagne*, hope chest, *le pot au lait*, Utopia, millennium; day –, golden-dream; dream of Alnaschar; airy hopes, fool's paradise; *mirage* &c. (*fallacies of vision*) 443; fond hope.

beam –, ray –, gleam –, glimmer –, dawn –, flash –, star- of hope; cheer; bit of blue sky, silver lining of the cloud, bottom of Pandora's box, balm in Gilead.

anchor, sheet-anchor, main-stay; staff &c. (*support*) 215; heaven &c. 981.

V. hope, trust, confide, rely on, put one's trust in, lean upon; pin one's -hope, – faith- upon &c. (*believe*) 484.

feel –, entertain –, harbour –, indulge –, cherish –, feed –, foster –, nourish –, encourage –, cling to –, live in- hope &c. *n.*; see land; feel –, rest- -assured, – confident &c. *adj.*

presume; promise oneself; expect &c. (*look forward to*) 507.

hope for &c. (*desire*) 865; anticipate.

be -hopeful &c. *adj.*; look on the bright side of, view on the sunny side, make the best of it, hope for the best; put -a good, – a bold, – the best- face upon; keep one's spirits up; take heart, – of grace; be of good -heart, – cheer; flatter oneself, lay the flattering unction to one's soul.

859. [Absence, want, or loss of hope.] **Hopelessness.—N.** hopelessness &c. *adj.*; despair, desperation; despondency &c. (*dejection*) 837; pessimism.

hope deferred, dashed hopes; vain expectation &c. (*disappointment*) 509.

airy hopes &c. 858; forlorn hope; bad -job, – business; *enfant perdu*; gloomy –, black spots in the- horizon; slough of Despond, cave of Despair.

Job's comforter; bird of -bad, – ill-omen.

V. despair; lose –, give up –, abandon –, relinquish- -all hope, – the hope of; give -up, – over; yield to despair; falter; despond &c. (*be dejected*) 837; *jeter le manche après la cognée*.

inspire –, drive to- despair &c. *n.*; disconcert; dash –, crush –, shatter –, destroy- one's hopes; hope against hope.

Adj. hopeless, desperate, despairing, in despair, *au désespoir*, forlorn; inconsolable &c. (*dejected*) 837; broken-hearted.

out of the question, not to be thought of; impracticable &c. 471; past -hope, – cure, – mending, – recall; at one's last gasp &c. (*death*) 360; given -up, – over.

incurable, cureless, immedicable, remediless, beyond remedy; incorrigible; irre-parable, -mediable, -coverable, -versible, -trievable, -claimable, -deemable, -vocable; ruined, undone; immitigable.

unpromising, unpropitious; inauspicious, ill-omened, threatening, clouded over, lowering, ominous.

Phr. '*lasciate ogni speranza voi ch' entrate*'; its days are numbered; the worst come to the worst.

860. Fear.—N. fear, timidity, diffidence, want of confidence; apprehensive-, fearful-ness &c. *adj.*; solicitude,

catch at a straw, hope against hope, count one's chickens before they are hatched.

give –, inspire –, raise –, hold out-hope &c. n.; raise expectations; encourage, hearten, cheer, assure, reassure, buoy up, embolden; promise, bid fair, augur well, be in a fair way, look up, flatter, tell a flattering tale.

Adj. hoping &c. v.; in -hopes &c. n.; hopeful, confident; secure &c. (certain) 484; sanguine, in good heart, buoyed up, buoyant, elated, flushed, exultant, enthusiastic; utopian.

unsus-pecting, -picious; fearless, free –, exempt from- -fear, – suspicion, – distrust, – despair; undespairing, self-reliant.

probable, on the high road to; within sight of -shore, – land; promising, propitious; of –, full of- promise; of good omen; auspicious, de bon augure; reassuring; encouraging, cheering, inspiriting, looking up, bright, roseate, couleur de rose, rose-coloured.

Adv. hopefully &c. adj.

Int. God speed! good luck!

Phr. nil desperandum; never say die, dum spiro spero, latet scintillula forsan, all is for the best, spero meliora; the wish being father to the thought; 'hope told a flattering tale'; rusticus expectat dum defluat amnis.

anxiety, care, apprehension, misgiving; mistrust &c. (doubt) 485; suspicion, qualm; hesitation &c. (irresolution) 605.

nervous-, restless-ness &c. adj.; in-, dis-quietude; flutter, trepidation, fear and trembling, perturbation, tremor, quivering, shaking, trembling, throbbing heart, palpitation, ague fit, cold sweat; abject fear &c. (cowardice) 862; mortal funk, heart-sinking, despondency; despair &c. 859.

fright; affright, -ment; alarm, pavor, dread, awe, terror, horror, dismay, consternation, panic, scare, stampede [of horses].

intimidation, terrorism, reign of terror.

[Object of fear] bug-bear, -aboo; scarecrow; hobgoblin &c. (demon) 980; daymare, nightmare, Gorgon, Medusa, mormo, ogre, Hurlothrumbo, raw head and bloody bones, fee faw fum, bête noire, enfant terrible.

alarmist &c. (coward) 862.

V. fear, stand in awe of; be -afraid &c. adj.; have -qualms &c. n.; apprehend, sit upon thorns, eye askance; distrust &c. (disbelieve) 485.

hesitate &c. (be irresolute) 605; falter, funk, cower, crouch; skulk &c. (cowardice) 862; let 'I dare not' wait upon 'I would'; take -fright, – alarm; start, wince, flinch, shy, shrink; fly &c. (avoid) 623.

tremble, shake; shiver, – in one's shoes; shudder, flutter; shake –, tremble- -like an aspen leaf, – all over; quake, quaver, quiver, quail; get the wind up.

grow –, turn- pale; blench, stand aghast; not dare to say one's soul is one's own.

inspire –, excite- -fear, – awe; raise apprehensions; give –, raise –, sound- an alarm; alarm, startle, scare, cry 'wolf,' disquiet, dismay; fright, -en; affright, terrify; astound; frighten from one's propriety; frighten out of one's -wits, – senses, – seven senses; awe; strike -all of a heap, – an awe into, – terror; harrow up the soul, appal, unman, petrify, horrify.

make one's -flesh creep, – hair stand on end, – blood run cold, – teeth chatter; chill one's spine; take away –, stop- one's breath; make one -tremble &c.

haunt, obsess, beset; prey –, weigh- on the mind.

put in -fear, – bodily fear; terrorize, intimidate, cow, daunt, over awe, abash, deter, discourage; browbeat, bully; threaten &c. 909.

Adj. fearing &c. v.; frightened &c. v.; in -fear, – a fright &c. n.; haunted with the -fear &c. n.- of.

afraid, fearful; tim-id, -orous; nervous, diffident, coy, faint-hearted, tremulous, shaky, afraid of one's shadow, apprehensive, restless, fidgety; more frightened than hurt.

aghast; awe-, horror-, terror-, panic- -struck, -stricken; frightened to death, white as a sheet; pale, – as -death, – ashes, – a ghost; breathless, in hysterics.

inspiring fear &c. *v.*; alarming; formidable, redoubtable; perilous &c. (*danger*) 665; portentous; fear-ful, -some; dread, -ful; fell; dire, -ful; shocking; terri-ble, -fic; tremendous; horri-d, -ble, -fic; ghastly; awful, awe-inspiring, eerie, weird; revolting &c. (*painful*) 830.

Adv. *in terrorem.*

Int. 'angels and ministers of grace defend us!'

Phr. *ante tubam trepidat; horresco referens*, one's heart failing one, *obstupui steteruntque comæ et vox faucibus hæsit.*

861. [Absence of fear.] **Courage.—N.** courage, bravery, valour; resolute-, bold-ness &c. *adj.*; spirit, daring, gallantry, intrepidity; contempt –, defiance- of danger; derring-do; audacity; rashness &c. 863; dash; defiance &c. 715; confidence, self-reliance.

man-liness, -hood; nerve, pluck, mettle, game; heart, – of grace; spunk, gameness, grit, face, virtue, hardihood, fortitude; firmness &c. (*stability*) 150; heart of oak; bottom, backbone &c. (*perseverance*) 604a.

resolution &c. (*determination*) 604; tenacity, bull-dog courage.

prowess, heroism, chivalry.

exploit, feat, achievement; heroic -deed, – act; bold stroke.

man, – of mettle; hero, demigod, paladin, heroine, Amazon, Hector, Joan of Arc; lion, tiger, panther, bull-dog; game-, fighting-cock; bully, fire-eater &c. 863; dare-devil.

V. be -courageous &c. *adj.*; dare, venture, make bold; face –, front –, affront –, confront –, brave –, defy –, despise –, mock- danger; look in the face; look -full, – boldly, – danger- in the face; face; meet, – in front; brave, beard; defy &c. 715.

take –, muster –, summon up –, pluck up- courage; nerve oneself, take heart; take –, pluck up- heart of grace; hold up one's head, screw one's courage to the sticking place; come -to, – up to- the scratch; stand, – to one's guns, – fire, – against; bear up, – against; hold out &c. (*persevere*) 604a.

put a bold face upon; show –,

862. [Excess of fear.] **Cowardice.—N.** cowardice, pusillanimity; cowardliness &c. *adj.*; timidity, effeminacy.

poltroonery, baseness; dastard-ness, -y; abject fear, funk; Dutch courage; fear &c. 860; white feather, faint heart.

coward, poltroon, dastard, sneak, recreant; shy –, dunghill- cock; coistril, milksop, white-liver, nidget, cur, craven, one that cannot say 'Bo' to a goose; Bob Acres, Jerry Sneak.

alarm-, terror-, pessim-ist; runagate &c. (*fugitive*) 623; shirker.

V. quail &c. (*fear*) 860; be -cowardly &c. *adj.*, – a coward &c. *n.*; funk; cower, skulk, sneak; flinch, shy, fight shy, slink, turn tail; run away &c. (*avoid*) 623; show the white feather, have cold feet, show a yellow streak.

Adj. coward, -ly; fearful, shy; tim-id, -orous; skittish; poor-spirited, spiritless, soft, effeminate.

weak-minded; infirm of purpose &c. 605; weak-, faint-, chicken-, lily-. pigeon-hearted; yellow; white-, lily-, milk-livered; milksop, smock-faced; unable to say 'Bo' to a goose.

dastard, -ly; base, craven, sneaking, dunghill, recreant; unwar-, unsoldier-like.

'in face a lion but in heart a deer.' unmanned; frightened &c. 860.

Int. *sauve qui peut!* devil take the hindmost!

Adv. in fear and trembling, in fear of one's life, in a blue funk.

Phr. *ante tubam trepidat*, one's courage oozing out.

present- a bold front, face the music; envisage; show fight.

bell the cat, take the bull by the horns, beard the lion in his den, march up to the cannon's mouth, go through fire and water, run the gauntlet, go over the top.

give -, infuse -, inspire- courage; reassure, encourage, embolden, inspirit, cheer, hearten, nerve, put upon one's mettle, rally, raise a rallying cry; pat on the back, make a man of, keep in countenance.

Adj. courageous, brave; val-iant, -orous; gallant, intrepid; spirit-ed, -ful; high-spirited, -mettled; mettlesome, game, plucky; man-ly, -ful; resolute; stout, -hearted; iron-, lion-hearted; heart of oak; Penthesilean.

bold, - spirited; daring, audacious; fear-, daunt-, dread-, awe-less; un-daunted, -appalled, -dismayed, -awed, -blenched, -abashed, -alarmed, -flinching, -shrinking, -blenching, -apprehensive; confident, self-reliant; bold as -a lion, - brass.

enterprising, adventurous; ventur-ous, -esome; dashing, chival-rous; soldierly &c. (*warlike*) 722; heroic.

fierce, savage; pugnacious &c. (*bellicose*) 720.

strong-minded, hardy, doughty; firm &c. (*stable*) 150; determined &c. (*resolved*) 604; dogged, indomitable &c. (*persevering*) 604a.

up to, - the scratch; upon one's mettle; reassured &c. *v.*; un-feared, undreaded.

Phr. one's blood being up.

---

863. Rashness.—N. rashness &c. *adj.*; temerity, want of caution, im-prudence, indiscretion; over-confidence, presumption, audacity.

precipit-ancy, -ation; impetuosity; levity; foolhardi-hood, -ness; heed-, thought-lessness &c. (*inattention*) 458; carelessness &c. (*neglect*) 460; despera-tion; Quixotism, knight-errantry; fire-eating.

gam-ing, -bling; blind bargain, leap in the dark, fool's paradise; too many eggs in one basket.

desperado, rashling, mad-cap, dare-devil, Hotspur, fire-eater, bully, *bravo*, Hector, scapegrace, *enfant perdu*; Don Quixote, knight-errant, Icarus; adven-turer; gam-bler, -ester; dynamitard.

V. be -rash &c. *adj.*; stick at nothing, play a desperate game; run into danger &c. 665; play with -fire, - edge tools.

carry too much sail, sail too near the wind, ride at single anchor, go out of one's depth.

take a leap in the dark, buy a pig in a poke.

donner tête baissée; knock one's head against a wall &c. (*be unskilful*) 699; rush on destruction; kick against the

864. Caution.—N. caution; cautious-ness &c. *adj.*; discretion, prudence, cautel, heed, circumspection, calcula-tion, deliberation; safety first.

foresight &c. 510; vigilance &c. 459; warning &c. 668.

coolness &c. *adj.*; self-possession, -command; presence of mind, *sang-froid*; well-regulated mind; worldly wisdom, Fabian policy.

V. be -cautious &c. *adj.*; take -care, - heed, - good care; have a care; mind, - what one is about; be on one's guard &c. (*keep watch*) 459; make assurance double sure; ca' canny.

bespeak &c. (*be early*) 132.

think twice, look before one leaps, keep one's weather eye open, count the cost, look to the main chance, cut one's coat according to one's cloth; feel one's -ground, - way; see how the land lies &c. (*foresight*) 510; wait to see how the cat jumps; bridle one's tongue; *reculer pour mieux sauter* &c. (*prepare*) 673; let well alone, let sleeping dogs lie, *ne pas réveiller le chat qui dort*.

keep out of -harm's way, - troubled waters; keep at a respectful distance, stand aloof; keep -, be- on the safe side

pricks, tempt Providence, go on a for-lorn hope.

count one's chickens before they are hatched; reckon without one's host; catch at straws; trust to –, lean on- a broken reed.

Adj. rash, incautious, indiscreet, in-judicious; imprudent, improvident, temerarious; uncalculating; heedless; careless &c. (*neglectful*) 460; without ballast, heels over head; giddy &c. (*inattentive*) 458; wanton, reckless, wild, madcap; desperate, devil-may-care.

hot-blooded, -headed, -brained; head-long, -strong; break-neck; fool-hardy; hare-brained; precipitate, im-pulsive.

over-confident, -weening; ventur-esome, -ous; adventurous, Quixotic; fire-eating, cavalier; free-and-easy.

off one's guard &c. (*inexpectant*) 508.

Adv. post haste, *à corps perdu*, hand over head, *tête baissée*, head-foremost; happen what may.

Phr. neck or nothing, the devil being in one.

husband one's resources &c. 636. caution &c. (*warn*) 668.

Adj. cautious, wary, guarded; on one's guard &c. (*watchful*) 459; *cavendo tutus*; *in medio tutissimus*.

care-, heed-ful; cautelous, stealthy, chary, shy of, circumspect, prudent, canny, safe, non-committal, discreet, politic; sure-footed &c. (*skilful*) 698.

unenterprising, unadventurous, cool, steady, self-possessed; over-cautious.

suspicious, leery, vigilant.

Adv. cautiously, gingerly &c. *adj.*

Int. have a care! look out! *cave canem!*

Phr. *timeo Danaos; festina lente.*

---

865. Desire.—N. desire, wish, fancy, fantasy; want, need, exigency.

mind, inclination, leaning, bent, *animus*, partiality, *penchant*, predilection; propensity &c. 820; willingness &c. 602; liking, love, fondness, relish.

longing, hankering; solicitude, anx-iety; yearning, coveting; aspiration, ambition, vaulting ambition; eagerness, zeal, ardour, *empressement*, breathless impatience, over-anxiety; solicitude, impetuosity &c. 825.

appet-ite, -ition, -ence, -ency; sharp appetite, keenness, hunger, stomach, twist; thirst, -iness; drouth, mouth-watering; itch, -ing; prurience, *caco-ēthes*, cupidity, lust, concupiscence.

edge of -appetite, – hunger; torment of Tantalus; sweet –, lickerish- tooth; itching palm; longing –, wistful –, sheep's- eye.

avidity; greed, -iness; covetous-, ravenous-ness &c. *adj.*; grasping, crav-ing, canine appetite, rapacity; voracity &c. (*gluttony*) 957.

passion, rage, *furore*, mania, *manie*; inextinguishable desire; dips-, klept-, mon-omania.

[Person desiring] desirer, lover, *ama-*

866. Indifference.—N. indifference neutrality; coldness &c. *adj.*; uncon-cern, *insouciance*, *nonchalance*; want of -interest, – earnestness; anorexy, in-appetency; apathy &c. (*insensibility*) 823; supineness &c. (*inactivity*) 683; disdain &c. 930; recklessness &c. 863; inattention &c. 458.

V. be -indifferent &c. *adj.*; stand neuter; take no interest in &c. (*insensi-bility*) 823; have no -desire &c. 865, – taste, – relish- for; not care for; care nothing -for, – about; not care a -straw &c. (*unimportance*) 643 -about, – for; not mind.

set at naught &c. (*make light of*) 483; spurn &c. (*disdain*) 930.

Adj. indifferent, cold, frigid, luke-warm; cool, – as a cucumber; uncon-cerned, *insouciant*, phlegmatic, *pococu-rante*, easy-going, devil-may-care, care-less, listless, lackadaisical, feckless; half-hearted; un-ambitious, -aspiring, -desirous, -solicitous, -attracted.

un-attractive, -alluring, -desired, -de-sirable, -cared for, -wished, -valued, all one to.

insipid &c. 391; vain.

Adv. for aught one cares;

teur, votary, devotee, aspirant, solicitant, candidate; cormorant &c. 957; sycophant.

[Object of desire] *desideratum*; want &c. (*requirement*) 630; 'consummation devoutly to be wished'; attraction, magnet, allurement, fancy, temptation, seduction, lure, fascination, *prestige*, height of one's ambition, idol; whim, ·sey; maggot; hobby, -horse.

Fortunatus's cap, wishing cap, love potion.

V. desire; wish, – for; be -desirous &c. *adj.*; have a -longing &c. *n.*; hope &c. 858.

care for, affect, like, list; take to, cling to, take a fancy to; fancy; prefer &c. (*choose*) 609.

have -an eye, – a mind- to; find it in one's heart &c. (*be willing*) 602; have a fancy for, set one's eyes upon; cast a sheep's eye –, look sweet- upon; take into one's head, have at heart, be bent upon; set one's -cap at, – heart upon, – mind upon; covet.

want, miss, need, lack, desiderate, feel the want of; would fain -have, – do; would be glad of.

be -hungry &c. *adj.*; have a good appetite, play a good knife and fork; hunger –, thirst –, crave –, lust –, itch –, hanker –, run mad- after; raven –, die- for; burn to.

desiderate; sigh –, cry –, gape –, gasp –, pine –, pant –, languish –, yearn –, long –, be on thorns –, hope- for; aspire after; catch at, grasp at, jump at.

woo, court, solicit; fish –, spell –, whistle –, put up- for; ogle.

cause –, create –, raise –, excite –, provoke- desire; whet the appetite; appetize, titillate, allure, attract, take one's fancy, tempt; hold out -temptation, – allurement; tantalize, make one's mouth water, *faire venir l'eau à la bouche*.

gratify desire &c. (*give pleasure*) 829.

Adj. desirous; desiring &c. *v.*; orectic, appetitive; inclined &c. (*willing*) 602; partial to; fain, wishful, optative; anxious, wistful, curious; at a loss for, sedulous, solicitous.

craving, hungry, sharp-set, peckish,

Int. never mind.

867. Dislike.—N. dis-like, -taste, -relish, -inclination, -placency.

reluctance; backwardness &c. (*unwillingness*) 603.

repugnance, disgust, queasiness, turn, nausea, loathing; avers-eness, -ation, -ion; abomination, antipathy, abhorrence, horror; mortal –, rooted- -antipathy, – horror; hatred, detestation; hate &c. 898; animosity &c. 900; hydrophobia.

sickener; gall and wormwood &c. (*unsavoury*) 395; shuddering, cold sweat.

V. dis-, mis-like, -relish; mind, object to; have rather not, not care for; have –, conceive –, entertain –, take- -a dislike, – an aversion- to; have no -taste, – stomach- for.

shun, avoid &c. 623; eschew; withdraw –, shrink –, recoil- from; not be able to -bear, – abide, – endure; shrug the shoulders at, shudder at, turn up the nose at, look askance at; make a -mouth, – wry face, – grimace; make faces.

loathe, nauseate, abominate, detest, abhor; hate &c. 898; take amiss &c. 900; have enough of &c. (*be satiated*) 869.

cause –, excite- dislike; disincline, repel, sicken; make –, render- sick; turn one's stomach, nauseate, wamble, disgust, shock, stink in the nostrils; go against the -grain, – stomach; stick in the throat; make one's blood run cold &c. (*give pain*) 830; pall.

Adj. disliking &c. *v.*; averse to, loth, adverse; shy of, sick of, out of conceit with; disinclined; heart-, dog-sick; queasy.

disliked &c. *v.*; uncared for, unpopular; out of favour; repulsive, repugnant, repellent; abhorrent, insufferable, fulsome, nauseous; loath-some, -ful; offensive; disgusting &c. *v.*; disagreeable &c. (*painful*) 830; unsavoury &c. 395.

Adv. *usque ad nauseam.*

Int. faugh! foh! ugh!

868. Fastidiousness.—N. fastidious ness &c. *adj.*; nicety, meticulosity,

ravening, with an empty stomach, esu-rient, lickerish, thirsty, athirst, parched with thirst, pinched with hunger, fam-ished, dry, drouthy; hungry as a ⌐hunter, – hawk, – horse, – church mouse.

greedy, – as a hog; over-eager, vora-cious; ravenous, – as a wolf; open-mouthed, covetous, rapacious, grasp-ing, extortionate, exacting, sordid, *alieni appetens*; insati-able, -ate; un-quenchable, quenchless; omnivorous.

unsatisfied, unsated, unslaked.

eager, avid, keen; burning, fervent, ardent; agog; all agog; breathless; impatient &c. (*impetuous*) 825; bent –, intent –, set- -on, – upon; mad after, *enragé*, rabid, dying for, devoured by desire.

aspiring, ambitious, vaulting, sky-aspiring.

desirable; popular; desired &c. *v.*; in demand; pleasing &c. (*giving pleasure*) 829; appeti-zing, -ble; tantalizing.

Adv. wistfully &c. *adj.*; fain.

Int. would -that, – it were! O for! *esto perpetua!* if only!

Phr. the wish being father to the thought; *sua cuique voluptas*; *hoc erat in votis*, the mouth watering, the fingers itching; *aut Cæsar aut nullus*.

hypercriticism, difficulty in being pleased, *friandise*, epicurism, *omnia suspendens naso*.

discrimination, discernment, good taste, perspicacity.

epicure, gourmet.

[Excess of delicacy] prudery, prud-ishness, primness.

V. be -fastidious &c. *adj.*; split hairs, discriminate, have a sweet tooth.

mince the matter; turn up one's nose at &c. (*disdain*) 930; look a gift horse in the mouth, see spots on the sun.

Adj. fastidious, meticulous, exacting, nice, delicate, *délicat*, finical, finicky, difficult, dainty, lickerish, squeamish, thin-skinned; s-, queasy; hard -, diffi-cult- to please; querulous, particular, over-particular, straitlaced, prudish, prim, scrupulous; censorious &c. 932; hypercritical, discriminating, discern-ing, perspicacious.

Phr. *noli me tangere*.

869. Satiety.—N. satiety, satisfac-tion, saturation, repletion, glut, sur-feit; weariness &c. 841.

spoiled child; *enfant gâté*; too much of a good thing, *toujours perdrix*; *crambe repetita*.

V. sate, satiate, satisfy, saturate; cloy, quench, slake, pall, glut, gorge, surfeit; bore &c. (*weary*) 841; tire &c. (*fatigue*) 688; spoil.

have -enough of, – quite enough of, – one's fill, – too much of; be -satiated &c. *adj.*

Adj. satiated &c. *v.*; overgorged; *blasé*, used up, sick of, heart-sick.

Int. enough! hold! *eheu jam satis!*

4°. CONTEMPLATIVE AFFECTIONS

870. Wonder.—N. wonder, marvel; astonish-, amaze-, wonder-, bewilder-ment; amazedness &c. *adj.*; admira-tion, awe; stup-or, -efaction; stound, fascination; sensation; surprise &c. (*inexpectation*) 508; cynosure.

note of admiration; thaumaturgy &c. (*sorcery*) 992.

V. wonder, marvel, admire; be -sur-prised &c. *adj.*; start; stare; open -, rub -, turn up- one's eyes; gloar; gape, open one's mouth, hold one's breath;

871. [Absence of wonder.] **Expec-tance.—N.** expectan-ce, -cy &c. (*expec-tation*) 507; calmness, composure, tran-quillity, serenity, coolness, imperturb-ability &c. 826.

nine days' wonder.

V. expect &c. 507; not -be surprised, – wonder &c. 870; *nil admirari*, make nothing of.

Adj. expecting &c. *v.*; unamazed, astonished at nothing; *blasé* &c. (*weary*) 841; unimaginative, calm, serene, im-

look –, stand- -aghast, – agog; look blank &c. (*disappointment*) 509; *tomber des nues*; not believe one's -eyes, – ears, – senses.

not be able to account for &c. (*unintelligible*) 519; not know whether one stands on one's head or one's heels.

surprise, astonish, amaze, astound; dumbfound, -er; startle, dazzle; strike, – with -wonder, – awe; electrify; stun, stupefy, petrify, confound, bewilder, flabbergast; stagger, throw on one's beam ends, fascinate, turn the head, take away one's breath, strike dumb; make one's -hair stand on end, – tongue cleave to the roof of one's mouth; make one stare.

take by surprise &c. (*be unexpected*) 508.

be -wonderful &c. *adj.*; beggar –, baffle- description; stagger belief.

Adj. surprised &c. *v.*; aghast, all agog, breathless, agape; open-mouthed; awe-, thunder-, moon-, planet-struck; spell-bound; lost in -amazement, – wonder, – astonishment; struck all of a heap, unable to believe one's senses, like a duck in thunder.

wonderful, wondrous; surprising &c. *v.*; unexpected &c. 508; un-heard of; mysterious &c. (*inexplicable*) 519; miraculous; *foudroyant.*

in-describable, -expressible, -effable; un-utterable, -speakable.

monstrous, prodigious, stupendous, marvellous; in-conceivable, -credible; in-, un-imaginable; strange &c. (*uncommon*) 83; passing strange.

striking &c. *v.*; over-whelming; wonder-working.

Adv. wonderfully &c. *adj.*; fearfully; for a –, in the name of-wonder; strange to say; *mirabile -dictu, – visu*; to one's great surprise.

with -wonder &c. *n.*, – gaping mouth, – open eyes, – upturned eyes; eyes starting out of one's head.

Int. lo, – and behold! O! hey-day! halloo! what! indeed! really! surely! humph! hem! good -lack, – heavens, – gracious! – lord! by jove! gad so! well a day! dear me! only think! lack-a-daisy! my -stars, – goodness! gracious goodness! goodness gracious! mercy on us! heavens and earth! God bless me! bless -us, – my heart! odzookens! O *gemini!* adzooks! hoity-toity! strong! Heaven save –, bless- the mark! can such things be! zounds! 'sdeath! what -on earth, – in the world! who would have thought it! &c. (*inexpectation*) 508; fancy! did you ever? you don't say so! what do you say to that! how now! where am I? well I'm blowed! &c.

Phr. *vox faucibus hæsit*; one's hair standing on end.

872. Prodigy.—N. prodigy, phenomenon; wonder, -ment; genius, marvel, miracle; freak, monster &c. (*unconformity*) 83; curiosity, lion, infant prodigy, sight, spectacle; *jeu* –, *coup- de théâtre*; gazing-stock; sign; portent &c. 512.

bursting of a -shell, – bomb; volcanic eruption, peal of thunder; thunder-clap, -bolt.

what no words can paint; wonders of the world; *annus mirabilis*; *dignus vindice nodus.*

perturbable &c. 826; expected &c. *v.*; foreseen.

common, ordinary &c. (*habitual*) 613

Int. no wonder; of course; why not?

───────────

5°. INTRINSIC AFFECTIONS*

873. Repute.—N. distinction, mark, name, figure; repute, reputation, char-

874. Disrepute.—N. disrepute, discredit; ill-, bad- -repute, -name, -odour,

* Or personal affections derived from the opinions or feelings of others.

acter; good –, high- repute; note, notability, notoriety, *éclat*, 'the bubble reputation,' vogue, celebrity; fame, famousness; renown; popularity, *aura popularis*; esteem, approval, approbation &c. 931; credit, *succès d'estime*, *prestige*, talk of the town; name to conjure with.

glory, honour; lustre &c. (*light*) 420; illustriousness &c. *adj.*

account, regard, respect; reputableness &c. *adj.*; respectability &c. (*probity*) 939; good -name, – report; fair name.

dignity; stateliness &c. *adj.*; solemnity, grandeur, splendour, nobility, majesty, sublimity.

rank, standing, brevet rank, precedence, *pas*, station, place, *status*; position, – in society; order, degree, *locus standi*, caste, condition.

greatness &c. *adj.*; eminence; height &c. 206; importance &c. 642; pre-, super-eminence; high mightiness, primacy; top of the -ladder, – tree.

elevation; ascent &c. 305; super-, ex-altation; dignification, aggrandizement.

dedication, consecration, enthronement, canonization, apotheosis, deification, celebration, enshrinement, glorification.

hero, man of mark, great card, celebrity, champion, worthy, lion, *rara avis*, notability, somebody; man of rank &c. (*nobleman*) 875; pillar of the -state, – society, – church.

chief &c. (*master*) 745; first fiddle &c. (*proficient*) 700; scholar &c. 492; cynosure, mirror; flower, pink, pearl; paragon &c. (*perfection*) 650; choice and master spirits of the age; *élite*; star, sun, constellation, galaxy.

ornament, honour, feather in one's cap, halo, aureole, nimbus; halo –, blaze- of glory; blushing honours; laurels &c. (*trophy*) 733.

memory, posthumous fame, niche in the temple of fame; immor-tality, -tal name; *magni nominis umbra*.

V. be conscious of glory; be proud of &c. (*pride*) 878; exult &c. (*boast*) 884; be vain of &c. (*vanity*) 880.

be -distinguished &c. *adj.*; shine &c.

-favour; disapprobation &c. 932; ingloriousness, derogation; a-, de-basement; abjectness &c. *adj.*; degradation, dedecoration; 'a long farewell to all one's greatness'; odium, obloquy, opprobrium, ignominy.

dishonour, disgrace; shame, humiliation; scandal, baseness, vileness; perfidy, turpitude &c. (*improbity*) 940; infamy.

tarnish, taint, defilement, pollution; stain, blot, spot, blur, stigma, brand, reproach, imputation, slur.

crying –, burning- shame; *scandalum magnatum*, badge of infamy, blot in one's escutcheon; bend –, bar- sinister; champain, point champain; by-word of reproach; Ichabod.

argumentum ad verecundiam; sense of shame &c. 879.

V. be -inglorious &c. *adj.*; incur -disgrace &c. *n.*; have –, earn- a bad name; put –, wear- a halter round one's neck; disgrace –, expose- oneself.

play second fiddle; lose caste; pale one's ineffectual fire; recede into the shade; fall from one's high estate; keep in the background &c. (*modesty*) 881; be conscious of disgrace &c. (*humility*) 879; look -blue, – foolish, – like a fool; cut a -poor, – sorry- figure; laugh on the wrong side of the mouth; make a sorry face, go away with a flea in one's ear, slink away.

cause -shame &c. *n.*; shame, disgrace, put to shame, dishonour; throw –, cast –, fling –, reflect- dishonour &c. *n.* upon; be a -reproach &c. *n.* to; derogate from.

tarnish, stain, blot, sully, taint; discredit; degrade, debase, defile; beggar; expel &c. (*punish*) 972.

impute shame to, brand, post, stigmatize, vilify, defame, slur, cast a slur upon, hold up to shame, send to Coventry; tread –, trample- under foot; show up, drag through the mire, heap dirt upon; reprehend &c. 932.

bring low, put down, snub; take down a peg, – lower, – or two.

obscure, eclipse, outshine, take the shine out of; throw –, cast- into the shade; overshadow; leave –, put- in the background; push into a corner,

(*light*) 420; shine forth, figure; make –, cut- a -figure, – dash, – splash.

rival, surpass; out-shine, -rival, -vie, -jump; emulate, vie with, eclipse; throw –, cast- into the shade; overshadow.

live, flourish, glitter, scintillate, flaunt; gain –, acquire- honour &c. *n.*; play first fiddle &c. (*be of importance*) 642; bear the -palm, – bell; lead the way; take -precedence, – the wall of; gain –, win- -laurels, – spurs, – golden opinions &c. (*approbation*) 931; graduate, take one's degree, pass one's examination, win a -scholarship, – fellowship.

make -a, – some- -noise, – noise in the world; leave one's mark, exalt one's horn, star, have a run, be run after; enjoy popularity, come -into vogue, – to the front; raise one's head.

enthrone, signalize, immortalize, deify, exalt to the skies; hand one's name down to posterity.

consecrate; dedicate to, devote to; enshrine, inscribe, blazon, lionize, blow the trumpet, crown with laurel.

confer –, reflect- honour &c. *n.* on; shed a lustre on; redound to one's honour, ennoble.

give –, do –, pay –, render- honour to; honour, accredit, pay regard to, dignify, glorify; sing praises to &c. (*approve*) 931; look up to; exalt, aggrandize, elevate, nobilitate.

Adj. distinguished, *distingué*, noted; of -note &c. *n.*; honoured &c. *v.*; popular; fashionable &c. 852.

put one's nose out of joint; put out, – of countenance.

upset, throw off one's centre; discompose, disconcert; put to the blush &c. (*humble*) 879.

Adj. disgraced &c. *v.*; blown upon; shorn of -its beams, - one's glory; overcome, down-trodden; loaded with -shame &c. *n.*; in -bad repute &c. *n.*; out of -repute, – favour, – fashion, – countenance; at a discount; under -a cloud, – an eclipse; unable to show one's face; in the -shade, – background; out at elbows, down in the world, down and out.

inglorious; nameless, renownless, obscure, unknown to fame; un-noticed, -noted, -honoured, -glorified.

shameful; dis-graceful, -creditable, -reputable; despicable; questionable; unbecoming, unworthy; derogatory; degrading, humiliating, *infra dignitatem*, dedecorous; scandalous, infamous, too bad, unmentionable; ribald, opprobrious; arrant, shocking, outrageous, notorious, shady.

ignominious, scrubby, dirty, abject, vile, beggarly, pitiful, low, mean, shabby; base &c. (*dishonourable*) 940.

Adv. to one's shame be it spoken.

Int. fie! shame! for shame! *pro pudor! O tempora! O mores!* ough! *sic transit gloria mundi!*

---

in good odour; in –, in high- favour; reput-, respect-, credit-able.

remarkable &c. (*important*) 642; notable, notorious; celebrated. renowned, in every one's mouth, talked of; fam-ous, -ed; far-famed; conspicuous, to the front; foremost; in the -front rank, – ascendant.

imperishable, deathless, immortal, never fading, *ære perennius*; time-honoured.

illustrious, glorious, splendid, brilliant, radiant; bright &c. 420; full-blown; honorific.

eminent, prominent; high &c. 206; in the zenith; at the -head of, – top of the tree; peerless, of the first water; superior &c. 33; super-, pre-eminent.

great, dignified, proud, noble, honourable, worshipful, lordly, grand, stately, august, princely, imposing, solemn, transcendent, majestic, sacred, sublime, heaven-born, heroic, *sans peur et sans reproche*; sacrosanct.

Int. hail! all hail! *ave! viva! vive!* long life to! glory –, honour- be to!

Phr. one's name -being in every mouth, – living for ever; *sic itur ad astra, fama volat, aut Cæsar aut nullus*; not to know him argues oneself unknown; none but himself could be his parallel, *palmam qui meruit ferat*.

875. Nobility.—N. nobility, rank, condition, distinction, optimacy, blood, *pur sang*, birth, high descent, order; quality, gentility; blue blood of Castile; *ancien régime*.

high life, *haut monde*; upper -classes, – ten thousand; *élite*, aristocracy, great folks; fashionable world &c. (*fashion*) 852; salariat.

peer, -age; House of -Lords, – peers; ¹ords, – temporal and spiritual; *noblesse*; ᵇaronage, knightage; noble, -man; lord, ⁻ling; grandee, *magnifico, hidalgo*; don, ᴸship; aristocrat, swell, three-tailed bashaw; gentleman, squire, squireen, patrician, laureate.

gentry, gentlefolk; squirarchy, better sort, *magnates, primates, optimates.*

king &c. (*master*) 745; prince, crown prince, *Dauphin*; duke; marquis, -ate; earl, viscount, baron, thane, banneret; baronet, -cy; knight, -hood; count, armiger, laird; sig-, seig-nior; esquire, boyar, margrave, vavasour, sheik, emir, ameer, scherif, *pasha*, effendi, sahib.

queen &c. 745; princess, begum, duchess, marchioness; countess &c.; lady, dame.

personage –, man- of -distinction, – mark, – rank; nota-bles, -bilities; celebrity, big-wig, magnate, great man, star; *magni nominis umbra*; 'every inch a king'; grand Panjandrum.

V. be -noble &c. *adj.*

Adj. noble, exalted; of -rank &c. *n.*; princely, titled, patrician, aristocratic; high-, well-born; of gentle blood; genteel, *comme il faut*, gentlemanlike, courtly &c. (*fashionable*) 852; highly respectable.

Adv. in high quarters.

877. Title.—N. title, honour; knighthood &c. (*nobility*) 875.

royal –, serene- highness, excellency, grace; lordship, worship, Rt. Hon., rever-ence, -end; esquire, sir; madam, *madame*; master, mistress, Mr., Mrs., *signor, señor, Mein Herr, mynheer*;

876. Commonalty.—N. commonalty, democracy; obscurity; low -condition, – life, – society, – company; *bourgeoisie*; mass of -the people, – society; Brown, Jones, and Robinson; Tom, Dick, and Harry; lower –, humbler- -classes, – orders; vulgar –, common- herd; rank and file, *hoc genus omne*; the -many, – general, – crowd, – people, – populace, – multitude, – million, – masses, – mobility, – peasantry; king Mob; proletariat, *fruges consumere nati*, great unwashed; man in the street.

mob; rabble, – rout; chaff, rout, horde, *canaille*; scum –, *residuum* –, dregs- of -the people, – society; swinish multitude, *fæx populi*; *profanum* –, *ignobile- vulgus*; vermin, riff-raff, tag-rag and bobtail; small fry.

commoner, one of the people, democrat, plebeian, republican, proletary, *prolétaire, roturier*, Mr. Snooks, *bourgeois, épicier*, Philistine, cockney; *grisette, demi-mondaine.*

peasant, countryman, boor, carle, churl; vill-ain, -ein; serf, kern, tyke, tike, chuff, ryot, fellah; long-shore-man; swain, clown, hind; clod, -hopper; hobnail, yokel, hick, rube, cider squeezer, bog-trotter, bumpkin; plough-man, -boy; rustic, chawbacon, tiller of the soil; hewers of wood and drawers of water, groundling; gaffer, loon, put, cub, Tony Lumpkin, looby, lout, underling; *gamin*, guttersnipe, street arab, mudlark; rough, rowdy, ruffian, roughneck; pot-wallopper, slubberde-gullion; vulgar –, low- fellow; cad, curmudgeon.

upstart, *parvenu, nouveau-riche*, skip-jack; nobody, – one knows; *hesterni quirites, pessoribus orti; bourgeois gentil-homme, novus homo*, snob, gent, mush-room, no one knows who, adventurer; man of straw.

beggar, panhandler, gaberlunzie, muckworm, mudlark, *sans-culotte*, raff, tatterdemalion, caitiff, ragamuffin, Pariah, outcast of society, tramp, weary Willie, bum, vagabond, *chiffon*

your –, his- honour; handle to one's name.

decoration, laurel, palm, wreath, garland, bays, medal, ribbon, riband, blue ribbon, *cordon*, cross, crown, coronet, star, garter; feather, – in one's cap; chevron, epaulet, *épaulette*, colours, cockade; livery; order, arms, armorial bearings, shield, scutcheon, crest, reward &c. 973.

---

nier, rag-picker, Cinderella, cinderwench, scrub, jade; boots, gosscon.

Goth, Vandal, Hottentot, savage, barbarian, Yahoo; unlicked cub, rough diamond.

barbar-ousness, -ism; Bœotia.

V. be -ignoble &c. *adj.*, – nobody &c. *n.*

Adj. ignoble, common, mean, low, base, vile, sorry, scrubby, beggarly, below par; no great shakes &c. (*unimportant*) 643; home-ly, -spun; vulgar, low-minded; snobbish, *parvenu*.

plebeian, proletarian; of -low, – mean- -parentage, – origin, extraction; low-, base-, earth-born, low bred; mushroom, dunghill, risen from the ranks: unknown to fame, obscure, untitled.

rustic, uncivilized; lout-, boor-, clown-, churl-, brut-, raff-ish; rude, unlicked, unpolished.

barbar-ous, -ian, -ic, -esque; cockney, born within sound of Bow bells.

underling, menial, servile, subaltern.

Adv. below the salt.

---

878. Pride.—N. dignity, self-respect, *mens sibi conscia recti*.

pride; haughtiness &c. *adj.*; high notions, *hauteur*; vainglory, crest; arrogance &c. (*assumption*) 885; pomposity &c. 882.

proud man, highflier; fine -gentleman, – lady; *grande dame*.

V. be -proud &c. *adj.*; put a good face on; look one in the face; stalk abroad, perk oneself up; presume, swagger, strut; rear –, lift up –, hold up- one's head; hold one's head high, look big, take the wall, 'bear like the Turk no rival near the throne,' carry with a high hand; ride the –, mount on one's- high horse; set one's back up, bridle, toss the head; give oneself airs &c. (*assume*) 885; boast &c. 884.

pride oneself on; glory in, take a pride in; pique –, plume –, hug- oneself; stand upon, be proud of; put a good face on; not -hide one's light under a bushel, – put one's talent in a napkin; not think small beer of oneself &c. (*vanity*) 880.

Adj. dignified; stately; proud, -crested; lordly, baronial; lofty-minded; high-souled, -minded, -mettled, -handed, -plumed, -flown, -toned.

---

879. Humility.—N. hum-ility, -bleness; meek-, low-ness; lowli-ness, -hood; abasement, self-abasement, -effacement; submission &c. 725; resignation; condescension; affability &c. (*courtesy*) 894.

modesty &c. 881; verecundity, blush, suffusion, confusion; sense of -shame, – disgrace; humiliation, mortification; let -, set- down.

V. be -humble &c. *adj.*; deign, vouchsafe, condescend; humble –, demean- oneself; stoop, – to conquer; carry coals; submit &c. 725; submit with a good grace &c. (*brook*) 826; yield the palm.

lower one's -tone, – note; sing small, draw in one's horns, sober down; hide one's -face, – diminished head; not dare to show one's face, take shame to oneself, not have a word to say for oneself; feel –, be conscious of- -shame, – disgrace; drink the cup of humiliation to the dregs; eat -humble pie, – one's words, – dirt; be humiliated, receive a snub.

blush -for, – up to the eyes; redden, change colour; colour up; hang one's head, look foolish, feel small.

render humble; humble, humiliate;

haughty, paughty, insolent, lofty, high, mighty, swollen, puffed up, flushed, blown; vain-glorious; purse-proud, fine; proud as -a peacock, Lucifer; bloated with pride.

supercilious, disdainful, bumptious, magisterial, imperious; high -handed, - and mighty; overweening, consequential; arrogant &c. 885; unblushing &c. 880.

stiff, -necked; starch; perked -, stuck- up; in buckram, straitlaced; prim &c. (*affected*) 855.

on one's -high horses, - tight ropes, -high ropes; on stilts; *en grand seigneur.*

Adv. with head erect, with one's nose in the air.

Phr. *odi profanum vulgus et arceo.*

---

let -, set -, take -, tread -, frown-down; snub, abash, abase, make one sing small, strike dumb; teach one -his distance, - his place; take down a peg, - lower; throw -, cast- into the shade &c. 874; stare -, put- out of countenance; put to the blush; confuse, ashame, mortify, disgrace, crush; send away with a flea in one's ear.

get a set down.

Adj. humble, lowly, meek; modest &c. 881; humble-, sober-minded; unoffended; submissive &c. 725; servile &c. 886.

condescending; affable &c. (*courteous*) 894.

humbled &c. *v.*; bowed down, resigned; abashed, ashamed, dashed; out of countenance; down in the mouth; down on one's -knees, - marrow-bones; humbled in the dust, brow-beaten; chap-, crest-fallen; dumbfoundered, flabbergasted, struck all of a heap.

shorn of one's glory &c. (*disrepute*) 874.

Adv. with -downcast eyes, - bated breath, - bended knee; on all fours, on one's feet.

under correction, with due deference.

Phr. I am your -obedient, - very humble- servant; my service to you.

880. Vanity.—N. vanity; conceit, -edness; self-conceit, -complacency, -confidence, -sufficiency, -esteem, -love, -approbation, -praise, -glorification, -laudation, -gratulation, -applause, -admiration; *amour-propre*; selfishness &c. 943.

airs, pretensions, mannerism; egotism; prigg-ism, -ishness; coxcombry, gaudery, vainglory, elation; pride &c. 878; ostentation &c. 882; assurance &c. 885.

vox et præterea nihil; cheval de bataille.

ego-ist, -tist; peacock, coxcomb &c. 854; Sir Oracle &c. 887.

V. be -vain &c. *adj.*, - vain of; pique oneself &c. (*pride*) 878; lay the flattering unction to one's soul.

have -too high, - an overweening-opinion of -oneself, - one's talents; blind oneself as to one's own merit; not think -small beer, - *vin ordinaire*- of oneself; put oneself forward; fish

881. Modesty.—N. modesty; humility &c. 879; diffidence, timidity; retiring disposition, unobtrusiveness, bashfulness &c. *adj.*; *mauvaise honte*; blush, -ing; verecundity; self-knowledge.

reserve, constraint; demureness &c. *adj.*; blushing honours.

V. be -modest &c. *adj.*; retire, reserve oneself; give way to; draw in one's horns &c. 879; hide one's face.

keep -private, - in the background, - one's distance; pursue the noiseless tenor of one's way, 'do good by stealth and blush to find it fame,' hide one's light under a bushel, cast a sheep's eye.

Adj. modest, diffident; humble &c. 879; timid, timorous, bashful; shy. nervous, skittish, coy, sheepish, shame-faced, blushing, over-modest.

unpreten-ding, -tious; un-obtrusive, -assuming, -ostentatious, -boastful, -aspiring; poor in spirit.

for compliments; give oneself airs &c. (*assume*) 885; boast &c. 884.

render -vain &c. *adj.*; inspire with -vanity &c. *n.*; inflate, puff up, turn up, turn one's head.

Adj. vain, – as a peacock; conceited, assured, overweening, pert, forward, perky; vain-glorious, high-flown; ostentatious &c. 882; puffed up, inflated, flushed.

out of countenance &c. (*humbled*) 879.

reserved, constrained, demure.

Adv. humbly &c. *adj.*; quietly, privately; without -ceremony, – beat of drum; *sans façon*.

self-satisfied, -confident, -sufficient, -flattering, -admiring, -applauding, -glorious, -opinionated; *entêté* &c. (*wrong-headed*) 481; wise in one's own conceit, pragmatical, overwise, pretentious, priggish; egotistic, -al; *soi-disant* &c. (*boastful*) 884; arrogant &c. 885.

un-abashed, -blushing; un-constrained, -ceremonious; free and easy.

Adv. vainly &c. *adj.*

Phr. how we apples swim!

---

882. Ostentation.—N. ostentation, display, show, flourish, parade, *étalage*, pomp, array, state, solemnity; dash, splash, glitter, strut, swank, side, swagger, pomposity; preten-se, -sions; showing off; fuss.

magnificence, splendour; *coup d'œil*; grand doings.

coup de théâtre; stage -effect, – trick; clap-trap; *mise en scène*; *tour de force*; chic.

demonstration, flying colours; tomfoolery; flourish of trumpets &c. (*celebration*) 883; pageant, -ry; spectacle, exhibition, procession; turn –, set- out; grand function; *fête*, gala, field-day, review, march past, promenade, insubstantial pageant.

dress; court –, full –, evening –, ball –, fancy- dress; tailoring, millinery, man-millinery, frippery; foppery, equipage.

ceremon-y, -ial; ritual; form, -ality; etiquette; punct-o, -ilio, -iliousness; starched-, stateli-ness.

mummery, solemn mockery, mouth honour.

attitudinarian; fop &c. 854.

V. be -ostentatious &c. *adj.*; come –, put oneself- forward; attract attention, star it.

make –, cut- a -figure, – dash, – splash; strut, blow one's own trumpet; figure, – away; make a show, – display; glitter.

show -off, – one's paces; parade, march past; display, exhibit, put forward, hold up; trot –, hang- out; sport, brandish, blazon forth; dangle, – before the eyes.

cry up &c. (*praise*) 931; *prôner*, flaunt, emblazon, prink, set off, mount, have framed and glazed.

put a good, – smiling- face upon; clean the outside of the platter &c. (*disguise*) 544.

Adj. ostentatious, showy, dashing, pretentious; ja-, jau-nty; grand, pompous, palatial; high-sounding; turgid &c. (*big-sounding*) 577; garish, gorgeous; gaudy, – as a -peacock, – butterfly, – tulip; flaunting, flashing, flaming, glittering; gay &c. (*ornate*) 847; colourful.

splendid, magnificent, sumptuous.

theatrical, dramatic, spectacular, scenic, ceremonial, ritual, -istic.

solemn, stately, majestic, formal, stiff, ceremonious, punctilious, starch-ed, -y.

en grande tenue, in best bib and tucker, in Sunday best, *endimanché.*
Adv. with -flourish of trumpet, – beat of drum, – flying colours, – a
brass band.
ad captandum vulgus.

883. Celebration.—N. celebration, solemnization, jubilee, diamond
jubilee, commemoration, ovation, pæan, triumph, jubilation.

triumphal arch, bonfire, salute; salvo, – of artillery; *feu de joie,*
flourish of trumpets, *fanfare*, colours flying, illuminations, fireworks.

inauguration, installation, presentation; *début*, coming out, birthday anniversary, bi-, ter-, centenary; silver –, golden –, diamond-
wedding, -day; coronation; Lord Mayor's show; harvest home, red
letter day, festival; trophy &c. 733; *Te Deum* &c. *(thanksgiving)* 990;
fête &c. 882; holiday &c. 840.

V. celebrate, keep, signalize, do honour to, commemorate, solemnize,
hallow, mark with a red letter, hold high festival, maffick.

pledge, drink to, toast, hob and nob.

inaugurate, install, instate, induct, chair.

rejoice &c. 838; kill the fatted calf, hold jubilee, roast an ox, fire
a salute.

Adj celebrating &c. *v.*; commemorative, celebrated, immortal.

Adv. in -honour, – commemoration, – celebration of.

Int. hail! all hail! *io -pæan, – triumphe!* 'see the conquering hero
comes!'

884. Boasting.—N. boasting &c. *v.*; boast, vaunt, crake; preten-ce,
-sions; puff, -ery; flourish, *fanfaronnade*; gasconade; bluff, swank,
brag, -gardism; bravado, bunkum, Buncombe; highfalutin; jact-itation,
-ancy; bounce, rant, bluster; venditation, vapouring, rodomontade,
bombast, fine talking, tall talk, magniloquence, teratology, heroics;
jingoism, Chauvinism; exaggeration &c. 549; gas, hot air.

vanity &c. 880; *vox et præterea nihil*; much cry and little wool,
brutum fulmen.

exultation; glorification; flourish of trumpets; triumph &c. 883.

boaster; bragg-art, -adocio; hot air merchant; Gascon, *fanfaron,*
pretender, fourflusher, *soi-disant*; windbag, blowhard, bluffer; chau-
-inist; blusterer &c. 887; charlatan, jack-pudding, trumpeter; puppy
&c. *(fop)* 854.

V. boast, make a boast of, brag, vaunt, puff, show off, flourish, crake,
crack, trumpet, strut, swagger, vapour, bluff; draw the long bow.

exult, crow over, neigh, chuckle, triumph; glory, gloat, jubilate;
throw up one's cap; talk big, *se faire valoir, faire claquer son fouet,*
take merit to oneself, make a merit of, sing *Io triumphe*, holloa before
one is out of the wood.

Adj. boasting &c. *v.*; magniloquent, flaming, Thrasonic, stilted, gas-
conading, braggart, boastful, pretentious, *soi-disant*; vain-glorious &c.
(conceited) 880.

elate, -d; jubilant, triumphant, exultant; in high feather; flushed, -
with victory; cock-a-hoop; on stilts.

vaunted &c. *v.*

Adv. vauntingly &c. *adj.*; with a brass band.

Phr. 'let the galled jade wince.'

885. [Undue assumption of superiority.] **Insolence.—N.** insolence; haughtiness &c. *adj.*; arrogance, airs; overbearance, brashness, bumptiousness, contumely, disdain; domineering &c. *v.*; tyranny &c. 739.

impertinence; cheek, nerve, sauce; sauciness &c. *adj.*; flippancy, dicacity, petulance, procacity, bluster; swagger, -ing &c. *v.*; bounce; terrorism; jingoism, chauvinism.

as-, pre-sumption; beggar on horseback; usurpation.

impudence, assurance, audacity, self-assertion, hardihood, front, face, brass; shamelessness &c. *adj.*; effrontery, hardened front, face of brass.

assumption of infallibility.

malapert, saucebox &c. (*blusterer*) 887.

V. be -insolent &c. *adj.*; bluster, vapour, swagger, swell, give oneself airs, snap one's fingers, kick up a dust; swear &c. (*affirm*) 535; rap out oaths; roister.

arrogate; as-. pre-sume; make -bold, - iree; take a liberty, give an inch and take an ell.

domineer, bully, dictate, hector; lord it over, bulldoze; *traiter de haut, regarder de haut en bas*; exact; snub, huff, beard, fly in the face of; put to the blush; bear –, beat- down; browbeat, intimidate; trample –, tread- -down, - under foot; dragoon, ride roughshod over, terrorize.

out-face, -look, -stare, -brazen, -brave; stare out of countenance; brazen out; lay down the law; teach one's grandmother to suck eggs; assume a lofty bearing; talk –, look- big; put on big looks, act the *grand seigneur*; mount –, ride- the high horse; toss the head, carry with a high hand.

tempt Providence, want snuffing.

Adj. insolent, haughty, arrogant, imperious, magisterial, dictatorial, arbitrary; high-handed, high and mighty; contumelious, supercilious, overbearing, intolerant, domineering; overweening, high-flown.

flippant, pert, cavalier, saucy, forward, impertinent, fresh, malapert.

precocious, assuming, would-be, bumptious.

bluff; brazen-, -browed, -faced, shameless, aweless, unblushing, unabashed; bold-, bare-faced; dead –, lost- to shame.

886. Servility.—N. servility; slavery &c. (*subjection*) 749; obsequiousness &c. *adj.*; subserviency; abasement; pros-tration, -ternation; genuflexion &c. (*worship*) 990; fawning &c. *v.*; tuft-hunting, time-serving, flunkeyism; sycophancy &c. (*flattery*) 933; humility &c. 879.

sycophant, parasite, yes-man; toad, -y, -eater; tuft-hunter; snob, flunkey, lap-dog, spaniel, lickspittle, smell-feast, *Græculus esuriens*, hanger on, stooge, *cavaliere servente*, led captain, carpet knight; time-server, fortune-hunter, Vicar of Bray, Sir Pertinax Mac Sycophant, pick-thank; flatterer &c. 935; doer of dirty work; *âme damnée*, tool; reptile; slave &c. (*servant*) 746; courtier; sponge, jackal; truckler.

V. cringe, bow, stoop, kneel, bend the knee; fall on one's knees, prostrate oneself; worship &c. 990.

sneak, crawl, crouch, cower, truckle to, grovel, fawn, toady, lick the feet of, kiss the hem of one's garment.

pay court to; feed –, fatten –, batten-on; dance attendance on, pin oneself upon, hang on the sleeve of, *avaler des couleuvres*, keep time to, fetch and carry, do the dirty work of.

go with the stream, follow the crowd, worship the rising sun, hold with the hare and run with the hounds.

Adj. servile, obsequious; supple, - as a glove; soapy, oily, pliant, cringing, fawning, slavish, grovelling, snivelling, mealy-mouthed; beggarly, sycophantic, parasitical; abased, abject, prostrate, down on one's marrow-bones; base, mean, sneaking; crouching &c. *v.*

Adv. hat –, cap- in hand.

impudent, audacious, presumptuous, free and easy, devil-may-care, rollicking; janty, jaunty; roistering, blustering, hectoring, swaggering, vapouring; thrasonic, fire-eating, 'full of sound and fury.'

Adv. insolently, with a high hand; *ex cathedrâ*.

Phr. one's bark being worse than his bite.

887. Blusterer.—N. bluster-, swagger-, vapour-, roister-, brawl-er; brazen-face; *fanfaron*; braggart &c. (*boaster*) 884; bully, terrorist, rough, rough-neck; hooligan, hoodlum, larrikin, ruffian; Mo-hock, -hawk; drawcansir, swashbuckler, Captain Boabdil, Sir Lucius O'Trigger, Thraso, Pistol, Parolles, Bombastes Furioso, Hector, Chrononhotonthologos; jingo; desperado, dare-devil, fire-eater; fury &c. (*violent person*) 173; rowdy.

puppy &c. (*fop*) 854; prig; Sir Oracle, dogmatist, *doctrinaire*, stump orator, jack-in-office; saucebox, malapert, jackanapes, minx; bantam-cock.

SECTION III. SYMPATHETIC AFFECTIONS

1°. SOCIAL AFFECTIONS

888. Friendship. — N. friendship, amity; friendliness &c. *adj.*; brotherhood, fraternity, sodality, confraternity, sorosis, sisterhood; harmony &c. (*concord*) 714; peace &c. 721.

firm -, staunch -, intimate -, familiar -, bosom -, cordial -, tried -, devoted -, lasting -, fast -, sincere -, warm -, ardent- friendship.

cordiality, fraternization, *entente cordiale*, good understanding, *rapprochement*, sympathy, fellow-feeling, response, welcomeness; *camaraderie*.

affection &c. (*love*) 897; favouritism; goodwill &c. (*benevolence*) 906; partiality.

acquaintance, familiarity, intimacy, intercourse, fellowship, knowledge of; introduction.

V. be -friendly &c. *adj.*, - friends &c. 890, - acquainted with &c. *adj.*; know; have the ear of; keep company with &c. (*sociality*) 892; hold communication -, have dealings -, sympathize- with; have a leaning to; bear good will &c. (*benevolence*) 906; love &c. 897; make much of; befriend &c. (*aid*) 707; introduce to.

set one's horses together; hold out -, extend- the right hand of friendship, - fellowship; become -friendly &c. *adj.*; make -friends &c. 892 with; break the ice, be introduced to; make -, pick -, scrape- acquaintance with; get into favour, gain the friendship of.

shake hands with, fraternize, embrace; receive with open arms, throw oneself into the arms of; meet half way, take in good part.

Adj. friendly; amic-able, -al; well affected, unhostile, neighbourly, brotherly, fraternal, sisterly, sympathetic, harmonious, hearty, cordial, warm-hearted, devoted

889. Enmity.—N. enmity, hostility, unfriendliness &c. *adj.*; discord &c. 713.

alienation, estrangement; dislike &c. 867; hate &c. 898; antagonism.

heartburning; animosity &c. 900; malevolence &c. 907.

V. be -inimical &c. *adj.*; keep -, hold- at arm's length; be at loggerheads; bear malice &c. 907; fall out; take umbrage &c. 900; harden the heart, alienate, estrange.

Adj. inimical, unfriendly, hostile; at -enmity, - variance, - swords points, - daggers drawn, - open war with; up in arms against; in bad odour with.

on bad -, not on speaking- terms; cool; cold, -hearted; estranged, alienated, disaffected, irreconcilable.

friends –, well –, at home –, hand in hand- with; on -good, - friendly, – amicable, – cordial, – familiar, – intimate- -terms, – footing; on -speaking, – visiting- terms; in one's good -graces, – books.

acquainted, familiar, intimate, thick, hand and glove, hail fellow well met, free and easy; welcome.

Adv. amicably &c. *adj.*; with open arms; *sans cérémonie*; arm in arm.

890. Friend.—N. friend, – of one's bosom, intimate acquaintance, neighbour, well-wisher; *alter ego*; best –, bosom –, fast- friend; *amicus usque ad aras*; *fidus Achates*; *persona grata*.

favourer, *fautor*, patron, backer, Mæcenas; tutelary saint, good genius, advocate, partisan, sympathiser; ally; friend in need &c. (*auxiliary*) 711.

associate, compeer, comrade, mate, companion, *confrère*, *camarade*, *confidante*, colleague; old –, crony; side-kick; chum, buddy, bunkie, roommate, pal; play-fellow, -mate; classmate, schoolfellow; bedfellow, -mate; maid of honour.

compatriot; fellow –, countryman, – townsman.

shop-, ship-, mess-mate; fellow –, boon –, pot- companion; co-partner.

Arcades ambo, Pylades and Orestes, Castor and Pollux, Nisus and Euryalus, Damon and Pythias, *par nobile fratrum*.

host, Amphitryon, Boniface; guest, visitor, frequenter, *habitué*; *protégé*.

891. Enemy.—N. enemy; antagonist, foeman; open –, bitter- enemy; opponent &c. 710; back friend.

public enemy, enemy to society, traitor, anarchist &c. 742; *persona non grata*.

Phr. every hand being against one.

892. Sociality.—N. soci-ality, -ability, -ableness &c. *adj.*; social intercourse; consociation; inter-course, -community; consort-, companion-, fellow-, comrade-ship; clubbism; *esprit de corps*.

conviviality; good -fellowship, – company, *camaraderie*; joviality, jollity, *savoir-vivre*, festivity, festive board, merry-making; loving cup; hospitality, heartiness; cheer.

welcome, -ness; greeting; hearty –, warm –, welcome- reception; urbanity &c. (*courtesy*) 894; intimacy, familiarity.

good –, jolly- fellow, good mixer, Rotarian; *bon enfant*.

social –, family- circle; circle of acquaintance, *coterie*, society, company.

social -gathering, – *réunion*; assembly &c. (*assemblage*) 72; party, entertainment, reception, *levée*, at home, *conversazione*, soirée, matinée, evening –, morning –, afternoon –, garden –, dinner –, tea –, cocktail- party; symposium, sing-song; kettle-, drum; *partie carrée*, dish of tea, *ridotto*, rout. house-

893. Seclusion. Exclusion.—N. seclusion, privacy; retirement; concealment; reclusion, recess; snugness &c. *adj.*; delitescence; rustication, *rus in urbe*; solitude; solitariness &c. (*singleness*) 87; isolation; loneliness &c. *adj.*; estrangement from the world, anchoritism, voluntary exile; aloofness.

cell, hermitage; convent &c. 1000; *sanctum sanctorum*; study, library, den; hide-out.

depopulation, desertion, desolation; wilderness &c. (*unproductive*) 169; howling wilderness; rotten borough, Old Sarum.

exclusion, excommunication, banishment, exile, ostracism, proscription; cut, – direct; dead cut.

inhospit-ality, -ableness &c. *adj.*; un-, dis-sociability; domesticity, Darby and Joan.

recluse, hermit, eremite, cenobite; anchor-et, -ite; Simon Stylites; Troglodyte, Timon of Athens, Santon, *solitaire*, ruralist, disciple of Zimmermann, closet cynic. Diogenes; outcast, pariah-

warming; ball, prom, hop, dance, *thé dansant*; festival &c. (*amusement*) 840; wedding breakfast; 'the feast of reason and the flow of soul.'

visit, -ing; round of visits; call, morning call; interview &c. (*interlocution*) 588; assignation; tryst, -ing place; appointment.

club &c. (*association*) 712.

V. be -sociable &c. *adj.*; know; be -acquainted &c. *adj.*; associate –, sort –, keep company –, walk hand in hand -with; eat off the same trencher, club together, consort, bear one company, join; make acquaintance with &c. (*friendship*) 888; make advances, fraternize, embrace; intercommunicate.

be –, feel –, make oneself- at home with; make free with; crack a bottle with; take pot luck with, receive hospitality, live at free quarters.

visit, pay a visit; interchange -visits, – cards; call -at, – upon; leave a card; drop in, look in; look one up, beat up one's quarters.

entertain; give a -party &c. *n.*; be at home, see one's friends, hang out, keep open house, do the honours; receive, – with open arms; welcome; give a warm reception &c. *n.* to; kill the fatted calf.

Adj. sociable, companionable, clubbable, clubby, conversable, cosy, cosey, chatty, conversational; homiletical.

convivial; fest-ive, -al; jovial, jolly, hospitable.

welcome, – as the roses in May; *fêté*, entertained.

free and easy, hail fellow well met, familiar, on visiting terms, acquainted.

social, neighbourly; international, cosmopolitan, gregarious.

Adv. *en famille*, in the family circle; *sans -façon*, – *cérémonie*, arm in arm.

castaway, outsider, pilgarlic; wastrel, foundling, orphan.

V. be –, live- secluded &c. *adj.*; keep –, stand –, hold oneself- -aloof, – in the background; keep snug; shut oneself up; deny –, seclude- oneself; creep into a corner, rusticate, *aller planter ses choux*; retire, – from the world; hermetize, take the veil; abandon &c. 624;

cut, – dead; refuse to -associate with, – acknowledge; look cool –, turn one's back –, shut the door- upon; repel, blackball, excommunicate, exclude, exile, expatriate; banish, outlaw, maroon, ostracize, proscribe, cut off from, send to Coventry, keep at arm's length, draw a cordon round; boycott, blockade, lay an embargo on, isolate.

depopulate; dis-, un-people.

Adj. secluded, sequestered, retired, delitescent, private, bye; out of the -world, -way; in a backwater; 'the world forgetting by the world forgot.'

snug, domestic, stay-at-home.

unsociable; un-, dis-social; inhospitable, cynical, inconversable, unclubbable, *sauvage*, eremetic.

solitary; lone-ly, -some; isolated, single.

excluded, estranged; unfrequented; uninhabit-able, -ed; tenantless; un-tenanted, -occupied; abandoned; deserted, – in one's utmost need; unfriended; kith-, friend-, home-less; lorn, forlorn, desolate.

un-visited, -introduced, -invited, -welcome; under a cloud, left to shift for oneself, derelict, outcast, outside the gates.

banished &c. *v.*; under an embargo;

Phr. *noli me tangere.*

---

894. Courtesy.—N. courtesy; respect &c. 928; good -manners, – behaviour, – breeding; manners; politeness &c. *adj.*; *bienséance*, urbanity, comity, gentility; gentle –, breeding; polish, presence, cultivation, culture; civili-ty, -zation; amenity, suavity; good -temper, – humour; amiability, easy temper, complacency, soft tongue,

895. Discourtesy.—N. discourtesy; ill-breeding; ill –, bad –, ungainly- manners; insuavity; grouchiness; uncourteousness &c. *adj.*, tactlessness; rusticity, inurbanity; illiberality, incivility, displacency.

disrespect &c. 929; procacity, impudence; barbar-ism, -ity; misbehaviour, brutality, blackguardism, conduct un-

mansuetude; condescension &c. (*humility*) 879; affability, complaisance, *prévenance*, amiability, gallantry, chivalry; pink of -politeness, – courtesy.

compliment; fair -, soft -, sweet-words; honeyed phrases, flattering remarks, ceremonial; salutation, reception, presentation, introduction, *accueil*, greeting. recognition; welcome, *abord*, respects, *devoir*, regards, remembrances; kind -regards, – remembrances; love, best love, duty; deference.

obeisance &c. (*reverence*) 928; bow, courtesy, curtsy, scrape, *salaam*, *kowtow*, bowing and scraping; kneeling; genuflexion & c. (*worship*) 990; obsequiousness &c. 886; capping, shaking hands &c. *v.*, grip of the hand, embrace, hug, squeeze, *accolade*, loving cup, *vin d'honneur*, pledge; love token &c. (*endearment*) 902; kiss, buss, salute.

mark of recognition, nod; 'nods and becks and wreathed smiles'; valediction &c. 293; condolence &c. 915.

V. be -courteous &c. *adj.*; show -courtesy &c. *n.*

mind one's P's and Q's, behave oneself, be all things to all men, conciliate, speak one fair, take in good part; make -, do- the amiable; look as if butter would not melt in one's mouth; mend one's manners.

receive, do the honours, usher, greet, hail, bid welcome; welcome, – with open arms; shake hands; hold out -, press -, squeeze- the hand; bid God speed; speed the parting guest; cheer, serenade.

salute; embrace &c. (*endearment*) 902; kiss, – hands; drink to, pledge, hob and nob; move to, nod to; smile upon.

uncover, cap; touch -, take off- the hat; doff the cap; pull the forelock; present arms; make way for; bow; make one's bow; scrape, curtsy, courtesy; bob a -curtsy, – courtesy; kneel; bow -, bend- the knee; salaam, *kowtow*.

visit, wait upon, present oneself, pay one's respects, pay a visit &c. (*sociability*) 892; dance attendance on &c. (*servility*) 886; pay attentions to; do homage to &c. (*respect*) 928.

becoming a gentleman, *grossièreté, brusquerie*; vulgarity &c. 851.

churlishness &c. *adj.*; spinosity, perversity; moroseness &c. (*sullenness*) 901*a*.

bad-, ill-temper; sternness &c. *adj.*; austerity; moodishness, captiousness &c. 901; cynicism; tartness &c. *adj.*; acrimony, acerbity, virulence, asperity.

scowl, black looks, frown; short answer, rebuff; hard words, contumely; unparliamentary language, personality.

bear, bruin, brute, grouch, blackguard, beast; unlicked cub; frump, cross-patch; saucebox &c. 887.

V. be -rude &c. *adj.*; insult &c. 929; treat with discourtesy; take a name in vain; make -bold, – free- with; take a liberty; stare out of countenance, ogle, point at, put to the blush.

cut; turn -one's back upon, – on one's heel; give the cold shoulder; keep at -a distance, – arm's length; look -cool, – coldly, – black- upon; show the door to, send away with a flea in the ear.

lose one's temper &c. (*resentment*) 900; sulk &c. 901*a*; frown, scowl, glower, pout; snap, snarl, growl.

render -rude &c. *adj.*; brut-alize, -ify.

Adj. dis-, un-courteous; uncourtly; ill-bred, -mannered, -behaved, -conditioned; unbred; unmanner-ly, ed; im-, un-polite; un-polished, -civilized, -genteel; ungentleman-like, -ly; unladylike; blackguard; vulgar &c. 851; dedecorous; foul-mouthed, -spoken; abusive.

un-civil, -gracious, -ceremonious; cool; pert, forward, obtrusive, impudent, rude, saucy, precocious; insolent &c. 885.

repulsive; un-complaisant, -accommodating, -neighbourly, -gallant; in-affable; un-gentle, -gainly; rough, rugged, bluff, blunt, gruff; churl-, boor-, bear-ish; brutal, *brusque*; stern, harsh, austere; cavalier.

tart, sour, crabbed, sharp, short, trenchant, sarcastic, crusty, biting, caustic, virulent, bitter, acrimonious, venomous, contumelious; snarling &c, *v.*; surly, – as a bear; perverse; grim.

prostrate oneself &c. (*worship*) 990. give –, send- one's duty &c. *n.* to.

render -polite &c. *adj.*; polish, civil-ʰze, humanize.

sullen &c. 901*a*; peevish &c. (*irascible*) 901.

Adv. discourteously &c. *adj.*; witʰ -discourtesy &c. *n.*, – a bad grace.

Adj. courteous, polite, civil, mannerly, urbane; well-behaved, -mannered, -bred, -brought up, gently bred, of gentle -breeding, – manners, good-mannered, polished, civilized, cultivated; refined &c. (*taste*) 850; gentlemanlike &c. (*fashion*) 852; gallant, chivalrous, on one's good behaviour.

fine –, fair –, soft- spoken; honey-mouthed, -tongued; oily, unctuous, bland, suave; obliging, conciliatory, complaisant, complacent; obsequious &c. 886.

ingratiating, winning; gentle, mild; good-humoured, cordial, gracious, amiable, tactful, addressful, affable, genial, friendly, familiar; neighbourly.

Adv. courteously &c. *adj.*; with a good grace; with -open, – out-stretched- arms; *à bras ouverts*; *suaviter in modo*, in good humour.

Int. hail! welcome! well met! *ave!* all hail! good -day, – morning &c., – morrow! God speed! *pax vobiscum!* may your shadow never be less! *chin-chin!*

896. Congratulations.—**N.** con-, gratulation; felicitation; salute &c. 894; condolence &c. 915; compliments of the season; good –, best- wishes.

V. con-, gratulate; felicitate, compliment; give –, wish one- joy; tender –, offer- one's congratulations; wish -many happy returns of the day, – a merry Christmas and a happy new year.
congratulate oneself &c. (*rejoice*) 838.

Adj. con-, gratulatory.

897. Love.—**N.** love; fondness &c. *adj.*; liking; inclination &c. (*desire*) 865; regard, dilection, admiration, fancy.

affection, sympathy, fellow-feeling; tenderness &c. *adj.*; heart, brotherly love; benevolence &c. 906; attachment.

yearning, tender passion, *affaire de cœur, amour* gallantry, passion, flame, devotion, fervour, enthusiasm, transport of love, rapture, enchantment, infatuation, adoration, idolatry.

narcissism, Œdipus complex, Electra complex.

Cupid, Venus, Eros; myrtle; true lover's knot; love -token, – suit, – affair, – tale, – story; the old story, plighted love; courtship &c. 902; *amourette*.

maternal love.

attractiveness, charm; popularity; favourite &c. 899.

lover, suitor, follower, admirer, adorer, wooer, amoret, beau, sweet-

898. Hate.—**N.** hate, hatred, ᴠialε of hate; Hymn of Hate.

dis-affection, -favour; alienation, estrangement, coolness; enmity &c. 889; animosity &c. 900.

umbrage, pique, grudge; dudgeon, spleen; bitterness, – of feeling; ill –, bad- blood; acrimony; malice &c. 907; implacability &c. (*revenge*) 919.

repugnance &c. (*dislike*) 867; odium, unpopularity; loathing, detestation, antipathy; object of -hatred, – execration; abomination, aversion, *bête noire*; enemy &c. 891; bitter pill; source of annoyance &c. 830.

V. hate, detest, abominate, abhor, loathe; recoil –, shudder- at; shrink from, view with horror, hold in abomination, revolt against, execrate; scowl &c. 895; disrelish &c. (*dislike*) 867.

owe a grudge; bear -spleen, – a grudge, – nᴛalice &c. (*malevolence*) 907; conceive ₐn aversion to.

heart, inamorato, swain, young man, flame, love, truelove; leman, Lothario, gallant, paramour, *amoroso, cavaliere servente*, captive, *cicisbeo; caro sposo*, Don Juan, sheik, ladies' man, squire of dames, Knave of Hearts.

inamorata, lady-love, idol, darling, duck, Dulcinea, angel, goddess, *cara sposa*; mistress.

betrothed, affianced, *fiancée*.

flirt, *coquette*; amorette; pair of turtle doves; abode of love, *agapemone*.

V. love, like, affect, fancy, care for, take an interest in, be partial to, sympathize with; be -in love &c. *adj.*- with; have –, entertain –, harbour –, cherish- a -love &c. *n.* for; regard, revere; take to, bear love to, be wedded to; set one's affections on; make much of, feast one's eyes on; hold dear, prize, treasure; hug, cling to, cherish, pet, caress &c. 902.

burn; adore, idolize, love to distraction, *aimer éperdument*; dote -on, – upon:

take a fancy to, fall for, be stuck on, look sweet upon; become -enamoured &c. *adj.*; fall in love with, lose one's heart; desire &c. 865.

excite love; win –, gain –, secure –, engage- the -love, – affections, – heart; take the fancy of; have a place in –, wind round- the heart; attract, attach, endear, charm, fascinate, captivate, bewitch, seduce, enamour, enrapture, turn the head.

get into favour; ingratiate –, insinuate –, worm- oneself; propitiate, curry favour with, pay one's court to, make a date with, *faire l'aimable*, set one's cap at, flirt, coquet.

Adj. loving &c. *v.*; fond of; taken –, struck- with; smitten, bitten; attached to, wedded to; enamoured; charmed &c. *v.*; in love; love-sick; over head and ears in love.

affectionate, tender, sweet upon, sympathetic, loving, fond, amorous, amatory; erotic, uxurious, ardent, passionate, rapturous, devoted, motherly.

loved &c. *v.*; beloved; well –, dearly- beloved; dear, precious, darling, pet, little; favourite, popular.

congenial; to –, after- one's -mind, – taste, – fancy, – own heart. in one's good -graces &c. (*friendly*) 888; dear as the apple of one's eye, nearest to one's heart.

lovable, adorable; lovely, sweet; attractive, seductive, winning; charming, engaging, interesting, enchanting, captivating, fascinating, intriguing, bewitching; amiable, like an angel, angelic, seraphic.

excite –, provoke- hatred &c. *n.*; be -hateful &c. *adj.*; stink in the nostrils; estrange, alienate, repel, set against, sow dissension, set by the ears, envenom, incense, irritate, rile, ruffle, vex; horrify &c. 830.

Adj. hating &c. *v.*; abhorrent; averse from &c. (*disliking*) 867; set against. bitter &c. (*acrimonious*) 895; implacable &c. (*revengeful*) 919.

un-loved, -beloved, -lamented, -deplored, -mourned, -cared for, -endured, -valued; disliked &c. 867.

crossed in love, forsaken, rejected, love-lorn, jilted.

obnoxious, hateful, odious, abominable, repulsive, offensive, shocking; disgusting &c. (*disagreeable*) 830.

invidious, spiteful; malicious &c. 907. insulting, irritating, provoking.

[Mutual hate] at -daggers drawn, – swords points; not on speaking terms &c. (*enmity*) 889.

Phr. no love lost between.

---

899. Favourite.—N. favourite, pet, cosset, minion, idol, jewel, spoiled child, *enfant gâté*; led captain; crony; fondling; apple of one's eye, man after one's own heart; *persona grata*.

love, dear, darling, duck, honey, jewel; mopsey, moppet; sweetheart &c. (*love*) 897.

general –, universal- favourite; idol of the people; matinée idol, movie –, radio- star.

900. Resentment.—N. resentment, displeasure, animosity, anger, wrath, indignation; vexation, exasperation, bitter resentment, wrathful indignation.

pique, umbrage, huff, miff, soreness, dudgeon, acerbity, virulence, bitterness, acrimony, asperity, spleen, gall; heart-burning, -swelling; rankling.

ill –, bad- -humour, – temper; irascibility &c. 901; ill blood &c. (*hate*) 898; revenge &c. 919.

excitement, irritation; warmth, bile, choler, ire, fume, pucker, dander, ferment, ebullition; towering -passion, – rage, *acharnement*, angry mood, taking, pet, tiff, passion, fit, tantrums.

burst, explosion, paroxysm, storm, rage, fury, desperation; violence &c. 173; fire and fury; vials of wrath; gnashing of teeth, hot blood, high words.

scowl &c. 895; sulks &c. 901a.

[Cause of umbrage] affront, provocation, offence; indignity &c. (*insult*) 929; grudge, crow to pluck, sore subject; red rag to a bull; *casus belli*.

Furies, Erinys, Eumenides, Alecto, Megæra, Tisiphone.

buffet, slap in the face, box on the ear, rap on the knuckles.

V. resent; take -amiss, – ill, – to heart, – offence, – umbrage, – huff, – exception; take in -ill part, – bad part, – dudgeon; *ne pas entendre raillerie*; breathe revenge, cut up rough.

fly –, fall –, get- into a -rage, – passion; bridle –, bristle –, froth –, fire –, flare- up; open –, pour out- the vials of one's wrath.

pout, knit the brow, frown, scowl, lower, snarl, growl, gnarl, gnash, snap; redden, colour; look -black, – black as thunder, – daggers; bite one's thumb; show –, grind- one's teeth; champ the bit.

chafe, mantle, fume, kindle, fly out, take fire; boil, – over; boil with -indignation, – rage; rage, storm, foam; vent one's -rage, – spleen; lose one's temper, stand on one's hind legs, stamp the foot, kick up a row, fly off the handle, cut up rough; stamp –, quiver –, swell –, foam- with rage; burst with anger; raise Cain, breathe fire and fury.

have a fling at; bear malice &c. (*revenge*) 919.

cause –, raise- anger; affront, offend; give -offence, – umbrage anger; hurt the feelings; insult, discompose, fret, ruffle, nettle, heckle, huff, pique; excite &c. 824; irritate, stir the blood, stir up bile; sting, – to the quick; rile, provoke, chafe, wound, incense, inflame, enrage, aggravate, add fuel to the flame, fan into a flame, widen the breach, envenom, embitter, exasperate, infuriate, kindle wrath; stick in one's gizzard; rankle &c. 919.

put out of humour; put one's -monkey, – back- up; set –, get- one's back up; raise one's -gorge, – dander, – choler; work up into a passion; make -one's blood boil, – the ears tingle; throw into a ferment, madden, drive one mad; lash into -fury, – madness; fool to the top of one's bent; set by the ears.

bring a hornet's nest about one's ears.

Adj. angry, wrath, irate; ire-, wrath-ful; cross &c. (*irascible*) 901; sulky &c. 901a; bitter, virulent; acrimonious &c. (*discourteous*) &c. 895; violent &c. 173.

warm, burning; boiling, - over; fuming, raging; foaming, - at the mouth; convulsed with rage.

offended &c. *v.*; waxy, *acharné*; wrought, worked up; indignant, hurt, sore, peeved; set against.

fierce, wild, rageful, furious, mad with rage, fiery, infuriate, rabid, savage; relentless &c. 919.

flushed with -anger, - rage; in a -huff, - stew, - fume, - pucker, - passion, - rage, - fury; on one's high ropes, up in arms; in high dudgeon;

Adv. angrily &c. *adj.*; in the height of passion; in the heat of -passion, - the moment.

Int. *tantæne animis cœlestibus iræ!* marry come up! zounds! 'sdeath!

Phr. one's -blood, - back, - monkey- being up; *fervens difficili bile jecur*; the gorge rising, eyes flashing fire; the blood -rising, - boiling; *hæret lateri lethalis arundo.*

901. Irascibility.—N. irascibility, temper; crossness &c. *adj.*; susceptibility, procacity, petulance, irritability, tartness, acerbity, protervity; pugnacity &c. (*contentiousness*) 720.

excitability &c. 825; bad -, fiery -, crooked -, irritable &c. *adj.*- temper; *genus irritabile*, hot blood.

ill humour &c. (*sullenness*) 901a; asperity &c., churlishness &c. (*discourtesy*) 895.

huff &c. (resentment) 900; a word and a blow.

Sir Fretful Plagiary; brabbler, Tartar; shrew, vixen, virago, termagant, dragon, scold, Xanthippe; porcupine; spit-fire; fire-eater &c. (*blusterer*) 887; fury &c. (*violent person*) 173.

V. be -irascible &c. *adj.*; have a -temper &c. *n.*, - devil in one; fire up &c. (*be angry*) 900.

Adj. irascible; bad-, ill-tempered; irritable, susceptible; excitable &c. 825; thin-skinned &c. (*sensitive*) 822; fretful, fidgety; on the fret.

hasty, over-hasty, quick, warm, hot, testy, touchy, techy, tetchy; like -touchwood, - tinder; huffy; pet-tish, -ulant; waspish, snapp-y, -ish, peppery, fiery, passionate, choleric, shrewish, 'sudden and quick in quarrel.'

querulous, captious, mood-y, -ish; quarrelsome, contentious, disputatious; pugnacious &c. (*bellicose*) 720; cantankerous, exceptious; restive &c. (*perverse*) 901a; churlish &c. (*discourteous*) 895.

cross, - as -crabs, - two sticks, - a cat, - a dog, - the tongs; like a bear with a sore head; fractious, peevish, *acariâtre*.

in a bad temper; sulky &c. 901a; angry &c. 900.

resent-ful, -ive; vindictive &c. 919.

Int. pish!

901a. Sullenness.—N. sullenness &c. *adj.*; morosity, spleen; churlishness &c. (*discourtesy*) 895; irascibility &c. 901.

moodiness &c. *adj.*; perversity; obstinacy &c. 606; torvity, spinosity; crabbedness &c. *adj.*

ill -, bad- -temper, - humour; sulks, dudgeon, mumps, doleful dumps, doldrums, fit of the sulks, *bouderie*, black looks, scowl; huff &c. (*resentment*) 900.

V. be -sullen &c. *adj.*; sulk; frown, scowl, lower, glower, grouse, grouch, crab, gloam, pout, have a hang-dog look, glout.

Adj. sullen, sulky; ill-tempered, -humoured, -affected, -disposed; in an ill, - a bad, - a shocking- -temper, - humour; out of -temper, -

humour; knaggy, torvous, crusty, crabbed; sore as a boil; surly &c.
(*discourteous*) 895.

moody; spleen-ish, -ly; splenetic, cankered.

cross, -grained; perverse, wayward, humoursome; restive; cantankerous, refractory, intractable, exceptious, sinistrous, deaf to reason,
unaccommodating, rusty, crusty, froward.

dogged &c. (*stubborn*) 606.

grumpy, glum, grim, grum, morose, frumpish; in the -sulks &c. *n.*;
out of sorts; scowl-, glower-, growl-ing.

peevish &c. (*irascible*) 901.

902. [Expression of affection or love.] Endearment.—N. endearment, caress; blandish-, blandi-ment; *épanchement*, fondling, billing
and cooing, dalliance.

embrace, salute, kiss, buss, smack, osculation, deosculation; amorous
glances; ogle, side glance, sheep's eyes.

courtship, wooing, suit, addresses, the soft impeachment; love-
making; an affair; serenading; caterwauling.

flirting &c. *v.*; flirtation, gallantry; coquetry, spooning.

true lover's knot, plighted love, engagement, betrothal; love -tale,
— token, — letter; *billet-doux*, valentine.

honeymoon; Strephon and Chloe, 'Arry and 'Arriet.

V. caress, fondle, pet, dandle, nurse; pat, — on the -head, — cheek;
chuck under the chin, smile upon, coax, wheedle, cosset, coddle, cocker;
make -of, — much of, pamper; cherish, foster, kill with kindness.

clasp, hug, cuddle; fold —, strain- in one's arms; nestle, nuzzle, neck,
embrace, kiss, buss, smack, blow a kiss; salute &c. (*courtesy*) 894.

bill and coo, spoon, toy, dally, flirt, coquet; galli-, gala-vant; philander; make love; pay one's -court, — addresses, — attentions- to;
serenade; court, woo; set one's cap at; be —, look- sweet upon; ogle,
cast sheep's eyes upon; *faire les yeux doux*.

fall in love with, win the affections &c. (*love*) 897; die for.

propose; make —, have- an offer; pop the question; plight one's
-troth, — faith; become -engaged, — betrothed.

Adj. caressing &c. *v.*; 'sighing like furnace'; love-sick, spoony.
caressed &c. *v.*

903. Marriage.—N. marriage, matrimony, wedlock, union, intermarriage,
vinculum matrimonii, nuptial tie, knot.

married state, coverture. bed, cohabitation.

match; betrothment &c. (*promise*)
768; wedding, nuptials, Hymen, bridal;
e-, spousals; leading to the altar &c.
v.; nuptial benediction, *epithalamium*.

torch —, temple- of Hymen; hymeneal altar; honeymoon.

bride, bridegroom; brides-maid,
-man.

best —, grooms-man, page, usher.

married -man, — woman, — couple;
neogamist, Benedick, partner, spouse,
mate, yokemate; husband, man, con-

904. Celibacy.—N. celibacy, singleness, single blessedness; bachelor-hood,
-ship; miso-gamy, -gyny.

virginity, *pucelage*; maiden-hood,
-head.

unmarried man, bachelor, Cœlebs,
agamist, old bachelor; miso-gamist,
-gynist; celibate.

unmarried woman, spinster; maid,
-en; virgin, *femme sole*, old maid; bachelor girl; nun &c.

V. live single; keep bachelor hall.

Adj. un-married, -wedded; wife-,
spouse-less; single, virgin, celibate.

905. Divorce.—N. divorce, -ment;
separation; judicial separation, separ-

sort, baron; old –, good- man; wife of one's bosom; help-meet, -mate, rib, better half, grey mare, old woman, good wife; *femme couverte*; squaw, lady; matron, -age, -hood; man and wife; wedded pair, Darby and Joan.

affinity, soul-mate.

mono-, bi-, di-, deutero-, tri-, polygamy; mormonism; poly-andry; Turk, Bluebeard.

ate maintenance; *separatio a -mensâ et thoro,* – *vinculo matrimonii.*

widowhood, viduage, viduity, weeds. widow, -er; relict; dowager; *divorcée*; cuckold.

V. live -separately, – apart; separate, divorce, disespouse, put away; wear the horns.

_____

unlawful –, left-handed –, companionate –, morganatic –, ill-assorted- marriage; *mésalliance; mariage de convenance*; an affair.

match-maker, marriage broker, matrimonial agent.

V. marry, wive, take to oneself a wife; be -married, – spliced; go –, pair- off; wed, espouse, lead to the hymeneal altar, take 'for better, for worse,' give one's hand to, bestow one's hand upon; remarry; intermarry.

marry, join, handfast; couple &c. (*unite*) 43; tie the nuptial knot; give -away, – in marriage; affy, affiance; betroth &c. (*promise*) 768; publish –, bid- the banns; be asked in church.

Adj. married &c. *v.*; one, – bone and one flesh.

marriageable, nubile.

engaged, betrothed, affianced.

matrimonial, marital, conjugal, connubial, wedded; nuptial, hymeneal, spousal, bridal.

Phr. the grey mare the better horse.

2°. DIFFUSIVE SYMPATHETIC AFFECTIONS

906. Benevolence.—N. benevolence, Christian charity; God's -love, – grace; good-will; philanthropy &c. 910; unselfishness &c. 942.

good -nature, – feeling, – wishes; kind-, kindli-ness &c. *adj.*; lovingkindness, benignity, brotherly love, charity, humanity, fellow-feeling, sympathy; goodness –, warmth- of heart; *bonhomie*; kind-heartedness; amiability, milk of human kindness, tenderness; love &c. 897; friendship &c. 888.

toleration, consideration, generosity; mercy &c. (*pity*) 914.

charitableness &c. *adj.*; bounty, alms-giving; good works, beneficence, the luxury of doing good.

acts of kindness, a good turn; good –, kind- -offices, – treatment.

good Samaritan, sympathizer, well-wisher, philanthropist, *bon enfant*; altruist.

V. be -benevolent &c. *adj.*; have one's heart in the right place, bear good will; wish -well, – God speed;

907. Malevolence.—N. malevolence; bad intent, -ion; un-, dis-kindness; ill -nature, – will, – blood; acrimony; bad blood; enmity &c. 889; hate &c. 898; malignity; malice, – aforethought, -prepense; maliciousness &c. *adj.*; spite, despite; resentment &c. 900.

uncharitableness &c. *adj.*; incompassionateness &c. 914*a*; gall, venom, rancour, rankling, virulence, mordacity, acerbity; churlishness &c. (*discourtesy*) 895.

hardness of heart, heart of stone, obduracy; cruelty; cruelness &c. *adj.*; brutality, savagery; fer-ity, -ocity; barbarity, inhumanity, immanity, truculence, ruffianism; evil eye, cloven -foot, – hoof; inquisition; torture.

ill –, bad- turn; affront &c. (*disrespect*) 929; outrage, atrocity; ill usage; intolerance, bigotry, persecution; tender mercies [ironical]; 'unkindest cut of all.'

V. be -malevolent &c. *adj.*; bear –, harbour- -spleen, – a grudge, – mal

view –, regard- with an eye of favour;
take in good part; take –, feel- an
interest in; be –, feel- interested- in;
sympathize with, feel for; fraternize
&c. (*be friendly*) 888.

enter into the feelings of others, do
as you would be done by, meet half-
way.

treat well; give comfort, smooth the
bed of death; do -good, – a good turn;
benefit &c. (*goodness*) 648; render a
service, be of use; aid &c. 707.

Adj. benevolent; kind, -ly; well-
meaning; amiable; obliging, accommodating, indulgent, considerate, gracious, complacent, good-humoured.

warm-, soft-, kind-, tender-, large-,
broad-hearted; merciful &c. 914; philanthropic &c. 910; charitable, beneficent, humane, benign, benignant;
bount-eous, -iful &c. 816.

good-, well-natured; spleenless;
sympath-izing, -etic; complaisant &c.
(*courteous*) 894; kindly, well-meant,
-intentioned.

fatherly, motherly, brotherly, sisterly; pat-, mat-, frat-ernal; friendly &c.
888.

Adv. with -a good intention, – the
best intentions.

Int. God speed! much good may it
do!

ice; betray –, show- the cloven foot;
hurt &c. (*physical pain*) 378; annoy
&c. 830; injure, harm, wrong; do -harm,
– an ill office- to; outrage; disoblige,
malign, plant a thorn in the breast.

molest, worry, harass, haunt, harry,
bait, tease, throw stones at; play the
devil with; hunt down, dragoon, hound;
persecute, oppress, grind; maltreat;
ill-treat, -use.

wreak one's malice on, do one's
worst, break a butterfly on the wheel;
dip –, imbrue- one's hands in blood;
have no mercy &c. 914a.

Adj. male-, unbene-volent; unbenign;
ill-disposed, -intentioned, -natured,
-conditioned, -contrived; evil-minded,
-disposed.

malicious; malign, -ant; rancorous;
de-, spiteful; mordacious, caustic,
bitter, envenomed, acrimonious, virulent; un-amiable, -charitable; maleficent, venomous, grinding, galling.

harsh, disobliging; un-kind, -friend-
ly, -gracious; treacherous; inofficious;
invidious; uncandid; churlish &c. (*un-
courteous*) 895; surly, sullen &c. 901a.

cold, -blooded, -hearted; hard-, flint-
marble-, stony-hearted; hard of heart,
unnatural; ruthless &c. (*unmerciful*)
914a; relentless &c. (*revengeful*) 919.

cruel; brut-al, -ish; savage, – as a
-bear, – tiger; ferine, feral, ferocious;
inhuman; barbarous, fell, untamed, tameless, truculent, incendiary;
bloodthirsty &c. (*murderous*) 361; atrocious.

fiend-ish, -like; demoniacal; diabolic, -al; devilish, infernal,
hellish, Satanic.

Adv. malevolently &c. *adj.*; with -bad intent &c. *n.*

908. Malediction.—N. malediction, malison, curse, imprecation,
denunciation, execration, anathema, ban, proscription, excommunication, commination, thunders of the Vatican, fulmination, aspersion,
vilification, vituperation, scurrility.

abuse; foul –, bad –, strong –, unparliamentary- language, Limehouse; Billingsgate, sauce, evil speaking; cursing &c. *v.*; profane
swearing, oath.

threat &c. 909; more bark than bite; invective &c. (*disapprobation*)
932.

V. curse, accurse, imprecate, damn, swear at; slang; curse with bell,
book and candle; invoke –, call down- curses on the head of; devote
to destruction.

execrate, beshrew, scold; anathematize &c. (*censure*) 932; hold up
to execration, denounce, proscribe, excommunicate, fulminate, thunder
against; threaten &c. 909; curse up hill and down dale.

curse and swear; swear, – like a trooper; fall a cursing, rap out an oath, damn, cuss.

Adj. curs-ing, -ed &c. *v.*; maledictory.

Int. woe to! beshrew! *ruat cœlum!* ill –, woe- betide! confusion seize! damn! confound! blast! curse! devil take! hang! out with! a plague –, out- upon! aroynt! *honi soit!*

Phr. *delenda est Carthago.*

909. Threat.—N. threat, menace; defiance &c. 715; abuse, minacity, intimidation; fulmination; commination &c. (*curse*) 908; gathering clouds &c. (*warning*) 668.

V. threat, -en; menace; snarl, growl, gnarl, mutter, bark, bully; defy &c. 715; intimidate &c. 860; keep –, hold up –, hold out- *in terrorem*; shake –, double –, clinch- the fist at; thunder, talk big, fulminate, use big words, bluster, look daggers.

Adj. threatening, menacing; mina-tory, -cious; comminatory, abusive; *in terrorem*; ominous &c. (*predicting*) 511; defiant &c. 715; under the ban.

Int. *væ victis!* at your peril! do your worst!

910. Philanthropy. — N. philanthropy; altruism, humanit-y, -arianism; universal benevolence; *deliciæ humani generis*; cosmopolitanism, utilitarianism, the greatest happiness of the greatest number, social science, sociology.

common weal, public welfare, socialism, communism.

patriotism, civism, nationality, love of country, *amor patriæ*, public spirit.

chivalry, knight errantry; generosity &c. 942.

philanthropist, altruist &c. 906; utilitarian, Benthamite, socialist, communist, cosmopolite, citizen of the world, *amicus humani generis*; knight errant; patriot.

Adj. philanthropic, altruistic, humanitarian, utilitarian, cosmopolitan; public-spirited, patriotic; humane, large-hearted &c. (*benevolent*) 906; chival-ric, -rous, generous &c. 942.

Adv. *pro -bono publico, – aris et focis.*

Phr. *'humani nihil a me alienum puto.'*

911. Misanthropy.—N. misanthropy, incivism; egotism &c. (*selfishness*) 943; moroseness &c. 901a; cynicism; defeatism.

misanthrope, misanthropist, egotist, cynic, man-hater, Timon, Diogenes.

woman-hater, misogynist.

Adj. misanthropic, antisocial, unpatriotic; egotistical &c. (*selfish*) 943; morose &c. 901a.

912. Benefactor. — N. benefactor, saviour, good genius, tutelary saint, patron, guardian angel, fairy godmother, good Samaritan; *pater patriæ*; salt of the earth &c. (*good man*) 948; auxiliary &c. 711.

913. [Maleficent being.] Evil-doer. —N. evil- doer, – worker; wrong doer &c. 949; mischief maker, marplot; oppressor, tyrant; firebrand, incendiary, pyromaniac, anarchist, destroyer, Hun, *Boche*, Vandal, iconoclast; communist; terrorist, *apache*, gunman, gangster, racketeer.

savage, brute, ruffian, barbarian, semi-barbarian, caitiff, desperado; Mo-hock, -hawk; bludgeon man, bully, rough, hooligan, larrikin, dangerous classes, ugly customer; thief &c. 792.

cockatrice, scorpion, hornet; viper, adder; snake, – in the grass;

serpent, cobra, asp, rattlesnake, anaconda; canker-, wire-worm; locust, Colorado beetle; torpedo; bane &c. 663.

cannibal; Anthropophag-us, -ist; bloodsucker, vampire, ogre, ghoul, gorilla; vulture; gyr-, ger-falcon.

wild beast, tiger, hyæna, butcher, hangman; cut-throat &c: (*killer*) 361; blood-, sleuth-, hell-hound.

hag, hellhag, beldam, Jezebel.

monster; fiend &c. (*demon*) 980; homicidal maniac, devil incarnate, demon in human shape; Frankenstein's monster.

harpy, siren, vampire; Furies, Eumenides &c. 900.

Attila, scourge of the human race.

Phr. *fœnum habet in cornu.*

3°. SPECIAL SYMPATHETIC AFFECTIONS

914. Pity.—N. pity, compassion, commiseration; bowels, – of compassion; condolence &c. 915; sympathy, fellow-feeling, tenderness, yearning, forbearance, humanity, mercy, clemency, exorability; leniency &c. (*lenity*) 740; charity, ruth, long-suffering.

melting mood; *argumentum ad misericordiam*; quarter, grace, *locus pœnitentiæ.*

sympathizer, champion, partisan.

V. pity; have –, show –, take- pity &c. *n.*; commiserate, compassionate; condole &c. 915; sympathize; feel –, be sorry –, yearn- for; weep, melt, thaw, enter into the feelings of.

forbear, relent, relax, give quarter, wipe the tears, *parcere subjectis*, give a *coup de grâce*, put out of one's misery; be cruel to be kind.

raise –, excite- pity &c. *n.*; touch, soften; melt, – the heart; appeal to one's better feelings; propitiate, disarm.

ask for -mercy &c. *n.*; supplicate &c. (*request*) 765; cry for quarter, beg one's life, kneel; deprecate.

Adj. pitying &c. *v.*; pitiful, compassionate, sympathetic, touched. merciful, clement, ruthful; humane; humanitarian &c. (*philanthropic*) 910; tender. – hearted, – as a chicken; soft, – hearted; unhardened; lenient &c. 740; exorable, forbearing; melting &c. *v.*; weak.

Int. for pity's sake! mercy! have –, cry you- mercy! God help you! poor -thing, – dear, – fellow! woe betide! *quis talia fando temperet a lachrymis!*

Phr. one's heart bleeding for; *haud ignara mali miseris succurrere disco.*

914a. Pitilessness.—N. pitilessness &c. *adj.*; inclemency; inexorability, hardness of heart; inflexibility; severity &c. 739; malevolence &c. 907.

V. have no –, shut the gates of- mercy &c. 914; give no quarter.

Adj. piti-, merci-, ruth-, bowel-less; unpitying, unmerciful, inclement; in-, un-compassionate; inexorable, inflexible; harsh &c. 739; cruel &c. 907; unrelenting &c. 919.

915. Condolence.—N. condolence; lamentation &c. 839; sympathy, consolation.

V. condole with, console, sympathize &c. 914, share one's misery; feel for; express –, testify- pity; afford –, supply- consolation; lament &c. 839- with; send one's condolences.

4°. RETROSPECTIVE SYMPATHETIC AFFECTIONS

916. Gratitude. — N. gratitude, thankfulness, gratefulness, feeling of obligation.

acknowledgment, recognition thanksgiving, giving thanks.

thanks, praise, benediction; pæan; *Te Deum* &c. (*worship*) 990; grace, – before, – after- meat; thank-offering. requital.

V. be -grateful &c. *adj.*; thank; give –, render –, return –, offer –, tenderthanks &c. *n.*; acknowledge, requite.

feel –, be –, lie- under an obligation; *savoir gré*; not look a gift horse in the mouth; never forget, overflow with gratitude; thank –, bless- one's stars; fall on one's knees.

Adj. grateful, thankful, obliged, beholden, indebted to, under obligation.

Int. thanks! many thanks! gramercy! much obliged! thank you! thank Heaven! Heaven be praised!

917. Ingratitude.—N. ingratitude, thanklessness, oblivion of benefits; unthankfulness.

'benefits forgot'; thankless -task, – office.

V. be -ungrateful &c. *adj.*; forget benefits; look a gift horse in the mouth;

Adj. un-grateful, -mindful, -thankful; thankless, ingrate, wanting in gratitude, insensible of benefits.

forgotten; un-acknowledged, -thanked, -requited, -rewarded; ill-requited,

Int. thank you for nothing! *'et tu, Brute !'*

---

918. Forgiveness.—N. forgiveness, pardon, condonation, grace, remission, absolution, amnesty, oblivion; indulgence; reprieve.

conciliation; reconciliation &c. (*pacification*) 723; propitiation.

excuse, exoneration, quittance, release, indemnity; bill -, act -, covenant -, deed- of indemnity; exculpation &c. (*acquittal*) 970.

longanimity, placability, forbearance; *amantium iræ*; *locus pœnitentiæ*.

V. forgive, – and forget; pardon, condone, think no more of, let bygones be bygones, shake hands; forget an injury, bury the hatchet; clean the slate.

excuse, pass over, overlook; wink at &c. (*neglect*) 460; bear with; allow -, make allowances- for; let one down easily, not be too hard upon, pocket the affront; blot out one's transgression.

let off, remit, absolve, give absolution, reprieve; acquit &c. 970.

beg -, ask -, implore- pardon &c. *n.*; conciliate, propitiate, placate; make up a quarrel &c. (*pacify*) 723; let the wound heal.

919. Revenge.—N. revenge, -ment; vengeance; avenge-ment, -ance; sweet revenge, *vendetta*, death-feud, eye for an eye, blood for blood, a Roland for an Oliver; retaliation &c. 718; day of reckoning.

rancour, vindictiveness, implacability; malevolence &c. 907; ruthlessness &c. 914a.

avenger, vindicator, Nemesis, Eumenides.

V. re-, a-venge; take -, have one's-revenge; breathe -revenge, – vengeance; wreak one's -vengeance, – anger; give no quarter.

have -accounts to settle, – a crow to pluck, – a rod in pickle; pay off old scores.

keep the wound green; harbour -revenge, – vindictive feeling; bear malice; rankle, – in the breast; have at one's mercy.

Adj. revenge-, venge-ful; vindictive, rancorous; pitiless &c. 914a; ruthless, rigorous, avenging, retaliative.

unforgiving, unrelenting; inexorable, stony-hearted, implacable; relent-, remorse-less.

æternum servans sub pectore vulnus; rankling, immitigable.

Adj. forgiving, placable, conciliatory. forgiven &c. *v.*; un-resented, -avenged, -revenged.

Adv. cry you mercy.

Phr. *veniam petimusque damusque vicissim*; more in sorrow than in anger.

Phr. *manet -cicatrix,* – *altâ mente repostum.* revenge is sweet.

————

920. Jealousy.—N. jealous-y, -ness; jaundiced eye, heartburning; green-eyed monster; yellows; Juno.

V. be -jealous &c. *adj.*; view with -jealousy, – a jealous eye.

Adj. jealous, – as a Barbary pigeon; jaundiced, yellow-eyed, horn-mad.

921. Envy.—N. envy; enviousness &c. *adj.*; rivalry; *jalousie de métier.*

V. envy, covet, lust after, crave, burst with envy, regard with envious eyes.

Adj. envious, invidious, covetous; *alieni appetens.*

SECTION IV.　MORAL AFFECTIONS

1°.　MORAL OBLIGATIONS

922. Right.—N. right; what -ought to, – should- be; fitness &c. *adj.*; *summum jus.*

justice, equity; equitableness &c. *adj.*; propriety; fair play, impartiality, measure for measure, give and take, *lex talionis*, square deal.

Astræa, Nemesis, Themis.

scales of justice, even-handed justice, retributive justice, *suum cuique*; clear stage –, fair field- and no favour; Queensberry rules.

morals &c. (*duty*) 926; law &c. 963; honour &c. (*probity*) 939; virtue &c. 944.

V. be -right &c. *adj.*; stand to reason. see -justice done, – one righted, – fair play; do justice to; recompense &c. (*reward*) 973; hold the scales even, give and take; serve one right, put the saddle on the right horse; give -every one, – the devil- his due; *audire alteram partem.*

deserve &c. (*be entitled to*) 924.

Adj. right, good; just, reasonable; fit &c. 924; equ-al, -able, -itable; even-handed, fair, – and square.

legitimate, justifiable, rightful; as it -should, – ought to- be; lawful &c. (*permitted*) 760, (*legal*) 963.

deserved &c. 924.

Adv. rightly &c. *adj.*; in -justice, – equity, – reason.

without -distinction of, – regard to, – respect to- persons; upon even terms.

Int. all right!

923. Wrong. — N. wrong; what -ought not to, – should not- be; *malum in se*; unreasonableness, grievance; shame.

injustice; unfairness &c. *adj.*; iniquity, foul play, partiality, leaning; favour, -itism; nepotism, party spirit, partisanship; undueness &c. 925; unlawfulness &c. 964.

robbing Peter to pay Paul &c. *v.*; the wolf and the lamb; vice &c. 945.

a custom more honoured in the breach than the observance.

V. be -wrong &c. *adj.*; cry to heaven for vengeance.

do -wrong &c. *n.*; be -inequitable &c. *adj.*; favour, lean towards; encroach; impose upon; reap where one has not sown; give an inch and take an ell; rob Peter to pay Paul.

Adj. wrong, -ful; bad, too bad; unjust, -fair; in-, un-equitable; unequal, partial, one-sided.

objectionable; un-reasonable, -allowable, -warrantable, -justifiable; not cricket, not playing the game; improper, unfit; unjustified &c. 925; illegal &c. 964; iniquitous, criminal; immoral &c. 945; injurious &c. 649.

in the wrong, – box.

Adv. wrongly &c. *adj.*

Phr. it will not do; this is too bad.

————

924. Dueness.—N. due, -ness; right, privilege, prerogative, prescription, title, claim, pretension, demand, birthright.

immunity, licence, liberty, franchise; vested -interest, – right; licitness.

sanction, authority, warranty, charter; warrant &c. (*permission*) 760; constitution &c. (*law*) 963; tenure; bond &c. (*security*) 771.

deserts, merits, dues.

claimant, appellant; plaintiff &c. 938.

V. be -due &c. *adj.* to, – the due &c. *n.* of; have -right, – title, – claim- to; be entitled to; have a claim upon; belong to &c. (*property*) 780.

deserve, merit, be worthy of, richly deserve.

demand, claim; call upon –, come upon –, appeal to- for; re-vendicate, -claim; exact; insist -on, – upon; challenge; take one's stand, make a point of, require, lay claim to, assert, assume, arrogate, make good; substantiate; vindicate a -claim, – right; make out a case.

give –, confer- a right; sanction, entitle; authorize &c. 760; sanctify, legalize, ordain, prescribe, allot.

give every one his due &c. 922; pay one's dues; have one's -due, – rights; stand upon one's rights.

use a right, assert, enforce, put in force, lay under contribution.

Adj. having a right to &c. *v.*; entitled to; claiming; deserving, meriting, worthy of.

privileged, allowed, sanctioned, warranted, authorized; ordained, prescribed, constitutional, chartered, enfranchised.

prescriptive, presumptive; absolute, indefeasible; un-, in-alienable; imprescriptible, inviolable, unimpeachable, unchallenged; sacrosanct.

due to, merited, deserved, condign, richly deserved, *emeritus*.

allowable &c. (*permitted*) 760; lawful, licit, legitimate, legal; legalized &c. (*law*) 963.

square, unexceptionable, right; equitable &c. 922; due, *en règle*; fit, -ting; correct, proper, meet, befitting, becoming, seemly; decorous; creditable, up to the mark, right as a trivet; just –, quite- the thing; *selon les règles*.

Adv. duly, *ex officio, de jure*; by -right, – divine right; as is -fitting, – proper, – fitting and proper; *jure divino, Dei gratiâ*, in the name of.

Phr. *civis Romanus sum.*

925. [Absence of right.] Undueness —N. undueness &c. *adj.*; *malum prohibitum*; impropriety; illegality &c. 964.

falseness &c. *adj.*; emptiness –, invalidity- of title; illegitimacy.

loss of right, disfranchisement, forfeiture.

usurpation, assumption, tort, violation, breach, encroachment, presumption, seizure, stretch, exaction, imposition, lion's share.

usurper, pretender, Carlist; impostor.

V. be -undue &c. *adj.*; not be -due &c. 924.

infringe, encroach, trench on, exact; arrogate, – to oneself; give an inch and take an ell; stretch –, strain- a point; usurp, violate, do violence to; sail under false colours.

dis-franchise, -entitle, -qualify; invalidate.

relax &c. (*be lax*) 738; misbehave &c. (*vice*) 945; misbecome.

Adj. undue; unlawful &c. (*illegal*) 964; unconstitutional, *ultra vires*; illicit; un-authorized, -warranted, -allowed, -sanctioned, -justified; un-, dis-entitled, -qualified; un-privileged, -chartered.

illegitimate, bastard, spurious, false; usurped, tortious.

un-deserved, -merited, -earned; unfulfilled.

forfeited, disfranchised.

improper; un-meet, -fit, -befitting, -seemly; un-, mis-becoming; seemless; *contra bonos mores*; not the thing, out of the question, not to be thought of; preposterous, pretentious, would- be.

926. Duty.—N. duty, what ought to be done, moral obligation, account-ableness, liability, *onus*, responsibility; bounden –, imperative- duty; call, – of duty.

allegiance, fealty, tie; engagement &c. (*promise*) 768; part; function, calling &c. (*business*) 625.

morality, morals, decalogue; case of conscience; conscientiousness &c. (*probity*) 939; conscience, inward monitor, 'still small voice within, sense of duty, tender conscience.

dueness &c. 924; propriety, fitness, seemliness, amenableness, decorum; the -thing, – proper thing; the -right, – proper- thing to do.

[Science of morals] eth-ics, -ology; ʌleon-, are-tology; moral –, ethical-philosophy; casuistry, polity.

observance, fulfilment, discharge, performance, acquittal, satisfaction, redemption; good behaviour.

V. be -the duty of, – incumbent &c. *adj.* on, – responsible &c. *adj.*; behoove, become, befit, beseem; belong –, pertain- to; fall to one's lot; devolve on; lie -upon, – on one's head, – at one's door; rest -with, – on the shoulders of.

take upon oneself &c. (*promise*) 768; be –, become- -bound to, – sponsor for; be responsible for; incur a -responsibility &c. *n.*; be –, stand –, lie- under an obligation; have to answer for, owe it to oneself.

impose a -duty &c. *n.*; enjoin, require, exact; bind, – over; saddle with, prescribe, assign, call upon, look to, oblige.

927. Dereliction of Duty.—N. dere; liction of duty; fault &c. (*guilt*) 947-sin &c. (*vice*) 945; non-observance, -performance, -co-operation; neglect, carelessness, laziness, incompetence, eye-service, relaxation, infraction, violation, transgression, failure, evasion, indolence; dead letter.

slacker, loafer, striker, non-co-operator.

V. violate; break, – through; infringe; set -aside, – at naught; trample -on, – under foot; slight, neglect, evade, renounce, forswear, repudiate; wash one's hands of; escape, transgress, fail; call to account &c. (*disapprobation*) 932.

927a. Exemption.—N. exemption, freedom, irresponsibility, immunity, liberty, licence, release, exoneration, excuse, dispensation, absolution, franchise, renunciation, discharge; exculpation &c. 970; *ægrotat.*

V. be -exempt &c. *adj.*

exempt, release, acquit, discharge, quit-claim, remise, remit; free, set at liberty, let off, pass over, spare, excuse, dispense with, give dispensation, license; stretch a point; absolve &c; (*forgive*) 918; exonerate &c. (*exculpate*) 970; save the necessity.

Adj. exempt, free, immune, at liberty, scot free; released &c. *v.*; unbound, unencumbered; irresponsible, unaccountable, not answerable; excusable.

———

enter upon –, perform –, observe –, fulfil –, discharge –, adhere to –, acquit oneself of –, satisfy- -a duty, – an obligation; act one's part, redeem one's pledge, do justice to, be at one's post; do duty; do one's duty &c. (*be virtuous*) 944.

be on one's good behaviour, mind one's P's and Q's.

Adj. obligatory, binding; imperative, peremptory; stringent &c. (*severe*) 739; behooving &c. *v.*; incumbent –, chargeable- on; under obligation; obliged –, bound –, tied- by; saddled with.

due –, beholden –, bound –, indebted- to; tied down; compromised &c. (*promised*) 768; in duty bound.

amenable, liable, accountable, responsible, answerable.

right, meet &c. (*due*) 924; moral, ethical, casuistical, conscientious, ethological.

Adv. with a safe conscience, as in duty bound, on one's own responsibility, at one's own risk, *suo periculo*; *in foro conscientiæ*; *quamdiu se bene gesserit*; at one's post, on duty.

Phr. *dura lex sed lex.*

2°, MORAL SENTIMENTS

928. Respect.—N. respect, regard, consideration; courtesy &c. 894; attention, deference, reverence, honour, esteem, estimation, veneration, admiration; approbation &c. 931.

homage, fealty, obeisance, genuflexion, kneeling, prostration; obsequiousness &c. 886; salaam, *kowtow*, bow, presenting arms, salute.

respects, regards, duty, *devoirs*, *égards*.

devotion &c. (*piety*) 987.

V. respect, regard; revere, -nce; hold in reverence, honour, venerate, hallow; esteem &c. (*approve of*) 931; think much of; entertain –, bear-respect for; have a high opinion of; look up to, defer to; pay -attention, – respect &c. *n.*- to; do –, render- honour to; do the honours, hail; show courtesy &c. 894; salute, present arms; do –, pay- homage to; pay tribute to, kneel to, bow to, bend the knee to; fall down before, prostrate oneself, kiss the hem of one's garment; worship &c. 990.

keep one's distance, make room, observe due decorum, stand upon ceremony.

command –, inspire- respect; awe, impose, overawe, dazzle.

Adj. respecting &c. *v.*; respectful, deferential, decorous, reverential, obsequious, ceremonious, bare-headed, cap in hand, on one's knees; prostrate &c. (*servile*) 886.

respected &c. *v.*; in high -esteem, – estimation; time-honoured, venerable, *emeritus*.

Adv. in deference to; with -all, – due, – the highest- respect; with submission.

saving your -grace, – presence; *salva sit reverentia*; *pace tanti nominis*.

Int. hail! all hail! *esto perpetua!* may your shadow never be less!

929. Disrespect. — N. dis-respect, -esteem, -estimation, -favour, -repute; low estimation; disparagement &c. (*dispraise*) 932, (*detraction*) 934.

irreverence; slight, neglect; *spretæ injuria formæ*; superciliousness &c. (*contempt*) 930.

vilipendency, contumely, affront, dishonour, insult, indignity, outrage, discourtesy &c. 895; practical joking; scurrility, scoffing, sibilation; ir-, derision; mockery; irony &c. (*ridicule*) 856; sarcasm.

hiss, hoot, gibe, flout, jeer, scoff, gleek, taunt, sneer, quip, fling, wipe, slap in the face.

V. hold in disrespect &c. (*despise*) 930; misprize, disregard, slight, undervalue, depreciate, trifle with, set at naught, pass by, push aside, overlook, turn one's back upon, laugh in one's sleeve; be -disrespectful &c. *adj.*, – discourteous &c. 895; treat with -disrespect &c. *n.*; set down, browbeat.

dishonour, desecrate, insult, affront, outrage.

speak slightingly of; disparage &c. (*dispraise*) 932; vilipend, call names; throw –, fling- dirt; drag through the mud, point at, indulge in personalities; make -mouths, – faces; bite the thumb; take –, pluck- by the beard; toss in a blanket, tar and feather.

have –, hold- in derision; deride, scoff, sneer, laugh at, snigger, ridicule, gibe, mock, jeer, taunt, twit, niggle, gleek, gird, flout, fleer; roast, turn into ridicule; guy, burlesque &c. 856; laugh to scorn &c. (*contempt*) 930; smoke; fool; make -game, – a fool, – an April fool- of; play a practical joke; rag; lead one a dance, run the rig upon, have a fling at, scout, hiss, hoot, mob.

Adj. disrespectful; aweless, irreverent; disparaging &c. 934; insulting &c. *v.*; supercilious &c. (*scornful*) 930; rude, derisive, contemptuous, sarcastic; scurri-le, -lous; contumelious.

un-respected, -worshipped, -envied, -saluted; un-, dis-regarded;
Adv. disrespectfully &c. *adj.*

930. Contempt.—N. contempt, disdain, scorn, sovereign contempt; despi-sal, -ciency; vilipendency, contumely; slight, sneer, spurn, by-word.

contemptuousness &c. *adj.*; scornful eye; smile of contempt; derision &c. (*disrespect*) 929.

[State of being despised] despisedness.

V. despise, contemn, scorn, disdain, feel contempt for, view with a scornful eye, disregard, slight, not mind; pass by &c. (*neglect*) 460.

look down upon; hold -cheap, – in contempt, – in disrespect; think -nothing, – small beer- of; make light of; underestimate &c. 483; esteem -slightly, – of small or no account; take no account of, care nothing for; set no store by; not care a -straw &c. (*unimportance*) 643; set at naught, laugh in one's sleeve, snap one's fingers at, shrug one's shoulders, turn up one's nose at, pooh-pooh, damn with faint praise; sneeze –, whistle –, sneer- at; curl up one's lip, toss the head, *traiter de haut*; laugh at &c. (*be disrespectful*) 929.

point the finger of –, hold up to –, laugh to- scorn; scout, hoot, flout, hiss, scoff at.

turn -one's back, – a cold shoulder- upon; tread –, trample- -upon, – under foot; spurn, kick; fling to the winds &c. (*repudiate*) 610; send away with a flea in the ear.

Adj. contemptuous; disdain-, scorn-ful; withering, contumelious, supercilious, cynical, haughty, bumptious, cavalier; derisive.

contemptible, despicable; pitiable; pitiful &c. (*unimportant*) 643; despised &c. *v.*; down-trodden; unenvied.

Adv. contemptuously &c. *adj.*

Int. a fig for &c. (*unimportant*) 643; bah! never mind! away with! hang it! fiddle-de-dee!

---

931. Approbation.—N. approbation; approv-al, -ement; sanction, advocacy; nod of approbation; esteem, estimation, good opinion, golden opinions, admiration; love &c. 897; appreciation, regard, account, popularity, *kudos*, credit; repute &c. 873.

commendation, praise; laud, -ation; good word; meed –, tribute- of praise; encomium; eulog-y, -ium; *éloge*, panegyric; homage, hero worship; benediction, blessing, benison.

applause, plaudit, clap; clapping, – of hands; accl-aim, -amation; cheer; pæan, hosannah; shout –, peal –, chorus –, thunders- of -applause &c.; Kentish fire; Prytaneum; blurb.

V. approve; think -good, – much of, – well of, – highly of; esteem, value, prize; set great store -by, – on.

do justice to, appreciate; honour, hold in esteem, look up to, admire; like &c. 897; be in favour of, wish God speed; hail, – with satisfaction.

stand –, stick- up for; uphold, hold

932. Disapprobation.—N. disapprobation, -val; improbation; dis-esteem, -valuation, -placency; odium; dislike &c. 867; dissent &c. 489.

dis-praise, -commendation; blame, censure, obloquy; detraction &c. 934; disparagement, depreciation; denunciation; condemnation &c. 971; ostracism; boycott; black-list, -ball; *index -expurgatorius, – librorum prohibitorum.*

animadversion, reflection, stricture, objection, exception, criticism; sardonic -grin, – laugh; sarcasm, insinuation, innuendo; bad –, poor –, left-handed- compliment.

satire; sneer &c. (*contempt*) 930; taunt &c. (*disrespect*) 929; cavil, carping, censoriousness; hypercriticism &c. (*fastidiousness*) 868.

reprehension, remonstrance, expostulation, reproof, reprobation, admonition, increpation, reproach; rebuke, reprimand, castigation, jobation, lecture, curtain lecture, blow up, wigging, dressing, – down; rating, scolding, trim-

up, countenance, sanction; clap -, pat- on the back; keep in countenance, en- dorse, give credit, recommend; mark with a white -mark, – stone.

commend, praise; be-, laud; com- pliment, pay a tribute, bepraise; clap, – the hands; applaud, cheer, acclaim, acclamate, encore; panegyrize, eulo- gize, cry up, *prôner*, puff; extol, – to the skies; magnify, glorify, exalt, boost, swell, make much of; flatter &c. 933; bless, give a blessing to; have -, say- a good word for; speak -well, – highly, – in high terms- of; sing -, sound -, chaunt -, resound- the praises of; sing praises to; cheer -, applaud- to the -echo, – very echo.

redound to the -honour, – praise, – credit- of; do credit to; deserve -praise &c. *n.*; recommend itself; pass muster.

be -praised &c.; receive honourable mention; be in -favour, – high favour- with; ring with the praises of, win golden opinions, gain credit, find favour with, stand well in the opinion of; *laudari a laudato viro.*

Adj. approving &c. *v.*; in favour of; lost in admiration.

commendatory, complimentary, ben- edictory, laudatory, panegyrical, eulo- gistic, encomiastic, acclamatory, lavish of praise, uncritical.

approved, praised &c. *v.*; un-cen- sured, -impeached; popular, in good odour; in high esteem &c. (*respected*) 928; in -, in high- favour.

deserving -, worthy of- praise &c. *n.*; praiseworthy, commendable, of estima- tion; good &c. 648; meritorious, estim- able, creditable, plausible, unimpeach- able; beyond all praise.

Adv. commendably, with credit, to admiration; well &c. 618; with three times three.

Int. hear, hear! well done! *brav-o! -a! -i! bravissimo! euge! macte virtute!* so far so good, that's right, quite right; *op- time!* one cheer more; may your shad-- ow never be less! *esto perpetua!* long life to! *viva! evviva!* God speed! *valete et plaudite! encore! bis!*

Phr. *probatum est.*

———

ming; correction, set down, rap on the knuckles, *coup de bec*, rebuff; slap, – on the face; home thrust, hit; frown, scowl, black look.

diatribe; jeremiad; *tirade*, philippic.

clamour, outcry, hue and cry; hiss, -ing; sibilation, cat-call; execration &c. 908.

chiding, upbraiding &c. *v.*; expro- bration, abuse, vituperation, invective, objurgation, contumely, personal re- marks; hard -, cutting -, bitter- words.

evil-speaking; bad language &c. 908; personality.

V. disapprove; dislike &c. 867; la- ment &c. 839; object to, take excep- tion to; be scandalized at, think ill of; view with -disfavour, – dark eyes, – jaundiced eyes; *nil admirari*, dis- value, improbate.

frown upon, look grave; bend -, knit- the brows; shake the head at. shrug the shoulders; turn up the nose &c. (*contempt*) 930; look -askance, – black upon; look with an evil eye; make a wry -face, – mouth- at; set one's face against.

dis-praise, -commend, -parage; de- precate, speak ill of, not speak well of, slate, condemn &c. (*find guilty*) 971.

blame; lay -, cast- blame upon; censure, *fronder*, reproach, pass censure on, reprobate, impugn.

remonstrate, expostulate, recrimin- ate.

reprehend, chide, admonish; bring -, call- -to account, – over the coals, – to order; take to task, reprove, lecture, bring to book; read a -lesson, – lecture- to; rebuke, correct.

reprimand, chastise, castigate, lash, blow up, trounce, trim, *laver la tête*, overhaul; give it one, – finely; gibbet.

accuse &c. 938; impeach, denounce; hold up to -reprobation, – execration; expose, brand, gibbet, stigmatize; show -, pull -, take- up; cry 'shame' upon; be outspoken; raise a hue and cry against.

execrate &c. 908; exprobrate, speak daggers, vituperate; abuse, – like a pickpocket; scold, rate, objurgate, up- braid, fall foul of; jaw; rail, – at, – in good set terms; bark at; anathematize, call names; call by -hard, – ugly- names; a-, re-vile; vili-fy, -pend; bespatter; backbite; clapperclaw; rave –, thunder –, fulminate-against; load with reproaches; lash with the tongue.

exclaim –, protest –, inveigh –, declaim –, cry out –, raise one's voice- against.

decry; cry –, run –, frown- down; clamour, hiss, hoot, mob, ostracize; draw up –, sign- a round robin; black-ball, -list.

animadvert –, reflect- upon; glance at; cast -reflection, – re-proach, – a slur- upon; insinuate, damn with faint praise; 'hint a fault and hesitate dislike'; not to be able to say much for.

scoff at, point at; twit, taunt &c. (disrespect) 929; sneer at &c. (despise) 930; satirize, lampoon; defame &c. (detract) 934; depre-ciate, find fault with, criticize, cut up; pull –, pick- to pieces; take exception; cavil; peck –, nibble –, carp- at; be -censorious &c. adj.; pick -holes, – a hole, – a hole in one's coat; make a fuss about.

take –, set- down; snub, snap one up, give a rap on the knuckles; throw a stone -at, – in one's garden; have a -fling, – snap- at; have words with, pluck a crow with; give one a -wipe, – lick with the rough side of the tongue.

incur blame, excite disapprobation, scandalize, shock, revolt; get a bad name, forfeit one's good opinion, be under a cloud, come under the ferule, bring a hornet's nest about one's ears.

take blame, stand corrected; have to answer for.

Adj. disapproving &c. v.; scandalized.

disparaging, condemnatory, damnatory, denunciatory, reproach-ful, abusive, objurgatory, clamorous, vituperative; defamatory &c. 934.

satirical, sarcastic, sardonic, cynical, dry, sharp, cutting, biting, severe, virulent, withering, trenchant, hard upon; censorious, criti-cal, captious, carping, hypercritical; fastidious &c. 868; sparing of –, grudging- praise.

disapproved, chid &c. v.; in bad odour, blown upon, unapproved; unblest; at a discount, exploded; weighed in the balance and found wanting.

blameworthy, reprehensible &c. (guilt) 947; to –, worthy of-blame, answerable, uncommendable, exceptionable, not to be thought of, bad &c. 649; vicious &c. 945.

un-lamented, -bewailed, -pitied.

Adv. with a wry face; reproachfully &c. adj.

Int. it is too bad! it -won't, – will never- do! marry come up! Oh! come! 'sdeath!

forbid it Heaven! God –, Heaven- forbid! out –, fie- upon it! away with! tut! O tempora! O mores! shame! fie, – for shame! out on you!

tell it not in Gath!

933. Flattery.—N. flattery, adula-tion, gloze; bland-ishment, -iloquence; cajolery; fawning, wheedling &c. v.; captation, coquetry, sycophancy, ob-sequiousness, flunkeyism, toad-eating, tuft-hunting; snobbishness.

incense, honeyed words, flummery; bun-kum, -combe; blarney, placebo, but-

934. Detraction.—N. detraction, dis-paragement, depreciation, vilification, obloquy, scurrility, scandal, defama-tion, aspersion, traducement, slander, calumny, obtrectation, evil-speaking, backbiting, scandalum magnatum.

personality, libel, squib, lampoon, skit, pasquinade; chronique scandaleuse.

ter; soft -soap, – sawder; rose water.

voice of the charmer, mouth honour; lip-homage; euphemism; unctuousness &c. *adj.*

V. flatter, praise to the skies, puff; wheedle, cajole, glaver, coax; fawn, – upon; humour, gloze, soothe, pet, coquet, slaver, butter; be-spatter, -slubber, -plaster, -slaver; lay it on thick, overpraise; earwig, cog, collogue; truckle –, pander *or* pandar –, pay court- to; court; creep into the good graces of; curry favour with, hang on the sleeve of; fool to the top of one's bent; lick the dust.

lay the flattering unction to one's soul, gild the pill, make things pleasant.

overestimate &c. 482; exaggerate &c. 549.

Adj. flattering &c. *v.*; adulatory; mealy-, honey-mouthed; honeyed; smooth, – tongued; soapy, oily, unctuous, blandiloquent, specious; fine-, fair-spoken; plausible, servile, sycophantic, fulsome; courtier-ly, -like.

Adv. *ad captandum.*

---

935. Flatterer.—N. flatterer, adulator; eu-logist, -phemist; optimist, encomiast, *laudator*, whitewasher, booster.

toad-y, -eater; sycophant, courtier, pickthank, Sir Pertinax MacSycophant; *flâneur, prôneur;* puffer, touter, *claqueur;* claw-back, ear-wig, doer of dirty work; parasite, hanger on &c. (*servility*) 886.

---

937. Vindication.—N. vindication, justification, warrant; exoneration, exculpation; acquittal &c. 970; whitewashing.

extenuation; pallia-tion, -tive; softening, mitigation.

reply, defence; recrimination &c. 938.

apology, gloss, varnish; plea &c. 617; salvo; excuse, extenuating circumstances; allowance, – to be made; *locus pœnitentiæ.*

apologist, vindicator, justifier; defendant &c. 938.

justifiable charge, true bill.

sarcasm, cynicism; criticism (*disapprobation*) 932; invective &c. 932; envenomed tongue; *spretæ injuria formæ.* detractor &c. 936.

V. detract, derogate, decry, depreciate, disparage; run –, cry- down; minimize, make light of; belittle, sneer at &c. (*contemn*) 930; criticize, pull to pieces, pick a hole in one's coat, asperse, cast aspersions, blow upon, bespatter, blacken; vili-fy, -pend; avile; give a dog a bad name, brand, malign, backbite, libel, lampoon, traduce, slander, defame, calumniate, bear false witness against; speak ill of behind one's back.

'damn with faint praise, assent with civil leer; and without sneering, others teach to sneer.'

fling dirt &c. (*disrespect*) 929; anathematize &c. 932; dip the pen in gall, view in a bad light.

Adj. detracting &c. *v.*; defamatory, detractory, derogatory; disparaging, libellous; scurril-e, -ous; abusive; foulspoken, -tongued, -mouthed; slanderous; calumni-ous, -atory; sar-castic, -donic; satirical, cynical.

---

936. Detractor.—N. detractor, reprover; cens-or, -urer; cynic, critic, caviller, carper, wordcatcher.

defamer, backbiter, slanderer, knocker, Sir Benjamin Backbite, lampooner, satirist, traducer, libeller, calumniator, dearest foe, dawplucker, Thersites; Zoilus; good-natured –, candid- friend [satirically]; reviler, vituperator, castigator; shrew &c. 901.

disapprover, *laudator temporis acti.*

---

938. Accusation. — N. accusation, charge, imputation, slur, inculpation, exprobration, delation; crimination; in-, ac-, re-crimination; *tu quoque* argument; invective &c. 932.

de-nunciation, -nouncement; libel, challenge, citation, arraignment; im-, ap-peachment; indictment, bill of indictment, true bill; lawsuit &c. 969; condemnation &c. 971.

gravamen of a charge, head and front of one's offending, *argumentum ad hominem;* scandal &c. (*detraction*) 934; *scandalum magnatum.*

V. justify, warrant; be an -excuse &c. *n.*- for; lend a colour, furnish a handle; vindicate; ex-, dis-culpate; acquit &c. 970; clear, set right, exonerate, whitewash.

extenuate, palliate, excuse, soften, apologize, varnish, slur, gloze; put a -gloss, – good face- upon; mince; gloss over, bolster up, help a lame dog over a stile.

advocate, defend, plead one's cause; stand –, stick –, speak- up for; contend –, speak- for; bear out, keep in countenance, support; plead &c. 617; say in defence; plead ignorance; confess and avoid, propugn, put in a good word for.

take the will for the deed, make allowance for, do justice to; give -one, – the Devil- his due.

make good; prove -the truth of, – one's case; be justified by the event.

Adj. vindicat-ed, -ing &c. *v.*; vindicat-ive, -ory; palliative; exculpatory; apologetic.

excusable, defensible, pardonable; veni-al, -able; specious, plausible, justifiable.

Phr. *'honi soit qui mal y pense.'*

accuser, prosecutor, plaintiff, complainant, petitioner; relator, informer; appellant.

accused, defendant, prisoner, panel, co-, respondent; litigant.

V. accuse, charge, tax, impute, twit, taunt with, reproach.

brand with reproach; stigmatize, slur; cast a -stone at, – slur on; incriminate; inculpate, implicate; call to account &c. (*censure*) 932; take to -blame, – task; put in the black book.

inform against, indict, denounce, arraign; im-, ap-peach; have up, show up, pull up; challenge, cite, lodge a complaint; prosecute, bring an action against &c. 969.

charge –, saddle- with; lay to one's -door, – charge; lay the blame on, bring home to; cast –, throw- in one's teeth; cast the first stone at.

have –, keep- a rod in pickle for; have a crow to pluck with.

trump up a charge.

Adj. accusing &c. *v.*; accusat-ory, -ive; imputative, denunciatory; re-, criminatory.

accused &c. *v.*; suspected; under -suspicion, – a cloud, – *surveillance*; in -custody, – detention; in the -lock up, – watch house, – house of detention.

accusable, imputable; in-defensible, -excusable; un-pardonable, -justifiable; vicious &c. 945.

Int. look at home; *tu quoque* &c. (*retaliation*) 718.

3°. MORAL CONDITIONS

939. Probity.—**N.** probity, integrity, rectitude; uprightness &c. *adj.*; honesty, faith; honour; good faith, *bona fides*; purity, clean hands.

fairness &c. *adj.*; fair play, justice, equity, impartiality, principle; grace.

constancy; faithfulness &c. *adj.*; fidelity, loyalty; incorrupt-ion, -ibility.

trustworthiness &c. *adj.*; truth, candour, singleness of heart; veracity &c. 543; tender conscience &c. (*sense of duty*) 926.

punctil-iousness, -io; delicacy, nicety; scrupul-osity, -ousness &c. *adj.*; scruple; point, – of honour; punctuality.

dignity &c. (*repute*) 873; respectabiiity, -bleness &c. *adj.*; gentleman; man of -honour, – his word; *fidus*

940. Improbity. **N.** improbity; dishon-esty, -our; deviation from rectitude; disgrace &c. (*disrepute*) 874; fraud &c. (*deception*) 545; lying &c. 544; bad –, Punic- faith; *mala –, Punica- fides*; infidelity; faithlessness &c. *adj.*; Judas kiss, betrayal; scrap of paper.

breach of -promise, – trust, – faith: prodition, disloyalty, divided allegiance, treason, high treason; apostasy &c. (*tergiversation*) 607; non-observance &c. 773.

shabbiness &c. *adj.*; villainy; base-ness &c. *adj.*; abjection, debasement, turpitude, moral turpitude, laxity, trimming, shuffling.

perfidy; perfidiousness &c. *adj.*;

Achates, preux chevalier, galantuomo; truepenny, trump, brick; true Briton, white man, sportsman.

court of honour, a fair field and no favour; *argumentum ad verecundiam.*

V. be -honourable &c. *adj.*; deal -honourably, – squarely, – impartially, – fairly; speak the truth &c. (*veracity*) 543; tell the truth and shame the devil, *vitam impendere vero*; show a proper spirit, make a point of; do one's duty &c. 944; play the game.

redeem one's pledge &c. 926; keep –, be as good as- one's -promise, – word; keep faith with, not fail

give and take, *audire alteram partem*, give the devil his due, put the saddle on the right horse.

redound to one's honour.

Adj. upright; honest, – as daylight; veracious &c. 543; virtuous &c. 944; honourable; fair, right, just, equitable, impartial, even-handed, square; fair –, open- and aboveboard.

constant, – as the northern star; faithful, loyal, staunch; true, – blue, – to one's colours, – to the core, – as the needle to the pole; true-hearted, trust-y, -worthy; as good as one's word, to be depended on, incorruptible.

manly, straightforward &c. (*ingenuous*) 703; frank, candid, open-hearted.

conscientious, tender - conscienced, right-minded; high-principled, -minded; scrupulous, religious, strict; nice, punctilious, correct, punctual; respect-, reput-able; gentlemanlike.

inviol - able, - ate; un - violated, -broken, -betrayed; un-bought, -bribed.

innocent &c. 946; pure; stainless; un-stained, -tarnished, -sullied, -tainted, -perjured; uncorrupt, -ed; unde-filed, -praved, -bauched; *integer vitæ scelerisque purus*; *justus et tenax propositi.*

chivalrous, jealous of honour, *sans peur et sans reproche*; high-spirited.

supra-mundane, unworldly, over-scrupulous.

Adv. honourably &c. *adj.*; *bona fide*; on the square, in good faith, honour bright, *foro conscientiæ*, with clean hands; by fair means.

treachery, double-dealing; unfairness &c. *adj.*; knavery, roguery, rascality, foul-play; jobb-ing, -ery; Tammany, graft; venality, nepotism; corruption, job, shuffle, fishy transaction, barratry; sharp practice, heads I win, tails you lose; mouth-honour &c. (*flattery*) 933.

V. be -dishonest &c. *adj.*; play false; break one's -word, – faith, – promise, jilt, betray, forswear; shuffle &c. (*lie*) 544; live by one's wits, sail near the wind; play with marked cards.

disgrace –, dishonour –, demean –, degrade- oneself; derogate, stoop, grovel, sneak, lose caste; sell oneself, go over to the enemy; seal one's infamy.

Adj. dishon-est, -ourable; un-conscientious, -scrupulous; fraudulent &c. 545; knavish; disgraceful &c. (*disreputable*) 874; wicked &c. 945.

false-hearted, disingenuous; unfair, one-sided; double, -tongued, -faced; time-serving, crooked, tortuous, insidious, Machiavellian, dark, slippery; questionable; fishy; perfidious, treacherous, perjured.

infamous, arrant, foul, base, vile, low, ignominious, blackguard.

contemptible, abject, mean, shabby, little, paltry, dirty, scurvy, scabby, sneaking, grovelling, scrubby, rascally, pettifogging; beneath one; not cricket.

low-minded, -thoughted; base-minded.

undignified, indign; unbe-coming, -seeming, -fitting; de-rogatory, -grading; *infra dignitatem*; ungentleman-ly, -like; un-knightly, -chivalric, -manly, -handsome; recreant, inglorious.

corrupt, venal; debased, mongrel.

faithless, of bad faith, false, unfaithful, disloyal; untrustworthy; trust-, troth-less; lost to shame, dead to honour.

Adv. dishonestly &c. *adj.*; *malâ fide*, like a thief in the night, by crooked paths; by foul means.

Int. *O tempora! O mores!*

---

941. Knave.—**N.** knave, rogue, villain; Scapin, rascal; Lazarillo de Tormes; bad man &c. 949; blackguard &c. 949.

traitor, betrayer, arch-traitor, conspirator, stool pigeon, Judas, Catiline; reptile, serpent, snake in the grass, wolf in sheep's clothing, sneak, Jerry Sneak, tell-tale, squealer, mischief-maker, trimmer; renegade &c. (*tergiversation*) 607; truant, recreant; sycophant &c. (*servility*) 886.

942. Disinterestedness.—N. disinterestedness &c. *adj.*; generosity; liberal-ity, -ism; altruism; benevolence &c. 906; elevation, loftiness of purpose, exaltation, magnanimity; chival-ry, -rous spirit; heroism, sublimity.

self-denial, -abnegation, -effacement, -sacrifice, -immolation, -control &c. (*resolution*) 604; stoicism, devotion, martyrdom, *suttee*.

labour of love.

V. be -disinterested &c. *adj.*; make a sacrifice, lay one's head on the block; put oneself in the place of others, do as one would be done by, do unto others as we would men should do unto us.

Adj. disinterested; unselfish; self-denying, -sacrificing, -devoted; generous.

handsome, liberal, noble; noble-, high-minded; princely, great, high, elevated, lofty, exalted, spirited, stoical, magnanimous; great-, large-hearted, chivalrous, heroic, sublime.

un-bought, -bribed; uncorrupted &c. ⟨*upright*⟩ 939.

943. Selfishness.—N. selfishness &c. *adj.*; self-love, -indulgence, -worship, -interest; ego-tism, -ism; egocentrism, narcissism; *amour propre* &c. (*vanity*) 880; nepotism.

worldliness &c. *adj.*; world wisdom.

illiberality; meanness &c. *adj.*

time-server; tuft-, fortune-hunter; self-seeker; jobber, worldling; egotist, egoist, monopolist, nepotist, profiteer; temporizer, trimmer; dog in the manger, charity that begins at home.

V. be -selfish &c. *adj.*; please –, indulge –, coddle- oneself; consult one's own -wishes, – pleasure; look after one's own interest; feather one's nest; take care of number one, have an eye to the main chance, know on which side one's bread is buttered; give an inch and take an ell; wangle.

Adj. selfish; self-seeking, -indulgent, -interested; wrapped up –, centred- in self; egotistic, -al; egoistical; egocentric.

illiberal, mean, ungenerous, narrowminded; mercenary, venal; covetous &c. 819.

unspiritual; earthly, -minded; mundane; worldly, -minded, -wise; timeserving.

interested; *alieni appetens sui profusus*.

Adv. ungenerously &c. *adj.*; to gain some private ends; from selfish –, interested- motives.

Phr. *après nous le déluge*.

944. Virtue.—N. virtue; virtuousness &c. *adj.*; morality; moral rectitude; integrity &c. (*probity*) 939; nobleness &c. 873.

morals; ethics &c. (*duty*) 926; cardinal virtues.

merit, worth, desert, excellence, credit; self-control &c. (*resolution*) 604; self-denial &c. (*temperance*) 953.

well-doing; good -actions, – behaviour; discharge –, fulfilment –, performance- of duty; well-spent life; innocence &c. 946.

V. be -virtuous &c. *adj.*; practise -virtue &c. *n.*; do –, fulfil –, perform –,

945. Vice. — N. vice; evil -doing, – courses; wrong doing; wickedness, viciousness &c. *adj.*; iniquity, peccability, demerit; sin, Adam; old –, offending- Adam.

immorality, impropriety, indecorum, scandal, laxity, looseness of morals; want of -principle, – ballast; obliquity, backsliding, infamy, demoralization, pravity, depravity, pollution; hardness of heart; brutality &c. (*malevolence*) 907; corruption &c. (*debasement*) 659; knavery &c. (*improbity*) 940; profligacy; lust &c. 961; flagrancy, atrocity; cannibalism.

discharge- one's duty; redeem one's pledge &c. 926; act well, – one's part; fight the good fight; acquit oneself well; command –, master- one's passions; keep -straight, – in the right path.

set -an, – a good- example; be on one's -good, – best- behaviour.

Adj. virtuous, good; innocent &c. 946; meritorious, deserving, worthy, desertful, correct; dut-iful, -eous; moral; right, -eous, -minded; well-intentioned, creditable, laudable, commendable, praiseworthy; above –, beyond- all praise; excellent, admirable; sterling, pure, noble.

exemplary; match-, peer-less; saintly, -like; heaven-born, angelic, seraphic, godlike.

Adv. virtuously &c. *adj.*; *e merito.*

infirmity; weakness &c. *adj.*; weakness of the flesh, frailty, imperfection; error; weak side; foible; fail-ing, -ure; crying –, besetting- sin; defect, deficiency, shortcoming; cloven foot.

lowest dregs of vice, sink of iniquity, Alsatian den; *gusto picaresco.*

fault, crime; criminality &c. (*guilt*) 947.

sinner &c. 949.

V. be -vicious &c. *adj.*; sin, commit sin, do amiss, err, transgress; misdemean –, forget –, misconduct- oneself; mis-do, -behave; fall, lapse, slip, trip, offend, trespass; deviate from the -line of duty, – path of virtue &c. 944; take a wrong course, go astray; hug a -sin, – fault; sow one's wild oats.

render -vicious &c. *adj.*; demoralize, brutalize; corrupt &c. (*degrade*) 659.

Adj.* vicious; sinful; sinning &c. *v.*; wicked, iniquitous, bad, immoral, unrighteous, wrong, criminal; naughty, incorrect; undut-eous, -iful.

unprincipled, lawless, disorderly, *contra bonos mores*, indecorous, unseemly, improper; dissolute, profligate, scampish; unworthy; worth-, desert-less; disgraceful, recreant; reprehensible, blameworthy, uncommendable; dis-creditable, -reputable.

base, sinister, scurvy, foul, gross, vile, black, grave, facinorous, felonious, nefarious, shameful, scandalous, infamous, villainous, of a deep dye, heinous; flag-rant, -itious; atrocious, incarnate, accursed.

Mephistophelian, satanic, diabolic, hellish, infernal, stygian, fiend-ish, -like, hell-born, demoniacal, devilish.

mis-created, -begotten; demoralized, corrupt, depraved.

evil-minded, -disposed; ill-conditioned; malevolent &c. 907; heart-, grace-, shame-, virtue-less; abandoned, lost to virtue; unconscionable; sunk –, lost –, deep –, steeped- in iniquity.

incorrigible, irreclaimable, obdurate, reprobate, past praying for; culpable, reprehensible &c. (*guilty*) 947.

unjustifiable; in-defensible, -excusable; inexpiable, unpardonable, irremissible.

weak, frail, lax, infirm, imperfect, indiscreet; demoralizing, degrading.

Adv. wrong; sinfully &c. *adj.*; without excuse.

Int. *O tempora! O mores!*

---

946. Innocence. — N. innocence; guiltlessness &c. *adj.*; incorruption, impeccability.

clean hands, clear conscience, *mens sibi conscia recti.*

innocent, new born babe, lamb, dove.

V. be -innocent &c. *adj.*; *nil conscire sibi nullâ pallescere culpâ.*

947. Guilt.—N. guilt, -iness; culpability; crimin-ality, -ousness; deviation from rectitude &c. (*improbity*) 940; sinfulness &c. (*vice*) 945; peccability.

mis-conduct, -behaviour, -doing, -deed; malpractice, fault, sin, error, transgression; dereliction, delinquency; indiscretion, lapse, slip, trip, *faux pas,*

* Most of these adjectives are applicable both to the act and to the agent.

acquit &c. 970; exculpate &c. (*vindi-cate*) 937.

Adj. innocent, not guilty; unguilty; guilt-, fault-, sin-, stain-, blood-, spotless; clear, immaculate; *rectus in curiâ*; un-spotted, -blemished, -erring; undefiled &c. 939; unhardened, Saturnian; Arcadian &c. (*artless*) 703.

in-, un-culpable; unblam-ed, -able; blameless, inerrable, above suspicion; irrepr-oachable, -ovable, -ehensible; un-exceptionable, -objectionable, -impeachable; salvable; venial &c. 937.

harmless; in-offensive, -noxious, -nocuous; dove-, lamb-like; pure, harmless as doves; innocent as -a lamb, – the babe unborn; more sinned against than sinning.

virtuous &c. 944; un-reproved, -impeached, -reproached.

Adv. innocently &c. *adj.*; with clean hands; with a -clear, – safe- conscience.

948. Good Man. — **N.** good man, worthy.

good woman, goddess, *madonna*, virgin.

model, paragon &c. (*perfection*) 650; good example; hero, demigod, seraph, angel; innocent &c. 946; saint &c. (*piety*) 987; benefactor &c. 912; philanthropist &c. 910; Aristides.

brick, trump, rough diamond, ugly duckling.

salt of the earth; one in ten thousand; one of the best.

Phr. *si sic omnes!*

peccadillo; flaw, blot, omission; fail-ing, -ure.

offence, trespass; mis-demeanour, -feasance, -prision; tort; mal-efaction, -feasance, -versation; crime, felony.

enormity, atrocity, outrage; deadly –, mortal –, unpardonable- sin; died without a name.

corpus delicti.

Adj. guilty, to blame, culpable, peccable, in fault, censurable, reprehensible, blameworthy, uncommendable, illaudable; weighed in the balance and found wanting; exceptionable, objectionable.

Adv. *in flagrante delicto*; red-handed, in the very act.

---

949. Bad Man.—**N.** bad man, wrongdoer, worker of iniquity; evil-doer &c. 913; sinner; the -wicked &c. 945; bad example.

rascal, scoundrel, villain, miscreant, caitiff; wretch, reptile, viper, serpent, cockatrice, basilisk, urchin; tiger, monster; devil &c. (*demon*) 980; devil incarnate; demon in human shape, Nana Sahib; hell-hound, -cat; rake-hell.

bad woman, jade, Jezebel, adultress, &c. 962.

scamp, scapegrace, rip, runagate, ne'er-do-well, reprobate, *roué*, rake; limb; one who has sold himself to the devil, fallen angel, *âme damnée, vaurien*, *mauvais sujet*, loose fish, sad dog; lost –, black- sheep; castaway, recreant, defaulter; prodigal &c. 818; libertine &c. 962.

rough, rowdy, ugly customer, ruffian, hoodlum, bully; Jonathan Wild; hangman; incendiary; thief &c. 792; murderer &c. 361.

culprit, delinquent, criminal, malefactor, misdemeanant; felon; convict, jail-bird, ticket-of-leave man; outlaw.

blackguard, *polisson*, loafer, sneak; raps-, ras-callion; cullion, mean wretch, varlet, kern, *âme-de-boue, drôle*; cur, dog, hound, whelp, mongrel; lown, loon, runnion, outcast, vagabond; rogue &c. (*knave*) 941; scum of the earth, riff-raff; *Arcades ambo*.

Int. sirrah!

950. Penitence.—**N.** penitence, contrition, compunction, repentance, remorse; regret &c. 833.

self-reproach, -reproof, -accusation,

951. Impenitence.—**N.** impenitence, irrepentance, recusance.

hardness of heart, seared conscience, induration, obduracy.

-condemnation, -humiliation; stings –, pangs –, qualms –, prickings –, twinge –, twitch –, touch –, voice- of conscience; compunctious visitings of nature.

acknowledgment, confession &c. (*disclosure*) 529; apology &c. 952; recantation &c. 607; penance &c. 952; resipiscence.

awakened conscience, deathbed repentance, *locus pœnitentiæ*, stool of repentance, cutty stool.

penitent, Magdalen, prodigal son, returned prodigal, a sadder and a wiser man.

V. repent, be sorry for; be -penitent &c. *adj.*; rue; regret &c. 833; think better of; recant &c. 607; knock under &c. (*submit*) 725; plead guilty; sing -*miserere*, – *de profundis*; cry *peccavi*; own oneself in the wrong; acknowledge, confess &c. (*disclose*) 529; humble oneself; beg pardon &c. (*apologize*) 952; turn over a new leaf, put on the new man, turn from sin; reclaim; repent in sackcloth and ashes &c. (*do penance*) 952; learn by experience.

Adj. penitent; repenting &c. *v.*; repentant, contrite; consciencesmitten, -stricken; self-accusing, -convicted.

penitenti-al, -ary; chastened, reclaimed; not hardened; unhardened.

Adv. *meâ culpâ.*

Phr. *peccavi; erubuit; salva res est; vous l'avez voulu, Georges Dandin.*

V. be -impenitent &c. *adj.*; steel –, harden- the heart; die -game, – and make no sign.

Adj. impenitent, uncontrite, obdurate; hard, -ened; seared, recusant; unrepentant; relent-, remorse-, grace-, shrift-less.

lost, incorrigible, irreclaimable.

unre-claimed, -formed; unrepented, unatoned.

---

952. Atonement.—N. atonement, reparation; compromise, composition; compensation &c. 30; quittance, quits; indemni-ty, -fication; expiation, redemption, reclamation, conciliation, propitiation.

amends, apology, *amende honorable*, satisfaction; peace –, sin –, burnt- offering; scapegoat, sacrifice.

penance, fasting, maceration, sackcloth and ashes, white sheet, shrift, flagellation, lustration; purga-tion, -tory.

V. atone, – for; expiate; propitiate; make -amends, – good; reclaim, redeem, repair, ransom, absolve, purge, shrive, do penance, stand in a white sheet, repent in sackcloth and ashes.

set one's house in order, wipe off old scores, make matters up; pay the -forfeit, – penalty.

apologize, beg pardon, express regret, *faire amende honorable*, give satisfaction; come –, fall- down on one's -knees, – marrow bones.

Adj. propitiatory, expiatory; sacrific, -ial, -atory; piacul-ar, -ous.

4°. MORAL PRACTICE

953. Temperance.—N. temperance moderation, sobriety, soberness.

forbearance, abnegation; self-denial, -restraint, -control &c. (*resolution*) 604.

frugality; vegetarianism, teetotalism, total abstinence, prohibition; abst-inence, -emiousness, asceticism &c. 955; system of -Pythagoras, – Cornaro; Pythagorism, Stoicism.

954. Intemperance.—N. intemperance; sensuality, animalism, carnality; pleasure; effeminacy, silkiness; luxur-y, -iousness; lap of -pleasure, – luxury.

indulgence; high-, free- living, inabstinence, self-indulgence; voluptuousness &c. *adj.*; epicur-ism, -eanism; sybaritism.

vegetarian; Pythagorean, gymnosophist; teetotaler &c. 958; abstainer.

V. be -temperate &c. *adj.*; abstain,
forbear, refrain, deny oneself, spare;
know when one has had enough; take
the pledge; look not upon the wine
when it is red.

Adj. temperate, moderate, sober,
frugal, sparing; abst-emious, -inent;
within compass; measured &c. (*sufficient*) 639.

Pythagorean; vegetarian; teetotal,
pussy-foot.

_____

dissipation; licentiousness &c. *adj.*,
debauchery; crapulence.

revel-s, -ry; debauch, carousal, jollification, drinking bout, wassail, Saturnalia, orgies; excess, too much; intoxication &c. 959.

Circean cup; drug habit &c. 663.

V. be -intemperate &c. *adj.*; indulge,
exceed; live -well, - high, - on the fat
of the land; give a loose to -indulgence
&c. *n.*; dine not wisely but too well;
wallow in -voluptuousness &c. *n.*;
plunge into dissipation.

revel, rake, live hard, run riot, sow
one's wild oats; slake one's -appetite,
- thirst; swill; pamper.

Adj. intemperate, inabstinent, intoxicated &c. 959; sensual, self-
indulgent; voluptuous, luxurious, licentious, wild, dissolute, rakish,
fast, debauched.

brutish, crapulous, swinish, piggish, porcine, hoggish, bestial.

Paphian, Epicurean, Sybaritical; bred -, nursed- in the lap oi
luxury; indulged, pampered, full-fed.

954a. Sensualist.—N. Sybarite, voluptuary, Sardanapalus, man of
pleasure, carpet knight; epicure, -an; *gourm-et, -and*; gormandizer,
gutling, glutton, pig, hog; votary -, swine- of Epicurus; sensualist;
Heliogabalus; free -, hard- liver; libertine &c. 962; hedonist.

955. Asceticism.—N. asceticism, puritanism, sabbatarianism; cynicism, austerity; total abstinence.

mortification, maceration, sackcloth and ashes, flagellation; penance
&c. 952; fasting &c. 956; martyrdom.

ascetic; anchor-et, -ite; martyr; *Heautontimorumenos*; hermit &c.
(*recluse*) 893; puritan, sabbatarian, cynic.

Adj. ascetic, austere, puritanical; cynical; over-religious.

956. Fasting. — N. fasting; xerophagy; famishment, starvation; banting.

fast, *jour maigre*; fast -, banyan-
day; Lent, quadragesima; Rama-dan,
-zan; spare -, meagre- diet; lenten
-diet, - entertainment; *soupe maigre*,
short -rations, - commons; Barmecide
feast; hunger strike.

V. fast, starve, clem, famish, perish
with hunger; dine with Duke Humphrey; make two bites of a cherry.

Adj. lenten, quadragesimal; unfed;
starved &c. *v.*; half-starved; fasting
&c. *v.*; hungry &c. 865.

_____

957. Gluttony.—N. gluttony; greed;
greediness &c. *adj.*; voracity.

epicurism; good -, high- living;
edacity, gulosity, crapulence; gutt-,
guzz-ling; over-indulgence.

good cheer, blow out; feast &c. (*food*)
298; gastronomy.

epicure, *bon vivant, gourmand*; glutton, cormorant, hog, belly-god, Apicius,
gastronome, gormandizer.

V. gormandize, gorge; over-gorge,
-eat- oneself; engorge, eat one's fill,
cram, stuff, stodge, glut, satiate;
gutt-le, guzz-le; bolt, devour, gobble
up; gulp &c. (*swallow food*) 298; raven,
eat out of house and home.

have the stomach of an ostrich;

play a good knife and fork &c. (*appetite*) 865.
pamper, indulge.

Adj. gluttonous, greedy; gormandizing &c. *v.*; edacious, omnivorous, crapulent, swinish, voracious, devouring. pampered; over-fed, -gorged.

958. Sobriety.—**N.** sobriety; teetotalism, temperance &c. 953.

water-drinker; teetotal-er, -ist; abstainer, Good Templar, Rechabite, band of hope; prohibitionist, pussyfoot.
V. take the pledge.
Adj. sober, – as a judge; dry, on the water wagon.

959. Drunkenness.—**N.** drunkenness &c. *adj.*; intemperance; drinking &c. *v.*; inebri-ety, -ation; ebri-ety, -osity; befuddlement; insobriety; intoxication; temulency, bibacity, wine-bibbing; com-, potation; deep potations, bacchanals, *bacchanalia*, libations.

oino-, dipso-mania; *delirium tremens,* d.t.; alcohol, -ism.

drink; alcoholic drinks, alcohol, booze; gin, blue ruin, grog, brandy, port wine; punch, -bowl; cup, rosy wine, flowing bowl; drop, – too much; dram; beer, wine, spirits &c. (*beverage*) 298; cocktail, nip, peg; stirrup cup.

drunkard, sot, toper, tippler, bibber, wine-bibber; hard –, gin –, dram- drinker; soak, soaker, sponge, tun; love-, toss-pot; thirsty soul, reveller, carouser; Bacchanal, -ian; Bacch-al, -ante; devotee to Bacchus, dipsomaniac.

V. get –, be- drunk &c. *adj.*; see double; take a -drop, – glass- too much; drink, tipple, tope, booze, bouse, guzzle, swill, soak, sot, lush, bib, swig, carouse; sacrifice at the shrine of Bacchus; take to drinking; drink -hard, – deep, – like a fish; have one's swill, drain the cup, splice the main brace, take a hair of the dog that bit you.

liquor, – up; wet one's whistle, take a whet; lift one's elbow; crack a –, pass the- bottle; toss off &c. (*drink up*) 298; go to the -ale, – public-house.

make one -drunk &c. *adj.*; inebriate, fuddle, fuzzle, get into one's head.

Adj. drunk, tipsy; intoxicated; inebri-ous, -ate, -ated; in one's cups; in a state of -intoxication &c. *n.*; temulent, -ive; fuddled, mellow, cut, boosy, fou, fresh, merry, elevated, squiffy; plastered, befuddled, sozzled; flush, -ed; flustered, disguised, groggy, beery; topheavy; pot-valiant, glorious; potulent; over-come, -taken; whittled, screwed, tight, primed, oiled, corned, raddled, sewed up, lushy, nappy, muddled, muzzy, bosky, obfuscated, maudlin; crapulous, dead –, blind- drunk.

inter pocula; in –, the worse for- liquor, having had a drop too much, half seas over, three sheets in the wind; under the table, blind to the world, one over the eight.

drunk as -a piper, – a fiddler, – a lord, – Chloe, – an owl, – David's sow, – a wheelbarrow.

drunken, bibacious, bibulous, sottish; given –, addicted- to -drink, – the bottle; toping &c. *v.*; wet.

Phr. *nunc est bibendum.*

960. Purity.—**N.** purity; decency, decorum, delicacy; continence, chastity, honesty, virtue, modesty, shame; pudicity, *pucelage*, virginity.

vestal, virgin, Joseph, Hippolytus; Lucretia, Diana; prude.

961. Impurity.—**N.** impurity; uncleanness &c. (*filth*) 653; immodesty; grossness &c. *adj.*; indelicacy, indecency; impudicity; obscenity, ribaldry, smut, bawdry, *double entendre, équivoque*; Aretinism; pornography.

Adj. pure, undefiled, modest, delicate, decent, decorous; *virginibus puerisque*; chaste, continent, virtuous, honest, Platonic.

concupiscence, lust, carnality, flesh, salacity; pruriency, lechery, lasciviency, lubricity, lewdness.

incontinence, intrigue, *faux pas*; *amour, -ette*; gallantry; debauchery, libertinism, *libertinage*, fornication; *liaison*; wenching, venery, dissipation.

seduction; defloration, defilement, abuse, violation, rape; incest.

social evil, harlotry, stupration, whoredom, concubinage, cuckoldom, adultery, advoutry, *crim. con.*; free love.

seraglio, harem, zenana; brothel, bagnio, stew, bawdy-house, *lupanar*, house of ill fame, *bordel*, kip.

V. be -impure &c. *adj.*; intrigue; debauch, defile, assault, attack, seduce; prostitute; abuse, violate, deflower; commit -adultery &c. *n.*

Adj. impure; unclean &c. *(dirty)* 653; not to be mentioned to ears polite; immodest, shameless; in-decorous, -delicate, -decent; loose, suggestive, *risqué*, coarse, gross, broad, free, equivocal, smutty.

fulsome, ribald, obscene, bawdy, pornographic.

concupiscent, prurient, lickerish, rampant, lustful; carnal, -minded; lewd, lascivious, lecherous, libidinous, erotic, ruttish, salacious; Paphian; voluptuous; incestuous.

unchaste, light, wanton, licentious, adulterous, debauched, dissolute; of -loose character, – easy virtue; frail, gay, riggish, incontinent, meretricious, rakish, gallant, dissipated; no better than she should be; on the -town, – streets, – *pavé*, – loose.

adulterous, incestuous, bestial.

962. Libertine.—N. libertine; voluptuary &c. 954*a*; rake, debauchee, loose fish, rip, rake-hell, fast man; *intrigant*, gallant, seducer, fornicator, lecher, satyr, goat, whoremonger, *paillard*, adulterer, gay deceiver, Lothario, Don Juan, Bluebeard.

adulteress, advoutress, courtesan, prostitute, strumpet, tart, hustler, chippy, broad, harlot, whore, punk, *fille de joie*; woman, – of the town; street-walker, Cyprian, miss, piece; frail sisterhood, fallen woman; demirep, wench, trollop, trull, baggage, hussy, drab, bitch, jade, skit, rig, quean, mopsy, slut, minx, harridan; woman -of easy virtue &c. (*unchaste*) 961; wanton, fornicatress; Jezebel, Messalina, Delilah, Thaïs, Phryne, Aspasia, Lais, *lorette, cocotte, petite dame, grisette; demimondaine*; white slave.

concubine, mistress, fancy woman, kept woman, doxy, *chère amie, bona roba*.

pimp; pand-er, -ar; bawd, *conciliatrix*, procuress, mackerel; wittol.

5°. INSTITUTIONS

963. Legality.—N. legality; legitimacy, -teness, legitimization.

legislature; law, code, *corpus juris*, constitution, pandect, charter, act, enactment, statute, rule; canon &c. (*precept*) 697; ordinance, institution, regulation; by-, bye-law, rescript; decree &c. (*order*) 741; *ordonnance*;

964. [Absence or violation of law.] **Illegality.—N.** lawlessness; breach -, violation- of law; disobedience &c. 742; unconformity &c. 83.

arbitrariness &c. *adj.*; antinomy, violence, brute force, despotism, outlawry.

mob -, lynch -, club -, Lydford -

standing order; *plébiscite* &c. (*choice*) 609.

legal process; form, -ula, -ality; rite; arm of the law; *habeas corpus.*

[Science of law] jurisprudence, nomology; legislation, codification.

equity, common law; *lex* -, *lex non-scripta,* unwritten law; law of nations, international law, *jus gentium; jus civile;* civil -, criminal -, canon -, statute -, ecclesiastical- law; *lex mercatoria.*

constitutional-ism, -ity; justice &c. 922.

V. legalize, legitimize; enact, ordain; decree &c. (*order*) 741; pass a law; legislate; codify, formulate; authorize.

Adj. legal, legitimate; according to law; vested, constitutional, chartered, legalized; lawful &c. (*permitted*) 760; statut-able, -ory; legislat-orial, -ive.

Adv. legally &c. *adj.;* in the eye of the law; *de jure.*

martial -, drumhead- law; *coup d'état; le droit du plus fort; argumentum ad baculum.*

illegality, informality, unlawfulness, illegitimacy, bar sinister.

trover and conversion; smuggling, boot-legging, rum-running, poaching; simony.

speakeasy, speakie, blind pig.

V. offend against -, violate- the law; set the law at defiance, ride rough-shod over, drive a coach and six through a statute; make the law a dead letter, take the law into one's own hands.

smuggle, run, poach.

Adj. illegal; prohibited &c. 761; not allowed, unlawful, illegitimate, illicit, contraband, actionable.

unchartered, unconstitutional; un-warrant-ed, -able; unauthorized; informal, unofficial; in-, extra-judicial.

lawless, arbitrary; despotic, -al; summary, irresponsible; un-answer-able, -accountable.

null and void; a dead letter.

Adv. illegally &c. *adj.;* with a high hand, in violation of law.

965. Jurisdiction. [Executive.]—**N.** jurisdiction, judicature, administration of justice, soc; executive, commission of the peace; magistracy &c. (*authority*) 737.

judge &c. 967; tribunal &c. 966; municipality, corporation, bailiwick, shrievalty; lord lieutenant; lord -, mayor, city manager, alderman &c. 745; sheriff, bailie, shrieve, chief -, constable; police, - force; constabulary, bumbledom.

officer; proctor, high -, commissioner; bailiff, tipstaff, bum-bailiff, catchpoll, beadle; police-man, -constable, -sergeant; *sbirro, alguazil, gendarme,* kavass, *lictor,* macebearer, *huissier,* bedel.

press-gang; exciseman, gauger, custom-house officer, *douanier.*

coroner, edile, ædile, portreeve, paritor; *posse comitatus.*

V. judge, sit in judgment.

Adj. executive, administrative, municipal; inquisitorial, causidical; judic-atory, -iary, -ial; juridical.

Adv. *coram judice.*

966. Tribunal.—N. tribunal, court, board, bench, judicatory, curia; court of -justice, - law, - arbitration; inquisition; guild.

justice -, judgement -, mercy- seat; woolsack; bar, - of justice; dock; forum, hustings, *bureau,* drum-head; jury-, witness-box.

senate-house, town-hall, theatre; House of -Lords, - Commons.

assize, eyre; ward-, burgh-mote; superior courts of Westminster; court of -record, - oyer and terminer, - assize, - appeal, - error; High court of -Judicature, - Appeal; Judicial Committee of the Privy Council; Star-Chamber; Court of -Chancery, - King's *or* Queen's Bench, - Exchequer, - Common Pleas, - Probate, - Arches, - Admiralty, - Criminal Appeal; Lords Justices' -, Rolls -, Vice-Chancellor's -,

Stannary –, Divorce –, Palatine –, ecclesiastical –, county –, police-court; sessions; quarter –, petty- sessions; court -leet, – baron, – of pie poudre, – of common council; board of green cloth.

court-martial; drum-head court-martial; *durbar,* divan; Areopagus; *rota.*

Adj. judicial &c. 965; appellate; curial.

967. Judge.—N. judge; justi-ce, -ciar, -ciary; chancellor; justice –, judge- of assize; recorder, common serjeant; puisne –, assistant – county court- judge; conservator –, justice- of the peace, J.P.; court &c. (*tribunal*) 966; grand –, petty –, coroner's- jury; panel, juror, juryman; twelve men in a box; magistrate, police magistrate, stipendiary, the great unpaid, beak; his -worship, – honour, – lordship; deemster, moderator.

Lord -Chancellor, – Justice; Master of the Rolls, Vice-Chancellor; Lord Chief -Justice, – Baron; Mr. Justice; Baron, – of the Exchequer.

jurat, assessor; arbi-ter, -trator; umpire; refer-ee, -endary; revising barrister; domesman; censor &c. (*critic*) 480; official –, receiver.

archon, tribune, prætor, *ephor,* syndic, *podestà,* mullah, ulema, mufti, cadi, kadi; Rhadamanthus.

litigant &c. (*accusation*) 938.

V. adjudge &c. (*determine*) 480; try a -case, – prisoner.

Adj. judicial &c. 965. **Phr.** 'a Daniel come to judgment.'

968. Lawyer.—N. lawyer, jurist, legist, civilian, pundit, publicist, jurisconsult, legal adviser, advocate; barrister, – at law; counsel, -lor; King's *or* Queen's counsel; K.C.; Q.C.; silk gown, leader; junior, – counsel; stuff gown, serjeant-at-law, bencher; tubman; judge &c. 967.

bar, legal profession, gentleman of the long robe; junior –, outer –, inner- bar; Inns of Court; equity draftsman, conveyancer, pleader, special pleader.

solicitor, attorney, proctor; notary, – public; scrivener, cursitor; writer, – to the signet; S.S.C.; limb of the law; pettifogger.

V. practise -at, – within- the bar; plead; call –, be called- -to, – within- the bar; take silk.

Adj. learned in the law; at the bar; forensic.

969. Lawsuit.—N. lawsuit, suit, action, cause, petition; litigation; dispute &c. 713.

citation, arraignment, prosecution, impeachment; accusation &c. 938; presentment, true bill, indictment.

apprehension, arrest; committal; imprisonment &c. (*restraint*) 751.

writ, summons, subpœna, *-duces tecum, latitat, nisi prius; habeas corpus.*

pleadings; declaration, bill, claim; *procès-verbal,* bill of right, information, *corpus delicti;* affidavit, state of facts; answer, replication, plea, demurrer, rebutter, rejoinder; surre-butter, -joinder.

suitor, party to a suit; litigant &c. 938; libellant.

hearing, trial; verdict &c. (*judgment*) 480; appeal, – motion; writ of error; *certiorari.*

case, decision, precedent, ruling; decided case, reports.

V. go to –, appeal to the- law; bring to -justice, – trial, – the bar; put on trial, pull up; accuse &c. 938; prefer –, file- a claim &c. *n.*; take the law of, inform against.

serve with a writ, cite, apprehend, arraign, sue, prosecute, bring an action against, indict, impeach, attach, distrain, commit; arrest; summon, -s; give in charge &c. (*restrain*) 751.

empanel a jury, implead, join issue; close the pleadings; set down for hearing.

try, hear a cause; sit in judgment; adjudicate &c. 480.

Adj. litigious &c. (*quarrelsome*) 713; *qui tam; coram –, sub- judice.*

Adv. *pendente lite.*

Phr. *adhuc sub judice lis est.*

970. Acquittal. — N. acquit-tal, -ment; clearance, exculpation, exoneration; discharge &c. (*release*) 750; *quietus,* absolution, compurgation, reprieve, re-,spite; pardon &c. (*forgiveness*) 918.

[Exemption from punishment] impunity, immunity.

V. acquit, exculpate, exonerate, clear; absolve, whitewash, assoil, discharge, release; liberate &c. 750;

reprieve, respite; pardon &c. (*forgive*) 918; let off, – scot free.

Adj. acquitted &c. *v.*; un-condemned, -punished- -chastised; recommended to mercy.

971. Condemnation.—N. condemnation, conviction, proscription, damnation; death warrant; penalty &c. 974. attain-der, -ture, -tment.

V. condemn, convict, cast, bring home to, find guilty, damn, doom, sign the death warrant, sentence pass sentence on, attaint, confiscate, proscribe, sequestrate; non-suit.

disapprove &c. 932; accuse &c. 938. stand condemned.

Adj. condem-, dam-natory; condemned &c. *v.*; non-suited &c. (*failure*) 732; self-convicted.

Phr. *mutato nomine de te fabula narratur.*

---

972. Punishment. — N. punishment, punition; chast-isement, -ening; correction, castigation.

discipline, infliction, trial; judgement; penalty &c. **974;** retribution; thunderbolt, Nemesis; requital &c. (*reward*) 973; penology; retributive justice.

lash, scaffold &c. (*instrument of punishment*) 975; imprisonment &c. (*restraint*) 751; chain gang; transportation, banishment, expulsion, deportation, exile, involuntary exile, ostracism; penal servitude, hard labour; galleys &c. 975; beating &c. *v.*; flagellation, fustigation, ga-ntlet, *strappado, estrapade, bastinado, argumentum ad baculum,* stick law, rap on the knuckles, box on the ear; blow &c. (*impulse*) 276; stripe, cuff, kick, buffet, pummel; slap, – in the face; wipe, douse; *coup de grâce;* torture, rack; picket, -ing; *dragonnade;* capital punishment, extreme penalty; execution; hanging &c. *v.*; de-capitation, -collation; *garrotte;* electrocution, lethal chamber; crucifixion, impalement; martyrdom, *auto-da-fé; noyade; hara-kiri,* happy despatch.

V. punish; chast-ise, -en; castigate, correct, inflict punishment, administer correction, deal retributive justice.

visit upon, pay; pay –, serve- out; settle with, get even with, get one's own back; do for; make short work of, give a lesson to, strafe, serve one right, make an example of; have a rod in pickle for; give it one.

strike &c. 276; deal a blow to, administer the lash, smite; slap, – the face; smack, cuff, box the ears, spank, thwack, thump, beat, lay on, swinge, buffet; thresh, thrash, pummel, drub, leather, trounce, baste, belabour; lace, – one's jacket; dress, give a -dressing, – down; trim, warm, wipe, tund, cob, bang, strap, comb, lash, lick, larrup, whallop, whop, flog, scourge, whip, birch, cane, give the stick, switch, flagellate, horsewhip, *bastinado*, towel, rub down with an oaken towel, rib roast, dust one's jacket, fustigate, pitch into, lay about one, beat black and blue; beat to a -mummy, – jelly; give a black eye; hit on the head; sandbag.

tar and feather; pelt, stone, lapidate; mast-head, keelhaul.

execute; bring to the -block, – gallows; behead; de-capitate, -collate; guillotine; hang, turn off, gibbet, bowstring, hang, draw and quarter; shoot; decimate; burn; electrocute; break on the wheel, crucify; em-, im-pale; flay; lynch; put to death.

torture; put -on, – to- the rack; picket.

banish, exile; trans-, de-port; expel, ostracize; rusticate; drum out; dismiss, -bar, -bench; strike off the roll, unfrock; post.

suffer, – for, – punishment; be -flogged, – hanged &c.; come to the gallows, dance upon nothing, die in one's shoes; be rightly served.

Adj. punishing &c. *v.*; penal; puni-tory, -tive; inflictive, castigatory; punished &c. *v.*

Int. *à la lanterne!*

973. Reward.—N. reward, recompense, remuneration, prize, meed, guerdon, reguerdon; indemni-ty, -fication, price; quittance; compensation; reparation, *ersatz*, assythment, redress; retribution, reckoning, acknowledgment, requital, amends, sop; atonement; consideration, return, *quid pro quo*; salvage, perquisite; vail &c. (*donation*) 784; *douceur*, bribe, bait, baksheesh, tip; hush-, smart-money; blackmail; carcelage; *solatium*.

allowance, salary, stipend, wages; pay, -ment; emolument; tribute; batta, shot, scot; premium, fee, *honorarium*; hire.

crown &c. (*decoration of honour*) 877.

V. re-ward, -compense, -pay, -quite; re-, munerate; compensate; fee, tip, bribe; pay one's footing &c. (*pay*) 807; make amends, indemnify, atone; satisfy, acknowledge.

get for one's pains, reap the fruits of.

Adj. remunerat-ive, -ory; munerary, compensatory, retributive, reparatory.

974. Penalty.—N. penalty; retribution &c. (*punishment*) 972; pain, pains and penalties; *peine forte et dure*; penance &c. (*atonement*) 952; the devil to pay.

fine, mulct, amercement; forfeit, -ure; escheat; damages, deodand, sequestration, confiscation, *premunire*.

V. penalize, fine, mulct, amerce, sconce, confiscate; sequest-rate, -er; escheat; estreat, forfeit.

975. [Instrument of punishment.] **Scourge.—N.** scourge, rod, cane, stick; ra-, rat-tan; birch, – rod; rod in pickle; switch, ferule, cudgel, truncheon; rubber hose.

whip, lash, strap, thong, cowhide, knout; cat, – o'-nine-tails, *sjambok*, quirt; rope's end.

pillory, stocks, whipping-post; cuck-, duck-ing stool; brank; triangle, wooden horse, maiden, thumbscrew, boot, rack, wheel, iron heel; treadmill, crank, galleys.

scaffold; block, axe, *guillotine*; stake; cross; gallows, gibbet, Tyburn tree; drop, noose, rope, halter, bowstring;

electric chair, lethal chamber.

house of correction &c. (*prison*) 752.

gaol-, jail-er; executioner; hang-, heads-man; Jack Ketch; lyncher.

Section V. RELIGIOUS AFFECTIONS

1°. Superhuman Beings and Regions

976. Deity.—N. Deity, Divinity; God-head, -ship; Omnipotence, Providence.

[Quality of being divine] divin-eness, -ity.

God, Lord, Jehovah, *Deus*; The -Almighty, – Supreme Being, – First Cause; *Ens Entium*; Author –, Creator- of all things; Author of our being; The -Infinite, – Eternal; The All-powerful, -wise, -merciful, -holy; The Omni-potent, -scient.

[Attributes and perfections] infinite -power, – wisdom, – goodness, – justice, – truth, – love, – mercy; omni-potence, -science, -presence; unity, immutability, holiness, glory, majesty, sovereignty, infinity, eternity.

The -Trinity, – Holy Trinity, – Trinity in Unity, – Triune God, Three in One and One in Three.

God the Father; The -Maker, – Creator, – Preserver.

[Functions] creation, preservation, divine government; The-ocracy, -archy; providence; ways –, dealings –, dispensations –, visitations- of Providence.

God the Son, Jesus, Christ; The -Messiah, – Anointed, - Saviour, – Redeemer, – Mediator, – Intercessor, – Advocate, – Judge; The Son of -God, – Man, – David; The Only Begotten; The Lamb of God, The Word; Em-, Im-manuel; The -King of Kings and Lord of Lords, – King of Glory, – Prince of Peace, – Good Shepherd, – Way, – Truth, – Life, – Bread of Life, – Light of the World; The -Lord our, – Sun of- Righteousness.

The -Incarnation, – Hypostatic Union, – Word made Flesh.

[Functions] salvation, redemption, atonement, propitiation, mediation, intercession, judgment.

God the Holy Ghost, The Holy Spirit, Paraclete; The -Comforter, – Consoler, – Spirit of Truth, – Dove.

[Functions] inspiration, unction, regeneration, sanctification, consolation.

eon, æon, special providence, *Deus ex machinâ*; *Avatar*.

V. create, uphold, preserve, govern &c.

atone, redeem, save, propitiate, mediate &c.

predestinate, elect, call, ordain, bless, justify, sanctify, glorify &c.

Adj. almighty, holy, hallowed, sacred, divine, heavenly, celestial; messianic; sacrosanct; all-powerful, -wise, -seeing, -knowing; omnipotent, omniscient; supreme.

super-human, -natural; ghostly, spiritual, hyperphysical, unearthly; the-istic, -ocratic, deistic; anointed.

Adv. *jure divino*, by divine right; *Deo volente*, D.V.

977. [Beneficent spirits.] Angel.—N. angel, archangel; heavenly host, choir invisible, host of heaven, sons of God; Michael, Gabriel &c.; seraph, -im; cherub, -im; ministering spirit, morn-

978. [Maleficent spirits.] Satan.- N. Satan, the Devil, Lucifer, Ahrimanes, Belial; Sammael, Zamiel, Beelzebub, the Prince of the Devils; Mephistopheles, his satanic majesty.*

* The slang expressions 'the -deuce, – dickens, – old Gentleman; old -Nick, – Scratch, – Horny, – Harry, – Gooseberry,' have not been inserted in the text.

ing star; saint, *Madonna*; Our Lady, the Blessed Virgin, the Virgin Mary.

Adj. angelic, seraphic, cherubic.

-common enemy, – angel of the bottomless pit; Abaddon, Apollyon, Mammon.

fallen angels, unclean spirits, devils; the -rulers, – powers- of darkness; inhabitants of Pandemonium; demon &c. 980.

diabolism; devil-ism, -ship, -dom, -ry, -worship; *diablerie*; satanism, manicheism; the cloven foot; black magic &c. 992.

Adj. satanic, diabolic, devilish, infernal, hell-born.

the tempter; the evil -one, – spirit; the -author of evil, – wicked one, – old Serpent; the Prince of -darkness, – this world, – the power of the air: the -foul, – arch- fiend; the devil incarnate; the

*Heathen, Mythological and other fabulous Deities and Powers**

979. Jupiter.—N. god, -dess; heathen gods and goddesses; Pantheon; Jupiter, Jove, Zeus, Apollo, Mars, Mercury, Neptune, Vulcan, Bacchus, Pluto, Saturn, Cupid, Eros, Pan; Juno, Ceres, Proserpina, Diana, Minerva, Pallas Athene, Venus, Aphrodite, Vesta; The Fates &c. 601.

Allah, Brahma, Vishnu, Siva, Shiva, Krishna, Juggernaut, Buddha; Ra, Isis, Osiris; Belus, Bel, Baal, Asteroth &c.; Thor, Odin; Mumbo Jumbo; good –, tutelary- genius; demiurge, familiar, – spirit; Sibyl; fairy, fay; sylph, -id; Ariel, peri, nymph, nereid, dryad, oread, sea-maid, Banshee, Benshie, Ormuzd; Oberon, Titania, Mab, hamadryad, naiad, mermaid, kelpie, Ondine, nix, nixie, sprite; denizens of the air; pixy &c. (*bad spirit*) 980.

mythology; heathen –, fairy- mythology; Lemprière, folklore.

Adj. fairy-, sylph-like; sylphic.

980. Demon.—N. demon, -ry, -ism, -ology; evil genius, fiend, familiar, – spirit, devil; bad –, unclean- spirit; cacodemon, incubus, Frankenstein's monster, succubus and succuba, Titan, Shedim, Mephistopheles, Asmodeus, Moloch, Belial, Ahriman, fury, The Furies &c. 900; harpy; Friar Rush.

vampire, ghoul; af-, ef-freet; afrite; ogre, -ss; gnome, gin, djinn, imp, deev, *lamia*; bo-gie, -gle; nis, kobold, flibbertigibbet, fairy, brownie, pixy, elf, dwarf, urchin, Puck, Robin Goodfellow; lepre-, cluri-chaune; troll, dwerger, sprite, oaf, changeling, bad fairy, nixe, pigwidgeon, Will-o'-the-wisp; Erl King.

[Supernatural appearance] ghost, spectre, apparition, genie, spirit, shade, shadow, vision, phantom &c. 443; materialization (*spiritualism*) 992; hob-, goblin; wraith, spook, werwolf, boggart, banshee, *loup-garou, lemures*; evil eye.

nisse, necks; mer-man, -maid, -folk; siren, Lorelei; satyr, faun.

Adj. supernatural, weird, uncanny, unearthly, spectral; ghost-ly, -like; elf-in, -like; fiend-ish, -like; impish, demoniacal; haunted.

981. Heaven.—N. heaven; kingdom of -heaven, – God; heavenly kingdom; throne –, presence- of God; inheritance of the saints in light.

Paradise, Eden, abode of the blessed; Holy City, New Jerusalem; celestial bliss, glory.

[Mythological -heaven] Olympus; [– paradise] Elysium, Elysian fields, Arcadia, bowers of bliss, garden of the Hesperides, Islands of the Blessed;

982. Hell.—N. hell, bottomless pit, place of torment; habitation of fallen angels; Pandemonium, Abaddon, Domdaniel.

hell fire; everlasting -fire, – torment; lake of fire and brimstone; fire that is never quenched, worm that never dies.

purgatory, limbo, gehenna, abyss.

[Mythological hell] Tartarus, Hades, Avernus, Styx, Stygian creek, pit of Acheron, Cocytus, Phlegethon, Lethe;

* Only a selection of those best known to literature is included.

happy hunting-ground; third –, seventh- heaven; Valhalla (Scandinavian); Nirvana (Buddhist).

future state, eternity, eternal life, life after death, eternal home, resurrection, translation; resuscitation &c. 660; apotheosis, deification.

Adj. heavenly, celestial, supernal, unearthly, from on high, paradisiacal, beatific, elysian, Olympian, Arcadian.

infernal regions, *inferno*, shades below, realms of Pluto.

Pluto, Rhadamanthus, Erebus, Charon, Cerberus; Tophet.

Adj. hellish, infernal, stygian.

___

2°. RELIGIOUS DOCTRINES

983. [Religious Knowledge.] Theology.—N. Theology (natural and revealed); Theo-gony, -sophy; Divinity; Hagio-logy, -graphy; Caucasian mystery; monotheism; religion; religious -persuasion, – sect, – denomination; cult; creed &c. (*belief*) 484; articles –, declaration –, profession –, confession- of faith.

theolog-ue, -ian; divine, schoolman, canonist, monotheist.

Adj. theological, religious; canonical; denominational; sectarian &c. 984.

983a. Orthodoxy.—N. orthodoxy; strictness, soundness, religious truth, true faith; truth &c. 494.

Christian-ity, -ism; Catholic-ism, -ity; 'the faith once delivered to the saints'; hyperorthodoxy &c. 984; iconoclasm.

the Holy –, the Orthodox- Church; Catholic –, Universal –, Apostolic –, Established- Church; temple of the Holy Ghost; Church –, body –, members –, disciples –, followers- of Christ; Christian, – community; true believer; canonist &c. (*theologian*) 983; Christendom, collective body of Christians, the Church Militant.

canons &c. (*belief*) 484; thirty-nine articles; Apostles' –, Nicene –, Athanasian- Creed; Church Catechism; textuary.

Adj. orthodox, sound, literal, strict, faithful, catholic, schismless, Christian, evangelical, scriptural, divine, monotheistic; true &c. 494.

High –, Low –, Broad –, Free- Church; ultramontanism; monasticism; pap-ism, -istry; papacy; Anglican-, Catholic-, Roman-ism; popery, Scarlet Lady, Church of Rome, Greek Church; Christian Science, The Church of Christ Scientist.

984. Heterodoxy. [Sectarianism.] N. heterodoxy; error &c. 495; false doctrine, heresy, schism; schismatic-ism, -alness; recusancy, backsliding, apostasy; atheism &c. (*irreligion*) 989.

bigotry &c. (*obstinacy*) 606; fanaticism, iconoclasm; hyperorthodoxy, precisianism, bibliolatry, hagiolatry, sabbatarianism, puritanism; idolatry &c. 991; superstition &c. (*credulity*) 486; dissent &c. 489.

sectar-ism, -ianism; nonconformity; secularism; syncretism; religious sects; the clash of creeds.

protestant-, advent-, Arian-, Erastian-, Calvin-, quaker-, method-, anabapt-, Pusey-, tractarian-, ritual-, Origen-, Sabellian-, Socinian-, De-, The-, mon-, material-, positiv-, latitudinarian-ism &c.

pagan-, heathen-, ethic-ism; mythology; animism; poly-, di-, tri-, pantheism; dualism; heathendom.

Juda-, Gentil-, Mahometan-, Islam-, Turc-, Brahmin-, Hindoo-, Buddh-, Lama-, Confucian-, Shinto-, Sabian-, Gnostic-, Soofee-, Hylothe-, Mormon-ism.

Theosophy; Spiritualism, Occultism.

heretic, antichrist; pagan, heathen; pai-, pay-nim; *giaour*; gentile; pan-, poly-theist; idolator; misbeliever, apostate, backslider.

bigot &c. (*obstinacy*) 606; fanatic, dervish, abdal, iconoclast.

latitudinarian, limitarian, Deist, Theist, Unitarian; positivist, materialist; agnostic, skeptic &c. 989.

schismatic; sectar-y, -ian, -ist; seceder, separatist, recusant, dissenter; non-conformist, -juror; Huguenot, Protestant; orthodox dissenter, Congregationalist, Independent; Episcopalian, Presbyterian; Lutheran, Calvinist, Quaker, Methodist, Wesleyan; Ana-, Baptist; Dunker; Mormon, Latter-day Saint, Irvingite, Sandemanian, Glassite, Erastian; Sub-, Supra-lapsarian; Gentoo, Antinomian, Swedenborgian, Adventist, Plymouth Brother; Theosophist &c.

Catholic, Roman Catholic, Romanist, papist, ultramontane; Old Catholic, tractarian, Anglican, Puseyite, ritualist; Puritan.

Jew, Hebrew, Rabbist; Mahometan, Mohammedan, Mussulman, Moslem, Islamite, Osmanli; Brahm-in, -an; Parsee, Sofi, Soofee; Buddhist; Zoroastrian, Magi, Gymnosophist, fire-worshipper, Sabian, Gnostic, Sadducee, &c.

Adj. heterodox, heretical; un-orthodox, -scriptural, -canonical; antiscriptural, apocryphal; un-, anti-christian; schismatic, recusant, iconoclastic; sectarian; dis-senting, -sident; secular &c. (*lay*) 997.

pagan; heathen, -ish; ethnic, -al; gentile, painim; pan-, polytheistic; agnostic, skeptic.

Judaical, Mohammedan, Moslem, Brahminical, Buddhist &c. *n.* Romish, Protestant &c. *n.*

bigoted &c. (*prejudiced*) 481, (*obstinate*) 606; superstitious &c. (*credulous*) 486; fanatical; idolatrous &c. 991; visionary &c. (*imaginative*) 515.

985. Revelation.—N. revelation, inspiration, *afflatus*.

Word, – of God; Scripture; the -Scriptures, – Bible, – Book of Books; Holy -Writ, – Scriptures; inspired writings, Gospel.

Old Testament, Septuagint, Vulgate, Pentateuch; Octateuch; the -Law, – Jewish Law, – Prophets; major –, minor- Prophets; Hagio-grapha, -logy; Hierographa; Apocrypha.

New Testament; Gospels, Evangelists, Acts, Epistles, Apocalypse, Revelations.

Talmud; Mishna, Masorah.

prophet &c. (*seer*) 513; evangelist, apostle, disciple, saint; the –, the Apostolical- fathers; Holy Men of old, inspired -writers, – penmen.

Adj. scriptural, biblical, sacred, prophetic; evangel-ical, -istic; apostolic, -al; inspired, theopneustic, apocalyptic, ecclesiastical canonical, textuary.

986. Pseudo-Revelation.*—N. the -Koran, – Alcoran; Ly-king, Shaster, Vedas, Zendavesta, Vedidad, Purana, Edda; Go-, Gau-tama; Book of Mormon.

[False prophets and religious founders] Buddha, Zoroaster, Zerdhusht, Confucius, Mahomet.

[Idols] golden calf &c. 991; Baal, Moloch, Dagon.

* See note on page 378.

3°. Religious Sentiments

987. Piety.—N. piety, religion, theism, faith; religiousness, holiness &c. *adj*; saintship; religionism; sanctimony &c. (*assumed piety*) 988; reverence &c. (*respect*) 928; humility, veneration, devotion; prostration &c. (*worship*) 990; grace, unction, edification; sancti-ty, -tude; consecration.

spiritual existence, odour of sanctity, beauty of holiness.

theopathy, beatification, adoption, regeneration, conversion, justification, sanctification, salvation, inspiration, bread of life; Body and Blood of Christ.

believer, convert, theist, Christian, devotee, pietist; the -good, – righteous, – just, – believing, – elect; Saint, *Madonna.*

the children of -God, – the kingdom, – light.

V. be -pious &c. *adj.*; have -faith &c. *n.*; believe, receive Christ; revere &c. 928; worship &c. 990; be -converted &c.

convert, edify, sanctify, hallow, keep holy, beatify, regenerate, inspire, consecrate, enshrine.

Adj. pious, religious, devout, devoted, reverent, godly, heavenly minded, humble; pure, – in heart; noly, spiritual, pietistic; saint-ly, -like; seraphic, sacred, solemn.

believing, faithful, Christian, Catholic.

elected, adopted, justified, sanctified, regenerated, inspired, consecrated, converted, unearthly, not of the earth.

988. Impiety.—N. impiety; sin &c. 945; irreverence; profan-eness &c. *adj*, -ity, -ation; blasphemy, desecration, sacrilege; scoffing &c. *v.*

[Assumed piety] hypocrisy &c. (*falsehood*) 544; pietism, cant, pious fraud; lip-devotion, -service, -reverence; misdevotion, formalism, austerity; sanctimon-y, -iousness &c. *adj.*; pharisaism, precisianism; sabbat-ism, -arianism; *odium theologicum*, sacerdotalism; bigotry &c. (*obstinacy*) 606, (*prejudice*) 481.

hardening, backsliding, declension, perversion, reprobation, apostasy, recusancy.

sinner &c. 949; scoffer, blasphemer; sacrilegist; worldling; hypocrite &c. (*dissembler*) 548; Scribes and Pharisees; Tartufe, Maw-worm.

bigot; saint [ironically]; Pharisee, sabbatarian, formalist, methodist, puritan, pietist, precisian, religionist, devotee, ranter, fanatic, wowser.

the -wicked, – evil, – unjust, – reprobate; son of -men, – Belial, – the wicked one; children of darkness.

V. be -impious &c. *adj.*; profane, desecrate, blaspheme, revile, scoff; swear &c. (*malediction*) 908; commit sacrilege.

snuffle; turn up the whites of the eyes; idolize.

Adj. impious; irreligious &c. 989; desecrating &c. *v.*; profane, irreverent, sacrilegious, blasphemous.

un-hallowed, -sanctified, -regenerate; hardened, perverted, reprobate.

hypocritical &c. (*false*) 544; canting, pietistical, sanctimonious, unctuous, pharisaical, over-righteous, righteous over much.

bigoted, fanatical &c. 481 & 606; priest-ridden.

Adv. under the -mask, cloak, – pretence, – form, – guise- of religion.

989. Irreligion.—N. irreligion, indevotion; ungodliness &c. *adj.*; laxity, quietism, apathy, indifference, passivity.

scepticism, doubt; un-, dis-belief; incredul-ity, -ousness &c. *adj.*; want of -faith, – belief; pyrrhonism; doubt &c. 485; agnosticism.

atheism, deism; hylotheism; materialism; positivism; nihilism.

infidelity, freethinking, antichristianity, rationalism.

atheist, anti-christian, sceptic, unbeliever, deist, infidel, pyr-rhonist; *giaour*, heathen, alien, gentile, Nazarene; *esprit fort*, free-thinker, latitudinarian, rationalist; materialist, positivist, nihilist, agnostic.

V. be -irreligious &c. *adj.*; disbelieve, lack faith; doubt, question &c. 485.

dechristianize; serve Mammon, love darkness better than light.

Adj. irreligious; in-, un-devout; devout-, god-, grace-less; un-godly, -holy, -sanctified, -hallowed; atheistic, without God.

sceptical, free-thinking; un-believing, -converted; incredulous, faithless, lacking faith; deistical; un-, anti-christian.

worldly, mundane, earthly, carnal, unspiritual; worldly &c.-minded.

Adv. irreligiously &c. *adj.*

4°. Acts of Religion

990. Worship.—N. worship, adoration, devotion, aspiration, latria, homage, service, humiliation; kneeling, genuflexion, prostration.

prayer, invocation, supplication, rogation, intercession, orison, holy breathing; petition &c. (*request*) 765; collect, litany, Lord's prayer, paternoster, *Ave Maria*, rosary; bead-roll; latria, dulia, hyperdulia, vigils; revival; cult.

thanksgiving; giving -, returning- thanks; grace, praise, glorifica-tion, benediction, doxology, hosanna; h-, allelujah; *Te Deum, non nobis Domine, nunc dimittis*; pæan.

psalm, -ody; hymn, plainsong, chant, chaunt, response, anthem, motet; antiphon, -y.

oblation, sacrifice, incense, libation; burnt -, votive -, thank-offering; offertory, collection.

discipline; self-discipline, -examination, -denial; fasting.

divine service, office, duty; morning prayer; mass, matins, evensong, vespers, compline; holy day &c. (*rites*) 998.

worshipper, congregation, communicant, celebrant.

V. worship, lift up the heart, aspire; revere &c. 928; adore, do serv-ice, pay homage; humble oneself, kneel; bow -, bend- the knee; fall -down, - on one's knees; prostrate oneself, bow down and worship, recite the rosary.

pray, invoke, supplicate; put -, offer- up -prayers, - petitions; beseech &c. (*ask*) 765; say one's prayers, tell one's beads.

return -, give- thanks; say grace, bless, praise, laud, glorify, magnify, sing praises; give benediction, lead the choir, intone, chant, sing.

propitiate, offer sacrifice, fast, deny oneself; vow, offer vows, give alms.

work out one's salvation; go to church; attend -service, - mass; communicate &c. (*rite*) 998.

Adj. worshipping &c. *v.*; devout, devotional, reverent, pure, solemn; fervid &c. (*heartfelt*) 821.

Int. h-, allelujah! hosanna! glory be to God! O Lord! pray God that! God -grant, - bless, - save, - forbid! *sursum corda*.

991. Idolatry.—N. idol-atry, -ism; demon-ism, -olatry; idol -, demon -, devil -, fire- worship; zoolatry, fetishism, Mari-, Bibli-, ecclesi-, heli-olatry.

deification, apotheosis, canonization; hero worship.

sacrifices, hecatomb, holocaust; human sacrifices, immolation, mactation, infanticide, self-immolation, *suttee.*

idol, golden calf, graven image, fetish, *avatar,* Juggernaut, joss, *lares et penates;* Baal &c. 986.

idolater &c. *n.*

V. worship -idols, – pictures, – relics; put on a pedestal, bow down to, prostrate oneself before, make sacrifice to; deify, canonize, idolize.
Adj. idolatrous.

992. Sorcery.—N. sorcery; superstition; occult -art, – sciences; black –, magic; the black art, necromancy, theurgy, thaumaturgy; demon-ology, -omy, -ship; *diablerie,* bedevilment; witch-craft, -ery; glamour; fetis-hism, -ism; ghost dance; hoodoo, voodoo; Shamanism [Esquimaux], vampirism; conjuration; bewitchery, exorcism, enchantment, incantation, obsession, possession, mysticism, second sight, mesmerism, animal magnetism; od –, odylic- force; electro-biology, *clairvoyance;* spiritualism, spirit-rapping, table-turning; thought reading, telepathy, thought transference, automatic writing, *planchette,* ouija board; crystal gazing; spirit manifestation, materialization, astral body, ectoplasm &c.

divination &c. *(prediction)* 511; sortilege, ordeal, *sortes Virgilianæ, -biblicæ,* hocus-pocus &c. *(deception)* 545; oracle &c. 513.

V. practice -sorcery &c. *n.;* cast a -horoscope, – nativity; conjure, exorcise, charm, enchant; be-witch, -devil; overlook, look on with the evil eye; entrance, mesmerize, magnetize; fascinate &c. *(influence)* 615; taboo; wave a wand; rub the -ring, – lamp; cast a spell; call up spirits, – from the vasty deep; raise spirits from the dead; raise –, lay- ghosts; command genii.

Adj. magic, -al; mystic, weird, cabalistic, talismanic, phylacteric, incantatory; charmed &c. *v.*

993. Spell.—N. spell, charm, incantation, exorcism, weird, cabala, exsufflation, cantrap, runes, abracadabra, hocus-pocus, open *sesame,* counter-charm, Ephesian letters, bell, book and candle, Mumbo Jumbo, evil-eye, fee-faw-fum.

talisman, amulet, periapt, telesm, phylactery, philtre, wish-bone, merry-thought, mascot, scarab, swastika; fetish; *agnus Dei.*

wand, caduceus, rod, divining rod, lamp of Aladdin, magic carpet, seven-league boots; magic ring; wishing –, Fortunatus's- cap.

994. Sorcerer.—N. sorcerer, magician; thaumat-, the-urgist; conjuror, necromancer, seer, wizard, witch; fairy &c. 980; *lamia,* hag, warlock, charmer, exorcist, voodoo, mage, diviner, dowser; cunning –, medicine- man, witch doctor; Shaman, figure-flinger, ecstatica, medium, *clairvoyant,* mesmerist, hypnotist; *deus ex machinâ;* astrologer; soothsayer &c. 513.

Katerfelto, Cagliostro, Merlin, Comus, Mesmer; Hecate, Circe, Lilith, siren, weird sisters; witch of Endor.

5°. Religious Institutions

995. Churchdom.—N. church, -dom; ministry, apostleship, priesthood, prelacy, hierarchy, church government, christendom, pale of the church.

clerical-, sacerdotal-, episcopalian-, ultramontan-ism; Theocracy; ecclesiolog-y, -ist; priestcraft, *odium theologicum*.

monach-ism, -y; monasticism, monkhood.

[Ecclesiastical offices and dignities] pontificate, primacy, archbishopric, archiepiscopacy; prelacy; bishop-ric, -dom; episcop-ate, -acy; see, diocese; deanery, stall; canon-ry, -icate; prebend, -aryship; benefice, incumbency, glebe, advowson, living, cure, – of souls; rectorship; vicar-iate, -ship; pastor-ate, -ship; deacon-ry, -ship; -curacy; chaplain, -cy, -ship; cardinal-ate, -ship; abbacy, presbytery.

holy orders, ordination, institution, consecration, induction, reading in, preferment, translation, presentation.

popedom, papacy; the -Vatican, – apostolic see, – see of Rome; religious sects &c. 984.

council &c. 696; conclave, college of cardinals, convocation, synod, consistory, chapter, vestry, presbytery; sanhedrim, *congé d'élire*; ecclesiastical courts, consistorial court, court of Arches.

V. call, ordain, induct, prefer, translate, consecrate, present, elect, bestow.

take -orders, – the veil, – vows.

Adj. ecclesi-astical, -ological; clerical, sacerdotal, priestly, prelatical, pastoral, ministerial, capitular, theocratic; hierarchical, archiepiscopal; episcopal, -ian; canonical; mon-astic, -achal; monkish; abbati-al, -cal; pontifical, papal, apostolic; ultramontane, priest-ridden.

---

996. Clergy.—N. clergy, clericals, ministry, priesthood, presbytery, the cloth, the pulpit.

clergyman, divine, ecclesiastic, churchman, priest, presbyter, hierophant, pastor, shepherd, minister, clerk in holy orders; father, – in Christ; *padre, abbé, curé*; patriarch; reverend; black coat; confessor; sky pilot.

dignitaries of the church; ecclesi-, hier-arch; eminence, reverence, elder, primate, metropolitan, archimandrite, archbishop, bishop, prelate, diocesan, suffragan, dean, subdean, archdeacon, prebendary, canon, rural dean, rector, parson, vicar, perpetual curate, residentiary, beneficiary, incumbent, chaplain, curate, – in charge; deacon, -ess; preacher; lay reader, lecturer; capitular; missionary, propagandist, Jesuit, revivalist, field preacher.

churchwarden, sidesman; clerk, precentor, choir; almoner, *suisse*, verger, beadle, sexton, sacristan; acol-yth, -othyst, -yte; thurifer; chorister, choir boy.

[Roman Catholic priesthood] Pope, *Papa*, Holy Father, pontiff, high priest, cardinal; ancient -, flamen; confessor, penitentiary; spiritual director.

cenobite, conventual, abbot, prior, monk, friar, lay brother, beadsman, mendicant, pilgrim, palmer; canon-regular, -secular; Jesuit, Franciscan, Friars minor, Minorites; Observant, Capuchin, Dominican, Carmelite; Augustinian; Gilbertine; Austin-, Black-, White-, Grey-, Crossed-, Crutched-Friars; Bonhomme, Carthusian, Benedictine, Cistercian, Trappist, Cluniac. Premonstratensian, Maturine; Templar. Hospitaller.

997. Laity.—N. laity, flock, fold, congregation, assembly, brethren, people.

temporality, secularization.

layman, civilian; parishioner, catechumen; secularist.

V. secularize.

Adj. secular, lay, laical, civil, temporal, profane.

---

abb-, prior-, canon-ess; mother superior; *religieuse,* nun, sister, *béguine,* novice, postulant.

[Under the Jewish dispensation] prophet, priest, high priest, Levite; Rabbi, -n; scribe.

[Mohammedan &c.] mullah, ulema, imaum, sheik; so-fi, -phi; mufti, hadji, muezzin, dervish; fa-kir, -quir; brahmin, gooroo, druid, bonze, santon, abdal, Lama, talapoin, caloyer &c.

V. take orders &c. 995.

Adj. the -, the very -, the Right- Reverend; ordained, in orders, called to the ministry.

998. Rite.—N. rite; ceremon-y, -ial; ordinance, observance, function, duty; form, -ulary; solemnity, sacrament; incantation &c. (*spell*) 993; service, psalmody &c. (*worship*) 990; liturgies.

ministration; preach-ing, -ment; predication, sermon, homily, exhortation, lecture, discourse, pastoral.

baptism, christening, chrism, immersion; baptismal regeneration; font; circumcision.

confirmation; imposition -, laying on- of hands; churching, purification, ordination &c. (*churchdom*) 995; excommunication.

Eucharist, Lord's supper, communion; the -, the holy- sacrament; celebration, high celebration; *missa cantata;* offertory; introit; consecration; con-, tran-substantiation; real presence; elements, bread and wine; mass; high -, low -, dry- mass.

matrimony &c. 903; burial &c. 363; visitation of the sick.

seven sacraments, impanation extreme unction, last rites. *viaticum,* invocation of saints, canonization, transfiguration, auricular confession; fasting; maceration, flagellation, sackcloth and ashes; penance &c. (*atonement*) 952; absolution; telling of beads, reciting the rosary, processional; thurification, incense, holy water, aspersion.

relics, rosary, beads, reliquary, host, cross, rood, crucifix, pax, pix, pyx, *agnus Dei,* censer, thurible, patera, urceole; chalice, patten, Holy Grail, sangrail; seven-branch candle stick, monstrance, sacring bell.

ritual, rubric, canon, ordinal; liturgy, prayer-book, book of common prayer, pietas, euchology, litany, lectionary; missal, breviary, massbook, bead-roll.

psalter; psalm -, hymn- book; hymn-al, -ology; psalmody.

ritual-, ceremonial-ism; sabbat-ism, -arianism; ritualist, sabbatarian.

holyday, feast, fast; Sabbath, Passover, Pentecost; Advent, Christmas, Noël, Epiphany, Lent, Shrove Tuesday, Ash Wednesday, Maundy Thursday; Passion -, Holy- week; Good Friday, Easter, Ascension Day, Whitsuntide; Trinity Sunday, Corpus Christi; All-Saints' -, - Souls'-Day; Candle-, Lam-, Martin-, Michael-mas; hogmanay; Rama-dan, -zan; Bairam &c. &c.

V. perform service, do duty, minister, officiate, baptize, dip, sprinkle; confirm. lay hands on; give -, administer -, take -, receive -. attend -, partake of- the -sacrament, - communion; communicate; celebrate mass; administer -, receive- extreme unction; anele, shrive, absolve, confess; do penance; genuflect; cross oneself, make the sign of the cross.

excommunicate, ban with bell, book and candle.

preach, sermonize, predicate, lecture.

Adj. ritual, -istic; ceremonial, liturgic; baptismal, eucharistical; paschal.

999. Canonicals.—N. canonicals, vestments; robe, gown, Geneva gown, frock, pallium, surplice, cassock, dalmatic, scapulary, cope. scarf, tunicle, chasuble, alb, *alba*, stole; fan-on, -nel; tonsure, cowl, hood; calo-te, -tte; bands; capouch, amice, orarium, ephod; apron, lawn sleeves, pontificals, pall; mitre, tiara, triple crown; shovel –, cardinal's-hat; biretta; crosier; pastoral staff; costume &c. 225.

1000. Temple.—N. place of worship; house of -God, – prayer.

temple, cathedral, minster, church, kirk, chapel, meeting-house, bethel, tabernacle, conventicle, *basilica*, fane, holy place, chantry, oratory.

synagogue; mosque; marabout; pantheon; pagoda; joss-house; dagobah, tope; kiosk.

parsonage, rectory, vicarage, manse, deanery, glebe, church house; Vatican; bishop's palace; Lambeth.

altar, shrine, sanctuary, Holy of Holies, *sanctum sanctorum*, sacr-arium, -isty; communion –, holy –, Lord's- table; table of the Lord; pyx; baptistery, font; piscina, stoup; aumbry; sedile; reredos; rood-loft, – screen; jube.

chancel, quire, choir, nave, aisle, transept, lady chapel, vestry, crypt, cloisters, porch; triforum, clerestory, churchyard, *golgotha*, calvary, Easter sepulchre; stall, pew, sitting; pulpit, ambo, lectern, reading-desk, confessional, prothesis, credence, baldachin, *baldacchino*; jesse, apse, belfry; chapter-house; presbytery.

monastery, priory, abbey, friary, convent, nunnery, cloister.

Adj. claustral, cloistered; monast-ic, -erial; conventual.

INDEX

N.B.: The numbers refer to the headings under which the words or phrases occur. When the same word or phrase may be used in various senses, the several headings under which it, or its synonyms, will be found, according to those meanings, are indicated by the words printed in Italics. These words in Italics are not intended to explain the meaning of the word or phrase to which they are annexed, but only to assist in the required reference.

When the word given in the Index is itself the title or heading of a category, the number of reference is printed in blacker type, thus: **abode 189.**

---

accipient 785
acclamation
assent 488
approbation 931
acclimatize 370, 613
acclivity 217
accloy 641
accolade 894
accommodate
suit 23
adjust 27
aid 707
reconcile 723
give 784
lend 787
– oneself to 82
accommodation
space 180
accommodating
kind 906
accompaniment
adjunct 39
coexistence **88**
musical 415
accompany
add 37
coexist 88
concur 120
music 416
accompli, fait – 729
accomplice 711
accomplish
execute 161
complete 729
succeed 731
accomplishment
490, 698
accompts 811
accord
uniform 16
agree 23
music 413
assent 488
concord 714
grant 760
give 784
of one's own – 602
according
– as *qualification*
469
– to *evidence* 467
– to circumstances
8
– to law 963
– to rule
conformably 82
– rumour 527
accordingly
logically 476
accordion 417
accost 586

accoucheur 631, 662
accouchement 161
account *list* 86
adjudge 480
description 594
credit 805
money - 811
fame 873
approbation 931
call to – 932
find one's – in
useful 644
success 731
make no – of 483,
930
not – for 519
on – of *motive* 615
behalf 707
on no – 536
send to one's – 361
take into – 457,
469
small – 643
to one's – 780
turn to –
improve 658
use 677
success 731
gain 775
– as *deem* 484
– book 551
– for 155, 522
– with 794, 807
accountable
liable 177
debit 811
duty 926
accountant 801, 811
certified public –
811
accounts **811**
accouple 43
accoutred
armed 717
accoutrement
dress 225
appliance 633
equipment 673
accoy 174
accredit
commission 755,
759
money 805
honour 873
accredited 484, 613
– to 755, 759
accretion 35, 46
accrimination 938
accroach 789
accrue *add* 37
result 154

acquire 775
be received 785,
810
accubation 213
accueil 894
accultural 658
accumbent 213
accumulate
collect 72
store 636
redundance 641
accurate 494
– *knowledge* 490
accurse 908
accursed
disastrous 649
undone 828
vicious 945
accusation **938**
accuse
disapprove 932
charge 938
lawsuit 969
accustom 613
ace *small* 32
unit 87
within an – 197
aceldama *kill* 361
arena 728
acephalous 59
acerbate 659, 835
acerbity
acrimony 395
sourness 397
rudeness 895
spleen 900, 901
malevolence 907
acervate 72
acetous 397
acetylene 388
acharné 900
Achates, fidus –
890, 939
ache *physical* 378
mental 828
Acheron
pit of – 982
Acherontic
moribund 360
gloomy 837
achievable 470
achieve *end* 67
produce 161
do 680
accomplish 729
achievement 551,
861
Achilles, heel of –
vulnerable 665
achromatism **429**
acicular 253

acid 397
acid test 463
acknowledge
answer 462
assent 488
disclose 529
avow 535
consent 762
observe 772
pay 807
thank 916
repent 950
reward 973
acknowledged
custom 613
acme 210
– of perfection **650**
Acology 662
acolyte 996
acomous 226
aconite 663
acoustic 418
– organs 418
acoustics 402
acquaint
– oneself with **539**
– with 527
acquaintance
knowledge 490
information 527
friend 890
make – with **888**
acquiesce
assent 488
willing 488
consent 762
tolerate 826
acquire
develop 161
get 775
receive 785
– a habit 613
– learning 539
acquirement
knowledge 490
learning 539
talent 698
receipt 810
acquisition
knowledge 490
gain 775
acquit
liberate 750
exempt 927a
vindicate 937
innocent 946
absolve 970
acquit oneself
behave 692
– of a debt 807
– of a duty 926

Column 1 (ACQ)

– of an obligation 772
acquittal 506, 970
acquittance 771
acres *space* 180
  land 342
  property 780
Acres, Bob 862
acrid 392, 395
acridity 171
acrimony
  physical 171
  caustic 830
  discourtesy 895
  hatred 898
  anger 900
  malevolence 907
acroamatics 490
acrobat
  strength 159
  actor 599
  proficient 700
  mountebank 844
Acropolis 210
across 219, 708
acrostic 533, 561, 842
act *imitate* 19
  physical 170
  - *of a play* 599
  personate 599
  voluntary 680
  statute 697
  in the – 680, 947
  – a part *feign* 544
  – one's part 625, 926
  - upon
  physical 170
  mental 615
  take steps 680
  – up to 772
  – well one's part 944
  – without authority 738
acting *deputy* 759
actinic 420
actinometer 445
action *physical* 170
  voluntary **680**
  battle 720
  law 969
  line of – 692
  put in – 677
  suit the – to the word 550
  thick of the – 682
activate 171
actionable 964
active *physical* 171

Column 2 (ADA)

voluntary 682
– *service* 722
– *thought* 457
activity 682
actor
  impostor 548
  player 599
  agent 690
  affectation 855
Acts *record* 551
  Apostolic 985
actual *existing* 1
  present 118
  real 494
actuary 85, 811
actuate 175, 615
actum est 729
acu tetigisti, rem 465, 494
acuity 253
aculeate 253
acumen 498
acuminate 253
acupuncture 260
acustics 402
acute *energetic* 171
  physically violent 173
  pointed 253
  physically sensible 375
  musical tone 410
  perspicacious 498
  cunning 702
  strong feeling 821
  morally painful 830
  – *angle* 244
  – *ear* 418
  – *note* 410
acutely 31
acuteness 465
ad
  – *eundem* 27
  – *hominem* 79
  – *infinitum* 105
  – *instar* 82
  – *interim* 106
  – *lib* 705
  – *rem* 23
A.D. 106
adage 496
adagio *music* 415
  slow 275
Adam *sin* 945
  – 's *apple* 250
adamant 159, 323
adapt 23, 27
  – *oneself to* 82
adaptable
  conformable 82

Column 3 (ADI)

useful 644
add *increase* 35
  join 37
  numerically 85
  – *up* 811
addendum 39
adder 913
addict *habit* 613
adding machine 85
additament 39
addition
  extrinsical 6
  increase 35
  adjunction **37**
  thing added 39
  arithmetical 85
addle *barren* 169
  incomplete 730
  abortive 732
  – the *wits*, 475, 503
addlehead 501
addleheaded 499
address
  residence 189
  direction 550
  speech 582
  speak to 586
  skill 698
  request 765
  – *oneself to* 673
addresses
  courtship 902
addressful 894
adduce
  bring to 288
  evidence 467
addulce 834
ademption 789
adenoid 250
adenology 329
adept 700
adequate *power* 157
  sufficient 639
  for a purpose 644
adhere *stick* 46
  – to 604a, 613
  – to an obligation 772
  – to a duty 926
adherent
  follower 711
adhesive, 46, 327, 352
adhibit 677
adhortation 695
adieu *departure* 293
  loss 776
adipocere 356
adipose 355
adit *orifice* 260
  conduit 350

Column 4 (ADM)

passage 627
adjacent 197
adjection 37
adjective 39
adjoin 197, 199
adjourn 133
adjudge 480
adjudicate 480
adjunct
  thing added **39**
  accompaniment 88
  aid 707
  auxiliary 711
adjuration 535
adjure 765, 768
adjust *adapt* 23
  equalize 27
  order 58
  prepare 673
  settle 723, 762
  – *differences* 774
adjutage 260, 350
adjutant
  auxiliary 711
  military 745
adjuvant *helping* 707
  auxiliary 711
admeasurement 466
adminicle 467
administer
  utilize 677
  conduct 693
  exercise authority 737
  distribute 786
  – *correction* 972
  – *oath* 768
  – *sacrament* 998
  – to *aid* 707
  give 784
administration of justice 965
administrative 737, 965
administrator 694
admirable 648, 944
admiral 745
Admiralty, court of – 966
admirari, nil – 871, 932
admiration
  wonder 870
  love 897
  respect 928
  approval 931
admired disorder 59
admirer 897
admissible

aery 317
Æsculapius 662
Æsop 846
æsthetic
  sensibility 375
  beauty 845
  taste 850
æstival 125
æternum servans
  sub pectore vul-
  nus 919
ætiology [*see* etiol-
  ogy]
afar 196
affable 879, 894
affair *event* 151
  topic 454
  business 625
  battle 720
  love 902, 903
  – of honour 720
affaires, chargé d' –
  758
affaire de cœur 897
affect *relate to* 9
  tend to 176
  qualify 469
  feign 544
  touch 824
  desire 865
  love 897
affectation **855**
affected with
  feeling 821
  disease 655
affectibility 822
affecting 830
affection 821, 897
affections **820**
affettuoso 415
affiance 768, 858
affianced 897, 903
affiche 531
affidation 769
affidavit
  affirmation 535
  record 551
  lawsuit 969
affiliation
  relation 9
  kindred 11
  attribution 155
affine 11
affinitive 9
affinity 9, 17
  mate 903
affirmation **535**, 488
affix *add* 37
  sequel 39
  fasten 43
  letter 561

[392]

afflation 349
afflatus 349, 597,
  985
afflict 830
  – with illness 655
affliction *pain* 828
  infliction 830
  adversity 735
affluence
  sufficiency 639
  prosperity 734
  wealth 803
affluent *river* 348
afflux 286
afford *supply* 784
  wealth 803
  yield 810
  sell for 812
  – *aid* &c. 707
afforestation 371
affranchise
  make free of 748
  liberate 750
affray 720
affreet 980
affriction 331
affright 860
affront *molest* 830
  provocation 900
  insult 929
  – *danger* 861
affuse 337
afield 186
afire 382
afloat *extant* 1
  unstable 149
  going on 151
  ship 273
  navigation 267
  ocean 341
  news 532
  preparing 673
  keep oneself – 734
  set – *publish* 531
afoot *on hand* 625
  preparing 673
  astir 682
afore 116
aforementioned 116
aforesaid
  preceding 62
  repeated 104
  prior 116
aforethought 611
aforetime 116
afraid 860
  be – *irresolute* 605
  – to say *uncertain*
  475
afresh 104, 123
Afric heat 382

Afrikander 57
afrite 980
aft 235
after *in order* 63
  in time 117
  too late 135
  rear 235
  pursuit 622
  be – *intention* 620
  pursuit 622
  go – *follow* 281
  – all *for all that* 30
  qualification 469
  on the whole 476
  – time 133
after acceptation
  516
after-age 124
after-clap 509
after-crop 65, 168
after-dinner 117
after-glow 40, 65,
  420
after-growth 65
after-life 152
aftermath
  sequel 65
  fertile 168
  profit 775
aftermost 235
afternoon 126
  – *farmer* 683
after-part 65, 235
after-piece 599
after-taste 65, 390
after-thought
  thought 451
  memory 505
  change of mind
  607
after-time 121
afterwards 117
aga 745
agacerie 615
again 90, 104
  – and again 136
  come – *periodic* 138
  fall off – 661
  live – 660
against
  counteraction 179
  anteposition 237
  provision 673
  *voluntary opposi-
  tion* 708
  chances – 473
  declaim – 932
  false witness – 934
  go – 708
  set – *actively* 898
  set one's face –

  764, 932
  stand up – *resist*
  719
raise &c. one's
  voice – 489
  – one's will 744
  – one's expecta-
  tion 508
  – the grain *difficult*
  704
  painful 830
  dislike 867
  – the stream 704
  – the time when
  510
  – one's will 744
  – one's wishes 603
agamist 904
agape *open* 260
  curious 455
  expectant 507
  wonder 870
Agapemone 827,
  897
agate 847
age *time* 106
  period 108
  long time 110
  era 114
  present time 118
  oldness 128
  advanced life **128**
  of – 131
  from age to – 112
age quod agis! 682
agency
  physical **170**
  instrumentality
  631
  means 632
  employment 677
  voluntary action
  680
  direction 693
  commission 755
agenda 625, 626
agent *physical* 153
  intermediary 228
  voluntary **690**
  consignee 758
  – provocateur 615
agentship 755
ages: for – 110
  – ago 122
agglomerate 46, 72
agglutinate 46
aggrandize
  in degree 35
  in bulk 194
  honour 873
aggravate

increase 35
vehemence 173
exaggerate 549
render worse 659
distress 835
exasperate 900
aggravating 830
aggravation 835
aggregate 50, 72, 84
aggregation 46
aggression 716
aggressor 726
aggrieve 649, 830
aggroup 72
aghast
  disappointed 509
  fear 860
  wonder 870
agile 274, 682
agio 813
agiotage 794
agitate *move* 315
  inquire 461
  activity 682
  excite the feelings
  824
  – *a question* 476
agitation [*see* agitate]
  changeableness
  149
  energy 171
  motion **315**
  in – *preparing* 673
agitator *leader* 694
aglet 554
agley, gang – 732
aglow 382, 420
agnate 11
agnition 762
agnomen 564
agnostic 487
agnosticism 984, 989
agnus Dei 993, 998
ago 122
  not long – 123
agog *expectant* 507
  desire 865
  wonder 870
agoing 682
  set – 707
agonism 720
agonizing 824, 830
agony 378, 828
  – *of death* 360
  – *of excitement* 825
agrarian 371
agree *accord* 23
  concur 178

assent 488
concord 714
consent 762
compact 769
compromise 774
– in opinion 488
– with *salubrity* 656
agreeable
  comfortable 82
  physically 377
  mentally 829
agreeably to 82
agreement 23 [*see* agree]
  compact 769
agrestic 371
agriculture 371
agronomy 371
aground *fixed* 150
  in difficulty 704
  failure 732
ague-fit 860
aguets, aux –
  expectation 507
  ambush 530
aguish *cold* 383
ah me! 839
aha! *rejoicing* 838
ahead 234, 280
  go – *progression* 282
  shoot – *transcursion* 303
  activity 682
  rock – 665, 667
Ahrimanes 978, 980
aid 707, 906
  by the – of 631, 632
aide-de-camp 711, 745
aidless 160
aigrette 847
aiguille 253
aiguillette 747, 847
aigulet 847
ail 655, 828
aileron 267, 273
ailment 655
aim 278, 620, 675
  – *a blow at* 716
aimable 894
  faire l' – 897
aimer éperdument 897
aimless *without*
  motive 615a
  chance 621
air *unsubstantial* 4
  broach 66

lightness 320
gas 334
atmospheric **338**
wind 349
tune 415
appearance 448
refresh 689
demeanour 692
fashionable 852
beat the – 645
fill the – 404
fine – *salubrity* 656
fish in the – 645
fowls of the – 366
in the – 527
rend the – 404
take – 531
air-balloon 273
air base 728
air-commodore 745
aircraft 273, 726
air-drawn 515
airdrome 273
air-force 726
air-gun 727
airing 266
air-mail 273
airman 269
airmanship 698
air-marshal 745
air-passage 351
air-pipe 351
airport 273, 292, 728
air-pump 349
air-raid 716
airs *affectation* 855
  pride 878
  vanity 880
  arrogance 885
air-shaft 351
air service 267
airship 273, 726
air-tight 261
airways 267
airworthy 273, 664
airy [*see* air]
  windy 349
  unimportant 643
  gay 836
  – *hopes* 858, 859
  give to – *nothing*
  a local habitation &c. 515
aisle *passage* 260
  way 627
  in a church 1000
ait 346
ajar *open* 260
  discordant 713
ajee 217

ajutage 260, 350
akimbo *angular* 244
  stand – 715
akin *related* 9
  consanguineous 11
  similar 17
al fresco 220
alabaster *white* 430
alack! 839
alacrity *willing* 602
  active 682
  cheerful 836
Aladdin's lamp 993
alar 267
alarm *warning* 668
  notice of danger
  669
  fear 860
  cause for – 665
  give an – *indicate*
  550
alarmist 862
alarum. 114, 550, 669
alas! 839
alate 267
alb 999
albeit 30
albert
  chain 847
albification 430
albinescence 430
albinism 430
albino 443
album 593, 596
albumen
  semi-liquid 352
  protein 357
Alcaic 597
alcaid 745
alcalde 745
alcazar 189
alchemy 144
alcohol 959
Alcoran 986
alcove 191, 252
Aldebaran 423
alderman 745
ale 298
alea, jacta est – **601**
aleatory 665
Alecto 173
alectryomancy 511
alehouse 189
  go to the – 959
alembic
  conversion 144
  vessel 191
  furnace 386
  laboratory 691
alentours 197
alert *watchful* 457,

antithesis
  contrast 14
  difference 15
  opposite 237
  style 574, 577
antitoxin 662
antitype 22
antler 253
antonomasia
  metaphor 521
  nomenclature 564
antonym 14
antrum 252
anvil *support* 215
  on the –
  intended 620
  in hand 625
  preparing 673
anxiety *pain* 828
  fear 860
  desire 865
anxious expectation
  507
any *some* 25
  part 51
  no choice 609a
  at – *price* 604a
  at – *rate*
  certain 474
  true 494
  at all hazards 604
anybody 78
anyhow 460, 627
anything one
  knows, for – 491
aorist 109, 119
aorta 350
apace *early* 132
  swift 274
apache 913
apart 44, 87
  set – 636
  wide – 196
apartment 191
  –s 189
  –s to let
  imbecile 499
apathetic 275
apathy
  indifference 866
  insensibility 823
  irreligion 989
ape *imitate* 19
Apelles 559
aperçu 596
aperture 260
apex 210
aphasia 583
aphelion 196
aphonic 403
aphony 581

aphorism 496
Aphrodite 845, 979
apiary 370
apiculture 370
Apicius 957
apiece 79
apish 19, 499
aplanatic 429
aplomb
  stability 150
  self-possession
  498
  resolution 604
Apocalypse 985
Apocrypha 985
apocryphal
  uncertain 475
  erroneous 495
  heterodox 984
apodictic 478
apodosis 67
apogee 210
apograph 21
Apollo *sun* 318
  music 416
  luminary 423
  beauty 845
  god 979
  magnus – 500, 695
Apollyon 978
apologue
  metaphor 521
  teaching 537
  description 594
apology *excuse* 617
  vindication 937
  penitence 950
  atonement 952
apophthegm 496
apophysis 250
apoplexy 158, 655
aporetic 487
aposiopesis 585
apostasy
  recantation 607
  dishonour 940
  heterodoxy 984
apostate
  convert 144
  turncoat 607
  impiety 988
apostle *teacher* 540
  disciple 541
  inspired 985
  –'s creed 983a
apostolic 985
  – church 983a
  – see 995
apostrophe
  address 586
  soliloquy 589

  appeal 765
apothecary 662
  –'s weight 319
apothegm 496
apotheosis
  resuscitation 163
  canonization 873
  heaven 981
  hero worship 991
apozem 335, 384
appal 830, 860
appanage
  property 780
  gift 784
apparatus 633
apparel 225
apparent
  visible 446
  appearing 448
  probable 472
  manifest 525
  heir – 779
apparition
  fallacy of vision
  443
  spirit 980
apparitor 534
appeach 938
appeal 586, 765
  court of – 966
  – to arms 722
  – motion 969
  – from Philip
  drunk to Philip
  sober 658
  – to *call to witness*
  467
  – to for (*claim*) 924
appear 446, 525
  – for 759
  – in print 591
appearance 448
  make one's – 292
  to all – 448
  probable 472
appearances
  keep up – 852
appease 174
appellant 924, 938
appellate 966
appellation 564
append *add* 37
  sequence 63
  hang 214
appendage 39
appendectomy 662
appendix
  adjunct 39
  sequel 65
  end 67
  book 593

appertain
  related to 9
  component 56
  belong 777
  property 780
appetite 865
  tickle the –
  savoury 394
appetizing 865
  exciting 824
applaud 931
apple – of discord
  713
  golden –
  allurement 615
  – of one's eye *good*
  648
  love 897
  favorite 899
  – off another tree
  15
  how we –s swim!
  880
apple-green 435
apple-pie order 58
appliance *use* 677
  –s *means* 632
  machinery 633
applicable *relevant*
  23
  useful 644
  expedient 646
applicability 9
applicant 767
application *study*
  457
  metaphor 521
  use 677
  request 765
apply, *use* 677
  – a match 384
  – the match to
  train 66
  – the mind 457
  – a remedy 662
appoggiatura 413
appointment
  employment 625
  order 741
  charge 755
  assignment 786
  interview 892
appointments
  gear 633
apportion *arrange*
  60
  disperse 73
  allot 786
apportionment 786
appositeness 9
apposition

ment 24
topic 454
discussion 476
meaning 516
have the best of
an – 478
argumentum
ad baculum
compel 744
lawless 964
punish 972
-- ad crumenam
800
-- ad hominem
reasoning 476
accuse 938
– ad verecundiam
939
Argus-eyed 441, 459
argute 498
aria 415
arianism 984
arid 340
unproductive 169
uninteresting 841
Ariel *courier* 268
swift 274
messenger 534
spirit 979
arietation 276
arietta 415
aright *well* 618
Ariman [see Ahri-
manes]
ariolation 511
arioso 415
aris et focis, pro –
defence 717
philanthropy 910
arise *exist* 1
begin 66
happen 151
mount 305
appear 446
– from 154
Aristarchus 850
Aristides
good man 948
aristocracy
power 737
fashion 852
nobility 875
Arithmancy 511
arithmetic 85
ark *abode* 189
asylum 666
arm *part* 51
power 157
instrument 633
provide 637

prepare 673
war 722
weapon 727
make a long – 200
– chair 215
– in arm
together 88
friends 888
sociable 892
– of the law 963
– of the sea 343
armada 726
Armageddon 720,
722
armament 673, 727
armed 717
– at all points 673
– force 726
– guard 664
armet 717
armful 25
armiger 875
armigerent 726
armigerous 722
armilla 247, 847
armillary sphere
466
armipotent 157
armistice
cessation 142
respite 672
pacification 723
armless 158
armlet *ring* 247
gulf 343
ornament 847
armorial bearings
550, 877
armour *cover* 223
defence 717
arms 727
buckle on one's –
673
– plated 223
armoured
– car 726
– cruiser 726
– train 726
armoury *store* 636
workshop 691
arm's length
at – 196
keep at –
repel 289
defence 717
enmity 889
seclusion 893
discourtesy 895
arms 727 [see arm]
heraldry 550
war 722

honours 877
clash of – 720
deeds of – 720
with folded – 681
in – *infant* 129
throw oneself into
the – of 666, 888
under – 722
up in – *active* 682
discord 713
resistance 719
resentment 900
enmity 889
Armstrong gun 727
army *collection* 72
multitude 102
troops 726
aroma 400
around 227
lie – 220
arouse *move* 615
excite 824
– oneself 682
aroynt *begone* 297
malediction 908
arquebusade 662
arquebuse 727
arraign 938, 969
arrange
set in order 60
plan 626
compromise 774
– with creditors
807
– itself 58
arrange – matters
pacify 723
– music 413, 416
– in a series 69
– under 76
arrangement 23, **60**
[see arrange]
order 58
temporary – 111
arrant *identical* 31
manifest 525
notorious 531
bad 649
disreputable 874
base 940
arras 847
array *order* 58, 60
series 69
assemblage 72
multitude 102
dress 225
prepare 673
adorn 847
ostentation 882
battle – 722
arrear, in – 53, 808

arrears *debt* 806
arrectis auribus
hear 418
expect 507
arrest *stop* 142
restrain 751
in law 969
– the attention 457
arrière-pensée
after-thought 65
mental reservation
528
motive 615
set purpose 620
arrival 292
arrive *happen* 151
reach 292
complete 729
– at a conclusion
480
– at the truth 480a
arrogant *severe* 739
proud 878
insolent 885
arrogate 885, 924
– to oneself
undue 925
arrondissement 181
arrosion 331
arrow *swift* 274
missile 284
arms 727
broad – 550
arrow-head
form 253
writing 590
'Arry and 'Arriet
902
ars celare artem
698
arsenal *store* 636
workshop 691
arsenic 663
arson 384
art *representation*
554
business 625
skill 698
cunning 702
fine – 850
work of – 845, **847**
– gallery 556
artery 350, 627
artes, hæ tibi
erunt – 627
artesian well 343
artful 544, 702
– dodge 545, 702
article *thing* 3
part 51
matter 316

give 784
allot 786
– as cause 155
– a duty 926
– places 60
essignat 800
assignation 892
place of – 74
assignee *donee* 785
assimilate
uniform 16
resemble 17
imitate 19
agree 23
transmute 144
assist 707
– at 186
assistant 711
assister *be present*
186
assize *measure* 466
tribunal 966
justice of – 967
associate *mix* 41
unite 43
collect 72
accompany 88
colleague 690
auxiliary 711
friend 890
– with 892
association
[*see* associate]
relation 9
combination 48
co-operation 709
partnership 712
– of ideas
intellect 450
thought 451
intuition 477
hint 514
– football 840
assoil *acquit* 970
assonance
music 413
poetry 597
assort *arrange* 60
assortment 72, 75
assuage 174, 834
assuetude 613
assume *believe* 484
suppose 514
falsehood 544
take 789
insolent 885
right 924
– authority 737
– a character 554
– command 741
– a form 144

– the offensive 716
assumed name 565
assumption
[*see* assume]
severity 739
hope 858
usurpation 925
assurance
speculation 156
certainty 474
belief 484
assertion 535
promise 768
security 771
hope 858
vanity 880
insolence 885
make – double
sure *safe* 664
caution 864
assuredly
assent 488
assythment 973
astatic 320
asterisk 550
astern 235
put the engines –
275
fall – 283
asteroid 318
Asteroth 979
asthenia 160
astigmatism 443
astir 682
set – 824
astonish 870
astonished
– at nothing 871
astonishing
great 31
astound *excite* 824
fear 860
surprise 870
astra, sic itur ad –
360, 873
Astræa 922
astraddle 215
astragal 847
astral 318
– body 317, 992
– influence 601
– plane 317
astray 475, 495
go – *deviate* 279
sin 945
astriction 43
astride 215
astringent 195
astrolabe 466
astrologer 994

astrology 511
astromancy 511
astronomy 318
astute 498, 702
asunder 44, 196
as poles – 237
asylum *hospital* 663
retreat 666
defence 717
asymptote 290
at, be – 620
up and – them!
716
ataghan 727
atavism 145, 163
ataxia 158
atelier 556, 691
athanasia 112
Athanasian creed
983a
athanor 386
atheism 989
atheist 487
Athenae 979
Athens, owls to –
641
athirst 865
athlete *strong* 159
gladiator 726
athletic *strong* 159
strenuous 686
– sports
contest 720
games 840
athwart
oblique 217
crossing 219
opposing 708
Atkins, Tommy 726
Atlantis 515
Atlas *arrangement*
60
list 86
strength 159
support 215
maps 554
atmosphere
circumambience
227
air 338
painting 556
atmospheric blue
438
atoll 346
atom *small* 32, 193
atomic energy 157
atomizer 336
atoms
crush to – 162
atomy 193

atonement
restitution 790
expiation 952
amends 973
religious 976
atony 160
atrabilious 837
atramentous 431
atrium 191
atrocity
malevolence 907
vice 945
guilt 947
atrophy
shrinking 195
disease 655
decay 659
Atropos 601
attach *join* 43
love 897
legal 969
– importance to
642
attaché
employé 746
diplomatic 758
– case 191
attack *singing* 580
disease 655
assault 716
debauch 961
attaghan 727
attain *arrive* 292
succeed 731
– majority 131
attainable 470
attainder
taint 651
at law 971
attainment
knowledge 490
learning 539
skill 698
attar 400
attemper 41, 174
attempered 820
attempt 675
vain – 732
– impossibilities
471
attend
accompany 88
be present 186
follow 281
apply the mind
457
medically 662
aid 707
serve 746
– to business 625
– to orders 743

attendance on
dance – 886
attendant
[see attend]
attention 457
care 459
respect 928
attract – 882
call to – 457
call – to 550
give – 418
pay –s to 894
pay one's –s to
902
attenuate
decrease 36
weaken 158
reduce 195
rarefy 322
attenuated 203
attest
bear testimony 467
affirm 535
adjure 768
attested copy 771
attic *simple* 42
garret 191
summit 210
style 578
wit 842
taste 850
Attila 913
attire 225
attitude
circumstance 8
situation 183
posture 240
attitudinarian 882
attitudinize 855
attollent 307
attorney
consignee 758
at law 968
power of – 755
attract
bring towards 288
induce 615
allure 865
excite love 897
– the attention
457
visible 446
attraction
[see attract]
natural power 157
bring towards
288
attractive
[see attract]
pleasing 829
beautiful 845

attrahent 288
attribute
speciality 79
accompaniment
88
power 157
–s of the Deity 976
– to 155
attribution 155
attrite 330
attrition 330, 331
attroupement 72
attune *music* 415
prepare 673
attuned to
habit 613
attunement 23
auburn 433
A.U.C. 106
auction 796, 840
auctioneer 758, 796
auctorial 599
audacity
courage 861
rashness 863
insolence 885
audible 402
become – 418
scarcely – 405
audience
hearing 418
conversation 588
before an – 599
audire alteram
partem
counter-evidence
468
right 922
justice 939
audit
numeration 85
examination 461
accounts 811
auditive 418
auditor
hearer 418
accountant 811
auditorium 189, 588
auditory
sound 402
hearing 418
theatre 599
– apparatus 418
au fait 698
au fond 5
auf Wiedersehen
293
Augean
– stable 653
– task 704
auger 262

aught 51
for – one cares
unimportant 643
indifferent 866
for – one knows
ignorance 491
conjecture 514
augment
increase 35
thing added 39
expand 194
augur 513
– well 858
augurate 511
augury 512
august 873
Augustinian 996
auk 366
auld lang syne 122
aulic council 696
aumbry 1000
aunt 11
aura *wind* 349
sensation 380
aurea mediocritas
628
aureate 436
aureola 420
aureole 420, 873
aureolin 436
auribus, arrectis –
418
auricular *hearing*
418
clandestine 528
– confession 998
auri sacra fames
819
aurist 662
aurora
dawn 125
light 420, 423
twilight 422
– australis 423
– borealis 423
Auroral 236
ausculation 418
auspice *omen* 512
auspices
influence 175
prediction 511
protection 664
direction 693
aid 707
under the – of 693,
737
auspicious
opportune 134
prosperous 734
hopeful 858
austerity

harsh taste 395
severe 739
discourteous 895
ascetic 955
pietism 988
austral 237
austromancy 511
authentic 467
certain 474
true 494
authentication
evidence 467
security 771
author 164, 593
projector 626
dramatic – 599
– of our being 976
– of evil 978
– 's proof 591
authoritative 474,
741
authority
testimony 467
sage 500
informant 527
power **737**
permission 760
right 924
ensign of – 747
person in – 745
do upon one's own
– 600
authorized *due* 924
legalized 963
authorship
production 161
style 569
writing 590
autobiography 594
autocar 272
autochthonous 188
autocracy 737, 739
autocrat 745
autocratic 600, 737
auto-da-fé 384, 972
autograph 550, 590
Autolycus *thief* 792
pedlar 797
automaniac 504
automatic 601, 633
- pistol 727
- writing 992
automaton 554, 601
automobile 272
automobilist 268
automotive 266
autonomasia 521
autonomy 737, 748
autopsy
post-mortem 363
vision 441

autoptical 446, 525
autotype 558
autumn 126
auxiliary 711
  additional 37
  helpful 707
  – forces 726
avail *benefit* 618
  useful 644
  succeed 731
  of no – 645
  – oneself of 677
avalanche *fall* 306
  snow 383
  redundance 641
avaler des couleu-
  vres 725, 886
avant-coureur 64,
  673
avant-propos 64
avarice 819
avast! *stop* 142, 265
  desist 624
  forbid 761
avatar *change* 140
  deity 976
  idol 991
avaunt! 297, 449
ave! *honour* 873
  courtesy 894
Ave maria 990
avenge 919
avenue
  plantation 371
  way 627
aver 535
average *mean* 29,
  628
  médiocre 651
  – circumstances
  736
  take an – 466
Averni, facilis de-
  scensus – 217,
  665
Avernus 982
averruncate 297,
  301
aversion *unwilling-*
  ness 603
  dislike 867
  hate 898
avert 706
  – the eyes 442
aviary 370
aviation 267
aviator 269
avidity *avarice* 819
  desire 865
aviette 273
avile 932, 934

avion 273
aviso 532
avocation 625
avoidance 623
avoidless 474, 601
avoirdupois 319
avolation 623, 671
avouch 535, 768
avow *assent* 488
  disclose 529
  assert 535
avulsion 44, 301
avuncular 11
await *future* 121
  be kept waiting
  133
  impend 152
  expect 507
awake *attentive* 457
  careful 459
  intelligent 498
  active 682
  – to life immortal
  360
awaken *inform* 527
  excite 824
  – the attention 457
  – the memory 505
award *adjudge* 480
  give 784
aware 490
away 187, 196
  break – 623
  fly – 293
  move – 287
  take – from 789
  get &c. – 671
  throw &c. –
  eject 297
  reject 610
  waste 638
  relinquish 782
  – from *unrelated* 10
  – with! 930, 932
  do – with *undo* 681
  abrogate 756
awe *fear* 860
  wonder 870
  respect 928
aweless *fearless* 861
  insolent 885
  disrespectful 929
awful 31, 860
  – silence 403
awhile 111
awkward
  inelegant 579
  inexpedient 647
  unskilful 699
  difficult 704
  painful 830

ugly 846
vulgar 851
ridiculous 853
– squad 701
awl 262
awn 253
awning 223, 424
awry *oblique* 217
  distorted 243
  evil 619
axe *edge tool* 253
  impulse 276
  weapon 727
  for beheading 975
  have an – to grind
  702
Axinomancy 511
axiom 496
axiomatic 474
axis *support* 215
  centre 222
  rotation 312
axle 312
  wheel and – 633
axle load 466
axletree 215
ay 488
ayah 746, 753
aye *ever* 112
  yes 488
azimuth
  horizontal 213
  direction 278
  measurement 466
  – circle 212
azoic 358
azote 663
azotic 657
azure 438
azygous *single* 87

B

Baal 979, 986
Babbittry 851
babble *rivulet* 348
  faint sound 405
  unmeaning 517
  talk 584, 588
babbler 501
babbling
  foolish 499
babe 129
  innocent as the –
  unborn 946
Babel *confusion* 59
  discord 414
  tongues 560
  jargon 563
  loquacity 584

baboon 846
baby *infant* 129
  fool 501
  – linen 225
babyhood 127
babyish 499
baccarat 840
bacchanals 959
Bacchus 979
  drink 959
bachelor 904
  – of arts 492
  – girl 374
bacillus 193
back *rear* 235
  shoulder 250
  aid 707
  behind one's –
  latent 526
  hidden 528
  come – 292
  give – 790
  fall – *relapse* 661
  go – 283
  go – from *retract*
  773
  have at one's – 215
  hold – *avoid* 623
  keep – *reserve* 636
  look – 505
  on one's – *impo-*
  tent 158
  horizontal 213
  failure 732
  pat on the –
  incite 615
  encourage 861
  approve 931
  pay – *retaliate* 718
  put – *deteriorate*
  659
  restore 660
  send – 764
  take – again 790
  carry one's
  thoughts – 505
  some time – 122
  spring – 277
  trace – 505
  turn – 283
  turn one's – 283
  turn one's – upon
  repel 289
  inattention 458
  avoid 623
  oppose 708
  seclusion 893
  discourtesy 895
  disrespect 929
  contempt 930
  set one's – against

balanced 150, 242
balbucinate 583
balbutiate 583
balcony 250
theatre 599
bald *bare* 226
style 575
uninteresting 841
ugly 846
plain 849
baldachin 223, 1000
balderdash 517, 577
baldric 230, 247
bale *bundle* 72
load 190
ladle 270
evil 619
– out 297
baleful 649
balister 727
balize 550
balk *disappoint* 509
deceive 545
hinder 706
Balkanize 713
ball *globe* 249
missile 284
shot 727
dance 840
party 892
– at one's feet 731, 737
keep up the – 143, 682
ballad 415, 597
– monger 597
ballast
compensation 30
weight 319
wisdom 498
safety 666
without – *rash* 863
vicious 945
ballerina 599
ballet 599, 840
ballet-dancer 599
ballistics
projectiles 284
war 722
arms 727
ballon d'essai 463
balloon 273, 726
balloonist 269
balloonry 267
ballot 535, 609
ball-room 840
balm *moderate* 174
fragrance 400
remedy 662
relief 834
Balmoral *boot* 225

balmy
sleep 683
balneal 337
balourdise 699
balsam 662
balsamic
salubrious 834
balustrade
support 215
inclosure 232
bam 544
bambino 129
bamboozle 545
ban *exclude* 55
prohibit 761
denounce 908
under the – 909
– with bell, book, and candle 998
banal 613, 843
band *ligature* 45
assemblage 72
filament 205
belt 230
ring 247
music 415, 416, 417
party 712
shackle 752
– of hope 958
– together 709
– with 720
bandage 43, 45
support 215
cover 223
remedy 662
restraint 752
the eyes -d 442
bandana 225
bandbox 191
banded together 178, 713
bandit 792
bandog 664, 668
bandolier 636
bandore 417
bandrol 550
bands 999
bandurria 417
bandy
exchange 148
agitate 315
– about 531
– legged 243
– words 476, 588
bane 619, **663**
baneful 649
bang *impel* 276
sound 406
beat 972
bangle 847

banish *eject* 297
seclude 893
punish 972
banister 215
banjo 417
bank *acclivity* 217
side of lake 342
store 636
sand 667
fence 717
money 802
sea – 342
– of elegance 800
– holiday 840
– up 670
banker 797, 801
game 840
bank-note 800
bankruptcy 732, 808
banlieue 197, 227
banner 550
enlist under the -s of 707
raise one's – 722
banneret 875
banns
forbid the – 761
publish the –
ask 765
marriage 903
banquet 298, 840
banquette 717
banshee 979, 980
bantam cock 887
banter 842, 856
banterer 844
banting 956
bantling 129, 167
banyan *stint* 640
fast 956
baptism *name* 564
rite 998
Baptist 984
baptistery 1000
bar *except* 38
exclude 55
hotel 189
line 200
support 215
inclosure 232
close 261
music 413
hindrance 706
insignia 747
prison 752
prohibit 761
ingot 800
tribunal 966
legal profession 968
– sinister *flaw* 651

disrepute 874
illegal 964
crossing the – 360
Barabbas 792
baragouin 517
barb *spike* 253
nag 271
– the dart *pain* 830
barbacan 717
barbarian
uncivilized 876
evil-doer 913
barbaric 851, 876
barbarism
neology 563
bad style 579
vulgarity 851
discourtesy 895
barbarous
unformed 241
plebeian 876
maleficent 907
barbette 717
barbican 717
barbouillage 590
barcarolle 415
bard 416, 597
bare *mere* 32
nude 226
manifest 525
disclose 529
scanty 640
– back 226
– bone 203
– faced *deceitful* 544, *insolent* 885
– foot 226, 804
- headed 928
scud under - poles 704
- possibility 473
- supposition 514
bargain
compact 769
barter 794
cheap 815
into the - 37
- for 507
- and sale *transfer of property* 783
barge 273
bargee 269
baritone 408
bark *rind* 223
strip 226
ship 273
yelp 412
- at *threaten* 909
censure 932
more - than bit 908

- worse than bite 885
barker 767
barleycorn
little 193
Barleycorn, Sir
John - 298
barm *leaven* 320
bubbles 353
Barmecide feast
956
barmy 320, 503
barn 189
barnacles 445
barndoor fowl 366
barograph 206, 338
barometer *air* 338
measure 466
consult the - 463
baron *peer* 875
husband 903
court - 966
- of the Exchequer
967
baronet 875
baronial 878
baroque 853
baroscope 338
barouche 272
barque 273
barrack 189
barracoon 717
barrage 407, 717
barratry 940
barred 219, 440
barrel 191, 249
- organ 417
barren 169, 645
barricade *fence* 232
obstacle 706
defence 717
prison 752
barrier [*see* barri-
cade]
barring *save* 38
excluding 55
except 83
- out *resist* 719
disobey 742
barrister 968
revising - 967
barrow
mound 206
vehicle 272
grave 363
barter
reciprocate 12
interchange 148
commerce **794**
barytone 408
basal 215

bas-bleu
scholar 492
affectation 855
base
site 183
lowest part **211**
support 215
bad 649
cowardly 862
shameful 874
servile 886
dishonourable 940
vicious 945
- ball 840
- born 876
- coin 800
- note 408
- of operations
plan 626
attack 716
- viol 417
baseball diamond
213
baseboard 211
based on *ground of*
belief 467
baseless 2, 4
basement *cellar* 191
lowest part 207,
211
bash 276
bashaw 739, 745
bashful 881
bashi bazouk 726
basilica 1000
basilisk *sight* 441
cannon 727
serpent 949
basin *dock* 189
vessel 191
hollow 252
plain 344
basinet 717
basis
lowest part 211
support 215
preparation 673
bask *physical enjoy-
ment* 377
warmth 382
prosperity 734
moral enjoyment
827
basket 191
- of 190
bas-relief 250, 557
bass *music* 415
- note 408
- viol 417
basset horn 417
bassinet 191, 215

bassoon 417
basso-profondo 408
basso-rilievo 250,
557
bastard 545, 925
baste *beat* 276
punish 972
Bastille 752
bastinado 972
bastion 717
bat 276, 727
batch 25, 72
bate *diminish* 36
subtract 38
reduce price 813
bated breath
with - *faint sound*
405
expecting 507
hiding 528
whisper 581
humble 879
bath 337, 652
public -s 652
warm - 386
- room 191, 652
Bath chair 272
bathe *immerse* 300
plunge 310
water 337
bathos 497
bathysphere 208
batik 440
batman 637
bâton *support* 215
sceptre 747
batrachian 366
batta 973
battalion 726
batten
feed 298
stage lighting 599
- down the
hatches 261
- on 886
batter *destroy* 162
beat 276
battered 659, 688
battering-ram 276
battering-train 727
battery *electric* 153
artillery 726
guns 727
floating - 726
plant a - 716
battle 720, 722
half the - 642
win the - 731
- array *order* 60
prepare 673
war 722

- axe 727
- cruiser 726
- cry 550, 722
- field *arena* 728
- ground *discord*
713
- ship 726
- with *oppose* 708
battledore and
shuttlecock
interchange 148
game 840
battlement 257, 717
battre
- la campagne
nonsense 497
diffuse style 573
excitable 825
- l'eau avec un
bâton 645
- le fer sur l'en-
clume 134
- la générale 669
se - contre des
moulins 645
ne - que d'une aile
683
battology
repeat 104
diffuse style 573
battue *pursuit* 622
attack 716
kill 361
bauble 643, 840
bavardage 517, 584
bawd 962
bawdy, - house 961
bawl 411
bawn 189
bay *concave* 252
gulf 343
cry 412
brown 433
at - *danger* 665
difficulty 704
defence 717, **719**
bring to - 716
- the moon 645
- window 260
bayadère 599
bayard 271
bayonet *kill* 361
attack 716
weapon 727
crossed -s 708
at the point of the
- *war* 722
severity 739
coercion 744
bays *trophy* 733
crown 877

accordant 23
proper 646
beautiful 845, 847
due 924
becripple 158
bed lodgment 191
layer 204
support 215
garden 371
marriage 903
brought to - 161
death - 360
smooth the - of death 707
go to - 265, 683
keep one's - 655
- of down 687
~ gown 255
- maker 746
- out 371
- ridden 655
- room 191
- of roses 377, 734
put to - with a shovel 363
- time 126
bedarken 421
bedaub 223
bedazzle 420
bedding 215
bedeck 847
bedel 965
bedesman
[see beadsman]
bedevil derange 61
sorcery 992
bedew 339
bedight 847
bedim 421, 422
bedizen clothe 225
ornament 847
vulgar 851
Bedlam
- broke loose 59
candidate for - 504
be-dog 281
Bedouin 792
bedraggled 59
bedwarf 195
bee 690
busy - 682
swarm like -s 102
- in one's bonnet 503
- in a bottle 407
- line 246, 278
-'s wax 352
beef-eater 726
beef-headed 499
beehive 250

Beelzebub 978
beer 298
beery 959
beetle overhang 206, 214
project 250
blind as a - 442
Colorado - 913
- head 501
befall 151
befit agree 23
expedient 646
due 924, 926
befog 353, 528
befool mad 503
deceive 545
befooled
victimized 732
before in order 62
in time 116
presence 186
in space 234
precession 280
preference 609
set - one 525
- Christ 106
- long 132
- mentioned 62, 116
- now 122
- one's eyes 446, 525
- one's time 132
- you could -turn round, - say Jack Robinson 113
beforehand
prior 116
early 132
foresight 510
resolve - 611
befoul 653
befriend 707, 888
befuddlement 959
beg Turk 745
ask 765
- one's bread 765
poor 804
- leave 760
- one's life 914
- pardon 952
- the question 477
beget 161
begetter 166
beggar idler 683
petitioner 767
poor 804
degrade 874
low person 876
sturdy - 792

- description 83, 870
- my neighbour 840
- on horseback 885
beggared
bankrupt 808
beggarly mean 643
vile 874
vulgar 876
servile 886
- account of empty boxes 640, 804
begging
go a -
too much 641
useless 645
offered 763
free 748
- letter 765
begilt 847
begin 66
- again 104
beginner 541
beginning 66
begird 227, 229
beglerbeg 745
begone
depart 293
ejection 297
abrogate 756
- dull care 836
Begotten, the only - 976
begrime 653
begrudge
unwilling 603
refuse 764
stingy 819
beguile mislead 495
deceive 545
reconcile 831
- the time
inaction 681
amusement 840
béguine 996
begum 745, 875
behalf 618, 707
in - of 759
behave oneself
conduct 692
fashion 852
courtesy 894
behaviour 692
on one's good - 894, 944
behead 361, 972
behemoth 192
behest 741
behind

in order 63
in space 235
sequence 281
- the age 124, 491
- one's back 187
speak ill of - one's back 934
- the bars 751
- the scenes
cause 153
unseen 447
cognizant 490
latent 526
hidden 528
playhouse 599
- time 133
behindhand
late 133
shortcoming 304
adversity 735
insolvent 808
behold 441, 457
beholden 916, 926
beholder 444
behoof 618
behoove 926
being 1, 3
created - 366
human - 372
time - 106
Bel 979
belabour 276, 972
belated late 133
ignorant 491
belaud 931
belay join 43
restrain 706
belch 297
beldam 130, 913
beldame 173
beleaguer 716
bel esprit 844
belfry 206, 1000
Belial 978, 980
son of - 988
belie deny 536
falsify 544
contradict 708
belief 484, 488
easy of - 472
hug a - 606
believe
[see belief]
suppose 514
reason to - 472
- who may 485
not - one's senses 870
believer
religious 987
true - 983a

bespeak *early* 132
  evidence 467
  indicate 516
  engage 755
  ask for 765
bespeckle 440
bespot 440
besprinkle 41, 440
best 648, 650
  all for the –
  good 618
  prosper 734
  content 831
  hope 858
  bad is the – 649
  do one's –
  care 459
  try 675
  activity 682
  exertion 686
  have the – of it 731
  make the – of it
  over-estimate 482
  use 677
  submit 725
  compromise 774
  take easily 826
  hope 858
  the – 800
  to the – of one's
  belief 484
  – bib and tucker
  prepared 673
  ornament 847
  ostentation 882
  – friends 890
  – intentions 906
  – man 903
  – part 31, 50
  – seller 731
  make the – of
  one's time 684
bestead 644
bestial 954, 961
bestir oneself
  activity 682
  haste 684
  exertion 686
bestow 784
  – one's hand 903
  – thought 451
bestraddle 215
bestrew 73
bestride 206, 215
bet 621
betake oneself to
  journey 266
  business 625
  use 677
bête, pas si – 498
bête noire *bane* 663

fear 860
hate 898
bethel 1000
bethink 451, 505
bethral 749, 751
betide 151
betimes 132
betoken
  evidence 467
  predict 511
  indicate 550
betray *disclose* 529
  deceive 545
  dishonour 940
  – *itself visible* 446
betrayer 941
betrim 673
betroth 768, 903
betrothed 897
better *good* 648
  improve 658
  appeal to one's –
  feelings 914
  get – *health* 654
  improve 658
  refreshment 689
  restoration 660
  get the – of, 479,
  702, 731
  think – of 658, 950
  seen – days
  deteriorate 659
  adversity 735
  poor 804
  – half 903
  only – than noth-
  ing 651
  – sort 875
  for – for worse
  choice 609
  marriage 903
between 228
  – cup and lip 111
  far – 198
  lie – 228
  – the lines 526
  vibrate – two ex-
  tremes 149
  – ourselves 528
  – two fires 665
  – maid 746
betwixt 228
bevel 217
  – gearing 633
bever 298
beverage 298
bévue 732
bevy 72, 102
bewail *regret* 833
  lament 839
beware 665, 668

bewilder
  put out 458
  uncertainty 475
  astonish 870
bewitch
  fascinate 615
  please 829
  excite love 897
  exorcise 992
bey 745
beyond *superior* 33
  distance 196
  go – 303
  – compare 31, 33
  – control 471
  – one's depth 208,
  519
  – expression 31
  – one's grasp 471
  – hope 731, 534
  – the mark 303,
  641
  – measure 641
  – possibility 471
  – praise
  perfect 650
  approbation 931
  virtue 944
  – price 814
  – question 474, 494
  – reason 471
  – remedy 859
  – seas 57
bezel 217
bhang 663
bias *influence* 175
  tendency 176
  slope 217
  prepossession 481
  disposition 820
bib *pinafore* 225
  drink 959
bibber *weep* 839
  toper 959
bibble-babble 584
bibelot 847
bibendum, nunc
  est – 959
Bible 985
  – oath 535
biblioclasm 162
bibliography 593
bibliolatry
  learning 490
  heterodoxy 984
  idolatry 991
bibliomancy 511
bibliomania 490
bibliomaniac 492
bibliophile 492
bibliopole 593

bibliotheca 593
bibulous 298, **959**
bicameral 90
bicapital 90
bice 435, 438
bicentenary 98,
  138, 883
bicker *flutter* 315
  quarrel 713
bicolour 440
biconjugate 91
bicuspid 91
bicycle 272
bid *order* 741
  offer 763
  – the banns 903
  – defiance 715
  – fair *tend* 176
  probable 472
  promise 511
  hope 858
  – a long farewell
  624
  – for *intend* 620
  offer 763
  request 765
  bargain 794
bidder 767
bide *wait* 133
  remain 141
  take coolly 826
  – one's time 133
  watch 507
  inactive 681
bidet 271
biennial
  periodic 138
  plant 367
bienséance 852, **894**
bier 363
bifacial 90
bifarious 90
bifid 91
bifold 90
biform 90
bifurcate 91, 244
big *in degree* 31
  in size 192
  wide 194
  look – *defy* 715
  proud 878
  insolent 885
  talk – 885, **909**
  – sounding
  loud 404
  words 577
  affected 855
  – swollen 194
  – with 161
  – with the fate **of**
  511

Column 1 (BIG)

bigamy 903
biggin 191
bight 343
bigot *positive* 474
  prejudice 481
  obstinate 606
  heterodox 984
  impious 988
bigotry 907
bigwig *scholar* 492
  sage 500
  nobility 875
bijou *goodness* 648
  beauty 845
  ornament 847
bilander 273
bilateral 90, 236
bilbo 727
bilboes 752
  put into – 751
bile 900
bilge *base* 211
  convex 250
  yawn 260
  – water 653
bilingual 560
bilious 837
bilk
  disappoint 509
  cheat 545
  steal 791
bill *list* 86
  hatchet 253
  placard 531
  ticket 550
  paper 593
  plan 626
  weapon 727
  money order 800
  money account 811
  charge 812
  in law 969
  true – 969
  – and coo 902
  – of exchange 771
  – of fare *food* 298
  plan 626
  – of indictment 938
  –s of mortality 360
  – of sale 771
billet *locate* 184
  ticket 550
  apportion 786
billet *epistle* 592
  – doux 902
billfold 191
billhook 253
billiard – ball 249
  – room 191

[412]

Column 2 (BIR)

– table *flat* 213
billiards 840
Billingsgate 563, 908
billion 98
billow *sea* 348
  river 341
billy-cock 225
billy-goat 373
bimetallism 800
bin 191
binary 89
bind *connect* 43
  cover 223
  compel 744
  condition 770
  obligation 926
  – hand and foot 751
  – oneself 768
  – over 744
  – up wounds 660
binding 744
bine 367
binnacle 693
binocular 445
binomial 89
biogenesis 161
biograph 448
biography 594
biology 357, 359
bioscope 448
biota 357
biparous 89
bipartite 44, 91
biplane 273
biplicity 89
biquadrate 96
birch *flog* 972
  – rod 975
bird 366
  kill two –s with one stone 682
  –'s eye view 441, 448
  –s of a feather 17
  the – has flown 187, 671
  – in hand 777, 781
  – of ill omen
  omen 512
  warning 668
  hopeless 859
  – of passage 268
  – of prey 739
  a little – told me 527
birdcage 370
birdlime *glue* 45
  trap 545
biretta 999

Column 3 (BIT)

birth *beginning* 66
  production 161
  paternity 166
  nobility 875
  – place 153
  – right 924
birthday 138, 883
  – suit 226
birthmark 848
bis *repeat* 104
  approval 931
biscuits, s'embarquer sans – 674
bise 349
bisection 68, **91**
bishop *punch* 298
  clergy 996
  –'s palace 1000
  –'s purple 437
bishopric 995
bisque 33
bissextile 138
bistoury 253
bistre 433
bisulcate 259
bit
  small quantity 32
  part 51
  interval 106
  curb 752
  just a – 26
  – by bit
  by degrees 26
  by instalments 51
  in detail 79
  slowly 275
  – between the teeth 600, 719
bitch *animal* 366
  female 374
  clumsy 699
  fail 732
  impure 962
bite *eat* 298
  physical pain 378
  cold 385
  cheat 545
  dupe 547
  etch 558
  mental pain 830
  – the dust 725
  – in 259
  – the thumb 900, 929
  – the tongue 392
biter bit 718
biting *pain* 378
  cold 383
  pungent 392
  painful 830
  discourteous 895

Column 4 (BLA)

  censorious 932
bitten 897
bitter *beer* 298
  cold 383
  taste 392, 395
  painful 830
  acrimonious 895
  hate 898
  angry 900
  malevolent 907
  – end 67
  – ender 606, 710, 832
  – pill 735
  – words 932
bitterly *greatly* 31
bitterness
  [*see bitter*]
  pain 828
  regret 833
bitumen 356a
bituminous coal 388
bivouac
  encamp 184
  camp 189
  repose 265
  watch 668
bi-weekly 138
bizarre 83, 853
blab 529
blabber 584
black *colour* 431
  crime 945
  look – *feeling* 821
  discontent 832
  angry 900
  – art 992
  – and blue
  beat 972
  – board 590
  – book 938
  – eye 848, 972
  – in the face
  swear 535
  excitement 821, 824
  – flag 722
  – hole *crowd* 72
  prison 752
  – lead 556
  – letter *old* 124
  barbarism 563
  print 591
  – list 932
  – looks
  discourteous 895
  sullen 901a
  disapprove 932
  magic 992
  – mail *theft* 791

booty 793
bribe 973
– sheep 949
– spots in the horizon 859
– swan 83
– and white
  chiaroscuro 420
  colourless 429
  record 551
  writing 590
  prove that – is white 477
blackamoor 431
  wash a – white 471
blackball 55, 893, 932
blackcoat 996
blacken [*see* black]
  defame 934
blackguard
  vulgar 851
  rude 895
  base 940
  vagabond 949
blackleg 792
black Maria 727
blackness 431
blacksmith 690
bladder 191
blade *edge tool* 253
  man 373
  instrument 633
  sharp fellow 682
  proficient 700
  sword 727
  fop 854
blague 545
blain 250, 848
blame 155, 932
  lay – on 938
  take – 932
blameless 946
blameworthy
  disapprove 932
  vice 945
  guilt 947
blanc-bec 701
blanch 429, 430
blancmange 298
bland 174, 894
blandiloquence 933
blandishment
  inducement 615
  endearment 902
  flattery 933
blank 2, 4
  empty 187
  simple 849
look –
  disappointed 509

discontent 832
wonder 870
point – 576
– cartridge 158
– verse 597
blanket 223, 384
  wet – 174
  toss in a – 929
blare 404, 412
blarney 933
blasé 841, 869
blasphemy 988
blast
  destroy 162
  explosion 173
  wind 349
  sound 404
  adversity 735
  curse 908
– furnace 386
blatant *loud* 404
  cry 412
  silly 499
blather 584
blatter 412
blaze *heat* 382
  light 420
  mark 550
  excitement 824
– abroad 531
blazer 225
blazing
  luminary 423
blazon *publish* 531
  repute 873
  ornament 847
  ostentation 882
blé: manger son –
  en herbe 818
bleach 429, 430
bleak 383
blear-eyed 443
bleary 422
bleat 412
bleed
  physical pain 378
  remedy 662
  spend money 809
  extort money 814
  moral pain 828
  make the heart – 830
– freely *liberal* 816
bleeding
  hemorrhage 299
  remedy 662
– heart 828
blemish
  imperfection 651
  injure 659

ugly 846
defect 848
blench *avoid* 623
  whiten 821
  fear 860
blend 41, 48
– with 714
bless
  give pleasure 829
  approve 931
  divine function 976
  worship 990
– my heart 870
– one's stars 838, 916
blessed 827
  abode of the – 981
blessedness
  single – 904
blessing *good* 618
  approval 931
blessings 734
blest 827
– with 177
bletonism 511
blight
  deteriorate 659
  adversity 735
– hope 509
blighty 189
blimp 273
blind 223
  shade 424
  cecity 442
  inattentive 458
  ignorant 491
  conceal 528
  screen 530
  deception 545
  instinctive 601
  pretext 617
  insensible 823
  drunk 959
– alley 261
– bargain
  uncertain 475
  purposeless 621
  rash 863
– the eyes *hide* 528
  deceive 545
– hookey 840
– lead the blind 538
– man's buff 840
– man's holiday
  evening 126
  dark 421, 422
– to one's own merit 880

– to the world 959
– of one eye 443
– reasoning 486
– side *prejudice* 481
  credulity 486
  obstinacy 606
blinders 424, 443
blindness 442
blind pig 964
blink *wink* 443
  neglect 460
  falter 605
  avoid 623
– at *blind to* 442, 458
blinkard 443
blinker 424, 530
bliss 827
  celestial 981
blister 250
blithe 836
blizzard 349
bloat 194
bloated
  expanded 194
  misshapen 243
  convex 250
– with pride 878
blob 250
block *mass* 192
  support 215
  dense 321
  hard 323
  fool 501
  engraving 558
  writing 590
  hinder 706
  execution 975
  bring to the – 972
  wood – 558
– of buildings 189
– out 230, 240, 673
– printing 591
– up 261, 706
blockade
  surround 227
  close 261
  restrain 751
  exclude 893
blockhead 501
blockhouse 717
blockish 499
blond 429, 430
blood
  consanguinity 11
  fluid 333
  kill 361
  fop 854
  nobility 875
  dye with –

severe 739
hands in – *cruel* 907
in the – 5
life – 359
new – 658, 824
spill – *war* 722
– for blood 919
– boil *excite* 824, 825
 anger 900
– run cold 830, 860
– heat 382
– horse 271
– hound 913
– letting 297, 662
– poisoning 655
– red 434
– stained 361
– sucker 789, 913
– thirsty
 murderous 361
 cruel 907
– up *excited* 824
 angry 900
bloodless 160
 peace 721
 virtue 946
bloody [*see* blood]
 red 434
 unclean 653
 cruel 907
bloom *youth* 127
 flower 367
 blue 438
 health 654
 prosperity 734
bloomer 495
bloomers 225
blooming 654, 845
blossom
 flower 154, 161, 367
 prosperity 734
blot *blacken* 431
 error 495
 obliterate 552
 dirty 653
 blemish 848
 disgrace 874
 guilt 947
– out *destroy* 162
 forgive 918
blotch 848
blouse 225
blow *expand* 194
 knock 276
 wind 349
 unexpected 508

disappointment 509
 evil 619
 action 680
 get wind 688
 failure 732
 prosper 734
 pain 828, 830
come to –s 720, 722
deal a – at 716
deal a – to 972
 death – 360, 361
– for blow 718
– one's brains out 361
– the coals 824
– down 162
– the fire 384
– the gaff 529
– hole 351
– the horn 416
– hot and cold
 lie 544
 irresolute 605
 tergiversation 607
 caprice 608
– a kiss 902
– off *disperse* 73
– out *food* 298
 darken 421
 gorge 957
– over *past* 122
– pipe 349, 727
– the trumpet 873
– one's own trumpet 882
– up *destroy* 162
 eruption 173
 inflate 194
 wind 349
 excite 824
 objurgate 932, 934
blower 349
blowhard 884
blown [*see* blow]
 fatigued 688
 proud 878
 storm – over 664, 721
– upon 874, 932
blow-out 406
blowzy *swollen* 194
 red 434
blubber *fat* 356
 cry 839
Blücher boot 225
bludgeon 727
– *man* 726, 913
blue *sky* 338
 colour 438

learned 490
bit of – *hope* 858
look –
 disappointed 509
 feeling 821
 discontent 832
 disrepute 874
out of the – 508
swear till all's – 535
true – 543, 939
– book 86, 551
– blood 875
– devils 837
– jacket 269
– light 550, 669
– pencil 174, 596
– moon 110
– Peter 293, 550
– and red 437
– ribbon 733, 877
– ruin 959
– stocking
 scholar 492
 affectation 855
– and yellow 435
Bluebeard
 marriage 903
 libertine 962
blueness 438
blues 837, 840
bluff *violent* 173
 high cliff 206
 blunt 254
 deceive 545
 boasting 884
 insolent 885
 discourteous 895
blunder *error* 495
 absurdity 497
 awkward 699
 failure 732
– upon 156
blunderbuss 727
blunderhead 701
blunderheaded 499
blunt *weaken* 160
 inert 172
 moderate v. 174
 obtuse 254
 benumb 376
 damp v. 616
 plain-spoken 703
 cash 800
 deaden 823
 discourteous 895
– tool 645
– witted 499
bluntness 254
blur
 imperfect vision

443
 dirt 653
 blemish 848
 stigma 874
blurb 931
blurred
 invisible 447
blurt out 529, 582
blush *flush* 382
 redden 434
 feel 821
 humbled 879
 modest 881
at first – *see* 441
 appear 448
 manifest 525
put to the –
 humble 897
 browbeat 885
 discourtesy 895
blushing honours 873, 881
bluster *violent* 173
 defiant 715
 boasting 884
 insolent 885
 threaten 909
blusterer 887
blustering [*see* bluster]
 windy 349
Bo to a goose, not say – 862
boa 225
Boanerges 540
boar 366, 373
board *layer* 204
 support 215
 food 298
 hard 323
 council 696
 attack 716
 tribunal 966
festive – 892
go by the – 158, 162
go on – 293
on – 186, 273
preside at the – 693
– of trade 621
– school 542
boarder 188
boarding-house 189
boards 599, 728
boast 884
not much to – of 651
boasting 884
boaston 840
boat 273

in the same – 88
– race 720
boating 267
boatman 269
boatswain 269
bob *depress* 308
 leap 309
 oscillate 314
 agitate 315
 money 800
 – a curtsy 894
 – for *fish* 463
Bobadil, Captain –
 887
bobbed
 hair 53
bobbin 312
bobbing *fuel* 388
bobbish 654
bobby *police* 664
bobsleigh 272
bobsleighing 840
bobtailed 53
bocage 367
bocca, per amusare
 la – 394
Boche 913
boddice 225
bode 511
bodega 189
bodily
 substantially 3
 wholly 50
 material 316
 – enjoyment 377
 – fear 860
 – pain 378
bodkin
 go between 228
 perforator 262
body *substance* 3
 whole 50
 assemblage 72
 frame 215
 matter 316
 party 712
 in a – *together* 88
 – and blood of
  Christ 987
 – clothes 225
 – colour 556
 – of doctrine 490
 – forth 554
 – guard 717, 753
 – of knowledge
  490
 – politic
  mankind 372
  authority 737
 keep – and soul
  together 654

– of water 438
Bœotian *rustic* 371
 stupid 499
 fool 501
 vulgar 851
 ignoble 876
Boer 371
bog 345, 653
 – trotter 876
boggart 980
boggle *hesitate* 605
 awkward 699
 difficulty 704
bogie 980
 truck 272
bogle 980
bogus 545
Bohemian
 unconventional 83
 nomad 268
 ungenteel 851
boil *violence* 173
 effervesce 315
 bubble 353
 heat 382, 384
 ulceration 655
 excitement 824,
  825
 anger 900
 – down 195
boiler 386
boisterous
 violent 173
 hasty 684
 excitable 825
bold *prominent* 250
 unreserved 525
 vigorous 574
 brave 861
 make – with 895
 show a – front 715,
  861
 – faced 885
 – push *essay* 675
 – relief *visible* 446
 – stroke *plan* 626
 success 731
bole 50
bolero 840
bollard 45
bolshevik 146, 742
bolshevist 737, 742
bolster *support* 215
 repair 658
 aid 707
 – up *vindicate* 937
bolt *sift* 42
 fasten 43
 fastening 45
 close 261
 move rapidly 274

propel 284
run away 623
escape 671
hindrance 706
shaft 727
disobey 742
shackle 752
 thunder – 872
 – the door 761
 – food 298, 957
 – in 751
 – upright 212
bolthead 191
bolus *mouthful* 298
 remedy 662
bomb 404, 727
 – proof 664, 717
 – vessel 726
bombard 716
bombardier 726
bombardon 417
bombast
 unmeaning 517
 magniloquence
  577
 ridiculous 853
 boasting 884
 exaggeration 549
Bombastes Furioso
 887
bomber
 aeroplane 726
bombilation 404
bon – **de augure**
 858
 – enfant *social* 892
  kindly 906
 – gré mal gré 601
 – marché 815
 – mot 842
 – naturel 836
 – ton 852
 – vivant 957
 – voyage 293
bona – **fides**
 veracity 543
 probity 939
 – roba 962
bonanza 641, 784
 wealth 803
bonbon 396
bond *relation* 9
 tie 45
 compact 769
 security 771
 money 800
 right 924
 – of union 9, 45
 government – 802
 Liberty – 802
bondage 749

bonded together
 712
bonds [*see* bond]
 fetters 752
 funds 802
 in – *service* 746
 tear asunder one's
  – 750
 – of harmony 714
bondsman 746
bone *strength* 159
 dense 321
 hard 323
 bred in the – 5
 feel it in one's –
  510
 – of contention
  713, 720
 one – and one flesh
  903
 – to pick *difficulty*
  704
 discord 713
 – setter 662
bonehouse 363
boner 495
bones [*see* bone]
 corpse 362
 music 417
 break no – 648
 make no – 602,
  705
boneyard 363
bonfire 382
 festivity 840
 celebration 883
 make a – of 384
bonhomie 703, 906
bonhomme 996
Boniface 890
bonne 746, 753
 – bouche *end* 67
 pleasant 377
 savoury 394
 saving 636
 à la – heure 602,
  831
 de – volonté 602
bonnet 225
bonny 836, 845
bono: cui –
 intention 620
 utility 644
 inutility 645
 pro – publico **644,**
  910
bonus *extra* 641
 gift 784
 money 810
bony 323
bonze 996

breach *crack* 44
  gap 198
  quarrel 713
  violation 925
  custom honoured
    in the – 614
  – of faith 940
  – of law 83, 964
  – of the peace 713
bread 298
  beg – 765
  selfish 943
  quarrel with –
    and butter 699
  – of idleness 683
  – of life *Christ* 976
  piety 987
  – upon the waters
    638
  – and wine 998
breadbasket 191
breadth 202
  chiaroscuro 420
break
  fracture 44
  discontinuity 70
  change 140
  gap 198
  carriage 272
  crumble 328
  disclose 529
  cashier 756
  violate 773, 927
  bankrupt 808
  – away 623
  – bread 298
  – bulk 297
  – camp 293
  – of day *morning*
    125
  twilight 422
  – down *destroy*
    162
  fall short 304
  decay 659
  fail 732
  dance 840
  – one's fetters 614
  – forth 295
  – ground 66
  – a habit 614
  – the heart *pain*
    828, 830
  dejection 837
  – the ice 888
  – in *ingress* 294
  domesticate 370
  teach 537
  tame 749
  – in upon *derange*
    61

inopportune 135
hinder 706
– a lance 716, 722
– a law 83
– loose 671, 750
– one's neck
powerless 158
die 360
– the neck of
  task 676
  success 731
– the news 529
– no bones 648
– of 660
– off *cease* 142
relinquish 624
abrogate 756
– out *begin* 66
violent 173
disease 655
excited 825
– the peace 173,
  720
– Priscian's head
  568
– prison 750
– the ranks 61
– short 328
– silence 582
– the teeth 579
– the thread 70
– through the
  clouds *visible*
  446
disclose 529
– through a cus-
  tom 614
– up *disjoin* 44
decompose 49
end 67
revolution 146
destroy 162
– up of the system,
  360, 655
– on the wheel
  physical pain 378
  mental pain 830
  punishment 972
– with 713
– with the past
  146
– word *deceive* 545
improbity 940
breaker
  of horses 268
  reef 346
  wave 348
breakers 348, 667
  surrounded by –
    704
  – ahead 665

breakfast 298
breakneck
  precipice 217
  rash 863
breakwater
  refuge 666
  obstruction 706
breast *interior* 221
  confront 234
  convex 250
  mind 450
  oppose 708
  soul 820
  at the – 129
  in the – of 620
  – the current 719
  – high 206
breastplate 717
breastwork 717
breath *instant* 113
  breeze 349
  life 359
  animality 364
  faint sound 405
  with bated – 581
  hold – *quiet* 265
  expect 507
  wonder 870
  not a – of air 265,
    382
  out of – 688
  in the same – 120
  shortness of – 688
  take – 265, 689
  take away one's –
    unexpected 508
  fear 860
  wonder 870
breathe *exist* 1
  blow 349
  live 359
  faint sound 405
  evince 467
  mean 516
  inform 527
  disclose 529
  utter 580
  speak 582
  refresh 689
  – freely 827, 834
  – one's last 360
  not – a word 528
breathing time 687,
  723
breathless
  voiceless 581
  out of breath 688
  feeling 821
  fear 860
  eager 865
  wonder 870

– attention 457
– expectation 507
– impatience 865
– speed 684
bred in the bone 820
breech 235
– loader 727
breeches 225
  wear the – 737
  – buoy 666
  – maker 225
  – pocket
  money 800, 802
breed *kind* 75
  multiply 161
  progeny 167
  animals 370
  rear 537
breeding 161, 852,
  894
breeze *wind* 349
  discord 713
breezy 836
brethren 997
breve 413
brevet
  warrant 741
  commission 755
  permit 760
  – rank 873
breviary 998
brevier 591
brevity 201, 572
brew 41, 673
brewing
  impending 152
  storm – 665
bribe *equivalent* 30
  tempt 615
  offer 763
  gift 784
  buy 795
  expenditure 809
  reward 973
bric-à-brac 847
brick *hard* 323
  pottery 384
  material 635
  trump 939, 948
  make -s without
    straw 471
  – colour 434
brickbat 727
bricklayer 690
bride 903
bridewell 752
bridge 45, 627
  – over *join* 43
  facilitate 705
  make peace 723
  compromise 774

bumpkin 876
bumptious
  proud 878
  insolent 885
  contemptuous 930
bun 298
bunch *collection* 72
  protuberance 250
  – light 599
bunchbacked 243
Buncombe
  [*see* bunkum]
Bund 712
bundle *packet* 72
  go 266
  – on 275, 684
  – out 297
bung 263
  – up 261
bungalow 189
bungle 59, 699
bungler 701
bunion 259
bunk 186, 215
bunker 191
bunkie 890
bunkum *lie* 544
  style 577
  boast 884
  flattery 933
bunting 550
buoy *raise* 307
  float 320
  hope 858
buoyant
  floating 305
  light 320
  elastic 325
  prosperous 734
  cheerful 836
  hopeful 858
bur *clinging* 46
  sharp 253
  rough 256
  in engraving 558
burden *lading* 190
  weight 319
  melody 413
  poetry 597
  too much 641
  clog 706
  oppress 828
  care 830
  – the memory 505
  – of a song
  repetition 104
burdensome
  [*see* burden]
  hurtful 649
  labouring 686
bureau *chest* 191

office 691
shop 799
tribunal 966
bureaucracy 737
bureaucrat 694
burgee 550
burgeon
  [*see* bourgeon]
burgess 188
burgh 189
burgher 188
burghmote 966
burglar 792
  – alarm 669
burglary 791
burgomaster 745
burgrave 745
burial 363
buried *deep* 208
  imbedded 229
  hidden 528
  – in a napkin 460
  – in oblivion 506
burin 553
burke 361
burlesque
  imitation 19
  travesty 21
  absurdity 497
  misrepresent 555
  drama 599
  comic 853
  ridicule 856
burletta 599
burly 192
burn *near* 197
  rivulet 348
  hot 382
  consume 384
  near the truth
    480*a*
  excited 825
  love 897
  punish 972
  – the candle at
    both ends
  waste 638
  exertion 686
  prodigal 818
  – daylight 683
  – one's bridges 604
  – one's fingers 699
  – in 384
  – out 385
  – to 865
burner 423
burning [*see* burn]
  passion 821
  angry 900
  – glass 445
  – with curiosity

455
  – pain 378
  – shame 874
burnish *polish* 255
  shine 420
  beautify 845
burnous 225
burnt [*see* burn]
  red 434
  – offering 952, 990
burr 410
burrock 706
burrow *lodge* 184
  excavate 252
bursar 801
bursary 802
burst *disjoin* 44
  instantaneous 113
  explosion 173
  brittle 328
  sound 406
  paroxysm 825
bubble –
  disclosure 529
  all over 729
ready to –
  replete 641
  excited 824
  – of anger 900
  – away 623
  – of eloquence 582
  – of envy 921
  – into a flame 825
  – forth *begin* 66
  expand 194
  be seen 446
  –ing with health
    654
  – with grief 839
  – in 294
  – of laughter 838
  – out 295
  – upon *arrive* 292
  unexpected 508
  – into tears 839
burthen
  [*see* burden]
bury *enclose* 229
  inter 363
  conceal 528
  – the hatchet 918
  – one's talent 528
busboy 746
busby 225
bush *branch* 51
  jungle 344
  shrub 367
  beat about the –
    629
bushel *much* 31
  multitude 102

receptacle 191
size 192
hid under a – 460
not hide light un-
  der a – 878
bush-fighting 720
bushing 224
bushranger 792
bushy 256
business *event* 151
  topic 454
  occupation 625
  commerce 794
  full of – 682
  man of –
  proficient 700
  consignee 758
  mind one's –
  incurious 456
  attentive 457
  careful 459
  let alone 748
  send about one's
    297
  stage – 599
business-like
  orderly 58
  business 625
  active 682
  practical 692
  skilful 698
buskin *dress* 225
  drama 599
buss *boat* 273
  courtesy 894
  endearment 902
bust 554
bustle *energy* 171
  dress 225
  agitation 315
  activity 682
  haste 684
  difficulty 704
bustling
  [*see* bustle]
  eventful 151
busy 682
busybody 532, 682
but
  on the other hand
    30
  except 83
  limit 233
  qualifying 469
  – now 118
butcher *kill* 361
  provisions 637
  evil-doer 913
butler 746
butt *cask* 191
  push 276

aim 620
attack 716
laughing-stock 857
– in 294, 682
– end 67
butte 206
butter 356
flattery 933
– bread on both sides 641
– not melt in mouth 894
buttered *side*
know – *skill* 698
selfish 943
not know – 699
butter-fingers 701
butterfly
variegated 440
fickle 605
beauty 845
gaudy 882
break – on wheel
waste 638
spite 907
butter-scotch 396
buttery 636
buttock 235
button *fasten* 43
fastening 45
little 193
hanging 214
knob 250
trifle 643
ake by the – 586
– hole 586
– up *close* 261
restrain 751
– up one's pockets 808
buttoned-up
reserved 528
buttonholer 841
buttons *page* 746
button-top
useless 645
buttress
strengthen 159
support 215
defence 717
butyraceous 355
buxom 836
buy 795
– a pig in a poke 621
– and sell 794
buzz *hiss* 409
insect cry 412
publish 531
news 532

buzzard *fool* 501
blind as a – 442
between hawk and –
agitation 315
worry 828
by *alongside* 236
instrumental 631
go – *pass* 303
– air mail 684
– and by 121, 132
– the card 82
– the hour &c.
hire 788
– itself 87
– means of 632
– no means 32
have – one 637, 777
– my troth &c. 535
– the way
à propos 9
beside the purpose 10
parenthetical 134
– wire 684
– wireless 684
bye *departure* 293
sequestered 893
bygone 122, 506
let –s be bygones 918
by-law 963
by-name 565
by-path 279
by-play 527, 550
byre 189
byssus 256
bystander 197, 444
byway 627
by-word
maxim 496
cant term 563
reproach 574
contempt 930

C

C 3 160
cab 272
cabal *plan* 626
confederacy 712
cabala 526, 993
cabalistic 528, 992
cabaret 599
cabasset 717
cabbage 791
caber, tossing the – 840
cabin 189, 191

cabined, cribbed, confined 751
cabinet
photograph 554
receptacle 191
workshop 691
council 696
– picture 556
cable 45, 205
news 531, 532
slip – 623
telegraphic – 534
cabman 268, 694
caboose 386
cabriolet 272
cacation 299
cache 189, 530, 636, 666
cachet 550
lettre de – 751
cachexy 160, 655
cachinnation 838
cacique 745
cackle *of geese* 412
chatter 584
talk 588
laugh 838
cacodemon 980
cacoëthes 613, 865
– loquendi 584
– scribendi 590
cacography 590
caconym 563
cacophony
stridor 410
discord 414
style 579
Cacus 792
den of – 791
cad *servant* 746
vulgar 851
plebeian 876
cadastre 86, 466
cadaverous
corpse 362
pale 429
hideous 846
caddie 746
caddy 191
cadeau 784
cadence *pace* 264
fall 306
sound 402
music 415
cadenza 415
cadet *junior* 129
soldier 726
officer 745
cadge 765
cadger *idler* 683
beggar 767

huckster 797
cadi 967
cadit quæstio 479
cadmium 439
cadre 726
caduceus 993
caducity
fugacity 111
age 128
impotence 158
decay 659
cæcum 261
Cæsar 745
aut – aut nullus
ambition 865
fame 873
cæsura
disjunction 44
discontinuity 70
cessation 142
interval 198
cætera desunt 53
cæteris paribus 27
café 189
cafeteria 189
caftan 225
cage *receptacle* 191
restrain 751
prison 752
Cagliostro 548, 994
cahotage 59, 315
Cain 361
mark of – 550
raise – 825
caique 273
cairn 363, 550
caisse
grand – 417
caisson 191
caitiff *churl* 876
ruffian 913
villain 949
cajolery
imposition 544, 545
persuasion 615
flattery 933
cake *stick* 46
food 298
consolidate 321
sweet 396
– walk 840
calabash 191
calamity *evil* 619
adversity 735
suffering 830
calamo, currente – 590
calash *cap* 225
vehicle 272
calcedony 847

– appetite 865
canister 191
canker *disease* 655
  deterioration 659
  bane 663
  pain 830
canned goods 670
cannel coal 388
cankered
  sullen 901*a*
cankerworm 663
  evil-doer 913
  care 830
cannibal 913
cannibalism 945
cannon
  collision 276
  loud 404
  arms 727
  – fodder 726
  –'s mouth *war* 722
  courage 861
cannonade 716
cannonball 249, 274
cannoneer 726
cannot 471
cannular 260
canny 498, 702
  ca' – 864
canoe 273
  paddle one's own
  – 748
canon *rule* 80
  ravine 198
  music 415
  belief 484
  precept 697
  priest 996
  rite 998
  – law 697
canonical
  regular 82
  inspired 985
  ecclesiastical 995
canonicals 999
canonist 983
canonization
  repute 873
  deification 991
  rite 998
canonry 995
canopy 223
  – of heaven 318
canorous 413
cant *oblique* 217
  jerk 276
  hypocrisy 544
  neology 563
  impiety 988
cantabile 415
cantankerous 901,

901*a*
cantata 415
  missa – 998
cantatrice 416
canteen 189, 191
canter 266, 274
  win at a – 705
canterbury
  receptacle 191
Canterbury tale
  546
cantharides 171
canticle 415
cantilever 215
canting 855
cantle 51
cantlet 32, 51
canto 597
canton 181, 737
cantonment 184,
  189
cantrap 993
canty 836
canvas *sail* 267
  picture 556
  under press of –
  274
canvass
  investigate 461
  discuss 476
  dissert 595
  solicit 765
canvasser 767
canyon 350
canzonet 415, 597
caoutchouc 325
cap *be superior* 33
  height 206
  summit 210
  cover 223
  hat 225
  retaliate 718
  complete 729
  salute 894
  fling up one's –
  838
  Fortunatus's – 993
  set one's – at 897,
  902
  – and bells 844
  – fits 23
  – in hand
  request 765
  servile 886
  respect 928
  – of maintenance
  747
capability
  endowment 5
  power 157
  skill 698

facility 705
capacious *space* 180
  – memory 505
capacity
  endowment 5
  power 157
  space 180
  size 192
  intellect 450
  wisdom 498
  office 625
  talent 698
cap-à-pie
  complete 52
  armed –
  prepared 673
  defence 717
  war 722
caparison 225
cape *height* 206
  cloak 225
  projection 250
capella, alla – 415
caper *leap* 309
  dance 840
capful *quantity* 25
  small 32
  – of wind 349
capillament 205
capillary
  hairlike 205
  thin 203
capital *city* 189
  top 210
  letter 561
  important 642
  excellent 648
  money 800
  wealth 803
  make – out of
  pretext 617
  acquire 775
  print in –s 642
  – messuage 189
  – punishment 972
capitalist 803
capitation 85
  – tax 812
capitol 189, 717
capitular 995, 996
capitulate 725
capnomancy 511
capon 373
caponize 38, 158
capote 225
capouch 999
capper 548
capriccio *music* 415
  whim 608
caprice 608

out of – 615*a*
capricious
  irregular 139
  changeable 149
  irresolute 605
  whimsical 608
capriole 309
capsize 218, 731
capsized 732
capstan 307, 633
capstone 210
capsular 252
capsule *vessel* 191
  tunicle 223
  medicine 662
captain 269, 745
captandum, ad –
  sophistry 477
  deception 545
  affectation 855
  ostentation 882
  flattery 933
captation 933
captious
  capricious 608
  irascible 901
  censorious 932
caption
  taking 789
  beginning 66
  heading 564
captivate
  induce 615
  restrain 751
  please 829
captivated 827
captivating 829, **897**
captive
  prisoner 754
  adorer 897
  lead – 749
  make – 751
  – balloon 273
captivity 751
capture 789
Capuchin 996
caput 696
  – mortuum 645,
  653
caquet 584
car 272
carabineer 726
carack 273
caracole 309
caracoler 266
carafe 191
caramel 396
carambole 276
carapace 717
cara sposa 897
carat 319

cartes sur table 525, 543
Carthago, delenda est – 908
Carthusian 996
cartilage
  dense 321
  hard 323
  tough 327
cartography 466, 554
cartoon 21, 556
cartoonist 559
cartouche
  ammunition 727
  ornament 847
cartridge 727
cartulary 86, 551
caruncle 250
carve *cut* 44
  make 161
  form 240
  sculpture 557
  apportion 786
  – one's way 282
carvel 273
carver 559
caryatides 215
Cary's chickens, Mother – 668
cascade 348
case *state* 7
  box 191
  sheath 223
  topic 454
  argument 476
  specification 527
  grammar 567
  affair 625
  patient 655
  law-suit 969
  be the – 1, 494
  in good – 654, 734
  in –
  circumstance 8
  event 151
  supposition 514
  make out a – 467, 924
  – in point 23, 82
caseation 321
caseharden
  strengthen 159
  habituate 613
case-hardened
  callous 376, 823
  obstinate 606
casemate 189, 717
casement 260
casern 189
cash *money* 800

pay 807
in – 803
pay – for 795
  – account 811
  – book 551
  – box 802
  – down 807
  – register 85, 553, 802
cashier *dismiss* 756
  treasurer 801
casing 223
casino 712; 840
cask 191
casket 191
casque 717
Cassandra 513, 668
cassation 552
casserole 191
Cassiopeia's chair 318
cassock 999
cast *mould* 21
  small quantity 32
  spread 73
  tendency 176
  form 240
  throw 284
  tinge 428
  aspect 448
  drama 599
  reject 610
  plan 626
  company 712
  give 784
  allot 786
  condemn 971
  give one a – 707
  set on a – 621
  – about for 463
  – accounts 811
  – adrift *disperse* 73
  eject 297
  liberate 750
  dismiss 756
  – anchor 265, 292
  – aside 460
  – aspersions 934
  – away 610, 638
  lost 732
  – behind one
  forget 506
  refuse 764
  relinquish 782
  – away care 836
  – off clothes 645
  – of countenance 448
  – of the dice 156
  – in a different

mould 18
– dishonour &c. upon 874
  – to the dogs 162
  – down 308, 837
  – in the eye 443
  – the eyes back 122
  – eyes on 441
  – the eyes over 457
  – a gloom 837
  – off a habit 614
  – iron 323
  resolute 604
  – in one's lot with 609
  – lots 621
  – lustre upon 420
  – of mind 820
  – a nativity 511, 992
  – one's net 463
  – off *divest* 226
  disused 678
  dismiss 756
  relinquish 782
  – over-board 678
  – the parts 60
  – reflection upon 932
  – in the same mould 17
  – a shade 421
  – the skin 226
  – a slur 874
  accuse 938
  – a spell 992
  – off trammels 750
  – up *add* 85
  happen 151
  eject 297
castanet 417
castaway *exile* 893
  reprobate 949
caste 75, 873
  lose – 940
castellan 746, 753
castellated 717
caster *cruet* 191
  wheel 312
castigate 932, 972
castigator 936
casting 21
casting – vote 480
  – weight 28, 30
castle *at chess* 148
  abode 189
  defence 717
  – in the air *impossible* 471

imagination 515
  hope 858
Castle of Indolence 683
castor *hat* 225
Castor and Pollux 89, 890
castrametation 189, 722
castrate *subduct* 38
  impotent 158
casual *extrinsic* 6
  chance 156
  uncertain 475
  lax 773
casualty *event* 151
  killed 361
  evil 619
  misfortune 735
casuist 476
casuistry
  sophistry 477
  falsehood 544
  duty 926
casus belli
  quarrel 713
  irritation 824, 900
casus fœderis 770
cat *nine lives* 359
  animal 366
  keen sight 441
  fall on one's feet 734
  cross 901
  gib –, tom – *male* 373
  rain –s and dogs 348
  let – out of bag 529
  – boat 273
  – burglar 792
  – call *whistle* 417
  disapproval 932
  –'s cradle 219
  – and dog life 713
  as the – jumps
  event 151
  see how the – jumps 510
  fickleness 607
  caution 864
  – o' nine tails 975
  – in pattens 652
  –'s paw *dupe* 547
  instrumental 631
  use 677
  auxiliary 711
catabasis 36
catachresis 521, 523

cataclysm
  convulsion 146
  destruction 162
  deluge 348
catacomb 363
catacoustics 402
catadupe 348
catafalque 363
catalectic 597
catalepsy 265, 376, 683
catalogue 60, 86
catalysis 49, 140
catamaran 273, 726
catamenial 138, 299
cataphonics 402
cataplasm 662
catapult 284, 726, 727
cataract
  waterfall 348
  blindness 442, 443
catarrh 299
catastrophe
  disaster 619
  finish 729
  misfortune 735
  end 67
catch *imitate* 19
  fastening 45
  song 415
  detect 480a
  joke 497
  gather the meaning 518
  cheat 545
  receive 785
  take 789
  by −es 70
  no great − 651
  − at *willing* 602
  desire 865
  − the attention 457
  − one's death 360
  − a disease 655
  − the ear 418
  − the eye 446
  − fire 384
  − a glimpse of 441
  − an idea 498
  − the infection
  excitation 824
  − a likeness 554
  − a sound 418
  − at straws
  overrate 482
  credulous 486
  unskilful 699
  rash 863

− by surprise 508
− a Tartar *dupe* 547
  retaliate 718
− in a trap 545
− tripping 480a
− up 789
catching
  infectious 657
catchpenny
  deceiving 545
  trumpery 643
  cheap 815
catchpoll 965
catchword 550
catechism 461, 484
  church − 983a
catechize 461
catechumen 541, 997
categorical
  positive 474
  demonstrative 478
  affirmative 535
categorically true 494
category 7, 75
  in the same − 9
catena 69
catenary 245
catenation 69
cater 298, 637
caterpillar tractor 271
caterwaul
  cat-cry 412
  discord 414
  courting 902
cates 298
catgut 417
− scraper 416
cathartic 652
cathedrâ, ex −
  affirm 535
  school 542
  authority 737
  audacity 885
cathedral 1000
Catherine wheel 840
catholic
  universal 78
  religious 987
− church 983a
  Roman − 984
catholicon 662
Catiline 941
catopsis 441
catoptrics 420
catoptromancy 511
cattle 271, 366

− truck 272
catwalk 273, 627
Caucasian mystery 983
caucus 696
caudal 67, 235
caudate 214
caudex 215
Caudine forks 162
cauf 370
caught tripping 491
caulk 660
cause *source* **153**
  law-suit 969
  final − 620
  take up the − of 707
  tell the − of 522
  −d by 154
causeless
  casual 156
  aimless 621
causerie 588
causeway 627
causidical 965
caustic
  energetic 171
  feeling 821
  painful 830
  gruff 895
  malevolent 907
  − *curve* 245
cautel 864
cautelâ, ex abundanti − 664
cautery 384
caution *warn* 668
  prudence 864
  security 771
  want of − 863
cavalcade 69, 266
cavalier
  horseman 268
  rash 863
  insolent 885
  discourteous 895
  contemptuous 930
cavaliere servente
  servile 886
  lover 897
cavalry 726
cavatina 415
cave *dwelling* 189
  cell 191
  cavity 252
  − *canem* 864
  − of Adullam 624, 832
  − in *hollow* 252
  submit 725
caveat

  warning 668
  command 741
− emptor 769
cavendo tutus 664, 864
cavern [*see* cave]
cavernous 252
caviare 392, 393
  − to the general 850
cavil *sophistry* 477
  dissent 489
  censure 932
caviller 936
cavity 252
caw 412
cayak 273
cayenne 392, 393
cazique 745
cease 142
  − to breathe 360
  − to exist 2
ceaseless 112
cecity 442
cede *submit* 725
  relinquish 782
  give 784
ceiling 206, 210, 223
celare artem, ars − 698
cela va sans dire
  conformity 82
  consequence 154
celebrant 990
celebration **883**, 998
celebrity 873, 875
celerity 274
celeste 417
celestial
  physical 318
  religious 976
  heaven 981
celibacy **904**
cell *abode* 189
  receptacle 191
  cavity 221, 252
  prison 752
  hermitage 893
cellar 191
cellaret 191
cello 417
cellular 191, 252
cement
  medium 45
  unite 43, 46, 48
  covering 223
  hard 323
  material 635
  − a party 712
cemented
  concord 714

cry 411
aid 707
pleasure 827
relief 834
mirth 836
rejoicing 838
amusement 840
courage 861
sociality 892
welcome 894
applaud 931
good – *hope* 858
high living 957
cheerfulness 836
cheerless 830, 837
cheeseparings
  remains 40
  dirt 653
  economy 817
chef de cuisine
  servant 746
chef-d'œuvre 648,
  698
cheka 696
chemin
  – de fer
    game 840
  – faisant 270
chemise 225
chemist 662
Chemistry 144
  organic – 357
cheque 800
chequer 440
  – roll 86
cherchez la femme
  155
chère amie 962
cherish *aid* 707
  love 897
  endearment 902
  – a belief 484
  – feelings &c. 821
  – an idea &c. 451
cheroot 392
cherry
  – red 434
  two bites of a –
    overrate 482
    roundabout 629
    clumsy 699
cherry-cheeked
  845
cherry-coloured
  434
cherub 977
Cheshire cat 838
chess 840
chessboard 440
chest 191, 802
chestnut-colour 433

cheval-de-bataille
  plea 617
  plan 626
  vanity 880
cheval-glass 445
chevalier 875
  – d'industrie 792
chevaux de frise
  253, 717
chevron
  angle 217
  indication 550
  badge 747
  decoration 877
chew 298
  – the cud 451
  – tobacco 392
chiaroscuro
  light 420
  grey 432
  painting 556
chiasma 43
chic 845, 882
chicane
  sophistry 477
  deceit 545
  cunning 702
chicken 129, 366
  – in every pot 733
  count –s before
    hatched 858,
    863
  tender as a – *soft*
    324
    sensitive 822
    compassionate
    914
chickenhearted 862
chide 932
chief *principal* 642
  master 745
  evidence in – 467
  – constable 765
  – part 31
Chief Justice 967
chiefdom 737
chieftain 745
chiffonnier 876
chiffonnière 191
chignon 225
chilblain 383
child
  infant 129
  offspring 167
  fool 501
  – of God 987
  –'s play 643, 705
  with – 161
childbirth 161
childhood 127
childish

credulous 486
  foolish 499
  feeble 575
  – treble 581
childlike 703
chiliad 98
chill *cold* 383
  render cold 385
  indispose 616
  – the spine 830,
    860
chillies 393
Chiltern Hundreds
  757
chime
  repetition 104
  roll 407
  resonance 408
  melody 413
  – in with *agree* 23
  conform 82
  assent 488
  concord 714
chimera 83, 515
chimney 260, 351
  – corner 189
  – pot 249
china 384, 557
China to Peru 180
chine 235
chinese white 430
chink *gap* 198
  sound 408
  money 800
chip *small* 32
  detach 44
  bit 51
  reduce 195
  – of the old block
    similar 17
    copy 21
    offspring 167
chippy 962
Chirography 590
Chirology 550
Chiromancy 511
chirp
  bird-note 412
  sing 416
  cheerful 836
  rejoice 838
chirrup [see chirp]
chirurgery 662
chisel
  fabricate 161
  form 240
  sharp 253
  sculpture 557
chit 129, 193
chit-chat 588
chitterlings 221

chivalry *war* 722
  tenure 777
  courage 861
  courtesy 894
  philanthropy 910
  honour 939
  generosity 942
chlamys 225
chloroform 376, 823
chlorophyl 435
chlorotic 655
chock full 52
chocolate
  food 298
  colour 433
choice *will* 600
  election 609
  excellent 648
  absence of – **609a**
  by – 600
  – spirits 873
  – of words 569
choir *sing* 416
  church music 996
  church 1000
  – boy 996
  – invisible 360,
    977
choke *close* 261
  stifle 361
  redundant 641
  hinder 706
  –full *complete* 52
  replete 639
  –off 706
choler 900
choleric 901
choose 609
  do what one –s **748**
chop *disjoin* 44
  change 140
  – logic 476
  – up 201
chopfallen 837
chopper 330
chopping
  large 192
  – sea 348
chops *mouth* 66
  jaws 231
  food 298
chorale 415
chord 413
chore 625
choreography 840
chorister 416, 996
chorography 183
chorus
  shout 411
  song 415
  singers 416

clear-obscure 420
cleat 45
cleavage
  cutting 44
  structure 329
cleave *sunder* 44
  adhere 46
  bisect 91
cleaver 253
cledge 342
clef 413
cleft *divided* 44
  bisected 91
  chink 198
in a – stick
  difficulty 704
clem 956
clement
  lenient 740
  long-suffering
  826
  compassionate
  914
clench *compact* 769
  retain 781
  take 789
clepe 564
clepsydra 114
clerestory 191, 1000
clergy 996
clerical 995, 996
– error 495
– staff 746
clerk *scholar* 492
  recorder 553
  writer 590
  helper 711
  servant 746
  agent 758
  clergy 996
  articled – 541
– in holy orders
  995
– of works 694
clerkship
  commission 755
cleromancy 511
clever
  intelligent 498
  skilful 698
  smart 842
  too – by half 702
clew *ball* 249
  interpretation 522
  indication 550
seek a – 461
click 406
client
  dependant 746
  customer 795
clientship

subjection 749
cliff *height* 206
  vertical 212
  steep 217
  land 342
climacteric 128
climate *region* 181
  weather 338
  fine – 656
climatology 338
climax
  supremacy 33
  summit 210
  culmination 729
climb 305
– on the band-
  wagon 731
clime 181
clinal 217
clinch *fasten* 43
  close 261
  certify 474
  pun 563
  complete 729
  clutch 781
  snatch 789
– an argument 47
– the fist at 909
clincher 479
cling *adhere* 46
– to *near* 197
  willing 602
  persevere 604*a*
  habit 613
  observe 772
  desire 865
  love 897
– to hope 858
– to one another
  709
clinic 662
clink
  resonance 408
  stridor 410
  prison 752
clinker *brick* 384
  dirt 653
clinometer
  oblique 217
  angle 244
clinquant
  ornament 847
  vulgar 851
Clio 594
clip *shorten* 201
– the wings
  powerless 158
  speed 264
  slow 275
  useless 645
  hinder 706

prohibit 761
– one's words 583
clipper 273
clipping
  small piece 51
clique *conclave* 696
  party 712
cloaca *conduit* 350
  foul 653
Cloacina 653
cloak *dress* 225
  conceal 528
  disguise 530
cloaked 223
cloche 371
clock 114
clockwork 633
by – *uniform* 16
  order 58
  regular 80
clod *lump* 192
  earth 342
  fool 501
  bungler 701
clodhopper 876
clodpated
  stupid 499
clog *shoe* 225
  hinder 706
– *dance* 840
cloison 228
cloisonné 557
cloister *arcade* 189
  way 627
  restraint 751
  convent 1000
close *similar* 17
  tight 43
  end 67
  field 181
  court 189
  near 197
  narrow 203
  shut 261
  dense 321
  warm 382
  hidden 528
  concise 572
  taciturn 585
  complete 729
  stingy 819
  examine –ly 457
keep – *hide* 528
  retain 781
tread – upon 281
– the door upon
  restrain 751
– the ears 419
– the eyes
  die 360
  not see 442

– one's eyes to
  not attend 458
  set at naught 773
– at hand
  to-morrow 121
  imminent 152
  near 197
– the hand
  refuse 764
– in upon 290
– inquiry 461
–ly packed 72
– prisoner 754
– quarters 197
  approach 286
  attack 716
  battle 722
– one's ranks 673
– study
  thought 451
  attention 457
– up 197, 290
– with *cohere* 46
  assent 488
  attack 716
  contend 720
  consent 762
  compact 769
close-mouthed 585
closet
  receptacle 191
  ambush 530
closeted with
  conference 588
  advice 695
close-up 197
closure 142, **261**
clot *solidify* 321
  earth 342
cloth *vocation* 625
  napkin 652
  clergy 996
clothes 225
  grave – 363
– basket 191
clothier 225
Clotho 601
clotpoll 501
clotted 352
cloud
  assemblage 72
  multitude 102
  mist 353
  shade 424
  screen 530
break through the
  –s 446
drop from the –s
  508
in a – 475, 528
in the –s

comfit 396
comfort
　pleasure 377
　delight 827
　content 831
　relief 834
　give – 906
comfortable
　pleasing 829
comforter
　covering 223
Comforter 976
comfortless
　painful 830
　dejected 837
comic *wit* 842
　ridiculous 853
　– opera 599
　– strips 531
coming [*see* come]
　impending 152
　– events
　　prediction 511
　– out 883
　– time 121
comitia 696
comity 894
comma 142
　inverted –s 550
command *high* 206
　requisition 630
　authority 737
　order **741**
　possess 777
　at one's –
　　obedient 743
　– belief 484
　– of language
　　writing 574
　　speaking 582
　– of money 803
　– one's passions
　　944
　– respect 928
　– one's temper
　　826
　– a view of 441
commandant 745
commandeer 744,
　789
commander 269
commanding
　[*see* command]
　important 642
commando 726
commandment 697
comme deux
　gouttes d'eau 17
comme il faut
　taste 850
　fashion 852

genteel 875
commemorate 883
commence 66
commencement de
　la fin *end* 67
　destruction 162
commend 931
　– the poisoned
　　chalice 544
commendable 944
commensurate
　accordant 23
　numeral 85
　adequate 639
comment
　reason 476
　judgment 480
　interpretation 522
　criticize 595
commentary 595
commentator 492,
　524, 527
commerce
　conversation 588
　barter 794
　cards 840
commercial 811
　– arithmetic 811
　– traveller 758
commère 599
commination 908,
　909
commingle 41
comminute 330
commiserate 914
commissariat 637
commissary
　provisions 637
　consignee 758
commission
　task 625
　delegate **755,** 759
　Royal – 696
　– of the peace 965
commissioner 758
commissionaire
　doorkeeper 263
　messenger 534
　consignee 758
commissure 43
commis-voyageur
　758
commit *do* 680
　delegate 755
　cards 840
　arrest 969
　– an absurdity 853
　– oneself to a
　　course 609
　– to the flames
　　384

　– to memory 505
　– oneself
　　clumsy 699
　　promise 768
　– to prison 751
　– sin 945
　– to writing 551
committee
　council 696
　consignee 758
　(*director* 694)
commix 41
commode 191
commodious 644
commodity 798
commodore 745
common
　general 78
　ordinary 82
　plain 344
　habitual 613
　trifling 643
　base 876
　in – *related* 9
　　participate 778
　right of – 780
　short –s 640
　tenant in – 778
　make – cause 709
　– consent 488
　– council 966
　– course 613
　– herd 876
　– law *old* 124
　　law 697, 963
　– measure 84
　– origin 153
　– parlance 576
　– place 82
　– place book
　　record 551
　　compendium 596
　– saying 496
　– sense 498
　– sewer 653
　– stock 778
　– weal
　　mankind 372
　　good 618
　　utility 644
　　philanthropy 910
Common Pleas
　Court of – 966
commonalty 876
commoner 876
commonplace
　usual 82
　known 490
　plain 576
　habit 613
　unimportant 643

dull 843
commons 298
commonwealth
　territory 181
　community 372
　authority 737
commorant 188
commotion 315
communalism 778
commune
　township 181
commune with 588
　– oneself 451
communibus annis
　29
communicant 990
communicate
　join 43
　tell 527
　correspond 592
　give 784
　sacrament 998
communication
　news 532
　of disease 657
　oral – 582, 588
communion
　discourse 588
　society 712
　participation 778
　sacrament 998
　hold – with 888
　– table 1000
communiqué 527
communism 737
communist
　party 712
　rebel 742
　participation 778
　philanthropy 910
　evil doer 913
community
　party 712
　– at large 372
　– of goods 778
commutation
　compensation 30
　substitution 147
　interchange 148
　compromise 774
　barter 794
commutual 12
compact
　joined 43
　united 87
　receptacle 191
　small 193
　compressed 195
　compendious 201
　dense 321
　bargain **769**

[437]

COM · COM · COM · COM

compages
whole 50
structure 329
compagination 43
companion *match*
17
accompaniment
88
ladder 305
friend 890
companionable 892
companionship 892
companionway 305
company
assembly 72
actors 599
party, partnership 712
troop 726
sociality 892
bear – 88
in – *with* 88
comparable 9
comparative 464
degree 26
– *anatomy* 368
comparatively 32
compare 464
– *notes* 695
comparison 464
compartition 44
compartment
part 51
region 181
place 182
cell 191
carriage 272
compass
degree 26
space 180
surround 227
measure 466
intend 620
guidance 693
achieve 729
box the –
direction 278
rotation 312
keep within –
moderation 174
fall short 304
economy 817
points of the – 236
in a small – 193
– *about* 229
– *of thought* 498
compassion 914
object of – 828
compatible
consentaneous 23
possible 470

[438]

compatriot
inhabitant 188
friend 890
compeer *equal* 27
friend 890
compel 744
compellation 564
compendency 43
compendious 201
compendium 596
book 593
compensate
make up for 30
requite 973
compensation 30
compère 599
competence
power 157
sufficiency 639
skill 698
wealth 803
competition
opposition 708
contention 720
competitor
opponent 710
combatant 726
candidate 767
compilation
collect 72
book 593
compendium 596
compile 54
complacent
pleased 827
content 831
courteous 894
kind 906
complain 839
complainant 938
complaint
illness 655
murmur 839
lodge a – 938
– *without cause*
839
complaisant
lenient 740
courteous 894
kind 906
complement
adjunct 39
remainder 40
part 52
arithmetic 84
complementary
correlation 12
colour 428
complete
entire 52
accomplish 729

compact 769
– *answer* 479
– *circle* 311
in a – *degree* 31
completeness 52
completion 729
complex 59
complexion
state 7
colour 428
appearance 448
compliance
conformity 82
obedience 743
consent 762
observance 772
complicate
derange 61
complicated
disorder 59
convolution 248
complice 711
complicity 709
compliment
courtesy 894, 896
praise 931
poor – 932
–s *of season* 896
complimentary
free 815
complot 626
comply [*see* compliance]
compo *coating* 223
material 635
component 56
componere lites
723, 724
comport
– *oneself* 692
– *with* 23
compos mentis 502
compose
make up 54, 56
produce 161
moderate 174
music 416
write 590
printing 591
pacify 723
assuage 826
composed
self-possessed 826
composer
music 413
composite 41
composition 54
[*see* compose]
combination 48
piece of music 415
picture 556

style 569
writing 590
building material
635
compromise 774
barter 794
atonement 952
compositor
printer 591
compost 653
composure 826, 871
compotation 959
compote 298
compound
mix 41
combination 48
limited space 182
enclosure 232
compromise 774
– *arithmetic* 466
– *for substitute* 147
barter 794
comprador 637
comprehend
compose 54
include 76
know 490
understand 518
comprehension [*see*
comprehend]
intelligence 498
comprehensive 76
complete 50
general 78
wide 192
– *argument* 476
compress
contract 195
curtail 201
condense 321
remedy 662
compressible 322
comprise 76
comprobation
evidence 467
demonstration 478
compromise
dally with 605
mid-course 628
taint 659
danger 665
pacify 723
compact 769
compound 774
atone 952
compromised
promised 768
compter 799
compte rendu
record 551
accounts 811

confer *advise* 695
 give 784
 – benefit 648
 – power 157
 – privilege 760
 – right 924
 – with 588
conference [*see*
 confer]
 council 696
confess *assent* 488
 avow 529
 penitence 950,
 998
 – and avoid 937
confession [*see*
 confess]
 auricular – 998
 – of faith 983
confessional 1000
confessions
 biography 594
confessor 996
confidant 711
confidante
 servant 746
 friend 890
confidence
 trust 484
 hope 858
 courage 861
 in – 528
 – trick 545
confident 535
configuration 240
confine
 region 182
 circumscribe 229
 limit 231, 233
 imprison 751
confined
 narrow judgment
 481
 ill 655
confinement
 childbed 161
confines of
 on the – 197
confirm
 corroborate 467
 assent 488
 consent 762
 compact 769
 rite 998
confirmed 150
 – habit 613
confiscate *take* 789
 condemn 971
 penalty 974
confiture 396
conflagration 382,

 384
conflexure 245
conflict
 opposition 708
 discord 713
 contention 720
conflicting
 contrary 14
 counteracting 179
 – evidence 468
confluence
 junction 43
 convergence 290
 river 348
conflux
 assemblage 72
 convergence 290
conform *assent* 488
 – to rule 494
conformable 23,
 178
conformation 54,
 240
conformity 82, 178
confound
 disorder 61
 destroy 162
 not discriminate
 465a
 perplex 475
 defeat 731
 astonish 870
 curse 908
confounded
 great 31
 bad 649
confraternity
 party 712
 friendship 888
confrère
 colleague 711
 friend 890
confrication 331
confront *face* 234
 compare 464
 oppose 708
 resist 719
 – danger 861
 – witnesses 467
confucianism 984
Confucius 986
confuse *derange* 61
 perplex 458
 obscure 519
 not discriminate
 465a
 abash 879
confused *disorder*
 59
 invisible 447
 uncertain 475

 style 571
confusion
 [*see* confuse]
 – seize 908
 – of tongues 560,
 563
 – of vision 443
 – worse-con-
 founded 59
confutation 479
congé 293, 756
 – d'élire 995
congeal *dense* 321
 cold 385
congeneric
 similar 17
 included 76
congenial
 related 9
 agreeing 23
 concord 714
 love 897
congenital 5, 820
congeries 72
congestion 641
conglaciation 385
conglobation 72
conglomerate
 cohere 46
 assemblage 72
 council 696
 dense 321
conglutinate 46
congratulate 896
 – oneself 838
congratulation 896
congregation
 assemblage 72
 worshippers 990
 laity 997
Congregationalist
 984
congress
 assembly 72
 convergence 290
 conference 588
 council 696
Congressional
 Medal 733
Congressional
 Record 551
congreve *fuel* 388
 – rocket 727
congruous
 agreeing 23
 (*expedient* 646)
conical *round* 249
 pointed 253
conjecture 475, 514
conjoin 43
conjoint 48

conjointly 37
conjugal 903
conjugate
 words 562
 grammar 567
 – in all its tenses
 &c. 104
conjugation
 junction 43
 pair 89
 phase 144
 grammar 567
conjunction 43
 in – with 37
conjuncture
 contingency 8
 occasion 134
conjure *deceive* 545
 entreat 765
 sorcery 992
 name to – with
 873
 – up *recall* 505
 – up a vision 505
conjuror
 deceiver 548
 sorcerer 994
**connaître le des-
 sous des cartes**
 490
connate
 intrinsic 5
 kindred 11
 cause 153
connatural
 uniform 16
 similar 17
connect *relate* 9
 link 43
connection
 [*see* connect]
 kin 11
 in – with 9
connections
 cards 840
connective 45
conned, well – 490
connive
 overlook 460
 co-operate 709
 allow 760
connoisseur
 critic 480
 scholar 492
 taste 850
connotate 550
connote 516, 550
 imply 526
connubial 903
connuted 9
conoscente 850

conquer 731
conquered
 (*failure* 732)
conquering hero
 comes 883
conqueror 731
consanguinity **11**
consciarecti, mens–
 pride 878
 innocence 946
conscience
 knowledge 490
 moral sense 926
 in all – *great* 31
 affirmation 535
 awakened – 950
 qualms of – 603
 clear – 946
 stricken – 950
 tender – 926
 honour 939
conscientious 926
 scrupulous 939
 – objector 489
conscious
 intuitive 450
 knowledge 490
 – of disgrace 874
 – of glory 873
conscript 726
conscription 744
consecrate *use* 677
 dedicate 873
 sanctify 987
 holy orders 995
consecration
 rite 998
consectary 478
 – reasoning 476
consecution 63
consecutive
 following 63
 continuous 69
 – fifth 414
consecutively
 slowly 275
consensus 488
 – of opinion 23
consent *assent* 488
 compliance **762**
 with one – 178
consentaneous
 agreeing 23
 (*expedient* 646)
consequence
 event 151
 effect 154
 importance 642
 in – 478
 of no – 643
 take the –s 154

consequent 63
consequential
 deducible 478
 arrogant 878
consequently
 reasoning 476
 effect 154
conservation
 permanence 141
 storage 636
 preservation 670
conservatism 141,
 670
conservative 141,
 712
 – policy 681
conservatoire 542
conservator
 of the peace 967
conservatory
 receptacle 191
 floriculture 371
 furnace 386
 store 636
conserve 396, 636
consider *think* 451
 attend to 457
 examine 461
 adjudge 480
 believe 484
considerable
 in degree 31
 in size 192
 important 642
considerate
 careful 459
 judicious 498
 benevolent 906
consideration
 purchase money
 147
 thought 451
 idea 453
 attention 457
 qualification 469
 inducement 615
 importance 642
 gift 784
 benevolence 906
 respect 928
 requital 973
 deserve – 642
 in – of
 compensation 30
 reasoning 476
 on – 658
 take into –
 thought 451
 attention 457
 under –
 topic 454

inquiry 461
 plan 626
considered, all
 things –
 collectively 50
 judgment 480
 premeditation 611
 imperfection 651
consign
 transfer 270
 commission 755
 property 783
 give 784
 – to the flames 384
 – to oblivion 506
 – to the tomb 363
consignee **758**
consignor 796
consignment
 commission 755
 gift 784
 apportionment
 786
consilience 178
consist
 – in 1
 – of 54
consistence
 density 321
consistency
 uniformity 16
 agreement 23
consistently with
 82
consistory
 council 696
 church 995
consolation
 relief 834
 condole 915
 religious 976
console
 table 215
Consoler
 the – 976
consolidate
 unite 46, 48
 condense 321
consols 802
consommé 298
consonant
 agreeing 23
 musical 413
 letter 561
consort
 accompany 88
 associate 892
 spouse 903
 – with 23
consortium 23
consortship 892

conspection 441
conspectus 596
conspicuous
 visible 446
 famous 873
conspiracy 626
conspirator 626
 traitor 941
conspire
 concur 178
 co-operate 709
constable
 policeman 664
 governor 745
 officer 965
constant
 fixed 5
 uniform 16
 continuous 69
 regular 80
 continual 112
 frequent 136
 regular 138
 immutable 150
 exact 494
 persevering 604*a*
 obey 743
 faithful 939
 – flow 69
constellation
 stars 318
 luminary 423
 glory 873
consternation 860
constipation
 closure 261
 density 321
constituency 181,
 737
constituent 51, 56
constitute
 compose 54, 56
 produce 161
constitution
 nature 5
 state 7
 composition 54
 structure 329
 charter 924
 law 963
constitutional
 walk 266
 – government **737**
constrain
 compel 744
 restrain 751
 abash 881
constraint 195
constrict 195, 706
constringe 195
construct 161

aid 707
give 784
contribution 784
  lay under – 789,
  924
contrition
  abrasion 331
  regret 833
  penitence 950
contrivance 633
contrive
  produce 161
  plan 626
  – *to succeed in* 731
contriving
  cunning 702
control
  power 157
  influence 175
  regulate 693
  authority 737
  restrain 751
  board of – 696
  under –
  obedience 743
  subjection 749
controller of
  currency 801
controls 273, 693
controversial
  discussion 476
  discordant 713
controversialist
  476, 726
controversy
  disagreement 24
  discussion 476
  debate 588
  contention 720
controvert
  deny 536
controvertible
  uncertain 475
  debatable 476
  untrue 495
contumacy
  obstinacy 606
  disobedience 742
contumely
  arrogance 885
  rudeness 895
  disrespect 929
  scorn 930
  reproach 932
contund 330
contuse 330
conundrum *pun*
  520
  riddle 533
  wit 842
convalescence 654,

660
convection 270
convenance
  mariage de – 903
convene 72
conveniences 632
convenient 646, 705
convent 1000
conventicle
  assembly 72
  council 696
  chapel 1000
convention
  agreement 23
  assembly 72
  rule 80
  council 696
  precept 697
  treaty of peace
  723
  compact 769
  –s *of society* 852
conventional 82,
  613
conventual 996,
  1000
convergence 290
convergent 286
conversable
  talk 588
  sociable 892
conversant
  know 490
  skilful 698
conversation 588
conversational
  loquacious 584
  interlocution 588
  sociable 892
conversazione 588,
  892
converse
  reverse 14
  talk 588
conversely 468
conversion 144
  trover and – 964
convert
  change to 140, 144
  opinion 484
  tergiversation 607
  religion 987
  – *to use* 677
convertible 13, 27
  – terms 522
convexity 250
convey
  transfer 270
  mean 516
  assign 783
  – *away* 791

– the knowledge
  of 527
conveyance
  [*see* convey]
  vehicle 272
conveyancer 968
conveyancing 783
convict
  convince 484
  condemned 949
  condemn 971
convicted, self –
  950
conviction
  confutation 479
  belief 484
  prove guilty 971
convince
  belief 484
  confute 479
  teach 537
convivial 892
convocate 72
convocation
  council 696
  church 995
convoke 72
convolution
  coil 248
  rotation 312
convoy
  accompany 88
  transfer 270
  guard 664
  escort 753
convulse
  derange 61
  violent 173
  agitate 315
  bodily pain 378
  mental pain 830
convulsed with
  – *laughter* 838
  – *rage* 900
convulsion
  [*see* convulse]
  disorder 59
  revolution 146
  in –s 315
coo 412
cook *heat* 384
  falsify 544
  improve 658
  prepare 673
  servant 746
  too many –s 699
  – *accounts* 811
cool *moderate* 174
  cold 383
  refrigerate 385
  grey 432

dissuade 616
cautious 864
indifferent 866
unamazed 871
unfriendly 889
discourteous 895
look – upon
  unsocial 893
take –ly 826
– down 826
– one's heels
  kept waiting 133
  inaction 681
cooler 387
coolheaded
  judicious 498
  unexcitable 826
coolie
  bearer 271
  military 726
coolness
  insensibility 823
  estrangement 898
coon-can 840
coop *abode* 189
  restrain 751
  prison 752
co-operation
  physical 178
  voluntary 709
  participation 778
co-operator 690, 71?
co-optation 609
co-ordinate
  equal 27
  arrange 60
  measure 466
cootie 653
cop 664
copal 356a
coparcener 778
copartner
  accompanying 88
  participator 778
  associate 890
copartnership
  co-operation 709
  party 712
cope *equal* 27
  oppose 708
  contend 720
  canonicals 999
copia verborum
  diffuse 573
  loquacious 584
coping stone
  top 210
  completion 729
copious
  diffuse style 573
  abundant 639

coportion 778
copper *money* 800
  policeman 664
copper-coloured
  433, 439
copper-plate
  engraving 558
  writing 590
coppice 367
coprolite 653
copse 367
copula 45
copulation 43
copy
  imitate 19
  facsimile 21
  prototype 22
  news 532
  record 551
  represent 554
  write 590
  for the press 591
  plan 626
  − *book* 22
copyhold 780
copyist
  imitator 19
  artist 559
  writer 590
copyright 780
coquet *lie* 544
  change the mind
  607
  affected 855
  endearment 902
  flattery 933
  − *with*
  irresolute 605
coquette
  affected 854, 855
  flirt 897
coquillage 847
coracle 273
coral 847
  − *reef* 667
coram judice
  jurisdiction 965
  lawsuit 969
cor Anglais 417
corbeille 191
corbel 215
cord *tie* 45
  filament 205
cordage 45
cordated 245
cordial
  pleasure 377
  dram 392
  willing 602
  remedy 662
  feeling 821

[444]

grateful 829
friendly 888
courteous 894
cordiform 245
cordite 727
cordon
  inclosure 232
  circularity 247
  decoration 877
  − bleu 733, 746
  − sanitaire
    safety 664
  preservation 670
corduroy 259
cordwainer
  shoemaker 225
  artificer 690
core *gist* 5
  source 153
  centre 222
  gist 642
  true to the − 939
coriaceous 327
Corinthian 850
co-rival
  [*see* corrival]
cork *plug* 263
  lightness 320
  − jacket 666
  − up *close* 261
  restrain 751
corking pin 45
corkscrew
  spiral 248
  perforator 262
  circuition 311
cormorant
  desire 865
  gluttony 957
corn
  projection 250
Cornaro 953
cornea 441
corned 959
cornelian 847
corneous 323
corner *place* 182
  receptacle 191
  angle 244
  monopoly 777
  − *creep into a* −
    893
  in a dark − 528
  drive into a − 706
  push into a − 874
  rub off −s 82
  − *turn a* − 311
  turn the − 658
  − stone
  support 215
  importance 642

defence 717
cornet *music* 417
  officer 745
cornice 210
corniculate 253
cornification 323
Cornish hug 545
corno 417
cornopean 417
cornucopia 639
cornute
  projecting 250
  sharp 253
corollary
  adjunct 39
  deduction 480
corona 247
coronach 839
coronation
  enthronement 755
  celebration 883
coroner 363, 965
  −'s *jury* 967
coronet *hoop* 247
  insignia 747
  title 877
corporal
  corporeal 316
  officer 745
corporate 43
  − *body* 712
corporation
  bulk 192
  convex 250
  association 712
  jurisdiction 965
corporeal 3, 316,
  364
  − hereditaments
    780
corporeity 316
corps *assemblage* 72
  troops 726
  à − *perdu*
    haste 684
    rash 863
  − de reserve 636
corpse 362
corpulence 192
corpus 316
  − Christi 998
  − delicti
    guilt 947
    lawsuit 969
  − juris
    precept 697
    law 963
corpuscle
  small 32
  little 193
corradiation

focus 74
  convergence 290
corral 232, 370
correct
  orderly 58
  true 494
  inform 527
  disclose 529
  improve 658
  repair 660
  due 924
  censure 932
  honourable 939
  virtuous 944
  punish 972
  − ear 416, 418
  − memory 505
  − reasoning 476
  − style
  grammatical 567
  elegant 578
correction
  [*see* correct]
  house of − 752
  under − 879
corrective 662
corregidor 745
correlation
  relation 9
  reciprocity 12
correspondence
  correlation 12
  similarity 17
  agreement 23
  writing 592
  − *course* 537
correspondent
  messenger 534
  journalist 593
  consignee 758
corresponding
  similar 17
  agreeing 23
corridor *region* 181
  place 191
  passage 627
  − train 272
corrigendum 495
corrigible 658
corrival 726
corrivalry 720
corrivation 348
corroborant 662
corroboration
  evidence 467
  assent 488
corrode *burn* 384
  erode 659
  afflict 830
corrosive
  [*see* corrode]

creditable *right* 924
creditor 805
credo quia
    impossibile 486
credulity 486
credulous person
    dupe 547
creed *belief* 484
    theology 983
    Apostles' – 983*a*
creek *interval* 198
    water 343
creel 191
creep *crawl* 275
    tingle 380
    (*inactivity* 683)
    – in 294
    – into a corner 893
    – into the good
        graces of 933
    – out 529
    – upon one 508
    - with
        multitude 102
        redundance 641
creeper 367
creeping
    sensation 380
    – thing 366
creese 727
cremation
    of corpses 363
    burning 384
crematorium 363,
    386
crematory 386
crème de la crème
    648
Cremona 417
crenate 257
crenelle 257
crenulate 257
creole 57
crêpe 248, 839
crepidam, ultra –
    471
crepitation 406
crepuscule
    dawn 125
    dusk 422
crescendo
    increase 35
    musical 415
crescent
    growing 35
    street 189
    curve 245
cresset 423, 550
crest *supremacy* 33
    summit 210
    pointed 253

tuft 256
sign 550
armorial 877
pride 878
on the – 33
crest-fallen
    dejected 837
    humble 879
crevasse 198, 667
crevice 198
crew *assemblage* 72
    inhabitants 188
    mariners 269
    party 712
crib *bed* 215
    key 522
    granary 636
    steal 791
    parsimony 819
cribbage 840
cribbed, confined,
    cabined – 751
cribble 260
cribriform 260
Crichton,
    Admirable –
        scholar 492
        perfect 650
        proficient 700
crick *pain* 378
cricket *game* 840
    not – 940
    – ground 213
crier 534
    send round the –
        531
crim. con. 961
crime 945, 947
criminal 923, 945
    culprit 949
    – *law* 963
    court of – appeal
        966
criminality 947
criminate 938
crimp *crinkle* 248
    notch 257
    brittle 328
    deceiver 548
    take 789
    steal 791
crimple 258
crimson 434, 821
cringe *submit* 725
    subject 749
    servility 886
crinite 256
crinkle *angle* 244
    convolution 248
    roughen 256
    fold 258

crinoline 225
cripple *disable* 158
    weaken 160
    injure 659
crippled
    disease 655
crisis
    conjuncture 8
    present time 118
    opportunity 134
    event 151
    strait 704
    excitement 824
    bring to a – 604
    come to a – 729
crisp *rumpled* 248
    rough 256
    brittle 328
    style 572
Crispin 225
criss-cross 219
cristallomantia 511
criterion *test* 463
    evidence 467
    indication 550
crithomancy 511
critic *judge* 480
    taste 850
    detractor 936
critical
    contingent 8
    opportune 134
    discriminating
        465
    important 642
    dangerous 665
    difficult 704
    censorious 932
criticism
    judgment 480
    dissertation 595
    disapprobation
        932
    detraction 934
critique
    [*see* criticism]
croak *cry* 412
    hoarseness 581
    stammer 583
    warning 668
    discontent 832
    lament 839
croaker 832, 837
Croat 726
crochet 847
crock 191
crockery 384
crocodile tears 544
crocus *yellow* 436
Crœsus 803
croft 189, 232

Croix de Guerre 733
cromlech 363, 551
crone *veteran* 130
    fool 501
crony *friend* 890
    favourite 899
crook *curve* 245
    deviation 279
    thief 792
crooked
    sloping 217
    distorted 243
    angular 244
    latent 526
    crafty 702
    ugly 846
    dishonourable 940
    – *path* 704
    – *temper* 901
    – *ways* 279
croon 580
crop
    stomach 191
    harvest 154
    shorten 201
    eat 298
    vegetable 367
    store 636
    gather 775
    take 789
    second – 167, 775
    – out *visible* 446
    disclose 529
    – up *begin* 66
    take place 151
    reproduction 163
cropper *fall* 306
croquet *game* 840
    – ground *level* 213
croquette 298
crosier 747, 999
cross *mix* 41
    across 219
    pass 302
    grave 363
    oppose 708
    failure 732
    disaster 735
    refuse 764
    pain 830
    decoration 877
    fretful 901
    punishment 975
    rites 998
    fiery – 722
    proclaim at the –
        roads 531
    red – 662
    –ed bayonets 708
    – breed 83
    – cut 628

cub *young* 129
  vulgar 851
  clown 876
  unlicked – 241
cubby-hole 191
cube
  three dimensions
  92, 93
  form 244
cubicle 191
cubist 556
cubit 200
cucking stool 975
cuckold 905
cuckoldom 961
cuckoo
  imitation 19
  repetition 104
  sound 407
  cry 412
cuddle 197, 902
cudgel *beat* 276
  weapon 727
  punish 975
  take up the –s
  aid 707
  attack 716
  contention 720
  – one's brains
  think 451
  imagine 515
cue *hint* 527
  watchword 550
  plea 617
  rôle 625
  take one's – from
  695
  in proper – 698
cuff *sleeve* 225
  blow 276
  punishment 972
cui bono 644, 645
cuique voluptas
  sui – 865
cuirass 717
cuirassier 726
cuisine 298
  batterie de – 957
culbute
  inversion 218
  fall 306
cul-de-lampe
  engraving 558
  ornament 847
cul-de-sac
  concave 252
  closed 261
  difficulty 704
culinary 298
  – art 673
cull *dupe* 547

choose 609
  take 789
cullender 260
cullibility 486
cullion 949
cully *deceive* 545,
  547
culm 388
culminate
  maximum 33
  height 206
  top 210
  complete 729
culpability *vice* 945
  guilt 947
culprit 949
cult 983
cultivate *till* 365,
  371
  sharpen 375
  improve 658
  prepare 673
  aid 707
cultivated
  courteous 894
  – *taste* 850
cultivator 371
culture
  knowledge 490
  improvement 658
  taste 850
  politeness 894
culverin 727
culvert 350
cum multis aliis 37,
  102
cumber *load* 319
  obstruct 706
cumbersome
  incommodious
  647
  disagreeable 830
cummerbund 225
cumulative 72
  increasing 35
  assembled 72
  – evidence 467
  – vote 609
cumulus 353
cunctando restituit
  rem 681
cunctation 133
cuneiform 244
  – character 590
cunning
  prepense 611
  sagacious 698
  artful 702
  – fellow 700
  – man 994
cup *vessel* 191

hollow 252
  beverage 298
  remedy 662
  trophy 733
  tipple 959
  between – and lip
  111
  in one's –s 959
  – that cheers &c.
  298
  – of humiliation
  879
  dash the – from
  one's lips 509
  – too low 837
cupbearer 746
cupboard 191
cupellation 384
Cupid *beauty* 845
  love 897
  gods 979
cupidity
  avarice 819
  desire 865
cupola *height* 206
  roof 223
  dome 250
cup-tossing 621
cur *dog* 366
  coward 862
  sneak 949
curable 658, 660,
  662
curacy 995
curare 663
curate 996
curative 660
curator 694, 758
curb *moderate* 174
  slacken 275
  dissuade 616
  restrain 751
  shackle 752
curb exchange 621
curbstone 233
curd *density* 321
  pulp 354
  (*cohere* 46)
curdle *condense* 321
  (*cohere* 46)
  make the blood –
  830
curdled 352
cure *reinstate* 660
  remedy 662
  preserve 670
  benefice 995
curé 996
cureless 859
curfew 126
curia 966

curio 847
curiosa felicitas 698
curiosity
  unconformity 83
  inquiring 455
  phenomenon 872
curious
  exceptional 83
  inquisitive 455
  true 494
  beautiful 845
  desirous 865
curiously *very* 31
curl *bend* 245
  convolution 248
  hair 256
  cockle up 258
  badge 747
  – up one's lip 930
curling *game* 840
curmudgeon
  miser 819
  plebeian 876
currency
  publicity 531
  money 800
current *existing* 1
  usual 78
  present 118
  happening 151
  flow 264
  of water 348
  of air 349
  rife 531, 532
  language 560
  habit 613
  danger 667
  account – 811
  against the – 708
  go with the – 82
  pass –
  believed 484
  fashion 852
  stem the – 708
  – belief 488
  – of events 151
  – of ideas 451
  – of time 109
currente calamo
  590
curricle 272
curriculum 537
curry *food* 298
  rub 331
  condiment 392,
  393
  – favour with
  love 897
  flatter 933
curry-comb 370
curse *bane* 663

adversity 735
painful 830
malediction 908
cursed bad 649
cursitor 968
cursive 590
cursory
  transient 111
  inattentive 458
  hasty 684
  take a – view of
    457
  neglect 460
curst 901a
curt short 201
  concise 572
  taciturn 585
curtail retrench 38
  shorten 201
  –ed of its fair pro-
    portions
  distorted 243
  ugly 846
curtain 223
  shade 424
  hide 528, 530
  theatre 599
  fortification 717
  behind the –
    invisible 447
    inquiry 461
    knowledge 490
  close the – 528
  raise the – 529
  rising of the – 448
  – lecture 932
  – raiser 66, 599
curtsy
  stoop 308, 314
  submit 725
  polite 894
curule 696
curvature 245
curvet leap 309
  turn 311
  oscillate 314
  agitate 315
curvilinear 245
  – motion 311
cushion pillow 215
  soft 324
  relief 834
cushy 829
cusp angle 244
  sharp 253
cuspidor 191
cuss 908
custard 298
custodes? quis cus-
  todiet – 459
custodian 753

custody safe 664
  captive 751
  retention 781
  in – prisoner 754
  accused 938
  take into – 751
custom old 124
  habit 613
  barter 794
  sale 796
  tax 812
  fashion 852
  – honoured in
    breach 614
customary
  [see custom]
  regular 80
customer 795
custom-house 799
  – officer 965
custos 753
  – rotulorum 553
cut divide 44
  bit 51
  discontinuity 70
  interval 198
  curtail 201
  layer 204
  form 240
  notch 257
  blow 276
  eject 297
  reap 371
  physical pain 378
  cold 385
  neglect 460
  carve 557
  engraving 558
  road 627
  attack 716
  portion 786
  affect 824
  mental pain 830
  dance step 840
  decline acquaint-
    ance 893
  discourtesy 895
  tipsy 959
  – short 628
  unkindest – of all
    pain 828
    malevolence 907
  – across 302
  – adrift 44
  – along 274
  have a – at 716
  – away 274
  – a whetstone with
    a razor
    sophistry 477
    waste 638

misuse 679
  – both ways 468
  – capers 309
  – according to
    cloth
  economy 817
  caution 864
  – and come again
  repeat 104
  enough 639
  – dead 893
  – direct 893
  – down destroy 162
  shorten 201
  fell 308
  kill 361
  – down expenses
    817
  – and dried
  arranged 60
  prepared 673
  – a figure
  appearance 448
  fashion 852
  repute 873
  display 882
  – the first turf 66
  – the ground from
    under one
  confute 479
  hinder 706
  – to the heart 824,
    830
  – ice with
    influence 175
  – of one's jib 448
  – jokes 842
  – the knot 705
  – off subduct 38
  disjoin 44
  kill 361
  impede 706
  bereft 776
  secluded 893
  – off with a shil-
    ling 789
  – open 260
  – out surpass 33
  stop 142
  substitute 147
  plan 626
  – out for 698
  – out work
    prepare 673
    direct 693
  – to pieces
    destroy 162
    kill 361
  – a poor figure 874
  – to the quick 830
  – up root and

branch 162
  – up rough 900
  – and run 274
  depart 293
  escape 623
  – short stop 142
  destroy 162
  shorten 201
  silence 581
  – one's stick
  depart 283
  avoid 623
  – one's own throat
    699
  – and thrust 716
  – in two 91
  – up divide 44
  destroy 162
  pained 828
  give pain 830
  discontented 832
  dejected 837
  censure 932
  what one will – up
    for 780
  – one's way
    through 302
cutaneous 223
cute 698
cuticle 223
cutlass 727
cutlery 253
cut-purse 792
cutter 273
cut-throat
  killer 361
  evil-doer 913
cutting sharp 253
  cold 383
  path 627
  affecting 821
  painful 830
  reproachful 932
cuttings
  excerpta 596
  selections 609
cutty stool 950
cwt. 98, 319
cyanogen 438
cyanide of potas-
  sium poison 661
cycle time 106
  period 138
  circle 247
  ride 266
  vehicle 272
  – car 272
cyclist 268
cycloid 247
cyclometer 200
cyclone

rotation 312
wind 349
cyclopædia
  knowledge 490
  book 593
Cyclopean
  strong 159
  huge 192
Cyclops
  monster 83
  mighty 159
  huge 192
  dupe 547
cygne
  chant du – 360
  – noir 650
cylindric 249
cyma 847
cymbal 417
cymbalo 417
cymophanous 440
cynic
  misanthrope 911
  detractor 936
  ascetic 955
  closet – 893
cynical
  contemptuous 930
  censorious 932
  detracting 934
cynicism
  discourtesy 895
  contempt 930
cynosure *sign* 550
  direction 693
  wonder 870
  repute 873
Cynthia of the
  minute 149
cypher [*see* cipher]
cypress
  interment 363
  mourning 839
Cyprian 962
cyst 191
czar 745

D

da capo 104
dab *small* 32
  paint 223
  slap 276
  clever 700
dabble *water* 337
  dirty 653
  meddle 682
  fribble 683
dabbled *wet* 339
dabbler 493

dachshund 366
dacoit 792
dactyl 597
dactylogram 467
dactyliomancy 511
dactylonomy
  numeration 85
  symbol 550
dad 166
daddy 166
dado 211
dædal
  variegated 440
dædalian
  convoluted 248
  artistic 698
daft 503
dagger 727
  look –s *anger* 900
  threat 909
  air drawn – 515
  plant – in breast
  give pain 830
  speak –s 932
  at –s drawn
  opposed 708
  discord 713
  enmity 889
  hate 898
daggle *hang* 214
  dirty 653
dagobah 1000
Dagon 986
daguerreotype
  represent 554
  paint 556
dahabeah 273
Dail Eireann 696
daily
  frequent 136
  periodic 138
  – *occurrence*
  normal 82
  habitual 613
  – *paper* 531
dainty *food* 298
  savoury 394
  pleasing 829
  delicate 845
  tasty 850
  fastidious 868
dairy 191, 370
  – maid 746
dais *support* 215
  throne 747
daisy
  fresh as a – 654
  – pied 847
dale 252
dally *delay* 133
  irresolute 605

inactive 683
amuse 840
fondle 902
dalmatic 999
Daltonism 443
dam *parent* 166
  close 261
  pond 343
  obstruct 706
damage *evil* 619
  injure, spoil 659
  price 812
damages 974
damascene 440
damask 434
dame
  woman 374
  teacher 540
  lady 875
damn
  malediction 908
  condemn 971
  – with faint
    praise 932, 934
damnable 649
damnatory
  disapprove 932
  condemn 971
damnify
  damage 649
  spoil 659
damnosa hereditas
  663
Damocles
  sword of – 667
Damon and
  Pythias 890
damozel 129
damp
  moderate 174
  moist 339
  cold 385
  sound 405
  dissuade 616
  hinder 706
  depress 837
  dull 843
  – the sound 408a
damper 387
damsel
  youth 129
  female 374
Dan to Beersheba
  52, 180
Danaë 803
Danaos, timeo –
  doubt 485
  caution 864
dance
  jump 309
  oscillate 314

agitate 315
rejoice 838
sport 840
sociality 892
lead the – 175
lead one a –
  run away 623
  circuit 629
  difficult 704
  practical joke 929
  St. Vitus' – 315
  – attendance
    waiting 133
    follow 281
    servant 746
    petition 765
    servility 886
  – the back step
    283
  – upon nothing
    972
  – the war dance
    715
dance-band 417
dance-music 415
dander 900
Dandie Dinmont
  366
dandiprat 193
dandle 902
dandruff 653
dandy
  ship 273
  fop 854
dandyism 855
danger 665
  in – *liable* 177
  source of – 667
  – past 664
  – signal 669
dangerous
  [*see* danger]
  – classes 913
  – illness 655
  – person 667
dangle *hang* 214
  swing 314
  display 882
dangler 281
Daniel *sage* 500
  judge 967
dank 339
Dannemora 752
danseuse 599
dapper
  little 193
  elegant 845
dapple 433
dappled 440
darbies
  handcuffs 752

Darby and Joan
secluded 893
married 903
dare *defy* 715
face danger 861
– *not* 860
– *say probable* 472
believe 484
suppose 514
dare-devil
courage 861
rash 863
bluster 887
daring 861
unreserved 525
– *imagination* 515
dark
obscure 421
dim 422
black 431
blind 442
invisible 447
unintelligible 519
latent 526
joyless 837
insidious 940
in the –
ignorant 491
leap in the –
experiment 463
chance 621
rash 863
keep – *hide* 528
– *ages* 491
– *cloud* 735
view with – eyes
932
– *lantern* 423
darkly
see through a
glass – 443
darkness [*see* dark]
421
children of – 988
love – better than
light 989
powers of – 978
darky 431
darling *beloved* 897
favourite 899
darn 660
dart *swift* 274
propel 284
missile 727
– to and fro 684
Dartmoor 752
Darwinism 357
dash
small quantity 32
mix 41
swift 276

fling 284
mark 550
courage 861
cut a – *repute* 873
display 882
– *at resolution* 604
attack 716
– *board* 666
– *cup from lips* 761
– *down* 308
– *hopes*
disappoint 509
fail 732
dejected 837
despair 859
– *on* 274
– *off paint* 556
write 590
active 682
haste 684
– *of the pen* 590
dashed [*see* dash]
humbled 879
dashing
fashionable 852
brave 861
ostentatious 882
dastard 862
data *evidence* 467
reasoning 476
supposition 514
date *time* 106
chronology 114
datum 673
daub *cover* 223
paint 428
misrepresent 555
dirt 653
daughter 167
daunt 860
dauntless 861
Dauphin 875
davenport 191, 215
davit 214
Davus sum non
Œdipus
unintelligent 499
artless 703
dull 843
Davy Jones' locker
310
dawdle *tardy* 133
slow 275
inactive 683
dawk 534
dawn
precursor 64
begin 66
priority 116
morning 125
light 420

dim 422
glimpse 490
dawplucker 936
day
period 108
present time 118
light 420
all – 110
clear as –
certain 474
intelligible 518
manifest 525
close of – 126
decline of – 126
denizens of the –
366
good old –'s 122
have had its – 124
one fine – 119
open as – 703
order of the – 613
red letter – 642
see the light of –
446
– *after day*
diuturnal 110
frequent 136
– *by day*
repeatedly 104
time 106
periodic 138
– *after the fair*
135
–s gone by 122
– of judgment 121
happy as the – is
long 827, 836
– and night
frequent 136
labour – and night
686
–s numbered
transient 111
death 360
– one's own 731
– of rest 687
– star 423
– after to-morrow
121
– before yesterday
122
–s of week 138
all in –'s work 625
daybed 215
daybook *record* 551
accounts 811
daybreak
morning 125
dim 422
day-dream
fancy 515

hope 858
day-labourer 690
daylight 125, 420
see – *intelligible*
518
– *saving* 114
daymare 859
daze 420
dazed 376
dazzle
light 420
blind 422, **443**
put out 458
astonish 870
awe 928
dazzling
[*see* dazzle]
beautiful 845
de: – die in diem
time 106
periodic 138
– facto 1
– fond en **comble**
52
– novo 104
– omnibus **rebus**
81
– profundis 821
deacon 996
deaconry 995
dead *complete* 52
inert 172
colourless 429
lifeless 360
insensible 376
– against
contrary 14
oppose 708
more – than **alive**
688
– asleep 683
– beat
powerless 158
– certainty 474
– colour 556
– cut 893
– drunk 959
– failure 732
– flat 213
– heat 27
– languages 560
– letter
impotent 158
unmeaning 517
useless 645
laxity 738
exempt 927
illegal 964
– level 16
– lift *exertion* 686
difficulty 704, **706**

kill 361
play havoc 659
punish 972
decipher 522
decision
  judgment 480
  resolution 604
  intention 620
  law case 969
decisive
  certain 474
  proof 478
  commanding 741
  take a – step 609
deck *floor* 211
  beautify 847
declaim 531, 582
  – against 932
declamatory
  style 577
  speech 582
declaration
  affirmation 535
  law pleadings 969
  – of faith
  belief 484
  theology 983
  – of war 713
declaratory
  meaning 516
  inform 527
declare
  publish 531
declension
  [*see* decline]
  grammar 567
  backsliding 988
declensions 5
declination
  [*see* decline]
  deviation 279
  measurement 466
  rejection 610
decline *decrease* 36
  old 124
  weaken 160
  descent 306
  grammar 567
  be unwilling 603
  reject 610
  disease 655
  become worse 659
  adversity 735
  refuse 764
  - of day 126
  – of life 128
declivity *slope* 217
  descent 306
decoction 335, 384
decode 522
decollate 972

décolleté 226
decoloration 429
decomposition 49
deconsecrate 756
decontrol 158
décor 448, 599
decoration
  insignia 747
  ornament 847
  title 877
decorative 556
decorous
  [*see* decorum]
  fashionable 862
  proper 924
  respectful 928
decorticate 226
decorum
  fashion 852
  duty 926
  purity 960
décousu
  discontinuous 70
  failure 732
decoy *attract* 288
  deceive 545
  deceiver 548
  entice 615
decrease 36, 195
decree
  judgment 480
  order 741
  law 963, 969
decrement
  decrease 36
  thing deducted 40a
  contraction 195
decrepit *old* 128
  weak 158, 160
  disease 655
  decayed 659
decrepitate 406
decrescendo 36
decretal 741
decry *underrate* 483
  censure 932
  detract 934
decumbent 213
decuple 98
decursive 306
decurtation 201
decussation 219
dedecorous
  disreputable 874
  discourteous 895
dedicate *use* 677
  inscribe 873
deduce *deduct* 38
  infer 480
deducible
  evidence 467

proof 478
deduct *retrench* 38
  deprive 789
  subtract 813
deduction
  [*see* deduce]
  decrement 40a
  reasoning 476
deed *evidence* 467
  record 551
  act 680
  security 771
  –s of arms 720
  – without a name
  947
deem 484
deemster 967
deep *great* 31
  profound 208
  sea 341
  sonorous 404
  cunning 702
  plough the – 267
  – colour 428
  – in debt 806
  – game 702
  – knowledge 490
  – mourning 839
  – note 408
  – potations 959
  – reflection 451
  – sense 821
  – sigh 839
  – study 457
  in – water 704
deepen 35
deep-dyed
  intense 171
  black 431
  vicious 945
deep-felt 821
deep-laid *plan* 626
deep-mouthed
  resonant 408
  bark 412
  thrilling 821
deep-musing 458
deep-read 490
deep-rooted
  stable 150
  strong 159
  belief 484
  habit 613
  affections 820
deep-sea 208
deep-seated 208,
  221
deer 366
  in heart a – 862
deev 980
deface

destroy form 241
  obliterate 552
  injure 659
  render ugly 846
defalcation
  incomplete 53
  contraction 195
  shortcoming 304
  non-payment 808
defame *shame* 874
  censure 932
  detract 934
defamer 936
defatigation 841
default
  incomplete 53
  shortcoming 304
  neglect 460
  insufficiency 640
  debt 806
  non-payment 808
  in – of 187
  judgment by – 725
defaulter *thief* 792
  non-payer 808
  rogue 949
defeasance 756
defeat
  confute 479
  succeed 731
  failure 732
  – one's hope 509
defeatism 911
defecate 652
defecation 299
defect
  decrement 40a
  incomplete 53
  imperfect 651
  failing 945
defection
  relinquishment
  624
  disobedience 742
defective
  incomplete 53
  insufficient 640
  imperfect 651
defence
  plea 462
  resist **717**
  vindication 937
  first line of – 726
defenceless
  impotent 158
  weak 160
  exposed 665
defendant 938
defensible *safe* 664
  excusable 937
defensive alliance

712
defer 133
  – to *assent* 488
  submit 725
  respect 928
deference
  obedience 743
  humility 879
  courtesy 894
  respect 928
defiance 715, 909
  threat 909
  in – *opposition* 708
  set at – *disobey* 742
  – of danger 861
deficiency
  [*see* deficient]
  vice 945
deficient
  inferior 34
  incomplete 53
  shortcoming 304
  insufficient 640
  imperfect 651
deficit
  incompleteness 53
  debt 806
defigure 846
defile
  interval 198
  march 266
  dirt 653
  spoil 659
  shame 874
  impure 961
define
  specify 79
  limit 233
  explain 522
  name 564
definite
  [*see* define]
  visible 446
  certain 474
  exact 494
  intelligible 518
  manifest 525
  perspicuous 570
definition
  interpretation 522
definitive *final* 67
  affirmative 535
  decided 604
deflagration 384
deflate 195
deflation
  currency 800
deflect
  curve 245
  deviate 279
deflower

spoil 659
violate 961
defluxion
  egress 295
  flowing 348
defœdation 653,
  659
deform 241
deformity
  distortion 243
  ugliness 846
  blemish 848
defraud *cheat* 545
  swindle 791
defray 807
deft *suitable* 23
  clever 698
defunct 360, 362
defy 715
  disobey 742
  threaten 909
  – danger 861
dégagé *free* 748
  fashion 852
degenerate 659
deglutition 298
degradation
  deterioration 659
  shame 874
  dishonour 940
degree 26
  term 71
  honour 873
  by –s 26
  by slow –s 275
degustation 390
dehiscence 260
dehort
  dissuade 616
  advise 695
dehydrate 340
Dei gratiâ 924
deification 873, 981
deify
  honour 873
  idolatry 991
deign
  condescend 762
  consent 879
Deism
  heterodoxy 984
  irreligion 989
Deity 976
  tutelary – 664
dejection
  excretion 299
  melancholy **837**
déjeuner 298
délabrement 162
delaceration 659
delation 938

delator 527
delay 133
dele 552
delectable
  savoury 394
  agreeable 829
delectation 827
delectus 562
delegate
  transfer 270
  commission 755
  consignee 758
  deputy 759
delenda est
  Carthago
  destroy 162
  curse 908
delete 162
deleterious
  pernicious 649
  unwholesome 657
deletion 552
deletory
  destructive 162
deliberate
  slow 275
  think 451
  attentive 457
  leisure 685
  advise 695
  cautious 864
deliberately
  [*see* deliberate]
  late 133
  with premedi-
  tation 611
delicacy *weak* 160
  slender 203
  dainty 298
  brittleness 328
  texture 329
  savoury 394
  colour 428
  exact 494
  scruple 603
  ill health 655
  difficult 704
  pleasing 829
  beauty 845
  taste 850
  fastidious 868
  honour 939
  pure 960
  delicate ear 418
délice 377
delicious *taste* 394
  pleasing 829
delicti, corpus –
  guilt 947
  lawsuit 969
delicto, in

flagrante – **947**
delight
  pleasure 827
  pleasing 829
Delilah 962
delimit 233
delineate
  outline 230
  represent 554
  describe 594
delineator 559
delineavit 556
delinquency 304,
  947
delinquent 949
deliquation 335
deliquesce 36
deliquescence 335
deliquium
  paralysis 158
  fatigue 688
delirant reges
  plectuntur
  Achivi 739
delirium
  raving 503
  passion 825
  – tremens 503,
  959
delitescence
  invisible 447
  latency 526
  seclusion 893
deliver
  transfer 270
  utter 580, 582
  birth 662
  rescue 672
  liberate 750
  give 784
  relieve 834
  – as one's act **and**
  deed 467
  – the goods 729
  – judgment 480
  – a speech 582
deliverance 672
delivery
  [*see* deliver]
  bring forth 161
  cash on – 807
dell 252
Delphic oracle
  prophetic 513
  equivocal 520
  latent 526
delta 342
delude *error* 495
  deceive 545
deluge *crowd* 72
  water 337

flood 348
redundance 641
delusion
  [*see* delude]
  insane 503
  self – *credulous*
  486
delve *dig* 252
  till 371
  – into *inquire* 461
demagogue
  director 694
  malcontent 710
  rebel 742
demagogy 737
demand
  inquire 461
  order 741
  ask 765
  price 812
  claim 924
  in – *require* 630
  desire 865
  saleable 796
demarcation 233
dematerialize 317
demean oneself
  conduct 692
  humble 879
  dishonour 940
demeanour
  aid 448
  conduct 692
  fashion 852
demency 503
démenti 536
dementia 503
demerit 945
demesne
  abode 189
  property 780
demi- 91
demigod *hero* 861
  angel 948
demigration 266
demijohn 191
demi-jour 422
demi-lune 717
demi-mondaine
  plebeian 876
  licentious 962
demirep 962
demise *death* 360
  transfer 783
  lease 787
demisemiquaver
  413
demission 756
demit 757
demiurge
  deity 979

demivolt 309
demobilize 73
democracy *rule* 737
  commonalty 876
Democrats
  party 712
Democritus 838
demoiselle 129
demolish 479
demon *violent* 173
  bane 663
  devil **980**
  – in human shape
  913, 949
  – worship 991
demoniacal
  malevolent 907
  furious 824
  wicked 945
demonology
  demons 980
  sorcery 992
demonstration
  number 85
  proof **478**
  manifest 525
  ostentation 882
  ocular – 441, 446
demonstrative
  manifest 525
  indicative 550
  vehement 825
demonstrator 524
demoralize
  unnerve 158
  spoil 659
  vicious 945
Demosthenes 582
demotic 590
demulcent
  mild 174
  soothing 662
demur
  disbelieve 485
  dissent 489
  unwilling 603
  hesitate 605
  without – 602
demure
  grave 826
  sad 837
  affected 855
  modest 881
demurrage 133
demurrer 969
den *abode* 189
  study 191, 893
  sty 653
  prison 752
  – of thieves 791

denary 98
denaturalize
  corrupt 659
denaturalized
  abnormal 83
dendriform 242, 367
dendrology 369
denial
  negation 536
  refusal 764
  self– 953
denigrate 431
denization 748
denizen
  inhabitant 188
  freeman 748
  –s of the air 979
  –s of the day 366
Denmark, rotten in
  the state of –
  526
denomination
  class 75
  name 564
  sect 712
  religious – 983
denominational
  dissent 489
  theological 983
  – education 537
denominator 84
denote
  specify 79
  mean 516
  indicate 550
dénouement
  end 67
  result 154
  disclosure 529
  completion 729
denounce
  curse 908
  disapprove 932
  accuse 938
dense
  crowded 72
  ignorant 493
density **321**
dent 252, 257
dental 561
denticulated 253,
  257
dentifrice 652
dentistry 662
denude 226
denuded *loss* 776
  – of
  insufficient 640
denunciation
  [*see* denounce]
deny *dissent* 489

negative **556**
refuse 764
– oneself
  avoid 623
  seclude 893
  temperate 953
  ascetic 990
Deo volente 470,
  976
deobstruct 705
deodand 974
deodorize 399
  clean 652
deontology 926
deoppilation 705
deorganization 61
deosculation 902
depart 293
  – from
  deviate 15, 279
  relinquish 624
  – this life 360
departed
  non-existent 2
department
  class 75
  region 181
  business 625
departure 293
  new – 66
  point of – 293
depend *hang* 214
  contingent 475
  – upon
  be the effect of 154
  evidence 467
  trust 484
  – on circumstan-
  ces 475
depended on, to
  be –
  certain 474
  reliable 484
  honourable 939
dependency 777,
  780
dependent
  effect 154
  liable 177
  hanging 214
  puppet 711
  servant 746
  subject 749
deperdition 776
dephlegmation 340
depict 554, 556
  describe 594
depilation 226
depilatory 662
depletion 638, 640
deplorable *bad* 649

conduct 692
complete 729
command 741
happy – 972
– case 191
– food 298
– rider 534
desperado
rash 863
blusterer 887
evil-doer 913
desperate *great* 31
violent 173
impossible 471
resolved 604
difficult 704
excitable 825
hopeless 859
rash 863
anger 900
despicable
trifling 643
shameful 874
contemptible 930
despise 930
– *danger* 861
despite 30, 907
in – 708
despoil *injure* 659
take 789
rob 791
despond 837, 860
despot 745
despotism
authority 737
severity 739
arbitrary 964
despumate 652
desquamation 226
dessert 298
dessous des cartes
cause 153
latent 526
secret 533
connaître le – 490
dessus dessous
sens – 218
destination *end* 67
arrival 292
intention 620
destiny *chance* 152
fate 601
fight against – 606
destitute
insufficient 640
poor 804
refuge for – 666
destrier 726
destroy
demolish 162
injure 659

– hopes 859
– life 361
destroyed
[*see* destroy]
inexistent 2
failure 732
destroyer **165**
warship 726
evil-doer 913
destructive
bad 649
destructor 383
desuetude **614**
disuse 678
desultory
disordered 59
fitful 70
multiform 81
irregular in time
139
changeable 149
deviating 279
agitated 315
desume 788
detach 44
detached
irrelated **10**
loose 47
detachment
part 51
army 726
detail *describe* 594
special portions
79
allot 786
ornament 847
attention to –
457, 459
in – 51
details
minutiæ 32
unimportant 643
detain 781
detect 480*a*
detective 527, 664
detention 133, 751,
781
house of – 752
in house of – 938
détenu 754
deter *dissuade* 616
alarm 860
deterge *clean* 652
detergent
remedy 662
deterioration **659**
determinate
special 79
exact 474
conclusive 480
intended 620

determine *end* 67
define 79
cause 153
direction 278
satisfy 462
make sure 474
judge 480
discover 480*a*
resolve 604
determined
resolute 604
determinism 601
deterration 529
detersion 652
detersive 662
detest *dislike* 867
hate 898
detestable 649
dethronement
anarchy 738
abrogation 756
detonate
explode 173
sound 406
detortion *form* 243
meaning 523
détour *curve* 245
circuit 629
detract *subduct* 38
underrate 483
defame 934
slander 938
detraction 934
detractor 936
detrain 292
detriment
evil 619
deterioration 659
detrimental 649
detrition 330
detritus
fragments 51
deposit 270
powder 330
detrude
cast out 297
cut down 308
detruncate 38
deuce *two* 89
devil 978
play the – 825
– is in him 608
deuced *great* 31
painful 830
deus 976
– ex machinâ
aid 707
auxiliary 711
deity 976
sorcerer 994
deuterogamy 903

devastate
destroy 162
havoc 659
develop
increase 35
produce 161
expand 194
evolve 313
development **144**,
154
devexity
bending 217
curvature 245
deviate *vary* 20*a*
change 140
turn 279
diverge 291
circuit 629
– from 15
– from rectitude
940
– from virtue **945**
deviation **279**
device *motto* 550
expedient 626
artifice 702
devil
seasoned food 392
evil-doer 913
bad man 949
Satan 978
demon 980
fight like –s 722
have a – 503
machinations of
the – 619
play the – with
injure 659
malevolent 907
printer's – 591
raise the – 825
– may care
rash 863
indifferent 866
insolent 885
give the – his due
right 922
vindicate **937**
fair 939
– in one
headstrong **863**
temper 901
– to pay
disorder 59
violence 173
evil 619
failure 732
penalty 974
– take 908
– take the hind-
most

run away 623
haste 684
cowardice 862
–'s tattoo 407
devilish *great* 31
bad 649
malevolent 907
devious *curved* 245
deviating 279
circuitous 311
devisable 270
devise *imagine* 515
plan 626
bequeath 784
devised by the
enemy 546
devisee *possess* 779
receive 785
deviser 164
devitalize 158
devoid *absent* 187
empty 640
not having 777a
devoir *courtesy* 894
respect 928
devolve 783
– on 926
devote *destine* 601
employ 677
consecrate 873
– to destruction
908
– the mind to 457
– oneself to 604
devoted
habit 613
ill-fated 735
obedient 743
undone 828
friendship 888
love 897
devotee
zealot 682
aspirant 865
pious 987
fanatic 988
devotion [see de-
votee, devoted]
love 897
piety 987
worship 990
self – 942
devour
destroy 162
eat 298
gluttony 957
devoured by
feeling 821
devouring element
382
devout 987, 990

devoutless 989
devoutly 821
dew 339
shake as –drops
from lion's
mane 483
dewy eve 126
dexterous 238, 698
dextrality **238**
dey 745
dhow 273
diable:
avoir le – au corps
503
– à quatre
disorder 59
violence 173
loud 404
excitement 825
tirer le – par la
queue 804
diablerie 978, 992
diabolic
bad 649
malevolent 907
wicked 945
Satanic 978
Diacoustics 402
diacritical 550
diadem 747, 847
diaeresis 49
diagnosis 465, 655
diagnostic
special 79
experiment 463
indication 550
(intrinsic 5)
diagonal 217
diagram 554
dial 114
as the – to the sun
veracious 543
faithful 772
dialect 563
dialectic
argument 476
language 560
dialogism 586
dialogue 588
diameter 202
diametrically
opposite
contrariety 14
contraposition
237
diamond
lozenge 244
type 591
goodness 648
ornament 847
rough – 703

– cut diamond
cunning 702
retaliation 718
– jubilee 883
– wedding 883
Diana *moon* 318
chaste 960
goddess 979
diapason 413
diaper 847
diaphanous 425
diaphonics 402
diaphoresis 299
diaphragm 68, 228
diaporesis 475
diarchy 737
diarrhœa 299
diary 114, 551
diastole 194
diatessaron 413
diathermancy 384
diathesis
nature 5
state 7
temperament 820
diatonic 413
diatribe 932
dibble
perforator 262
till 371
dibs *money* 800
dicacity 885
dice 156, 621
on the – 470
dicer 621
false as –'s oaths
546
dichotomy
bisect 91
angle 244
dichroism 440
dichromatic 443
dickens 978
dicker 794
dicky 215, 225
dictaphone 553
dictate
write 590
enjoin 615
advise 695
authority 737
command 741
–s of society 852
dictator 694, 745
dictatorial
dogmatic 481
wilful 600
insolent 885
dictatorship 737,
739
diction 569

dictionary
list 86
words 562
book 593
dictum
judgment 480
maxim 496
affirmation 535
command 741
didactic 537
didder 383
diddle 545, 791
Diddler, Jeremy –
792
diduction 44
die *mould* 22
expire 360
engraving 558
hazard of the –
621
never say – 604a
not willingly let –
670
– away
vanish 4
decrease 36
cease 142
the – is cast 601
– with ennui 841
– for *desire* 865
endearment 902
– game 951
– hard
obstinate 606
resist 719
– in harness 143,
604a
– in the last ditch
604a
– with laughter
838
– from the mem-
ory 536
– and make no
sign 951
– out 2, 4
– of a rose in aro-
matic pain 822
– in one's shoes
972
– a violent death
361
– hard 710, 832
dies non *never* 107
rest 687
diet *food* 298
council 696
spare – 956
dietetics 662
differ 15
discord 713

agree to – 489
beg to – 489
– in opinion 489
– toto cœlo
  contrary 14
  dissimilar 18
  dissent 489
difference 15
  [*see* differ]
  numerical 84
  perception of –
  465
  split the – **774**
  – engine 85
different 15
  multiform 81
  – time **119**
differentia 15
differential 15, 84
  – calculus 85
differentiate 79, 465
differentiation
  calculation 85
  discrimination
  465
difficult 704
  – to please 868
difficulties
  poverty 804
  in – 806
difficulty 704
  question 461
diffide 485
diffident 860, 881
diffluent 348
diffraction 420
  – grating 445
diffuse *mix* 41
  disperse 73
  publish 531
  style 573
diffuseness 104, **573**
dig *deepen* 208
  excavate 252
  till 371
  – out 461
  – the foundations
  673
  – up 455, 480*a*
digamy 903
digest *arrange* 60
  boil 384
  think 451
  compendium 596
  plan 626
  prepare 673
  brook 826
diggings 189
dight *dress* 225
  ornament 847
digit 84

digitate 44
digitated 253
digladiation 720
dignify 873
dignitary
  clergy 996
dignity
  glory 873
  pride 878
  honour 939
dignus vindice
  nodus
  unintelligible 519
  difficulty 704
  prodigy 872
digress
  deviate 279
  style 573
digression
  circuit 629
dihedral 89
  – angle 244
dijudication 480
dike *gap* 198
  fence 232
  furrow 259
  gulf 343
  conduit 350
  defence 717
dilaceration 44
dilapidation 659
dilate
  increase 35
  swell 194
  widen 202
  rarefy 322
  expatiate 573
dilatory
  slow 275
  inactive 683
dilection 897
dilemma
  uncertain 475
  logic 476
  choice 609
  difficulty 704
dilettante 492, 850
dilettantism
  knowledge 490
diligence
  coach 272
diligent
  active 682
  – thought 457
dilly-dally
  irresolution 605
  inactivity 683
dilucidation 522
diluent 335
dilute *weaken* 160
  water 337

diluvian 124
dim *dark* 421
  faint 422
  invisible 447
  unintelligible 519
dime 800
dimension 192
dimidiate 91
diminish
  lessen 36
  contract 195
  – the number 103
diminutive 32, 193
diminuendo
  decreasingly 36
  music 415
dimness 422
dimple 252, 257
dimsightedness 443
  unwise 499
din 404
  – in the ear
  repeat 104
  drum 407
  loquacity 584
dine 298
  – with Duke
    Humphrey 87
ding 408
ding-dong
  repeat 104
  chime 407
dining-car 272
dining-room 191
dingle 252
dingy *boat* 273
  dark 421, 422
  colourless 429
  black 431
  gray 432
dinner 298
  – jacket 225
  – party 892
dint *power* 157
  concavity 252
  blow 276
  by – of
  instrumentality
  631
dio, sub – 220, 338
diocesan 996
diocese 181, 995
Diogenes
  recluse 893
  cynic 911
  lantern of –
  inquiry 461
dioptrics 420
diorama *view* 448
  painting 556
diorism 465

dip *slope* 217
  concavity 252
  ladle 270
  direction 278
  insert 300
  descent 306
  plunge 310
  water 337
  candle 423
  baptize 998
  – one's hands into
  take 789
  – into
  glance at 457
  inquire 461
  learn 539
diphthong 561
diploma
  evidence 467
  commission 755
diplomacy
  artfulness 702
  mediation 724
  negotiation 769
diplomatist
  messenger 534
  expert 700
  consignee 758
dipper 191
dipsomania
  insanity 503
  desire 865
  drunkenness 959
dipsomaniac 504
diptych 86, 551
dire *hateful* 649
  disastrous 735
  grievous 830
  fearful 860
direct
  straight 246
  teach 537
  artless 703
  command 741
  – attention to 457
  – one's course
  motion 278
  pursuit 622
  – the eyes to 441
direction
  [*see* direct]
  tendency **278**
  indication 550
  management **693**
  precept 697
directly *soon* 132
director
  teacher 540
  theatre 599
  manager **694**
  master 745

– of the budget 801
directorship 737
directory *list* 86
  council 696
diremption 44
direption 791
dirge
  funeral 363
  song 415
  lament 839
dirigible balloon 273, 726
dirk 727
dirt 653
  throw –
  defame 874
  disrespect 929
  – cheap 815
  like – under one's feet 749
dirty *dim* 422
  opaque 426
  unclean 653
  disreputable 874
  dishonourable 940
  – end of stick 699
  – sky 353
  – weather 349
  do – work
  servile 886
  flatterer 935
diruption 162
dis aliter visum
  disappointment 509
  necessity 601
disability
  impotence 158
disable 158
  weaken 160
disabuse 527, 529
disaccord 713
disadvantage
  evil 619
  inexpedience 647
  at a – 34
  lie under a – 651
disadvantageous 647, 649
disaffection
  dissent 489
  enmity 889
  hate 898
disaffirm 536
disagreeable 830, 867
disagreement
  difference 15
  incongruity **24**
  dissent 489

discord 713
disallow 761
disannul 756
disappearance **449**
disappointment
  balk **509**
  fail 732
  discontent 832
disapprobation 706, **932**
disapprover 936
disarm *disable* 158
  weaken 160
  reconcile 831
  propitiate 914
disarrange 61
disarray
  disorder 59
  undress 226
disaster *evil* 619
  failure 732
  adversity 735
  calamity 830
disastrous *bad* 649
disavow 536
disband
  separate 44
  disperse 73
  liberate 750
disbar
  abrogate 756
  punish 972
disbarment 55
disbelief 485, 487
  religious 989
disbench 756, 972
disbowel 297
disbranch 44
disburden
  facilitate 705
  – one's mind 529
  – oneself of 782
disburse 809
disc 220, 234
discard *eject* 297
  relinquish 624
  disuse 678
  abrogate 756
  refuse 764
  repudiate 773
  surrender 782
  – from one's thoughts 458
discarded 495
disceptation 476
discern *see* 441
  know 490
discernible 446
discernment 498, 368
discerption 44

discharge
  violence 173
  propel 284
  emit 297
  excrete 299
  sound 406
  acquit oneself 692
  complete 729
  liberate 750
  abrogate 756
  pay 807
  exempt 927a
  acquit 970
  – a duty 926, 944
  – a function
  business 625
  utility 644
  – itself *egress* 295
  river 348
  – from the memory 506
  – from the mind 458
  – an obligation 772
discind 44
disciple *pupil* 541
  votary 711
  Christian 985
disciplinarian
  master 540
  martinet 739
discipline
  order 58
  teaching 537
  training 673
  restraint 751
  punishment 972
  religious 990
disclaim *deny* 536
  repudiate 756
  abjure 757
  refuse 764
disclosure 480a, **529**
discoid *layer* 204
  frontal 220
  flat 251
discoloration 429
discoloured
  shabby 659
  ugly 846
  blemish 848
discomfit 731
discomfiture 732
discomfort
  physical 378
  mental 828
discommend 932
discommode
  hinder 706
  annoy 830

discommodious 645, 647
discompose
  derange 61
  put out 458
  hinder 706
  pain 830
  disconcert 874
  anger 900
discomposure 828
disconcert
  derange 61
  distract 458
  disappoint 509
  hinder 706
  discontent 832
  confuse 879
disconcerted
  hopeless 859
disconformity 83
discongruity 24
disconnected
  style 575
disconnection
  irrelation 10
  disjunction 44
  discontinuity 70
disconsolate 837
discontent **832**
discontinuance
  cessation 142
  relinquishment 624
discontinuity **70**
discord
  difference 15
  disagreement 24
  of sound **414**
  of colour 428
  dissension **713**
discount
  decrease 36
  decrement 40a
  money **813**
  at a –
  disrepute 874
  disapproved 932
discountenance
  disfavour 706
  refuse 764
discourage
  dissuade 616
  sadden 837
  frighten 860
discourse
  teach 537
  speech 582
  talk 588
  dissert 595
  sermon 998
discourtesy **895**

punish 972
- from the mind
452, 458
dismount
arrive 292
descend 306
render useless 645
disnest 185
disobedience 742
non-observance
773
disoblige 907
disorder
confusion **59**
derange 61
turbulent 173
disease 655
-ed intellect 503
disorderly
unprincipled 945
disorganize
derange 61
destroy 162
spoil 659
disorganized 59
disown 536
dispair 44
disparage
underrate 483
disrespect 929
dispraise 932
detract 934
disparity
different 15
dissimilar 18
disagreeing 24
unequal 28
isolated 44
dispart 44
dispassionate 826
- opinion 484
dispatch
[*see* despatch]
dispel *scatter* 73
destroy 162
displace 185
repel 289
dispensable
useless 645
dispensary 662
dispensation
[*see* dispense]
command 741
licence 760
relinquishment
782
exemption 927*a*
-s of Providence
976
dispense
disperse 73

give 784
apportion 786
retail 796
- with
disuse 678
permit 760
exempt 927*a*
cannot be -d with
630
dispeople
eject 297
expatriate 893
disperse
separate 44
scatter 73
diverge 291
waste 638
dispersion 73
- of light 420
chromatic - 428
dispirit
discourage 616
sadden 837
displacement
derange 61
remove **185**
transfer 270
displacency
dislike 867
incivility 895
disapprobation
932
displant 185
display *appear* 448
show 525
parade 882
displease 830
displeasure 828
anger 900
displosion 173
displume 789
disport 840
disposal
[*see* dispose]
at one's - 763, 777
dispose
arrange 60
tend 176
induce 615
- of *use* 677
complete 729
relinquish 782
give 784
sell 796
disposed 620
disposition
nature 5
order 58
arrangement 60
inclination 602
mind 820

dispossess
transfer 783
take away 789
- oneself of 782
dispraise 932
dispread 73
disprize 483
disproof
counter-evidence
468
confutation 479
disproportion
irrelation 10
disagreement 24
disprove 479
disputable 475, 485
disputant 710, 726
disputatious 901
dispute
discuss 476
doubt 485
deny 536
discord 713
in - 461
disqualification
incapacitate 158
useless 645
unprepared 674
unskilful 699
disentitle 925
disquiet
changeable 149
agitation 315
excitement 825
uneasiness 828
give pain 830
disquietude
apprehension 860
disquisition 539,
595
disregard
overlook 458
neglect 460
make light of 483
insensible to 823,
826
disrespect **929**
contempt 930
- of time 115
disrelish 867, 898
disreputable 874
vicious 945
disrepute 874, 929
disrespect 929
despise 930
disrobe 226
disruption
disjunction 44
destruction 162
discord 713
dissatisfaction

disappointment
509
sorrow 828
discontent 832
dissect
anatomize 44, 49
investigate 461
dissemblance 18
dissemble 544
dissembler 548
disseminate
scatter 73
pervade 186
publish 531
teach 537
dissension 713
sow - 898
dissent
disagree **489**
refuse 764
heterodoxy 984
dissentient 15
dissentious 24
dissertation 595
disservice
disadvantage 619
useless 645
disserviceable 649
dissever 44
dissidence
disagreement 24
dissent 489
discord 713
discontent 832
heterodoxy 984
dissilience 173
dissimilarity 18
dissimulate 544
dissipate *scatter* 73
destroy 162
pleasure 377
prodigality 818
amusement 840
intemperance **954**
dissolute 961
dissocial 893
dissociate 44
dissociation
irrelation 10
separation 44
dissolute 961
profligate 945
intemperate 954
dissolution
[*see* dissolve]
decomposition 49
destruction 162
death 360
dissolve *vanish* 2, **4**
liquefy 335
disappear 449

abrogate 756
dissolving views
  448, 449
dissonance
  disagreement 24
  unmusical 414
  discord 713
dissuasion 616
dissyllable 561
distaff
  – side 374
distain *dirty* 653
  ugly 846
distal 196
distance 196
  overtake 282
  go beyond 303
  defeat 731
  angular – 244
  keep at a –
    discourtesy 895
  keep one's –
    avoid 623
    modest 881
    respect 928
  teach one his – 879
  – of time
    long time 110
    past 122
distaste 867
distasteful 830
distemper 299, 428
  colour 428
  painting 556
  disease 655
distend 194
distended 192
distich 89, 597
distil *come out* 295
  extract 301
  evaporate 336
  drop 348
distinct
  disjoined 44
  audible 402
  visible 446
  intelligible 518
  manifest 525
  express 535
  articulate 580
distinction
  difference 15
  discrimination
    465
  style 578
  fame 873
  rank 875
  – without a differ-
    ence 27
distinctive 15
  – feature 79

distinctness 15
distingué 852, 873
distinguish
  perceive 441
  discriminate 465
  – by the name of
    564
distinguishable 15
distinguished
  superior 33
  repute 873
Distinguished
  Service Cross
  733
distortion
  obliquity 217
  twist **243**
  of vision 443
  misinterpret 523
  falsehood 544
  misrepresent 555
  ugly 846
distract 458
distracted
  confused 475
  insane 503
  excited 824
distraction
  passion 825
  love to – 897
distrain *take* 789
  appraise 812
  attach 969
distrait 458
distraught 824
distress
  distraint 789
  poverty 804
  affliction 828
  cause pain 830
  signal of – 669
distressingly
  excessively 31
distribute
  arrange 60
  disperse 44, 73
  allot 786
district 181
  – council 696
distrust
  disbelief 485
  fear 860
distrustful 487
disturb
  derange 61
  change 140
  agitate 315
  excite 824
  distress 828, 830
disturbance 59
disunion

discord 24
  separation 44
  disorder 59
  discord 713
disuse
  desuetude 614
  relinquish 624
  unemploy **678**
disused
  old 124
disvalue 932
ditch
  inclosure 232
  trench 259
  water 343
  conduit 350
  defence 717
  to the last – 606
ditch-water 653
ditheism 984
dither 315
dithyramb
  music 415
  poetry 597
dithyrambic 503
ditto 13, 104
  say – to 488
ditty 415
  – box 191
diurnal 138
diuturnity 110
diva 416
divagate 279, 629
divan *sofa* 215
  council 696
  throne 747
  tribunal 966
divaricate *differ* 15
  bifurcate 91
  diverge 291
dive *swim* 267
  fly 267
  plunge 306, 310
  – into *inquire* 461
divellicate 44
diver 208
divergence
  difference 15
  variation 20a
  disagreement 24
  deviation 279
  separation **291**
divers *different* 15
  multiform 81
  many 102
  – coloured 440
diverse 15
diversify
  very 20a
  change 140
diversion

change 140
  deviation 279
  pleasure 377
  amusement 840
diversity
  difference 15
  irregular 16c
  dissimilar 18
  multiform 81
  – of opinion 489
divert *turn* 279
  deceive 545
  amuse 840
  – the mind 452,
    458
divertissement
  diversion 377
  drama 599
  amusement 840
Dives 803
divest *denude* 226
  take 789
  – oneself of
    abrogate 756
    relinquish 782
divestment 226
divide *differ* 15
  separate 44
  part 51
  arrange 60
  arithmetic 85
  bisect 91
  vote 609
  apportion 786
dividend *part* 51
  number 84
  portion 786
divina particula
  auræ 450
divination
  prediction 511
  sorcery 992
divine *predict* 511
  guess 514
  perfect 650
  of God 976, 983,
    983a
  clergyman 996
divine afflatus 515
  – right
    authority 737
    due 924
  – service 990
diving 840
diving-bell 208
divining-rod 550,
  993
Divinity *God* 976
  theology 983
divisible
  number 84

division
  [*see* divide]
  part 51
  class 75
  arithmetic 85
  discord 713
  military 726
divisor 84
divorce
  separation 44
  relinquish 782
  matrimonial 905
Divorce Court 966
divulge 529
divulsion 44
divvy 786
dixi 535
dizen 847
dizzard 501
dizzy
  dimsighted 443
  confused 458
  vertigo 503
  – height 206
  – round 312
djerrid 727
djinn 980
do *fare* 7
  suit 23
  produce 161
  cheat 545
  act 680
  complete 729
  succeed 731
  I beg 765
  all one can – 686
  plenty to – 682
  thing to – 625
  – away with
  destroy 162
  eject 297
  abrogate 756
  – battle 722
  – one's bidding
    743
  – business 625
  – to death 361
  – as done by 906,
    942
  – for *destroy* 162
  kill 361
  conquer 731
  serve 746
  punish 972
  – good 906
  – harm 907
  – honour 873
  – into
  translate 522
  – justice to 595
  – like 19

– little 683
– no harm 648
– nothing 681
– nothing but 136
– one's office 772
– as others do 82
– over 223
– as one pleases
  748
– a service
  useful 644
  aid 707
– up 660
have to – with
  680, 692
– without 678
– the work 686
– wrong 923
docere, pisces na-
  tare – 641
docile *domesticated*
  370
  learning 539
  willing 602
docimastic 463
dock *diminish* 36
  cut off 38
  port 189
  shorten 201
  edge 231
  store 636
  tribunal 966
docked
  incomplete 53
docker 690
docket
  list 86
  evidence 467
  note 550
  record 551
  security 771
dockyard 691
doctor
  learned man 492
  restore 660
  remedy 662
  after death the –
    135
  – accounts 811
  when –s disagree
    475
doctrinaire
  positive 474
  pedant 492
  affectation 855
  blusterer 887
doctrinal 537
doctrinarian 514
doctrine *tenet* 484
  knowledge 490
document 551

documentary
  evidence 467
dodder 315
doddering 128
dodecahedron 244
dodge *change* 140
  shift 264
  deviate 279
  oscillate 314
  pursue 461
  avoid 623
  stratagem 702
dodger, artful – 792
dodo 366
  extinct as the –
    122
Doe, John 4
doe *swift* 274
  deer 366
  female 374
doer
  originator 164
  agent 690
doff 226
  – the cap 894
dog *follow* 281
  animal 366
  male 373
  pursue 622
  wretch 949
  cast to the –s
  reject 610
  disuse 678
  abrogate 756
  relinquish 782
  fire – 386
  go to the –s
  destruction 162
  fail 732
  adversity 735
  poverty 804
  sea – 269
  watch –
  safety 664
  warning 668
  keeper 753
  hair of – that bit
    you 959
  let sleeping –s lie
    141
  – in manger 706,
    943
  –tired 688
  –s of war 722
dog-cart 272
dog-cheap 815
dog-days 382
doge 745
dogged
  obstinate 606
  valour 861

  sullen 901*a*
dogger 273
doggerel
  verse 597
  ridiculous 851,
    853
dog-hole 189
dog Latin 563
dogma *tenet* 484
  theology 983
dogmatic
  certain 474
  positive 481
  assertion 535
  obstinate 606
dogmatist 887
dog's ear 258
dog robber 746
dog-sick 867
dog-star 423
dog-trot 275
dog-weary 688
doily 652
doing
  up and – 682
  what one is – 625
doings
  events 151
  actions 680
  conduct 692
doit *trifle* 643
  coin 800
dolce far niente 681
doldrums
  dejection 837
  sulks 901*a*
dole
  small quantity 32
  scant 640
  give 784
  allot 786
  parsimony 819
  grief 828
doleful 837
  – dumps 901*a*
doll *small* 193
  image 554
dollar 800
dolman 225
dolmen 363, 551
dolorem, infandum
  renovare – 833
dolorous 830
dolour
  physical 378
  moral 828
dolphin 341
dolt 501
doltish 499
domain
  class 75

region 181
property 780
Domdaniel 982
dome *high* 206
  roof 223
  curvature 245
  convex 250
Domesday book
  list 86
  record 551
domesman 967
domestic
  inhabitant 188
  home 189
  interior 221
  servant 746
  secluded 893
  – *animals* 366
domesticate
  locate 184
  acclimatize 613
  – *animals* 370
domicile 189
domiciled 186
domiciliary 188
  – *visit* 461
dominant 175
  note in music 413
domination 737
dominical 998
domineer
  tyrannize 739
  insolence 885
Domini, anno – 106
Dominican 996
Dominie 540
dominion 181, 737
domino *dress* 225
  mask 530
  game 840
domn 745
don *put on* 225
  scholar 492
  teacher 540
  noble 875
Don Juan 897
donation 784
done *finished* 729
  work – 729
  – for *spoilt* 659
  failure 732
  – up
  impotent 158
  tired 688
  have – with
  cease 142
  relinquish 624
  disuse 678
donee 785
donjon 717, 752
donkey *ass* 271

fool 501
talk a –'s hind leg
  off 584
donna 374
Donnybrook Fair
  disorder 59
  discord 713
donor 784
donzel 746
doodle 501
doom *end* 67
  fate 152
  destruction 162
  death 360
  judgment 480
  necessity 601
  sentence 971
  – sealed
  death 360
  adversity 735
doomed 735, 828
doomsday
  end 67
  future 121
  till – 112
door *entrance* 66
  cover 223
  brink 231
  barrier 232
  opening 260
  passage 627
  at one's – 197
  beg from door to –
  765
  bolt the – 666
  close the – upon
  751
  death's – 360
  keep within –s 265
  lie at one's – 926
  lock the – 666
  open a – to
  liable 177
  open the – to
  receive 296
  facilitate 705
  permit 760
  show the – to
  eject 297
  discourtesy 895
  – mat 652
doorkeeper 263
doorway 260
dope 376, 545, 663
doquet
  security 771
Dorado, El – 803
Doric mode 413
dormant
  inert 172
  latent 526

asleep 683
dormer 260
dormeuse 272
dormir debout,
  conte à – 843
dormitive 841
dormitory 191
dormouse 683
dorp 189
dorsal 235
dorser 191
dorsum 235, 250
dory 273
dose *quantity* 25
  part 51
  medicine 662
  apportion 786
dosser 191
dossier *bundle* 72
  record 551
dossil 223, 263
dot *small* 32
  place 182
  little 193
  variegate 440
  mark 550
  dowry 780
  on the – 113
dotage 128, 499
dotard 130, 501
dotation 784
dottle 40, 645
dote *drivel* 499, 503
  – upon 897
douanier 965
double
  similar 17
  increase 35
  duplex 90
  substitute 147
  fold 258
  turn 283
  finesse 702
  march at the – 274
  see –
  dim sight 443
  drunk 959
  – acrostic
  letters 561
  wit 842
  – dutch 519
  – entry 811
  – the fist 909
  – march 684
  – meaning 520
  – a point 311
  in – quick time
  274
  – reef topsails 664
  – sure 474
  work – tides 686

– up
  render powerless
  158
double bar 747
double-bass 417
doublecross 545
double-dealing
  lie 544
  cunning 940
double-distilled 171
double-dyed 428
double-eagle 800
double-edged 90,
  171
double entendre
  ambiguity 520
  impure 961
double-faced
  lie 544
  cunning 702, 940
double-headed 90
double-minded 605
double-shotted 171
doublet 225
double-tongued
  lie 544
  cunning 702, 940
doubt
  uncertain 475
  disbelieve 485
  sceptic 989
doubtful 475
  more than – 473
  – meaning
  unintelligible 519
doubtless
  certain 474
  belief 484
  assent 488
douceur 784, 973
douche 337
dough 324, 354, 800
doughty 861
dour 739
douse
  immerse 310
  splash 337
  blow 972
Dove
  Holy Ghost 976
dove
  innocent 946
  roar like sucking ·
  174
dovecote 189
dovetail
  agree 23
  join 43
  intersect 219
  intervene 228
  angle 244

insert 300
dowager 374, 905
dowdy 653, 851
dower 780, 803, 810
dowerless 804
down
  below 207
  light 320
  bear – upon 716
  bed of –
    pleasure 377
    repose 687
  come – 306
  get – 306
  go –
    sink 306
    calm 826
  keep – 36
  money – 807
  take –
    lower 308
    rebuff 874
    humble 879
  – on one's mar-
    row-bones 886
  – in the mouth 837
  – and out 874
  – in price 815
  go – like a stone
    310
  be – upon
    attack 716
    severe 739
downcast 306, 837
  – eyes 879
downfall
  destruction 162
  fall 306
  failure 732
  misfortune 735
downhill 217, 306
  go –
    adversity 735
downpour 348
downright
  absolute 31
  manifest 525
  sincere 703
downs 206, 344
down-trodden
  submission 725
  vanquished 732
  subject 749
  dejected 837
  disrepute 874
  contempt 930
downwards 306
downy
  smooth 255
  plumose 256
  soft 324

dowry 780, 784
dowse 276
dowser 994
doxology 990
doxy 962
doyen 128
doyley 652
doze 683
dozen 98
drab *colour* 432
  slut 653
  hussy 962
drabble 653
drachm 319
Draco 694, 739
draff 653
draft [*see also*
  draught]
  multitude 102
  drawing 554, 556
  write 590
  abstract 596
  plan 626
  cheque 800
  credit 805
  – off *displace* 185
  transfer 270
draft-horse 271
drag *carriage* 272
  crawl 275
  traction 285
  impediment 706
  put on the – 275
  – a chain
    tedious 109, 110
    exertion 686
    subjection 749
  – into
    implicate 54
    compel 744
  – through mire
    disrepute 874
    disrespect 929
  – on *tedious* 110
  – into open day
    531
  – towards
    attract 288
  – slow length
    long 200
    weary 841
draggle 285, 653
  – tail 59
drag-net
  all sorts 78
dragoman 524
dragon *monster* 83
  violent 173
  animal 366
  irascible 901
dragonnade

attack 716
  punish 972
dragoon
  soldier 726
  compel 744
  insolent 885
  worry 907
drain
  flow out 295
  empty 297
  dry 340
  conduit 350
  waste 638
  clean 652
  unclean 653
  exhaust 789
  dissipate 818
  – the cup
  drink 298
  drunken 959
  – the cup of
    misery 828
  – into 348
  – pipe 249
  – of resources 640
drake *male* 373
  fire – 423
dram *drink* 298
  pungent 392
  stimulus 615
  – drinking 959
drama 599
dramatic 599
  ostentation 882
  – author 599
  – critic 599
  – poetry 597
dramatis personæ
  mankind 372
  play 599
  agents 690
  party 712
drapery 225, 847
drast 645
drastic 171
draught
  [*see also* draft]
  depth 208
  traction 285
  drink 298
  stream of air 349
  delineation 554,
    556
  plan 626
  physic 662
  troops 726
  – off 73
draughts
  game 840
draughtsman
  artist 559

draw *equality* 27
  compose 54
  pull 285
  delineate 554, 556
  – aside 279
  – off the attention
    458
  – back
  deduction 40a
  regret 283
  avoid 623
  – breath
  refresh 689
  feeling 821
  relief 834
  – a cheque 800
  – a curtain 424
  – down 153
  – forth 677
  – from 810
  – on futurity 132
  – in one's horns
    tergiversation 607
    humility 879
  – in 195
  – an inference 480
  – the line 465
  – lots 621
  – near *time* 121
    approach 286
  – off *eject* 297
    hinder 706
    take 789
  – on *time* 121
    event 151
    induce 615
  – out
    protract 110
    late 133
    prolong 200
    extract 301
    discover 480a
    exhibit 525
    diffuse style 573
  – over *induce* 615
  – a parallel 9
  – the pen through
    552
  – a picture 594
  – profit 775
  – and quarter 972
  – the sword
    attack 716
    war 722
  – the teeth of 158
  – together
    assemble 72
    co-operate 709
  – towards 288
  – up *order* 58
    stop 265

[468]

write 590
– up a statement 594
– upon *money* 800
– the veil 528
drawback *evil* 619
  imperfection 651
  hindrance 706
  discount 813
drawbar 45
drawbridge
  way 627
  escape 671
  raise the – 666
drawcansir 887
drawee 800
drawer
  receptacle 191
  artist 559
  – of water 690
drawers
  dress 225
drawhead 45
drawing
  delineation 554, 556
  prize 810
drawing-room
  assembly 72
  room 191
  fashion 852
drawl *prolong* 200
  creep 275
  in speech 583
  sluggish 683
drawn *equated* 27
  – battle
  – irresistibly 601
  pacification 723
  incomplete 730
dray 272
  – horse 271
drayman 268
dread 860
dreadful *great* 31
  bad 649
  dire 830
  depressing 837
  fearful 860
dreadless 861
dreadnought
  warship 726
dream
  unsubstantial 4
  error 495
  fancy 515
  sleep 683
  golden – 858
  – of *think* 451
  intend 620
  – on other things

458
dreamer
  madman 504
  imaginative 515
dreamy
  unsubstantial 4
  inattentive 458
  sleepy 683
dreary
  monotonous 16
  solitary 87
  melancholy 830, 837
dredge *collect* 72
  extract 301
  raise 307
dregs
  remainder 40
  refuse 645
  dirt 653
  – of the people 876
  – of vice 945
drench *drink* 298
  water 337
  redundance 641
  – with *physic* 662
drencher 248
drenching rain 348
dress
  uniformity 16
  agree 23
  equalize 27
  clothes 225
  prepare 673
  ornament 847
  ostentation 882
  full – 852
  – circle 599
  – the ground 371
  – up *falsehood* 544
  represent 554
  – wounds 662
  – to advantage 847
dress-coat 225
dresser
  sideboard 215
  surgeon 662
dressing 932, 972
  – room 191, 599
dressing-gown 225
dressmaker 225
dribble 295, 348
driblet 25, 32
drift
  accumulate 72
  distance 196
  motion 264
  flying 267
  float 267
  transfer 270

direction 278
deviation 279
approach 286
wind 349
meaning 516
intention 620
snow – 383
drifter 273
drifting 605
driftless 621
drill *fabric* 219
  bore 260
  auger 262
  teach 537
  prepare 673
  – hall 191
drink
  swallow 296
  liquor 298
  tipple 959
  – one's fill
  enough 639
  – in *imbibe* 296, 298
  – in learning 539
  – to *celebrate* 883
  courtesy 894
drinking-bout 954
drink-money 784
drip 295, 348
dripping *wet* 339
  fat 356
drive *airing* 266
  impel 276
  propel 284
  break in 370
  urge 615
  haste 684
  direct 693
  attack 716
  compel 744
  – at *mean* 516
  intend 620
  – a bargain
  barter 794
  parsimony 819
  – care away 836
  – a coach and six through 83
  – into a corner
  difficult 704
  hinder 706
  defeat 731
  subjection 749
  – to despair 859
  – matters to an extremity 604
  – from *repel* 289
  – one hard 716
  – home 729
  – in 300

– to the last **133**
– out 297
– trade
  business 625
  barter 794
drivel *slobber* 297
  imbecile 499
  mad 503
  rubbish 517
driveller 501, 584
driver 268
  director 694
driving rain 348
drizzle 348
droil 683
droit du plus fort 744
drôle *cards* 840
drôle 949
  – de corps 844
drollery
  amusement 840
  wit 842
  ridiculous 853
dromedary 271
drone *slow* 275
  sound 407, 412, 413
  inactive 683
drool 297
droop
  weak 160
  hang 214
  sink 306
  disease 655
  decline 659
  flag 688
  sorrow 828
  dejection 837
drop *small quantity* 32
  discontinue 142
  powerless 158
  bring forth 161
  spherule 249
  emerge 295
  fall 306
  trickle 348
  relinquish 624
  discard 782
  gallows 975
  let – 308
  ready to –
  fatigue 688
  – asleep 683
  – astern 283
  – from the cloud 508
  – dead **360**
  – by drop
  by degrees 26

in parts 51
~ in the bucket 32
~ in upon 674
– into a good
  thing 734
– into the grave
  360
– a hint 527
– all idea of 624
– in *arrive* 292
  immerse 300
  sociality 892
– the mask 529
– off *decrease* 36
  die 360
  sleep 683
– in the ocean
  trifling 643
– the subject 458
– too much 959
dropping fire 70
drop-scene 599
dropsical 194, 641
droshki 272
dross
  remainder 40
  slag 384
  trash 643, 645
  dirt 653
drought
  dryness 340
  insufficiency 640
drouth *desire* 865
drove
  assemblage 72
  multitude 102
drover 370
drown
  affusion 337
  kill 361
  ruin 731, 732
– care 840
– the voice 581
drowsy *slow* 275
  sleepy 683
  weary 841
drub
  defeat 731, 732
  punish 972
drudge *labour* 686
  worker 682, 690
drug
  render insensible
  376
  superfluity 641
  trash 643
  remedy 662
  bane 663
– in the market
  815
drugget

cover 223
clean 652
preserve 670
druggist 662
druid 996
drum
  repeat 104
  cylinder 249
  sound 407
  music 417
  party 892
  beat of –
  signal 550
  alarm 669
  war 722
  command 741
  parade 882
  ear – 418
  muffled –
  funeral 363
  non-resonance
  408a
– and fife band 417
– fire 407
– out 972
drum-head 964,
  966
drum-major 745
drummer 416
drunken 959
  reel like a – man
  315
drunkenness 959
dry *arid* 340
  style 575, 576, 579
  hoarse 581
  scanty 640
  preserve 670
  exhaust 789
  tedious 841
  dull 842
  thirsty 865
  cynical 932
  teetotal 958
  run – 640
  with – eyes 823
– dock 189
– joke 842
– land 342
– the tears 834
– up 340, 638
dryad 979
dry-as-dust
  antiquarian 122
  dull 843
dryness 340
dry-nurse
  teach 537
  teacher 540
  aid 707
dry-point 558

dry-rot
  dirt 653
  decay 659
  bane 663
dualism 984
duality 89
duarchy 737
dub 564
dubious 475
ducat 800
duce 745
duchess 745, 875
duchy 181
duck *stoop* 308
  plunge 310
  water 337
  darling 897, 899
  play –s and
  drakes
  recoil 277
  prodigality 818
–'s egg
  zero 101
– in thunder 870
ducking-stool 975
duckling 129
duck-pond 370
duct 350
ductile
  elastic 325
  flexible 324
  trimming 607
  easy 705
  docile 743
dud 158, 727
dude 854
duds 225
dudgeon
  dagger 727
  discontent 832
  churlishness 895
  hate 898
  anger 900
  sullenness 901a
due
  expedient 646
  owing 806
  proper 924, 926
  give his – to
  right 922
  vindication 937
  fair 939
  in – course 109
  occasion 134
– respect 928
– sense of 498
– time
  soon 132
– to
  cause and effect
  154, 155

  give – weight 465
duel 720
duellist 726
dueness 924
duenna
  teacher 540
  guardian 664
  keeper 753
dues 812
duet 415
duff 298
duffer
  bungler 701
  smuggler 792
dug 250
dug-out
  old man 130
  boat 273
  defence 717
duke *ruler* 745
  noble 875
dulce domum 189
dulcet
  sweet 396
  sound 405
  melodious 413
  agreeable 829
dulcify 174, 396
dulcimer 417
Dulcinea 897
dulcorate 396
dulia 990
dull *weak* 160
  inert 172
  moderate 174
  blunt 254
  insensible 376,
  381
  sound 405
  dim 422
  colourless 429
  ignorant 493
  stolid 499
  style 575
  inactive 683
  unapt 699
  callous 823
  dejected 837
  weary 841
  prosing 843
  simple 849
– of hearing 419
– sight 443
dullard 501
dullness 843
duly 924
duma 696
dumb 581
– animal 366
– show 550
– waiter 307

strike –
ignorant 493
astonish 870
humble 879
dumbfounder
disappoint 509
silence 581
astonish 870
humble 879
dummy
substitute 147
impotent 158
speechless 581
inactive 683
dump *music* 415
store 636
lament 839
undersell 796
dumpling 298
dumps
discontent 832
dejection 837
sulk 901a
dumpy *little* 193
short 201
thick 202
dun *dim* 422
colourless 429
grey 432
importune 765
creditor 805
dunce
ignoramus 493
fool 501
dunderhead 501
dune 206
dung 653
dungeon 752
dunghill
dirt 653
cowardly 862
baseborn 876
– *cock* 366
Dunker 984
dunt 716
duo 415
duodecimal 99
duodecimo
little 193
book 593
duodenary 98
duologue
interlocution 588
drama 599
dupe
credulous 486
deceive 545
deceived **547**
duplex 90, 189
duplicate
imitate 19

copy 21
double 90
tally 550
record 551
redundant 641
pawn 805
duplication
imitation 19
doubling **90**
repetition 104
duplicature
fold 258
duplicity
duality 89
falsehood 544
dura lex sed lex 926
durable
long time 110
stable 150
durance 141, 751
in – 754
duration 106
contingent – **108a**
infinite – 112
durbar
conference 588
council 696
tribunal 966
duress
compulsion 744
restraint 751
during 106
– *pleasure &c.*
108a
durity 323
dusk
evening 126
half-light 422
dusky
dark 421
black 431
dust *levity* 320
powder 330
corpse 362
trash 643
dirt 653
money 800
come to –
die 360
*come down with
the* – 807
humbled in the –
879
kick up a – 885
level with the –
162
lick the –
submit 725
fail 732
make to bite the –
731

turn to –
deorganized 358
die 360
– *in the balance*
643
throw – *in the*
eyes
blind 442
deceive 545
plead 617
– *one's jacket* 972
duster 652
dust-bin, dust-hole
191, 645
fit for the –
useless 645
dirty 653
spoilt 659
dustman 653
cleaner 652
dust-storm 330
dusty
powder 330
dirt 653
Dutch
double – 519
high – 519
– *auction* 796
– *courage* 862
Dutchman, flying
515
dutiful 944
duty
business 625
work 686
tax 812
courtesy 894
obligation **926**
respect 928
worship 990
rite 998
do one's –
virtue 944
on – 680, 682
duumvirate 737
Duval, Claude –
792
D.V. 470, 976
dwarf
lessen 36
small 193
elf 980
dwell
reside 186
abide 265
– *upon*
descant 573
dweller 188
dwelling 184, 189
dwindle *lessen* 36
shrink 195

dyad 89
dye 428
dying 360
dyke [*see* dike]
dynamic energy
157
dynamics 276
dynamitard 863
dynamite 727
dynamo 153
dynasty 737
dysentery 299
dyspepsia 655
dysphony 581

E

each 79
– *to each* 786
– *other* 12
– *in his turn* 148
eager
willing 602
active 682
ardent 821
desirous 865
– *expectation* **507**
eagle
standard 550
money 800
– *boat* 726
– *eye sight* 441
intelligence 498
– *winged swift* **274**
insignia 747
eagre 348
ean 161
ear 418
corn 154
come to one's –**s**
527
din in the –
loud 404
drum 407
all – 418
have the – *of*
belief 484
friendship 888
lend an –
hear 418
attend 457
meet the – 418
nice – 418
no – 419
offend the – 410
pick up the –**s**
attention 457
expectation 507
put about one's –**s**
308

quick – 418
reach one's –s 527
ring in the – 408
set by the –s
discord 713
hate 898
resentment 900
split the –s 404
together by the –s
discord 713
contention 720
up to one's –s
redundancy 641
active 680, 682
willing – 602
word in the – 586
– for music 416,
418
in at one – out at
the other
inattention 458
forget 506
not for –s polite
961
make the –s tingle
anger 900
– ache 378
ear-drum 418
earl 875
earless 419
earliness 132
early 132
get up – 682
earmark 550
earn 775
earnest *willing* 602
determined 604
emphatic 642
pledge 771
pay in advance
809
eager 821
in –
affirmation 535
veracious 543
strenuous 682
ear-piercing 410
ear-ring 847
ear-shot 197
out of – 405
ear-splitting 404
earth *ground* 211
world 318
land 342
corpse 362
what on –
inquiry 461
wonder 870
– closet 653
earthenware
baked 384

sculpture 557
earthling 372
earthly 318
end of one's –
career 360
of no – use 645
earthly-minded
943, 989
earthquake 146,
173
earthwork 717
earwig *flatter* 933,
935
ear-witness 467
ease *bodily* 377
style 578
leisure 685
facility 705
mental 827
content 831
at one's –
prosperous 734
mind at –
cheerful 836
set at – *relief* 834
take one's – 687
– off *deviate* 297
– one of *take* 789
easel *support* 215
painting 556
– picture 556
easement
property 780
relief 834
easily
[*see* easy]
let one down – 918
– accomplished
705
– deceived 486
– persuaded 602
East 236, 278
Easter *period* 138
rite 998
– Monday
holiday 840
– offering
gift 784
– sepulchre 1000
easy *gentle* 275
style 578
facile 705
make oneself –
about 484
take it –
inactive 683
inexcitable 826
– ascent 217
– of belief 472
– chair
support 215

repose 687
– circumstances
803
– going
willing 602
irresolute 605
lenient 740
inexcitable 826
contented 831
indifferent 866
– sail
moderate 174
slow 275
– temper 894
– terms 705
– to understand
518
– virtue 961
eat *food* 298
tolerate 826
– dirt 725, 879
– one's fill
enough 639
gorge 957
– heartily 298
– one's words 879
– out of house and
home *take* 789
prodigal 818
gluttony 957
– of the same
trencher 892
– one's words 607
eatables 298
eaten up with 820
eau, battre l' – 645
faire venir l' – à la
bouche 865
mettre de l' – dans
son vin 174
eaves 250
eavesdropper 455,
527
eavesdropping 418,
532
ébauche 626
ebb *decrease* 36
contract 195
regress 283
recede 287
waste 638
spoil 659
low – 36
low 207
depression 308
insufficient 640
– and flow 314
– of life 360
ebb-tide *low* 207
dry 340
ebony 431

ebriety 959
ebullient
violent 173
hot 382
excited 824
ebullition
energy 171
violence 173
agitation 315
heating 384
excitation 825
anger 900
écarté 840
ecce
– iterum Crispinⁱᵉ
104
– signum 550
eccentric 220
irregular 83
foolish 499
crazed 503, 504
capricious 608
ecchymosis 299
ecclesiastic
church 995
clergy 996
ecclesiastical
canonical 985
– court 966
– law 963
ecclesiolatry 991
écervelé 458
échafaudage 673
échappée 840
échapper belle 671
échelon 279
echo *imitate* 19
copy 21
repeat 104
reflection 277
resonance 408
answer 462
assent 488
applaud to the –
931
awake –es 404
éclaircissement 522
éclat 873
eclectic 609
eclipse *surpass* 33
disappearance
449
hide 528
outshine 873, **874**
partial – *dim* 422
total – *dark* 421
under an –
invisible 447
out of repute **874**
ecliptic 318
eclogue 597

economic pressure
751
economy
order 58
conduct 692
frugality **817**
animal – 359
écorcher les oreilles
410
ecphorize 615
écru 433
ecstasis 683
ecstasy
frenzy 515
transport 821
rapture 827
ecstatic 829
ecstatica 994
ectoplasm 992
ectype 21
ecumenical 78
edacity 957
Edda 986
eddy
whirlpool 348
current 312
danger 667
Eden 827
edge *energy* 171
height 206
brink **231**
sidle 279
advantage 731
cutting – 253
on – 256, 507
take the – off 174
– of hunger 865
– in 228
– one's way 282
edge-tools 253
play with – 863
edgewise 217
edging
obliquity 217
border 231
ornament 847
edible 298
edict 741
edification
building 161
teaching 537
learning 539
piety 987
edifice 161
edifying *good* 648
edile 965
edit
publication 531
condense 596
revise 658
edition, new – 658

editor 593
educate 537
educated 490
self – 490
education
teaching 537
knowledge 490
man of – 492
higher – 490
educational 537,
542
educe *extract* 301
discover 480a
educt 40
eduction 40a
edulcorate 396, 652
eel 248
wriggle like an –
315
eerie 860
efface
delete 162
disappear 449
obliterate 552
– from the
memory 506
effect
consequence **154**
product 161
impression 375
complete 729
carry into – 692
with crushing –
162
in – 5
take – 731
to that – 516
effective
capable 157
useful 644
effectuation 729
expedient 646
effects 780, 798
effectual 731
effectually 52
effectuate 729
effeminate
weak 160
womenlike 374
timorous 862
sensual 954
effeminize 158
effendi 875
effervesce
energy 171
violence 173
agitate 315
bubble 353
excited 825
effervescent 338
effete *old* 128

weak 160
useless 645
spoiled 659
efficacious
[*see* efficient]
efficient
power 157
agency 170
utility 644
skill 698
effigy 21, 554
effleurer *skim* 267,
460
efflorescence 330
effluxion of time
109
effluence *egress* 295
flow 348
effluvium 334, 398
efflux 295
efformation 240
effort 686
effreet 980
effrontery 885
effulgence 420
effuse
pour out 295, 297
excrete 299
speech 582
loquacity 584
effusion of blood
361
effusive 573
eft 366
eftsoons 117
egad 535
égards 928
egesta 299
egestion 297
egg *beginning* 66
cause 153
food 298
walk among –s
704
too many –s in
one basket
unskilful 699
(*imprudent* 863)
– and dart
ornament 847
– on 615
egg-shaped 247,
249
ego *intrinsic* 5
speciality 79
immaterial 317
non – 6
egocentrism 943
egotism
vanity 880
cynicism 911

selfishness 943
egregious
exceptional 83
absurd 497
exaggerated 549
important 642
egregiously 31, 33
egress **295**
Egyptian darkness
421
eheu! fugaces
labuntur anni
111
eiderdown 223
eidouranion 318
Eiffel tower 206
eight *number* 98
boat 273
representative **759**
eisteddfod 72, 416
eighty 98
either *choice* 609
happy with – **605**
ejaculate
propel 284
utter 580
ejection 185, **297**
ejecta 299
ejector 349
eke *also* 37
– out *complete* **52**
spin out 110
ekka 272
El Dorado 803
elaborate
improve 658
prepare 673
laborious 686
work out 729
elaine 356
élan 276
elapse 109, **122**
elastic fluid **334**
elasticity
power 157
strength 159
energy 171
spring **325**
elate *cheer* 836
rejoice 838
hope 858
vain 880
boast 884
elbow *angle* 244
projection 250
push 276
at one's –
near 197
advice 695
lift one's –

drink 959
out at –s
  undress 226
  poor 804
  disrepute 874
– one's way
  progress 282
  pursuit 622
  active 682
elbow-chair 215
elbow-grease 331
elbow-room 180,
  748
elder *older* 124
  aged 128
  veteran 130
  clergy 996
elect *choose* 609
  good 648
  predestinate 976
  pious 987
  clergy 996
election
  numerical 84
  necessity 601
electioneering 609
elector 745
electorate 737
Electra complex
  897
electric
  swift 274
  sensation 821
  excitable 825
  car 272
– blue 438
– chair 974
– light 423
– piano 417
electrician 599, 690
electricity 157, 388
electrify
  unexpected 508
  excite 824
  astonish 870
electro-biology 992
electrocution 972
electrolier 214, 423
electrolyze 49
electro-magnetism
  157
electromobile 272
electron 32
electroplate 223
electrotype 21, 591
electuary 662
eleemosynary 784
elegance
  in style 578
  beauty 845
  taste 850

Bank of – 800
elegy *interment* 363
  poetry 597
  lament 839
element
  component 56
  beginning 66
  cause 153
  matter 316
in one's –
  facility 705
  content 831
devouring – 382
out of its – 195
elementary 42
– education 537
– school 542
elements
  Eucharist 998
elench 477
elephant
  large 192
  carrier 271
  white – *bane* 663
elevated
  tipsy 959
elevation
  height 206
  vertical 212
  raising **307**
  plan 554
– of style 574
  improvement 658
  glory 873
– of mind 942
  angular – 244
élève 541
eleven 98
  representative 759
eleventh hour
  evening 126
  late 133
  opportune 134
elf *infant* 129
  little 193
  imp 980
elicit *cause* 153
  draw out 301
  discover 480*a*
  manifest 525
eligible 646
Elijah's mantle 63
eliminant 299
eliminate
  subduct 38
  simplify 42
  exclude 55
  weed 103
  extract 301
  reject 610
elision **44, 201**

élite *best* 648
  distinguished 873
  aristocratic 875
elixation 384
elixir 662
– of life 471
elk 223
ell 200
take an –
  take 789
  insolence 885
  wrong 923
  undue 925
  selfish 943
ellipse 247
ellipsis *shorten* 201
  style 572
ellipsoid 247, 249
elocation 185, 270
elocution 582
éloge 931
elongation 196, 200
elopement 623, 671
eloquence 574, 582
else 37
elsewhere 187
elucidate 522
elude
  sophistry 477
  avoid 623
  escape 671
  succeed 731
  palter 773
elusive 545
elusory 546
elutriate 652
elysian 829, 981
Elysium 827, 981
elytron 223
Elzevir edition 193
emaciation 195,
  203, 640
emanate 151
  go out of 295
  excrete 299
– from 544
emanation 398
emancipate
  facilitate 705
  free 748, 750
emasculate
  impotent 158
embalm
  interment 363
  perfume 400
  preserve 670
– in the memory
  505
embankment
  esplanade 189
  refuge 666

fence 717
embar 229
embargo
  stoppage 265
  prohibition 761
  exclusion 893
embark
  transfer 270
  depart 293
– in *begin* 66
  engage in 676
embarquer sans
  biscuits, s' – **674**
embarras de
– choix 609
embarrass 641,
  704, 706
embarrassed 804,
  806
embarrassing **475**
embase 659
embassy
  errand 532
  commission **755**
  consignee 758
embattled
  arranged 60
  leagued 712
  war array **722**
embed
  locate 184
  base 215
  enclose 221
  insert 300
embellish 847
embers 384
embezzle 791
embitter
  deteriorate 659
  aggravate 835
  acerbate 900
emblazon
  colour 428
  ornament 847
  display 882
emblem 550, **747**
embody
  join 43
  combine 48
  form a whole 50
  compose 54
embolden
  hope 858
  encourage 861
embolism 228, 261,
  300
embonpoint 192
embosomed
  lodged 184
  interjacent 228
  circumscribed 229

emboss *convex* 250
  ornament 847
embouchure 260
embowel 297
embrace
  cohere 46
  compose 54
  include 76
  enclose 227
  choose 609
  take 789
  friendship 888
  sociality 892
  courtesy 894
  endearment 902
  – an offer 762
embrangle 61
embranglement 713
embrasure 257, 260
embrocation 662
embroider
  variegate 440
  lie 544
  ornament 847
embroidery
  adjunct 39
  exaggeration 549
embroil *derange* 61
  discord 713
embroilment 59
embrown 433
embryo
  beginning 66
  cause 153
  in – *destined* 152
  preparing 673
embryology 357
embryonic 193, 674
embus 293
embusqué 603
emendation 658
emerald *green* 435
  jewel 847
emerge 295, 446
emergency
  circumstance 8
  event 151
  difficulty 704
emeritus 500, 928
emersion 295, 446
emery
  sharpener 253
  – paper
  smooth 255
emetic *remedy* 662
émeute 742
emication 420
emigrant 57, 268
emigrate 266, 295
emigré 268, 295
eminence

height 206
  fame 873
  church dignitary 996
eminent domain 744
eminently 33
emir 745, 875
emissary
  messenger 534
  consignee 758
emission 297
emit *eject* 297
  publish 531
  voice 580
  – vapour 336
Emmanuel 976
emmet 193
emollient 662
emolument
  acquisition 775
  receipt 810
  remuneration 973
emotion 821
  –al appeal 824
  –al drama 599
empale 260, 972
empanel 86, 969
empathy 515
emperor 745
emphasis 580
emphatic 535, 642
emphatically 31
empierce
  perforate 260
  insert 300
empire 737, 789
  – day 840
empiric 548
empirical 463, 675
empiricism 463
emplane 293
employ
  business 625
  use 677
  servitude 749
  commission 755
  in one's – 746
  – one's capital in 794
  – oneself 680
  – one's time in 625
employé
  servant 746
  agent 758
employer 795
empoison 659
emporium 799
empower
  power 157

commission 755
  accredit 759
  permit 760
empress 745
empressement
  activity 682
  emotion 821
  desire 865
emprise 676
emption 795
emptor 795
  caveat – 769
empty *clear* 185
  vacant 187
  deflate 195
  drain 297
  ignorant 491
  waste 638
  deficient 640
  useless 645
  beggarly account of – boxes
  poverty 804
  – one's glass 298
  – purse 804
  – sound 517
  – stomach 865
  – title *name* 564
  undue 925
  – words 546
empty-handed 640
empty-headed 491
empurple 437
empyrean *sky* 318
  blissful 829
empyreuma 41
empyrosis 384
emulate *imitate* 19
  goodness 648
  rival 708
  compete 720
  glory 873
emulsion 352
emunctory 350
en – bloc 50
  – masse 50
  – passant
  parenthetical 10
  transient 111
  à propos 134
  – rapport 9
  – règle *order* 58
  conformity 82
  – route
  journey 266
  progress 282
enable 157
enact *drama* 599
  action 680
  conduct 692

complete 729
  order 741
  law 963
enallage 521
enamel *coating* 223
  painting 556
  ornament 847
enameller 559
enamour 897
encage 751
encamp 184, 189
encampment 184
encaustic 556
enceinte
  with child 161
  region 181
  inclosure 232
enchafe 830
enchain 751
enchant *please* 829
enchanted 827
enchanting 845, 897
enchantment
  sorcery 992
enchase 43, 259
enchiridion 593
enchorial 188
encincture 229
encircle 76, 227, 311
enclave *close* 181
  boundary 233
enclose 227, 229
enclosure
  region 181
  envelope 232
  fence 752
encomiast 935
encomium 931
encompass 227, 233
  –ed with difficulties 704
encore 104, 931
encounter
  undergo 151
  clash 276
  meet 292
  withstand 708
  contest 720
  – danger 665
  – risk 621
encourage
  animate 615
  aid 707
  comfort 834
  hope 858
  embolden 861
encroach
  transcursion 303
  do wrong 923

infringe 925
encumber 704, 706
encumbrance
  clear of – 807
encyclical 531
encyclopædia 490,
  593
  walking – 700
encyclopædical
  general 78
  – knowledge 490
encysted 229
end
  termination **67**
  effect 154
  object 620
  at an – 142
  come to its – 729
  one's journey's –
    292
  on – 212
  put an – to
  destroy 162
  kill 361
  begin at the
    wrong – 699
  – one's days 360
  –s of the earth 196
  – to end *space* 180
  touching 199
  length 200
  – of life 360
  – in smoke 732
  – of one's tether
  sophistry 477
  ignorant 491
  insufficient **640**
  difficult 704
endamage 649
endanger 665
endear 897
endearment 902
endeavour
  pursuit 622
  attempt 675
  use one's best –
    686
  – after 620
endemic
  special 79
  interior 221
  disease 657
endimanché 847,
  882
endless
  multitudinous
    102
  infinite 105
  perpetual 112
endlessly 16
endlong 200

endocrine 221
endogenous 367
endorse
  evidence 467
  assent 488
  compact 769
  - *a bill* 800
  approve 931
endorsement 550
endosmose 302
endow
  confer power 157
endowed with
  possessed of 777
endowment
  intrinsic 5
  power 157
  talent 698
  gift 784
endrogynous 83
endue 157
endure *time* 106
  last 110
  persist 143
  continue 141
  undergo 151
  feel 821
  submit to 826
  unable to – 867
  – for ever 112
  – *pain* 828
enduring
  indelible 505
endwise 212
enemy *time* 841
  foe 891
  the common – 978
  thing devised by
    the – 546
  – to society 891
energumen 504
energy *power* 157
  strength 159
  physical **171**
  resolution 604
  activity 682
enervate 158, 160
enfant, bon – 906
  – gâté
  prosperity 734
  satiety 869
  favourite 899
  – perdu
  hopeless 859
  reckless 863
  – terrible
  curiosity 455
  artless 703
  object of fear 860
enfeeble 160
enfeoff 780, 783

Enfield rifle 727
enfilade
  lengthwise 200
  pierce 260
  pass through 302
enfold 229
enforce *urge* 615
  advise 695
  compel 744
  require 924
enfranchise
  free 748
  liberate 750
  permit 760
enfranchised 924
engage
  bespeak 132
  induce 615
  undertake 676
  do battle 722
  commission 755
  promise 768
  compact 769
  I'll –
  affirmation 535
  – the attention
    457
  – with 720
engaged
  marriage 903
  be – 135
  – in *attention* 457
engagement
  business 625
  battle 720
  betrothal 902
engaging
  pleasing 829
  amiable 897
engender 161
engine 153, 633
engine-driver 268
engineer 690, 694,
  726
engineering 633
engird 227
English 188
  broken – 563
  king's – 560
  murder the king's
    – 568
  plain –
  intelligible 518
  interpreted 522
  style 576
  – *horn* 417
engorge
  swallow 296
  gluttony 957
engorgement
  too much 641

engrail 256
engrave
  furrow 259
  mark 550
  – in the memory
    505
engraver 559
engraving 21, 22,
  558
engross *write* 590
  possess 777
  – the thoughts
  thought 451
  attention 457
engrossed in
  thought 451
engulf
  destroy 162
  plunge 310
  swallow up 296
enhance
  increase 35
  improve 658
enharmonic 413
enigma
  question 461
  secret 533
enigmatic
  uncertain 475
  unintelligible **517**
  obscure 519
énigme, mot d' –
  522
enjoin *advise* 695
  command 741
  prescribe 926
enjoy
  physically 377
  possess 777
  morally 827
  – health 654
  – popularity 873
  – a state 7
enkindle *heat* 384
  excite 824
enlarge
  increase 35
  swell 194
  in writing 573
  liberate 750
  – the mind 537
enlarged views 498
enlighten
  illumine 420
  inform 527
  teach 537
enlightened
  knowledge 490
enlist *engage* 615
  war 722
  commission 755

under the ban-
ners of 707
– into the service
677
enliven
delight 829
cheer 836
amuse 840
enmity 889
ennoble 873
ennui 841
enormity
crime 947
enormous *great* 31
big 192
– number 102
enough *much* 31
no more! 142
sufficient 639
moderately 651
satiety 869
know when one
has had – 953
– in all conscience
641
– to drive one
mad 830
– and to spare 639
enounce 535, 580
enrage 830, 900
enragé 865
enrapture
excite 824
beatify 829
love 897
enraptured 827
enravish 829
enravished 827
enravishment 824
enrich
improve 658
wealth 803
ornament 847
enrobe 225
enroll *list* 86
record 551
– troops 722
commission 755
ens *essence* 1
Ens Entium 976
ensample 22
ensanguined 361
ensconce
conceal 528
safety 664
ensconced
located 184
ensemble 50
enshrine
circumscribe 229
repute 873

sanctify 987
– in the memory
505
ensiform 253
ensign
standard 550
officer 726
master 745
– of authority 747
ensilage 637
enslave 749
ensnare 545
ensue *follow* 63, 117
happen 151
ensure 474
entablature 210
entail *cause* 153
tie up property
781
entangle
interlink 43
derange 61
ravel 219
entrap 545
embroil 713
entangled
disorder 59
– by difficulties
704
entend, cela s' – 613
entente
agreement 23
alliance 714
friendship 888
enter *go in* 294
appear 446
note 551
accounts 811
– into the compo-
sition of 56
– into details
special 79
describe 594
– into an engage-
ment 768
– into the feelings
of 914
– into the ideas of
understand 518
concord 714
– in *converge* 290
– the lists
attack 716
contention 720
– the mind 451
– a profession 625
– into the spirit of
feel 821
delight 827
– upon 66
– into one's views

488
enterprise
pursuit 622
undertaking 676
commercial – 794
enterprising
active 171, 682
courageous 861
entertain
bear in mind 457
support 707
amuse 840
sociality 892
– doubts 485
– feeling 821
– an idea 451
– an opinion 484
entertainment 840
pleasure 377
repast 298
entêté 481, 606
enthral
subjection 749
restraint 751
enthrone 873
enthronement 755
enthusiasm
language 574
willingness 602
feeling 821
hope 858
love 897
enthusiast
madman 504
obstinate 606
active 682
enthusiastic
imaginative 515
sensitive 822
excitable 825
sanguine 858
enthymeme 476
entice 615
enticing 829
entire *whole* 50
complete 52
continuous 69
– horse 373
entirely *much* 31
entitle *name* 564
give a right 924
entity 1
entoil 545
entomb *inter* 363
imprison 751
Entomology 368
entourage 88, 183,
227
entozoon 193
entrails 221
entrain 293

entrammel 751
entrance
beginning 66
ingress 294
way 627
enrapture 827,
829
magic 992
give – to 296
entranced 515
entrancement 824
entrap 545
entre nous 528
entreat 765
entrée
reception 296
dish 298
give the – 296
have the – 294
– dish 191
entremet 298
entrepôt 636, 799
entrepreneur 599
entresol 191
entrust
commission 755
give 784
credit 805
entry *beginning* 66
ingress 294
record 551
entwine *join* 43
intersect 219
convolve 248
enucleate 522
enumerate 85
– among 76
enumeration 86
enunciate
inform 527
affirm 535
voice 580
envelop 225
envelope 223, 232
envenom
deprave 659
exasperate 835
hate 898
anger 900
envenomed
bad 649
insalubrious **657**
painful 830
malevolent 907
– tongue 934
environ 227
environment 183
environs 197
in such and such –
183
envisage 515, 861

envoy
messenger 534
consignee 758
envy 921
enwrap 225
enzyme 320
Eolian harp 417
Eolus 349
eon 976
épanchement
manifest 525
artless 703
endearment 902
epact 641
épaulette
badge 550, 747
ornament 847
decoration 877
éperdu 824
épergne 191
ephemeral 111
ephemeris
calendar 114
record 551
book 593
Ephesian letters
993
ephialtes
physical pain 378
hindrance 706
mental pain 828
ephod 999
ephor 967
epic 594, 597
epicedium 839
epicene 81, 83
epicier 876
epicure
fastidious 868
sybarite 954a
glutton 957
epicurean 954
Epicurus, system
of – 954
epicy-cle, -cloid
247
epidemic
general 78
disease 655
insalubrity 657
epidermis 223
epigenesis 161
epigram 496, 842
epigrammatic 572
epigrammatist 844
epigraph 550
epilepsy 315, 655
epilogue
sequel 65
end 67
drama 599

èpingles, tiré à
quatre – 855
Epiphany 998
episcopal 995
Episcopalian 984
episcopate 995
episode
adjunct 39
discontinuity 70
interjacence 228
episodic
irrelative 10
style 573
epistle 592
Epistles 985
epistrophe 104
epistyle 210
epitaph 363
epithalamium 903
epithem 662
epithet 564
epitome
miniature 193
short 201
concise 572
epizoötic 657
epoch *time* 106
instant 113
date 114
present time 118
epode 597
eponym 564
epopœa 597
epos 594
epulation 298
epulotic 662
epuration 652
equable 16, 922
equal *even* 27
equitable 922
– *chance* 156
– *times* 120
– *to power* 157
equality 13, **27**
equalize 213
equanimity 826
equate 27, 30
equations 85
equator 68, 318
equatorial 68, 236
equerry 746
equestrian 268
equibalanced 27
equidistant 68
equilibration 27
equilibrist 599
equilibrium 27
equine *carrier* 271
horse 366
equinox 125, 126
equip 225, 673

equipage
vehicle 272
instruments 633
display 882
equiparent 27
equipment 633
equipoise &c. 27, 30
equiponderate 30
equitable *wise* 498
just 922
due 924
honourable 939
– *interest* 780
equitation 266
equity *right* 922
honour 939
law 963
in – 922
– *draftsman* 968
equivalent
identical 13
equal 27
compensation 30
substitute 147
translation 522
equivocalness
dubious 475
double meaning
520
impure 961
equivocate
sophistry 477
palter 520
lie 544
equivocation
[*see* equivocate]
without – 543
équivoque
double meaning
520
impure 961
era *time* 106, 108
date 114
eradicate
destroy 162
extract 301
erase *destroy* 162
obliterate 331, 552
Erastian 984
erasure 552
Erato 416
ere 116
– *long* 132
– *now* 116
past 122
Erebus *dark* 421
hell 982
erect *build* 161
vertical 212
raise 307
with head – 878

– *the scaffolding*
673
erewhile 116, 122
ergatocracy 737
ergo 476
ergotism 480
ergotize 485
eriometer 445
Erinys 900
Erl King 980
ermine
badge of authority
747
ornament 847
erode 36, 659
Eros 897, 979
erosion 36
erotic 897, 961
err – *in opinion* **495**
– *morally* 945
errand
message 532
business 625
commission 755
errand-boy 534
errant 279
erratic
irregular 139
changeable 149
wandering 279
capricious 608
erratum 495
erroneous 495
error *fallacy* **495**
vice 945
guilt 947
court of – 966
writ of – 969
ersatz 973
erst 122
erubescence 434
erubuit salva res
est 95
eruct 297
eructate 297
erudition 490, 539
eruption
upheaval 146
violence 173
egress 295, 297
disease 655
volcanic – 872
escadrille 726
escalade
mounting 305
attack 716
escalator 307
escalop 248
escapade
absurdity **497**
freak 608

euthanasia 360
euthenics 658
evacuate
quit 293
excrete 295
emit 297
evacuation 299
evade *sophistry* 477
avoid 623
not observe 773
exempt 927
evagation 279
evanescent
small 32
transient 111
little 193
disappearing 449
evangelical 983*a*,
985
Evangelists 985
evanid 160
evaporable 334
evaporate
unsubstantial 4
transient 111
vaporize 336
evaporation 340
evasion
sophistry 477
concealment 528
falsehood 544
untruth 546
avoidance 623
escape 671
cunning 702
non-observance
773
dereliction 927
eve 126
on the − of
transient 111
prior 116
future 121
evection 61
even
uniform 16
equal 27
still more 33
regular 138
level 213
straight 246
flat 251
smooth 255
although 469
in spite of 708
− course 628
− now 118
− so
for all that 30
yes 488
− temper 826

− terms 922
− tenor
uniform 16
order 58
continuity 58
pursue the −
tenor
continue 143
avoid 623
business 625
be − with
retaliate 718
pay 807
get − with 972
even-handed 922,
939
evening **126**
shades of − 422
− classes 537
− star 423
evenness 16
evensong 126, 990
event 151
bout 720
in the − of
circumstance 8
expectation 507
supposition 514
justified by the −
937
eventful 151
remarkable 642
stirring 682
eventide 126
eventual 121
eventuality **151**
eventually
effect 154
ever 16, 112
did you − ? 870
− and anon 136
− changing 149
− recurring 104
ever so 31
− little 32
− long 110
− many 102
evergreen
continuous 69
lasting 110
always 112
fresh 123
everlasting 112
− life 152
− fire 982
evermore 112
eversion 218
evert 140
every 78
− hand against
one 891

− day
conformity 82
frequent 136
habit 613
− description 81
− inch 50
in − mouth
assent 488
news 532
repute 873
− other 138
in − quarter 180
in − respect 494
on − side 227
at − turn 186
− whit 52
everybody 78
everyone 78
− his due 922
− in his turn 148
everywhere 180,
186
evict 297
evidence **467**
disclose 529
ocular − 446
évidence, en − 446
evident
concrete 3
visible 446
certain 474
manifest 525
evidently 516
evil *harm* **619**
badness 649
impious 988
− day
prepare for − 673
adversity 735
− eye *vision* 441
malevolence 907
disapprobation
932
demon 980
sorcery 992
spell 993
− favoured 846
− fortune 735
− genius 980
− hour 135
− one 978
− plight 735
through − report
&c. 604*a*
− star 649
evil-doer **913**
evil-doing 945
evil-minded 907,
945
evil-speaking
malediction 908

censure 932
detraction 934
evince *show* 467
prove 478
disclose 529
eviscerate 297, 301
eviscerated 4
evoke *cause* 153
call upon 765
excite 824
evolution
numerical 85
production 161
motion 264
extraction 301
circuition 311
turning out **313**
organization 357
training 673
action 680
military −s 722
evolve
discover 480*a*
evolved from 154
[*and see*
evolution]
evulgate 531
evulsion 301
evivva! 931
ewe 366, 374
− lamb 366
ewer 191
ex
− animo 602
− cathedra 542
− officio 494, 924
− parte 467
− pede Herculem
82
− post facto 122,
133
− tempore
instant 113
occasion 134
exacerbate
increase 35
exasperate 173
aggravate 659,
835
exact *similar* **17**
special 79
true 494
style 572
require 741
tax 812
insolence 885
claim 924, 926
− meaning 516
− memory 505
− observance 772
− truth 494

exacting
severe 739
discontented 832
grasping 865
fastidious 868
exaction
[*see* exact]
undue 925
exactly
just so 488
exaggeration
increase 35
expand 194
overestimate 482
magnify **549**
misrepresent 555
exalt
increase 35
elevate 307
extol 931
– one's horn 873
exalté 504
tête –e 503
exalted *high* 206
repute 873
noble 875
magnanimous
942
examination
[*see* examine]
evidence 467
undergo – 461
examine 457, 461
example
pattern 22
instance 82
bad – 949
good – 948
make an – of 972
set a good – 944
exanimate
dead 360
supine 683
exarch 745
exasperate
exacerbate 173
aggravate 835
enrage 900
excavate 252
excecation 442
exceed *surpass* 33
remain 40
transgress 303
intemperance 954
excel *surpass* 33
– in *skilful* 698
excellence 648, 944
excellence, par –
642
excellency 877
excelsior 305

except *subduct* 38
exclude 55
reject 610
exception
unconformity 83
qualification 469
exemption 777a
disapproval 932
take –
qualify 469
resent 900
exceptionable
bad 649
guilty 947
exceptional
original 20
extraneous 57
unconformable 83
in an – degree 31
exceptious 901,
901a
exceptis
excipiendis 469
excern 297
excerpt 609
excerpta *parts* 51
compendium 596
selections 609
excerption 609
excess
remainder 40
redundance 641
intemperance 954
excessive 31
exchange
reciprocity 12
interchange 148
transfer 783
barter 794
mart 799
bill of – 771
rate of – 800
– blows &c.
retaliation 718
battle 720
Exchequer 802
Baron of – 967
Court of – 966
– bill 800
excise 812
exciseman 965
excision 38
excitability **825,**
901
excitation 824
excite *energy* 171
violence 173
- *morally* 824
– attention 457
– desire 865
– hope 811

– an impression
375
– love 897
excited fancy 515
excitement 824, 825
anger 900
exclaim 411
– against 932
exclamation 580
mark of – 550
exclude
leave out 42, 55
reject 610
prohibit 761
banish 893
exclusion **55, 57**
exclusive
simple 42
omitting 55
special 79
irregular 83
forbidding 761
– of 38
– possession 777
– thought 457
excogitate 451, 515
excommunicate
banish 893
curse 908
rite 998
excoriate 226
excrement
excretion 299
dirt 653
excrescence
projection 250
blemish 848
excreta
excretion 299
dirt 653
excretion 297, 299
excruciating 378,
830
exculpate
forgive 918
vindicate 937
acquit 970
excursion 266, 311
excursionist 268
excursive
deviating 279
- *style* 573
excursus 595
excuse *plea* 617
forgive 918
exempt 927a
vindicate 937
execrable 649, 830
execrate 898, 908
execution
music 416

action 680
conduct 692
signing 771
observance 772
punishment 972
carry into –
complete 729
put in –
undertaking 676
executioner 975
executive
conduct 692
direction 693
authority 737
judicature 965
executor 690
to one and his
&c., *property*
780
exegetical 522
exemplar 22
exemplary 944
exemplify
quote 82
illustrate 522
exempt *free* 748
dispensation 927a
– from *absent* 187
unpossessed 777a
exemption
exception 83
qualification 469
deliverance 672
permission 760
non-possession
777a
non-liability **927**
exenterate 297
exequatur 755
exequies 363
exercise
operation 170
teach 537
task 625
use 677
act 680
exert 686
– authority **737**
– discretion 609
– the intellect **451**
– power 157
exergue 231
exert *use* 677
– authority **737**
– oneself 686
exertion 171, **686**
exfoliate 226
exhalation
ejection 297
excretion 299
vapour 336

186
up to one's –s
  641
have one's –s
  about one 459
– askance 860
–s draw straws 683
an – for an – 718,
  919
– glistening 824
in the – of the law
  963
– of the master
  693
– of a needle 260
–s open
  attention 457
  care 459
  intention 620
–s opened
  disclosure 529
–s out 442
eye-ball 441
eyebrows 256
eyeglass 445
eyelashes 256
eyeless 442
eyelet 260
eyelid 223
eye-shade 443
eye-sight 441
eyesore 846, 848
eye-teeth
  have cut one's –
    adolescence 131
    skill 698
    cunning 702
eye-wash 544
eye-witness
  spectator 444
  evidence 467
eyot 346
eyre 966
eyry 189

F

Fabian policy
  delay 133
  inaction 681
  caution 864
fable *error* 495
  metaphor 521
  fiction 546
  description 594
fabric *state* 7
  effect 154
  texture 329
fabricate
  composition 54

make 161
invent 515
falsify 544
fabrication *lie* 546
fabula narratur, de
  te – *retaliate* 718
  condemn 971
fabulist 594
fabulous
  enormous 31
  imaginary 515
  untrue 546
  exaggerated 549
faburden 413
façade 234
face *exterior* 220
  covering 223
  front 234
  aspect 448
  oppose 708
  resist 719
  brave 861
  impudence 885
  change the – of
    146
  fly in the – of
    disobey 742
  put a good – upon
    sham 545
    calm 826
    cheerful 836
    hope 858
    pride 878
    display 882
    vindicate 93
  in the – of
    presence 186
    opposite 708
  look in the –
    see 441
    proud 878
  make –s
    distort 243
    ugly 846
    disrespect 929
  on the – of
    manifest 525
  show –
    present 186
    visible 446
  not show –
    disreputable 874
    bashful 879
  to one's – 525
  wry – 378
  – about 279
  set one's – against
    708
  – of the country
    344
  on the – of the

earth
  space 180
  world 318
  – to face *front* 234
  contraposition
    237
  manifest 525
  – of the thing
    appearance 448
facet 220
facetiæ 842
facetious 842
facia 234
facile *willing* 602
  irresolute 605
  easy 705
facile princeps 33
facilis descensus
  Averni
  sloping 217
  danger 665
facilitate 705
facility *skill* 698
  easy **705**
facing *covering* 223
facinorous 945
façon de parler 521,
  549
fac-simile 21, 554
fact *existence* 1
  event 151
  certainty 474
  truth 494
  in – 535
faction 712, 713
factious 24
factitious 545, 546
factor
  numerical 84
  director 694
  consignee 758
factory 691
factotum
  agent 690
  manager 694
  employé 758
facts *evidence* 467
  summary of – 594
  at variance with –
    471
facula 420
faculties 450
  in possession of
    one's – 502
faculty
  power 157
  profession 625
  skill 698
facundity 582
fad 481, 608
faddle 683

fade *vanish* 4
  transient 111
  become old 124
  droop 160
  grow dim 422
  lose colour 429
  disappear 449
  spoil 659
  – from the
    memory **506**
fade 391
fadge 23
fæces 299, 653
fæx populi 876
fag *cigarette* 392
  labour 686
  fatigue 688
  drudge 690, **746**
  – end
    remainder 40
    end 67
faggot 72, 388
fagots et fagots 15,
  465
faïence 557
fail *droop* 160
  shortcoming 304
  be confuted 479
  illness 655
  not succeed 732
  not observe 773
  not pay 808
  dereliction 927
failing [see fail]
  incomplete 53
  insufficient 640
  vice 945
  guilt 947
  – heart 837
  – luck 735
  – memory 506
  – sight 443
  – strength 160
failure **732**
  heart – 360
fain *willing* 602
  compulsive **744**
  wish 865
fainéant 683
faint 32
  impotent **158**
  weak 160
  sound 405
  dim 422
  colour 429
  swoon 688
  – heart *fear* 860
  cowardice 862
  damn with –
    praise 930, **932**,
    934

pleased 827
fascination [*see*
fascinate]
infatuation 825
desire 870
fascine 72
Fascisti 712
fas et nefas, per –
604a, 631
fash 830
fashion
state 7
form 240
custom 613
method 627
ton **852**
after a –
middling 32
after this – 627
follow the – 82
be in the – 488
man of – 852
set the –
influence 175
authority 737
for –'s sake 852
fast *joined* 43
steadfast 150
rapid 274
fashionable 852
intemperate 954
not eat 956
worship 990
rite 998
stick – 704
– asleep 683
– by 197
– day 956
– friend 890
– and loose
sophistry 477
falsehood 544
irresolute 605
tergiversation 607
caprice 608
– man *fop* 854
libertine 962
fasten *join* 43
hang 214
restrain 751
– on the mind 451
– a quarrel upon
713
– upon 789
fastening 45
fast-handed 819
fastidious
censorious 932
fastidiousness **868**
fasting
insufficiency 640

worship 990
penance 952
abstinence **956**
fastness
asylum 666
defence 717
fat *corpulent* 192
expansion 194
unctuous 355
oleaginous 356
kill the –ted calf
celebration 883
sociality 892
– in the fire
disorder 59
violence 173
– of the land
pleasure 377
enough 639
prosperity 734
intemperance 95
fata – Morgana
occasion 134
ignis fatuus 423
– obstant 601
fatal 361
– disease 655
fatalism 601
fatality 601
fate *end* 67
necessity 601
chance 621
be one's – 156
sure as – 474
Fates 601, 979
fat-head 501
father *eldest* 128
paternity 166
priest 996
Apostolical –s 985
gathered to one's
–s 360
heavy – 599
– upon 155
Father, God the –
976
fatherland 189
fatherless 158
fatherly 906
fathom
length 200
investigate 461
solve 462
measure 466
discover 480a
knowledge 490
fathomless 208
fatidical 511
fatigation 688
fatigue **688**
fatras 643

fatten
expand 194
improve 658
prosperous 734
– on *parasite* 886
– upon
feed 298
fatuity 4, 499
fatuous 517
fat-witted 499
faubourg 227
fauces 231
faucet 252
faugh! 867
fault
break 70
error 495
imperfection 651
failure 732
vice 945
guilt 947
at –
uncertain 475
ignorant 491
unskilful 699
find – with 932
faultless 650, 946
faulty 495, 651
faun 980
fauna 366
faut: comme il –
taste 850
fashion 852
il s'en – bien 489
tant s'en – 536
faute 732
– de mieux
substitution 147
necessity 601
fauteuil 215
fautor 890
faux pas
error 568
failure 732
misconduct 947
intrigue 961
favour
resemble 17
badge 550
letter 592
aid 707
indulgence 740
permit 760
gift 784
partiality 923
appearances in –
of 472
get into –
friendship 888
love 897
in – *repute* 873

approbation **931**
in – of
approve 931
under – of 760
view with – 906
– with 784
favourable
occasion 134
willing 602
good 648
aid 707
– prospect **472**
– to 709
take a – turn
improve 658
prosperity **734**
favourably
well 618
favourer 890
favourite
pleasing 829
beloved 897, **899**
favouritism
friendship 888
wrong 923
fawn *colour* 433
cringe 749, 886
flatter 933
fay 979
fealty
obedience 743
duty 926
respect 928
fear **860**
fearful
painful 830
timid 862
fearfully 31, 870
fearless *hope* 858
courage 861
fearsome 860
feasible 470, 705
feast *period* 138
repast 298
pleasure 377
revel 840
rite 998
– one's eyes 897
feast of reason
conversation 588
– and flow of soul
sociality 892
feat *action* 680
courage 861
– of arms 720
– of strength **159**
feather
class 75
tuft 256
light 320
trifle 643

ornament 847
decoration 877
in full –
  prepared 673
  prosperous 734
  rich 803
hear a – drop 403
in high –
  health 654
  cheerful 884
pleased with a –
  840
– in one's cap
  honour 873
  decoration 877
– one's nest
  prepare 673
  prosperity 734
  wealth 803
  economy 817
  selfish 943
– the oar 698
– in the scale 643
feather-bed 324
feathered tribes
  366
feathery 256
featly 682
feature
  character 5
  component 56
  form 240
  appearance 448
  press 531
  lineament 550
– in 56
features
  face 234
febrifuge 662
febrile 382, 825
fecal 653
fecit 556
feckless 866
feculence 653
fecund 168
fecundate 161
federal council 696
– penitentiary 752
federalism 737
federation 48, 709,
  712
fee *possession* 777
  property 780
  pay 809
  reward 973
feeble *weak* 160
  illogical 477
feeble-minded 497,
  605
feebleness
  style **575**

feed *eat* 298
  supply 637
– the flame 707
fee-faw-fum
  bugbear 860
  spell 993
feel *sense* 375
  touch 379
  emotion 821
– for *try* 463
  benevolence 906
  pity 914
  condole with 915
– the pulse 461
– the want of 865
– one's way
  essay 675
  caution 864
feeler 379
  inquiry 461
  experiment 463
feeling 698, **821**
feet *low* 207
  walkers 266
at one's –
  near 197
  subjection 749
  humility 879
fall at one's –
  submit 725
fall on one's –
  prosper 734
lick the – of
  servile 886
light upon one's –
  safe 664
spring to one's –
  307
throw oneself at
  the – of
  entreat 765
feign 544, 546
feigned 545
feint 545
felicitas, curiosa –
  698
felicitate 896
felicitous
  agreeing 23
  - *style* 578
  skilful 698
  successful 731
  pleasant 829
felicity 827
feline *cat* 366
  stealthy 528
  cunning 702
fell *destroy* 162
  mountain 206
  lay flat 21
  skin 223

lay low 308
moor 344
dire 860
malevolent 907
fellah 876
felloe 231
fellow *similar* 17
  equal 27
  companion 88
  dual 89
  man 373
  scholar 492, 541
fellow-commoner
  541
fellow-companion
  890
fellow-countryman
  890
fellow-creature 372
fellow-feeling
  friendship 888
  love 897
  benevolence 906
  pity 914
fellowship
  partnership 712
  distinction 873
  friendship 888
  companionship
  890
  good – 892
fellow-student 541
fellow-worker 690
felly 231
felo-de-se 361
felon 949
felonious 945
felony 947
felt *texture* 219
  heart– 821
felucca 273
female 374
feme coverte 903
feme sole 904
feminality
  weakness 160
  woman 374
feminine 374
feminism 374
femme de chambre
  746
fen 345
fence *enclose* 232
  evade 544
  defence 717
  fight 720
  prison 752
  thief 792
– round 229
– with a question
  528

fenced 770
fenceless 665
fencible 726
fencing 840
feneration 787
fend 717
fender 717
Fenian 710, 742
fenum habet in
  cornu 668, 913
feodal 780
feodality 737, 777
feoff *property* 780
feoffee 779, 785
feoffer 784
feræ naturæ 366
feral 907
ferine 907
ferment
  disorder 59
  energy 171
  violence 173
  agitation 315
  lightness 320
  effervesce 353
  emotion 821
  excitement 824,
  825
  anger 900
fermentation,
  acetous – 397
fern 367
ferocity 173, 907
Ferrara
  sword 727
ferret out 461, 480*a*
ferro-concrete 635
ferrule 223
ferry 270, 627
ferry-boat 273
ferry-man 269
fertile 161, 168
– imagination **515**
ferule 975
  come under the –
  932
fervent *hot* 382
  desirous 865
– hope 858
fervid *hot* 382
  heartfelt 821
  excited 824
fervour *heat* 382
  animation 821
  love 897
festal *eating* 298
  social 892
fester 653, 655
festina lente 864
festival
  music 416

filigree 219
filings 330
fill *complete* 52
  occupy 186
  contents 190
  stuff 224
  provision 637
  eat one's – 957
  have one's –
    enough 639
  satiety 869
  – the bill 229
  – an office
    business 625
  government 737
  – out
    expand 194
  –ed to overflow-
    ing 641
  – one's pocket 803
  – time 106
  – up *compensate*
    30
  compose 54
  close 261
  restore 660
  – up the time
    inaction 681
fille
  – de chambre 746
  – de joie 962
filled
  – to overflowing
    641
filler 532
fillet *band* 45
  filament 205
  circle 247
  insignia 550
  ornament 847
fillibeg 225
filling 224
fillip
  impulse 276
  propulsion 284
  stimulus 615
  excite 824
filly 271
film *layer* 204
  opaque 426
  semitransparent
    427
  – over the eyes
    dim sight 443
  cinema 448
  ignorant 491
filmy *texture* 329
filter *percolate* 295
  clean 652
filth 653
  –y *lucre* 800

filtrate 652
fimbriated 256
fin 267
final *ending* 67
  conclusive 474
  completing 729
  court of – appeal
    474
  – cause 620
  – stroke 729
  – touch 729
finale *end* 67
  completion 729
finality 67, 729
finally
  for good 141
  on the whole 476
finance 800, 811
  minister of – 801
financier 801
finch 366
find
  eventuality 151
  adjudge 480
  discover 480a
  acquire 775
  – one's account in
    644
  – the cause of 522
  – a clue to 480a
  – to one's cost 509
  – credence 484
  – it in one's heart
    602
  – in *provide* 637
  – the key of 522
  – the meaning 522
  – means 632
  – oneself *be* 1
    present 186
  – out 480a
  – vent 671
  – one's way 731
  – one's way into
    294
finding
  judgment 480
fine *small* 32
  large 192
  thin 203
  rare 322
  not raining 340
  exact 494
  good 648
  beautiful 845
  adorned 847
  proud 878
  mulct 974
  in – *end* 67
  after all 476
  – air 656

  – arts 554
  – feather 159, 654
  – feeling 850
  – frenzy 515
  – gentleman
    fop 854
  proud 878
  – grain 329
  – lady 854, 878
  one – morning 106
  some – morning
    119
  – powder 330
  – talking
    overrate 482
  boast 884
  – writing 577
  – time of it 734
  – voice 580
fine-draw 660
fine-fingered 698
fine-spoken 894,
  933
fine-spun *thin* 203
  sophistry 477
fine-toned 413
finem, respicere –
  510
finery 847, 851
finesse *tact* 698
  artifice 702
  taste 850
finger *touch* 379
  hold 781
  lay the – on
  point out 457
  discover 480a
  lift a – 680
  not lift a – 681
  point the – at 457
  turn round one's
    little – 737
  –'s breadth 203
  at one's –s' end
    near 197
  know 490
  remember 505
  – on the lips
    aphony 581
  taciturnity 585
  – in the pie
    cause 153
  interfere 228
  act 680
  active 682
  co-operate 709
fingerling 193
finger-post 550
finger-print 467
finger-stall 223
fingle-fangle 643

finical
  trifling 643
  affected 855
  fastidious 868
finicky 855, 868
finikin 643
finis 67
  – coronat opus
    729
finish *lend* 67
  symmetry 242
  complete 729
  skill 698
finished
  absolute 31
  perfect 650
  skilled 698
finishing
  – stroke 361
  – touch 729
finite 32
fiord 343
fire *energy* 171
  heat 382
  make hot 384
  stoke 388
  vigour 574
  discharge 756
  enthusiasm 821
  excite 824, 825
  catch – 384
  hell – 982
  on – 382
  open – *begin* 66
  play with – 863
  signal – 550
  take –
    excitable 825
  angry 900
  between two –s
    665
  under – 665, 722
  – at 716
  – the blood 824
  – and fury 900
  – the first shot 716
  – of genius 498
  – off 284
  – a salute 883
  – and sword 162
  – up *excite* 825
  anger 900
  – a volley 716
  go through – **and**
    water
    resolution 604
  perseverance 604a
  courage 861
fire-alarm 669
fire-annihilator 385
fire-arms 727

smoothness 255
slow 275
leaf 367
sign 550
path 627
infirm 655
inactive 683
tired 688
weary 841
lower one's – 725
red – *alarm* 669
yellow –
  warning 668
  alarm 669
– man 668
– ship 726
– of truce 723
flag-bearer 534
flagellation
  penance 952
  asceticism 955
  flogging 972
  rite 998
flagelliform 205
flageolet 417
flagitious 945
flagon 191
flagrant
  great 31
  manifest 525
  notorious 531
  atrocious 945
flagrante
– *bello* 722
– *delicto*
  sure enough 474
  act 680
  guilt 947
flagration 384
flagstaff *tall* 206
  signal 550
flail 276
flair 450, 698
flake 204
  snow – 383
– white 430
flam 544
flambé 732
flambeau 423
flamboyant 577
flame *fire* 382
  light 420
  luminary 423
  passion 824, 825
  love 897
  catch the –
  emotion 821
  consign to the –s
    384
  add fuel to the –
    173

[492]

in –s 382
– up 825
–coloured
  red 434
  orange 439
flame-projector 727
flamen 996
flaming *violent* 173
  feeling 821
  excited 824
  ostentatious 882
  boasting 884
flâneur 935
flange *support* 215
  rim 231
  projection 250
flank *side* 236
  protect 664
flannel 384
flap *adjunct* 39
  hanging 214
  move to and fro
    315
– the memory 505
flapdoodle 517
flapper *girl* 129
flapping *loose* 47
flare *violent* 173
  glare 420
  light 423
– up
  excited 824, 825
  angry 900
flaring *colour* 428
flash *instant* 113
  violent 173
  fire 382
  light 420
  eyes – *fire* 900
– lamp 550
– light 423
– across the mem-
    ory 505
– on the mind
  thought 451
  disclose 529
  impulse 612
– note 800
– in the pan
  unsubstantial 4
  transientness 111
  impotent 158
  unproductive 169
  failure 732
– tongue 563
– up *excited* 824
– upon
  unexpected 508
– of wit 842
flashing
  ostentatious 882

flashy
  gaudy colour 428
  style 577
  ornament 847
  vulgar 851
flask 191
flat *inert* 172
  abode 189
  story 191
  low 207
  horizontal 213
  vapid 391
  low tone 408
  musical note 413
  positive 535
  dupe 547
  back-scene 599
  shoal 667
  bungler 701
  poor 804
  insensible 823
  dejected 837
  weary 841
  dull 843
  simple 849
  fall – 732
– contradiction
    536
– iron 255
– refusal 764
flatfoot 664
flatness 251
flatter *deceive* 545
  cunning 702
  please 829
  grace 845
  encourage 858
  approbation 931
  adulation 933
– oneself
  probable 472
  hope 858
– the palate 394
flatterer 935
flattering
– remarks 894
– tale
  hope 858
– unction to one's
  soul
  content 831
  vain 880
  flattery 933
flattery 544, 933
flatulent
  gaseous 334
  air 338
  wind 349
- *style* 573, 575
flatus 334, 349
flaunt 873, 882

flaunting *vulgar* 851
  gaudy 428
  unreserved 525
flautist 416
Flavian amphi-
  theatre 728
flavour 390
flavouring 393
flavous 436
flaw *break* 70
  crack 198
  error 495
  imperfection 651
  blemish 848
  fault 947
– in an argument
    477
flaxen 436
flay *divest* 226
  punish 972
flea *jumper* 309
  dirt 653
– in one's ear
  repel 289
  eject 297
  refuse 764
  disrepute 874
  abashed 879
  discourteous 895
  contempt 930
flea-bite 643
flea-bitten 440
fleck 32
flecked 440
flection 279
fled *escaped* 671
fledge 673
fledgling 123
flee *avoid* 623
fleece *tegument* 223
  strip 789
  rob 791
  impoverish 804
  surcharge 814
fleet *ridicule* 856
  insult 929
fleet *ships* 273
  swift 274
  navy 726
Fleet *prison* 752
fleeting 4, 111
flesh *bulk* 192
  animal 364
  mankind 372
  carnal 961
  gain - 194
  ills that – is heir
    to *evil* 619
  disease 655
  in the – 359
  one – 903

way of all – 360
weakness of the –
  945
– and blood
  substance 3
  materiality 316
  animality 364
  affections 820
make the – creep
  pain 830
  fear 860
flesh-colour 434
flesh-pots 298
  – of Egypt 734,
  803
fleshly 316
fleur-de-lis 847
fleuron 847
flexible 324, 705
flexion
  curvature 245
  fold 258
  deviation 279
flexuous 248
flexure 245, 258
flibbertigibbet 980
flicker
  changing 149
  waver 314
  flutter 315
  light 420
  dim 422
flickering 139
flier 621
flies *theatre* 599
flight *flock* 102
  volitation 267
  swiftness 274
  departure 293
  avoidance 623
  escape 671
  – lieutenant 745
put to –
  propel 284
  repel 717
  vanquish 731
– of fancy 515
– of stairs 305,
  627
– of time 109
flighty *inattentive*
  458
  mad 503
  fanciful 515
flim-flam 544, 608
flimsy *unsubstan-*
  tial 4
  weak 160
  rarity 322
  soft 324
  sophistical 477

trifling 643
finch *swerve* 607
  avoid 623
  fear 860
  cowardice 862
fling *propel* 284
  jig 840
  jeer 929
have one's –
  active 682
  laxity 738
  freedom 748
  amusement 840
– aside 782
have a – at
  attack 716
  resent 900
  disrespect 929
  censure 932
– away *reject* 610
  waste 638
  relinquish 782
– down 308
– to the winds
  destroy 162
  not observe 773
flint *hard* 323
flint-hearted 907
flintlock 727
flip *beverage* 298
flippant *fluent* 584
  pert 885
flipper *paddle* 267
flirt *propel* 284
  coquet 607, 854
  love 897
  endearment 902
– a fan 855
flit *elapse* 109
  changeable 149
  move 264
  travel 266
  swift 274
  depart 293
  run away 623
flitter
  small part 32
  changeable 149
  flutter 315
flitting 111
float *establish* 150
  navigate 267
  boat 273
  buoy up 305
  lightness 320
before the –s
  on the stage 599
– on the air 405
– before the eyes
  446
– bonds 788

– in the mind
  thought 451
  imagination 515
floater 683
floating
  [*see* float]
  rumoured 532
– battery 726
– capital 805
– debt 806
– dock 189
flocculent
  woolly 256
  soft 324
  pulverulent 330
flock
  assemblage 72
  multitude 102
  laity 997
–s and herds 366
– together 72
floe *ice* 383
flog 972
  hasten 684
flood *much* 31
  crowd 72
  river 348
  abundance 639
  redundance 641
  prosperity 734
stem the – 708
– of light 420
– of tears 839
flood-gate
  limit 233
  egress 295
  conduit 350
open the –s
  eject 297
  permit 760
flood-light 423,
  599
flood-mark 466
flood-tide
  increase 35
  complete 52
  height 206
  advance 282
  water 337
floor *level* 204
  base 211
  horizontal 213
  support 215
  overthrow 731
ground – 191
flop 315
Flora 369
floral 367
florescence 154
floriculture 371
florid *colour* 428

  red 434
– *style* 577
  health 654
florist 371
floss 256
flotilla 273, 726
flotsam and jetsam
  73
flounce
  trimming 231
  jump 309
  agitation 315
flounder
  change 149
  toss 315
  uncertain 475
  bungle 699
  difficulty 704
  fail 732
flour 330
flourish
  brandish 314, **315**
  exaggerate 549
  language 577
  speech 582
  prosper 618
  healthy 654
  prosperous **734**
  ornament 847
  repute 873
  display 882
  boast 884
– of trumpets
  loud 404
  cheerfulness **836**
  publish 531
  ostentation 882
  celebrate 883
  boast 884
flout 929, 936
flow *course* 109
  hang 214
  motion 264
  stream 348
  murmur 405
  abundance **639**
– from
  result 154
– of ideas **451**
– in 294
– into *river* **348**
– out 295
– over 641
– of soul
  conversation **588**
  affections 820
  cheerful 836
  social 892
– with the tide
  705
– of time 109

[493]

– of words 582, 584
flower *essence* 5
  produce 161
  vegetable 367
  prosper 734
  beauty 845
  ornament 847
  repute 873
  – of age 131
  – of flock 648
  – of life 127
  – painting 556, 559
flowering plant 367
flowers
  anthology 596
  – of rhetoric 577
flowing
  [*see* flow]
  – periods 578
fluctuate
  change 149
  oscillate 314
  irresolute 605
flue *opening* 260
  air-pipe 351
  down 320
  dust 653
fluent
  differential 84
  fluid 333
  stream 348
  - *language* 578
  speech 584
fluff 256
  little bit of – 374
fluid 333
  – in motion 347
fluidity 333
fluke *hook* 244
  chance 621
flummery
  unmeaning 517
  flattery 933
flunk 732
flunkey
  servant 746
  servile 886
flunkeyism 933
flurry *hurry* 684
  agitation 821
  excitability 825
flush *flat* 251
  flood 348
  heat 382
  light 420
  colour 428
  red 434
  abundant 639
  wash 652

health 654
feeling 821
passion 825
rejoicing 838
in liquor 959
– of cash 803
flushed
  [*see* flush]
  excited 824
  cheerful 836
  hopeful 858
  proud 878
  vain 880
  – with rage 900
  – with success 731
  – with victory 884
fluster
  distract 458
  move 821
  excite 824, 825
flustered *tipsy* 959
flute
  furrow 259
  music 417
flutter
  variable 149
  agitation 315
  gamble 621
  hurry 684
  emotion 821
  excite 824, 825
  fear 860
fluvial 348
flux
  conversion 144
  motion 264
  liquefaction 335
  flow 348
  – and reflux 314
  – of time 109
flux de paroles 584
fluxion 84
fluxions 85
fly *vanish* 4
  time 109
  transient 111
  burst 173
  minute 193
  wings 267
  vehicle 272
  swift 274
  depart 293
  break 328
  lose colour 429
  shun 623
  – to arms 722
  – at 716
  – back 277
  – in the face of *oppose* 708
  resist 719

disobey 742
insolence 885
– in the face of facts 481, 606
– from 623
– kites
  borrow 788
  credit 805
  not pay 808
– off 291
– in the ointment 651
– open 260
– out *violent* 173
excitable 825
angry 900
fly-blown 653
fly-boat 273
flyer 269
flying [*see* fly]
  – colours
  success 731
  display 882
  celebrate 883
  – boat 273, 726
  – column 726
  – field 728
  – fish 83
  – machine 273
  – officer 745
  – rumour 532
fly-leaf
  interjacent 228
  book 593
fly-wheel 312
foal 129, 271
foam *violent* 173
  boil 315
  spray 353
  excitement 824, 825
  – with rage 900
fob 191
  – off 545
focal 222
focis, pro aris et – 717
focus 74
  centre 222
  furnace 386
  bring into a –
  collect 72
  convergence 290
  in – *visible* 446
  out of – *dim* 447
  – the thoughts 457
fodder 298
foe 891
fœderis, casus – 770
föhn 349
fœnum habet in

cornu 668, 913
fœtor 401
fœtus 129, 153
fog 353, 475
  in a – 528
  London – 436
fogey 501, 857
foggy
  opaque 426
fog-signal 668, 669
foh! 867
foible 945
foil *contrast* 14
  lamina 204
  baffle 706
  weapon 727
  defeat 731
foiled 732
foin 276
foist *ship* 273
  – in 228
  – upon 545
folâtre 836
fold *fold* 39
  bisect 91
  inclosure 232
  plait **258**
  prison 752
  congregation 997
  – one's arms 681
  – in one's arms 902
  – up 225
foliaceous 204
foliage 367
foliate 85
foliated 204
folio 593
folk 372
folk-dance 840
folk-lore 124, 979
folk-song 597
follicle *cyst* 191
  hollow 252
follicular 260
follow
  - *in order* 63
  conform to 82
  - *in time* 117
  - *in motion* 281
  understand 518
  pursue 622
  obey 743
  – advice 695
  – the dictates of 615
  – the example of 19
  – from
  result from 154
  be proved by 478

- implicitly 486, 695
- the lead of
  co-operate 709
- suit *imitate* 19
- the trail 461
- up
  continue 143
  persevere 604a
follower
  [*see* follow]
  successor 65
  learn 541
  servant 746
  lover 897
folly
  building 189
  irrationality **499**
  act of –
  mismanagement
  699
foment
  stimulate 173
  warm 384
  promote 707
  excite 824
  relieve 834
fond 897
- hope 858
fondle 902
fondling 899, 902
fondness
  desire 865
fondre en larmes
  839
fons et origo 153
font *origin* 153
  type 591
  rite 998
  altar 1000
food 298
  preparation of –
  673
- for the mind 454
- for powder 726
fool 501
  pudding 354
  deceive 545
  ridicule 856
  disrespect 929
  make a – of
    oneself
  bungle 699
  motley – 844
  play the –
  folly 499
  amusement 840
-'s errand
  deceived 545
  unskilful 699
-'s mate 732

–'s paradise
  unsubstantial 4
  misjudgment 481
  disappoint 509
  hope 858
  rash 863
- to the top of
  one's bent
  excite 824
  anger 900
  flatter 933
- away money 818
- away time 683
foolhardy 863
fooling 842
foolish 499
  act –ly 699
  look –
  disrepute 874
  shame 879
foolscap 550, 559
foot
  length 200
  stand 211
  metre 597
  at the – of 207
  keep on –
  continue 143
  support 251
  provide 637
  prepare 673
  not stir a – 681
  on – *existing* 1
  during 106
  journey 266
  topic 454
  business 625
  preparing 673
  active 682
  put one's – down
  resolved 604
  put one's – in
  undertake 676
  bungle 699
  set – on land 342
  trample under –
  930
- the bill 807
- by foot 51
  one – in the grave
  age 128
  death 360
  it *journey* 266
  dance 309
  at –'s pace 275
foot-ball
  subjection 749
  game 840
footboy 746
footfall
  motion 264

  indication 550
  stumble 732
footing
  circumstances 8
  rank 71
  influence 175
  situation 183
  foundation 211
  support 215
  payment 809
  friendly – 888
  get a –
  location 184
  be on a –
  state 7
  pay one's – 807
footlights 599
footman 746
footmark 551
footpad 792
foot-passenger 268
footpath 627
foot pound 466
footprint 551
foot-soldier 726
foot-warmer 386
footsore 688
footstep 551
footstool 215
foozle 732
fop 854
foppery 882
foppish 855
for *cause* 155
  tendency 176
  reason 476
  motive 615
  intention 620
  preparation 673
  have –
  price 812
- all that
  notwithstanding
  30
  qualification 469
- all the world
  like 17
- aught one
  knows 156
- better for worse
  78
- ever 112
- example 82
- form's sake 82
- good
  complete 52
  diuturnity 110
  permanence 141
- the most part
  great 31
  general 78

  special 79
- the nonce 118
- nothing 815
- a season 106
- a time 111
- the time being
  106
forage
  food 298
  provision 637
  steal 791
forage-cap 225
foramen 260
foraminous 260
forasmuch as
  relating to 9
  cause 155
  reason 476
  motive 615
foray *attack* 716
  robbery 791
forbear
  avoid 623
  spare 678
  lenity 740
  sufferance 826
  pity 914
  abstain 953
  forbearance 918
forbid 761
  God –
  dissent 489
  deprecation **766**
  censure 932
  prayer 990
forbidden fruit
  seduction 615
  prohibition **761**
forbidding
  ugly 846
force *corps* 72
  power 157
  strength **159**
  agency 170
  energy 171
  violence 173
  cultivate 371, **707**
  cascade 348
- *of style* 574
  urge 615
  exertion 686
  compulsion **744**
  armed – 726
  brute – 964
  put in – 924
- of argument **476**
- of arms 744
- of character 82**0**
- down the throat
  severe 739
  compel 744

frankincense 400
frantic
violent 173
delirious 503
excited 824
fraternal
brother 11
concord 714
friendly 888
fraternity
[*see* fraternal]
party 712
fraternize
co-operate 48, 709
agree 714
sympathize 888
associate 892
fratricide 361
Frau 374
fraud
falsehood 544
deception 545
pretender 548
dishonour 940
pious – 988
fraught *full* 52
pregnant 161
possessing 777
– with danger 665
fray *rub* 331
battle 720
in the thick of
the – 722
frayed 659
frazzle
beaten to a – 732
freak 608, 872
– of Nature 83
freckle 848
freckled 440
fredaine 840
free
detached 44
unconditional 52
liberate 672
unobstructed 705
at liberty 748, 750
gratis 815
liberal 816
insolent 885
exempt 927a
impure 961
– balloon 273
– and easy
cheerful 836
adventurous 863
vain 880
insolent 885
friendly 888
sociable 892
– fight 720

– from
simple 42
never – from 613
– gift 784
– from imperfec-
tion 650
– lance 726
– land 748
– liver 954a
– love 961
make – of 748
– play 170, 748
– quarters
cheap 815
hospitality 892
– space 180
– stage 748
– trade
commerce 794
– translation 522
– will 600
make – with
frank 703
take 789
sociable 892
uncourteous 895
freebooter 792
freeborn 748
freedman 748
freedom 748
free-handed 816
freehold 780
freely
willingly 602
freeman 748
freemasonry
unintelligible 519
secret 528
sign 550
co-operation 709
party 712
free-spoken 703
freethinker 989
freeze
benumb 381
cold 385
– the blood 830
freezing 383
– mixture 387
freight *lade* 184
cargo 190
transfer 270
freightage 812
freighter 273
freight train 272
French
peddler's – 563
– and English 840
– horn 417
– leave *avoid* 623
freedom 748

– polish 847
frenetic 503
frenzy
madness 503
imagination 515
excitement 825
frequency 136
frequent
in number 104
in time 136
in space 186
habitual 613
visit 892
fresco *cold* 383
painting 556
al –
out of doors 220
in the air 338
fresh *additional* 37
new 123
flood 348
cold 383
colour 428
remembered 505
unaccustomed 614
good 648
healthy 654
impertinent 885
tipsy 959
– breeze 349
– colour 434
– news 532
freshen 658, 689
freshet 348
freshman 541
freshwater 851
freshwater sailor
701
fret *suffer* 378
grieve 828
gall 830
discontent 832
sad 837
ornament 847
irritate 900
– and fume 828
fretful 901
fret-work 219
friable 328, 330
friandise 868
friar 996
–'s lantern 423
– Rush 980
Black –s 996
friary 1000
fribble
slur over 460
trifle 643
dawdle 683
fop 854
fricassee 298

frication 331
friction *force* 157
obstacle 179
rubbing 331
on – wheels 705
friend 711, **890**
candid – 936
next – 759
friendless 893
friendly 714, **894**
friends, be – 888
see one's – 892
friendship 9, **888**
frieze 210
frigate 726
fright
cards 840
alarm 860
frightful 31, 830,
846
frightfully 31
frightfulness 860
frigid
cold 383
- *style* 575
callous 823
indifferent 866
frigidarium 387
frigorific 385
frill 231, 248
*frills and furbe-
lows* 847
fringe
border 231
lace 256
exaggeration 549
ornament 847
frippery
trifle 643
ornament 847
finery 851
ridiculous 853
ostentation 882
frisk *prance* 266
leap 309
search 461
gay 836
amusement 840
frisky 682, 836
frith *chasm* 198
strait 343
forest 367
fritinancy 412
fritter *small* 32
– *away lessen* 36
waste 638
– *away time* 683
fritters 298
frivolous
unreasonable 477
foolish 499

fetid 401
  bad 649
  abhorrent 867
  adulatory 933
  impure 961
fulvid 436
fulvous 436
fumble
  derange 61
  handle 379
  grope 463
  awkward 699
fumbler 701
fume
  violent 173
  exhalation 334,
    336
  froth 353
  heat 382
  odour 398
  excitement 824,
    825
  anger 900
  in a –
    discontented 832
  –s of fancy 515
fumid 426
fumigate
  vaporize 336
  cleanse 652
fumigator 388
fumo, dare pondus
  – 481
fun 827, 840, 842
  make – of 856
funambulist 700
function
  algebra 84
  office 170
  business 625
  utility 644
  pomp 882
  rite 998
  duty 926
functionary
  director 694
  consignee 758
functus officio 756
fund *store* 636
  sinking – 802
fundamental
  intrinsic 5
  base 211
  support 215
  – bass 413
  – note 413
fundamentally 31
funds 800
  in – 803
  public – 802
funebrial 363

funeral 363
  – pace 275
  – march 415
funereal
  interment 363
  dismal 837
fungiform 249
fungology 369
fungosity 250
fungus
  projection 250
  vegetable 367
  fœtor 401
  bane 663
funicle 205
funicular 627
funk 860, 862
  – hole 530
funnel *opening* 260
  conduit 350
  air-pipe 351
funnel-shaped 252
funny *odd* 83
  boat 273
  humorous 842
  comic 853
fur *covering* 223
  hair 256
  warm 384
  dirt 653
furacious 791
furbelow 231
furbish
  improve 658
  prepare 673
  adorn 847
furcated 244
furcation 91
furcular 244
furfur 653
furfuraceous 330
Furies *anger* 900
  evil-doers 913
  demons 980
furious *violent* 173
  haste 684
  passion 825
  anger 900
furiously 31
furl 312
furlong 200
furlough 760
furnace 386
  workshop 691
  like a – *hot* 382
  sighing like –
    lament 839
    in love 902
furnish
  provide 637
  prepare 673

give 784
  – aid 707
  – a handle 617
  – its quota 784
furniture 633
  – van 272
furor
  insanity 503
  passion 825
furore
  emotion 820, 821
  passion 825
  desire 865
furrow 259
further
  added 37
  distant 196
  aid 707
  go – and fare
    worse
    worse 659
    bungle 699
  not let it go – 528
furthermore 37
furtive
  clandestine 528
  stealing 791
furuncle 250
fury *violence* 173
  excitation 825
  anger 900
  demon 980
furze 367
fuscous 433
fuse *join* 43
  combine 48
  heat 382, 384
  torch 388
fuselage 215
fusel oil 356
fusiform 244, 253
fusil 727
fusileer 726
fusillade 361, 716
fusion *union* 48
  heat 384
  co-operation 709
fuss *agitation* 315
  activity 682
  haste 684
  difficulty 704
  excitement 825
  ostentation 882
  kick up a – 173
  make a – about
    importance 642
    lament 839
    disapprove 932
fussy *crotchety* 481
  bustling 682
  excitable 825

fustian
  absurd 497
  unmeaning 517
  - *style* 577, 579
fustigate 972
fusty 124, 401, **653**
futhorc 590
futile 497, 645
future 121
  eye to the – 510
  – possession **777**
  – state
    destiny 152
    heaven 981
futurity **121**
fuzzle 959
fuzzy 447

G

gab 584
  gift of the – **582**
gabardine 225
gabble 517, 583
gabelle 812
gaberlunzie 876
gabion 717
gable *side* 236
  – end 67
Gabriel 977
gaby 501
gad
  about 266, 268
gadget 626
gad-so 870
gaff 727
gaffer *old* 130
  man 373
  clown 876
gag
  closure 261
  render mute 403,
    581
  dramatic 599
  muzzle 751
  imprison 752
gage *measure* 466
  security 771
  throw down the –
    715
gaggle 412
gag-man 844
gaieté de cœur 836
gaiety
  [see gay] 836
gaillard 844
gain
  increase 35
  advantage 618
  skilful 698

acquisition **775**
- the confidence of 484
- credit 931
- one's ends 731
- ground
  progress 282
  improve 658
- head 175
- laurels 873
- learning 539
- over 615
- a point 731
- private ends 943
- the start
  priority 116
  early 132
- strength 35
- time
  protract 110
  early 132
  late 133
- upon
  approach 286
  pass 303
  become a habit 613
- a victory 731
gainful *useful* 644
gainless 645
gainsay 536
gait 264, 627
gaiter 225
gala 840, 882
galactic circle 318
galantuomo 939
galavant 902
galaxy
  assemblage 72
  multitude 102
  stars 318
  luminary 423
  glory 873
gale 349
Galen 662
galenicals 662
galimatias 497
galipot 191
galopade 840
galore 639
gall *hurt* 378
  bitter 395
  annoy 830
  anger 900
  malevolence 907
  dip the pen in -
  934
gallant *brave* 861
  courteous 894
  love 897
  licentious 961,

962
gallantry
  dalliance 902
gallanty-show 448, 840
galled jade wince, let the - 884
galleon 273
gallery *room* 191
  passage 260
  auditory 599
  museum 636
  picture - 556
galley *ship* 273
  punishment 972, 975
  work like a - *slave* 686
  - proof 591
galliass 273
Gallicism 563
galligaskin 225
gallimaufry 41
galliot 273
gallipot 191
gallivant 902
galloon 847
gallop
  pass away 111
  ride 266
  scamper 274
galloping consump- tion 655
galloway 271
gallows 361, 975
  come to the - 972
galoche 225
galore 102
galvanic
  excitable 825
galvanism 157
galvanize 824
gamache 225
Gamaliel
  brought up at the feet of - 492
gambade *leap* 309
  prank 840
gambado
  gaiter 225
  leap 309
gambit 66
gamble 156
gambling
  chance 621
  rashness 863
gambling-house 621
gamboge 436
gambol 309, 827, 840

game *lame* 160
  food 298
  animal 366
  savoury 394
  resolute 604
  persevering 604a
  aim 620
  gamble 621
  pursuit 622
  tactics 692
  amusement 840
  laughing-stock 857
  brave 861
make - of
  deceive 545
  ridicule 856
  disrespect 929
play the - 709, 939
- in one's hands
  easy 705
  succeed 731
  command 737
- to the last 604a
- at which two can play 718
- up 732
game-cock 726, 861
game-keeper 370, 753
gameness 861
gamesome 836
gamester
  chance 621
  play 840
  rash 863
gamey 392
gamin 876
gaming-house 621
gammer *old* 130
  woman 374
gammon 544, 545
gamut 413
gander 373
gang
  assemblage 72
  go 264
  party 712
- agley 732
ganger 690
gangrene 655
gangster 361, 913
gangway 260, 627
gantlet 972
run the -
  resolution 604
  dare 861
gaol 752
- delivery 672
gaoler 753, 975
gap 70, 198, 252

stand in the - **717**
gape *open* 260
  curiosity 455
  wonder 870
- for *desire* 865
gaping [*see* gape]
  expectant 507
gar 161
garage 191
garb 225
  under the - of **545**
garbage 653
garble
  take from 38
  exclude 55
  erroneous 495
  misinterpret **523**
  falsify 544
- accounts 811
garbled
  incomplete 53
garden *grounds* 189
  horticulture 371
  beautiful 845
  botanic - 371
  zoological - 370
- party 840
gardener 371
gardens *street* 189
Gargantua 192
gargle 337
gargoyle 350
garish
  light 420
  colour 428
  ugly 846
  ornament **847**
  vulgar 851
  display 882
garland
  circle 247
  sign 550
  trophy 733
  ornament 847
  decoration 877
garlic
  condiment 393
  fetid 401
garment 225
garner 636
garnet 847
  red 434
garnish
  addition 39
  prepare 673
  fee 809
  ornament **847**
garniture 225
garran 271
garret 191, 210
garrison

occupant 188
safety 664
defence 717
soldiers 726
garrotte
  render powerless
    158
  kill 361
  punishment 972
garrulity 584
garter
  fastening 45
  decoration 877
  – blue 438
garth 181
gas 334
  talk 482
  fuel 388
  boasting 884
  – balloon 273
  – stove 386
  – bomb 727
  – fitter 690
  – mask 717
  – projector 727
gasconade 884
gaseity 334
gaselier 214
gash *cut* 44
  interval 198
  wound 619
gasification 334,
    336
gaskins 225
gas-light 423
gasoline 388
gasometer 636
gasp *blow* 349
  droop 655
  fatigue 688
  at the last – 360
  – for *desire* 865
gasper 392
gastriloquism 580
Gastromancy 511
gastronomy 298,
    957
gate *beginning* 66
  inclosure 232
  mouth 260
  barrier 706
  water – 350
  –way *way* 627
  – keeper 263
gâté, enfant – 734
Gath, tell it not in –
  conceal 528
  disapprove 932
gather *collect* 72
  expand 194
  fold 258

[502]

conclude 480
acquire 775
take 789
– breath 689
– flesh 194
– from one
  information 527
– fruits 731
gathered
  – to one's fathers
    360
gathering
  assemblage 72
  abscess 655
  – clouds *dark* 421
  shade 424
  omen 512
  danger 665
  warning 668
  adversity 735
gathering-place 74
gauche *clumsy* 699
gaucherie 699, 851
gaud 847
gaudery 880
gaudy *colour* 428
  vulgar 851
  showy 882
gauge 466
  rain– 348
  wind– 349
gauger 965
gaunt *bulky* 192
  lean 203
  ugly 846
gauntlet *glove* 225
  armour 717
  fling down 715
  run the – 665, 972
  take up the – 720
gauntry 627
Gautama 986
gauze *shade* 424
  semitransparent
    427
gavel 72, 812
gavelkind 778
gavelock 633
gavot 840
gawky
  awkward 699
  ugly 846
  (*ridiculous* 853)
gay *colour* 428
  cheerful 836
  adorned 847
  showy 882
  dissipated 961
  – deceiver 962
  – world 852
gaze 441

gazebo 441
gazelle *swift* 274
gazette
  publication 531
  record 551
  in the –
    bankrupt 808
gazetteer
  list 86
  information 527
  record 551
gazing-stock
  ridiculous 857
  wondrous 872
géant, à pas de –
    274
gear *clothes* 225
  harness 633
  high – 274
  in – 673
  low – 275
  out of –
    disjoin 44
    derange 61
    useless 645
    unprepared 674
  – wheel 633
geese are swans,
  all his – 482
gehenna 982
geisha 599
Geist 498
gel 352
gelatin 352
gelatinify 352
geld 38, 158
gelding 271, 373
gelid 383
Geloscopy 511
gem 648, 847
geminate 90
Gemini *twins* 89
  O – ! 870
gemote 72
gendarme 726, 965
gender 75
genealogy 69, 166
general
  generic 78
  habitual 613
  officer 745
  the –
    commonalty 876
  things in – 151
  – breaking up 655
  – favourite 899
  – information 490
  – meaning 516
  – public 372
  – run 613
  – servant 690, 746

generalissimo 745
generality
  mean 29
  universal 78
generalize 476
generally speaking
    613
generalship 692,
    722
generate 161, 168
generation
  consanguinity 11
  period 108
  production 161
  mankind 372
  rising – 167
  spontaneous – 161
  wise in one's – 498
generator 164
generic 78
generosity
  giving 784
  liberality 816
  benevolence 906
  disinterestedness
    942
genesis
  beginning 66
  production 161
genet 271
Genethliacs 511
genetic 161
Geneva gown 999
genial
  productive 161
  sensuous 377
  warm 382
  willing 602
  delightful 829
  affable 894
geniality 836
geniculated 244
genie 980
genital 161
genitor 166
geniture 161
genius
  intellect 450
  talent 498
  skill 698
  proficient 700
  prodigy 872
  evil – 980
  good –
    friend 898
    benefactor 912
    spirit 979
  tutelary – 711
  – for 698
  – of a language
    560

- loci 664
genre 556, 559
gent 851, 876
genteel 852, 875
 - comedy 599
gentile 984, 989
gentility
 fashion 852
 rank 875
 politeness 894
gentium, jus - 963
gentle *moderate* 174
 slow 275
 domesticated 370
 faint sound 405
 lenient 740
 meek 826
 courteous 894
 - blood 875
 - breeding 894
 - hint 527
 - as a lamb 174
 - slope 217
gentlefolk 875
gentleman
 male 373
 squire 875
 man of honour
 939
 the old - 978
 walking - 599
gentlemanly 852
gently bred 894
Gentoo 984
gentry 875
 landed - 779
genuflexion
 bowing 308
 submission 725
 servility 886
 courtesy 894
 respect 928
 worship 990, 998
genuine 494, 648
genus 75, 901
 - irritabile vatum
 597
geodesist 85, 318
geodesy 318, 466
geography 183, 318
geoid 249
geology &c. 358
geomancer 513
geomancy 511
geometry 466
geoponics 371
georama 448
Georgics 371
geotic 318
gerfalcon 913
germ 153

german 11
 - band 417
 - silver 545
germane 23
germicide 662
germinal 153
germinate 161, 194,
 365
 - from 154
gerontic 128
gerrymander 545
gesso 556
gest 680
gestation
 propagation 161
 carriage 270
 maturation 673
gesticulate 550
gesture *hint* 527
 indication 550
get *become* 144
 beget 161
 acquire 775
 receive 810
 - ahead 35
 - ahead of 33
 - along 282
 - along with you
 ejection 297
 dismissal 756
 - at 480a
 - away 287
 - back
 retire 283
 regain 775
 - the best of 731
 - better 658
 - down
 swallow 298
 descend 306
 - you gone 297
 - into harness 673
 - by heart 505
 - home 292
 - in *collect* 72
 gather 775
 - loose 44
 - near 286
 - off *depart* 293
 escape 671
 - on *advance* 282
 prosper 734
 - out *eject* 297
 extract 301
 publish 531
 - over
 recover from 660
 succeed 731
 be content 831
 - over the ground
 274

 - for one s pains
 973
 - ready 673
 - rid of 672
 - a sight of 441,
 490
 - through
 end 67
 transact 692
 complete 729
 expend 809
 - to
 extend to 196
 arrive 292
 - together 72
 - into trouble 732
 - the wind up 860
 - up *produce* 161
 ascend 305
 raise 307
 learn 539
 fabricate 544
 prepare 673
 rise early 682
 foment 824
 - into the way of
 613
get-away 671
gewgaw
 trifle 643
 ornament 847
 vulgar 851
geyser 382, 386
ghastly
 pale 429
 hideous 846
 frightful 860
ghaut 203
ghetto 189
ghost *shade* 362
 fallacy of vision
 443
 soul 450
 writer 593
 apparition 980
 give up the - 360
 needs no - to tell
 us 525
 pale as a -
 colourless 429
 fear 860
 - dance 992
ghost-like
 ugly 846
ghostly
 intellectual 450
 supernatural 976,
 980
Ghost, Holy - 976
ghoul 913, 980
ghyll 348

giant
 large 192
 tall 206
 - refreshed
 strong 159
 refreshed 689
 -'s strides
 distance 196
 swift 294
giaour 984, 989
gibber 583
gibberish 517, **563**
gibbet
 brand 932
 execute 972
 gallows 975
gibble-gabble 584
gibbous 249, 250
gib-cat *male* 373
gibe 929
giblets 298
gibus 225
giddy
 inattentive 458
 vertiginous 503
 irresolute 605
 capricious 608
 bungling 699
giddy-head 501
giddy-paced 315
gift *power* 157
 talent 698
 given 784
 - of the gab 582
 look a - horse in
 the mouth
 fastidious 868
 ungrateful 917
gifted 698
gig 272, 273
gigantic
 strong 159
 large 192
 tall 206
giggle 838
giglamps 441
Gilbertian 842
Gilbertine 996
gild *coat* 223
 colour 439
 ornament 847
 - refined gold **641**
 - the pill
 deceive 545
 tempt 615
 please 829
 flatter 933
Gilead, balm in -
 834, 858
Giles's Greek, St. -
 563

gill 348
gillie 746
gilt 436, 847
– edged 648
gimbals 312
gimcrack
  weak 160
  brittle 328
  trifling 643
  ornament 847
  ridiculous 853
gimlet 262
gimp
  clean 652
  pretty 845
  decoration 847
gin *trap* 545
  instrument 633
  intoxicating 959
  demon 980
gin mill 189
gin palace 189
gingerbread
  weak 160
  vulgar 851
gingerly 174, 459, 864
gingle 408
gipsy
  wanderer 268
  wag 844
  – lingo 563
giraffe 206
girandole 423
girasol 847
gird *bind* 43
  strengthen 159
  surround 227
  jeer 929
  – up one's loins
  brace 159
  prepare 673
girder 45, 215
girdle *bond* 45
  encircle 227
  circumference 230
  circle 247
  put a – round the earth 311
girl 129, 374
girlhood 127
girt 45
girth
  bond 45
  circumference 230
gisarm 727
gist *essence* 5
  meaning 516
  important 642
git, ci – 363
gittern 417

give *yield* 324
  melt 382
  bestow 784
  discount 813
  – away 782, 784
  in marriage 903
  – back 790
  – birth to 161
  – with both hands 816
  – in charge
  restrain 751
  – chase 622
  – consent 762
  – one credit for 484
  – in custody 751
  – expression to 566
  – forth 531
  – the go by 623
  – a horse his head 748
  – in *submit* 725
  – into *consent* 762
  – light 420
  – the mind to 457
  – notice
  inform 527
  warn 668
  – it one
  censure 932
  punish 972
  – out *emit* 297
  publish 531
  bestow 784
  – over *cease* 142
  relinquish 624
  lose hope 859
  – place to
  substitute 147
  avoid 623
  – play to the imagination 515
  – points to 27
  – quarter 740
  – rise to 153
  – one the slip 671
  – security 771
  – and take
  reciprocate 12
  compensation 30
  interchange 148
  retaliation 718
  compromise 774
  barter 794
  equity 922
  honour 939
  – tongue 531
  – a turn to 140
  – one to under-

  stand 527
  – up
  not understand 519
  unwilling 603
  reject 610
  relinquish 624
  submit 725
  resign 757
  surrender 782
  restore 790
  hopeless 859
  – up the ghost 360
  – way *weak* 160
  brittle 328
  submit 725
  pine 828
  despond 837
  modest 881
given [see give]
  circumstances 8
  supposition 514
  received 785
  – over *dying* 360
  – time 134
  – to 613
giving 784
gizzard 191
  stick in one's – 900
glabrous 255
glacial 383
glaciate 385
glacier 383
glacis 217, 717
glad 827, 829
  give the – eye 441
  would be – of 865
  – tidings 532
gladden 834, 836
glade *hollow* 252
  opening 260
  shade 424
gladiator 726
gladiatorial 361, 713, 720
gladsome 827, 829
Gladstone bag 191
glair 352
glaive 727
glamour 992
glance *look* 441
  sign 550
  see at a – 498
  – at
  take notice of 457
  allude to 527
  censure 932
  – off *deviate* 279
  diverge 291
gland 221

glare *light* 420
  stare 441
  imperfect vision 443
  visible 446
glaring
  [see glare]
  great 31
  colour 428
  visible 446
  manifest 525
glass *vessel* 191
  smooth 255
  brittle 328
  transparent 425
  lens 445
  musical –es 417
  see through a – darkly 491
  – of fashion 852
  live in a – house
  brittle 328
  visible 446
  danger 665
  – too much 959
glass-coach 272
glasshouse 191, 371
Glassite 984
glassy [see glass]
  shining 420
  colourless 429
glaucous 435
glave 727
glaver 933
glaze 255
gleam *small* 32
  light 420
glean 609, 775
gleanings 636
glebe *land* 342
  ecclesiastical 995
  church 1000
glee *music* 415
  satisfaction 827
  merriment 836
gleek 929
glen 252
glengarry 225
glib *voluble* 584
  facile 705
glide *lapse* 109
  move 264
  travel 266
  fly 267
  – into
  conversion 144
glider 273
glimmer
  light 420
  dim 422
  visible 446

slight knowledge
490, 491
glimpse 441, 490
glint 420
glissade 306
glisten 420
glitter
shine 420
appear 446
illustrious 882
glittering
ornament 847
display 882
gloam 901*a*
gloaming 126, 422
gloar *look* 441
wonder 870
gloat 884
– *on look* 441
– *over* 441
pleasure 377
delight 827
globated 249
globe
sphere 249
world 318
on the face of the
– 318
– *trotter* 268
globule 32, 219
glomeration 72
gloom 421, 837
gloomy horizon 859
glorification 884
glorify
honour 873
approve 931
worship 990
glorious
illustrious 873
tipsy 959
glory
light 420
honour 873
heaven 981
King of – 976
– *in* 878, 884
– *be to God* 990
gloss *smooth* 255
sheen 420
interpretation 522
falsehood 546
plea 617
beauty 845
– *of novelty* 123
– *over*
neglect 460
sophistry 477
falsehood 544
vindicate 937
glossary 86, 562

glossographer 492
glossologist 492
glossology 560, 562
glossy [*see* gloss]
glottology 560
glout 901*a*
glove 225
take up the – 720
throw down the –
715
glow *warm* 382
shine 420
appear 446
colour 428
style 574
passion 821
glower
glare 443
discourteous 895
sullen 901*a*
glowing
[*see* glow]
orange 439
excited 824
beautiful 845
– *terms* 574
glow-worm 423
gloze 933, 937
glucose 396
glue *cement* 45
cementing 46
semiliquid 352
glum
discontented 832
dejected 837
sulky 901*a*
glut
redundance 641
satiety 869
gluttony 957
glutinous 352
glutton 954*a*, 957
gluttony **957**
glycerine 332, 356
glyphography 558
glyptography 558
glyptotheca 557
gnarl *protuberance*
250
anger 900
threat 909
gnarled 256, 321
gnash one's teeth
839, 900
gnat *little* 193
strain at a – &c.
caprice 608
gnaw *eat* 298
rub 331
injure 659
gnawing

– grief 828, 830
– pain 378
gnome 496, 980
gnomic 496
gnomon 114
Gnostic 984
go
cease to exist 2
energy 171, 682
move 264
recede 287
depart 293
fade 429
disappear 449
fashion 852
come and – 314
as things – 613
– about
turn round 311
published 531
undertake 676
– across 302
– after
in time 117
in motion 281
– ahead
energetic 171
precede 280
advance 282
active 682
– against 708
– astray 495
– away 293
– back 283, 624
– bad 659
– bail 771
– before 280
– between
interjacent 228
instrumental 631
mediate 631, 724
– beyond 303
– by the board
158
– about your
business
ejection 297
dismissal 756
– by
conform to 82
elapse 109
past 122
outrun 303
subterfuge 702
give the – by to
neglect 460
deceive 545
avoid 623
not observe 773
– by the name of
564

– deep into 461
– down *sink* 306
decline 659
– down with
believed 484
tolerated 826
content 831
– farther and **fare**
worse 659
– forth *depart* **293**
publish 531
– halves 91
– hand in hand
accompany 88
same time 120
– hard 704
– on ill 735
– in 294
– in for
resolution 604
pursuit 622
– into
ingress 294
inquire 461
dissert 595
– all lengths
complete 52
resolve 604
exertion 686
– mad 503
– near 286
– no further
keep secret 528
– for nothing
sophistry 477
unimportant **643**
– off *explode* **173**
depart 293
die 360
wither 659
marry 903
– on *time* 106
continue 143
advance 282
– on for ever **112**
– one better **303**
– out
cease 142
egress 295
extinct 385
– out of one's
head 506
– over
passage 302
explore 461
apostate 607
faithless 940
– to pieces 162
– on record **551**
– round 311
– shares **778**

– to sleep 683
– through
 meet with 151
 pass 302
 explore 461
 perform 599
 conduct 692
 complete 729
 endure 826
– to *extend* 196
 travel 266
 direction 278
 remonstrance 695
– up 305
– to war 722
– with
 assent 488
 concord 714
– with the stream
 conform 82
 servile 886
– from one's word
 773
goad 615
 hasten 684
goal *end* 67
 reach 292
 object 620
 reach the –
 complete 729
goat *substitute* 147
 jumper 309
 lecher 962
 he – *male* 373
 play the – 499
gob 269
gobang 840
gobbet
 small piece 32
 food 298
gobble *cry* 412
 gormandize 957
 eat 298
gobemouche 501,
 547
go-between 758
goblet 191
goblin 980
go-cart 272
GOD 976
 house of – 1000
 kingdom of – 981
 sons of – 977
 –'s acre 363
 – bless me! 870
 – bless you
 farewell 293
 – forbid 766
 –'s grace 906
 – grant 990
 – knows 491

–'s love 906
 for –'s sake 765
–'s will 601
– willing 470
god 979
 household –s 189
 tutelary – 664
goddess *love* 897
 good woman 948
 heathen 979
Godhead 976
godlike 944
godly 987
godsend *good* 618
 prosperity 734
Godspeed
 farewell 293
 hope 858
 courtesy 894
 benevolence 906
 approbation 931
goer *horse* 271
goes [*see* go]
 as one – 270
 here – 676
Gog and Magog 192
goggle 441
 – eyes 443
goggles 445
going [*see* go]
 general 78
 rumour 532
 – to happen 152
 – on
 incomplete 53,
 730
 current 151
 transacting 625
goitre 250
Golconda 803
gold *yellow* 436
 orange 439
 money 800
 write in letters
 of – 642
 worth its weight
 in – 648
gold certificate 800
golden [*see* gold]
 – age
 prosperity 734
 pleasure 827
 – apple 615
 – calf
 wealth 803
 idol 986
 idolatry 991
 – dream
 imagination 515
 hope 858
 – mean

 moderation 174
 mid-course 628
– opinions 931
– opportunity 134
– rule
 precept 697
– season of life
 127
– wedding 883
golf 840
Golgotha 363, 1000
Goliath 159, 192
goloshes 225
gondola 273
gondolier 269
gone [*see* go]
 past 122
 absent 187
 dead 360
– bad 653
– by 122
 antiquated 124
– out of one's rec-
 ollection 506
gonfalon 550
gong 417
goniometer 244,
 466
good
 complete 52
 palatable 394
 assent 488
 benefit **618**
 beneficial 648
 right 922
 virtuous 944
 pious 987
 as – as 197
 be so – as 765
 do – 906
 for –
 diuturnal 110
 permanent 141
 make –
 evidence 467
 provide 637
 restore 660
 complete 729
 substantiate 924
 vindicate 937
 atone for 952
 so far so – 931
 think – 931
 to the – 780
 turn to – account
 731
 what's the – 645
– actions 944
– at 698
– auspices 858
– behaviour

 contingent 108*a*
 duty 926
 virtue 944
 in one's – books
 888
– bye 293
 in – case 192
– chance 472
– cheer *food* 298
 cheerful 826
– circumstances
 803
– condition 192
– day
 arrival 292
 departure 293
 courtesy 894
– effect
 goodness 648
 beauty 845
– enough
 not perfect 651
 be – enough 765
 put a – face upon
 cheerful 836
 proud 878
– fellow 892
– fight *war* 722
 virtue 944
– for
 useful 644
 salubrious 656
– fortune 734
– Friday 998
– genius
 friend 890
 benefactor 912
 god 979
 in one's – graces
 888
– hand 700
– humour
 concord 714
 cheerfulness 836
 amuse 840
 courtesy 894
 kindly 906
– intention 906
– judgment 498
– lack! 870
– living
 food 298
 gluttony 957
– look-out 459
– looks 845
– luck 734
– man *man* 373
 husband 903
 worthy **948**
– manners 894
 much – may it do

906
- morrow 292
- name 873
- nature 906
- night 293
- for nothing
  impotence 158
  useless 645
in - odour
  repute 873
  approbation 931
- offices
  mediation 724
  kind 906
- old time 122
- omen 858
- opinion 931
take in - part
  pleased 827
  courteous 894
  kind 906
- pennyworth 815
- at the price 815
to - purpose 731
- repute 873
- sense 498
- society 852
- taste 578, 850
- temper 894
- thing 648
- time *early* 132
  opportune 134
  prosperous 734
- turn
  kindness 906
- understanding
  714
- wife
  woman 374
  spouse 903
- will
  willingness 602
  benevolence 906
- word
  approval 931
  vindication 937
- as one's word
  veracity 543
  observance 772
  probity 939
- works 906
goodie 652, 746
goodly
  great 31
  large 192
  handsome 845
good mixer 892
goodness
  [*see* good] **648**
  virtue 944
have the -

request 765
- *gracious!* 870
- of heart 906
goods *effects* 270,
  780
  merchandise 798
good taste 868
Goodwin sands 667
goody 374, 652, 746
gooroo 996
goose *hiss* 409
  game of - 840
  giddy as a - 458
  tailor's - 255
  kill the - with
    golden eggs
    699, 818
  a wild - chase 545
gooseberry
  old - 978
  play - 459
- eyes 441, 443
goosecap 501
goose egg 101
gooseflesh 383
goosequill 590
goose-skin 383
Gordian knot 59,
  704
gore *stab* 260
  blood 361
gorge *ravine* 198
  conduit 350
  fill 641
  satiety 869
  gluttony 957
  raise one's - 900
- the hook 602
gorge de pigeon 440
gorgeous
  colour 428
  beauty 845
  ornament 847
  ostentation 882
Gorgon 860
gorilla 913
gormandize 298,
  954a, 957
gorse 367
gory *red* 434
  murderous 361
  unclean 653
gospel
  certainty 474
  truth 494
  take for - 484
Gospels 985
gossamer
  filament 205
  light 320
  texture 329

gossip *news* 532
  babbler 584
  conversation 588
gossoon 876
Gotama 986
Goth 851, 876
Gotham, wise men
  of - 501
gothic
  amorphous 241
gouache 556
gouge *concave* 252
  perforator 262
goulash 298
gourd 191
gourmand 954a,
  957
gourmet 868, 954a
gout 378
goût, haut - 392
goutte d'eau, il se
  noyerait dans
  une - 699
govern 693, 737
  [*see* govern]
  ruling power 745
  divine - 976
  petticoat - 737
governess 540
governor
  tutor 540
  director 694
  ruler 745
  keeper 753
gowk 501
gown *dress* 225
  canonicals 999
gownsman 492
grab *take* 789
  miser 819
grabble 379
grace *style* 578
  permission 760
  concession 784
  elegance 845
  polish 850
  title 877
  pity 914
  forgiveness 918
  honour 939
  piety 987
  worship 990
  act of - 784
  God's - 906
  with a bad - 603
  with a good -
    willing 602
    courteous 894
  in one's good -s
    888
  heart of - 861

say - 990
submit with a
  good - 826
- before meat **916**
grâce: coup de -
  914
  la - 840
graceless
  inelegant 579
  ugly 846
  vicious 945
  impenitent 951
  irreligious 989
Graces 845
gracile 203
gracious
  willing 602
  courteous 894
  kind 906
  good - 870
grade *degree* 26
  arrange 60
  term 71
  ascent 217
  on the down - **658**
  on the up - **659**
gradatim
  gradually 26
  in order 58
  continuous 69
  slow 275
gradation
  degree 26
  order 58
  continuity 69
gradient 217
gradual *degree* 26
  continuous 69
  slow 275
graduate
  adjust 23
  calibrate 26
  arrange 60
  series 69
  measure 466
  scholar 492, **873**
graduated scale **466**
gradus 86, 562
Græculus esuriens
  886
graft *join* 43
  locate 184
  insert 300
  trees 371
  teach 537
  booty 794
  corruption **940**
Grail
  holy - 998
grain *essence* 5
  small 32

tendency 176
little 193
rough 256
weight 319
texture 329
powder 330
paint 428
temper 820
ornament 847
against the –
rough 256
unwilling 603
opposing 708
in the – 820
–s of allowance
qualification 469
doubt 485
like –s of sand
incoherent 47
gramercy 916
graminivorous 298
grammar
beginning 66
teaching 537
school 542
language **567**
bad – 568
comparative – 560
grammarian 492
gramme 319
gramophone 417,
418, 553
granary 636
grand
great 31
style 574
important 642
money 800
handsome 845
glorious 873
ostentatious 882
– climacteric 128
– doings 882
– duchy 181
– jury 967
en – seigneur
proud 878
insolent 885
en –e tenue
ornament 847
show 882
– piano 417
– style 556
– tour 266
– Turk 745
– vizier 694
grandam 130
grandchildren 167
grandee 875
grande dame 878
grandeur 873

grandfather 130,
166
grandiloquent 577
grandiose 577
grandmother 166
simple 501
teach – 538
grandsire 130, 166
grange 189
granite 323
granivorous 298
grano salis, cum
469, 485
grant *admit* 529
permit 760
consent 762
confer 784
God – 990
– a lease 771
granted 488
take for –
believe 484
suppose 514
grantee
possessor 779
receiver 785
granular 330
granulate 330
granule 32
grapes, sour –
unattainable 471
falsehood 544
excuse 617
grape-shot
attack 716
arms 727
graph 554
graphic
intelligible 518
painting 556
descriptive 594
graphite 332
graphito 556
graphology 590
graphometer 244
graphotype 558
grapnel 666
grapple
fasten 43
clutch 789
– with
- *a question* 461
- *difficulties* 704
oppose 708
resist 719
contention 720
grappling-iron
fastening 45
safety 666
grasp
comprehend 518

power 737
retain 781
seize 789
in one's – 737
possess 777
tight – *severe* 739
– at 865
– of intellect 498
grasping
miserly 819
covetous 865
grass 344, 367
let the – grow
under one's feet
neglect 460
inactive 683
not let the – &c.
active 682
grasshopper 309
grass-plat 371
grate *rub* 330
physical pain 378
stove 386
– on the ear
harsh sound 410
– on the feelings
830
grated
barred 219
grateful
*physically pleas-
ant* 377
agreeable 829
thankful 916
grater 260, 330
gratification
animal – 377
moral – 827
gratify 829
permit 760
please 829
grating [see grate]
lattice 219
harsh 713
gratis 815
gratitude **916**
gratuitous
inconsequent 477
supposititious
514
voluntary 602
payless 815
gratuity
gift 784
gratis 815
gratulate 896
gravaman 642
– of a charge 938
grave *great* 31
engrave 259, 558
tomb 363

important 642
composed 826
distressing 830
sad 837
heinous 945
beyond the – 360
look –
disapprove 932
rise from the – 660
silent as the – 403
sink into the – 360
on this side of the
– 359
– in the memory
505
– note 408
– trap 599
gravel
earth 342
material 635
puzzle 704
graven image 991
graveolent 398
graver 558
graving dock 189
gravitate
descend 306
weigh 319
– towards 176
gravity *force* 157
weight **319**
vigour 574
importance 642
sedateness 826
seriousness **837**
centre of – 222
specific –
weight 319
density 321
gravy 333
– boat 191
gray **432** [and *see*
grey]
graze *touch* 199
browse 298
rub 331
brush 379
grazier 370
gré, savoir – 916
grease
lubricate 332
oil 356
– the palm
tempt 615
give 784
pay 807
greasy 355
great *much* 31
big 192
glorious 873
magnanimous

land 342
plain 344
evidence 467
teach 537
motive 615
plea 617
above – 359
down to the – 52
dress the – 371
fall to the – 732
get over the – 274
go over the – 302
level with the –
  162
maintain one's –
  persevere 604a
play– 840
prepare the – 673
stand one's –
  defend 717
  resist 719
– bait 784
– cut from under
  one 732
– floor
  chamber 191
  low 207
  base 211
– on
  attribute 155
– plan 554
– of quarrel 713
– sliding from
  under one 665
– swell
  agitation 315
  waves 348
grounded
  stranded 732
  well– 490
  – on *basis* 211
  evidence 467
groundless
  unsubstantial 4
  illogical 477
  erroneous 495
groundling 876
grounds
  dregs 653
groundwork
  precursor 64
  cause 153
  basis 211
  support 215
  preparation 673
group
  marshal 60
  cluster 72
  – captain 745
grouping 60
grouse 832, 901a

grout 45
grove
  street 189
  glade 252
  wood 367
grovel
  below 207
  move slowly 275
  cringe 886
  base 940
grow
  increase 35
  become 144
  expand 194
  – from
  effect 154
  – into 144
  – less 195
  – taller 206
  – together 46
  – up 194
  – upon one 613
grower 164
growl *cry* 412
  complain 839
  discourtesy 895
  anger 900
  threat 909
growler *cab* 272
  discontented 832
  sulky 901a
grown up 131
growth [*see* grow]
  development 161
  - *in size* 194
  tumour 250
  vegetation 367
groyne 706
grub
  small animal 193
  food 298
  – up
  eradicate 301
  discover 480a
Grub-street writer
  593
grudge
  unwilling 603
  refuse 764
  stingy 819
  hate 898
  anger 900
  bear a – 907
  owe a – 898
grudging 603
  – praise 932
gruel 298
gruesome 846
gruff
  harsh sound 410
  discourteous 895

grum
  harsh sound 410
  morose 901a
grumble
  cry 411
  complain 832,
  839
grume 321, 354
grumous 321, 354
grumpy 901a
Grundy, Mrs. 852
grunt 412
  complain 839
guano 653
guarantee 768, 771
guard
  travelling 268
  safety 664
  defence 717
  soldier 726
  sentry 753
  advanced – 668
  mount –
  care 459
  safety 664
  off one's –
  inexpectant 508
  throw off one's –
  cunning 702
  on one's –
  careful 459
  cautious 864
  rear – 668
  – against
  prepare 673
  defence 717
  – ship 664, 726
guarda costa 753
guarded
  conditions 770
guardian
  safety 664
  defence 717
  keeper 753
  – angel
  helper 711
  benefactor 912
guardless 665
guard-room 752
gubernation 693
gubernatorial 737
gudgeon 547
guerdon 973
guernsey 225
guerre:
  nom de – 565
  – à outrance &c.
  722
guerilla 726
  – warfare 720
guess 514

guesswork 514
guest 890
  paying – 188
guet:
  mot de – 550
  –à-pens 545
guffaw 838
guggle
  gush 348
  bubble 353
  resound 408
  cry 412
guide
  pattern 22
  courier 524
  teach 537
  teacher 540
  indicate 550
  direct 693
  director 694
  advise 695
guide-book 527
guided by, be – 82
guideless 665
guide-post 550
guiding star 693
guild 712, 966
guildhall 799
guile
  deceit 544, 545
  cunning 702
guileless 543, 703
guillotine 972, **975**
guilt 947
guiltless 946
guilty:
  find – 971
  plead – 950
guindé 579
guinea 800
guipure 847
guisard 599
guise
  state 7
  dress 225
  appearance **448**
  plea 617
  mode 627
  conduct 692
guiser 599
guitar 417
gulch 198
gules 434
gulf
  interval 198
  deep 208
  lake **343**
gull 545, 547
gullet *throat* 260
  rivulet 348
gullible 486

gully *gorge* 198
　hollow 252
　opening 260
　conduit 350
gulosity 957
gulp *swallow* 296
　take food 298
　– down
　credulity 486
　submit 725
gum *fastening* 45
　fasten 46
　resin 356a
　– elastic 325
　– tree 367
gumbo 298
gummy 352
gumption 498
gun *report* 406
　weapon 727
　great – 626
　blow great –s 349
　sure as a – 474
gunboat 726
gunfire 404
gunlayer 284
gunman 361
gunner 726
gunnery
　warfare 722
　cannon 727
gunpowder
　warfare 722
　ammunition 727
　not invent – 665
　sit on barrel of –
　　501
gunroom 191
gun-shot 197
gunwale 232
gurge 312, 348
gurgle
　flow 348
　bubble 353
　faint sound 405
　resonance 408
gurgoyle 350
gush
　flow out 295
　flood 348
　exaggeration 482
　talk 584
gushing
　emotional 821
　impressible 822
gusset 43
gust *wind* 349
　physical taste 390
　passion 825
　moral taste 850
gustation 390

gustful 394
gustless 391
gusto [*see* gust]
　physical pleasure
　　377
　emotion 821
gut *destroy* 162
　opening 260
　strait 343
　eviscerate 297
　sack 789
　steal 791
gutling 954a
guts *inside* 221
guttapercha 325
gutter *groove* 259
　conduit 350
　vulgarity 851
guttersnipe 876
guttle 957
guttural
　letter 561
　inarticulate 583
guy
　fastening 45, 752
　fellow 373
　disrespect 929
　grotesque 853
guzzle
　gluttony 957
　drunkenness 959
gybe [*see* jibe]
gymkhana 720, 840
gymnasium 189
　school 542
　arena 728, 840
gymnast 159
gymnastics
　training 537
　exercise 686
　contention 720
　sport 840
gymnosophist
　abstainer 953
　sectarian 984
gynander 83
gynarchy 727
gynecæum 374
gynecology 662
gyniatrics 374
gynics 374
gyp 545, 746
gyre 311
gyrate 312
gyrfalcon 913
gyromancy 511
gyrostat 312
gysart 599
gyve 752

H

habeas corpus 963,
　969
haberdasher 225
habergeon 717
habiliment 225
habilitation 698
habit
　essence 5
　coat 225
　custom **613**
　want of – 614
　–s of business 682
　– of mind 820
habitant 188
habitat 189
habitation 189
habit-maker 225
habitual
　unvariable 16
　orderly 58
　ordinary 82
　customary 613
habituate 537, 613
habitude
　state 7
　habit 613
habitué 613
hacienda 189, 780
hack *cut* 44
　shorten 201
　horse 271
　writer 593
　worker 690
　literary – 593
hackle 44
hackney-coach 272
hackneyed
　known 490
　trite 496
　habitual 613
Hades 982
Hadji
　traveller 268
　priest 996
hæ tibi erunt artes
　627
hæret lateri lethalis
　arundo
　displeasure 828
　anger 900
haft 633
hag *age* 130
　ugly 846
　wretch 913
　witch 994
haggard
　insane 503
　tired 688
　wild 824

　ugly 846
haggis 298
haggle *cut* 44
　chaffer 794
Hagiographa 985
Hagiolatry 984
Hagiology 983, 985
haguebut 727
ha-ha *trench* 198,
　717
haik 225
hail *welcome* 292
　ice 383
　call 586
　rejoicing 838
　honour to 873
　celebration 883
　courtesy 894
　salute 928
　approve 931
　–fellow well met
　friendship 888
　sociality 892
hailstone 383
hair *small* 32
　filament 205
　roughness 256
　to a – 494
　–'s breadth
　near 197
　narrow 203
　–breadth escape
　danger 665
　escape 671
　–s on the head
　multitude 102
　make one's –
　　stand on end
　distressing 830
　fear 860
　wonder 870
hairless 226
hairy *rough* 256
halberd 727
halberdier 726
halcyon *calm* 174
　peace 721
　prosperous 734
　joyful 827, 829
hale 654
half 91
　– the battle
　important 642
　success 731
　– distance 68
　– a dozen *six* 98
　several 102
　see with – an eye
　intelligent 498
　intelligible 518
　manifest 525

– a gale 349
– and half
   equal 27
   mixed 41
   incomplete 53
– a hundred 98
– light 422
– measures
   incomplete 53
   vacillating 605
   mid-course 628
– moon 245
– price 815
– rations 640
- scholar 493
– seas over 959
– sight 443
– speed
   moderate 174
   slow 275
– truth 546
half-blind 443
half-blood
   mixture 41
   unconformity 83
   imperfect 651
half-frozen 352
half-hearted
   irresolute 605
   insensible 823
   indifferent 866
half-learned 491
half-melted 352
halfpenny
   trifle 643
half-starved
   insufficient 640
   fasting 956
half-way
   small 32
   middle 68
   between 228
go – *irresolute* 605
   mid-course 628
meet –
   willing 602
   compromise 774
half-witted 499, 501
hall *house* 189
   lobby 191
   mart 799
   music – 599
– of audience 588
– mark 550
hallelujah 990
halliard 45
halloo *cry* 411
   look here! 457
   call 586
   wonder 870
hallow

celebrate 883
respect 928
hallowed 976
hallucination
   error 495
   insanity 503
halo *light* 420
   glory 873
Halomancy 511
halser 45
halt *cease* 142
   weak 160
   rest 265
   go slowly 275
   lame 655
   fail 732
 at the – 265
halter *rope* 45
   restraint 752
   punishment 975
wear a – 874
with a – round
   one's neck 665
halting
   style 579
– place 292
halve [*see* half]
halves
do by –
   neglect 460
   not complete 730
not do by – 729
go – 778
ham *house* 189
hamadryad 979
hamlet 189
hammam 386, 652
hammer
   repeat 104
   knock 276
   stammer 583
under the –
   auction 796
between the – and
   the anvil 665
– at *think* 451
   work 686
– out *form* 240
   prepare 673
   complete 729
hammock 215
hamper *basket* 191
   obstruct 706
hamstring 158, 659
hanaper 802
hand
   measure of
    length 200
   side 236
   transfer 270
   man 372

organ of touch
   379
   indicator 550
   writing 590
   medium 631
   agent 690
   grasp 781
   transfer 783
at – *future* 121
   destined 152
   near 197
   useful 644
bad – 590
bird in – 781
come to – 292, 785
fold one's –s 681
give one's – to
   marry 903
good –
   writing 590
   skill 698
   proficiency 700
helping – 707, 711
hold in – 737
hold out the – 894
hold up the –
   vote 609
in –
   incomplete 53
   business 625
   preparing 673
   not finished 730
   possessed 777
   money 800
in the –s of
   authority 737
   subjection 749
lay –s on
   discover 480a
   use 677
   take 789
   rite 998
much on one's –s
   682
on one's –s
   business 625
   redundant 641
   not finished 730
   for sale 796
on the other – 468
no – in 623
poor – 701
put into one's –s
   784
put one's – to 676
ready to one's –
   673
shake –s 918
stretch forth one's
   – 680
take by the – 707

take in –
   teach 537
   undertake 676
time hanging on
   one's –s
   inaction 681
   leisure 685
   weary 841
try one's – 675
turn one's – 675
turn one's – to 625
under one's –
   in writing 590
   promise 768
   compact 769
– back 683
– cart 272
– of death 360
– down
   record 551
   transfer 783
have one's –s full
   682
– gallop 274
– glass 445
– and glove 709,
   888
– in hand
   joined 43
   accompanying 88
   same time 120
   concur 178
   co-operate 709
   party 712
   concord 714
   friend 888
   social 892
– to hand
   touching 199
   transfer 270
   fight 720, 722
– over head
   inattention 458
   neglect 460
   reckless 863
have a – in
   cause 153
   act 680
   co-operate 709
have one's – in
   skill 698
keep one's – in
   613
live from – to
   mouth
   insufficient 640
   unprepared 674
   poor 804
–s off! *avoid* 623
   leave alone 681
   prohibition 761

* over
  transfer 783
  give 784
  win –s down 731
  with the –s in the
    pockets 681
hand-bag 191
hand-barrow 272
handbook
  travel 266
  information 527
  book 593
handcuff 751, 752
handfast 903
handful
  quantity 25
  small 32
  few 103
handicap
  equalize 27
  inferiority 34
  encumber 706
  race 720
handicraft 625, 680
handicraftsman 690
  effect 154
  doing 680
handkerchief
  clothes 225
  cleaner 652
handle
  feel, touch 379
  name 565
  dissert 595
  plea 617
  instrument 633
  use 677
  manage 693
  furnish a – 937
  make a – of 677
  – a case 693
  – to one's name
    name 564
  honour 877
handmaid
  instrumentality
    631
  auxiliary 711
  servant 746
handpost 550
handsel
  begin 66
  security 771
  gift 784
  pay 809
handsome
  liberal 816
  beautiful 845
  disinterested 942
  – fortune 803
handspike 633

handstaff 727
handwriting
  signature 550
  autograph 590
  – on the wall
    warning 668
handy
  near 197
  useful 644, 646
  ready 673
  dexterous 698
hang
  pendency 214
  kill 361
  curse 908
  execute 972
  – about 133, 197
  – back 133, 623
  – in the balance
    133
  – in doubt 485
  – fire *late* 133
  cease 142
  unproductive 169
  inert 172
  slow 275
  reluctance 603
  inactive 683
  not finish 730
  fail 732
  refuse 764
  dullness 843
  – on hand 641
  – down the head
    837
  – over the head
    152
  – it! *regret* 833
  contempt 930
  – out a light 420
  – upon the lips of
    418
  – on
  accompany 88
  – out
  display 882
  entertain 892
  – over
  destiny 152
  height 206
  project 250
  – out a signal 550
  – on the sleeve of
  servant 746
  servility 886
  flattery 933
  – in suspense 605
  – by a thread 665
  – together
  joined 43
  cohere 46

concur 178
co-operate 709
– upon
  effect 154
  dependency 749
hangar 191, 273
hang-dog look 901a
hanged if, I'll be –
  489
hanger
  weapon 727
  suspender 45, 214
  pothooks and –s
    590
  – on
  accompaniment
    88
  servant 746
  servile 886
hanging [see hang]
  elevated 307
  ornament 847
  – look 846
hangman
  evil-doer 913
  bad man 949
  executioner 975
hank *tie* 45
hanker 865
hanky-panky 545
Hansard 551
hansom 272
hap 156
haphazard
  chance 156, 621
hapless
  unfortunate 735
  (*miserable* 828)
  (*hopeless* 859)
haply
  possibly 470
  (*by chance* 156)
happen 151
  – as it may
  chance 621
  – what may
  certain 474
  reckless 863
happening 151
happiness
  [see happy]
  the greatest – of
    the greatest
    number 910
happy *fit* 23
  opportune 134
  style 578
  glad 827
  cheerful 836
  – despatch 972
  – go lucky 674

– hunting grounds
  981
– returns of the
  day 896
– thought 842
– valley
  imagination 515
  delight 827
harangue 582
hara-kiri 972
harass
  fatigue 688
  vex 830
  worry 907
harbinger
  precursor 64
  omen 512
  informant 527
harbour
  abode 189
  haven 292
  refuge 666
  cherish 821
  natural – 343
  – a design 620
  in – 664
  – an idea 451
  – revenge 919
harbourless 665
hard *strong* 159
  dense 323
  physically insen-
    sible 376
  sour 397
  difficult 704
  severe 739
  morally insen-
    sible 823
  grievous 830
  impenitent 951
  blow – 349
  go –
  difficult 704
  failure 732
  adversity 735
  pain 828
  hit – 276
  look – at 441
  not be too – upon
    918
  strike –
  energy 171
  impulse 276
  try – 675
  work – 686
  – at it 682
  – bargain 819
  – of belief 487
  – to believe 485
  – by 197
  – case 735

HAR　　HAR　　HAR　　HAT

– cash 800	739	*music* 413	**harvest**
– earned 704	**hardihood** 861, 885	*colour* 428	*effect* 154
– and fast rule 80	**hardly**	*concord* 714	*profit* 618
– fought 704	*scarcely* 32	*peace* 721	*store* 636
– frost 383	deal – with 739	*friendship* 888	*acquisition* 775
– of hearing 419	– any *few* 103	**harness**	get in the –
– heart	– anything	*fasten* 43	*complete* 729
malevolent 907	*small* 32	*fastening* 45	*succeed* 731
vicious 945	*unimportant* 643	*accoutrement* 225	– home
impenitent 951	– ever 137	*yoke* 370	*celebration* 883
– hit 732	**hard-mouthed** 606	*instrument* 633	– time
– knocks 720	**hardness 323**	*restraint* 752	*autumn* 126
– life 735	– of heart 914*a*	in –	*exertion* 686
– lines	**hardship** 735	*prepared* 673	**has been** 122
adversity 735	**hardy**	*in action* 680	**hash** *mix* 41
severity 739	*strong* 159	*active* 682	*cut* 44
– liver 954*a*	*healthy* 654	*subjection* 749	*confusion* 59
– lot 735	*brave* 861	– up 293	*food* 298
– master 739	**hare** 274	**harp**	make a – 699
– measure 739	hold with the –	*repeat* 104	**hashish** 663
– names 932	and run with	*musical instru-*	**hasp** 43, 45
– necessity 601	the hounds	*ment* 417	**hassock** 215
– nut to crack 704	*fickle* 607	*weary* 841	**hastate** 253
– to please 868	*servile* 886	**Harpagon** 819	**haste**
– pressed	**hare-brained** 458,	**harper** 416	*velocity* 274
haste 684	863	**harpist** 416	*activity* 682
difficulty 704	**harem** 961	**harpoon** 727	*hurry* **684**
hindrance 706	**hariolation** 511	**harpsichord** 417	**hasten**
– put to it 704	**hark** 418, 457	**harpy**	*promote* **707**
– set 704	– back 283	*relentless* 739	**hasty**
– tack 298	**harl** 205	*thief* 792	*transient* 113
– task 703	**harlequin**	*miser* 819	*hurried* 684
– time 704	*changeable* 149	*evil-doer* 913	*impatient* 825
– up 704, 804	*nimble* 274	*demon* 980	*irritable* 901
– upon	*motley* 440	**harquebuss** 727	– pudding 298
attack 716	*pantomimic* 599	**harridan** 846, 962	**hat** 225
severe 739	*humorist* 844	**harrier** 366	cardinal's – 999
censure 932	**harlequinade** 599	**harrow**	send round the –
– winter 383	**harlot** 962	*agriculture* 371	765
– words	**harlotry** 961	– up the soul 860	shovel – 999
obscure 571	**harm**	**harrowing** 830	– in hand 886
rude 895	*evil* 619	**harry** *pain* 830	**hatch**
censure 932	*badness* 649	*attack* 716	*produce* 161
– work 686	*malevolence* 907	*persecute* 907	*gate* 232
– at work 682	**harmattan** 349	**Harry,** old – 978	*opening* 260
harden [see **hard**]	**harmless**	**harsh**	*chickens* 370
strengthen 159	*impotent* 158	*acrid* 171	*fabricate* 544
accustom 613	*good* 648	*sound* 410	*shading* 556
– the heart	*perfect* 650	*style* 579	*plan* 626
insensible 823	*salubrious* 656	*discordant* 713	*prepare* 673
enmity 889	*safe* 664	*severe* 739	– a plot 626
impenitence 951	*innocent* 946	*disagreeable* 830	**hatches, under –**
hardened	bear – 717	*morose* 895	*restraint* 751
impious 988	**harmonica** 417	*malevolent* 907	*prisoner* 754
– front	**harmonics** 413	– voice 581	*poor* 804
insolent 885	**harmonist** 413	**hart** 366, 373	**hatchet**
hardening	**harmonium** 417	**hartal** 142, 489	*cutting* 253
habit 613	**harmonize** 178, 416	**harum-scarum** 59,	bury the – 918
hard-featured 846	**harmony**	458	dig up the – 722
hard-fisted 819	*agreement* 23	**haruspice** 513	throw the helve
hard-headed 498,	*order* 58	**Haruspicy** 511	after the – 818

[514]

hatchet-faced 203
hatchment
  funeral 363
  arms 550
  record 551
hatchway 260
hate 867, **898**
hateful 649, 830
hath been, the
  time – 122
hatrack 215
hatred [*see* hate]
  object of – 898
hatter 225
  mad as a – 503
hatti-sheriff 741
hauberk 717
haud passibus
  æquis 28, 275
haugh 344
haughty
  proud 878
  insolent 885
  contemptuous 930
haul *drag* 285
  catch of fish &c.
  780
  – down one's flag
  725
  – in 10
haunch 236
haunt *focus* 74
  presence 186
  abode 189
  alarm 860
  persecute 907
  – the memory
  remember 505
  trouble 830
haunted 980
haut
  traiter de –
  insolence 885
  contempt 930
hautboy 417
haut-goût 392
haut-monde 875
hauteur 878
have *confute* 479
  ken 490
  possess 777
  – the advantage
  28, 33
  – at 716
  – no choice 609a
  – done! 142
  – to do with 9
  – no end 112
  – other fish to fry
  135
  – it

discover 480a
  believe 484
  – one to know 527
  – some knowledge
  of 490
  – nothing to do
  with 10
  – for one's own
  780
  – rather 609
  – one's rights 924
  – the start 116
  – in store 152, 637
  – to 620
  – up 638
  – it your own way
  submission 725
haven 292, 666
haversack 191
havoc
  destruction 162
  cry – *war* 722
  play – *spoil* 659
haw 583
hawk *spit* 297
  stammer 583
  eye of a – 498
  – about
  publish 531
  offer 763
  sell 796
  – at 716
  between – and
  buzzard 315,
  828
  know a – from a
  handsaw 465,
  698
hawker 796
hawk-eyed 441
hawking *chase* 622
hawser 45
hay while the sun
  shines, make –
  134
haycock 72
hazard
  chance 156, 621
  danger 665
  at all –s 604
  – a conjecture 514
  – a proposition
  477
haze *mist* 353
  uncertainty 475
  in a –
  hidden 528
hazel 433
hazy *opaque* 426
he 373
head *precedence* 62

beginning 66
  class 75
  summit 210
  coiffure 225
  lead 280
  froth 353
  person 372
  intellect 450
  topic 454
  wisdom 498
  picture 556
  nomenclature 564
  chapter 593
  direct 693
  director 694
  master 745
  at the – of
  direction 693
  authority 737
  repute 873
  bow the – 308
  bring to a – 729
  come into one's –
  451
  come to a – 729
  drive into one's –
  505
  gain – 175
  get into one's –
  thought 451
  learn 505
  belief 484
  intoxicate 959
  give a horse his –
  748
  hang one's – 879
  have in one's – 490
  from – to heels 52,
  200
  hit on the – 912
  knock on the –
  361
  knock one's –
  against
  impulse 276
  unskilful 699
  fail 732
  lie on one's – 926
  lift up one's – 878
  make – against
  oppose 708
  resistance 719
  success 731
  never entered
  into one's – 458
  have no – 506
  on one's – 218
  off one's – 503
  can't get out of
  one's – 505
  over – and ears

deep 641
  debt 806
  love 897
  put into one's –
  supposition 514
  information 527
  put out of one's –
  458
  run in the – 505
  not know whether
  one stands on –
  or heels
  uncertain 475
  wonder 870
  take into one's –
  thought 451
  caprice 608
  intention 620
  turn the – 824
  trouble one's –
  about 457
  as one's – shall
  answer for 768
  with – erect 878
  from – to foot 200
  – and front
  important 642
  – and front of
  one's offending
  provocation 830
  charge 938
  – over heels
  inversion 218
  rotation 312
  – light 423
  – line 591
  – and shoulders
  irrelevant 10
  complete 52
  haste 684
  make neither· **nor**
  tail of 519
  hold one's – up
  307
  – above water
  safe 664
  prosperous 734
  wealth 803
  with a – on 353
headache 378
head-dress 225
header 310
head-foremost
  violent 173
  rash 863
head-gear 225
heading *prefix* 64
  beginning 66
  indication 550
  title 564
headland

height 206
projection 250
headlong
hurry 684
rush 863
rush –
violence 173
headman 694
headmost
front 234
precession 280
head-piece
summit 210
intellect 450
helmet 717
ornament 847
headquarters
focus 74
abode 189
authority 737
head-race 350
heads
compendium 596
– or tails 156, 621
lay – together
advice 695
co-operate 709
– I win tails you
lose
unfair 940
headship 737
headsman 975
head-stone 363
headstrong
violent 173
obstinate 606
rash 863
headway *space* 180
navigation 267
progression 282
headwind 708
headwork 451
heady 606
heal *restore* 660
remedy 662
let the wound –
forgive 918
– the breach
pacify 723
healing art 662
health 654
picture of – 654
healthiness 655
health resort 189
healthy 656
heap *quantity* 31
collection 72
store 636
too many 641
heaps 102
rubbish – 645

hear
audition 418
be informed 527
not – of (refuse)
764
– a cause
adjudge 480
lawsuit 969
– hear! 931
– and obey 743
– out 457
hearer 418
hearing 418, 696
[*see* hear]
gain a – 175
give a – 418
hard of – 419
out of – 196
within – 197
hearken 457
hearsay 532
– *evidence* 467
hearse 363
heart
intrinsicality 5
interior 221
centre 222
mind 450
willingness 602
essential 642
affections 820
courage 861
love 897
man after one's
own – 899
with all one's –
438, 602
at – 820, 821
from bottom of –
543
beating – 821, 824
break the – 830
by –
memory 505
go to one's – 824
in good – 858
with a heavy –
603
know by – 490
lay to – 837
learn by – 539
lift up the – 990
lose – 837
lose one's – 897
nearest to one's –
897
not find it in one's
– 603
have a place in
the – 897
put one's – into

604
set one's – upon
604
take –
content 831
hope 858
courage 861
take to –
sensibility 822
discontent 832
dejection 837
anger 900
warm – 822
wind round the –
897
– bleeding for 914
to one's –'s con-
tent
willing 602
enough 639
success 731
pleasure 829
–'s core
mind 450
affections 820
– expanding 821
– failing one 837,
860
do one's – good
829
– of grace 858
– in hand 602
– leaping with joy
827, 838
– leaping into
one's mouth 824
– of oak
strong 159
hard 323
– in right place
906
– sinking *fear* 860
– and soul
completely 52
willing 602
resolute 604
exertion 686
feeling 821
– of stone 823, 907
– swelling 824
heartache 828
heart-breaking 821,
830
heart-broken 828
heartburning
discontent 832
regret 833
enmity 889
anger 900
jealousy 920
hearten 858, 861

heartfelt 821, **829**
hearth
home 189
fireplace 386
heartless 823, 945
heart-rending 830
heartsease 831
heart-shaped 245
heart-sick
dejection 837
dislike 867
satiety 869
heart-stricken 828
heart-strings, tear
the – 830
hearty
willing 602
healthy 654
feeling 821
cheerful 836
friendly 888
social 892
– laugh 838
– meal 298
– reception 892
heat *warmth* **382**
make hot 384
contest 720
excitement 824,
825
dead – 27
– of passion 900
– wave 382
heated imagination
515
heater 386
heath *moor* 344
plant 367
heathen 984, 989
– *mythology* 979
heathenish 851
heather *moor* 344
plant 367
heaume 717
heautontimoru-
menos 837, **955**
heave *raise* 307
emotion 821
– the lead 208,
466
– a sigh 839
– in sight 446
– to 265
heaven 827, **981**
call – to witness
535
in the face of –
525
light of – 420
move – and earth
686

will of – 601
– forfend! 766
– knows 475, 491
– be praised 838, 916
for –'s sake 765
heaven-born
  wise 498
  repute 873
  virtue 944
heaven-directed 498
heaven-kissing 206
heavenly
  celestial 318
  rapturous 829
  divine 976
  of heaven 981
  – bodies 318
  – host 977
  – kingdom 981
heavenly-minded 987
heavens 318
  – and earth! 870
Heaviside layer 338
heavisome 843
heavy *great* 31
  inert 172
  weighty 319
  stupid 499
  actor 599
  sleepy 683
  dull 843
  brutish 851
  – affliction 828
  – artillery 726
  – cost 814
  – dragoon 726
  – father 599
  – gaited 843
  – gun 727
  – hand
  clumsy 699
  severe 739
  – on hand 641
  – heart *loth* 603
  pain 828
  dejection 837
  – hours 841
  – on the mind 837
  – news 830
  – sea
  agitation 315
  waves 348
  – sleep 683
  – type 591
  – wet 298
heavy-laden 706, 828

hebdomadal 138
Hebe 845
hebetate 823, 826
hebetude
  imbecile 499
  insensible 823
  inexcitable 826
Hebrew
  unintelligible 519
  Jew 984
Hecate 994
hecatomb
  number 98
  sacrifice 991
heckle 830, 900
hectic 382, 821
Hector *brave* 861
  rash 863
  bully 885, 887
hedge
  compensate 30
  inclosure 232
  – in
  circumscribe 229
  hinder 706
  conditions 770
hedgehog 253
hedonism 377, 827
hedonist 954a
heed *attend* 457
  care 459
  beware 668
  caution 864
heedful 457
heedless
  inattentive 458
  neglectful 460
  oblivious 506
  rash 863
heel *support* 215
  lean 217
  deviate 279
  go round 311
  iron – 975
  lay by the –s 162
  turn on one's –
  go back 283
  go round 311
  avoid 623
  – of Achilles 665
heel-piece
  sequel 65
  back 235
  repair 660
heel-tap
  remainder 40
  dress 653
heels *lowness* 207
  at the – of
  near 197
  behind 235

cool one's – 681
follow on the – of 281
laid by the – 751
lay by the – 789
show a light pair of – 623
take to one's – 623
tread on the – of
  near 197
  follow 281
  approach 286
  – over head
  inverted 218
  hasty 684
  rash 863
heft *handle* 633
  exertion 686
hegemony
  influence 175
  direction 693
  authority 737
hegira [*see* hejira]
heifer 366
heigho! 839
height *degree* 26
  altitude 206
  summit 210
  at its –
  great 31
  supreme 33
  draw oneself up to his full – 307
  – finder 206
heighten
  increase 35
  elevate 307
  exaggerate 549
  aggravate 835
heinous 945
heir *futurity* 121
  posterity 167
  inheritor 779
heirloom 780
heirship 777
hejira 293
Helen of Troy 845
heliacal 318
helical 248
Helicon 597
helicon-horn 417
helicopter 273
Heliogabalus 954a
heliograph
  signal 550
  picture 554
heliography 550
  light 420
  painting 556
Helios 423

heliotrope 847
heliotype 558
helix 248
hell *abyss* 208
  gaming-house **621**
  gehenna **982**
  – upon earth
  misfortune 735
  pain 828
  – broke loose 59
hell-born 945, 978
hellebore 663
hell-hound 913, 949
hellish
  malevolent 907
  vicious 945
  hell 982
helluo librorum 492
helm *handle* 633
  sceptre 747
  (*authority* **737**)
  answer the – **743**
  at the – 693
  obey the – 705
  take the – 693
helmet 225, 717
helminthology 368
helmsman 269, **694**
helot 746
help *benefit* 618
  utility 644
  remedy 662
  aid 707
  servant 746
  give 784
  it can't be –ed
  submission 725
  never mind 823
  content 831
  God – you 914
  so – me God 535
  – oneself to 789
helper 711
helpless 158, 665
helpmate
  auxiliary 711
  wife 903
helter-skelter 59, 684
helve
  throw the – after the hatchet **818**
hem *edge* 231
  fold 258
  indeed! 870
  kiss the – of **one's** garment 886
  – in *enclose* **227**
  restrain 751
hemi- 91
hemisphere 181

days 840
in a – degree 31
– descent 875
– and dry
  stable 150
  safe 664
in – esteem 928
in – feather
  strong 159
  health 654
  cheerful 836
  boasting 884
– glee 836
– hand
  violent 173
  resolved 604
  authority 737
  severe 739
  pride 878
  insolence 885
  lawless 964
– jinks 840
ride the – horse
  878
– hat 225
  life *fashion* 852
  rank 875
  living
  intemperance 954
  gluttony 957
– mass 998
– mightiness 873
– and mighty
  pride 878
  insolence 885
– note 410
– notions 878
– places 210
– pressure
  energy 171
  excitation of
    feeling 824
– price 814
– priest 996
in – quarters 875
– relief 448
  repute 873
–ly respectable
  875
on the – road to
  way 627
  hope 858
on one's – ropes
  excitation 824
  pride 878
  anger 900
– seas 341
in – spirits 836
– tide *wave* 348
  prosperity 734
– time *late* 133

occasion 134
– in tone
  white 430
– treason
  disobedience 742
  dishonour 940
– words
  quarrel 713
  anger 900
high-ball 298
high-born 875
high-brow 492
higher 33
highest 210
highfalutin 884
high-flavoured 392
high-flier
  madman 504
  proud 878
high-flown
  imaginative 515
  style 577
  proud 878
  vain 880
  insolent 885
high-flying
  inattentive 458
  exaggerated 549
  ostentatious 822
highlands 206
high-low 225
high-mettled
  excitable 825
  brave 861
high-minded
  honourable 939
  magnanimous
    942
highness *title* 877
high-pitched 410
high-seasoned 392
high-souled 878
high-sounding
  loud 404
  words 577
  display 882
high-spirited 861,
  939
hight 564
high-toned 852
high-water
  completeness 52
  height 206
  water 337
– mark
  measure 466
highway 627
–s and byways
  627
– robbery 791
highwayman 792

high-wrought
  good 648
  prepared 673
  excited 824
hike 266
hilarity 836
hill *height* 206
  convexity 250
  ascent 305
  descent 306
  take to the –s 666
  –dwelling 206
hillock 206
hilt 633
hinc illæ lachrymæ
  155
hind *back* 235
  clown 876
on one's – legs
  elevation 307
  anger 900
– quarters 235
hinder 706
hindermost 67, 235
Hindooism 984
hindrance 706
hinge *fasten* 43
  fastening 45
  cause 153
  depend upon 154
  rotate 312
hinny 271
hint *reminder* 505
  suppose 514
  inform 527
  take a – 498
  – a fault &c. 932
hinterland 235
hip 236
have on the –
  confute 479
  success 731
  authority 737
  subjection 749
– hip, hurrah! 838
hipped [*see* hypped]
hippocentaur 83
Hippocrates 662
hippocratic 360
hippodrome
  drama 599
  arena 728
  amusement 840
hippogriff 83
Hippolytus 960
hippophagy 298
hippopotamus 192
hirdie-girdie 218
hire
  commission 755
  borrowing 788

  price 812
  reward **973**
  on – 763
hireling 746
hirsute 256
hispid 256
hiss *sound* 409
  animal cry 412
  disrespect 929
  contempt 930
  disapprobation
    932
hist! 585, 586
histology 329
historian 553
historic 594
historiette 594
historical:
– painter 559
– painting 556
historiographer **553**
historiography 594
history *past* 122
  record 551
  narrative 594
History, Natural
  357
histrionic 599
hit *chance* 156
  strike 276
  reach 292
  succeed 731
  censure 932
  (*punish* 972)
  good – 626
  make a – 731
– one's fancy **829**
– the mark 731
– off 554
– upon
  discover 480*a*
  plan 626
hitch
  fasten 43
  knot 45
  stoppage 142
  hang 214
  jerk 315
  harness 370
  difficulty 704
  hindrance 706
– up 293
hither 278, 292
  come – 286
hitherto 122
hive
  multitude 102
  location 184
  abode 189
  bees 370
  workshop 691

H.M.S. 726
hoar *aged* 128
　white 430
　– *frost* 383
hoard 636
hoarse
　husky 405
　harsh 410
　voiceless 581
　talk oneself – 584
hoary [*see* hoar]
hoax 545
hob *support* 215
　stove 386
　– and nob
　celebration 883
　courtesy 894
hobble
　limp 275
　awkward 699
　difficulty 704
　fail 732
　shackle 751
　– skirt 225
hobbledehoy 129
hobby
　crotchet 481
　pursuit 622
　desire 865
hobby-horse 272
hobgoblin
　fearful 860
　demon 980
hobo 268
hobnail 876
Hobson's choice
　necessity 601
　no choice 609a
　compulsion 744
hoc genus omne
　876
hock 771
hock shop 787
hockey 840
hockey rink 213
hocus 545
hocus-pocus
　interchange 148
　unmeaning 517
　cheat 545
　conjuration 992
　spell 993
hod
　receptacle 191
　support 215
　vehicle 272
hoddy-doddy 501
hodge-podge 41
hoe 272, 371
hog *animal* 366
　sensualist 954a

[520]

glutton 957
greedy as a – 865
go the whole – 604
hog's back 206
hogmanay 998
hogshead 191
hog-wash 653
hoist 307
　– the black flag
　722
　– a flag 550
　– on one's own
　petard
　retaliation 718
　failure 732
hoity-toity! 815,
　870
hold *cohere* 46
　contain 54
　remain 141
　cease 142
　go on 143
　happen 151
　receptacle 191
　cellar 207
　base 211
　support 215
　halt 265
　believe 484
　be passive 681
　defend 717
　power 737
　restrain 751
　prison 752
　prohibit 761
　possess 777
　retain 781
　enough! 869
　have a firm – 781
　have a – upon 175
　gain a – upon 737
　get – of 789
　quit one's – 782
　take – 175
　– aloof
　stay away 187
　distrust 487
　avoid 623
　– an argument
　476
　– authority 737
　– back *avoid* 623
　store 636
　hinder 706
　restrain 751
　retain 781
　miserly 819
　– one's breath
　wonder 870
　– converse 588
　– a council 695

– fast 751, 781
– forth *teach* 537
　speak 582
– good 478, 494
– one's ground
　141
– in hand 737
– one's hand
　cease 142
　relinquish 624
– hard 265
– up one's head
　861
– a lease 771
– a meeting 72
– off 623
– office 693
– on
　continue 141, 143
　persevere 604a
– out [*see below*]
– one's own
　preserve 670
　defend 717
　resist 719
– oneself in readi-
　ness 673
– in remembrance
　505
– both one's sides
　838
– a situation 625
– in solution 335
– to 602
– together 43, 709
– one's tongue
　403, 585
– up [*see below*]
– oneself up 307
hold out
　endure 106
　affirm 535
　persevere 604a
　resist 719
　offer 763
　brave 861
　– expectation
　predict 511
　promise 768
　– temptation 865
hold up
　continue 143
　support 215
　not rain 340
　aid 707
　rob 791
　display 882
　extol 931
　– one's hand
　sign 550
　threat 609

– to execration
　cures 908
　censure 932
– the mirror 525
– to scorn 930
– to shame 874
– to view 525
holder 779
holdfast 45
holding
　tenancy 777
　property 780
hole *place* 182
　hovel 189
　receptacle 191
　opening 260
　ambush 530
　– in one's coat 651
　– and corner
　place 182
　peer into – 461
　hiding 528, 530
　– to creep out of
　plea 617
　escape 671
　facility 705
holiday *leisure* 685
　repose 687
　amusement 840
　– task *easy* 705
holiness *God* 976
　piety 987
holloa 411
　– before one is out
　of the wood 884
hollow
　unsubstantial 4
　completely 52
　incomplete 53
　depth 208
　concavity 252
　channel 350
　– *sound* 408
　specious 477
　false 544
　voiceless 581
　beat – 731
　– truce 723
holm 346
holocaust
　kill 361
　sacrifice 991
　(*destruction* 162)
holograph 590
holster 191
holt 367
holus bolus 684
Holy *of God* 976
　pious 987
　keep – 987
　– breathing 990

hopper 191
horary 108
horde
  assemblage 72
  party 712
  commonalty 876
horizon
  distance 196
  view 441
  expectation 507
  appear on the –
    525
  gloomy – 859
horizontality 213
horn
  receptacle 191
  sharp 253
  music 417
  draw in one's –s
  recant 607
  submit 725
  humility 879
  exalt one's – 873
  wear the –s 905
  –s of a dilemma
  reasoning 476
  difficulty 704
  – in 294
  – mad 920
  – of plenty 639
hornbook 542
hornet
  evil-doer 913
  –'s nest
  pitfall 667
  difficulty 704
  adversity 735
  painful 830
  resentment 900
  censure 932
hornpipe 840
hornwork 717
horny 323
Horny, old – 978
horology 114
horoscope 511, 992
horresco referens
  860
horrible *great* 31
  noxious 649
  dire 830
  ugly 846
  fearful 860
horrid [*see* horrible]
  vulgar 851
horrida bella 722
horrific [*see*
  horrible]
horrified 828, 860
horrify 830, 860
horripilation 383

horrisonous 410
horror 860, 867
  view with – 898
horrors 837
  sup full of – 828
horror-stricken 828
hors de combat
  impotent 158
  useless 645
  tired out 688
  put – 731
hors-d'œuvre 298
horse *hang on* 214
  stand 215
  carrier 271
  animal 366
  male 373
  cavalry 726
  ride the high –
    885
  put the –s to 673
  put up one's –s at
    184
  put up one's –s
    together
  concord 714
  friendship 888
  take – 266
  to – 293
  war – 726
  work like a – 686
  – artillery 726
  – of another colour
    15
  – doctor 370
  – and foot 726
  – laugh 838
  – marine 701
  like a – in a mill
    613
  – racing
  pastime 840
  contention 720
  – soldier 726
  – track 627
horseback 266
horse-cloth 225
horseman 268
horsemanship
  riding 266
  skill 698
horseplay 856
horse power 466
horse-shoe 245
horse-whip 972
hortation 615, 695
hortative 537
horticulture 371
hortus siccus 369
hosanna 931, 990
hose

  stockings 225
  pipe 348, 350
  extinguisher 385
hosier 225
hospice 189, 662
hospitable 816, 892
hospital 189, 662
  in – 655
hospitality
  [*see* hospitable]
hospodar 745
host *collection* 72
  multitude 102
  army 726
  friend 890
  rite 998
  reckon without
    one's –
  error 495
  unskilful 699
  rash 863
  – of heaven 977
  – in himself 175
hostage 771
hostel 189
hostelry 189
hostile
  disagreeing 24
  opposed 708
  enmity 889
  in – array 708
  – meeting 720
hostilities 722
hostility 889
hostler 746
hot *violent* 173
  warm 382
  pungent 392
  red 434
  orange 439
  excited 824
  irascible 901
  make – 384
  – air 482, 884
  – bath 386
  – blood *rash* 863
  angry 900
  irascible 901
  blow – and cold
  inconsistent 477
  falsehood 544
  tergiversation 607
  caprice 608
  in – haste 684
  in – pursuit 622
  – water
  difficulty 704
  quarrel 713
  painful 830
  – water bottle 386
hot air merchant

  884
hot-bed *cause* 153
  centre 222
  workshop 691
Hotchkiss gun 727
hotchpotch
  mixture 41
  confusion 59
  participation 778
hotel 189
hot-headed 684,
  825
hothouse
  conservatory 371,
    636
  furnace 386
  workshop 691
hot-press 255
Hotspur 863
Hottentot 876
hough 659
hound *animal* 366
  hunt 622
  persecute 907
  wretch 949
  hold with the hare
    but run with the
    –s 607
  – on 615
houppelande 225
hour *period* 108
  point of time 113
  present time 118
  improve the shin-
    ing – 682
  one's – is come
  occasion 134
  death 360
  – after hour 110
hour-glass
  chronometer 114
  contraction 195
  narrow 203
Houri 845
hourly *time* 106
  frequent 136
  periodical 138
house *family* 166
  locate 184
  abode 189
  theatre 599
  make safe 664
  council 696
  firm 712
  before the – 454
  keep – 184
  eat out of – and
    home
  prodigal 818
  gluttony 957
  turn out of – and

the same a – years|
hence 460
hundredth 99
hundredweight 319
hunger 865
hunger-strike 956
hunks 819
hunt *inquiry* 461
  pursuit 622
  – after 622
  – in couples 709
  – down 907
  – out *inquiry* 461
  discover 480a
  – slipper 840
hunter *horse* 271
  killer 361
  pursuer 622
  place &c. – 767
hunting 361, 622
hunting-ground 840
  happy – 981
hurdle 272
hurdy-gurdy 417
hurl 284
  – against 716
  – defiance 715
hurler avec les
  loups 82, 714
Hurlothrumbo 860
hurly-burly 315
hurrah 411, 836,
  838
hurricane 349, 667
  – deck 210
hurry *haste* 684
  excite 825
  – forward 684
  – off with 789
  – on 615
  – of spirits 821
  – up 684
hurst 367
hurt
  physical pain 378
  evil 619
  maltreat 649
  injure 659
  more frightened
  than – 860
  – the feelings
  pain 830
  anger 900
hurtful 649
hurtle 276
hurtless 648
husband
  store 636
  director 694
  spouse 903
husbandman 371

husbandry
  agriculture 371
  conduct 692
  economy 817
hush *moderate* 174
  stop 265
  silence 403
  taciturn 585
  – up
  conceal 528
  pacify 723
hush-money 30,
  973
husk 223, 226
husky *strong* 159
  dry 340
  faint sound 405
  hoarse 581
hussar 726
hussy 962
hustings
  school 542
  arena 728
  tribunal 966
hustle
  perturb 61
  push 276
  agitate 315
  activity 682
  hinder 706
hustler 682, 962
hut 189
hutch 189
huzza 838
hyacinth
  jewel 847
hyæna 913
hyaline 425
hybrid
  mixture 41
  exception 83
hydra
  monster 83, 366
  productive 168
  – headed 163
hydrant 348, 385
hydraulics 333, 348
hydroplane
  273
hydrodynamics
  333, 348
hydrography 341
hydrology 333
hydrolysis 49
hydromancy 511
hydromel 396
hydropathy 662
hydrophobia 867
hydrostatics 333
hyemal 383

hyetology 348
hygeian 656
hygiantics 670
hygienic 656, 670
hygre 348
hygrometry 339
hyle 316
hylism 316
hylotheism 984,
  989
Hymen 903
hymeneal 903
hymn *song* 415
  worship 990
  – of hate 898
hymn-book 998
hyoscine 663
hypallage 218
hyperbaton 218
hyperbola 245
hyperbole 549
hyperborean
  far 196
  cold 383
hypercriticism
  misjudgment 481
  discontent 832
  fastidiousness 868
  censure 932
hyperdulia 990
Hyperion 423, 845
  – to a satyr 14
hyperorthodoxy 984
hyperphysical 976
hypertrophy 194
hyphen 45
hypnology 683
hypnotic
  remedy 662
  sleep 683
hypnotize 376
hypocaust 386
hypochondriac
  madman 504
  low spirits 837
hypochondriasis
  837
hypocrisy
  falsehood 544
  religious – 988
hypocrite 548, 855
  play the – 544
hypostasis 1, 3
Hypostatic union
  976
hypothecate 771
hypothenuse 217
hypothesis 514
hypothesize 514
hypothetical 475,
  514

hypped *insane* 503
  dejected 837
hypsometer 206
Hyrcynian woo
  533
hysteria
  insanity 503
hysteric *violent* 173
hysterical
  spasmodic 608
  emotional 821
  excitable 825
hysterics 173
  in – *excited* 824
  frightened 860
hysteron proteron
  218

I

I 79
iambic 597
ibidem 13
Icarus
  navigator 269
  rash 863
  fate of – 306
ice *cold* 383
  refrigerate 385
iceberg 383
ice-bound 383
  restraint 751
ice-chest 387
ice-house 387
ice-yacht 273
Ichabod 874
ichnography 554
ichor 333
ichthyology 368
ichthyomancy 511
ichthyophagous 298
icicle 383
icon 554
iconoclasm 983a,
  984
iconoclast 165, **913**
iconography 554
icosahedron 244
id est 522
idea
  small quantity 32
  notion **453**
  give an – of 537
ideal *unreal* 2
  completeness 52
  erroneous 495
  imaginary 515
  perfect 650
ideality 450, 515
idée fixe 481

identification
identity 13
comparison 464
discovery 480*a*
identity 13
− *book* 206
Ideology 450
Ides of March 601
idiocrasy
essence 5
tendency 176
idiocy 499
idiom 560, 566
idiomatic 79
idiosyncrasy
essence 5
speciality 79
unconformity 83
tendency 176
temperament 820
idiot 501
tale told by an −
517
idiotic
foolish 499
idiotism
folly 499
phrase 566
idle *foolish* 499
trivial 643
slothful 683
lie − *inaction* 681
− *conceit* 842
− *hours* 681
be an − *man*
leisure 685
− *talk* 588
− *time away* 683
idler 683
Ido 560
idol *desire* 865
favourite 899
fetich 991
− *of the people*
899
idolater 984
idolatry 897, **991**
idolize *love* 897
impiety 988
idoneous 23
idyl 597
if *circumstance* 8
qualification 469
supposition 514
− *you please* 765
− *possible* 470
igloo 189
igneous 382
ignis fatuus
luminary 423
phantom 443

ignite 384
ignoble 876
ignominy 874, 940
ignoramus **493**
ignorance **491**
keep in − 528
plead − 937
ignoratio elenchi
477
ignore
neglect 460
incredulity 487
not known 491
repudiate 756,
773
ignotum per
ignotius 477
ilk 13
ill *evil* 619
badness 649
sick 655
go on − *fail* 732
adversity 735
look − 846
take −
discontent 832
anger 900
− *betide* 908
− *blood hate* 898
malevolence 907
− *at ease pain* 828
dejection 837
house of − *fame*
961
−*s that flesh is*
heir to evil 619
disease 655
− *humour*
anger 900
sullenness 901*a*
− *luck* 735
as − *luck would*
have it 135
− *off*
insufficient 640
adversity 735
poor 804
do an − *office to*
907
bird of − *omen*
668
− *repute* 874
− *turn evil* 619
spiteful 907
− *usage* 907
− *will* 907
wind bad 649
hindrance 706
adversity 735
ill-adapted 24
ill-advised

foolish 499
inexpedient 647
unskilful 699
ill-affected 901*a*
illapse
conversion 144
ingress 294
illaqueate 545
ill-assorted 24
illation 480
illaudable 947
ill-balanced 28
ill-bred 851, 895
ill-conditioned
bad 649
difficult 704
discourteous 895
malevolent 907
vicious 945
ill-conducted 699
ill-contrived
inexpedient 647
bad 649
unskilful 699
malevolent 907
ill-defined 447
ill-devised 499, 699
ill-digested 674
ill-disposed 901*a*,
907
illegality **964**
illegible 519
render − 552
− *hand* 590
illegitimate
deceitful 545
undue 925
illegal 964
ill-fated 735
ill-flavoured 395
ill-furnished 640
illiberal
narrow-minded
481
stingy 819
uncourteous 895
selfish 943
illicit 925, 964
ill-imagined 499,
699
illimited 105
ill-intentioned 907
illiterate 491, 493
ill-judged 499, 699
ill-judging 481
ill-made 243, 846
ill-mannered 851,
895
ill-marked 447
ill-matched 24
ill-mated 24

ill-natured 907
illogical 477, 495
ill-omened 605, 859
ill-proportioned 243
ill-provided 640
ill-qualified 699
ill-requited 917
ill-spent 645
ill-tempered 901
ill-timed 135
ill-treat *bad* 649
severe 739
malevolent 907
illuminant 388
illuminate
enlighten 420
colour 428
excite 824
ornament 847
illuminati 492
illumination
[*see* illuminate]
book-illustration
558
celebration 883
ill-use 907
ill-used 828
illusion
fallacy of vision
443
error 495
illusive, illusory
sophistical 477
erroneous 495
deceitful 545, **546**
illustrate
exemplify 82
interpret 522
represent 554
engravings 558
ornament 847
illustrious 873
image
likeness 17
copy 21
appearance **448**
idea 453
metaphor 521
representation
554
graven − *idol* 991
imagery *fancy* **515**
metaphor 521
representation
554
imaginable 470
imaginary
non-existing 2
fancied 515
− *quantity* 84
imagination **515**

imaum 745, 996
imbecile 158, 499
imbécile 501
imbecility 499
imbed [*see* embed]
imbedded 229
imbibe 296
  – learning 539
imbrangle 61
imbricated 223
imbroglio
  disorder 59
  difficulty 704
  discord 713
ìmbrue
  impregnate 300
  moisten 339
  – one's hands in
    blood
  killing 361
  war 722
  – the soul 824
imbue *mix* 41
  impregnate 300
  moisten 339
  tinge 428
  teach 537
ìmbued
  affections 820
  – with
  belief 484
  habit 613
  feeling 821
ìmburse 803
imitation
  copying **19**
  copy 21
  representation
    554
immaculate
  perfect 650
  clean 652
  innocent 946
immanent 5
immanity 907
Immanuel 976
immaterial
  unsubstantial 4
immateriality
  spiritual **317**
  trifling 643
immature 123, 674
immeasurable 31,
  105
immediate
  continuous 69
immediately 113,
  132
immedicabile
  vulnus 619
immedicable 859

immelodious 414
immemorial 124
  from time – 122
  – usage 613
immense *great* 31
  infinite 105
  - *size* 192
immerge⎱
immerse⎰
  introduce 300
  dip 337
immersed in 229
immethodical 59
immigrant *alien* 57
  entering 294
immigration 266,
  294
imminent 132, 152,
  286
immiscible 47
immission 296
immitigable
  hopeless 859
  revenge 919
immix 41
immobility 150, 265
immoderately 31
immodest 961
immolation
  killing 361
  giving 784
  sacrifice 991
immoral 923, 945
immortal
  perpetual 112
  glorious 873
  celebrated 883
immotile 265
immovable
  stable 150
  quiescent 265
  obstinate 606
immundicity 653
immunity
  health 656
  freedom 748
  right 924
  exemption **777a**,
    927a
immure 751
immutable
  stable 150
  deity 976
imo pectore, ab –
  821
imp 980
impact *contact* 43
  impulse 276
  insertion 300
impair 659
impale *transfix* 260

  execute 972
impalpable
  small 193
  powder 330
  intangible 381
impanation 998
impar sibi 608
imparity 28
impart *inform* 527
  give 784
impartial
  judicious 498
  neutral 628
  just 922
  honourable 939
  – opinion 484
impassable
  closed 261
  impossible 471
impasse 706
impassible 823
impassion 824
impassionable 822
impassioned
  - *language* 574
  excited 825
impassive 823
impatient 825
  – of control 742
impawn 771
impeach
  censure 932
  accuse 938
  go to law 969
impeachment,
  soft – 902
impeccability 650,
  946
impecunious 804
impede 706
impediment 706
  – in speech 583
impedimenta 633,
  780
impel *push* 276
  induce 615
impend
  future 121
  imminent 132
  destiny 152
  overhang 206
impenetrable
  closed 261
  solid 321
  unintelligible 519
  latent 526
impenitence 951
imperative
  require 630
  command 737,
    741

  severe 739
  duty 926
imperator 745
imperceptible
  small 32
  minute 193
  slow 275
  invisible 447
  latent 526
impercipient 376
imperdible 664
imperfect
  incomplete **53**
  failing 651
  vicious 945
imperfection 651
  inferiority 34
  vice 945
imperfectly 32
imperforate 261
imperial
  trunk 191
  beard 256
  authority **737**
imperil 665
imperious
  command 737
  proud 878
  arrogant 885
  – *necessity* 601
imperishable 112
  stable 150
  glorious 873
imperium in
  imperio 737
impermanent 111
impermeable
  closed 261
  dense 321
impersonal
  general 78
  neuter 316
impersonate 19,
  554
impersonator 19
imperspicuity 519
impersuasible 606
impertinent
  irrelevant 10
  insolent 885
imperturbable 823,
  826
impervious
  closed 261
  impossible 471
  insensible 823
  – to light 426
  – to reason 606
impetiginous 653
impetrate 765
impetuous

boisterous 173
hasty 684
excitable 825
rash 863
eager 865
impetus 276
impi 726
impiety 988
impignorate 771
impinge 276
implacable 848, 919
implant *insert* 300
  teach 537
implanted
  adventitious 6
implausible 473
implead 969
implement 633
impletion 52
implex 41
implicate *involve* 54, 526
  accuse 938
implicated *related* 9
  component 56
implication
  disorder 59
  meaning 516
  latency 526
implicit 526
  – *belief* 484
implore 765
imply *evidence* 467
  mean 516
  involve 526
impolicy 699
impolite 895
imponderable 4, 320
imporous 261, 321
import
  put between 228
  ingress 294
  take in 296
  insert 300
  mean 516
  imply 526
  be of consequence 642
importance 642
  greatness 31
  attach – to 642
  attach too much – to 482
  of no – 643
importune 765, 830
impose *order* 741
  awe 928
  – upon
  credulity 486
  deceive 545

be unjust 923
imposing
  important 642
  exciting 824
  glorious 873
imposition [*see* impose]
  undue 925
  – of hands 998
impossibile, credo quia – 486
impossibilities, seek after – 645
impossibility 471
impossible 471
  refusal 764
  – *quantity*
  algebra 84
impost 812
imposthume 655
impostor 548, 925
imposture 545
impotence 158
impotent conclusion 732
impound 751
impoverish
  weaken 160
  waste 638
  despoil 789
  render poor 804
impracticable
  impossible 471
  misjudging 481
  obstinate 606
  difficult 704
imprecation
  prayer 765
  curse 908
impregnable 159, 664
impregnate *mix* 41
  combine 48
  fecundate 161, 168
  insert 300
  teach 537
  – *with* 641
impresario 599
imprescriptible 924
impress *cause*
  sensation 375
  mark 550
  steal 791
  excite feeling 824
  – upon the mind
  memory 505
  teach 537
impressed with
  belief 484
  feeling 821

impressible
  motive 615
  sensibility 822
impression
  sensation 375
  idea 453
  belief 484
  printing 531
  mark 550
  engraving 558
  print 591
  emotion 821
  make an –
  act 171
  thought 451
impressionable 375, 822
impressive
  language 574
  important 642
  feeling 821, 824
imprimis 66
imprimit 558
imprint
  publisher 531
  indication 550
  – in the memory 505
imprison
  circumscribe 229
  restrain 751
  punish 972
improbability 473
improbate 932
improbity 940
impromptu 612
  – fait à loisir 673
improper
  incongruous 24
  foolish 499
  solecism 568
  inexpedient 647
  wrong 923
  unmeet 925
  vicious 945
  – *time* 135
impropriate 777, 789
impropriator 779
improve 658
  – the occasion 134
  – the shining hour 682
  – upon 658
improvement 658
improvident
  careless 460
  not preparing 674
  prodigal 818
  rash 863
improvisation

  music 415
improvisatore
  speech 582
  poetry 597
  impulse 612
improvise
  imagination 515
  impulse 612
  unprepared 674
improviste, à l' – 508, 612
improvisatrice 612
imprudent 460, 863
impudent 885, 895
impudicity 961
impugn *deny* 536
  attack 716
  blame 932
impugnation 708
impuissance 158
impulse *push* **276**
  sudden thought 612
  motive 615
  blind – 601
  creature of – **612**
  give an – to
  propel 284
  aid 707
impulsive [*see* impulse]
  intuitive 477
  excitable 825
  rash 863
impunity *escape* **671**
  acquittal 970
  with – *safely* 664
impurity 653, **961**
imputation
  ascribe 155
  slur 874
  accuse 938
in 221
  go – 294
  – as much as
  relation 9
  degree 26
  – the circumstances 8
  – doors 221
  – durancevile **751**
  – for
  – force 1
  undertake 676
  promise 768
  – re 9
  – and out 314
  –s and outs 182
in: – articulo 111
  – extenso *whole* **50**

character 820
ingrate 917
ingratiate 897
ingratiating 894
ingratitude **917**
ingredient 51, 56
ingress **294**
 forcible – 300
ingurgitate 296
ingustible 391
inhabile 699
inhabit 186
inhabitant **188**
inhale *receive* 296
 breathe 349
 smell 398
inharmonious
 discord 713
 – colour 428
 – sound 414
inhere 1
inherent 5, 820
inherit 775, 777
inheritance 780
 – of the saints 981
inherited
 intrinsic 5
inheritor 779
inhesion 5
inhibit *hinder* 706
 restrain 751
 prohibit 761
inhospitable 893
inhuman 907
inhume 363
inimaginable
 impossible 471
 improbable 473
 wonderful 870
inimical 708, 889
inimitable
 non-imitation 20
 supreme 33
 very good 648
 perfect 650
iniquity 923, 945
 worker of – 949
inirritability 826
initial 66
 – letter 558
initiate *begin* 66
 admit 296
 teach 537
initiated *skilful* 698
initiative 66
inject 300, 337
injection 662
injudicial 964
injudicious 499, 863
injunction

acquirement 630
advice 695
command 741
prohibition 761
injure *evil* 619
 damage 659
 spite 907
injuria formæ,
 spretæ – 846, 930
injury *evil* 619
 badness 649
 damage 659
injustice 923
ink 431
 pen and – 590
 before the – is dry 132
 – slinging 720
inkle 45
inkling
 knowledge 490
 supposition 514
 information 527
inkstand 590
inland 221
inlay 440, 847
inlet *beginning* 66
 interval 198
 opening 260
 ingress 294
 - *of the sea* 343
inly 221
inmate 188
inmost 221
 to the – core 822
 – soul 820
 – thoughts 451
inn 189
 – s of Court 968
innate 5, 601
innavigable 471
inner 221
 – coating 224
 – man *intellect* 450
 affections 820
innermost recesses 221
innings *land* 342
 acquisition 775
 receipt 810
innkeeper 601
innocence **946**
innocent *fool* 501
 good 648
 healthy 656
 artless 703
 guiltless 946
innocuous *good* 648
 healthy 656
 innocent 946

innominate 565
innovation
 variation 20a
 new 123
 change 140
innoxious
 salubrious 656
 innocent 946
innuendo *hint* 527
 censure 932
innumerable 105
innutritious 657
inobservance 773
inoccupation 681
inoculate
 insert 300
 teach 537
 influence 615
inodorous **399**
inoffensive 648, 946
inofficious 907
inoperative
 powerless 158
 unproductive 169
 useless 645
inopportune
 untimely 135
 inexpedient 647
inordinate 31, 641
inorganization **358**
inornate 849
inosculate *join* 43
 intersect 219
 convoluted 248
inquest 461
inquietude
 changeable 149
 uneasy 828
 discontent 832
 apprehension 860
inquinate 659
inquire 461
 – into 595
inquirer 461
inquiring mind 455
inquiry **461**
inquisition
 inquiry 461
 severity 739
 torture 907
 tribunal 966
inquisitive 455
inquisitorial
 prying 455
 inquiry 461
 severe 739
 jurisdiction 965
inroad *ingress* 294
 devastation 659
 invasion 716
inrolment 551

insalubrity **657**
insanity **503**
insatiable 865
inscribe 590, **873**
inscription 551
inscroll 551
inscrutable 519
insculpture 557
insculptured 558
insecable 43, 87
insect *minute* **193**
 animal 366
 – cry 412
insecure
 uncertain 475
 danger 665
insensate
 foolish 499
 insane 503
insensibility
 slow 275
 physical **376**
 moral **823**
 – of benefits 917
 – to the past 506
inseparable 43, 46
insert *locate* 184
 interpose 228
 enter 294
 put in 300
 record 551
 – itself 300
insertion **300**
 adjunct 39
 ornament 847
inservient 645
inseverable 43, **87**
inside 221
 – out 218
 turn – out 529
insidious
 deceitful 545
 cunning 702
 dishonourable **940**
insight 465, 490
insignia 550
 – of authority **747**
insignificant
 unmeaning 517
 unimportant 643
insincere 544, 855
insinuate
 intervene 228
 ingress 294
 insert 300
 latency 526
 hint 527
 ingratiate **897**
 blame 932
insipid
 style **575**

dull 840
insipidity
  tasteless **391**
  indifferent 866
insist *argue* 476
  command 741
  – upon *affirm* 535
  dwell on 573
  be determined 604
  contend 720
  compel 744
  conditions 770
  due 924
insnare 545
insobriety 959
insolation 382, 384
insolence 878, 885
insoluble *dense* 321
  unintelligible 519
insolvable 519
insolvent
  poverty 804
  debt 806
  non-payment 808
insomnia 682
insouciance
  thoughtlessness 458
  supineness 823
  indifference 866
inspan 293
inspect 441, 457
inspector 444
  inquisitor 461
  judge 480
  director 694
inspiration
  wisdom 498
  imagination 515
  poetry 597
  impulse 612
  motive 615
  feeling 821
  Deity 976
  revelation 985
  religious - 987
inspire *improve* 658
  prompt 615
  animate 824
  cheer 836
  – courage 861
  – hope 858
  – respect 928
inspirit *incite* 615
  animate 824
  encourage 861
inspiriting
  hopeful 858
inspissate 321, 352
instability 149
install *locate* 184

commission **755**
  celebrate 883
instalment
  portion 51
  payment 807, 809
instance
  example 82
  motive 615
  solicitation 765
instant *moment* 113
  present 118
  destiny 152
  required 630
  importance 642
  active 682
  lose not an – 684
  on the – 132
instantaneity 113
instanter 113, 132
instar omnium 17, 82
instate 883
instauration 660
instead 147
instep 245
instigate 615
instil *extrinsic* 6
  mix 41
  insert 300
  teach 537
instinct
  intellect 450
  intuition 477
  impulse 601
  – with *motive* 615
  possession 777
  brute – 450*a*
instinctive
  inborn 5
institute *begin* 66
  cause 153
  produce 161
  academy 542
  society 712
  – an inquiry 461
institution
  academy 542
  society 712
  political - 963
  church 995
institutor 540
instruct *teach* 537
  advise 695
  precept 697
  order 741
instructed 490
instructor 540
instrument
  implement **633**
  security 771
  musical – 417

optical – 445
  recording – 553
instrumental 631
  – music 415
instrumentalist 416
instrumentality 631
insuavity 895
insubordinate 742
insubstantial 4
  – pageant 882
insufferable
  painful 830
  dislike 867
insufficiency 640
insufflation 349
insular *unrelated* 10
  detached 44
  single 87
  local 181
  island 346
  prejudice 481
insulate 44
insulse 499, 843
insult *rudeness* 895
  offence 900
  disrespect 929
insulting 898
insuperable 471
  – obstacle 706
insupportable 830
insuppressible 173
insurance 768, 771
insure
  make sure 474
  obtain security 771
insurgent 742
insurmountable 471
insurrection 719, 742
insusceptible 823
  – of change 150
inswept 195
intact
  permanent 141
  perfect 650
  preserved 670
intaglio *mould* 22
  concave 252
  sculpture 557
  engraving 558
intangible *little* 193
  numb 381
integer 50, 84
integer vitæ scelerisque purus 939
integral 50
  – calculus 85
  – part 56
integrate 50

integrity *whole* **50**
  probity 939
  virtue 944
integument 223
intellect 450
  absence of – **450a**
  exercise of the – 451
intellectual 450
intelligence
  mind 450
  capacity **498**
  news 532
intelligencer 527
intelligentsia 492
intelligibility 518
intemperance 954
  drunkenness 959
intempestivity 135
intend 620
intendant 694
intended *will* 600
  predetermined 611
intense *great* 31
  energetic 171
  – colour 428
  – thought 457
intensification 35
intensify
  increase 35
  stimulate 171
intensity *degree* 26
  greatness 31
  energy 171
intensive culture 371
intent *attention* **457**
  will 600
  design 620
  active 682
  – upon *desire* **865**
  resolved 604
intention 620
  bad – 907
  good – 906
intently, look – **441**
intents and purposes, to all – 27, 52
inter 363
interact 12
inter: – *alia* 82
  – *nos* 528
interaction 170
interbreeding 41
intercalate 228
intercalation 300
intercede
  mediate 724
  deprecate 766

intercept
hinder 706
take 789
intercession
[*see* intercede]
worship 990
Intercessor 976
interchange 148
barter 794
– *visits &c.* 892
interchangeable 12
intercipient 706
interclude 706
intercommunication 527
intercommunity 892
interconnection 9
intercourse
copulation 43
friendship 888
sociality 892
verbal – 582, 588
intercurrence
interchange 148
interjacence 228
passage 302
interdependence 12
interdict 761
interdictive 55
interdigitate 219, 228
interest *concern* 9
influence 175
curiosity 455
advantage 618
importance 642
property 780
debt 806
excite 824
please 829
amuse 840
devoid of – 841
feel an – *in* 906
not know one's own – 699
make – *for* 707
place out at – *lend* 787
economy 817
take an – *in curiosity* 455
love 897
take no – *in insensibility* 823
indifference 866
want of – 866
interested
selfish 943
– *in* 457
interesting

[534]

lovable 897
interfere *disagree* 24
counteract 179
intervene 228
activity 682
thwart 706
mediate 724
interference
light 420
interfretted 219
interfusion 41
interim 106, 120
interior 221
painting 556
interjacence 68, **228**
interject 228, 300
interlace *join* 43
twine 219
interlacing 41
interlard 41, 228
interleave 228
interline
interpolate 228
write 590
interlineation 39
interlink 43, 219
interlocation 228
interlocking directorate 709
interlocution 588
interlocutor 582
interloper
extraneous 57
intervene 228
obstruct 706
interlude
time 106
dramatic 599
intermarriage 903
intermeddle 682, 706
intermeddling 724
intermediary 534
intermediate
mean 29
middle 68
intervening 228
ministerial 631
– *time* 106
intermedium
mean 29
link 45
intervention 228
instrument 631
interment 363
insertion 300
intermezzo 415
intermigration 266
interminable

infinite 105
eternal 112
long 200
intermingle 41
intermission 106, 142
intermit
interrupt 70
recur 138
discontinue 142
intermittence
time 106
intermix 41, 48
intermutation 148
intermural 278
intern 221
internal 5, 221
– *evidence* 467
international
reciprocal 12
sociality 892
– *law* 963
internecine 361
– *war* 722
internuncio 534, 758
interpel 142
interpellation
inquiry 461
address 586
summons 741
appeal 765
interpenetration
interjacence 228
ingress 294
passage 302
interpolation
adjunct 39
analytical 85
interpose 228
insertion 300
interpose
intervene 228
act 682
hinder 706
mediate 724
interposit 799
interplanetary 228
interpretation 522
interpreter 524
interrelation 9, 12
interregnum
intermission 106
transient 111
discontinuance 142
interval 198
laxity 738
interrogate 461
interrupt
discontinuity 70

cessation 142
hinder 706
interruption
derangement 61
interval 198
intersect 219
interspace 198, 221
intersperse 73, 228
interstellar 228
interstice 198
interstitial 221, **228**
intertexture
intersection 219
tissue 329
inter-twine, -twist
unite 43
cross 219
interval
– *of time* 106
– *of space* **198**
– *in music* 413
at –s
discontinuously 70
at regular –s 138
intervene
– *in order* 70
– *in time* 106
– *in space* 228
be instrumental 631
mediate 724
intervert 140, 279
interview 588, 892
intervolved 43
interweave *join* 43
cross 219
interjacence 228
interworking 170
intestate 552
intestine 221
inthral 749, 751
intimacy 9
intimate
personal 79
close 197
inside 221
tell 527
friendly 888, **892**
intimately
joined 43
intimidate
frighten 860
insolence 885
threat 909
intitule 564
into: *go* – 294
put – 300
run – 300
intolerable 830
intolerance

itinerary 266, 527
itur ad astra, sic –
 360
ivory 430
Ixion 312

J

jab 276
jabber
 unmeaning 517
 stammer 583
 chatter 584
jacent 213
jacet, hic – 363
jacinth 847
jack
 rotation 312
 ensign 550
 instrument 633
 money 800
Jack – Cade 742
 – Ketch 975
 – o' lantern 423
 – in office
 director 694
 bully 887
 – at a pinch 711
 – Pudding
 actor 599
 humorist 844
 boaster 884
 before one can say
 ' – Robinson'
 132
 – tar 269
 – of all trades 700
jack-a-dandy 844,
 854
jackal
 auxiliary 711
 servility 886
jackanapes 854,
 887
Jackass 271
jack-boot 225
jackdaw in pea-
 cock's feathers
 701
jacket 225
 cork – 666
Jacobin 710
Jacquerie 716, 719
jacta est alea 601
jactitation
 tossing 315
 boasting 884
jaculation 284
jade *horse* 271
 fatigue 688

low woman 876
scamp 949
drab 962
jag 257
jagged 244
jail 752
 – bird
 prisoner 754
 bad man 949
jailer 753, 975
jakes 653
jalousie de métier
 921
jam *squeeze* 43
 crowd 72
 food 298
 pulp 354
 sweet 396
 scrape 732
 – in *interpose* 228
jamb 215
jamboree 840
jammed in 751
jangle
 harsh sound 410
 quarrel 713
janissary 726
janitor 263
janty *gay* 836
 pretty 845
 stylish 852
 showy 882
 insolent 885
January 138
januis clausis 528
Janus *deceiver* 607
 tergiversation 607
 close the temple
 of – 723
Janus-faced 544
japan *coat* 223
 resin 356a
 ornament 847
jar *clash* 24
 vessel 191
 agitation 315
 stridor 410
 discord 713
 – upon the feel-
 ings 830
jardinière 191
jargon
 absurdity 497
 no meaning 517
 unintelligible 519
 neology 563
jarvey 694
jasper 847
jaundiced
 yellow 436
 prejudiced 481

dejected 837
jealous 920
view with – eyes
 disapprove 932
jaunt 266
jaunting car 272
jaunty [*see* janty]
javelin 727
jaw *chatter* 584
 scold 932
jaw-fallen 837
jaws *mouth* 231
 eating 298
 – of death 360
jay 584
jaywalker 701
jazz 415, 840
 – band 417
jealous of honour
 939
jealousy **920**
 suspicion 485
jecur, difficili bile –
 900
jeer 929
Jehovah 976
Jehu 268, 694
jejune *insipid* 391
 style 575
 scanty 640
 dull 843
jell 352
jelly 298, 352
 beat to a – 972
jemidar 745
jemmy *lever* 633
 dandy 854
je ne sais quoi
 exceptional 83
 what d'ye call 'em
 563
 beauty 845
jennet 271
jeopardy 665
jerboa 309
jeremiad
 lament 839
 invective 932
Jericho, send to –
 297
jerk *start* 146
 throw 284
 pull 285
 agitate 315
jerkin 225
jerks, by – 70
Jerry Sneak 862,
 941
jersey 225
Jerusalem
 the new – 981

Jessamy, Jemmy
 854
jesse 1000
jest *trifle* 643
 wit 842
jest-book 842
jester 844
jesting-stock 857
Jesuit *deceiver* 548
 priest 996
jesuitical 477, 544
Jesus 976
jet *stream* 348
 – black 431
jetsam 73, 782
jettison 782
jetty *protection* 250
 harbour 666
jeu
 le – n'en vaut pas
 la chandelle
 waste 638
 unimportant 643
 dear 814
 – d'esprit 842
 – de mots 842
 – de théâtre 599
jeune
 – premier 599
 – veuve 599
jewel *gem* 648
 ornament 847
 favourite 899
jewellery, false –
 545
Jezebel *wicked* 913
 wretch 949
 courtesan 962
jib *front* 234
 regression 283
 cut of one's –
 form 240
 appearance 448
jibe 140
jiffy 113
jig 840
jig-saw puzzle 840
jilt *disappoint* 509
 deceive 545
 deceiver 548
 cast off 756
 dishonour 940
jilted 898

at one – 113
– about 315
– at *willing* 602
pursue 622
hasten 684
consent 762
seize 789
desire 865
– to a conclusion
misjudge 481
credulous 486
– over 460
– up 307, 309
jumper 225
junction **43**
juncture
circumstance **8**
junction 43
period 134
jungle *disorder* 59
vegetation 367
junior 127, 541
– counsel 968
junk 273
junket *dish* 298
merry-making
840
Juno 920, 979
junta 696
junto 712
jupe 225
Jupiter **979**
jurare in verba ma-
gistri 481, 486
jurat 967
jure: de – *due* 924
legal 963
– divino *due* 924
God 976
juridical 965
jurisconsult 968
jurisdiction **965**
authority 737
Jurisprudence 963
jurist 480, 968
jury 967
empanel a – 969
– box 966
– mast
substitute 147
refuge 666
jus: summum –
922
– civile 963
– gentium 963
– nocendi 737
– et norma
loquendi 567
jussive 741
just *accurate* 494
right 922

equitable 939
pious 987
– as *similar* 17
same time 120
– do 639
– now 118
– out 123
– reasoning 476
– so 488
– then 113
– the thing
agreement 23
exact 494
– in time 134
juste milieu
middle 68
moderation 174
mid-course 628
justice
right 922
honour 939
magistrate 967
administration of
– 965
bring to – 969
court of – 966
do – to *eat* 298
duty 926
praise 931
vindicate 937
not do – to 483
retributive – 922,
972
– seat 966
justifiable 922, 937
justification
vindication 937
religious 987
justle *push* 276
contend 720
jut out 250
jute 205
jutty 250
juvenile 127
– lead 599
juxtaposition 199
j'y suis j'y reste
141

K

kadi 967
kail 840
kaiser 745
kaleidoscope 149,
445
kangaroo 309

Katerfelto 994
kavass 965
K.C. 968
keck 297
kedge *navigate* 267
anchor 666
keek 527
keel 211
– upwards 218
keelhaul 972
keen *energetic* 171
sharp 253
sensible 375
cold 383
intelligent 498
poignant 821
lament 839
witty 842
eager 865
– blast 349
keener 839
keen-eyed 441
keep *do often* 136
persist 141
continue 143
food 298
store 636
provision 637
refuge 666
preserve 670
citadel 717
custody 751
prison 752
observe 772
retain 781
celebrate 883
– alive 359, 670
– aloof 196, 623
– accounts 811
– an account with
805
– apart 44
– at it 143
– away 187
– back *late* 133
conceal 528
dissuade 616
not use 678
restrain 751
retain 781
– the ball rolling
143
– one's bed 655
– body and soul
together *life* 359
health 654
– within bounds
304
– close 781

– company 88
– one in counte-
nance
conformity 82
induce 615
aid 707
encourage 861
– one's counte-
nance
unexcitable 826
sad 837
– one's course 282
– an eye upon 459
– the field 722
– firm 150
– on foot
continuance 143
support 215
preparation 673
– from *conceal* **528**
refrain 623
not do 681
restrain 751
– going
continue 143
move 264
– one's ground 141
– one's hand in 613
– one's head above
water 731, 817
– hold 150
– holy 987
– house 184
– in ignorance 528
– in *restrain* 751
prohibit 761
– on one's legs **654**
– a good look out
for 507
– in mind 505
– moving 682
– off *avoid* 623
hinder 706
defend 717
resist 719
prohibition 761
– on *do often* 136
continue 143
persevere 604a
– to oneself 528
– in order 693
– out
- *of the way* 187
- *of harm's way*
864
– pace with 27,
120
– the peace **714**
– posted 527
– the pot boiling
143

[539]

– one's promise
772
– quiet 265
– a secret 528
– a shop 625
– in sight 459
– silence 585
– straight 944
– in suspense
uncertainty 475
irresolution 605
– in the thoughts
505
– time
punctual 132
music 416
– to 604*a*
– together 709
– under
authority 737
subjection 749
restraint 751
– up [*see below*]
– in view
attend to 457
remember 505
expect 507
– waiting 133
– watch 459
– one's word 939
ʀeep up
continue 143
preserve 670
stimulate 824
– appearances 852
– the ball 682, 840
– a correspond-
ence 592
– the memory of
505
– one's spirits 836
– with 274
keeper 370, **753**
keeping
congruity 23
in – 82
safe – *safety* 664
preservation 670
keepsake 505
keg 191
kelpie 979
kelson 211
kempt 652
ken 441, 490
beyond mortal –
360
kennel
assemblage **72**
hovel 189
ditch 259
conduit 350

Kentish fire 931
képi 225
kerb-stone 233
kerchief 225
wave a – 550
kern *quern* 330
low fellow 876
varlet 949
kernel *heart* 5
cause 153
central 222
important 642
kerosene 356
ketch
ship 273
Ketch, Jack – 975
kettle *vessel* 191
caldron 386
– drum *music* 417
tea-party 892
– of fish
disorder 59
difficulty 704
key *cause* 153
opener 260
music 413
colour 428
interpretation 522
indication 550
instrument 631,
633
*emblem of au-
thority* 747
deliver the –s of
the city 725
key-hole 260
key-note *model* 22
rule 80
music 413
key-stone
support 215
motive 615
importance 642
completion 729
khaki 225, 433
khan *inn* 189
governor 745
khedive 745
kibitka 272
kibitzer 682
kick *impulse* 276
recoil 277
assault 716
thrill 821
spurn 930
punish 972
– against
oppose 708
resist 719
– against the
pricks

useless 645
rash 863
unequal 28
superior 33
– up a dust
active 682
discord 713
insolent 885
– a row 900
– one's heels
kept waiting 133
nothing to do 681
– off 62
– up a row
violent 173
discord 713
– over the traces
742
kicking, alive and –
359
kickshaw *food* 298
trifle 643
kid *child* 129
progeny 167
leather 223
not to be handled
with – gloves
dirty 653
difficult 704
kidnap
deceive 545
take 789
steal 791
kidney *class* 75
kilderkin 191
Kilkenny cats 713
kill 361
– or cure 662
– the fatted calf
883
– the goose with
golden eggs 699
– with kindness
902
– the slain 641
– time 106
inactivity 683
amusement 840
– two birds with
one stone 682
killing **361**
delightful 829
kill-joy 706
kiln 386
kilowatt 466
kilt 225
kimbo 244
kimono 225
kin 75
kind *class* 75
benevolent 906

– regards 894
kinder-garten 542
kindle *cause* 153
produce 161
quicken 171
inflame 173
set fire to 384
excite 824
incense 900
kindling wood 388
kindred 9, 11
kine 366
kinematics 264
kinetic energy 157
king 745
every inch a –
authority 737
rank 875
–maker 694
King –'s Bench
752, 966
–'s birthday 268
–'s counsel 968
– Death 360
–'s English 560
–'s evidence 529
–'s highway 627
–'s ransom 648
– of Kings 976
kingcraft 693
kingdom
region 181
property 780
– of heaven 981
kingly 737
king-post 215
kink 248, 378, 608
kiosk 189, 1000
kip 961
kirk 1000
kirtle 225
kismet 601
kiss *touch* 199
courtesy 894
endearment 902
– the book 535
– the hem of one's
garment 928
– in the ring 840
– the rod 725
kit *class* 75
equipment 191
fiddle 417
–bag 191
kitcat 556
kitchen 191, 691
– maid 746
– range 386
kitchener 386
kitchenette 691
kite *fly* 273

bill 800
fly a – *credit* 805
insolvency 808
– balloon 273, 726
kith 11
kithless 87
kitten *animal* 366
young 129
bring forth 161
playful as a – 836, 840
kleptomania
insanity 503
stealing 791
desire 865
kleptomaniac 504
knack 698
get into the – 613
knacker 361
knag 706
knaggy 901*a*
knap 206
knapsack 191
knave 548, **941**
– of hearts 897
knavery
deception 545
cunning 702
improbity 940
vice 945
knead *mix* 41
mould 240
soften 324
stroke 379
knee *angle* 244
bend the –
stoop 308
submission 725
down on one's –s
humble 879
on one's –s
beg 765
respect 928
atone 952
on the –s of the gods 121, 152
knee-deep 208, 209
kneel *stoop* 308
submit 725
beg 765
servility 886
courtesy 894
ask mercy 914
respect 928
worship 990
knell 363
strike the death – 361
knickerbockers 225
knicknack 643, 847
knife 253

play a good – and fork *eat* 298
appetite 865
war to the – 708
knight 875
– errant
madman 504
defender 717
rash 863
philanthropist 910
–'s move 279
– service 777
– of the road 792
– Templar 712
knit 43
well – 159
– the brow
discontent 832
anger 900
disapprobation 932
knitting 847
knob *pendency* 214
ball 249
protuberance 250
knock *blow* 276
sound 406
hard –s 720
– at the door
death 360
request 765
– down
destroy 162
lay flat 213
lower 308
injure 659
dishearten 837
– on the head
kill 361
– one's head against 699
– off *complete* 729
– out 162
– over 162
– under 725
– up 688
knock-down argument 479
knocked
– to atoms 162
– on the head
failure 732
knocker 936
knock-kneed 243, 244
knoll 206
knot *ligature* 45
entanglement 59
group 72
intersection 219

round 249
dense 321
difficulty 704
hindrance 706
junto 712
ornament 847
marriage 903
true lover's – *love* 897
endearment 902
tie the nuptial – 903
knotted *rough* 256
knout 975
know *believe* 484
knowledge 490
friendly 888
associate 892
I'd have you to – 457, 535
not that one –s 491
– what one is about 698
– all 474
I – better 536
– no bounds
great 31
infinite 105
redundance 641
– for certain 484
– by heart 505
– one's own mind 604
– one's stuff 465
– one's way about 465
– nothing of 491
– what's what 698
– which is which 465
knowing 702
knowingly 620
knowledge **490**
[*and see* know]
acquire – 539
come to one's – 527
practical – 698
– of the world 698
known:
become – 529
make – *inform* 527
publish 531
well – 490
habitual 613
– as 564
– by 550
knuckle 244
– down 725
knuckle-duster 727

knurl 256
knurr and spell 840
kobold 980
Koh-i-noor 650
kopje 206
Koran 986
kotow *bow* 308
submission 725
courtesy 894
respect 928
kraal 189, 232
kraken 83
kris 727
Krishna 979
kudos 931
Ku klux klan 712
Kursaal 840
kyanize 670
kyles 343

L

laager 717
labarum 550
labefy 659
label 39, 550
labent 306
labial *lip* 231
letter 561
labitur et labetur 112, 143
labor hoc opus, **hic** – 704
laboratory 691
laborious
active 682
exertion 686
difficult 704
labour
parturition 161
work 680
exertion 686
hard –
punishment 972
mountain in – 638
– for 620
– of love
willing 602
amusement 840
disinterested 942
– party 712
– under *state* 7
disease 655
difficulty 704
feeling 821
affliction 828
– in vain
fall short 304
useless 645
– in one's voca-

tion 625
– unrest 832
laboured - *style* 579
prepared 673
– *study* 457
labourer 690
labouring
– man 690
– oar 686
labyrinth
disorder 59
convolution 248
secret 533
lac *number* 98
resin 356a
– of rupees 800
lace *stitch* 43
netting 219
ornament 847
– one's jacket 972
lacerable 328
lacerate 44
– the heart 830
laches 460, 773
Lachesis 601
lachrymæ, hinc
illæ – 830
lachrymatory gas
727
lachrymis, quis
temperet a – 914
lachrymose 837
lack *require* 630
insufficient 640
destitute 804
desire 865
– faith 989
– harmony 708
– preparation 674
– wit 501
lackadaisical
inactive 683
melancholy 837
indifferent 866
lackadaisy! 839,
870
lack-brain 499, 501
lacker [*see* lacquer]
lackey 746
lack-lustre 422, 429
laconic 572
lacquer
covering 223
resin 356a
adorn 847
lacrosse 840
lacteal 352
lacuna 198, 252
lacustrine 343
lad 129
ladder 305, 627

[542]

kick down the –
604
lade *load* 184
transfer 185
contents 190
dip 270
– out 297
laden 52
heavy – 828
– with 777
ladies' man 897
lading 190, 780
bill of – *list* 86
ladle *receptacle* 191
transfer 270
vehicle 272
lady *woman* 374
rank 875
wife 903
our – 977
– *day* 138
– help 746
–'s maid 746
lady chapel 1000
ladylike
womanly 374
fashionable 852
lady-love 897
lag *linger* 275
follow 281
dawdle 683
– behind 133
laggard 603, 683
lager *beer* 298
lagoon 343
laical 997
laid: – on one's
back 158
– by the heels 751
– low 160
– up 655
lair 189, 653
laird *master* 745
proprietor 779
nobility 875
Lais 962
laisse manger, cela
se – 394
laisser: – aller,
– faire
permanence 141
neglect 460
inaction 681
laxity 738
freedom 748
inexcitable 826
laity 997
lake *water* **343**
pink 434
– of fire and brim-
stone 982

Lama 745, 996
Lamaism 984
Lamarkism 357
lamb *infant* 129
animal 366
gentle 826
innocent 946
go out like a – 174
lion lies down
with – 721
Lamb of God 976
lambent
touching 379
– flame *heat* 382
light 420
Lambeth 1000
lame *incomplete* 53
impotent 158
weak 160
imperfect 651
disease 655
injury 659
failing 732
– conclusion
illogical 477
failure 732
help a – dog over
a stile *aid* 707
vindicate 937
– duck 808
– excuse 617
lamellar 204
lamentable *bad* 649
painful 830
sad 837
lamentably *very* 31
lamentation **839**
lamia 980, 994
lamina 51, 204
lamination 204
Lammas 998
lamp 423
rub the – 992
safety – 666
smell of the –
style 577
prepared 673
lamplighter
quick 682
lampoon 932, 934
lampooner 936
lanâ caprinâ, de –
643
lanary 636
lanate 255, 256
lance *pierce* 260
throw 284
spear 727
break a – with
attack 716
warfare 722

couch one's – **720**
– corporal 745
lancer 726
–'s *dance* 840
lancet 253, 262
lancinate 378, 830
land *arrive* 292
ground **342**
estate 780
gone to a better –
360
hug the – 286
make the – 286
on – 342
see – 858
– covered with
water 343
– flowing with
milk and honey
168
how the – *lies*
circumstances 8
experiment 463
foresight 510
in the – *of the*
living 359
landamman 745
landau 272
landed
– gentry 779
– estate 780
landgrave 745
landholder 779
landing field 273
landing-place 215,
292
landlady 779
land-locked 229,
343
landloper 268
landlord 779
land-lubber 343,
701
landmark
limit 233
indication 550
land-mine 727
landreeve 694
landscape
prospect 448
– gardening
agriculture 371
beauty 845
– painting 556
– painter 559
land-shark 792
land-slip 306
landsman 342
Landsturm 726
land-surveying 466
Landwehr 726

lane 189, 260, 627
langrel 727
lang-syne 122
language 560
  command of – 582
  strong –
    vigour 574
    malediction 908
languid *weak* 160
  inert 172
  slow 275
  - *style* 575
  inactive 683
  torpid 823
languish
  decrease 36
  ill 655
  inactive 683
  repine 828
  - for 865
languishing
  weak 160
  affected 855
languishment
  lament 839
languor
  [*see* languid]
lank 200
lanky 203, 206
lantern
  window 260
  lamp 423
  magic – 448
  - of Diogenes 461
  - jaws 203
lanterne, à la – 972
lanuginous 256
lanyard 45
Laodicean 822
lap *abode* 189
  support 215
  interior 221
  wrap 225
  encompass 227, 229
  drink 298
  - of luxury
    pleasure 377
    inactivity 683
    voluptuousness 954
lap-dog *animal* 366
  servile 886
lapel 39
lapidary 559
lapidate *kill* 361
  attack 716
  punish 972
lapidescence 323
lapis lazuli
  blue 438

jewel 847
lappet 39, 214
lapse *course* 109
  past 122
  conversion 144
  fall 306
  degeneracy 659
  relapse 661
  loss 776
  vice 945
  guilt 947
  - of memory 506
  - of time 109
lapsus calami 495
lapsus linguæ
  mistake 495
  solecism 568
  stammering 583
Laputa, college of –
  538
larboard 239
larceny 791
lard 356
lardaceous 355
larder 636
  contents of the –
  298
lares et penates
  home 189
  idols 991
large
  quantity 31
  size 192
  at – *diffuse* 573
  free 748
  become – 194
  - number 102
  - type 642
large-hearted
  liberal 816
  benevolent 906
  disinterested 942
larger 194
largest 784
largest portion 192
larghetto 275, 415
largiloquent 573
largo 275, 415
lariat 45, 247
lark *ascent* 305
  pleasure 827
  spree 840
  with the – 125
larmes:
  fondre en – 839
  - aux yeux 839
larmoyante,
  comédie – 599
larrikin 887, 913
larrup 972
larum 404, 669

larva 129
larynx 351
lascar 269
lasciate ogni spe-
  ranza 859
lascivious 961
lash *tie together* 43
  violence 173
  incite 615
  censure 932
  punish 972
  scourge 975
  under the – *com-*
    pelled 744
  subject 749
  - into fury 900
  - with the tongue 932
  - the waves 645
lass *girl* 129
lassitude 688, 841
lasso 45, 247
last *model* 22
  - *in order* 67
  endure 106
  durable 110
  - in time 122
  continue 141
  at – 133
  breathe one's –
    360
  game to the –
    604a
  never hear the –
    of 104
  - but one &c. 67
  die in the – ditch
    604a
  - for ever 112
  at the – extremity
    665
  - finish 729
  - gasp 360
  go to one's – home
    360
  on – legs *weak* 160
  dying 360
  spoiled 659
  adversity 735
  - resort 666
  - rites 998
  - shift 601
  - sleep 360
  - stage 67
  - straw 153
  - stroke 729
  - touch 729
  - word
    affirmation 535
    obstinacy 606
  - year &c. 122

latch 43, 45
latchet 45
latch-key 631
late *past* 122
  new 123
  tardy 133
  dead 360
  too – 135
lately 122, 123
latency 526
lateness 133
  - organism **153**
later 117
laterality 236
lateritious 434
latest 118
latet anguis in
  herbâ 667
lath 205
  thin as a – 203
lathe
  region 181
  machine 633
lather 332, 353
Latin
  au bout de son –
    704
  perdre son – **704**
  thieves' – 563
latitancy 528
latitat 969
latitude *extent* 180
  region 181
  breadth 202
  measurement **466**
  freedom 748
  - and longitude
    situation 183
latitudinarian 984, 989
latration 412
latria 990
latrines 653
latrociny 791
latter *sequent* 63
  past 122
Latter-day Saint 984
latterly 123
lattice *crossing* 219
  opening 260
laud 931, 990
laudable 944
laudanum 174
laudari a laudato
  viro 931
laudator 935
  - temporis acti
    past 122
    habit 613

discontent 832
detractor 936
laudatory 931
laugh 838
  make one – 853
  raise a – 840
  – at *ridicule* 856
  sneer 929
  (*undervalue* 483)
  – to scorn *defy* 715
  despise 930
  – in one's sleeve
  latent 526
  ridicule 856
  disrespect 929
  contempt 930
  – on the wrong
    side of one's
    mouth
  disappointed 509
  dejected 837
  in disrepute 874
laughable 853
laughing:
  no – matter 642
  – gas 376
laughing-stock 857
laughter-loving 836
launch *begin* 66
  boat 273
  propel 284
  – forth 676
  – into 676
  – into eternity
    360, 361
  – out 573
  – out against 716
laundress 652, 746
laundry *room* 191
  heat 386
  clean 652
  – maid 746
  – man 652
laureate 875
  poet – 597
laurel *trophy* 733
  glory 873
  decoration 877
  repose on one's –s
    265
lava *excretion* 299
  semiliquid 352
lavatory 652
lave *water* 337
  clean 652
lavender *colour* 437
laver la tête 932
lavish *profuse* 641
  give 784
  squander 818
  – of praise 931

law *regularity* 80
  statue 697
  permission 760
  legality 963
  court of – 966
  give the – 737
  go to – 969
  Jewish – 985
  lay down the –
  certainty 474
  affirm 535
  command 741
  learned in the –
    968
  set the – at
    defiance 964
  take the – into
    one's own
    hands 722, 742
  – of the Medes
    and Persians
    80, 141
  take the – of 969
law-abiding 743
lawful
  permitted 760
  due 924
  legal 963
lawgiver 694
lawless 59
  irregular 83
  mutinous 742
  non-observant 773
  vicious 945
  arbitrary 964
lawn *plain* 344
  grass 367
  agriculture 371
  – sleeves 999
  – tennis 840
lawsuit 969
lawyer 968
lax *incoherent* 47
  soft 324
  error 495
  - *style* 575
  remiss 738
  non-observance
    773
  dishonourable 940
  licentious 945
  irreligious 989
laxity 738
lay *moderate* 174
  place 184
  ley 344
  music 415
  poetry 597
  bet 621
  secular 997
  – about one

active 682
exertion 686
attack 716
contend 720
punish 972
– one's account for
  484
– apart
exclude 55
relinquish 782
– aside
neglect 460
reject 610
disuse 678
give up 782
– on the table 133
– the axe at the
  root of tree 162
– bare 529
– before 527
– brother 996
– by *store* 636
sickness 655
disuse 678
– to one's charge
  938
– claim to 924
– in the dust 162
– eggs 161
– at the door of
  155
– down [*see below*]
– at one's feet 763
– figure *nonentity* 4
model 22
representation
  554
– one's finger
  upon 480*a*
– the first stone 66
– the flattering
  unction to one's
  soul 831, 834
– the foundations
  153, 673
– ghosts 992
– hands on
use 677
take 789
rite 998
– under hatches
  751
– one's head on
  the block 942
– heads together
  695, 709
– in *eat* 298
store 636
provide 637
– on 972
open *divest* 226

opening 260
show 525
disclose 529
– oneself open to
  177
– out
horizontal 213
corpse 363
plan 626
expend 809
– oneself out for
  673
– over 133
– reader 996
– under restraint
  751
– in ruins 162
– siege to 716
– stress on 642
– to *attribute* 155
rest 265
– it on thick
cover 223
too much 641
flatter 933
-- together 43
– train 626
– up *store* 636
sickness 655
disuse 678
– waste 162
lay down *locate* 184
horizontal 213
assert 535
renounce 757
relinquish 782
pay 807
– one's arms
pacification 723
submission 725
– the law
certain 474
assert 535
command 741
insolence 885
– one's life 360
– a plan 626
layer 204
layette 225
layman 699, 997
laystall 653
lazaret 662
lazar-house 662
lazy 683, 927
lazzarone 683
lb. 319
lea *land* 342
plain 344
leach 335
lead *superiority* 33
in order 62

lee-shore 665, 667
leet, court – 966
lee-wall 666
leeward 236
lee-way *space* 180
  tardy 133
  navigation 267
  deviation 279
  progression 282
  shortcoming 304
left *residuary* 40
  sinistral 239
  over the – 545
  – alone 748
  – in the lurch 732
  – to shift for one-
   self 893
  pay over the –
   shoulder 808
left-handed
  clumsy 699
  – compliment 932
  – marriage 903
leg *support* 215
  walker 266
  thief 792
  best – foremost
   686
  fast as –s will
   carry 274
  have a – to stand
   on 470
  keep on one's –s
   654
  last –s *spoiled* 659
  fatigue 688
  light on one's –s
   734
  make a – 894
  not a – to stand on
  illogical 477
  confuted 479
  failure 732
  off one's –s
  propulsion 284
  on one's –s
  upright 212
  elevation 307
  speaking 582
  in health 654
  active 682
  free 748
  set on one's –s 660
  – bail 623
legacy 270, 780, 784
legal *permitted* 760
  legitimate 924
  relating to law
   963
  – adviser 968
  – estate 780

legality **963**
legate 534
legatee 779, 785
legation 755
legato 415
legend 551, 594
legendary
  imaginary 515
legerdemain 146,
  545
légèreté 605
leggings 225
leghorn hat 225
legible 518
  – hand 590
legion
  multitude 102
  army 726
legionary 726
legislation 693, 963
legislative assem-
  bly 696
legislator 694
legislature 693, 696
legist 968
legitimate *true* 494
  permitted 760
  right 922
  due 924
  legal 963
legume 367
lei 847
leisure **685**
  at one's – *late* 133
leisurely 275
leman 897
lemma 476
lemon *colour* 436
Lemprière 979
lemures 980
lend 787
  – aid 707
  – countenance 707
  – a hand 680
  – oneself to
  assent 488
  co-operate 709
  – on security 789
  – wings to 707
lender *creditor* 805
lending **787**
length **200**
  go all –s
  resolution 604
  activity 682
  exertion 686
  at – *in time* 133
  full – *portrait* 556
  go great –s 549
  – and breadth of
   50

– and breadth of
  the land
  space 180
  publication 531
  – of time 110
lengthen 35, 200
  – out
  diuturnity 110
  late 133
lengthwise 200
lengthy *long* 200
  diffuse 573
lenient
  moderate 174
  mild 740
  compassionate
   914
lenify 174
lenitive
  moderating 174
  remedy 662
  relieving 834
lenity **740**
lens 445
Lent 956, 998
lenten 956
lenticular 245, 250
lentor *slowness* 275
  spissitude 352
  inactivity 683
lentous 352
leonem, ex ungue –
  550
leonine verses 597
leopard
  variegated 440
  –'s spots
  unchanging 150
leprechaune 980
leprosy 655
lerret 273
lèse-majesté 742
less *inferior* 34
  subduction 38
  – than no time
   113
lessee
  possessor 779
  receiver 785
lessen
  – in quantity or
   degree 36
  – in size 195
  – an evil 658
lesson *teaching* 537
  warning 668
  give a – to
  punish 972
  read a – to
  censure 932
  say one's –

  memory 505
lessor 805
lest 623
let *hindrance* **706**
  permit 760
  lease 771
  lend 787
  sell 796
  apartments to –
  fool 499
  to – 763
  – alone *besides* **37**
  permanence 141
  quiescence 265
  avoid 623
  disuse 678
  inaction 681
  not complete 730
  free 748
  – be
  permanence 141
  continuance 143
  inaction 681
  – blood 297
  – 'I dare not' wait
   upon 'I would'
   605
  – down
  depress 308
  humble 879
  – down easily
  forgive 918
  – fall *drop* 308
  inform 527
  speak 582
  – fly *violence* 173
  propel 284
  – fly at 716
  – go *neglect* 460
  liberate 750
  relinquish 782
  restitution 790
  – in *interpose* 228
  admit 296
  trick 545
  – into *inform* 490
  disclose 529
  – one know 527
  – off *violent* 173
  propel 284
  permit 760
  forgive 918
  exempt 927a
  acquit 970
  – out *disperse* **73**
  lengthen 200
  eject 297
  disclose 529
  liberate 750
  – out at 716
  – pass 460

put – into 359
recall to – 660
see – 840
support – 359
take away – 361
tenant for – 779
– to come 152
– after death 981
– or death
  need 630
  important 642
  contention 720
– and spirit 682
Life, the 976
life-blood 5, 359
life-boat 273, 666
life-giving 168
lifeguards 726
lifeless 172, 360
lifelike 17
lifelong 110
life-preserver 666, 727
life-size 192
lifetime 108
life-weary 841
lift *raise* 307
  aid 707
  steal 791
  – cattle 791
  – up the eyes 441
  – a finger 680
  – hand against 716
  - one's head 734
  - up the heart 990
  - the mask 529
  - the voice
  shout 411
  speak 582
lift-smoke 840
ligament 45
ligation 43
ligature 45
light *state* 7
  small 32
  window 260
  velocity 274
  arrive 292
  descend 306
  levity 320
  kindle 384
  match 388
  luminosity **420**
  luminary 423
  - *in colour* 429
  white 430
  aspect 448
  knowledge 490
  interpretation 522
  unimportant 643

easy 705
gay 836
loose 961
blue – *signal* 550
bring to –
  discover 480a
  manifest 525
  disclose 529
children of – 987
come to – 529
false – 443
foot –s 599
half – 422
make – of
  underrate 483
  easy 705
  inexcitable 826
  despise 930
in one's own – 699
obstruct the – 426
side – 490
see the – *life* 359
  publication 531
transmit – 425
throw – upon 522
a – breaks in upon one 529
– under a bushel
  hide 528
  not hide 878
  modesty 881
– comedy 599
– cruiser 726
– fantastic toe 309
– upon one's feet 664
– heart 836
– of heel 274
– horse 726
– infantry 726
– purse 804
– and shade 420
– of truth 543
– up *illumine* 420
  excite 824
  cheer 836
– upon *chance* 156
  arrive at 292
  discover 480a
  acquire 775
Light of the World 976
lighten
  make light 320
  illume 420
  facilitate 705
lighter *boat* 273
lighterage 812
lighterman 269
light-fingered 791, 792

light-footed 274, 682
light-headed 503
lighthouse 550
lightless 421
light-minded 605
lightning
  velocity 274
  flash 420
  spark 423
  like greased – 113
lightsome
  luminous 420
  irresolute 605
  cheerful 836
ligneous 367
lignite 388
lignography 558
ligulate 205
like *similar* 17
  relish 394
  enjoy 377, 827
  wish 865
  love 897
  do what one –s 748
  look – 448
  we shall not look upon his – again 33
  – master like man 19
  – a pin in paper 58
likely 472
  think – 507
likeness 21, 554
  bad – 555
likewise 37
liking 865, 897
  have a – for 827
  to one's – 829
lilac *colour* 437
Liliputian 193
Lillith 994
lilt 416, 836
lily *white* 430
  beauty 845
  paint the – 641
lily-livered 862
limæ labor
  improve 658
  toil 686
limature 330, 331
limb *member* 51
  instrument 633
  scamp 949
  – of the law 968
limber 272, 324
limbo *prison* 751, 752
  pain 828

purgatory 982
lime *entrap* 545
  – *light* 423, 531, 599
Limehouse 908
limine, in – 66
limit *complete* 52
  end 67
  circumscribe 229
  boundary **233**
  qualify 469
  restrain 751
  prohibit 761
limitarian 984
limitation [*see* limit]
  estate 780, 783
limited
  - *in quantity* 32
  - *in size* 193
  to a – extent
  imperfect 651
limitless 105
limitrophe 197
limn 556
limner 559
limousine 272
limp *weak* 160
  slow 275
  supple 324
  fail 732
limpid 425
lin 343, 348
lincture 662
line *fastening* 45
  continuous 69
  ancestors 166
  descendants 167
  length 200
  no breadth 203
  string 205
  lining 224
  outline 230
  straight 246
  of steamers 273
  direction 278
  music 413
  appearance 448
  measure 466
  mark 550
  writing 590
  verse 597
  vocation 625
  army and navy 726
  boundary – 233
  draw the – 465
  drop a – to 526
  in a –
  continuous 69
  straight 246

- face 832, 837
- for 865
-headed *wise* 498
- life to *glory* 873
  approval 931
-lived 110
- odds *chance* 156
  improbability 473
  difficulty 704
- pending 110
- primer 591
- pull and strong
  pull 285
- range 196
- robe 968
- run *average* 29
  whole 50
  destiny 152
- sea 348
- and the short
  whole 50
  concise 572
-sighted
  dim-sighted 443
  wise 498
  foresight 510
- since 122
- spun 573
- standing
  diuturnal 110
  old 124
-suffering
  lenient 740
  inexcitable 826
  pity 914
- time 110
-winded 573
longanimity
  inexcitable 826
  forgiving 918
longevity 110, 128
longhead 500
longing 865
- lingering look
  behind 833
longinquity 196
longitude
  situation 183
  length 200
  measurement 466
longitudinal 200
longo intervallo
  discontinuity 70
  diuturnity 110
  distance 196
  interval 198
longshore-man
  waterman 269
  plebeian 876
longways 217
loo 840

looby *fool* 501
  bungler 701
  clown 876
look *small degree* 32
  see 441
  appearance 448
  attend to 457
- about 459, 461
- after 459, 693
- ahead 510
- alive 457, 684
- another way 442
- back 122
- beyond 510
- black *or* blue
  feeling 821
  discontent 832
  dejection 837
- down upon 930
- in the face
  sincerity 703
  courage 861
  pride 878
- foolish 874
- for 461, 507
- forwards 121,
  510
- here 457
- into 457, 461
- before one leaps
  864
- like 17, 448
- on 186
- out *view* 448
  attention 457
  care 459
  seek 461
  expect 507
  intention 620
  business 625
  danger 665
  warning 668
  caution 864
- over *examine*
  461
- round *seek* 461
- sharp 682
- to 459, 926
- through 461
- up *prosper* 734
  high price 814
  hope 858
  visit 892
- up to *repute* 873
  respect 928
  approbation 931
- upon as 480, 484
looker-on 444
looking-glass 445
loom *destiny* 152
  dim 422

  dim sight 443
  come in sight 446
  weave 691
- of the land 342
- up 31
loon *fool* 501
  clown 876
  rascal 949
loop 245, 247, 629
- the loop 245
loop-hole
  opening 260
  vista 441
  plea 617
  device 626
  escape 671
  fortification 717
loose *detach* 44
  incoherent 47
  pendent 214
  desultory 279
  illogical 477
  vague 519
- *style* 575
  lax 738
  free 748
  liberate 750
  debauched 961
give a - to
- *imagination* 515
  laxity 738
  permit 760
  indulgence 954
let - 750
on the - 961
screw - 713
- character 961
at a - end 685
- fish 949, 962
- morals 945
- rein 738
- suggestion 514
- thread 495
leave a - 460
take up a - 664
loosen 47, 750
loot 791, 793
lop 201
- and top 371
lopped
  incomplete 53
loppet 699
lop-eared 53
lop-sided 28
loquacity 584
loquendi
  cacoëthes - 584
  jus et norma - 567
  usus - 582
lorcha 273
Lord, lord

  ruler 745
  nobleman 875
  God 976
O - *worship* 990
- Chancellor 967
- of the creation
  372
-'s day 687
-s Justices 966,
  967
the - knows 491
- lieutenant 965
- of Lords 976
- of the manor
  779
- it over 737, 885
-'s prayer 990
-'s supper 998
-'s table 1000
lordling 875
lordly 873, 878
Lord Mayor 745,
  965
-'s show 883
lordship
  authority 737
  property 780
  title 877
  judge 967
lore 490, 539
Lorelei 980
lorette 962
lorgnette 445
lorication
  armour 717
loricated
  clothed 223
lorn 893
lorry 272
lose *forget* 506
  unintelligible 519
  fail 732
  loss 776
no time to - 684
- one's balance
  732
- breath 688
- caste 874, 940
- the clew 475,
  519
- colour 429
- one's cunning
  699
- the day 732
- flesh 195
- ground
  slow 275
  regression 283
  shortcoming 304
- one's head
  bewildered 475

- heart 837
- one's heart 897
- hope 859
- interest in 624
- labour 732
- one's life 360
- no time 682, 684
- oneself 475
- an opportunity 135
- one's reason 503
- sight of
  blind 442
  disappear 449
  neglect 460
  oblivion 506
  not complete 730
- one's temper 900
- time 683
- one's way
  wander 279
  uncertainty 475
  unskilful 699
  difficulty 704
losel 818
losing game 732, 735
loss *decrement* 40a
  death 360
  evil 619
  deterioration 659
  privation **776**
  at a –
  uncertain 475
  at a – for
  desiring 865
- of fortune 804
- of health 655
- of life 360
- of right 925
- of strength 160
lost *non-existing* 2
  absent 187
  invisible 449
  abstracted 458
  uncertain 475
  failure 732
  loss 776
  over-excited 824
  pain 828
  dejection 837
  impenitent 951
- in admiration 931
- in astonishment 870
- in iniquity 945
- labour 645
- to shame
  insolent 885
  improbity 940

bad man 949
- to sight 449
- in thought 458
- to virtue 945
lot *state* 7
  quantity 25
  group 72
  multitude 102
  necessity 601
  chance 621
  sufficient 639
  allotment 786
  be one's – 151
  cast –s 621
  cast in one's –
  with 609, 709
  fall to one's – 156
  in –s 51
  where one's – is
  cast 189
loth 603, 867
Lothario 897, 962
lotion *liquid* 337
  clean 652
  remedy 662
loto 840
lottery 156, 840
  put into a – 621
lotus-eater 683
loud 404, 525
  vulgar 851
lough 343
lounge 191, 683
- suit 225
loup
  hurler avec les –s 714
-garou 980
louse 653
lout 501, 701, 876
louvre 351
lovable 897
love *desire* 865
  courtesy 894
  affection **897**
  favourite 899
  abode of – 897
  labour of –
  willing 602
  inexpensive 815
  amusement 840
  disinterested 942
  God's – 906
  make – 902
  no – lost 713
- affair 897
- of country 910
- lock 256
  not for – or money 640, 814
love-knot *token* 550

love-lorn 898
lovely 845, 897
love-making 902
love-pot 959
love-potion 865
lover [*see* love]
love-sick 897, 902
love-story 897, 902
love-token 897, 902
loving-cup 892, 894
loving-kindness 906
low *small* 32
  not high 207
- *sound* 405
  moo 412
  vulgar 851
  disreputable 874
  common 876
  base 940
  bring – 308
- condition 876
- comedy 599
  at a – ebb
  small 32
  inferior 34
  depressed 308
  waste 638
  deteriorated 659
- fellow 876
- life 851
- note 408
- origin 876
- price 815
- spirits 837
- tide 207
- tone *black* 431
  mutter 581
- water *low* 207
  dry 340
  insufficient 640
  poor 804
low-born 876
low-brow 491
low-lands 207
low-minded 876, 940
lower *inferior* 34
  decrease 36
  overhang 214
  depress 308
  dark 421
  dim 422
  predict 511
  sad 837
  irate 900
  sulky 901a
- one's flag 725
- one's note 879
- orders 876
lowering 668, 859

lowly 879
lown 501, 949
lowness [*see* low]
  207
  humility 879
loy 272
loyal *obedient* 743
  observant 772
  honourable 939
lozenge 244, 662
L. s. d. 800
lubbard [*see* lubber]
lubber 683, 701
lubberly 192, 699
lubricant 332
lubrication 255, **332**
lubricity
  slippery 255
  unctuous 355
  impure 961
lucent 420
lucid
  luminous 420
  transparent 425
  intelligible 518
- *style* 570
- interval 502
lucidus ordo 58
lucifer 388
Lucifer 423, 978
lucimeter 445
luck *chance* 156, 621
  prosperity 734
  good – 858
luckless 735
lucky 134, 734
lucrative 775
lucre 775, 803
Lucretia 960
luctation 720
lucubration 451
luculent 420
lucus a non lucendo 18, 565
lud! O – 839
ludibrious 840
ludicrous 853
luff 267
lug *pull* 285
  ear 418
luge 272
luggage 270, 780
- van 272
lugger 273
lugubrious 837
lukewarm
  temperate 382
  irresolute 605
  torpid 823
  indifferent 866
lull *cessation* 142

store 636
– rifle 727
Magdalen 950, 962
mage 994
magenta 434
maggot *little* 193
  fancy 515
  caprice 608
  desire 865
maggoty
  capricious 608
  unclean 653
  – headed
  silly 499
  excitable 825
Magi *sage* 500
  sect 984
magic 175, 992
– lantern
  instrument 445
  show 448
magician 548, 994
magilp 356*a*
magisterial 878,
  885
magistery 330
magistracy 737, 965
magistrate 745, 967
magistrature 737
magistri, jurare in
  verba – 481
  nullius – 487
magma 41
Magna Charta 769
magna pars fui,
  quorum – 690
magnanimity 942
magnate 875
magnet *attract* 288
  desire 865
magnetism
  power 157
  influence 175
  attraction 288
  motive 615
  animal – 992
magnetize
  influence 175
  motive 615
  conjure 992
magni nominis
  umbra
  wreck 659
  repute 873
  rank 875
magnificent
  large 192
  fine 845
  grand 882
magnifico 875
magnifier 445

magnifique et pas
  cher 815
magnify
  increase 35
  enlarge 194
  over-rate 482
  exaggerate 549
  approve 931
  praise 990
magniloquent 577,
  884
magnitude 25, 31,
  192
magno conatu
  magnas nugas
  638, 643
Magnus Apollo 500
magpie 584
magsman 792
maharajah 745
maharani 745
mah jong 840
mahl-stick [*see*
  maulstick]
mahogany
  colour 433
Mahomet 986
Mahometan 984
maid *girl* 129
  servant 631, 746
  spinster 374, 904
  – of all work 690
  – of honour 890
maiden *first* 66
  girl 129
  punishment 975
  – speech 66
maidenhood 904
maidenly 374
maigre 956
mail *post* 270, 534
  armour 717
  – coach 272, 534
  – steamer 273
  – van 272, 534
maim 158, 659
main *tunnel* 260
  ocean 341
  conduit 350
  principal 642
  coup de – 680
  in the –
  intrinsically 5
  greatly 31
  on the whole 50
  principally 642
  with might and –
  686
  plough the – 267
main-chance 156
  good 618

important 642
  profit 775
  look to the –
  foresight 510
  skill 698
  economy 817
  caution 864
  selfish 943
main-force
  strength 159
  violence 173
  compulsion 744
mainland 342
main-part 31, 50
mainpernor 771
main-spring 153,
  633
mainstay
  support 215
  refuge 666
  hope 858
maintain
  permanence 141
  continue 143
  sustain 170
  support 215
  assert 535
  preserve 670
  – one's course
  persevere 604*a*
  – the even tenor of
  one's way 623
  – one's ground 717
maintenance
  [*see* maintain]
  assistance 707
  wealth 803
maintien 692
maison de santé
  662
maisonette 189
maître: coup de –
  goodness 648
  skill 698
  l'œil de – 459
majesté, lèse– 742
majestic 873, 882
majesty *king* 745
  rank 873
  deity 976
major *greater* 33
  officer 745
  –domo
  director 694
  retainer 746
  –general 745
  – key 413
  – part *great* 31
  all 50
majority
  superiority 33

multitude 102
  age 131
  join the – 360
majuscule 561
make
  constitute 54, 56
  render 144
  produce 161
  form 240
  arrive at 292
  complete 729
  compel 744
  – acquainted with
  527, 539
  – after 622
  – its appearance
  446
  – away with 162,
  361
  – believe 544, 545,
  546
  – the best of 725
  – bold to differ 489
  – a date with 897
  – choice of 609
  – fast 43
  – a fool of 853
  – for 278
  – one's fortune 734
  – fun of 842, 856
  – a fuss 642, 682
  – good
  compensation 30
  complete 52, 729
  establish 150
  evidence 467
  demonstrate 478
  provide 637
  restore 660
  - *one's escape* 671
  - *one's word* 772
  – a go of 731
  – haste 684
  – hay while the
  sun shines 134
  – interest 765
  – known 527
  – the land 292
  – light of 483, 705,
  934
  – oneself master
  of 539
  – money 775
  – a monkey of 853
  – much of 549, 642
  – no doubt 484
  – no secret of 525
  – no sign 526, 528
  – nothing of
  unintelligible 519
  not wonder 871

- of 902
- off 623, 671
- off with 791
- out *see* 441
  evidence 467
  demonstrate 478
  discover 480a
  know 490
  intelligible 518
  interpret 522
  due 924
- over 658, 783, 784
- peace 723, 724
- a piece of work 832
- things pleasant 702
- a present 784
- public 531
- a push 682
- ready 673
- a requisition 741, 765
- a speech 582
- a sucker of 853
- sure 150, 673
- terms 769
- time 110
- tracks 293
- towards 278
- up [*see below*]
- use of 677
- way 282
- one's way 302, 734
- way for 147, 623
- a wry face 867
make up
  complete 52
  compose 54
- accounts 811
- for 30
- matters 952
- one's mind
  judgment 480
  belief 484
  resolve 604
- a quarrel 723
- a sum 809
- to *approach* 286
  address 586
maker *artificer* 690
Maker, the - 976
makeshift 147, 617
make-weight
  inequality 28
  compensation 30
  completeness 52
making of, be the -
  utility 644

goodness 648
aid 707
mal du pays 833
mala fides 940
malachite 435
malacology 368
malade imaginaire 837
maladie du pays 833
maladministration 699
maladroit 699
malady 655
malaise 378, 828
malapert 885, 887
Malaprop, Mrs. - 565
malapropism 495
mal à propos 24, 135
malaria 657, 663
malconformation 243
malcontent 710, 832
male 159, 373
- animal 373
malediction 908
malefaction 947
malefactor 949
malefic 649
maleficent 907
- being 913
malevolence 907
malfeasance 647
malformed 241
malformation 243
malgré 179
- soi 603
malice *hate* 898
  spite 907
  bear - *revenge* 919
- aforethought 907
- prepense 907
malign *bad* 649
  malevolent 907
  detract 934
malignant 649, 907
malignity
  violence 173
malinger 544, 655
malison 908
malkin 653
mall *walk* 189
  club 276
malleable 324
mallet 276
malnutrition 655
mal-odour 401

malpractice 947
malt liquor 298
maltreat
  injure 649
  aggrieve 830
  molest 907
malum
- prohibitum 925
- in se 923
malversation 818, 947
Mameluke 726
mamelon 250
mamma 166
mammal 366
mammiform 250
mammilla 250
Mammon 803, 978
  serve - 989
mammoth 192
man *adult* 131
  mankind 372
  male **373**
  prepare 673
  workman 690
  servant 746
  courage 861
  husband 903
  make a - of 648, 861
  Son of - 976
  straight - 599
  to a - 488
  -at-arms 726
  one's - of business 758
  -'s estate 131
- in office 745
- in the street 876
  -of-war 273, 726
  -of-war's man 269
- at the wheel 694
- and wife 903
manacle 751, 752
manage 693
- to *succeed* 731
manageable 705
management
  conduct 692
  skill 698
manager
  stage - 599
  director 694
managery 693
manche après la cognée, jeter le - 859
manciple 637
mancipation 751
mandamus 741
mandarin 745

mandate 630, **741**
mandible 298
mandolin 417
mandragora 174
mandrel 312
manducation 298
mane 256
man-eater 361
manège 266, 370
manes 362
manet: altâ mente repostum 505
- cicatrix 919
manful *strong* 159
  resolute 604
  brave 861
manger 191
manger:
  cela se laisse - 394
- son blé en herbe 818
mangle
  separate 44
  smooth 255
  injure 659
mangled 53
mangy 655
man-hater 911
manhood 131, 861
mania *insanity* 503
  desire 865
maniac 504
manibus pedibus-que 686
manic 503
manic-depressive 503
manicure 847
manicheism 978
manichord 417
manie 865
maniéré 855
manifest
  list 86
  visible 446
  obvious 525
  disclose 529
manifestation **525**
manifesto 531
manifold 81, 102
manikin *dwarf* 193
  image 554
maniple 103
manipulate
  handle 379
  use 677
  conduct 692
manipulator 621
mankind **372**
manly
  adolescent 131

matross 726
matter *substance* 3
  material world
    316
  topic 454
  meaning 516
  type 591
  business 625
  importance 642
  pus 653
  no – 460
  what – 643
  what's the – 455,
    461
  – of course
  conformity 82
  certain 474
  habitual 613
  – in dispute 461
  – of fact *event* 151
  certainty 474
  truth 494
  language 576
  artless 703
  dull 843
  – in hand 454, 625
  – of indifference
    866
  – nothing 643
mattock 253
mattress 215
mature *old* 124
  adolescent 131
  conversion 144
  scheme 626
  perfect 650
  improve 658
  prepare 673
  complete 729
  – thought 451
maturely consid-
  ered 611
maturine 996
maturity [*see*
  mature]
  bring to – 729
matutinal 125
matzoon 298
maudlin
  inactive 683
  drunk 959
maugre 30
maukin 652
maul *hammer* 276
  hurt 649
maulstick 215
maund *basket* 191
  mumble 583
maunder
  diffuse style 573
  mumble 583

[558]

talk 584
lament 839
maundy
– *money* 784
– Thursday 988
Mauser rifle 727
mausoleum 363
mauvais
– *goût* 851
– quart d'heure
  828
– sujet 949
– ton 851
mauvaise:
– *honte*
  affectation 855
  modesty 881
– plaisanterie 851
mauve 437
maw 191
mawkish 391
Mawworm
  deceiver 548
  sham piety 988
maxim 80, **496**
Maxim gun 727
maximal 33
maximalist 742
maximum 33, 210
maxixe 840
may be 470
  as it – 156
May-day 138, 840
May-fly 111
mayhap 470
mayonnaise 298
mayor 745, 965
maypole 206
May-queen 847
mazard 298
maze
  disorder 59
  convolution 248
  enigma 533
  difficulty 704
  in a –
  uncertain 475
mazed 503
mazurka 840
me 317
me judice 484
meâ culpâ 950
mead *plain* 344
  sweet 396
meadow *plain* 344
  grass 367
  – land 371
meagre *small* 32
  incomplete 53
  thin 203
  - *style* 575

scanty 640
poor 643
– diet 956
meal *repast* 298
  powder 330
mealy-mouthed
  falsehood 544
  servile 886
  flattering 933
mean *average* **29**
  small 32
  middle 68, 228
  signify 516
  intend 620
  contemptible 643
  stingy 819
  shabby 874
  ignoble 876
  sneaking 886
  base 940
  selfish 943
  golden – 174
  take the – 774
  – nothing 517
  – parentage 876
  – time 114
  – wretch 949
meander
  convolution 248
  deviate 279
  circuition 311
  river 348
  – around Robin
    Hood's barn 279
meandering
  diffuse 573
meanest capacity
  499
  intelligible to the
    – 518
meaning **516**
meaningless 517
means
  appliances **632**
  property 780
  wealth 803
  by all – 602
  by any – 632
  by no – 536
  – of access 627
meantime 106
meanwhile 106
measurable 466
  within – *distance*
    470
measure *extent* 25
  degree 26
  moderation 174
  music 413
  compute 466
  verse 597

proceeding 626
action 680
apportion 786
angular – 244
full – 639
out of – 641
without – 641
– of inclinatio
  217
measured
  moderate 174
  sufficient 639
  temperate 953
measureless 105
measurement 25,
  466
measures
  have no – with **713**
  take – *plan* 626
  prepare 673
  conduct 692
  – of length 200
meat 298
  broken – 645
  one man's – is
    another man's
    poison 15
mechanic 690
mechanical 601,
  633
  – warfare 722
  – powers 633
mechanician 690
mechanism 633
medal
  record 551
  sculpture 557
  palm 733
  decoration 877
  – of Honor **733**
medallion 557
medallist 700
meddle 682
médecin tant pis
  837
médecine expec-
  tante 133, 662
Medes and Per-
  sians, law of the
    – 80, 141
mediæval 124
mediævalism 122
medial 29, 68
median 228
mediant 413
medias res, in – 68
  plunge – 300, **576**
mediation—*instru-
  mentality* 631
  intercession **724**
  deprecation 766

disregard distinc-
tion between –
791
mew *moult* 226
cry 412
– up 751
mewed up 229
mewl 412
mews 189
mezzanine floor
191, 599
mezzo rilievo
convex 250
sculpture 557
mezzo termine
middle 68
mid-course 628
compromise 774
Mezzofanti 492
mezzosoprano 416
mezzotint 420, 558
miasm 663
mica 425
micacious 204
mi-carême 840
Micawber 460
Michael 977
Michaelmas 998
Micomicon 515
microbe 193
microcosm 193
micrography 193,
441
micrometer 193
micro-organism
193
microphone 418
microscope 193, 445
microscopic 32, 193
mid 68
Midas 803
mid-course **628**
mid-day 125
midden 653
middle - *in degree*
29
- *in order* **68**
- *in space* 222,
228
– classes 736
– constriction 203
– course 29, 628
– man *director* 694
agent 758
– point 29
– term 68
compromise 774
middlemost 222
middling 29, 32, 68,
651
middy 225, 269

midge 193
midget 193
midland 342
midnight *night* 126
dark 421
– oil 539, 689
mid-progress 282
midriff 68, 228
midshipman 269,
745
midships 68
midst - *in order* 68
central 222
interjacent 228
in the – of
mixed with 41
doing 680
midsummer **125**
– day 138
midway 68
midwife
instrument 631
remedy 662
auxiliary 711
midwifery 161, 662
mien 448, 692
miff 900
might *power* 157
violence 173
energy 686
mightily 31
mighty *much* 31
strong 159
large 192
haughty 878
migraine 378
migrate 266, 295
mikado 745
milch cow
productive 168
animal 366
store 636
mild *moderate* 174
warm 382
insipid 391
lenient 740
calm 826
courteous 894
mildew 653, 663
mildewed
spoiled 659
mile 200
milestone 550
whistle jigs to a –
645
milieu, juste – 174,
628
militant 722
'church – 983a
military
warfare 722

soldiers 726
– authorities 745
– band 417
– power 737
– time 132
– train 726
militate against 708
militia 726
milk *moderate* 174
semiliquid 352
cows &c. 370
white 430
mild 740
– a he-goat into a
sieve 471
flow with – and
honey *plenty*
639
prosperity 734
pleasant 829
– of human kind-
ness 906
– the ram 645
– and water
weak 160
insipid 391
unimportant 643
imperfect 651
milk-livered 862
milksop
incapable 158
fool 501
coward 862
milky [*see* milk]
semitransparent
427
whiteness 430
– way 318
mill 330
notch 257
machine 633
workshop 691
fight 720
like a horse in a –
312
millennium
number 98
period 108
futurity 121
utopia 515
hope 858
millesimal 99
millet seed 193
milliard 98
milliner 225
man – 854
millinery *dress* 225
ornament 847
display 882
man – 855
million 98

multitude 102
people 372
populace 876
for the –
intelligible 518
easy 705
–s *money* 800
millionaire 803
mill-pond *level* 213
pond 343
store 636
mime 19, 599, 844
mimeograph 19
mimeotype 19
mimic 19
mimodrama 599
minacity 909
minaret 206
minatory 668
minauderie 855
mince *cut up* 44
slow 275
food 298
stammer 583
affected 855
extenuate 937
– the matter 868
not – the matter
affirm 535
artless 703
– the truth 544
mincemeat of
make – 162
mincing 855
– steps 275
mind *intellect* 450
attend to 457
take care 459
believe 484
remember 505
will 600
willing 602
purpose 620
warning 668
desire 865
dislike 867
bear in – 451, 457
bit of one's – 527
food for the – 454
give the – to 457
have a – 602, 865
in the –
thought 451
topic 454
willing 602
make up one's –
484, 604
never – *neglect* 460
unimportant 643
not – 866
out of – 506

set one's – upon
604
speak one's – 582,
703
to one's – *taste* 850
love 897
willing – 602
– one's book 539
~ one's business
456, 457
– at ease 826
make one's – *easy*
826
–'s eye 515
– what one is
about 864
minded 602, 620
mindful 457, 505
mindless
inattentive 458
imbecile 499
forgetful 506
insensible 823
mine
sap 162
hollow 252
open 260
snare 545
store 636
abundance 639
damage 659
attack 716
defence 717
explosive 727
dig a – *plan* 626
prepare 673
spring a –
unexpected 508
attack 716
– of information
700
–layer 726
–sweeper 726
–thrower 727
– of wealth 803
miner 252
sapper and – 726
mineral 358
– oil 356
mineralogy 358
Minerva 979
– in vita 603, 704
– press 577, 594
mingle 41
miniature *small* 193
portrait 556
– painter 559
Minié rifle 727
minikin 193
minim *small* 32
music 413

minimize 36, 483,
934
minimum *small* 32
inferior 34
minion 899
type 591
minister *instru-
mentality* 631
remedy 662
director 694
aid 707
deputy 759
give 784
clergy 996
rites 998
– to 746
ministerial
clerical 995
ministering spirit
977
ministration
direction 693
aid 707
rite 998
ministry
direction 693
aid 707
church 995
clergy 996
miniver 223
minnesinger 597
minnow 193
minor *inferior* 34
infant 129
– key 413
Minorites 996
minority *few* 103
youth 127
Minos 694
minotaur 83
minster 1000
minstrel 416, 597
minstrelsy 415
mint *mould* 22
workshop 691
wealth 803
– of money 800
minuend 38
minuet 415, 840
minus *less* 34
subtracted 38
absent 187
deficient 304
loss 776
in debt 806
non-payment 808
minuscule 561
minute
– *in degree* 32
– *of time* 108
instant 113

- *in size* 193
record 551
compendium 596
to the – 132
– account 594
– attention 457
minuteness
care 459
minutiæ 32, 79, 643
minx 887, 962
mirabile
– dictu &c. 870
mirabilis, annus –
872
miracle 83, 872
– play 599
miraculous 870
mirage 443
mire 653
mirror *imitate* 19
reflector 445
perfection 650
glory 873
hold up the – 525
hold the – up to
nature 554
magic – 443
mirth 836
misacceptation 523
misadventure 735
misadvised 699
misanthropy 911
misapply
misinterpret 523
misuse 679
mismanage 699
misapprehend 495,
523
misappropriate 679
misarrange 61
misbecome 925
misbegotten 243,
945
misbehave 851, 945
misbehaviour 895,
947
misbelief 485
misbeliever 487,
984
miscalculate
misjudge 481
err 495
disappoint 509
miscall 565
miscarry 732
miscegenation 41
miscellany
mixture 41
collection 72
generality 78
compendium 596

mischance 619, **735**
mischief 619
do – 649
make – 649
mischief-maker
913, 941
miscible 41
miscite 544
miscompute 481,
495
misconceive 495,
523
misconduct 699,
947
– oneself 945
misconjecture 481
misconstrue 523
miscorrect 538
miscount 495
miscreance 485
miscreant 949
miscreated 945
misdate 115
misdeed 947
misdemean 945
misdemeanant 949
misdemeanour 947
misdevotion 988
misdirect 538, 699
misdo 945
misdoing 947
misdoubt 485, 523
mise en scène
appearance 448
drama 599
display 882
misemploy 679
miser 819
–'s hoard 800
miserabile dictu 839
miserable *small* 32
contemptible 643
unhappy 828
miserably 31
miserere 215
sing – 950
misericordiam,
argumentum ad
– 914
miseries of human
life 828
miseris succurrere
disco 914
miserly 819
misery 828
put out of one's –
914
misestimate
misjudge 481
misfeasance 699,
947

slow 275
sufficient 639
cheap 815
temperate 953
– circumstances
mediocrity 736
modera\tely
imperfect 651
moderation [*see*
moderate] 174
mid-course 628
inexcitability 826
moderato *music*
415
moderator 174
lamp 423
director 694
mediator 724
judge 967
modern 123
music 415
art 556
modest *small* 32
modesty
humility **881**
purity 960
mock – 855
modicum *little* 32
allotment 786
modification
difference 15
variation 20a
change 140
qualification 469
modish 852
modulation
variation 20a
change 140
music 413
module 22
modulus 84
modus: – operandi
method 627
conduct 692
– in rebus 174
– vivendi 723
mogul 745
Mohammedan 984
Mohawk
swaggerer 887
evil-doer 913
moider 458, 475
moiety 51, 91
moil *active* 682, 686
exertion 686
moisture *wet* 337
humid **339**
mokes 219
molar 330
molasses 396
mole *mound* 206

prominence 250
colour 432
refuge 666
defence 717
spot 848
molecular 32
molecule 193
molehill *little* 193
low 207
trifling 643
molest *trouble* 830
molestation
damage 649
malevolence 907
mollia tempora 134
– fandi 588
mollify *allay* 174
soften 324
mollusk 366
mollycoddle 158
Molly Maguire 548
Moloch
slaughter 361
demon 980
heathen deity 986
molten 384
moment
- *of time* 113
importance 642
for the – 111
lose not a – 684
not have a – 682
on the spur of the
– 612
momentous 152
momentum 276
Momus 838
monachism 995
monad 193
monarch 745
monarchy 737
monastery 1000
monastic 995
monasticism 984
monetary 800
– arithmetic 11
money 800
wealth 803
bad – 800
command of – 803
for one's – 609
made of – 803
make – 775
raise – 788
save – 817
throw away one's
– 818
– to burn 641, 803
– burning one's
pocket 818
– coming in 810

– down 807
– going out 809
– market 800
– matters 811
– paid 809
–'s worth
useful 644
price 812
cheap 815
money-bag 800,
802
money-belt 802
money-broker 797
money-changer
797, 801
moneyed 803
moneyer 797
money-grubbing
775
moneyless 804
monger 797
mongrel
mixture 41
anomalous 83
dog 366
base 949
moniker 565
moniliform 249
monism 984
monition 527, 668
information 527
warning 668
monitor *hear* 418
oracle 513
pupil-teacher 540
director 694
adviser 695
war-ship 726
inward – 926
monitory
prediction 511
dissuasion 616
warning 668
monk 996
monkey
imitative 19
support 215
catapult 276
ridiculous 857
play the – 499
–jacket 225
– trick
absurdity 497
sport 840
– up 900
monkhood 995
monkish Latin 563
monochord 417
monochrome 429,
556
monocracy 737

monoculous 443
monode 445
monodrame 599
monody 597, 839
monogamist 904
monogamy 903
monogram
sign 550
cipher 533
diagram 554
letter 561
monograph
publication 531
writing 590
book 593
description 594
monolith 551
monolithic 983a
monologue
soliloquy 589
drama 599
monomachy 720
monomania 503
obstinacy 606
fanaticism 825
monomaniac 504
monomark 550
monoplane 273
monopolist 943
monopoly
restraint 751
possession 777
monostich 572
monosyllable 561
monotheism 983
monotonous
uniform 16
equal 27
repetition 104
permanent 141
- *style* 575
weary 841
dull 843
monotype 591
monsoon 349
monsieur 373
monster
exception 83
large 192
ugly 846
prodigy 872
evil-doer 913
ruffian 949
monstrance 998
monstrosity
[*see* monster]
distortion 243
monstrous
excessive 31
exceptional 83
huge 192

destroy 162
moxa 384
M.P. 696
Mr. 373, 877
Mrs. 374
MS. 22, 590
much 31
  make − of
    importance 642
  friends 888
  love 897
  endearment 902
  approval 931
  not say − for 932
  think − of 928, 931
  − ado *exertion* 686
  difficulty 704
  − ado about noth-
    ing
  over-estimate 482
  exaggerate 549
  unimportant 643
  unskilful 699
  − cry and little
    wool 884
  - the same
  identity 13
  similarity 17
  equality 27
  − *speaking* 584
mucid 352, 653
mucilage 352
muck 653
  run a − *kill* 361
  attack 716
  excitement 825
muckle 31
muckworm 819,
  876
mucor 653
mucosity 352
mucronate 253
muculent 352
mud *marsh* 345
  semiliquid 352
  dirt 653
  clear as − 519
  stick in the − 704
  − guard 666
muddle *disorder* 59
  derange 61
  inattention 458
  absurd 497
  difficulty 704
  failure 732
  − one's brains 475
muddled 959
muddle-headed 499
muddy *moist* 339
  dim 422
  opaque 426

colour 429
stupid 499
mudlark *dirty* 653
  commonally 876
muezzin 550, 996
muff *incapable* 158
  dress 225
  bungle 699
  bungler 701
muffettee 225
muffle *wrap* 225
  silent 403
  deaden 408a
  conceal 528
  voiceless 581
  stammer 583
muffled *faint* 405
  latent 526
  − drums
  funeral 363
  non-resonance
    408a
muffler 225, 384
mufti *undress* 225
  judge 967
  priest 996
mug *cup* 191
  face 234, 448
  pottery 384
  dupe 547
muggy *moist* 339
  dim 422
  opaque 426
mug-house 189
mugient 412
mugwump 607
mulatto
  mixture 41
  exception 83
mulct *steal* 791
  fine 974
mule *mongrel* 83
  beast of burden
    271
  obstinate 606
muleteer 694
muliebrity 374
mull
  prominence 250
  sweeten 396
mullah 967, 996
muller 330
mullion 215
mullioned 219
multifarious
  irrelevant 10
  diverse 16a
  multiform 81
multiferous 102
multifid
  divided 51

multifold 81
multiformity 81
multigenerous 81
multilateral 236,
  244
multilocular 191
multiloquence 582,
  584
multinomial 102
multiparous 168
multipartite 44
multiple 84, 102
multiplex 81
multiplicand 84
multiplicate 81
multiplication
  increase 35
  arithmetic 85
  multitude 102
  reproduction 163
  productiveness
    168
multiplicator 84
multiplicity 102
multiplier 84
multiply 35
multipotent 157
multisonous 404
multitude 72, 102
  the − 876
multum in parvo
  596
multure 330
mum 581, 585
  −'s the word 403
mumble *chew* 298
  mutter 583
Mumbo Jumbo
  979, 993
mummer 599
mummery
  absurdity 497
  imposture 545
  masquerade 840
  parade 882
mummify 363
mummy *dry* 340
  corpse 362
  beat to a − 972
mump *mutter* 583
  beg 765
mumper 767, 804
mumpish *sad* 837
mumps 837, 901a
munch 298
Munchausen 549
mundane
  world 318
  selfish 943
  irreligious 989
mundation 652

mundivagant 266
munerary 973
munerate 973
municipal 965
municipality 737
munificent 816
muniment
  evidence 467
  record 551
  defence 717
  security 771
munition
  materials 635
  defence 717
mural 717
murder 361
  − the King's Eng
    lish
  solecism 568
  stammering 583
  the − is out 529
murderer 361
muricated 253
murky *dark* 421
  opaque 426
  black 431
  gloomy 837
murmur *purl* 348
  sound 405
  voice 580
  complain 839
murmurer 832
murrain 655
Murray *travel* 266
  Lindley − 542
murrey 434
murrion 717
mus, nascitur ridi-
  culus − 509, 643
muscadine 400
muscle 159
muscular 159
muse 451
  [*and see* musing]
Muse *poetry* 597
  historic − 594
  unlettered − 579
musette 417
Muses, the − 416
museum
  collection 72
  store 636
mush 354
mushroom
  new 123
  fungus 367
  upstart 734
  low-born 876
  spring up like −s
    163
  − anchor 666

narrow-minded 481, 943
narrowness 203
narrows 343
nasal accent 583
nascent 66
nascitur: – *ridiculus mus* 509
– *a sociis* 82
naso, omnia suspendens – 868
nasty
  unsavoury 395
  foul 653
  offensive 830
  cheap and – 815
natâ, pro re – 770
natal *birth* 66
  indigenous 188
natation 267
natatorium 652
nathless 30
nation 372
national 188, 372
  – guard 726
nationality 372, 910
nations, law of 963
native
  inhabitant 188
  artless 703
  – accent 580
  – land 189
  – soil 189
  – tongue 560
nativity *birth* 66
  cast a –
  predict 511
  sorcery 992
natty 845
natura il fece e poi roppe la stampa 87
naturæ, vis medicatrix – 662
natural *intrinsic* 5
  musical note 413
  true 494
  fool 501
  – *style* 576, 578
  spontaneous 612
  not prepared 674
  artless 703
  simple 849
  – course of things 613
  – death *death* 360
  completion 729
  – impulse 601
  – meaning 516
  – order of things 82

– state 80
– turn 820
Natural – History 357
  – Philosophy 316
  – Theology 983
naturalist 357
naturalization
  conformity 82
  conversion 144
  location 184
naturalize
  habit 613
naturalized
  inhabitant 188
naturally 154
nature *essence* 5
  rule 80
  tendency 176
  world 318
  reality 494
  artlessness 703
  affections 820
  animated – 357
  organized – 357
  second – 613
  state of –
  naked 226
  raw 674
  in –'s garb 226
naught *nothing* 4
  zero 101
  bring to – 732
  set at –
  make light of 483
  opposition 708
  disobey 742
  not observe 773
  disrespect 929
  contempt 930
naughty 945
naumachia 720
nausea 841, 867
nauseate 395, 830
nauseous
  unsavoury 395
  unpleasant 830
  disgusting 867
nautch dancer 840
nautical 267
naval 267
  – authorities 745
  – engagement 720
  – forces 726
nave *middle* 68
  centre 222
  church 1000
navel 68, 222
navigation 267
navigator 269
navvy 673, 690

navy 273, 726
  – blue 438
nay 536
  – rather 14
Nazarene 989
naze 250
N.C.O. 745
ne plus ultra
  supreme 33
  complete 52
  distance 196
  summit 210
  limit 233
  perfection 650
  completion 729
neaf 781
neap 195, 207
  – tide 36, 340
near *like* 17
  - *in space* 197
  - *in time* 121
  soon 132
  impending 152
  approach 286
  stingy 819
  bring – 17
  draw – 197
  come – 286
  – one's end 360
  – at hand 132
  – the mark 32
  – run 32
  – side 239
  – sight 443
  – the truth 480*a*
  – upon 3
  sail – the wind
  skilful 698
  rash 863
nearly 32
nearness 197
neat *simple* 42
  order 58
  in writing 572, 576, 578
  clean 652
  spruce 845
  –'s foot oil 356
  – as a pin 58
neat-handed 698
neatherd 370
neb 250
nebula *stars* 318
  mist 353
nebular *dim* 422
nebulous *misty* 353
  obscure 519
necessarian 601
necessaries 630
necessarily 154
necessitate 630

necessity *fate* **601**
  requirement 630
  compulsion 744
  indigence 804
  make a virtue of – 698
neck
  contraction 195
  narrow 203
  make love 902
  break one's – 360
  – and crop
  completely 52
  turn out - 297
  – of land 342
  – and neck 27
  – or nothing
  resolute 604
  rash 863
neckcloth 225
necklace 247, 847
necks 980
necrology 360, 594
necromancer 548, 994
necromancy 992
necropsy 363
necroscopic 363
necrosis 49
nectar 394, 396
need *necessity* 601
  requirement 630
  insufficiency 640
  indigence 804
  desire 865
  friend in – 711
  in one's utmost – 735
needful
  necessary 601
  requisite 630
  money 800
  do the – *pay* 807
needle *sharp* 253
  perforator 262
  compass 693
  as the – to the pole
  veracity 543
  observance 772
  honour 939
  – in a bottle of hay 475
needle-gun 727
needle-shaped 253
needless 641
needle-witted 498
needlewoman 690
needlework 847
ne'er-do-well 949
nefarious 945

negation **536**, 764
negative
  inexisting 2
  contrary 14
  prototype 22
  quantity 84
  confute 479
  deny 536
  photograph 558
  refuse 764
  prove a – 468
neglect **460**
  disuse 678
  leave undone 730
  omit 773
  evade 927
  disrespect 929
  – of time 115
négligé 225, 674
negligence 460
negotiable 270
negotiate
  mediate 724
  bargain 769
  transfer 783
  traffic 794
negotiations
  breaking off – 713
negotiator 724, 758
negro 431, 746
negus
  drink 298
  king 745
neif 781
neigh *cry* 412
  boast 884
neighbour 197, 890
neighbourhood 183,
  197, 227
neighbourly
  aid 707
  friendly 888
  social 892
  courteous 894
neither 610
  – here nor there
  irrelevant 10
  absent 187
  – more nor less
  equal 27
  true 494
  – one thing nor
  another 83
nem. con. 488
Nemesis
  vengeance 919
  justice 922
  punishment 972
nemine contra-
  dicente 488
nemo me impune

lacessit 715
nenia 839
neogamist 903
neologism 123
neology **563**
neophyte 144, 541
neoteric 123
nepenthe 662, 836
nephelogy 353
nephew 11
nepotism
  nephew 11
  wrong 923
  dishonest 940
  selfish 943
Neptune 341
Nereid 341, 979
nerve 159, 861, 885
  exposed – 378
nerveless 158
nervous *weak* 160
  style 574
  timid 860
  modest 881
nescience 491
nest
  multitude 102
  cradle 153
  lodging 189
  – of boxes 204
nest-egg 636
nestle *lodge* 186
  safety 664
  endearment 902
nestling 129
Nestor *veteran* 130
  sage 500
  advice 695
net *remainder* 40
  receptacle 191
  intersection 219
  inclosure 232
  snare 545
  difficulty 704
  gain 775
  – *profit gain* 775
  receipt 810
nether 207
nethermost 211
netting 219
nettle *bane* 663
  sting 830
  incense 900
network
  disorder 59
  crossing 219
neuralgia 378
neurasthenia 655
neuritis 378
neurology 329
neurotic 662

neuter *matter* 316
  no choice 609a
  remain –
  irresolute 605
  stand –
  indifferent 866
neutral *mean* 29
  no choice 609a
  avoidance 623
  – tint
  colourless 429
  grey 432
  peace 721
neutrality
  mid-course 628
  peace 721
  insensibility 823
  indifference 866
neutralize
  compensate 30
  counteract 179
névé 383
never 107
  – say die
  persevere 604a
  cheerful 836
  hope 858
  it will – do
  inexpedient 647
  prohibit 761
  discontent 832
  disapprobation
  932
  –dying 112
  –ending 112
  –fading
  perpetual 112
  glory 873
  – forget 916
  – to be forgotten
  642
  – indebted 807
  – hear the last of
  841
  – mind
  neglect 460
  unimportant 643
  insensible 823
  indifferent 866
  contempt 930
  – more 107
  – a one 4
  – otherwise 16
  – to return 122
  – was seen the
  like 83
  – so 31
  – tell me 489
  – thought of 621
  – tired *active* 682
  – tiring

  persevering 604a
neverness **107**
nevertheless 30
new *different* 18
  additional 37
  novel 123
  unaccustomed 614
  – birth 660
  – blood *change* 140
  improve 658
  excite 824
  – brooms 614, 682
  – comer 57
  – conditions 469
  – departure 66
  – edition
  repetition 104
  reproduction 163
  improvement 658
  – ideas 537
  turn over a – leaf
  change 140
  repent 950
  give – life to 707,
  824
  view in a – light
  658
  put on the – man
  950
New Year's Day
  138
new-born 123, 129
Newcastle, carry
  coals to – 641
new-fangled
  unfamiliar 83
  change 140
  neology 563
new-fashioned 123
new-fledged 129
Newfoundland dog
  366
Newgate 752
new-gilt 847
new-model
  convert 144
  revolutionize **146**
  improve 658
newness **123**
news **532**
  – sheet 531
newsmonger
  curious 455
  informant 527
  news 532
newspaper 531, 551
  – correspondent
  758
newspaperman **534**
newt 366

contrary 14
dissimilar 18
– surrender 606, 717
– thank you 764
at – time 107
– wonder 871
Noah's ark 41, 72
nob 210
nobilitate 873
nobility 875
noble *great* 31
    important 642
    rank 873
    peer 875
    disinterested 942
    virtuous 944
noblesse 875
nobody
    unsubstantial 4
    zero 101
    absence 187
    low-born 876
    – knows
    ignorance 491
    – knows where
    distance 196
    – present 187
    – would think 508
noctambulation 266
noctivagant
    travel 266
    dark 421
noctograph 421
noctuary 421, 551
nocturnal
    night 126
    dark 421
    black 431
nocturne 415
nocuous 649
nod *wag* 314
    assent 488
    signal 550
    sleep 683
    command 741
    bow 894
    – of approbation 931
    – of assent 488
nodding to its fall 162, 306
noddle 210, 450
noddy 501
node 250
nodosity 250, 256
nods and becks and wreathed smiles 894
nodule 250
nodular 256

nodus, dignus vindice – 704
Noel 998
noggin 191
noise 402, 404
    – abroad 531
    make a – in the world 873
noiseless 403
noisome
    fetid 401
    bad 649
    unhealthy 657
nolens volens 601
noli me tangere
    defiance 715
    excitable 825
    fastidious 868
nolition 603
nolle prosequi 624
nolumus leges
    Angliæ mutari
    permanence 141
    continuance 143
    preservation 670
nom de: – guerre 565
    – plume 565
nomad 268
nomadic 266
Nomancy 511
nomenclature 564
nominal
    unsubstantial 4
    word 562
    name 564
    – price 815
nomination 564, 755
nominee 758
nominis umbra 4
Nomology 963
non:
    – compos mentis 503
    – constat 477
    – deficit alter 100
    – est inventus 187
    – hæc in fœdera 536, 610
    – nobis Domine 990
    – obstante 707
    – placet 489
    – possumus
    impossible 471
    obstinate 606
    refusal 764
    – nostrum tantas componere lites 471, 713

lex – scripta 963
    – semper erit
    æstas 111
    – sequitur 70, 477, 495
    ⌐ sum qualis eram 140, 160
non-addition 38
non-admission 55
nonage 127
nonagenarian 98
non-appearance 447
non-assemblage 73
non-attendance 187
nonce 118
    for the – 118, 134
nonchalance
    neglect 460
    insensibility 823
    indifference 866
non-coincidence 14
non-cohesive 47
non-com. 726
non-commissioned officer 745
non-committal 528, 864
non-completion 730
non-compliance 742, 764
nonconformity
    difference 15
    exception 83
    dissent 489
    sectarianism 984
non-content 489
non-cooperation 489, 927
nondescript 83
none 101
    – else 87
    – to spare 640
    – such
    superior 33
    exceptional 83
    very good 648
    – in the world 4
    – the worse 660
non-endurance 825
nonentity
    inexistence 2
    unsubstantial 4
    unimportant 643
non-essential 6, 643
non-existence 2
non-expectance 508
non-extension 180a
non-fulfilment 730, 732

– of one's hope 509
non-imitation 20
non-interference
    inaction 681
    freedom 748
nonius 466
non-juror 489, 98(
non-naturals 657
nonny 501
non-observance
    inattention 458
    desuetude 614
    infraction **773**
    dereliction 927
nonpareil 648
    type 591
non-payment 808
non-performance
    non-completion 730
    dereliction 927
non-plus
    uncertain 475
    difficulty 704
    conquer 731
non-preparation 674
non-prevalence 614
non-residence 187
non-resistance 725, 743
non-resonance 408a
nonsense
    absurdity 497
    unmeaning 517
    trash 643
    talk – *folly* 499
non-subsistence 2
non-success 732
nonsuch [*see* none]
nonsuit *defeat* 731
    fail 732
    condemn 971
nonum prematur in annum 133
non-uniformity 16a
noodle 501
nook *place* 182
    receptacle 191
    corner 244
noology 450
noon *mid-day* 125
noon-day *light* 420
    clear as –
    intelligible 518
    manifest 525
nooscopic 450
noose *ligature* 45
    loop 247

snare 545
  gallows 975
norma loquendi 567
normal
  intrinsic 5
  mean 29
  regular 82
  perpendicular 212
  – condition
  rule 80
normality 80, 502
Normand, répon-
  dre en – 544
Norns 601
North 278
  – and South 237
Northern 237
  – light 423
  – star 939
North-west
  passage 311
noscitur a sociis 82
nose *prominence*
  250
  smell 398
  with one's – in
  the air 878
  lead by the – 615,
  737
  led by the – 749
  not see beyond
  one's –
  misjudge 481
  folly 499
  unskilful 699
  speak through
  the – 583
  thrust one's – in
  interjacence 228
  busy 682
  under one's –
  present 186
  near 197
  manifest 525
  defy 715
  put one's – out of
  joint *defeat* 731
  disrepute 874
  – ring 847
nose-dive 306
nosegay 400, 847
nosey 455
nosology 655
nostalgia 833
nostril 351
  breath of one's –s
  359
  stink in the –s 401
nostrum 626, 662
not *negation* 536
  what is – 546

what ought – 923
  – at all 32
  – allowed 964
  – amiss 618, 651,
  845
  – any 101
  – bad 651
  – bargain for 508
  – a bit 536
  – to be borne 830
  – a Chinaman's
  chance 471
  – come up to 34
  – cricket 923
  – to be despised
  642
  it will – do 923
  – of the earth 987
  – expect 508
  – fail 939
  – far from 197
  – a few 102
  – fit to be seen 846
  – following 477
  – grant 764
  – guilty 946
  – to be had 471,
  640
  – having 187, 777*a*
  – hardened 950
  – hear of 764
  – included 55
  – know what to
  make of 519
  – a leg to stand
  on 158
  – likely 473
  – a little 31
  – matter 643
  – to mention 37
  – mind 823, 930
  – often 137
  – on your life 489
  – one 101
  – a particle 4
  – particular 831
  – pay 808
  – a pin to choose
  27
  – playing the
  game 923
  – within previous
  experience 137
  – to be put down
  604
  – quite 32
  – reach 304
  – right 503
  – sorry 827
  – a soul 101
  – on speaking

terms 889
  – the thing 925
  – to be thought of
  incogitancy 452
  impossible 471
  refusal 764
  hopeless 859
  undue 925
  disapprobation
  932
  – trouble oneself
  about 460
  – understand 519
  – vote 609*a*
  – wonder 871
  – for the world
  603, 764
  – worth
  trifling 643
  useless 645
nota bene 457
notabilia 642
notabilities 875
notable
  manifest 525
  important 642
  active 682
  distinguished 873
notables 875
notably 31
notary 553, 968
notation 85
notch 198, **257,** 550
note *cry* 412
  music 413
  take cognizance
  450
  remark 457
  explanation 522
  sign 550
  record 551
  printing 591
  epistle 592
  minute 596
  money 800
  fame 873
  change one's – 607
  make a – of 551
  of – 873
  take – of 457
  – of admiration
  870
  – of alarm 669
  – of preparation
  673
note-book
  memorandum 505
  record 551
  compendium 569
  writing 590
noted 490, 873

noteworthy
  great 31
  exceptional 83
  important 642
nothing *nihility* 4
  zero 101
  trifle 643
  come to – 304, **732**
  do – 681
  for – 815
  go for – 643
  good for – 646
  make – of
  under-estimate
  483
  fail 732
  take – by 732
  think of – 930
  worse than – 808
  – comes amiss 831
  – to do 681
  – to do with 764
  – doing 681
  – to go upon 471
  – in it 4
  – of the kind 18,
  536
  – loth 602
  – on 226
  – more to be said
  478
  – to signify 643
nothingness 2
notice *intellect* 450
  observe 457
  review 480
  information 527
  warning 668
  bring into – 525
  deserve – 642
  give –
  manifest 525
  inform 527
  indicate 550
  short – 111
  take – of 450
  this is to give –
  457
  worthy of – 642
  – is hereby given
  publication 531
  – to quit 782
noticeable 31
notification 527
notion *idea* 453
notional 515
notoriety 531, **873**
notorious
  known 490
  public 531
  famous 873

infamous 874
notturno 415
notwithstanding 30
nought [*see* naught]
noun 564
nourish 707
nourishment
  food 298
nous 498
nous avons changé
  tout cela 140
nouveau riche 123,
  734, 876
Nova Zembla 383
novation 609
novel
  dissimilar 18
  new 123
  unknown 491
  tale 594
novelette 594
novelist 594
novice
  ignoramus 493
  learner 541
  bungler 701
  religious 996
novitiate 539, 673
novocaine 376, 381
novus homo 57,
  876
now 118
  – and then 136
  – or never 134
noways 32
nowhere 187
nowise 32, 536
noxious 649, 657
noyade 361, 972
noyerait dans une
  goutte d'eau, il
  se – 699
nozzle
  projection 250
  opening 260
  air-pipe 351
nuance 15, 465
nubibus, in – 2, 515
nubiferous 353, 426
nubile 131, 903
nucleus *middle* 68
  cause 153
  centre 222
  kernel 642
nuda veritas 494
nude 226, 849
nudge 550
nudity 226
nugacity 499, 645
nugæ canoræ 517,
  842

nugas, magno co-
  natu magnas –
  643
nugatory 158
  unimportant 643
nuggar 273
nugget *mass* 192
  money 800
nuisance 619, 830
null 4
  – and void
  inexistence 2
  powerless 158
  unproductive 169
  illegal 964
  declare – and void
  abrogation 756
  non-observance
  773
nulla dies sine
  lineâ 682
nullâ pallescere
  culpâ, nil
  conscire sibi –
  946
nullah 198
nulli secundus 33
nullibiety 187
nullify *inexistence* 2
  compensate 30
  destroy 162
  abrogate 756
  not observe 773
  not pay 808
nullity 2, 4
nullius jurare in
  verba magistri
  487
numb
  physically insen-
  sible 376, 381
  morally insensible
  823
  –skull 493
number
  part 51
  abstract - **84**
  count 85
  plural 100
  - *of a magazine*
  &c. 593
  – among 76
  take care of – one
  943
  – of times 104
numbered: days –
  kill 360
  necessity 601
  hopeless 859
  – with the dead
  360

numberless 105
numbers *many* 102
  verse 597
numbness 375, **381**
numerable 85
numeral 84, 85
numeration **85**
numerator 84
numerical 85
numerose
  many 102
numerous 102
numismatics 800
numps 501
numskull 501
nun 996
nunc dimittis 990
nuncio 534, 758
nuncupation
  naming 564
nuncupatory
  informing 527
nundination 794
nunnery 1000
nuptials 903
nurse *remedy* 662
  preserve 670
  help 707
  servant 746
  custodian 753
  fondle 902
  put to – 537
nurseling 129
nursery *infancy* 127
  nest 153
  room 191
  garden 371
  school 542
  workshop 691
  – rhymes 597
  – tale 546, 594
nursing home 493
nurture *feed* 298
  educaie 537
  prepare 673
  aid 707
  – a belief 484
  – an idea 451
nut
  – to crack
  fanatic 504
  riddle 533
  difficulty 704
  – oil 365
nut-brown 433
nutmeg 393
nutmeg-grater 330
nuts 618, 829
nutshell *small* 32
  lie in a – 572
  little 193

compendium 596
nutation 314
nutriment 298
nutrition 707
nutritious *food* 298
  healthy 656
  remedy 662
nutty 499
nuzzle 902
nyctalopy 443
nymph *girl* 129
  woman 374
  mythology 979
  sea – 341
nystagmus 443

O

O! *wonder* 870
  discontent 932
  – for *desire* 865
oaf *fool* 501
  bungler 701
  changeling 980
oak *strong* 159
  heart of –
  hard 323
  brave 861
oakum 205
oar *paddle* 267
  oarsman 269
  instrument 633
  labouring – 686
  lie upon one's –s
  681
  ply the –
  navigate 267
  exert 686
  pull an – 680
  put in an – 228,
  682
  rest on one's –
  cease 142
  quiescence 265
  repose 687
  stroke – 693
oarsman 269
oasis *separate* 44
  exceptional 83
  land 342
oast-house 386
oath
  assertion 535
  bad language **908**
  on – 543
  rap out –s 885
  upon – 768
oatmeal 298
obbligato 88, 415
obduction 223

obdurate
obstinate 606
severe 739
malevolent 907
graceless 945
impenitent 951
obedience 743
obeisance *bow* 308
submission 725
courtesy 894
reverence 928
obelisk 206, 551
Oberon 979
obese 194
obesity 192
obey 743
be subject to 749
− a call 615
− the helm 705
− rules 82
obfuscate 421, 426
obfuscated
drunk 959
obit 360, 363
post − 360, 363
obiter dictum
irrelevant 10
occasion 134
interjacent 228
obituary 360, 594
object *thing* 3
matter 316
take exception 469
intention 620
ugly 846
disapprove 932
be an −
important 642
− to *dislike* 867
− lesson 82
objection 706, 932
no − 762
objectionable
inexpedient 647
wrong 923, 947
objective
extrinsic 6
material 316
objector
conscientious −
710
objurgate 932
oblate 201
− spheroid 249
oblation *gift* 784
religious - 990
oblectation 827
obligation
necessity 601
promise 768
conditions 770

debt 806
confer an − 648
feeling of − 916
under an − 916,
926
oblige *benefit* 707
compel 744
duty 926
obligé, bien −
refusal 764
obliged
necessity 601
grateful 916
duty 926
obligee 800
obliging
helping 707
courteous 894
kind 906
obliquation 279
obliquity
slope **217**
vice 945
− of judgment 481
− of vision 443
obliteration 552
− of the past 506
oblivion 506
nothingness 2
pardon 506
forgiveness 918
redeem from − 505
− of benefits 917
− of time 115
oblivious 506
oblong 200
− spheroid 249
obloquy
disrepute 874
disapprobation
932
detraction 934
obmutescence 581,
585
obnoxious
pernicious 649
unpleasing 830
hateful 898
− to *liable* 177
obnubilated 422
oboe 417
obreption 528
obscene 653, 961
obscurantist 421,
519, 710
obscure *dark* 421
dim 422
unseen 447
uncertain 475
unintelligible 519
eclipse 874

ignoble 876
obscurity *style* **571**
obscurum per
obscurius 519
obsecration 765
obsequies 363
obsequious
subject 749
servile 886
courteous 894
respectful 928
flattery 932
observance *rule* 82
attention 457
habit 613
practice 692
fulfilment **772**
duty 926
rite 998
observant
friar 996
observation
intellect 450
idea 453
attention 457
assertion 535
− *car* 272
observatory 318
observe [*see* observance, observa-
tion]
remark 457
− a duty 926
− rules 82
observer 444
obsess 860, 992
obsession 716
obsidional 716
obsolete *old* 124
words 563
effete 645
obstacle 179, 706
obstant, Fata − 601
obstetrician 631
obstetrics 161, 662
obstinacy 606
prejudice 481
obstipation 261
obstreperous 173,
404
obstruct *close* 261
hinder 706
− the passage of
light 426
− the view 424
obstructive
opponent 710
obstruent 706
obstupefaction 823
obstupui steterunt-
que comæ 860

obtain *exist* 1
prevail 78
get 775
− under false
pretences **791**
obtainable 470
obtenebration 421
obtestation 765
obtrectation 934
obtrude
interfere 228
insert 300
meddle 682
obtruncate 201
obtrusion 228, **706**
obtrusive
interfering 228
vulgar 851
rude 895
obtund *mitigate* **174**
blunt 254
deaden 376
paralyze 823
obturate 261
obturator 263
obtuse *blunt* 254
insensible 376
imbecile 499
dull 823
− *angle* 244
obtuseness 456*a*
obumbrate 421
obverse 234
obviate 706
obvious *visible* 446
evident 474
clear 518
manifest 525
ocarina 417
occasion
juncture 8
opportunity **134**
cause 153
befit the − 646
have − for 630
on the present −
118
on the spur of −
612
occasional 475
occasionally 136
occidental 236, **560**
occiput 235
occision 361
occlusion 261
unintelligible **919**
latent 526
hidden 528
− *art* 992
occultism 984
occultation 449, 528

– to be met with 136
ogee 847
Ogham 590
ogive 215
ogle *look* 441
  desire 865
  rude 895
  endearment 902
ogpu 696
ogre *bugbear* 860
  evil-doer 913
  demon 980
oil *lubricate* 332
  grease 355, **356**
  pour – on
  relieve 834
  – on the troubled
    waters 174, 714
  – lamp 423
  – stove 386
oilcloth 223
oiled *drunk* 959
oilskin 386
oil-painting 556
oily *smooth* 255
  greasy 355
  servile 886
  courteous 894
  flattery 933
oinomania 959
ointment
  grease 356
  remedy 662
O.K. 488
old 124
  of – 122
  – age 128
  die of – age 729
  – bachelor 904
  – clothes 225
  – fashioned 851
  – fogey 501, 857
  – joke 842
  – maid *cards* 840
  spinster 904
  – man *veteran* 130
  husband 903
  – man of the sea 706
  – Nick 978
  – school 124
  obstinate 606
  habit 613
  pay off – scores 718
  – song
  repetition 104
  trifle 643
  cheap 815
  – stager

veteran 130
  actor 599
  proficient 700
  – story
  repetition 104
  stale news 532
  love 897
  – times 122
  one's – way 613
  – woman *fool* 501
  wife 903
Oldbuck 122
olden 124
older 128
oldest inhabitant
  not in memory of – 137
old-fashioned 124, 851
oldness **124**
oleagine 356
oleaginous 355
oleomargarine 356
oleum addere camino 35, 173
olfactory 398
olid 401
oligarch 745
oligarchy 737
olio 41
olive-branch
  infant 129
  offspring 167
  pacification 723
olive-green 435
olla podrida 41
Olympiad 720
Olympus 981
ombre 840
ombres chinoises 448
omega *end* 67
omelet 298
omen **512**
ominate 511
ominous
  predicting 511
  indicating 550
  danger 665
  hopeless 859
omission
  incomplete 53
  exclusion 55
  neglect 460
  failure 732
  non-observance 773
  guilt 947
omitted 2, 187
omne tulit punctum 731

omnibus 272
omnifarious 81
omnific 168
omniform 81
omnigenous 81
omnipotence 157, 976
omnipresence 186, 976
omniscience 490, 976
omnium gatherum
  mixture 41
  confusion 59
  assemblage 72
omnivorous
  eating 298
  desire 865
  gluttony 957
omphalos 68
on *forwards* 282
  – account of 155
  – all accounts 52
  – that account 155
  – approval 463
  – an average 29
  – the brink of 32
  – the cards 152
  – foot *duration* 106
  event 151
  doing 170
  – the fire 730
  – all fours 13, 23
  – the other hand 30
  – one's head 218
  – the increase 35
  – a large scale 31
  – these lines 627
  – the move 264
  – the nail 118
  – no account 32
  – no occasion 107
  – a par 27
  – the part of 9
  – the point of 111
  – the present oc-
    casion 118
  – trial 463
  – the whole 50
on dit 532, 588
once *past* 119, 122
  seldom 137
  at – 113, 132
  – for all *final* 67
  infrequency 137
  tell one - 527
  determine - 604
  choose 609
  – in a blue moon 137

– more 90, 104
– over 457
– upon a time
  time 106
  different time **119**
  formerly 122
– in a way 137
Ondine 979
one *identical* 13
  whole 50
  unity 87
  somebody 372
  married 903
  all – to 823
  at – with *agree* 23
  concur 178
  concord 714
  make – of 186
  neither – nor the
    other 610
  of – accord 488
  – and all
  whole 50
  general 78
  unanimous 488
  from – to another
  transfer 783
  – thing with
    another 476
  – of the best 948
  – bone and one
    flesh 903
  – consent 178, 488
  – of these days 121
  – fell swoop 113, 173
  – fine morning 106
  – and a half 87
  – horse 643
  – idea 481
  – jump 113
  – leg in the grave 160
  as – man 488, 709
  – mind 178, 488
  – by one
  separately 44
  respectively 79
  unity 87
  both the – and
    the other 89
  the – or the other 609
  – over the eight 959
  – and the same 13
  on – side 217, 236
  – step 840
  – in ten thousand 648, 948
  – at a time 87

- or two 100
with – voice 488
– in a way 83
– way or another
627
at – with
agree 23
concur 178
concord 714
one-eyed 443
oneirocritic 524
oneiromancy 511
oneness 13
onerous *bad* 649
difficult 704
burdensome 706
troublesome 830
oneself 13
have all to – 777
kill – 361
take merit to –
884
take upon –
will 600
undertake 676
talk to – 589
true to – 604a
be – again 660
one-sided
misjudging 481
wrong 923
dishonourable 940
onion 393
onlooker 444
only *small* 32
simple 42
single 87
imperfect 651
if – 865
– think 870
– yesterday 123
only-begotten 87
onomancy 511
onomatopœia 560,
564
onset *beginning* 66
attack 716
onslaught 716
ontology 1
onus *burden* 706
duty 926
– probandi
uncertainty 475
doubt 485
onward 282
onychomancy 511
onyx 847
oof 800
ooze *emerge* 295
flow 348
semiliquid 352

[578]

– out
disclosure 529
opacity 426
opal 847
opalescent 427, 440
opaque 426
open *begin* 66
expand 194
unclose 260
manifest 525
reveal 529
frank 543
artless 703
break – 173
lay – 226
lay oneself – to
177
leave the matter –
705
pry – 173
throw – 296
– and above board
703, 939
– air 220, 338
– arms *willing* 602
friendship 888
social 892
courtesy 894
– the ball 62, 66
– a case 476
– country 344
in – court 525, 531
– a discussion 476
– to discussion 475
– the door to
cause 153
facilitate 705
permit 760
with – doors 531
– enemy 891
– eyes *see* 441
attention 457
discovery 480a
expectation 507
inform 527
undeceive 529
teach 537
predetermination
611
wonder 870
– fire 716
– house 892
– into
conversion 144
river 348
– the lips 529
– the lock 480a
– market 799
– one's mind 529
– order 194
– one's purse-

strings 809
– question 461,
475
– rupture 713
– sesame 260, 550,
631, 993
– the sluices 297
– space 180
– to suspicion 485
– to *liable* 177
facile 705
– the trenches 716
– up *begin* 66
disclose 529
– to the view 446
– war 722, 889
– the wound 824
opening
beginning 66
opportunity 134
space 180
gap 198
aperture **260**
open-handed 809,
816
open-hearted
veracious 543
artless 703
liberal 816
honourable 939
open-mouthed
cry 411
expectation 507
speak 582
loquacious 584
desire 865
wonder 870
opera *music* 415
poetry 597
drama 599
– glass 445
– hat 225
– house 599
opéra bouffe 599
operculum 261
operæ pretium est
646
operandi, modus
627, 692
operate *cause* 153
produce 161
act 170
work 680
– upon *motive* 615
operation
[see operate]
arithmetical – 85
in – 680
put in – 677
surgical – 662
operative

acting 170
workman 690
operator
surgeon 662
doer 690
operculated 261
operculum 223
operetta 415
operose 686, **704**
ophicleide 417
ophiology 368
ophiomancy 511
ophthalmia 443
ophthalmic 441
opiate 174
opine 484
opiniative 481
opiniator 606
opinion 484
give an – 480
have too high an –
of oneself 880
popular – 488
system of –s 484
wedded to an –
606
opinionate 481, **606**
opinionated 474
self– 880
opiniâtre 481
opinionist 474, **606**
opitulation 707
opium *soothe* 174
deaden sense 376
bane 663
opium-eater 683
oppidan 188
oppilation 706
opponent **710, 891**
opportune
well-timed 134
expedient 646
opportunism 605,
646
opportunity 134
lose an – 135
oppose *contrary* 14
counteract 179
evidence 468
clash 708
opposite 14
– scale 30
– side 237
opposition
[*see* oppose] **708**
the – 710
oppositionist 710
oppress *molest* 649
severe 739
malevolence 907
oppressed with

melancholy 837
oppressive *hot* 382
    painful 830
oppressor 739, 913
opprobrium 874
oppugnation 708,
    719
optative 865
optical 441
    – instruments **445**
    – lantern 448
optician 445
optics *light* 420, 445
optics *sight* 441
optimacy 875
optimates 875
optime! 931
optimism 482, 858
optimist 858
    flatterer 935
option 609
optional 600
optometer 445
optometry 445
opulence 803
opuscule 593
or *yellow* 436
    orange 439
    alternative 609
oracle 500, **513**
Oracle, Sir –
    positive 474
    vanity 880
    blusterer 887
oracular
    answering 462
    ambiguous 475
    wise 498
    prediction 511
oral *information*
    527
    voice 580
    speech 582
    – communication
    588
    – evidence 467
orange *round* 249
    colour **439**
orangery 371
orarium 999
oration 582
    funeral – 363
orator 582
oratorio 415
oratory
    speaking 582
    place of prayer
    1000
orb *region* 181
    circle 247
    luminary 423

eye 441
sphere of action
    625
– of day *sun* 318
    luminary 423
– of night 318
orbicular 247
orbit *circle* 247
    heavens 318
    path 627
orchard 371
orchestra
    music 415
    musicians 416
    instruments 417
    theatre 599
orchestral 415
orchestrate 60, 413,
    416
orchestration 413
orchestrelle 417
ordain
    command 741
    commission 755
    due 924
    legal 963
    God 976
    church 995
ordained *due* 924
    clergy 996
ordeal
    experiment 463
    trouble 828
    sorcery 992
    – of battle 722
order
    regularity **58**
    arrangement 60
    class 75
    record 551
    requisition 630
    direct 693
    command **741**
    money 800
    rank 873
    quality 875
    decoration 877
    law 963
    at one's – 743
    call to – 932
    in – 620
    keep in – 693
    money – 800
    out of – 651
    put in – 60
    recur in regular –
    138
    set in – 60
    set one's house
    in – 673
    standing – 613

in working – 673
– of the day
    conformity 82
    events 151
    habit 613
    plan 626
    command 741
    pass to the – of
    the day 624
orderless 59
orderly
    regular 58, 80
    arrange 60
    conformable 82
    servant 746
    – of succession 63
    – of things 80
orders, holy – 995
    in – 996
ordinal 998
ordinance
    command 741
    law 963
    rite 998
ordinary *usual* 82
    meal 298
    habitual 613
    imperfect 651
    ugly 846
    simple 849
    in – *store* 636
    lie in – 681
    – condition
    rule 80
    – course of things
    613
ordinate 466
ordination
    measurement 466
    command 741
    commission 755
    church 995
    rite 998
ordnance 727
ordonnance 963
ordure 653
ore 635
ore rotundo 577
oread 979
orectic 865
organ *music* 417
    voice 580
    instrument 633
    internal –s 221
    – point 413
organic *state* 7
    structural 329
    protoplastic 357
    – change 146
    – chemistry 357
    – remains 357

dead 329
organism 329
organist 416
organization 60
    production 161
    structure 329
    animated nature
    357
organize
    arrange 60
    produce 161
    plan 626
organized hypoc-
    risy 544
organology 329
orgasm 173
orgies 954
oriel *recess* 191
    corner 244
    window 260
    chapel 1000
Orient 236, 420
orifice
    beginning 66
    opening 260
oriflamme 550
Origenism 984
origin 66, 153
    derive its – 154
original
    dissimilar 18
    not imitated 20
    model 22
    initial 66
    individual 79
    exceptional 83
    cause 153
    invented 515
    unaccustomed **614**
    laughing-stock
    857
    return to – state
    660
originality 600
    want of – 843
originate *begin* 66
    cause 153
    invent 515
    – in 154
originator 164
originative 168
Orion's belt 318
orismology 562, **564**
orison *request* **765**
    worship 990
orlop deck 211
ormolu
    sham 545
    ornament 847
Ormuzd 979
ornament

palatial *palace* 189
　ostentatious 882
palatinate 181
palatine 745
Palatine Court 966
palaver
　unmeaning 517
　speech 582
　loquacity 584
　colloquy 588
　council 696
pale stake 45
　region 181
　inclosure 232
　limit 233
　dim 422
　colourless 429
　emotion 821
　frightened 860
　turn –
　lose colour 429
　emotion 821
　fear 860
　– of the church
　995
　– its ineffectual
　fire
　dim 422
　out of repute 874
pale-faced 429
paleography
　past 122
　philology 560
paleology past 122
　language 560
paleontology 368
paleozoic 124
palestric 686, 720
paletot 225
palette 556
palfrey 271
palimpsest 147, 528
palindrome
　inversion 218
　neology 563
paling 232, 752
palingenesia 163
palingenesis 660
palinode 597
palinody 607
palisade
　wall 212
　defence 717
　prison 752
pall covering 223
　mantle 225
　funeral 363
　disgust 395
　insignia 747
　weary 841
　dislike 867

satiety 869
　canonicals 999
palladium
　safety 664
Pallas 979
pall-bearer 363
pallet support 215
　painter's - 556
palliament 225
palliate
　moderate 174
　mind 658
　relieve 834
　extenuate 937
palliative 174
　remedy 662
pallid 429
pallium 999
pall-mall 840
pallone 840
pallor 429
palm
　measure of length
　200
　trophy 733
　steal 791
　laurel 877
　bear the – 873
　grease the –
　induce 615
　give 784
　itching – 865
　win the – 731
　– off, – upon 545
　– tree 367
palmated 257
palmer
　traveller 268
　clergy 996
palmist 513
palmistry 511
palmy
　prosperous 734
　pleasant 829
　– days
　prosperous 734
　pleasure 827
palpable
　material 316
　tactile 379
　obvious 446
　manifest 525
　– obscure 421
palpation 379
palpitate
　tremble 315
　colour 440
　emotion 821
　fear 860
palsy
　impotence 158

physical insensi-
　bility 376
　disease 655
　mental insensi-
　bility 823
palter
　falsehood 544
　shift 605
　elude 773
paltry small 32
　unimportant 643
　mean 940
paludal 345
pampas 344
pamper 902, 954,
　957
pamphlet 531, 593
pamphleteer 595
Pan 979
pan 191
panacea 662
panache 256, 847
panama hat 225
panary 636
pancake 298
pandar [see pander]
Pandean pipes 417
pandect
　knowledge 490
　dissertation 595
　compendium 596
　code 963
pandemonium 59,
　404, 982
　inhabitants of –
　978
pandemic 657
pander pimp 962
　– to instrument
　631
　help 707
　flatter 933
pandiculation
　expansion 194
　opening 260
　sleepy 683
Pandour 726
Pandora's box 619
　bottom of 858
paned 440
panegyric 931
panegyrize 482
panel list 86
　layer 204
　partition 228
　accused 938
　jury 967
　sliding – 545
panelling 847
pang 378, 828
Pangloss 492

panguid 355
panhandle 765, 767,
　876
panic 860
panier 225
Panjandrum 875
pannel 215
pannikin 191
pannier 191
panoply 717, 727
panopticon 752
panorama 448, 556
panoramic 78, 446
　– view 441
pansophy 490
pant heat 382
　fatigue 688
　emotion 821
　– for 865
pantaloon
　old man 130
　pantomimist 599
　buffoon 844
pantaloons 225
pantechnicon 272,
　636
pantheism 984
Pantheon 979, 1000
panther 861
pantile 223, 350
pantologist 492, 700
pantology 490
pantomime 550, 599
pantry 191, 636
pants 225
panurgy 698
pap 250, 354
papa father 166
Papa pope 996
papacy 984, 995
papal 995
paper cover 223
　white 430
　writing 590
　book 593
　security 771
　exist only on – 4
　– credit 805
　– money 800
　– pellet 643
　– war 476, 720
Paphian 954, 961
papilla 250
papistry 984
papoose 129
pappous 256
papula 250
papulose 250
papyrus 590
par 27
　above – 648

below – *low* 207
imperfect 651
– excellence 33
– nobile fratrum
alike 17
friends 890
de – le roi 737
– parenthèse 134
– pari refero 718
– value 812
parable
metaphor 521
teaching 537
description 594
parabola *curve* 245
parabolic
metaphorical 521
paracentesis 297
parachronism 115
parachute
balloon 273
means of safety
666
– *light* 423
Paraclete 976
parade *procession*
69, 266
walk 189
ostentation 882
paradigm 22, 567
Paradise *bliss* 827
heaven 981
in – 827
parados 717
paradox
absurdity 497
obscurity 519
difficulty 704
paradoxical 475,
519
paraffin 356
paragon
perfect 650
glory 873
good man 948
paragram
ambiguous 520
neology 563
paragraph *part* 51
phrase 566
article 593
paraleipsis 460
parallax 196
parallel
similarity 17
imitate 19
harmonious 178
– *position* 216
symmetry 242
draw a – 464
none but himself

can be his – 873
run – 178
parallelism 216
agreement 23
parallelogram 244
parallelopiped 244
paralogism 477
paralogize 477
paralysis
impotence 158
physical insensi-
bility 376
disease 655
moral insensi-
bility 823
paralyse 158, 376,
823
paramount
supreme 33
important 642
authority 737
lord – *master* 745
possessor 779
– *estate* 780
paramour 897
paranoia 503, 504
parapet 717
paraph 550
paraphernalia
machinery 633
belonging 780
paraphrase
imitation 19
copy 21
synonym 522
phrase 566
paraphrast 524
paraphrastic 19,
522
parasite *auxiliary*
711
servile 886
flatterer 935
parasitic
subjection 749
grasping 789
servile 886
parasol *covering* 223
shade 424
paratus:
in utrumque –
resolved 604
ready 673
semper – 673
parboil 384
parbuckle 633
Parcæ 601
parcel *part* 51
group 72
part and – 56
– out *arrange* 60

allot 786
parcels
property 780
parcere subjectis
740, 914
parch *dry* 340
heat 382
bake 384
parched with thirst
865
parchment
writing 590
security 771
parcity 819
pardi 535
pardon 506, 918
beg – 952
– me 489
pardonable 937
pare *cut* 38
reduce 195
peel 204
divest 226
– *down*
shorten 201
paregoric 662
parenchyma 316,
329
parent 166
– *ship* 726
parentage 11, 166
parenthesis
discontinuity 70
inversion 218
interjacence 228
by way of – 134
parenthetical
irrelative 10
pargeting 847
parhelion 423
pari passu 27, 120
Pariah
outlaw 83
commonalty 876
outcast 893
parian
sculpture 557
parietal 236
parietes 224
paring 32
parish 181
bring to the – 804
come upon the –
804
– council 696
parishioner 997
paritor 965
parity 17, 27
park *house* 189
plain 344
trees 367

artillery 727
pleasure ground
840
– *paling* 232
parkway 627
parlance 582
in common – 576
parlante 415
parlementaire 534,
723
parler:
facon de – 521
– à tort et à
travers
illogical 477
nonsense 497
parley *talk* 588
conference 695
mediation 724
parliament 696
parliamentary
securities 802
parlour 191
parlour-maid 746
parlous 665
Parnassus 597
parochial 181, 189
prejudiced 481
parody
imitation 19
copy 21
misinterpret 523
misrepresent 555
travesty 856
parole *speech* 582
on – *restraint* 751
prisoner 754
promise 768
Parolles 887
paronomasia
neology 563
ornament 577
paronymous 562
paroxysm
violence 173
agitation 315
emotion 825
anger 900
parquetry 440
Parr, Old – 130
parricide 361
parrot
imitation 19
repetition 104
loquacity 584
repeat as a – 505
parry *confute* 479
avert 623
defend 717
pars magna fui,
quorum – 690

parse 461, 567
Parsee 984
parsimony 819
parson 996
parsonage 1000
part *divide* 44
  portion 51
  diverge 291
  music 413
  book 593
  rôle 599
  function 625
  duty 926
act a – *action* 680
take an active –
  682
bear – in 709
component – 56
fractional – 100*a*
in – *a little* 32
for my – 79
on the – of 707
play a – in 175
principal – 642
take the – of 709
take – with 709
take a – in 680
take no – in 623
– company
  disjunction 44
  avoid 623
  quarrel 713
– and parcel 56
– by part 51
–song 415
– of speech 567
– with 782, 784
partake 778
– of the sacrament
  998
parte, ex – 481
parterre *level* 213
  cultivation 371
Parthis mendacior
  544
parti pris 611
partial *unequal* 28
  incomplete 51
  special 79
  misjudging 481
  unjust 923
– shadow 422
partiality
  preponderance 33
  desire 865
  friendship 888
  love 897
partially 32, 51
partible 44
particeps criminis
  690, 711

participate 709, 778
– in *be a doer* 680
participation 778
participator 690
particle 32, 330
parti-coloured 440
particular *item* 51
  event 151
  attentive 457
  careful 459
  exact 494
  capricious 608
  odd 851
  fastidious 868
in – 79
– account 594
– estate 780
particularize
  special 79
  describe 594
particularly 31, 33
particulars 79, 594
partie carrée 892
parting 44
partisan
  auxiliary 711
  weapon 727
  friend 890
  sympathizer 914
partisanship
  warped judgment
  481
  co-operation 709
  partiality 923
partition *wall* 228
  allot 786
partlet 366
partly 51
partner
  companion 88
  auxiliary 711
  sharer 778
  friend 890
  spouse 903
  sleeping – 683
partnership
  party 712
  join – with 709
parts *intellect* 450
  skill 698
  wisdom 498
parturition 161
parturiunt montes
  482, 509
party *assemblage* 72
  special 79
  person 372
  association **712**
  sociality 892
– spirit
  warped judgment

481
  cooperation 709
  wrong 923
– to *action* 680
  agent 690
  co-operate 709
– to a suit 969
– wall 228
parva componere
  magnis 464
parvenu
  new 123
  successful 734
  vulgar 851
  low-born 876
parvitude 193
pas *precedence* 62
  term 71
  precession 280
  rank 873
– de quatre 840
– seul 840
pas si bête 498
paschal 998
pasha 875
pashalic 737
pashaw 745
pasigraphie 560
pasigraphy 590
pasquinade 934
pass *conjuncture* 8
  be superior 33
  course 109
  lapse 122
  happen 151
  interval 198
  defile 203
  move 264
  transfer 270
  move through 302
  exceed 303
  vanish 449
  way 627
  difficulty 704
  thrust 716
  passport 760
  gratuity 815
– *as property* 783,
  784
barely – 651
let it – 460
make a – at 716
pretty – 704
– away
  cease to exist 2
  end 67
  transient 111
  past 122
  cease 142
  die 360
– by *course* 109

inattention 458
neglect 460
disrespectful 929
– comprehension
  519
– current 484
– an examination
  648, 873
– the eyes over
  457
– the fingers over
  379
– into one's hand
  785
– through one's
  hands 625
– into 144
– judgment 480
– a law 963
– in the mind 451
– muster
  conform to 82
  sufficient 639
  good 648
  approbation 931
barely – muster
  651
– under the name
  of 564
– off *be past* 122
  egress 295
– off for 544
– on 282
– an opinion 480
– to the order of
  the day 624
– out of 295
– over
  exclude 55
  cross 302
  give 784
  forgive 918
  exemption 927*a*
– over to 709
– and repass 302,
  314
– in review 457,
  461
– the Rubicon 609
– sentence on 971
– time *exist* 1
  time 106
  do nothing 681
– one's time in
  625
– to 144
– through
  event 151
  motion 302
– one's word **768**
passable *small* 32

unimportant 643
imperfect 651
pretty 845
passado 716
passage [*see* pass]
part 51
conversion 144
street 189
corridor 191
opening 260
navigation 267
moving through
302
music 413
- *in a book* 593
action 680
cut a – 260
force a – 302
– of arms 720
passant, en –
transit 270
incidentally 621
pass-book 811
passe: mot de –
550
passé
antiquated 124
aged 128
spoiled 659
passed away 122
passementerie 847
passenger 268
– *train* 272
passe-partout
key 260
instrument 631
passer by 444
passer le temps,
pour – 681
passeront pas, ilsne
717
passe-temps 840
passim
dispersed 73
place 182
situation 183
passing *very* 31
transient 111
– *bell* 363
– *strange* 870
– *word* 527
passion
emotion 820, 821
excitability 825
pain 828
desire 865
love 897
anger 900
ruling – 606
Passion-week 998
passionate

warm 825
irascible 901
passionless 823
passive *inert* 172
inaction 681
obedient 743
inexcitable 826
– *resister* 489
passivity 172, 989
pass-key 631
Passover 998
passport
indication 550
instrumentality
631
order 741
permission 760
pass-word
answer 462
sign 550
military 722
past 122
danger – 664
insensibility to
the – 506
obliteration of
the – 506
thing of the – 124
– *bearing* 830
– *comprehension*
519
– *cure* 859
– *dispute* 474
– *praying for* 945
– *one's prime* 128
– *recollection* 506
– *work*
useless 645
impaired 659
paste *attach* 43
cement 45
to cement 46
pulp 354
sham 545
tinsel 847
scissors and – 609
pastel 556
pasteurize 652
pasticcio 21, 41
pastil 400
pastime 840
pastor 996
pastoral
bucolic 370
music 415
poem 597
religious 995
sermon 998
pastorale 415
pastry *food* 298
sweets 396

pasturage
meadow 344
herbage 367
pasture *food* 298
pasty *tart* 298
like paste 352
pat *pertinent* 23
strike 276
(*expedient* 646)
– *on the back*
induce 615
comfort 834
encourage 861
approve 931
– *on the cheek* 902
– *on the head*
endearment 902
Patagonian 206
patch *small* 32
change 140
region 181
blemish 848
– *up restore* 660
compromise 774
patchwork
mixture 41
discontinuous 70
variegation 440
pate *summit* 210
brain 450
patefaction 260
patella 191
paten 191
patent *open* 260
manifest 525
licence 760
property 780
– *medicine* 662
pater 166
– *patriæ* 912
patera *cup* 191
sacramental 998
paterfamilias 166
paternal
father 166
benevolent 906
– *domicile* 189
paternity 166
paternoster 990
path *direction* 278
way 627
cross the – 706
secret – 530
pathetic 830
pathless
spacious 180
closed 261
difficult 704
pathognomonic 550
pathology 655, 662
pathos 821

pathoscopic 820
pathway 627
patience
perseverance 604
endurance 826
cards 840
patient *sick* 655
patisserie 298
patois 563
patriæ: amor – 910
pater – 912
patriarch
family 11
veteran 130
ancestors 166
priest 996
patriarchal
ancient 124
ancestral 166
patriarchate 737
patrician 875
patrilineal 11, 166
patrimony 780
patriot 910
patrol *walk* 266
safeguard 664
(*warning* 668)
patrolman 664
patron
auxiliary 711
customer 795
friend 890
benefactor 912
patronage
influence 175
aid 707
authority 737
patronize 693, 707
patronymic 564
patten 225, 998
patter *strike* 276
sound 407
meaningless 517
talk 584
stage 599
patterer 582
pattern *model* 22
perfection 650
ornament 847
– *after* 19
patte de
– *mouche* 590
– *velours* 544, **545**
patulous 194
patty 298
pauciloquy 585
paucity *small* 32
few 103
scanty 640
paughty 878
Paul Jones 792

peevish 895, 901
peg *grade* 71
  hang 214
  project 250
  drink 298, 959
  come down a –
    306
  let down a – 308
  not stir a – 265,
    681
  – away 682
  – to hang on 617
  – on *journey* 266
  – out *die* 360
Pegasus 271
pegomancy 511
pegs *legs* 266
peignoir 225
peindre, fait à –
  845
peine forte et dure
  974
pejorative 483
pelagic 341
pelerine 225
pelf *gain* 775
  property 780
  money 803
pelisse 225
Pelion, Ossa on –
  72, 319
pellet 249, 727
  paper – 643
pellicle 204, 223
pell-mell 59
pellucid 425
pelote 249
pelt *skin* 223
  dress 225
  throw 276
  attack 716
  punish 972
peltry 223
pemmican 298
pen *inclosure* 232
  write 590
  writer 593
  restrain 751
  imprison 752
  ready – 569
  slip of – 495, 568
  stroke of the –
    write 590
  authority 737
  command 741
  – in hand 590
  - and ink 590
  – name 565
  draw the –
    through 552
penal 972

– servitude 972
– settlement 752
penalty 974
  extreme – 972
penance 952, 974
  do – 998
penates, lares et –
  189, 991
penchant
  willing 602
  desire 865
  love 897
pencil *bundle* 72
  - *of light* 420
  write 590
pencil-drawing 556
pencraft 590
pendant *match* 17
  flag 550
  ornament 847
pendency *time* 106
  hanging 214
pendente lite 106
  uncertain 475
  lawsuit 969
pendule 114
pendulous 214, 314
pendulum 114, 214
  motion of a – 314
Penelope, work of –
  645, 730
penetralia 221
  – *mentis* 450, 820
penetrate
  ingress 294
  passage 302
  sagacity 498
  – the soul 824
penetrated with
  484, 821
penetrating
  sagacious 498
  feeling 821
  – glance 441
penfold 232
peninsula 342
penitence 950
penitentiary 752,
  996
pen-knife 253
penman 590
  inspired – 985
penmanship 590
pennant 550
pennate 267
penniless 804
pennon 550
penny 800
  not have a – 804
  cost a pretty – 814
  turn a – 775

no – no paternos-
  ter 812
in for a – in for a
  pound 768
– dreadful 594
– trumpet 410
– whistle 410
penny-a-liner 534,
  593
penny-a-lining 573
pennyweight 319
penny-wise 819
  – and pound fool-
    ish *caprice* 608
  waste 638
  prodigal 818
pennyworth 812
penology 972
penscript 590
pensée, arrière –
  528
penseroso 837
pensile 214
pension *income* 810
pensioner
  student 541
  servant 746
  receiver 785
pensive 451, 837
penstock 350
pent up 751
  – in one's mem-
    ory 505
pentagon 98, 244
pentahedron 244
pentameter 98, 597
Pentateuch 98, 985
Pentecost 998
Penthesilean 861
penthouse 189, 191
pentile 223
penultimate 67
penumbra 421
penurious 819
penury 804
peon 726
people
  kinsfolk 11
  multitude 102
  inhabit 186
  mankind 372
  commonalty 876
  laity 997
pep 171
  – up 171
pepastic 662
pepper *pungent* 392
  condiment 393
  attack 716
  – and salt 432,
    440

peppercorn 643
  – rent 815
peppery
  irascible 901
peptic 662
per 631
  – contra
    contrariety 14
    counter-evidence
    468
    opposition 708
  – procuratio 755
  – saltum 70, 113
  – se 87
peradventure 470
peragrate 266
perambulate 266
perambulator
  measure of length
    200
  vehicle 272
perceivable 446
perceive
  be sensible of 375
  see 441
  know 490
percentage 84, 813
perceptible 446
perception 453, 490
perceptive 375
perch *location* 184
  abide 186
  habitation 189
  length 200
  height 206
  support 215
  – up 307
perchance 156, 470
percipience 450
percolate 295, 348
percolator 191
percursory 458
percussion 276
  centre of – 222
percussive 277
perdition
  destruction 162
  ruin 732
  loss 776
perdre son Latin
  704
perdrix, toujours –
  841
perdu 528
  enfant – 859, 863
perdurable 110
perdy 535
peregrination 266
peregrinator 268
peremptory
  assertion 535

firm 604
  authoritative 737
  rigorous 739
  compulsory 744
  duty 926
  – denial 536
  – refusal 764
perennial
  continuous 69
  diuturnal 110
  - *plants* 367
perennius, ære –
  873
pererration 266
perfect
  great 31
  entire 52
  excellent 650
  complete 729
perfection 650
  bring to – 729
perfervidum in-
  genium 682
perfidy 874, 940
perflate 349
perforate 260
perforator 262
perforce 601, 744
perform
  produce 161
  do 170
  - *music* 416
  action 680
  achieve 729
  fulfil 772
  – a circuit 629
  – a duty 926
  – the duties of 625
  – a function 644
  – an obligation
   772
  – a part 599, 680
  – a service 998
performable 470
performance
  [*see* perform]
  effect 154
performer
  musician 416
  stage-player 599
  agent 690
  affectation 855
perfume 400
perfunctory 53, 460
pergola 191
perhaps 470, 514
peri 845, 979
periapt 993
pericranium 450
periculous 665
peridot 847

perihelion 197
peril 665
  at your – 909
  take heed at
   one's – 668
perilepsis 476
perimeter 230
period *end* 67
  point 71
  - *of time* 106, **108**
  recurrence 138
  at fixed –s 138
  well rounded –s
   577, 578
periodical
  recurring 138
  book 593
periodicity **138**
peripatetic 266, 268
periphery 230
periphrase 566, 573
periplus 267
periscope 441, 445
periscopic 446
  – lens 445
perish
  cease to exist 2
  be destroyed 162
  die 360
  decay 659
  – with cold 383
  – with hunger 956
perishable 111
perissology 573
peristaltic 248
peristyle 189
periwig 225
perjured 940
perjurer 548
perjury 544
perk *dress* 225
  – up *elevate* 307
  revive 689
perked up
  proud 878
perky 880
perlustration 441
permanence
  durability 110
  unchanging **141**
  unchangeable 150
permanent
  habitual 613
permeable 260
permeate
  insinuate 228
  pervade 186
  pass through 302
  –d with 613
permissible 760
permission **760**

permissive 760
permit 760
permitting
  weather &c. – 469,
   470
permutation
  numerical - 84
  change 140
  interchange 148
pernicious 649
pernicity 274
perorate
  diffuse style 573
peroration
  sequel 65
  end 67
  speech 582
perpend *think* 451
perpendicular 212
perpension
  attention 457
perpetrate 680
  – a pun &c. 842
perpetrator 690
perpetua, esto –
  928, 931
perpetual 112
  frequent 136
  – curate 996
  – motion 467
perpetuate 112
  continue 143
  establish 150
perpetuity 69, **112**
perplex *derange* 61
  distract 458
  uncertainty 475
  bother 830
perplexed 59, 248
perplexity
  disorder 59
  uncertainty 475
  unintelligibility
   519
  difficulty 704
perquisite 775, 973
perquisition 461
perron 627
perscrutation 461
persecute
  oppress 649
  annoy 830
  malevolence 907
perseverance 143,
  604a
Persides 215
persiflage 842, 856
persifleur 844
persist *duration* 106
  permanence 141
  continue 143

persevere 604a
persistence
  diuturnity 110
person 3, 372
  without distinc-
   tion of –s 922
persona grata 890,
  899
personable 845
personæ, dramatis
  – 599, 690
personage 372
personal
  [*see* person]
  special 79
  subjective 317
  – narrative 594
  – property 780
  – remarks 932
  – security 771
personality
  [*see* personal]
  discourtesy 895
  disrespect 929
  censure 932
  detraction 934
personalty 780
personate 19, 554
personify 521, 554
personnel 56, 590
perspective
  view 448
  expectation 507
  painting 556
  aerial – 428
  in – 200
perspicacity
  sight 441
  intelligence 498
  fastidiousness 868
perspicuity
  intelligibility 518
  style **570**
perspiration 295,
  299
  in a – 382
perstringe 457
persuadable 602
persuade *belief* 484
  induce 615
persuasibility
  willingness 602
persuasion
  class 75
  opinion 484
  teaching 537
  inducement 615
  religious – 983
persuasive
  reasoning 476
pert

vain 880
insolent 885
discourteous 895
pertain to
relate to 9
included under 76
power 157
belong 777
property 780
duty 926
perte de vue, à –
196, 447
pertinacity 604a
pertinent 9, 23
pertingent 199
perturbation
derange 61
ferment 171
agitation 315
emotion 821
excitation 824, 825
fear 860
pertusion 260
peruke 225
peruse 539
pervade
influence 175
extend 186
affect 821
– *the soul* 824
pervading spirit 820
perverse
obstinate 606
difficult 704
churlish 895
sulky 901a
perversion
sophistry 477
misinterpretation 523
misteaching 538
falsehood 544
untruth 546
injury 659
impiety 988
pervert 144, 607
[*see* perversion]
perverted 495
pervestigation 461
pervicacious 606
pervigilium 682
pervious 260
pessimism
overrate 482
underrate 483
dejection 837
hopeless 859
pessimist
[*see* pessimism]
coward 862

pessomancy 511
pessoribus orti 876
pest 663, 830
pester 830
pest-house 662
pestiferous 657
pestilence 655
pestle 330
pet *love* 897
favourite 899
anger 900
fondle 902
flatter 933
– *lamb* 366
petal 367
petard 727
hoist on one's own
– 718, 732
Peter to pay Paul:
borrow of – 788
rob – *steal* 791
wrong 923
–'s pence 784, 809
peter out 142
petit-maître 854
petite dame 962
petitio principii 477
petition 765, 969, 990
petitioner 767
petrel *warning* 668
petrify *dense* 321
hard 323
freeze 385
thrill 824
affright 860
astonish 870
petrol 388
petroleum 356
pétroleuse 384
petronel 727
petticoat *dress* 225
woman 374
– *government*
authority 737
pettifogger 968
pettifogging
sophistry 477
deception 545
litigious 713
dishonourable 940
pettish 901
petto, in –
mental 450
thought of 454
concealed 528
intention 620
petty *little* 32, 193
unimportant 643
– *cash* 800, 811
– *jury* 967

– larceny 791
– officer 745
– sessions 966
– treason 742
petulance 885, 901
petulant
- *language* 574
peu de chose 643
peu s'en faut 32
pew *cell* 191
church 1000
pewter 41
phaeton 272
Phaëthon 423
phalanx 712, 726
phantasm
unsubstantiality 4
illusion 443
appearance 448
imagination 515
phantasmagoria 448
phantasy 453, 515
phantom *unreal* 4
fallacy of vision 443
imaginary 515
pharisaical 544, 988
Pharisee 548, 988
pharmacy 662
pharos 550
phase *aspect* 8
transition 144
form 240
appearance 448
have many –s 149
assume a new –
144
view in all its –s
461
phasis 448
phasma 443
phenomenon
event 151
appearance 448
prodigy 872
phial 191
Phidias 559
philander 902
philanthropy 784, 906, 910
**Philip drunk to
Philip sober,
appeal from –**
658
philippic 932
Philistine 491, 876
philologist 492
philology 560
philomath 492
philomel 416

philosopher 492, 500
–'s stone
impossibility 471
perfect 650
remedy 662
wealth 803
philosophical
thoughtful 451
calm 826
philosophy
calmness 826
knowledge 490
Moral – 450
– of the Mind 450
philtre 993
phiz *face* 234
look 448
phlebotomy
ejection 297
remedy 662
Phlegethon 982
phlegm *viscid* 352
insensibility 823
phlegmatic
indifferent 866
phlogiston 382
pho! 497
Phœbus *sun* 318
luminary 423
phœnix
exception 83
reproduction 163
paragon 650
restoration 660
phonate 402
phonetic
sound 402
voice 580
speech 582
– *spelling* 561
phonics 402
phonograph 417, 418
phonography
sound 402
letter 561
writing 590
phonology 562
Phosphor 423
phosphorescence 420, 423
phosphorus 423
photo-engraving 558
photograph 17
photographer 556
photography 445
light 420
representation 554

PIT PLA PLA PLA

pitched battle 720
pitcher 191
pitchfork 272, 284
  rain −s 348
pitch-pipe 417
piteous 830
piteously *much* 31
pitfall 545, **667**
pith *gist* 5
  strength 159
  interior 221
  centre 222
  meaning 516
  important part
   642
pithless 158
pithy *meaning* 516
  concise 572
  vigorous 574
pitiable *bad* 649
  painful 830
  contemptible 930
pitied, to be − 828
pitiful
  unimportant 643
  bad 649
  disrepute 874
  pity 914
pitiless **914a**
  revengeful 919
pittance
  quantity 25
  dole 640
  allotment 786
  income 810
pitted 848
pituitous 352
pity 914
  express − 915
  what a −
  regret 833
  lament 839
  for −'s sake 914
pivot *junction* 43
  cause 153
  support 215
  axis 222, 312
pix *box* 191, 998
  assay 463
pixy 980
pizzicato 415
placable 918
placard 531
placate 723, 918
place
  circumstances 8
  order 58
  arrange 60
  term 71
  situation **182,** 183

locate 184
abode 189
office 625
rank 873
give − to 623
have − 1
in − 183
in − of 147
make a − for 184
out of − 185
take − 151
  − to one's credit
   805
  − itself 58
  − in order 60
  − upon record 551
  − under
  include 76
placebit, decies re-
  petita − 829
placebo 933
place-hunter 767
placeman 758
placet 488, 741
placid 826
placket 260
plagiarism
  imitation 19
  borrowing 788
  theft 791
plagiarist 792
Plagiary, Sir
  Fretful − 901
plagiedral 217
plague *disease* 655
  pain 828
  worry 830
plague-spot 657
plaguy 704, 830
plaid *shawl* 225
  variegation 440
plaidoyer 476
plain
  horizontal 213
  country **344**
  obvious 446
  meaning 518
  manifest 525
  style 576
  artless 703
  ugly 846
  simple 849
speak −ly 576
tell one −ly 527
  − English 576
  − dealing 543
  − interpretation
   522
  − question 461
  − sailing 705
  − sense 498

− speaking 525,
  703
 − terms
  intelligible 518
  interpreted 522
  language 576
 − truth 494
 − words 703
plainness **576**
plainsong 990
plain-spoken 525,
  703
plaint 411, 839
plaintiff 938
plaintive 839
plaisance
  [*see* pleasance]
plaisanterie 842
plaister 223
plait 219, 258
plan *itinerary* 266
  information 527
  representation
   554
  scheme **626**
  according to − 82
planchette 992
plane *horizontal* 213
  flat 251
  smooth 255
  fly 267
  aeroplane 273
  soar 305
  inclined − 633
planet *world* 318
  luminary 423
  fate 601
planet-struck
  adversity 735
  wonder 870
planimeter 466
planish 255
plank *board* 204
  programme 626
  path 627
  safety 666
plant *place* 184
  insert 300
  vegetable 367
  agriculture 371
  trick 545
  tools 633
  property 780
  − a battery 716
  − a dagger in the
   breast 830
  − oneself 184
  − a thorn in the
   side 830
plantation
  location 184

agriculture **371**
estate 780
planter 188
planter ses choux,
  aller − 893
plaque 204
plash *lake* 343
  stream 348
  sound 405, **408**
plashy 345
plasm 22
plasma 847
plasmic 240
plaster *cement* **45**
  covering 223
  remedy 662
  − up *repair* 660
plastered 959
plastic *alterable* **149**
  form 240
  soft 324
  − arts 557
plastron 717
plat *weave* 219
  ground 344
plate *dish* 191
  layer 204
  covering 223
  flat 251
  food 298
  engraving **558**
  − layer 690
  − printing **558,**
   591
plateau 213, 344
plated 545
platform
  horizontal 213
  support 215
  stage 542
  scheme 626
  arena 728
  − *orator* 582
platinum blond 430
platitude 517, 843
Platonic
  contemplative 451
  inexcitable 826
  chaste 960
  − bodies 244
Platonism 451
platoon 726
  − fire 716
platter 191
  layer 204
  flat 251
clean the outside
  of the − 544
plaudit 931
plausible
  probable **472**

[594]

sophistical 477
false 544
approbation 931
flattery 933
vindication 937
play *operation* 170
influence 175
scope 180
oscillation 314
music 416
drama 599
use 677
action 680
freedom 748
amusement 840
at – 840
bring into – 677
full – 175
full of – 836
in – 842
– along with 709
– one's best card
  686, 698
– of colours 440
– at cross pur-
  poses 59, 523
– a deep game 702
– the deuce 825
– the devil 907
– one false
  disappoint 509
  falsehood 544
  deception 545
– fast and loose
  falsehood 544
  irresolute 605
  tergiversation 607
  caprice 608
– on the feelings
  824
– first fiddle 642,
  873
– the fool
  folly 499
  clumsy 699
  amusement 840
  ridiculous 853
  ridicule 856
– for *chance* 621
– a game
  pursue 622
  conduct 692
  pastime 840
– the game 939
– into the hands
  of 709
– havoc 659
– hide and seek
  528, 623
– a joke 853
give – to the im-

agination 515
– of light 420
– the monkey 499
– off 545
– a part
  false 544
  drama 599
  action 680
– one's part 625,
  692
– second fiddle
  34, 749
– one a trick 509,
  545
– tricks with 699,
  702
– truant 623
– upon 545, 856
– with 460
– upon words
  misinterpret 523
  neology 563
  wit 842
play-boy 818
play-day 840
played out
  end 67
  fatigue 688
  completion 729
  failure 732
player
  musician 416
  actor 599
– *piano* 417
playfellow 890
playful 836
– *imagination* 515
playground 728,
  840
play-house 599
playmate 890
playsome 836
plaything
  trifle 643
  toy 840
  make a – of 749
playwright 599
plea
  defence 462
  argument 476
  excuse 617
  vindication 937
  lawsuit 969
plead *argue* 467
  plea 617
  beg 765
– one's cause 937
– guilty 950
pleader *lawyer* 968
pleading, special –
  477

pleadings 969
pleasance 189, 840
pleasant
  agreeable 829
  amusing 840
  witty 842
  make things –
  deceive 545
  induce 615
  please 829
  flatter 933
pleasantry 840, 842
please 829
  as you – 743
  do what one –s
  748
  if you –
  obedience 743
  consent 762
  request 765
– oneself 943
pleasurableness
  829
pleasure
  physical – 377
  will 600
  moral – 827
  dissipation 954
  at – 600
  at one's – 737
  during – 108a
  give – 829
  man of – 954a
  make a toil of –
  682
  take one's – 840
  will and – 600
  with –
  willingly 602
pleasure-giving 829
pleasure-ground
  demesne 189
  amusement 840
pleat 258
plebeian 851, 876
plébiscite 480, 609
plectrum 417
plectuntur Achivi
  739
pledge *affirmation*
  535
  promise 768
  security 771
  borrow 788
  drink to 883, 894
  hold in – 771
  take the – 958
– oneself 768
– one's word 768
pledget 263, 662
Pleiades 72, 318

plenary 31, 52
plenipotent 157
plenipotentiary
  consignee 758
  deputy 759
plentitude 639
  in the – of power
  159
plenty
  multitude 102
  sufficient 639
– to do 682
plenum *substance* 3
  matter 316
pleonasm
  repetition 104
  diffuseness 573
  redundance 641
plerophory 484
plethora 641
plexal 219
plexus 219
pliable 324
pliant *soft* 324
  irresolute 605
  facile 705
  servile 886
plicature 258
pliers 301, 781
plight *state* 7
  promise 768
  security 771
  evil – 735
– one's faith 902
– one's troth 768,
  902
plighted love 897,
  902
Plimsoll mark 466
plinth 211, 215
plod *journey* 266
  slow 275
  persevere 604a
  work 682
– along 143
plodding 604a, 682
  dull 843
plot – *of ground* 181
  plain 344
  story 594
  plan 626
  realty 780
  the – thickens
  assemblage 72
plough *furrow* 259
  agriculture 371
– the ground 673
– in 228
– the waves 267
– one's way 266
ploughboy

commonalty 876
ploughman 371
ploughshare 253
pluck *cheat* 545
  resolution 604
  persevere 604a
  reject 610
  take 789
  steal 791
  courage 861
  – up courage 861
  – a crow with 932
  – out 301
plug 261, 263
  – along 143
plum *number* 98
  sweet 396
  money 800
plumage 256
plumb *vertical* 212
  close 261
  measure 466
plumber 690
plumb-line 212
plum-coloured 437
plume *feather* 256
  ornament 847
  borrowed –s 545
  – oneself 878
plume
  coup de – 590
  nom de – 565
plumigerous 256
plummet 208, 212
plumose 256
plump
  instantaneous 113
  fat 192
  plunge 310
  unexpected 508
  – down 306
  – upon 292
plumper
  expansion 194
  vote 609
plunder 791, 793
plunderer 792
plunge
  revolution 146
  insert 300
  dive 306, **310**
  immerse 337
  hurry 684
  – into difficulties 704
  – into dissipation 954
  – headlong 684
  – into 676
  – in medias res 576, 604

– into sorrow 830
plunged
  – in debt 806
  – in grief 828
plunger 621
plurality **100**
plus 37
  plus fours 225
plush 256
Pluto 979, 982
  realms of – 982
Plutocracy 803
plutonic 382
Plutus 803
pluvial 348
ply *layer* 204
  fold 258
  use 677
  exert 686
  request 765
  – one's task 680
  – one's trade 625
  – a trade 794
Plymouth Brother 984
p.m. 114, 126
pneumatics 334, 338
pneumatology 450
pneumatoscopic 317
poach 791, 964
poacher 792
poachy 345
pock 250
pocket *place* 184
  pouch 191
  diminutive 193
  receive 785
  take 789
  money 800
  treasury 802
  brook 826
  button up one's – 808
  out of – 776, 806
  touch the – 800
  – the affront 725, 918
pocket-book 551
pocket-handker-chief 225
pocket-money 800
pocket-pistol
  bottle 191
pococurante 823, 866
pocula, inter – 959
pod 191, 223
podestà 967
podgy 201

poem 597
  book of –s 593
pœnitentiæ, locus –
  pity 914
  forgive 918
  vindicate 937
  repent 950
poesy 597
poet 597
poetaster 597, 855
poetic *style* 574
poetic frenzy 515
poetry **597**
pogrom 361
poignancy
  physical energy 171
  pain 378
  pungency 392
  feeling 821
point *condition* 8
  degree 26
  small 32
  end 67
  term 71
  poignancy 171
  no magnitude 180a
  place 182
  speck 193
  sharp 253
  topic 454
  mark 550
  vigour 574
  intention 620
  wit 842
  punctilio 939
  at the – of 197
  come to the –
  special 79
  attention 457
  reasoning 476
  plain language 576
  culminating – 210
  disputed – 713
  from all –s 180
  full of – 574
  give –s to 27
  go straight to the – 278
  in – *relative* 9
  agreeing 23
  conformable 82
  knotty – 704
  make a – of
  resolution 604
  contention 720
  compulsion 744
  conditions 770
  due 924

honour 939
  nice – 697
  on the – of 111, 121
  to the – 572, 642
  – an antithesis 578
  – at *direction* 278
  direct attention 457
  intend 620
  discourtesy 895
  disrespect 929
  censure 932
  – of attack 716
  at the – of the bayonet 173
  – of the compass 278
  – of convergence 74
  – of death 360
  – in dispute 461
  – of etiquette 852
  in – of fact 1
  – the finger of scorn 930
  – of honour 939
  – of land 250
  – a moral 537
  – out 155, 457, 527
  – to – race 720
  at the – of the sword
  violence 173
  severity 739
  compulsion 744
  – to *attribute* 155
  direction 278
  probable 472
  predict 511
  mean 516
  – of view 441, 448
point d'appui 215
point-blank
  direct 278
  plain language 576
  refusal 764
point-champain 874
pointed
  great 31
  sharp 253
  affirmation 535
  marked 550
  concise 572
  language 574
pointedly
  intention 620
pointer *dog* 366
  indicator 550

pointless 843
poise 27, 319, 852
  mental – 498
poison 659, 663
  – gas 722, 727
poisoned 655
  commend the –
    chalice 544
poisonous 657, 665
poke
  pocket 191
  pig in a –
  uncertain 475
  chance 621
  dawdle 683
  rash 863
  – at 276, 716
  – the fire 384
  – fun at 856
  – one's nose in
    682
  – out *project* 250
poker 386
  cards 840
polacca 273
polacre 273
polar 210
  cold 383
  – co-ordinates 466
polarization 420
polariscope 445
polarity
  duality 89
  counteraction 179
  contraposition
    237
pole *measure of*
  length 200
  tall 206
  summit 210
  axis 222
  punt 267
  rotation 312
  greasy – 840
  opposite –s 237
  from – to pole 180
pole-axe 727
polecat 401
pole-star 550, 693
polemic
  discussion 476
  discord 713
  contention 720
  combatant 726
polemoscope 445
police 965
  – court 966
  – magistrate 967
policeman 664, 965
policy 626, 692
polish *smooth* 255

rub 331
furbish 658
beauty 845
ornament 847
taste 850
politeness 894
– off *finish* 729
Polish bank 840
polished
  – *language* 578
  fashionable 852
  polite 894
polisson 949
polite 894
  offensive to ears –
    579
  – literature 560
  – society 852
politic *wise* 498
  cunning 702
  cautious 864
  body –
  mankind 372
  government 737
political economy
  692
politician
  director 694
  proficient 700
politics 702
polity *conduct* 692
  authority 737
  duty 926
polka 840
poll 85, 609
  – tax 812
pollard 193, 201
  tree 367
Poll-parrot 584
pollute *soil* 653
  corrupt 659
  disgrace 874
pollution
  disease 655
  vice 945
Pollyanna 858
polo 840
polonaise 840
poltroon 862
polyandry 903
polychord 417
polychromatic 428,
  440
polychrome 440,
  556
polygamy 903
polygastric 191
polyglot 522, 560
polygon
  buildings 189
  figure 244

polygraphy 590
polylogy 573
polymorphic 81
polyphonism 580
polypus 250
polyscope 445
polysyllable 561
polytheism 984
pomade 356
pomatum 356
pommel
  support 215
  round 249
  beat 972
Pomona 369
pomp 882
pom-pom 727
pomposity 882
pompous
  language 577
poncho 225
pond 343, 636
  fish – 370
ponder 451
ponderable 316,
  319
ponderation 319,
  480
ponderous 319
  - *style* 574, 579
  dull 843
pondus fumo, dare
  – 481
poniard 727
pons asinorum 519,
  704
pontifical 995
pontificals 999
pontificate 995
pontiff 996
pontoon
  vehicle 272
  boat 273
  way 627
pony 271
poodle 366
pooh, pooh!
  unimportance 643
  contempt 930
pool *lake* 343
  combination 709
  prize 775
  billiards 840
poop 235
poor *weak* 160
  - *reasoning* 477
  - *style* 575
  insufficient 640
  trifling 643
  indigent 804
  unhappy 828

cut a – figure **874**
  – hand 701
  – head 499
  – house 189
  – man 804
  – in spirit 881
  – stick 501
  – thing 914
poorly 160, 655
  – off 804
poor-spirited 862
pop *noise* 406
  unexpected 508
  – at 716
  – in *ingress* 294
  insertion 300
  – off *die* 360
  – a question 461
  – the question
  request 765
  endearment 902
  – upon *arrive* 29➤
  discover 480a
Pope
  infallibility 474
  priest 996
Popedom 995
Pope Joan 840
Popery 984
pop-gun *trifle* 643
popinjay 854
poplar *tall* 206
poppy *sedative* **174**
populace 876
popular
  in demand 865
  celebrated 873
  favourite 897
  approved 931
  – opinion 488
popularis, aura –
  873
popularize
  render intelligible
    518
  facilitate 705
  make pleasant
    829
populate 184
population 188, **372**
populi, vox –
  publication 531
  election 609
  authority 737
populous
  crowded 72
  multitude 102
  presence 186
porcelain
  baked 384
  sculpture 557

safety 664
preparation 673
precede
  superior 33
  - *in order* 62
  - *in time* 116
  - *in motion* 280
precedence 873
precedent
  [*see* precede]
  prototype 22
  precursor 64
  habit 613
  legal decision 969
  follow –s 82
precentor 694, 996
precept *adage* 496
  maxim **697**
  order 741
  permit 760
preceptor 540
precession 62, **280**
précieuse ridicule
  855
precinct *region* 181
  place 182
  environs 227
  boundary 233
precious *great* 31
  excellent 648
  valuable 814
  beloved 897
  – metals 800
  – stone 648, 847
precipice
  vertical 212
  slope 217
  dangerous 667
  on the verge of
  a – 665
precipitancy 684,
  863
precipitate
  early 132
  sink 308
  consolidate 321
  refuse 653
  haste 684
  rash 863
  – oneself 306
precipitous 217
précis 596
precise *exact* 494
preciosity 578
precisely
  literally 19
  assent 488
precisianism
  affectation 855
  heterodoxy 984
  over-religious 988

preclude 55, **706**
precocious
  early 132
  immature 674
  pert 885
  rude 895
precognition
  forethought 490
  knowledge 510
preconceived idea
  481
preconception 481
preconcert 611, 626
preconcertation 673
precursor
  - *in order* 62, **64**
  - *in time* 116
  predict 511
predatory 789, 791
predecessor 64
predeliberation
  510, 611
predella 215
predesigned 611
predestination
  fate 152
  necessity 601
  predetermination
  611
  Deity 976
predetermination
  611
predial
  land 342
  agriculture 371
  manorial 780
predicament 8, 75
predicate
  affirm 535
  preach 998
prediction **511**
predilection
  bias 481
  affection 820
  desire 865
predispose 615, 673
predisposed
  willing 602
predisposition 176,
  820
predominant 175,
  737
predominate 33
pre-eminent 33, 873
pre-emption 795
preen 847
pre-engage 132
pre-engagement
  768
pre-establish 626
pre-examine 461

pre-exist 1, 116
preface 62, 64
prefect 745, 759
prefecture 737
prefer *choose* 609
  – a claim 969
  – a petition 765
preference 62
preferment
  improvement 658
  ecclesiastical -
  995
prefigure 511
prefix 62, 64
  letter 561
pre-glacial 124
pregnable 158
pregnant
  producing 161
  productive 168
  predicting 511
  - *style* 572
  important 642
  – with meaning
  516
prehensile 789
prehension 789
pre-historic 124
pre-instruct 537
prejudge 481
prejudicate 481
prejudice
  misjudge 481
  evil 619
  detriment 659
prejudicial 481, 649
prelacy 995
prelate 996
prelation 609
prelection 537, 582
prelector 540
preliminaries:
  settle – 673
  – of peace 723
preliminary 62, 64
prelude 62, 64
  beginning 66
  music 415
premature 132, 674
premeditate 611,
  620
prémices 154
premier 694, 759
  – pas 66
premiership 693
premise *prefix* 62
  precede 116
  announce 511
premises
  precursor 64
  prior 116

ground 182
evidence 467
logic 476
premium
  debt 806
  receipt 810
  reward 973
  at a – 814
premonish 668
premonitory 511,
  668
Premonstratensian
  996
premonstration
  appearance 448
  prediction 511
  manifestation 525
premunire 742, 974
prendre la balle au
  bond 134
prenotion
  misjudgment 481
  foresight 510
prensation 789
prentice 541
prenticeship 539
preoccupancy
  possession 777
preoccupation
  inattention 458
preoption 609
preordain 152, 601
preparation **673**
  music 413
  instruction 537
  in – 730
  in course of – 626
preparatory
  preceding 62
prepare the way
  facilitate 705
prepared *expectant*
  507
  ready 698
preparing
  destined 152
prepense
  spontaneous **600**
  predetermined
  611
  intended 620
  malice – 907
prepollence 157
preponderance
  superiority 33
  influence 175
  dominance 737
prepossessed
  obstinate 606

prepossessing 829
prepossession
  prejudice 481
  possession 777
preposterous
  great 31
  absurd 497
  exaggerated 549
  ridiculous 853
  undue 925
prepotency 157
pre-Raphaelite 122, 124, 556
pre-require 630
pre-resolve 611
prerogative 737, 924
presage 511, 512
presbyopia 443
presbyter 996
Presbyterian 984
presbytery 995, 996, 1000
prescience 510
prescious 511
prescribe *direct* 693
  advice 695
  order 741
  entitle 924
  enjoin 926
prescript 697, 741
prescription
  remedy 662
prescriptive *old* 124
  unchanged 141
  habitual 613
  due 924
presence
  in space **186**
  appearance 448
  breeding 894
  in the – of
  near 197
  real – 998
  saving one's – 928
  – of God 981
  – of mind 826, 864
presence-chamber 191
present
  - *in time* 118
  - *in space* 186
  offer 763
  give 784
  church prefer-ment 995
  at – 118
  these –s 590, 592
  – arms 894, 928
  – a bold front 861

– a front 719
– itself *event* 151
  visible 446
  thought 451
– oneself
  presence 186
  offer 763
  courtesy 894
– to the mind 457, 505
– time **118**
  instant 113
– to the view 448
presentable 852
presentation 883, 894
presentiment
  instinct 477
  prejudgment 481
  foresight 510
presently 132
presentment
  information 527
  law proceeding 969
preservation
  continuance 141
  conservation **670**
  Divine attributes 976
preserve *sweets* 396
preserver 664
preshow 511
preside 693, 737
presidency 737
president 694, 745
press *crowd* 72
  closet 191
  weight 319
  public - 531
  printing 591
  book 593
  move 615
  compel 744
  offer 763
  solicit 765
  go to – 591
  under – of 744
  writer for the – 593
  – of business 682
  – one hard 716
  – in 300
  – on *course* 109
  progression 282
  haste 684
  – into the service 677, 707
  – out 301
press-agent 599
pressed: hard – 704

– for time 684
press-gang 965
pressing *need* 630
  urgent 642
pressure *power* 157
  influence 175
  weight 319
  urgency 642
  exertion 686
  adversity 735
  centre of – 222
  high – 824
  work under – 684
Prester John 515
prestidigitation 545
prestidigitator 548
prestige *bias* 481
  authority 737
  fascination 865
  fame 873
prestigiation 545
prestissimo 415
presto
  instantly 113
  music 415
prestriction 442
presumable 472
presume
  misjudge 481
  believe 484
  suppose 514
  hope 858
  pride 878
presumption
  [see presume]
  probability 472
  expectation 507
  rashness 863
  arrogance 885
  unlawfulness 925
presumptive
  probable 472
  supposed 514
  due 924
  heir – 779
  – evidence
  evidence 467
  probability 472
presumptuous 885
presuppose
  misjudge 481
  suppose 514
presurmise 510, 514
pretence
  imitation 19
  falsehood 544
  untruth 546
  excuse 617
  ostentation 882
  boast 884

pretend *assert* 535
  simulate 544, 546
pretended 545
pretender
  deceiver 548
  braggart 884
  unentitled 925
pretending 544
pretension
  ornament 577
  affectation 855
  due 924
pretentious
  affected 855
  vain 880
  ostentatious 882
  boasting 884
  undue 925
preterite 122
preterition **122**
preterlapsed 122
pretermit 460
preternatural 83
preterperfect 122
pretext 546, 617
pretty
  much 31
  imperfectly 651
  beautiful 845
  – fellow 501
  – good 651
  – kettle of fish, pass &c. 59, **704**
  – well *much* 31
  little 32
  trifling 643
preux chevalier 939
prevail *exist* 1
  superior 33
  general 78
  influence 175
  habit 613
  succeed 731
  – upon 615
prevailing 78
  – taste 852
prevalence
  [see prevail]
prevaricate 544
prévenance 894
prevenient 62, 132
prevention
  prejudice 481
  hindrance 706
  – of waste 817
preventive 55
preventorium 656
previous 116
  move the – question 624
  not within –

experience 137
prevision 510
pre-war 116
prewarn 668
prey *food* 298
  quarry 620
  booty 793
  victim 732, 828
fall a – to
  be defeated 732
  subjection 749
  – to grief 828
  – to melancholy
    837
  – on the mind
  excite 824
  regret 833
  fear 860
  – on the spirits
    837
price
  consideration 147
  value 648
  money **812**
  reward 973
  at any – 604*a*
  beyond – 814
  cheap at the – 815
  of great –
  good 648
  dear 814
  have one's – 812
price-current 812
priceless
  valueless 645
  dear 814
prick *sharp* 253
  hole 260
  sting 378
  sensation of touch
    380
  incite 615
  mental suffering
    830
  kick against the –s
  useless 645
  resistance 719
  – up one's ears
  hear 418
  curiosity 455
  attention 457
  expect 707
prickle 253, 380
pride
  ornament 847
  loftiness **878**
  take a – in 878
prie-dieu 215
priest 996
priestcraft 995
priesthood 995, 996

priest-ridden 988,
  995
prig *steal* 791
  puppy 854
  affected 855
  blusterer 887
priggish 855, 880
prim *affected* 855
  fastidious 868
  proud 878
prima: – donna
  actress 599
  important 642
  proficient 700
  – facie *sight* 441
  appearance 448
  probable 472
  - *meaning* 516
  manifest 525
primacy
  superiority 33
  celebrity 873
  church 995
primary
  original 20
  cause 153
  important 642
  – colour 428
  – education 537
primarily 66
primate 996
primates 875
prime
  primeval 124
  early 132
  teach 537
  important 642
  excellent 648
  prepare 673
  in one's – 131
  in the – of man-
    hood 159
  – cost *price* 812
  cheap 815
  – of life *youth* 127
  adolescence 131
  – and load 673
  – minister 694
  – of the morning
    125
  – mover 153
  – number 84
prime constituent 1
primed
  skilled 698
  tipsy 959
primer 542
primeval 124
  – forest 367
primigenous 124
primitive 124, 153

– colour 428
primogenial 66
primogeniture
  old 124
  age 128
  posterity 167
primordial 20, 124,
  153
primordinate 124
primrose-coloured
  436
primum:
  – mobile 153, 615
primus inter pares
  33
prince
  perfection 650
  master 745
  nobility 875
  – of darkness 978
princely
  authoritative 737
  liberal 816
  famous 873
  noble 875
  generous 942
princeps
  facile – 33
princess 745, 875
principal
  important 642
  director 694
  – part 31, 50
principality 181,
  780
principally 33
principia 66, 496
principiis obstare
  673
principle
  intrinsic 5
  rule 80
  cause 153
  element 316
  idea 453
  reasoning 476
  tenet 484
  maxim 496
  motive 615
  probity 939
  on – 615
  want of – 945
principled, high-
  939
prink 847, 882
print *copy* 21
  mark 550
  engraving 558
  letter-press 591
  out of – 552
printer 591

printing 531, **591**
  – telegraph 553
prior
  - *in order* 62
  - *in time* 116
  clergy 996
priori reasoning,
  a – 476
priority **116**, 234
priory 1000
Priscian's head,
  break – 568
prism
  angularity 244
  optical 445
  see through a –
    443
prismatic
  colour 428
  variegated 440
prison **752**
  cast into – 751
  in – 754
prisoner **754**, 938
  take – 751, 789
prison-house
  secrets of the –
    529, 533
pristine 20, 122
prithee 765
prittle-prattle 588
private *special* 79
  hidden 528
  secluded 893
  to gain some –
    ends 943
  in – 528
  keep – 881
  talk to in – **586**,
    588
  – road 627
  – soldier 726
privateer 726, **792**
privateering 791
privately 881
privation 776, 804
privative 789
privilege
  freedom 748
  permission 760
  exemption 777*a*
  due 924
privity 490
privy *hidden* 528
  latrines 653
  – to 490
Privy Council 696
prize *good* 618
  palm 733
  gain 775
  booty 793

agreement 23
elegance 578
expedience 646
fashion 852
right 922
duty 926
proprio motu 600
props 599
propter hoc 155
propugn
　resist 717
　vindicate 937
propulsion **284**
propylon 66
prore 234
prorogue 133
proruption 295
prosaic *usual* 82
　- *style* 575, 576
　dull 843
prosaism *prose* 598
proscenium
　front 234
　theatre 599
proscribe
　interdict 761
　banish 893
　curse 908
　condemn 971
prose
　diffuse style 573
　prate 584
　not verse **598**
　- run mad 577, 597
　- *writer* 598
prosecute
　pursue 622
　act 680
　accuse 938
　arraign 969
　- an inquiry 461
prosecutor 938
proselyte
　convert 144, 607
　learner 541
proselytism 537
proser 841
prosody 597
prosopopœia 521
prospect
　futurity 121
　view 448
　probability 472
　expectation 507
　*landscape paint-
　　ing* 556
　good - 858
　in - *intended* 620
prospective 121
prospector 463
prospectus *list* 86

foresight 510
compendium 596
scheme 626
prosper 618
prosperity **734**
prospicience 510
prosternation
　dejection 837
　servility 886
prostitute
　corrupt 659
　misuse 679
　impure 961
　courtesan 962
prostrate
　powerless 158
　destroyed 162
　low 207
　horizontal 213
　depress 308
　laid up 655
　exhausted 688
　dejected 837
　servile 886
　fall - 306
　- oneself
　　servile 886
　　obeisance 928
　　worship 990, 991
prostration
　[see prostrate]
　submission 725
　pain 828
prosy 841, 843
prosyllogism 476
protagonist
　actor 599
　proficient 700
protasis
　precursor 64
　beginning 66
　maxim 496
protean 149
protect *safe* 664
protected cruiser
　726
protective 717
protection
　influence 175
　defence 717
　restrain 751
protector 664, 717
　master 745
　keeper 753
protectorate 737,
　780
protégé *servant* 746
　friend 890
proteiform 149
protein 298
　semiliquid 352

organic 357
protervity 901
protest *dissent* 489
　assert 535
　deny 536
　refuse 764
　deprecate 766
　not observe 773
　not pay 808
　counter - 468
　enter a - 766
　under - 603, 744
　- against 708, 932
protestant 489, 764
Protestant 984
protested bills 808
Proteus 149
prothesis 1000
prothonotary 553
protocol *scheme* 626
　compact 769
protogram 572
protoplasm
　prototype 22
　material 316
　organization 357
protoplast 22
prototype **22**
　prediction 511
prototypal 20
protozoon 366
protract *time* 110
　late 133
　lengthen 200
　diffuse style 573
protreptical 615
protrude 250
protuberance 250
protypify 511
proud 873, 878
　- flesh 250
prove
　arithmetic 85
　turn out 151
　try 463
　demonstrate 478
　affect 821
　- one's case
　　vindication 937
　- true 494
provender 298, 637
proverb 496
proverbe *acting* 599
proverbial 490
provide
　furnish 637
　- against
　　prepare 673
　- against a rainy
　　day 817
provided

conditionally 8
qualification 469
supposition 514
well - 639
- for 803
providence
　foresight 510
　preparation 673
　*divine govern-
　　ment* 976
Providence 976
special - 711
waiter on - 683,
　831
provident
　careful 459
　wise 498
　prepared 673
providential
　opportune 134
　fortunate 734
province
　department 75
　region 181
　abode 189
　office 625
provincial
　[see province]
　prejudiced 481
　vulgar 851
provincialism
　neology 563
provision *food* 298
　supply **637**
　preparation 673
　wealth 803
　- merchant 637
provisional
　uncertain 475
　circumstances 8
　temporary 111
　preparing 673
provisions
　conditions 770
proviso 469, 770
provisory 111
provoke *cause* **153**
　incite 615
　excite 824
　vex 830
　anger 900
　- desire 865
　- hatred 898
provoquant 824
provost *master* **745**
　deputy 759
prow 234
prowess 861
prowl *walk* 266
　lurk 528
　- after 622

proximate
next 63
near 197
– *cause* 153
proximity *near* 197
adjacent 199
proximo 121
proximus ardet
danger 665, 667
proxy 634, 759
prude *affected* 855
chaste 960
prudent
careful 459
wise 498
economical 817
cautious 864
prudery 855, 868
prudish 739
prune
take away 38
lop 201, 371
repair 658
prunes and prisms
855
prunello, leather
or – 643
prurience 865, 961
Prussian blue 438
Prussic acid 663
pry *look* 441
curiosity 455
inquire 461
– into the future
510
Prytaneum 931
psalm 415, 990
psalm-book 998
psalmody 415, 998
psalter 998
psaltery 417
psephomancy 511
pseudo 17, 545
pseudoblepsis 443
pseudonym 565
pseudo-revelation
986
pseudoscope 445
pshaw
trifling 643
excitement 825
psychiatry 662
psychical 450
psycho-analysis
662
psychological
moment 824
Psychology 450
Psychomancy 511
psycho-therapy 662
ptisan 632

ptomaine poisoning
663
puberty 127
pubescent 131
public, general –
372
make – 531
– enemy 891
– good 644
– opinion 488
– press 531
– school 542
– spirit 910
– welfare 910
publican 637
publication **531**
production 161
book 593
public-house 189
go to the – 959
publicist 593, 595,
968
publicity 531
publicly rumoured
532
publico, pro bono –
644, 910
publish 531
– the banns 765,
903
publisher 593
puce 433, 437
pucelage *youth* 127
celibacy 904
purity 960
Puck 980
play – 699
pucker *fold* 258
anger 900
in a – 824
pudder
disorder 59
pudding *food* 298
soft 324
pulpy 354
sweets 396
in – time 132
Pudding, Jack –
599
puddle 343
pudicity 960
pudor, proh –
874
puerile *boyish* 129
foolish 499
feeble 575
trifling 643
puerperal 161
puff *inflate* 194
wind 349
tartlet 396

exaggerate 482
advertisement 531
pant 688
boast 884
praise 931
flatter 933
– of smoke 330
– out 194
– up *vanity* 880
puffed up
exaggerated 482
pride 878
puffer 935
puffery 884
puffy 194
pug *short* 201
dog 366
pugilist 726
pugh! 643
pugilism 720
pugilist 726
pugilistic 720
pugnacity 720, 901
puisné
posterior 117
young 127
puissant 157, 159
puke 297
pukka 494
pulchritude 845
pulcinella 599, 844
pule *cry* 411, 412
weep 839
pull *superiority* 33
influence 175
row 267
draw 285
printing 591
a long and a
strong – 709
strong – 636
– the check string
142
– different ways
713
– down 162, 308
– about one's ears
308
– in 751
– an oar 680
– out 301
– to pieces
separate 44
destroy 162
censure 932
detract 934
– upon the purse
814
– by the sleeve
505
– the strings 631

– through 660,
707
– together 709
– towards 288
– up *stop* 142
rest 265
root out 301
reprimand 932
accuse 969
– the wires 693
pulled down 160,
688
pullet 129
pulley 633
Pullman car 272
pullulate
produce 161
multiply 168
grow 194
pulmonary 349
pulmotor 349
pulp 354
pulpiness **354**
pulpit *rostrum* **542**
church 1000
the – 996
pulsate
periodic 138
oscillate 314
agitate 315
pulsation
feeling 821
pulse [*see* pulsate]
vegetable 367
feel the –
inquire 461
test 463
pulsion 276
pultaceous 354
pulverize 330
destroy 162
dust 358
pulverulence **330**
pulvil 400
pummel
[*see* pommel]
pump *shoe* 225
water supply 348
inquire 461
– up 349
pump-room
house 189
remedy 662
pun *similarity* 17
absurdity 497
ambiguity 520
wit 563, 842
punce 276
punch *mould* 22
perforate 260
perforator 262

nag 271
strike 276
beverage 298
engrave 558
vigour 574
Punch *buffoon* 844
  – and Judy 599,
   840
punchbowl
  vessel 191
  hollow 252
  tippling 959
puncheon
  vessel 191
  perforator 262
punchinello 599
punctated 440
punctilio 852
punctilious
  exact 494
  observant 772
  ostentation 882
  scrupulous 939
puncto 882
punctual *early* 132
  periodical 138
  exact 494
  observance 772
  scrupulous 939
punctuation 567
puncture 260
pundit
  learned man 492,
   500
  lawyer 968
pungency
  physical energy
   171
  taste 392
pungent *taste* 392
  odour 398
  vigour 574
  feeling 821
  wit 842
Punica fides 940
punishment 972
punition 972
punk 962
punkah 349
punnet 191
punster 844
punt 267, 273
punter 621
puny 193
pup *infant* 129
  give birth 161
  dog 366
pupil 541
  – *of the eye* 441
pupilage *youth* 127
  learning 539

pupillari, in statu –
  541
puppet *little* 193
  dupe 547
  effigy 554
  auxiliary 711
  tool 746
  make a – of 737
  be the – of 749
puppet-show 599,
  840
puppy *dog* 366
  fop 854
  braggart 884
  blusterer 887
puppyism 855
pur: – *sang* 875
Purana 986
purblind 443, 481
purchase
  support 215
  acquisition 775
  buy **795**
purchase-money
  147
purchaser 795
purdah 374, 530
pure *simple* 42
  true 494
  truthful 543
  – *style* 576, 578
  clean 652
  artless 703
  – *taste* 850
  honourable 939
  virtuous 944
  innocent 946
  chaste 960
  devout 987, 990
  – *accent* 580
  – *colour* 428
  – and *simple* 42
purée 298
purely 31, 32
purgation
  cleansing 652
  atonement 952
purgative 652
purgatory
  suffering 828
  atonement 952
  hell 982
purge *cast out* 297
  clean 652
  atone 952
purification 998
purify 652, 658
puris naturalibus,
  in – 226
purist *style* 578
  affected 855

Pharisee 988
Puritan 984, 988
puritanical
  strict 739
  affected 855
  ascetic 955
purity 960
  [*see* pure]
purl *drink* 298
  stream 348
  faint sound 405
  music 416
purlieus 197, 227
purloin 791
purple
  violet **437**
  insignia 747
  – and fine linen
   377
purport 516, 600
purpose 620
  at cross –s 523
  infirm of – 605
  to little or no –
   645
  on – 620
  serve a – 644
  to some – 731
  tenacity of – 604*a*
purposeless 621
purpure 437
purr 412
purse 800, 802
  long – 803
  put into one's –
   785
  – up 195
purse-bearer 801
purse-proud 878
purser 801
purse strings:
  draw the – 808
  open the – 809
pursuant to 620
pursue *continue* 143
  follow 281
  aim 622
  – a course 680
  – an inquiry 461
  – the tenor of
   one's way 625,
   881
pursuer 622
pursuit 622
pursuivant 534
pursy 194
purulent 653
purvey 637
purview 620
pus 653
Puseyite 984

push *exigency* 8
  impel 276
  progress 282
  propel 284
  essay 675
  activity 682
  haste 684
  come to the – **704**
  – aside 460, 929
  – forward 682, **707**
  – from 289
  – to the last 133
  – on *haste* 684
  – out *eject* 297
pushing 282, 284,
  682
pusillanimity 862
puss 366
  play – in the
   corner 148
pussy-foot 528, **958**
pustule 250, 848
put *place* 184
  fool 501
  cards 840
  clown 876
  neatly – 578
  – across 484
  – about
   turn back 283
   go round 311
   publish 531
  – aside
   exclude 55
   inattention **458**
   neglect 460
   disuse 678
  – away
   - *thought* 452
   relinquish 782
   divorce 905
  – back
   turn back 283
   deteriorate 659
   restore 660
  – before 527
  – by 636
  – a case 82, 514
  – in commission
   755
  – a construction
   on 522
  – on the cuff 806
  – down
   destroy 162
   record 551
   conquer 731
   compel 744
   pay 807
   humiliate 874
  – an end to **67**

end 67
stop 142
destroy 162
- *oneself* 361
- in force
complete 729
compel 744
- forth
expand 194
suggest 514
publish 531
assert 535
- *a question* 461
- *strength* 686
- forward
suggest 514
publish 531
ostentation 882
one's hand to
676
the horses to 673
in [*see below*]
- to inconvenience
647
- a mark upon 457
- one's nose out of
joint 33
- off *late* 133
divest 226
depart 293
plea 617
- on *clothe* 225
deceive 544
hasten 684
affect 855
- out [*see below*]
- on paper 551
- over 484, 731
- a question 461
- right 660
- the saddle on
the right horse
155
- the seal to 729,
769
- to [*see below*]
- together *join* 43
combine 48
assemble 161
- one's trust in
484
- up [*see below*]
- upon 545, 649
put in *arrive* 292
insert 300
- an affidavit 535
- hand 676
- one's head 514
- mind 505
- motion 264
- order 60

- the place of 147
- one's pocket 785
- practice 692
- remembrance
505
- shape 60
- trim 60, 673
- the way of 470
- a word 582, 588
put out
destroy 162
outside 220
extinguish 385
darken 421
*distract the atten-
tion* 458
uncertain 475
difficult 704
discontent 832
- of countenance
874
oneself - of court
sophistry 477
bungling 699
- of gear 158
- of one's head
458
- of joint 61
- of one's misery
914
- to nurse 707
- of order 59
put to *attribute* 155
request 765
- the blush 879
- death 361
- the door 261
- it 704
- one's oath 768
- press 591
- the proof 463
- the question 830
- the rack 830
- rights 60
- sea 293
- shame 874
- silence 581
- the sword 361
- task 677
- use 677
- the vote 609
put up *assemble* 72
locate 184
store 636
- to auction 796
- for 865
- a petition } 765
- a prayer } 990
- for sale 796
- a shutter 424
- the sword 723

- to 615
- with 147, 826
putative
attributed 155
believed 484
supposed 514
putid 643
putrefy 653
putrescence 49
putrid 653
putsch 742
puttee 225
putter 683
putting the weight
840
putty 45
puzzle *uncertain*
475
conceal 528
enigma 533
- out 522
puzzled 475, 533
puzzle-headed 499
puzzling 519
pyæmia 655
pyjamas 225
Pylades and
Orestes 890
pylon 206
pyramid *heap* 72
height 206
point 253
pyramids
billiards 840
pyre 363
pyriform 249
pyrology 382
pyromaniac 384,
504, 913
pyromancy 511
pyrometer 389
pyrotechnics 423
pyrotechny 382
Pyrrhic victory 814
pyrrhonism 487,
989
Pythagorean 953
Pythia *oracle* 513
Python, -ess 513
pyx *vessel* 191, 998
temple 1000

Q

Q-boat 726
Q.C. 968
Q.E.D. 478
quack *cry* 412
imposter 548

quackery
falsehood 544
want of skill 699
affectation 855
quacksalver 548
quad 189
quadragesima 956
quadrangle
four-sided 95
precinct 182
house 189
angular 244
quadrant 244, 247
quadrate with 23
quadratic 95
quadrature
four 95
angle 244
quadrennial 95
quadrible 96
quadrifid 97
quadriga 95, 272
quadrilateral
sides 236
angles 244
quadrille 840
quadripartition 97
quadrisection 97
quadrivalent 95
quadroon 41
quadruped 366
quadruplet 95
quadruplex 96
quadruplication 96
quære 461
quaff 298
- the bitter cup
828
quaggy 345
quagmire
marsh 345
dirty 653
difficult 704
quail 860, 862
quaint *odd* 83
pretty 845
ridiculous 853
quake *oscillate* 314
shake 315
cold 383
fear 860
quakery 826, 855
Quakerism 984
qualification
[*see qualify*]
power 157
modification 469
skill 698
discount 813
qualify *change* 140
modify 469

Column 1 (QUI)

- upon the fretful
  porcupine 256
quilt *covering* 223
  variegated 440
quinary 98
quincunx 98
quinquarticular 99
quinquennium 108
quinquesection 99
quinquifid 99
quint 98
quintain 620, 840
quintal 319
quinteron 41
quintessence 5
quintet 98, 415
quintuple 98
quinze 840
quip
  amusement 840
  wit 842
  ridicule 856
  disrespect 929
quire *singers* 416
  paper 593
  church 1000
quirk
  sophistry 477
  misjudgment 481
  caprice 608
  amusement 840
  wit 842
quirt 975
quis custodiet istos
  custodes? 459
quit *depart* 293
  relinquish 624
  pay 807
  - claim 927*a*
  - one's hold 782
  - of 776, 782
  - scores 807
qui-tam 969
quite 52
  - another thing
    10, 18
  - the reverse 14
  - the thing 23
quits *equal* 27
  atonement 952
be - with
  retaliation 718
  pay 807
quittance
  security 771
  payment 807
  forgiveness 918
  atonement 952
  reward 973
quiver
  receptacle 191

[610]

Column 2 (RAB)

  oscillation 314
  agitation 315
  shiver 383
  store 636
  feeling 821
  fear 860
in a - 821, 824
  - with rage 900
qui-vive 669
on the - 459
Quixote, Don -
  504, 863
Quixotic 515, 863
Quixotism 825
quiz 856, 857
quizzical 853
quo animo 620
quoad minus 30
quod *prison* 752
in - 754
quodlibet
  inquiry 461
  sophism 477
  wit 842
quoits 840
quondam 122
quorum 696
quot homines tot
  sententiæ 489,
  713
quota
  quantity 25
  contingent 786
  expenditure 809
furnish its - 784
quotation
  imitation 19
  conformity 82
  price 812
  - marks 550
quote 82
  evidence 467
quoth 535, 582
quotidian 138
quotient 84
quotum 25

R

Ra 423, 979
R's, three - 537
rabbet 43
Rabbi 996
Rabbist 984
rabbit
  productive 168
rabble 72, 876
rabid *insane* 502
  emotion 821
  eager 865

Column 3 (RAC)

  angry 900
rabies 503
raccroc 156
race *relation* 11
  sequence 69
  kind 75
  lineage 166
  run 274
  stream 348
  conduit 350
  pungency 392
  course 622
  business 625
  haste 684
  career 692
  opposition 708
  contention 720
run a - 720
run in a - 680
run one's - 729
one's - is run 360
  - prejudice 481
race-course 728
racehorse
  horse 271
  swift 274
racing car 272
rack *receptacle* 191
  frame 215
  cloud 353
  physical pain 378
  purify 652
  moral pain 828
  torture 830
  punish 972
  *instrument of
    torture* 975
on the - 507
  - one's brains
    thought 451
    imagination 515
  -rent 810
go to - and ruin
  735
racket
  agitation 315
  loud 404
  roll 407
  scheme 626
  discord 713
racket-court 840
racketeer 913
racketeering 361,
  792
racketing 682, 840
rackets 840
rackety *loud* 404
raconteur 594
racy *strong* 171
  pungent 392
  - style 574

Column 4 (RAG)

  feeling 821
raddle *weave* 219
raddled *tipsy* 959
radiance *light* 420
  beauty 845
radiant
  diverging 291
  glorious 873
  - heat 420
radiate 73, 291
radiation 420
radiator 386
radical
  essential 5
  complete 52
  algebraic root 84
  cause 153
  important 642
  reformer 658
  party 712
  - change 146
  - cure 662
  - reform 658
radically 31
radication 613
radio 532
radio-active 171
radio-activity 420
radio-graph 421,
  554
radiogram
  wireless 532
  X-ray 554
radiometer 445
radiomicrometer
  389
radiophone 418
radio star 899
radiotelegraph 534
radiotelephone 534
radium 423
radius 200, 202
radix 153
radoter 499
radoteur 501
raff 653, 876
raffle 156
Raffles
  thief 792
raft 273
rafter 215
rag 32
  tease 830, 856,
    929
ragamuffin 876
rage *violence* 173
  influence 175
  excitement 824,
    825
  fashion 852
  desire 865

repeat 104
– one's efforts 686
redoubt 717
redoubtable 860
redound to
  conduce 176
– one's honour
  glory 873
  approbation 931
  honour 939
redress *restore* 660
  remedy 662
  reward 973
red-tape 694, 739
reduce *lessen* 36
– *in number* 103
  weaken 160
  contract 195
  shorten 201
  lower 308
  subdue 731
  discount 813
– to ashes 384
– to demonstra-
  tion 478
– to a mean 29
– to order 60
– to poverty 804
– to powder 330
– the speed 275
– in strength 160
– to subjection 749
– to *convert* 144
– to writing 551
reduced [*see* reduce]
  impoverished 804
– to the last ex-
  tremity 665
– to a skeleton 659
– to straits 704
**reductio ad absur-
  dum** 476, 479
reduction
  [*see* reduce]
  arithmetical 85
  conversion 144
  at a – 815
– of temperature
  385
redundance
  diffuseness 573
  too much **641**
redundancy 104
reduplication 19, 90
re-echo *imitate* 19
  repeat 104
  resonance 408
reechy 653
reed *weak* 160
  pan 590
  arrow 727

trust to a broken –
  699
– *instrument* 417
reef *slacken* 275
  shoal 346
  danger 667
take in a – 664
double – topsails
  664
reefer 269
reek *gas* 334
  vaporize 336
  liquid 337
  hot 382
  fester 653
reeking 339, 653
reel *rock* 314
  agitate 315, 851
  dance 840
– back *yield* 725
re-embody
  junction 43
  combination 48
re-enter 245
re-entrant angle
  244
re-establish 660
re-estate 660
refashion 163
refect
  strengthen 159
refection
  meal 298
  refreshment 689
  (*restoration* 660)
refectory 191
refer to *relate* 9
  include 76
  attribute 155
  cite 467
  allude 521
  take advice 695
referable 9, 155
referee
  judgment 480
  judge 967
reference
  [*see* refer]
referendary 967
referendum 480,
  609
  ad – 461, 605
referrible 9, 155
refine *clean* 652
– upon 658
refined *colour* 428
  fashionable 852
refinement
  discrimination
  465
  wisdom 498

elegance 578, 845
  improvement 658
  taste 850
  over– 477
refit 660
reflect *imitate* 19
  think 451
– dishonour 874
– light 420
– upon *censure* 932
reflecting 498
reflection 408, 453
  light 420
reflector *mirror* 445
reflex *copy* 21
  recoil 277
  regressive 283
reflexion 21, 277
refluence *recoil* 277
  regress 283
reflux *decrease* 36
  recoil 277
  regress 283
  current 348
refocillate
  strengthen 159
  refresh 689
reform *convert* 144
  improve 658
reformatory 542,
  752
reformer 658
refound 144
refraction
  deviation 279
  light 420
  fallacy of vision
  443
refractory
  obstinate 606
  difficult 704
  mutinous 742
  ill-tempered 901a
refrain *poetry* 597
  avoid 623
  do nothing 681
  temperate 953
– from laughter
  837
– from voting
  609a
  repetition 104
refresh
  strengthen 159
  cool 385
  refit 658
  restore 660
  recruit 689
  relieve 834
– the memory 505

refreshing 377, **829**
refreshment
  food 298
  recruiting **689**
  delight 827
refrigeration
  anæsthetic 376
  making cold **385**
refrigerator **387**
reft 44
refuge **666**
refugee 268, 623
refulgence 420
refund 807
refurbish 673
refusal **764**
  pre-emption 795
refuse *remains* 40
  useless 645
  not consent 764
– assent 489
– to associate with
  893
– to believe 487
– to hear 460
refute 479
refuted 495
regain 775
– breath 689
regal 737
regale *feast* 298
  physical pleasure
  377
  refresh 689
  pleasing 829
  amusement 840
regalia 747
regality 737
regard
  relation 9
  view 441
  attention 457
  judge 480
  credit 873
  love 897
  respect 928
  approbation 931
  have – to 457
  merit – 642
  pay – to
  believe 484
  honour 873
– as 484
regardful 457, 459
regardless 458, **823**
regards 894, 928
regatta 720, 840
regency 755
regenerate
  reproduce 163
  restore 660

piety 987
regeneration
  divine function
  976
  baptismal – 998
regent 745, 759
regicide 361
régime
  circumstances 8
  conduct 692
  authority 737
  ancien – 875
regimen *diet* 298
  remedy 662
  conduct 692
regime: 72, 726
regimentals 225
region 181
register
  arrange 60
  list 86
  chronicle 114
  record 551, 553
registrar 553
registration 551
registry 114
règle: en – 924
regnant 175, 737
regni, anno – 106
regorge 790
regrade 283
regrate 777
regrater 797
regression 283
regret 833, 950
  express – 952
regretted, to be –
  833
reguerdon 973
regular
  uniform 16
  complete 52
  order 58
  arrangement 60
  rule 80
  conformity 82
  periodic 138
  symmetric 242
  habitual 613
  by – intervals 58
  – return 138
regulars 726
regulate
  adjust 23
  arrange 60
  direct 693
regulated by
  conformity 82
regulation 697, 963
regurgitate
  return 283

flow 348
  restore 790
rehabilitate 660,
  790
rehearse
  repeat 104
  try 463
  describe 594
  drama 599
  prepare 673
Reichsrath 696
reign 175, 737
  – of terror 739, 860
reimburse 790, 807
rein 752
  – in 275, 751
reincarnation 163
reindeer 271
re infectâ 304, 681
reinforce
  strengthen 159
  restore 660
  aid 707
reinforced concrete
  635
reinforcement
  addition 37
  adjunct 39
  materials 635
  provision 637
  aid 707
reinless 738
reins [*see* rein]
  direction 693
  give the – to
  facilitate 705
  lax 738
  permit 760
  hold the – 693
  take the – 737
  give – to the im-
  agination 515
reinstall 660
reinstate 660, 790
reinvest 790
reinvigorate 658,
  689
Reis Effendi 694
reiterate 104
reject
  exclude 55
  eject 297
  refuse 764
rejected
  hateful 898
rejection 610
rejoice *exult* 838
  amuse 840
  – the heart
  gratify 829
  cheer 836

– in 827
– in the name of
  564
rejoicing 838
rejoin *assemble* 72
  arrive 292
rejoinder
  answer 462
  law pleadings 969
rejuvenescence 660
rekindle
  ignite 384
  excite 824
relapse
  turn back 145,
  283
  fall back 661
relate *narrate* 594
  – to *refer* 9
related *kin* 11
relation 9
  kin 11
  narrative 594
relationship 9
relative 11, 464
  – position
relativity 9
relator
  accuser 938
relax *loose* 47
  weaken 160
  moderate 174
  slacken speed 275
  soften 324
  inactive 683
  repose 687
  misrule 738
  liberate 750
  relent 914
  – one's efforts 681
  – the mind 452
relaxation
  [*see* relax]
  amusement 840
  dereliction 927
relaxed *weak* 160
relay 635, 636
release *death* 360
  deliverance 672
  liberate 750
  exempt 760
  from engagement
  768a
  security 771
  restore 790
  repay 807
  forgive 918
  exempt 927*a*
  discharge 970
  deed of – 923
relegate *banish* 55

transfer 270
  remove 297
relent *moderate* **174**
  soften 324
  pity 914
relentless
  resolute 604
  severe 739
  wrathful 900
  malevolent 907
  revenge 919
  impenitent 951
relessee
  possessor 779
  receiver 785
relevancy 9, 23
relevé 298
reliable 474
reliance
  confidence 484
  hope 858
relic *remainder* 40
  reminiscence 505
  token 551
relics *corpse* 362
  sacred 998
relict 40, 905
relief
  prominence 250
  aid 707
  comfort **834**
  bas – 250, 557
  in strong – 446,
  525
relieve *improve* **658**
  aid 707
  comfort 834
relievo 250, 557
religieuse 996
religion 983, 987
  under the mask
  of – 988
religionist 988
religious
  honourable 939
  theological 983
  pious 987
  over– 955
  – education 537
  – persuasion 983
  – sects 984
religiously exact
  494
relinquish 757
  – hope 859
  – life 360
  – property 782
  – a purpose 624
  recant 607
relinquishment
  624, 782

répertoire 599
repertory 636
repetend
  arithmetical 84
  iteration 104
repetition 19, **104**
repine
  pain 828
  discontent 832
  regret 833
  sad 837
replace
  substitute 147
  locate 184
  restore 660
replenish 52, 637
repletion
  filling 639
  redundance 641
  satiety 869
replevin
  recovery **775**
  borrow 788
  restore 790
replica 21
replication
  answer 462
  law pleadings 969
reply 462, 937
répondre en
  Normand 544
report *noise* 406
  judgment 480
  inform 527
  publish 531
  news 532
  rumour 532
  record 551
  statement 594
  good – 873
  through evil re-
    port and good –
    604*a*
  – progress 527
reporter
  informant 527
  messenger 534
  recorder 553
  journalist 593,
    758
reports *law* 969
repose
  quiescence 265
  leisure 685
  rest **687**
  – confidence in
    484
  – on *support* 215
  evidence 467
  – on one's laurels
    142

[618]

reposit 184
repository 636
repostum, manet
  alta mente –
  919
repoussé 250
reprehend 932
reprehensible 945,
  947
represent *similar* 17
  imitate 19
  exhibit 525
  intimate 527
  declare 535
  denote 550
  delineate 554
  commission 755
  deputy 759
  – to oneself 515
representation
  [*see* represent]
  copy 21
  portrait **554**
  drama 599
representative
  typical 79
  commissioner 758
  deputy 759
  – government 737
  – of the people 696
  – of the press
  messenger 534
  writer 593
repress 751
  – one's feelings
    826
  – a smile **837**
reprieve
  respite 133, 970
  deliverance 672
  release 750
  pardon 918
reprimand 932
reprint
  copy 21
  repetition 104
  reproduce 163
reprisal
  retaliation 718
  resumption 789
reprise 40*a*
reproach
  disgrace 874
  blame 932
  accusation 938
reprobate
  disapproved 932
  vicious 945
  bad man 949
  sinner 988

reprobation 932,
  988
reproduce
  imitate 19
  repeat 104
  renovate 163
reproduction [*see*
  reproduce] 21,
  163
reproductive 163
reproof 932
reprover 936
reptile
  animal 366
  servile 886
  knave 941
  miscreant 949
republic
  country 181
  people 372
  government 737
  – of letters 560
republican
  party 712
  government 737
  commonalty 876
republicanism 737
repudiate
  exclude 55
  deny 489
  reject 610
  abrogate 756
  violate 773
  not pay 808
  evade 927
repugn 719
repugnance
  incongruity 24
  resistance 719
  dislike 867
  hate 898
repulse *recoil* 277
  repel 289
  resist 719
  failure 732
  refusal 764
repulsion 157, **289**
repulsive
  [*see* repulse]
  unsavoury 395
  painful 830
  ugly 846
  disliked 867
  discourteous 895
  hateful 898
repurchase 795
reputable 873, 939
reputation 873
repute **873**
request **765**
  in – 630

– permission 760
requiem 839
requies, nec mora
  nec – 682
requiescat in pace
  363, 723
require
  need 630
  insufficient 640
  exact 741
  compel 744
  price 812
  due 924
  duty 926
  – explanation 519
requirement **630**
requisite 630
requisition 741, 765
  put in – *use* 677
  order 741
requital
  retaliation 918
  gratitude 916
  punishment 972
  reward 973
reredos 1000
res ipsa loquitur
  525
rescind *cut off* 44
  abrogate 756
  refuse 764
rescission 44, 756
rescript *answer* 462
  transcript 590
  letter 592
  order 741, 963
rescriptive 761
rescue *preserve* 670
  deliver 672
  aid 707
research 461
  – student 541
reseat 660
resection 44
reseda 435
resemblance 17, 21
resent 900
resentful 901
resentment **900**
reservation
  location 184
  concealment 528
  mental – 477, 528
  equivocation 520
  untruth 546
  with a – 38, 770
reservatory 191,
  636
reserve
  concealment 528
  silence 585

revision, under –
673
revisit 186
revival
reproduction 163
restoration 660
worship 990
revivalist 996
revive
reproduce 163
improve 658
resuscitate 660
excite 824
revivify
reproduce 163
life 359
improve 658
resuscitate 660
revocable 605
revoir, au – 293
revoke 607, 756
revolt *resist* 719
disobey 742
shock 830
disapproval 932
– *against hate* 898
– *at the idea*
dissent 489
revolting
painful 830
revolution
periodicity 138
change **146**
rotation 312
disobedience 742
revolutionize 140,
146
revolve
[*see* revolution]
– *in the mind* 451
revolver 727
revue 599
intimate – 599
revulsion
reversion 145
revolution 146
inversion 218
recoil 277
reward 973
reword 104
Reynard
animal 366
cunning 702
rez-de-chaussée
191, 207
rhabdology 85
rhabdomancy 511
Rhadamanthus
967, 982
rhapsodical
irregular 139

imaginary 515
rhapsodist
fanatic 504
rhapsody
discontinuity 70
music 415
nonsense 497
fancy 515
poetry 597
rhetoric *speech* 582
flowers of – 577
rheum
excretion 299
fluidity 333
water 337
rhino 800
rhinoceros hide
376, 823
rhomb 244
rhumb 278
rhyme
similarity 17
verse 597
without – **or**
reason
absurd 497
caprice 608
motiveless 615a
rhymeless 598
rhymester 597
rhythm
periodicity 138
melody 413
elegance 578
verse 597
rhythmical
- *style* 578
Rialto 799
rib *support* 215
ridge 250
wife 903
ribald *vulgar* 851
disreputable 874
impure 961
riband
[*see* ribbon]
ribbed 259
ribbon *tie* 45
filament 205
record 551
decoration 877
–s *reins* 752
handle the – 693
ribroast 972
rich *savoury* 394
colour 428
language 577
abundant 639
wealthy 803
beautiful 845
ornament 847

– **man** 803
riches 803
richesses, embarras
de – 641, 803
richly *much* 31
– *deserve* 924
rick 72, 636
rickety *weak* 160
ugly 846
imperfect 651
rickshaw 272
ricochet 277
ricordo, non mi –
506
rid *deliver* 672
get – of *eject* 297
liberation 750
loose 776
relinquish 782
riddance 672, 776,
782
good – 776
riddle *arrange* 60
sieve 260
secret 533
clean 652
ride *get above* 206
move 266
break in 370
– *at anchor* 265
– *full tilt at* 622,
716
– *hard* 274
– *one's hobby* 622
– *rough shod*
violence 173
severity 739
insolence 885
illegality 964
– *out the storm*
664
– *and tie*
periodicity 138
journey 266
– *the whirlwind*
604, 737
rideau, lever de –
599
ridentem dicere
verum 836, 842
rider *appendix* 39
equestrian 268
rideret Heraclitus
853
ridge *narrow* 203
height 206
prominence 250
ridicule 856, 929
ridiculous
absurd 497
foolish 499

trifling 643
grotesque 853
ridiculousness 853
riding *district* 181
journey 266
ridotto 840, 892
rifacimento 104,
660
rife *existence* 1
general 78
influence 175
riff-raff *dirt* 653
commonalty 876
bad folk 949
rifle *musket* 727
plunder 791
– *shot* 406
rifled cannon 727
rifleman 726
rifler 792
rifles 726
rifle-shooting 840
rift 44, 198
– *within the lute*
651, 713
rig *dress* 225
prepare 673
frolic 840
strumpet 962
– *the market* 794
run the – *upon* 929
rigadoon 840
rigging *ropes* 45
gear 225
instrument 633
riggish 961
right *dextral* 238
straight 246
true 494
property 780
just **922**
privilege 924
duty 926
honour 939
virtuous 944
bill of – 969
by – 924
have a – to **924**
set – *inform* 527
disclose 529
that's – 931
– *about*
[*see below*]
– *ahead* 234
– *angle* 212
– *ascension* 466
– *away* 133
step in the – *direc-*
tion 644
– *hand* [*see below*]
– *itself* 660

– and boiled 298
– an ox 883
rob 354, 791
robber 792
robbery 791
robe 225, 999
robes – of state 747
Robin Goodfellow
980
Robinson
say Jack – 132
Robot 554
robust *strong* 159,
654
roc 83
rocaille 853
rock *firm* 150
oscillate 314
hard 323
land 342
safety 664
danger 667
build on a – 150
founded on a –
664
split upon a – 732
– ahead 665
–bound coast 342
– oil 356
rocket *rapid* 274
rise 305
light 423
signal 550
arms 727
fireworks 840
go up like a – and
come down like
the stick 732
rocking-chair 215
rococo 124, 853
rod *support* 215
measure 466
scourge 975
divining 993
kiss the – 725
sounding – 208
– of empire 747
– in pickle
prepared 673
accusation 938
punishment 972
scourge 975
rodeo 720, 840
rodomontade
exaggeration 482
unmeaning 517
boast 884
roe 366, 374
Roentgen rays 420
rogation
request 765

worship 990
rogue *cheat* 548
knave 941
scamp 949
–'s march 297
roguery 940
roguish
playful 840
Roi le veut, le –
741
roister 885
roisterer 887
Roland for an
Oliver
retaliation 718
revenge 919
barter 794
rôle *drama* 599
business 625
plan 626
conduct 692
roll *list* 86
fillet 205
convolution 248
rotundity 249
make smooth 255
move 264
fly 267
rotate 312
rock 314
flow 348
sound 407
record 551
money 800
strike off the –
756, 972
– along 312
– in the dust 731
– on the ground
839
– of honour 86
– in 639, 641
– on 109
– into one 43
– in riches 803
– up 312
– up in 225
– in wealth 803
roll-call 85
roller *fillet* 45
round 249
clothing 255
rotate 312
roller-coaster 840
rollers *billows* 348
rollick 836
rollicker 838
rollicking
frolicsome 836
blustering 885
rolling: – pin 249

– stock 272
– stone 312
Rolls: Master of
the –
recorder 553
judge 967
– Court 966
Roman candle 840
Roman Catholic
984
romance
music 415
absurdity 497
imagination 515
untruth 546
fable 594
Romanism 984
romantic
imaginative 515
art 556
sensitive 822
romanticism 515
Romanus sum,
civis – 924
Romany 563
Rome: Church of
984
do at – as the
Romans do 82
romp *violent* 173
game 840
rondeau *music* 415
poem 597
rondel 597
rondoletto 597
rood *area* 180
cross 998
– loft 1000
roof 189, 223
roofless 226
rook 791, 792
rookie 726
rookery *nests* 189
dirt 653
room *occasion* 134
space 180
lodge 186
chamber 191
plea 617
assembly – 840
in the – of 147
make – for
opening 260
respect 928
roommate 890
rooms
lodgings 189
roomy 180
roost 189
rule the – 737
rooster 366

root *algebraic* - 84
cause 153
place 184
abide 186
base 211
etymon 562
lie at the – of 642
pluck up by the
–s 301
strike at the – of
716
take –
influence 175
locate 184
habit 613
– and branch 52
cut up – and
branch 162
– out *eject* 297
extract 301
discover 480a
rooted
old 124
firm 150
located 184
habit 613
deep – 820
– antipathy 867
– belief 484
rope *fastening* 45
cord 205
freedom 748
scourge 975
give – enough 738
–'s end 975
– of sand
incoherence 47
weakness 160
impossible 471
– way 627
rope-dancer 700
rope-dancing 698
ropy 352
roquelaure 225
roric 339
rosâ, sub – 528
rosary 990, 998
Roscius 599
rose *pipe* 350
fragrant 400
red 434
beauty 845
bed of –s 377, 734
couleur de –
red 434
good 648
prosperity 734
hope 858
under the – 528
welcome as the –s
in May 829, 892

roseate *red* 434
 hopeful 858
rose-coloured
 hope 858
Rosetta stone 522
rosette 847
rose-water
 moderation 174
 flattery 933
 not made with –
  704
Rosicrucian
 order or *party*
  712
rosin *rub* 331
 resin 356a
Rosinante 271
roster 86
rostrum *beak* 234
 pulpit 542
rosy 434
 – *wine* 959
rosy-cheeked 845
rot *decompose* 49
 absurdity 497
 rubbish 517
 putrefy 653
 disease 655
 decay 659
rota 86, 138
Rotarian 892
rotate 138
rotation 312
 periodicity 138
rote, by – 505
 know – 490
 learn – 539
rôti 298
rôtisserie 189
rotogravure 531,
 558
rotten *weak* 160
 bad 649
 foul 653
 decayed 659
 – at the core
 deceptive 545
 diseased 655
 – borough 893
rotulorum, custos –
 553
rotund 249
rotunda 189
rotundity 249
roturier 876
roué 949
rouge 434, 847
rouge-et-noir 621
rough *violent* 173
 shapeless 241
 uneven 256

[624]

pungent 392
unsavoury 395
sour 397
sound 410
unprepared 674
fighter 726
ugly 846
low fellow 876
bully 887
churlish 895
evil-doer 913
bad man 949
cut up – 900
– *copy writing* 590
unprepared 674
– diamond
uncouth 241
unprepared 674
artless 703
vulgar 851
commonalty 876
good man 948
– draft 626
– guess 514
– it 686
– sea 348
– side of the
 tongue 932
– and tumble 59
– weather 173, 349
rough-cast 256
 covering 223
 shape 240
 scheme 626
 unpolished 674
rough-hew 240, 673
roughly
 nearly 197
rough-neck 876,
 887
roughness 256
rough-rider 268
roughshod over,
 ride – 739
roulade 415
rouleau
 assemblage 72
 cylinder 249
 money 800
roulette 621, 840
round *series* 69
 revolution 138
 – *of a ladder* 215
 curve 245
 circle 247
 rotund 249
 music 415
 fight 720
 all – 227
 bring – 660
 come –

periodic 138
recant 607
persuade 615
dizzy – 312
get – 660
go – 311
go one's –s 266
go the –
 publication 531
make the – of 311
run the – of 682
go the same – 104
turn – *invert* 218
 retreat 283
revolve 311
– assertion 535
– a corner 311
– dance 840
– game 840
– hand 590
– like a horse in a
 mill 613
– of the ladder 71
– number 84, 102
in – numbers 29,
 197
– pace 274
– of pleasures
 377, 840
– robin
 information 527
 petition 765
 censure 932
– and round 138,
 312
– sum 800
– terms 566
– trot 274
– up 370
– of visits 892
round about
 circumjacent 227
 deviation 279
 circuit 311
 amusement 840
 – phrases 573
 – way 279
rounded periods
 577, 578
roundelay 597
rounders 840
round-house 752
roundlet 247
round-shouldered
 243
roup 796
rouse 615, 824
 – oneself 682
rousing 171
rout *crowd* 72
 agitation 315

overcome 731
discomfit 732
rabble 876
assembly 892
put to the – 731
– out 652
route 627
 en – 270
 en – for 282
routine
 uniform 16
 order 58
 rule 80
 periodic 138
 custom 613
 business 625
rove *travel* 266
 deviate 279
rover *traveller* 268
 pirate 792
roving commission
 475
row *disorder* 59
 series 69
 violence 173
 street 189
 navigate 267
 discord 713
 – in the same
  boat 88
rowdy *vulgar* 851,
 876
 blusterer 887
 bad man 949
rowel 253, 615
rower 269
rowlock 215
royal 737
 – blue 438
 – highness 877
 – road 627, 705
Royal Academician
 559
royalist 737
royaliste que le roi,
 plus 33
royalty 737
Rt. Hon. 877
ruade *impulse* 276
 attack 716
ruat cœlum 908
rub *friction* 331
 touch 379
 difficulty 704
 adversity 735
 painful 830
 – off corners 82
 – down *lessen* 195
 powder 330
 – down with an
  oaken towel 972

saddle 215
in the – 673
– on 37, 43
– on the right
  horse
  discovery 480*a*
  skill 698
  right 922
  fair 939
– with *add* 37
  attribute 155
  quarter on 184
  clog 706
  impose a duty
   926
  accuse 938
– on the wrong
  horse 495, 699
– up 293
saddle-bags 191
Sadducee 984
sadness, in – 535
safe *cupboard* 191
  hiding place 530
  secure 664
  treasury 802
  cautious 864
– conduct 631
– conscience 926,
  946
– deposit 636
– keeping 670
– and sound 654
on the – side 864
safety 664
– bicycle 272
– curtain 599
- first 664, 864
– match 388
– valve 666
saffron *colour* 436
sag 214, 217, 245
saga 594
sagacious 498, 510
sage 498, **500**
– maxim 496
saggar 386
sagittal 253
sagittary 83
sagum 225
Sahara 169
sahib 373, 745, 875
saick 273
said *preceding* 62
  repeated 104
  prior 116
  it is – 532
  thou hast – 488
  more easily – than
   done 704
sail *navigate* 267

ship 273
set out 293
easy – 174
full – 274
press of – 274
shorten – 275
take in – 174
take the wind out
  of one's –s 706
too much – 863
under – 267
– before the wind
  734
– near the wind
  698
– too near the
  wind 863
sailing: plain – 705
– vessel 273
sailor 269
fair weather – 701
saint *angel* 977
  revelation 985
  piety 987
  false piety 988
  tutelary – 664
Saint Monday 840
saintly 944, 987
sais quoi, je ne –
  563
sake:
  for the – of 615,
   707
  for goodness – 765
salaam
  bow 308
  submit 725
  courtesy 894
  respect 928
salacity 961
salad 41
– oil 356
salade 717
salamander 386
salariat 875
salary 973
sale **796**
  bill of – 771
  for – *offer* 763
  barter 794
saleable 796
salebrosity 256
salesman 797
salient
  projecting 250
  sharp 253
  manifest 525
  important 642
– angle 244
– points 642
saline 392

saliva 299, 332
salivate 297
salle-à-manger 191
sallet 717
sallow
  colourless 429
  yellow 436
sally *issue* 293
  attack 716
  wit 842
sally-port 295, 717
salmagundi 41
salmi 298
salmon-coloured
  434
saloon 189, 191
salt *sailor* 269
  pungent 392
  condiment 393
  importance 642
  preserve 670
  money 800
  wit 842
below the – 876
worth one's – 644
– of the earth
  648, 948
– water 341
saltation 309
saltatory 315
saltimbanco 548
saltpetre 392, 727
saltum, per – 315
salubrity **656**
salutary 656
salutatory 582
salute
  allocution 586
  celebration 883
  courtesy 894
  kiss 902
  respect 928
salutiferous
  [*see* salutary]
salva:
– res est 664
– sit reverentia
  928
salvable 946
salvage
  acquisition 775
  tax 812
  discount 813
  reward 973
salvation
  preservation 670
  deliverance 672
  religious 976
  piety 987
  work out one's –
   990

salve *unguent* **356**
  remedy 662
  relieve 834
salver 191
salvo *exception* 83
  explosion 406
  qualification 469
  plea 617
  attack 716
  excuse 937
– of artillery
  celebration 883
Samaritan, good –
  906, 912
same 13
all the – to 823
in the – boat 709
in the – breath
  113, 120
go over the –
  ground 104
of the – mind 488
on the – tack 709
adds up to the –
  thing 27
at the – time 30,
  120
sameness 16
samiel 349
samisen 417
Sammael 978
samovar 191
sampan 273
sample 82, 463
Samson 159
sana, mens – 502
– in corpore sano
  827
sanation 660
sanative 662
sanatorium 662
sanctification 976
sanctify 926, 987
sanctimony 988
sanction
  permission 760
  dueness 924
  approbation 931
sanctitude 987
sanctity 987
sanctuary 666, 100
sanctum 191
– sanctorum
  abode 189
  privacy 893
  temple 1000
sand *powder* 330
–bag 727
built upon – **665**
–dance 840
sow the – 645

sax-horn 417
Saxon
  style 576, 578
saxophone 417
say *nearly* 32
  assert 535
  speak 560, 582
  you don't – so 870
  go without –ing
    525
  have one's – 535,
    582
  that is to – 522
  what do you – to
    that 870
  – by heart 505
  – no 489
  – nothing 585
  – to oneself 589
  – one's prayers
    990
  – what comes up-
    permost 612
saying 496, 535
sbirro 965
scabbard 191
  throw away the –
    resolution 604
  war 722
scabby 940
scabrous 256
scaffold
  support 215
  preparation 673
  execution 975
scagliola 545
scalawag 193
scald *burn* 384
  poet 597
scale *transcend* 31
  portion 51
  series 69
  term 71
  slice 204
  skin 223
  mount 305
  weigh 319
  gamut 413
  measure 466
  hold the –s 480
  turn the –
  reversion 145
  influence 175
  counter evidence
    468
  motive 615
  hold the –s even
    922
  –s of justice 922
  – the heights 305
  – the walls 716

–s falling from the
  eyes 441, 529
scalene 243
scallop 248, 257
scalp 226
scalpel 253
scamble 44
scamp *neglect* 460
  shirk 603
  rascal 949
scamped *sham* 545
scamper *speed* 274
  – off 623
scampish 945
scan *see* 441
  attend to 457
  inquire 461
  know 490
  prosody 597
scandal *news* 532
  obloquy 934
scandaleuse, chro-
  nique – 934
scandalize 932
scandal-monger
  532
scandalous 874, 945
scandalum magna-
  tum
  infamy 874
  detraction 934
  accusation 938
scandent 305
scansion 597
scant *small* 32
  few 103
  little 193
  narrow 203
  insufficient 640
scantling *model* 22
  scrap 32
  dimensions 192
scanty [*see* scant]
scape 671
scapegoat 147, 952
scapegrace 863, 949
Scapin 548, 941
scapulary 999
scar *shore* 342
  record 551
  blemish 848
scarab 993
scaramouch 844
scarce
  few 103, 137, 640
  make oneself – -
    187, 623
scarcely 32
  – any 103
  – anything 643
  – ever 137

scarcity 103
scare 860
scarecrow 846, 860
scarf 225, 999
scarfskin 223
scarify *notch* 257
  torment 830
scarlet 434
  – Lady 984
scarp *oblique* 217
  defence 717
scathe 649, 659
scatheless 650
scatter *derange* 61
  disperse 73
  diverge 291
  – to the winds
  destroy 162
  confute 479
scatterbrained 458,
  503
scatterling 268
scavenger 652
scenario 594, 626
scene
  appearance 448
  painting 559
  drama 599
  excitement 825
  – of action 728
  look behind the
    –s 461
scene-painter 559
scene-painting 556
scenery 448, 599
scenic 599, 882
  – railway 840
scenography 556
scent *smell* 398
  discovery 480a
  disbelieve 485
  knowledge 490
  sign 550
  trail 551
  get – of 527
  put on a new -
    279
  on the – 622
  throw off the –
    623
  on the right – 462
  – from afar 510
scent-bag 400
scent-bottle 400
scented 400
scentless 399
sceptre 747
  sway the – 737
schedule 86
schematist 626
scheme *draft* 554

  plan 626
schemer 626
scherif 745, 875
scherzo 415
schesis 7
schism *dissent* 489
  discord 713
  heterodoxy 984
schismless 983a
schistose 204
scholar 492, 541
scholarly 539
scholarship
  knowledge 490
  learning 539
  distinction 873
scholastic
  knowledge 490
  teaching 537
  learning 539
  school 542
scholiast 492, 522
scholium 496, 522
school
  herd 72
  multitude 102
  system of
    opinions 484
  knowledge 490
  teaching 537
  academy 542
  painting 556
  go to – 539
  send to – 537
schoolboy 129, 541
  familiar to every –
    490
schooldays 127
schoolfellow 541
schoolgirl 129, 541
schoolman 492, 983
schoolmaster 540
  – abroad 490, 537
schoolroom 191
schooner 273
schottische 840
sciatica 378
science 490, 698
scientific *exact* 494
scientist 476, 492
scimitar 727
scintilla *small* 32
  spark 420, 423
scintillate 446, 873
scintillation
  heat 382
  light 420
  wit 842
scintillula forsan,
  latet – 858
sciolism 491

scroll 86, 551
scrub *rub* 331
  bush 367
  clean 652
  dirty person 653
  commonalty 876
scrubby *small* 193
  trifling 643
  stingy 819
  disreputable 874
  vulgar 876
  shabby 940
scruff 235
scruple
  small quantity 32
  weight 319
  doubt 485
  reluctance 603
  probity 939
scrupulous
  careful 459
  incredulous 487
  exact 494
  reluctant 603
  fastidious 868
  punctilious 939
scrutator 461
scrutiny 457, 461
scrutoire 191
scud *sail* 267
  speed 274
  shower 348
  cloud 353
  – under bare
    poles 704
scuffle 720
scull *row* 267
  brain 450
scull-cap 225
scullery 191
scullion 746
sculpsit 558
sculptor 559
sculpture 240, **557**
scum *dirt* 653
  – of the earth 949
  – of society 876
scupper 350
scurf 653
scurrilous
  ridicule 856
  malediction 908
  disrespect 929
  detraction 934
scurry 274, 684
scurvy
  insufficient 640
  unimportant 643
  base 940
  wicked 945
scut 235

scutcheon
  standard 550
  honour 877
scutiform 251
scuttle *destroy* 162
  receptacle 191
  speed 274
  – along *haste* 684
Scylla and Charyb-
  dis, between –
  danger 665
  difficulty 704
Scyllam, incidit
  in – 699
scythe *pointed* 244
  sharp 253
'sdeath! *wonder* 870
  anger 900
  disapprobation
    932
se non è vero è ben
  trovato 546
sea *multitude* 102
  ocean 341
  at – 341
  uncertain 475
  erroneous 495
  go to – 293
  on the high –s 341
  heavy – 315
  the seven –s 341
  – of doubt 475
  – of troubles
    difficulty 704
    adversity 735
seaboard 342
seafarer 269
seafaring 267, 273
sea-fight 720
sea-girt 346
sea-going 267, 341
sea-green 435
seal
  matrix 22
  close 261
  evidence 467
  mark 550
  resolve 604
  complete 729
  compact 769
  security 771
  break the – 529
  under – 769
  – the doom of 162
  – one's infamy 940
  – the lips 585
  – of secrecy 528
  – up *restrain* 751
sealed:
  one's fate is – 601
  hermetically – 261

– book
  ignorance 491
  unintelligible 519
  secret 533
sealing-wax 356
seals *insignia* 747
sealskin 223
seam 43
sea-maid 979
sea-man 269
seamanship 692,
  698
sea-mark 550
seamless 50
seamstress 225,
  690
seamy side 651
séance 525, 696
sea-piece 556
seaplane 273, 726
sea-port 666
sear *dry* 340
  burn 384
  deaden 823
  – and yellow leaf
    128, 659
search *inquire* 461
searching
  severe 739
  painful 830
searchless 519
searchlight 423,
  726
seared conscience
  951
searing 830
seascape 556
sea-serpent 83
seaside 342
season *mix* 41
  time 106
  pungent 392
  accustom 613
  preserve 670
  prepare 673
seasonable 23, 134
seasoning 393
seasons 138
seat *place* 183
  locate 184
  abode 189
  support 215
  posterior 235
  parliament 693
  country – 189
  judgment – 966
  – of government
    737
  – of war 728
seated, firmly – 150
seaway 180

seaweed 367
seaworthy 273, 66
sebaceous 355
secant 219
secede *dissent* 489
  relinquish 624
  disobey 742
seceder
  heterodox 984
secern 297
seclusion **893**
second
  duplication 90
  - *of time* 108
  instant 113
  - *in music* 413,
    415
  abet 707
  play or sing a –
    416
  – best 651, 732
  – childhood 128,
    499
  – crop 168, 775
  – edition 104
  play – fiddle
    obey 743
    subject 749
    disrepute 874
  – nature 613
  – to none 33
  one's – self 17
  – rate 659
  – sight
    foresight 510
    sorcery 992
  – thoughts
    sequel 65
    thought 451
    improvement 658
  – youth 660
secondary
  inferior 34
  following 63
  imperfect 651
  deputy 759
  – education 537
  – evidence 467
  – school 542
seconder 711
second-hand
  imitation 19
  old 124
  deteriorated 659
  received 785
secondly 90
second-rate 651
secret *key* 522
  latent 526
  hidden 528
  riddle **533**

Column 1 (SEC)

in the – 490
keep a – 585
~ motive 615
– passage 627, 671
– place 530
– writing 590
secrétaire 191
secretary
 recorder 553
 writer 590
 director 694
 auxiliary 711
 servant 746
 consignee 758
– of state 694
– of the treasury 801
secrete *excrete* 297
 conceal 528
secretion 299
secretive 528
sect 75
 religious – 983, 984
sectarian
 dissent 489
 ally 711
 heterodox 984
sectary 489
section *division* 44
 part 51
 class 75
 chapter 593
 troops 726
sector *part* 51
 circle 247
secula seculorum, in – 112
secular
 centenary 98
 periodic 138
 laity 997
– education 537
secularism 984
secundum artem 82, 698
secure *fasten* 43
 bespeak 132
 belief 484
 safe 664
 restrain 751
 engage 768
 gain 775
 confident 858
– an object 731
securities 802–805
security *safety* 664
 pledge 771
 hope 858
lend on – 787
Sedan

[632]

Column 2 (SEE)

disaster 162
sedan chair 272
sedate
 thoughtful 451
 calm 826
 grave 837
sedative 174, 662
sedentary 265
sedge 367
sedile 1000
sediment *dregs* 653
sedimentary 40
sedition 742
seduce *entice* 615
 love 897
 debauch 961
seducer 962
seduction 829, 865
sedulous 682, 865
see *view* 441
 look 457
 believe 484
 know 490
 bishopric 995
we shall – 507
– after 459
– daylight 480a
– double 959
– fit 600, 602
– at a glance 498
– justice done 922
– life 840
– the light
 born 359
 published 531
– service 722
– sights 455
– through 480a, 498
– to *attention* 457
 care 459
 direction 693
– one's way
 foresight 510
 intelligible 518
 skill 698
 easy 705
seed *small* 32
 cause 153
 posterity 167
 grain 330
run to – *age* 128
 lose health 659
sow the – 673
seedling 129
seed-plot 168, 371
seed-time of life 127
seedy *weak* 160
 disease 655
 deteriorated 659

Column 3 (SEI)

exhausted 688
 needy 804
seeing that 8, 476
seek *inquire* 461
 pursue 622
 offer 763
 request 765
– safety 664
seek-sorrow 837
seel 217
seem 448
 as it –s good to 600
seeming 448
seemingly 472
seemless 846, 925
seemliness 926
seemly
 expedient 646
 handsome 845
 due 924
seep 295
seer *veteran* 130
 madman 504
 oracle 513
 sorcerer 994
see-saw 12, 314
seethe *wet* 339
 hot 382
 make hot 384
 excitement 824
seething caldron 386
segar 392
segment 44, 51
segnitude 683
s'égosiller 411
segregate
 not related 10
 separate 44
 exclude 55
segregated
 incoherent 47
seigneur, grand –
 pride 878
 insolence 885
seignior 745, 875
seigniority
 authority 737
 possession 777
 property 780
seigniory 737
seine net 232
seisin 777, 780
seismic 314
seismograph 553
seismometer 276, 314
seize 789, 791
– an opportunity 134

Column 4 (SEL)

seized with
 disease 655
 feeling 821
seizure 925
sejunction 44
seldom 137
select *choose* 609
 good 648
self 13, 79
–abasement 879
–accusing 950
–admiration 880
–applause 880
–appointed task 602
–assertion 885
–called 565
–command 604, 864
–communing 451
–complacency 836, 880
–confidence 880
–conquest 604
–conscious 855
–consultation 451
–contained 52
–control 604
–conviction
 belief 484
 penitent 950
 condemned 971
–counsel 451
–deceit *error* 495
–deception 486
–defence 717
–delusion 486
–denial
 disinterested 942
 temperance 953
 penance 990
–discipline 990
–effacement 879, 942
–esteem 880
–evident 474, 525
–examination 990
–existing 1
–government 748
–help 698
–immolation 991
–indulgence
 selfishness 943
 intemperance 954
–interest 943
–knowledge 881
–love 943
–luminous 423
–mastery 604
–opinioned 481
–possession

sanity 502
resolution 604
inexcitability 826
caution 864
−praise 880
−preservation 717
−reliance
resolution 604
hope 858
courage 861
−reproach 950
−respect 878
−restraint 953
−sacrifice 942
−satisfied 880
−seeking 943
−styled 565
−sufficient 880
−taught 490
−tormentor 837
−will 606
selfishness **943**
self-same 13
sell *convince* 484
absurdity 497
deception 545
untruth 546
sale 796
− for 812
− one's life dearly
719, 722
− off 796
− oneself 940
− out 796
seller 796
selon les règles 82
selvedge 231
semaphore 550
semblance
similarity 17
imitation 19
copy 21
probability 472
wear the − of
appearance 448
semeiology 522
semeiotics 550
semester 108
semi- 91
semi-barbarian 913
semibreve 413
semicircle 247
semicircular 245
semicolon 142
semi-diaphanous
427
semi-fluid 352
semi-liquidity **352**
semi-lunar 245
seminal 153
seminary 542

semination 673
semi-opaque 427
semi-pellucid 427
semiquaver 413
semitone 413
semi-transparency
427
sempervirent 110
sempiternal 112
sempstress 225, 690
senary 98
senate 696
senate-house 966
senator 695, 696
senatorship 693
senatus consultum
741
send 270, 284
− adrift 597
− away
repel 289
eject 297
refuse 764
− for 741
− forth 284, 531
− a letter to 592
− off 284
− out *eject* 297
− packing 289
commission 755
− word 527
senescence 128
seneschal
director 694
master 745
servant 746
seneschalship 737
senile 128
senility 158, 659
senior *age* 128
student 541
master 745
seniores priores 62,
280
seniority 124, 128
sennight 108
señor 373, 877
senora 374
sensation
physical sensi-
bility 375
emotion 821
wonder 870
sensational 574,
824
sensation drama
599
sensations of touch
380
sense 498, 516
deep − 821

horse − 498
in no − 565
accept in a par-
ticular − 522
− of duty 926
senseless
insensible 376
absurd 497
foolish 499
unmeaning 517
senses
external - 375
intellect 450
sanity 502
sensibility **375, 822**
sensible
material 316
wise 498
sensitive 375, 822
sensorial 821
sensorium 450
sensual 377, 954
sensualist 954*a*
sensuous
sensibility 375
pleasure 377
feeling 821
sentence
decision 480
maxim 496
affirmation 535
phrase 566
condemnation 971
sententious 572,
574
sentient 375, 821
sentiment 453
sentimental
sensitive 822
affected 855
sentinel } 263
sentry }
guardian 664
watch 668
keeper 753
separate *disjoin* 44
exclude 55
bisect 91
diverge 291
divorce 905
− the chaff from
the wheat
discriminate 465
select 609
− into elements 49
− maintenance 905
separation 44
separatist 489, 984
sepia 433
seposition 44, 55
sepoy 726

sept *kin* 11
class 75
clan 166
Septentrional 237
septet 415
septic 655, 657
septicæmia 655
septuagenarian 98
Septuagint 985
septum 228
sepulchral
interment 363
resonance 408
stridor 410
hoarse 581
sepulchre 363
whited − 545
sepulture 363
sequacious 63
sequacity *soft* 324
tenacity 327
sequel **65**, 117
sequela 65, 154
sequence
- *in order* **63**
- *in time* 117
motion **281**
logical − 476
sequent 63
sequester 789, **974**
sequestered 893
sequestrate
seize 789
condemn 971
confiscate 974
sequin 847
serac 383
seraglio 961
seraph 948, **977**
seraphic
blissful 829
virtuous 944
pious 987
seraphina 417
seraskier 745
sere and yellow
leaf 128
serein 339, 348
serenade *music* **415**
compliment 894
endearment 902
serene
pellucid 425
calm 826
content 831
imperturbable **871**
- *highness* 877
serf *slave* 746
clown 876
serfdom 749
sergeant 745

serial
  continuous 69
  periodic 138
  book 593
seriatim
  in order 58
  continuously 69
  each to each 79
  slowly 275
series 69, 84
sérieux, take au –
  843
serio-comic 853
serious *great* 31
  resolved 604
  important 642
  dejected 837
seriously 535
serjeant:
  common – 967
  –at-law 968
sermon *lesson* 537
  speech 582
  dissertation 595
  pastoral 998
  funeral – 363
sermonizer 584
seroon 72
serosity 333, 337
serpent
  tortuous 248
  snake 366
  hiss 409
  wind instrument
    417
  wise 498
  deceiver 548
  cunning 702
  evil-doer 913
  knave 941
  demon 949
  the old – 978
  great sea – 515
serpentine 248
serrated 244, 257
serried 72, 321
serum 333, 337
servant *instrumen-*
    tality 631
  help 711
  retainer **746**
  – of all work 690
serve *benefit* 618
  business 625
  utility 644
  aid 707
  warfare **722**
  obey 743
  servant 746
  – an apprentice-
    ship 539

– faithfully 743
– loyally 743
– notice 527
– out 972
– one right
  retaliation 718
  right 922
  punish 972
– as a substitute
  147
– one's turn 644
– with a writ 969
service *good* 618
  utility 644
  use 677
  warfare 722
  servitude 749
  worship 990
  rite 998
  hold – 363
  at one's – 763
  press into the –
    677
  render a – 644,
    906
serviceable 644, 648
serviette 652
servile 749, 876, **886**
servitor 746
servitorship 749
servitude 749
  penal – 972
sesame, open – 260
  watchword 550
  spell 993
sesqui- 87
sesquipedalia verba
  577
sesquipedalian 200
sess 812
sessile 46
session *council* 696
sessions *law* 966
sestet 597
set
  condition 7
  join 43
  coherence 46
  group 72
  class 75
  firm 150
  tendency 176
  place 184
  form 240
  sharpen 253
  direction 278
  go down 306
  dense 321
  stage 599
  habit 613
  prepare 673

gang 712
impose 741
make a dead – at
  716
– about 66, 676
– abroach 73
– one's affections
  on 897
– afloat 153, 531
– against
  oppose 708
  quarrel 713
  hate 898
  angry 900
– against one
  another 464
– agoing
  impulse 276
  propulsion 284
  aid 707
– apart
  separate 44
  exclude 55
  select 609
– aside
  displace 185
  disregard 458
  neglect 460
  negative 536
  reject 610
  disuse 678
  annul 756
  refuse 764
  not observe 773
  relinquish 782
  dereliction 927
– one's back up
  878
– before
  inform 527
  choice 609
– before oneself
  620
– by 636
– one's cap at
  897, 902
– on a cast 621
– down [*see below*]
– by the ears 898
– at ease 831
– an example
  model 22
  motive 615
– the eyes on 441
– one's face
  against
  oppose 708
  refuse 764
  disapprove 932
– the fashion
  influence 175

authority **737**
fashion 852
– fast 704
– on fire
  ignite 384
  excite 824
– on foot 66
– foot on 294
– forth *show* 525
  assert 535
  describe 594
– forward 293
– free 750
– going
  [*see* – agoing]
– one's hand to
  467
– one's heart upon
  604, 865
– at hazard 665
– in *begin* 66
  rain 348
– on its legs 150
– on one's legs 159,
  660
– in motion 264,
  677
– to music 416
– at naught
  make light of 483
  reject 610
  oppose 708
  defy 715
  disobey 742
  not observe 773
  dereliction 927
– no store by 483,
  930
– off
  compensation 30
  depart 293
  improve 658
  discount 813
  adorn 845
  display 882
– on 615
– in order 60
– out *arrange* 60
  begin 66
  depart 293
• *decorate* 845
  display 882
– over 755
– phrase 566
– a price 85, 812
– purpose 620
– at rest *end* 67
  answer 462
  adjudge 480
  complete 729
  compact 769

– right
inform 527
disclose 529
teach 537
reinstate 660
vindicate 937
– to rights 60
– sail 293
– the seal on 729
– one's seal to 467
– store by 642
– straight 246, 723
– the table in a
  roar 840
– one's teeth 604
– terms
manifest 525
phrase 566
style 574
– a trap for 545
– to 720, 722
– in towards 286
– up
printing 54
originate 153
strengthen 159
produce 161
upright 212
raise 307
successful 731
prosperous 734
– up shop 676
– upon
resolved 604
attack 716
desirous 865
– too high a value
  upon 482
– watch 459
– one's wits to
  work *think* 451
imagine 515
plan 626
– to work
undertake 676
impose 741
set-back 735
set down
record 551
unseat 756
humiliate 879
slight 929
censure 932
give one a –
confute 479
– as 484
– for 484
– a cause for
  hearing 969
– to 155
– in writing 551

setaceous 256
seton 662
setose 256
sett *lease* 771, 787
settee 215
setter 366
settle *regulate* 60
establish 150
be located 184
bench 215
come to rest 265
subside 306
kill 361
decide 480
choose 609
vanquish 731
consent 762
compact 769
pay 807
– accounts 807,
  811
– down 131
stability 150
moderate 174
locate oneself 184
– into 144
– matters 723
– preliminaries
  673
– property 781
– the question 478
– to sleep 683
– upon *give* 784
– with 807, 972
settled [*see* settle]
characteristic 5
ended 67
account – 811
– opinion 484
– purpose 620
settlement [*see*
  settle]
location 184
colony 188
dregs 653
compact 769
deed 771
property 780
strict – 781
settler 188
settlor 784
seven 98
–league boots 274,
  992
wake the –
  sleepers 404
seventy 98
sever 38, 44
several *special* 79
plural 100
many 102

– times 104
severalize 465
severally 44, 79
severalty 44
severance 38
severe
energetic 171
symmetry 242
exact 494
- *style* 576
harsh 739
painful 830
simple 849
critical 932
severely *very* 31
severity **739**
sew 43
sewage 299, 653
sewed up
drunk 959
sewer 350, 653
sewerage 652, 653
sewer-gas 663
sewing-silk 205
sex *kind* 75
women 374
fair – 374
sexagenarian 98,
  130
sexagenary 99
sextant 217, 244,
  247
sextet 98
sextodecimo 593
sexton 363, 996
sextuple 98
seyyid 745
sforzando 415
shabbiness 34
shabby *trifling* 643
deteriorated 659
stingy 819
mean 874
disgraceful 940
shabby-genteel 851
shack 189
shackle
fastening 45
hinder 706
restrain 751
fetter 752
shade *degree* 26
small quantity 32
manes 362
darkness 421
shadow **424**
colour 428
conceal 528
screen 530
paint 556
ghost 980

eye – 443
in the – 528, 874
shadow of a – 32,
  422
throw into the –
surpass 303
conceal 528
glory 873
throw all else into
  the – 642
thrown into the –
  34, 874
under the – of 664
without a – of
  doubt 474
shades:
– below 982
– of death 360
– of difference 15
– of evening 422
shading 421
– off 26
shadow
unsubstantial 4
copy 21
small 32
accompaniment
  88
thin 203
be behind 235
sequence 281
dark 421
shade 424
pursue 461, 622
dream 515
demon 980
fight with a – 699
follow as a – 281
partial – 422
without a – of
  turning 141
worn to a –
thin 203
worse for wear
  659
– of coming
  events 511
– forth *dim* 422
predict 511
metaphor 521
represent 554
may your – never
  be less
courtesy 894
respect 928
approbation 931
take the – for the
  substance
credulous 486
mistake 495
unskilful 699

-burst 404
-shock 655
– out 784, 807,
   809
shellac 356a
shellback 269
shell-fish 366
shelter 664, 666
– oneself under
   plea of 617
sheltie 271
shelve *defer* 133
   locate 184
   slope 217
   neglect 460
   disuse 678
shelving beach 217
shend 659
shepherd *tender of*
   sheep 370
   director 694
   pastor 996
Shepherd, the Good
   – 976
shepherd's dog 366
Sheppard, Jack –
   792
shere 32
sheriff 745, 965
Shetland pony 271
shew [*see* show]
shibboleth 550
shield
   heraldry 550
   safety 664
   buckler 666
   defend 717
   scutcheon 877
   look only at one
   side of the – 481
   reverse of the –
   235, 468
   under the – of 664
shift *change* 140
   convert 144
   substitute 147
   changeable 149
   chemise 225
   move 264
   transfer 270
   deviate 279
   prevaricate 546
   plea 617
   cunning 702
   last – 601
   make a – with
   147, 677
   put to one's –s
   704, 804
   ·· one's ground
   607

– off *defer* 133
– for oneself 692,
   748
left to – for one-
   self 893
– one's quarters
   264
– the scene 140
– to and fro 149
shifting [*see* shift]
   transient 111
   – sands 149
   – trust or use 783
shiftless 674, 699
shillelagh 727
shilling 800
   cut off with a –
   789
– shocker 594
shilly-shally 605
shimmer 420
shimmy
   dance 840
shindy 720
shine *light* 420
   beauty 845
   glory 873
   take the – out of
   874
   – in conversation
   588
   – forth 873
   – upon
   illumine 420
   aid 707
shingle 330
shingled
   hair 53
shingles 223
shining [*see* shine]
   – light *sage* 500
Shintoism 984
shiny 420
ship *lade* 190
   transfer 270
   vessel **273**
   take – 267, 293
   one's – coming in
   803
   – of the line 726
shipboard, on – 273
ship-load 31, 190
shipman 269
shipmate 890
shipment
   contents 190
   transfer 270
shippen 189
shipping 273
shipshape *order* 58
   conformity 82

skill 698
shipwreck
   destruction 162
   vanquish 731
   failure 732
shire 181
shirk 603, 623, 742
shirker 862
shirt 225
Shiva 979
shive 32, 204
shiver
   small piece 32
   divide 44
   destroy 162
   filament 205
   shake 315
   brittle 328
   cold 383
   fear 860
   go to –s 162
   – in one's shoes
   860
shivery *brittle* 328
   powdery 330
shoal
   assemblage 72
   multitude 102
   shallow 209
shoals *danger* 667
   surrounded by –
   difficulty 704
shoat 366
shock *sheaf* 72
   violence 173
   concussion 276
   agitation 315
   unexpected 508
   disease 655
   discord 713
   affect 821
   move 824
   pain 828
   give pain 830
   dislike 867
   scandalize 932
shocking *bad* 649
   painful 830
   ugly 846
   vulgar 851
   fearful 860
   disreputable 874
   hateful 898
   in a – temper 901a
shockingly *much* 31
shod 225
shoddy 645
shoe *support* 215
   dress 225
   hindrance 706
   stand in the –s of

commission **755**
   deputy 759
   where the –
   pinches
   badness 649
   difficulty 704
   opposition 708
   sensibility 822
   painful 830
shoemaker 225
shofle 272
shoful 792
shog 173
shoneen 855
shoot
   offspring 167
   expand 194
   dart 274
   propel 284
   kill 361
   sprout 365, **367**
   pain 378
   execute 972
   teach the young
   idea to – 537
   – ahead 282
   – ahead of 303
   – at 716
   – out beams 420
   – up *increase* 35
   prominent 250
shooting
   [*see* shoot]
   chase 622
   – pain 378
   – star 318, 423
shooting-coat 225
shop 795, 799
   keep a – 625, 794
   shut up – *end* 67
   cease 142
   relinquish 624
   rest 687
   smell of the – **851**
shopkeeper 797
shoplifter 792
shoplifting 791
shopman 797
shopmate 890
shopping 794, 795
shore
   support 215
   border 231
   land 342
   buttress 717
   hug the – 286
   on – 342
   – up 215, 670
shoreless 180
shorn *cut short* **201**
   deprived 776

– of its beams
422, 874
– lamb 828
short
  not long 201
  brittle 328
  concise 572
  uncivil 895
  come – of, fall – of
  inferior 34
  shortcoming 304
  insufficient 640
  in – 572, 596
  – allowance 640
  – answer 895
  – breath 688
  – by 201
  of cash 804
  – commons
  insufficiency 640
  fasting 956
  – circuit 279, 628
  – cut *straight* 246
  mid-course 628
  – distance 197
  – life and merry
  840
  – measure 53
  at – notice 111,
  132
  – of *small* 32
  inferior 34
  subtraction 38
  incomplete 53
  shortcoming 304
  insufficient 640
  – sea 348
  make – work of
  destroy 162
  active 682
  haste 684
  complete 729
  conquer 731
  punish 972
  shortage 53
shortcoming
  inequality 28
  inferiority 34
  motion short of
  304
  non-completion
  730
  deficiency 945
shorten 201
  – sail 275
shorthand 590
short-handed 651
shorthorn 366
short-lived 111
shortly *soon* 132
shortness 201

for – sake 572
shorts 225
short-sighted
  myopic 443
  misjudging 481
  foolish 499
short-story 594
short-winded 160,
  688
short-witted 499
shot *missile* 284
  report 406
  variegated 440
  guess 514
  war material 722,
  727
  price 812
  reward 973
  bad – 701
  exchange –s 720
  good – 700
  have a – at 716
  like a – 113
  off like a – 623
  pistol – 406
  random – 463, 621
  round – 727
  – in the locker 632
  not have a – in
  one's locker 804
  – and shell 722
shot-free 815
shot-gun 727
should be:
  no better than
  she – 961
  what – 922
shoulder
  support 215
  projection 250
  shove 276
  broad –ed 159
  cold – 289
  have on one's –s
  625
  on the –s of
  high 206
  elevated 307
  instrumentality
  631
  shrug the –s
  [*see* shrug]
  rest on the –s of
  926
  rub –s with no-
  bility 852
  take upon one's –s
  676
  – arms 673
  – a musket 722
  – to shoulder 709,

712
– to the wheel
604, 676
shoulder-knot 847
shoulder-strap 747
shout
  loud 404
  cry 411
  rejoice 838
shove 276
  give a – to
  aid 707
shovel
  receptacle 191
  transfer 270
  vehicle 272
  fire-iron 386
  cleanness 652
  put to bed with
  a – 363
  – away 297
shovel-hat 999
show *visible* 446
  appear 448
  draw attention
  457
  evidence 467
  demonstrate 478
  manifest 525
  entertainment 599
  parade 882
  dumb – 550
  make a – 544
  mere – 544
  peep– 840
  – off 525
  – one's cards 529
  – cause 527
  – one's colours,
  550
  – one's face
  presence 186
  manifest 525
  disclose 529
  – fight *defy* 715
  attack 716
  defend 717
  brave 861
  – forth 525
  – in front 303
  – one's cards 529
  – one's hand 529
  – a light pair of
  heels 623
  – itself 446
  – of 17, 472
  – off 882, 884
  – one's teeth 715
  – up *visible* 446
  manifest 525
  ridicule 856

  degrade 874
  censure 932
  accuse 938
shower
  assemblage **72**
  rain 348
  – bath 386
  – down
  abundance 639
  – down upon **784,**
  816
showman 524
showy *colour* 428
  beauty 845
  ornament 847
  fashion 852
  vulgar 851
  ostentatious 882
shrapnel 727
shred 32, 205
shredder 260
shrew 901
shrewd
  knowing 490
  wise 498
  cunning 702
shriek 410, 411
shrievalty 965
shrieve 965
shrift
  confession 529
  absolution 952
shriftless 951
shrill 410, 411
shrimp 193
shrine 363, 1000
  receptacle 191
shrink
  decrease 36
  shrivel 195
  go back 283, **287**
  unwilling 603
  avoid 623
  sensitive 822
  – from *fear* 860
  dislike 867
  hate 898
shrive 952, 998
shrivel 195
shrivelled *thin* 203
shroud *cover* 225
  funeral 363
  hide 528
  safety 664
  defend 717
  –ed in mystery
  519
shrouds 45
Shrove Tuesday
  998
shrub *plant* 367

plantation 371
shrug *sign* 550
– the shoulders
dissent 489
submit 725
discontent 832
dislike 867
contempt 930
disapprobation
932
shrunk 193, 195
shudder *cold* 383
fear 860
make one –
painful 830
– at *aversion* 867
hate 898
shuffle *mix* 41
derange 61
change 140
interchange 148
changeable 149
move slowly 275
agitate 315
falsehood 544
untruth 546
irresolute 605
recant 607
dance 840
improbity 940
, the cards
begin again 66
change 140
chance 621
prepare 673
patience and –
the cards 826
– off *run away* 623
– off this mortal
coil 360
– on 266
shuffler 548
shun 623, 867
shunt 270, 279
shunted
shelved 460
shut 261
– the door 761
– the door in one's
face 764
– the door upon
893
– one's ears 419,
487
– the eyes 442
– one's eyes to
not attend to 458
neglect 460
not believe 487
permit 760
not observe 773

– the gates of
mercy 914*a*
– in 751
– oneself up 893
– out 55, 761
– up shop *end* 67
cease 142
silence 403
relinquish 624
repose 687
– up *close* 261
confute 479
imprison 751
shutter 424
shuttle 314
shuttlecock 605
shy *deviate* 279
draw back 283
propel 284
avoid 623
fearful 860
cowardly 862
modest 881
fight – of 623
have a – at 716
– of belief 487
– cock 862
– of *doubtful* 485
unwilling 603
cautious 864
dislike 867
Shylock 787
Siamese twins 89
sib 11
Siberia 383
sibi gladio hunc
jugulo, suo – 718
sibilation *hiss* 409
disrespect 929
disapprobation
932
Sibyl *oracle* 513
ugly 846
Sibylline 511
– leaves 513
sic *imitation* 19
exact 494
si – omnes! 948
– transit gloria
mundi 111
– volo sic jubeo
600
– vos non vobis
791
siccity 340
sick *ill* 655
make one – 830,
867
visitation of the –
998
– at heart 837

– of *weary* 841
dislike 867
satiated 869
in –ness and in
health 604
sick-chamber 655
sicken *nauseate* 395
disease 655
pain 830
weary 841
disgust 867
sickener
too much 641
sickle 244, 253
sickly *weak* 160
sick-room 655
side
consanguinity 11
edge 231
laterality 236
party 712
ostentation 882
at one's – 197
on every – 227
on one – 243
on one's – 714
look only at one –
of the shield 481
pass from one – to
another 607
take up a – 476
wrong – up 218
– by side
accompaniment
88
near 197
laterality 236
party 712
from – to side 314
– with *aid* 707
co-operate 709
concord 714
side-arms 727
side-blow 702
sideboard 191
side-car 272
side-dish 298
side-drum 417
side-kick 890
side issue 643
sideling 279
sidelong 236
sideration 158
sidereal 318
– time 114
siderite 288
Sideromancy 511
side-saddle 215
side-scene 599
sideslip 267
sidesman 996

side-track 287
sidewalk 627
sideways 217, **236**
side-wind
oblique 217
circuit 629
cunning 702
sidle *oblique* 217
lateral 236
deviate 279
siege 716
lay – to 716
state of – 722
siege-train 727
siesta 683
sieve *sort* 60
perforate 260
clean 652
memory like a –
506
pour water into
a – 638, 818
stop one hole in
a – 819
sift *simplify* 42
sort 60
inquire 461
discriminate 465
clean 652
– the chaff from
the wheat 609
sigh 405, 839
– for 865
sighing like
furnace 902
sight *much* 31
multitude 102
vision 441
appearance 448
ugly 846
prodigy 872
at – 132, 441
dim – 443
in – 446
in – of 197, 441
in plain – 525
keep in – 457
within – of shore
858
sightless
blind 442
invisible 447
ugly 846
sightly 845
sights, see – 455
sightseeing 441
sightseer 444, **455**
sigil *seal* 550
evidence 769
sigmoidal 248
sign *attest* 467

omen 512
indication 550
record 551
write 590
compact 769
prodigy 872
give – of 525
make no – 585
– of the cross 998
–s of the times
indication 550
omen 512
warning 668
–s of the zodiac
318
signal *great* 31
sign 550
important 642
give the – 741
– of distress 669
signalize
indicate 550
glory 873
celebrate 883
signally 31
signal oil 356
signal-post 668
signature
*mark, identifica-
tion* 550
writing 590
compact 769
security 771
sign-board 550
signet
*mark, identifica-
tion* 550
sign of authority
747
compact 769
writer to the – 968
significant 642
[*see* signify]
evidence 467
important 642
signifies, what –
643
signify
forebode 511
mean 516
inform 527
signior 875
sign-manual 550,
590
signor 373, 877
signora 374
sign-painter 559
sign-painting 555
sign-post 550
signum, ecce – 550
sike 348

silence *disable* 158
no sound 403
confute 479
latency 526
concealment 528
aphony 581
taciturn 585
check 731
silencer 405, 408
silentio, sub –
silent 403
inattention 458
latent 526
silhouette
outline 230, 448
shadow 421
portrait 556
siliquose 191
silk 255, 324
– *gown*
barrister 968
– hat 225
make a – purse
out of a sow's
ear 471
silken repose 687
silkiness 954
sill 215
silly
credulous 486
imbecile 499
insane 503
silo 636
silt *deposit* 321
dirt 653
silvan 367
silver *bright* 420
white 430
grey 432
money 800
bait with a – hook
615
german – 545
– lining of the
cloud 858
– wedding 883
silver certificate
800
silver-toned 413
silviculture 371
simagrée 855
similarity 17
– of form 240
simile
similarity 17
comparison 464
metaphor 521
similitude 17, 21
simmer
agitation 315
boil 382, 384

excitement 824
simmering 825
simoleon 800
Simon Pure
the real – 494
Simon, Simple –
501, 547
Simon Stylites 893
simony 964
simoon 349, 382
simper *smile* 838
affectation 855
simple *mere* 32
unmixed 42
credulous 486
ignorant 493
silly 499
- *language* 576
herb 662
artless 703
unadorned 849
– *meaning* 516
simple-hearted 543
simpleness 42
Simple Simon 501,
547
simpleton 501
simplex munditiis
849
simplicity
[*see* simple] **849**
ignorance 491
simplify
[*see* simple]
elucidate 518
simply 32, 87
more – 522
simulacrum 19
simulate
resemble 17
imitate 19
cheat 544
simultaneous 120
sin 945, 947
sinapism 662
since *under the cir-
cumstances* 8
after 117
cause 155
reason 476
sincere
veracious 543
ingenuous 703
feeling 821
sine 217
sine: – curâ 831
– die 107, 133
– ictu 158
– quâ non
required 630
important 642

condition 770
sinecure 681
no – 682
sinew 159
sinewless 158
sinews of war 800
sinful 945
sing *bird* 412
resonance 408
music 416
voice 580
poetry 597
rejoice 838
– Io triumphe 884
– out 411
– praises
approve 931
worship 990
– in the shrouds
349
– small 879
singe 382, 384
singer 416
single *unmixed* 42
unit 87
secluded 893
unmarried 904
ride at – anchor
863
– combat 720
– entry
– file 69
– out 609
single-handed
one 87
easy 705
unassisted 706
single-minded 703
singleness
[*see* single]
– of heart 703, 939
– of purpose 604a,
703
single-stick 720
singlet 225
Sing Sing 752
sing-song 414, 892
singular *special* 79
exceptional 83
one 87
singularly *very* 31
sinister *left* 239
bad 649
vicious 945
bar –
imperfect 651
disrepute 874
sinistrality 239
sinistromanual 239
sinistrous

fail 732
slipper 225
hunt the – 840
slippery
   transient 111
   smooth 255
   greasy 355
   uncertain 475
   vacillating 607
   dangerous 665
   facile 705
   faithless 940
   – ground 667
slipshod 575
slipslop
   absurdity 497
   solecism 568
   weak language 575
slit *divide* 44
   chink 198
   furrow 259
slither 264
sliver 32
slobber *drivel* 297
   slop 337
   dirt 653
sloe *black* 431
slog 143
slogan 722
sloop 273
   –of-war 726
slop *spill* 297
   water 337
   dirt 653
slope *oblique* 217
   run away 623
sloppy *moist* 339
   marsh 345
   - *style* 575
slops *clothes* 225
slosh 337, 653
slot 44, 260
sloth 683
slouch *low* 207
   oblique 217
   move slowly 275
   inactive 683
slouching *ugly* 846
slough
   quagmire 345
   dirt 653
   difficulty 704
   adversity 735
   – of Despond 859
sloven *untidy* 59
   bungler 701
slovenly *untidy* 59
   careless 460
   - *style* 575
   dirty 653

awkward 699
vulgar 851
slow *tardy* 133
   inert 172
   moderate 174
   motion 275
   inactive 683
   wearisome 841
   dull 843
by – degrees 26
– movement
   music 415
march in – time 275
– as molasses in January 275
be – to
   unwilling 603
   not finish 730
   refuse 764
slow-coach 701
slowness 275
sloyd 537
slubber 653
slubberdegullion 876
sludge 653
slug *slow* 275
   inaction 681
   inactivity 683
   bullet 727
sluggard 275, 683
sluggish 172, 823, 843
sluice *limit* 233
   egress 295
   river 348
   conduit 350
   open the –s 297
slum 653
slumber 683
slump 304
slur *blemish* 848
   stigma 874
   gloss over 937
   reproach 938
   – over *neglect* 460
   slight 483
slush *marsh* 345
   semiliquid 352
   dirt 653
slut *untidy* 59
   female 374
   dirty 653
   unchaste 962
sly *stealthy* 528
   cunning 702
smack
   small quantity 32
   mixture 41
   boat 273

impulse 276
taste 390
thud 406
kiss 902
strike 972
– the lips
   pleasure 377
   taste 390
   savoury 394
   rejoice 838
   – of *resemble* 17
small
   – *in degree* 32
   – *in size* 193
   become – 195
   feel – 879
   of – account 643
   esteem of –
     account 930
   – arms 727
   – beer 643, 880, 930
   – coin 800
   – chance 473
   – fry 193, 643, 876
   – matter 643
   – number 103
   – part 51
   – pica 591
   in the – hours 125
   on a – scale 32, 193
   – talk 588
small-bore 727
small-clothes 225
smaller 34, 195
smallness 32
smalls 225
smalt 438
smart *pain* 378
   active 682
   clever 698
   feel 821
   grief 828
   witty 842
   pretty 845
   ornamental 847
   – pace 274
   – saying 842
   – under 821
smarten 847
smart-money 973
smash 162, 732
smasher 792
smatch 390
smatterer 493
smattering 491
smear *cover* 223
   soil 653
   blemish 848
smell 398

bad – 401
– of the lamp
   ornate style 577
   prepared 673
– powder 722
smell-feast 886
smelling-bottle 400
smelt *heat* 384
   prepare 673
smicker 838
smile 836, 838
   raise a – 840
   – at 856
   – of contempt 930
   – of fortune 734
   – upon *aid* 707
   courtesy 894
   endearment 902
smirch 431, 653
smirk 838
smite *maltreat* 649
   excite 824
   afflict 830
   punish 972
smith 690
smithereens 162
smitten *love* 897
   – with *moved* 615
smock 225, 258
smock-faced 862
smock-frock 225
smoke
   dust 330
   vapour 336
   heat 382
   tobacco 392
   discover 480a
   suspect 485
   unimportant 643
   dirt 653
   cure 670
   disrespect 929
   end in –
     shortcoming 304
     failure 732
   – the calumet of peace 723
   –ed glasses 424
   – screen 424
   – stack 260
smoking hot 382
smoking-jacket 225
smoking-room 191
smoky *opaque* 426
   dirty 653
smooth *uniform* 16
   calm 174
   flattery 213, 251
   not rough 255
   easy 705
   – the bed of death

707, 906
- down 174
- over 174
- the ruffled brow
of care 834
- sailing 705
- water *easy* 705
- the way 705
smooth-bore 727
smoothly, go on -
prosperous 734
smoothness 255
smooth-tongued
544, 933
smother
repress 174
kill 361
stifle sound 581
restrain 751
smoulder *inert* 172
burn 382
latent 526
smous 796, 797
smudge 431, 653,
848
smug *affected* 855
smuggle
introduce 228
steal 791
illegal 964
smuggler 792
smut
dirt 653
impurity 961
smutch 431
snack
small quantity 32
food 298
snacks, go - 778
snaffle 752
snag *projection* 250
sharp 253
danger 667
hindrance 706
snail *slow* 275
snake *undulation*
248
serpent 366
hissing 409
miscreant 913
scotch the - 640
- in the grass
hidden 528
deceiver 548
bad 649
source of danger
667
evil-doer 913
knave 941
snake-like
convoluted 248

snap *break* 44
eat 298
brittle 328
noise **406**
rude 895
- at *seize* 789
bite 830
censure 932
- of the fingers
trifle 643
- one's fingers at
defy 715
insolence 885
despise 930
- the thread 70
- up *seize* 789
- one up
censure 932
-shot 554
snap-dragon 840
snappish 901
snare *deception* 545
snarl *growl* 412
rude 895
angry 900
threaten 909
snatch
small quantity 32
seize 789
- at *pursue* 622
seize 789
- a grace beyond
the reach of art
845
- from one's grasp
789
- from the jaws of
death 662, 672
- from under
one's nose 702
- a verdict 545,
702
snatches, by - 70
sneak *hide* 528
coward 862
servile 886
base 940
knave 941
bad man 949
- off, - out of 623
sneer *disparage* 929
contempt 930
blame 932
sneeze *blow* 349
snuffle 409
- at *despise* 930
sneezed at, not to
be - 642
snick 32, 51
snicker 838
sniff *blow* 349

odour 398
discovery 480a
sniffle 349
snigger *laugh* 838
ridicule 856
disrespect 929
sniggle 545
snip
small quantity 32
cut 44
short 201
tailor 225
sniping 716
snippet 32
snip-snap 713
snip-snap-snorem
840
snivel *weep* 839
snivelling
servile 886
snob *vulgar* 851
plebeian 876
servile 886
snobbishness
flattery 933
snood
headdress 225
circle 247
snooker 840
Snooks, Mr. - 876
snooze 683
snore 411, 683
snort 411, 412
snout 250
snow *ship* 273
ice 383
white 430
snow-ball 72
snow-blindness 443
snow-drift 72
snow-shoe 272
snow-storm 383
snozzle 250
snub *short* 201
hinder 706
cast a slur 874
humiliate 879
bluster 885
censure 932
snub-nosed 243
snuff *blow* 349
pungent 392
odour 398
up to - 698, 702
go out like the -
of a candle 360
- out 162, 421
- up 296, 398
snuff-colour 433
snuffing, want -
pert 885

snuffle *blow* 349
hiss 409
stammer 583
hypocrisy 988
snuffy 653
snug *closed* 261
comfortable 377
safe 664
prepared 673
content 831
secluded 893
keep - 528, 893
make all - 673
snuggery 189
snugness 827
so *similar* 17
very 31
therefore 476
method 627
- be it 488, 762
- far so good 618
- let it be 681
- much the better
831, 838
- much the worse
832, 835
- to speak 17, 521
soak *immerse* 300
water 337
moist 339
drunkenness 959
- up 340
So-and-so, Mr. -
neology 563
soap *lubricate* 332
oil 356
cleanser 652
soapy *unctuous* 355
servile 886
flattery 933
soar *great* 31
height 206
fly 267
rise 305
sob 839
sober *moderate* 174
wise 498
sane 502
style 576
grave 837
temperate 953
abstinent 958
- down 174, 502
humility 879
in - sadness
affirmation 535
- senses 502
- truth *fact* 494
sober-minded 502
calm 826
humble 879

song *music* 415
  poem 597
  death – 360, 839
  love– 597
  for a mere – 815
  no – no supper 812
  old – 643
songster 416
soniferous 402
sonnet 597
sonneteer 597
sonorous *sound* 402
  loud 404
  language 577
sons of:
  – Belial 988
  - God 977
Soofeeism 984
soon *transient* 111
  future 121
  early 132
  too – for 135
sooner: – or later
  another time 119
  future 121
  – said than done
    704
soot 431, 653
sooth 511
  in good – 543
soothe
  allay 174
  relieve 834
  flatter 933
soothing
  faint sound 405
  – syrup 174
soothsay 511
soothsayer 513, 994
soothsaying 511
sop
  small quantity 32
  food 298
  fool 501
  inducement 615
  reward 973
  – to Cerberus 458
  – in the pan 615
soph 492, 541
Sophi 745, 996
sophism 477, 497
sophist *scholar* 492
  dissembler 548
sophister 492
  student 541
sophistical 477
sophisticate *mix* 41
  debase 659
sophisticated
  spurious 545
sophistry 477

sophomore 541
soporific 683, 841
soporous 683
soprano 410, 416
sorbet 298
sorcerer 994
sorcery 992
sordes 653
sordet 417
sordid *stingy* 819
  covetous 865
sordine 417
sore
  bodily pain 378
  disease 655
  mental suffering
    828, 830
  discontent 832
  anger 900
  – as a boil 901*a*
  – place 822
  – subject 830, 900
sorely *very* 31
s'orienter 278
sorites 476
sorority 712
sorrel 433, 434
sorrow 828
  give – words 839
sorry *trifling* 643
  grieved 828
  mean 876
  make a – face 874
  cut a – figure 874
  be – for 750, 914
  in a – plight 732
  – sight 830, 837
sort *degree* 26
  arrange 60
  kind 75
  – with
    sociality 892
sortable }
sortance }
  agreement 23
sortes
  chance 156, 621
  – Virgilianæ
  sorcery 992
sortie 716
sortilege
  prediction 511
  sorcery 992
sortilegy 621
sortition 621
sorts, out of –
  ill-health 655
  sulky 901*a*
S.O.S. 669, 707
so-so *small* 32
  trifling 643

imperfect 651
sostenuto 415
sot *fool* 501
  drunkard 959
sot à triple étage
  501
sotto voce
  faint sound 405
  conceal 528
  voiceless 581
sou *money* 800
  qui n'a pas le –
    804
soubrette 599, 746
sough *conduit* 350
  noise 405
  cloaca 653
soul *essence* 5
  person 372
  intellect 450
  genius 498
  affections 820
  cure of –s 995
  flow of – 588
  not a – 187
  not dare to say
    one's – is his
    own *subjection*
    749
  fear 860
  – of wit 572
  have one's whole
    – in his work
    686
soulless 683, 823
soul-mate 903
soul-sick 837
soul-stirring 821,
  824
sound *great* 31
  conformable 82
  stable 150
  strong 159
  fathom 208
  bay 343
  noise 402
  investigate 461
  measure 466
  true 494
  wise 498
  sane 502
  good 648
  perfect 650
  healthy 654
  solvent 803
  orthodox 983*a*
  catch a – 418
  safe and – 654,
    670
  – the alarm
    indication 550

  warning 668
  alarm 669
  fear 860
  – asleep 683
  full of – and fury
    unmeaning 517
  insolent 885
  – the horn 416
  – of limb 654
  – locator 726
  – mind 502
  – the praises of
    931
  – the note of prep-
    aration 673
  – reasoning 476
  – a retreat 283
  – sleep 683
  – a trumpet
    publish 531
    alarm 669
  – of wind 654
sounding: big –
  577
  – brass 517
sounding-board 417
soundings 208
soundless
  unfathomable 208
  silent 403
soup 298, 352
soupçon 32, 41
soufflé 298
sour *acid* 397
  discontented 832
  embitter 835
  uncivil 895
  sulky 901
  – grapes
    impossible 471
    excuse 617
  – the temper 830
source *beginning* 66
  cause 153
sourdet 417
sourdine 417
  à la – *noiseless* 403
  concealed 528
sourdough 463
soured 832
sourness 397
sous tous les
  rapports 52
souse 310, 337
South *direction* 278
  North and –
  opposite 237
Southern
  antipodes 237
  – Cross 318
souvenir 505

display 882
–board 666
splay 291
–footed 243
spleen
  melancholy 837
  hatred 898
  anger 900
  sullen 901a
  harbour – 907
spleenless 906
splendour
  bright 420
  beautiful 845
  glorious 873
  display 882
splenetic 837, 901a
splice *join* 43
  cross 219
  interjacent 228
  repair 660
  – the main brace
  tipsy 959
spliced, be –
  marriage 903
splint 215
splinter
  small piece 32
  divide 44
  filament 205
  brittle 328
split *divide* 44
  discontinuity 70
  bisect 91
  brittle 328
  divulge 529
  quarrel 713
  fail 732
  portion 786
  laugh 838
  – the difference
    29, 774
  – the ears ⎫ 404
  – the head ⎭ 410
  – hairs
  discriminate 465
  sophistry 477
  fastidiousness 868
  – upon a rock 732
  – one's sides 838
splutter *energy* 171
  spit 297
  stammer 583
  haste 684
spoil *vitiate* 659
  hinder 706
  lenity 740
  plunder 791
  booty 793
  deface 846
  satiate 869

– sport 706
– trade 708
spoiled child 869,
  899
– of fortune 734
spoiler 792
spoke *radius* 200
  tooth 253
  obstruct 706
  put a – in one's
  wheel *render*
  powerless 158
  hinder 706
spokesman 524,
  582
spolia opima 793
spoliate 791
spoliative 793
spondee 597
spondulics 800
sponge *moisten* 339
  dry 340
  pulp 354
  clean 652
  despoil 791
  hanger on 886
  drunkard 959
  apply the –
  obliterate 552
  non-payment 808
  – out 552
sponging-house 752
spongy *porous* 252
  soft 324
  marshy 345
sponsion 771
sponsor
  witness 467
  security 771
  be – for
  promise 768
  obligation 926
sponsorship 771
spontaneous
  voluntary 600
  willing 602
  impulsive 612
spontoon 727
spoof 545
spook 980
spool 312
spoon
  receptacle 191
  ladle 272
  bill and coo 902
  born with a silver
  – in one's mouth
  734
Spoonerism 218,
  853
spoonful 25, 32

spoon-like 252
spoon-meat 298
spoony *foolish* 499
  lovesick 902
spoor 551
sporadic 73, 137,
  657
spore 330
sport *killing* 361
  chase 622
  amusement 840
  show off 882
  in – *pastime* 840
  humour 842
  the – of 749
  – of fortune 735
sporting *killing* 361
  contention 720
  amusement 840
  – dog 366
sportive 836, 840
sports 686
sportsman 361, 622,
  840
sportulary 784, 785
sportule 784
sporule 330
spot *place* 182
  discover 480a
  mark 550
  dirt 653
  blemish 848
  blot 874
  on the –
  instantly 113
  present time 118
  soon 132
  in one's presence
  186
spotless *perfect* 650
  clean 652
  innocent 946
spot light 423, 599
spots in the sun,
  see – *fastidious*
  868
spotted
  variegated 440
  damaged 659
spousal 903
spouse 88, 903
spouseless 904
spout *egress* 295
  flow out 348
  conduit 350
  speak 582
  act 599
  pawn 771, 787,
  788
sprag 215
sprain 158, 160

sprat to catch a:
  – herring 794
  – whale 699
sprawl *length* 200
  horizontal 213
  descend 306
spray *sprig* 51
  vaporizer 336
  foam 353
spread *enlarge* 35
  disperse 73
  broadcast 78
  expanse 180
  expand 194
  diverge 291
  feast 298
  publish 531
  – abroad 531
  – canvas 267
  – out 194
  – sail 267
  – a shade 421
  – to 196
  – the toils 545
spree 840
spretæ injuria
  formæ *ugly* 846
  disrespect 929
  detraction 934
sprig *branch* 51
  child 129
  shillelagh 727
sprightly 836, 842
spring *early* 125
  source 153
  strength 159
  velocity 274
  recoil 277
  fly 293
  leap 309
  elasticity 325
  rivulet 348
  instrument 633
  store 636
  –s of action 615
  – back 277
  – to one's feet 307
  – from 154
  – a leak 651, 659
  – a mine
  destroy 162
  unexpected 508
  attack 716
  – a project 626
  – up *begin* 66
  event 151
  grow 194
  ascend 305
  visible 446
  hot – 382
  – upon 789

starch *stiff* 323
  viscid 352
  affected 855
  proud 878
Star Chamber 966
starched
  ostentatious 882
stare *look* 441
  curiosity 455
  wonder 870
  make one – 870
  – out of counte-
    nance
  humiliate 879
  insolent 885
  discourteous 895
  – one in the face
  destiny 152
  manifest 525
  Death –s one in
    the face 360
**stare super anti-
  quas vias**
  continue 143
  habit 613
  preservation 670
  inaction 681
star-gazing 318
staring 446
stark *very* 31
  sheer 32
  complete 52
  hard 323
  – blind 442
  – naked 226
stark staring 31
  manifest 525
  – mad 503
starlight 422
starlike
  pointed 253
starry 318
stars [*see* star]
  worlds 318
  bless one's – 916
  – in the firmament
  multitude 102
  – and stripes 550
start *begin* 66
  sudden change
    146
  arise 151
  impulse 276
  move 284
  depart 293
  leap 309
  unexpected 508
  suggest 514
  crack 659
  offer 763
  fear 860

wonder 870
get the –
  precede 280
  success 731
  give a – to 276
have the –
  prior 116
  early 132
  get before 280
  – afresh 66
  – a doubt 485
  – game 622
  – off 293
  – a question 461
  – up *project* 250
  arise 305
  appear 446
starting: – hole
  plea 617
  – point
  departure 293
  reasoning 476
  eyes – out of one's
    head 870
startle *doubt* 485
  unexpected 508
  excite 824
  fear 860
  wonder 870
startling 508
startlish 825
starts, by fits and –
  608
starvation 640, 956
starve *cold* 383, 385
  poverty 804
  parsimony 819
  fast 956
starveling *thin* 203
  insufficient 640
  poor 804
state *condition* **7**
  speciality 79
  nation 372
  inform 527
  affirm 535
  government 737
  realm 780
  ostentation 882
  robes of – 747
  secretary of – 694
  – of affairs 151
  –'s evidence 529
  – of facts
  description 594
  lawsuit 969
  – paper 551
  – room 191
  – of siege 722
statecraft 693
stated periods, at –

138
stately *grand* 873
  proud 878
  pompous 882
statement 535, 594
statemonger 694
state prison 752
states-general 696
statesman 694
statesmanlike 698
statesmanship 692,
  693
static 404
Statics *strength* 159
  gravity 319
station *degree* 26
  term 71
  place 182
  situation 183
  locate 184
  rank 873
stationary
  permanent 141
  quiescent 265
stationery 590
station-house 752
statist 694
statistics 85, 86
statu:
  in – pupillari 127
  in – quo 141, 660
statuary 557, 559
statue 554
  still as a – 265
stature 206
status *position* 8
  terms 71
  situation 183
  repute 873
status quo
  past 122
  unchanged 145
  restoration 660
  – ante bellum 145
statute 697, 963
staunch *health* 654
  reinstate 660
  honest 939
  – belief 484
stave *music* 413,
  415
  contention 720
  – in *concave* 252
  hole 260
  – off 133, 706
stay *remain* 106
  wait 133
  continue 141
  stop 142
  dwell 186
  support 215

  not move 265
  prevent 706
  – away 187
  – one's hand
  cease 142
  relinquish 624
  rest 687
  – at home 893
stayed [*see* staid]
stays *corset* 225
stead 644
  in the – of
  substitution 147
  commission 755
  deputy 759
  stand one in
    good – 644
steadfast *stable* 150
  persevering 604a
  – belief 484
  – thought 457
steady *uniform* 16
  regular 80
  periodic 138
  stable 150
  persevering 604a
  unexcitable 826
  cautious 864
steal 791
  – along 275, 528
  – away 623
  – on the ear 405
  – a march
  prior 116
  early 132
  precede 280
  deceive 545
  active 682
  cunning 702
  – upon one 508
stealing 791
stealth 528
  do good by – &c.
    881
stealthy 528
  cunning 702
  caution 864
steam *navigate* 267
  gas 334
  vaporize 336
  bubbles 353
  under – 267
  under sail and –
    274
  – car 272
  – up 171
  get the – up 673
steamboat 273
**steam-hammer to
  crack a nut**
  waste 638

silent 403
- less 467
- life *matter* 316
painting 556
- more
superior 33
evidence 467
- small voice 405
in - water 714
still-born 360, 732
stillroom 636
stillicidium 348
stilted
elevated 307
- *style* 577
ridiculous 853
affected 855
boasting 884
stilts *support* 215
on - *high* 206
elevated 307
hyperbolical 549
proud 878
boasting 884
stimulant 662
stimulate
energy 171
violence 173
incite 615
excite 824
stimulating
suggestive 514
stimulus 615
sting *pain* 378
tingle 380
poison 663
excite 824
mental suffering
830
anger 900
stinging
pungent 392
stingo 298
stingy 819
stink 401
- in the nostrils
unpleasant 830
dislike 867
hate 898
stink-bomb 727
stink-pot 401
stint *degree* 26
limit 233
scanty 640
begrudge 819
stintless 639
stipend *salary* 973
stipendiary
subject 749
receiving 785
magistrate 967

stipple
variegate 440
painting 556
engraving 558
stipulate 769, 770
- for 720
stipule 51
stir *energy* 171
move 264
agitation 315
excite 375
activity 682
jail 752
emotion 824
make a - 642, 682
- about 682
- the blood 824,
900
- up dissension
713
- the embers 163,
824
- the feelings 824
- the fire 384
- a question 461,
476
- one's stumps
266, 682
- up *mix* 41
violent 173
excite 824
stirps *kin* 11
source 153
paternity 166
stirring *events* 151
important 642
active 682
- news 532
stirrup
support 215
with a foot in the
- 293
stirrup-cup 293, 959
stitch *junction* 43
pain 378
work 680
- in time 132
- of work 686
stive 384
stiver 800
stoat 401
stoccado 717
stock *kinship* 11
quantity 25
origin 153
paternity 166
collar 225
soup 298
fool 501
habitual 613
materials 635

store 636
property 780
merchandise 798
money 800
in - 777
laughing - 857
lay in a - 637
take - *inspect* 457
accounts 811
- exchange 799
- still 265
- in trade
means 632
store 636
property 780
merchandise 798
- with 637
stockade 717
stocked, well - 639
stock exchange 621
stock-farm 370
stocking 225
hoard 800
stock-jobbing 794
stock operator 621
stocks *prison* 752
funds 802
punishment 975
on the -
business 625
preparation 673
incomplete 730
- and stones 316,
823
stocky 201
stodge 957
stoicism
insensibility 823
inexcitability 826
disinterested 942
temperance 953
stoke 388
stoker 268
stole 999
stolen: - away 671
- goods 793
stolid 499, 843
stomach *pouch* 191
taste 390
brook 826
desire 865
not have the - to
603
turn the - 830
- of an ostrich 957
stomacher 225
stone *heavy* 319
dense 321
hard 323
kill 361
lithography 558

material 635
attack 716
weapon 727
punish 972
corner - 642
go down like a -
310
cast the first - at
938
heart of - 823, **907**
key- 642
musical -s 417
no - unturned
461, 686
philosopher's -
662
precious - 648
stepping - 627
throw a - at
attack 716
censure 932
accuse 938
throw -s at 907
tomb- 363
mark with a
white - 642
throw a - in one's
own garden 699
- dead 360
- of Sisyphus 645
stone-blind 442
stone-coloured 432
stone-deaf 419
stone's throw 197
stoneware 384
stony 323
stony-hearted 907,
919
stooge 711, 746, **886**
stook 72
stool 215
between two -s
704
- of repentance
950
- pigeon 527, **548**
stoop *slope* 217
lower 308
humble 879
servile 886
dishonourable 940
- to conquer 702
stop *end* 67
cease 142
close 261
rest 265
silent 403
danger 665
inaction 681
hinder 706
prohibit 761

long 200
narrow 203
furrow 259
light 420
stripe 440
mark 550
streaked 219, 440
stream *assemble* 72
move 264
– *of fluid* **347**
– *of water* 348
– *of air* 349
– *of light* 420
abundance 639
against the – 708
with the –
conformity 82
progression 282
assent 488
facility 705
concord 714
fashion 852
servility 886
– **of events** 151
– **of time** 109
streamer *flag* 550
streaming 47, 73
streamlet 348
street 189, 627
man in the – 876
streets:
ːn the open – 525
on the – 961
street-walker 962
strength
quantity 25
degree 26
greatness 31
vigour **159**
energy 171
tenacity 327
animality 364
put all one's –
into 686
lose – 655
tower of – 717
– **of mind** 604
strengthen 35
strengthless 160
strenuous
persevering 604a
active 682
exertion 686
Strephon and Chloe
902
stress *emphasis* 580
requirement 630
importance 642
strain 686
difficulty 704
by – *of* 601

lay – **on** 476
– **of circumstances**
compulsion 744
– **of weather** 349
stretch *expanse* 180
expand 194
extend 200
exaggerate 549
exertion 686
encroach 925
at a – 69
mind on the – 451
on the – 686
upon the – 457
– **away to** 196
– **forth one's hand**
680, 789
– **of the imagina-**
tion 515, 549
– **the meaning** 523
– **a point** 83, 303
exaggerate 549
severity 739
permit 760
not observe **773**
undue 925
exempt 927a
– **to** *distance* 196
length 200
stretcher 215, 272
strew 73
striæ, striated 259,
440
stricken *pain* 828
terror– 860
be – by 655
– **in years** 128
strict
in conformity 82
exact 494
severe 739
conscientious 939
orthodox 983a
– **inquiry** 461
– **interpretation**
522
– **search** 461
– **settlement** 780
strictly speaking
literally 19
exact 494
interpreted 522
stricture
constriction 203
hindrance 706
censure 932
stride *distance* 196
motion 264
walk 266
strident 410
strides: make – 282

rapid – 274
stridor **410**
strife 713, 720
strigil 652
strike *operate* 170
hit 276
resist 719
disobey 742
impress 824
beat 972
– **at** 716
– **a balance**
equalize 27
mean 29
pay 807
– **a bargain** 769,
794
– **a blow** *act* 680
– **dumb** *dumb* 581
excitement 824
wonder 870
humble 879
– **the eye** 457
– **the first blow**
716
– **one's flag** 725
– **hard** 171
– **all of a heap**
824, 860
– **home** 171
– **in with**
imitate 19
assent 488
cooperate 709
– **the iron while it**
is hot 134
– **a light** 384, 420
– **the lyre** 416
– **the mind** 457
– **out something**
new 146, 515
– **off** *exclude* 55
– **one** 451
– **out** *exclude* 55
destroy 162
invent 515
obliterate 552
scheme 626
– **off the roll** 756,
972
– **at the root of**
162
– **root** 150
– **sail** 275
– **tents** 293
– **terror** 860
– **up** 416
– **with wonder** 870
striker 927
striking 525
– **likeness** 554

strikingly
greatly 31
string *tie* 43
ligature 45
continuity 69
filament 205
musical note 413
– **together** 60, 69
stringed instru-
ments 417
stringent
energetic 171
authoritative **737**
strict 739
compulsory 744
strings: *music* 417
leading – 541
pull the – 175, 693
two – **to one's bow**
632
stringy 205, 327
strip *adjunct* 39
narrow 203
filament 205
divest 226
take 789
rob 791
stripe *length* 200
variegation 440
mark 550
badge 747
blow 972
stripling 129
stripped *poor* 804
strive *endeavour*
675
exert 686
contend 720
– **against** 720
stroke *impulse* **276**
touch 379
mark 550
evil 619
expedient 626
disease 655
action 680
success 731
painful 830
at a – 113
good – 626
– **of death** 360
– **of the pen**
writing 590
command 741
– **of policy** 626
– **of time** 113
– **of work** 686
– **the wrong way**
256
stroll 266
strolling player 599

subaction 330
subahdar 745
subalpine 206
subaltern
  inferior 34
  soldier 726
  officer 745
  servant 746
  plebeian 876
subaqueous 208
subastral 318
subaudition 527
subcommittee 696
subconscious 317
subcontrary 237
subcutaneous 221
subdean 996
subdichotomy 91
subdititious 147
subdivide 44
subdivision
  part 51
  class 75
  military 726
  realty 780
subdolous 702
subdominant 413
subdual 731
subduction 38
subdue *calm* 174
  succeed 731
subdued
  morally 826
sub-editor 593
subitaneous 113
subito 113
subjacent 207
subject *dominate*
  175
  liable 177
  topic 454
  meaning 516
  servant 746
  enthral 749
  - of dispute 713
  - to examination
  461
  - of inquiry 461
  - of thought 454
  - to 469, 475
subjection 749
subjective
  intrinsic 5
  immaterial 317
  intellectual 450
subjoin 37
subjugate 731, 749
subjugation 732,
  824
subjunctive 37
sublapsarian 984

sublation 38
sublevation 307
sub-lieutenant 745
sublimate
  elevate 307
  lighten 320
  vaporize 336
sublime *high* 206
  language 574
  beauty 845
  glory 873
  magnanimous
  942
  from the - to the
  ridiculous 853
subliminal 317
sublineation 550
sublunary 318
submarine
  deep 208
  ship 273
  warship 726
  - chaser 726
  - warfare 722
submediant 413
submerge
  destroy 162
  immerse 300
  plunge 310
  steep 337
submersible 273,
  726
submersion 208
subministration
  707
submission **725**
  obedience 743
submissive
  tractable 705
  enduring 826
  humble 879
submit to arbitra-
  tion 774
submonish 695
submultiple 84
subordinate
  inferior 34
  unimportant 643
  subject 749
subordination 58
suborn 615, 795
subpœna 741, 969
subreption
  falsehood 544
  acquisition 775
subrogation 147
subscribe
  assent 488
  aid 707
  agree to 769
  give 784

subscript 39, 65
subscription
  gift 784
subsequent
  - *in order* 63
  - *in time* 117
subserviency
  servility 886
subservient
  instrumental 631
  aid 707
  subject 749
subside 36, 306
subsidiary *aid* 707
  servant 746
subsidy
  assistance 707
  gift 784
  pay 809
subsist *exist* 1
  continue 141
  live 359
subsistence 298
subsoil 221, 342
substance
  existence 1
  thing 3
  quantity 25
  inside 221
  matter 316
  texture 329
  important part
  642
  wealth 803
  in - 596
  man of - 803
substantial
  existing 1
  hypostatic 3
  material 316
  dense 321
  true 494
  - *meaning* 516
substantiality **3**
substantially
  intrinsically 5
  - *true* 494
substantiate 467,
  924
substantive 1, 3
substitute
  inferior 34
  change 147
  means **634**
  deputy 759
substitution **147**
substratum
  substance 3
  layer 204
  base 211
  support 215

interior 221
  materiality 316
substructure 211
subsultory 315
subsume 54
subtend 237
subterfuge 617
  sophistry 477
  lie 546
  cunning 702
subterranean 208
subtile *light* 320
  rare 322
  - *texture* 329
subtilize *rarefy* **322**
  sophistry 477
subtle *slight* 32
  light 320
  cunning 702
  - point 704
  - reasoning 476
subtlety 477, 498
subtraction
  subduction 38
  arithmetic 85
  taking 789
subtrahend 38, 84
suburb *town* 189
  near 197
  environs 227
subvention
  support 215
  aid 707
  gift 784
subversion 146
subvert *destroy* 162
  invert 218
  depress 308
subway 627
  - train 272
succedaneum 147
succeed *follow* 63
  posterior 117
  success 731
  transfer 783
  - to *acquire* 775
succès d'estime 873
success **731**
succession
  sequence 63
  continuity 69
  repetition 104
  posteriority 117
  transfer 783
  in quick - 136
  in regular - 138
  - of ideas 451
  - of time 109
successless 732
successor 65, 117
succinct 572

suo: – periculo 926
– sibi gladio hunc
jugulo
absurdity 479
retaliation 718
sup *small quantity*
32
feed 298
– full of horrors
828
super *theatrical* 599
superable 470
superabound 641
superadd 37
superannuated 128
superb 845
supercargo 694
supercherie 545
supercilious
proud 878
insolent 885
disrespectful 929
scornful 930
superdreadnought
726
supereminence
648, 873
supererogation 641,
645
superexaltation 873
superexcellence
648
superfetation 37,
168
Superficial
shallow 209
outside 220
misjudging 481
ignorant 491
– extent 180
Superficies 220
superfine 648
superfluitant 305
superfluity 40, 641
superfluous 645
superhuman 650,
976
superimpose 223
superimposed 206
superincumbent
206, 319
superinduce
change 140
cause 153
produce 161
superintend 693
superintendent 694
superior *greater* 33
– *in size* 194
important 642
good 648

director 694
superiority 33
superjunction 37
superlative 33
superlatively good
648
superman 33
supernal 206, 210,
981
supernatant 206,
305
supernatural 976,
980
– aid 707
supernumerary
adjunct 39
theatrical 599
reserve 636
redundant 641
superpose 37, 223
supersaturate 641
superscription 550,
590
supersede
substitute 147
disuse 678
relinquish 782
supersensible 317
superstition
credulity 486
error 495
religion 984
superstratum 220
superstructure 729
supertax 812
supertonic 413
supervacaneous
641
supervene
extrinsic 6
be added 37
succeed 117
happen 151
supervise 693
supervisor 694
supination 213
supine
horizontal 213
inverted 218
sluggish 683
mentally torpid
823
suppeditate 637
supper 298
supplant 147
supple *soft* 324
servile 886
supplement
addition 37
adjunct 39
completion 52

publication 531
book 593
suppletory 37
suppliant 765, 767
supplicate *beg* 765
pity 914
worship 990
supplies
materials 635
aid 707
money 800
supply *store* 636
provide 637
give 784
– aid 707
– deficiencies 52
– the place of 147
– and transport
726
support *perform* 170
sustain 215
evidence 467
preserve 670
aid 707
feel 821
endure 826
vindicate 937
– life 359
supporter 711
–s *heraldic* 550
suppose 514
supposing 469
supposition 514
supposititious 546
suppress
destroy 162
conceal 528
silent 581
restrain 751
suppression of
truth 544
suppuration 653
suppute 85
supralapsarian 984
supramundane 939
supremacy 33, 737
supreme 33
summit 210
authority 737
in a – degree 31
Supreme Being 976
surbate 659
surbated 688
surcease 142
surcharge 641
– and falsify 811
surcingle 45
surcoat 225
surd *number* 84
deaf 419
silent letter 561

sure *certain* 474
belief 484
safe 664
make – against
673
make – of
inquire 461
take 789
you may be – 535
to be – *assent* 488
on – ground 664
security 771
sure-footed
careful 459
skilful 698
cautious 864
surely 488, 602, 870
sureness 474
surety 474, 664
surf 348, 353
surface *outside* 220
texture 329
below the – 526
lie on the – 518,
525
skim the – 460
Surface, Joseph –
548
surfeit 641, 869
surge *swarm* 72
swell 305
rotation 312
wave 348
surgeon 662
surgery 662
surgit amari
aliquid 651
surly *gruff* 895
sullen 901a
unkind 907
surmise 514
surmount *be*
superior 33
tower 206
transcursion 303
ascent 305
– a difficulty
overcome 731
surmountable 470
surname 564
surpass
be superior 33
grow 194
go beyond 303
outshine 873
surplice 999
surplus 40, 641
surplusage 641
surprint 550
surprise
non-expectation

tenter-hook 214
on –s 507
tenth 99
tenths
tithe 812
tent-pegging 840
tents, O Israel, to
your – 722
tenue, en grande –
847, 882
tenuity
smallness 32
thinness 203
rarity 322
tenuous
shadowy 4
tenure
possession 777
property 780
due 924
tepee 189
tepefaction 384
Tephramancy 511
tepid 382
tepidarium 386
ter quaterque
beatus 827
teratology
unconformity 83
distortion 243
altiloquence 577
boasting 884
tercentenary 98,
138, 883
terceron 41
terebration 260
teres atque rotun-
dus 249
in seipso – 650
tergiversation 283,
607
term *end* 67
place in series **71**
period of time 106
limit 233
word 562
name 564
lease 780
termagant 901
terminal 67, 233,
292
terminate 67, 292
limit 233
termination 154
termine, mezzo –
628
terminology 562
terminus *end* 67
limit 233
arrival 292
termless 105

terms [*see* term]
circumstances **8**
reasoning 476
pacification 723
conditions 770
bring to – 723
come to –
assent 488
pacify 723
submit 725
consent 762
compact 769
couch in – 566
on friendly – 888
in no measured –
574
ternary 93
ternion 92
Terpsichore 416,
840
terra: – cotta
baked 384
sculpture 557
– firma
support 215
land 342
safety 664
– incognita 491
terrace *houses* 189
level 213
terrain 181
terraqueous 318
terre verte 435
terrene 318, 342
terrine 191
terrestrial 318
terrible 860
terribly *greatly* 31
terrier *list* 86
auger 262
dog 366
terrific 31, 830, 860
terrify 860
territorial *land* 342
soldier 726
territory 181, 780
terror 860
King of –s 360
reign of – 739, 828
terrorem, in – 860,
909
terrorism 860
insolence 885
terrorist
coward 862
blusterer 887
evil-doer 913
terse 572
tertian *periodic* 138
tertiary *three* 92
tertium quid

dissimilar 18
mixture 41
combination 48
unconformable 83
tesselated 440, 847
tesseræ
mosaic 440
counters 550
test 463
testa, voce di – 410
testament 771
Testament 985
tester *bedstead* 215
sixpence 800
testify 467, 550
testimonial 551
testimony 467
testy 901
tetanus 315
tetchy 901
tête: – baissée 863
– exaltée 503
– montée 503, 825
–à-tête *two* 89
near 197
confer 588
tether *fasten* 43
locate 184
restrain 751
means of restraint
752
go beyond the
length of one's
– 738
tethered *firm* 150
tetrachord 413
tetractic 95
tetrad 95
tetrahedral 95
tetrahedron 244
tetrarch 745
text *prototype* 22
topic 454
meaning 516
printing 591
–book 542, 596
textile 219, 329
textuary 983*a*, 985
texture *mixture* 41
roughness 256
fabric **329**
Thais 962
Thalia 599
Thalmud 985
Thames on fire
set the – 471
never set the –
501, 701
thane *nobility* 875
thank 916
no – you 764

– one's stars 838
– you for nothing
917
thankful 916
rest and be – 265,
831
thankless
painful 830
ungrateful 917
thank-offering 916,
990
thanks to 155
thanksgiving
gratitude 916
worship 990
that 79
– is 118
– is to say 79
– being so 8
at – time 119
thatch *roof* 223
thaumatrope 445
thaumaturgist 994
thaumaturgy 992
thaw *melt* 335
heart 382
heating 384
calm the mind 826
pity 914
Thearchy
authority 737
Deity 976
theatre
spectacle 441
school 542
drama 599
arena 728
amusement 840
tribunal 966
théâtre: coup de –
appearance 448
prodigy 872
display 882
jeu de – 448, 872
nom de – 565
theatrical 599
affected 855
ostentatious 882
Theban, learned –
492
theca 223
thé dansant 840
theft 775, 791
theism 984, 987
theistic *of God* 976
theme *topic* 454
dissertation 595
Themis 922
then *time* 106
therefore 476
thence

627
thorough-going 52
thoroughly, do –
729
thorough-paced 31
thorp 189
though
  compensation 30
  qualification 469
  opposition 708
thought *little* 32
  reflection **451**
  idea 453
  give a – to 457
  not to be – of
  610, 761
  organ of – 450
  quick as – 274
  seat of – 450
  subject of – 454
  want of – 458
  who would have –
  it? 508
  – of 454
thoughtful 451, 498
thoughtless
  incogitant 452
  inattentive 458
  careless 460
  improvident 674
thoughts:
  – that breathe 574
  – elsewhere 458
thousand 98, 102
  one in a – 648,
  948
thralldom 749, 751
thrash 972
Thraso 887
Thrasonic 884, 885
thread
  arrange 60
  series 69
  weak 160
  filament 205
  pass *through* 302
  not have a dry –
  339
  hang by a – 665
  life hangs by a –
  360
  worn to a – 659
  – one's way 266,
  302
threadbare 226, 659
threadpaper 203
threat **909**
threaten
  future 121
  destiny 152
  danger 665

threatening
  warning 668
  unhopeful 859
three 93
  – in one and one
  in – 976
  sisters – 601
  go through – hun-
  dred and sixty
  degrees 311
  – sheets in the
  wind 959
  times three
  number 98
  approbation 931
threefold 93
three-score 98
  – years and ten
  128
three-tailed
  bashaw
  master 745
  nobility 875
threne 839
threnody 839
thresh 972
  – out 461
threshold
  beginning 66
  edge 231
  at the – *near* 197
  – of an inquiry 461
thrice 93
  – happy 827
  –told tale 573
thrid 302
thrift
  prosperity **734**
  gain 775
  economy 817
thriftless 818
thrill
  physical pain 378
  touch 380
  feeling 821
  excitation 824
thrilling
  pleasing 829
  painful 830
thrive **734**
throat *opening* 260
  pipe 350, 351
  cut the – 361
  force down the –
  739
  stick in one's –
  581, 585
  take by the – 789
throb 315, 821
throbbing: – heart
  860

– pain 378
throe
  revolution 146
  violence 173
  agitation 315
  physical pain 378
  agony 828
  birth– 161
throne *abode* 189
  seat 215
  *emblem of au-
  thority* 747
  ascend the – 737
  occupy the – 737
  power behind
  the – 526
  – of God 981
throng 72
throttle
  render powerless
  158
  close 261
  kill 361
  seize 789
  – down 275
through
  owing to 154
  viâ 278
  by means of 631
  get – 729
  go – one 824
  wet – 339
  – thick and thin
  complete 52
  violence 173
  perseverance 604a
throughout 50, 52
  – the world 180
throw *impel* 276
  propel 284
  exertion 686
  – oneself into the
  arms of 666
  – away *reject* 610
  waste 638
  relinquish 782
  – back 145
  – cold water on
  616
  – of the dice 156
  – doubt upon 485
  – down 162, 308
  – oneself at the
  feet of 725
  – good money
  after bad 818
  – in 228
  – off [*see below*]
  – open 260, 296
  – out [*see below*]
  – over *destroy* 162

– overboard
  exclude 55
  destroy 162
  eject 297
  abrogate 756
  – on paper 590
  – away the scab-
  bard 722
  – into the shade
  superior 33
  lessen 36
  surpass 303
  important 642
  – a tub to catch a
  whale 545
  – up [*see below*]
  – a veil over 528
throw off 297
  – all disguise 529
  – one's guard 508
  – the mask 529
  – the scent
  misdirect 538
  avoid 623
throw out 284, 297
  eject 297
  – a feeler 379
  – of gear
  disjoin 44
  derange 61
  – a hint 527
  – a suggestion 514
throw up *eject* 297
  resign 757
  – one's cap 884
  – the game 624
throwing stick 727
thrown out 704
thrum 416
thrush 416
thrust *push* 276
  attack 716
  – in *insert* 300
  (*interpose*) 228
  – one's nose in 682
  – out 55
  – down one's
  throat 744
  – upon 784
thud 406, 408a
thug *murderer* 361
  thief 792
thumb *touch* 379
  bite the – 929
  one's fingers all –
  699
  rule of –
  experiment 463
  unreasoning 477
  essay 675
twiddle one's –

inaction 381
leisure 685
weariness 841
– immemorial 122
– of life
duration 106
now 118
age 128
– out of mind 122
– to spare 685
– after time 104
– up 111, 134
– was 122
there being –s
when 136
timeful 134
time-honoured
old 124
repute 873
respected 928
time-keeper 114
time-recorder 553
timeless 135
timelessness 112
timely 132, 134
timeo Danaos 485, 864
timeous 134
time-piece 114
time-pleaser 607
timetable 266
times *present* 118
events 151
hard - 735
many – 136
– out of number 104
time-serving
tergiversation 607
cunning 702
servility 886
improbity 940
selfishness 943
time-worn *old* 124
age 128
deteriorated 659
timid *fearful* 860
cowardly 862
humble 881
timist 607
Timocracy 803
Timon of Athens
wealth 803
seclusion 893
misanthrope 911
timorous [*see* timid]
tin *preserve* 670
money 800
– *hat* 717
tinct 428
tinctorial 428

tincture
small quantity 32
mixture 41
colour 428
tinctured
disposition 820
tinder *fuel* 388
irascible 901
tine 253
tinge
small quantity 32
mix 41
colour 428
tingent 428
tingle *pain* 378
touch 380
emotion 821
make the ears –
900
tink 408
tinker
repair 660
tinkle
faint sound 405
resonance 408
tinkling cymbal 517
tinnient 408
tinsel *glitter* 420
sham 545
ornament 847
frippery 851
tinsmith 690
tint 428
tintamarre 404
tintinnabulary 408
tiny 32, 193
– *bit* 32
tip *end* 67
summit 210
cover 223
give 784
reward 973
on –*toe high* 206
expect 507
– *off* 527
– the wink 550
tip-cat 840
tippet 214, 225
tipple 298, 959
tippler 959
tipstaff 965
tipsy 959
tip-top 210, 648
tirade 582, 932
tire *dress* 225
fatigue 688
worry 830
weary 841
tiré à quatre épin-
gles 850
tirer d'affaire 672

se – 731
Tiresias 513
tiresome [*see* tire]
Tisiphone 173, 900
tissue *whole* 50
assemblage 72
matted 219
texture 329
tit *small* 193
pony 271
tit for tat 718
Titan 159, 980
Titania 979
titanic 192
titbit 298, 394, 829
tithe *tenth* 99
tax 812
tithing 181
titillate 840, 865
titillation 377, 380
titivate 847
title
indication 550
name 564
printing 591
right to property
780
distinction **877**
right 924
titled 875
title-deed 771
title-page 66
titter 838
tittle 32
to a – 494
tittle-tattle 532, 588
titubancy 315
titubate 306, 732
titular 562, 564
tmesis 218
T.N.T. 727
to *direction* 278
lie – 681
– all intents and
purposes 27, 52
– a certain degree
32
– come 121, 152
– the credit of 805
– crown all 33, 642
– do 59
– the end of the
chapter 52
– the end of time
112
– and fro 12, 314
– the full 52
– a great extent
31
– the letter 19
– a man 78

– the point 23
– the purpose 23
– a small extent 32
– some extent 26
– be sure 488
– this day 118
– wit 79
toad 649, 846
– under a harrow
378
toad-eater 886, **935**
toad-eating
flattery 933
toadstool 367
toady 886
toast *roast* 384
celebrate 883
tobacco 392
toboggan 272, 840
toby *jug* 191
toccata 415
tocsin 669
tod 319
to-day 118
toddle 266, 275
toddy 298
toe 211
on the light fan-
tastic 309, 840
toes turn up the –
die 360
toff 854
toffee 396
toga 225, 747
assume the –
virilis 131
together 88, 120
come – 290
get – 72
hang – 709
lay heads – 695
– with 37, 88
toggery 225
toil
activity 682
exertion 686
– of a pleasure 682
–s *trap* 545
toilet 225
– *water* 400
toilette 225
en grande – 847
toilsome 686, **704**
toilworn 688
token 550
give – 525
– of remembrance
505
told, do what one
is – 743
tolderolloll 838

music 417
punishment 975
triangular duel 720
triarchy 737
tribe *race* 11
assemblage 72
class 75
clan 166
tribulation 828
tribunal 966
tribune
rostrum 542
judge 967
tributary *river* 348
giving 784
tribute
compensation 30
donation 784
money paid 809
reward 973
pay – to 928, 931
trice 113, 633
– up 43
in a – 113
trichotomy 94
trichroism 440
trick *deception* 545
trait 550
habit 613
contrivance 626
skill 698
artifice 702
- *at cards* **775**
play –s
bungle 699
cunning 702
amusement 840
ridicule 856
– of fortune 509
– out 847, 851
–s of the trade 702
trickery *deceit* 545
finery 851
trickle 295, 348
trickster
deceiver 548
cunning 702
rogue 792
tricksy *cheery* 836
pretty 845
ornamented 847
tricolour
variegated **440**
flag 550
tricycle 272
trident 92, 341
triennial
periodical 138
plant 367
triennium 92
trifid 94

trifle *small* 32
neglect 460
folly 499
unimportant 643
not to be –d with
744
not stick at –s 604
– time away 683
– with *neglect* 460
deceive 545
disrespect 929
trifler 460, 501
trifling 499, 643
wit 842
triforium 1000
triform 92
trifurcate 94
trigamy 903
trigger 633
draw the – 722
**Trigger, Sir Lucius
O' –** 887
trigon 244
trigonometry 244
trihedral 93
trilateral 236, 244
trilogistic 93
trilogy 93
drama 599
trill *stream* 348
sound 407
music 416
trillion 98
trim *state* 7
adjust 27
dress 225
form 240
lie 544
waver 605
change sides 607
clean 652
beautify 845
adorn 847
scold 932
flog 972
in – order 58
trimmer *fickle* 607
apostate 941
selfish 943
trimming
border 231
ornament 847
dishonesty 940
trinal 92
trine 93
trinitrotoluene 727
trinity 92
– Sunday 998
Trinity, Holy – 976
trinket 643, 847

Trinkgeld 784
trinal 93
trinomial 92
trio *three* 92
music 415
triolet 597
trip *jaunt* 266
run 274
fall 306
leap 309
mistake 495
bungle 699
fail 732
vice 945
guilt 947
– up *deceive* 545
overthrow 731
tripartition 94
triplane 273
triple 93
– crown 747, 999
triplet *three* 92
verse 597
triplex 93
triplication 93
triplicity 93
tripod 215
tripos 461
tripotage 588
tripping [*see* trip]
style 578
nimble 682
caught – 491
**trippingly on the
tongue** 584
Triptolemus 371
trireme 273
trisection 94
triste 837
tristful 837
trisulcate
trisected 94
furrow 259
trite
known 490
conventional 613
– *saying* 496
tritheism 984
Triton *sea* 341
– among the
minnows
superior 33
huge 192
important 642
trituration 330
**trium literarum,
homo** – 792
triumph
success 731
trophy 733
exult 838

celebrate 883
boast 884
triumvirate 92, **737**
triune 92
Triune God 976
trivet 215, 386
right as a – 650,
924
trivia 643
trivial
unmeaning **517**
trifling 643
useless 645
troat 412
trocar 262
trochaic 597
trochee 597
trochilic 312
trodden: down–
749
well – 613, **677**
Troglodyte 893
troika 92
troll
roll 312
fairy 980
trollop 962
trolley 272
– *omnibus* 272
trombone 417
tronk 752
troop 72, 726
raise –s 722
– *carrier*
aeroplane 726
trooper 726
lie like a – 544
swear like a – 908
troop-ship 726
trop, de – 641
trope 521
**Trophonius, cave
of** – 837
trophy 551, **733**
tropical 382
troposphere 338
trot 266, 274
– out 525, 882
troth *belief* 484
veracity 543
promise 768
by my – 535
plight one's – 902
trothless 544, 940
trotters 266
trottoir 627
troubadour 597
trouble *disorder* 59
derange 61
exertion 686
difficulty 704

adversity 735
pain 828
painful 830
bring into – 649
get into – 649, 732
in – 619, 735
take – 686
– one's head
about 682
– one for 765
– oneself 686
troubled waters,
fish in – 704
troublesome 686,
704, 830
troublous 59, 173
– times 713
trough hollow 252
trench 259
conduit 350
trounce 932, 972
troupe 72
trousers 225
trousseau 225
trouvaille 775
trouvère 597
trover 775, 964
trow think 451
believe 484
know 490
trowel 191
troy-weight 319
truant absent 187
runaway 623
idle 682
apostate 941
truce cessation 142
deliverance 672
peace 721
pacification 723
flag of – 724
trucidation 361
truck summit 210
vehicle 272
barter 794
truck driver 268
truck farm 371
truckle to
submit 725
servile 886
flatter 933
truckle-bed 215
truck-load 31
truckman 268
truculent 907
trudge 266, 275
truditur dies die
109
true real 1
straight 246
assent 488

accurate 494
veracious 543
faithful 772
honourable 939
orthodox 983a
– bill
vindicate 937
accuse 938
lawsuit 969
see in its –
colours 480a
– meaning 516
– to nature 17
– to oneself 604a
– saying 496
– to scale 494
true-hearted 543,
939
true-love 897
true-lover's knot
897, 902
true-penny 939
truism axiom 496
unmeaning 517
trull 962
truly very 31
assent 488
really 494
indeed 535
trump perfect 650
honourable 939
good man 948
turn up –s 731
– card device 626
success 731
– up falsehood 544
accuse 938
trumped up 468,
545, 546
trumpery 517, 643
trumpet music 417
war cry 722
boast 884
flourish of –s
ostentation 882
celebration 883
boasting 884
ear– 418
penny –
skill 410
sound of –
alarm 669
speaking – 418
– blast 404
– call 550, 741
– forth 531
trumpeter
musician 416
messenger 534
boaster 884
trumpet-toned 410

trumpet-tongued
404, 531
truncate 201, 241
truncated 53
truncheon
weapon 727
staff of office 747
instrument of
punishment 975
trundle 284, 312
trunk whole 50
origin 153
paternity 166
box 191
trunk-hose 225
trunnion
support 215
projection 250
truss tie 43
pack, packet 72
support 215
trust
belief 484
combination 709
property 780
credit 805
hope 858
– to a broken reed
699
– to the chapter of
accidents 621
trustee
consignee 753
possessor 779
treasurer 801
trustful 484
trustless 940
trustworthy
certain 474
belief 484
- memory 505
veracious 543
honourable 939
truth
exactness 494
veracity 543
probity 939
arrive at the –
480a
in – certainly 474
love of – 543
of a – 535, 543
prove the – of 937
religious – 983a
speak the – 529,
543
in very – 543
Truth, Spirit of –
976
truthless 544
trutination 319

try experiment 463
adjudge 480
endeavour 675
use 677
lawsuit 969
– a case 967
– a cause 480
– conclusions
discuss 476
quarrel 713
contend 720
– one's hand 675
– one's luck 621
– one 704
– out 463
– the patience 830
– a prisoner 967
– one's temper 824
– one's utmost 686
trying 688, 704
tryst 892
trysting-place 74
tsar [see czar]
tu quoque 718
– argument
counter-evidence
468
confutation 479
accuse 938
tub 101
– thumper 582
– to a whale 545,
617
tuba 417
tubam trepidat,
ante – 860, 862
tubby 202
tube 260
test – 144
tubercle 250
tuberculous 655
tuberosity 250
tubman 968
tubular 260
tubulated 260
tubule 260
tuck fold 258
dagger 727
– in locate 184
eat 298
insert 300
tucker 225
tuft collection 72
rough 256
tufted 256
tuft-hunter 886,
943
tuft-hunting 886,
933
tug ship 273
pull 285

effort 686
- of war 720, 722
athletic sport 840
tuition 537
tulip *variegated* 440
gaudy 882
tumble *derange* 61
destruction 162
fall 306
agitate 315
fail 732
rough and – 59
– down 665
tumbler *athlete* 159
glass 191
actor 599
buffoon 844
tumbrel 272
tumefaction 194
tumid
expanded 194
- *style* 577
tumour
expansion 194
prominence 250
tumult *disorder* 59
agitation 315
revolt 742
emotion 825
tumultuous 59, 173
tumulus 363
tun *receptacle* 191
large 192
drunkard 959
tunable 413
tund 972
tundra 344
tune 402, 415
in – 413
out of –
unmusical 414
imperfect 651
deteriorated 659
put in –
prepare 673
concord 714
to the – of
quantity 25
payment 807
price 812
– up 416
tuneful *music* 413
poetry 597
-- nine 416, 597
tuneless 414
tunic 225
tunicle 999
tuning-fork 417
tunnage 192
tunnel *concave* 252
opening 260

passage 627
tup 366, 373
turban 225
turbary 267
turbid 426, 653
turbinated 248, 312
turbine 153
turbulence
violence 173
agitation 315
excitation 825
turbulent 59
Turcism 984
tureen 191
turf *lawn* 344
grass 367
fuel 388
gambling 621
races 720
race-course 728
amusement 840
turgid
expanded 194
- *style* 577
redundant 641
ostentatious 882
Turk
polygamist 903
grand – 745
'bear like the – no
rival near the
throne' 878
turkey-trot 840
Turkish bath 386,
652
turlupinade 842
turmoil
confusion 59
violence 173
agitation 315
turn *state* 7
crisis 134
period of time 138
change 140
tendency 176
form 240
curve 245
blunt 254
stroll 266
deviate 279
circuition 311
rotate 312
aptitude 698
affections 820
emotion 821
dance 840
nausea 867
by –s 138, 148
come in its – 138
each in its – 148
meet one at

every – 641
take a favourable
– 658
give one a –
aid 707
excite 824
do a good – 648,
906
ill – 907
in – 58, 138
one's luck –s 735
serve one's – 644
to a – 494
take a wrong – 732
– about 148
– to account 677,
775
– adrift 73, 297
– aside *change* 140
deviate 279
hinder 706
– one's attention
from 458
– away *eject* 297
not look 442
avoid 623
dismiss 756
relinquish 782
– back 145, 283
– one's back upon
oppose 708
refuse 764
disrespect 929
contempt 930
– the brain 503
– of the cards 156
– colour 821
– a corner
go round 311
succeed 731
– the corner 140,
658
– a deaf ear to
deaf 419
refuse 764
– down 258
– of expression 566
– the eyes upon
441
– for 698
– from *repent* 950
– to good account
658
– one's hand to
625
– the head
induce 615
excite 824
astonish 870
vanity 880
hate 898

– on one's heel
avoid 623
discourtesy 895
– the house out
window 713
– in *go to bed* 683
– inside out 529
– into
conversion 144
translate 522
- *money* 796
- *ridicule* 856
– of mind 820
– the mind to 457
– off 972
– on the tap 297
– the other cheek
725
– out *become* 144
happen 151
exterior 220
clothes 225
carriage 272
eject 297
strike 719
- *well* 731
- *ill* 732
dismiss 756
display 882
– over [*see below*]
– a penny 775
– round
inversion 218
revolve 311
rotate 312
recant 607
- *one's little
finger* 737
– the scale
unequal 28
superior 33
change 140
reverse 145
cause 153
counter-evidence
468
induce 615
– the stomach
395, 867
– the tables 14,
718
– of the table 156
– tail *go back* 283
run away 623
cowardice 862
– the tide 145
– of the tide 145,
218
– topsy turvy 61,
218
– and turn about

ubiquity 186
U-boat 726
Ucalegon, proxi-
  mus ardet – 667
udder 191
ugh! 867
ugliness 846
ugly 846
  – customer *source*
  of danger 667
  evil-doer 913
  bad man 949
  – duckling 948
  call by – names
  932
  take an – turn 732
uhlan 726
ukase 741
ukulele 417
ulcer *disease* 655
  care 830
ulema 967, 996
uliginous 352
ullage 53, 190
ulster 225
ulterior
  additional 37
  extraneous 57
  - *in time* 121
  - *in space* 196
  – motive 615
ultima ratio 744
  – regum 722
ultima Thule 196
ultimate 67
ultimately 121, 133,
  151
ultimatum
  definite 474
  intention 620
  requisition 630
  terms 770
ultimo 122
ultra 31, 33
  – vires 925
  ne plus – 729
  – crepidam 471
ultramarine 438
ultramontane
  foreign 57
  distant 196
  heterodox 984
  church 995
ultramundane 196
ultra-violet rays
  420
ululation 412, 839
Ulysses 702
umbilicus 222
umbra 421
  magni nominis –

659
umbrage *shade* 424
  hatred 898
  take – *anger* 900
umbrageous 421
umbrella
  covering 223
  shade 424
  protection 666
umpire
  judgment 480
  mediator 724
  judge 967
unâ voce 488
unabashed
  bold 861
  vain 880
  insolent 885
unabated 31
unable 158
  – to say 'No' 605
unacceptable 830
unaccommodating
  disagreeing 24
  disagreeable 830
  discourteous 895
  sulky 901a
unaccompanied 87
unaccomplished
  730
unaccountable
  exceptional 83
  unintelligible 519
  irresponsible 927a
  arbitrary 964
unaccustomed
  unusual 83
  unused 614
  unskilful 699
unachievable 471
unacknowledged
  489, 917
unacquainted 491
unacquired 777a
unadmonished 665
unadorned 576, 849
  beauty – 845
unadulterated 42,
  494, 652
unadventurous 864
unadvisable 647
unadvised 665, 699
unaffected
  genuine 494
  sincere 543
  – *style* 578
  obstinate 606
  artless 703
  insensible 823
  simple 849
  taste 850

unafflicted 831
unaided *weak* 160
unalarmed 861
unalienable 924
unallayed 159
unallied 10
unallowable 923
unallowed 925
unalloyed 42
  – happiness 827
  – truth 494
unalluring 866
unalterable 150
unaltered 13, 150
unamazed 871
unambiguous 518
unambitious 866
unamiable 907
unanimated 823
unanimity 23, 488,
  714
unannexed 44
unanswerable
  demonstrative 478
  irresponsible 927a
  arbitrary 964
unanswered 478
unanticipated 508
unappalled 861
unappareled 226
unapparent 526
unappeasable 173
unappetizing 395
unapplied 678
unappreciated 483
unapprehended 491
unapprehensive 861
unapprized 491
unapproachable
  great 31
  infinite 105
  distant 196
unapproached 33
unappropriated 782
unapproved 932
unapt
  incongruous 24
  important 158
  unskilful 699
unarmed 158
unarranged 59, 674
unarrayed 849
unascertained 475,
  491
unasked 602, 766
unaspiring 866, 881
unassailable 664
unassailed 748
unassembled 73
unassisted 160, 706
  – eye 441

unassociated 44
unassuming 881
unatoned 951
unattached 44
unattackable 664
unattainable 471
unattained 732
unattempted 623
unattended 87
  – to 460
unattested 468
unattracted
  indifferent 866
unattractive 866
unauthenticated
  unproved 468
  uncertain 475
  error 495
unauthoritative 475
unauthorized
  prohibited 761
  undue 925
  lawless 964
unavailing 645, **732**
unavenged 918
unavoidable 474,
  601
unavowed 489
unawakened 683
unaware 491, 508
  take –s 674
unawed 861
unbalanced 28
unbar 750
unbearable 830
unbeaten 123
unbeauteous 846
unbecoming
  incongruous 24
  disreputable 874
  undue 925
  dishonourable 940
  – a gentleman **895**
unbefitting 24, **925,**
  940
  [*see* unbecom-
  ing]
unbegotten 2
unbeguile 527, 529
unbegun 67, 674
unbelief 485, 989
unbeloved 898
unbend
  straighten 246
  repose 687
  – the mind 452
unbending 323
unbenevolent 907
unbenign 907
unbeseeming 851.
  940

unbesought 766
unbetrayed 939
unbewailed 932
unbiassed 498, 748
unbidden 600, 742
unbigoted 498
unbind 44, 750
unblamable 946
unblamed 946
unblemished 650,
  946
unblenching 861
unblended 42
unblest 735, 932
  – with 777a
unblown 674
unconmenced 67
unblushing
  proud 878
  vain 880
  imprudent 885
unboastful 881
unbodied 317
unboiled 674
unbolt 750
unbookish 491
unborn 2, 152
unborrowed 787,
  788
unbosom oneself
 , 529
' unbought
  not bought 796
  honorary 815
  honourable 939
  unselfish 942
unbound 748, 927a
unbounded 105
unbrace 160, 655
unbreathed 526
unbred 895
unbribed 939, 942
unbridled
  violent 173
  lax 738
  free 748
unbroken
  entire 50
  continuous 69
  preserved 670
  unviolated 939
unbruised 50
unbuckle 44
unburden
  – one's mind 529
unburdened 705
unburied 362
unbusinesslike 699
unbuttoned 748
uncalculating 863
uncalled for

redundant 641
useless 645
not used 678
uncandid 544, 907
uncanny 846, 980
uncanonical 984
uncared for
  neglected 460
  indifference 866
  disliked 867
  hated 898
uncase 226
uncaught 748
uncaused 156
unceasing 112
uncensured 931
unceremonious
  880, 895
uncertain
  irregular 139
  not certain 475
  doubtful 485
  in an – degree 32
uncertainty 475
unchain 44, 750
unchained 748
unchallenged 488,
  924
unchangeable 150,
  604a
unchanged 16, 141
unchanging 5
uncharitable 907
unchartered 925,
  964
unchaste 961
unchastised 970
unchecked 748
uncheckered 141
uncheerful 837
unchivalric 940
unchristian 984,
  989
uncial 590
uncinated 244
uncircumscribed
  180
uncircumspect 460
uncivil 851, 895
uncivilized 876, 895
unclaimed 748
unclassical 851
uncle *kin* 11
  my –'s
  pawnshop 787
unclean 653
  – spirit 978, 980
uncleanness 653
unclipped 50
unclog 705, 750
unclose 260, 750

unclothe 226
unclouded 420, 446
unclubbable 893
unclutch 790
uncoif 226
uncoil 313
uncoloured
  achromatic 429
  true 494
uncombed 653, 851
uncombined
  simple 42
  incoherent 47
uncomeatable 471
uncomely 846
uncomfortable 828,
  830
uncommenced 67
uncommendable
  blamable 932
  bad 945
  guilt 947
uncommensurable
  24
uncommon 31, 83,
  137
uncommonly 31
uncommunicated
  781
uncommunicative
  528
uncompact 322
uncompassionate
  914a
uncompelled 748
uncomplaisant 764
uncompleted
  incomplete 53
  unfinished 730
  failure 732
uncomplying 742,
  764
uncompounded 42
uncompressed 320,
  322
uncompromising
  conformable 82
  severe 739
unconcealable 525
unconceived
  uncreated 2
  unintelligible 519
unconcern 823, 866
unconcocted 674
uncondemned 970
unconditional
  complete 52
  free 748
  permission 760
  consent 762
  release 768a

unconducive 175a
unconfined 748
unconfirmed 475
unconformity
  disagreement 24
  irregularity 83
unconfused
  methodical 58
  clear 518
unconfuted 478,
  494
uncongealed 333
uncongenial 24, 657
unconnected
  irrelative 10
  disjointed 44
  discontinuous 70
  illogical 477
unconquerable
  strong 159
  persevering 604a
  – will 604
unconquered 719
unconscientious
  940
unconscionable
  excessive 31
  unprincipled 945
unconscious
  ignorant 491
  insensible 823
unconsenting 603,
  764
unconsidered 452
unconsolable 837
unconsolidated 47
unconsonant 24
unconspicuous 447
unconstitutional
  925, 964
unconstrained 748,
  880
unconsumed 40
uncontested 474
uncontradicted 488
uncontrite 951
uncontrollable
  violent 173
  necessity 601
  emotion 825
uncontrolled
  free 748
  excitability 825
uncontroverted 488
unconventional 83,
  614
unconversant 491,
  699
unconverted
  dissenting 489
  irreligious 989

[682]

unforfeited 781
unforgettable 505
unforgiving 919
unforgotten 505
unformed 241, 674
unfortified
pure 42
powerless 158
unfortunate
ill-timed 135
failure 732
adversity 735
unhappy 828
– woman 962
unfounded 546
unfrequent 137
unfrequented 893
unfriended
powerless 158
secluded 893
unfriendly
opposed 708
hostile 889
malevolent 907
unfrock 756, 972
unfrozen 382
unfruitful 169
unfulfilled 773, 925
unfurl
unfold 313
– a flag 525, 550
unfurnished 640, 674
ungainly 846, 895
ungallant 895
ungarnished 849
ungathered 678
ungenerous 819, 943
ungenial 657
ungenteel 851, 895
ungentle 173, 895
ungentlemanly
vulgar 851
rude 895
dishonourable 940
ungifted 499
unglorified 874
unglue 47
ungodly 989
ungovernable
violent 173
disobedient 742
passionate 825
ungoverned 748
ungraceful
– language 579
ugly 846
vulgar 851
ungracious 895, 907
ungrammatical 568

ungranted 764
ungrateful 917
ungratified 832
ungrounded
unsubstantial 4
erroneous 495
ungrudging 816
unguarded
neglected 460
spontaneous 612
unprepared 674
in an – moment
unexpectedly 508
unguem, ad – 494, 650
unguent 356
unguibus et rostro 686
unguided
ignorant 491
impulsive 612
unskilled 699
unguilty 946
unhabitable 187
unhabituated 614
unhackneyed 614
unhallowed 988, 989
unhand 750
unhandseled 123
unhandsome 940
unhandy 699
unhappy
adversity 735
pain 828
dejected 837
make – 830
unharbored 185
unhardened
tender 914
innocent 946
penitent 950
unharmonious 24, 414
unharness 750
unhatched 674
unhazarded 664
unhealthy 655, 657
unheard of
exceptional 83
improbable 473
ignorant 491
wonderful 870
unheated 383
unheed, -ed 460
unheeding 458
unhesitating
belief 484
resolved 604
unhewn 241, 674
unhindered 748

unhinge 61, 158
unhinged
impotent 158
insane 503
failure 732
unhitch 44
unholy 989
unhonoured 874
unhook (44)
unhoped 508
unhorsed 732
unhostile 888
unhouse 297
unhoused 185
unhurt 670
unicorn
monster 83
carriage 272
unideal *existing* 1
no thought 452
true 494
unification 48, 87
uniform
homogeneous 16
simple 42
orderly 58
regular 80
dress 225
symmetry 242
livery 550
uniformity 16
unilluminated 421
unimaginable 471, 473
wonderful 870
unimaginative 576, 843, 871
unimagined 1, 494
unimitated 20
unimpaired 670
unimpassioned 826
unimpeachable
certain 474
true 494
due 924
approved 931
innocent 946
unimpeached 931, 946
unimpeded 705, 748
unimportance 643
unimpressed 838
unimpressible 823
unimproved 659
unincreased 36
unincumbered
easy 705
exempt 927a
uninduced 616
uninfected 652
uninfectious 656

uninflammable 385
uninfluenced
obstinate 606
unactuated 616
free 748
uninfluential 172, 175a
uninformed 491
uningenuous 544
uninhabit, -able, -ed 187, 893
uninitiated 491, 699
uninjured
perfect 650
healthy 654
preserved 670
uninjurious 656
uninquisitive 456
uninspired 823
uninstructed 491
unintellectual 452, 499
unintelligent 499
unintelligibility **519**
unintelligible 519
– style 571
render – 538
unintentional
necessary 601
undesigned 621
uninterested 456, 841, 843
unintermitting
unbroken 69
durable 110
continuing 143
persevering 604a
uninterrupted
continuous 69
perpetual 112
unremitting 143
unintroduced 893
uninured 614
uninvented 526
uninvestigated 491
uninvited 893
uninviting 830
union
agreement 23
junction 43
combination 48
concurrence 178
workhouse 189
party 712
concord 714
marriage 903
unionist 712
union-jack 550
union-pipes 417
unique
dissimilar 18

free 748
unretracted 535
unrevenged 918
unreversed 143
unrevoked 143
unrewarded 806,
　917
unrhymed 598
unriddle 480a, 529
unrig 645
unrighteous 945
unrip 260
unripe
　young 127
　sour 397
　immature 674
unrivalled 33
unroll *evolve* 313
　display 525
unromantic 494
unroot 301
unruffled
　calm 174
　quiet 265
　unaffected 823
　placid 826
unruly *violent* 173
　obstinate 606
　discbedient 742
unsaddle 756
unsafe 665
unsaid 526
unsaleable
　useless 645
　selling 796
　cheap 815
unsaluted 929
unsanctified 988,
　989
unsanctioned 925
unsated 865
unsatisfactory
　inexpedient 647
　bad 649
　displeasing 830
　discontent 832
unsatisfied 832, 865
unsavouriness 395
unsay *recant* 607
unscanned 460
unscathed 654
unschooled 491
unscientific 477
unscoured 653
unscriptural 984
unscrupulous 940
unseal 529
unsearched 460
unseasonable 24,
　135
unseasoned 614,

674
unseat 756
unseemly
　inexpedient 647
　ugly 846
　vulgar 851
　undue 925
　vicious 945
unseen
　invisible 447
　neglected 460
　latent 526
unseldom 136
unselfish 942
unseparated 46
unserviceable 645
unsettle *derange* 61
unsettled
　mutable 149
　displaced 185
　uncertain 475
　– in one's mind
　503
unsevered 50
unsex 146
unshaded 525
unshaken 159
　– *belief* 484
unshapely 846
unshapen 241
unshared 777
unsheathe
　– the sword 722
unsheltered 665
unshielded 665
unshifting 143
unship 185, 297
unshocked 823
unshorn 50
unshortened 200
unshrinking 604,
　861
unsifted 460
unsightly 846
unsinged 670
unskilfulness 699
unslaked 865
unsleeping 604a,
　682
unsmooth 256
unsociable 893
unsocial 893
unsoiled 652
unsold 777
unsoldierlike 862
unsolicitous 866
unsolved 526
unsophisticated
　simple 42
　genuine 494
　artless 703

unsorted 59
unsought
　avoided 623
　unrequested 766
unsound
　illogical 477
　erroneous 495
　deceptive 545
　imperfect 651
　– mind 503
unsown 674
unsparing
　abundant 639
　severe 739
　liberal 816
　with an – hand
　818
unspeakable 31,
　870
unspecified 78
unspent 678
unspied 526
unspiritual 316, 989
unspoiled 648
unspotted
　clean 652
　beautiful 845
　innocent 946
unstable 218
　changeable 149
　uncertain 475
　irresolute 605
　precarious 665
　– equilibrium 149
unstaid 149
unstained
　clean 652
　honourable 939
unstatesmanlike
　699
unsteadfast 605
unsteady
　mutable 149
　irresolute 605
　in danger 665
unstinted 639
unstinting 816
unstirred 823, 826
unstopped
　continuing 143
　open 260
unstored 640
unstrained
　turbid 653
　relaxed 687
　– meaning 516
unstrengthened 160
unstruck 823
unstrung 160
unstudied 460
unsubject 748

unsubmissive 742
unsubservient
　useless 645
　inexpedient 647
unsubstantial 4
　weak 160
　rare 322
　erroneous 495
　imaginary 515
unsubstantiality 4
unsuccessful 732
unsuccessive 70
unsuitable
　incongruous 24
　(*inexpedient* 647)
　– time 135
unsullied *clean* 652
　honourable 939
　(*guiltless* 946)
unsung 526
unsupplied 640
unsupported
　weak 160
　(*unassisted* 706)
　– by evidence 468
unsuppressed 141
unsurmountable
　471
unsurpassed 33
unsusceptible 823
unsuspected
　latent 526
unsuspecting
　belief 484
　hopeful 858
unsuspicious
　belief 484
　artless 703
　hope 858
unsustainable 495
unsweet 395
unswept 653
unswerving
　straight 246
　direct 278
　persevering 604a
unsymmetric 83
unsymmetrical 59,
　243
unsystematic 59
untainted *pure* 652
　healthy 654
　honourable 939
untalked of 526
untamed 851, 907
untarnished 939
untasted 391
untaught 491, 674
untaxed 815
unteach 538
unteachable 499,

699
untenable
  powerless 158
  illogical 477
  undefended 725
untenanted 187, 893
unthanked 917
unthankful 917
unthawed 321, 383
unthinkable 471
unthinking
  unconsidered 452
  involuntary 601
unthought of 452, 460
unthreatened 664
unthrifty
  unprepared 674
  prodigal 818
unthrone 756
untidy 59, 653
untie 44, 750
  – the knot 705
until 106
  – now 118
untilled 674
untimely 135
  – end 360
untinged 42
untired 689
untiring 604a
untitled 876
untold
  countless 105
  uncertain 475
  latent 526
  secret 528
untouched
  disused 678
  insensible 823
untoward
  ill-timed 135
  bad 649
  unprosperous 735
  unpleasant 830
untraced 526
untracked 526
untractable 606, 699
untrained
  unaccustomed 614
  unprepared 674
  unskilled 699
untrammelled 705, 748
untranslatable 523
untranslated 523
untravelled 265
untreasured 640
untried *new* 123

not decided 461
untrimmed 674, 849
untrodden *new* 123
  impervious 261
  not used 678
untroubled 174, 721
untrue 495, 546
untrustworthy
  uncertain 475
  erroneous 495
  danger 665
  dishonourable 940
untruth 544, **546**
untunable 414
unturned 246
untutored
  ignorant 491
  unprepared 674
  artless 703
untwine 313
untwist 313
unused
  new 123
  unaccustomed 614
  unskilful 699
unusual 83
unusually *very* 31
unutterable 31, 519, 870
unvalued
  underrated 483
  undesired 866
  disliked 898
unvanquished 748
unvaried
  continuing 143
  - *style* 575, 576
unvarnished
  true 494
  - *style* 576
  unreserved 703
  simple 849
  - *tale* 494, 543
unvarying 16, 143
unveil 525, 529
unventilated 261
unveracious 544
unversed 491
unvexed 831
unviolated 939
unvisited 893
unwakened 683
unwarlike 862
unwarmed 383
unwarned 508, 665
unwarped judg-
ment 498
unwarrantable 923
unwarranted
  illogical 477

undue 925
  illegal 964
unwary 460
unwashed 653
  great – 876
unwatchful 460
unwavering 604a
unweakened 159
unwearied
  persevering 604a
  indefatigable 682
  refreshed 689
unwedded 904
unweeded garden 674
unweeting 491
unweighed 460
unwelcome 830, 893
unwell 655
unwept 831
unwholesome 657
unwieldy
  large 192
  heavy 319
  cumbersome 647
  difficult 704
  ugly 846
unwilling 489
unwillingness 603
unwind *evolve* 313
unwiped 653
unwise 499
unwished 866
unwithered 159
unwitting
  ignorant 491
  involuntary 601
unwittingly 621
unwomanly 373
unwonted 83, 614
unworldly 939
unworn 159
unworshipped 929
unworthy
  shameful 874
  vicious 945
  – of belief 485
  – of notice 643
unwrap 246
unwrinkled 255
unwritten
  latent 526
  obliterated 552
  spoken 582
  – law 697, 963
unwrought 674
unyielding
  tough 323
  resolute 604
  obstinate 606

resisting 719
up
  aloft 206
  vertical 212
  effervescing 353
  excited 824
  the game is – **735**
  prices looking –
  814
  time – 111
  – in arms
  prepared 673
  active 682
  opposition 708
  attack 716
  resistance 719
  warfare 722
  – and at them **716**
  – and doing 682
  – and down 314
  – on end 212
  – in 698
  – to [*see below*]
  all – with
  destruction 162
  failure 732
  adversity 735
up to
  time 106
  power 157
  knowing 490
  skilful 698
  brave 861
  – the brim 52
  – date 123
  – one's ears **641**
  – one's eyes **641**
  – the mark
  equal 27
  sufficient 639
  good 648
  due 924
  – snuff 702
  – this time
  time 106
  past 122
Upas tree 663
upbear 215, 307
upbraid 932
upcast 307
upgrow 206
upgrowth 194, **305**
upheaval 146
upheave 307
uphill
  acclivity 217
  ascent 305
  laborious 686
  difficult 704
uphoist 307
uphold

deviating 279
vague
  unsubstantial 4
  uncertain 475
  unreasoning 477
  unmeaning 517
  obscure 519
  - *language* 571
  - suggestion 514
vail *panel* 228
  donation 784
  reward 973
vain *unreal* 2
  unprofitable 645
  unvalued 866
  conceited 880
  in - *failure* 732
  labour in -
  come short 304
  useless 645
  fail 732
  take a name in -
    895
  - attempt 732
  use - efforts 645
  - expectation 509
vainglorious
  haughty 878
  vain 880
  boasting 884
vaivode 745
valance 231
vale 252
  - of years 128
valeat quantum 467
valediction 293, 894
valedictory 293
valentine 902
valet 631, 746
valet
  - de chambre 746
  - de place 524, 527
valetudinarian 655, 656
Valhalla 981
valiant 861
valid *confirmed* 150
  powerful 157
  strong 159
  true 494
  sufficient 639
  - reasoning 476
valise 191
valley 252
  - of the shadow of death 360
vallum 717
valoir, se faire - 884
valorem, ad - 812
valour 861

valuable 644, 648
value *colour* 428
  measure 466
  estimate 480
  importance 642
  utility 644
  goodness 648
  price 812
  approbation 931
  of priceless - 814
  set a - upon 482
  - received 810
  -s *painting* 556
valueless 645
valve *stop* 263
  conduit 350
  safety - *safety* 664
  refuge 666
  escape 671
vamp *change* 140
  music 416
  - up *improve* 658
  restore 660
  prepare 673
vampire 913, 980
vampirism 789, 992
van *beginning* 66
  front 234
  wagon 272
  in the - 234
  precession 280
van-courier 64
Vandal
  destroyer 165
  vulgar 851
  commonalty 876
  evil-doer 913
vandalism 851
vandyke 257
Vandyke brown 433
vane *wind* 349
  indication 550
vanguard 234
vanish
  unsubstantial 4
  transient 111
  disappear 449
vanishing 32, 193
vanity *useless* 645
  conceit 880
  - bag 191
Vanity Fair 852
vanquish 731
vantage ground
  superiority 33
  power 157
  influence 175
  height 206
vapid *insipid* 391
  - *style* 575
vaporization 336

vaporous
  imaginary 515
  opaque 426
vapour *gas* 334
  bubbles 353
  fancy 515
  boast 884
  insolence 885
  - bath 386, 652
vapourer 887
vapours
  dejection 837
variable 149, 605
variance
  difference 15
  disagreement 24
  discord 713
  at - *enmity* 889
  at - with 489
variant 15
variation
  difference 15
  diverseness 20a
  number 84
  chance 140
  music 415
varied 15
variegated 16a, 440
variegation 440
variety
  difference 15
  class 75
  multiformity 81
  exception 83
  entertainment 599
variform 81
various 15, 102
  - places 182
  - times 119
varlet 949
varnish
  overlay 223
  resin 356a
  sophistry 477
  falsehood 544
  painting 556
  decorate 847
  excuse 937
vary *differ* 15
  dissimilar 18
  variation 20a
  change 140
  fluctuate 149
vascular *cells* 191
  holes 260
  pipes 350
vase 191
vassal 746
vassalage 749
vast *great* 31
  spacious 180

  large 192
  - learning 490
vasty deep 341
vat 191
Vatican 995, 1000
  thunders of the - 908
vaticination 511
vatum, genus irritabile - 901
vaudeville 599, 840
vault
  cellar 191
  curve 245
  leap 309
  tomb 363
  store 636
  - of heaven 318
vaulted 245, 252
vaulting 33, 865
vaunt 884
vaurien 949
vavasour
  possessor 779
  nobleman 875
V.C. 733
vection 270
Vedas 986
vedette 668
Vedidad 986
veer
  change 140
  deviate 279
  go back 283
  change intention 607
vegetability 365
vegetable 367
  - kingdom 367
  - life 365
  - oil 356
  - physiology 369
vegetarian 298, 953
vegetate 365
  exist 1
  grow 194
  stagnate 265
  inactive 681, 683
  insensible 823
vegetation 365
vehemence
  violence 173
  feeling 821
  emotion 825
vehement
  - *language* 574
vehicle
  carriage 272
  instrument 631
veil *covering* 225
  shade 424

vindicator 919
vindictive 901, 919
vine 367
  – grower 371
vinegar 397
  – aspect 846
vinery 191
vineyard 371, 691
vingt et un 840
vintage 371, 636
vintner 637
viol 417
violate
  disobey 742
  non-observance
    773
  undue 925
  dereliction 927
  ravish 961
  – a law 83
  – the law 964
  – a usage 614
violence 173
  arbitrary 964
  do – to *bad* 649
  non-observance
    773
  undue 925
violent 173
  excitable 825
  – death 360, 361
  in a – degree 31
  lay – hands on 789
violet 437
violin 417
violinist 416
violoncello 417
viper *snake* 366
  bane 663
  evil-doer 913
  bad man 949
  – in one's bosom
    667
virago 901
virent 435
vires acquirit
  eundo
  increase 35
  energy 171
  velocity 274
virescence 435
Virgilianæ, sortes –
  621
virgin *new* 123
  girl 129
  woman 374
  spinster 904
  good 948
  pure 960
  – forest 367
  – soil

ignorance 491
untilled 674
the – Mary 977
virginals 417
virginibus
  puerisque 960
viribus, totis – 686
viridity 435
virile
  adolescent 131
  strong 159
  manly 373
virtu 850
  article of – 847
virtual 2, 5
  – image 443
virtue *power* 157
  courage 861
  goodness **944**
  purity 960
  by – of 157, 631
  in – of 737
  make a – of neces-
    sity *no choice*
    609a
  skill 698
  submit 725
  compromise **774**
  bear 826
virtueless 945
virtuoso 416, 850
virtuous 944, 960
virulence
  energy 171
  noxiousness 649
  insalubrity 657
  discourtesy 895
  anger 900
  malevolence 907
virulent 932
virum volitare per
  ora 531
virus 655, 663
vis:
  – comica 842
  – conservatrix 670
  – inertiæ
  power 157
  inertness 172
  insensibility 823
  – medicatrix 660,
    662
  – mortua 157
  – a tergo 284
  – viva 157
visa 488
visage 234, 448
vis-à-vis *front* 234
  opposite 237
  carriage 272
viscera 221

viscid 352
viscount 875
viscous 352
vise 781
Vishnu 979
visibility **446**
visible 446
  be – 448
  become – 448
  darkness – 421
  – radiation 420
vision *sight* **441**
  phantasm 443
  dream 515
  spectre 980
  organ of – 441
visionary
  inexistence 2
  unsubstantial 4
  impossible 471
  imaginary 515
  heterodox 984
visionless 442
visit *arrival* 292
  social 892
  courtesy 894
  – upon 972
  pay a surprise –
    674
visitation
  disease 655
  adversity 735
  suffering 828
  –s of Providence
    976
  – of the sick 998
visiting:
  – card 550
  on – terms 888,
    892
visitor *incomer* 294
  director 694
  friend 890
visor 530
vista
  convergence 260
  sight 441
  appearance 448
  expectation 507
visual 441
  – organ 441
vitability 359
vitæ, elixir – 662
vital *life* 359
  important 642
vitality
  stability 150
  strength 159
  life 359
vitalize 359
vitals 221

vitam impendere
  vero 535, 939
vitamines 298
vitiate 659
vitiated 655
viticulture 371
vitreous 323, 425
vitrify 323
vituperate 908, 932
vituperator 936
viva! 873, 931
vivace *music* 415
vivacious
  active 682
  sensitive 822
  cheerful 836
vivamus, dum
  vivimus – 840
vivandière 797
vivarium 370
vivâ voce 582
vive *glory be to* 873
  on the qui – 824
vivendi
  modus – 723
  – causa 359
vivid *energetic* **171**
  sensibility 375
  light 420
  colour 428
  distinct 518
  – memory 505
vivify 159, 359
vivisection 378
vixen *fox* 366
  female 374
  shrew 901
viz. [*see* videlicet]
vizier *director* 694
  mask 530
  shield 717
  deputy 759
vizor 530
vobis, sic vos non –
  791
vocable 562
vocabulary 562
vocal 415, 580
  – training 537
vocalist 416
vocalize 580
vocation 625
voce, sotto – 581
vociferation
  loud 404
  cry 411
  voice 580
vogue *custom* **613**
  fashion 852
  fame 873
vogue la galère

[693]

wait 133, 681
lie in – for 530
– for 507
– impatiently 133
– on *accompany* 88
aid 707
– to see how the
wind blows 607
– upon *serve* 746
call on 894
waiter *servant* 746
– on Providence
neglect 460
inactive 683
content 831
waiting 507
be kept – 133
waiting-maid 746
waitress 746
waits 416
waive *defer* 133
not choose 609a
not use 678
waiwode 745
wake *sequel* 65
rear 235
funeral 363
trace 551
excite 824
amusement 840
in the – of 281
enough to – the
dead 404
– the thoughts
457
– up 824
wakeful
careful 459
active 682
Walhalla 981
walk *region* 181
lane 189
move 266
business 625
way 627
conduct 692
arena 728
– one's chalks
293, 623
– the earth 359
– of life 625
–ed off one's legs
688
– off with 791
– over the course
705, 731
– in the shoes of
19
walker 268
walking gentleman
599

wall *vertical* 212
parietes 224
inclosure 232
refuge 666
obstacle 706
defence 717
prison 752
driven to the –
704
go to the –
destruction 162
die 360
fail 732
pushed to the –
601
take the – 873,
878
wooden –s 726
–eyed 442
– in 229, 751
wallah 746
wallet 191
wallop 315
wallow *low* 207
plunge 310
rotate 312
– in 377, 641
– in the mire 653
– in riches 803
– in voluptuous-
ness 954
wallsend 388
Wall-street 799
– slang 563
waltz 415, 840
wamble
vacillate 149
oscillate 314
dislike 867
wampum 800
wan 429, 837
wand *sceptre* 747
magic 993
wave a – 992
wander *move* 264
journey 266
deviate 279
delirium 503
the attention –s
458
wanderer 268
wandering
exceptional 83
– Jew 268
wane
decrease 36
age 128
contract 195
decay 659
one's star on the –
735

wax and – 140
wangle 943
want
inferiority 34
shortcoming 304
requirement 630
insufficiency 640
poverty 804
desire 865
wanted 187
wanting
incomplete 53
absent 187
imbecile 499
found –
imperfect 651
disapproval 932
guilt 947
wantless 639
wanton
unconformable 83
capricious 608
unrestrained 748
amusement 840
rash 863
impure 961
wapentake 181
war 722
at – 24, 720
at – with 708, 722
declare – 713
man of – 726
seat of – 728
– correspondent
534, 593
– of words 588,
720
warble 416
war-cry *alarm* 669
defiance 715
war 722
ward *part* 51
parish 181
safety 664
asylum 666
dependent 746
restraint 751
watch and – 459,
753
– off 706, 717
war-dance 715
warden
guardian 664
master 745
deputy 759
warder
perforator 262
porter 263
guardian 664
keeper 753
wardmote 966

wardrobe 191, 225
ward-room 191
war-drum 417
wardship 664
ware
warning 668
merchandise 798
warehouse 636, 799
warfare 722
discord 713
war-horse 726
warlike 722
warlock 994
warm
violent 173
hot 382
make hot 384
red 434
orange 439
wealthy 803
ardent 821
excited 824
angry 900
irascible 901
flog 972
– bath 386
– the blood 824
– the cockles of
the heart 829
– imagination 515
– man 803
– reception
repel 717
welcome 892
– up 658, 660
– work 686
warm-hearted
feeling 821
sensibility 822
friendship 888
benevolence 906
warming 384
warming-pan
locum tenens 147
heater 386
preparation 673
warmth
vigorous languag
574
warn *dissuade* 616
caution 668
– off 761
warning *omen* 512
dissuasion 616
caution 668
give – *dismiss* 678
relinquish 782
– voice *alarm* 668
warp *change* 140
tend 176
contract 195

find its – 302
gather – 267
get into the – of 613
go one's – 293
go your – 297
let it have its – 681
it must have its – 601
have one's own – 748
in a – 828, 900
in the – near 197
in the – of 706, 708
make – 302
make one's –
journey 266
progression 282
passage 302
prosperity 734
make – for
substitution 147
opening 260
turn aside 279
avoid 623
facilitate 705
courtesy 894
on the – 282
place in one's – 763
put in the – of 470, 537
see one's – 490
show the – 693
under – *move* 264
sail 267
progression 282
depart 293
wing one's – 267
– in 294
long – off 196
have – on 267
– out 295
– of speaking 521
– of thinking 484
not know which – to turn 475
Way, the – 976
wayfarer 268
wayfaring 266
waylay 545, 702
wayless 261
ways 692
in all manner of – 278
– and means 632, 800
wayward
changeable 149

obstinate 606
capricious 608
sullen 901a
waywode 745
wayworn 266, 688
wayzgoose 840
weak *feeble* 160
water 337
insipid 391
illogical 477
foolish 499
- *style* 575
irresolute 605
trifling 643
lax 738
compassionate 914
vicious 945
– point 477, 651
expose one's –
point 479
– side 499, 945
weaken
decrease 36, 38
enfeeble 160
refute 468
weaker vessel 374
weak-headed 499
weak-hearted 862
weak-kneed 725
weakness 160
– of the flesh 945
weal 618
common – 644
weald 367
wealth 780, 803
wean 484, 614
– from 616
– one's thoughts from 506
weanling 129
weapon 727
weaponless 158
wear *decrease* 36
clothes 225
deflect 279
use 677
– away *cease* 142
deteriorate 659
– the breeches 737
– off 142, 614
– on 109
– out 659, 688
– and tear
decrease 36
waste 638
injury 659
exertion 686
weariness 841
wearing 841
– apparel 225

wearisome
laborious 686
fatiguing 688
painful 830
weary *fatigue* 688
painful 828
sad 837
ennuyant 841
– flat, stale, and unprofitable 843
– waste 344
– Willie 876
weasand 260, 351
weasel asleep,
catch a – 471, 682
weather 338
keep one's – eye open 864
rough – 173, 349
– the storm
stability 150
recover 660
safe 664
succeed 731
weather permitting 469, 470
weather-beaten
weak 160
damaged 659
fatigue 688
weather-bound 751
weathercock
changeable 149
wind 349
indication 550
fickle 607
weathered 659
weather-gauge 338
weather-glass 338
weather-proof 654, 664
weatherwise 338
foresight 510
weave *produce* 161
interlace 219
– a tangled web 704
weazen 193
web
complexity 59
intersection 219
texture 329
wed 48, 903
wedded: – pair 903
– to *belief* 484
habit 613
loving 897
– to an opinion
misjudgment 481
obstinacy 606
wedding 903

– breakfast 892
– day 883
wedge *join* 43
angular 244
sharp 253
instrument 633
thin edge of the *begin* 66
insinuate 228
cunning 702
– in 228
wedged in 751
wedlock 903
wee 193
weed *exclude* 55
few 103
plant 367
agriculture 371
cigar 392
trifle 643
clean 652
– out 297, 301
weeds *dress* 225
useless 645
mourning 839
widowhood 905
weedy 203, 643
week 108
weekly 138
– paper 531
ween *judge* 480
believe 484
know 490
weeny 32
weep 839, 914
weet 480, 490
weetless 491
weft, warp and – 329
weigh *influence* 175
lift 307
heavy 319
ponder 451
under – [*see* way]
– anchor 293
– carefully 465
– down 649, 749
– on the heart 830
– heavy on 649
– on the mind
regret 833
dejection 837
fear 860
– with 615
weighed and found wanting 34, 932
weighing machine 319
weight
influence 175
gravity 319

inquiry 461
reasoning 476
where 186, 461
– am I? 870
whereabouts 183, 197
whereas 9, 476
whereby 631
wherefore
attribution 155
inquiry 461
reasoning 476
motive 615
wherein 221
whereness 186
whereupon 106, 121
wherever 180, 182
wherewith 632, 800
wherret 830
wherry 273
whet *sharpen* 253
meal 298
incite 615
excite 824
take a –
tipple 959
– the appetite 865
– the knife 673
whether or not 609
whetstone, cut a – with a razor 638
which:
at – time 119
know – is which 465
whiff 349, 825
whiffle 349
Whig 712
while *time* 106
in a – 132
worth – 646
– away time
inaction 681
pastime 840
– speaking of 9, 134
whilom 122
whilst 106
whim *fad* 481
fancy 515
caprice 608
wit 842
desire 865
whimper 839
whimsey 515, 865
whimsical [*see* whim] 853
whimwham 608, 643
whin 367
whine 411, 839
whinyard 727

whip *collect* 72
coachman 268
strike 276
stir up 315
urge 615
hasten 684
director 694
flog 972
scourge 975
– and spur 274
– away 293
– hand 731, 737
– in 300
– on 684
– off 293
– up 789
whipcord 205
whipper-in 694
whippersnapper 129
whipping-post 975
whipster 129
whir *rotate* 312
sound 407
whirl *rotate* 312
flurry 825
whirligig 312
whirlpool *rotate* 312
agitation 315
water 348
danger 667
whirlwind
disorder 59
agitation 315
wind 349
reap the –
product 154
fail 732
ride the –
resolution 604
authority 737
whisk *rapid* 274
circuition 311
agitation 315
– off 297
whisker 256
whisket 191
whisky
vehicle 272
drink 298
whisper
faint sound 405
tell 527
conceal 528
stammer 583
stage – 580
– about
disclose 529
publish 531
– in the ear
voice 580
whist *hush* 403

cards 840
whistle *wind* 349
hiss 409
play music 416
musical instrument 417
clean as a –
thorough 52
perfect 650
neatly 652
pay too dear for one's –
inexpedient 647
unskilful 699
dear 814
police – 669
wet one's –
drink 298
tipple 959
– at 930
– for *request* 765
desire 865
– jigs to a milestone 645
– for want of thought
inaction 681
whit *small* 32
whit-leather 327
Whit-Monday 840
white 430
– of the eye 441
– feather 862
– flag 723
– frost 383
– heat 382
– horses 348
– lie *equivocal* 520
concealment 528
untruth 546
plea 617
– liver 862
– as a sheet 860
– slave 962
stand in a – sheet 952
mark with a – stone 642, 931
whitechapel
vehicle 272
Whitefriars 996
whiteness 430
whitewash
cover 223
whiten 430
cleanse 652
ornament 847
justify 937
acquit 970
whitewashed
get – 808

whitewasher 935
white wings 652
whitey-brown 433
whither
tendency 176
direction 278
inquiry 461
whitlow 655
whittle 44, 253
whittled
drunk 959
Whitsuntide 998
whiz 409
who 461
– goes there? 669
– would have thought? 508, 870
whoa! 265
whole *entire* 50
healthy 654
make – 660
as a – 50
on the – 476, 480
go the – hog 729
the – time 106
– truth
truth 494
disclosure 529
veracity 543
wholesale
large scale 31
whole 50
abundant 639
trade 794
wholesome 656
wholly 50, 52
whoop 411
war – 715, 722
whop *flog* 972
whoopee 840
whopper *lie* 546
whopping *huge* 192
whore 962
whoredom 961
whoremonger 962
whorl 248
why *cause* 153
attribution 155
inquiry 461
indeed 535
motive 615
– not 868
wibble-wabble 314
wick 388, 423
wicked 945
the – *bad men* 949
impious 988
the – one 978
wicker 219
wicket 66, 260

wide 202
- apart 15
-awake *hat* 225
intelligent 498
- away 196
- berth 748
- of the mark
distance 196
deviation 279
error 495
- of *distant* 196
- open 194, 260
- of the truth 495
- world 180, 318
in the - world 180
widen 194
- the breach 713, 900
wide-spread
great 31
dispersed 73
space 180
expanded 194
widow 905
widowhood 905
width 202
wield
brandish 315
handle 379
use 677
- authority 737
- the sword 722
wieldy 705
wife 903
wig 225
wigging 932
wiggle 315
wight 373
wigwam 189
wild 851
unproductive 169
violent 173
plain 344
inattentive 458
mad 503
shy 623
unskilled 699
excited 824, 825
untamed 851
rash 863
angry 900
licentious 954
run - 825
- animals 366
- beast *fierce* 173
evil-doer 913
- goose chase
caprice 608
useless 645
unskilful 699
- imagination 515

[700]

sow one's - oats
grow up 131
improve 658
amusement 840
vice 945
intemperance 954
Wild, Jonathan -
thief 792
bad man 949
wilderness
disorder 59
unproductive 169
space 180
solitude 893
wild-fire 382
spread like -
violence 173
influence 175
expand 194
publication 531
wile 545, 702
wilful
voluntary 600
obstinate 606
will
volition **600**
resolution 604
testament 771
gift 784
at - 600
at one's own
sweet - 608
have one's own -
600, 748
make one's - 360
tenant at - 779
- be 152
- for the deed
774, 937
- of Heaven 601
- he nil he 601
- power 600
- and will not 605
- you 765
Will o' the wisp
luminary 423
imp 980
willing or unwilling
601
willingness 602
willow 839
willy-nilly 601, 744
wilted 659
wily 702
wimble 262
wimple 225
win 731, 775
- the affections
897
- golden opinions
931

- the heart 829
- laurels 373
- out 33
- over *belief* 484
induce 615
content 831
wince
bodily pain 378
emotion 821
excitement 825
mental pain 828
flinch 860
winch 307, 633
wind *convolution*
[*see below*]
velocity 274
blast **349**
life 359
against the - 278, 708
before the - 278, 734
cast to the -s
repudiate 610
disuse 678
not observe 773
relinquish 782
close to the - 278
fair - 705
to the four -s 180
get - 531
get the - up 860
see how the -
blows
direction 278
experiment 463
foresight 510
fickle 607
in the - 151, 152
lose - 688
sail near the -
direction 278
skill 698
sharp practice 940
outstrip the - 274
preach to the -s
645
raise the - 775
scatter to the -s
756
see where the -
lies 698
short -ed 688
sport of -s and
waves 315
sound of - and
limb 654
take the - out of
one's sails
render powerless
158

hinder **706**
defeat 731
touched in the -
655
what's in the - ?
461
- ahead **708** '
- bag 584
in the -'s eye **278**
- the horn 416
hit between - **and**
water 659
- and weather
permitting
qualification **469**
possibility 470
wind *blast* [*see
above*]
convolution 248
deviate 279
circuition 311
- round the heart
897
- up *strengthen* **159**
prepare 673
complete 729
- *accounts* 811
windbag 884
wind instruments
417
wind-bound 706
windfall 618
wind-gauge 349
wind-gun 727
winding 248, 311
winding-sheet 363
**windings and turn-
ings** 248
wind-jammer 273
windlass 307, 633
windless 688
windmill 312
tilt at -s 638
window 260
make the -s shake
loud noise 404
- dressing 544
wind-pipe 351
wind-up 67
windward, to - **236**,
278
windy 349
wine 298, 959
put new - into old
bottles 699
look upon the -
when it is red
953
wine-bibbing 959
wine-cooler 387
wineglass 191

Column 1 (WRI)

small 32
wriggle 314, 315
  – into 294
  – out of 671
wright 690
wring *twist* 248
  pain 378
  clean 652
  torment 830
  – from
  extract 301
  compel 744
  take 789
  – one's hands 839
  – the heart 830
wringing *wet* 339
wrinkle *fold* 258
  hint 527
wrinkled 128
wrist 781
wristband 225
writ 741, 969
Writ, Holy – 985
write *compose* 54
  style 569
  writing 590
  – down *record* 551
  – music 416
  – off 624
  – out 590
  – prose 598
  – to 592
  – upon 595
  – word 527
writer 590, 593
  dramatic – 599
  pen of a ready –
  569
  – to the Signet
  968
writhe *distort* 243
  agitate 315
  pain 378
writing **590**, 593
  put in – 551
  – in cipher 590
written, it is – 601
wrong *error* 495
  evil 619
  injury 649
  spite 907
  improper **923**
  vice 945
  go – 732
  in the – *error* 495,
  923
  own oneself in
  the – 950
  – box 699, 704
  wrong 923
  – course 945

Column 2 (YAR)

begin at the – end
  699
  – in one's head
  503
  in the – place 647
  – side out 145, 218
  – side up 218
  – side of the wall
  665
  – sow by the ear
  699, 732
  – step 732
wrong-doer 949
wrong-doing 945
wrongful 923
wrong-headed 481
wrought:
  highly –
  prepared 673
  complete 729
  – iron 323
  – out 729
  – up *excited* 824
  angry 900
wry 217, 243
  – face *pain* 378
  discontent 832
  lamentation 839
  ugly 846
  disapproval 932
wynd 189
wyvern 83

X

X-rays 420, 554
xanthic 436
Xanthippe 901
xebec 273
xenogenesis 161
xerophagy 956
xylography 558
xylophone 417
x, y, z 491

Y

yacht 273
yachting 267
yachtsman 269
yager 726
Yahoo 876
yammer 839
yap 412
yard *abode* 189
  length 200
  enclosure 232
  workshop 691
yardarm to yard-
  arm 197
yare 682

Column 3 (YER)

yarn *filament* 205
  story 532
  untruth 546
  exaggeration 549
  mingled – 41
  spin a long – 549
  diffuse style 573
yarr 412
yashmak 225
yataghan 727
yaup 411
yaw 279
yawl *ship* 273
  cry 412
yawn *open* 260
  sleepy 683
  tired 688
  weary 841
yawning *gulf* 198,
  260
yclept 564
yea *more* 33
  assent 488
yean 161
year 106, 108
  – in and – out 104
  since the – one
  124
  all the – round 110
  – after year 104
  tenant from – to
  year 779
yearling 129
yearly 138
yearn 828, 837
  – for *desire* 865
  pity 914
yearning *love* 897
years 128
  in – 128
  tenant for – 779
  – ago 122
  come to – of dis-
  cretion 131
  – old 128
yeast *leaven* 320
  bubbles 353
yell *cry* 411
  scream 839
yellow 436
  – flag 668
  – streak 862
  – and red 439
yellow-eyed 920
yellowness **436**
yelp 412
yeoman 371, 373
  – of the guard 726
  –'s service 644
yeomanry 726
yerk *strike* 276

Column 4 (ZAM)

yes 488, 762
yes-man 886
yesterday *past* 122
  of – *new* 123
yet *in compensation*
  30
  exception 83
  time 106
  prior 116
  past 122
  qualification 469
yeux doux, faire les
  – 902
yield *soft* 324
  harvest 636
  submit 725
  consent 762
  resign 782
  furnish 784
  gain 810
  price 812
  – assent 488, 762
  – one's breath 360
  – to despair 859
  – up the ghost 360
  – the palm 34, 879
  – to temptation
  615
yielding *soft* 324
  facile 705
  submissive 725
yodel 580
yoicks 622
yoke *join* 43
  vinculum 45
  couple 89
  subject 749
  means of restraint
  752
  rivet the – 739
yokel 701, 876
yokemate 903
yonder 79, 196
yore 122
Yorkshireman 702
you: – don't say so
  870
  –'re another 718
young 127
  – man *lover* 897
younger generation
  127
youngster 129
younker 129
youth **127**, 129
Yule log 388

Z

Zadkiel 513
zambo 41
Zamiel 978